E1XM

World's First and Only

Building off of a 25-year tradition of manufacturing the finest high-end tabletop receivers in the world, the E1 is designed without compromise to give you direct access to news, sports and music from around the world.

_ AM/FM/SW/XM Satellite Ready Radio
_ Frequency Coverage: 100-30,000 KHz, includes shortwave, medium wave AM broadcast band and longwave; 76-90, 87-108 MHz FM broadcast band; XM Satellite Ready Radio
_ Reception Modes: AM, FM-stereo, Single Sideband (selectable USB/LSB) and CW
_ Digital Display: large 5.7 inch square, 240 x 320 pixel, dot matrix display. Shows all modes and selected functions
_ Programmable Memories: 500 user programmable with alpha labeling plus 1200 user definable country memories, for a total of 1700
_ Memory Scan Function
_ Digital Phase Lock Loop (PLL) Synthesized Tuning with Direct Digital Synthesis (DDS) for drift-free frequency stability and finest tuning resolution
_ Dual Conversion Superheterodyne Circuit: results in minimized interference through superior selectivity Excellent Sensitivity: yielding a true high-performance receiver
_ High Dynamic Range: allowing for detection of weak signals in the presence of strong signals
_ Selectable Bandwidths: 7.0, 4.0, 2.5 kHz for excellent selectivity
_ Single Sideband Synchronous AM Detector: selectable USB/LSB or double sideband to minimize adjacent frequency interference and fading distortion of AM signals
_ IF Passband Tuning: an advanced tuning feature that functions in AM and SSB. Greatly helps reject interference
_ Tuning Modes: variable-rate tuning knob, direct keypad frequency entry, up/down pushbuttons and auto-tuning
_ Direct Shortwave Band Entry, allows instant access to the shortwave band of choice
_ Selectable AGC: fast and slow mode
_ Display Backlighting: evenly lit backlight enables display viewing under all lighting conditions
_ Dual Programmable Clocks With WWV Auto-Setting
_ Dual-Event Programmable ON/OFF Timers: can be used for recording or 'alarm clock' function
_ Power Source: 4 "D" Batteries (not included); AC Adapter (included)
_ Dimensions: 13"W x 7-1/2"H x 2-1/2"D
_ Weight: 4 lb 3 oz.

XM Satellite Radio subscription and antenna sold separately.

etón®
RE_INVENTING™ RADIO
www.etoncorp.com

2006 Passport® to

World Band Radio

International Broadcasting Services, Ltd.

ISSN 0897-0157

OUR READER IS THE MOST IMPORTANT PERSON IN THE WORLD!

Editorial

Editor in Chief	Lawrence Magne
Editor	Tony Jones
Assistant Editor	Craig Tyson
Consulting Editor	John Campbell
Founder Emeritus	Don Jensen
PASSPORT REPORTS	George Heidelman, Lawrence Magne, Dave Zantow, George Zeller
WorldScan® Contributors	Azizul Alam Al-Amin (Bangladesh), Gabriel Iván Barrera (Argentina), David Crystal (Israel), Alok Dasgupta (India), Graeme Dixon (New Zealand), Nicolás Eramo (Argentina), Paulo Roberto e Souza (Brazil), Alokesh Gupta (India), Jose Jacob (India), *Jembatan DX/* Juichi Yamada (Japan), Anatoly Klepov (Russia), Marie Lamb (U.S.), Célio Romais (Brazil), Nikolai Rudnev (Russia), David Walcutt (U.S.)
WorldScan® Software	Richard Mayell
Laboratory	Robert Sherwood
Artwork	Gahan Wilson, cover
Graphic Arts	Bad Cat Design; Mike Wright, layout
Printing	Tri-Graphic Printing

Administration

Publisher	Lawrence Magne
Associate Publisher	Jane Brinker
Offices	IBS North America, Box 300, Penn's Park PA 18943, USA; www.passband.com; Phone +1 (215) 598-9018; Fax +1 (215) 598 3794; mktg@passband.com
Advertising & Media Contact	Jock Elliott, IBS Ltd., Box 300, Penn's Park PA 18943, USA; Phone +1 (215) 598-9018; Fax +1 (215) 598 3794; media@passband.com

Bureaus

IBS Latin America	Tony Jones, Casilla 1844, Asunción, Paraguay; schedules@passband.com
IBS Australia	Craig Tyson, Box 2145, Malaga WA 6062; addresses@passband.com
IBS Japan	Toshimichi Ohtake, 5-31-6 Tamanawa, Kamakura 247-0071; Fax +81 (467) 43 2167; ibsjapan@passband.com

Library of Congress Cataloging-in-Publication Data

Passport to World Band Radio.
1. Radio Stations, Shortwave—Directories. I. Magne, Lawrence
TK9956.P27 2005 384.54'5 05-22739
ISBN 0-914941-61-5

Opener credits: M. Guha (pp. 10, 38, 384); M. Wright (pp. 60, 72, 84, 94, 98, 156, 160, 182, 190, 206, 234, 294, 362, 404, 414); R. Sherwood (p. 212).

Tune in the world with Icom

IC-R75 *Tune in the world!* • 30 kHz - 60.0 MHz • AM, FM, S-AM, USB, LSB, CW, RTTY • 101 Alphanumeric Memory Channels • Twin Passband Tuning (PBT) • Synchronous AM Detection (S-AM) • DSP with Noise Reduction Auto Notch Filter • Triple Conversion • Up to Two Optional Filters • Front Mounted Speaker • Large Display • Well Spaced Keys and Dials • PC Remote Control with Optional Icom RSR75 Software for Windows® • And Many Other Features

Handheld Receivers

IC-R3 • 500 kHz – 2.45 GHz* • AM, FM, WFM, AM-TV, FM-TV • 450 Alphanumeric Memories • CTCSS with Tone Scan • 4 Level Attenuator • Antenna with BNC Connector • 2" Color TFT Display with Video and Audio Output Jacks • Lithium Ion Power

IC-R5 • 150 kHz – 1.3 GHz* • AM, FM, WFM • 1250 Alphanumeric Memories • CTCSS & DTCS Decode • Weather Alert • Dynamic Memory Scan • Icom's Hot 100 Preprogrammed TV & Shortwave Channels • Weather Resistant • AA Ni-Cds & Charger

IC-R20 • 150 kHz – 3.3 GHz* • AM, FM, WFM, USB, LSB, CW • 1250 Alphanumeric Memories • CTCSS & DTCS Decode • Dual Watch • Audio Recorder • Weather Alert • Dynamic Memory Scan • Icom's Hot 100 Preprogrammed TV & Shortwave Channels • Lithium Ion Power

All Icom receivers are PC programmable. See your dealer for details.

AMATEUR | AVIONICS | LAND MOBILE | MARINE | **RECEIVER** | WWW.ICOMAMERICA.COM

*Cellular frequencies blocked on US versions.
©2005 Icom America Inc. The Icom logo is a registered trademark of Icom Inc. All other trademarks remain the property of their respective owners. All specifications are subject to change without notice or obligation. 7642

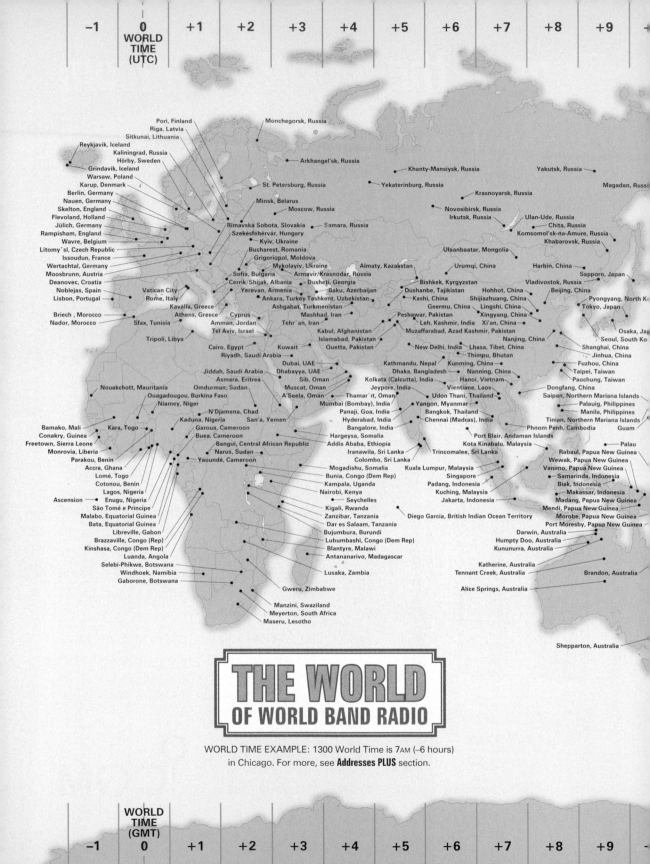

THE WORLD
OF WORLD BAND RADIO

WORLD TIME EXAMPLE: 1300 World Time is 7AM (–6 hours)
in Chicago. For more, see **Addresses PLUS** section.

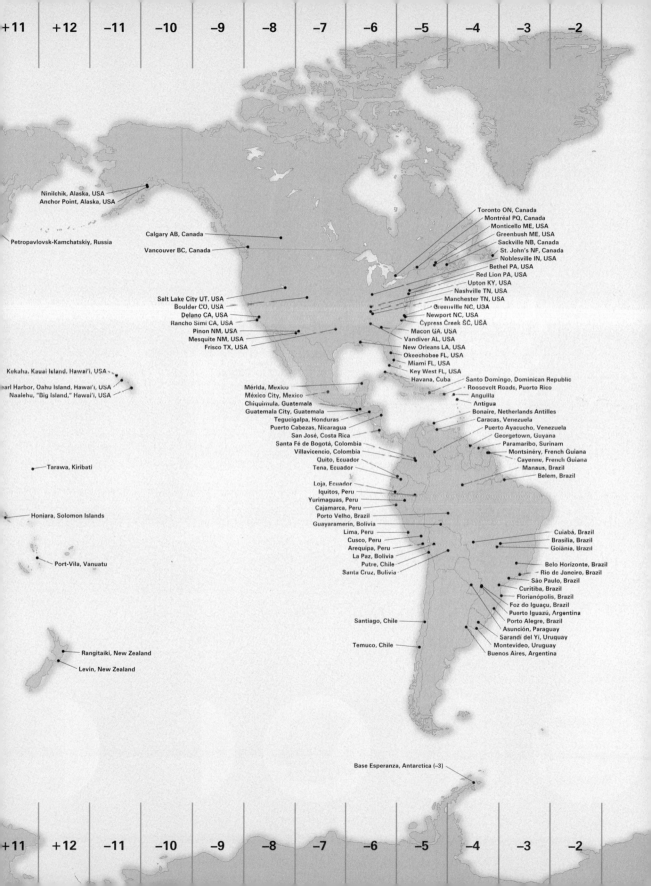

Re_Inventing Radio through Innovation

The E1XM is the world's first radio to combine AM, FM, Shortwave, and XM Satellite Radio Ready technology into one ultra-high-performance unit.

XM Satellite Radio subscription and antenna sold separately.

E1XM

AM/FM/Shortwave/XM Satellite Ready Radio

Building off of a 25-year tradition of manufacturing the finest high-end tabletop receivers in the world, the E1 is designed without compromise to give you direct access to news, sports and music from around the world.

_ AM/FM/Shortwave/XM Satellite Ready Radio
_ Frequency Coverage: 100-30,000 KHz, includes shortwave, medium wave AM broadcast band and longwave; 76-90, 87-108 MHz FM broadcast band; XM Satellite Ready Radio
_ Reception Modes: AM, FM-stereo, Single Sideband (selectable USB/LSB) and CW
_ Digital Display: large 5.7 inch square, 240 x 320 pixel, dot matrix display. Shows all modes and selected functions
_ Programmable Memories: 500 user programmable with alpha labeling plus 1200 user definable country memories, for a total of 1700
_ Memory Scan Function
_ Digital Phase Lock Loop (PLL) Synthesized Tuning with Direct Digital Synthesis (DDS) for drift-free frequency stability and finest tuning resolution
_ Dual Conversion Superheterodyne Circuit: results in minimized interference through superior selectivity
_ Excellent Sensitivity: yielding a true high-performance receiver
High Dynamic Range: allowing for detection of weak signals in the presence of strong signals
_ Selectable Bandwidths: 7.0, 4.0, 2.5 kHz for excellent selectivity
_ Single Sideband Synchronous AM Detector: selectable USB/LSB or double sideband to minimize adjacent frequency interference and fading distortion of AM signals
_ IF Passband Tuning: an advanced tuning feature that functions in AM and SSB. Greatly helps reject interference
_ Tuning Modes: variable-rate tuning knob, direct keypad frequency entry, up/down pushbuttons and auto-tuning
_ Direct Shortwave Band Entry, allows instant access to the shortwave band of choice
_ Selectable AGC: fast and slow mode
_ Display Backlighting: evenly lit backlight enables display viewing under all lighting conditions
_ Dual Programmable Clocks With WWV Auto-Setting
_ Dual-Event Programmable ON/OFF Timers: can be used for recording or 'alarm clock' function
_ Superior Audio Quality via a bridged type audio amplifier, providing high output power with battery operation
_ Power Source: 4 D Batteries (not included); AC Adapter (included)
_ Dimensions: 13"W x 7-1/2"H x 2-1/2"D
_ Weight: 4 lb 3 oz.

E1

AM/FM/Shortwave/DAB Ready Radio

Satellite radio brings premium music, news, and sports radio directly to you. The E1 is the world's first radio to combine AM, FM, Shortwave, and DAB (Digital Audio Broadcasting) technology into one ultra-high-performance unit. The finest portable in the world, the E1 offers powerful reception through its digitally synthesized PLL tuner with synchronous detector, passband tuning, selectable bandwidth filters. Offering rich sound, the latest in radio technology, 1700 station presets, and memory scan function, the E1 is designed without compromise, giving you direct access to news, sports, and music from around the world.

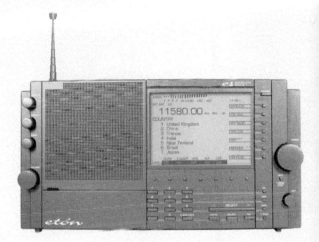

www.etoncorp.com

China's Radio: Size Matters

by Manosij Guha

China has had the world's longest continuous civilization for over 4,000 years. Its twenty-odd provinces, five autonomous regions, four municipal provinces and two special administrative regions are home to windy plateaus, towering mountains, arid deserts and majestic rivers. Size and diversity make it more like a continent than a country.

Its Confucian outlook has been a Petri dish for artistic refinement and scientific achievement. This was evident early in China's history, but much of China's great civilization was undone in the 19th and early 20th centuries by internal strife, wars, famines and foreign occupation.

Only after World War Two was China able to reassert its sovereignty, albeit under the aegis of communism. In the two decades that followed, everyday life came under strict scrutiny. Personal freedom was circumscribed, while tens of millions perished from famine and purges.

Markets Freer than Citizens

A change in communist leadership in 1978 resulted in market-driven policies that have turned China into the fastest-growing economy in world history. Inefficient collective farms, state-run industries and other Marxist nostrums have given way to free markets and burgeoning private enterprise.

Affordable chic: Copycat designer chic graces China's catwalks as well as sidewalks. M. Guha

There has also been a resurgence of travel and private personal ownership—all indicators of a healthy society. For the ordinary citizen with an improved quality of life and earning potential, this has ushered in an era of good cheer. But this outward prosperity has not yet translated into intellectual and creative freedom. China's media are tightly controlled by the central government, which also limits access to foreign news by restricting rebroadcasting and satellite receivers, jamming foreign world band broadcasts and blocking websites.

Liu Min, who prefers her English name April, is a twentysomething web designer. With her chic appearance and exotic Hebei features, she could easily be mistaken for a model on the catwalks of Beijing. She muses, "For young people, it is really bad. Things move really very slowly. I have decided not to worry about politics and move on." This is common sentiment among the young and restless in China's metropolises—at least during the current dawning of a consumer society.

China's government jams foreign broadcasts and blocks websites.

As economic growth has not been matched by political reform, there is great disparity between urban and rural China. Rampant corruption, epidemics, pollution and environmental degradation have stolen China's economic thunder in the hinterland. This has given rise to bloody protests, along with large-scale migration to the wealthy eastern coast.

China's exports to the United States have grown by 1,600 percent over the past 15 years, while U.S. exports to China have grown by only 415 percent. M. Guha

The Forbidden City was *verboten* to the public for 500 years. Its ramparts and moats reflect Chinese society, which is both multilayered and restrictive.   M. Guha

Nuclear Minuet

Chinese saber rattling towards Taiwan has acquired unsettling overtones. The People's Republic considers the island to be a renegade province that must be reunited with the mainland, by force if necessary. Most Taiwanese and Americans beg to differ.

China has threatened to invade should Taiwan move towards independence. Simultaneously, it has greatly expanded its capacity to take offensive military action beyond the mainland. In 2005 this lurched beyond diplomatic poker. A senior Chinese general threatened to launch preemptive nuclear destruction of American cities should the United States appear ready to defend Taiwan from a Chinese attack.

Operator attends to transmitting apparatus inside the studios of JQAK, Manchuria, in October 1930.
Simon Green/Eric Shackle Collection, Radio Heritage Foundation

Although this threat was scarcely mentioned in the American media, months later the Bush administration greatly upgraded American ties with India, which along with Japan is one of China's major rivals in the region. Subsequently, the administration played its follow-up hand by moving to improve military ties with China.

EARLY RADIO IN CHINA

The history of radio in China is as checkered as the internal turmoil, invading armies, occupation forces and puppet governments. Broadcasting was found to be an effective complement to the war culture by offering official information, instructions and propaganda.

Americans Establish First Stations

Nonetheless, the first station in China was actually a commercial enterprise established by no less than an American. Prof. Chia-shih Hsu, writing in *Broadcasting in Asia and the Pacific*, explains that the Yank, Mr. P. Osborn, was simply a businessman. In December 1922, along with his Chinese friend Mr. Tseng, he set up the station with a 50 Watt transmitter in Shanghai's Tai Lai department store.

A second station was established on January 23, 1923 in cooperation with a local news-

East meets West in the former Portuguese territory of Macau.
M. Guha

paper that also provided the first newscast. It used the callsign XRO and identified as the "Continent News-China Radio," indicating joint ownership with "Continent News," a leading newspaper in the city. However, the station had been established illegally, which presumably explains its premature demise that July.

The third station in China's early radio market was also founded by Americans—the firm of Kellogg Switchboard Supply Company—and based in Shanghai. It fired up a year later, in April 1924.

The imperial government in China did not take up broadcasting until 1927, when they constructed stations in Tientsin and Beijing (then Peking) under the Ministry of Communications. Several provincial governments followed suit with their own facilities.

Nationalist Era Boosts Radio

During the pre-communist era, the most notable development in Chinese broadcasting came under the Kuomintang (Nationalist Party) government at their national capital in the eastern city of Nanjing. First off the block was the 100 Watt XOH in October 1927. With the rising importance of the Nationalist government in China, the station moved up in stature a year later to become the Central Broadcasting Station on August 1, 1928 under callsign XKM.

When the Japanese invaded Shanghai on January 28, 1932 the station began its first international broadcast in Japanese. Called XGOA, it was quickly dubbed "the bush warbler of Nanjing" because of its noisy transmissions. Later that year, on August 13, 1932, a 75 kW transmitter—mighty power in those days—appeared under yet another callsign, XGOP. Following tests, it became a powerful voice throughout the whole of China and Southeast Asia. When the capital, Nanjing, fell to the Japanese in 1937, the Chinese government hastily relocated to Chongqing. Yet, the Central Broadcasting Station never once left the air.

The station resumed normal operation in March 1939 when its broadcasts were ex-

China's new affluence has not percolated down to its vast rural population, which still ekes out a subsistence living. M. Guha

Re_Inventing Radio through Design

The S350 family of field radios brings a
blend of the best of yesterday and today.

S350 Deluxe

High-Performance Field Radio with Stereo Headphones

For S350 devotees the deluxe model combines a sporty new exterior with the same unrivalled functionality.

_ Highly sensitive analog tuner with digital display
_ Large, full range speaker with bass & treble control
_ Clock, alarm, and sleep timer
_ Built-in antennas and connections for external antennas
_ Headphones included
_ Dimensions: 12-1/2"W x 7"H x 3-1/2"D
_ Weight: 3 lb. 4 oz.
_ Power Source: 4 D or AA Batteries (not included) or AC Adapter (included)
_ Available colors: Metallic Red, Black
■ ■

Improvements over S350:

_ FM- stereo via headphones (included)
_ AM/Shortwave Frequency Lock
_ Set clock and alarm
_ Operates on 4D or 4AA batteries

S350

Ruggedly Retro

The S350 blends the best of yesterday and today. With the look of a retro field radio sporting a rugged body and military-style controls – the S350 also features today's innovation for excellent AM, FM, and Shortwave reception and a large, full-range speaker for clear sound.

_ AM/FM/Shortwave radio reception
_ Highly sensitive and selective analog tuner circuitry
_ Liquid Crystal Display (LCD), for frequency and clock display.
_ Digital clock with selectable 12/24 hour format
_ Wake-up timer (use as radio-play alarm clock)
_ Power failure backup feature
_ Sleep timer
_ Main tuning knob and independent fine-tuning control knob
_ Dimensions: 10-3/4"W x 7"H x 3-18-1/2"D
_ Weight: 3 lb. 2 oz.
_ Power Source: 4 D Batteries (not included) or AC Adapter (included)

Synthetic Wall: This section of the Great Wall was built especially for tourists, like an attraction at a theme park.   M. Guha

metropolises of Shanghai, Tientsin, Beijing, Hanchow and Canton.

During this time radio played a tremendous role in mobilizing the Chinese population. It was the only medium of communication between people in free areas with compatriots in Japanese-occupied zones. Radio not only conveyed government propaganda, but like today's Internet it also provided information for clandestine newspapers and underground fighters.

After V-J Day the Central Broadcasting Network quickly established itself in newly liberated territories, increasing medium-wave AM affiliates from 39 to 72. Reflecting its new role, the network was renamed the Broadcasting Corporation of China. In 1949, after the Communist Party came to power in China, the station, along with what was left of the Nationalist government, relocated to the island redoubt of Taiwan.

Occupiers Expand Broadcasting

The Japanese occupation of Manchuria, a region along the country's east coast, provided a thrust for radio broadcasting in China. In September 1931, the Japanese invaded Manchuria, renamed it Manchukuo and installed Pu Yi, the last Manchu king, to head a puppet regime. Bernardo Bertolucci's critically acclaimed film "The Last Emperor" portrays this in fascinating detail.

As the civil war among Nationalists, Communists and Japanese progressed, a plethora of stations expanded, closed down or changed hands in rapid succession. Most operated at low power on mediumwave AM, but a few were on longwave or world band.

As detailed by declassified internal documents of the Japanese Imperial Government, in March 1925 experimental broadcasts were conducted at the Radiophone Institution in the Kanto agency under the Dalian maritime bureau. In July the station was solidified as JQAK on a 500 Watt mediumwave AM transmitter on 645 kHz, identifying as the Dalian Broadcasting Station. Manchukuo's first station, it began in earnest on August 6 with news, music, lectures, weather

panded. A month earlier an external service, XGOX, had also launched, identifying itself as Central Shortwave Radio. It targeted not only neighboring Japan, but also Germany, Europe and North America. A year later it saw further expansion and was renamed the International Broadcasting Station.

After the end of World War Two, it reverted to its earlier location in Nanjing. By then, the broadcasting apparatus of the Nationalist government was the center of a network of ten affiliated stations within China.

Before and during the War, there were 81 broadcast and point-to-point stations—11 run by the Nationalist government, three by the Ministry of Communications, 18 by provincial and local governments, two by the military, and 47 by private organizations. Private stations huddled mainly in the

and public announcements. There was a listener's license fee of one yen, renewable each year.

Adrian Peterson, eminent radio historian, writes that in 1927 a station with the same call letters, JQAK, existed at Port Arthur—also known by the Chinese name of Lushun. Not very far from the present-day city of Dalian, it used 5 kW on 770 kHz medium-wave AM.

Around that same time, radio broadcasting started in the then-British colony of Hong Kong. Radio Hong Kong was established on June 30, 1928 by a band of radio amateurs, and was formally inaugurated on February 1, 1929 under the office of the governor-general. Using callsign ZBW, it operated primarily in English with 250 Watts on mediumwave AM.

On August 19, 1932 the French settlement in Shanghai started its own 250 Watt station using callsign XFFZ. The Portuguese colony of Macau wasn't far behind when it fired up radio facilities in August 1933.

Hong Kong, Manchukuo Add World Band

In 1935 Radio Hong Kong had its international debut when it added its first world band transmitter, ZBW2. It managed to remain on the air throughout the Japanese occupation.

Meanwhile, by 1934, under the direction of the Japanese Army of North China and the provisional Chinese government, all broadcasting matters in Manchukuo were entrusted to the Japan Broadcasting Corporation (NHK). The NHK also dealt with construction and management of stations under Japanese control, such as Nanjing, Hankou, Hangzhou and Suzhou—also Beijing, which had become a large 50 kW operation.

In early 1935 the Manchuria Telephone and Telegraph Company launched a station on mediumwave AM using callsign MTCY. It had a mighty transmitter of 100 kW—one of three behemoths manufactured by the Nippon Electric Company. According to the internal publication *NEC Corp 1899-1999*, "In

China's economic boom has come at the cost of its environment. Its pristine landscape is being steadily denuded.   M. Guha

response to subsequent requests for higher power equipment, Nippon Electric began designing 100kW broadcasting equipment in 1933. The 100 kW broadcasting equipment was delivered to the Hsinking [today's Changchun] Broadcasting Station of the Manchuria Telegraph and Telephone Corporation in 1934."

These innovative transmitters were extremely large and an engineering marvel. The remaining two units were installed as part of the Japanese system in Seoul, Korea and Minxiong (Minhsiung), Taiwan. The latter, which survived American strafing during World War Two, has been preserved and still works.

The mediumwave AM facility in Lushan, Manchukuo, was upgraded to include a 10 kW shortwave transmitter and a new studio.

Japanese announcer
Hara Kiyoko was the
first announcer for the
Communists. She often
rode a donkey to reach
the cave studio.   CRI

Operating under callsign JDY, its first world band transmission aired on July 16, 1937.

The end of that year was marked with much fanfare, thanks to a special "Bells on New Year's Eve" program on December 31, 1937. This was relayed by all stations in Manchuria as well as in Tianjin and Shanghai, along with Taipei and Seoul in Japanese-occupied Taiwan and Korea.

Test broadcasts from a new 20 kW world band transmitter at Manchukuo's MTCY began in June 1939, and a second such transmitter was added two years later. Much of

Wei Lin, CRI's first announcer, retired in 1983.
Nevertheless, she volunteered to do part-time work for
CRI's English Service.   CRI

this type of Japanese broadcasting prowess was also showcased at the 1938 Olympic Games in Tokyo.

COMMUNIST-ERA RADIO

The Communist Party of China, supported by the Soviet Comintern, established its first radio station on September 5, 1945 at a temple about 19 miles from Yan'an in northern Shaanxi province. Using only 300 Watts, it identified as the Yan'an Hsin Hua (New China) Broadcasting Station. It was on the air two hours a day with programs intended for Kuomintang-held territories.

Overseas broadcasts started a couple of months later on December 3, 1945 after Japanese announcer Hara Kiyoko arrived at the studio on a donkey. A second station, Chang Kiakow (Kalgan) Hsin Hua Broadcasting Station, began about the same time in the northeastern Hopeh (Hebei) province. As the civil war progressed, yet another station was set up at the foot of the Taihang mountains in the village of Shahe, also in Hebei province.

Wolves Prowl Debut in English

Broadcasts were expanded to three hours in 1947, and a 20-minute English segment was added on September 11. At 8:40 PM local time the voice of communist-controlled

CRI Towers: CRI's state-of-the-art headquarters are unmistakable along Beijing's western horizon.
CRI

China reached the outside world in English for the first time. Its studio was in a cave so primitive that announcers carried flashlights to keep wolves at bay.

News was read by a young pigtailed woman named Wei Lin, now in her early eighties. "The studio was in a doorless cave with no proper equipment," reminisces Wei, "and only a kerosene lantern for lighting. Whenever we started broadcasting, we had to hang up a coarse felt blanket to keep out the bleating of nearby sheep."

Tape recorders did not exist then, nor did any music library except for a lone recording of the Triumphal March from the opera Aïda. Other singing was simply done live into the microphone.

People's Republic Inaugurates Broadcasting

When the People's Republic was founded in 1949, the station followed the government to Beijing and was renamed the Central People's Broadcasting Station. It broadcast 15 and a half hours a day over a network of 89 transmitters at 49 stations. Seventeen were new stations, with the remainder having been confiscated from the defeated Kuomintang.

Programming consisted mostly of news, editorials from newspapers, lectures on natural sciences and Marxism-Leninism. Entertainment included revolutionary and folk songs, as well as drama and Russian music. As now, it was mandatory for all provincial and local stations to relay news, commentaries and other political programming from the Central Station.

Despite an equipment shortage, radio experienced major growth in the 1950s, expanding to 122 stations by 1959 and 151 by 1967. By 1970 the Central People's Broadcasting Station had mushroomed to 713 mediumwave AM, 307 world band and one FM transmitter. Forty-six of these world band transmitters were operated by the China Press Agency, a subsidiary of Xinhua, for transmitting the daily news file to domestic and foreign audiences.

Collective Listening to Wired Broadcasts

A byproduct of inadequate radio facilities in the 1950s was wired broadcasting. To educate often-illiterate masses, all factories, schools, offices and the People's Liberation Army were required to have human broadcast monitors. They would listen to news from the central and provincial stations, then absorb political instructions and other announcements. Afterwards, they would rehash this material over loudspeakers connected to rudimentary studios supervised by local party cells. Citizens were "encouraged" to listen collectively.

This clunky scheme was later upgraded to a wired broadcasting network where audio from a central receiver was amplified and distributed over the existing loudspeaker network. Soon, loudspeakers invaded every sphere of social life, creating a constant din that few could avoid.

Since then, the Central People's Broadcasting Station has become known internationally as China National Radio (although its Chinese on-air name is still CPBS), and is one of three central media organizations that include China Radio International and China Central Television. The State Administration of Radio, Film and Television controls all broadcasting, including studios and transmitters.

World Band Is Domestic Mainstay

China has one of the most extensive domestic networks in the world. Though world band is the mainstay, FM and mediumwave

AM are increasingly being used to cater to new audiences with different program streams. From its studios in downtown Beijing, China National Radio produces nine streams for a national audience, with dedicated channels for news, business, music, culture and minority programming.

Minority programs consist of three one-hour daily broadcasts in Korean, five in Mongolian, and four in Kazakh, Uighur and Tibetan. Additionally, there are stations dedicated to broadcasts for Taiwan and Vietnam.

No less than five stations along the eastern seaboard are dedicated to broadcasts for Taiwan. Best known is Voice of the Strait, operated by the People's Liberation Army from Fuzhou, capital of Fujian province in southeastern China just across from Taiwan. Broadcasting on world band, FM and mediumwave AM, programs are mainly in Chinese and Amoy, a language common to Fujian as well as Taiwan.

Thirty regional stations affiliated with China National Radio operate from the various provinces, autonomous regions and municipalities. There is extensive use of world

CONFISCATED AMERICAN TRANSMITTER

In the well stocked radio museum inside the CRI headquarters, it's hard to miss an old transmitter proudly on display. A plaque explains, "The BC-610E transmitter was first used at the New China (Xinhua) Broadcasting Station in northern Shaanxi Province during the late 1940s. It was left by the American military observation group during China's War of Liberation. When the Kuomintang organized attacks on the Liberation Army in Yan'an, the transmitter was transported to SheXian county in Hebei Province. Later, it was shipped to Pingshan in Hebei Province and used by the Shanbei New China Broadcasting Station. After liberation, it was used in Beijing until 1965."

This was effectively CPBS' first transmitter, and is remarkably similar to another transmitter at a radio museum near Taipei in Taiwan.

This American transmitter was one of the first used by Communist forces in China.

M. Guha

Re_Inventing Radio through Necessity

Crank it up or plug it in.
Batteries not required.

FR300
All-In-One

This all-in-one unit offers functionality and versatility that makes it ideal for emergencies. The FR300 provides you with AM/FM Radio, TV-VHF, NOAA, built-in flashlight, and cell phone battery life when you need it most. A great everyday flashlight, the two white LED lights help illuminate your pathway during an emergency, or use the red LED as a flashing beacon.

_ AM/FM/TV-VHF, NOAA radio reception
_ Built-in power generator recharges the internal rechargeable Ni-MH battery (Included)
_ Can be powered from four different sources:
  1. The built-in rechargeable Ni-MH battery that takes charge from the dynamo crank and from an AC adapter (AC adapter not included)
  2. 3 AA batteries (Not included)
  3. The AC adapter alone (AC adapter not included)
  4. The dynamo crank alone, even with no battery pack installed
  Built-in white LED light source
_ Cell-phone charger output jack 3.5mm (various cell phone plug tips included)
_ Incorporates a fine-tuning control knob superimposed on the main tuning control knob
_ Built-in 2 white LED light source and one flashing red LED
_ Siren
_ Weather Alert
_ Dimensions: 6-1/2"W x 6"H x 2-1/2"D
_ Weight: 1 lb. 3 oz.

FR250
Multi-Purpose

Stay informed and prepared for emergencies with this self-powered 3-in-1 radio, flashlight and cell-phone charger — no batteries required. The Hand-Crank Power Generator gives you unlimited power for AM/FM Radio, 7 International Shortwave Bands, Built-in flashlight, and cell phone battery life when you need it most.

_ AM/FM/Shortwave radio reception
_ Built-in power generator recharges the internal rechargeable Ni-MH battery (Included)
_ Can be powered from four different sources:
  1. The built-in rechargeable Ni-MH battery that takes charge from the dynamo crank and from an AC adapter (AC adapter not included)
  2. 3 AA batteries (Not included)
  3. The AC adapter alone (AC adapter not included)
  4. The dynamo crank alone, even with no battery pack installed
_ Built-in white LED light source
_ Cell-phone charger output jack 3.5mm (various cell phone plug tips included)
_ Incorporates a fine-tuning control knob superimposed on the main tuning control knob
_ Built-in 2 white LED light source and one flashing red LED
_ Siren
_ Dimensions: 6-1/2"W x 6"H x 2-1/2"D
_ Weight: 1 lb. 3 oz.

etón®
RE_INVENTING™ RADIO
www.etoncorp.com

band, along with FM and mediumwave AM. All stations relay China National Radio from Beijing, along with their own programs.

Radio Peking Becomes China Radio International

China's external service, Radio Peking, began broadcasting on April 10, 1950 in English, Vietnamese, Indonesian, Burmese and Thai for seven hours daily to neighboring countries. Also, 17 and a half hours a week were in five Chinese dialects for Southeast Asia and overseas Chinese.

After the Korean war, the external service was further expanded, and by 1956 Chinese broadcasts had grown to 45 and a half hours a week. Also added were transmissions to Cambodia and Laos, English to Asia and the Middle East, and English and Spanish to Europe. Arabic, Farsi, Turkish and French were added in 1957 and 1958.

YUNNAN RADIO CONTINUES UPGRADING

Yunnan province's first station, Yunnan Radio in Kunming, appeared in 1932 during Japanese occupation. Situated in the old part of town, it was located in a small building that is now engulfed by a government housing estate. Operating under callsign XGOY, it made do with a modest 250 Watt world band transmitter.

On April 13, 1953 the station morphed into the Yunnan People's Broadcasting Station. Eventually, in 1990, it moved to its present home next to Yunnan TV in a fortified complex guarded by soldiers.

Sheng Hong Peng has been a senior reporter at the Yunnan station for many years. He reminisces, "At first the main program was in Chinese. Now, we are focused on minorities' programs in five languages. The first programs were reading newspaper clippings in those languages for 30 minutes each. That changed when news from outside the local newspapers was covered."

Sheng Hong Peng.   M. Guha

Remembering the difficulties in field reporting in those days, he recalls, "We used very large tape recorders of Chongsun brand. Sometimes we would go on a field trip to Dali with smaller Japanese-made tape machines. We would travel for five days to reach the

remote areas, sometimes by bus, bullock carts or by simply walking. Sometimes it took one month to produce such a program. From those areas, a letter took a week to reach the station. Telegraph, and then, later, telephone, changed all that."

Variety of World Band Offerings

YPBS and CRI blanket the region and globe from two transmitter sites near Kunming.   YPBS

The station has 100 employees and airs two services on world band: a minority language service three times a day on 6937 kHz, and morning and evening broadcasts to Vietnam on 6035 kHz.

Radio Peking continued as the external service until 1983, when it was renamed Radio Beijing, reflecting the correct Chinese intonation of its capital city. Ten years later, on January 1, 1993, it adopted its present name of China Radio International (CRI).

CRI now broadcasts to the world daily in 38 foreign languages and five Chinese dialects for a total of 211 program-hours. To adequately cater to its expanded role as a major international broadcaster, CRI moved in 1997 to a new landmark skyscraper in the western part of Beijing. State-of-the-art digital facilities, provided by Siemens Austria, include central control, data storage, live broadcast systems and recording workstations. An impressive array of sophisticated studios in an ergonomic setting complete a picture of coolness.

Using the best of mixing consoles and microphones from Studer, Beyer Dynamic and Shure, the studios are used in live or re-

World band facilities nearest to Kunming are located in the villages of Lantau and Anning.

Lantau is only ten miles (15 km) away and is for domestic broadcasting. It originally housed one 20 kW world band transmitter and another of 50 kW, both probably of Russian origin. However, these were being upgraded during our visit in the summer of 2005 and, sure enough, improved signals began to appear by September. Co-located are a pair of mediumwave AM transmitters— 200 kW and 300 kW—shared between domestic and external services.

Yangyue Hao is not just a studio engineer—she also announces YPBS' traffic bulletins. M. Guha

Yunnan Radio and TV lies alongside a busy highway.
M. Guha

Anning, 20 miles (35 km) from Kunming, is larger and newer, with two 100 kW and two 500 kW transmitters to relay China Radio International, as well as Radio France Internationale's French programs to Southeast Asia. The 500 kW transmitters, made in the United States by Continental Electronics, were installed in 1994, while the 100kW senders were made by Japan's NEC.

CRI transmitters in the Kunming area are used to reach Africa, the Middle East, South and Southeast Asia, the Far East, Australia and the Pacific in two dozen languages.

cording configurations. In keeping with this work culture, most producers and announcers multitask—writing as well as recording, with everyone editing their own audio as a "one-person team." Finished programs are sent by file transfer to the central server where they are queued for eventual playout.

As production and transmission workflow is totally digital, a quiet efficiency prevails, especially in the CRI News Center. CRI employs about 2,000 people, mostly young computer-savvy professionals wired into an intranet. They churn out a phenomenal output 24/7, liberally using the Internet for research, communication and dissemination.

Added to the mix are audio and video feeds from China's official Xinhua news agency, Associated Press, CNN and Reuters. Incoming news is edited and fed into a centralized news pool, ready for use by the various language departments.

Wang Ling produces CRI's popular "Listener's Garden" from this state-of-the-art studio. CRI

Executives Describe CRI

The suave, soft-spoken Wang Lei is deputy director of CRI's English. He wears many hats, among them that of the department's news minder. He explains, "We are a news station, we try to be objective and neutral. We do enjoy a lot of press freedom in China.

"We, of course, have our own editorial policy. We do not have any restrictions on reporting. We can do any program as long as we do it properly. We not only report good news, but a lot of bad news."

Lin Shaowen is the other deputy director, sharing editorial responsibilities with Yang Lei. He interjects, "It is not in the Chinese culture to criticize. We might criticize a particular policy, but not the person."

News input is supplemented by CRI's foreign correspondents and bureaus. CRI opened its first overseas office in Tokyo on December 2, 1980, and subsequently expanded to 39 correspondents in 28 bureaus in as many countries. In the United States, the main CRI office is in Washington, with a satellite office in New York to cover the United Nations.

There is also an exchange program for producers and announcers who work with the Canadian Broadcasting Corporation and Australian Broadcasting Corporation. This provides CRI with a reliable source of experienced foreign staff.

Wang Lei fills in on the *raison d'être* of CRI. He explains, "There are a lot of changes in China, and we are building on that. We are trying to be interactive, more responsive with greater variety, and use foreign staff to anchor shows to attract the younger audience."

"China believes in gradual changes. Even five years ago it was unimaginable," says Lin Shaowen in a trademark baritone from his days as CRI correspondent in New York. "The gradual change started in 1978. Reports on corruption, accountability of public officials, decentralization in decision making—we are building a system with China's characteristic, that's what we are talking about."

CRI's Angels: Staff from CRI's large English Service stike an Apple-friendly pose.   CRI

Yang Lei continues, "Most of all, as China's role becomes bigger on the world stage we are trying to build interest in China and the changes that are happening here. That is a tremendous job that we have to do."

Lin Shaowen elaborates, "Young Chinese people have a lot of interest in the outside world. Overall economic growth is great, but there is disparity in some parts of the country. Eighty percent of the leadership is trying to bridge the rich-poor divide with equitable distribution of wealth. People in general have a better life than before."

Information Central—Master Control

Once an entire program is ready for broadcast, it is transferred to a bank of servers in the master control room, which is the nerve center for all operations. Located at the ground level of the building, it also the most secure wing, with armed PLA soldiers on guard round the clock.

With its banks of LCD panels and control desks, it could easily fit into the Johnson Space Center. Most functions are automated, with a lone engineer standing by at all times "just in case." There are five work shifts with four to five employees each, with video cameras in each studio so control room operators can peer in.

Recorded programs—six streams having 200 hours of programs in 43 languages—are sent by FTP to 16 servers in a totally automated playl-ist. Distribution of programs in the capital region is by fiber optic.

Large satellite antennas outside the building uplink to Sinosat-1 and Asiasat-3S, which feed domestic relay and world band transmitters across the country. Another antenna uplinks to three more satellites for distribution to CRI's many relay locations overseas.

CRI is a chief information source in English, the *lingua franca* of the world's elites.

English Service, Pride of The Fleet

Since the end of the Cold War, official American and European international broadcasters have been cutting back on English, particularly over world band. As in other areas where China has been taking over from the West, CRI has not let this opportunity pass it by. It has been systematically moving to be the chief information source for the world's elites in their *lingua franca* of English. Using world band and other audio delivery media, CRI enhances audience rapport by sending regular newsletters and feedback forms to listeners.

Thus it is that in China, where English is not even a second language, the English Service is CRI's most prized possession, occupying fully five floors. It employs 120 people,

including 40 to prepare programs and 48 to tend the website. Output of 136.5 hours of programs per day focuses on news, but includes a variety of features.

CRI English Service Deputy Director Yang Lei comments: "Many western listeners have a prejudice against us. They think we project the Chinese government only. We are trying to change that image by being a professional broadcaster and by covering every major international issue."

With news and features like "RealTime Beijing" and "Listeners' Garden," programming has improved markedly by any credible standard—and especially when compared to such Cultural Revolution soporifics as, "People of the world unite to defeat the U.S. imperialists and all their running dogs!"

RADIO BEIJING'S FINEST HOUR

On June 3, 1989 Chinese armed forces suppressed the Tiananmen Square pro-democracy protest. Although best remembered is the young man who stopped a tank with his body, another courageous incident has gone relatively unreported.

On June 4 an announcer at Radio Beijing's English Department broke in with this report:

> "This is Radio Beijing. Please remember June the third, 1989. A most tragic event happened in the Chinese capital, Beijing. Thousands of people, most of them innocent civilians, were killed by fully armed soldiers when they forced their way into the city. Among the killed are our colleagues at Radio Beijing."

He went on to describe the horrors of that day, then was arrested. Although unconfirmed, it is believed the reader or at least the scriptwriter was Wu Xiaoyang, son of one of China's most senior Communist Party officials. Wu is now a director at Hong Kong's Phoenix Satellite Television.

Radio Prague had a similar golden moment as Warsaw Pact invaders marched into that city in 1968, and similar incidents have surfaced on world band radio over the years. Each underscores that no matter how rigorously staffs are trained to parrot propaganda, at crucial moments the better among them will choose decency over career expediency.

The Gate of Heavenly Peace was once used to address crowds.   M. Guha

Radio Beijing's Tiananmen report, via satellite relay of a world band pickup, can be heard in full at http//www.albany.edu/talkinghistory/arch2001jan-june.html.

—*World DX Club* et al.

Affable Yang Lei is CRI-English's acting director while Mme. Li Peng is on study leave. Once CRI's UN correspondent in New York, his English is impeccable. M. Guha

Yang Lei candidly admits, "Earlier on, listeners, especially during the Cultural Revolution, criticized us as propaganda. But we don't receive letters like that anymore. This is an indication of the quality of our programming."

How many listeners does CRI have? Nobody knows—it's impossible to ascertain without credible surveys in target countries. In 2002 the station received 168,000 letters from listeners in more than 100 countries, but audience letters have been shown to be meaningless to measure listenership.

Still, CRI may have at least a feel for overall world band audience potential in the United States and Canada. Etón markets the lion's share of world band radios in North America, and nearly all Etón products are manufactured in China by Tecsun and Degen. Assume product life of roughly ten years, and *voilà!*—except that how frequently these radios are tuned to CRI still remains anybody's guess.

DELIVERY OPTIONS
EXPAND AUDIENCE

CRI uses world band transmission facilities with powers ranging from 100 to 500 kW; these dot the official transmitter map of the country, from Beijing in the east to Kashi in the extreme northwest. Some are run in conjunction with the associated regional station, but others are strictly for CRI programs. Complementing these are mediumwave AM transmitters that reach neighboring countries from 13 sites.

Some world band transmitters do double duty by jamming foreign broadcasts. Such activity has been documented from Beijing, Lingshi, Kashi and Ürümqi, while transmitters at Dongfang are solely for jamming.

ALLISS antennas are known for their flexibility and sturdiness. According to Reporters without Borders, these have been affixed by Thales, a French defense contractor, to transmitters near the city of Kashi in the Xinjiang autonomous region in the extreme northwest of the country. Some are for jamming foreign broadcasts, although many aren't. There are about a dozen similar sites strategically located around the country.

Recently there has been a furor over the jamming of "Sound of Hope," an expatriate station based in Mountain View, California. It airs news and cultural programs to China for four hours a day from a powerful world band transmitter in Taiwan. This jamming, which uses music or programming lifted from China National Radio, has been monitored at various Chinese locations, including the Xinjiang autonomous region and the cities of Dalian and Fuzhou.

JRC NRD-545

Legendary Quality. Digital Signal Processing. Awesome Performance.

With the introduction of the NRD-545, Japan Radio raises the standard by which high performance receivers are judged.

Starting with JRC's legendary quality of construction, the NRD-545 offers superb ergonomics, virtually infinite filter bandwidth selection, steep filter shape factors,
a large color liquid crystal display, 1,000 memory channels, scan and sweep functions, and both double sideband and sideband selectable synchronous detection. With high sensitivity, wide dynamic range, computer control capability, a built-in RTTY demodulator, tracking notch filter, and sophisticated DSP noise control circuitry, the NRD-545 redefines what a high-performance receiver should be.

- LSB, USB, CW, RTTY, FM, AM, AMS, and ECSS (Exalted Carrier Selectable Sideband) modes.

- Continuously adjustable bandwidth from 10 Hz to 9.99 kHz in 10 Hz steps.

- Pass-band shift adjustable in 50 Hz steps up or down within a ±2.3 kHz range.

- Noise reduction signal processing adjustable in 256 steps.

- Tracking notch filter, adjustable within ±2.5 kHz in 10 Hz steps, follows in a ±10 kHz range even when the tuning dial is rotated.

- Continuously adjustable AGC between 0.04 sec and 5.1 sec in LSB, USB, CW, RTTY, and ECSS modes.

- 1,000 memory channels that store frequency, mode, bandwidth, AGC, ATT, and (for channels 0–19) timer on/off.

- Built-in RTTY demodulator reads ITU-T No. 2 codes for 170, 425, and 850 Hz shifts at 37 to 75 baud rates. Demodulated output can be displayed on a PC monitor through the built-in RS-232C interface.

- High sensitivity and wide dynamic range achieved through four junction-type FETs with low noise and superior cross modulation characteristics.

- Computer control capability.

- Optional wideband converter unit enables reception of 30 MHz to 2,000 MHz frequencies (less cellular) in all modes.

JRC *Japan Radio Co., Ltd.*

Japan Radio Company, Ltd., New York Office —
2125 Center Ave., Suite 208, Fort Lee, NJ 07024
Voice: 201 242 1882   Fax: 201 242 1885

Japan Radio Company, Ltd. — Nittochi Nishi-Shinjuku Bldg.
10-1 Nishi-Shinjuku 6 chome, Shinjuku-ku, Tokyo 160-0023, Japan
Voice: 81 3 3348 3858   Fax: 81 3 3348 3938

Similar jamming is also directed against the India-based "Voice of Tibet," BBC World Service, Voice of America, Radio Free Asia, All India Radio, Radio Taiwan International, and to some extent the programs of "The Voice of Han" and other stations.

Relays Boost Overseas Signals

China's strategic location and armada of powerful transmitters has made it an ideal site for relays of foreign broadcasters. Powerful world band transmitters in Xi'an, Kashi, Kunming, and Beijing relay Radio Canada International, Radio France Internationale, Radio Exterior de España and Voice of Russia for several hours a day. Radio France Internationale and Voice of Russia additionally use mediumwave AM relays in Dongfang and Kunming to reach southern China and Southeast Asia. Also, a mediumwave AM transmitter of Radio 6 in Hong Kong relays the BBC World Service round the clock.

In turn, CRI programs are "swap" or otherwise relayed by world band transmitters at Sackville, Canada; Havana, Cuba; Bonaire, Netherlands Antilles; Montsinéry, French Guiana; Brasília, Brazil; Santiago, Chile; Bamako, Mali; Meyerton, South Africa;

Issoudun, France; Noblejas, Spain; Cerrik, Albania; and the Russian cities of Moscow, St. Petersburg and Samara.

On mediumwave AM, CRI is relayed by high-powered transmitters in Albania, Lithuania, Luxembourg and Moldova.

High Hopes for DRM

Both China Radio International and China National Radio have renewed their commitment to Digital Radio Mondiale (DRM). Hosting a conference on this technology, Chinese radio authorities showcased local Zhejiang Radio and TV Group to demonstrate DRM's potential. A new DRM-capable transmitter from Thales was used to demonstrate world band, while an existing 10-year old Harris DX 10 mediumwave AM unit was converted to DRM.

Local Placement Targets Youth

CRI, although a leading world broadcaster, can also be heard through local placement on FM and mediumwave AM in dozens of major international cities. "Young people don't listen to shortwave. That's why we devote a lot of effort to the web, plus we buy a lot of time on local stations around the

VOA: OUTSOURCE NEWS TO CHINA?

The Voice of America shortly hopes to implement a proposal to move the overnight news shift from Washington to Hong Kong. Night-shift employees who lose jobs in Washington would be transferred to other jobs, but the announcement nevertheless has created a stir among VOA's unionized employees—as well as on Capitol Hill.

Director Defends Decision

Jennifer Janin directs the VOA News Center in Hong Kong, its only news center outside Washington. She quickly denies any wrongdoing, explaining, "We have had this office in Hong Kong for many years. VOA has many bureaus across the world, and most correspondent bureaus have only two people. We are slightly larger, being the only news center outside Washington DC. We are hiring only eight people to do editorial tasks."

The main purpose of the overnight shift is to gather news from East Asia for use in the VOA's evening Asian programs, most of which begin around 1100 or 1200 World Time. Ms. Janin emphasizes, "Modern technology allows us to work from anywhere. So, it doesn't matter if we are in DC or Hong Kong. Even the time difference works to our advantage."

VOA Hong Kong bureau with empty desks waiting for new hires. M. Guha

From VOA management's perspective, it makes sense for Asian news to be gathered from Hong Kong, rather than Washington. Too, one editor would remain overnight in Washington to oversee the work of the eight staffers in Hong Kong.

Labor costs, of course, are much cheaper in China. Although the proposed job shuffle would involve only eight employees, it would save the VOA almost $300,000, including health care benefits. Nevertheless, the concept of having foreigners in a communist country gathering news for America's official voice guarantees that this issue will remain controversial for some time.

Local announcer at the VOA's small but sophisticated studio in Hong Kong. M. Guha

In three years Starbucks expects to have more stores in tea-drinking China than in the United States.   M. Guha

world," explains Yang Lei, acting director of CRI's English service.

CRI has been taking its expansion into local placement seriously over the last few years, and has set up an Overseas Development Office to oversee this activity. Currently, 202 hours of CRI programs in 28 languages and dialects air through local placement in more than 60 countries in the Americas, Europe, Africa, Asia and Oceania.

Young PLA soldiers maintain order in China's restrictive but secure society.   M. Guha

China Radio International has also renewed and extended its agreement with World Radio Network, the London-based global transmission provider. Through WRN, CRI's daily programs are heard on FM in Berlin and Moscow and on mediumwave AM in London and St. Petersburg, as well as across western Europe, southwest Russia, Ukraine and Romania.

CRI's programs in English, French, German and Russian are also carried on WRN's feeds to international news networks, then distributed worldwide via satellite, cable, local FM, wireless applications and the Internet. WRN also distributes CRI on key platforms such as Sirius Satellite Radio in the United States and Sky Digital in the United Kingdom and Ireland.

CRI has concluded a separate agreement to be heard on FM in Los Angeles, San Diego and New York, in addition to its existing liaison with WUST-AM in Washington. Additionally, more than ten other radio stations in North America and Europe carry "Real-Time China," a radio magazine specially produced for local rebroadcast.

CRI has also concluded a multi-year agreement with a satellite company which has a strong footprint over the Pacific, Atlantic and Indian Oceans. CRI will then be able to reach listeners in almost every corner of the globe in eight different languages over 36 satellite audio channels.

CRI Targets Domestic Audience

Since early 1984, CRI has been operating a "home" service to the Beijing area on FM and mediumwave AM. This has since been expanded to major cities across China: Shanghai, Guangzhou, Wuhan, Dalian and Xi'an. It serves an ostensibly young domestic audience with news, music and weather, but mainly it helps listeners hone their English-language skills without having to tune to foreign broadcasts.

CRI has also upped its informational role in Beijing by launching a new domestic mediumwave AM channel, CRI Newsradio, on 900 kHz. Aimed at expatriates in China, it repackages existing foreign language programs into a 24-hour stream of current affairs, finance, sports and entertainment.

Repackaging its foreign language output for the online community, CRI launched Inet Radio, its first online station, on July 14, 2005. Available at www.inetradio.cn, this narrowcasts in Chinese, English, German and Japanese with information, entertainment, music and language lessons.

Faith among the faithless: Devout Christians come out of the woodwork to worship quietly.   M. Guha

Also, www.crienglish.com is being developed as a one-stop portal for almost everything Chinese. This well-designed and media-rich site provides archived CRI audio streams, as well as program transcripts complemented by photos and illustrations.

Size matters. China is huge and growing in almost every sense, and this means there's available funding for a national broadcast voice second to none. PASSPORT's Tony Jones explains, "There's enough money for virtually all platforms: world band, mediumwave AM—particularly in Europe and Asia—satellite, Internet and FM."

China Aids Broadcasters

Coupled with its soft-power approach to emerging superpower status, the Chinese government also practices a unique brand of transmitter diplomacy. Here, grants of radio broadcasting equipment and expertise are factored into the overall political approach to allies.

> **There is funding for a world voice second to none.**

Recent beneficiaries have included Albania, Cuba, Equatorial Guinea and Zimbabwe. Grants to most nations have been benevolent, but Zimbabwe has used its aid to jam radio signals it doesn't like.

Beijing Radio Targets Cellphones

There are more mobile phones in China than people in the United States—some 350 million. Leaving no platform unturned, domestic broadcaster Beijing Radio has bought four 900 Watt Harris DAB 660 transmitters to broadcast six digital programs with moving images.

Foreign Policy Underscores Persuasion

Grateful Eastern European statesmen have emphasized that Western broadcasts, jammed though most were, did more to bring down the Iron Curtain than any other single activity. But with the Cold War generation of international broadcasting managers and experts now retired or eased aside, this success has been all but forgotten. While armies of democratic nations are on the march at great cost, Western international broadcasting is being shortchanged or turned over to PR and commercial radio mavens.

The pace of construction for the 2008 Olympics has been so rapid that the IOC has asked it to slow down.   M. Guha

China appears to be treading along a wiser path. Although the reasoning behind its ongoing armed forces buildup remains murky, those assets have thus far remained within the country while Chinese global influence has been accomplished, instead, through increasingly effective international broadcasts.

Re_Inventing Radio through Necessity
Crank it up or plug it in.
Batteries not required.

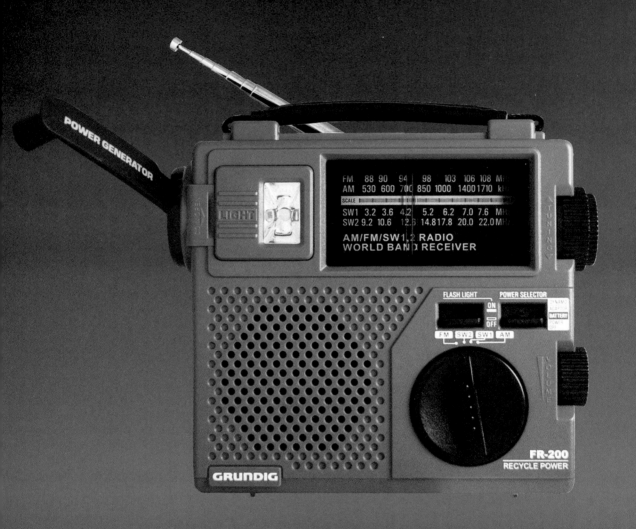

FR200
Crank it Up

Without the need for batteries, this self-powered 2-in-1 radio and flashlight helps you stay informed and prepared for emergencies. The Hand-Crank Power Generator gives you power for AM/FM radio, access to 12 international Shortwave bands, and a built-in LED flashlight.

_ AM/FM/Shortwave Radio Reception
_ Built-in power generator recharges the internal rechargeable Ni-MH battery (Included)
_ Can be powered from four different sources:
  1. The built-in rechargeable Ni-MH battery that takes charge from the dynamo crank and from an AC adapter (AC adapter not included)
  2. 3 AA batteries (Not included)
  3. The AC adapter alone (AC adapter not included)
  4. The dynamo crank alone, even with no battery pack installed
_ Built-in white LED light source
_ Dimensions: 6-1/2"W x 5-3/4"H x 2-1/4"D
_ Weight: 1 lb. 2 oz.
_ Available colors: Metallic Blue, Metallic Red, Sand

Mini 300PE
Compact and Power-Packed

Small enough to fit into your pocket, the Mini 300PE world-band radio makes a perfect travel companion. Its oversized telescopic antenna provides great AM/FM reception for camping, hiking, listening to sports, or just relaxing in the backyard. Also pulling in 7 shortwave bands, you will have access to both local and international news and music wherever you go.

_ Built-in clock, alarm, and sleep functions
_ Large easy-to-read LCD screen
_ Protective travel case and ear buds
_ Dimensions: 2-1/2"W x 4-1/2"H (not including 2-1/4" antenna stub) x 3/4"D
_ Weight: 4.5 oz.
_ Power Source: 2 AA Batteries
_ Available colors: Metallic Blue, Metallic Red, Yellow, Metallic Bronze, Metallic Pearl

Tibet: Making Waves Atop The World

by Manosij Guha

Sprawled across the towering Himalayas at an average of 15,000 feet, Tibet is the top of the world. Its lofty peaks include Mount Everest, while mountain lakes and glaciers give birth to such mighty waterways as the Yangtze and Indus. Once the remotest region in the world, its doors are opening to the world partly because of China's forcible occupation.

Lamas Supreme for Centuries

Since the 7th century Tibet has practiced its own brand of Buddhism that relies on incarnate religious leaders or lamas. Supreme is the Dalai Lama or "Ocean of Wisdom," with the Panchen Lama a close second in hierarchy and importance.

Tibet has attracted adventurers, invaders and ascetics with equal

gusto to imbibe its untold riches—material or otherwise. The devout-
ness of the people and their adherence to a code of nonviolence has
made them easy prey for marauding invaders, who since early times
have streamed across the nation's unguarded frontiers.

Tibet gradually acquired a spirit of nationhood, but the resulting kingdom was fractured by internecine rivalry. In a tumultuous history, it
has been conquered by powerful Chinese and Mongolian neighbors and
has twice dallied as a short-lived independent entity.

British Endorse Chinese Rule

More recently, Tibet became an unwitting pawn of Czarist Russia and
the British Empire in India, with each player wanting to bring the vast
kingdom under its sphere of influence. Both powers sent emissaries
to curry favor from the Dalai Lama—the temporal as well as spiritual
head.

The 1890 Sikkim-Tibet convention aimed at opening border trade was
rejected by Tibet, which ultimately led to a British military expedition
by Sir Francis Younghusband in 1904. Starting from his base in northeastern India—with 1,000 troops augmented by 10,000 servants and
4,000 yaks—he quickly overran the Gyantse fort in central Tibet.

Younghusband awaited word from the Tibetan government in Lhasa.
When none was forthcoming, he marched into Lhasa to find that the
Dalai Lama had taken refuge among his own people in Mongolia. The
British then established permanent missions in Lhasa and the western
city of Gartok.

In order to end Russian influence in the region, the Sino-British Agreement of 1906 was signed. As it provided a basis for permanent Chinese
rule over Tibet, this document between two foreign empires sealed
Tibet's fate.

Gyatsola Pass, at 17,126
feet, is only partway up
the high road to Lhasa.
M. Guha

> Radio became
> a key player
> in upheavals
> plaguing Tibet.

In high-rise Tibet, even
valleys and plateaus
can sock travelers with
mountain sickness.
M. Guha

Miss Wenxin produces such English programs as "Holy Tibet" at Xizang Radio-CTB. Xizang Radio

Radio Arrives, but not Broadcasts

Despite Tibetan rejection of modern civilization, during the 1930s fascinating new technology appeared: a point-to-point radio transmitter. This newfangled medium was to become a key player in upheavals that were to plague this isolated kingdom.

"Radio" entered the Tibetan vocabulary in 1934, when a new word for it had to coined. This happened when the Chinese emperor of the Qing dynasty sent General Huang Mu-sung on a condolence mission to commemorate the passing of the 13th Dalai Lama. Along with him came Tibet's first wireless transmitter. When the general returned to China, he left the contraption behind under the care of a trusted Chinese operator who worshiped its every bolt and capacitor.

Sir Basil's Drowned Transmitter

This flyspeck radio monopoly ended in 1936 with the arrival of the British Political Mission under Sir Basil Gould. With him came more up-to-date radio equipment so the Tibetan government could communicate with outlying officials. Alas, the Chinese radio operator's attachment to the old transmitter was so strong that he was reduced to tears.

Glowing obituaries in 2002 marked the death of Lieutenant-Colonel Sir Evan Nepean, Bart, the mission's radio operator. In both

the Weekly Telegraph and The Guardian, these provided anecdotal accounts of how wireless operations started in the remote region.

Nepean was a subaltern serving in the Peshawar District Signals in the North West Frontier province of India, in what is present-day Pakistan. He was assigned to the mission to Tibet in the summer of 1936, along with Lieutenant Sidney Dagg of the Royal Signals and Hugh Richardson, Britain's last diplomatic envoy in Lhasa.

The mission had been proposed by the government of Tibet, then temporarily under Regency rule between Dalai Lamas. The government wanted Britain to mediate for the return of the Panchen Lama, the second-most senior religious leader in Tibet, who had fled to China after falling out with the 13th Dalai Lama.

Nepean took to Lhasa a point-to-point transmitter built in the signals regiment's workshops at Rawalpindi, also in present-day Pakistan, along with a privately built receiver. This and all his other radio equipment was carried across the 14,600 foot (4,450 meter) Nathu-La pass from Sikkim in northeastern India into Tibet by a party of 50 men and 25 pack animals.

En route, the transmitter was accidentally dropped into a river and had to be rebuilt. Then the 120 pound (54 kilo) battery charging engine refused to work at Tibet's high altitude. Some returned to India to build a hand-cranked charger, then carried it back to Tibet. Given the altitude and distances involved, all this was no mean task.

Nepean set up his tent, transmitter and receiver in the Deyki Lingka garden, the mission's base. The aerial was supported by a 40 foot (12 meter) mast, and regular contact was kept up with India on 30 meters shortwave. Among other things, he helped to film the mission with a 16 mm movie camera and played soccer as a member of the "Mission Marinots" team against "Lhasa United."

However, radiocommunication on such a small scale was grossly inadequate, and many "Western" improvements were rolled back because of rivalry between the 13th Dalai Lama and the Panchen Lama.

Roosevelt Provides New Transmitters

Matters came to a head in 1942 when Chinese Nationalist troops took advantage of poor communication to penetrate deep into eastern Tibet. When President Roosevelt's envoys visited Lhasa later that year, Tibetan authorities had new radio transmitters high on their wish list. The hope was to set up wireless communications throughout the region, starting with the invasion-prone reaches of Chamdo, Gartok, Nagchuka, Tsona and Rima.

Their wish was realized. Three transmitters and five receivers were donated by the American government, and there was more: The British added two wireless sets and battery chargers, along with much-needed training of wireless operators.

Operator training was first undertaken in Lhasa, but eventually a number of young ethnic Tibetans from adjoining India were added. These served not only as radio operators in Lhasa, but also for the Tibetan army in the eastern province of Kham in present-day Sichuan. Thus, despite the reluctance of Tibetans to modernize, defense requirements kick-started wireless communication which led to the development of Tibetan broadcast radio.

Broadcasting Finally Begins

Radio equipment donated by the American government served a dual purpose. Besides being a communication lifeline to the far reaches of Tibet's vast territory, the same infrastructure was also used to initiate broadcasting to the public. In 1945 the United States government followed up its earlier aid with three broadcast studios, along with technicians to install equipment and train Tibetan journalists.

It was fully five years, in January 1950, before the station, Radio Lhasa, put out its first programs. It aired only half an hour each day at 5:00 PM local time—mostly news in

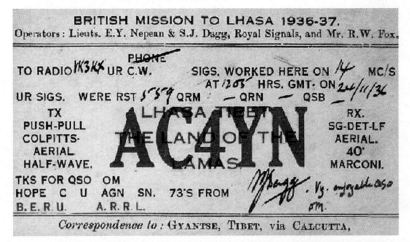

Verifications don't get much better than this card from Tibet's "drowned transmitter."

E1XM
World's First and Only

The E1XM is designed without compromise to give you direct access to news, sports and music from around the world.

_ AM/FM/Shortwave/XM Satellite Rea Radio
_ 1700 station presets
_ Digitally synthesized PLL tuner with synchronous detector
_ Passband tuning, selectable ban width filters and Selectable Sing Sideband (SSB) reception
_ Dual conversion superheterodyn circuit design

E10
AM/FM/Shortwave Radio

Intelligence meets performance in the E10. The E10 provides sophisticated tools for listening to news, sports, and music from around the world.

_ Shortwave range of 1711 – 29,9! KHz
_ 550 programmable memories wi memory page customization
_ Manual and auto scan, direct ke pad frequency entry, ATS
_ Clock with alarm, sleep timer, ar snooze functions

E100
AM/FM/Shortwave Radio

The E100 features a sleek design complimented by a portable physique. This little marvel is packed with all the latest radio features you want and it's small enough to fit in your coat pocket!

_ Shortwave range of 1711 – 29,9! KHz
_ 200 programmable memories
_ Memory page customization
_ Manual and auto scan, direct ke pad frequency entry

S350 Deluxe
High-Performance Field Radio with Stereo Headphones

For S350 devotees the deluxe model combines a sporty new exterior with the same unrivalled functionality.
_ FM- stereo via headphones (included)
_ AM/Shortwave Frequency Lock
_ Set clock and alarm

_ Highly sensitive analog tuner wi digital display
_ Large, full range speaker with bass & treble control
_ Clock, alarm, and sleep timer
_ Built-in antennas and connectio for external antennas
_ Available colors: Metallic Red, Black
■ ■

S350
Ruggedly Retro

With the look of a retro field radio sporting a rugged body and military-style controls – the S350 also features today's innovation for excellent AM, FM, and Shortwave reception and a large, full-range speaker for clear sound.

_ AM/FM/Shortwave Radio recepti
_ Highly sensitive and selective an log tuner circuitry
_ Liquid Crystal Display (LCD), for frequency and clock display.
_ Digital clock with selectable 12/2 hour format

G2000A
AM/FM/Shortwave Radio by F.A. Porsche

_ Protective case
_ Autoscan and direct keypad tuning
_ 20 customizable station presets
_ Dual alarms, and sleep timer

G1000A AM/FM/Shortwave Radio (not pictured)

G4000A
AM/FM/Shortwave Radio

_ SSB (Single Side Band)
_ 40 customizable station presets
_ Autoscan & direct keypad tuning
_ Alarm & sleep timer functions

FR200
Crank it Up

Without the need for batteries, this self-powered 2-in-1 radio and flashlight helps you stay informed and prepared for emergencies.

_ AM/FM/Shortwave Radio Reception
_ Built-in power generator recharges the internal rechargeable Ni-MH battery (Included)
_ Built-in white LED light source
_ 12 international bands
_ Available colors: Metallic Blue, Metallic Red, Sand
■ ■ ■

FR250
Multi-Purpose

Stay informed and prepared for emergencies with this self-powered 3-in-1 radio, flashlight and cell-phone charger — no batteries required.

AM/FM/Shortwave Radio Reception
_ Built-in power generator recharges the internal rechargeable Ni-MH battery (Included)
Cell-phone charger output jack 3.5mm (various cell phone plug tips included)
_ Built-in 2 white LED light source and one flashing red LED

FR300
All-In-One

This all-in-one unit offers functionality and versatility that makes it ideal for emergencies.

_ Weather alert

_ AM/FM/TV-VHF/NOAA Radio Reception
_ Built-in power generator recharges the internal rechargeable Ni-MH battery (Included)
_ Cell-phone charger output jack 3.5mm (various cell phone plug tips included)
_ Built-in 2 white LED light source and one flashing red LED

Mini 300PE
Compact and Power-Packed

Small enough to fit into your pocket, the Mini 300PE world-band radio makes a perfect travel companion.

_ Built-in clock, alarm, and sleep functions
_ Large easy-to-read LCD screen
_ Protective travel case and ear buds
_ Available colors: Metallic Blue, Metallic Red, Yellow, Metallic Bronze, Metallic Pearl
■ ■ ■ □

Drumming up support: Unlike in Tibet, traditional singing and dancing are cultural staples among Tibetan exiles. M. Guha

Tibetan and English, along with a newscast in Chinese read by Phuntsok Tashi Takla, the Dalai Lama's brother-in-law.

Radio Lhasa was used for official pronouncements, especially during major events. The first was the installation of the 14th Dalai Lama, which ran: "We have the honor to announce that Radio Lhasa will broadcast an announcement of the enthronement of His Holiness the Dalai Lama, the ruler of Tibet, together with a proclamation of the Tibetan government to the Tibetan people and the world, on Friday, November 17, 1950, at 5:45 PM Indian Standard Time."

As Tibet did not have its own time zone, the use of Indian Standard Time was commonplace. Today, "Beijing Time" is mandated for use throughout Tibet, putting Lhasa, despite its western location, in the same time zone as Perth, Australia.

Shortly afterwards, the Tibetan government set up a second station in Chamdo province towards the east, then a third in the town of Nagchuka in northeastern Tibet.

World Band Radios Commonplace

Since the mid-1930s it appears that a number of households in Lhasa and the other

big cities of Shigatse and Gyantse have had world band radios. The uncluttered airwaves provided clear reception not only of Radio Lhasa, but also Radio Peking, All India Radio and other stations broadcasting to the region.

Such was the zeal for radio reception that some enterprising individuals even built their own receivers, while aristocrats and lamas used their wealthier Muslim friends and business associates to monitor news from Indian broadcasts. This freedom of information is a far cry from present-day Tibet, where listening to unapproved broadcasts can mean confiscation of the receiver, denial of privileges and jail time.

Chinese Invasion Obliterates Identity

Just under a year after the launch of Radio Lhasa, the invading People's Liberation Army reached the city. This brought independent Tibet's broadcasting experiments to an abrupt end.

Peace proved to be elusive, given the widespread destruction, and about the only thing Tibetans were liberated of was their independence. Tibet's small and ill-equipped army was quickly overrun, and by the summer of 1951 Chinese troops were marching into the capital Lhasa.

Thus began the darkest chapter in Tibetan history. The invasion and its aftermath lead to 1.2 million deaths, massive destruction of historical edifices, wholesale atrocities against civilians, and the obliteration of Tibet's traditions and way of life. The nation was robbed of any sense of national identity.

The 16-year-old Dalai Lama was forced to come to terms with the Chinese, and tried to maintain an uneasy coexistence with the occupying forces. Nevertheless, the outlying provinces of Kham and Amdo were stripped from Tibet and annexed by the adjoining Chinese provinces of Sichuan, Gansu and Yunnan. Even now tensions between ethnic Tibetans and Chinese settlers continue to arise in these areas, usually over the great cultural and economic disparities between them.

Afterwards, the Chinese began in earnest to impose communist norms, whereupon the very essence of Tibetan life—Buddhism—came under threat. In 1956, the siege and bombing of Lithang Monastery in Kham sparked a revolt that transformed the region into a tinderbox of armed uprising. Khampa tribesmen, known for their martial skill, took to the hills to wage a guerrilla campaign.

Tibet Today

The Chinese Communist Party is now the ultimate political and administrative authority in Tibet. The region's party secretary is the key figure, and effectively runs the government of the Tibet Autonomous Region.

But this degree of control from Beijing didn't happen quickly or without a price. Monasteries which had been the epicenter of Tibetan life were destroyed en masse in the 1960s and 1970s during the "Great Proletarian Cultural Revolution." Countless Tibetan lives were lost, with notorious outrages being committed on Buddhist priests and nuns.

The Chinese authorities continue to suppress Tibetan identity. They closely monitor and punish monasteries viewed as hubs for Tibetan autonomy or the Dalai Lama, who

continues to live in neighboring India. "They even translate the songs that we sing to check if there's anything subversive" says a recent escapee, whose name roughly translates into "Happy Flower."

But happiness is the one thing she is not about, having left behind her entire family that she is unlikely to see again for years to come. "In school, all teachers are Chinese and we are taught hardly any Tibetan. We are encouraged to use Chinese pronunciation of Tibetan words. Our traditional dances have been changed to match the Chinese opera."

Nearly 3,000 Tibetans flee to Nepal every year, usually in winter when there is heavy snowfall along the southern border. She explains, "We took a bus to Shigatse, the

The Gyantse Kumbum's serene surroundings contrast with the historic battle fought below between the Tibetans and the British. M. Guha

Souvenir shops and an army camp have altered the aura of Tibet's revered Potala Palace. M. Guha

now comprise a 50 million dollar enterprise where even senior monks have been downgraded to tour guides and tourists get priority over Tibetan pilgrims.

Nowhere is this more obvious than at Lhasa's magnificent Potala palace, which is getting a 21 million dollar facelift. The magnificent edifice was once home to the Dalai Lama, and it is here that many of his predecessors are interred. For ordinary Tibetans, the palace is a venerated pilgrimage destination, but they are allowed to climb to the hilltop palace for only a few hours a day. All other times are reserved for high-paying tourists.

The Potala once bisected the capital into Tibetan and Chinese quarters. Now, rapid sinocization has replaced traditional markets and thoroughfares with broad avenues and shopping malls. Even the area before the venerated Jokhang temple now sports a large square that serves as a glorified bus depot and resting place for tourists.

One of the jewels of Chinese development in Tibet is the ongoing construction of a railway line from Lhasa to Xinning in western China. Touted as the highest railway in the world, it is expected to open in 2007, bringing an end to the isolation of the region while giving a massive boost to economic expansion. It would only facilitate migration of settlers from China, who lured by

new economic opportunities and incentives, have already been arriving in increasing numbers—to the point where Tibetans, like native Americans two centuries ago, are becoming a minority in their own land.

Autonomy or Independence?

The Dalai Lama, who continues to push for Tibetan independence, was awarded the Nobel Peace Prize in 1989. Since then there have been intermittent indirect contacts between China and the Dalai Lama as they seek some sort of workable solution.

Chinese pressure has meant apathy from world powers, which has forced the Dalai Lama to abandon outright Tibetan nationhood. Instead, he now advocates a nonviolent, negotiated solution and accepts the notion of genuine autonomy for Tibet under Chinese sovereignty. China, in turn, questions his claim that he does not seek full independence.

On the eve of his 70th birthday and after 50 years of Chinese rule, the Dalai Lama explained, "I once again want to reassure the Chinese authorities that as long as I am responsible for the affairs of Tibet, we remain fully committed to the Middle Way Approach of not seeking independence for Tibet and are willing to remain within the People's Republic of China. I am convinced that in the long run such an approach is of

Listening is only half the fun...
POPULAR COMMUNICATIONS
is the other half

The World's most authoritative monthly magazine for Shortwave Listening and Scanner Monitoring. Read by more active listeners world-wide.

You'll find features on scanner monitoring of police, fire, utility, and aircraft communications; international shortwave listening; CB radio; amateur radio; FRS; GMRS; monitoring radio digital communications including CW, RTTY, SITOR, etc; AM/FM commercial broadcasting; weather and communications satellites; telephone equipment and accessories; radio nostalgia; alternative radio; clandestine radio; and military radio.

Subscribe today and SAVE over 58% off the newsstand price (Save even more off 2- and 3-year subscriptions).

FOR FASTER SERVICE FAX 1-516-681-2926

Name _____ Call _____

Address _____

City _____ State _____ Zip _____

☐ **1 year 12 issues........$28.95**   ☐ **2 years 24 issues........$51.95**   ☐ **3 years 36 issues........$74.95**
Save $30.93   *Save $67.81*   *Save $104.69*

Canada/Mexico–one year $38.95, two years $71.95, three years $104.95. **U.S Dollars**
Foreign Air post–one year $48.95, two years $91.95, three years $134.95. **U.S Dollars**

Credit Card # _____ Exp. Date _____

☐ Check   ☐ Money Order   ☐ MasterCard   ☐ VISA   ☐ AMEX   ☐ Discover

Allow 6 to 8 weeks for delivery   PASS 06

Popular Communications, 25 Newbridge Road, Hicksville, NY 11801 Telephone (516) 681-2922
www.popular-communications.com

Woman's tribal splendor on display in the exile center of Dharamsala.   M. Guha

second largest city of Tibet. Then we continued on foot in small groups for 20 days on old mountain paths. We traveled through the treacherous terrain at night, hiding by day from army patrols. Once we came very close to being discovered, but we remained quiet and hid in the shadows."

Only the rich can afford the steep smugglers' fee of 1,000 yuan (about 132 dollars); the rest attempt to flee solo. Ironically, it is those in high places—party officials, police and cadres—who are most likely to send their children to India for a proper education and to learn Tibetan religion and culture.

Those who aren't caught arrive at a reception center on the outskirts of the Nepal-

IKE'S SECRET WAR

The relative stillness of the airwaves above this remote kingdom was shattered in the 1950s, when radio was resurrected by the CIA's then-biggest covert aid package for any nation. Although targeted to Tibetan nationalists, the program was a stepchild of the "lost China" concerns of the time.

Hardy tribesmen from eastern Tibet were recruited as operatives and trained at camps in Saipan, Colorado and, later, Nepal. When the Tibetan resistance was ready, the CIA began to drop parachute missions in small batches into Tibet. Radio equipment formed a key part of these airdrops, as the aim was to set up a rudimentary communications backbone to aid in the insurgency that was to follow. Soon the air was filled with coded messages, which were later followed by high-speed burst transmissions initially hand-keyed on magnetic tape.

Eisenhower Follows Leader's Escape

Many uprisings that followed were fraught with misfortune and inadequacy. In 1959, after a failed anti-Chinese insurgency, the 14th Dalai Lama fled Tibet and set up a government-in-exile in India. His escape was monitored by CIA operatives who were able to brief President Eisenhower on the spiritual leader's daily progress to India.

The Dalai Lama's request for asylum and the Indian Prime Minister's ready response were then transmitted worldwide by two CIA-trained monks using a transmitter powered by a hand-cranked generator. So dramatic was the escape of the Dalai Lama and his entourage disguised as soldiers that it has been immortalized in the 1997 Hollywood blockbuster "Kundun" by director Martin Scorsese.

Rebels Centered in Colorado and India

Buoyed by the success of the two radio operators in central Tibet, the CIA was now keen to step up its involvement. A top secret training facility was built at Camp Hale, a disused World War Two military base high in Colorado's Rocky Mountains. By the time the camp ceased to function in October 1964, some 259 Tibetans had been trained there. Following the debacle of the Sino-Indian War of 1962, Indian Prime Minister Nehru turned for help to

ese capital of Kathmandu. It is run by the Tibetan government-in-exile in cooperation with UNHCR. However, the Nepalese government, which considers China to be an important ally, does not allow refugees to tarry before they are packed off for India.

The Indian government provides travel documents and identity papers recognized by several countries. These allow Tibetan exiles to travel internationally. However, most proceed to pay homage to the Dalai Lama in Dharamsala, then go off to an institute of higher learning with branches throughout India. The government-in-exile provides material and moral support, while every exile pays a nominal "voluntary" tax.

New Invaders

In the 1980s, under international pressure, China eased its grip on Tibet, introducing Open Door reforms and boosting investment. This has translated to large scale development of its western hinterland, with upgrades to basic infrastructure, communications, roads and mining. But Tibetans have had little say in any of these projects.

Today's tourism and ongoing modernization stand in stark contrast to Tibet's former isolation. Ironically, some of the well-known religious centers, which were once anathema during the cultural revolution, have been resurrected and renovated at great effort and expense to cater to the "new invaders"—tourists. These venerated institutions

America, which responded swiftly. India then became an active partner in Tibet's pro-independence movement.

According to the Los Angeles Times, citing declassified intelligence documents released by the State Department, the CIA gave the Tibetan exile movement 1.7 million dollars a year through much of the 1960s. The funding was part of the agency's effort to undermine the governments of communist nations, notably China and the Soviet Union.

Amid allegations that the Dalai Lama was on Washington's payroll, Tibetan exiles have acknowledged that they once received support from American intelligence. Moreover, the Dalai Lama in his 1990 autobiography, *Freedom in Exile*, admitted that his brothers made contact with the CIA in 1956.

All indications are that these contacts ended decades ago. Nevertheless, China continues to accuse the Dalai Lama of being an agent of foreign forces seeking to separate Tibet from China.

Nixon Nixes Support

All covert American aid ended abruptly when then-President Richard Nixon made his historic opening to China in 1972.

This came as a hammer blow to Tibetan exiles, who had long trusted America to uphold their movement as an effective force. Indeed, so distraught were Tibetan fighters when urged by the Dalai Lama to lay down arms, a number chose instead to throw themselves into a river and drown.

The Dalai Lama now advocates autonomy for Tibet under Chinese rule. M. Guha

Antenna mast pierces the sky at Lhasa's broadcasting complex. M. Guha

Broadcasting Station"—"Xizang Guangbo Dientai," Xizang being Chinese for China-Tibet.

Xizang Radio is headquartered in a fortified complex in the shadow of the Potala Palace in bustling central Lhasa. Across the road on a smaller hill are its FM transmitter towers. Since 2002 the station has offered four program streams totaling over 78 hours. These include a Tibetan news channel, a news channel in Chinese, a channel in the Kham dialect and the FM outlet—"City Life."

Tibetan language programs, initially nine hours a day, have been extended to 21 hours. New programs in Kham and Amdo dialects are also being added to counter foreign world band stations. When not carrying its own programs, the station airs Tibetan programs from China National Radio's Minorities Service in Beijing—these are aired in one-hour segments four times a day.

Xizang Radio has five departments with 227 employees and a handful of stringers. Forty Tibetan journalists from the region, as well as from Tibetan areas in the Chinese provinces of Qinghai and Sichuan, have been trained in Beijing to staff the expanded network.

The Beijing government, as well as provincial and municipal administrations, have supplied the station with equipment and materials, along with more than 200 technicians drawn mostly from party cadres. Over the years the Tibet region itself has invested a over ten million dollars to develop its broadcasting infrastructure.

benefit to the Tibetan people for their material progress."

Radio Changes After Chinese Victory

Immediately following Chinese military victory, broadcasting in Tibet, as in China proper, used wired loudspeakers. To this end, the "Tibet Wired Radio Station" ("Lhasa Cable Broadcasting Station") was founded in 1953.

Chinese-ruled Tibet didn't go wireless until New Year's Day of 1959, when radio broadcasting was inaugurated in Tibetan and Chinese. The station was known variously as "Tibetan People's Radio Station" and "Lhasa People's Broadcasting Station," but in March it finally settled on "China-Tibet

World Band Preferred

Given the vastness of the region and its mountainous terrain, world band appears to be the preferred mode of coverage. Broadcasts are carried on 13 transmitters, each rated at 100 kW—eight in Tibetan, and five in Chinese.

These are also aired by 300 kW and 1,000 kW mediumwave AM transmitters. That Megawatt monster is also used to carry China Radio International's service in Hindi and Urdu. It puts in a sizeable signal to targets in northern India and Pakistan, much to the chagrin of official broadcasters in those countries. Over the last decade its programs have been available via satellite to 1,475 ground stations linking 75 county-level FM relay stations, bringing radio to 83 percent of the population.

For greater Lhasa, programs in FM stereo include catchy programming and English-language lessons to attract a youthful audience. These are simulcast on the Internet as the "Sound of China Tibet" at www.tibetradio.cn.

Besides the two mediumwave AM transmitters in Lhasa, Tibet has a 1 kW medium-wave AM operation, the Shannan People's Broadcasting Station, in the eastern city of Nedong. There are also two 50 kW world band transmitters in Xian and one in Lingshi in neighboring Chinese provinces. These have occasionally been used not only to augment existing program streams, but also to reach local ethnic Tibetans.

The adjoining Chinese province of Qinghai also broadcasts its own programs in Tibetan. These emanate from 15 kW and 50 kW shortwave transmitters and a higher-power mediumwave AM unit in Xinning.

Self-Censorship Widespread

Running Xizang Radio's impressive operation is the debonair managing director Phur-phu Dorji, who agreed to be interviewed at some risk to his career. Dorji started as a junior journalist, when he spent four years being trained at a Beijing college with follow-up training at journalism school.

Speaking through a translator, he reminiscences, "In the beginning all news was written by hand. There were no computers. News from the field was sent by telex. When phone lines became prevalent, telex was replaced by fax. Now email has replaced all these. Stringers and freelancers send news from remote places, while research is mostly conducted over the Internet."

He adds, "There is total freedom to report and the news coverage is restricted to Tibet, with news drawn from the official Chinese news agency Xinhua for the rest of the country and the world."

Dorji states that he is unaware of jamming of foreign broadcasts to Tibet. However, when pressed he responds, "Every country does that. It is better to leave such political things out." Then, in a quick repartee, he interjects, "I normally ask the questions, but this is the first time I am answering questions—and so many of them!"

Responding to international interest and tourism, Xizang Radio has introduced a twice-daily 20-minute broadcast in English called Holy Tibet. It also airs "Broadcast for Tibetan Compatriots Outside of China" twice daily in Tibetan with news, features, literature and the arts. Other programs include "The Sound of China Tibet," "Transfer Singing," "Date of Tibet," "A Story of the King Garsar," "Tibet Opera," "Entertainment Place," and "Enter into Tibet."

These are popular even among non-Tibetans, and reception reports have been received from as far afield as East Asia, Africa and Europe—chiefly Finland, the United States, Japan and India. But replies to listener's letters and reports have been slow. "Reception reports sometimes do not get answered promptly, as English speaking freelancers need to hired to attend to them," explains Dorji.

Tsering Wangchuk, a journalist and presenter with Xizang Radio from 1988 to 1993, gives a different view to Reporters without Borders. Now living in exile in Dharamsala, he says, "Chinese journalists, most of whom are members of the CCP, are running those media. They enforce drastic censorship and impose editorial decisions about which no discussion is possible."

He also said that every day the editor gave journalists instructions about what events they should cover. The editorial staff, which in 1993 was made up of three Tibetan journalists and 17 Chinese, was expected to "inform listeners about the positive side of the Chinese authorities' work." Any news about the activities of the government in exile, the Dalai Lama, religious freedom or human rights was strictly banned from

E10
AM/FM/Shortwave Radio

Intelligence meets performance in the E10. The E10 provides sophisticated tools for listening to news, sports, and music from around the world.

_ Shortwave range of 1711 – 29,99 KHz
_ 550 programmable memories w memory page customization
_ Manual and auto scan, direct ke pad frequency entry, ATS
_ Clock with alarm, sleep timer, ar snooze functions

E100
AM/FM/Shortwave Radio

The E100 features a sleek design complimented by a portable physique. This little marvel is packed with all the latest radio features you want and it's small enough to fit in your coat pocket!

_ Shortwave range of 1711 – 29,9 KHz
_ 200 programmable memories
_ Memory page customization
_ Manual and auto scan, direct ke pad frequency entry

S350
Ruggedly Retro

With the look of a retro field radio sporting a rugged body and military-style controls – the S350 also features today's innovation for excellent AM, FM, and Shortwave reception and a large, full-range speaker for clear sound.

_ AM/FM/Shortwave Radio recept
_ Highly sensitive and selective an log tuner circuitry
_ Liquid Crystal Display (LCD), for frequency and clock display.
_ Digital clock with selectable 12/. hour format

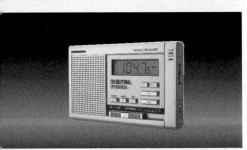

G1000A
AM/FM/Shortwave Radio

Small enough to fit in a coat pocket, yet powerful enough to capture eight Shortwave bands, the G1000A also features a digital frequency readout and alarm.

_ AM, FM-stereo and 8 shortwave bands
_ Analog tuning with digital frequency readout
_ Clock, alarm and sleep timer (1– 119 minutes)
_ Digital display shows frequency, time, sleep time and symbols fo sleep timer and alarm activatio

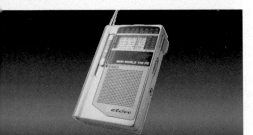

Mini 100PE
AM/FM/Shortwave Radio

Small enough to fit in your palm, yet powerful enough to receive AM/FM/Shortwave bands, the Mini 100PE is the perfect personal radio.

_ 6 Shortwave bands
_ Classic analog tuning dial
_ Belt clip, earphones, and soft pr tective pouch (included)

FR300
All-In-One

This all-in-one unit offers functionality and versatility that makes it ideal for emergencies.

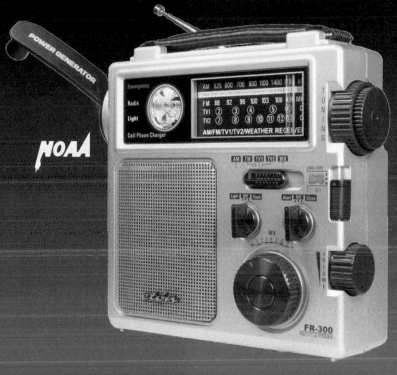

_ AM/FM/TV-VHF, NOAA radio reception
_ Built-in power generator recharges the internal rechargeable Ni-MH battery (Included)
_ Can be powered from four different sources:
  1. The built-in rechargeable NI-MH battery that takes charge from the dynamo crank and from an AC adapter (AC adapter not included)
  2. 3 AA batteries (Not included)
  3. The AC adapter alone (AC adapter not included)
  4. The dynamo crank alone, even with no battery pack installed
_ Built-in white LED light source
_ Cell-phone charger output jack 3.5mm (various cell phone plug tips included)
_ Incorporates a fine-tuning control knob super-imposed on the main tuning control knob
_ Built-in 2 white LED light source and one flashing red LED
_ Siren
_ Weather Alert
_ Dimensions: 6-1/2"W x 6"H x 2-1/2"D
_ Weight: 1 lb. 3 oz.

FR200
Crank it Up

Without the need for batteries, this self-powered 2-in-1 radio and flashlight helps you stay informed and prepared for emergencies.

_ AM/FM/Shortwave Radio Reception
_ Built-in power generator recharges the internal rechargeable Ni-MH battery (Included)
_ Built-in white LED light source
_ 12 international bands
_ Available colors: Metallic Blue, Metallic Red, Yellow, Sand, Pearl

the airwaves. "We were all afraid. Anyone who defies the censors can expect the worst."

This presumably explains widespread self-censorship in Tibet and the relatively small number of journalists in prison.

> Anyone who
> defies the
> censors can
> expect the
> worst.

Voice for The Voiceless

It was not until May 14, 1996 that an independent Tibetan station, "Voice of Tibet," was launched, thanks to financing by a collective of three Norwegian NGOs. The station was the brainchild of a group of Tibetan journalists who had noticed a tightening of controls at the Chinese border, making it increasingly difficult to bring news into Tibet. It was initially hosted by the Far Eastern Broadcasting Association (FEBA), a Christian broadcaster, from its world band transmitter in the Seychelles.

Chinese officials reacted by threatening to jam all FEBA programs. So, later that year the Tibetans left FEBA for leased-time facilities in Kazakhstan, Central Asia.

Originally the station's daily 15-minute program consisted of five minutes of international news plus a feature on international human rights and the situation in Tibet. Once more funding became available, the "Voice of Tibet" moved transmissions to higher-powered shortwave facilities closer to its target area. Daily output was increased to half an hour in January 1997, and by March 1999 this had risen to three 45-minute transmissions.

Offices in India near Dalai Lama

Studios and editorial offices of the "Voice of Tibet" are currently located in India's picturesque Dharamsala, which has terrain similar to that of Tibet. A winding road, plied by madcap Indian taxi drivers, leads to the exile complex. Referred to as the "Library" by locals, it lies along the route to the Dalai Lama's residence further uphill in Mcleodganj.

Once a remote area nestled high in the Himalayas of northern India, it has now fallen prey to tourist traffic resulting from their leader's celebrity status.

Karma Nazee Yeshi is editor in chief of this independent radio voice, which operates from a small office and a rudimentary studio with a staff of five. "We are the only station with programs edited and produced entirely by Tibetans. The 'Voice of Tibet' seeks to promote ethnic awareness among the Tibetan minority in China. We are the voice of the voiceless, which is our slogan." He adds, "Sometimes listeners from Tibet are brave enough to call us. They ask us to improve our signal. We try our best despite the jamming by the Chinese authorities."

Even though it is independently funded, much of the "Voice of Tibet's" content is derived from the government-in-exile located at its doorstep. Production at the original studios in Oslo was too costly, so the Norway office is now used only for fund-raising.

Every evening the "Voice of Tibet" airs a half-hour newscast in Tibetan, followed by 15 minutes of news in Mandarin (Standard Chinese) presented by staffers drawn from recent escapees who speak the language fluently. Tibetan journalists stationed elsewhere, notably in New Delhi and Kathmandu, also contribute stories.

"Voice of Tibet" focuses mainly on developments inside Tibet and activities within exile institutions. Twice a week it airs the Dalai Lama's latest public speeches, and there are features on Tibetan culture, history, education, medicine, music and folklore.

Producers use rudimentary digital workstations to edit programs. To keep content fresh, the final product is sent as an Internet file transfer to the transmitting station an hour before the broadcast. When Internet connectivity is poor, transfer is made by slow and costly dial-up.

Schedule Fluid to Counter Jamming

For now, the "Voice of Tibet" broadcasts to Tibet at 1103-1148, 1215-1300, 1305-1350 and 1433-1518 World Time from a location in Central Asia; and to northern India at 1400-1430 and 1530-1600 from a site in the Southern Hemisphere. The number of daily broadcasts can vary, depending on financial resources, while frequencies change often in an effort to counter jamming. "We try our best to smuggle the latest frequency information into Tibet by using very innovative means," adds station editor Yeshi.

Fund raising is underway for an updated rebroadcast of the evening service the next morning. For those outside the target area who can't catch the world band transmission, archived audio, along with current world band times and frequencies, are available at www.vot.org.

Just as the Soviet Union found out during the decades of the Cold War, world band can be transmitted such that it gets through even the most persistent of jamming—even if only partially. After that, buzz takes over to gnaw away at the underpinnings of the ruling power structure.

Karma Yeshi Nazee manages the "Voice of Tibet" exile station from secluded Dharamsala, India.   M. Guha

JAMMING—RADIO'S CHINESE CHECKERS

In the absence of credible domestic media and press freedom, foreign world band broadcasts play a crucial role. Tibetans listen to these at great peril, and their listening is further complicated by skywave and groundwave jamming on a scale unmatched since the Cold War.

China generally jams foreign radio broadcasts by transmitting its own domestic programs on the same frequency, but at times simply airs Chinese music or just plain noise. Even so, it has been uniquely creative in its choice of program "feeds" to overwhelm external broadcasts it deems objectionable.

Jammers Try Australian, Canadian Audio

For example, to jam the "Voice of Tibet" Chinese transmitters in 1997 began airing heavily modulated audio from Beijing's Easy FM, produced jointly with the Australian press group AWA Australia Technology. This stopped after the Australian group protested.

In December 1998 it was the turn of Radio Canada International, which was being "swap" relayed by a transmitter in Xian. RCI officials complained to the Chinese and the practice ceased the next day. RCI continues to be relayed by Xian.

China's jamming effort, like that of the former Soviet Union, is massive and well funded—but not always well run. As one example, in 1996 a private Cambodian station found itself being mistakenly jammed, even though Tibetan is quite different from Cambodian.

Group Says Jammers Built by French

Reporters Without Borders, in an article dated July 5, 2005, offered a detailed expose of Chinese jamming. The American-based Radio Free Asia and Voice of America and the Indian-based "Voice of Tibet" are the main world band stations broadcasting Tibetan-language programming to Tibet, and each is systematically jammed.

The article points out that thanks to the acquisition of sophisticated ALLISS antennas from the French company Thales Broadcast & Multimedia (formerly Thomson-CSF), Chinese authorities have improved their jamming capabilities. Installed above all in the far northwestern city of Kashi, they are used to jam international radio signals, as well as for legitimate broadcasting.

"Voice of Tibet" has beamed nightly broadcasts to Tibet for over a decade.   M. Guha

Radio Free Asia broadcasts on ten different frequencies in an attempt to get around this censorship, but they are all systematically jammed by diffuse noise or music. The authorities recently installed new jamming towers in Pemba (Chamdo prefecture), and since then most residents in the groundwave of these jammers have been unable to receive the VOA.

World band jamming is far less effective outside jamming groundwave zones, so those living in or visiting the countryside have a much better chance of tasting forbidden radio fruit. To help overcome this, authorities have distributed new radio sets to the population in the Kardze region on the grounds that they are of "better quality" than older radios. But they are actually built so they cannot be tuned to international stations without modification.

Politics Limit Counter-Jamming Options

Radio Free Asia and the Voice of America reach audiences in part by using numerous strategically placed transmitters for each broadcast. Location is especially important for "twilight immunity," which in concert with sophisticated frequency management can successfully thwart skywave jamming.

Tenzin Peldon is equally adept at mixing audio and being chief reporter at the "Voice of Tibet."
M. Guha

However, the "Voice of Tibet," perceived by many countries as politically dicey, is limited in its choice of transmitting locations. Oystein Alme, project manager of the "Voice of Tibet," laments, "We have been broadcasting for nine years now, and China has attempted for as many years to jam our transmissions. Especially for 'Voice of Tibet,' with very limited financial resources and beaming into a politically sensitive area, it is hard to 'beat the jammers on a permanent basis'."

Nevertheless, the mouse sometimes manages to roar. "For the last few years," he goes on, "we have been able to do adjustments that have improved our ability to compete and often beat the signal of the China jammers."

The Voice of America has been jammed by the Chinese since it first went on the air and the American government, which owns the station, has complained to authorities in Beijing on several occasions. Chinese officials have always denied being behind the jamming. In 1997 a delegation of VOA technicians even went to China in an attempt to find a solution, but the discussions led nowhere and jamming continues with a vengeance.

Silver Lining: Jamming Boosts Credibility

But in all this there is a bright spot. Similar negotiations with the Soviet Union succeeded four decades ago, whereupon jamming of the VOA ceased.

The unforseen rub: Listeners were certain there had to be a quid pro quo to satisfy the Russians, so they assumed the VOA had agreed to be less hard-hitting and controversial. American officials insisted there was no such deal, but the very fact that jamming ceased caused the VOA's credibility to drop within the USSR.

"Voice of Tibet" staff gathers for a rare group photo.
Voice of Tibet

E10
AM/FM/Shortwave Radio

Intelligence meets performance in the E10. The E10 provides sophisticated tools for listening to news, sports, and music from around the world.

_ Shortwave range of 1711 – 29,9 KHz
_ 550 programmable memories w memory page customization
_ Manual and auto scan, direct ke pad frequency entry, ATS
_ Clock with alarm, sleep timer, a snooze functions

E100
AM/FM/Shortwave Radio

The E100 features a sleek design complimented by a portable physique. This little marvel is packed with all the latest radio features you want and it's small enough to fit in your coat pocket!

_ Shortwave range of 1711 – 29,9 KHz
_ 200 programmable memories
_ Memory page customization
_ Manual and auto scan, direct ke pad frequency entry

S350
Ruggedly Retro

With the look of a retro field radio sporting a rugged body and military-style controls – the S350 also features today's innovation for excellent AM, FM, and Shortwave reception and a large, full-range speaker for clear sound.

_ AM/FM/Shortwave Radio recept
_ Highly sensitive and selective ar log tuner circuitry
_ Liquid Crystal Display (LCD), for frequency and clock display.
_ Digital clock with selectable 12/. hour format

S350 Deluxe
High-Performance Field Radio with Stereo Headphones

For S350 devotees the deluxe model combines a sporty new exterior with the same unrivalled functionality.
_ FM- stereo via headphones (included)
_ AM/Shortwave Frequency Lock
_ Set clock and alarm

_ Highly sensitive analog tuner w digital display
_ Large, full range speaker with bass & treble control
_ Clock, alarm, and sleep timer
_ Built-in antennas and connectio for external antennas
_ Available colors: Metallic Red, Black

E1XM

The E1XM is the world's first radio to combine AM, FM, Shortwave, and XM Satellite Radio Ready technology into one ultra-high-performance unit.

- AM/FM/Shortwave/XM Satellite Ready Radio
- 1700 station presets
- Digitally synthesized PLL tuner with synchronous detector
- Passband tuning, selectable bandwidth filters and Selectable Single Sideband (SSB) reception
- Dual conversion superheterodyne circuit design
- Stereo line-level audio inputs and outputs and external antenna connections
- Dual Clocks and programmable timers
- Headphone jack
- Built-In Antenna: telescopic antenna for AM, FM and Shortwave reception
- External Antenna Connection for the addition of auxiliary antennas
- Calibrated LCD signal strength meter
- High Dynamic Range: allowing for the detection of weak signals in the presence of strong signals
- Power Source: 4 "D" Batteries (not included); AC Adapter (included)
- Dimensions: 13"W x 7-1/2"H x 2-1/2"D
- Weight: 4 lb 3 oz.

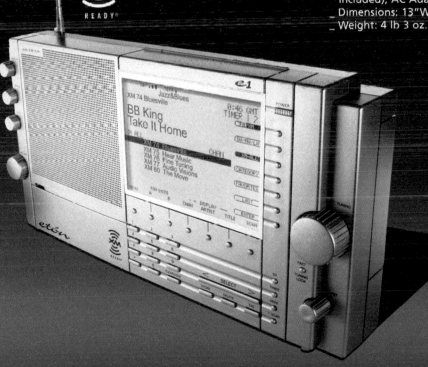

Compleat Idiot's Guide to Getting Started

The Three "Musts"

World band isn't your everyday radio—it require special receivers and also operates differently. So, here are three "musts" to enjoy it to full advantage.

"Must" #1: World Time and Day

World band schedules use a single time. World band is global, with stations beaming 24/7 from nearly every time zone. Imagine the chaos if each station's schedule were given in its local time to listeners worldwide.

Solution: *World Time*—a single time zone for the entire planet.

World Time, or Coordinated Universal Time (UTC), replaces the virtually identical Greenwich Mean Time (GMT) as the global standard. It uses the 24-hour format, so 2 PM is 14:00 ("fourteen hundred") hours, and strictly speaking leading zeroes are shown (e.g., "08:00," read as "oh-eight-hundred hours," not "8:00"). In the military, it is often called "Zulu" or "Zulu Time."

Most major international broadcasters announce World Time at the hour. On the Internet, it's shown at various sites, including http://time5.nrc.ca/webclock_e.shtml. Around North America, World Time is also announced over standard time stations WWV in Colorado, WWVH in Hawaii and CHU in Ottawa. WWV and WWVH use world band on 5000, 10000 and 15000 kHz, with WWV also on 2500 and 20000 kHz. CHU ticks away on 3330, 7335 and 14670 kHz.

See the "Setting Your Clock" sidebar to adjust your 24-hour clock. For example, if you live in the eastern United States, *add* five hours winter (four hours summer) to your local time to get World Time. So, if it is 8 PM EST (the 20th hour of the day) in Miami, it is 01:00 hours World Time.

Don't forget to "wind your calendar," because at midnight a new *World Day* arrives. This can trip up even experienced listeners—sometimes radio stations, too. So if it is 9:00 PM EST Wednesday in New York, it is 02:00 hours World Time *Thursday*.

Bottom line for getting started: Get a radio with a 24-hour clock or buy a separate clock.

Citizen's Navitach Chronograph Chrono features time and date for 22 different world time zones.

"Must" #2: Finding Stations

PASSPORT shows station schedules three ways: by country, time of day and frequency. By-country is best for tuning to a given station. "What's On Tonight"—the time-of-day section—is like *TV Guide* and has program descriptions. Quick-access Blue Pages show what you might be hearing when you're dialing around the bands.

World band frequencies are usually given in kilohertz (kHz), but some stations use Megahertz (MHz). The only difference is three decimal places, so 6170 kHz is the same as 6.17 MHz, 6175 kHz identical to 6.175 MHz, and so on.

FM and other stations keep the same spot on the dial, day and night— webcast URLs, too, sort of. But things are different on international airwaves. World band radio is like a global bazaar where a variety of

> For one world there's one time: World Time (UTC).

PASSPORT'S THREE-MINUTE START

Too swamped to read the owner's manual? Try this:

1. Night time is the right time, so wait until evening when signals are strongest. In a concrete-and-steel building put your radio by a window or balcony.

2. Make sure your radio is plugged in or has fresh batteries. Extend its telescopic antenna fully and vertically. Set the DX/local switch (if there is one) to "DX," but otherwise leave the controls the way they came from the factory.

3. Turn on your radio. Set it to 5900 kHz and begin tuning slowly toward 6200 kHz. You should hear stations from around the world.

Other times? Read "Best Times and Frequencies for 2006," below.

merchants come and go at various times of the day and night. So, where you once tuned in a French station, hours later you might find a Russian roosting on that same spot.

Or on a nearby perch. If you suddenly hear interference from a station on an adjacent channel, it doesn't mean something is wrong with your radio; another station has probably fired up on a nearby frequency. There are more stations on the air than available space, so sometimes they try to outshout each other.

To cope with this, purchase a radio with superior adjacent-channel rejection—selectivity, as it's commonly known—and lean towards models with synchronous selectable sideband. Passport Reports tests these and other features and tells you which models can hack it.

Because world band is full of surprises from one listening session to the next, experienced listeners like to stroll through the airwaves. Daytime, you'll find most stations above 11500 kHz; at night, below 10000 kHz, but there are interesting exceptions.

If a station can't be found or fades out, there is probably nothing wrong with your radio or the schedule. World band stations are located on *terra firma*, but because of the earth's curvature their signals eventually impact the atmosphere's sky-high ionosphere.

When the ionosphere is suitably energized, it deflects these signals back down, after which they bounce off oceans or soil and sail once again back up to the ionosphere.

This process of bouncing up and down, like a dribbled basketball, continues until the signal finally arrives at your radio. However, if the ionosphere at any one "bounce point" isn't in a bouncing mood—like the weather, this varies daily and seasonally—the signal disappears into space instead of bouncing back to earth. That's great for travelers to Uranus, but for the rest of us it's a key reason a scheduled signal might be audible one hour, gone the next.

The ionosphere is also why world band radio is so unencumbered—its signals don't rely on cables or satellites or the Internet, just layers of ionized gases which have enveloped our planet for eons. This also means that, unlike the Internet, world band usage can't be traced.

The ionosphere also allows world band to be free from regulation, taxes and fees. And, like domestic public radio, it is largely devoid of ads. Analog world band radio is also the single most effective vehicle to get around jamming used by governments and during emergencies. This makes it the ultimate among media alternatives for circumventing censorship.

WORLD TIME CLOCKS

Some radios include a World Time clock displayed fulltime—this is handiest. Other radios may have World Time clocks, but to see time when the radio is on you have to press a button.

Because World Time is 24-hour format, digital is easier to read than analog hands. MFJ Enterprises makes several 24-hour clocks—conventional or atomic-synchronized, some with seconds displayed numerically—from $9.95 to $79.95 at MFJ and radio dealers. Sharper Image also offers clocks for under $50.

Other 24-hour clocks, often targeted to professionals, can run up to $2,000. Pricier models typically display seconds and even split-seconds numerically, while many synchronize with an official atomic clock standard. There are even wristwatches that give World Time in analog or digital format.

La Crosse Technology's affordable WS-8117 displays World Time, date, day and outdoor/indoor temperature. In North America its clock is kept exact by radio control.

SETTING YOUR CLOCK TO WORLD TIME

PASSPORT's "Addresses PLUS" chapter lets you figure out local time in other countries by adding or subtracting from World Time. Use that section to ascertain local time within a country you are hearing.

Here is the opposite: what to add or subtract from your local time to get World Time. For example, if you live near Chicago and it's 7:00 AM in the winter, the list below shows World Time as six hours later—13:00.

In the summer, with saving time in effect, World Time is only five hours later—noon, or 12:00. That's because World Time, unlike Chicago time, doesn't change with the seasons. So, once you've set your clock for World Time, you're done. You won't have to fool with it again unless the batteries go dead.

In many parts of the world you can also tune to stations that broadcast nothing but World Time. In and around North America try WWV in Colorado on 2500, 5000, 10000, 15000 and 20000 kHz; also, Canada's CHU on 3330, 7335 and 14670 kHz. In the Pacific tune to WWVH in Hawaii on 2500, 5000, 10000 and 15000 kHz.

WHERE YOU ARE	TO DETERMINE WORLD TIME
North America	
Newfoundland St. John's NF, St. Anthony NF	Add 3½ hours, 2½ summer
Atlantic St. John NB, Battle Harbour NF	Add 4 hours, 3 summer
Eastern New York, Miami, Toronto	Add 5 hours, 4 summer
Central Chicago, Mexico City, Nashville, Winnipeg	Add 6 hours, 5 summer
Mountain Denver, Salt Lake City, Calgary	Add 7 hours, 6 summer
Pacific San Francisco, Vancouver	Add 8 hours, 7 summer
Alaska	Add 9 hours, 8 summer
Hawaii	Add 10 hours
Central America & Caribbean	
Bermuda	Add 4 hours, 3 summer
Barbados, Puerto Rico, Virgin Islands	Add 4 hours
Bahamas, Cuba	Add 5 hours, 4 summer
Jamaica	Add 5 hours
Costa Rica	Add 6 hours

Europe

United Kingdom, Ireland, Portugal	Same time as World Time winter, subtract 1 hour summer
Continental Western Europe; parts of Central and Eastern Continental Europe	Subtract 1 hour, 2 hours summer
Elsewhere in Continental Europe: Belarus, Bulgaria, Cyprus, Estonia, Finland, Greece, Latvia, Lithuania, Moldova, Romania, Russia (Kaliningradskaya Oblast), Turkey, Ukraine	Subtract 2 hours, 3 summer
Moscow	Subtract 3 hours, 4 summer

Mideast & Africa

Côte d'Ivoire, Ghana, Guinea, Liberia, Mali, Morocco, Senegal, Sierra Leone	World Time exactly
Angola, Benin, Chad, Congo, Nigeria, Tunisia	Subtract 1 hour
Egypt, Israel, Jordan, Lebanon, Syria	Subtract 2 hours, 3 summer
South Africa, Zambia, Zimbabwe	Subtract 2 hours
Ethiopia, Kenya, Kuwait, Saudi Arabia, Tanzania, Uganda	Subtract 3 hours
Iran	Subtract 3½ hours, 4½ summer

Asia & Australasia

Pakistan	Subtract 5 hours
India	Subtract 5½ hours
Bangladesh, Sri Lanka	Subtract 6 hours
Laos, Thailand, Vietnam	Subtract 7 hours
China (including Taiwan), Malaysia, Philippines, Singapore	Subtract 8 hours
Japan, Korea	Subtract 9 hours
Australia: *Victoria, New South Wales, Tasmania*	Subtract 11 hours local summer, 10 local winter (midyear)
Australia: *South Australia*	Subtract 10½ hours local summer, 9½ hours local winter (midyear)
Australia: *Queensland*	Subtract 10 hours
Australia: *Northern Territory*	Subtract 9½ hours
Australia: *Western Australia*	Subtract 8 hours
New Zealand	Subtract 13 hours local summer, 12 hours local winter (midyear)

E1XM

The E1XM is the world's first radio to combine AM, FM, Shortwave, and XM Satellite Radio Ready technology into one ultra-high-performance unit.

_ AM/FM/Shortwave/XM Satellite Ready Radio
_ 1700 station presets
_ Digitally synthesized PLL tuner with synchronous detector
_ Passband tuning, selectable bandwidth filters and Selectable Single Sideband (SSB) reception
_ Dual conversion superheterodyne circuit design
_ Stereo line-level audio inputs and outputs and external antenna connections
_ Dual clocks and programmable timers
_ Headphone jack
_ Built-In antenna: telescopic antenna for AM, FM and Shortwave reception
_ External antenna connection for the addition of auxiliary antennas
_ Calibrated LCD signal strength meter

E10
AM/FM/Shortwave Radio

Intelligence meets performance in the E10. The E10 provides sophisticated tools for listening to news, sports, and music from around the world.

_ Shortwave range of 1711 – 29,9 KHz
_ 550 programmable memories w memory page customization
_ Manual and auto scan, direct ke pad frequency entry, ATS
_ Clock with alarm, sleep timer, ar snooze functions

E100
AM/FM/Shortwave Radio

The E100 features a sleek design complimented by a portable physique. This little marvel is packed with all the latest radio features you want and it's small enough to fit in your coat pocket!

_ Shortwave range of 1711 – 29,9 KHz
_ 200 programmable memories
_ Memory page customization
_ Manual and auto scan, direct ke pad frequency entry

S350
Ruggedly Retro

With the look of a retro field radio sporting a rugged body and military-style controls – the S350 also features today's innovation for excellent AM, FM, and Shortwave reception and a large, full-range speaker for clear sound.

_ AM/FM/Shortwave Radio reception
_ Highly sensitive and selective analog tuner circuitry
_ Liquid Crystal Display (LCD), for frequency and clock display.
_ Digital clock with selectable 12/24 hour format

G2000A
AM/FM/Shortwave Radio by F.A. Porsche

Drive through the airwaves and get breaking news from this stylish AM/FM/Shortwave Radio—designed by legendary F.A. Porsche.

_ Protective case
_ Autoscan and direct keypad tuning
_ 20 customizable station presets
_ Dual alarms, and sleep timer

FR200
Crank it Up

Without the need for batteries, this self-powered 2-in-1 radio and flashlight helps you stay informed and prepared for emergencies.

_ AM/FM/Shortwave Radio Reception
_ Built-in power generator recharges the internal rechargeable Ni-MH battery (Included)
_ Built-in white LED light source
_ 12 international bands
_ Available colors: Metallic Blue, Metallic Red, Sand

FR300
All-In-One

This all-in-one unit offers functionality and versatility that makes it ideal for emergencies.

_ Weather alert

_ AM/FM/TV-VHF/NOAA Radio Reception
_ Built-in power generator recharges the internal rechargeable Ni-MH battery (Included)
_ Cell-phone charger output jack 3.5mm (various cell phone plug tips included)
_ Built-in 2 white LED light source and one flashing red LED

BEST TIMES AND FREQUENCIES FOR 2006

With world band, dialing randomly within the shortwave range might get you nothing but dead air. That's because world band stations transmit only on limited segments within the shortwave spectrum. Some of these are alive and kicking only by day, while others don't spring to life until night. Time of year also counts.

World band is always active, but most signals are strongest evenings because they're aimed your way. But that's just for starters. Much of the juicy stuff is heard beyond prime time when, thanks to shortwave's scattering properties, signals beamed elsewhere appear on good receiving setups.

Experienced station hunters especially enjoy the hour or two on either side of dawn. Because propagation is different then, you may hear parts of the world that normally elude. Try after lunch, too—especially towards sunset. After midnight also can be interesting, especially winters.

Fine Print and Slippery Excuses: Treat this time and frequency guide like a good weather forecast: helpful, but not holy writ. Nature, as always, has a mind of its own, and world band is nature's radio.

This guide is most accurate if you're north of the African and South American continents. Even then, what you hear will vary depending on such things as your location, where the station transmits from, the time of year and your radio hardware (*see* Propagation in PASSPORT's glossary).

☞ Fourteen official frequency segments are allocated for world band radio. Broadcasters also operate "out of band" as secondary users, provided they don't cause harmful interference to such primary users as fixed-service utility stations.

☞ "Night" refers to your local hours of darkness, give or take.

Night—Very Limited Reception
Day—Local Reception Only

2 MHz (120 meters) **2300-2495 kHz**—overwhelmingly domestic stations, plus 2496-2504 kHz for time stations only.

Night—Limited Reception
Day—Local Reception Only

3 MHz (90 meters) **3200-3400 kHz**—overwhelmingly domestic broadcasters, but also some international stations.

Unlike the Internet, world band usage can't be traced.

Day and Night—Good-to-Fair in Europe and Asia except Summer Nights; Elsewhere, Limited Reception Night

4 MHz (75 meters) **3900-4050 kHz**—international and domestic stations, primarily not in or beamed to the Americas; 3900-3950 kHz mainly Asian and Pacific transmitters; 3950-4000 kHz also includes European and African transmitters; 4001-4050 kHz currently out-of-band.

Night—Fair Reception
Day—Regional Reception Only

5 MHz (60 meters) **4750-4995 kHz** and **5005-5100 kHz**—mostly domestic stations, plus 4996-5004 kHz for time stations only; 5061-5100 kHz currently out-of-band.

Night—Excellent Reception
Day—Regional Reception Only

6 MHz (49 meters) **5730-6300 kHz**—5730-5899 kHz and 6201-6300 kHz currently out-of-band.

Night—Good Reception
Day—Mainly Regional Reception

7 MHz (41 meters) **6890-6990 kHz** and **7100-7600 kHz**—6890-6990 kHz and 7351-7600 kHz currently out-of-band; 7100-7300 kHz no American-based transmitters and few transmissions targeted to the Americas. Some years hence, the 7100 kHz lower parameter may shift to 7200 kHz, with 7200-7300 kHz rather than 7100-7300 kHz being for outside the Americas.

> World band is nature's radio, and nature has a mind of its own.

Day—Fair Reception Winter; Regional Reception Summer
Night—Good Reception Summer

9 MHz (31 meters) **9250-9995 kHz**—9250-9399 kHz and 9901-9995 kHz currently out-of-band, plus 9996-10004 kHz for time stations only.

Day—Good Reception
Night—Variable Reception Summer

11 MHz (25 meters) **11500-12200 kHz**—11500-11599 kHz and 12101-12200 kHz currently out-of-band.

13 MHz (22 meters) **13570-13870 kHz**

15 MHz (19 meters) **15005-15825 kHz**—15005-15099 kHz and 15801-15825 kHz currently out-of-band, plus 14996-15004 kHz for time stations only.

Day—Good Reception
Night—Limited Reception Summer

17 MHz (16 meters) **17480-17900 kHz**

19 MHz (15 meters) **18900-19020 kHz**—few stations use this segment.

Day—Variable Reception
Night—Little Reception

21 MHz (13 meters) **21450-21850 kHz**

Day—Rare, if Any, Reception
Night—No Reception

25 MHz (11 meters) **25670-26100 kHz**

Bangladeshi listener Azizul Alam al-Amin initiates his cousin Turjo into world band at a tender age.

Md. Azizul Alam al-Amin

World band stations cope with the ionosphere's changeability by operating within different frequency ranges, depending on the season and time of day. This changeability is part of the fun, as it allows you to eavesdrop on a serendipitous roster of signals not intended for your part of the world. Sometimes stations from exotic locales—places you don't ordinarily hear—become surprise arrivals, thanks to the ionosphere's free spirit.

Bottom line for getting started: You've already done it by getting Passport. Now, polish your wanderlust!

"Must" #3: The Right Radio

Choose carefully, but start off affordably. If you just want to hear major stations, you'll do fine with a moderately priced portable. If you want something better, portatop models excel with tough signals and have superior audio quality. But top-rated tabletop receivers are aimed at experienced and demanding users. Pass on these pricey models until you're sure you want a Maserati instead of a Mazda.

Select a radio with digital frequency display. This makes digging out stations much easier—all radios in Passport Reports have digital displays, but analog display (slide-rule-tuning) models still abound. Some low-cost hybrids have analog tuning with digital frequency display, but most radios with digital display use synthesized tuning. This is the way to go, as synthesized tuning usually adds such handy tuning aids as presets and keypads.

Tuning range? Get a radio that covers at least 4750-21850 kHz with no significant frequency gaps or "holes." Otherwise, it may miss some stations.

You won't need an exotic outside antenna unless you're using a tabletop model. All portables, and to some extent portatops, are designed to work well off their built-in telescopic antennas. If you want to enhance weak-signal sensitivity, either clip several yards or meters of insulated wire onto that antenna, or use one of the portable active antennas evaluated in Passport Reports.

Bottom line for getting started: Avoid cheap radios, as they suffer from one or more major defects—but don't break the bank.

Prepared by Jock Elliott, Tony Jones and Lawrence Magne.

Re_Inventing Radio through Innovation

E1XM

The E1XM is the world's first radio to combine AM, FM, Shortwave, and XM Satellite Radio Ready technology into one ultra-high-performance unit.

_ AM/FM/Shortwave/XM Satellite Ready Radio
_ 1700 station presets
_ Digitally synthesized PLL tuner with synchronous detector
_ Passband tuning, selectable bandwidth filters and Selectable Single Sideband (SSB) reception
_ Dual conversion superheterodyne circuit design
_ Stereo line-level audio inputs and outputs and external antenna connections
_ Dual Clocks and programmable timers
_ Headphone jack
_ Built-In Antenna: telescopic antenna for AM, FM and Shortwave reception
_ External Antenna Connection for the addition of auxiliary antennas
_ Calibrated LCD signal strength meter
_ Power Source: 4 "D" Batteries (not included); AC Adapter (included)
_ Dimensions: 13"W x 7-1/2"H x 2-1/2"D
_ Weight: 4 lb 3 oz.

First Tries:
Ten Easy
Catches

The stronger a station, the more likely it is to attract listeners. Fortunately, the loudest stations often have the best programs—in English, too. Here are ten of these heard pretty much worldwide.

All times and days are in World Time (UTC). "Winter" and "summer" refer to seasons in the Northern Hemisphere, where summer takes place in the middle of the year.

EUROPE
France

Radio France Internationale has never broadcast much in English, but what it airs is good and popular with listeners. Though RFI now only targets listeners in Africa, the Middle East and South Asia, thanks to the scattering effect of shortwave it reaches a much wider audience.

☞ RECOMMENDED PROGRAM: All are first-rate.

North America: Although it has been several years since RFI suspended English to North America, it is still audible in the United States and Canada. Best by far is the 0700-0800 broadcast for West Africa from the RFI relay in Gabon. It's widely heard in parts of North America—especially toward the east. Winter on 11725 kHz, summer on 15605 kHz.

Middle East: 1400-1500 on 17515 kHz winter, and 15615 or 17515 kHz summer; also 1600-1730 winter on 11615 kHz and summer on 15605 kHz.

South Asia: 1400-1500 on 7180 or 9580 kHz via a transmitter in China. Also well heard in western parts of *Southeast Asia* and *Australia*.

Africa: RFI's popular broadcasts to Africa are audible at 0400-0430 winter weekdays on 7315 and 9555 or 11995 kHz, and summer on 7315 or 9805 kHz; 0500-0530 weekdays on any two channels from 9825, 11850, 11995, 13680 15155 and 15160 kHz; 0600-0630 winter weekdays on 9865 and 17800 kHz, and summer on 11665 and 15160 kHz; 0700-0800 winter on 11725 kHz, and summer on 15605 kHz; 1200-1230 on 15275 (winter), 17815 (summer) and 21620 kHz; 1600-1700 on any four frequencies from 7170, 9730, 11615, 15160, 15365, 15605, 17605 and 17850 kHz; and 1700-1730 winter on 15605 kHz, replaced summer by 17605 kHz.

> Loud stations often have the best programs.

Germany

Deutsche Welle is one of Europe's top broadcasters, with interesting programs and top-notch production. Once a bastion of news and related topics, it now offers a broad menu that includes folk, pop and classical music. The station no longer beams to North America and

Nigerian Rabi Gwandu enlivens programs at widely heard Deutsche Welle, one of the world's most respected stations.
DW

Starting young: DW's Susanne Henn with a curious youngster at DW's open day in Bonn.   DW

Australasia, but English transmissions targeted elsewhere scatter to listeners throughout the globe.

☞ RECOMMENDED PROGRAMS: "A World of Music" and "Inside Europe."

North and Central America: Best in the eastern and southern United States and the Caribbean is the broadcast for West Africa at 2100-2200. Try 9615 and 11690 kHz winter, and 11865 and 15205 kHz summer.

Europe: 0600-1000 and 1300-1600 year-round on 6140 kHz.

Southern Africa: 0500-0600 winter—summer in the Southern Hemisphere—on 12035 kHz, and midyear on 9630 kHz. The evening transmission airs at 2000-2100 winter on 12025 kHz, and midyear on 7130 kHz.

East Asia: 2200-2300, winter on 6180 kHz and summer on 7115 and 9720 kHz.

Southeast Asia: 2300-2400 winter on 6070, 9555, and 9815 kHz; replaced summer by 5955, 9890 and 15135 kHz.

Australasia: There's nothing specifically beamed to Australasia, but some of the frequencies for Southeast Asia provide adequate reception when there's no interference from other stations.

Netherlands

Radio Netherlands—the English service of **Radio Nederland Wereldomroep**—produces excellent programs despite a modest budget. Unapologetically controversial, its strong focus on social issues makes it an interesting alternative.

☞ RECOMMENDED PROGRAMS: "Research File" and "Wide Angle."

North America: (East) 1200-1300 (one hour earlier in summer) on 11675 kHz; 1900-2100 (weekends only) on 15525 kHz winter, and 17735 kHz summer; and 0000-0100 winter on 6165 kHz, replaced summer by 9845 kHz; *(Central)* 1900-2100 (weekends only) on 15315 kHz; and 0100-0200 winter on 6165 kHz, replaced summer by 9845 kHz; *(West):* 1900-2100 (weekends only) on 17725 kHz winter, and 17660 kHz summer; 0400-0500 summer on 6165 and 9590 kHz; and 0500-0600 winter on 6165 kHz.

Southern Africa: 1800-1900 on 6020 kHz, and 1900-2100 on 7120 kHz.

East and Southeast Asia: 1000-1100 winter on 7315, 9795 and 12065 kHz; and summer on 12065, 13710 and 13820 kHz—some are also well heard in parts of Australasia.

Australasia: 0500-0600 winter on 11710 kHz, and 1000-1100 midyear on 9790 kHz. Also, see preceding item.

Russia

The **Voice of Russia** continues to air a wide range of cultural and other offerings reflecting the country's past and present. Friendly announcers and entertaining music help the VoR maintain popularity with its audience.

☞ RECOMMENDED PROGRAMS: "Christian Message from Moscow" and "Music and Musicians."

Eastern North America: Winter, 0200-0600 on 7180 kHz, 0300-0500 on 7350 kHz, and 0400-0600 on 7150 kHz; summer, 0100-0500 on 9665 kHz (7180 kHz in autumn), 0200-0400 on 9860 kHz, and 0300-0500 on 9880 kHz (5900 kHz in autumn). Winter

E1XM

The E1XM is the world's first radio to combine AM, FM, Shortwave, and XM Satellite Radio Ready technology into one ultra-high-performance unit.

_ AM/FM/Shortwave/XM Satellite Ready Radio
_ 1700 station presets
_ Digitally synthesized PLL tuner with synchronous detector
_ Passband tuning, selectable bandwidth filters and Selectable Single Sideband (SSB) reception
_ Dual conversion superheterodyne circuit design
_ Stereo line level audio inputs and outputs and external antenna connections
_ Dual Clocks and programmable timers
_ Headphone jack
_ Built-In Antenna: telescopic antenna for AM, FM and Shortwave reception
_ External Antenna Connection for the addition of auxiliary antennas
_ Calibrated LCD signal strength meter

FR250
Multi-Purpose

Stay informed and prepared for emergencies with this self-powered 3-in-1 radio, flashlight and cell-phone charger — no batteries required.

_ AM/FM/Shortwave Radio Reception
_ Built-in power generator recharges the internal rechargeable Ni-MH battery (Included)
_ Cell-phone charger output jack 3.5mm (various cell phone plug tips included)
_ Built-in 2 white LED light source and one flashing red LED

S350
Ruggedly Retro

With the look of a retro field radio sporting a rugged body and military-style controls – the S350 also features today's innovation for excellent AM, FM, and Shortwave reception and a large, full-range speaker for clear sound.

_ AM/FM/Shortwave Radio reception
_ Highly sensitive and selective analog tuner circuitry
_ Liquid Crystal Display (LCD), for frequency and clock display.
_ Digital clock with selectable 12/24 hour format

etón®
RE_INVENTING™ RADIO
www.etoncorp.com

afternoons, try frequencies for Europe—some make it to eastern North America.

Western North America: Winter, 0200-0500 on 12010 (from 0400), 15425, 15475 and 15595 kHz; and 0500-0600 on 12010, 15425 and 15595 kHz. Summer, 0100-0500 on 15455, 15555 and 15595 kHz.

Europe: Winter, 1800-1900 on 7290 kHz; 1900-2000 on 6175, 6235, 7290 and 7400 kHz; and 2000-2200 on 6145 (till 2100), 6235, 7290, 7300 (from 2100) and 7330 kHz. Summer, 1700-1800 on 9890 kHz; 1800-1900 on 9480, 9890 and 11630 (or 9820) kHz; and 1900-2100 on 7380 (till 2000), 9890, 12070 (or 7310) and (from 2000) 15455 (or 7330) kHz [5950 and 6175 kHz (winter), 9480 and 11675 (summer) and 7390 and 9820 kHz (autumn) are also available weekends during the first hour].

Middle East: Winter, 1600-1700 on 6005 and 9830 kHz, and 1700-1900 on 9830 kHz. Summer, 1500-1600 on 7325 and 11985 kHz, 1600-1700 on 11985 and 15540 kHz, and 1700-1800 on 11985 kHz.

Southern Africa: 1800-2000 (one hour earlier in summer) on 11510 kHz.

Southeast Asia: Winter, 0800-1000 on 17495, 17525 and 17570 kHz; and 1500-1600 on 6205 and 11500 kHz. Summer, 0700-0900 on 17495 and 17525 kHz; 1400-1500 on 7390 kHz; and 1500-1600 on 7390 and 11500 kHz.

Australasia: Winter, 0600-0900 on 21790 kHz; 0600-1000 on 17665 kHz; and 0800-1000 on 17495, 17525 and 17570 kHz. Midyear, 0500-0900 on 21790 kHz; 0700-0900 midyear on 17495, 17525 and 17635 kHz.

United Kingdom

The **BBC World Service** continues to lose its bite. Not only was there zero improvement in program quality in 2005, but transmissions were reduced to Europe and—yet again!—the Americas.

With the entire BBC undergoing major restructuring, including layoffs and reassignments, the World Service has received its share of knocks. Outsourcing of production is also taking a toll, further reducing the development of inhouse talent.

Yet, there are still worthy programs, some one-of-a-kind. Grab 'em while you can!

☞ RECOMMENDED PROGRAMS: "Charlie Gillett," "One Planet" and "Reporting Religion."

North America: With the closure of the BBC's Antigua relay in March 2005, and the rescheduling of transmissions for the Caribbean and Central America, reception of BBC broadcasts in North America has been drastically reduced. Worse, the service to South America, previously audible in parts of the United States, has also been reduced to just two hours a day.

Listeners in the southern and southwestern United States often hear broadcasts for the Caribbean: 1000-1100 on 6195 kHz, 1100-1200 on 11865 kHz; 1200-1300 on 9605 and 11865 kHz; 1300-1400 on 15190 kHz; 2100-2130 weekdays on 15390 kHz (11675 kHz in summer); 2100-2200 on 11675 kHz (15390 kHz in summer); and 2200-0100 and 0300-0400 on 5975 kHz. Transmissions for South America are at 1200-1300 on 15190 kHz, and 0200-0300 on 5975, 9825 and 12095 kHz.

Some daytime frequencies for Europe, Africa and the Mideast manage to reach North America— particularly during summer. But times vary, depending on your location and the time of year. Early morning in western North America, tune to the BBC's East Asia stream on 9740 kHz (1000-1600); reception is especially good on the West Coast.

Europe: (Western) Winter, 0400-0800 on 6195 and 9410 kHz; 1400-1700 Saturday on 6195 kHz; and 1700-2200 on 6195 and 9410 kHz; summer, 0400-0700 on 6195, 9410 and 12095 kHz (times vary for each frequency); 1300-1600 Saturday on 12095 kHz; 1600-1900 on 9410 and 12095 kHz; and 1900-2100 on 6195 and 9410 kHz. *(Central and Southeast)* 0400-0700 and 1500-1900 (one hour earlier summer) on 6195, 9410, 12095, 15565 and 17640 kHz (times vary for each channel).

Middle East: 0200-2000 (summer, till 1900). Key frequencies—times for each vary seasonally—are 9410, 11760, 12095, 15310, 15565, 15575 and 17640 kHz. The 12095, 15565 and 17640 kHz frequencies are mainly for Eastern Europe, but can be heard in northern parts of the Mideast.

Southern Africa: 0300-2200 on, among others, 3255, 6005, 6190, 11940, 12095 and 21470 kHz—times vary for each channel.

East and Southeast Asia: 0000-0300 on 6195 (till 0200), 9740 (till 0100), 15280 and 15360 kHz; 0300-0500 on 15280, 15360, 17760 and 21660 kHz; 0500-0800 on 11955, 15280 (till 0530), 15360, 17760 and 21660; 0800-0900 on 6195 (winter), 9740 (winter), 11955 (summer), 15280 (winter), 17760 and 21660 kHz; 0900-1030 on 6195, 9605, 9740, 15280 (winter), 15360 (summer), 17760 and 21660 kHz; 1030-1400 on 6195, 9740 and (summer) 17760 kHz; 1400-1600 on 6195, 7160, 9740 and (summer) 11750 kHz; 1600-1700 on 3915, 6195 and 7160 kHz; and 1700-1800 (to Southeast Asia) on 3915 and 7160 kHz. Local mornings, it's 2100-2200 on 3915, 5965, 6110 (winter), 6195 and (summer) 11945 kHz; 2200-2300 on 5965, 5990, 6195, 7105, 9740 and 11955 kHz; and 2300-2400 on 3915, 5965, 6195, 7105, 9740, 11955 and (summer) 15280 kHz.

Australasia: Like North America, Australasia is no longer an official target for BBC broadcasts. However, some transmissions for Southeast Asia are easily heard in Australia and New Zealand. Best bets: 0500-0800 on 11955 and 15360 kHz, and 0800-1600 on 9740 kHz (midyear, the first transmission continues to 0900, while 9740 kHz starts one hour later). At 2200-2300, 12080 kHz is also available for the southwestern Pacific.

ASIA
China

China Radio International is gradually filling the void left by the BBC World Service and other declining broadcasters. Its numerous transmitting sites on home soil and overseas relays in Europe, Africa and the Americas guarantee top-notch reception just about everywhere on an everyday radio.

Even the prime minister complains about the BBC World Service these days, but Charlie Gillett keeps folks tuning in.   Philip Ryalls

It offers interesting programs and an upbeat style, and is a leading force in international broadcasting.

☞ RECOMMENDED PROGRAMS: "RealTime Beijing" and "Voices from Other Lands."

Eastern North America: 0000-0200 on 6020 and 9570 kHz; 0100-0200 on 6005 (winter), 6080 and 9580 kHz; 0300-0400 on 9690 kHz; 1000-1100 summer on 6040 kHz; 1100-1200 winter on 5960 kHz, and summer on 6040 kHz; 1300-1400 on 9570 and (summer) 9650 and 15260 kHz; 1300-1500 winter on 15230 kHz; and 2300-2400 on 5990 (better to the south), 6040 (winter) and (summer) 6145 kHz.

Western North America: 0000-0200 on 6020 and 9570 kHz; 0100-0200 on 6005 (winter), 6080 and (summer) 9790 kHz; 0300-0400 on 9690 and 9790 kHz, 0400-0500 on 6090 (summer), 6190 (winter), 9560 (summer) and 9755 kHz; 0500-0600 on 5960 (winter), 6090 (summer), 6190 and (summer) 9560 kHz; 0600-0700 winter on 6115 kHz; 1100-1200 summer on 11750 kHz; 1300-1400 winter on 11885 kHz; 1400-1600 on 13675

China Radio International apparently wants to be heard—no matter how! Its focus on English is transforming it into a key information source in the world's *lingua franca*.   CRI

(winter) and 13740 kHz; and 2300-2400 winter on 11970 kHz, replaced summer by 13680 kHz.

Europe: 0000-0200 winter on 7345 kHz, and summer on 13600 kHz; 0600-0700 summer on 17490 kHz; 0700-0900 on 11855 (winter), 13710 (summer) and 17490 kHz (winter from 0800); 0900-1100 on 17490 kHz; 1100-1200 on 13650 (summer), 13665 (winter) and 17490 kHz; 1200-1300 on 13650 (summer), 13665 (winter), 13790 and 17490 kHz; 1300-1400 on 13610 (winter), 13790 and (summer) 17490 kHz; 1400-1500 winter on 9700, 9795 and 13610 kHz, and summer on 13790, 17490 and 17650 kHz; 1500-1600 winter on 9435 and 9525 kHz, and summer on 11965, 13640 and 17490 kHz; 1600-1700 winter on 7255, 9435 and 9525 kHz, and summer on 11940, 11965, 13760 and 17490 kHz; 1700-1800 winter on 6100 and 7255 kHz, and summer on 9695,

11940 and 13760 kHz; 1800-1900 winter on 6160 kHz, and summer on 9695, 11940 and 13760 kHz; 1900-2000 winter on 6160 kHz, and summer on 11940 kHz; and 2000-2200 on 5960, 7190, 7285, 9600 and (summer) 9800 and 11790 kHz. A relay via Moscow can be heard winter at 2200-2300 on 7170 kHz, and summer on 7175 kHz.

Middle East: 1900-2100 on 7295 and 9440 kHz.

Southern Africa: 1500-1600 on 6100 kHz; 1600-1800 on 6100, 9570 and 11900 kHz; and 2000-2130 on 11640 kHz.

Southeast Asia: 1200-1300 on 9730 and 11980 kHz; and 1300-1400 on 11980 kHz.

Australasia: 0900-1100 on 15210 and 17690 kHz; 1200-1300 on 11760 and 9760 or 15415 kHz; and 1300-1400 on 11760 and 11900 kHz.

China (Taiwan)

Compared to its radio cousin in Beijing, **Radio Taiwan International** offers more variety in its broadcasts. News reporting is balanced by cultural and entertainment features, and overall presentation is more relaxed.

☞ RECOMMENDED PROGRAM: "Jade Bells and Bamboo Pipes."

North America: (East and Central) 0200-0300 on 5950 and 9680 kHz; *(West)* 0300-0400 and 0700-0800 on 5950 kHz.

Europe: 1800-1900 on 3955 kHz; and 2200-2300 winter on 9355 kHz, replaced summer by 15600 kHz.

Middle East: There is nothing specifically targeted at the Mideast, but try the 2200-2300 broadcast to Europe via RTI's North American relay.

Asia: (East) 0200-0300 on 15465 kHz, and 1200-1300 on 7130 kHz; *(Southeast)* 0200-0300 on 11875 kHz; 0300-0400 on 15320 kHz; 1100-1200 on 7445 kHz, and 1400-1500 on 15265 kHz; *(South)* 1600-1700 on 11815 kHz.

Australasia: 0800-0900 on 9610 kHz.

E1XM

The E1XM is the world's first radio to combine AM, FM, Shortwave, and XM Satellite Radio Ready technology into one ultra-high-performance unit.

_ AM/FM/Shortwave/XM Satellite Ready Radio
_ 1700 station presets
_ Digitally synthesized PLL tuner with synchronous detector
_ Passband tuning, selectable bandwidth filters and Selectable Single Sideband (SSB) reception
_ Dual conversion superheterodyne circuit design
_ Stereo line-level audio inputs and outputs and external antenna connections
_ Dual Clocks and programmable timers
_ Headphone jack
_ Built-In Antenna: telescopic antenna for AM, FM and Shortwave reception
_ External Antenna Connection for the addition of auxiliary antennas
_ Calibrated LCD signal strength meter

E10
AM/FM/Shortwave Radio

Intelligence meets performance in the E10. The E10 provides sophisticated tools for listening to news, sports, and music from around the world.

_ Shortwave range of 1711 – 29,999 KHz
_ 550 programmable memories with memory page customization
_ Manual and auto scan, direct keypad frequency entry, ATS
_ Clock with alarm, sleep timer, and snooze functions

S350
Ruggedly Retro

With the look of a retro field radio sporting a rugged body and military-style controls – the S350 also features today's innovation for excellent AM, FM, and Shortwave reception and a large, full-range speaker for clear sound.

_ AM/FM/Shortwave Radio reception
_ Highly sensitive and selective analog tuner circuitry
_ Liquid Crystal Display (LCD), for frequency and clock display.
_ Digital clock with selectable 12/24 hour format

AES
AMATEUR ELECTRONIC SUPPLY
47 Years
Serving Hams

etón®
RE-INVENTING™ RADIO
www.etoncorp.com

Japan

Like China Radio International, **Radio Japan** uses overseas relays to ensure global coverage. News reporting homes in on Asia and the Pacific, and is nicely complemented by music and entertainment.

☞ RECOMMENDED PROGRAM: "Japan Music Archives."

Eastern North America: Best: 0000-0100 on 6145 kHz, and 1000-1200 on 6120 kHz, all via the Canadian relay at Sackville, New Brunswick.

Western North America: 0100-0200 on 17825 kHz; 0500-0600 on 6110 kHz; 0600-0700 winter on 11690 kHz, and summer on 13630 kHz; 1500-1600 on 9505 kHz; 1700-1800 on 9535 kHz; and 2100-2200 on 17825 kHz. Listeners in Hawaii can tune in at 0600-0700 on 17870 kHz, and 2100-2200 on 21670 kHz.

Europe: 0500-0600 on 5975 kHz; 0500-0700 on 7230 kHz; 1000-1100 on 17585 kHz; 1700-1800 on 11970 kHz; and 2100-2200 on 6055 (summer), 6090 (winter) and 6180 kHz.

Middle East: 0100-0200 on 6030 (winter), 5960 (summer) and 17560 kHz; and 1000-1100 on 17720 kHz.

Southern Africa: 1700-1800 on 15355 kHz.

Asia: 0000-0015 on 13650 and 17810 kHz; 0100-0200 on 11860, 15325, 17810 and 17845 kHz; 0500-0600 on 15195 and 17810 kHz; 0600-0700 on 11715, 11740, 11760 and 15195 kHz; 1000-1200 on 9695 and 11730 kHz; 1400-1500 on 7200 and 9875 (or 11730) kHz; and 1500-1600 on 6190, 7200 and 9875 (or 11730) kHz. Transmissions to Asia are often also heard in other parts of the world.

Australasia: 0100-0200 on 17685 kHz; 0300-0400 on 21610 kHz; 0500-0700 and 1000-1100 on 21755 kHz; 1400-1500 on 11840 kHz; and 2100-2200 on 6035 kHz.

NORTH AMERICA
Canada

Over the past couple of years **Radio Canada International** has cut back on broadcasts to the United States and western Europe while expanding its reach to other continents. Asia is now well served via relays in China, Japan and South Korea, while Africa is covered by transmitters in Europe, China, the United Arab Emirates and Canada itself.

Most of RCI's English programs continue to be produced by its parent organization, the domestic Canadian Broadcasting Corporation. Several are long-running listener favorites.

☞ RECOMMENDED PROGRAMS: "The Vinyl Café" and "Global Village."

North America: The continuing consolidation of RCI broadcasts to North America and the Caribbean leaves much of western North America without a reliable signal, while the Caribbean and southern United States are strongly favored. In winter, the morning broadcast airs at 1400-1700 on 9515, 13655 and 17820 kHz. Summer, it's one hour earlier on 9515, 13655 and 17800 kHz. During winter, evening broadcasts air at 2300-2400 on 6100 kHz (East Coast), and 0000-0200 on 9755 kHz. There's only one broadcast in summer: 0000-0200 on 9755 and 13710 kHz. Also for the southern United States and Caribbean there's a relay of CBC domestic programs at 2000-2300 winter on 15180 kHz, and 1900-2200 summer on 17765 kHz.

Europe: 2100-2200 winter on 5850 and 9770 kHz; and 2000-2100 summer on 5850, 11765 and 15325 kHz.

Middle East: Try 2100-2200 winter on 5850 kHz, and 2000-2100 summer on 11765 kHz.

Southern Africa: Try 2000-2100, winter on 13730 kHz and summer on 15420 kHz.

Asia: (East) 1200-1330 winter on 7105 kHz (replaced by 9725 kHz at 1300), summer on 9660 kHz; and 2230-2300 winter on 6160 kHz, summer on 9870 kHz; *(Southeast)* 0000-0100 winter on 9880 kHz, summer on 9690 kHz; 1200-1300 winter on 9665 kHz, summer on 15170 kHz; and 2230-2300 winter on 7195 and 9730 kHz, summer on 9525 and 12035 kHz; *(South)* 1500-1600 winter on 9635 and 11975 kHz; replaced summer by 11675, 15360 and 17720 kHz.

United States

Will the English broadcasts of the **Voice of America** survive, or are they doomed to death by a thousand cuts? Shorter transmissions, fewer frequencies, and program repeats every hour or two do not bode well for its future, especially with China Radio International grabbing abandoned VOA audiences.

The Voice of America was authoritatively credited with being one of the top reasons the West won the Cold War—and, unlike armies, it did so affordably and without loss of life. But its onetime professional sophistication and caliber of influence has all but disappeared, and with it the VOA as a ubiquitous world voice.

There is a belief within the VOA that politicians and members of the VOA's parent organization, the IBB, intend to totally eliminate the station and use its funds for other radio and television ventures. With the IBB increasingly subject to political influence and journalists pressured to tow the line, it's difficult to be optimistic about the future of this elder statesman of the world's airwaves.

☞ RECOMMENDED PROGRAM: "Country Hits USA."

North America: The VOA can still be heard in North America, albeit far less than it used to be. Closest to home is a 30-minute broadcast in "Special" (slow speed) English to the Caribbean and South America at 0130 Tuesday through Saturday (weekday evenings in the Americas) on 7405, 9775 and 13740 kHz. The African Service can also be heard in parts of North America; try 0400-0500 on 9575 kHz; 0500-0630 winter on 6035 kHz; and 1900-2200 winter on 15580 kHz, replaced summer by 15445 kHz.

Middle East: 0900-1200 winter on 15615 and 17555 kHz; summer on 9520, 15205 and 17745 kHz; and 1500-1700 winter on 9685, 11835 and 15255 kHz; summer on 9700 (from 1600), 9825, 15195 and 15445 kHz.

Southern Africa: 0300-0600 (till 0630 winter) on 4930 kHz; 1600-1700 on 4930, 15240 (winter) and (midyear) 17895 kHz; 1700-1800 on 15240 (or 15410) kHz; and 1800-2200 on 4930 and 15240 (or 15410) kHz.

East and Southeast Asia: 1200-1300 winter on 6110, 9645, 9760, 11705, 11715 and 15665 kHz; summer on 6160, 9645, 9760 and 15240 kHz; 1300-1500 winter on 6110, 9645, 9760, 11705 and (from 1400) 15425 kHz; summer on 6160 (from 1400), 9645 (till 1400) and (from 1400) 15185 kHz; 1500-1600 winter on 9645, 11780 and 13735 kHz; summer on 13690 and 15105 kHz; 1600-1700 weekdays on 6160, 9645 (winter) and 9760 kHz; and 2200-0100 on 7215, 9890 (winter), 15185, 15290, 15305 (till 2400), 17740 and (summer) 17820 kHz.

Australasia: 1200-1400 on 9645 kHz; 1400-1500 midyear on 15185 kHz; 1400-1600 winter on 9645 kHz; 1600-1700 winter weekdays on 9645 kHz; and 2200-0100 on 17740 kHz.

Mary Morningstar hosts the VOA's popular "Country Hits USA." VOA

> The VOA was a top reason the Cold War was won.

Prepared by Tony Jones and the staff of Passport to World Band Radio.

FR200
Crank it Up

Without the need for batteries, this self-powered 2-in-1 radio and flashlight helps you stay informed and prepared for emergencies.

_ AM/FM/Shortwave Radio Reception
_ Built-in power generator recharges the internal rechargeable Ni-MH battery (Included)
_ Built-in white LED light source
_ 12 international bands
_ Available colors: Metallic Blue, Metallic Red, Sand

■ ■ ■

FR250
Multi-Purpose

Stay informed and prepared for emergencies with this self-powered 3-in-1 radio, flashlight and cell-phone charger — no batteries required.

_ AM/FM/Shortwave Radio Reception
_ Built-in power generator recharges the internal rechargeable Ni-MH battery (Included)
_ Cell-phone charger output jack 3.5mm (various cell phone plug tips included)
_ Built-in 2 white LED light source and one flashing red LED

E1

The E1 is the world's first radio to combine AM, FM, Shortwave, and Satellite Radio Ready technology into one ultra-high-performance unit.

_ AM/FM/Shortwave/Satellite Ready Radio
_ 1700 station presets
_ Digitally synthesized PLL tuner with synchronous detector
_ Passband tuning, selectable bandwidth filters and Selectable Single Sideband (SSB) reception
_ Dual conversion superheterodyne circuit design
_ Stereo line-level audio inputs and outputs and external antenna connections
_ Dual Clocks and programmable timers
_ Headphone jack
_ Built-In Antenna: telescopic antenna for AM, FM and Shortwave reception
_ External Antenna Connection for the addition of auxiliary antennas
_ Calibrated LCD signal strength meter
_ High Dynamic Range: allowing for the detection of weak signals in the presence of strong signals

Mini 300PE
Compact and Power-Packed

Small enough to fit into your pocket, the Mini 300PE world-band radio makes a perfect travel companion.

_ Built-in clock, alarm, and sleep functions
_ Large easy-to-read LCD screen
_ Protective travel case and ear buds
_ Available colors: Metallic Blue, Metallic Red, Yellow, Metallic Bronze, Metallic Pearl

E10
AM/FM/Shortwave Radio

Intelligence meets performance in the E10. The E10 provides sophisticated tools for listening to news, sports, and music from around the world.

_ Shortwave range of 1711 – 29,999 KHz
_ 550 programmable memories with memory page customization
_ Manual and auto scan, direct keypad frequency entry, ATS
_ Clock with alarm, sleep timer, and snooze functions

E100
AM/FM/Shortwave Radio

The E100 features a sleek design complimented by a portable physique. This little marvel is packed with all the latest radio features you want and it's small enough to fit in your coat pocket!

_ Shortwave range of 1711 – 29,999 KHz
_ 200 programmable memories
_ Memory page customization
_ Manual and auto scan, direct keypad frequency entry

S350
Ruggedly Retro

With the look of a retro field radio sporting a rugged body and military-style controls – the S350 also features today's innovation for excellent AM, FM, and Shortwave reception and a large, full-range speaker for clear sound.

_ AM/FM/Shortwave Radio reception
_ Highly sensitive and selective analog tuner circuitry
_ Liquid Crystal Display (LCD), for frequency and clock display.
_ Digital clock with selectable 12/24 hour format

S350 Deluxe
High-Performance Field Radio with Stereo Headphones

For S350 devotees the deluxe model combines a sporty new exterior with the same unrivalled functionality.
_ FM- stereo via headphones (included)
_ AM/Shortwave Frequency Lock
_ Set clock and alarm

_ Highly sensitive analog tuner with digital display
_ Large, full range speaker with bass & treble control
_ Clock, alarm, and sleep timer
_ Built-in antennas and connections for external antennas
_ Available colors: Metallic Red, Black

www.nevada.co.uk

Ten of the Best: 2006's Top Shows

World band has some of the juiciest shows around, and here are ten top examples. Times and days are in World Time—"winter" and "summer" refer to seasons in the Northern Hemisphere, where summer takes place in the middle of the year.

"Charlie Gillett"
BBC World Service

There's no need to be a world music buff to enjoy "Charlie Gillett." Origi-nally known as "World of Music," it has been honed to perfection and is now rightly named after its host.

Apart from the rare live perfor-mance, all music is taken off CDs and there's no end of variety—the sublime voice of Ladino singer Yasmin Levy, Nour el Ain's "Egyptian flamenco" or Guinea's Jali Moussa Jawara. But it's not only current art-ists; there are also evergreens like

Amália Rodriguez's "Tudo Esto é Fado," and Vinicius de Moraes and Maria Creuza's "A Garota de Ipanema." If you like music because it's good—popularity be damned—you'll feast at "Charlie Gillett."

Americas: Winter, *Caribbean* listeners can tune in at 0132 Thursday (local Wednesday evening) on 5975 kHz; summer, it's one hour earlier on the same frequency. Also heard in the southern *United States.*

Europe: Winter, 1932 Wednesday on 6195 and 9410 kHz; summer, one hour earlier on 9410 and 12095 kHz .

Middle East: Winter, 0832 Wednesday on 11760 kHz; with repeats at 1432 on 12095 and 15575 kHz, and 1932 on 5975 kHz. Summer, one hour earlier at 0732 on 11760 kHz; 1332 on 11760 and 15575 kHz; and 1832 on 12095 kHz.

Southern Africa gets two Wednesday slots: 0732 on 6190 and 11940 kHz; and 1332 on 6190, 11940 and 21470 kHz.

East Asia: 0232 Wednesday (one hour earlier in summer) on 15280 and 15360 kHz; repeated at 0732 on 15360, 17760 and 21660 kHz. *Southeast Asia* has the same Wednesday slots: 0132 summer on 6195 and 15360 kHz; 0232 winter on 15360 kHz; and 0732 on 11955, 15360 and 17760 kHz.

There's officially nothing for *Australasia*, but 0732 Wednesday on 11955 and 15360 kHz can provide fair-to-good reception.

> **Musical archives reach back to the earliest days of recording.**

"The Research File"
Radio Netherlands

Few of world band's long-running science shows have maintained their popularity like Radio Netherlands' "The Research File." It's a thoroughly un-boring half hour with lean, tight production.

Topics range from nuclear fusion and pharmaceuticals testing to hypnotherapy and autism. All covered with panache and expertise.

As Dutch science masters the sea, so Radio Netherlands masters science in one of world band's long-running shows.   Corbis

North America: (East) 1227 Monday (one hour earlier in summer) on 11675 kHz, with a repeat at 0027 on 6165 kHz (summer on 9845 kHz); *(Central)* 0127 Tuesday (Wednesday evening in the Americas) on 6165 kHz (summer on 9845 kHz). *(West)* 0527 Tuesday (Monday evening local date) on 6165 kHz (summer one hour earlier on 6165 and 9590 kHz).

There's nothing for *Europe* or the *Middle East*, but there are three slots for *southern Africa*: 1827 Monday on 6020 kHz, 2000 Monday on 7120 kHz, and 1900 Thursday on 7120 kHz.

East and *Southeast Asia:* 1027 Monday on 7315 (winter), 9785 (winter), 12065, and (summer) 13710 and 13820 kHz. *Australasia:* Monday at 0527 winter on 11710 kHz, and 1027 midyear on 9790 kHz; channels for Asia can also provide good reception.

"Music and Musicians"
Voice of Russia

Digital Age it may be, but there's a surprising amount of good music on analog world band. Among the best hangouts is "Music and Musicians," 47 minutes of classical music aired each week over the Voice of Russia.

The station's musical archives reach back to the earliest days of recording. Add to this the thriving music scene in today's Moscow, and there's hardly any limit to what you can hear. Because some of the cuts are new or unusual, they are often complemented by short interviews, anecdotes and informative tidbits.

North America: Winter, 0411 Sunday (Saturday evening local American date) on 7180, 7150, 7350, 12010, 15425, 15475 and 15595 kHz; summer, one hour earlier on 9665 (7180 kHz in autumn), 9860, 9880, 15455, 15555 and 15595 kHz.

Europe has two Saturday slots: Winter, 1811 on 5950, 6175 and 7290 kHz; and 2111 on 6235, 7290, 7300 and 7330 kHz; summer, 1711 on 7390, 9820 and 9890 kHz; and 2011 on 9890, 12070 (or 7310) and 15455 (or 7330) kHz.

Middle East: Winter, 1811 Saturday on 9830 kHz; summer, one hour earlier on 11985 kHz.

Southern Africa: 1811 Saturday (one hour earlier in summer) on 11510 kHz.

Southeast Asia: Winter, 0811 Monday on 17495, 17525 and 17570 kHz; summer, one hour earlier on 17495 and 17525 kHz.

Re_inventing Radio through Design, Innovation, Necessity

E1XM

The E1XM is the world's first radio to combine AM, FM, Shortwave, and XM Satellite Radio Ready technology into one ultra-high-performance unit.

_ AM/FM/SW/XM Satellite Ready Radio
_ 1700 station presets
_ Digitally synthesized PLL tuner with synchronous detector
_ Passband tuning, selectable bandwidth filters and Selectable Single Sideband (SSB) reception
_ Dual conversion superheterodyne circuit design

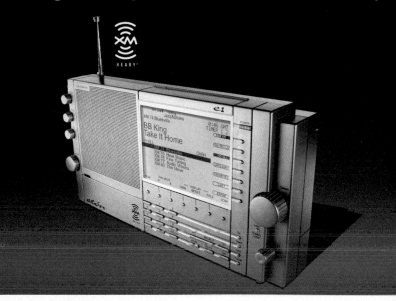

E10
AM/FM/Shortwave Radio

Intelligence meets performance in the E10. The E10 provides sophisticated tools for listening to news, sports, and music from around the world.

_ Shortwave range of 1711 – 29,999 KHz
_ 550 programmable memories with memory page customization
_ Manual and auto scan, direct keypad frequency entry, AIS
_ Clock with alarm, sleep timer, and snooze functions

E100
AM/FM/Shortwave Radio

The E100 features a sleek design complimented by a portable physique. This little marvel is packed with all the latest radio features you want and it's small enough to fit in your coat pocket!

_ Shortwave range of 1711 – 29,999 KHz
_ 200 programmable memories
_ Memory page customization
_ Manual and auto scan, direct keypad frequency entry

S350
Ruggedly Retro

With the look of a retro field radio sporting a rugged body and military-style controls – the S350 also features today's innovation for excellent AM, FM, and Shortwave reception and a large, full-range speaker for clear sound.

_ AM/FM/Shortwave Radio reception
_ Highly sensitive and selective analog tuner circuitry
_ Liquid Crystal Display (LCD), for frequency and clock display.
_ Digital clock with selectable 12/24 hour format

Radioworld®

etón®
RE_INVENTING™ RADIO
www.etoncorp.com

Rick Fulker, editor of "A World of Music," in his listening room at Deutsche Welle headquarters in Bonn.

DW

Australasia: Winter, 0811 Monday on 17495, 17525, 17570, 17665 and 21790 kHz, midyear, one hour earlier on 17495, 17525, 17635 and 21790 kHz.

"Reporting Religion"
BBC World Service

Islamic fundamentalism, separation of church and state, creationism—all underscore that religion is once again on the global front burner. Keeping an eye on nearly all aspects of it is the BBC World Service's "Reporting Religion."

Scrupulously fair, the show nevertheless exposes the downside of current religious practices: faith influencing political and judicial decisions, for example, or missionary zeal exacerbating environmental or cultural degradation. "Reporting Religion" is honest with an open mind—no blind faith.

Americas: Listeners in the *Caribbean* can tune in at 2332 Saturday (one hour earlier in summer) on 5975 kHz; or 1132 Sunday on 11865 kHz. Reception should also be possible in much of the southern *United States.* On the West Coast, listen to the 1132 Sunday edition to Asia on 9740 kHz.

Europe has two Saturday editions which are one hour earlier in summer, but which use the same channels all year. Winter, it's

0532 Saturday on 6195 and 9410 kHz; and 1932 Saturday (sometimes replaced by the last part of an extended "Play of the Week") on 6195 and 9410 kHz (12095 kHz is also available in summer).

Middle East: Winter, 0432 Saturday and 0332 Sunday on 11760 kHz; and 0532 Sunday on 9410 and 11760 kHz. In summer, all are one hour earlier, but on the same frequencies.

Southern Africa: 0832 Sunday on 6190, 11940 and 21470 kHz.

East Asia: 2232 Saturday (local Sunday in the target area) on 5965 kHz; 0532 Sunday on 15360, 17760 and 21660 kHz; and 1132 Sunday (sometimes replaced by the last part of an extended "Play of the Week") on 9740 kHz. *Southeast Asia* has the same slots, but on different frequencies: 2232 Saturday on 5990, 6195, 7105 and 9740 kHz; 0532 Sunday on 9740, 11955 and 15360 kHz; and 1132 Sunday on 6195 and 9740 kHz.

There's officially nothing for *Australasia,* but reception at 1132 Sunday on 9740 kHz should be more than adequate in many areas.

"Global Village"
CBC/Radio Canada International

If the BBC's "Charlie Gillett" is the salon version of world music, then "Global Village" is its festival. Interviews, reports, live performances and a fine selection of recordings make this all-embracing show an extravaganza.

"Global Village" seamlessly combines traditional folk music and today's world music. It's aired to North America at 0105 Sunday (local Saturday evening) on 9755 and (summer) 13710 kHz; and to East Asia at 1205 Thursday, winter on 7105 and 9665 kHz, and summer on 9660 and 15170 kHz.

"A World of Music"
Deutsche Welle

"Unusual classical music" can mean reaching for the dial or stuffing cotton in your ears. Not so with Deutsche Welle's "A World of Music." It airs gems you're unlikely to hear elsewhere and which you'll probably enjoy more than another earful of Bizet or Rossini. For example, to celebrate the rebuilding of the Church of Our Lady in Dresden destroyed in World War II, the show once offered weeks of exquisite baroque and other fine music from that city.

Deutsche Welle doesn't target *North America*, but in the eastern and southern United States there's often good reception of the 2100-2200 transmission to West Africa. Luckily, "A World of Music" is part of the Monday broadcast at this time, so try 2130 on 9615 and 11690 kHz in winter, and 11865 and 15205 kHz in summer.

Europe: 0730, 0930 and 1430 Tuesday on 6140 kHz.

There's nothing for the *Middle East*, but listeners in *Southern Africa* can tune in at 0530 Tuesday, winter on 12035 kHz, and midyear on 9630 and 9700 kHz.

East Asia—like the Middle East—misses out, but *Southeast Asia* gets its chance at 2330 Monday (Tuesday morning local date). Winter frequencies are 6070, 9555 and 9815 kHz; and are replaced summer by 5955, 9890 and 15135 kHz.

There's nothing specifically scheduled to *Australasia*, but reception of the 2330 broadcast to Southeast Asia should be adequate, especially to the west.

"Voices from Other Lands" China Radio International

The format is simple: a one-on-one interview with foreigners who are visiting or working in China.

It works. Businesspeople, architects, teachers, historians, grizzled voyagers—they all have interesting tales to relate. "Voices from Other Lands" handles these in a relaxed and chatty 20 minutes that mixes interviews with discussions.

North America: 2333 Wednesday on 5990 (nominally to the Caribbean), 6040 (winter), 6145 (summer), 11970 (winter) and

(summer) 13680 kHz. All other airings are Thursday, World Time: 0033 (Wednesday evening local American date) on 6020 and 9570 kHz; 0133 on 6005 (winter), 6020, 6080, 9570, 9580 and (summer) 9790 kHz; 0333 on 9690 and 9790 kHz; 0433 on 6090 (summer), 6190 (winter), 9560 (summer) and 9755 kHz; 0533 on 5960 (winter), 6090 (summer), 6190 and (summer) 9560 kHz; 0633 winter on 6115 kHz; 1333 on 9570, 9650 (summer), 11885 (winter), 15230 (winter) and (summer) 15260 kHz; 1433 winter on 13675 and 15230 kHz, and year round on 13740 kHz; and 1533 on 15230 (winter) and 13740 kHz.

All broadcasts to other areas are aired Thursday.

Europe: 0033 and 0133 winter on 7345 kHz, and summer on 13600 kHz; 0633 summer on 17490 kHz; 0733 winter on 11855 kHz; and summer on 13710 kHz; 0833 on 11855 (winter), 13710 (summer) and 17490 kHz; 0933 on 17490 kHz; 1233 on 13650 (summer), 13665 (winter), 13790 and 17490 kHz; 1333 on 13610 (winter), 13790 and (summer) 17490 kHz; 1433 winter on 9700, 9795 and 13610 kHz; and summer on 13790, 17490 and 17650 kHz; 1533 winter on 9435 and 9525 kHz; and summer on 11965, 13640 and 17490 kHz; 1633 winter

CRI's studios are among the world's best. They are home to some excellent shows, including "Voices from Other Lands."   M. Guha

Barbara Gruber and Helen Seeney prepare "Inside Europe." If something interesting is going on, they're sure to flush it out.   DW

on 7255, 9435 and 9525 kHz; and summer on 11940, 11965, 13760 and 17490 kHz; 1733 winter on 6100 and 7255 kHz; and summer on 9695, 11940 and 13760 kHz; 1833 winter on 6160 kHz, and summer on 9695, 11940 and 13760 kHz; 1933 winter on 6160 kHz; and summer on 11940 kHz; 2033 and 2133 on 5960, 7190, 7285, 9600 and (summer) 9800 and 11790 kHz; and 2233 winter on 7170 kHz; and summer on 7175 kHz.

Middle East: 1933 and 2033 on 7295 and 9440 kHz.

Southern Africa: 1533 on 6100 kHz; 1633 on 6100, 9570 and 11900 kHz; and 2033 on 11640 kHz.

There's nothing for *East Asia*, but listeners in *Southeast Asia* have two slots: 1233 on 9730 and 11980 kHz; and 1333 on 11980 kHz.

Australasia: 0933 on 15210 and 17690 kHz; 1233 on 9760 (or 15415) and 11760 kHz; and 1333 on 11760 and 11900 kHz.

"One Planet"
BBC World Service

"One Planet" is the BBC World Service's window on environmental and development issues. Pragmatic and nonpartisan, it's also a good listen. Warhorse issues such as global warming and garbage disposal are complemented by under-the-radar topics

like nuclear science in agriculture or fires in underground coal seams.

Americas: Winter, listeners in the *Caribbean* can choose between 2206 Thursday and 0206 Friday (Thursday evening in the Americas) on 5975 kHz; summer, one hour earlier, it's 2106 on 15390 kHz, and 0106 on 5975 kHz. These should also provide reasonable reception in the southern *United States*. On the West Coast, 9740 kHz at 1506 Thursday provides easy reception, although part of the BBC's East Asian stream.

Europe has two Thursday editions, both one hour earlier in summer but using the same channels all year. Winter, it's at 1506 on 12095 and 15565 kHz; and 2006 on 6195 and 9410 kHz. The first is best heard in central and eastern Europe, with the second favoring listeners farther west.

The *Middle East* also has two Thursday editions: winter, 0906 on 11760 kHz; and 1406 on 12095 kHz; summer, 0806 on 11760 kHz; and 1506 on 15310 kHz.

Southern Africa gets three Thursday slots: 0806 on 6190, 11940 and 21470 kHz; 1606 on 3255 (or 11940), 6190 and 21470 kHz; and 2106 on 3255, 6005 and 6190 kHz.

East Asia also has three Thursday offerings: 0206 summer on 15280 and 15360 kHz; 0306 winter on 15280, 17760 and 21660 kHz; 0806 on 15280 (winter), 15360 (summer), 17760 and 21660 kHz; and 1506 on 9740 and (summer) 11750 kHz. *Southeast Asia* has the same slots, but on different frequencies: 0206 summer and 0306 winter on 15360 kHz; 0806 winter on 6195 and 9740 kHz, and summer on 11955 and 15360 kHz; and 1506 on 6195 and 9740 kHz.

There's officially nothing for *Australasia*, but it's often audible anyway at 0806 Thursday—winter on 9740 kHz and midyear on 11955 and 15360 kHz. There's also a repeat at 1506 the same day on 9740 kHz.

"Inside Europe"
Deutsche Welle

There are several solid programs about Europe, but the most ample is Deutsche

E1XM

The E1XM is the world's first radio to combine AM, FM, Shortwave, and XM Satellite Radio Ready technology into one ultra-high-performance unit.

_ AM/FM/Shortwave/XM Satellite Ready Radio
_ 1700 station presets
_ Digitally synthesized PLL tuner with synchronous detector
_ Passband tuning, selectable bandwidth filters and Selectable Single Sideband (SSB) reception
_ Dual conversion superheterodyne circuit design
_ Stereo line-level audio inputs and outputs and external antenna connections
_ Dual Clocks and programmable timers
_ Headphone Jack
_ Built-In Antenna: telescopic antenna for AM, FM and Shortwave reception
_ External Antenna Connection for the addition of auxiliary antennas
_ Calibrated LCD signal strength meter

F10
AM/FM/Shortwave Radio

Intelligence meets performance in the E10. The E10 provides sophisticated tools for listening to news, sports, and music from around the world.

_ Shortwave range of 1711 – 29,999 KHz
_ 550 programmable memories with memory page customization
_ Manual and auto scan, direct keypad frequency entry, ATS
_ Clock with alarm, sleep timer, and snooze functions

E100
AM/FM/Shortwave Radio

The E100 features a sleek design complimented by a portable physique. This little marvel is packed with all the latest radio features you want and it's small enough to fit in your coat pocket!

_ Shortwave range of 1711 – 29,999 KHz
_ 200 programmable memories
_ Memory page customization
_ Manual and auto scan, direct keypad frequency entry

C.CRANE

etón®
RE_INVENTING™ RADIO
www.etoncorp.com

> **Nukes to immigration, surprise is part of the fun.**

Clair Cavanagh, senior producer of "Wide Angle." News fades, but Cavanagh unearths issues behind today's and potentially tomorrow's events. RNW

Welle's weekly "Inside Europe." Topics for this 55-minute offering range from business and social issues to natural heritage to music. Be it Berlin, Paris or a small Welsh village, if there's something interesting afoot, "Inside Europe" will flush it out.

The station no longer beams to *North America*, but try 0605 Sunday when the show is aired to West Africa. Best bet is 15440 kHz in winter, and 17860 kHz in summer, both via the Deutsche Welle relay station in Rwanda. Good reception is most likely in the southern United States and Caribbean.

Europe: 0705, 0905 and 1405 Saturday and 0605 Sunday on 6140 kHz.

There's nothing for the *Middle East*, but listeners in *Southern Africa* can tune in at 2005 Saturday, winter on 6145 and 12025 kHz, and midyear on 7130, 11895, 13780 and 15205 kHz.

East Asia: A truncated 25-minute version is available at 2205 Saturday (Sunday local date in the target area), winter on 6180 kHz, and summer on 7115 and 9720 kHz. It's also heard in parts of *Southeast Asia*, which otherwise would be left out. In *Australasia*, reception is limited to western parts of Australia.

"Wide Angle"
Radio Netherlands

The incorporation of Radio Netherlands' "Wide Angle" into the new "Saturday Connection" show on October 30, 2005 allowed "Wide Angle" greater flexibility than it formerly enjoyed. No longer restricted to a fixed time or length, the program can now offer an even broader view of issues behind the news.

Topics run the gamut: Iran's nuclear activities, immigrant workers in the Netherlands, social conditions in Bolivia, suicide bombers. Surprise is part of the fun.

It's always aired Saturday, local date in the target areas. Since "Wide Angle" no longer occupies a fixed slot, these are the start times for "The Saturday Connection":

North America: (East) 1200 (one hour earlier in summer) on 11675 kHz; 1930 and 2030 winter on 15525 kHz, summer on 17735 kHz; and 0000 winter on 6165 kHz, summer on 9845 kHz; *(Central)* 1930 and 2030 on 15315 kHz, and 0107 winter on 6165 kHz, summer on 9845 kHz; *(West)* 1930 and 2030 winter on 17725 kHz, summer on 17660 kHz; 0400 summer on 6165 and 9590 kHz; and 0500 winter on 6165 kHz.

There's nothing for *Europe* or the *Middle East*, but *southern Africa* gets 1800 on 6020 kHz, and 1930 and 2030 on 7120 kHz.

East and *Southeast Asia:* 1000 on 7315 (winter), 9795 (winter), 12065, and (summer) 13710 and 13820 kHz. *Australasia:* 0500 winter on 11710 kHz, and 1000 midyear on 9790 kHz; channels for Asia can also provide good reception.

Prepared by the staff of PASSPORT TO WORLD BAND RADIO.

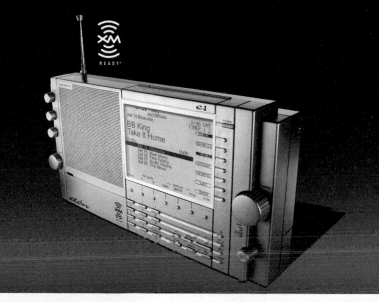
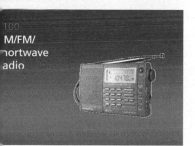

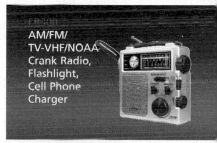
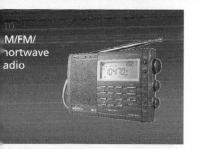
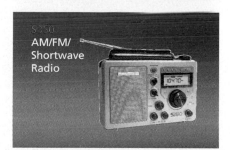
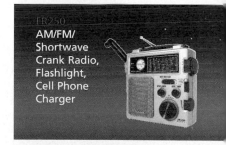
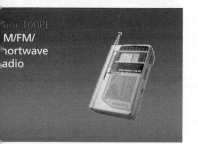

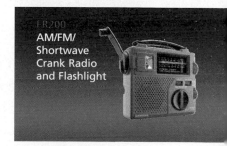

How to Choose a World Band Radio

Some electronic products are commodities. Use a little horse sense and you'll find what you want.

Not so world band receivers, which can vary greatly from model to model. As usual money talks, but even that's a fickle barometer. Fortunately, many perform well and we rate them accordingly. Yet, even among models with comparable star ratings it helps to read the fine print.

Squeezed-in Stations

World band radio offers hundreds of channels, each shoehorned five kilohertz away from the other. That's more crowded than FM or mediumwave AM, and it gets worse: Global treks wear down signals, causing fading and reduced strength. To cope with these challenges, a world band radio has to perform electronic gymnastics.

Some succeed, others don't.

This is why PASSPORT REPORTS was created. At International Broadcasting Services we've independently tested hundreds of world band radios, antennas and accessories since 1977. These evaluations include rigorous hands-on use by listeners, plus specialized lab tests developed over the years. These form the basis of PASSPORT REPORTS, and for some popular premium receivers and antennas there are also soup-to-nuts Radio Database International White Papers®.

If Etón's Mini 300PE is lost or stolen, you're not out much.

Four-Point Checklist

✔ **Price.** Want to hear big stations, or do you prefer gentler voices from exotic lands? Powerful evening signals, or weaker stations by day? Decide, then choose a radio that slightly surpasses your needs—this helps ensure against disappointment without spending too much.

Once the novelty of world band wears thin, most people give up on cheap radios—they're clumsy to tune, often receive poorly and can sound terrible. That's why we don't cover analog-readout models. Yet, even some models with digital frequency readout can disappoint.

Most find satisfaction with digital-readout portables selling for $65–150 in the United States or €60-130 in the United Kingdom, and having a rating of ✪✪¾ or more. If you're looking for elite performance, shoot for a portable or portatop rated ✪✪✪¾ or better for roughly twice as much.

That's if you're practical. If you want bragging rights, a five-star tabletop or a professional model tops a plasma TV or Porsche any day.

> A five-star model tops a plasma TV or Porsche any day.

✔ **Location**. Signals are usually strongest around Europe, North Africa and the Near East, almost as good in eastern North America. Elsewhere in the Americas, or in Hawaii or Australasia or the Middle East, spring for a receiver with superior sensitivity to weak signals—some sort of accessory antenna helps, too.

✔ **Features**. Divide features between those for performance and those that impact operation (see sidebars), but don't judge too much by

PASSPORT'S STANDARDS

At International Broadcasting Services we have been analyzing shortwave equipment since 1977. Our reviewers, and no one else, write and edit everything in PASSPORT REPORTS. Our lab tests are performed by an independent laboratory recognized as the world's leader. (For more on this, please see the Radio Database International White Paper, *How to Interpret Receiver Lab Tests and Measurements*.)

The review process is completely separate from equipment advertising, which is not allowed in PASSPORT REPORTS. Our team members may not accept review fees from manufacturers, nor may they "permanently borrow" radios. International Broadcasting Services does not manufacture, sell or distribute world band radios or related hardware.

PERFORMANCE FEATURES

A signal should sound pleasant, not just be audible. To help, some radios have features to ward off unwanted sounds or improve audio quality. Of course, just because a feature exists doesn't mean it functions properly, but PASSPORT REPORTS checks this out.

Reception "Musts"

Full world band coverage from 2300-26100 kHz is best, but 3200-21850 kHz or even 4750-21850 kHz is usually okay. Less coverage? Look over "Best Times and Frequencies for 2006" elsewhere in PASSPORT to ensure that major world band segments are fully covered.

Synchronous selectable sideband helps knock out adjacent-channel interference and reduce fading distortion. This advanced feature is found on a few portables, as well as most tabletop and professional models. PASSPORT REPORTS indicates which work well.

Especially if a receiver doesn't have synchronous selectable sideband, it benefits from two or more *bandwidths* to reduce adjacent-channel interference. Some premium models have both this and synchronous selectable sideband—a killer combo.

Double (or multiple) conversion helps reject unwanted noises—images, unwanted growls, whistles and dih-dah sounds. Few cheaper models have it.

Spit and Polish

Tone controls are a plus, especially continuous with separate bass and treble. For world band reception, *single-sideband* (SSB) isn't important, but is essential for utility or "ham" signals. The main use for world band is to hear the American Forces Radio and Television Service.

Tabletop models flush out stubborn signals, but they're for veterans and are overkill for casual listening. Look for a tunable *notch filter* to zap howls; *passband offset* (also called *passband tuning* and *IF shift*) for superior adjacent-channel rejection and audio contouring, especially in conjunction with synchronous selectable sideband; and multiple *AGC* decay rates. At electrically noisy locations a *noise blanker* is essential, although performance varies greatly.

Digital signal processing (DSP) attempts to enhance reception quality. Until recently it has been much smoke, little fire, but it's improving. Watch for more DSP receivers to appear, but don't worship at their altar.

With portables and portatops an *AC adaptor* reduces operating costs and may improve weak-signal performance. Some are poorly made and cause hum or buzzing, but most are okay. With tabletop models an *inboard AC power supply* is preferable but not essential.

Digital Transmission

Looking ahead, *digital shortwave transmission* from Digital Radio Mondiale (www.drm.org) is being implemented, although as a practical matter ready-to-use receivers are not yet available. The only DRM portable to date was sold in Europe for €860 (about $1,000)—it performed abominably. It is nominally still available, but appears to be more like an Elvis sighting.

Early DRM adopters with a technical bent and a suitable PC should look for models shown as DRM Ready in PASSPORT REPORTS. Whatever the ultimate fate of DRM, it will be years, if then, before existing analog transmissions are phased out in favor of digital. Not only does DRM have shortcomings, there are also some 600 million people who listen on traditional world band radios. None of these work with DRM.

features. Radios with relatively few features sometimes outperform those tricked out with seductive goodies.

✔ **Where to buy?** Whether you buy in a store, by phone or on the Internet makes little difference. That's because world band receivers don't test well in stores except in the rare showroom with an outdoor antenna. Even then, long-term satisfaction is hard to gauge from a spot test, so check at different times.

One thing you can nail down in a store is ergonomics—how intuitive is the radio to operate? You can also get a thumbnail idea of world band fidelity by listening to mediumwave AM stations or a muscular world band station.

Internet purchases from foreign countries are usually hassle-free, although don't expect enforceable warranties. Too, packets are sometimes refused by customs because of trademark and other legal considerations.

HANDY THINGIES

A "must" to find stations quickly is *digital frequency readout*, found on models tested by PASSPORT REPORTS. Too, a *24-hour World Time clock* to know when to tune in; many receivers include them. Best is if time can be read while the frequency is being displayed.

If your radio doesn't include a World Time clock, there are standalone 24-hour clocks and watches. Seconds displayed numerically are a nice touch so you can be alert for station IDs.

Other handy features: direct-access tuning by *keypad* and station *presets* ("memories"); and any combination of a *tuning knob*, up/down *slewing controls* or *"signal-seek" scanning* to search for stations. A few models have handy *one-touch presets* buttons, like a car radio. Quick access to *world band segments* (meter bands) is another time saver.

Presets are important because world band stations don't stay on the same frequency all day. Being able to store a station's multiple frequencies makes it easier to find whenever you want. With sophisticated receivers, presets should be able to store not only frequency, but also such parameters as bandwidth, mode and AGC.

Useful but less important is an *on/off timer*—some even come with built-in recorders. Also, look for an *illuminated display* and a good *signal-strength indicator*, either as an analog meter or a digital display.

Travelers like portables with *power-lock switches* or *recessed power buttons* so the radio won't go on by itself in luggage. The locks on some Chinese portables don't disable display illumination.

If ergonomics stand out, bad or good, PASSPORT REPORTS says so. But few controls doesn't necessarily mean handier operation. Some receivers with many controls are easier to operate than comparable receivers with few controls—especially if operation involves complex software menus.

Sony's ICF-SW07, though small, includes nearly every desirable feature.

Portables for 2006

Portables are world band's meat and potatoes. They are handy, affordable and usually do the trick whether at home or away.

In Europe and eastern North America evening signals come in well, so virtually any well-rated portable is okay. Elsewhere or daytime, when broadcasts may be more interesting but weaker, a good portable can be boosted by an accessory antenna.

Digital Broadcasts

So far there's been only one portable for DRM digital broadcasts, but it apparently didn't go into production. Indeed, no portable is even DRM ready—equipped to receive digital world band broadcasts after being connected to a PC. But if you're experimental, take heart. Modification instructions for some models are at www.drmrx.org/

receiver_mods.html. You'll also need DRM software: €60 from www. drmrx.org/purchase.php.

Three Categories

Think of pocket portables like cellphones, compacts like Palm-type handhelds and large portables like laptop PCs. You can't go wrong with a $150 compact rated at three or more stars, but lesser models can cut that in half or less.

Top end goes for five hundred dollars. That's for near-tabletop performance with satellite reception thrown in—more than you need, but for sure not more than you want.

Friendly skies? Pocket models are ideal, and their limited speaker audio can be overcome with earpieces. Yet, slightly larger "compact-compacts" sometimes perform better, sell for less and are small and light enough for most.

> Find major updates to the 2006 PASSPORT REPORTS at www. passband.com.

Longwave

The longwave band is still used for domestic broadcasts in Europe, North Africa and Russia. If you live or travel in rural areas there, long-wave coverage may be a plus. Otherwise, forget it.

Fix or Toss?

Portables aren't meant to be friends for life and are priced accordingly. The most robust models are usually not ready for the landfill until a decade or two of use, whereas pedestrian portables may give only a few years of regular service. Rarely are any worth fixing outside warranty except top end models.

If you receive a DOA portable, insist upon an immediate exchange without a restocking fee—manufacturers' repair facilities tend to have a disappointing record. If out-of-warranty service is a priority, consider a tabletop model.

Shelling Out

Street prices are cited, including European and Australian VAT/GST where applicable. These vary plus or minus, so take them as the general guide they are meant to be. Shortwave specialty outlets and some other retailers usually have attractive prices, but duty-free shopping is not always the bargain you might expect.

David Heim, electronics deputy editor at *Consumer Reports* and quoted in *Reader's Digest*, suggests, "Look for stuff that's been factory refurbished." In North America refurbished Grundig and Etón portables are occasionally available—these are cited in PASSPORT REPORTS—and try pot luck if you are near a Sony outlet store.

WHAT TO LOOK FOR

• **AC adaptor.** Those provided by the manufacturer are usually best and should be free from hum and noise—those that aren't are cited under "Con." Some are multivoltage and operate almost anywhere in the world. ☞ Beware of "switching" type power supplies, as these disrupt radio signals. In principle no radio manufacturer should be offering switching power supplies for use with radios, but it sometimes happens and in California it can be the law. PASSPORT REPORTS points these out.

• **Adjacent-channel rejection—I: *selectivity, bandwidth*.** World band stations are about twice as tightly packed as ordinary mediumwave AM stations. So, they tend to slop over and interfere with each other—DRM digital broadcasts are even worse. Radios with superior selectivity are better at rejecting interference, but at a price: better selectivity also means less high-end ("treble") audio response and muddier sound. So, having more than one bandwidth allows you to choose between tighter selectivity (narrow bandwidth) when it is warranted, and more realistic audio (wide bandwidth) when it is not.

• **Adjacent-channel rejection—II: *synchronous selectable sideband*.** With powerful stations "out in the clear," this has little audible impact. However, for tough catches it improves listening quality by minimizing selective-fading distortion and adjacent-channel interference. *Bonus:* it also helps reduce distortion with fringe mediumwave AM stations at twilight and even at night.

• **Ergonomics.** Some radios are a snap to use because they don't have complicated features. Yet, even sophisticated models can be designed to operate intuitively. Choose accordingly—there's no reason to take the square root and cube it just to hear a radio station.

• **Single-sideband demodulation.** If you are interested in hearing non-broadcast short-wave signals—"hams" and utility stations—single-sideband circuitry is *de rigueur*. Too, the popular low-powered American Forces Radio-Television Service requires this.

• **Speaker audio quality.** Unlike many portatop and tabletop models, few portables have rich, full audio through their speakers. However, some are much better than others, and with a model having line output you can connect amplified PC speakers for pleasant home listening.

• **Tuning features.** Models with digital frequency readout are so superior to analog that these are now the only radios normally tested by PASSPORT. Look for such handy tuning aids as direct-frequency access via keypad, station presets (programmable channel memories), up-down tuning via tuning knob and/or slew keys, band/segment selection, and signal-seek or other (e.g., presets) scanning. These make the radio easier to tune—no small point, given that a hundred or more channels may be audible at a time.

• **Weak-signal sensitivity.** Sensitivity is important if you live in a weak-signal location or tune exotic or daytime stations. Most portables have enough sensitivity to pull in major stations during prime time if you're in such places as Europe, North Africa or eastern North America.

• **World Time clock.** In 24-hour format, this is a "must." You can obtain these separately, but many radios have them built in; the best provide time whether the radio is on or off. However, many portable radios' clocks tend to gain or lose time if not reset periodically. In North America and beyond, the official shortwave time stations WWV on 2500, 5000, 10000, 15000 and 20000 kHz and CHU on 3330, 7335 and 14670 kHz are ideal for this; the Pacific is also served by WWVH in Hawaii on 2500, 5000, 10000 and 15000 kHz.

We try to stick to plain English, but specialized terms can be useful. If you come across something that's not clear, flip to PASSPORT's glossary.

What PASSPORT's Ratings Mean

Star ratings: ✪✪✪✪✪ is best. Stars reflect overall performance and meaningful features, plus to some extent ergonomics and perceived build quality. Price, appearance, country of manufacture and the like are not taken into account. To facilitate comparison, portable rating standards are quite similar to those used for the portatop, tabletop and professional models reviewed elsewhere in this PASSPORT.

A rating of at least ✪✪½ should please most who listen to major stations regularly during the evening. However, for casual use on trips virtually any small portable may suffice.

Passport's Choice. La crème de la crème. Our test team's personal picks of the litter—models we would buy or have bought for our personal use. Unlike star ratings, these choices are unapologetically subjective.

✪: A relative bargain, with decidedly more performance than the price would suggest.

Tips for Using This Section

Models are listed by size; and, within size, in order of world band listening suitability. Street selling prices are cited, including VAT/GST where applicable.

Unless otherwise indicated, each model has:

- Keypad tuning, up/down slew keys, station presets and signal-seek tuning/scanning.
- Digital frequency readout to the nearest kilohertz or five kilohertz.
- Coverage of the world band shortwave spectrum from at least 3200–26100 kHz.
- Coverage of the usual 87.5–108 MHz FM band, but not the Japanese and other FM bands below 87 MHz.

- Coverage of the AM (mediumwave) band in selectable 9 and 10 kHz channel increments from about 530–1705 kHz. No coverage of the 153–279 kHz longwave band.
- Adequate image rejection, almost invariably resulting from double-conversion circuitry.

Unless otherwise indicated, each model lacks:

- Single-sideband demodulation.
- Synchronous selectable sideband. However, when it is present the unwanted sideband is rejected approximately 25 dB via phase cancellation, not IF filtering.
- If 24-hour clock included, lacks tens-of-hours leading zero that properly should be displayed with World Time (UTC).

POCKET PORTABLES
Perfect for Travel, Marginal for Home

Pocket portables weigh around half pound, or 0.2 kg, and are between the size of an audio cassette jewel box and a handheld calculator. They operate off two to four "AA" (UM-3 penlite) batteries. These diminutive models are ideal to carry on your person, but listening to tiny speakers can be tiring. If you plan to listen for long periods or to music, opt for using headphones or earpieces, or look into one of the better compact models.

Best by far is the Sony ICF-SW100 series, but it's been discontinued and is getting harder to find. There has been nothing else like it in the history of world band radio, nor may we ever see its likes again. So, if you want this little Spook's Friend, get it while you can.

✪✪✪ (see ☞) *Passport's Choice*
Sony ICF-SW100E

Price (as available): *ICF-SW100E:* £159.95 in the United Kingdom. €269.00 in Germany. ¥45,100 as available in Japan. *ACE-30 220V AC adaptor:* £24.95 in the United Kingdom. €25.50 in Germany.

HAVE RADIO, WILL TRAVEL

Getting Past Airport Annie

Even in times of high alert, air travel with a world band radio is almost always trouble-free if common-sense steps are taken. To minimize the odds of delay at airport security, remember that their job is to be paranoid about you, so it's prudent to be paranoid about them.

- Answer all questions honestly, but don't volunteer information or joke around. Friendly banter can get you into the Dreaded Search corner.

- The nail that sticks out gets hammered first. Good security focuses on the unfamiliar or unusual, no matter how innocuous it may seem to you. Be gray.

- Bring a portable, not a portatop or tabletop—terrorists like big radios (they don't call them boom boxes for nothing). Best by far is a pocket or compact model.

- Stow your radio in a carry-on bag, not in checked luggage or on your person. Don't stuff it at the bottom, wrapped in clothing, like you're trying to hide something. Equally, it's usually best not to place it out in the open where it can be seen. However, if you decide to put a small radio into the manual inspection basket at the security portal, have it playing softly with earbuds or earphones attached, as though it were a Walkman you're listening to. Place any world band accessories, extra batteries, guides and instruction books in your checked luggage, or at least in a separate carry-on bag.

- Before entering the terminal, or at least before entering the security area, preset the radio to any popular FM music station, then keep batteries inside the radio so you can demonstrate that it actually works. Don't mention world band or shortwave unless queried.

- If asked what the radio is for, say for your own listening. If they persist, reply that you like to keep up with news and sports while away, and leave it at that. Don't volunteer information about alarm, snooze or other timer facilities, as timers can be components in bombs.

- If traveling in zones of war or civil unrest, or off the beaten path in parts of Africa or South America, take a radio you can afford to lose and which fits inconspicuously inside a pocket.

- If traveling to Bahrain, avoid taking a radio which has "receiver" visible on its cabinet. Security personnel may think you're a spy.

- If traveling to Malaysia, Bahrain or Saudi Arabia, don't take a model with single-sideband capability—or at the very least take steps to disguise this capability so it is not visually apparent. If things get dicey, point out that you listen to news and sports from the popular American AFRTS station, which transmits only in the single-sideband mode. (PASSPORT can be used to authenticate this.)

Theft? Radios, cameras, binoculars, laptops and other glitzy goodies are almost always stolen to be resold. The more worn the item looks—affixing scuffed stickers helps—the less likely it is to be confiscated by corrupt inspectors or stolen by thieves.

Tuning Local Stations Overseas

Mediumwave AM channel separation in the Americas is 10 kHz, elsewhere 9 kHz. When choosing a radio for traveling between these zones, try to select a model that tunes both norms. FM differs too, so Americans should select a model which can tune FM in increments of 0.1 MHz or less.

Pro: Tiny, easily the smallest tested, but with larger-radio performance and features. High-tech synchronous selectable sideband generally performs well, reducing adjacent-channel interference and selective-fading distortion on world band, longwave and mediumwave AM signals, while adding slightly to weak-signal sensitivity and audio crispness (*see* Con). Single bandwidth, especially when synchronous selectable sideband is used, exceptionally effective at adjacent-channel rejection. Relatively good audio, provided supplied earbuds or outboard audio are used (*see* Con). FM stereo through earbuds. Numerous helpful tuning features, including keypad, two-speed slew, signal-seek-then-resume scanning (*see* Con), five handy "pages" with ten station presets each. Station presets can display station name. Tunes in relatively precise 0.1 kHz increments. Good single-sideband performance (*see* Con). Good dynamic range. Worthy ergonomics for size and features. Illuminated display. Clock for many world cities, which can be made to work as a *de facto* World Time 24-hour clock (*see* Con). Timer and sleep delay. Travel power lock. Japanese FM (most versions) and longwave bands. Outboard passive reel accessory antenna aids slightly in weak-signal reception (*see* Con). Weak battery indicator; about 16 hours from a set of batteries (*see* Con).

Con: Hard to find dealers with remaining new stock. Tiny speaker, although innovative, has mediocre sound, limited loudness and little tone shaping. Closing clamshell reduces speaker loudness and high-frequency response. Weak-signal sensitivity could be better, although included outboard active antenna helps. Expensive. No tuning knob. Clock not readable when station frequency displayed. As "London Time" is used by the clock for World Time, the summertime clock adjustment cannot be used if World Time is to be displayed accurately. Rejection of images, and 10 kHz "repeats" when synchronous selectable sideband off, could be better. In some urban locations, FM signals from 87.5 to 108 MHz can break through into world band segments with distorted sound, e.g. between 3200 and 3300 kHz. Synchronous selectable sideband tends to

A legacy of Sony's legendary founder, the ICF-SW100 is the ultimate in high-tech mini radios.

lose lock if batteries weak, or if NiCd cells are used. Synchronous selectable sideband alignment can vary with temperature, factory alignment and battery voltage, causing synchronous selectable sideband reception to be slightly more muffled in one sideband than the other. Batteries run down faster than usual when radio off. Tuning in 0.1 kHz increments means that non-synchronous single-sideband reception can be mis-tuned by up to 50 Hz, so audio quality varies. Signal-seek scanner sometimes stops 5 kHz before a strong "real" signal. No meaningful signal strength indicator. Mediumwave AM reception only fair. Mediumwave AM channel spacing adjusts peculiarly. Flimsy battery cover. No batteries (two "AA" required).

☞ The above star rating reflects mediocre speaker audio quality. Through earpieces, the rating rises to ✪✪✪⅛.

☞ In early production samples, the cable connecting the two halves of the "clamshell" case tended to lose continuity with extended use because of a very tight radius and an unfinished edge; this was successfully resolved with a design change in 1997. Owners of early units who encounter this problem should go to www.tesp.com/sw100faq.htm for repair tips.

Verdict: The ICF-SW100E' synchronous selectable sideband and effective bandwidth filter provide superior adjacent-channel rejection. Speaker and, to a lesser extent, weak-signal sensitivity keep it from being all it could have been. Yet, this Japanese-made gem rules the pocket category, and even outperforms most compact models.

This jewel among world band radios is a shoehorned wonder, but is getting harder to find anymore. Although world band radio was a priority for Sony founder Akio Morita, it no longer appears to be on the radar screen of Sony's replacement management. For now the 'SW100E continues to be available from outlets in Japan and parts of Europe (exporters as of presstime include wsplc.com and thieCom.de) but don't hold your breath.

★★★ *Passport's Choice*
Sony ICF-SW100S

Price (as available): €298.00 in Germany.

Verdict: This discontinued version, even harder to find new than the ICF-SW100E, includes an outboard active antenna, an AC adaptor that adjusts automatically to worldwide voltages, wall (mains) plugs for European and American sockets, and a high-quality travel case for the radio and

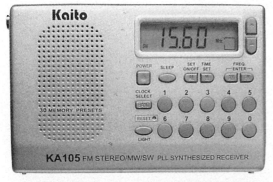

The Kaito KA105 is available in China as the Degen DE105. Rugged and affordable, but with pedestrian performance.   D. Zantow

accessories. Otherwise, it is identical to the Sony ICF-SW100E, above.

☞ Performance of the supplied active antenna is similar to that of the Sony AN-1 antenna reviewed elsewhere in PASSPORT REPORTS.

★★
Degen DE105, Kaito KA105

Price: *KA105:* $59.95 in the United States. $59.00CAD in Canada.

Pro: Reasonably good selectivity from single bandwidth. Good voice-audio quality, with ample volume, for a small speaker (*see* Con). A number of helpful tuning features, including keypad (*see* Con), up/down slew (*see* Con) and "signal seek" frequency scanning; also, 30 station presets, of which ten are for world band with others divided between FM and mediumwave AM. Above-average weak-signal sensitivity. Dual-zone 24-hour clock (*see* Con) with clock radio/alarm and sleep delay. Illuminated display via non-timed pushbutton. Clicky keys have superior tactile feel. LCD has excellent contrast. Low battery consumption. Weak-battery indicator. Battery cover hinged to avoid loss. Travel power lock (*see* Con). FM in stereo through earbuds, included (*see* Con). Build quality appears superior for price class, and manufacturer has solid if relatively brief construction history. Telescopic antenna swivels and rotates (*see* Con). Reset control for microprocessor and memory. Insertable elevation tab, attached to carrying strap, tilts radio to handier operating angle. Includes short external wire antenna accessory. *Kaito:* Tough, attractive matte aluminum alloy face plate. 120V AC adaptor (*see* Con). Mediumwave AM 9/10 channel steps user-selectable, tunes up to 1710 kHz. *Degen:* Available in either slate blue or silver.

Con: World band coverage of 5950–15600 kHz misses 17 and 21 MHz segments, skips chunks of 6 and 15 MHz, and omits lesser 25, 19, 5, 4, 3 and 2 MHz segments. Single-conversion IF circuitry results in poor image rejection. Speaker audio bereft of low-frequency ("bass") response. Audio through earbuds may be stronger in one channel at lower volume, whether in mono or stereo. No tuning knob. Keypad not in standard telephone format. Tunes world band only in 5 kHz steps and displays in nonstandard XX.XX/XX.XX$_5$ MHz format. Slow microprocessor lock time while slew tuning degrades bandscanning. No signal-strength indicator. Clock doesn't display when frequency is shown. Mediumwave AM coverage of 520–1620 kHz omits 1625–1705 kHz. Mediumwave AM suffers slightly from LCD digital hash. FM has so-so sensitivity, mediocre capture ratio and some tendency to overload. FM audio distorted through earbuds. Because telescopic antenna exits from cabinet's side, it can't tilt to the right for optimum FM reception. Travel power lock does not disable LCD illumination. Two "AA" batteries not supplied. *Kaito:* Minor hum with AC adaptor.

Verdict: This Chinese travel portable is as tough and well built as anything near its price. Except for the lack of single-sideband to hear the American Forces Radio and Television Service, it makes a rugged choice for areas of turmoil. Otherwise, the larger Degen/Kaito siblings DE1101/KA1101 and DE1102/KA1102 cover more frequencies, perform significantly better and cost little more.

Etón's Mini 300 PE is small, popular and inexpensive. Also sold under other names, its performance is a mixed bag.

✪⅝ ✪
Etón Mini 300PE, Grundig Mini 300PE, Tecsun R-919

Price: *Mini 300PE:* $39.95 in the United States. $39.99CAD in Canada. £24.95 in the United Kingdom. €27.95 in Germany.

Pro: Weak-signal sensitivity quite reasonable. Pleasant room-filling audio for such a small package (*see* Con). Clock/alarm-timer with sleep delay (*see* Con). FM in stereo with earbuds, included. Low battery consumption. Available in five colors. Soft carrying case affixes to belt or purse strap. Two "AA" batteries included.

Con: Analog-tuned with digital frequency counter, so tunes only by thumbwheel, which is somewhat touchy. Does not tune 120, 75, 90, 60, 15, 13 and 11 meter segments; misses small bits of tuned world band segments. Single-conversion IF circuitry results in poor image rejection. Audio lacks bass response. Frequency drift with changes in temperature. Telescopic antenna does not rotate or swivel. Antenna's plastic base protrudes even when antenna collapsed. Displays in nonstandard XX.XX/XX.XX$_5$ MHz format. Display not illuminated. Minor drift when hand grasps back of cabinet. Frequency counter noise slightly audible when finger placed over LCD during mediumwave AM reception. Some FM overloading in strong-signal environments. Clock in 12-hour format, displays only when radio off. No port for AC adaptor, much less the adaptor itself. *North America:* Toll-free tech support.

Verdict: Best of the really inexpensive portables, even though it comes up short on daytime frequency coverage, lacks display illumination and its clock isn't in World Time format. But thanks to true pocket size, nice weak-signal sensitivity and decent audio quality it is hard to resist for casual use on trips.

Degen's DE205 is dirt cheap in China, yet offers digital frequency readout and superior build quality. There seems to be no plan to offer it elsewhere.

✪½ ℰ
Degen DE205

Price: ¥76 (under $10) in China, but currently not available elsewhere.

Pro: Build quality appears superior for price class, and manufacturer has solid if relatively brief construction history. Reasonably good dynamic range for class. Ample volume (*see* Con). Clock with clock-radio (*see* Con). LCD has good contrast when viewed from below or head-on. Illuminated display (*see* Con). Low battery consumption. Battery cover hinged to avoid loss. FM 70–109 MHz coverage includes 76–90 MHz Japanese FM band and 70–74 MHz portion of 66–74 MHz low band still used within some former Warsaw Pact countries. Telescopic antenna swivels and rotates (*see* Con). Insertable elevation tab, attached to carrying strap, tilts radio to handier operating angle.

Con: Try finding one! Analog-tuned with digital frequency counter, so tunes only by thumbwheel, which operates smoothly. Unhandy and archaic "FM/MW/SW1/SW2" switch required for tuning within ranges 5450–10200 kHz *vs.* 11350–18180 kHz or *vice versa*. Does not tune 120, 75, 90, 60, 15, 13 or 11 meter segments. Mediocre speaker audio, although reasonable for size. Single-conversion IF circuitry results in poor

image rejection. Poor selectivity. Mediocre weak-signal sensitivity; improves greatly if ten feet or three meters of wire are clipped to telescopic antenna. Frequency drift with changes in temperature. Frequency counter omits last digit so, say, 5995 kHz appears as either 5.99 or 6.00 MHz. Readout at least 1 kHz high on world band, 2 kHz high on mediumwave AM on our unit. Clock in 12-hour format only, doesn't display when radio is on. No signal-strength indicator. Display illumination dim. Slight digital hash at times on shortwave. Digital hash degrades mediumwave AM weak-signal reception. Mediumwave AM 525–1620 kHz coverage omits 1625–1705 kHz portion of the X-band; mediocre selectivity; mediocre sensitivity; and inferior spurious-signal rejection on mediumwave AM. Pedestrian FM in mono only, with mediocre sensitivity, dynamic range and capture ratio. Telescopic antenna exits from the cabinet's side it can't tilt to the right for optimum FM reception. Two "AA" batteries not included. No AC adaptor, carrying pouch or earbuds; aftermarket AC adaptor would require uncommon 5V DC output (4.5V DC with correct pin type and center-pin negative, such as Kaito provides for the KA105, suffices).

☞ Shortwave tuning ranges (5.95–9.95 and 11.65–17.90 MHz) marked on back of panel are pessimistic; actual tuning ranges are significantly better: 5.45–10.20 and 11.35–18.18 MHz.

☞ Don't confuse the Degen DE205 with the analog-readout Grundig YB205 distributed in North America by Kaito (but not, ironically, by Grundig's North American distributor, Etón).

Verdict: Degen's DE205 is the cheapest world band radio tested that has digital frequency readout, and it outperforms a number of models that cost more. Equally encouraging, visual inspection suggests its build quality is superior to that of other tested cheaps.

✪½
Kaiwa KA-818, Tecsun R-818

Price: $34.95 or less as available in the United States and elsewhere.

Pro: Reasonable weak-signal sensitivity for low-cost pocket model. Clock with timer/alarm (*see* Con).

Con: Analog-tuned with digital frequency counter, so tunes only by thumbwheel, which is somewhat touchy. Does not tune 120, 75, 90, 60, 22, 15, 13 or 11 meter segments; misses some expanded coverage of other world band segments. Single-conversion IF circuitry results in poor image rejection. Frequency drift with changes in temperature. Frequency counter completely omits last digit so, say, 9575 kHz appears as either 9.57 or 9.58 MHz. Clock in 12-hour format only, displays only when radio off. Display not illuminated. Mediocre speaker audio quality. Telescopic antenna does not rotate or swivel. Mediumwave AM lacks weak-signal sensitivity. Pedestrian FM, with spurious signals. On one of our new units the telescopic antenna immediately fell apart. Two "AA" batteries not included. Few vendors in America and Europe. Warranty only 90 days in United States and various other countries.

Verdict: Performance brings up the rear, but price, size and alarm make this Chinese-made model worth consideration for casual use on trips—if you can find one.

Tecsun's R818 is sometimes made for other firms under their names. Inexpensive, but hardly worth it.

✪¼
Kchibo KK-C300, Sharper Image SN400

SN400: $29.95 in the United States. *KK-C300:* Roughly equivalent to $20 in East Asia.

Pro: Helpful tuning features include up/down slew and "signal seek" frequency scanning; also, world band segment selection and 30 station presets (*see* Con), of which ten are for world band with others divided between FM and mediumwave AM. Clicky keys have superior tactile feel. Timed LCD illumination (*see* Con). Travel power lock (*see* Con). Dual-zone clock (*see* Con) with sleep delay. FM stereo through earbuds (*see* Con), included. Mediumwave AM 9/10 kHz switch. Telescopic antenna rotates and swivels. Elevation panel. Superior carrying pouch (*see* Con).

Con: Digital buzz often degrades, and sometimes obliterates, world band reception. World band coverage of 5950–15600

kHz misses 17 and 21 MHz segments, skips chunks of 6 and 15 MHz, and omits lesser 25, 19, 5, 4, 3 and 2 MHz segments. No keypad or tuning knob. Slow microprocessor lock time while slew tuning degrades bandscanning. Single-conversion IF circuitry results in poor image rejection. Speaker audio bereft of low-frequency ("bass") response. Peculiar battery replacement/AC adapter procedure to retain memory data. Tunes world band only in 5 kHz steps and

The Kchibo KK-C300's name is more impressive than its performance. It has also been sold as the Sharper Image SN400.   D. Zantow

displays in nonstandard XX.XX/XX.XX₅ MHz format. Presets accessible only serially via up/down carousel. Mediumwave AM coverage of 520–1620 kHz omits 1625–1705 kHz. FM has so-so sensitivity, mediocre capture ratio and some tendency to overload. FM audio distorted through earbuds. Audio through earbuds may be a skosh stronger in one channel. Both clocks only in 12-hour format and neither displays when frequency is shown. No signal-strength indicator. Travel power lock does not deactivate LCD illumination button. No AC adaptor, and no indication of required polarity for an aftermarket adaptor. Two "AA" batteries not included. Carrying pouch has slight tire odor. *Sharper Image:* Warranty only 90 days.

Verdict: Sharp, this isn't. No low price can't justify the digital buzz that plagues world band reception, and important world band frequencies can't be tuned. Made in China.

✪¼
Kaide KK-989

Price: $24.95 as available in the United States.

Pro: Very small, ideally sized for air travel and has handy built-in belt clip. Clock with timer/alarm (*see* Con).

Cheap and nicely sized for travel, the Kaide KK-989 is nonetheless a performance dud. It is the worst pocket portable tested.

Con: Mediocre weak-signal sensitivity; helps considerably to clip a few yards of wire to the built-in antenna. Tinny audio. Analog-tuned with digital frequency counter, so tunes only by thumbwheel, which is very touchy. Does not tune 120, 75, 90, 60, 15, 13 or 11 meter segments; omits coverage of nearly all the 1605–1705 kHz mediumwave AM X-band; which frequencies are missed varies with battery voltage and from sample to sample. Single-conversion IF circuitry results in poor image rejection. Frequency counter completely omits last digit so, say, 9575 kHz appears as either 9.57 or 9.58 MHz. Clock in 12-hour format only, displays only when radio off. Display not illuminated. Telescopic antenna does not rotate or swivel. If hand is placed on rear of cabinet, world band drifts considerably; mediumwave AM drifts, too, but less badly. Frequency counter buzzes faintly on mediumwave AM; if finger placed over LCD display, buzz becomes strong and is also audible on lower world band frequencies. FM overloads in presence of strong signals, remediable by shorting antenna (which also reduces weak-signal sensitivity). Mediocre FM weak-signal sensitivity. Poor mediumwave AM weak-signal sensitivity. When first turned on, radio always reverts to FM band. FM in mono only. Three "AAA" batteries not included; "AAA" cells require more frequent replacement than standard "AA" cells, raising the cost of operation. No port for AC adaptor. In the United States, no warranty information comes with radio; best purchased from dealer who will swap if DOA. Although radio purchased from U.S. dealer, operating instructions only in Chinese. Country of manufacture not indicated on radio or box, but almost certainly is China.

Verdict: Nicely sized, and priced for every budget. Yet, with a long roster of significant drawbacks the Kaide KK-989 is a dud.

COMPACT PORTABLES
Nice for Travel, Okay for Home

Compacts are hugely popular, and no wonder. They offer a value mix of affordable price, worthy performance, manageable size and acceptable speaker audio. They tip in at one to two pounds, under a kilogram, and are typically sized less than 8 × 5 × 1.5 inches, or 20 × 13 × 4 cm. Like pocket models, they feed off "AA" (UM-3 penlite) batteries—but, usually, more of them. They travel almost as well as pocket models, but sound better through their larger speakers. They can also suffice for home use.

✪✪✪¼ *Passport's Choice*
Sony ICF-SW07

Price: $399.95 in the United States. £219.95 in the United Kingdom. €389.00 in Germany. ¥50,100 (domestic version)/¥55,400 (overseas version) in Japan.

Pro: Best non-audio performance among travel-worthy compact portables. Attractive and unusual styling. High-tech synchronous selectable sideband generally performs well and is straightforward to operate; reduces adjacent-channel interference and selective-fading distortion on world band, longwave and mediumwave AM signals while adding slightly to weak-signal sensitivity. Unusually small and light for a compact model when used without accessory antenna. Numerous tuning aids, including pushbutton access of frequencies for four stations stored on a replaceable ROM, keypad, two-speed up/down slew, 20 station presets (ten for world band) and "signal-seek, then resume" tuning. Clamshell design aids in handiness of operation, and is further helped by illuminated LCD readable from a wide variety of angles. Hump on the rear panel places the keypad at a convenient operating angle. Comes with AN-LP2 outboard "tennis racquet" antenna, commendably effective in raising the 'SW07's weak-signal sensitivity to excellent on world band; this antenna, unlike the Sony AN-LP1 optional accessory antenna for other receivers, has automatic preselector tuning, simplifying operation. Good single sideband performance (*see* Con). Clock covers most international time zones, as well as UTC (*see* Con). Outstanding reception of weak and crowded FM stations, with limited urban FM overloading resolved by variable-level attenuator. FM stereo through earbuds, included. Japanese

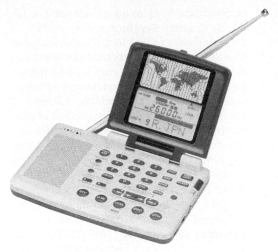

Best bet for lightweight travel with no-compromise technology is Sony's ICF-SW07. Except for speaker audio it excels at just about everything.

FM (most versions) and longwave bands. Above-average reception of mediumwave AM band. Travel power lock. Closing the clamshell does not interfere with speaker performance. Low-battery indicator. Presets information is non-volatile, can't be erased when batteries changed. Presets and time zone readout can be user-programmed to display six-character alphanumeric readout on LCD. Two turn-on times for alarm/clock radio. Sleep delay. Battery cover hinged to avoid loss, although AN-LP1 antenna battery cover not hinged. AC adaptor, albeit only single-voltage (e.g., 120V in version for North America).

Con: Only one bandwidth, surprising at this price—even some under-$100 models now provide two bandwidths. Pedestrian audio quality through small speaker, with relatively narrow audio-frequency response and above-average "hiss." Audio fidelity diminished, even with earbuds, in part because of the lack of a second, wider, bandwidth and meaningful tone control. No tuning knob. On our latest sample, the telescopic antenna would break its internal case mounting. Display shows time and tuned frequency, but not both simultaneously. Tuning resolution of 0.1 kHz above 1620 kHz means that non-synchronous single-sideband reception can be mis-tuned by up to 50 Hz, allowing audio fidelity to suffer. Synchronous selectable sideband tends to lose lock if batteries weak or if NiCd cells used. Synchronous selectable sideband alignment can vary with temperature, factory alignment and battery voltage, causing synchronous selectable sideband reception to be slightly more muffled in one sideband than the other. No meaningful signal-strength indicator, an unusual shortcoming at this model's price. LCD frequency/time numbers relatively small for size of display. AN-LP2 accessory antenna has to be physically disconnected for proper mediumwave AM reception. 1621–1705 kHz portion of American AM band and 1705–1735 kHz potential public service segment are erroneously treated as shortwave, although this does not harm reception quality. Low battery indicator misleadingly shows batteries as dead immediately after fresh batteries are installed; clears up when radio is turned on. No batteries (two "AA" required for radio, two more for antenna). UTC displays as "London" time even summer during DST, when London is an hour ahead of UTC; best is to re-label "London" as "UTC" and not display that zone at DST; however, the DST key can change UTC to UTC +1 in error if user is not careful.

Verdict: Speaker audio and sticker shock aside, this Japanese-made model is still the best compact portable for travel. It also passes the Caribbean Palm Frond Test as an effective prop for attracting friendly strangers. Clamshell open and antenna unfurled, the Sony ICF-SW07 is a great conversation-starter, especially among the intellectually curious . . . or, sometimes, the curiously intellectual.

DRM Modifiable

✪✪✪⅛ ℰ *Passport's Choice*
Sony ICF-SW7600GR

Price: *ICF-SW7600GR:* $159.95 in the United States. $329.99CAD in Canada. £173.93 in the United Kingdom. €159.00 in Germany. $509.00AUD in Australia. ¥33,600 in Japan. *MW 41-680 120V regulated AC adaptor (aftermarket, see below):* $19.95 in the United States.

Pro: One of the great values in a meaningful world band radio. Far and away the least-costly model available with high-tech synchronous selectable sideband; this generally performs well, reducing adjacent-channel interference and selective-fading distortion on world band, longwave and mediumwave AM signals (*see* Con). Single bandwidth, especially when synchronous selectable sideband is used, exceptionally effective at adjacent-channel rejection. Seemingly robust—similar predecessor had superior quality of components and assembly for price class, and held up unusually well. Numerous helpful tuning features, including keypad, two-speed up/down slew, 100 station presets and "signal-seek, then resume" tuning. For those with limited hearing of high-frequency sounds, such as some men over the half-century mark, speaker audio quality may be preferable to that of Grundig G4000A/Yacht Boy 400PE (*see* Con). Single-sideband performance arguably the best of any portable; analog clarifier, combined with LSB/USB switch, allow single-sideband signals (e.g., AFRTS, utility, amateur) to be tuned with uncommon precision, and thus with superior carrier phasing and the resulting natural-sounding audio. DRM modifiable (see www.drmrx.org/receiver_mods.html). Dual-zone 24-hour clock with single-zone readout, easy to set. Slightly smaller and lighter than most other compact models. Outboard reel passive wire antenna accessory aids slightly with weak-signal reception. Simple timer with sleep delay. Illuminated LCD has high contrast when read head-on or from below. Travel power lock. Superior reception of difficult mediumwave AM stations. Superior FM capture ratio aids reception when band congested, including helping separate co-channel stations. FM stereo through earpieces or headphones. Japanese FM (most versions) and longwave bands. Superior battery life. Weak-battery indicator. Stereo line output for recording, FM home transmitters and outboard audio systems. Battery cover hinged to avoid loss. Automatically provides power for optional AN-LP1 active antenna.

Con: Audio lacks tonal quality for pleasant world band or mediumwave AM music reproduction, and speaker audio tiring for any type of FM program. Weak-signal sensitivity, although respectable, not equal to that of the top handful of top-rated portables; helped considerably by extra-cost Sony AN-LP1 active antenna reviewed elsewhere in this edition. Image rejection adequate, but not excellent. Three switches, including those for synchronous selectable sideband, located unhandily at the side of the cabinet. No tuning knob. Slow microprocessor lock time while slew tuning degrades bandscanning. No meaningful signal-strength indicator. Synchronous selectable sideband holds lock decently, but less well on weak signals than in Sony's larger models; too, it tends to lose lock even more if batteries weak or if NiCd cells used. Synchronous selectable sideband alignment can vary with temperature, factory alignment and battery voltage, causing synchronous selectable sideband reception to be slightly more muffled in one sideband than the other. No AC adaptor included. In North America the optional Sony AC-E60A 120V AC "switching" adaptor causes serious interference to radio signals and, incredibly, is labeled "Not for use with radios"; Universal Radio offers its own MW 41-680 to remedy this, and presumably other firms will be offering something similar in due course. Reader reports indicate Sony's recommended 240V AC adaptor also causes serious interference to radio signals. Radio's adaptor socket is of an unusual size, making it difficult to find a suitable third-party AC adaptor. 1621–1705 kHz portion of American AM band and 1705–1735 kHz potential public-service segment are erroneously treated as shortwave, although this does not harm reception quality. Even though it has a relatively large LCD, same portion of display is used for clock and frequency digits; thus, clock doesn't display when frequency is shown, although pressing the EXE key allows time to replace frequency for nine seconds. No earphones or earpieces. No batteries (four "AA" needed).

Verdict: The robust Sony ICF-SW7600GR provides excellent bang for the buck, even though it is manufactured in high-cost Japan. Its advanced-tech synchronous selectable sideband is a valuable feature that

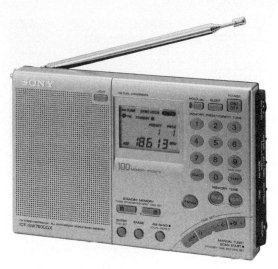

The Sony ICF-SW7600G is today's best buy in a compact portable. It is the only model anywhere near its price with synchronous technology to reduce fading and interference.

other portable manufacturers have yet to engineer properly—even some professional models costing thousands of dollars still haven't got it right. To find this useful operating feature at this price is without parallel.

Top drawer single-sideband reception for a portable, too, along with superior tough-signal FM and mediumwave AM reception. But it has warts: Musical audio quality through the speaker is only *ordinaire* and Sony of America's recommended adaptors should be avoided.

★★★ ✰ *Passport's Choice*
Degen DE1102, Kaito KA1102

Price: *Kaito:* $99.95 in the United States. $99.95CAD in Canada.

Pro: Unusually small and light for a sophisticated compact model; only a skosh larger and one ounce (28 grams) heavier than its simpler sibling '1101. Two bandwidths, both well chosen. A number of helpful tuning features, including keypad, up/down slew (1 or 5 kHz steps for world band, 1 or 9/10 kHz for mediumwave AM), carousel selector for 49-16 meter segments, and "signal seek" frequency scanning (*see* Con) and memory

When price is crucial but performance can't be mediocre, look to the Degen DE1102. In North America it's sold as the high-value Kaito KA1102.   D. Zantow

scanning; also, ten 19-preset "pages" provide a total of 190 station presets, of which 133 can be used for shortwave (*see* Con). Auto-store function automatically stores presets; works on all bands. Tunable BFO allows for precise signal phasing during single-sideband reception (*see* Con). No muting during manual shortwave bandscanning in 1 or 5 kHz steps, or mediumwave AM bandscanning in 1 kHz steps. PLL and BFO relatively free from drift during single-sideband operation (*see* Con). Above-average weak-signal sensitivity and image rejection. Little circuit "hiss." Superior speaker audio quality, intelligibility and loudness for size. Build quality appears superior for price class, and manufacturer has solid if relatively brief construction history. Four-LED signal-strength indicator for mediumwave AM and shortwave (*see* Con); three-level signal-strength indicator for FM (fourth LED becomes stereo indicator). World Time 24-hour clock displays seconds numerically when radio is off; when on, time (sans seconds) flashes on briefly when key is held down; user may choose 12-hour format, instead. Unusually appropriate for use in the dark, as display and keypad illuminated by pleasant blue light which works only in dark (*see* Con). Clicky keys have superior tactile feel. LCD has excellent contrast when viewed from sides or below. Alarm with sleep delay (*see* Con). Travel power lock. Rechargeable NiMH batteries (3 × "AA"), included, can be charged within the radio; station presets and time not erased during

charging. Switchable bass boost supplements high-low tone switch, significantly improves FM audio (*see* Con). Low battery consumption except with FM bass boost. Battery-level indicator. Battery cover hinged to avoid loss. Superior FM weak-signal sensitivity. Excellent FM capture ratio aids reception when band congested, including helping separate co-channel stations. FM in stereo through earbuds, included (*see* Con). FM 70–108 MHz coverage includes 76–90 MHz Japanese FM band and 70–74 MHz portion of 66–74 MHz low band still used within some former Warsaw Pact countries (*see* Con). Full coverage of mediumwave AM band. Includes short external wire antenna accessory, which in many locations is about the most that can be used without generating overloading. Available in black or aluminum colors. *Degen:* AC adaptor (220V). *Kaito:* AC adaptor (120V).

Con: Speaker audio, except FM, lacks low-frequency ("bass") response as compared to larger models. Bass-boost circuit, which could relieve this on world band, works only on FM. Dynamic range, although roughly average for a compact portable, not anywhere equal to that of the sibling '1101; overloads easily with a significant outdoor antenna, although much less often with the built-in antenna or a short outboard antenna. Not so straightforward to operate as some other portables; for example, single-sideband mode works only when presets "page 9" is selected (or SSB button is held in manually), even if no presets are to be chosen (in any event, presets don't store mode); otherwise, "ERR" is displayed; manufacturer says this is to prevent its Chinese consumers, who are unfamiliar with single sideband, from turning on the BFO accidentally and thus becoming confused. Slight warble in audio with ECSS reception, varies with how many signal-strength LEDs are being illuminated; LEDs can't be turned off. Volume at earphone jack sometimes inadequate with weak or undermodulated signals; variable-level earphone jack misleadingly described as "line out." Power button activates a 99-minute sleep delay; to turn the radio on fulltime, a second key must be pressed immediately afterwards. No tuning knob. No

LSB/USB switch. Displays in nonstandard XX.XX/XX.XXx MHz format. Signal-strength indicator overreads. Little-used 2 MHz (120 meter) world band segment not covered. Clock doesn't display when frequency is shown, although pushbutton allows time to replace frequency briefly. Always-on LCD/keypad illumination with AC adaptor, as described in owner's manual, did not function on test sample. LCD/keypad illumination dim and uneven. FM IF produces images 21+ MHz down.

Verdict: An exceptional price and performance winner from Degen, with superior build. Just don't expect much in the way of low-end audio.

The Etón/Grundig G4000A, a listener favorite, is straightforward to use with standout audio quality.

DRM Modifiable

★★★ ⓔ *Passport's Choice*
Etón G4000A, Grundig G4000A, Grundig Yacht Boy 400PE

Price: *G4000A:* $149.95 in the United States. $199.99CAD in Canada. $279.00AUD in Australia. *YB400PE (as available):* $169.00 in Canada. *Refurbished units, as available:* $99.95 in the United States. $169.00CAD in Canada.

Pro: Speaker audio quality tops in size category for those with sharp hearing. Two bandwidths, both well-chosen. Ergonomically superior, a pleasure to operate. A number of helpful tuning features, including keypad, up/down slew, 40 station presets, "signal seek" frequency scanning and scanning of station presets. Signal-strength indicator. Dual-zone 24-hour clock, with one zone shown at all times; however, clock displays seconds only when radio is off. Illuminated display. Alarm with simple sleep delay. Tunable BFO allows for superior signal phasing during single-sideband reception (*see* Con). DRM modifiable (see www. drmrx.org/receiver_mods.html). Outboard reel passive wire antenna accessory aids slightly with weak-signal reception. Generally superior FM performance, especially in weak-signal locations. FM in stereo through earpieces. Longwave. AC adaptor. *G4000A:* Excellent hardside leather travel case. *North America:* Toll-free tech support.

Con: Circuit noise ("hiss") can be slightly intrusive with weak signals. No tuning knob. At many locations there can be breakthrough of powerful AM or FM stations into the world band spectrum. Keypad not in telephone format. No LSB/USB switch, and single-sideband reception is below par. Battery consumption slightly above norm. No batteries (six "AA" needed).

☞ Refurbished units reportedly include gift and similar returns from department stores and other outlets where customers tend to be unfamiliar with world band radio. Everything but the radio itself is supposed to be replaced. Limited availability.

Verdict: This most popular of Grundig's digital-readout portables offers superior audio quality, ease of use and a roster of other virtues. So it's hardly surprising that this Chinese-made receiver is unusually popular for enjoying world band programs, including music. Tough FM catches, too, although single-sideband isn't all it could be.

★★⅞ (*see* ☞) ⓔ
Degen DE1103, Kaito KA1103

Price: *Kaito:* $109.95 in the United States. $109.00CAD in Canada.

Pro: Two bandwidths, both well chosen (*see* Con). Helpful tuning features include tuning knob (*see* Con), keypad (*see* Con), world

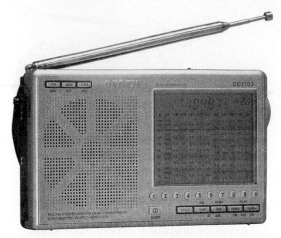

The Degen DE1103, available in North America as the Kaito KA1103, is a solid performer for its price and size. Alas, ergonomics are hostile.

band segment up/down carousel, "signal seek" (pause, resume) frequency scanning and presets scanning; also, sixteen "pages" holding 16 presets each provide 256 station presets, plus another dozen to select among world band segments (alternatively, "pages" may be bypassed for quick-access tuning, reducing available presets to 100). Presets store mode (*see* Con). Tuning knob not muted when tuned, facilitating bandscanning (*see* Con). Scanner works better than most. Radio can return to last-tuned frequency within ten world band segments, as well as FM and mediumwave AM. Superior dynamic range for a compact portable—better than that of DE1102/KA1102, and even approaching that of DE1101/KA1102 (*see* Con). Tunable BFO (*see* Con) allows for precise signal phasing during single-sideband reception. Relatively free from drift during single-sideband operation. Above-average sensitivity aided by quiet circuitry. Using dual conversion, image rejection is above average (*see* Con). Speaker audio quality, although limited, fairly good except during single-sideband reception (*see* Con). Four-level signal-strength indicator (*see* Con). World Time 24-hour clock (*see* Con). Display and keypad illumination is about as good as it gets: During battery operation, it

can be switched not to go on; otherwise, it is automatically activated by any of various controls, including those for tuning, and stays on for a full 15 seconds. Clicky keys with superior tactile feel (*see* Con). Sleep delay. Two-event timer. NiMH batteries (4 × "AA"), included, slowly rechargeable within radio. Travel power lock. Station presets and time not erased during battery charging or replacement. Battery-level indicator. Battery cover hinged to avoid loss. Superior FM sensitivity. Excellent FM capture ratio aids reception when band congested, including helping separate co-channel stations. FM in stereo through earbuds, included (*see* Con). Stereo audio line output, has appropriate level. Coverage of 76–108 MHz includes Japanese FM band. Longwave (*see* Con) tunes down to 100 kHz. Elevation panel. Includes short external wire antenna accessory. Available in black or aluminum colors. *Degen:* AC adaptor (220V). *Kaito:* AC adaptor (120V).

Con: Hostile ergonomics include having to operate two controls to change volume; nonstandard single-row keypad; small keys; stiff slider controls; only one knob tuning rate (1 kHz, slow) for world band and mediumwave AM; and no center detent for fine-tuning (tunable BFO) thumbwheel. Pseudo-analog LCD "dial," a pointless gimmick that takes up space which could have been used to display useful information and provide proper keypad layout. No up/down slew controls. No tone control except "news-music" switch that works only on FM. No LSB/USB switch. Single-sideband has audible distortion, seemingly from AGC. Image rejection, although fairly good, not all that it could be for a model with enough dynamic range to handle some outboard antennas. Slight microprocessor noise when tuning knob turned—a small price to pay to avoid bandscan limitations brought about by muting. Even though dynamic range superior, AGC seemingly swamped by exceptionally powerful signals, causing lowered volume; switching attenuator to "LO" allows volume to return to normal level. Signal-strength indicator overreads and does not operate on FM. Clock doesn't display when frequency is shown, although pushbutton allows time to replace frequency briefly. Presets do not store bandwidth. Longwave less convenient to access than other bands.

☞ The '1103 merits three stars for performance, but only two for ergonomics (*see* Evaluation).

☞ Unlike the sibling DE1101/KA1101 and DE1102/KA1102, the '1103's AC adaptor jack uses standard center-pin-positive polarity.

Verdict: Dreadful ergonomics and a wasted LCD make this a model to approach with caution. Yet, the Degen DE1103/Kaito KA1103 is a solid and versatile performer at a surprisingly low price. If you can endure its ergonomic shortcomings, the '1103 offers excellent performance value.

Sony's long-discontinued ICF-SW55 occasionally pops up new in Europe. Good audio, not much else.

✪✪⅞
Sony ICF-SW55

Price (as available): €379–430 in Germany. ¥45,000 in Japan.

Pro: Audio quality. Dual bandwidths. Logical controls. Innovative tuning, with alphabetic identifiers for groups ("pages") of stations; some like this approach. Weak-signal sensitivity a bit better than most. Demodulates single-sideband signals (*see* Con). Reel-in antenna, AC adaptor, earbuds and cord for external DC power. Signal/battery strength indicator. Local and World Time clocks, one displayed separately from frequency. Snooze/alarm. Five-event (daily only) timer. Illuminated display. Longwave and Japanese FM.

Con: Page tuning system cumbersome for some. Spurious-signal rejection in higher segments not commensurate with price. Wide bandwidth rather broad for receiver lacking synchronous selectable sideband. Tuning increments of 0.1 kHz and frequency readout of 1 kHz compromise single-sideband reception. BFO pulling reportedly causes audio quavering; not found in our test units. Display illumination dim and uneven. High battery consumption.

Verdict: Overpriced, but if you like the Sony ICF-SW55's operating scheme and want a small portable with good audio quality,

this discontinued veteran is a respectable performer in its size class. But this Japanese-made unit, still available here and there (e.g., thieCom.de and bolger.de) as "new old stock," lacks synchronous selectable sideband—a major plus found on newer Sony and Etón models.

✪✪⅞
Sangean ATS 909, Sangean ATS 909W, Sangean ATS 909 "Deluxe," Roberts R861

Price: *ATS 909:* $259.95 in the United States. $299.00CAD in Canada. £139.95 in

Sangean's flagship ATS 909 is ahead of the pack for single-sideband reception.

the United Kingdom. €168.00 in Germany. *ATS 909W:* €168.00 in Germany. *ATS 909 "Deluxe":* $289.90 in the United States. *Multivoltage AC adaptor:* £16.95 in the United Kingdom. €30.00 in Germany. *R861:* £169.00 in the United Kingdom.

Pro: Exceptionally wide range of tuning facilities, including hundreds of world band station presets (one works with a single touch) and tuning knob. Tuning system uses 29 "pages" and alphanumeric station descriptors for world band. Two voice bandwidths. Tunes single-sideband signals in unusually precise 0.04 kHz increments without having to use a fine-tuning control, making this one of the handiest and most effective portables for listening to these signals (*see* Con). Shortwave dynamic range slightly above average for portable, allowing it to perform unusually well with an outboard antenna (*see* Con). Travel power lock. 24-hour clock shows at all times, and can display local time in various cities of the world (*see* Con). Excellent 1–10 digital signal-strength indicator. Low-battery indicator. Clock radio feature offers three "on" times for three discrete frequencies. Sleep delay. FM sensitive to weak signals (see Con) and performs well overall, has RDS feature, and is in stereo through earpieces, included. Illuminated display. Superior ergonomics, including tuning knob with tactile detents. Longwave. *ATS 909W:* 76–108 MHz coverage includes Japanese FM band. *ATS 909 (North American units), ATS 909 "Deluxe" and Roberts:* Superb, but relatively heavy, multivoltage AC adaptor with North American and European plugs. ANT-60 outboard reel passive wire antenna accessory aids slightly with weak-signal reception. Sangean service provided by Sangean America on models sold under its name. *ATS 909 "Deluxe," available only from C. Crane Company:* Enhanced tuning knob operation and elimination of muting between stations when bandscanning.

Con: Weak-signal sensitivity with built-in telescopic antenna not equal to that of comparable models; usually remediable with ANT-60 accessory antenna (provided) or other suitable external antenna. Tuning knob tends to mute stations during bandscanning; C. Crane Company offers a "Deluxe" modification to remedy this. Larger and heavier than most compact models. Signal-seek tuning, although flexible and relatively sophisticated, tends to stop on few active shortwave signals. Although scanner can operate out-of-band, reverts to default (in-band) parameters after one pass. When entering a new page, there is an initial two-second wait between when preset is keyed and station becomes audible. Although synthesizer tunes in 0.04 kHz increments, frequency readout only in 1 kHz increments. Software oddities; e.g., under certain conditions, alphanumeric station descriptor may stay on full time. Page tuning system enjoyed by some users, but cumbersome for others. Speaker audio quality only so-so, not aided by three-level treble-cut tone control. No carrying handle or strap. The 24-hour clock set up to display home time, not World Time, although this is easily overcome by not using world-cities-time feature or by creative setup of World/Home display to London/Home. Clock does not compensate for daylight (summer) time in each displayed city. FM can overload in high-signal-strength environments, causing false "repeat" signals to appear; capture ratio average. Heterodyne interference, possibly related to the digital display, sometimes interferes with reception of strong mediumwave AM signals. Battery consumption well above average. No batteries (four "AA" required). Elevation panel flimsy.

☞ Frequencies pre-programmed into "pages" vary by country of sale. It helps to keep a couple of empty pages to aid in editing, deleting or changing pre-programmed page information.

Verdict: While many models are similar to others being offered, this compact from Sangean marches to its own drummer. Relatively high battery consumption and insufficient weak-signal sensitivity lower its standing as a portable, and our star rating reflects this. Yet, when it is used as a *de facto* tabletop connected to household current and an outboard antenna, it becomes worthy of a three-star rating—even if not as a genuine portable. In part, this is because its circuitry is more capable than those of most other compact portables in handling the increased signal load from an outboard antenna.

As a result, this feature-laden model has a visible and enthusiastic following among radio aficionados for whom portability is not *de rigueur*. Like the tabletop Icom IC-R75, it is a favorite for tuning utility and ham signals, as it offers superior single-sideband performance at an attractive price. The '909 is also the only Sangean model still made exclusively in Taiwan.

✪✪⅞
Sangean PT-80, Grundig Yacht Boy 80

Price: *Sangean:* $159.95 as available in the United States. $209.00CAD in Canada. *Grundig:* Around €129.00 as available in Germany.

Pro: Excellent world band selectivity (*see* Con). Worthy sensitivity and image rejection. Numerous helpful tuning features,

The Sangean PT-80 is perfectly adequate, but relatively dear for what it does.

including tuning disc-type knob with raised dots (*see* Con); nicely located up/down slew-scan keys; 18 world band presets; 9 additional presets each for longwave, FM and mediumwave AM; "auto arrange" scanning of presets from low-to-high frequency;

SATELLITE PRICE BEATER: WORLD BAND CAR RADIO

Over the years PASSPORT has tested car radios with significant world band coverage, and found two things in common: At any given time only one model or group of similar models is readily available; and performance differences among brands and models are not great.

Sony offers an ever-changing line of sensibly priced car stereos, usually with cassette players, that cover most world band segments. They differ in various ways, but world band circuitry thus far has been shared. These are available in the United States and Canada from Durham Radio in Ontario (www.durhamradio.com, $209.95–$289.00CAD or roughly US$165–235). In the recent past these have also been peddled in the Middle East, Australia and South Asia.

Armchair reasoning has long pointed to world band car radio as a juicy untapped market. So, some years back Philips and Becker undertook serious marketing campaigns within the United States. The results were discouraging, although they predate the recent buzz generated by satellite radio.

World band car radio doesn't begin to offer the fidelity or breadth of drivetime content of satellite. Still, when compared to XM and Sirius, world band is a bargain—with nary a dime in monthly fees. And in times of crisis it stands alone in being beyond the control of official or other gatekeepers who wish to limit information.

Sony offers various world band car radios, including the XR-CA660. These are usually available in Russia, the Middle East, South Asia, Australia and North America. Durham Radio

auto entry of presets (see Con); meter-segment selector; and selectable 5 kHz/1 kHz tuning steps on shortwave. For size, generally pleasant speaker audio in all bands (see Con). Single-sideband demodulation (see Con), with precise analog +/–1.5 kHz fine-tuning thumbwheel. No muting with tuning disc, aids bandscanning. Unusually attractive, sheathed in tan leather. Flip-open leather case excellent at protecting front, top and rear of the receiver (see Con). Leather case affixed to receiver with snaps and magnetic catches, so nearly impossible to misplace. Frequency easy to read, with decent-sized digits and good contrast. Illuminated LCD (see Con). Travel power lock (see Con). Tuning-disc lock. Superior mediumwave AM performance. On FM, superior capture ratio and worthy sensitivity. Dual-zone clock in 12 or 24 hour format (see Con). Alarm/clock radio with sleep delay. Rubber feet on bottom to prevent slipping. Stereo indicator (see Con). Battery cover hinged to avoid loss. Keys have good feel (see Con). Low battery indicator. Reset control for microprocessor and memory. Outboard reel passive wire antenna accessory aids slightly with weak-signal reception. Longwave. Earbuds. *Sangean (North America):* 120V AC adaptor (see Con).

Con: During single-sideband reception, circuit "pulling" during strong modulation peaks causes annoying warbling in audio. Just enough drift at times to prompt occasional tweaking during single-sideband reception. World band and mediumwave AM audio slightly muffled; becomes clearer if station off-tuned by 1 kHz or so, which also can reduce adjacent-channel interference. Limited dynamic range; tends to overload with significant external antenna; attenuator helps, but also reduces signal considerably. (Better to skip attenuation and use the outboard reel antenna, letting out just enough wire to give good reception.) Attenuator doesn't work on mediumwave AM or longwave; however, in unusual circumstances this can be a convenience. Birdies. Tuning disc has some "play," and raised dots can irritate finger during lengthy bandscanning sessions. Long-stroke keys need to be depressed fully to make contact.

No meaningful signal-strength indicator. Spurious signal rejection wanting; at one test location, and alone among several radios there, the PT-80 occasionally had a point-to-point voice transmission puffing away in the background throughout the entire shortwave spectrum. When radio on, displays either frequency or time, but not both at once. FM stereo indicator worked at some test locations, but not all. External antenna jack functions only on shortwave; however, this can also be a convenience. No audio line output. Auto entry of presets does not function on world band. Leather case: 1) sags when used as an elevation panel; 2) has no holes for speaker on front, just on back, so audio is muffled when case closed; and 3) does not protect receiver's sides or bottom. Travel power lock does not deactivate LCD illumination key. No batteries (four "AA" required). *Sangean:* Country of origin, China, not shown on radio, manual or box. Instructions for setting clocks may confuse newcomers, as both clocks are referred to as being for "local time," not UTC, and the manual's mention of UTC mis-states it as "Universal Time Coordinated" instead of Coordinated Universal Time (however, the PT-50's manual gets it right). *Sangean (North America):* 120V AC adaptor generates minor hum.

☞ Grundig version not found at retail as of presstime, but may still be available at some smaller German stores. Sangean version becoming difficult to locate in the United States, as well.

Verdict: This entry from Sangean is pleasant performer on world band and superior on mediumwave AM and FM. Its main drawbacks: single-sideband reception with "warbling" audio, and no meaningful signal-strength indicator.

With an external antenna, the sibling Sangean ATS 909 gets the nod, mainly for superior single-sideband performance, dual bandwidths, signal-strength indicator and sophisticated presets. However, as a true portable for only occasional single-sideband listening the PT-80 holds its own, plus it doesn't mute during bandscanning and costs much less.

★★⅞ ☺ *Passport's Choice*

Degen DE1101, Kaito KA1101

The Degen DE1101/Kaito KA1101 is easily the best choice in or near its price class. A knockout bargain, its size nonetheless limits loudspeaker music quality.
D. Zantow

Price: *Kaito:* $54.95 in the United States. $79.95CAD in Canada.

Pro: Exceptional dynamic range for a compact portable. Unusually small and light for a compact model. Two bandwidths, both well chosen. A number of helpful tuning features, including keypad, up/down slew and "signal seek" frequency scanning (*see* Con); also, 50 station presets of which ten are for 3,000–10,000 kHz and ten for 10,000–26,100 kHz; others are for FM, FML and mediumwave AM. Above-average weak-signal sensitivity and image rejection. Little circuit "hiss." Superior intelligibility and loudness for size. World Time 24-hour clock displays seconds numerically when radio is off; when on, time (sans seconds) flashes on briefly when key is held down. Illuminated display, works only in dark. Clicky keys have superior tactile feel. LCD has excellent contrast when viewed from sides or below. Alarm with sleep delay (*see* Con). AC adaptor (120V Kaito, 220V Degen). Rechargeable NiMH batteries (3 × "AA"), included, can be charged within the radio; station presets and time not erased during charging. Low battery consumption. Battery-level indicator. Battery cover hinged to avoid loss. Travel power lock. Superior FM weak-signal sensitivity. Excellent FM capture ratio aids reception when band congested, including helping separate co-channel stations. FM in stereo through earbuds, included. "FML" covers 76–90 MHz Japanese FM band and 70–74 MHz portion of 66–74 MHz low band still used within some former Warsaw Pact countries. Line output socket (separate from earphone socket) for recording, FM home transmitters and outboard audio systems. Available in gray or aluminum colors. *Kaito:* Mediumwave AM 9/10 channel steps user-selectable, tunes up to 1710 kHz.

Con: Speaker audio quality lacks low-frequency ("bass") response as compared to larger models. Power button activates a 99-minute sleep delay; to turn the radio on fulltime, a second key must be pressed immediately afterwards. Station presets, slew and scanning require pressing bandswitch carousel button up to four times when tuning from below 10 MHz to above 10 MHz and *vice versa*. No tuning knob. Tunes world band only in 5 kHz steps and displays in nonstandard XX.XX/XX.XX₅ MHz format. Digital buzz under some circumstances, such as when antenna is touched. Spurious signals can appear when user's hand is pressed over back cover. With our unit, microprocessor locked up when batteries removed for over a day; resolved by pressing tiny reset button. No signal-strength indicator (what appears to be an LED tuning indicator is actually an ambient-light sensor to disable LCD illumination except when it's dark). Clock doesn't display when frequency is shown, although pushbutton allows time to replace frequency briefly. Little-used 2 MHz (120 meter) world band segment not covered. On Degen unit tested, FM sounded best when tuned 50 kHz above nominal frequency on LCD; this would appear to be a sample-to-sample issue. *Degen:* Upper limit of mediumwave AM tuning is 1620 kHz, rather than the 1705 kHz band upper limit in the Americas, Australia and certain other areas. Mediumwave AM tunes only in 9 kHz steps, making it ill-suited for use in the Americas.

☞ The Kaito version comes with the proper 120V AC adaptor for North America, where-

HANDY HANDHELD?

Icom IC-R20 Wideband

The popularity and frequency coverage of handheld scanners keep marching on. Some even cover world band, where they've traditionally performed poorly. But Icom's interesting new IC-R20 handheld looks on paper as if it can overcome this unfortunate history.

At around US$500/£350 the 'R20 is costlier than nearly any dedicated world band portable. And at about 1.5 inches (14 cm) and 11.3 ounces (0.32 kg), it is on the beefy side for a handheld. Yet, it is comfortably within the norm for compact world band portables.

Broad Coverage, Novel Monitoring Aid

The 'R20 comes powered by a rechargeable lithium ion battery pack. Ordinary alkaline or other "AA" batteries, or the supplied AC adaptor, also may be used.

Frequency coverage is generous. In the United States, where eavesdropping on cellular bands is *verboten*, it tunes 150 kHz–822 MHz, 851–867 MHz and 896–3305 MHz. Elsewhere, or within the United States for government use, it tunes unimpeded from 150 kHz to 3305 MHz. Reception modes are typical: AM, FM, FM-wide, LSB, USB and CW—all user-selected in carousel fashion. The 'R20 tunes and displays in precise 10 Hz increments, but our unit's readout was off by up to 200 Hz.

A neat tuning-related feature is "dual watch," which allows scanning aficionados to monitor two signals simultaneously. Alas, this multitasking goodie doesn't work with world band.

Sensitivity, Dynamic Range Fall Short

Manufacturers drool at the thought of wideband receivers, as it reduces the number of models which have to be engineered, manufactured, inventoried and marketed. Problem is, wideband designs have yet to provide world band performance that's competitive with ordinary world band radios. Evolving technology may overcome this in time, but for now this "wideband curse" remains a fundamental drawback.

Here, the portable 'R20 disappoints—only powerful signals are suitably audible with the telescopic antenna. Another letdown is that although the antenna swivels a couple of different ways, it tends to flop over when fully extended.

The 'R20's dynamic range is significantly limited, so a serious outboard antenna tends to introduce overloading. Tweaking the RF gain control and single-step 30 dB attenuator can help, but not always.

Sensitivity within the mediumwave AM band is similar with the receiver's inboard ferrite rod antenna, while FM broadcasts fare little better. However, image and spurious-signal rejection are both commendable.

Unexpected Bandwidth Rescues World Band

The 'R20 has three bandwidths, each assigned by the received mode so none can be selected independent of mode. Alas, the bandwidth for the AM mode, which includes world band, is a whopping 12 kHz. This is far too wide except for reasonably strong stations in the clear.

The bandwidth for single sideband/CW, around 3 kHz, comes to the rescue. Although it is much too wide for CW, it allows for worthy ECSS reception (*see* glossary) of world band

and mediumwave AM stations. Other than a bit of a low-level buzz mixed in, single side-band/ECSS performs well, aided in part by the 'R20's stability.

The lone single-sideband bandwidth thus rescues the 'R20 for world band reception—*if* you're willing to tune signals by ECSS, a tiresome proposition. Synchronous selectable sideband, which the 'R20 lacks, does the same thing better and more easily.

Speaker audio is good considering the radio's size. However, it lacks punch when used outdoors or where it's noisy.

Built-in Digital Recorder

Although the 'R20 has issues with world band reception, in many other respects it is an intriguing device.

For starters, it comes with a built-in digital audio recorder, like on a telephone answering machine. Three settings are available—one, two and four hours—with great differences in playback quality. The four-hour option is distorted, while the middle (normal) setting is better but still not pleasant. The 65-minute "fine" choice is hardly high fidelity, but fares nicely for world band.

There is no line output to transfer internally recorded audio to an outboard device, such as a tape recorder or CD burner, for permanent retention. However, 65-minute recordings transfer decently through the earphone jack.

Ergonomics Typical for Handheld

Unilluminated, the 'R20's large LCD is not easy to read. Thankfully, this is overcome by effective illumination that can be selected for continuous operation.

Keys have good tactile response. Otherwise, ergonomics are characteristic of a handheld configuration which limits "real estate" available for controls. Tuning is by knob, keypad, up/down slewing and a thousand presets in increments of .01, .1, 5, 6.25, 8.33, 9, 10, 12.5, 15, 20, 25, 30, 50 and 100 kHz.

Glitch: Our receiver failed to power up twice, even with the AC adaptor in use. The only recourse to bring it back to life was to disconnect the adaptor, remove the battery pack, then wait a minute or so.

Scanner à Go-Go, World Band à So-So

The new Icom IC-R20 has much to commend it, even as it fails to break the "wideband curse." It makes a tempting choice for scanning signals on VHF and above, and offers built-in recording. For certain niche applications, including low-profile field surveillance, these characteristics can come together to make it a best-of-breed choice.

For world band, though, the 'R20 is mainly an adjunct to scanning and for inboard recording.

Icom's wideband IC-R20 features built-in recording.

as the Degen version comes with a 220V AC adaptor suitable for most other parts of the world. Both are safe when used "as is," or with a Franzus or other recognized 120V-to-220V or 220V-to-120V AC converter. However, according to unconfirmed reports, the Degen version ordered by Americans from a vendor in Hong Kong comes with a 220-to-120V AC converter that appears to pose a fire hazard.

Verdict: The Degen DE1101, sold in North America as the Kaito KA1101, is a knock-out bargain. Engineered and manufactured in China, it is one of the smallest compact models tested, and has exceptional dynamic range. It comes with an enviable grab-bag of features and accessories, right down to inboard rechargeable batteries. But if you want music-quality audio, be prepared to use earpieces.

✪✪¾
Etón E10, Tecsun PL-550

Price: *Etón:* $129.95 in the United States. $149.99CAD in Canada. £69.95 in the United Kingdom. €129.00 in Germany

Pro: Superior audio quality for size. Numerous helpful tuning features include 1/5 kHz knob, 5/100 kHz up/down slew, world band segment selector (covers all 14 segments), signal-seek scanning, keypad and 550 sta-

The Etón E10 offers agreeable audio. It costs slightly less than sibling G4000A, which is a better overall performer.   D. Zantow

tion presets clustered within pages. Fully 500 presets are for general use (*see* Con), including world band; the other 50 are for the "Automatic Tuning System" (ATS), which installs strong FM and mediumwave AM stations (not world band) into presets, like when setting up a VCR. Presets pages programmable to hold 10, 20, 25 or 50 presets per page. Audio muting scarcely noticeable when tuning by knob. Respectable world band and mediumwave AM sensitivity, with low circuit noise. Overloading, which can appear with a substantial external antenna, controllable by two levels of attenuation via a three-position switch. Two well-chosen bandwidths for program listening (*see* Con). Generally worthy ergonomics, including keys with positive-action feel (*see* Con). World Time clock (*see* Con) with alarm, clock radio (two on/off 30-minute timers), snooze and sleep delay (*see* Con); may also be set to 12-hour format. Clock reads out separately from frequency. Clock operates after batteries removed. LCD large and easy to read. Display illumination can either fade out in five seconds, be switched off before the five seconds have expired, or stay on fulltime when button held down more than five seconds. Five-level signal-strength indicator (*see* Con). External antenna jack for world band and FM. Novel 455/450 kHz IF control shifts images by 10 kHz (*see* Con). Rubber pads on bottom reduce sliding when elevation panel in use. Worthy FM sensitivity for superior fringe reception. Japanese FM band. Weak-battery indicator. Includes worthy travel pouch, stereo earbuds and outboard reel passive wire antenna. Numerous user-defined software functions, including page definitions for presets, FM frequency coverage and battery type (1.6V normal *vs.* 1.3V rechargeable). Travel power lock (*see* Con). Elevation panel. *Etón:* Two "AA" alkaline batteries included. Stylish curved front panel, albeit silver colored. Toll-free tech support. *Tecsun:* Regulated 220V AC adaptor and four "AA" nickel metal hydride cells that recharge inside the radio.

Con: Single-conversion circuitry allows for images, although these are weaker than usual even without the novel image-shifting control. Image-shifting control eliminates most image interference, but complicates operation. When image-shifting control adjusted from 455 kHz IF with wide bandwidth to the 450 kHz alternative to escape image interference, only the narrow bandwidth functions; too, when returning to the 455 kHz IF, the narrow bandwidth appears even if the wide bandwidth had originally been in use. Narrow bandwidth too broad for many DX situations. Signal-strength indicator overreads somewhat. Antenna-tuning control seems pointless: does not work with external antenna; yet, with telescopic antenna appears to require only initial tweaking—no adjusting thereafter. No audio line output for tape recording. Signal-seek scan rate is slow, and scanner stops only at strongest stations. Entering presets data unnecessarily complicated. Some keys relatively small for large fingers. Telescopic antenna, with fixed-height base, does not allow for full vertical positioning when radio laid flat; partially remedied by elevation panel. Travel power lock does not deactivate timers or LCD illumination key. Clock when in 24-hour format does not show leading tens-of-hours zero. Power switch needs to be held down for a second for radio to stay on fulltime; otherwise, sleep-delay function eventually turns off radio. FM frequency readout slightly off on one sample. *Etón:* Recessed keys not as easy as most to engage. On our unit from the brief initial production run, there were three issues that may not appear in later production: at one spot on tuning knob rotation an increment (1/5 kHz) was consistently skipped; tuning knob slid off shaft easily; silver paint wore through near antenna base.

☞ With early Tecsun units, the travel pouch emitted a powerful odor of old tires. This was not found with early samples of the newer Etón version, and thus presumably is being remedied with the Tecsun version, as well.

Verdict: This model offers unusually pleasant program listening and is loaded with useful goodies, even if it does not demodulate single-sideband signals. There are some questionable features, but the good points are significant while negatives are mainly small potatoes.

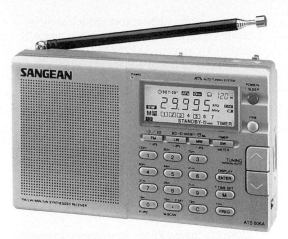

The Sangean ATS 606A was to be superceded by a smaller version of the ATS 909. However, increased competition has dampened Sangean's world band presence.

✪✪¾ Ⓒ
Sangean ATS 606AP, Sangean ATS 606A, Panasonic RF-B55, Roberts R876, Sanyo MB-60A

Price: *ATS 606AP:* $139.95 in the United States. $159.99CAD in Canada. €102.00 in Germany. *ATS 606A:* €95.00 in Germany. *RF-B55:* £109.95 in the United Kingdom. *R876:* £129.99 in the United Kingdom. *MB-60A:* R1,000.00 in South Africa.

Pro: Relatively diminutive for a compact model. Single bandwidth reasonably effective at adjacent-channel rejection, while providing reasonable audio bandwidth. Speaker audio quality better than most for size (*see* Con). Weak-signal sensitivity at least average. Various helpful tuning features, including keypad, 54 station presets, slew, signal-seek tuning and meter band selection. Keypad has superior feel and tactile response. Easy to operate. Longwave. Dual-zone 24-hour clock. Illuminated LCD. Alarm. Sleep delay. Travel power lock (*see* Con). Multi-level battery strength indicator; also, weak-battery warning. Stereo FM through earphones or earbuds. Above-average FM weak-signal sensitivity and selectivity. Above-average capture ratio aids reception when band congested, including helping separate co-channel stations.

Memory scan. Rubber feet reduce sliding while elevation panel in use. *R876 and ATS 606AP:* UL-approved 120/230V AC adaptor, with American and European plugs, adjusts to proper AC voltage automatically. *ATS 606AP:* ANT-60 outboard reel passive wire antenna accessory aids slightly with weak-signal reception. In North America, service provided by Sangean America to models sold under its name. *RF-B55:* Cabinet and controls not painted, so should maintain their appearance unusually well. Country of manufacture (Taiwan) specified on radio and box.

Con: No tuning knob. Speaker audio quality lacks low-frequency ("bass") response as compared to larger models. Clock not readable while frequency displayed. No meaningful signal-strength indicator. Keypad not in telephone format. Travel power lock doesn't disable LCD illumination button. No carrying strap or handle. No batteries (three "AA" needed). *ATS 606AP:* Country of manufacture (China) not specified on radio or box. *RF-B55:* No AC adaptor or outboard reel antenna included, although the owner's manual says that the radio is supposed to come with an "external antenna." Not available within the Americas.

Sangean's **ATS 505P** is an okay compact model that demodulates single-sideband signals.

Verdict: This classic continues to hold its own among travel-friendly compact models. Now, it is available in separate Chinese-made and Taiwanese-made versions.

✪✪⅝
Sangean ATS 505P, Sangean ATS 505, Roberts R9914

Price: *ATS 505P:* $129.95 in the United States. $159.00CAD in Canada. £79.95 in the United Kingdom. €105.00 in Germany. $199.00AUD in Australia. *ATS 505:* €95.00 in Germany. *R9914:* £59.99 in the United Kingdom. IAC adaptor: £16.95 in the United Kingdom.

Pro: Numerous helpful tuning features, including two-speed tuning knob, keypad, station presets (*see* Con), up/down slew, meter-band carousel selection, signal-seek tuning and scanning of presets (*see* Con). Automatic-sorting feature arranges station presets in frequency order. Analog clarifier with center detent and stable circuitry allows single-sideband signals to be tuned with uncommon precision and to stay properly tuned, thus allowing for superior audio phasing for a portable (*see* Con). Illuminated LCD. Dual-zone 24/12-hour clock. Alarm with sleep delay. Modest battery consumption. Nine-level battery-reserve indicator. Travel power lock (*see* Con). FM stereo through earbuds, included. Longwave. AC adaptor. *ATS 505P:* Tape measure antenna.

Con: Bandwidth slightly wider than appropriate for a single-bandwidth receiver. Large for a compact. Only 18 world band station presets, divided up between two "pages" with nine presets apiece. Tuning knob tends to mute stations during bandscanning by knob, especially when tuning rate is set to fine (1 kHz); muting with coarse (5 kHz) tuning is much less objectionable. Keys respond slowly, needing to be held down momentarily rather than simply tapped. Stop-listen-resume scanning of station presets wastes time. Pedestrian overall single-sideband reception because of excessively wide bandwidth and occasional distortion caused by AGC timing. Clock does not display independent of frequency. No meaningful signal-

MAKE YOUR PORTABLE "HEAR" BETTER

Regardless of which portable you own, you can boost weak-signal sensitivity on the cheap. How cheap? Nothing, for starters.

Look for "sweet spots" to place your radio: near windows, appliances, telephones, building I-beams and the like. If your portable has an AC adaptor, try that, then batteries; sometimes the adaptor works better, sometimes batteries. Places to avoid are near computers and appliances with microprocessors; also, light dimmers, non-incandescent lighting and cable TV or telephone lines. Sometimes power lines and cords can be noisy, too.

Outdoor Antenna Optional

An outdoor antenna shouldn't be needed with a portable. But it can help, especially with models lacking in weak-signal sensitivity with their built-in telescopic antennas. With compact and pocket models, simplest is often best—sophisticated or big antennas can cause "overloading." Run several meters or yards of ordinary insulated wire to a tree, then clip one end to your set's telescopic antenna with an alligator or claw clip available from RadioShack and such. It's fast and cheap, yet effective.

If you are in a weak-signal location, such as central or western North America or Australia, and want signals to be more audible, even better is to erect an inverted-L (so-called "longwire") antenna. Also sometimes called random-length antennas, they are available in the United States at RadioShack (278–758, $9.99) and worldwide at radio specialty outlets. Powerful versions can be constructed from detailed instructions in the RDI White Paper, PASSPORT *Evaluation of Popular Outdoor Antennas*. Antenna length is not critical, but keep the lead-in wire reasonably short.

Use an outdoor antenna only when required—disconnect during thunder, snow or sand storms, and when the radio is off. And don't touch any connected antenna during dry weather, as discharged static electricity might damage the radio.

Creative Indoor Solutions

All antennas work best outdoors, away from electrical noises inside the home. If your supplementary antenna has to be indoors, run it along the middle of a window with Velcro, tape or suction cups. In a reinforced-concrete building which absorbs radio signals, you can affix a telescopic car antenna so it sticks outdoors, like a wall flagpole. These are all but invisible, but work because they reach away from the building.

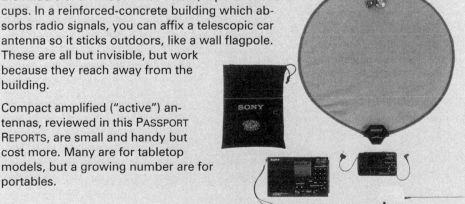

Compact amplified ("active") antennas, reviewed in this PASSPORT REPORTS, are small and handy but cost more. Many are for tabletop models, but a growing number are for portables.

Sony's AN-LP1 is designed for travel, but also works at home. J. Brinker

strength indicator. No carrying handle or strap. Country of manufacture (China) not specified on radio or box. Travel power lock does not deactivate LCD illumination key. No batteries (four "AA" needed).

Verdict: An okay portable that demodulates single-sideband signals.

✪✪⅝ ✐
Sony ICF-SW35

Price: $89.95 in the United States. $149.99CAD in Canada. £79.95 in the United Kingdom. €99.00 in Germany. $269.00AUD in Australia. ¥16,500 in Japan. *AC-E45HG 120V AC adaptor:* $19.95 in the United States.

Pro: Superior reception quality, with excellent adjacent-channel rejection (selectivity) and image rejection. Fifty world band station presets, which can be scanned within five "pages." Signal-seek-then-resume scanning works unusually well. Two-speed slew. Illuminated display. Dual-zone 24-hour clock. Dual-time alarm. Sleep delay. Travel power lock. FM stereo through earpieces, not included. Weak-battery indicator. Japanese FM (most versions) and longwave bands.

When it was first introduced, the Sony ICF-SW35 had price appeal. Alas, by now it has lost its competitive edge.

Con: No keypad or tuning knob. Synthesizer muting and poky slew degrade bandscanning. Speaker audio quality clear, but lacks low-frequency response ("bass"). Clock not displayed independent of frequency. LCD lacks contrast when viewed from above. No jacks for recording or outboard antenna. AC adaptor is extra and pricey. No batteries (three "AA" required).

Verdict: The Sony ICF-SW35 has superior rejection of images, which are the bane of most other under-$100 models. This Chinese-made compact lacks a keypad, which is partially overcome by a large number of station presets and effective scanning. Overall, a decent choice only if you listen to a predictable roster of stations.

New for 2006
✪✪½ ✐
Degen DE1105, Kaito KA1105

Price: *DE1105:* Under $65, including shipping, via eBay; insurance extra. *KA1105:* See ☞, below.

Pro: One thousand presets (*see* Con) within ten "pages" (*see* Con); presets do not erase if batteries removed or exhausted. Other handy tuning features include keypad, signal-seek scanning, automatic tuning system (ATS) and up/down slewing. Also, a knurled wheel with un-muted variable-rate tuning shifts from slow (1 kHz) to fast (5 kHz) increments when rotated quickly (*see* Con). Worthy sensitivity and selectivity. Double conversion provides effective image rejection. Dynamic range resists overloading. Buttons have excellent tactile feel (*see* Con). LCD and most buttons illuminate when touched or tuning wheel turned. Ten-level signal strength indicator accurate and precise for price class. Internal automatic NiMH battery recharging virtually eliminates having to purchase batteries. Three-level battery-strength indicator, seconds as battery-charging indicator. Radio shuts down if batteries too low. Clock selectable between 12-hour and 24-hour formats; seconds displayed numerically (*see* Con). Worthwhile FM sensitivity and selectivity. FM in stereo with earpieces. Bass boost, albeit only on FM with earpieces. FM 70-108

MHz includes Japanese band. Three alarms with sleep delay. Travel power lock. Hinged battery cover prevents loss. Includes soft carrying case, two "AA" NiMH batteries, earbuds, accessory wire antenna and 220V AC adaptor. Build quality seems above average for price. Displays ambient (e.g., room) temperature (*see* Con).

Con: Potentially confusing presets "page" system and user setup. Power button activates 99-minute sleep timer bypassed only by quickly pushing another button. World band coverage from 5800 to 26100 kHz, although reasonable, misses 5, 4, 3 and 2 MHz (60, 75, 90 and 120 meter) segments and 5730-5795 kHz end of 6 MHz (49 meters). Because only one (narrow) bandwidth provided, world band and mediumwave AM audio quality only fair with earpieces and internal speaker. Except for frequency/clock, LCD information small and hard to see. Buttons undersized. Keypad not in standard telephone format. Tuning wheel operates only in slow (1 kHz) increments within many "out-of-band" frequency zones. Clock shares display with frequency, so you can see one or the other but not both at once. Clock setting erases when batteries removed or exhausted. Mediumwave AM sensitivity only fair. No external antenna or audio line-out jacks. Temperature only in Celsius. *DE1105:* No meaningful warranty outside China. Owner's manual only in Chinese, although one eBay vendor provides a condensed manual in English.

☞ As of late 2005 Kaito had not announced that it would offer the '1105. Nevertheless, based on past actions there is a chance that a Kaito KA1105 will materialize in 2006 and include a 120V AC adaptor and an English-language owner's manual.

Verdict: The Chinese-made Degen DE1105 is a solid performer within its price class. Size and features make it especially welcome for use on trips, but for similar money Kaito/Degen offer better choices.

Evaluation of New Model: The new Degen DE1105 is the latest in their evolving series of travel-sized compact world band portables. Each provides superior performance,

The DE1105 is Degen's newest offering, but it is not equal to the earlier and cheaper Degen DE1101. Sold in North America as the Kaito KA1105.   D. Zantow

features and build quality for the price and size, and the '1105 is no exception.

The '1105 tunes the usual and Japanese FM bands, mediumwave AM and the shortwave spectrum from 5800–26100 kHz. This is ample for most, but omits the 5, 4, 3 and 2 MHz (60, 75, 90 and 120 meter) segments and the 5730–5795 kHz end of 6 MHz (49 meters). PASSPORT's Blue Pages give an idea of what's missed.

Handy Tuning

The '1105 sports a variety of handy tuning features, including no less than one thousand presets allocated among ten "pages" of a hundred presets each. Presets don't erase if battery power is lost, and there's an automatic tuning system to make data entry more convenient.

Other tuning aids include a keypad—alas, not in telephone format—plus signal-seek scanning and up/down slewing. Even better, there's a knurled tuning wheel with variable-rate tuning that shifts from slow (1 kHz) to fast (5 kHz) when rotated quickly. It isn't muted, either—a real plus when band-scanning.

There is a tuning quirk that's sometimes handy, sometimes not. Outside predefined world band segments using the wheel's fast (5 kHz) setting, the radio leaps to the next segment like a wallaby on steroids. For example, after 7400 kHz it suddenly jumps to 9100 kHz. Bandscanning 7405–9095 kHz in 5 kHz steps thus is limited to up/down slewing, although the tuning wheel's slow rate (1 kHz) still works.

Initial setup can be an ergonomic challenge. This has to be done immediately after battery insertion, after which there is little time allowed to complete the task. Another ergonomic drawback is the power switch, which is actually a "forced sleep timer." To turn on the radio normally, the exit key must be pushed within two seconds of the power button. If not, the radio shuts off in 99 minutes.

The sibling DE1103/KA1103's volume control is an ergonomic abomination shared with the tuning knob. Ditto the '1105, but thankfully it can be ignored because on this model there is also a normal volume control.

Traveler's Friend

A digital clock shows in 24-hour (World Time) or 12-hour (AM/PM) format. Although it shares display space with the frequency readout, it provides seconds numerically. There's also a three-setting alarm and sleep delay.

If you hate buying batteries, this is yet another Degen to make you rejoice. Two "AA" NiMH cells are supplied and recharge inside the radio whenever the AC adaptor is connected. It's a great feature made even better because the charge cycle is automatically timed. With the '1105 you won't have to replace batteries for years.

Another nice touch is that the LCD and buttons automatically illuminate when a key is touched or the tuning wheel is turned. This is ideal for gloomy hotel rooms, moonlit beaches and electrical failures.

Yet, the '1105's travel orientation results in compromises. For example, a small case

means that much displayed information is undersized and hard to read. Buttons and keys are itsy, too, although with excellent feel.

Worthy Overall Performance

World band sensitivity is at least average with the telescopic antenna, which unfortunately doesn't swivel. The signal-strength indicator uses a number of bars and is unusually accurate, especially for this price class.

Only one bandwidth is provided, a major letdown from other and similarly priced Degen models. It separates stations nicely, but its narrowness compromises world band audio quality. On the other hand, dual conversion virtually eliminates image signals and no microprocessor noise is audible. Dynamic range is quite reasonable, too.

FM selectivity is effective in keeping stations apart, and sensitivity is equally commendable. There is also marginally effective bass boost for FM stereo through earpieces. Mediumwave AM, though, performs less well: Sensitivity is wanting and the lone bandwidth muffles audio.

The DE1105 continues Degen's tradition of value with quality. Its size and features are great for travel and, bandwidth and software aside, performance is solid.

✪✪½
Etón E100, Tecsun PL-200

Price: *Etón:* $99.95 in the United States. $99.99CAD in Canada. £59.95 in the United Kingdom. €79.00 in Germany.

Pro: Handy size for travel. Very good weak-signal sensitivity. Above-average dynamic range. Superior audio for size, aided by hi/lo tone switch. Several handy tuning aids, including keypad; tuning knob in 1 kHz segments for world band/MW AM (*see* Con); 200 station presets, with eight pages where user selects how many presets per page; world band segment selector; and slew buttons (5 kHz world band increments, 9/10 kHz MW AM increments). Illuminated LCD, easy to read. World Time clock (see Con) with alarm, clock radio, snooze and sleep delay; may also be set to 12-hour format. Clock reads out separately from frequency. Signal-seek scanner searches world band segments or preset channels (see Con). Five-level signal/battery strength indicator, works well. Keys have positive-action feel (see Con). FM stereo with earbuds, included. Japanese FM. Travel power lock. Telescopic antenna swivels and rotates. Setting to allow for optimum performance from either regular or rechargeable batteries. Elevation panel. Microprocessor reset control. *Etón:* Excellent hardside leather travel case. Two "AA" alkaline batteries included. Stylish curved front panel, silver colored. Toll-free tech support. Owner's manual unusually helpful for newcomers. *Tecsun:* 220V AC adaptor/battery charger and rechargeable "AA" batteries included. Softside travel case protects better than most. Choice among three colors (red, gray, silver).

Con: Single-conversion IF circuitry results in mediocre image rejection. Signal-seek scanner progresses slowly. Some muting when tuning by knob or slewing, slows down bandscanning. Tuning knob has no selectable 5 kHz step option. Power button activates 90-minute sleep delay; works as full-time "on" control only if held down for two seconds, a minor inconvenience; there is an additional three seconds to boot up, so basically it takes five seconds to turn on. World band frequencies on all Etón and Tecsun samples displayed 1 kHz high. Small, cramped keys. No jacks for line output or external antenna. *Etón:* No AC adaptor included. On our early sample the tuning knob rubbed the cabinet slightly.

Verdict: A spit-and-polish offering for tuning major stations at home or away.

✪✪⅜
Etón YB 550PE, Grundig YB 550PE, Tecsun PL-230

Price: *Grundig:* $79.95 in the United States. $79.95CAD in Canada. £69.95 in the United Kingdom. *Etón:* €79.00 in Germany.

Etón's E100 is sensibly priced, with numerous performance pluses and useful features. However, image rejection is mediocre.

Pro: Very good selectivity. Above-average dynamic range. Several handy tuning aids, including 200 station presets with eight pages where user selects how many presets per page; also, world band segment selector. For world band, slew buttons tune in 5 kHz increments, while a fine tuning (encoder) thumbwheel tunes shortwave and mediumwave AM in 1 kHz increments. Illuminated LCD (see Con). World Time clock (see Con) with alarm, clock radio and sleep delay; may also be set to 12-hour format. Clock readout separate from frequency display, shows whether radio on or off.

The Etón/Grundig YB500PE is stylish and inexpensive, but lacks sensitivity and image rejection.

Signal-seek scanner searches world band segments or preset channels (*see* Con). Five-level signal/battery strength indicator, works well. FM stereo with earbuds, included. Japanese FM. Travel power lock. Telescopic antenna swivels and rotates (*see* Con). Setting to allow for optimum performance from either regular or rechargeable batteries. *YB 550PE and PL-230:* Generally pleasant audio (*see* Con). Stylish. Removable elevation panel (*see* Con). LCD easy to read. *PL-230:* AC adaptor/battery charger and rechargeable "AA" batteries included. *YB 550PE:* Three "AA" alkaline batteries included. *North America (Grundig YB 550PE):* Toll-free tech support.

Con: Weak-signal sensitivity only fair. Single-conversion IF circuitry results in mediocre image rejection. Signal-seek scanner stops only on very strong signals. Power button activates 90-minute sleep delay; works as full-time "on" control only if held down for two seconds, a minor inconvenience. Takes an additional five seconds to fully turn on (or boot up). Small, cramped keys. *YB 550PE:* No AC adaptor included. *YB 550PE and PL-230:* Audio crispness on FM through earpieces not fully up to Grundig standard. Keypad has oddly placed zero key. Telescopic antenna placement on right side disallows tilting to left. Illumination dim. Snap-on elevation panel must be removed to replace batteries. Battery cover comes loose easily if elevation panel not attached.

The Sony ICF-SW40, like the later Degen DE1103 and Kaito KA1103, uses a pseudo-analog frequency "dial."

One of our two units displayed FM 50 Hz high, whereas world band frequencies on both samples were 1 kHz high.

☞ The Tecsun PL-230 is essentially identical to the YB 550PE except for color and the inclusion of rechargeable batteries and an AC adaptor/charger.

Verdict: Under-$100 radios used to look blah and often sounded that way, but no more. These stylish portables are straightforward to use and full of software conveniences. However, images and weak-signal sensitivity keep them from reaching their full potential.

○○⅜
Sony ICF-SW40

Price: $119.95 in the United States. *AC-E45HG 120V AC adaptor:* $19.95.

Pro: Technologically unintimidating for analog traditionalists, as its advanced digital tuning circuitry is disguised to look like slide-rule, or analog, tuning. World Time 24-hour clock. Two "on" timers and sleep delay. Travel power lock. Illuminated LCD. Japanese FM band (most versions).

Con: Single bandwidth is relatively wide, reducing adjacent-channel rejection. No keypad. Lacks coverage of 1625–1705 kHz portion of North American and Australian mediumwave AM band and 1705–1735 kHz potential public service segment. AC adaptor, much-needed, is extra and overpriced. No batteries (three "AA" required).

Verdict: If you're turned off by things digital and complex, Sony's Japanese-made ICF-SW40 will feel like an old friend. Otherwise, forget it.

○○⅜
Sangean ATS 404, Sangean ATS 404P, Roberts R881

Price: *ATS 404:* $79.95 in the United States. $89.99CAD in Canada. €67.00 in Germany. *ATS 404P:* €77.00 in Germany. *ADP-808 120V AC adaptor:* $10.95 in the United States. *Roberts:* £54.95 in the United Kingdom.

Pro: Superior weak-signal sensitivity. Several handy tuning features. Stereo FM through earpieces, included. Dual-zone 24/12-hour clock displays seconds numerically. Alarm with sleep delay. Travel power lock. Illuminated LCD. Battery indicator. *ATS 404P:* Includes ANT 60 accessory antenna.

Con: Single-conversion IF circuitry results in poor image rejection. No tuning knob. Overloading, controllable by shortening telescopic antenna on world band and collapsing it on mediumwave AM band. Picks up some internal digital "buzz." Tunes only in 5 kHz increments. No signal-strength indicator. Frequency and time cannot be displayed simultaneously. Travel power lock does not disable LCD illumination. No handle or carrying strap. AC adaptor extra. Country of manufacture (China) not specified on radio or box. No batteries (four "AA" needed).

Verdict: Look elsewhere.

⊕⅞ ✐
Kchibo KK-E200

Price: $64.95 as available in the United States.

Pro: Pleasant audio for size and price. Various helpful tuning features, including keypad (*see* Con), 12 world band station presets (*see* Con), up/down slew, meter-band carousel selection and signal-seek tuning. High-contrast illuminated LCD (*see* Con) indicates which preset is in use. Agreeable selectivity and weak-signal sensitivity for price class. World Time clock with sleep delay. Travel power lock (*see* Con). AC adaptor (*see* Con). FM stereo through earbuds, included. Pleasant FM performance for price and size class. Control to reset microprocessor and memory. Battery cover hinged to avoid loss (*see* Con).

Con: Single-conversion IF circuitry results in mediocre image rejection. Dynamic range mediocre, sometimes overloads even with built-in antenna. Does not receive important 7305–9495 kHz chunk of world band spectrum. Does not receive 1621–1705 kHz portion of expanded AM band in the

Sangean's **ATS 404** is not up to that company's usual standard. It is now outclassed by similarly priced and cheaper models.

Americas and Australia and the 1705–1735 kHz potential public service segment. No tuning knob. Tunes world band only in 5 kHz steps and displays in nonstandard XX.XX/ XX.XX₅ MHz format. Unhandy carouseling "MW/SW1/SW2/FM" control required when shifting from tuning within 2300–7300 kHz *vs.* 9500–26100 kHz range or *vice versa*. No signal strength indicator. Annoying one-second pause when tuning from one channel to the next. Only six station presets for each of the four "bands" (FM/MW-AM/

Only a few years back something like the stylish Kchibo **KK-E200** could arouse interest. Not anymore—its performance falls short. J. Brinker

SW1/SW2). Dreadful mediumwave AM performance, with circuit noise drowning out weak stations and degrading stronger ones. AC adaptor sometimes produces slight hum. Elevation panel flimsy; also, hard to open with short fingernails. Clock doesn't display when frequency is shown, although pushbutton allows time to replace frequency. No alarm or other awakening function. Keypad not in telephone format. Fragile battery-cover hinge pins snap off easily. LCD illumination only fair. Travel power lock doesn't disable LCD light button. Using 9/10 kHz mediumwave AM channel switch erases station presets and clock setting. No weak-battery indicator; radio goes abruptly silent when batteries weaken. No batteries (three "AA" needed). Box claims "fancy leather cover," but it is ordinary vinyl. No indication of country of manufacture (China) on product, box or manual. "Chinglish" owner's manual occasionally puzzles. Warranty only 90 days in North America.

Verdict: The stylish Kchibo KK-E200 comes with useful accessories omitted on models costing much more. Its speaker audio quality is pleasant for its size and price, too. Although it lacks full frequency coverage, has no alarm and is overly muted for bandscanning, the 'E200 is cheap and an eyeful.

The Grundig G2000B uses Porsche styling to great effect. Performance is another matter.

★⅞

Grundig G2000B "Porsche Design," Grundig Porsche P2000, Grundig Yacht Boy P2000

Price: *G2000B:* $79.95 in the United States. $79.99CAD in Canada. £89.95 in the United Kingdom. *P2000:* £84.95 in the United Kingdom. $199.00AUD in Australia. *G2ACA 120V AC adaptor:* $12.95 in the United States.

Pro: One of the most functionally attractive world band radios on the market. Generally superior ergonomics include a handy flip-open leather protective case that seconds as an elevation panel. Leather case excellent at protecting front, top and rear of the receiver (*see* Con). Leather case affixed to receiver with snaps and magnetic catches, so nearly impossible to misplace. Superior adjacent-channel rejection—selectivity—for price and size class. Keypad (in proper telephone format), handy meter-band carousel control, signal-seek and up/down slew tuning. Twenty station presets, of which ten are for world band and the rest for FM and mediumwave AM stations. FM stereo through earpieces, included. World Time 24-hour clock. Timer/alarm with sleep delay. Illuminated display. Travel power lock. Reset control for microprocessor and memory. *North America:* Toll-free tech support.

Con: Pedestrian audio. Weak-signal sensitivity mediocre between 9400–26100 kHz, improving slightly between 2300–7400 kHz. Single-conversion IF circuitry results in poor image rejection. Does not tune such important world band ranges as 7405–7550 and 9350–9395 kHz. Tunes world band only in 5 kHz steps and displays in nonstandard XX.XX/XX.XX$_5$ MHz format. No tuning knob. Annoying one-second pause when tuning from one channel to the next. Old-technology SW1/SW2 switch complicates tuning. Protruding power button can get in the way of nearby slew-tuning and meter-carousel keys. Using 9/10 kHz mediumwave AM channel switch erases station presets and clock setting. Leather case makes it difficult to retrieve folded telescopic antenna. Leather case does not protect bottom or sides of radio. Magnetic catches weak on leather case. No carrying strap. Signal-strength

COMING UP: ETÓN E5

In the first half of 2005 Degen leaked news of a forthcoming compact portable, the DE1106. But Degen later shifted gears and announced they had sold the '1106's rights to another firm.

Months later, and *voilà!*—the '1106 is to surface in 2006 as the Etón e5. We tested a prototype only one squeak before PASSPORT's deadline, so findings are brief and preliminary. Even then, its performance, features and frequency coverage are obviously close to the kindred Degen DE1103/Kaito KA1103—even down to inboard-rechargeable batteries.

As tested in embryonic form, the Etón E5 appears to be a worthy performer with oodles of handy tuning features. Rechargeable batteries, too.

Improved over Degen Offerings

But there are improvements, as well. First, the e5's keypad is in standard telephone layout, unlike the DE1105/KA1105's single row of buttons. Second, gone is the '1103's pseudo-analog dial. Third, unlike the cockamamie setup on the '1103, two dedicated buttons control volume.

The e5 includes a genuine tuning knob, albeit with only a 1 kHz tuning rate. However, up/down slewing buttons incorporate a 5 kHz rate.

The e5 has 100 "pages" of seven presets each—700 in all, enough for even the most enthusiastic listener. They are easy to use, thanks to a row of seven buttons for one-touch access to each page; these also instantly jump to major world band segments. Finally, there is a programmable four-character alpha tag atop each page.

Bugaboos? When first powered up after purchase—or if left totally unpowered for some time—the e5 defaults to FM with blasting volume. Also, the LCD has mediocre contrast and brightness, sometimes making it a strain to see. We've mentioned these points to Etón, so production samples might fare better.

An AC adaptor/charger and a travel case are included. Prices are expected to be $149.95 in the United States and $199.99CAD in Canada.

Etón is expanding its Porsche series of world band radios with the portatop P'7131 (right), $299.95, and the forthcoming portable P'7132. These initial Porsche offerings reportedly will be watched carefully, with lessons learned being applied to an expanded and tweaked series of models later in 2006.

indicator nigh useless. Clock not displayed separately from frequency. No batteries (three "AA" required).

☞ At present there are no plans to sell this model under the Etón name.

Verdict: This German-styled, Chinese-manufactured portable is awash in tasteful design, but performance is another story.

✪¾ ✇
Grundig G1000A, Tecsun DR-910

Price: *Grundig:* $49.95 in the United States. $49.99CAD or more in Canada.

Pro: Clock/timer with sleep delay (*see* Con). Illuminated LCD has bigger digits than most models of this size. Elevation panel. FM in stereo with earbuds, included. Two "AA" batteries included. Superior carrying case. *North America:* Toll-free tech support.

Con: Analog-tuned with digital frequency counter, so tunes only by thumbwheel, which is slightly touchy. Does not tune 120, 75, 90, 60, 15 and 11 meter segments; misses a small amount of expanded coverage of 41 and 31 meter segments. Single-conversion IF circuitry results in poor image rejection. Audio lacks bass response. Frequency drift with changes in temperature. Clock in 12-hour format, displays only when radio off. Displays in nonstandard XX.XX/XX.XX₅

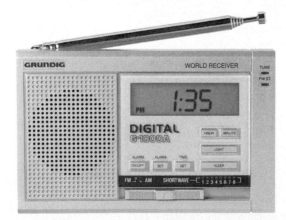

The inexpensive Grundig G1000A is no ball of fire. But, unlike most low-cost alternatives, it has a solid warranty and tech support.

MHz format. "Play" in bandswitch allows wiggling to slightly alter frequency readout. FM overloads in presence of strong signals, remediable by shorting antenna (which also reduces weak-signal sensitivity). On our units, FM frequency misread by 100 kHz (half a channel). If finger placed over LCD display, buzzing audible on mediumwave AM and lower world band frequencies.

Verdict: More spit and polish, and better daytime frequency coverage, than truly cheaper alternatives. It's also backed up by a solid warranty from a reputable company. The G1000A occupies a spot between "throwaway" models that are passable performers, and more highly rated models that cost more.

✪¾
Sangean PT-50, Grundig Yacht Boy 50

Price: *Sangean:* $79.95 as available in the United States. $99.00CAD in Canada. *Grundig:* Around €78.00 as available in Germany.

Pro: Unusually attractive, sheathed in tan leather. Flip-open leather case excellent at protecting front, top and rear of the receiver (*see* Con). Leather case affixed to receiver with snaps and magnetic catches, so nearly impossible to misplace. Two clocks, with separate display windows for home time and World Time. Changing home time to summer (savings) setting does not alter World Time. Handy disc to select time in any of 24 world zones (*see* Con). 24 or 12 hour clock format (*see* Con). Illuminated display. Reasonably clean, pleasant speaker audio for size (*see* Con). Travel power lock (*see* Con). FM in stereo through earpieces (*see* Con). Generally good mediumwave AM performance (*see* Con). Low-battery indicator. Stereo indicator (*see* Con). Battery cover hinged to avoid loss. Keys "clicky," with excellent feel. Alarm/clock radio with sleep delay and snooze. Rubber feet on bottom to prevent slipping. Reset control for microprocessor and memory.

Con: Analog-tuned with digital frequency counter, so tunes only by thumbwheel, which is slightly touchy. Bandswitch must be adjusted when going from one world band segment to another, complicating operation. World band coverage omits 5730–5795 kHz portion of 49 meters; 6890–6990 and 7535–7600 kHz portions of 41 meters; 9250–9305 kHz portion of 31 meters; and all of 120, 90, 75, 60, 15, 13 and 11 meters. Frequency display nonstandard, being in Megahertz and reading out only to the nearest 10 kHz; thus, 6155 kHz shows as 6.15 and/or 6.16 MHz. Single-conversion IF circuitry results in poor image rejection. World band sensitivity and selectivity only fair. No external antenna socket. Speaker audio weak in bass. Audio amplifier lacks punch; stations with weak audio hard to hear, or break into distortion. Frequency drift with changes in temperature. Time-format selection applies to World and home displays alike, so 24 hours can't be used for World Time and 12 hours for home. Small LCDs with thin characters for size of radio. FM performance ordinaire, with mediocre capture ratio; in strong-signal situations there can be overloading. FM stereo indicator worked at some test locations, but not all. Pedestrian spurious-signal rejection on mediumwave AM. No meaningful signal-strength indicator. Bandswitch designates world band segments as 1–7 rather than as MHz. No AC adaptor (needs 3–6V DC, center negative), batteries (two "AA" required) or earpieces. No audio line output. Leather case: 1) collapses when used as elevation panel; 2) no perforations over speaker, so case has to be opened for listening; 3) does not protect receiver's sides or bottom; 4) when case closed, telescopic antenna can only be extended roughly horizontally, to the left; and 5) even when open, case blocks folded telescopic antenna and there is no cabinet detent for finger, so unfolding antenna is cumbersome (best is not to push antenna into the cabinet's snap-in antenna catch). Travel power lock does not deactivate LCD illumination key. *Sangean:* Country of origin, China, not shown on radio, manual or box.

☞ Grundig version not found at retail as of presstime, but may still be available at some smaller German stores. Sangean version becoming difficult to locate in the United States, as well.

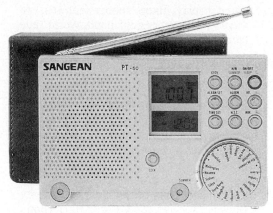

Like most Sangean models, the relatively new PT-50 is a decent offering, yet priced above comparable alternatives.

Verdict: Great clock, so-so radio. Unusually handy as a multi-zone timepiece and a class-act eyeful. Yet, by today's yardstick the '50's radio performance and features are inferior to various other models priced comparably or lower.

✪¾
Lowe SRX-50

Price (as available): Around £30.00 in the United Kingdom.

Pro: Five world band station presets, plus ten station presets for mediumwave AM and FM. Relatively simple to operate. Illumi-

The Lowe SRX-50 was thought to have long since vanished, but in late 2005 some units resurfaced on dealer shelves in the United Kingdom.

nated display. Alarm/snooze features. FM stereo via earpieces, included. World Time clock. Longwave.

Con: Substandard build quality. Does not tune important 5800–5895, 15505–15695, 17500–17900 and 21750–21850 kHz segments. No tuning knob; tunes only via presets and multi-speed up/down slewing/scanning. Tunes world band only in coarse 5 kHz steps. Even-numbered frequencies displayed with final zero omitted; e.g., 5.75 rather than conventional 5.750 or 5750. Poor image rejection. Mediocre selectivity. Does not receive 1605–1705 kHz portion mediumwave AM band. No signal-strength indicator. No travel power lock. Clock not shown independent of frequency display. Mediumwave AM tuning increments not switchable, which makes for inexact tuning in the Americas. Power switch shows no "off," although "auto radio" power-switch position performs comparable role. No AC adaptor.

Verdict: Although thoroughly outclassed by newer low-cost models, this apparently "new old stock" sometimes surfaces at retail in the U.K. Sometimes promoted simply as "SRX-50."

New for 2006
✪⅝
Anjan A-1004

Price: $31.90 including shipping and insurance from China via eBay.

Pro: Appears to be solidly made; includes a beefy aluminum front panel in lieu of the customary plastic. Almost totally free from the digital buzzing that plagues many other analog-tuned models with digital frequency readout. Reasonable sensitivity for price class. LCD illumination, unusually effective (*see* Con). Pleasant room-filling audio for such a small package (*see* Con). In some respects, tuning wheel superior for price class (*see* Con). Antenna swivels. Clock/alarm function (*see* Con). Insertable elevation tab, attached to carrying strap, tilts radio to handier operating angle. Build quality appears to be above average for class.

Con: Analog-tuned with digital frequency counter, so tunes only by thumbwheel; this has some backlash and tends to be touchy. Single-conversion IF circuitry results in poor image rejection, particularly noticeable with a short outboard antenna. Audio lacks any trace of bass. World band coverage omits the 2, 3, 4, 5 and 26 MHz (120, 90, 75, 60 and 11 meter) world band segments. Always defaults to FM when first turned on. Frequency display nonstandard, being in Megahertz and reading out only to the nearest 10 kHz; thus, 6155 kHz shows as 6.15 and/or 6.16 MHz. Volume control touchy, especially on FM. Some batteries fit so tight as to be almost impossible to insert. Battery cover not hinged. Clock only in 12-hour format. Does not tune 1640–1710 kHz portion of the mediumwave AM band. Mediumwave AM sensitivity poor. FM sensitivity marginal. FM in mono only. No travel lock. Button must be kept depressed for LCD to be illuminated. Batteries (2 × "AA") and AC adaptor not included.

Verdict: The Anjan A-1004's metal front panel helps it stand apart from most portables. This classy touch appears to be characteristic of what seems to be above-average build quality within its price class. Audio, too, is okay, while overall performance is about as much as you'll find among cheap analog models with digital frequency readout.

Still, this is no breakthrough model. Image rejection and selectivity are lousy, there's overloading, tuning coverage isn't quite complete, frequency readout is imprecise and controls can be touchy. FM and mediumwave AM performance are both wanting, too.

Consider this as one of the better portables you can risk losing on trips—or as a gift.

Evaluation of New Model: Another new kid on the block is the Chinese manufacturer Anjan. Its new A-1004 uses traditional analog tuning coupled to a crude digital frequency counter—hardly the handiest system, but inexpensive and dependable. It suffices, although tuning can be a touchy exercise that's compounded by a nine-position bandswitch. Another annoyance: The radio defaults to FM when turned on.

Although the volume control requires steady fingers, audio sounds clean with plenty of punch and nearly no trace of digital buzz. Sensitivity is adequate, but selectivity and image rejection are mediocre and overloading is a real problem. Bottom line: stations often sound much worse than they should.

World band coverage excludes the tropical bands and the scarcely used 26 MHz band. In this price range, that's adequate. However, mediumwave AM stops around 1630 kHz, and that band's sensitivity is only suitable for local signals. FM fares little better.

The LCD is nicely illuminated, a plus for travel. However, the battery cavity is undersized to the point where some cells are nigh impossible to insert, much less remove. No batteries come with the set, but it includes a clip-on wire antenna, earbuds and a cloth travel pouch.

Except for a genuine aluminum front panel, the Anjan A-1004 is stone-hearth basic. Yet, it is one of the better choices among the cheaps.

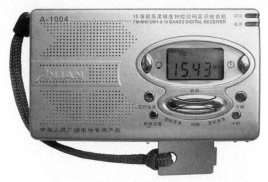

The only thing unusual about the new Anjan A-1004 is its styling. Performance is strictly basic, but it is nonetheless one of the better cheaps. D. Zantow

★½
jWIN JX-M14

Price: $29.95 or less in the United States.

Pro: Handy small size for travel. Clock with timer/alarm (see Con). Elevation panel. Earbuds included (in separate bubble pack).

Con: Mediocre weak-signal sensitivity; helps considerably to clip a few yards of wire to the built-in antenna. Mediocre selectivity. Analog-tuned with digital frequency counter, so tunes only by thumbwheel, which is stiff. Does not tune 120, 75, 90, 60, 15, 13 or 11 meter segments; misses a small amount of expanded coverage of 49 and 41 meter segments. Single-conversion IF circuitry results in poor image rejection. Audio lacks bass response. Frequency counter completely omits last digit so, say, 9575 kHz appears as either 9.57 or 9.58 MHz. Clock in 12-hour format only, displays only when radio off. Display not illuminated. If hand is placed on rear of cabinet, world band drifts up to 10 kHz. Frequency drift with changes in temperature. LCD buzzes on medium-wave AM; if finger placed over LCD, buzz also audible on lower world band frequencies. Mediumwave weak-signal sensitivity uninspiring. FM overloads in strong-signal environments, remediable by shorting antenna (which also reduces weak-signal sensitivity). When first turned on, radio always reverts to FM band. FM in mono only. Two "AA" batteries not included. Warranty in the United States only 90 days and requires $12 advance payment for "return shipping"; add to that the owner's cost to ship, and war-

The jWIN JX-M14 is passable and cheap—little else. Millions of marginal radios like this are being churned out in China. D. Zantow

ranty is of dubious value; best purchased from dealer who will swap if DOA.

Verdict: At almost a throwaway price, the Chinese-made jWIN JX-M14 is a passable portable for casual use on trips or as a stocking stuffer, provided a hank of wire is clipped on to give world band signals a boost.

✪½
Kchibo KK-S320

Price: $ 54.95 as available in the United States.

Pro: Even more compact than its costlier KK-E200 cousin, with better mediumwave AM performance and greater audio crispness. Agreeable weak-signal sensitivity. Sleep delay (*see* Con) and single-event on/off timer. High contrast LCD indicates which preset is in use. AC adaptor. FM stereo via earbuds, included.

Con: No coverage of 120, 90, 75, 60, 16, 15, 13 and 11 meter (2, 3, 4, 5, 17, 19, 21 and 25 MHz) segments, with only partial coverage of 49 and 19 meters (6 and 15 MHz). No keypad or tuning knob; other tuning alternatives cumbersome, especially with "out-of-band" frequencies. Only five station presets for each of the three "bands" (FM/MW-AM/SW). "Signal seek" scanning works only within limited frequency segments.

Kchibo's KK-S320 has cumbersome tuning, limited world band coverage and is a dubious performer. Cheap, but you can do better.

Radio cannot be turned on permanently; rather, the power button activates the 90-minute-or-less sleep-delay timer, forcing the radio to turn itself off after no more than an hour and a half. After radio powers up, slew buttons cannot be used nor the frequency displayed, until the user presses a preset or band key once, or presses the display key three times. Poor dynamic range, with overloading a major problem at night. Poor adjacent-channel selectivity. "Floating birdie" sometimes appears in various world band segments. Single-conversion IF circuitry results in mediocre image rejection. Does not receive 1621–1710 kHz portion of expanded mediumwave AM band in the Americas. Tunes world band only in 5 kHz steps. Displays only in nonstandard XX.XX/XX.XX₅ MHz format. Display not illuminated. Clock uses 12-hour format, not suitable for World Time. Elevation panel hard to open. Clock doesn't display when frequency is shown, although pushbutton allows time to replace frequency. No travel power lock. No signal-strength indicator. No weak-battery indicator; radio goes abruptly silent when batteries start to flag. No batteries included (three "AA" needed). Microprocessor sometimes freezes up, requiring activation of reset button; this also erases the station presets and clock setting stored in memory. No indication of county of manufacture (China) on product, box or manual. "Chinglish" owner's manual occasionally puzzles. FM performance pedestrian. Not easily purchased in the Americas or most other parts of the world. Warranty period not yet apparent.

Verdict: Conveniently smaller than its KK-E200 cousin, and priced to move. Yet, the KK-S320's cumbersome tuning, inadequate shortwave coverage and rudimentary world band performance make it a dubious choice.

Not Acceptable
Coby CX-CB91

Price: $19.95 in the United States. $7–20 or equivalent elsewhere worldwide.

Pro: Clock (*see* Con) with clock radio function (*see* Con). Antenna swivels and rotates.

Battery cover hinged to prevent loss (*see* Con). Earbuds (*see* ☞).

Con: Tuning knob feels as if it were connected to a rubber band, making the finding of stations a hit-and-miss frustration. Does not tune most of the crucial 6 MHz segment and some 7 MHz channels; also misses 2, 3, 4, 5 and 25 MHz segments. Mediocre weak-signal sensitivity. Fair-to-poor selectivity. Poor dynamic range and image rejection. Frequency counter omits last digit so, say, 9995 kHz appears as either 9.99 or 10.00 MHz. Clock only in 12-hour format. Clock radio allows only FM stations to heard. FM distorted and overloads, with poor sensitivity, mediocre capture radio and inaccurate frequency readout. FM not in stereo via earbuds (*see* ☞). LCD emits digital buzz that diminishes reception. DX/local switch has little expected effect. Display not illuminated. Construction quality poor. Batteries difficult to insert and remove. No batteries (two "AA" required).

☞ **Warning:** *Minor increase in volume causes audio to suddenly become extremely loud. Exercise great care when inserting and using earpieces.*

Verdict: Worst of the cheaps. Not acceptable when used with earpieces.

Evaluation of New Model: With tuning so hopeless and earpiece audio that can be unexpectedly painful, this Chinese model is unfit for human consumption.

LAP PORTABLES
Pleasant for Home, Acceptable for Travel

A lap portable is for use primarily around the home and yard, plus on occasional trips. They are large enough to perform well, usually sound better than compact models, yet are not too big to fit into a carry-on or briefcase. Most take 3–4 "D" (UM-1) or "C" (UM-2) cells, plus sometimes a couple of "AA" (UM-3) cells for memory backup.

These are typically just under a foot wide—that's 30 cm—and weigh in around 3–5 pounds, or 1.4–2.3 kg. For air travel, that's

The Coby CX-B91 is the first radio we've rated as Not Acceptable. Earpieces can emit unexpected and potentially harmful blasts of audio.

okay if you are a dedicated listener, but a bit much otherwise.

The Etón E1 makes it a whole new ball game for 2006, but ticket price isn't cheap.

New for 2006
✪✪✪✪⅜ *Passport's Choice*
Etón E1

Price: *E1:* $499.95 in the United States. $599.95CAD in Canada. £399.95 in the United Kingdom. €499.95 in Germany. *AudioVox CNP1000 XM antenna with cable:* about $50.00 in the United States. *KOK1-to-SO-239 antenna jack adaptor:* $7.95 in the United States. *KOK1 male connector (for raw antenna cable):* $4.95 in the United States. *Universal Portable Large Portable Stand:* $10.95 in the United States.

Pro: Good overall audio quality, aided by separate bass and treble controls (*see* Con). Overall receiver distortion generally superior (*see* Con). Full three Watt (nominal) audio amplifier with AC adaptor. To reduce drain, audio amplifier's current draw automatically drops by half with batteries. Agreeable ergonomics, including keys with superior tactile response. Passband tuning (PBT, a/k/a IF shift), a first for a portable; performance excellent. Synchronous selectable sideband holds lock unusually well; reception enhancement aided by tweaking passband tuning. Synchronous double sideband overcomes selective fading distortion and enhances fidelity during twilight and darkness (mixed skywave/groundwave) reception of fringe mediumwave AM stations. Wide (20 kHz) dynamic range good; IP3 excellent with preamp off, good when on (see Con). Blocking good. Phase noise good, although still intrudes >80 dB down. Sensitivity/noise floor good-to-excellent with preamp off, excellent-to-superb with 10 dB preamp on. Three well-chosen voice/music bandwidths with skirt selectivity and ultimate rejection that are excellent or better. Image rejection approaches professional caliber. Excellent first IF rejection. Tuning and display in 10 Hz steps, exceptionally precise for a portable; 100 Hz and 1 kHz tuning steps also selectable. No chuffing or muting when tuning. Octave filters provide good front end selectivity by tabletop standards, which is exceptional for a portable. Single sideband performance above average for a portable, aided by excellent frequency stability. Signal-strength indicator, with 21 bars, uncommonly accurate from S3 through S9 +60 dB even by professional receiver standards. Includes virtually every tuning method available, including frequency/presets scanning, up/down slewing, keypad frequency selection, keypad selection of world band segments and a tuning knob. Tuning knob has variable-rate incremental tuning (VRIT); for many this makes bandscanning more convenient (see Con). 1,700 easy-to-use presets don't erase if batteries removed; 500 of these presets allow for user-written ID tags, while the remainder have permanent factory-created country ID tags. Frequency may be entered on keypad in kHz or MHz. Audio line output jack (in stereo on FM/XM) with suitable level to feed external amplifier/speaker system, recorder or home FM transmitter; also, external speaker jack and separate jack for earpieces. Audio line input jack allows radio to be used as amp/speaker for CD players and the like (see Con). Useful battery status indicator. User-selectable slow/fast AGC decay adjustment; a third AGC option, "Auto," aids bandscanning by switching from slow to fast when radio tuned. Squelch. Telescopic antenna long and robust (see Con). Switches for internal/external antennas (if radio sounds "deaf," ensure these are in correct positions). Clock displays separately from frequency (see Con). Two-event timer with selectable on and off times. Snooze and sleep timer functions. Overall FM performance above average, including excellent sensitivity aided by switchable FM preamp (17 dB). Japanese 76–90 MHz FM band. Three-level LCD illumination (see Con). Travel power lock. Well-written printed owner's manual; also appears on CD-ROM along with quick-start guide. *United States and Canada:* XM ready, easily implemented (see Con). Atomic-type clock automatically kept accurate by XM or world band WWV/WWVH (but not longwave WWVB) (see Con). XM module easily removable for future uses or modes. One year parts and labor warranty. Excellent toll-free tech support. *Elsewhere, including EU:* New version under consideration would replace XM facility with one for DAB.

Con: No carrying handle or strap, or even provision for one to be user-affixed. When 2.5 kHz bandwidth used with BFO (or certain PBT settings with wider bandwidths), audio suffers from harshness resulting from high-order distortion products. Muted-sounding audio comes off as somewhat lifeless; needs to be crispier to reach fidelity potential. Narrow (5 kHz) dynamic range/IP3 poor, although IP3 improves to fair with preamp off. Because of the mechanical tuning encoder, the tuning knob, although precise, feels slightly "grizzly" when rotated. No rubber grip around tuning knob's circumference. Front-mounted battery access door difficult to open. Telescopic antenna flops over when moved from fully erect position. Dot-matrix LCD has limited useful viewing angle and lacks contrast in bright rooms or with illumination off; best contrast is found at angle provided by large Universal Radio or similar stand, although built-in elevation panel also helps some. Non-standard external antenna connector, and no adaptor or plug included; manufacturer states it hopes to implement a solution in due course. Variable-rate tuning, which some users don't care for, cannot be disabled. Mediumwave AM lacks directional reception, as telescopic antenna is used instead of the usual ferrite-rod antenna. Included AC adaptor produces minor hum with earpieces or line output; better aftermarket replacement hard to come by because of high amperage requirement. Lacks certain features—such as tunable notch, noise blanker and non-voice narrow bandwidths—found on tabletop receivers. No PC interface. No attenuator or RF gain control, although neither seems to be needed. No dedicated buttons for presets. Does not respond if LSB/USB/DSB button pushed when receiver in AM-sync mode; straight AM mode has to be selected first, and only then LSB/USB/DSB. Potentially ultra-precise atomic-type clock doesn't display seconds; local time option in 24-hour format only. Line input jack requires above-average audio level to perform properly. Paint on knobs, buttons and cabinet could eventually wear through. Four "D" cells not included. Like essentially all other world band portables, not designed to receive DRM digital broadcasts. *United States and Canada:* XM reception requires purchase of separate outboard antenna and payment of monthly XM fee. Significant current consumption when XM in use, restricting portability. Outboard XM antenna/cable can't be docked onto radio, further complicating portability. XM reception not possible when traveling outside United States and Canada. *United States:* Not designed for reception of HD Radio digital broadcasts.

Verdict: The stylish new Etón E1 has a combination of features and performance never before found in a portable. It does just about everything you could wish for now that the Sony ICF-2010 and ICF-SW77 are officially discontinued.

The E1 is different enough in look and feel from the Sony ICF-2010/2001D and ICF-SW77 that some may feel like they're trading in their soulmate for Paris Hilton. Especially when such all-looks, no guts wonders as the bygone Grundig Classic 960 spring to mind.

No way. Superficialities and expectations psychology aside, performance and features of the E1 are right up there with the very best portables of your and yore. Indeed, the E1 goes further by actually narrowing the preexisting gap between portables and serious tabletop receivers.

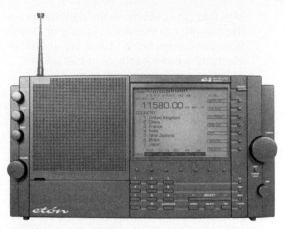

Etón's new E1 is a pleasant surprise. Few expected it to equal the performance of the legendary Sony ICF-2010, but it has—and then some.

Not enough? For North America there's XM satellite reception, too—provided you cough up for an accessory antenna and monthly XM fee. And a proposed separate version for Europe is scheduled to tune DAB in lieu of XM.

Evaluation of New Model: For world band veterans, there is only one question: Does Etón's E1 stand up to the discontinued Sony ICF-2010/2001D, or even the Sony ICF-SW77?

On the surface there is plenty of fuel for cynicism—the manufacturer has obviously focused on appearance and image, even leaving off something as un-chichi but practical as a handle. Yet, Bang & Olufsen manages to be similarly oriented and offer outstanding products.

Too, a few years back there were QA issues at Etón's Tecsun factory in China. Compare this with the consistently dependable '2010, many of which have operated faithfully for well over a decade. It was manufactured to lofty standards in Japan.

Banging 'em out in Bangalore

Putting aside appearance—Dolly Parton belts 'em out as well as Patsy Cline ever did—it will be years before we know how the E1 holds up. But there is an unexpected sign that QA could be on the right track: Unlike any prior device from Grundig or Etón, it is manufactured not in China, but at Bharat Electronics headquartered in Bangalore. Etón describes this as one of India's most sophisticated factories, with over 18,000 employees and 50 years of a strong industrial base. Its background reportedly includes the design and manufacture of electronic systems for the Indian armed forces.

Will this new partnership help assure superior QA and engineering? Only time will tell, but Etón states that the move is to enhance R&D and to avoid being tied to the fortunes of any one country. For now, they see their new Indian arrangement as providing a new home to engineer and manufacture a variety of midrange and higher-end world band and satellite receivers.

The E1 has quite a history behind it. Several years ago it was conceived as a German-designed Grundig Satellit 900 that likely was to be manufactured in Portugal. Parts shortages and other difficulties put it on the back burner until it was re-engineered, reportedly in part by the prestigious R.L. Drake Company in the United States.

Throughout all this it continued to be known as the Satellit 900, the latest in a long line of Grundig "Satellit" premium portables that never actually picked up satellites. Yet, no sooner than the Satellit 900's design was enhanced to pick up satellites than the Satellit moniker was dropped. Go figure.

The E1 tunes everything from 100 kHz longwave through 30 MHz at the top of the shortwave spectrum. FM coverage is equally generous—either the Japanese 76–90 MHz band or the customary 87.5–108 MHz band can be selected.

XM for North America, DAB for Europe

Not enough? In North America try XM satellite radio, operating at 2.3 GHz. The E1 contains much of what is needed, but for actual reception you'll also have to buy an optional plug-and-play outboard antenna and pay XM its usual monthly fee. Outside North America XM isn't offered, so for Europe and possibly beyond Etón plans to offer

a DAB version, instead. It will be distributed by Etón's new German office that oversees sales throughout Europe.

DRM? It didn't make the cut. Etón appears to be skeptical of DRM's potential, but continues to keep a wet finger to the wind.

XM performs nicely on the E1, and it's easy to operate using an excellent menu of program options. As expected, the mouse-type outboard antenna/cable has to be fastidiously aimed and have a reasonably unfettered signal path.

At some locations these are greater issues than elsewhere. At a rural home in the northeastern United States, for example, world band reception is pretty consistent in any room. Yet, XM yields grudging reception in only a few rooms. Apartment dwellers should be especially leery of XM if they don't have at least one window with an unobscured view of the faraway southern sky.

XM restricts portability, too. For starters, battery consumption with XM is painfully steep; most will find it okay only for now-and-again listening. Also, the outboard satellite antenna and cable can't be docked onto the radio, making it yet another gizmo to carry around.

The required four "D" cells do not install from the rear, as you might expect. Rather, there is a door at the lower corner of the front panel. It doesn't yield its battery treasure readily, but once accomplished it reveals a contrast control for the LCD, a reset button for microprocessor lockups and a computer connector. Electronic sleuths and hackers will have a field day trying to divine the potential of that connector which, for now, appears to be a mystery. Otherwise, the E1 has no PC interface.

Fortunately, a three-prong, one ampere AC adaptor is included. Thankfully, it uses a transformer and thus avoids radio interference inherent in switching-type power supplies. The adaptor works as expected, but minor hum comes through with good earpieces or line output into quality audio gear. None of this is audible with the built-in speaker, and it disappears altogether when batteries are used.

Operating Features, Ergonomics

This radio is a pleasure to use. With virtually all tuning methods available, the E1 is both flexible and straightforward to tune without even reading the owner's manual.

The Sangean ATS 909's minimum tuning step is 40 Hz. That has been as precise as it gets this side of a tabletop superset. Yet, the E1 goes it one better with a 10 Hz minimum step that's even shown on the LCD.

In part because of this, there is no audible chuffing or muting when tuning. The E1 thus provides the seamless tuning of analog with the convenience and precision of digital frequency synthesis.

For faster bandscanning there are also user-selectable 100 Hz and 1 kHz steps. Another bandscanning convenience is variable-rate incremental tuning (VRIT)—the faster you tune, the faster the rate that stations zip by. The only rub is that not everybody likes VRIT, and it can't be switched off.

Of the fully 1,700 station presets, 500 can include a user-entered alphanumeric tag. The remaining 1,200 have a specific country permanently burned onto the top line of each "page"; these lack tag-entry capability. Either way, entering data into presets is exceptionally straightforward and user-friendly. You can even tag presets with a "T" (T Scan) to limit scanning to these presets. Finally, a non-volatile EEPROM system is used, so presets never erase.

Signal-seek scanning allows the owner to unearth signals in VFO, Memory or Country modes. This is most useful and can work in concert with the squelch control. The scan stop is a five-second automatic resume, or it can stay put until the chosen signal drops off.

The tuning knob is free from backlash and wobble, but its mechanical encoder causes it to have a slight "grizzly" feel when rotated. The knob also lacks a rubber tread around the edge to improve grip. Like most modern receivers it has no flywheel effect.

The large LCD uses a dot matrix layout, which allows much useful information to be displayed. Dot matrix is inherently flexible,

so there's no "LISB" for "USB" as on the Satellit 800, for example. Yet, the LCD has a limited useful viewing angle, and the contrast is only so-so regardless of the contrast control's setting. Best contrast is at about the angle provided by Universal Radio's large radio stand or something similar (if you're into woodworking, imagine the E1 resting on an oil-rubbed walnut stand). But even the built-in elevation panel helps.

Indeed, with high ambient light the LCD becomes virtually unreadable without the illumination turned on. Alas, even that gets washed out once ambient light gets bright enough, making the LCD almost unreadable.

The clock appears in the upper right corner of the LCD and displays separately from the frequency. Either World Time (GMT) or local time can be shown, but not both at once. Local time appears only in 24 hour mode—no AM/PM. The sleep timer can be programmed from one to 99 minutes in one-minute steps, and there is a two-event timer with programmable on and off times.

The signal-strength indicator is of a caliber found on professional receivers. It is dead-to-nuts accurate from S3 through S9 +60 dB, and uses an unusually long 21-bar digital display. The S-unit scale is shown for world band, although on FM it vanishes.

A phone jack provides line audio output for a recorder or audio amplifier. This also can feed an FM home microtransmitter, so received world band stations can be enjoyed on ordinary radios throughout your property. The audio line output level is appropriate and in stereo on FM and XM, but no patch cord is included.

There's also an audio input jack to play, say, a CD player through the E1's amp and speaker. Nice idea, but it takes an above-average line level to work properly.

Experienced world band veterans know that a proper antenna is a key to listening success. Yet, most portables have telescopic antennas that look like rejects from dollar stores. Not so the E1. Its antenna is long, which helps pull in signals, and husky enough to withstand years of use. Still, as with the Satellit 800 there's a downside: When moved from vertical, the antenna flops over like George Washington's tree.

Design, Features Boost Performance

In general the E1's audio is quite pleasant by portable standards, and is aided by separate bass and treble controls. The audio amplifier has plenty of punch, too: It puts out a nominal three Watts with the AC adaptor, although this is sensibly halved with batteries. There is even a jack for an outboard amplifier/speaker. This is in addition to the jack for earpieces, so it bypasses anti-blast resistors normally used with earpiece outputs.

Still, this mellow audio would profit from more crispness. Panelists variously volunteered that the audio, while good overall, has a tendency to sound muffled, harsh, muted or somewhat lifeless: four ways of saying the same thing. Also, with the 2.5 kHz bandwidth—and sometimes with wider filters and passband tuning—some buzzy-sounding harmonic distortion is audible even with batteries, although overall receiver distortion fares well.

NUMBERS: TOP PORTABLES

	Etón E1	Sony ICF-SW77
Max. Sensitivity/Noise Floor	0.15 μV **S**/–132 dBm **E** (4)	0.16 μV **S**/–133 dBm **E** (1)
Blocking	123 dB **G**	121 dB **G**
Bandwidths *(Shape Factors)*	8.0 *(1:1.45* **S***)*, 5.0 *(1:1.6* **E***)*, 2.5 *(1.7,* **E***)*	6.0 *(1:1.9* **E***)*, 3.3 *(1:2.0* **G***)* kHz
Ultimate Rejection	80 dB **E** (5)	70 dB **G**
Front-End Selectivity	**G** (6)	— (2)
Image Rejection	>90 dB **S**	80 dB **E**
First IF Rejection	75 dB **E**	80 dB **E**
Dynamic Range/IP3 (5 kHz)	55 dB **P**/–50 dBm **P** (7)	64 dB **F**/–37 dBm **F**
Dynamic Range/IP3 (20 kHz)	87 dB **G**/–2 dBm **G** (8)	82 dB **F**/–10 dBm **G**
Phase Noise	113 dBc **G**	122 dBc **E**
AGC Threshold	0.3 μV **G** (9)	2.0 μV **G**
Overall Distortion, sync	2.6% **G** (10)	2.3% **E**/3.3% **G** (3)

IBS Lab Ratings: **S** Superb   **E** Excellent   **G** Good   **F** Fair   **P** Poor

(1) Sensitivity varies considerably by frequency at 2 MHz and between 10–29.9 MHz; *viz.*, from 0.16 μV to 1.40 μV **S** - **G**. Noise floor varies by frequency from –133 dBm to –117 dBm **E** - **G**. Neither measurement could be made at 5 MHz because of spurious responses, noise and leakage.

(2) Cannot be determined.

(3) Wide/narrow bandwidths.

(4) Preamp on; 0.28 μV **E**/–126 **G** with preamp off.

(5) Phase noise prevents accurate measurement beyond 80 dB.

(6) Octave filters, unusually good for a portable.

(7) Preamp on; 57 dB **P**/–39 dBm **P** with preamp on.

(8) Preamp on; 88 dB **G**/+7 dBm **E** with preamp off.

(9) Preamp on; 0.9 μV **S** with preamp off.

(10) Harmonic distortion includes several high-order products.

In the Department of No Good Deed Goes Unpunished, this wouldn't be noticed were the E1's audio output of lesser caliber. For this, there's no more relevant example than the famous Sony ICF-2010/ICF-2001D. When it first came out, there was some digital buzz in the audio, but it mysteriously disappeared in subsequent production. Why? Instead of fixing the buzz, Sony added a simple low-pass audio filter to keep it from being heard. Even though this also lopped off some music sounds, no one noticed because the audio circuit and speaker were so pedestrian to begin with. The difference was virtually imperceptible.

Bandwidths of 2.5, 5 and 8 kHz are well chosen, with excellent-to-superb skirt selectivity. Ultimate rejection measurement is limited by the presence of phase noise at 80 dB, but even then is better than on some costly tabletop receivers.

The E1's synchronous selectable sideband performs superbly, stubbornly holding onto carrier lock then releasing it when tuning starts. Tweaking the passband tuning helps optimize the tradeoff between interference rejection and audio fidelity.

The dynamic duo of sync and PBT really enhances listening pleasure, and you'll search in vain for any other portable that comes close. One ergonomic nit: no mid-position dimple to make PBT operation handier, although it can be toggled on and off by pushbutton.

There's also synchronous double sideband. This is less important than selectable sideband, but it can do wonders to improve fidelity under certain conditions. For example, around twilight and during darkness fringe mediumwave AM stations tend to arrive by both groundwave and skywave. As the skywave travels a slightly longer path, the two waves become out of phase to varying degrees. When this phase cancellation is smack on the carrier frequency, the result is selective fading distortion that can be so extreme as to render a strong signal unintelligible for under a second to over a minute. Synchronous selectable sideband can resolve this, but synchronous double

sideband does even better if there's no adjacent-channel interference.

The E1 has commendable sensitivity, and for additional kick there's a switchable 10 dB preamplifier. This poses a potential problem, as high sensitivity can lead to overloading. Yet, even with dismal narrow dynamic range there was no overloading during tests using serious outdoor antennas. This helps explain why there is no attenuator or RF gain control.

Image rejection approaches professional caliber, so stations 910 kHz away don't cause varied-pitch whistles and "ghost" modulation. These images, long a curse of shortwave, are simply banished.

Another apparent first for a portable: The E1 has real octave front-end filtering—0.1 to 1 MHz, 1 to 2 MHz, 2 to 4 MHz, 4 to 8 MHz, 8 to 16 MHz and 16 to 30 MHz. If you listen from where there are close-by powerful transmitters any type, any frequency front-end filtering can keep them from disrupting reception. We have tested tabletop supersets lacking good front-end selectivity, and their manufacturers tell us, "it's too costly." Well, for much less money it exists on the E1, so somehow it can be done.

The automatic gain control (AGC) works properly, with no audible quirks. The two selectable decay times are fast (300 ms) and slow (3 seconds); a third setting, auto, defaults to the slow setting but switches to fast during tuning to enhance bandscanning.

Reception of non-voice modes, such as CW and RTTY, is compromised by the lack of truly narrow bandwidths. However, single sideband performs well by portable standards, although a less-harsh BFO beat note would help for serious amateur and utility DXing. Bottom line, this receiver is as oriented to broadcast reception as the Icom IC-R75 is to utility and ham signals. Pay your money, take your choice.

Superior FM, No AM Loopstick

FM is in stereo via earpieces and line output. It is no slouch. Sensitivity is above average, and for DX gain there's a switchable 17 dB preamplifier. It even receives Japanese FM.

However, the mediumwave AM band is a weak spot, as there is no ferrite rod antenna to provide directional reception. Instead, it shares the same telescopic antenna used for world band and FM. This makes an outboard accessory loop antenna *de rigueur* for DXing.

Although remediable, it's a pity—the E1 otherwise has superior mediumwave AM fidelity and DX reception. Perhaps Etón's focus on advanced technology has caused it to overlook what C. Crane and GE have known for years: There is gold to be had with long-distance AM receivers.

Nearly every $10 radio comes with a ferrite rod antenna, so why not a model that costs 50 times more? Even better is the example of the former Tandberg Portable 41—a button allowed the user to choose between telescopic and ferrite-rod antennas.

Surprising Omissions

There's no carrying handle of any kind—not even places when one can be attached. In comparison, the Sony ICF-2010/2001D came with a shoulder strap that could be cut down into a handle. Even the giant Satellit 800 has an impressive carrying handle.

Etón insists this is the result of months of consideration, after which it was decided to treat the E1 more like Kim Komando's laptop PC than a portable radio. Whether this is excessive belly-button gazing or inspired thinking, only time will tell. But the E1 won't be a genuine portable until it can be carried around by other than the scruff of the neck.

The lack of headphones is also surprising. These come with the Satellit 800, same price, and the much-cheaper S350DL.

All bands use the same external antenna jack. Alas, it is anything but what is normally used for world band, so an adaptor is needed that mates with plugs that come with accessory antennas. Some radio-oriented firms carry adaptors, most others don't, and one doesn't come with the radio. Etón says it is aware of the issue and looking into a solution.

The E1's plastic case is painted—knobs, speaker grille and all. How this rubbery-feeling paint will hold up under regular use remains to be seen.

The 77-page owner's manual is well written, with a comprehensive table of contents. There is also a CD-ROM with the same manual and an additional quick-start guide. All this fits into Etón's established pattern of customer support in North America: toll-free help from knowledgeable company employees in California, and a full year's warranty instead of the 90 days that has been creeping into the consumer electronics industry like bad acne. Hopefully, Europeans will receive a similar level of TLC from Etón's new office in Germany.

Best Portable Tested

QA is always an issue with a new model, especially one as sophisticated as the E1. That having been said, our early production unit didn't have a single quality hiccup and visual inspection looks promising. Still, only Father Time can be the ultimate judge.

It's been a years-long wait for the E1, originally dubbed the Satellit 900 (think "Longhorn" becoming "Vista"), to the point where it began to look like the Elvis One. But like old port finally pulled from the cellar, the wait is over and with it the anticipation.

Quirks and all, Etón's new E1 sounds good, performs magnificently and is straightforward to operate. Imponderables of QA aside, it blows away all previous "kings of the heap" portables.

DRM Modifiable
✪✪✪¾
Sony ICF-SW77

Price: €499.00 as available in Germany.

Pro: A rich variety of tuning and other features, including sophisticated "page" tuning that some enjoy but others dislike; includes 162 station presets, two-speed tuning knob, signal-seek tuning (*see* Con), keypad tuning and meter-band access. Synchronous selectable sideband is exceptionally handy to operate; it significantly reduces selective-fading distortion and adjacent-channel interference on world band, longwave and mediumwave AM signals; although the sync chip part number was changed not long back, its performance is virtually unchanged (see Con). Two well-chosen bandwidths (6.0 kHz and 3.3 kHz) provide superior adjacent-channel rejection. Excellent image rejection and first-IF rejection, both 80 dB. Excellent-to-superb weak-signal sensitivity (noise floor –133 dBm, sensitivity 0.16 microvolts) in and around lower-middle portion of shortwave spectrum where most listening is done (see Con). Weak-signal sensitivity still excellent (noise floor –130 dBm, sensitivity 0.21 microvolts) within little-used 120 meter segment (see Con). Superb overall distortion, almost always under one percent. Dynamic range (82 dB) and third-order intercept point (–10 dBm) fairly good at 20 kHz separation (see Con). Tunes in very precise 0.05 kHz increments; displays in 0.1 kHz increments; these and other factors make this model superior to any other portable for single-sideband reception, although portatop and tabletop models usually fare better yet. Continuous separate bass and treble tone controls, a rarity. DRM modifiable (see www.drmrx.org/receiver_mods.html). Two illuminated multi-function liquid crystal displays. Dual-zone clock, displays separately from frequency. Station name appears on LCD when station presets used. 10-level signal-strength indicator (see Con). Excellent stability, less than 20 Hz drift after ten-second warmup. Flip-up chart for calculating time differences. VCR-type five-event timer controls radio and optional outboard recorder alike. Superior FM audio quality. Stereo FM through earpieces, included. Travel power lock. Japanese FM (most versions) and longwave bands. AC adaptor, hum-free. Outboard reel passive wire antenna accessory aids slightly with weak-signal reception. Antenna connector included. Rubber strip helps prevent sliding.

Con: No longer distributed by Sony outside Germany; given past practice, it may not be available even in Germany once present supplies are exhausted. "Page" tuning system relatively complex to operate; many

Sony's ICF-SW77, like so much else at the once-dynamic Sony Corporation, is fading into the sunset. Now available new only in Germany, but soon even those units will have been sold. *¡Adíos, amigo!*

find that station presets can't be accessed simply. World band and mediumwave AM audio slightly muffled even when wide bandwidth in use. Synthesizer chuffing degrades reception quality during bandscanning by knob. Dynamic range (64 dB) and third-order intercept point (–37 dBm) only fair at 5 kHz separation. Weak-signal sensitivity varies from fair to superb, depending on where between 2 and 30 MHz receiver is being tuned. Synchronous selectable sideband holds lock reasonably. Synchronous selectable sideband tends to lose lock if batteries weak, or if NiCd cells are used. Synchronous selectable sideband alignment can vary with temperature, factory alignment and battery voltage, causing synchronous selectable sideband reception to be slightly more muffled in one sideband than the other. Signal-seek tuning skips over weaker signals. Flimsy 11-element telescopic antenna (the older version of the 'SW77 had nine elements). LCD characters small for size of receiver. Display illumination does not stay on with AC power. Unusual tuning knob design disliked by some. On mediumwave AM band, relatively insensitive, sometimes with spurious sounds during single-sideband reception; this doesn't apply to world band reception, however. Mundane reception of difficult FM signals. Signal-strength indicator grossly overreads, covering only a 20 dB range with maximum reading at only 3 microvolts. AGC threshold, 2 microvolts (good). Painted surfaces can wear off with heavy use. No batteries (four "C" required).

Verdict: The Japanese-made Sony ICF-SW77 has been a strong contender among portables since it was improved some time back. After the Sony ICF-2010 was discontinued a few years ago, the '77 became uncontested as the top portable.

The '77 has always been tops among portables for single-sideband reception, beating out even the legendary '2010. It's also one of the very few models with continuously tuned bass and treble controls. Ergonomics, however, are a mixed bag; so if you're interested consider trying it out first.

The '77 is now available only in Germany, where thieCom.de and others export worldwide. Don't be surprised if it ceases to be offered there once existing supplies are sold, so if you want this exceptional receiver now's the time to spring into action.

✪✪½
Roberts R827

Price: *Roberts:* £159.95 in the United Kingdom.

The predictable Roberts R827 is available only in the United Kingdom, but is manufactured in China by Sangean.

Pro: Superior overall world band performance. Numerous tuning features, including 18 world band station presets. Two bandwidths for good fidelity/interference tradeoff. Analog clarifier with center detent and stable circuitry allows single-sideband signals to be tuned with uncommon precision, thus allowing for superior audio phasing for a portable (*see* Con). Illuminated display. Signal-strength indicator. Dual-zone 24-hour clock, with one zone displayed separately from frequency. Alarm/timer with sleep delay. Travel power lock. FM stereo through earpieces. AC adaptor. Longwave.

Con: Tends to mute when tuning knob turned quickly, making bandscanning difficult. Keypad not in telephone format. Touchy variable control for single-sideband fine tuning. Does not come with tape-recorder jack. No batteries (four "D" and three "AA" needed). Country of manufacture (now China) not specified on radio or box.

Verdict: This is a decent, predictable radio—performance and features, alike—and reasonably priced. Sangean no longer makes this model under its own name, and we were unable to find out whether they will continue to manufacture it for Roberts once the existing inventory is exhausted.

New Versions for 2006

✪✪⅜   🄮 (*see* ☞)

Passport's Choice
Etón S350DL, Tecsun BCL-3000, Etón S350, Grundig S350, Tecsun BCL-2000

Price: *Etón S350DL (red or black):* $149.95 in the United States. $149.99CAD in Canada. *Grundig/Etón S350 (silver):* $99.95 in the United States. $99.99CAD in Canada. £69.95 in the United Kingdom. €89.00 in Germany. *PAL-to-F adaptor for external FM antenna:* $2.29 in the United States. *Franzus FR-22 120>220V AC transformer for BCL-2000:* $15–18 in the United States.

Pro: Speaker audio quality substantially above norm for world band portables. Separate bass and treble tone controls, a rarity at any price, help shape audio frequency response. Reasonably powerful audio, helpful for where ambient noise is at least average. Two bandwidths, well-chosen, provide effective and flexible adjacent-channel rejection *vis-à-vis* audio fidelity. Sensitive to weak signals. No synthesizer, so exceptionally free from circuit noise ("hiss") and no chuffing while tuning. Relatively intuitive to operate, even for newcomers. World Time clock (*see* Con) with alarm, clock radio and sleep delay; may also be set to 12-hour format. Four-level (eight bar) signal-strength indicator. Battery-level indicator (*see* Con). Low battery consumption, combined with four "D" cells, greatly reduces need for battery replacement. Most comfortable carrying handle of any world band radio tested; also, seconds as a shoulder strap. Easy-to-read LCD has large numbers, high contrast, is visible from a variety of angles and is brightly illuminated. LCD illumination may be left on fulltime or timed to turn off. FM reception quality slightly above average. FM in stereo through headphones. Sturdy, flexible telescopic antenna. RCA phono sockets provide stereo line output for recording, home FM transmitters and outboard audio systems. Mediumwave AM reception better than most. *S350DL:* Full-size padded headphones for insertion into stereo headphone jack. Battery cavity allows for four "AA" cells in addition to, or in lieu of, the usual four "D" cells; user-switchable between "AA" and "D," for example to select "AA" should "D" cells die. *S350DL/S350:* Supplied outboard 120V AC adaptor can be left behind on trips, making it lighter than BCL-2000. *S350DL/BCL-2000:* Attractive, especially with snazzy red cabinet (black is the other option). LCD automatically illuminates whenever the tuning knob is turned. *BCL-3000/BCL-2000:* Built-in 220V AC power supply eliminates need for outboard AC adaptor. *North America:* Toll-free tech support.

Con: Analog-tuned with digital frequency counter, so tunes only by pair of concentric (fast/slow) knobs; thus, it lacks such helpful tuning aids as station presets, keypad and scanning. Unhandy "MW/SW1/SW2/SW3" switch must accessed often to tune mediumwave AM and shortwave spectra; switch

The Etón S350DL is an upgrade to the basic S350 that's still available for less than the 'DL. Both versions boast much-improved frequency stability, along with exceptional audio.

can be touchy, affecting frequency readings. Analog tuning uses string-pulley-gear hardware to turn variable capacitors, which results in frequency drift typically under 2 kHz on the DL version, along with some play and backlash—drift much improved over units produced before mid-2005; manufacturer advises same improved tuning incorporated in regular S350, seemingly since Q3/2005. Single-conversion IF circuitry results in poor image rejection. Power button activates 90-minute sleep-delay timer; works as full-time "on" control only if held down three seconds (*see* third ☞, below). Some user-correctable nighttime overloading in strong-signal parts of the world. Does not tune relatively unused 2 MHz (120 meter) tropical world band segment. Clock not displayed independent of frequency, but button allows time to replace frequency for three seconds. Clock tends to be off slightly over time. Nominal 30 MHz low-pass filter has such high apparent insertion loss as to be useless except as a *de facto* attenuator. Battery-level indicator gives little warning before radio becomes inoperative. Batteries (4 × "D") not included. *S350/S350DL:* AC adaptor less handy than built-in power supply. Minor but audible hum from speaker, headphones and line output with supplied 120V AC adaptor. *S350/BCL-2000:* Poor visual indication of adjustment position of black knobs (volume, tone and RF gain); user-remediable with light paint or Wite-Out. *BCL-3000/BCL-2000:* Nominally tunes mediumwave AM 520–1610 kHz; although actual tuning is more generous, it misses at least the 1650–1705 kHz portion of the band as defined in North America and some other parts of the world; also misses the 1705–1725 kHz potential public-service segment. Available only in and from China. *BCL-3000:* Available only in black, at least as of presstime.

☞ *©* applies only to S350, BCL-3000 and BCL-2000.

☞ Beware of a quasi-counterfeit Chinese clone, the "ECB 2000"—also, possibly the "ECB 3000."

☞ Initial BCL-2000 production samples, sold in China in early 2003, would always turn off after 90 minutes or less. This was remedied in subsequent production, but there's a Rube Goldberg solution for early units: have the radio turn off during the 30 minutes the clock radio stays on. For example, 60–85 minutes before the clock radio is programmed to go on, press the power button once so the radio will go off in 90 minutes. The radio will then stay on indefinitely until the power button is pressed again. The S350/S350DL/BCL-3000 have never suffered from this problem.

Verdict: The Grundig/Etón S350/S350DL—sold in China as the Tecsun BCL-2000/BCL-3000—is full of welcome surprises, as well as the other variety. Its flaws are obvious and real: images, no single-sideband demodulation, a paucity of tuning aids and some frequency drift. So, it receives a modest star rating. It's not for DXing, and is useless with most utility and ham signals.

Why, then, is it a "Passport's Choice"? Because for pleasant and affordable listening to world band news, music and entertainment it is hard to beat—audio quality just isn't equaled by any other portable. If you want something that sounds as good but performs better, dig deep and spring for a Grundig Satellit 800 portatop.

Evaluation of New Version: The new "DL" version, available in black or eye-popping

red, comes with the same headphones found on the much costlier Grundig Satellit 800 portatop. These sound pleasant and have a generously long cord.

S350DL: A Battery of Batteries

All versions use four long-lasting "D" cells, but the DL version goes this one step better: It can hold four additional "AA" cells. As there's no microprocessor to back up, these aren't included for the usual reason. Instead, because the radio has such low current drain, it needs fewer battery changes than most other models. So, weight-conscious travelers can use smaller "AA" cells instead of beefy "D" cells.

This novel setup also provides user-switchable backup to flagging "D" cells. Sound familiar? Early Volkswagen Beetles came with a small second gas tank to take over from the main tank when the driver turned a valve. *Le plus ça change…*

All versions come with a handy black carrying strap that doubles as a comfortable padded handle. There's also a 24/12-hour clock-radio timer—not displayed independent of frequency, but a button shows the time for three seconds.

Tuning: Pluses and Minuses

All versions use analog tuning coupled to an LCD to provide digital frequency readout. Tuning is only by two-speed knob and a pair of switches with three "bands" for shortwave: roughly 2925–8150 ("SW1"), 7840–17325 ("SW2") and 16835–28495 ("SW3") kHz. No station presets, no slewing, no scanning, no keypad, no RS232 port.

The concentric two-speed (4:1) knob tunes fast and easy, although with some annoying backlash and play—a steady and patient hand helps. That's because the analog tuning scheme uses a vintage tuning arrangement of string, gears and pulleys connected to potentially drifty variable capacitors. This allows for world band frequency drift of up to 1–2 kHz—passable, as the radio doesn't demodulate single-sideband signals, and much improved over S350 units built before Q3/2005.

Yet, this tuning scheme has advantages. It precludes rhythmic "synthesizer chuffing" during tuning, which helps when dialing up and down looking for stations. Also, world band sensitivity with the built-in telescopic antenna is very good, partly because the tuning circuitry is so quiet. Hiss and other noises found with synthesized tuning circuits just aren't there.

Ergonomics are reasonable, including a high-contrast LCD with easily visible digits, battery-level display and four-level signal-strength indicator (eight bars, but they operate in pairs).The LCD's illumination stays on for up to eight seconds or continuously—ideal for dialing around in the gloom.

Great Audio, Mixed Performance

Audio quality stands out. It is markedly superior, and more powerful than most. This is aided by continuous bass and treble controls—a rarity, even among costly models. For enjoyable program listening this makes all the difference, and contrasts with models that appeal to enthusiasts but can be hard on the ears.

Yet, all is not milk and honey. Poor image rejection allows annoying "ghost" signals to be heard at reduced strength some 910 kHz below fundamental signals. It's unfortunate that the new DL version didn't incorporate double conversion to alleviate this. Too, there is minor hum when the supplied 120V AC adaptor for North America is used.

Dynamic range isn't all that great, either, although for most it is adequate. Thus, there can be overloading when powerful signals are on nearby frequencies, especially if an accessory antenna is in use. The "SW LPF" switch is nominally a 30 MHz low-pass filter and helps by acting as a *de facto* attenuator, the apparent if unintended result of insertion loss. It or the RF gain control reduce overloading—and sensitivity—as does shortening the telescopic antenna.

Selectivity profits from two well-chosen bandwidths. These provide flexibility in balancing interference rejection, where narrow bandwidths are helpful, against audio fidelity that's enhanced by wider bandwidths.

Mediumwave AM has worthy sensitivity, directionality from the built-in ferrite rod antenna, flexible and appropriate selectivity, and of course commendable audio quality. Still, whistles tend to appear within the band. FM sensitivity is quite good, while selectivity and capture ratio are at least average. There is only slight overloading in the presence of powerful nearby transmitters.

Build quality, which two years back looked promising, has thus far withstood the test of time. That includes the robust telescopic antenna.

Oiled Wheel

For years there was a tendency to look to the squeaky wheel when designing world band radios. The result was models that excelled with tough signals sought by radio aficionados vocal about their enthusiasm. Meanwhile, audio fidelity and other points of interest to the listening public took a back seat.

This made sense to a point, as enthusiasts spend generously on their passion. But the discipline of the market has been influencing manufacturers in a broader direction. Some high-end models are being retired, while program-oriented portables are becoming better and more widely available.

In North America, for example, for every radio hobbyist there appear to be perhaps a hundred who solely enjoy content. Indeed, surveys have shown that the vast majority of world band listeners focus on several favorite stations, and only secondarily try out new offerings.

The Etón S350DL, Grundig/Etón S350 and their Tecsun cousins are not for chasing DX rarities or utility and ham signals. But for enjoyable listening to world band stations, they have excellent sound and performance that, image rejection aside, zero in nicely on that mission.

WORLD BAND CASSETTE RECORDERS

What happens if your favorite show comes on at an inconvenient time? Why, tape it, of course, with a world band cassette recorder—just like on your VCR.

Two models are offered, and there's no question which is better: the Sony. Smaller, too, so it is less likely to raise eyebrows among airport security personnel. But there's a whopping price difference over the Sangean, and the Sony is getting hard to find.

✪✪✪⅛ *Passport's Choice*
Sony ICF-SW1000T, Sony ICF-SW1000TS

Price (as available): *ICF-SW1000T:* €439.00 in Germany. *AC-E30HG 120V AC adaptor:* $19.95. *ICF-SW1000TS:* ¥46,000 in Japan.

Pro: Built-in recorder in rear of cabinet, with two events of up to 90 minutes each, selectable in ten-minute increments. Relatively compact for travel, also helpful to avoid airport security hassles. High-tech synchronous selectable sideband; this generally performs well, reducing adjacent-channel interference and selective-fading distortion on world band, longwave and mediumwave AM signals while adding slightly to weak-signal sensitivity (*see* Con). Single bandwidth, especially when synchronous selectable sideband is used, exceptionally

If you want to record programs automatically, like on a VCR, Sony's ICF-SW1000T can't be beat. Trouble is, try to find one.

effective at adjacent-channel rejection. Numerous helpful tuning features, including keypad, two-speed up/down slew, 32 station presets and signal-seek scanning. Thirty of the 32 station presets are within three easy-to-use "pages" so stations can be clustered. Weak-signal sensitivity above average up to about 16 MHz. Demodulates single-sideband signals (*see* Con). World Time 24-hour clock, easy to set (*see* Con). Sleep delay. Illuminated LCD readable from a wide variety of angles. Travel power lock, also useful to keep recorder from being inadvertently switched on while cabinet being grasped (*see* Con). Easy on batteries. Records on both sides of tape without having to flip cassette (provided FWD is selected along with the "turning-around arrow"). Auto record level (*see* Con). "ISS" switch helps radio avoid interference from recorder's bias circuitry. FM stereo through earphones; earbuds included. Japanese FM (most versions) and longwave bands. Outboard reel passive wire antenna accessory aids slightly with weak-signal reception. Dead-battery indicator. Lapel mic (*see* Con). *ICF-SW1000TS:* AC adaptor (100V AC only). AN-LP1 active antenna.

Con: Discontinued and thus hard to find, although some stocks remain. Pedestrian speaker audio quality. Synchronous selectable sideband tends to lose lock if batteries not fresh, or if NiCd cells are used. Synchronous selectable sideband alignment can vary with temperature, factory alignment and battery voltage, causing synchronous selectable sideband reception to be slightly more muffled in one sideband than the other. No tuning knob. Clock not readable when radio switched on except for ten seconds when key is pushed. No meaningful signal-strength indicator, which negates its otherwise obvious role for traveling technical monitors. No recording-level indicator or tape counter. Slow rewind. Fast forward and reverse use buttons that have to be held down. No built-in mic; outboard (lapel) mic is mono. Reception is interrupted for a good two seconds when recording first commences. No pause control. Single lock deactivates controls for radio and recorder alike; separate locks would have been preferable. Tuning resolution of

0.1 kHz allows single-sideband signals to be mis-tuned by up to 50 Hz. Frequency readout to 1 kHz, rather than 0.1 kHz tuning increment. Lacks flip-out elevation panel; instead, uses less handy plug-in tab. FM sometimes overloads. Telescopic antenna exits from the side, which limits tilting choices for FM. Misleading location of battery springs makes it easy to insert one of the two "AA" radio batteries in the wrong direction, albeit to no ill effect. No batteries (three "AA" required, two for radio and one for recorder). *ICF-SW1000T:* 120V AC or other adaptor costs extra (avoid Sony multivoltage adaptors, as they don't provide enough torque for starting tape drive).

Verdict: Strictly speaking, Sony's pricey ICF-SW1000T/ICF-SW1000TS is the world's only true world band cassette recorder—past or present. Made in Japan, it is an innovative little package with surprisingly good battery life and build quality. The rub is that it was disconti nued in 2004 and has become difficult to find (e.g., at exporter thieCom.de).

★★½ 𝓔

Sangean ATS-818ACS, Sangean ATS-818ACS "Deluxe," Roberts RC828

Price: *ATS-818:* $219.95 in the United States. $249.99CAD in Canada. €168.00 in Germany. *ATS-818 "Deluxe":* $249.95 in the United States. *AC adaptor:* £16.95 in the United Kingdom. *RC828:* £219.95 in the United Kingdom.

Pro: Built-in cassette recorder. Price low relative to competition. Superior overall world band performance. Numerous tuning features, including 18 world band station presets. Two bandwidths for good fidelity/interference tradeoff. Analog clarifier with center detent and stable circuitry allows single-sideband signals to be tuned with un-common precision, thus allowing for superior audio phasing for a portable (*see* Con). Illuminated display. Signal-strength indicator. Dual-zone 24-hour clock, with one zone displayed separately from frequency. Alarm/timer with sleep delay. Travel power lock. Stereo through earpieces. Longwave.

Sangean's ATS-818ACS records programs, albeit not with the panache of the Sony ICF-SW1000T. Nevertheless, the '818ACS is readily available and costs far less.

Built-in condenser mic. *Most versions:* AC adaptor. *ATS818ACS "Deluxe," available only from C. Crane Company:* Eliminates muting between stations when bandscanning; also, RCA jack for external antennas.

Con: Recorder has no multiple record ing events, just one "on" time (quits when tape runs out). Tends to mute when tuning knob turned quickly, making bandscanning difficult (the C. Crane Company offers a $20.00/$29.95 modification to remedy this). Wide bandwidth a bit broad for world band reception without synchronous selectable sideband. Keypad not in telephone format. Touchy single-sideband clarifier. Recorder has no level indicator and no counter. Fast-forward and rewind controls installed facing backwards. No batteries (four "D" and three "AA" needed). Country of manufacture (now China) not specified on radio or box.

Verdict: A great buy, although recording is only single-event with no timed "off."

The PASSPORT portable-radio review team: Lawrence Magne and David Zantow; also, Tony Jones, with laboratory measurements performed independently by Rob Sherwood. Additional feedback from David Crystal, Toshimichi Ohtake, Craig Tyson and George Zeller.

BIG HANDFUL, BIG PERFORMANCE

Portatops aren't as small as portables nor as rugged as tabletop models. Yet, they offer performance and fidelity approaching that of good tabletops, but without sticker shock. And, like portables, they work anywhere off batteries.

✪✪✪✪⅜ *Passport's Choice*

Grundig Satellit 800, Tecsun HAM-2000

Price (as available): *S800 (repacked/reconditioned):* $399.95 including 120V AC adaptor and headphones in the United States. £399.00 including dual-voltage AC adaptor and headphones in the United Kingdom. *S800 (new):* €849.00 including dual-voltage AC adaptor and headphones in Germany. *HAM-2000 (new):* ¥3,500 (about $435) in China.

Pro: Superior, room-filling tonal quality with continuous bass and treble controls. Full-size padded headphones. Excellent synchronous selectable sideband, with 27 dB of unwanted-sideband rejection to reduce interference and selective-fading distortion with world band, longwave and mediumwave AM signals. Synchronous selectable sideband also boosts recoverable audio from faint signals and halves overall distortion to 2.4% in AM mode on audio frequencies from 100–3,000 Hz. Three voice/music bandwidths: 7 kHz, 5.8 kHz and 2.6 kHz. Bandwidths generally have excellent shape factors and ultimate rejection; all are selectable independent of mode (or dependent, if user prefers), and function with synchronous selectable sideband. Slow/fast AGC decay (*see* Con). Numerous helpful tuning aids, including 70 tunable station presets that store many variables (*see* Con); also, presets may be scanned (*see* Con). Excellent ergonomics, including many dedicated, widely spaced controls; exceptionally smooth knob tuning aided by ball bearings (*see* Con); and foolproof frequency entry. Superb LCD with large, bold characters and high contrast clearly viewed from virtually any angle (*see* Con). Analog signal-strength indicator (*see* Con). Single-sideband reception above portable norm (*see* Con), with rock-solid frequency stability and 50 Hz tuning increments. High- and low-impedance inputs for 0.1–30 MHz external antennas. With built-in telescopic antenna, weak-signal shortwave sensitivity equal to or better than that of top-rated portables. Weak-signal shortwave sensitivity with external antenna can be boosted by setting switch to "whip" to add preamplification (sometimes generates overloading). Superior blocking performance aids consistency of weak-signal sensitivity. Generally superior dynamic range and third-order intercept point. Two-event on/off timer and two 24-hour clocks (*see* Con). Large, tough telescopic antenna includes spring-loaded detents for vertical, 45-degree and 90-degree swiveling; also rotates freely (*see* Con). Versatile display and signal strength meter illumination choices. FM—mono through built-in speaker, stereo through outboard speakers, headphones and line output—performs well, although capture ratio only average and nearby FM transmitters may cause overloading. Longwave. Built-in ferrite rod antenna for 0.1–1.8 MHz. Covers 118–137 MHz aeronautical band, but only in AM mode

Grundig's Satellit 800 is out of production but still available, usually as a repack. It will be missed, as there's nothing else quite like it.

and without synchronous selectable sideband. Excellent long carrying handle. AC adaptor—120V AC or 220V AC, depending on country of sale; otherwise, alkaline batteries need changing every 35 hours or so. Battery-strength indicator (*see* Con). Rack-type handles protect front panel. *North America:* Superior repairs in and out of one-year warranty by R.L. Drake Company. Excellent toll-free tech support.

Con: Huge (20⅜ inches—517 mm—wide) and weighty (15 pounds or 6.8 kg with batteries). Cabinet and components of portable-radio quality. Synthesizer phase noise, only fair, slightly impacts reception of weak-signals adjacent to powerful signals and in other circumstances. Lacks notch filter, noise blanker, passband tuning and digital signal processing (DSP) found on some tabletops. When ungrounded (e.g., AC adaptor not connected to a grounded AC socket) and powered by batteries, vigorous "hash" when tuning knob being turned within portions of mediumwave AM band. Each key push must each be done within three seconds, lest receiver wind up mis-tuned or in unwanted operating mode. No signal-seek frequency scanning. Signal strength indicator greatly underreads. Outboard AC adaptor in lieu of inboard power supply. Single sideband's 50 Hz synthesizer increments allow tuning to be out of phase by up to 25 Hz, diminishing audio fidelity. Fast AGC decay setting handy for bandscanning, but sometimes causes distortion with powerful signals; remedied by using slow AGC when not bandscanning. Numerous modest birdies on longwave, mediumwave AM, shortwave and FM bands; few cause heterodyne interference to world band signals. Ergonomics, although excellent, not ideal; e.g., no rows and columns of dedicated buttons for station presets. Sharp bevel on tuning knob. Neither clock displays when frequency shown; instead, pushbutton replaces frequency with time for three seconds. Both clocks only in 24-hour format and neither displays seconds numerically. For faint-signal DXing, recoverable audio with an outboard antenna, although good, not fully equal to that of most tabletop models. Using built-in antenna, sensitivity to weak signals not of DX caliber in mediumwave AM band; remedied by using Terk AM Advantage or similar accessory. Some frontal (only) radiation of digital noise from LCD, rarely a problem in actual use. When receiver leaned backward, telescopic antenna, if angled, spins rearward. Battery-strength indicator doesn't come on until immediately before radio mutes from low battery voltage. Misleading location of battery spring clips makes it easy to insert half the batteries in wrong direction, albeit to no permanent ill effect. Battery cover may come loose if receiver bumped in a specific and unusual manner. Antenna switches located unhandily on rear panel. "USB" on LCD displays as "LISB." No schematic or repair manual available, making service difficult except at authorized repair facility. No batteries (6 "D" needed).

The Satellit 800 sports a genuine S-meter.

☞ Prior to 2003 there were a number of batches manufactured with an above-average defect rate. Since then production quality has settled down.

☞ Refurbished units reportedly include gift and similar types of returns from department stores and other outlets where customers tend to be unfamiliar with world band radio. Refurbishing is done at Drake's facility in Ohio.

Verdict: Big Bertha. The beefy Grundig Satellit 800/Tecsun HAM-2000 offers near-tabletop performance at a near-portable price. Great audio quality and ergonomics, and it receives well with just its telescopic antenna. With pricing down and quality up, this receiver commands unusual attention. But it's no longer in production, so get it while you can.

▤ An *RDI WHITE PAPER* is available for this model.

Radios for Emergencies

When the facade of civilization is stripped away, trusted information is invaluable. For this, nothing delivers like world band radio.

World band is unfettered, soaring direct without wires or gatekeepers. That's because it bounces off heavenly layers invulnerable to manipulation—no satellites, no cables, no local towers. Even jamming often doesn't succeed.

What to Look for

If you already have a world band portable or portatop, look no further. Extra batteries allow it to serve nicely in a crisis.

No radio? Consider getting one now—not after a crisis, when anything decent is sold out. Best is a three-star or better portable that works for both routine listening and emergency use. Look through adjacent pages—the choice is vast.

Favor models that process single-sideband signals, explained in PASSPORT's glossary. These can eavesdrop on some aeronautical and other "utility" communications, and possibly the low-powered American Forces Radio and Television Service. Also, avoid battery hogs and look for illuminated LCDs, *de rigeur* for tuning in the dark—illuminated keypads help, too.

What to avoid? Cheap radios lacking digital frequency readout. Their imprecise dials make stations hard to find, they don't demodulate single-sideband signals and most are marginal performers. Also, think twice about windup radios. They have advantages, but all are rudimentary performers. Best is to treat them as backups or for family members.

Among windups only the Freeplay Summit meets minimum testing requirements at PASSPORT. However, we've bent the rules to include one analog-tuned series because it outsells all others combined. It also can be obtained quickly at local stores like Bed, Bath & Beyond.

> **World band is unfettered, soaring direct without wires or gatekeepers.**

Make Sure It Works

An emergency radio has to actually work during a crisis. To check, go outdoors and tune in foreign stations that are weak but intelligible. Head to your safe room and compare how those same frequencies come in. If reception is similar, you're all set for the inevitable day of reckoning. If not, put up a simple outdoor wire antenna, such as Radio Shack's "Outdoor Antenna Kit" (278-758). Cut it to a convenient length, then run the feedline into your room without damaging the insulation. Or check out compact antennas reviewed in PASSPORT REPORTS.

Either way, keep PASSPORT nearby so you'll know what's on.

✪¼
Freeplay Summit (International), Freeplay Summit (USA)

Price: *Summit (International):* $129.99CAD in Canada. £59.99 in the United Kingdom. €119.95 in Germany. *Summit (USA):* $99.95 or less in the United States.

Pro: Relatively technologically advanced for an emergency radio, including five world band presets and 25 more for other bands. Powered by rechargeable battery pack which, in turn, is

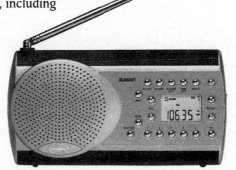

The Freeplay Summit offers modern tuning features, but performance is lackluster.

juiced three ways: foolproof cranked alternator, solar energy and AC adaptor. NiMH battery pack replaceable, although nominally radio runs even if pack no longer takes a charge. Reasonably pleasant audio quality. Timed LCD illumination. Low-battery and crank-charge indicators. World Time 24-hour clock with alarm and sleep functions can also display in 12-hour format. Accessory reel antenna and AC adaptor. Travel power lock. Mediumwave AM tunes in 9/10 kHz steps. FM includes NTSC (North American) channel 6 TV audio. Longwave. More stylish than most. *Summit (International):* AC adaptor adjusts to line voltage (110–240V AC) anywhere in the world (*see* Con). Three types of power plugs for different countries; also, carrying pouch. *Summit (USA):* 120V AC adaptor, works well.

Con: Slow battery recharge; full replenishment requires 24 hours with AC adaptor, 40 hours using sunlight, or 40 minutes of carpal-crunching cranking. Poor sensitivity on world band using built-in but undersized telescopic antenna; reel-in accessory antenna, included, helps slightly. Lacks non-radio emergency features found on some other windup radios. Poor selectivity. Poor image rejection. Shortwave coverage of 5.95–15.6 MHz omits 2, 3, 4, 5, 17, 19, 21 and 25 MHz (120, 90, 75, 60, 16, 15, 13 and

MCRADIO: MILLIONS SOLD

Grundig FR-200, Etón FR-250, Tecsun Green-88

World band radios can be major sellers. For example, there have been millions of Grundig FR-200 and Etón FR-250 radios reportedly sold in North America in recent years, and it's growing. A Tecsun version is being offered in China and Etón has just opened a new facility in Europe.

These sibling models succeed thanks to ubiquitous advertising, widespread availability and bargain pricing. They are powered not by ordinary batteries, but by a replaceable NiMH battery pack charged by crank-driven dynamo. Even if the battery pack dies the dynamo can power the radio.

Phone Recharger

A key non-radio feature of the '250 is its cellphone recharger—imagine having had this at the World Trade Center on 9/11! It includes a short cable and adapter plugs for popular phones.

The front panel sport s a bright flashlight to keep the boogie man at bay—in a blackout this could be as important as the radio. The '200 uses a bulb, while the '250 goes one better with long-life LEDs that second as a flashing red light. For hiking, traveling or bouncing around car trunks there's a rugged canvas bag with magnetic catch. The '250 also includes a siren to make neighborhood dogs bark.

Basic World Band

The '200 has two shortwave "bands" of 3.2–7.6 MHz and 9.2–22 MHz. These include nearly all world band segments, which in a national emergency could be the only source for credible news.

Alas, the frequency readout crams hundreds of world band stations into a wee couple of inches (five centimeters) of analog dial space and the tuning knob has play. Global signals can be hunted down only by ear, and even then it's hard to tell whether you're hearing the station's real signal or its image 900 kHz or so down. However, there's a fine tuning control to help out.

11 meter) world band segments, along with lower end of 6 MHz (49 meters) and upper end of 15 MHz (19 meters). Inconvenient to tune, with no keypad, no tuning knob and "signal-seek" scanning that stops only at very powerful stations; this essentially leaves only single-speed (slow) up/down slewing and five world band presets to navigate the airwaves. No volume knob or slider; level adjustable only through up/down slew controls. Mutes for a second whenever slew button pressed, an annoyance when bandscanning. Does not continuously display frequency—reverts back to clock after ten seconds. Tunes world band only in 5 kHz steps and displays in nonstandard XX.XX MHz/XX.XX₅ MHz format. LCD hard to read in low light without illumination, which fades away after only four seconds. FM overloads in strong-signal environments. One of the two units we purchased new was defective. No handle or carrying strap. *Summit (International):* Multivoltage

AC adaptor disturbs reception with vigorous noise and hum; best is either to replace it with an aftermarket transformer or to keep it unplugged except to charge battery pack.

☞ "International" and "USA" are informal terms used to differentiate between two *defacto* versions. Freeplay products have changed North American and other distributors frequently in recent months, so check with dealers for current warranty information.

Verdict: Yes, world band performance is mediocre. And, yes, it is bereft of most tuning aids and non-radio emergency features. Still, the Chinese-made Freeplay Summit is the most acceptable emergency radio we have come across, and it performs reasonably on FM and mediumwave AM.

_____

The PASSPORT *emergency radio review team: David Zantow and Lawrence Magne.*

Enter the new FR-250. It has seven separate world band segments nicely spread out and augmented by a fine tuning knob. Coverage omits the 3, 4, 5, 19 and 21 MHz (90, 75, 60, 15 and 13 meter) segments included on the '200, but it's a good tradeoff. As on the '200, the tuning knob has play.

Audio quality is pleasant with both models, but otherwise reception quality is elemental. Sensitivity to weak world band signals is marginal—so is selectivity and image rejection. As to single-sideband signals, forget it.

FM, in mono only, includes NTSC (North American) channel 6 TV audio. FM overloads in strong-signal environments, but otherwise both it and mediumwave AM perform reasonably well.

The FR-200 and FR-250 don't send radio hearts aflutter. But they suffice for emergencies, are widely available and affordable. Both come with a one-year warranty and superior product support.

Price: *Grundig FR-200:* $39.95 in the United States. $49.99CAD in Canada. Around €30 in Europe. *Etón FR-250:* $49.95 in the United States. $69.99CAD in Canada. *AC adaptor (110-120V AC to 4.5V DC):* $12.95 in the United States. $12.95CAD in Canada.

The FR-250 is Etón's latest low-cost emergency radio.

Tabletop Receivers for 2006

Tabletop receivers excel at flushing out faint stations swamped by competing signals. That's why they are prized by radio aficionados known as "DXers," an old telegraph term meaning long distance. But tabletop models aren't for everybody, and it shows. Even in prosperous North America and Europe, tabletop unit sales have been subject to increased competitive pressure from quality portables.

Virtually all cost more than portables or portatops, yet they're less expensive than professional receivers also reviewed in PASSPORT REPORTS. But there's a good reason for this. For the price of a tabletop you tend to get not only excellent performance, but also superior construction and ruggedness. They are also relatively easy to service and are backed up by knowledgeable repair facilities.

What you rarely find in a tabletop is reception of the everyday 87.5–108 MHz FM band. For this, look to a portatop or portable.

Tabletops Relieve Location Challenges

Not only DXers find tabletop sets to be desirable. Like portatop and professional models, they are ideally suited for where signals tend to be weak—western and midwestern North America, for example, or Australia and New Zealand.

Even elsewhere there can be a problem when signals pass over or near the magnetic North Pole, which periodically erupts into geomagnetic fury. To check, place a string on a globe—a conventional map won't do—between your location and the station's transmitter as shown in the Blue Pages. If the string passes near or above latitude 60% north, beware.

Antennas Rarely Overload Tabletops

One reason most tabletop receivers do so well is they accept outboard specialty antennas without the side effects these can cause with portables.

It's hard to overstate the benefit of a worthy, properly erected accessory antenna placed outdoors or, in a pinch, on a balcony or window. Just as a sailboat zips along with a proper sail, so, too, a receiver benefits from an antenna that can grab more signals. Test results and ratings of a wide variety of antennas—small and large, indoor and out—are detailed elsewhere in this Passport Reports.

Daytime Signals Grow in Importance

Some programs formerly aired during evening prime time are now heard, instead, by day. These tend to be weaker, especially when not beamed your way, but they are also among the most interesting. Thanks to the scattering properties of shortwave you can eavesdrop on many of these "off-beam" signals, but it's harder. This is where a superior receiver's longer reach comes in.

But not always. Say, you have a portable with a modest outdoor antenna and reception is still being disrupted by electrical noise—nearby dimmers, digital thingies and whatnot. Reception may not benefit from a tabletop model, as its superior circuitry boosts noise just as much as signals.

However, even here there may be an out. An active loop antenna, such as those reviewed in Passport Reports, can potentially improve signal-to-noise ratio because of its ability to be aimed away from noise sources. So, you may profit from a good tabletop model even in the face of some local electrical noise—provided you have the right antenna.

Apartment Solutions

In high-rise buildings, portables can disappoint. Reinforced concrete soaks up signals, while nearby broadcast, cellular and other transmitters can interfere.

Here, a good bet for reception of tough world band stations is a well-rated tabletop or portatop fed by a suitable antenna. Experiment with something like a homebrew insulated-wire antenna along, or just outside, a window or balcony. Or try an everyday telescopic car antenna that angles out, like a wall flagpole, from a window or balcony ledge.

You can also amplify your homebrew antenna with a good active preselector. Even simpler are factory-made amplified ("active") antennas that have reception elements and amplifiers in separate modules. Both solutions are covered in Passport Reports.

If you don't live in an apartment, consider a first-rate passive (unamplified) outdoor wire antenna, usually under $100. Performance findings and installation tips are detailed in the Radio Database International White Paper, *Popular Outdoor Antennas*, and summarized in Passport Reports.

DRM Digital Broadcasts

Some tabletop models come "DRM ready" to receive digital world band broadcasts being tested by broadcasters and manufacturers.

However, "DRM ready" isn't "Plug and Play." Today's receivers can reproduce DRM transmissions only when connected to a PC with separately purchased DRM software. For this combo to perform properly, it's best to use an outboard antenna located for minimum pickup of digital noise from the computer setup. Shielded cables help, too.

If DRM is important to you, there is another option. Some non-DRM-ready tabletop models can be modified to reproduce DRM signals—see www.drmrx.org/receiver_mods.html. This is one step removed from "DRM ready," but it helps ensure your new receiver won't become technologically limited in the years to come.

When DRM comes in with a powerful signal free from interference and the broadcaster uses a high bit rate, it results in virtually local-quality audio fidelity—to this extent, the lofty claims made by DRM's proponents are spot-on. However, lost amidst this optimism are DRM's shortcomings. These include inferior long-distance (multi-hop) performance; susceptibility to disruption by noise and interference, including jamming; and creation of wideband interference to analog stations on nearby frequencies.

Yet, DRM is a work in progress with powerful backers, so results are likely to improve over time. Bottom line, it may make sense to favor a receiver with some potential to reproduce DRM.

Shortwave's Hidden Offerings

Although virtually all shortwave listeners enjoy world band, some also seek out "utility" and "ham" signals nestled between world band segments. These have reception challenges and rewards of their own and, unlike world band, don't require much in the way of receiver audio quality. This allows some receivers to stand out even when their world band audio isn't inspiring. The Icom IC-R75 and Japan Radio NRD-545 are two popular examples.

Other top-rated tabletop models perform solidly with all kinds of signals.

Price vs. Performance

Top-rated tabletop models cost well over the equivalent of $1,000, and they cut the mustard. The Icom IC-R75 isn't quite in that league, but its price-performance ratio has made it a popular choice, especially for utility and "ham" reception. Indeed, in mid-2005 Icom America discontinued the 'R75, only to revive it months later after an avalanche of protest from American dealers and listeners.

Complete Findings Now Available

Our unabridged laboratory and hands-on test results for each receiver are too exhaustive to reproduce here. However, they are available for selected current and classic models as Passport's Radio Database International White Papers—details are elsewhere in this Passport.

Tips for Using this Section

Receivers are listed in order of suitability for listening to difficult-to-hear world band stations; important secondary consideration is given to audio fidelity, ergonomics and perceived build quality. Street selling prices are cited, including British and Australian VAT/GST where applicable. Prices vary, so take them as the general guide they are meant to be.

Unless otherwise stated, all tabletop models have the following characteristics. See Passport's glossary for terms used.

- Digital frequency synthesis and display.
- Full coverage of at least the 155–29999 kHz longwave, mediumwave AM and shortwave spectra—including all world band frequencies—but no coverage of the FM broadcast band (87.5–108 MHz). Models designed for sale in certain countries have reduced shortwave tuning ranges.
- A wide variety of helpful tuning features.
- Synchronous selectable sideband via high-rejection IF filtering (not lower-rejection phase cancellation), which greatly reduces adjacent-channel interference and selective-fading distortion.

☞ ECSS: Many tabletop models can tune to the nearest 10 Hz or even 1 Hz, allowing the operator to use the receiver's single-sideband circuitry to manually phase its BFO (internally generated carrier) with the station's transmitted carrier. Called "ECSS" (exalted-carrier, selectable-sideband) tuning, this can be used in lieu of synchronous selectable sideband. However, in addition to the relative inconvenience of this technique, unlike synchronous selectable sideband, which re-phases continually and perfectly, ECSS is always slightly out of phase. This causes at least some degree of harmonic distortion to music and speech, while tuning to the nearest Hertz can generate slow-sweep fading (for this reason, mis-phasing by two or three Hertz may provide better results).

- Proper demodulation of modes used by non-world-band shortwave signals, except for models designed to be sold in certain countries. These modes include single sideband (LSB/USB) and CW ("Morse code"); also, with suitable ancillary devices, radioteletype (RTTY), frequency shift key (FSK) and radiofax (FAX).
- Meaningful signal-strength indication.
- Illuminated display.

What PASSPORT's Rating Symbols Mean

Star ratings: ✪✪✪✪✪ is best. Stars reflect overall performance and meaningful features, plus to some extent ergonomics and perceived build quality. Price, appearance, country of manufacture and the like are not taken into account. With tabletop models there is a slightly greater emphasis on the ability to flush out tough, hard-to-hear signals, as this is one of the main reasons these sets are chosen. Nevertheless, to facilitate comparison the tabletop rating standards are very similar to those used for the professional, portatop and portable models reviewed elsewhere in this Passport.

Passport's Choice. La crème de la crème. Our test team's personal picks of the litter—models we would buy or have bought for our personal use. Unlike star ratings, these choices are unapologetically subjective.

✐: A relative bargain, with decidedly more performance than the price would suggest. However, none of these receivers is cheap.

Retested for 2006
DRM Ready

✪✪✪✪✪ 📄 *Passport's Choice*
AOR AR7030 PLUS, AOR AR7030 PLUS/DRM, AOR AR7030, AOR AR7030/DRM

Price (receivers): *AR7030 PLUS:* $1,499.95 in the United States. £949.00 or less in the United Kingdom. €1,198.00 in Germany. *AR7030:* £799.00 or less in the United Kingdom. €1,039.00 in Germany. *AR7030/DRM:* £949.00 in the United Kingdom. *AR7030 PLUS/DRM:* £1,099.00 in the United Kingdom. €1,579.00 in Germany.

Price (options, all versions): *Optional Mu-Rata ceramic bandwidth filters:* $59.95–79.95 each plus installation in the United States. £29.99–39.99 each including installation each in the United Kingdom. €49.00 each plus installation in Germany. *Optional Collins mechanical bandwidth filters:* $99.95 each plus installation each in the United States. £74.00 each including installation in the United Kingdom. €95.00–99.95 each plus installation in Germany. *FL124 daughter board for up to three crystal filters:* US$59.95 plus $25.00 installation in the United States. £24.99 including installation in the United Kingdom. €50.00 plus installation in Germany. *FL-624 Bolger aftermarket daughter board for up to six crystal filters:* contact Bolger-Funk in Germany for price. *XTL2.4 crystal filter, 2.4 kHz bandwidth:* £79.00 including installation in the United Kingdom; special-order part from AOR Japan, so requires waiting period. *Aftermarket (Icom, Kenwood, JRC, Inrad, Kiwa et al.) 455 kHz crystal bandwidth filters:* equivalent of $150–300 each plus installation worldwide, depending on filter and vendor. *SM7030 service kit:* $89.95 in the United States. £39.95 in the United Kingdom. €98.00 in Germany. *BP123 inboard rechargeable battery with inboard recharger (nominally results in minor performance drop-off):* $99.99 in the United Kingdom. €179.00 in Germany. *Add DRM to existing '7030 or '7030 PLUS:* £200.00 in the United Kingdom.

AOR's AR7030 has been tweaked for years. It is now the best tabletop model.

Price (options, AR7030 PLUS and AR7030 PLUS/DRM): *UPNB7030 notch filter:* $339.95 plus $25.00 installation in the United States. £163.00 including installation in the United Kingdom. €280.70 plus installation in Germany.

Price (options, AR7030 and AR7030/ DRM): *NB7030 noise blanker & notch filter:* £198.00 including installation in the United Kingdom. €298.00 plus installation in Germany.

Pro: In terms of overall performance for program listening, as good a receiver as we've ever tested. With one exception (*see* Con), exceptionally quiet circuitry enhances DXing and weak-signal listening, alike. Superb world band and mediumwave AM audio quality when used with a first-rate outboard speaker or audio system. Synchronous selectable sideband performs exceptionally well at reducing distortion caused by selective fading, as well as at diminishing or eliminating adjacent-channel interference; also has synchronous double sideband. Superb dynamic range and third-order intercept point at both wide (+11 dBm at 20 kHz, approaching +20 dBm at 50 kHz) and narrow (–3 dBm at 5 kHz) separation. Superb image rejection (102 dB). Superb first IF rejection (99 dB). Superb AGC threshold with preamp on. Four voice bandwidths (AR7030 & AR7030/DRM 2.3, 7.0, 8.2 and 10.3 kHz), using cascaded ceramic filters; optional filters can raise total to six bandwidths—ceramic, mechanical or crystal (crystal filters require optional daughter board) (*see* Con). Bandwidths using ceramic filters have excellent shape factors and superb ultimate rejection. Sensitivity to weak signals excellent (–131 dB noise floor, 0.2 &V sensitivity) with preamp on (*see* Con: *AR7030 & AR7030/DRM*). Advanced tuning and operating features aplenty, including passband tuning. Optional tunable audio (AF) notch filter and noise blanker; notch extremely effective, with little loss of audio fidelity. Automatically self-aligns and centers bandwidth filters—whether ceramic, mechanical or crystal—for optimum performance, then displays measured bandwidth of each. Remote keypad (*see* Con). Accepts two antennas. IF output. World Time 24-hour clock displays seconds, calendar and timer/sleep-delay. Outstanding performance with local, distant and multipath twilight-fringe mediumwave AM signals. Superior service at U.K. factory [AOR (UK)] and U.S. distributor (Universal Radio). Website (www.aoruk.com/7030bulletin. htm) provides technical updates and information. Owner's manual available online (www.aoruk.com/manuals.htm). *AR7030 PLUS & AR7030 PLUS/DRM:* 400 scannable presets, instead of 100, with 14-character alphanumeric readout for station names (*see* Con). Bandwidth choices (2.3, 4.6, 6.6 and 9.8 kHz) preferable to those of AR7030 & AR7030/DRM. Optical encoder for tuning inherently more reliable than mechanical encoder on AR7030 & AR7030/DRM (*see* Con). *AR7030/DRM and AR7030 PLUS/DRM:* Receives digital (DRM) world band broadcasts by connecting its 12 kHz IF output to a PC with separately obtained DRM software.

Con: Unusually convoluted ergonomics, including tree-logic operating scheme, especially in the PLUS version; once the initial glow of ownership has passed, some find this to be tiresome. No keypad on receiver; instead, keypad is part of an infrared wireless remote control which has to be aimed carefully at receiver's front or back. Although the remote can operate from across a room, LCD characters too small to be seen from such a distance. LCD omits certain useful information, such as signal strength, when radio in various status modes. Front end selectivity only fair. When four standard ceramic bandwidth filters are used with two optional mechanical filters, ultimate rejection, although superb with widest three bandwidths, cannot be measured beyond –80/–85 dB on narrowest three bandwidths because of phase noise; still, ultimate rejection is excellent or better with these configurations. Optional Collins filters measure as having poorer shape factors (1:1.8 to 1:2) than standard MuRata ceramic filters (1:1.5 to 1:1.7). LCD emits some digital electrical noise, a potential issue only if an amplified (active) antenna is used with its pickup element (e.g. telescopic rod) placed near receiver. 2.3 kHz bandwidth has some circuit noise (hiss) in single sideband or ECSS modes. Uses outboard AC adaptor instead of built-in power supply. *AR7030 & AR7030/DRM:* Unusual built-in preamplifier/attenuator design links both functions, so receiver noise rises slightly when preamplifier used in +10 dB position, or attenuator used at –10 dB setting. Lacks, and would profit from, a bandwidth of around 4 or 5 kHz; optional Collins mechanical bandwidth filter of 3.5 kHz (nominal at –3 dB, measures 4.17 kHz at –6 dB) thus worth considering. Only 100 presets and no alphanumeric readout. Mechanical tuning encoder occasionally skips frequency increments, especially if it has not been used for awhile. Not available from North American distributor. *AR7030 PLUS & AR7030 PLUS/DRM:* Tuning knob feel only fair.

Verdict: Radio Beemer.

Engineered by John Thorpe and manufactured in England, the AR7030 is a smashing performer, with audio quality that can be a pleasure hour after hour. And it's even better and more robust in its PLUS incarnation.

But there is a catch. Like BMW's iDrive, many functions are shoehorned into a tree-logic control scheme that only a digigeek or cost accountant could love. The resulting ergonomics are uniquely hostile—especially in the PLUS version—even if operation ultimately is not that difficult to master. *Best bet:* Before buying, either lay hands on a '7030 or read the free online owner's manuals (www.aoruk.com/pdf/7030m.pdf and www.aoruk.com/pdf/fpu.pdf).

Ergonomics aside, for serious DXing the '7030 is today's top performer on the scotch side of a professional receiver, but there's more. With a suitable outboard speaker it is also the best sounding receiver at any price for world band and mediumwave AM program listening under a wide range of reception conditions.

Evaluation of latest version: The PLUS version of the AR7030 we tested this year is from AOR's latest production. Overall, it performs comparably to earlier production samples. Yet, there are a number of signs of nuanced evolution—enough for potential buyers to give it a fresh look.

The Bourns optical tuning encoder in the latest PLUS is more reliable than its mechanical predecessor and tunes more consistently. Nevertheless, an optical encoder is like driving by wire—it reduces tuning feel, especially when turned quickly.

Properly designed and implemented, optical encoders typically have a much longer useful life than those with mechanical contacts. Given that outside the UK you can't take the '7030 to a corner electronics shop for repair, this can be a decisive feature. In that same vein, the volume and < > encoders are now more reliable. The all-important "information central" LCD likewise has been improved, offering a skosh more contrast to counteract eyestrain during tree-logic operation.

In the past a number of '7030 owners reportedly experienced failure of the earphone jack's audio-routing contact. Either the jack didn't switch back to the speaker after the phone plug was removed or the connection was intermittent. Neither problem appeared on our latest unit.

Still, not all changes to the '7030 have been positive. When using the 2.3 kHz bandwidth for single-sideband or ECSS reception, there is now modest circuit noise (hiss). This varies with signal modulation, and adjusting the AGC, attenuator and preamp controls doesn't help. Of the half dozen or so samples of the '7030 we have tested over the years, this is the first such encounter.

When the tuning encoders were upgraded, starting with serial number 102050, the '7030 quit being produced with a die-cast shield around the DDS/synthesizer. Nominally, this is because stress from the shield was causing a bad transistor connection. However, this reduces RF shielding, so there is now slightly more RF hash emanating from the LCD. Fortunately, this is a non-issue unless an active antenna's receiving element is placed close to the '7030's front panel.

Otherwise, performance is pretty much as before. Passport's measuring standard for IP3 is more conservative than some others. Yet, the '7030's IP3 measurements continue to be superb even if they don't yield the bigger numbers resulting from the measuring standard used by the manufacturer.

The AOR AR7030 is the undisputed king among nonprofessional tabletops. In the past the '7030 earned Passport's top rating, but it is now a skosh better and more dependable. With superb overall performance and virtually the best audio in a world band receiver, the '7030 has morphed into a serious temptation.

Provided you can accept its "radio iDrive."

📄 An *RDI WHITE PAPER* is available for this model.

NUMBERS: TOP TABLETOPS		
	AOR AR7030 PLUS	**Japan Radio NRD-545**
Max. WB Sensitivity/Noise Floor	0.2 µV **E**/–131 dBm **E**[1]	0.2 µV **E**/–130 dBm **E**[4]
Blocking	>125 dB **E**	>127 dB **E**
Shape Factors, voice BWs	1:1.5–1:1.7 **E**	1:1.1 **S**
Ultimate Rejection	90 dB **S**	65 dB **G**
Front-End Selectivity	**F**	**E**
Image Rejection	102 dB **S**	>75 dB **E**
First IF Rejection	99 dB **S**	>90 dB **S**
Dynamic Range/IP3 (5 kHz)	82 dB **E**/–3 dBm **S**	66 dB **F**/–31 dBm **F**[5]
Dynamic Range/IP3 (20 kHz)	91 dB **E**/+11 dBm **S**	NA[6,7]
Phase Noise	129 dBc **E**	118 dBc **G**
AGC Threshold	0.7 µV **S**[2]	2 µV **G**
Overall Distortion, sync	0.5–3% **S**-**G**[3]	0.1–7% **S**-**P**[3]
Stability	2 Hz **S**	20 Hz **G**
Notch filter depth	55 dB **S**	37 dB **G**[8]

IBS Lab Ratings: **S** Superb   **E** Excellent   **G** Good   **F** Fair   **P** Poor

(1) Preamplifier on. With preamp off: 0.35 µV **E**/–126 dBm **G**.
(2) Preamplifier on. With preamp off: 2 µV **G**.
(3) Usually <1% **S**.
(4) NRD-545SE: 0.16 **S**/–133 dBm **E**.
(5) NRD-545SE: 73 dB **G**/–23 dBm **G**.
(6) Not measurable at 20 kHz separation. At 10 kHz: 80 dB **F** **G**/–10 dBm **F** **G**.
(7) NRD-545SE: 89 dB **G**/+1 dBm **E**.
(8) DSP notch tunes only 100–2,500 Hz.

✪✪✪½
Japan Radio NRD-545

Price: $1,799.95 in the United States. $3,700.00CAD as available in Canada. £1,299.00 in the United Kingdom. €1,798.00 in Germany. $3,589.00AUD in Australia. *NVA-319 external speaker:* $199.95 in the United States. £199 in the United Kingdom. €259.00 in Germany. *CHE-199 VHF-UHF converter:* $369.95 in the United States. £289 in the United Kingdom. €398.00 in Germany. *CGD-197 frequency stabilizer:* $99.95 in the United States. €149.00 in Germany.

DSP receivers usually give sticker shock, but Japan Radio's NRD-545 is relatively affordable. Superior build quality and ergonomics, too.

Pro: Superior build quality, right down to the steel cabinet with machined screws. Easily upgraded by changing software ROMs. Fully 998 bandwidths provide unprecedented flexibility. Razor-sharp skirt selectivity, especially with voice bandwidths. Outstanding array of tuning aids, including 1,000 station presets (*see* Con). Wide array of reception aids, including passband offset, excellent manual/automatic tunable notch, and synchronous selectable sideband having good lock. Superb reception of single-sideband and other "utility" signals. Demodulates C-Quam AM stereo signals, which then need to be fed through an external audio amplifier, not provided (the headphone jack can't be used for this, as it is monaural). Highly adjustable AGC in all modes requiring BFO (*see* Con). Tunes in ultra-precise 1 Hz increments, although displays only in 10 Hz increments. Ergonomics, including the physical quality of tuning knob and other controls, among the very best. Some useful audio shaping. Computer interface with free NRDWIN software (*see* Con); among other things, is effective at processing RTTY signals. Virtually no spurious radiation of digital "buzz." Hiss-free audio-out port for recording or feeding low-power FM transmitter to hear world band around the house. Internal AC power supply is quiet and generates little heat. Power cord detaches handily from receiver, like on a PC, making it easy to replace. Includes a "CARE package" of all needed metric plugs and connectors, along with a 12V DC power cord.

Con: Ultimate rejection only fair, although average ultimate rejection equivalent is 10–15 dB better; this unusual gap comes about from intermodulation (IMD) inside the digital signal processor, and results in audible "monkey chatter" under certain specific and uncommon reception conditions. Audio quality sometimes tough sledding in the unvarnished AM mode—using synchronous selectable sideband helps greatly. No AGC adjustment in AM mode or with synchronous selectable sideband, and lone AGC decay rate too fast. Dynamic range only fair. Synchronous selectable sideband sometimes slow to kick in. Notch filter won't attenuate heterodynes (whistles) any higher in pitch than 2,500 Hz AF. Noise reduction circuit only marginally useful. Signal-strength indicator overreads at higher levels. Frequency display misreads by up to 30 Hz, especially at higher tuned frequencies, and gets worse as the months pass by. Station presets don't store synchronous AM settings. Audio amplifier lacks oomph with some poorly modulated signals. No IF output, nor can one be retrofitted. NRD Win software, at least the current v1.00, handles only uploads, not downloads, and works only on com port 1 that is usually already in use. World Time 24-hour clock doesn't show when frequency displayed. No tilt bail or feet. Anti-reflective paint on buttons and knobs becomes shiny with wear.

Verdict: In many ways Japan Radio's NRD-545 is a remarkable performer, especially for utility and tropical-bands DXing. With its first-class ergonomics and the fine feel of superior construction quality, it is always a pleasure to operate. Yet, more is needed to make this the ultimate receiver it could be. By now Japan Radio should have issued a ROM upgrade to remedy at least some of these long-standing issues, but contrary to urban legend *nada* as yet.

Whether "monkey chatter" and other manifestations of DSP overload are an issue varies markedly from one listening situation to another—some hear it, others never do. It depends on the specifics of the signal being received, what part of the world you are in and your own aural perceptions. Among our panelists, all noticed it eventually, but reaction varied from "no big deal" to howls of derision. Reader feedback suggests that most don't find it to be a significant drawback.

✪✪✪½
Japan Radio "NRD-545SE"

Price: *NRD-545SE:* $1,899.00 in the United States. *Retrofit to change an existing receiver to "SE":* $104.00 plus receiver shipping both ways.

Pro: Dynamic range, 5 kHz, improves from 66 dB to 73 dB. Occasional enhancement of tough-signal reception.

Con: Not available outside North America. *With 8 kHz replacement filter:* Audio bandwidth reduced by 20 percent at the high end. *With 6 kHz replacement filter (not tested):* Audio bandwidth reduced by about 40 percent at the high end.

☞ For all except those who largely confine their listening to tough DX or utility catches, the 8 kHz filter is a preferable choice over the 6 kHz option.

Verdict: Sherwood Engineering, an American firm, replaces the stock DSP protection filter with one of two narrower filters of comparable quality. In principle, this should provide beaucoup decibels of audible improvement in the "monkey chatter" sometimes encountered on the '545 from adjacent-channel signals. Perhaps, but we couldn't hear the difference. What was noticed, instead, was an unwelcome reduction in audio crispness with world band signals—as well as, of course, with mediumwave AM reception.

The '545 is best suited to non-broadcast-listening applications, anyway, so for some DXers the Sherwood modification provides a modestly positive tradeoff. For these, the aural drawback of the Sherwood modification can be less important than its 7 dB improvement in dynamic range and occasional enhancement of tough-signal reception.

But if your main interest is in listening to world band programs, this modification is not the way to go.

Improved for 2006
✪✪✪½ ✆
Icom IC-R75 (Kiwa)

Price (Kiwa modifications): *Synchronous detector upgrade:* $45.00 in the United States. *Audio upgrade:* $35.00 in the United States. *Audio "Hi-Fi" upgrade:* $35.00 in the United States.

Pro: Synchronous detection performance improved slightly, with synchronous selectable sideband actually being somewhat functional with narrow bandwidth. Added high-end audio response marginally improves fidelity with wider IF bandwidth settings. Generally high-quality parts and installation. Prompt turnaround.

Con: When synchronous detector loses lock during deep fades, there is a heterodyne squeal or warble not evident before modification; slow AGC setting occasionally helps ameliorate this. Slight increase in audible hiss with narrow bandwidth settings. Modifications not readily undone and may invalidate Icom's warranty, although in practice this may not be enforced.

☞ Kiwa's regular $35 audio upgrade extends the audio response of the audio amplifier, but doesn't impact the record (line) output. For yet another $35 the "hi-fi" upgrade provides even better audio—through the record (line) output, as well as speaker and headphones. The 'hi-fi' upgrade normally results in a 4.3 kHz bandwidth, but 5.5 kHz is an available alternative; we chose this (shown on our invoice as "5.3 kHz").

Verdict: Of the three tested Kiwa modifications for the popular Icom IC-R75, the audio "Hi-Fi" is the most useful. Runner up is the synchronous detector upgrade, which provides minor but useful improvement. All are reasonably priced but are best deferred until the factory warranty has expired.

Observations with Modified Receiver:
The small American firm of Kiwa Electronics offers a number of modifications to help overcome the 'R75's world band performance deficiencies. The synchronous detector upgrade uses a small "potted" cube affixed to the back microprocessor shield. As two pins of the sync chip are lifted and wired to the module, undoing the modification is no mean task.

The regular audio upgrade is achieved by changing a few capacitors and alters the internal audio amplifier circuit, but not audio through the tape-recording (line) port. This is less difficult to undo than the sync mod, but requires yeoman soldering skills.

The "Hi-Fi" modification alters four resistor values. These change the filter width of the audio preamplifier/filter prior to the main audio amplifier, improving high-end audio response. This impacts not only the receivers's speaker and headphone performance, but also that of the record "line" output. Although it doesn't totally cure the 'R75's bassy audio, it offers a noticeable and welcome improvement when the standard and wide bandwidths are in use.

The stock 'R75's synchronous selectable sideband performance is pitiful. While the Kiwa upgrade doesn't turn this sow's ear into a silk purse or even a cotton tote bag, there is a degree of audible improvement and the price is right.

For the "Hi-Fi" upgrade Kiwa removes surface-mounted resistors before installing discrete replacement components. This is the best procedure, but it also makes the modification virtually impossible to undo. Consequently, any of these options is best put off until after the manufacturer's warranty expires. Unless the tech at Icom is in a magnanimous mood, these could well invalidate the receiver's warranty.

Just as the 'R75 has become popular because of its price, so, too, have Kiwa modifications. The Sherwood SE-3 Mk III D device works wonders, but costs nearly as much as the receiver, making it a non-starter. Viewed in that context, the modest improvements provided by Kiwa's upgrades become both interesting and affordable.

✪✪✪✪⅜ ✪
Icom IC-R75

Price: *Receiver with UT-106 DSP accessory:* $599.95 in the United States. *Icom Replacement Bandwidth Filters (e.g., FL-257 3.3 kHz):* $159.95 in the United States. *SP-23 amplified audio-shaping speaker:* $169.95 in the United States.

Pro: Dual passband offset acts as variable bandwidth and a form of IF shift (*see* Con). Reception of faint signals alongside powerful competing ones aided by excellent ultimate selectivity and good blocking. Excellent front-end selectivity, with seven filters for the shortwave range and more for elsewhere. Two levels of preamplification, 10 dB and 20 dB, can be switched off. Excellent weak-signal sensitivity and good AGC threshold with +20 dB preamplification. Superior rejection of spurious signals, including images. Excellent stability, essential for unattended reception of RTTY and certain other types of utility transmissions. Excels in reception of utility and ham signals, as well as world band signals tuned via "ECSS" technique. Ten tuning steps. Can

Icom's IC-R75 was discontinued in 2005, then revived within months after howls from dealers and consumers. Value priced, it excels with non-broadcast signals.

tune and display in exacting 1Hz increments (*see* Con). Adjustable UT-106 DSP audio accessory with automatic variable notch filter, normally an extra-cost option, helps to a degree in improving intelligibility, but not pleasantness, of some tough signals; also, it reduces heterodyne ("whistle") interference. Fairly good ergonomics, including smooth-turning weighted tuning knob; nice touch is spinning finger dimple, even if it doesn't spin very well. "Control Central" LCD easy to read and evenly illuminated by 24 LEDs with dimmer. Adjustable AGC—fast, slow, off. Tuning knob uses reliable optical encoder normally found only on professional receivers, rather than everyday mechanical variety. Low overall distortion. Pleasant and hiss-free audio with suitable outboard speaker; audio-shaping amplified Icom SP-20, although pricey, works well for a number of applications. 101 station presets. Two antenna inputs, switchable. Digital bar graph signal-strength indicator, although not as desirable as an analog meter, is unusually linear above S-9 and can be set to hold a peak reading briefly. Audio-out port for recording or feeding low-power FM transmitter to hear world band around the house. World Time 24-hour clock, timer and sleep delay (*see* Con). Tunes to 60 MHz, including 6 meter VHF ham band. Tilt bail (*see* Con).

Con: Synchronous detector virtually nonfunctional; operates reasonably only with modification by user or specialty firm, or by addition of a specialized auxiliary device. Dual passband offset usually has little impact on received world band signals and is inoperative when synchronous detection is in use. DSP's automatic variable notch tends not to work with AM-mode signals not received via "ECSS" technique (tuning AM-mode signals as though they were single sideband). Mediocre audio through internal speaker, and no tone control to offset slightly bassy reproduction that originates prior to the audio stage; audio improves to pleasant with an appropriate external speaker, especially one that offsets the receiver's slight bassiness. Suboptimal audio recovery with weak AM-mode signals having heavy fading; largely remediable by

"ECSS" tuning and switching off AGC. Display misreads up to 20 Hz, somewhat negating the precise 1 Hz tuning. Keypad requires frequencies to be entered in MHz format with decimal or trailing zeroes, a pointless inconvenience. Some knobs small. Uses outboard AD-55 "floor brick" 120V AC adaptor in lieu of internal power supply; adaptor's emission field may be picked up by nearby indoor antennas or unshielded antenna lead-in wiring, which can cause minor hum on received signals (remediable by moving antenna or using shielded lead-in cable). AC adaptor puts out over 17.5V while the receiver is designed to run off 13.8V, so receiver runs hot and thus its component reliability suffers; dropping input voltage to 13–14V eliminates this shortcoming. Can read clock or presets IDs or frequency, but no more than one at the same time. RF/AGC control operates peculiarly. Tilt bail lacks rubber protection for furniture surface. Keyboard beep appears at audio line output. No schematic provided.

Verdict: The Japanese-made Icom IC-R75, formerly $800 in the United States, is now a tempting value. It is first-rate for unearthing tough utility and ham signals, as well as world band signals received via manual ECSS tuning (*see* glossary)—the receiver's exacting frequency steps facilitate tuning world band signals as though they were single sideband. For these applications nothing else equals it on the sunny side of a kilobuck.

It is less of an unqualified success for listening to world band broadcasts. Its hopeless synchronous detector performance is only very slightly improved by modifications from specialty firms like Kiwa (see preceding review). Sherwood's SE-3 Mk III D accessory brings the 'R75's fidelity to life by entirely replacing the synchronous and audio circuits, but it costs almost as much as the receiver and complicates operation.

To almost everyone's surprise, Icom abruptly discontinued the smart-selling 'R75 in the first half of 2005. Then—apparently in reaction to thumping protests from dealers and customers—they reintroduced it at a slightly higher price in the third quarter.

Improved for 2006
DRM Ready

✪✪✪✪¼

Ten-Tec RX-350D

Price: *RX-350D:* $1,199.00 in the United States. £999.00 in the United Kingdom. $2,175.00AUD in Australia. *302R external keypad/tuning knob:* $139.00 in the United States. £129.00 in the United Kingdom. *307B external speaker:* $98.00 in the United States. £89.00 in the United Kingdom.

It took years, but Ten-Tec finally and quietly implemented the upgrade they've been promising for the RX-350D. It's a real help in taming cross-modulation.

Pro: DRM ready (a modification, not tested by us, for pre-"D" versions of the RX-350 is described at http://home.satx.rr.com/ka5jgv/RX-350Mod.htm). Receiver is unlikely to become dated for some time, as many aspects of performance and operation can be readily updated, thus far and presumably always for free, by downloading revised firmware from the manufacturer's website (*see* Con); except for clock, all memory, including for firmware, is non-volatile and thus not dependent on battery backup. Lowest-cost tabletop model available with genuine DSP bandwidth filtering. A superb choice of no less than 34 bandwidths, including at least a dozen suitable for world band reception. Numerous helpful tuning features—front-panel tuning knob; up/down frequency and band slew; 1024 station presets divided into eight banks with alpha-numeric station indicators; sophisticated scanning; optional keypad/tuning knob; and two VFOs. Optional external keypad/tuning knob is handy, comfortable and works well (*see* Con); it allows for frequency entry not only in Megahertz, but also in kilohertz via the enter key if the leading zero is entered first for frequencies under 10000 kHz. Tuning knobs on receiver and outboard keypad both use a reliable optical encoder normally found only on professional receivers, rather than the everyday mechanical variety. Tunes and displays in ultra-precise 1 Hz increments (*see* Con). Superior close-in (5 kHz separation) dynamic range/IP3. Excellent passband offset works in all non-FM modes, providing (in addition to the handy AML/AMU settings) selectable sideband for the synchronous detector (*see* Con). Generally worthy ergonomics with large display and

seven useful tuning steps; also, bandwidths and station presets conveniently selectable by knob (*see* Con), and controls have good tactile feel—especially the large, weighted metal tuning knob with rubber edging (*see* Con). Punchy, above-average audio with low overall distortion adds to enjoyment of music and enhances intelligibility, especially with suitable external speaker (*see* Con). Audio-out port for recording or feeding low-power FM transmitter to hear world band around the house. Unlike a number of other DSP receivers, does not make static crashes sound harsh; additionally, DSP noise reduction feature can moderate static noise a bit more. DSP noise reduction also of some use in improving aural quality of certain received signals (*see* Con). Receiver emits very little radiated digital "buzz," so inverted-L antennas with single-wire feedlines and proximate loop antennas don't suffer from noise pickup. Rock stable, essential for unattended reception of RTTY and certain other types of utility transmissions. Notch filter automatic, effective over a wide range (0.1 to over 8.0 kHz AF), and can attenuate more than one heterodyne at a time (*see* Con). AGC threshold, originally poor, improved to excellent in latest version. Signal-strength indicator unusually accurate (*see* Con). Soft and hard microprocessor resets provide useful flexibility in case receiver's "computer" gets its knickers in a twist. AC power supply is inboard, where it belongs, and does not run hot. Tilt bail places receiver at handy angle for operation (*see* Con). Timer.

Con: Synchronous selectable sideband loses lock easily during fades, albeit without causing whistling. RF preamplifier cannot be switched off to help prevent overloading. Our receiver froze up periodically; also, when going from memory channels back to a VFO, display showed invalid frequencies in the 45 to 94 MHz range (*see* ☞). Significant phase noise kept us from meaningfully measuring dynamic range/IP3 at 20 kHz separation; it also precluded plausible skirt-selectivity and ultimate rejection measurements. Circuit hiss with widest bandwidths, a common syndrome with DSP receivers, although the noise reduction feature helps. Spectrum display of marginal utility—limited visual indication, poor contrast, significant time lag and it mutes the receiver during sweep; potentially the most useful range shown in the owner's manual is 120 kHz, but this does not appear in the receiver's menu. Keypad costs extra, even though it is virtually a necessity; it also comes with a remote tuning knob that some may find redundant and which adds to size and cost. Optional outboard keypad has intermittent frequency-entry hesitation. On one unit the display misread up to 30 Hz, somewhat negating the precise 1 Hz tuning; other samples did better. Ineffective noise blanker—DSP, not IF—unnecessarily complicated to turn on as instructed via menu (not indicated in the owner's manual, but the key combination of Alt NR can turn it on more simply), and its 1–7 adjustment needs to be at 5 or above to really work. AM- mode signals, whether received in the conventional AM mode or synchronous, sound harsh with fast AGC. No AGC off. Friction when turning knobs, at least with samples tested; remediable by easing knobs slightly away from front panel (with tuning knob, remove rubber edging to access hex screw). Passband offset requires many turns of the knob to shift the setting significantly with AM-mode or synchronous (SAM) reception, although not in other modes. Automatic notch filter can't be tuned manually in CW and RTTY reception modes, so the notch automatically impacts the desired signal along with any heterodyne(s). As tested in the revised-hardware version to improve front-end selectivity, sensitivity poor on mediumwave AM and even worse on longwave. Signal-strength indicator's format, using numeric decibels and a short displayed scale, generally disliked by panelists. Noise reduction not adjustable, and solitary setting sometimes reduces intelligibility. Audio control in original version required more than three turns from soft to loud, although revised version uses the traditional single turn; however, as a result the audio scale display shows 25 percent when the control is set to 100 percent. Unusual 9-pin-to-9-pin serial cable needed to download software not included with receiver. A number of commonly used controls are on the left, inconvenient for northpaws. No IF output. User reports in the past have told of display illumination flickering, then failing, necessitating a $55 factory repair; display board is made in China. Tilt bail lacks protective rubber sheathing. Neither speaker wire can connect to ground, so an external speaker should not have a grounded cabinet (the 307B is appropriate in this regard).

☞ Two of our three units tested suffered from periodic freezing, or lockup, and occasional peculiar display readings. All were resolved by turning the receiver off, then back on again after no more than ten minutes, but re-downloading the firmware made no difference. The manufacturer insists these are sample defects, although to us it appears to have the earmarks of an inherent, but remediable, firmware cause.

Verdict: Although the Ten-Tec RX-350 has been improved for 2006, some issues remain which keep it from achieving the level of performance found on, say, the AOR AR-7030 PLUS. Nonetheless, Ten-Tec's operating system is more user-friendly and flexible than that of the '7030, making the '350 a more appropriate choice for a variety of users.

Changes in Revised Version: A major problem with the production RX-350 was local mediumwave AM stations cross-modulating with other local stations—even world band stations 4 MHz and below. Ten-Tec years ago to resolve this by adding a high-pass filter to attenuate mediumwave and longwave signals, but this improvement didn't materialize until perhaps 2004, and even then it was stealth-like—not even dealers appear to have been informed, and its public discovery was essentially by chance in 2005.

One of the receiver's main shortcomings thankfully has been cleared up, even if not in the most sophisticated and effective of fashions.

Passport's star rating has been adjusted to reflect this upgrade, which is based on what we tested when Ten-Tec added the upgrade to an existing unit some time back.

Availability limited for 2006

✪✪✪✪
Icom IC-R8500A

Price: *IC-R8500A-02 (U.S. version, cellular reception blocked):* discontinued. *ICF-8500A (unblocked):* $1,649.95 for government use or export in the United States. $2,599.00CAD in Canada. £1,149.00 in the United Kingdom. €1,398.00 in Germany. $3,480.00AUD in Australia. *CR-293 frequency stabilizer:* $269.95 in the United States. £89.99 in the United Kingdom. €109.00 in Germany. *External speakers:* Up to three Icom speakers available worldwide, with prices ranging from under $65 to $220 or equivalent. *Aftermarket Sherwood SE-3 Mk III D:* $549.00 in the United States. *Aftermarket BHT DSP noise canceller (www.radio.bhinstrumentation.co.uk/index.html):* under £90 in the United Kingdom.

Pro: Wide-spectrum multimode coverage from 0.1–2000 MHz includes longwave, mediumwave AM, shortwave and scanner frequencies. Physically very rugged, with professional-grade cast-aluminum chassis and impressive computer-type innards. Generally superior ergonomics, with generous-sized front panel having large and well-spaced controls, plus outstanding tuning knob with numerous tuning steps. 1,000 station presets and 100 auto-write presets have handy naming function. Superb weak-signal sensitivity. Pleasant, low-distortion audio aided by audio peak filter. Passband tuning ("IF shift"). Unusually readable LCD.

Tunes and displays in precise 10 Hz increments. Three antenna connections. Clock-timer, combined with record output and recorder-activation jack, make for superior hands-off recording of favorite programs, as well as for feeding a low-power FM transmitter to hear world band around the house.

Con: No longer available to the public in the United States, North Korea and certain other countries, although Canadian mail-order firms have been known to ship the unblocked version to customers in the United States. No synchronous selectable sideband. Bandwidth choices for world band and other AM-mode signals leap from a very narrow 2.7 kHz to a broad 7.1 kHz with nothing between, where something is most needed; third bandwidth is 13.7 kHz, too wide for world band, and no provision is made for a fourth bandwidth filter. Only one single-sideband bandwidth. Unhandy carousel-style bandwidth selection with no permanent indication of which bandwidth is in use. Poor dynamic range, surprising at this price point. Passband tuning ("IF shift") does not work in the AM mode, used by world band and mediumwave AM-band stations. No tunable notch filter. Built-in speaker mediocre. Uses outboard AC adaptor instead of inboard power supply.

☞ Also tested with Sherwood SE-3 Mk III D aftermarket accessory, which proved to be outstanding at adding selectable synchronous sideband. This combo also provides passband tuning in the AM mode which is used by nearly all world band stations. Adding the SE-3 and replacing the widest

Icom's IC-R8500A is no longer available to the American public, but remains on sale elsewhere.

bandwidth with a 4 to 5 kHz bandwidth filter dramatically improve performance on short-wave, mediumwave AM and longwave.

Verdict: The large Icom IC-R8500 is a scanner that happens to cover world band, rather than *vice versa*.

As a standalone world band radio, this Japanese-made wideband receiver makes little sense. Yet, it is well worth considering if you want an all-in-one scanner that also serves as a shortwave receiver.

Change for 2006: The IC-R8500 version available to the public in the United States was blocked by law so it could not receive the 824–849 and 869–894 MHz cellular bands. However, it was discontinued in 2005.

In some other countries the unblocked version continues to be offered, which makes sense given that spread-spectrum and other digital cellular signals are virtually impossible for unauthorized persons to unscramble. Whether Icom will continue manufacturing that unblocked version remains to be seen.

DRM Modifiable

✪✪✪✪
AOR AR5000A+3

Price: *AR5000A+3 (cellular-blocked version) receiver:* $2,499.95 in the United States. *AR5000A+3 (full-coverage version) receiver:* $2,599.95 in the United States. $3,799.00CAD in Canada. £1,799.00 in the United Kingdom. €2,298.00 as available

in Germany. *Collins 6 kHz mechanical filter (recommended):* $99.95 in the United States. £76.00 in the United Kingdom. *SDU-5600 spectrum display unit:* $1,449.95 in the United States. $2,099CAD in Canada. €1,155.00 in Germany.

Pro: Ultra-wide-spectrum multimode coverage from 0.01–3,000 MHz includes longwave, mediumwave AM, shortwave and scanner frequencies. Helpful tuning features include 2,000 station presets in 20 banks of 100 presets each. Narrow bandwidth filter and optional Collins wide filter both have superb skirt selectivity (standard wide filter's skirt selectivity unmeasurable because of limited ultimate rejection). Synchronous selectable and double sideband (*see* Con). Front-end selectivity, image rejection, IF rejection, weak-signal sensitivity, AGC threshold and frequency stability all superior. Exceptionally precise frequency readout to nearest Hertz. Most accurate displayed frequency measurement of any receiver tested to date. Superb circuit shielding results in virtually zero radiated digital "buzz." IF output (*see* Con). DRM modifiable; see www.aoruk.com/drm.htm#ar5000_drm or www.drmrx.org/receiver_mods.html. Automatic Frequency Control (AFC) works on AM-mode, as well as FM, signals. Owner's manual, important because of operating system, unusually helpful.

Con: Synchronous detector loses lock easily, especially if selectable sideband feature in use, greatly detracting from the utility of this high-tech feature. Substandard rejection of unwanted sideband with selectable synchronous sideband. Overall distortion rises when synchronous detector used. Ultimate rejection of "narrow" 2.7 kHz bandwidth filter only 60 dB. Ultimate rejection mediocre (50 dB) with standard 7.6 kHz "wide" bandwidth filter, improves to an uninspiring 60 dB when replaced by optional 6 kHz "wide" Collins mechanical filter. Installation of optional Collins filter requires expertise, patience and special equipment. Poor dynamic range. Cumbersome ergonomics. No passband offset. No tunable notch filter. Needs good external speaker for good audio quality. World Time

Best of the easily found broadband tabletops is AOR's AR5000A +3. Prepare to dig deep.

24-hour clock does not show when frequency displayed. IF output frequency 10.7 MHz instead of standard 455 kHz.

Verdict: Unbeatable in some respects, inferior in others—it comes down to what use you will be putting the radio. The optional 6 kHz Collins filter is strongly recommended, but it should be installed by your dealer at the time of purchase. Although some AOR receivers are engineered and made in the United Kingdom, this model is designed and manufactured in Japan.

✪✪✪✪
Palstar R30C/Sherwood, Palstar R30CC/Sherwood

Price: *Sherwood SE-3 Mk III D:* $549.00 in the United States. *Palstar R30C/CC:* See below.

Pro: SE-3 provides nearly flawless synchronous selectable sideband, reducing adjacent-channel interference while enhancing audio fidelity. Foolproof installation; plugs right into the Palstar's existing IF output.

Con: Buzz occasionally heard during weak signal reception. SE-3 costs roughly as much as a regular Palstar receiver.

Verdict: If you're going to spend $550 to upgrade a $575–650 receiver, you may as well spring for another model.

✪✪✪⅛ ⊘
Palstar R30C, Palstar R30CC

Price: *R30C:* $575.00 in the United States. $799.00CAD in Canada. *R30CC:* $650.00 in the United States. $869CAD in Canada. *SP30 speaker:* $59.95 in the United States. $89.00CAD in Canada. £59.95 in the United Kingdom.

☞ We tested the CC, but not the C version. The C uses a MuRata filter in the wide position and a Collins mechanical filter in the narrow setting. That same narrow Collins filter is used in the CC version, but there's also a Collins filter in the wide position.

Pro: Generally good dynamic range. Overall distortion averages 0.5 percent, superb, in

VW Beetle: The Palstar R30C and R30CC offer simplicity that appeals to folks weary of ten-thumbs operation and scrambled microprocessors.

single-sideband mode (in AM mode, averages 2.9 percent, good, at 60% modulation and 4.4 percent, fair, at 95% modulation) (*see* Con, *R30CC*). Every other performance variable measures either good or excellent in Passport's lab, and birdies are virtually absent. Excellent AGC performance with AM-mode and single-sideband signals. Robust physical construction of cabinet and related hardware. Microprocessor section well shielded to minimize radiation of digital "buzz." Features include selectable slow/fast AGC decay (*see* Con), 20–100 Hz/100–500 Hz VRIT (slow/fast variable-rate incremental tuning) knob, 0.5 MHz slew and 455 kHz IF output. One hundred non-volatile station presets, using a generally well-thought-out scheme (*see* Con); they store frequency, bandwidth, mode, AGC setting and attenuator setting; also, presets displayed by channel number or frequency. Excellent illuminated analog signal-strength meter reads in useful S1–9/+60 dB standard and is reasonably accurate (*see* Con). LCD and signal-strength indicator illumination can be switched off. Also operates from ten firmly secured "AA" internal batteries (*see* Con). Lightweight and small (*see* Con). Good AM-mode sensitivity within longwave and mediumwave AM bands. Audio line output has suitable level and is properly located on back panel. Self-resetting circuit breaker for outboard power (e.g., AC adaptor); fuse used with internal batteries and comes with spare fuses. Tilt bail quite useful (*see* Con). Optional AA30A and AM-30 active antennas, evaluated elsewhere in this Passport Reports. *R30C:* Pleasant audio quality with wide (7.7 kHz) bandwidth (*see* Con). *R30CC:* Virtually superb skirt selectivity (1:1.4 wide and 1:1.5 narrow) and ultimate rejection (90 dB); bandwidths measure 6.3 kHz and 2.6 kHz, using Collins mechanical filters. Adjacent-channel 5 kHz heterodyne whistles largely absent with wide bandwidth (see Con, R30CC). Audio quality pleasant with wide bandwidth (see Con).

Con: No keypad for direct frequency entry, not even as an outboard mouse-type option; only some of the very cheapest of portables now don't come with or offer a keypad. No 5 kHz tuning step choice to aid in bandscanning. Lacks control to hop from one world band segment to another; instead, uses 0.5 MHz fast-slew increments. No synchronous selectable sideband without pricey Sherwood SE-3 Mk III D aftermarket accessory (see preceding review). ECSS tuning can be up to 10 Hz out of phase because of 20 Hz minimum tuning increment. Mechanical tuning encoder play gives tuning knob sloppy feel, making precise ECSS tuning difficult; an optical encoder might have helped avoided this while adding to reliability. Lightweight plastic tuning knob lacks mass to provide good tuning feel. Lacks features found in top-gun receivers, such as tunable notch filter, noise blanker, passband tuning and adjustable RF gain. Recovered audio fine with most signals, but with truly weak signals is not of the DX caliber found with top-gun receivers. No visual indication of which bandwidth is being used. No tone controls. Small identical front-panel buttons, including the MEM button which if accidentally pressed can erase a preset. Station presets not as intuitive or easy to select as with various other models; lacks frequency information on existing presets during memory storage. No AGC off. No RF gain control. Uses AC adaptor instead of built-in power supply. High battery consumption. Batteries frustratingly difficult to install, requiring partial disassembly of the receiver and care not to damage speaker connections or confuse polarities. Receiver's lightness and tilt bail's lack of rubber sheathing allow it to slide around, especially when tuning knob pushed to change VRIT increments; the added weight of batteries helps slightly. Unsheathed tilt bail digs into some surfaces. Mono headphone jack produces output in only one ear of stereo 'phones (remedied by user-purchased mono-to-stereo adaptor). Signal-strength meter illumination dims when volume turned high with AM-mode signals; LCD illumination unaffected. Three bulbs used for illumination are soldered into place, making replacement difficult, although they should last a very long time. R30C: Wide bandwidth slightly broad for a model lacking synchronous selectable sideband, often allowing adjacent-channel (5 kHz) heterodyne whistles to be heard; largely remedied by detuning 1–2 kHz, which unlike with some receivers doesn't significantly increase distortion. R30CC: Intermittent microphonics in AM mode when using narrow bandwidth and internal speaker. Audio frequency response with wide filter makes for slightly muffled audio as compared with R30C; largely remedied by detuning 1–2 kHz, which unlike with some receivers doesn't significantly increase distortion.

☞ Works best when grounded.

Verdict: Although the Ohio-made Palstar R30C/CC receivers are conspicuously lacking in tuning and performance features, what they set out to do, they tend to do to a high standard. If you can abide the convoluted battery installation procedure and don't mind having to add an outboard antenna, either version can work as a field portable.

Nevertheless, these receivers lack a distinct identity. Although audio is fairly pleasant, especially in the original and discontinued basic version, there isn't synchronous selectable sideband that's needed to make it a premium listener's radio. Audio quality in the current versions' narrow setting tend to sound muffled.

The lack of operating features is especially disappointing—not even a keypad, something routinely found on portables costing a fraction as much. And the lack of signal-tweaking features, along with pedestrian weak-signal recovered audio, preclude serious DX use.

Yet, as Saab likes to point out, not everybody fits neatly into standard categories. One size doesn't fit all, and to that end the R30C/CC's straightforward concept and physical robustness make it a clear alternative.

✪✪✪¾ *C* 📄
Yaesu FRG-100 (as available)

Price: *FRG-100:* $599.95 in the United States. $899.00CAD in Canada. £449.00 in the United Kingdom. *TCXO-4 frequency stabilizer:* $99.00 in the United States. £45.00 in the United Kingdom. *Universal Radio SWL Remote and RCU-1400 remote control:* $89.90 in the United States.

Pro: Commendable performance in many respects. Includes three bandwidths, a noise blanker, selectable AGC, two attenuators, the ability to select 16 pre-programmed world band segments, two clocks, on-off timers, 52 tunable station presets that store frequency and mode data, a variety of scanning schemes and an all-mode squelch.

Con: No factory-provided keypad for direct frequency entry, although a two-part user-installable aftermarket infrared keypad system is available in most countries by post from an American source (Universal Radio);

The slow-selling Yaesu FRG-100 has been discontinued for years, but continues to be available.

it also allows for remote control of a variety of receiver functions, although not volume. No synchronous selectable sideband. Lacks features found in "top-gun" receivers: passband tuning, notch filter, adjustable RF gain. Simple controls and display, combined with complex functions, can make certain operations confusing. Dynamic range only fair. Uses AC adaptor instead of built-in power supply.

Verdict: Every year we think the FRG-100 will cease to be available, yet year after year it soldiers on. Why? It is an incredibly slow seller. Given this, it could well continue to be available for another year or so.

BUILD YOUR OWN

Most shortwave kits are novelties or regenerative radios. But there is one exception: Ten-Tec's small 1254 world band radio, $195. Parts quality for this superheterodyne appears to be excellent, while assembly runs at least 24 hours. It has 15 station presets, but lacks keypad, signal-strength indicator, synchronous selectable sideband, tilt bail, LSB/USB settings and adjustable AGC. Tuning increments are 500 Hz for single sideband and 5 kHz for AM-mode, plus there is an analog clarifier for tweaking between increments.

Phase noise, front-end selectivity, and longwave and mediumwave AM sensitivity are poor. Bandwidth is a respectable 5.6 kHz, and there is worthy ultimate rejection, image rejection, world band sensitivity, blocking, AGC threshold and frequency stability. Dynamic range and first IF rejection are fair, while overall distortion is good—with an external speaker, audio is pleasant.

The Ten-Tec 1254 is a fun weekend project, and the manufacturer's track record for hand-holding means that when you're through the radio should really work.

The spirit of Heathkit lives on in the Ten-Tec 1254. A fun project, and it really works.

In the tradition of the Yaesu FRG-7 that started it all, this minimalist model is sparse on factory-provided features. Yet, the FRG-100 succeeds in delivering worthy performance within an attractive price class.

📖 An *RDI WHITE PAPER* is available for this model.

★★★ ✪
Yaesu VR-5000

Price: *VR-5000 Receiver, including single-voltage AC adaptor:* $599.95 in the United States. $899.00CAD or more in Canada. £579.00 in the United Kingdom. €649.00 in Germany. $1,399.00AUD in Australia. *DSP-1 digital notch, bandpass and noise reduction unit:* $119.95 in the United States. $199.00CAD in Canada. £94.95 in the United Kingdom. €98.00 in Germany. *DVS-4 16-second digital audio recorder:* $44.95 in the United States. $80.00CAD in Canada. £29.95 in the United Kingdom. €39.00 in Germany. *FVS-1A voice synthesizer (as available):* $44.95 in the United States. $75.00CAD in Canada. £39.95 in the United Kingdom. €55.00 in Germany. *RadioShack 22-504 aftermarket 120V AC>13.8V DC power supply:* $39.99 in the United States.

Pro: Unusually wide frequency coverage, 100 kHz through 2.6 GHz (U.S. version omits cellular frequencies 869–894 MHz). Two thousand alphanumeric-displayed station presets, which can be linked to any of up to 100 groupings of presets. Up to 50 programmable start/stop search ranges. Large and potentially useful "band scope" spectrum display (*see* Con). Bandwidths have superb skirt selectivity, with shape factors between 1:1.3 and 1:1.4. Wide AM bandwidth (17.2 kHz) allows local mediumwave AM stations to be received with superior fidelity (*see* Con). Flexible software settings provide a high degree of control over selected parameters. Sophisticated scanning choices, although they are of limited use because of false signals generated by receiver's inadequate dynamic range (*see* Con). Dual-receive function, with sub-receiver circuitry feeding "band scope" spectrum display; when display not in use, two signals may be monitored simultaneously, provided they are within 20 MHz of each other. Sensitivity to weak signals excellent-to-superb within shortwave spectrum, although combined with receiver's inadequate dynamic range this tends to cause overloading when a worthy antenna is used (*see* Con). Appears to be robustly constructed. External spectrum display, fed by receiver's 10.7 MHz IF output, can perform very well for narrow-parameter scans (*see* Con). Two 24-hour clocks, both of which are shown except when spectrum display mode is in use; one clock tied into an elementary map display and database of time in a wide choice of world cities. On-off timer allows for up to 48 automatic events. Sleep-delay/alarm timers. Lightweight and compact. Multi-level display dimmer. Optional DSP unit includes adjustable notch filtering, a bandpass feature and noise reduction (*see* Con). Tone control. Built-in "CAT" computer control interface (*see* Con). Control and memory backup/management software available from www.g4hfq.co.uk.

Con: Exceptionally poor dynamic range (49 dB at 5 kHz separation, 64 dB at 20 kHz) and IF/image rejection (as low as 30 dB) for a tabletop model; for listeners in such high-signal parts of the world as Europe, North Africa and eastern North America, this shortcoming all but cripples reception of shortwave signals unless a very modest antenna is used; the degree to which VHF-UHF is degraded depends *inter alia* upon the extent of powerful transmissions in the

Yaesu's VR-5000 offers wide coverage at a narrow price. Unsurprisingly, world band performance falls woefully short.

vicinity of the receiver. No synchronous selectable sideband, a major drawback for world band and mediumwave AM listening, but not for shortwave utility/ham, VHF or UHF reception. Has only one single-side-band bandwidth, a relatively broad 4.0 kHz. Wide AM bandwidth (17.2 kHz) of no use for shortwave reception. For world band listening, the middle (8.7 kHz) AM bandwidth lets through adjacent-channel 5 kHz heterodyne, while narrow bandwidth (consistently 3.9 kHz, not the 4.0 kHz of the SSB bandwidth) produces muffled audio. Line output level low. Audio distorts at higher volume settings. Limited bass response. Audio hissy, especially noticeable with a good outboard speaker. DSP-1 option a mediocre overall performer and adds distortion. Phase noise measures 94 dBc, poor. AGC threshold measures 11 microvolts, poor. No adjustment of AGC decay. Single-sideband AGC decay too slow. Most recent sample's (firmware v1u.17) tuning encoder sometimes has rotational delay that requires three clicks instead of one to commence down-frequency tuning when reversing direction from clockwise to counterclockwise. Mediocre tuning-knob feel. Signal-strength indicator has only five levels and overreads; an alternative software-selectable signal-strength indicator—not easy to get in and out of—has no markings other than a single reference level. Built-in spectrum display's dynamic range only 20 dB (–80 to –100 dBm), with a very slow scan rate. Single-sideband frequency readout of latest sample more accurate, but after warmup LSB is still 70 Hz and USB 100 Hz off. Long learning curve: Thirty buttons (often densely spaced, lilliputian and multifunction)—along with carouseling mode/tune-step selection and a menu-driven command scheme—combine to produce ergonomics that are not intuitive. Only one low-impedance antenna connector, inadequate for a wideband device that calls for multiple antennas. Longwave sensitivity mediocre. Clocks don't display seconds numerically. Marginal display contrast. Although four LEDs used for backlighting, the result is unevenly distributed. Uses AC adaptor instead of built-in power supply; adaptor and receiver

both tend to run warm. Repeated micro-processor lockups, sometimes displayed as "*ERROR* LOW VOLTAGE," even though the receiver now comes with a 7.2V NiCd battery pack to help prevent this; unplugging set for ten minutes resolves problem until it occurs again, but the only permanent solution appears to be replacing the receiver's AC adaptor with a properly bypassed and regulated non-switching AC adaptor/DC power supply of at least one ampere that produces no less than 13.5V DC—certainly no less than 13.2V DC—and no more than 13.8V DC (we use a lab power supply, but in North America the RadioShack 22-504 appears promising). Even with aforementioned battery, clock has to be reset if power fails. Squelch doesn't function through audio line output (for recording, etc.). Line output gain is somewhat low. Sub-receiver doesn't feed line output. Computer interface lacks viable command structure, limiting usefulness. Tilt feet have inadequate rise. Owner's manual (0104q-DY) doesn't cover all receiver functions, so user has to learn much by trial and error. *United States:* Based on our recent experiences, customer support appears to be indifferent.

Verdict: With existing technology, DC-to-daylight receivers which provide excellent shortwave performance are costly to produce, and thus expensive.

The relatively affordable wideband Yaesu VR-5000 tries to overcome this. This Japanese-made model acts as a VHF/UHF scanner as well as a shortwave receiver, but falls woefully shy for world band reception in strong-signal parts of the world. Elsewhere, it fares better on shortwave, especially if a modest antenna is used. VHF/UHF performance depends on the number and strength of local transmitters.

DRM Modifiable

★★★ ✪
AKD Target HF-3M, NASA HF-4/HF-4E/S, SI-TEX NAV-FAX 200

Price: *HF-3M/HF-4/HF-4E:* £149.95 in the United Kingdom. *HF-4E/S:* £159.95 in the United Kingdom. €298.00 in Germany. *PA30*

Priced more like a portable is the Target HF-3M, sold in North America as the SI-TEX NAV-FAX 200.

antenna: €45.50 in Germany. *NAV-FAX 200 (www.si-tex.com):* $399.00 in the United States. *SI-TEX ACNF 120V AC adaptor:* $19.95 in the United States.

Pro: Superior rejection of images. High third-order intercept point for superior strong-signal handling capability. Bandwidths have superb ultimate rejection. *HF-4/HF-4E/HF-4E/S:* Two AM-mode bandwidths. DRM modifiable (www.drmrx. org/receiver_mods.html). Illuminated LCD. *Except NAV-FAX 200:* Comes with DOS software for weatherfax ("WEFAX") reception using a PC; software upgrade may be in the offing. *NAV-FAX 200:* Comes with Mscan Meteo Pro Lite software (www.mscan.com) for WEFAX, RTTY and NAVTEX reception using a PC with Windows XP or earlier. Comes with wire antenna and audio patch cable. Two-year warranty, with repair facility in Florida.

Con: No keypad, and variable-rate tuning knob is difficult to control. Broad skirt selectivity. Single-sideband bandwidth relatively wide. Volume control fussy to adjust. Synthesizer tunes in relatively coarse 1 kHz increments, supplemented by an analog fine-tuning "clarifier" control. Only ten station presets. Single sideband requires both tuning controls to be adjusted. No synchronous selectable sideband, notch filter or passband tuning. Frequency readout off by 2 kHz in single-sideband mode. Uses AC adaptor instead of built-in power supply. No clock, timer or sleep-delay feature. *HF3M:* Bandwidths not selectable independent of mode. Only AM-mode bandwidth functions for world band reception. LCD not illuminated. *Except NAV-FAX 200:* Apparently not available outside United Kingdom.

Verdict: Pleasant world band performance at an affordable price, although numerous features are absent and operation is more frustrating than on many other models. Logical for yachting.

The PASSPORT *tabletop-model review team consists of Lawrence Magne and David Zantow, with George Zeller; also, David Crystal, George Heidelman, Tony Jones, Chuck Rippel and David Walcutt, along with Craig Tyson. Laboratory measurements by J. Robert Sherwood.*

COMING UP: AOR TO OFFER DSP MODEL?

AOR (UK) is seriously contemplating the engineering and eventual manufacture of a 0.x-30 MHz DSP tabletop receiver. Should it materialize, release is expected to be "some way off," according to the manufacturer—years, although at this embryonic juncture nobody seems to have a feel for just how many years.

Assuming DRM becomes truly viable, the proposed receiver is scheduled to include a 12 kHz IF output to aid in deciphering DRM. Should the contemplated receiver get approved for development, the engineering team would likely consist of veteran John Thorpe working in concert with other engineers in the United Kingdom.

AOR states that the existing AR7030 series is scheduled to stay in production for a considerable period of time—at least until the release of a new model, and possibly beyond.

Professional Receivers for 2006

Tired of the same old?
Tickle these.

Professional receivers are for intelligence, military and commercial operations. While only a few are engineered for shortwave and world band, these are unbeatable for flushing out tough signals. They also eavesdrop magnificently on military, civilian and espionage utility signals.

Elite professional receivers also find their way into homes with Porsches and yachts, but for more than big-bucks status. After all, anybody can drive a Meisterwagen, but who can master a receiver designed for snooping on terrorists and rogue states?

Yet, most civilian owners are simply exacting individuals who keep a low profile. Nearly all are dedicated radio aficionados, while others want the ultimate "information central" for when the unthinkable takes place. Some even purchase decoding accessories and software to interface with their supersets.

What about espionage operatives? While intelligence agencies are prime users of such receivers at official sites, portables are *de rigueur* to enhance deniability in the field. Some, enthusiastic about their work, keep sophisticated radio gear at home but almost never while on the outside.

Three Flavors

There are three key categories of professional receivers: easy for human operation, complex for human operation and no human operation.

The first is ideal for personnel with minimal training. After all, if an AWACS radioman is disabled, uncomplicated operation allows comrades to take over. But operational simplicity also means performance compromises, so these receivers are not covered here.

The second category goes to the other extreme, with "no holds barred" features and performance. This type is for skilled operators and is included in PASSPORT REPORTS.

Simplest are "black box" professional receivers with virtually no controls. These operate remotely or from computers, often at official surveillance facilities. We don't cover these, as some of the best are sold only to U.S. Federal agencies or NATO organizations. Indeed, some are so hush-hush that even manufacturers' names are aliases.

Nevertheless, there is a small but enthusiastic civilian market for consumer-grade versions. These are evaluated elsewhere in PASSPORT REPORTS.

Two Available Models

Professional receivers are physically and electrically robust, with resistance to hostile environments and rough handling. Additionally, components are consistent so board swapping and other field repairs can be done easily and without compromising performance.

The two professional models in PASSPORT REPORTS replace the erstwhile consumer-grade Icom IC-R71A analyzed in a still-available Radio Database International White Paper. Years ago, the tabletop 'R71A was used by the U.S. National Security Agency for offshore surveillance *i.a.* near the Korean Peninsula, but it was not manufactured to NATO spec and had other limitations. Thankfully, models designed to replace it are as good as it gets for shortwave DXing.

Professional receivers tested by PASSPORT continue to be officially classified as "NLR"—no license required—so they're not subject to U.S. Government export controls. Still, there may be a wait. If you want one as a gift, check out availability well in advance.

Find major updates to the 2006 Passport Reports at www.passband.com.

Digital Reception

One tested model, from Ten-Tec, is engineered to receive DRM digital world band broadcasts. While the Watkins-Johnson equivalent isn't DRM ready, this appears to be only because nobody has yet made public a modification procedure.

DRM requires that the receiver interface with a PC using separately purchased DRM software (www.drmrx.org).

Good Antenna a "Must"

Top-rated, properly erected antennas are a "must" for professional receivers. For test findings and installation tips, read the Radio Database International White Paper, *Evaluation of Popular Outdoor Antennas.* There are also antenna reviews in PASSPORT REPORTS.

If reception at your location is disrupted by nearby electrical noise even with a suitable antenna, a better receiver might be a waste of money. Before buying, try eliminating the source of noise or repositioning your antenna. If all else fails, try a Wellbrook active antenna.

Volts with Jolts

Professional receivers are rugged and typically include MOV surge protection. Nevertheless, it helps to plug a serious radio into a non-MOV surge arrestor, such as Zero-Surge (www.zerosurge.com) and Brick Wall (www.brickwall.com).

Any receiver's outdoor antenna should be fed through a static protector. This is especially so with the Watkins-Johnson WJ-8711A when it's not equipped with the 8711/PRE option. Even then, it's wise to disconnect outdoor antennas whenever a thunderstorm threatens.

DSP Audio

Most professional and a few consumer-grade receivers use DSP (digital signal processing) audio. In principle, there is no reason DSP audio quality can't equal that of conventional models. But a multi-stage DSP receiver is complex, requiring gobs of pro-

cessing horsepower. Today's DSP receivers fall a bit short, one result being that static crashes tend to sound harsher.

Helping offset this is recoverable audio, which with tough DX signals tends to be slightly better with DSP professional receivers. This is why these are not strangers to "DXpeditions," where the most stubborn of radio signals are sought out.

For world band, the Sherwood SE-3 fidelity-enhancing accessory is nearly a "must" for current and discontinued professional receivers. While it doesn't fundamentally resolve the DSP audio issue, it helps significantly. It also provides high-quality synchronous selectable sideband, a major plus. Downsides are cost, operating complexity and a BFO not as stable as those on some professional receivers.

Tips for Using this Section

Professional receivers are listed in order of suitability for listening to difficult-to-hear world band stations. Important secondary consideration is given to audio fidelity, ergonomics and reception of utility signals. Build quality is superior unless otherwise indicated. Selling prices, street, are as of when we go to press, and include European VAT and Australian GST where applicable.

Unless otherwise stated, all professional models have the following characteristics. Refer to PASSPORT's glossary to understand specialized terms.

- Digital signal processing, including digital frequency synthesis and display.
- Full coverage of at least the 5-29999 kHz VLF/LF/MF/HF portions of the radio spectrum, encompassing all the long-wave, mediumwave AM and shortwave portions—including all world band frequencies—but no coverage of the standard FM broadcast band (87.5-108 MHz).
- A wide variety of helpful tuning features, including tuning and frequency display in 1 Hz increments.
- Synchronous selectable sideband via high-rejection IF filtering (not lower-rejection phasing), which greatly reduces

adjacent-channel interference and fading distortion. On some models this is referred to as "SAM" (synchronous AM).

☞ **ECSS:** Professional models tune to the nearest 1 Hz, allowing the user to use the receiver's single-sideband circuitry to manually phase its BFO (internally generated carrier) with the station's transmitted carrier. Called "ECSS" (exalted-carrier, selectable-sideband) tuning, this can be used with AM-mode signals in lieu of synchronous selectable sideband. However, in addition to the relative inconvenience of this technique, unlike synchronous detection, which rephases continually and essentially perfectly, ECSS is always slightly out of phase. This causes at least some degree of harmonic distortion to music and speech, while tuning to the nearest Hertz can generate slow-sweep fading (for this reason, high-pass audio filtering or mis-phasing by two or three Hertz may provide better results).

- Proper demodulation of modes used by non world band—utility and amateur—shortwave signals. These modes include single sideband (LSB/USB and sometimes ISB) and CW ("Morse code"); also, with suitable ancillary devices, radioteletype (RTTY), frequency shift key (FSK) and radiofax (FAX).
- Meaningful signal-strength indication.
- Illuminated display.
- Superior build quality, robustness and sample-to-sample consistency as compared to consumer-grade tabletop receivers.
- Audio output for recording or low-power FM retransmission to hear world band around your domicile.

What PASSPORT's Rating Symbols Mean

Star ratings: ✪✪✪✪✪ is best. Stars reflect overall performance and meaningful features, plus to some extent ergonomics and perceived build quality. Price, appearance, country of manufacture and the like are not taken into account. With professional models there is a strong emphasis on the ability to flush out tough, hard-to-hear signals, as this is usually the main reason these sets are chosen by world band enthusiasts. Nevertheless, to facilitate comparison professional receiver rating standards are very similar to those used for the tabletop, portatop and portable models reviewed elsewhere in this PASSPORT.

Passport's Choice. La crème de la crème. Our test team's personal picks of the litter—models we would buy or have bought for our personal use. Unlike star ratings, these choices are unapologetically subjective.

✪✪✪✪✪ *Passport's Choice*
Watkins-Johnson WJ-8711A

Price (receiver, factory options; single-quantity prices change often): *WJ-8711A:* $5,500.00 plus shipping worldwide. *871Y/SEU DSP Speech Enhancement Unit:* $1,200.00. *8711/PRE Sub-Octave Preselector:* $1,100.00. *871Y/DSO1 Digital Signal Output Unit:* $1,150.00.

Price (aftermarket options): *Hammond RCBS1900517BK1 steel cabinet and 1421A mounting screws and cup washers:* $120-140 in the United States from manufacturer

The Watkins-Johnson WJ-8711A is about as good as it gets, and is priced accordingly.

(www.hammondmfg.com/rackrcbs.htm) or Newark Electronics (www.newark.com). *Sherwood SE-3 MK III accessory:* $549.00 plus shipping worldwide.

Pro: Proven robust. BITE diagnostics and physical layout allows technically qualified users to make most repairs on-site. Users can upgrade receiver performance over time by EPROM replacement. Exceptional overall performance. Unsurpassed reception of feeble world band DX signals, especially when mated to the Sherwood SE-3 synchronous selectable sideband device and the WJ-871Y/SEU noise-reduction unit (*see* Con). Unusually effective "ECSS" reception, tuning AM-mode signals as though they were single sideband. Superb reception of

non-AM mode "utility" stations. Generally superior audio quality when coupled to the Sherwood SE-3 fidelity-enhancing accessory, the W-J speech enhancement unit and a worthy external speaker (*see* Con). Unparalleled bandwidth flexibility, with no less than 66 outstandingly high-quality bandwidths. Trimmer on back panel allows frequency readout to be user-aligned against a known frequency standard, such as WWV/WWVH or a laboratory device. Extraordinary operational flexibility—virtually every receiver parameter is adjustable. One hundred station presets. Synchronous detection, called "SAM" (synchronous AM), reduces selective-fading distortion with world band, medium-wave AM and longwave signals, and works even on very narrow voice bandwidths

NUMBERS: PROFESSIONAL RECEIVERS

	Watkins-Johnson WJ-8711A	Ten-Tec RX-340
Max. WB Sensitivity/Noise Floor	0.13 μV, Ⓢ/–136 dBm, Ⓔ	0.17 μV, Ⓢ/–130 dBm, Ⓔ[1]
Blocking	123 dB, Ⓖ	109 dB, Ⓕ
Shape Factors, voice BWs	1:1.21–1:1.26, Ⓢ	1:1.15–1:1.33, Ⓢ
Ultimate Rejection	>80 dB, Ⓔ	70 dB, Ⓖ
Front-End Selectivity	Ⓕ/Ⓔ[2]	Ⓔ
Image Rejection	80 dB, Ⓔ	>100 dB, Ⓢ
First IF Rejection	— [3]	>100 dB, Ⓢ
Dynamic Range/IP3 (5 kHz)	74 dB, Ⓖ/–18 dBm, Ⓔ	55 dB, Ⓕ/–39 dBm, Ⓕ
Dynamic Range/IP3 (20 kHz)	99 dB, Ⓢ/+20 dBm, Ⓢ	86 dB, Ⓖ/+7 dBm, Ⓔ
Phase Noise	115 dBc, Ⓖ	113 dBc, Ⓖ
AGC Threshold	0.1 μV, Ⓟ	0.3 μV, Ⓖ[4]
Overall Distortion, sync	8.2%, Ⓟ	2.6%, Ⓖ
Stability	5 Hz, Ⓢ	5 Hz, Ⓢ
Notch filter depth	58 dB, Ⓢ	58 dB, Ⓢ

IBS Lab Ratings: Ⓢ Superb   Ⓔ Excellent   Ⓖ Good   Ⓕ Fair   Ⓟ Poor

(1) Preamp on. With preamp off, 0.55 μV, Ⓖ/–122 dBm, Ⓖ.
(2) Ⓕ standard/Ⓔ with optional preselector.
(3) Adequate, but could not measure precisely.
(4) Preamp on. With preamp off, 1.3 μV, Ⓔ

(*see* Con). Rock stable. Built-in preamplifier. Tunable notch filter. Effective noise blanking. Highly adjustable scanning of both frequency ranges and station presets. Easy-to-read displays. Large tuning knob. Unusually effective mediumwave AM performance. Can be fully and effectively computer and remotely controlled. Passband shift (*see* Con). Numerous outputs for data collection from received signals, as well as ancillary hardware; includes 455 kHz IF output, which makes for instant installation of Sherwood SE-3 accessory and balanced line outputs (connect to balanced hookup to minimize radiation of digital "buzz"). Remote control and dial-up data collection; Windows control software available from manufacturer. Among the most likely of all world band receivers tested to be able to be retrofitted for eventual reception of digital world band broadcasts. Inboard AC power supply, which runs unusually cool, senses incoming current and automatically adjusts to anything from 90-264 VAC, 47-440 Hz—a plus during brownouts or with line voltage or frequency swings. Superior-quality factory service (*see* Con). Comprehensive and well-written operating manual, packed with technical information and schematic diagrams. Hammond aftermarket cabinet is exceptionally robust.

Con: Static crashes and modulation-splash interference sound noticeably harsher than on analog receivers, although this has been improved in latest operating software. Synchronous detection not sideband-selectable, so it can't reduce adjacent-channel interference (remediable by Sherwood SE-3). Basic receiver has mediocre audio in AM mode; "ECSS" tuning or synchronous detection, along with the speech enhancement unit (W1 noise-reduction setting), required to alleviate this. Some clipping distortion in the single-sideband mode. Complex to operate to full advantage. Circuitry puts out a high degree of digital "buzz", relying for the most part on the panels for electrical shielding; one consequence is that various versions emanate digital "buzz" through the non-standard rear-panel audio terminals, as well as through the signal-strength meter and front- panel headphone jack—this problem is lessened when the Sherwood SE-3 is used. Antennas with shielded (e.g., coaxial) feedlines are less likely to pick up receiver-generated digital "buzz." Passband shift operates only in CW mode. Jekyll-and-Hyde ergonomics: sometimes wonderful, sometimes awful. Front-panel rack "ears" protrude, with the right "ear" getting in the way of the tuning knob; fortunately, these are easily removed. Mediocre front-end selectivity, remediable by 8711/PRE option (with minor 2.5 dB insertion loss); e.g. for those living near mediumwave AM transmitters. 871Y/SEU option reduces audio gain and is extremely difficult to install; best to have all options factory-installed. Signal-strength indicator's gradations in dBm only. No DC power input. Keypad lettering wears off with use; replacement keys available at under $8 each. Each receiver is built on order (David Shane at 1-800/954-3577), so it can take up to four months for delivery. Factory service can take as much as two months. Cabinet extra, available from Hammond and Premiere. Plastic feet have no front elevation and allow receiver to slide around. Available only through U.S. manufacturer, DRS Technologies (www.drs.com); receiver and factory options have been subjected to a number of price increases since 2000.

Verdict: The American-made WJ-8711A is, by a skosh, the ultimate machine for down-and-dirty world band DXing when money is no object.

Had there not been digital "buzz," inexcusable at this price—and had there been better audio quality, a tone control, passband shift and synchronous selectable sideband—the '8711A would have been even better, especially for program listening. Fortunately, the Sherwood SE-3 accessory remedies virtually all these problems and improves DX reception, to boot; W-J's optional 871Y/SEU complements, rather than competes with, the SE-3 for improving recovered audio.

Overall, the WJ-8711A DSP, properly configured, is as good as it gets. It is exceptionally well-suited to demanding connoisseurs with the appropriate financial wherewithal—provided they seek an extreme degree of manual receiver control.

Retested for 2006
DRM Ready
✪✪✪✪✪ *Passport's Choice*
Ten-Tec RX-340

Price: $3,950.00 in the United States. £3,299.00 in the United Kingdom. $7,650AUD in Australia. *Hammond RCBS1900513GY2 or RCBS1900513BK1 13" deep cabinet (www.hammondmfg.com/rack-rcbs.htm):* $99.95 in the United States. *Ten-Tec #307G (gray) external speaker:* $98.00 in the United States. *Ten-Tec #307B (black) external speaker:* £89.00 in the United Kingdom. *Sherwood SE-3 MK III accessory:* $549.00 plus shipping worldwide.

Pro: Appears to be robust (*see* Con). BITE diagnostics and physical layout allows technically qualified users to make most repairs on-site. Users can upgrade receiver performance over time by replacing one or another of three socketed EPROM chips (currently v1.10A). Superb overall performance, including unsurpassed readability of feeble world band DX signals, especially when mated to the Sherwood SE-3 device; in particular, superlative image and IF rejection, both >100 dB. Few birdies. Audio quality usually worthy when receiver coupled to the Sherwood SE-3 accessory and a good external speaker. Average overall distortion in single-sideband mode a breathtakingly low 0.2 percent; in other modes, under 2.7 percent. Exceptional bandwidth flexibility, with no less than 57 outstandingly high-quality bandwidths having shape factors of 1:1.33 or better; bandwidth distribution exceptionally good for world band listening and DXing, along with other activities (*see* Con). Receives digital (DRM) world band broadcasts by connecting it to a PC using DRM software purchased separately; *see* www.tentec.com/TT340DRM.htm. Tunes and displays accurately in ultra-precise 1 Hz increments. Extraordinary operational flexibility—virtually every receiver parameter is adjustable; for example, the AGC's various time constants have 118 million possible combinations, plus pushbutton AGC "DUMP" to temporarily deactivate AGC (*see* Con). Worthy front-panel ergonomics, valuable

given the exceptional degree of manual operation; includes easy-to-read displays (*see* Con). Also, large, properly weighted rubber-track tuning knob with fixed dimple and Oak Grigsby optical encoder provide superior tuning feel and reliability; tuning knob tension user-adjustable for personalized feel. Attractive front panel. Two hundred station presets, 201 including the scratchpad. Synchronous selectable sideband, called "SAM" (synchronous AM), reduces selective-fading distortion, as well as diminishes or eliminates adjacent-channel interference, with world band, mediumwave AM and longwave signals; with earlier software lock was easily lost, but from v1.10A it now holds lock acceptably (*see* Con). Built-in half-octave preselector comes standard. Built-in preamplifier (*see* Con). Adjustable noise blanker, works well in most situations (*see* Con). Stable as Gibraltar, as good as it gets. Tunable DSP notch filter with exceptional depth of 58 dB (*see* Con). Passband shift (passband tuning) works unusually well (*see* Con). Unusually effective "ECSS" reception by tuning AM-mode signals as though they were single sideband. Superb reception of "utility" (non-AM mode) stations using a wide variety of modes and including fast filters for delay-critical digital modes. Highly adjustable scanning of both frequency ranges and station presets. Can be fully and effectively computer and remotely controlled (*see* Con). Numerous outputs for data collection and ancillary hardware, including 455 kHz IF-out for instant hookup of Sherwood SE-3 accessory. Remote control and dial-up data collection. Superb analog signal-strength indicator (*see* Con). Inboard AC power supply senses incoming current and automatically adjusts to anything from 90-264 VAC, 48-440 Hz—a plus during brownouts or with line voltage or frequency swings. Superior control of fluorescent display dimming (*see* Con). Factory repair service is reasonably priced by professional standards, with relatively prompt turnaround. Comprehensive and well-written operating manual, packed with technical information and schematic diagrams.

Con: DSP microprocessor limitations result in poor dynamic range and fair IP3 at 5 kHz

Ten-Tec's RX-340 is superb. It is virtually the equal of Watkins-Johnson's offering, but costs less.

signal spacing. Blocking, phase noise and ultimate rejection all pretty good, but not of professional caliber. Complex to operate to full advantage. Static crashes sound harsher than on analog receivers. Not all bandwidths available in all modes. Spurious signals noted around 6 MHz segment (49 meters) at night at one test location having superb antennas. Synchronous selectable sideband, although improved over early production, doesn't hold lock quite as well as some other models. When 9-10 dB preamplifier turned on, AGC acts on noise unless IF gain reduced by 10 dB. Notch filter does not work in AM, synchronous selectable sideband or ISB modes. Synchronous selectable sideband loses lock relatively easily; e.g., if listening to one sideband and there is a strong signal impacting the other sideband, lock can be momentarily lost. Passband shift tunes only plus or minus 2 kHz and does not work in the ISB or synchronous selectable sideband modes; remediable with Sherwood SE-3. As the receiver comes from the manufacturer, audio quality and the synchronous selectable sideband's lock not all they could be; both profit from Sherwood SE-3 accessory and a good outboard speaker. Occasional "popping" sound, notably when synchronous selectable sideband or ISB in use—DSP overload? No AGC off except by holding down DUMP button. Noise blanker not effective at some test locations; for example, other receivers work better in reducing noise from electric fences. Audio power, especially through headphones, could be greater. With stereo headphones, one channel of headphone audio cuts out near full volume; also, at one position at lower volume. On our unit, occasional minor buzz from internal speaker.

Keypad not in telephone format; rather, uses computer keyboard numeric-keypad layout. Some ergonomic clumsiness when going back and forth between the station presets and VFO tuning; too, "Aux Parameter" and "Memory Scan" knobs touchy to adjust. Signal-strength indicator illuminated less than display. Digital "buzz" from fluorescent display emits from front of receiver, although not elsewhere. Standard serial cable does not work for computer control; instead, connector DB-25 pins have to be custom wired. On a units we tested awhile back, the stick-on decal with front-panel markings peeled loose above the main display, and pushing it back into place didn't help; this was not a problem on earlier units, nor was it a problem on the unit just tested for this edition. No DC power input. Cabinet extra.

Verdict: With an exceptional degree of manual control, the Ten-Tec RX-340, when coupled to fidelity-enhancing hardware, is a superb DSP receiver for those who want no-compromise performance for years to come.

It is technologically advanced, and can interface with a PC to receive digital (DRM) world band broadcasts. The '340 is a sensible value, too—with bells and whistles, it costs considerably less than a fully equipped WJ-8711A.

Findings for 2006: No significant changes were found in our latest unit.

The PASSPORT professional-model review team consists of Tony Jones, Lawrence Magne, Chuck Rippel, David Walcutt, David Zantow and George Zeller. Laboratory measurements by J. Robert Sherwood.

Receivers for PCs

Matchmaker's Delight

It's great to have knobs and keys to dig out signals, but not always. A dedicated core of radio enthusiasts prefer "black boxes" controlled by a PC. Official surveillance organizations, too, as their receivers, like some spooks, rarely interact with people.

As with a good marriage, mating a receiver with a PC allows each to enhance the other. Yet, this synergy can be offset by drawbacks, such as hardware complication and instability. There can also be radio interference from PC monitors, cables and so on. Professional receiving facilities are set up to overcome these challenges, but at home it's a lot tougher.

DRM Digital Reception

"DRM ready" receivers can process Digital Radio Mondiale (DRM) world band and other broadcasts, which are emerging from an advanced "beta zone." These require separately purchased DRM software, and eventually you may also need software updates (www.drmrx.org).

A major advantage of a PC controlled receiver for DRM is that it is already within or connected to a computer. Standalone receivers have to be tethered to a separate PC to process DRM signals.

The Icom IC-PCR1000 can be modified for DRM— see www.drmrx.org/receiver_mods.html. This is one step removed from "DRM ready," but helps ensure that it won't fall behind the technological curve should DRM ultimately succeed.

> **Like marriage, mating receivers with PCs offers synergies and headaches.**

Our tests take place using Windows XP-Pro and XP-Home. If you're using Mac or Linux, check manufacturers' websites for the growing roster of non-Windows software. For long-term ownership remember that once a receiver becomes discontinued it eventually may not work to full advantage with new or revised computer operating systems. This can be overcome by retaining the ability to use legacy OS.

No matter how carefully a PC controlled receiver is tested, its performance depends partly on your computer's configuration. This increases the odds that you will encounter an unwelcome surprise, so it's always best to purchase on a returnable basis.

DRM Ready
✪✪✪✪⅜ *Passport's Choice*
WiNRADiO G303i, WiNRADiO G303i-PD/P, WiNRADiO G303e, WiNRADiO G303e-PD/P

Price: *G303i:* $499.95 in the United States. $699.00CAD in Canada. £329.95 i n the United Kingdom. *G303i-PD/P:* $599.95 in the United States. $799.00CAD in Canada. £389.95 in the United Kingdom. €698.00 in Germany. *G303e (external, not tested):* $599.95 in the United States. £389.95 in the United Kingdom. *G303e-PD/P (external, not tested):* $699.95 in the United States. £449.95 in the United Kingdom. €875.00 in Germany. *DRM Decoder/Demodulator plugin:* $49.95 in the

The WiNRADiO G303's "front panel" is actually a PC monitor window, complete with spectrum display.

United States. £32.95 in the United Kingdom. *Advanced Digital Suite (full):* $199.95 in the United States. £129.95 in the United Kingdom. €198.00 in Germany. *WiNRADiO DRM plugin (special version of DRM software):* €60.00 worldwide from www.drmrx.org/purchase.php.

Pro: Plug and play aids setup. Once receiver is installed, the included software loads without problem; software updates available for free from manufacturer's website, and open source code allows for development of third-party software. With optional plugin (software), receives digital (DRM) world band broadcasts. Superb stability. Tunes and displays in ultra-precise 1 Hz increments. A thousand station presets, which can be clustered into any of 16 groups (*see* Con—Other). Excellent shape factors (1:1.6, 1:1.8) for 5.0 kHz and 3.2 kHz bandwidths aid selectivity/adjacent-channel rejection; 1.8 kHz bandwidth measures with good shape factor (1:2.3); many additional bandwidths available in the PD/P version, and perform similarly. Excellent shortwave sensitivity (0.21 &V)/noise floor (–130 dBm), good mediumwave AM and long-wave sensitivity (0.4 &V)/noise floor (–125 dBm). Potentially excellent audio quality (see below). Excellent dynamic range (90 dB) and third-order intercept point (+5 dBm) at 20 kHz signal separation points (*see* Con—AGC/AVC). Phase noise excellent (*see* Con—AGC/AVC). Image rejection excellent. Spurious signals essentially absent. Screen, and operation in general, unusually pleasant and intuitive. Single-sideband performance

generally excellent (*see* Con—AGC/AVC). AGC fast, medium, slow and off. Spectrum display shows real-time signal activity, performs commendably and in particular provides signal strength readings to within plus or minus 3 dB. Spectrum scope sweeps between two user-chosen frequencies, displays the output while receiver mutes, then a mouse click can select a desired "peak"; it works quickly and well, and when the step size is set to small (e.g., 1 kHz), resolution is excellent and quite useful, resolving signals having as little as 350 Hz separation. Large signal-strength indicator highly accurate, as good as we've ever tested; displays both as digitally and as a digitized "analog meter"; reads out in "S" units, dBm or microvolts. Two easy-to-read on-screen clocks for World Time and local time, display seconds numerically, as well as date. Superior, timely and free factory assistance via email, seemingly throughout the week. *G303i-PD/P:* Continuously adjustable bandwidths from 1Hz to 15 kHz (single sideband/ECSS 1 Hz to 7.5 kHz), with bandwidth presets, aid greatly in providing optimum tradeoff between audio fidelity and adjacent-channel interference rejection. AVC settings, limited to "on-off" in standard version, allow for control over decay and attack times. Improved audio quality in some test configurations. Demodulates ISB signals used by a small proportion of utility stations. SINAD and THD indicators. AF squelch for FM mode.

Pro/Con—Sound: Outstanding freedom from distortion aids in providing good audio quality with appropriate sound cards/chips and speakers; sound quality and level can run the gamut from excellent to awful, depending on the PC's sound card or chipset, which needs to be full duplex. Sound Blaster 16 cards are recommended by manufacturer, but not all models work. During our tests the $130 Sound Blaster Audigy 2 performed with considerable distortion—it doesn't offer full duplex operation for the line input—whereas the $43 Sound Blaster PCI 512 worked splendidly. (ISA sound cards perform terribly; quite sensibly, these are not recommended by the manufacturer.) All input settings for the audio card need to be carefully set to match the settings within the receiver's software. If wrong, there may

The entire WiNRADiO G303i is shoehorned into a PC plug-in card.

be no audio or it may be grossly distorted. Indeed, a sound card isn't always necessary, as some sound chipsets commonly found within PCs produce excellent audio with the G303i. Another reason the chipset may be preferable is that Sound Blaster manuals recommend that if there is an audio chipset on the motherboard, it first be disabled in the BIOS and all related software uninstalled—potentially a Maalox Moment. However, even with a suitable board or chipset installed, the user must carefully set the AGC and AVC (automatic volume control, termed "Audio AGC" on the G303i)

for distortion-free audio. Powerful amplified speakers provide room-filling sound and allow the AVC to be kept off, thus reducing band noise that can be intrusive when it is on.

Con—AGC/AVC: Weak-signal reception can be compromised by the AGC, which "sees" 10–15 kHz of spectrum within the IF upon which to act. So, if an adjacent world band channel signal is 20 dB or more stronger than a desired weak signal, the AGC's action tends to cause the adjacent signal to mask the desired signal. Inadequate gain with the AVC ("Audio AGC") off, but the aggressive

NUMBERS: TOP PC RECEIVERS

	WiNRADiO G303i (G313i)	Ten-Tec RX-320D
Sensitivity, World Band	0.21 (0.3 µV **E**)	0.31 to 0.7 µV **E**-**F**[1]
Noise Floor, World Band	–130 dBm **E** (–126 dBm **G**)	–126 to –119 dBm **G**-**F**[2]
Blocking	120 dB **G** (116 dB **G**)	>146 dB **S**
Shape Factors, voice BWs	1:1.6 **E**-1:2.4 **G** (1:1.7 **E**-1:2.4 **G**)	n/a[3]
Ultimate Rejection	70 dB **G** (75 dB **E**)	60 dB **G**
Front-End Selectivity	**G** (**F**)	**F**
Image Rejection	85 dB **E** (75 dB **E**)	60 dB **G**
First IF Rejection	52 dB **F** (51 dB **F**)	60 dB **G**
Dynamic Range/IP3 (5 kHz)	45 dB **P**/–62 dBm **P** (43 dB, **P**/–62 dBm **P**)	n/a[3]
Dynamic Range/IP3 (20 kHz)	90 dB **E**/+5 dBm **E** (85 dB **G**/+2 dBm **E**)	n/a[3]
Phase Noise	124 dBc **E**[4] (120 dBc **E**)	106 dBc **F**
AGC Threshold	2.7 to 8.0 µV **G**-**P** (18 µV **P**[5])	4.0 µV **F**
Overall Distortion, voice	<1.0% **S** (<1.0% **S**[6])	<1% **S**
Stability	5 Hz, **S** (10 Hz **E**)	80 Hz, **G**
Notch filter depth	n/a (30 dB **G**)	n/a

IBS Lab Ratings: **S** Superb   **E** Excellent   **G** Good   **F** Fair   **P** Poor

(1) Excellent 60 meters and up.
(2) Good 60 meters and up.
(3) Could not be measured accurately because of synthesizer noise and spurious signals, but appears to be very good.
(4) Worse at close-in measurement.
(5) 0.3 µV **G** with AVC enabled at –3 dB.
(6) See writeup, Con: DSP audio.

AVC adds listening strain with single-side-band signals, as it tends to increase band noise between words or other modulation peaks. Powerful outboard amplified speakers help reduce the need for the additional audio gain brought about by the AVC and thus are desirable, but be prepared for jumps in volume when you tune to strong stations. Reception sometimes further improves if the AGC is switched off and IF gain is manually decreased, but the operator then has to "ride" the volume control to smooth out major fluctuations. Manual ECSS tuning frequently helps, too. During moments of transient overload, the AVC can contribute to the creation of leading-edge "pops" with powerful signals (slightly more noticeable in the PD/P version). Single-sideband performance, particularly within crowded amateur bands, can be even more audibly compromised by the aforementioned out-of-passband AGC action. Dynamic range/IP3 at 5 kHz signal separation points couldn't be measured with AGC on, as test signals trigger the AGC and keep the receiver from going into overload; measurement with the AGC off resulted in exceptionally poor numbers (45 db/–62 dBm). Phase noise poor when measured close-in for the same reason.

Con—Other: No synchronous selectable sideband, and double-sideband "AMS" mode loses lock easily. First IF rejection only fair. Front-end selectivity, although adequate for most uses, could be better. Station presets ("memory channels") store only frequency and mode, not bandwidth, AGC or attenuation settings. No passband offset or tunable notch filter. Emits a "pop-screech" sound when first brought up or when switching from standard to professional demodulator. Uses only SMA antenna connection, typically found on handheld devices rather than tabletop receivers; an SMA-to-BNC adapter is included, but for the many shortwave antennas with neither type of plug a second adaptor or changed plug is needed. On our sample, country of manufacture not found on receiver, box or enclosed printed matter; however, website indicates manufacturing facility is in Melbourne, Australia. Erratum sheet suggests that a discone antenna be used; this is fine for reception above roughly

25 MHz; however, in our tests we confirmed that conventional shortwave antennas provide much broader frequency coverage with the G303i, just as they do with other shortwave receivers.

☞ Minimum of 1 GHz Pentium recommended by manufacturer, although in the process of checking this out we obtained acceptable results using vintage 400 MHz and 500 MHz Pentium II processors with Windows 2000. However, if your PC is multitasking, then 2 GHz or more helps keep the PC from bogging down. Primary testing was done using various desktop Pentium IV PCs at 1.5–2.4 GHz, 256–512 MHz RAM and Windows 2000, XP-Home and XP-Pro operating systems. WiNRADiO operating software used during tests were v1.07, v1.14, v1.25 and v1.26.

Verdict: The G303 is among the best PC receivers tested, especially in the preferred Professional Demodulator version. It can also be configured for reception of DRM digital broadcast signals, and is a pleasure to operate.

The G303 provides laboratory-quality spectrum displays and signal-strength indication. These spectrum-data functions are top drawer, regardless of price or type of receiver, and that's just the beginning of things done well. The few significant warts: AGC/AVC behavior, possible audio hassles during installation, and the absence of synchronous selectable sideband.

Nevertheless, WiNRADiO's G303 is an excellent value among tested PC controlled receivers for world band reception. Although its costlier G313 sibling has certain advantages, for most the G303 is fully its equal for world band reception.

New for 2006   DRM Ready
✪✪✪✪⅛
WiNRADiO G313i, WiNRADiO G313e

Price: *G313i:* $999.95 in the United States and worldwide. £599.95 in the United Kingdom. *G313i-180 (to 180 MHz):* €1,229.00 in Germany. *G313e (external, not tested):* $1,199.95 in the United States and worldwide. *DRM Decoder/Demodulator plugin:*

$49.95 in the United States. £32.95 in the United Kingdom. *Advanced Digital Suite (full):* $199.95 in the United States and worldwide. £129.95 in the United Kingdom. €198.00 in Germany. *Frequency Extension (to 180 MHz, at time of purchase from factory):* $249.95 in the United States and worldwide. £149.95 in the United Kingdom. *Mini-Circuits BLP-30 BNC-to-BNC 30 MHz low-pass filter:* $32.95 in the United States.

Pro: Unlimited bandwidths—DSP bandwidths continuously variable in one Hertz increments from 1 Hz through 15 kHz (LSB/USB through 7.5 kHz). Bandwidth "presets" enhance ergonomics. Spectrum display either wideband (*see* Con) or narrowband; narrow allows for first-rate test and measurement of audio-frequency response of AM or single-sideband mode signals, spectra of data transmissions, frequency accuracy, amplitude modulation depth, frequency deviation, THD (total harmonic distortion) and SINAD (signal plus noise plus distortion to noise plus distortion ratio). Unlimited station presets—one thousand per file, each of which can be clustered into any of 16 groups; number of files limited only by hard disk capacity, so virtually no limit to presets. Station presets store frequency, IF shift, bandwidth and mode (*see* Con). Four VFOs. Large signal-strength indicator as linear as any other tested to date. Signal-strength indicator displays both digitally and as a digitized "analog meter." Signal-strength indicator reads out in "S" units, dBm or microvolts. Manufacturer's website, unusually helpful, includes downloadable calibration utility for signal-strength indicator. Open source code allows for third-party development of software. Includes DSP electronics for audio, so sound card acts only as an optional audio amplifier (*see* Con) (*cf.* WiNRADiO G303), or 313's audio output can feed outboard audio system. Superb level of overall distortion (*see* Con: DSP audio). Notch filter, tunable 0–7500 Hz, has good (30 dB) rejection (*see* Con). Synchronous double sideband to help overcome selective fading distortion and enhance fidelity during twilight and darkness (mixed skywave/groundwave) reception of fringe mediumwave AM stations (*see* Con).

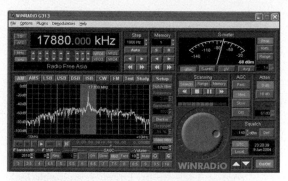

WiNRADiO G313 software display. It offers users more flexibility than can be extracted from most traditional hardware receivers.

Integrated audio recorder, a convenience for those without ReplayRadio or similar. Integrated IF recorder stores spectrum slice for subsequent analysis of received signals, and to "re-receive" the same swath of signals over and again experimenting with, for example, IF bandwidth, notch filter and noise blanker settings (*see* Con). Plug and play receiver software installed with no problems with XP Pro and XP Home. Does not overuse computer resources even while multitasking. Excellent shape factors at wider voice bandwidths (*see* Con). Excellent ultimate rejection. Excellent image rejection. Excellent phase noise as measured in lab (*see* Con). Spurious signals essentially nil. Screen, and operation in general, unusually pleasant and intuitive (*see* Con). Automatic frequency control (AFC) with FM and AM mode signals. Optional DRM reception. Demodulates ISB signals used by some utility stations. Single-step (18 dB) attenuator. Receiver incremental tuning (RIT) aids with transceiving. Two easy-to-read clocks displayed on screen for World Time; also, second clock for local time (*see* Con); both show seconds numerically, as well as day and date. FM mode squelch. Excellent owner's manual. Superior, timely and free factory assistance via email, seemingly throughout the week.

Con: DSP audio causes static crashes and local noise to sound unusually harsh, potentially increasing listening fatigue. Synchronous detector lacks meaningful selectable sideband, IF shift notwithstanding. Poor AGC threshold contributes to reduced audibility of weak signals; remediable by enabling switchable AVC at –3 dB, although this also increases pumping with single-sideband signals. AGC gain determined by all signals within the 15 kHz first IF filter, so background noise and audio can change in concert with on/off (e.g., CW) activity from adjacent carriers within the 15 kHz filter window; this can be an issue with utility and ham monitoring, but only rarely disturbs world band signals. Mediocre front-end selectivity, largely remediable by adding a Mini-Circuits BLP-30 or other outboard ~30 MHz low-pass filter. Poor close-in (5 kHz separation) dynamic range/IP3. Bandwidth shape factors slip from excellent at wider bandwidths (e.g., 6 kHz) to fair at narrower voice bandwidths (e.g., 1.9 kHz). Phase noise or a kind of local oscillator noise keeps CW bandwidths (e.g., 0.5 kHz) from being measurable at –60 dB; consequently, CW shape factors also not measurable. Significant audible distortion if computer-screen volume turned up high; remediable if level not adjusted beyond "6"; sound card or outboard audio amplifier can provide additional volume if needed. Cyclical background sound, which doesn't vary with carrier-BFO phasing, in manual ECSS mode. Mixed ergonomics—some functions a pleasure, others not. Tuning-steps in 5 kHz increments (world band channel spacing) impractical with mouse scroll wheel, as three keys have to be held down simultaneously; instead, up/down screen slew arrows can be used. Some screen icons small for typical PC displays/video cards. Real-time (always active) spectrum analyzer coverage width limited to 20 kHz (+/– 10 kHz), a pity given the exceptional resolution and analytical capabilities. IF recorder bandwidth also limited to 20 kHz. Tunable notch filter includes adjustable notch breadth, a creative but marginal option that complicates notch use. Notch filter takes unusually long to adjust properly using keypad, and small indicators make it prone to operating errors with GUI. First IF rejection only fair. Wideband spectrum analyzer not in real time, has disappointing resolution and thus of minor utility. SMA antenna connection; SMA-to-BNC adapter included, but for the many shortwave antennas with neither type

of plug a second adaptor or changed plug is needed. Station presets don't store AGC or attenuator values. Noise blanker only marginally effective. Local-time (secondary) clock displays only in 24-hour format—no AM/PM.

Verdict: With audio processing independent of the host PC—and heaps of additional goodies—the Australian WiNRADiO G313 is in many ways a solid improvement over the lower-cost WiNRADiO G303.

Alas, there's a hefty price to be paid for not using the PC sound card for audio processing: DSP harshness that aggravates static crashes and more. This limits its appeal, especially for tropical band and mediumwave AM DXing, but how much depends on your hearing and listening preferences.

The G313 is tempting for DRM, and it has excellent synchronous detection for alleviating selective fading distortion—a serious issue with dusk-to-dawn fringe analog mediumwave AM reception. But its selectable sideband capability is effectively nonexistent, and the "IF shift" doesn't help. This is a huge drawback in a kilobuck receiver, given that effective synchronous selectable sideband can be found on a $150 portable.

So, the G313's price/performance ratio is uninspiring for listening to broadcasts or monitoring utility/ham signals. But it excels with signal analysis and storage, thanks to a high-resolution spectrum analyzer with excellent test, measurement and recording capabilities. Add to that a highly linear and adjustable signal-strength indicator, and you can see why this model is spot-on for certain professional/surveillance applications. This also explains the kilobuck price, dirt cheap by professional standards.

Better for most world band listeners is the sibling WiNRADiO G303. How it sounds is partly a function of the host PC's sound card, but its audio is usually less tiring than that of the G313—particularly with static.

And it costs half as much.

Evaluation of New Model: In recent years WiNRADiO's G303 has been the best PC receiver tested at Passport. Yet, it has a number of points which could be better, so the new G313 has raised eyebrows.

The most apparent change over the cheaper '303 is in how audio is generated: It uses its own DSP instead of the PC's sound card. (The external version, not tested, nominally requires a 16-bit sound card.) Audio quality, freed from the vagaries of differing sound cards, is more predictable. Output can be directed from the '313 to outboard audio equipment or, using the included phone-plug cable, routed back to the computer's sound card line input.

The '313 is resource-friendly, too. With one modest test configuration—1.5 GHz Pentium IV, 512 MB RAM and XP Home—other applications ran simultaneously without slowing down.

Screen Offers Many Options

Just about every tuning feature is included, and the "operation central" screen is generally pleasant to view and use. Many icons are large, while the frequency displays to the nearest Hertz with big, easy-to-read digits.

However, IF bandwidth, volume, IF shift and notch adjustment indicators are small to the point where squinting testers made operating mistakes; superior-graphics screens and video cards help, but only to a point. Alternatively, use the easy-to-see virtual slider—its up-down arrows appear clearly when the mouse is moved between them. Keyboard commands are also dependable, even if retro.

Like on the '303, files of up to one thousand station presets each can be clustered into 16 groups. The number of files is limited only by hard drive capacity, so as a practical matter presets are unlimited—tens of thousands, if the spirit moves you. Also, these, unlike presets on the '303, store not only frequency and mode but also bandwidth and IF shift. Not AGC or attenuator settings, though.

Scanning is either through chosen presets or within a designated frequency range. However, contrary to what's suggested in the otherwise excellent owners manual, the mouse scroll wheel does not readily tune in 5 kHz steps. Instead, the Shift +Ctrl and Alt keys have to be held down while the wheel is rotated. Using screen arrows is handier.

The World Time (UTC) clock shows seconds, day and date, and is displayed independent of the frequency readout. There's another clock for local time, but it's only in 24-hour format—no AM/PM—and unlike on the '303 it shares display space normally occupied by World Time. So, you can see one time or the other, but not both at once.

Selectivity choices are essentially infinite. On all modes except LSB and USB, choices are in single-Hertz steps from 1 Hz to 15 kHz (LSB and USB stop at 7.5 kHz). Continuing a tradition from earlier models, there is also a row of bandwidth "presets" to enhance ergonomics.

However, ergonomics for some other activities could be better. For example, passband tuning requires right clicking and holding down the mouse key while sitting the cursor on the middle of a signal on the real-time display.

Great Spectrum Analyzer, "Meter"

The visual spectrum analyzer is arguably the chief reason to reach into your Levis for a '313. It operates two ways: wideband and narrowband. Wide coverage is not real-time, nor does it have meaningful resolution or any other significant virtue. Obviously, that's not where the good stuff is.

Rather, it's the real-time narrow option that has the goodies. It offers superb resolution, resolving signals with less than 200 Hz separation. It also allows for test and measurement of the audio-frequency response of AM-mode or single-sideband signals, spectra of data transmissions, frequency accuracy, amplitude modulation depth, frequency deviation, THD (total harmonic distortion) and SINAD (signal plus noise plus distortion to noise plus distortion ratio).

Taken together, this is meaty stuff, but there's a catch: Coverage width is limited to a mere 20 kHz. Obviously, there's a tradeoff between coverage width and such other variables as resolution. Yet, some moderately wider user-selectable choices are urgently needed if this spectrum analyzer is to achieve its superb potential.

The large signal-strength indicator is in a league of its own. For starters, it is as linear as any we've seen, and displays either as a digital indicator or a digitized "analog meter." Readings are in any of the three measurement standards: "S" units, dBm or microvolts. It can also be set to show peak, "RMS" (normal) or minimum/maximum (pointer added for the minimum reading). As if all this weren't enough, WiNRADiO's website offers a downloadable calibration utility to bring the signal-strength indicator to spot-on accuracy.

All this makes for the ultimate in "'S' meters." Taken together with the spectrum analyzer's functions, this turns the '313 into a powerful niche device for signal analysis. For the public, this analysis has limited appeal. But for certain engineering and surveillance activities, this capability and precision are most relevant.

An inboard recorder, like ReplayRadio set to What U Hear, records onto disk whatever station is tuned in. But it has a more interesting function: to capture a 20 kHz swath of received spectrum in real time, then store it on disk for future playback. Any mode, any bandwidth can be used.

Alas, with only 20 kHz of coverage it's like a Maybach with a Kia four-banger. It is too limited when compared to, say, the RF Space SDR-14's 150 kHz.

Performance Characteristics Vary

The '313 generally acquits itself nicely in the lab. Ultimate rejection, non-narrow-bandwidth skirt selectivity, image rejection, phase noise, sensitivity/noise floor and stability are all excellent or good, while overall distortion is superb. However, some important measurements disappoint: First IF rejection is only fair, while close-in (5 kHz) dynamic range is downright poor. Front-end selectivity is merely fair, but improves if an outboard ~30 MHz low-pass filter is added.

Unsurprisingly, real-life listening tends to confirm lab findings; say, in the lack of image or other spurious signals. But not always. For example, even though close-in dynamic range measures poorly there was no trace of overloading, even with significant outdoor antennas. Also, although phase noise measures well, phase noise or a kind of local oscillator noise causes an audible rumble with strong signals; it also compromises measurement of –60 dB CW bandwidths. The noise blanker, not rated in the lab, provided comparatively modest relief.

Synchronous double sideband ("AMS") is primarily for twilight and nighttime reception of fringe mediumwave AM stations chockablock with selective fading distortion. However, the '313 lacks the primary virtue of synchronous detection: selectable sideband. This major drawback is especially regrettable, as circuitry already exists to tie into AMS for proper selectable sideband.

Listeners can approximate synchronous selectable sideband with ECSS (*see* glossary). Alas, with ECSS rhythmic circuit noise is sometimes audible in the background—something not noticed with ECSS on the '303. Fortunately, normal single-sideband reception is free from this anomaly.

The AVC (software AGC, or SAGC) has to be adjusted carefully for each mode during setup. If the reference level is placed too high, nasty distortion occurs. The user can also tinker with the attack and decay times—slow, medium and fast—for each AVC "preset." Of course, distortion can result if the AVC is inadvertently set to the wrong mode.

Adjustable AVC is independent of the adjustable (also fast/medium/slow) AGC, and it's the combined action of both functions that impacts reception and audio quality. For example, AVC has the potential to elevate AGC threshold from poor to good. Still, while all this user control over AGC behavior will delight some, others will find it to be too much of a good thing.

Just as with the '303, nasty distortion can rear its head if the '313's main volume control is placed above the "6" position. If this level is inadequate, then volume can be increased using outboard audio or sound card adjustments.

DSP receivers tend to produce relatively harsh audio with static crashes—sometimes local noise, fading distortion and modulation splash, too. Most ears adjust to this in the short run, but over time any distortion increases listening fatigue.

Here, the G313i seriously disappoints. Apparently so much processing power is gobbled up by inboard DSP audio that there's not enough left to provide audio equal to that of the cheaper G303, which uses the PC sound card for audio. Even by the modest current state of audio in DSP receivers, the '313 sounds harsh. Whether this is a big deal, little deal or no deal depends on your hearing and how much you're bothered by such things. Otherwise, audio quality is quite good, provided the various controls are adjusted properly.

An audio notch filter tunes plus or minus 7.5 kHz, which is ideal, and when used properly it has good depth. However, it is not automatic like on some tabletop and professional DSP receivers.

It also takes longer to adjust properly than any other notch we've tested. In part that's because notch breadth (not tuning width) is adjustable from 1 Hz to 3 kHz, not fixed around 200 Hz like most other good notch filters. Possibly an adjustment as wide as 3 kHz is useful for selective content removal in surveillance and signal-analysis applications. But for the usual heterodyne reduction it's another who-needs-it adjustment to complicate what otherwise would be a straightforward tweak.

A nonstandard SMA antenna connector is used, although an SMA-to-BNC adapter is included. Still, many will need a different or additional converter for SO239/PL259 plugs, or your existing antenna lead-in plug can be replaced with a BNC or SMA.

Spectrum swath aside, the WiNRADiO's new G313 series is a knockout for analyzing a rich variety of signal and spectrum vari-

ables. But for world band DXing, program listening and chasing utility and ham signals, its G303 sibling offers audio that's less fatiguing—and it's half the price.

DRM Ready

★★★★ © *Passport's Choice*
Ten-Tec RX-320D

Price: *RX-320D:* $329.00 plus shipping worldwide. £239.00 in the United Kingdom. €449.00 in Germany. $668.00AUD in Australia. *DRM software:* €60.00 worldwide from www.drmrx.org/purchase.php. *Third-party control software:* Free-$99 worldwide.

Pro: The "D" version's 12 kHz IF output allows the receiver to receive digital (DRM) world band broadcasts by using DRM software purchased separately. Superior dynamic range. Apparently superb bandwidth shape factors (*see* Con). In addition to the supplied factory control software, third-party software is available, often for free, and may improve operation. Up to 34 bandwidths with third-party software. Tunes in extremely precise 1 Hz increments (10 Hz with tested factory software); displays to the nearest Hertz, and frequency readout is easily user-aligned. Large, easy-to-read

Ten-Tec's RX-320D provides a tempting ratio of price to performance. Superior service, too.

digital frequency display and faux-analog frequency bar. For PCs with sound cards, outstanding freedom from distortion aids in providing good audio quality with most but not all cards and speakers. Fairly good audio, but with limited treble, also available through radio for PCs without sound cards. Superb blocking performance helps maintain consistently good world band sensitivity. Passband offset (*see* Con). Spectrum display with wide variety of useful sweep widths (*see* Con). World Time on-screen clock (*see* Con). Adjustable AGC decay. Thousands of station presets, with first-rate memory configuration, access and sorting—including by station name and frequency. Only PC-controlled model tested which returns to last tuned frequency when PC turned off. Superior owner's manual. Outstanding factory help and repair support.

Con: No synchronous selectable sideband, although George Privalov's Control Panel Program now automates retuning of drifty AM-mode signals received as "ECSS." Some characteristic "DSP roughness" in the audio under certain reception conditions. Synthesizer phase noise measures only fair; among the consequences are that bandwidth shape factors cannot be measured exactly. Some tuning ergonomics only fair as compared with certain standalone receivers. No tunable notch filter. Passband offset doesn't function in AM mode. Signal-strength indicator, calibrated 0–80, too sensitive, reading 20 with no antenna connected and 30 with only band noise being received. Mediocre front-end selectivity can allow powerful mediumwave AM stations to "ghost" into the shortwave spectrum, thus

degrading reception of world band stations. Uses AC adaptor instead of built-in power supply. Spectrum display does not function with some third-party software and is only a so-so performer. Mediumwave AM reception below 1 MHz suffers from reduced sensitivity, and longwave sensitivity is atrocious. No internal speaker on outboard receiver module. World Time clock tied into computer's clock, which may not be accurate without periodic adjustment. Almost no retail sources outside the United States.

☞ PASSPORT's four-star rating is for the RX-320D with third-party control software. With factory software the rating is marginally lower.

Verdict: The American-made Ten-Tec RX-320D is one of the best PC controlled receivers tested. Yet, even with DRM software it is value priced. It is also less chancy to install to full operating advantage than the WiNRADiO G303i.

New for 2006
DRM Ready
✪✪✪⅝
RFSPACE SDR-14

Price: *RFSPACE SDR-14:* $999.95 in the United States. *Comet HS-10 SMA-to-SO-239 antenna adapter cable:* $17.99 in the United States.

Pro: Excellent spectrum display shows, with audio ("demodulation"), up to a 150 kHz slice of radio spectrum; this can also be recorded to disk and played back in any mode or bandwidth (*see* Con). Worthy sensitivity. DSP bandwidth filtering feels razor sharp and performs beautifully. Relatively free from overloading. Stable. Tunes and displays down to 1 Hz increments. Passband tuning (*see* Con). Three-level attenuator, labeled as RF gain control. Adjustable AGC decay and hang times. Good quality, flexible USB cable. Receives 30–260 MHz minus front end filtering or amplification (*see* Con). Third-party software development supported. Spectra-Vue software nominally has Linux server support (not tested), in addition to Windows. World Time (UTC) clock shows date and day

The new RFSPACE SDR-14 excels at spectrum recording—not listening or DXing.

of the week. Build quality appears solid. One year warranty. Fifteen day return privilege when ordered from the manufacturer. Helpful PDF operating manual (*see* Con).

Con: AC adaptor's switching circuitry emits noise that disrupts reception even with outdoor antenna and shielded lead-in. Initial installation not always successful, necessitating troubleshooting with or without the assistance of the manufacturer; however, manufacturer's phone number and street address aren't published. SMA antenna connector, with no adaptor included for non-SMA antenna plugs; for most shortwave antennas an adaptor or new antenna plug is required. No synchronous selectable or double sideband, tunable notch filter, presets or scanning. Passband tuning operates only in LSB and USB modes and is complex to use. Noise blanker performs marginally, and no DSP noise reduction offered. Inadequate front end filtering, so mediumwave AM stations may bleed through slightly to impact world band listening. With demodulation, spectrum display limited to 150 kHz maximum bandwidth. Marginally useful 30–260 MHz reception, with an abundance of spurious signals that not even maximum attenuation can overcome. Requires a speedy computer with large disk capacity to use to full benefit; even then, heavy resource drain may impact multitasking. Harsh audio quality in AM mode. About a half-second lag when operating controls and when listening (demodulation, see story). No power switch, even though manufacturer recommends receiver be powered down when not in use. Operation manual, only on CD, not printed as a book.

☞ The included switching AC adaptor is appalling and should be substituted with a non-switching type. Requirements are 12V DC output, one ampere minimum rating, center (tip) positive.

☞ Tested: firmware .014, SpectraVue 1.30.

Verdict: The RFSPACE SDR-14 is a niche device that does one thing very well: recording a slice of spectrum for later playback and analysis. Here, its advantage over the WiNRADiO G313 is that the slice may be up to 150 kHz, rather than 20 kHz.

However, this broader coverage comes at a price. The SDR-14, unlike the G313, requires a speedy processor and substantial disk—especially in a multitasking environment. And it is nowhere as flexible outside its niche as the G313.

However appropriate the SDR-14 is for spectrum analysis, it is a dismal choice for world band listening or DXing.

Evaluation of New Model: Job One before considering a SDR-14 is to take hard look at what you want a receiver for. This is not your grandfather's Oldsmobile—nor the Jetsons' car, either. It is very specific in what it does, and beyond that it is decidedly limited.

Job Two is to consider your target computer. This receiver may be small, but it chews up PC resources faster than a hungry goat. For multitasking this means something up-to-date and powerful, with generous disk capacity.

Recommended PC resources are a 2.2 GHz Pentium IV or better with 512 MB RAM, Windows 2000 or XP, 16-bit Sound Blaster or compatible card, AGP 14x video card with 64 MB or more of RAM. Linux is also supported, at least nominally and to a point, but we stuck with Windows for testing.

A USB 2.0 port is desirable, but 1.1 functions properly. A mouse with scroll wheel is also recommend, as it acts as a tuning "knob." So far, so good, provided you won't be doing heavy multitasking or using resource-heavy background utilities.

Schwarzedisker

But the main objective is not to run short of hard drive capacity. When capturing data within a 150 kHz slice, the SDR-14 slurps up 52 Gigabytes in 24 hours. So if plans are to capture lots of data, you'll need a seriously large drive or RAID combo.

If the computer is to be dedicated to receiver use, you can squeak by with the nominal minimum of 1GHz P3, 256 MB RAM, 16-bit Sound Blaster or compatible card, AGP video card with 32 MB RAM, USB 1.1 port and Windows 98SE/2000/ME/XP.

The supplied CD includes a 63-page PDF operation guide that's much more informative than the skimpy companion printed booklet—oddly, at this price point, the main guide isn't supplied in book form. Most owner's manuals are of limited usefulness, but you really need to read this guide before installing the receiver. So, Job Three is to print it out.

The required SpectraVue software should be installed before any hardware is plugged in. The black box receiver then can be powered up and the USB cable and antenna connected. A USB driver, included, is the last software to be loaded once the SDR-14 is on.

With luck you'll be ready to continue, but we found that even prudent installation did not always result in a working receiver. So, there's at least some chance you'll need to troubleshoot with or without the assistance of the manufacturer.

For this or other technical support there's an email address, e-fax and post box outside Atlanta, Georgia. However, there's no street address on the receiver's cabinet, box, manuals or even website. And forget griping about toll-free phone support from Bangalore. RFSPACE has no published phone number—toll-free or otherwise—and searches come up empty.

The included switching-type AC adaptor creates obnoxious digital noise that covers the entire shortwave spectrum. An antenna placed some distance from the receiver and using a shielded lead-in usually only reduces the noise. However, a better adaptor eliminates the problem completely (*see* ☞, above).

Like some PC accessories left on fulltime, the SDR-14 has no power switch. But there's a catch: The manufacturer recommends that the unit be powered down when not in use. So there's no excuse for not having a power switch, especially as this little black box costs a thousand dollars.

Next, the system needs to be configured properly, using the input source bar. As with many sophisticated PC devices there are many setup choices that are important. So,

follow your printed PDF operating manual carefully as you proceed, step-by-step, through setup.

Once setup is finished, hit the "Start" button to tune around and enter frequencies on the keypad. There are two tuning modes: center frequency and demod frequency. Center is for the usual bandscanning, with the mouse scroll wheel being the most handy alternative.

Spectrum Display Time Shifting

There are seven available SpectraVue spectrum displays, but option 2D FFT is likely to be of most significance. It is one of the best we've come across, and shows modulation peaks with commendable precision and sensitivity. The scale can be adjusted as well.

The major limitation is the maximum amount of spectrum that can be looked at or recorded at any one time. It is restricted to a slice of no greater than 150 kHz with receive (demodulation) active. This is much better than the 20 kHz limit on the WiNRADiO G313, but not enough for all applications.

The receiver can look over more of the radio spectrum—even the receiver's entire 30 MHz tuning range—but only sans demodulation/reception. So, if you want to look and listen, the limit is still 150 kHz.

The SDR-14 can record up to 150 kHz of spectrum, then when it's played back you can listen to and adjust every function for every signal within that slice. It's just as though you were bandscanning 150 kHz of spectrum live.

The recording is a high-quality but disk-gobbling .wav file. Fortunately, you can indicate how large a file can get before recording stops, and you may then continue by generating additional files within the same listening session. There's also a timer to automatically limit run time.

A separate signal-strength indicator reads out in either dBm or "S" units. It performs adequately, but is not in the same league as that on the WiNRADiO G313.

Depending on your PC's configuration, there can be a split-second lag between clicking on a function and when the function starts. Demodulation also lags by the same amount, so there's an echo when listening simultaneously to the same station on a nearby receiver.

Performance Varies

Sensitivity is fine, being on a par with other top-drawer receivers. Overloading is rarely a problem at most setups, too, but just in case there is a three-step attenuator labeled "RF gain."

Something really neat is an LED that glows when there's overloading—and there is a screen warning, too. Both warnings are genuinely useful when recording the spectrum while not listening; otherwise, the stored file could turn out to be a mishmash of unintelligible signals.

Alas, the SDR-14 is deficient in front-end selectivity. Powerful local mediumwave AM signals sometimes ghost into the shortwave spectrum, bothering world band reception. Even maximum attenuation does not resolve this. Nevertheless, the receiver's image rejection passes muster.

Selectivity is DSP and a real plus. Its bandwidth range is dependent on mode and is adjustable in 100 Hz increments:

Passband tuning is only for single-sideband, and adjusting it is a chore. Instead of one simple control, along either side of the bandwidth selection there is a Low Cutoff Frequency and a High Cutoff Frequency. This is similar to "IF shift" on the original version of the Icom IC-R71, rather than what's normally thought of as passband tuning.

Alas, there's no tunable notch control—manual or automatic. No synchronous selectable or double sideband, either. There is a DSP noise blanker, but it performs marginally no matter how much its control is tweaked.

Just as bandwidth can be adjusted, so, too, can AGC decay and hang times. This arrangement is much simpler and straight-forward—even if less flexible—than the AGC/AVC duo on the G313.

Audio quality is very pleasant in single-sideband modes. However, world band and other AM-mode audio has audible distortion, especially during fades. Tweaking the AGC doesn't help.

The SDR-14 improves as a world band listening device if you're willing to use ECSS (*see* glossary). Precise 1 Hz tuning steps and stability of under 30 Hz from cold start make for quality audio—provided your ears are sensitive enough to harmonic distortion to allow for precise phasing of the transmitted carrier and the receiver's internally generated carrier. Like the SDR-14's nominal passband tuning, this takes the long road to Rome.

If you are looking for a place to store your favorite stations into nice, handy presets, you can stop. The SDR-14/SpectraVue package has no provision for station presets or scanning facilities at all. None, *nada*, zip. Compare this with the same-priced WiN-RADiO G313, with its tens of thousands of presets, or cheap portables with dozens.

The full-bore tuning range of the SDR-14 is between 75 kHz and 30 MHz. This corresponds to the SMA antenna jack marked as 0.1 to 30 MHz.

Another SMA antenna jack is marked "Direct Input," for tuning up to 260 MHz—well above the normal upper tuning limit. This bonus reception works on harmonics and is

Mode	Minimum	Maximum
AM	200 Hz	20 kHz
WFM	Fixed	at 20 kHz
FM	7.5 kHz	30 kHz
USB*	1 kHz	17 kHz
LSB*	1 kHz	17 kHz
CW	100 Hz	1 kHz
DSB	1 kHz	17 kHz
*Passband tuning available.		

explained in the operating manual. However, it is done without the usual bandpass filtering, and it shows: In our tests, stray shortwave signals ghosted in to bother desired VHF signals. Even strong FM broadcasts and VHF public service transmissions popped up as spurious signals. So, think of this function like a limited-service spare tire. If you want better results, try external bandpass filtering or preselection.

The RFSPACE SDR-14 package is for spectrum viewing and recording, and to that extent competes directly with the WiNRADiO G313. But for world band listening, move on.

DRM Modifiable

✪✪✪ ⊘
Icom IC-PCR1000

Price: *IC-PCR1000 (as available):* $399.95 in the United States. $699.00CAD in Canada. £319.99 in the United Kingdom. €479.00 in Germany. $799.00AUD in Australia. *UT-106 DSP Unit:* $139.95 in the United States. £82.00 in the United Kingdom. €99.00 in Germany. $172.00AUD in Australia.

Pro: Wideband frequency coverage. Spectrum display with many useful sweep widths for shortwave, as well as good real-time performance. Tunes and displays in extremely precise 1 Hz increments. Comes with reasonably performing control software (*see* Con). Excellent sensitivity to weak signals. AGC, adjustable, performs

well in AM and single-sideband modes. Nineteen banks of 50 memories each, with potential for virtually unlimited number of memories. Passband offset (*see* Con). Powerful audio with good weak-signal readability and little distortion (*see* Con). DRM modifiable (http://www.drmrx.org/receiver_mods.html).

Con: Poor dynamic range. Audio quality, not pleasant, made worse by presence of circuit hiss. No line output to feed PC sound card and speakers, so no alternative to using receiver's audio. No synchronous selectable sideband. Only two AM-mode bandwidths—8.7 kHz (nominal 6 kHz) and 2.4 kHz (nominal 3 kHz)—both with uninspiring shape factors. Synthesizer phase noise, although not measurable, appears to be only fair; among the effects of this are that bandwidth shape factors cannot be exactly measured. Mediocre blocking slightly limits weak-signal sensitivity when frequency segment contains powerful signals. Tuning ergonomics only fair as compared with some standalone receivers. Automatic tunable notch filter with DSP audio processing (UT-106, not tested) an extra-cost option. Lacks passband offset in AM mode. Uses AC adaptor instead of built-in power supply. Spectrum display mutes audio when single-sideband or CW signal being received. No clock. Mediocre inboard speaker, remediable by using outboard speaker. Sparse owner's manual.

☞ The 'PCR1000 sometimes comes with a seasoned version of Bonito RadioCom software as a free bonus. RadioCom provides more-flexible audio shaping and the ability to record programs onto hard drives, but its improved current version costs extra.

Verdict: Among tested PC-controlled receivers, the Japanese-made Icom IC-PCR1000 is not the strongest world band performer. However, it is the most appropriate for wideband frequency coverage. Its spectrum display is a solid performer, as well. For all that, it is attractively priced.

The affordable Icom IC-PCR1000 is targeted at those who want broadband frequency coverage.

Robert Sherwood and David Zantow, with Lawrence Magne.

WHERE TO FIND IT: INDEX TO TESTED RADIOS

PASSPORT REPORTS evaluates nearly every digitally tuned receiver on the market. Here's where each is found, with those that are new, forthcoming, revised, rebranded or retested in **bold**.

Comprehensive PASSPORT® Radio Database International White Papers® are available for the many popular premium receivers. Each RDI White Paper®—$6.95 in North America, $9.95 airmail elsewhere, including shipping—contains virtually all our panel's findings and comments during hands-on testing, as well as laboratory measurements and what these mean to you. These unabridged reports are available from key world band dealers, or contact our 24-hour VISA/MC order channels for immediate shipment (www.passband. com, autovoice +1 215/598-9018, fax +1 215/598 3794), or write PASSPORT RDI White Papers, Box 300, Penn's Park, PA 18943 USA.

▤ *Radio Database International White Paper*® available.

Aerial Acrobatics

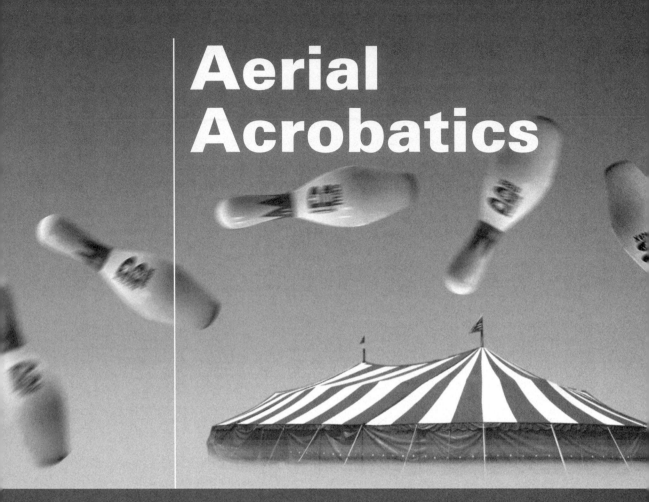

Back when Elvis sightings were real and Vaseline was for hair, nearly anybody could soup up a car with everyday tools.

No more, and the same goes for radios and electrified antennas. With chips, geeky software and connections a gnat can't solder, they are as hostile to tinkering as David Letterman is to saunas.

But sturdy wire antennas are still around, and they're the best way to boost world band reception without a grant from NASA. As a bonus they respond to creative experimentation like bees to fallen apples.

First, three truths:

• *Location, location.* If you can't put a wire antenna outdoors, consider a compact (see next article). Erect safely and for best performance.

- *Matchmaker, matchmaker.* Simple antennas for simple portables, sophisticated antennas for the rest.
- *Signal-to-noise:* Boosting signals isn't enough. Success requires that signals be enhanced relative to electrical and receiver noise. The result—more signal, proportionately less noise—improves the signal-to-noise ratio.

When Better Antennas Help

No surprise—stations already booming in aren't going to do better with an improved antenna. Your receiver's signal-strength indicator may read higher, but its automatic-gain control (AGC) ensures that what you hear isn't going to sound much different than before.

With all portables but premium models, forget sophisticated antennas—outdoor or in, passive or active. Make do with the radio's built-in telescopic antenna, or for more oomph use a simple inverted-L antenna (see below) or the compact Sony AN-LP1 or AOR WL500 evaluated in the next article.

At the other extreme, a first-rate remote antenna is as essential to elite receivers as power fuel is at NASCAR. So, tabletop and professional receivers usually don't have built-in antennas. After all, these aren't out in the fresh air where they can grab signals and avoid indoor electrical noises.

> **Good antennas provide more signal, less noise.**

Volksantenna

Inverted-L antennas are simple, flexible and inexpensive. Inconspicuous, too, as they have no unsightly traps and, being end-fed, their feedlines are usually next to the house rather than dangling out in the open. For most radios they provide excellent results, and are even reasonable for omnidirectional mediumwave AM reception.

Rough-and-ready inverted-Ls are cheap and usually rate three stars, sometimes four. Among those available in the United States is Radio Shack's $10 Outdoor Antenna Kit (278-758) with wire, insulators and other bits. Add loose change for a claw/alligator clip or other connector.

World band and specialty outlets often stock inverted-L antennas, as well as such add-ons as baluns (*see* glossary) and antenna tuners. These are made from superior materials and priced accordingly; for example, £26 for the Watson SWL-DX1 and £40 for the Moonraker Skywire. Others are creative end-fed variants of the classic inverted-L.

At full length, a typical inverted-L antenna can be too long for many portables, causing overloading from hefty incoming signals. Experiment, but usually the less costly the portable, the shorter the inverted-L antenna. Unlike other antenna types, the inverted-L can be readily shortened to avoid overloading or to fit a yard.

Longwires Reduce Fading

Acres aplenty?

Lengthy inverted-L antennas, detailed in the RDI White Paper on outdoor antennas, can be over 200 feet, or 60 meters. These homebrew skyhooks are readily assembled from parts found at world band and amateur radio outlets and flea markets.

They qualify as genuine longwire antennas, thanks to their having one or more wavelengths (see glossary). This helps reduce fading—something shorter antennas can't do—while improving the signal-to-noise ratio.

Pitfalls

A good antenna static protector is essential during nearby thunderstorms, windy snowfalls and sandstorms. These generate electrical charges that can seriously damage your radio.

Some of the best protectors are made by Alpha Delta Communications. It's also a good idea to have a surge arrestor or UPS on the power line, too—just like with a PC.

Most Americans don't encounter legal prohibitions on erecting world band antennas. However, covenants and deed restrictions, increasingly common in gated and other communities, can limit choices. Regardless, the Golden Rule of Aerials applies: Outdoor antennas should be neither unsightly nor particularly visible. If you want to annoy neighbors, put out plastic flamingos.

Most wire antennas are robustly constructed to withstand ice buildup during storms, but wire sometimes stretches. Bungee straps or pulley counterweights help.

Performance Freebie

You don't bathe in dirty water, so don't put your antenna where it is electrically "dirty." Place your antenna, like Superman, up, up and away from electrical lines, cables and other noise sources. Once out in the fresh air, it will reduce the "noise" portion of the signal-to-noise ratio.

Fight Noise and *Defacto* Jamming

Emerging digital technologies are creating so much RF pollution that antenna location is becoming a key performance variable. One, broadband over power lines (BPL), is particularly odious because it acts, in effect, as a government-sanctioned jammer of

LONG AND SHORT OF IT

Accessory antennas come in two flavors: unamplified or "passive" (usually outdoor), and amplified or "active" (indoor, outdoor or both). An unamplified antenna uses a wire or rod receiving element which sends radio signals straight to the receiver. All antennas in this article are unamplified and fairly long.

Amplified or active antennas have receiving elements that are shorter, but enhanced by electronic boost. Certain models even outperform big outdoor antennas, at least with staticky signals below 5 MHz.

As yards shrink and restrictive covenants grow, limited-space amplified antennas are becoming more popular. Even landed homeowners sometimes prefer them because they are so inconspicuous and easy to erect.

But amplified antennas have potential drawbacks. First, their short receiving elements usually don't provide the signal-to-noise enhancement of lengthier elements. Second, antenna amplifiers can generate noise of their own. Third, antenna amplifiers can overload, with results like when a receiver overloads . . . a mighty mumbling mishmash up and down the dial. Indeed, if antenna amplification is excessive it can overload the receiver, too.

Finally, amplified compact antennas often have mediocre front-end selectivity. This can allow local mediumwave AM signals to get jumbled in with world band signals.

the one type of mass information governments can't fully control: world band radio. Fortunately, BPL is not yet widespread and hopefully never will be, but it can be fought by careful antenna placement.

Even though BPL's technology and economics haven't excited markets, official Washington continues to push hard for its implementation. So, it's ironic that information on homebrew antennas that can counteract BPL is on a U.S. government site (www.rfa.org/english/support/anti-jamming). It is intended for listeners living under the yoke of totalitarianism.

Safe Installation

Safety is Rule One during installation. Avoid falls or making contact with potentially lethal electrical utility and other lines. If you want to be fried, go to the beach.

There's much more to this than can be covered here, but it's detailed in the RADIO DATABASE INTERNATIONAL report, *Evaluation of Popular Outdoor Antennas*. Also, check out www.universal-radio.com/catalog/sw_ant/safeswl.html.

What's Best?

For that RDI White Paper we've also tested a number of popular outdoor wire antennas, three of which are summarized here. All are dipoles which rely on traps for frequency resonance, but a variety of mounting layouts are used:

- End-fed sloper, with the antenna about 30 degrees from horizontal.

- Center-fed tapered wing, with a tall (about 20 feet or 6 meters) mounting amidships, plus two lower mountings.
- Center-fed horizontal, hung between two points of comparable height.

PASSPORT's star ratings mean the same thing regardless of whether an antenna is active or passive, big or little, indoor or out. This helps when you're trying to compare one type of antenna with another in this article or the next.

Nevertheless, passive antennas are more tricky than actives to evaluate properly. That's because performance is more dependent on such imponderables as local soil, moisture and bedrock.

So, don't hold back from "rolling your own" or buying something that, tests be damned, you think might do well at your location. There are countless designs on the market, and most wire antennas are frugal and forgiving.

Indeed, in the real world of tradeoffs and compromises the clincher is usually yard availability. Also, some wire antennas are almost kits, while others arrive ready to put up. Do you really have time or patience for the former?

✪✪✪✪¾ *Passport's Choice*
Alpha Delta DX-Ultra

Price: $129.95 in the United States. $179.00CAD in Canada. Coaxial cable extra.

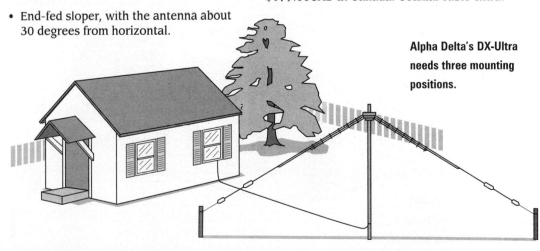

Alpha Delta's DX-Ultra needs three mounting positions.

Pro: Best overall performer of any antenna tested, passive or active. Little variation in performance from one world band segment to another. Rugged construction. Comes with built-in static protection. Wing design appropriate for certain yard layouts. Covers mediumwave AM band.

Con: Assembly a major undertaking, with stiff wire having to be bent and fed through spacer holes, then affixed. Unusually lengthy, 80 feet or 25 meters. Coaxial cable lead-in not included. Relatively heavy, adding to erection effort. Warranty only six months.

Verdict: The Alpha Delta DX-Ultra rewards sweat equity—it is really more of a kit than a finished product. First, you have to purchase the needed lead-in cable and other hardware bits, then assemble, bend and stretch the many stiff wires, section-by-section.

Because the wire used should outlast the Pyramids, assembly is a trying and unforgiving exercise. Each wire needs to be rigorously and properly affixed, lest it slip loose and the erected antenna comes tumbling down, as it did at one of our test sites.

While all outdoor antennas require yard space, the Ultra is the longest manufactured antenna tested. It is also relatively heavy, making installation an even more tiresome chore than it already is. In ice-prone climates, be sure any trees or poles attached to the antenna are sturdy. And don't even think about using a chimney.

But if you have yard space and don't object to assembly and erection hurdles, you are rewarded with a robust performer. It is outmatched only by hugely long inverted-L aerials and costly professional-grade antennas.

✪✪✪½ *Passport's Choice*
Alpha Delta DX-SWL Sloper

Price: $89.95 in the United States. $149.00CAD in Canada. Coaxial cable and static protector extra.

Pro: Rugged construction. Sloper design uses traps to keep the length down to 60 feet (18 meters), make it suitable for certain yard layouts. Covers mediumwave AM band.

Con: Requires assembly, a significant exercise. Does not include static protection. Coaxial cable lead-in not included. Warranty only six months.

☞ A greatly shortened version, the 40-foot (12 meter) DX-SWL-S (not tested), is available for $69.95, with coaxial cable and static protector extra. Its nominal coverage is 3.2–22 MHz, omitting the little-used 2 MHz (120 meter) world band segment. Although both Sloper versions nominally don't cover the 25 MHz (11 meter) world band segment, our measurements of the full-length Sloper show excellent results there (25650–26100 kHz).

Verdict: An excellent choice where space is limited, but it's a chore to assemble.

The Alpha Delta DX-SWL Sloper mounts easily from a handy tree.

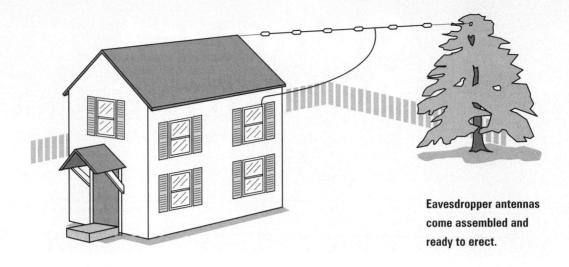

Eavesdropper antennas come assembled and ready to erect.

✪✪✪✪⅛ *Passport's Choice*
Eavesdropper Model T, Eavesdropper Model C

Price: *Model T:* $89.95, complete, in the United States. *Model C:* $89.95 in the United States. Coaxial cable extra.

Pro: Unusually compact at 43 feet or 13 meters, it fits into many yards. Comes with built in static protection. One-year warranty, after which repairs made "at nominal cost." *Model T:* Easiest to install of any Passport's Choice antenna—unpack, and it's ready to hang. Comes with ribbon lead-in wire, which tends to have less signal loss than coaxial cable. *Model C:* Easier than most to install, with virtually everything in cluded and assembled but the coaxial cable lead-in.

Con: Some performance drop within the 2 MHz (120 meter) and 3 MHz (90 meter) tropical world band segments. *Model C:* Coaxial cable lead-in not included.

☞ Eavesdropper also makes the $89.95 sloper antenna, not tested by us, similar to the Alpha Delta DX-SWL Sloper. It comes with a static arrestor, but no coaxial cable lead-in.

Verdict: If your teeth gnash when you see "Some Assembly Required," take heart. The Eavesdropper T, unlike Alpha Delta alterna-

tives, comes "ready to go" and is straightforward to erect. At most, you might want to get a pair of bungee straps to provide flexibility at the ends.

The size is user-friendly, too—the result of a compromise. There's no getting around the rule that the longer the antenna, the more likely it is to do well at low frequencies. Eavesdropper's designer, the late Jim Meadow, once told PASSPORT that he found few folks tuning below 4.7 MHz, but many people with limited yard space. So, he shrunk the Eavesdropper by focusing on performance above 4.7 MHz, yet allowed it to function decently lower down.

Our tests confirm this. The Eavesdropper horizontal trap dipoles perform quite nicely above 4.7 MHz, with a notch less gain than Alpha-Delta models in the 2 MHz and 3 MHz tropical world band segments.

In practice the ribbon lead-in wire used by the T version works well, using phasing to help cancel out electrical noise. Too, it stands up to the elements and usually has less signal loss than coaxial cable used by its C sibling.

Prepared by Stephen Bohac, Jock Elliott, Tony Jones, Lawrence Magne, David Walcutt and George Zeller.

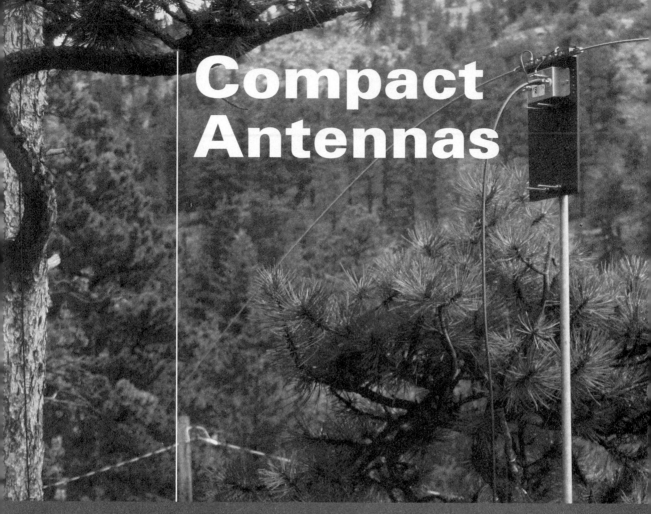

Compact Antennas

Do you enjoy world band by day, when signals are weaker, or elusive stations anytime? If so, put an accessory antenna near the head of your wish list.

Best are outdoor wire antennas that are unamplified—*passive*. Trouble is, they are lengthy, a pain to erect (think "big trees") and require yard space. But if you lack acreage, face community restrictions or are allergic to high-wire gymnastics, consider a compact antenna.

Compacts have a small rod, loop or wire receiving element to grab signals. But these are not big enough to have much oomph, so an amplifier is used to make up the difference. The antenna then becomes *active*, and today nearly all compact antennas are active.

These antennas have always been ideal for townhouses, apartments and hotels. But with detached houses now occupying more available lot size, even large homes may not have space for a passive wire antenna.

Greatly Improved

Early amplified antennas were noisy, overloaded easily, generated harmonic "false" signals and suffered if placed outdoors. They quickly earned a reputation for failing to deliver.

Things have changed. Now you can choose from several great performers. While compact antennas still don't fully equal their outdoor wire cousins, the gap has narrowed considerably. Indeed, a few occasionally outperform passive wire antennas in lower frequencies during high-static months.

The best compact antennas work surprisingly well and are unobtrusive.

Proximate *vs.* Remote

Compact antennas are either proximate or remote. A proximate has its receiving element on an amplifier box near the receiver. A remote model, whether active or passive, allows the receiving element to be mounted farther away—either indoors or, with some models, outdoors where reception tends to be superior.

Remote units are the way to go, as the receiving element can be put where electrical noise is weak but radio signals are strong. Proximate models give no such choice unless the receiver itself is placed where reception is best.

Some receivers emit electrical noise, usually from the front panel digital display. So, if you must use a proximate antenna put it behind or alongside the radio.

Yaesu's G-5500 twin-axis rotor mates well with the highly rated Wellbrook ALA 1530.

Loops Reduce Local Noise

Proximate loop antennas and indoor-remote loops are the least prone to receive local electrical noise. They are also less likely to pick up thunderstorm static and can be aimed away from electrical noise. All this improves the all-important signal-to-noise ratio—especially within lower frequency segments.

Wellbrook loops are especially effective because they can be outdoors and, unlike some other loops, are balanced. During high-static months their superior signal-to-noise ratios can make the difference between hearing static and understanding what's being said.

Travel Loops Best for Portables

Most active antennas are designed for table-top models, but not all. The Sony AN-LP1, great for home and on trips, is an exception-al value for use with nearly any portable. Another choice is the AOR WL500—pricier and less handy for trips, but an impressive performer. If price is paramount look into Degen's DE31.

Passive Compact

Often the first thing to go in an emergency is electricity. Batteries sometimes fill in, but nothing beats not needing electricity in the first place.

The R.F. Systems GMDSS-1 is that most unusual of antennas: short, yet with no electronic amplification. And it is tough enough to withstand serious abuse without flinching.

Preselection *vs.* Broadband

Broadband electronic amplifiers can cause all sorts of mischief. Some add noise and spurious signals, especially from the

INSTALLATION TIPS

When a remote compact antenna is installed properly it can perform very well. The bad news is that if you have room outdoors to mount it properly, you may also have room for a passive wire antenna that will perform better, yet. Probably cheaper, too.

Here are tips on placement of weather-resistant remote models, but creativity rules—experiment, experiment.

- Outdoors, put the receiving element in the clear, away from objects. Metal degrades performance, so especially keep it away from metal and use a nonconductive mast or capped PVC pipe. Optimum height from ground is usually around 10–25 feet or 3–8 meters. Here, "ground" refers to electrical ground—not only *terra firma*, but also reinforced concrete roofs and the like.

  Or try a tree. Although sap is electrically conductive, this is a reasonable fallback, especially with hardwood deciduous varieties. Keep leaves away from the receiving element.

- When yard placement is impractical, place the receiving element outdoors as far as you dare. In a high-rise building consider using a balcony or just outside a window. For example, if the receiving element is a rod, point it away from the building 45 degrees or so, like a flagpole. If you're on the top floor the roof may also be a good bet.

  If outdoor placement is impractical at your house, try the attic if the roof isn't metal. With large Wellbrook models, especially rotor-equipped, this beats having it hog an entire room.

- If all else fails affix the receiving element against the inside-center of a large window. Radio signals, like light, sail right through glass.

mediumwave AM band. Yet others overload a receiver with too much gain.

A partial fix is tunable or switchable prese-lection. This helps keep unwanted signals at bay by limiting the band of frequencies which get full amplification. Problem is, they almost always have controls that need tweaking. A high-pass filter or band rejec-tion filter (e.g., from Kiwa Electronics or Par Electronics) can also help keep powerful mediumwave AM stations from ghosting in to disturb world band.

How Much Oomph?

One way to judge an active antenna is sim-ply by how much gain it provides. That's like judging a car only by its horsepower.

An active antenna should provide signal levels similar to those from a good pas-sive wire antenna. With less gain, receiver circuit noise can become audible. Too much gain and the receiver's circuitry—maybe the antenna's, too—can become dysfunctional. Like Smucker's, it needs to be just right.

When Your Antenna Arrives

There are a number of things you can do to make your antenna reach its potential.

Active antennas work best off batteries, which avoid hum and buzz caused by AC mains power. But if your antenna uses an AC adaptor, keep it and electrical cords away from the receiving element and feed-line. If there's hum anyway, try substituting a higher-end AC adaptor from Radio Shack or other supplier.

Antenna performance is one part technol-ogy, another part geography-geology and a third part installation. We report on the first and give tips on the third. Yet, much depends on the second—local conditions. You can enhance those odds by placing the receiving element at various locations. Jerry-rig the antenna until you're satisfied the best spot has been found, then nail it down for good.

Finally, if your radio has multiple antenna inputs try each to see which works best.

What PASSPORT's Ratings Mean

Star ratings: ✪✪✪✪✪ is best for any type of antenna, but in reality even the best of compact antennas don't yet merit more than four stars when compared against long passive antennas. To help in deciding, star ratings for compact antennas can be compared directly against those for "lasso" antennas found elsewhere in this PASSPORT REPORTS. Stars reflect overall world band performance and meaningful features, plus to some extent ergonomics and build qual-ity. Price, appearance, country of manufac-ture and the like are not taken into account.

Passport's Choice. La crème de la crème. Our test team's personal picks of the litter—models we would buy or have bought for our personal use. Unlike star ratings, these choices are unapologetically subjective.

✪: A relative bargain, with decidedly more performance than the price would suggest. Active antennas are listed in descending order of merit. Unless otherwise indicated each has a one-year warranty.

✪✪✪✪   *Passport's Choice*
Wellbrook ALA330S

Outdoor-indoor. Active, remote, broad-band, 2.3–30 MHz

Price: *ALA 330S:* £189.00 plus £10.00 shipping in the United Kingdom and Eire. £189.00 plus £30.00 shipping elsewhere. *Upgrade kit '330 to '330S:* £80.00 plus £10.00 shipping in the United Kingdom and Eire. £80.00 plus £15.00 shipping else-where.

Pro: Best signal-to-noise ratio, including at times reduced pickup of thunderstorm static, on all shortwave frequencies, of any active model tested; low-noise/low-static pickup characteristics most notice-able below 8 MHz, especially during local summer, when it sometimes outperforms sophisticated outdoor wire antennas. Bal-anced loop design inherently helps reduce pickup of local electrical noise; additionally,

The Wellbrook ALA 330S can be mounted outdoors, as at this Rocky Mountain location, or indoors.   R. Sherwood

aluminum loop receiving element can be affixed to a low-cost TV rotor to improve reception by directionally nulling local electrical noise and, to a lesser degree, static. On occasion, rotatability also can slightly reduce co-channel shortwave interference below 4MHz, sometimes 5 MHz. Superior build quality, including rigorous weatherproofing (see Con). Supplied 117V AC adaptor (Stancor STA-300R) among best tested for not causing hum or buzzing (see Con). Although any large loop is inherently susceptible to inductive pickup of local thunderstorm static, during our tests of the prior and new versions the antenna's amplifier has never suffered static damage during storms; indeed, even nearby one kilowatt shortwave transmissions have not damaged it. Protected circuitry, using an easily replaced 315 mA slow-blow fuse. Threaded flange on "S" version improves mounting of loop receiving element (see Con). Superior factory support.

Con: Only moderate gain for reception within such modest-signal areas as Western Hemisphere, Asia and Australasia—a drawback only with receivers having relatively noisy circuitry. Slightly less gain than ALA 1530 within little-used 2.3–2.5 MHz (120 meter) tropical world band segment, a drawback only with receivers having relatively noisy circuitry. Mediumwave AM gain significantly inferior to that of the '1530. Flange for loop receiving element has metric pipe threading; most U.S. users will need to re-thread. Loop receiving element, about one meter across, is large and cumbersome to ship, although loop is slightly smaller than in the prior version. Mounting mast and optional rotor add to cost and complexity. BNC connector at the receiving element's base is open to the weather and thus needs to be user-sealed with Coax Seal, electrical putty or similar. Encapsulated amplifier makes repair impossible. Manufacturer cautions against allowing high winds to stress mounting flange, or sunlight to damage head amplifier; however, one of our units survived 90+ mph Rocky Mountain winds until the locally procured pipe coupling to which we had attached the antenna snapped. Adaptor supplied for 117V AC runs hot after being plugged in for an hour or two, while amplifier tends to run slightly warm. No coaxial cable supplied. Available for purchase or export only two cumbersome ways: via Sterling cheque or International Money Order through the English manufacturer (www.wellbrook.uk.com), or with credit card via an English dealer's unsecured email address (sales@shortwave.co.uk).

☞ The manufacturer offers a kit to convert the earlier ALA 330 to the improved "S" version. Recommended.

Verdict: The more we use this antenna, the more we like it, especially for its ability to reduce the impact of static and noise on weak signals below 8 MHz. If its dimensions and purchase hurdles don't deter you, you will not find a better active model than the Welsh-made Wellbrook ALA 330S.

For limited-space situations, and even to complement passive wire antennas on large properties, the '330S is hard to equal. However, if your receiver tends to sound "hissy" with weak signals, then it probably needs an antenna which gives even more gain than the '330S so it can overcome internal receiver noise. Of course, with top-rated tabletop models this is not an issue.

For best reception the antenna should be mounted outdoors, away from the house and atop a rotor. However, this is more important with the ALA 1530 model (*see* below) when used for longwave and mediumwave AM reception. In the real world of limited options, reasonable results on shortwave are sometimes obtained even indoors sans rotor or with manual rotation, provided the usual caveats are followed for placement of the reception element. But there's no getting around the laws of physics: The Wellbrook loop is an antenna, and all antennas work much better when not shielded by absorptive materials or placed near sources of electrical interference.

What's not to like? An ordering procedure that's inconvenient and démodé. There are no dealers outside the United Kingdom, and as there is still no secure way for those beyond U.K. borders to order by credit card on the Internet.

Overall, the '330S isn't in the same league as top-rated outdoor wire antennas. However, it can outperform even those antennas with some static-prone signals or when local electrical noise is a problem—provided it is erected properly.

✪✪✪⅛ *Passport's Choice*
Wellbrook ALA 1530, Wellbrook ALA 1530P

Outdoor-indoor. Active, remote, broadband, 0.15–30 MHz

Price: *ALA 1530:* £159.00 plus £10.00 shipping in the United Kingdom and Eire. £159.00 plus £30.00 shipping elsewhere. *ALA 1530P (not tested):* £159.00 plus £10.00 shipping in the United Kingdom and Eire. £159.95 plus £30.00 shipping elsewhere. *Yaesu G-5500/G-5500B twin-axis rotor:* $639.95 in the United States. $1,060.00CAD

Wellbrook's ALA 1530 excels with tough mediumwave AM signals, as well as world band stations.   R. Sherwood

in Canada. £559.00 in the United Kingdom. €659.00 in Germany.

Pro: Covers at comparable levels of performance not only shortwave, but also mediumwave AM and longwave nominally down to 150 kHz—but actually down to 30 kHz with reduced sensitivity (*see* Con); other Wellbrook models offer longwave coverage down to 50 kHz (LA 5030, 50 kHz–30 MHz indoor model) or 10 kHz (LFL 1010, 10 kHz–10 MHz outdoor model). Mediumwave AM and longwave performance superb when '1530 coupled to a Yaesu G-5500/G-5500B rotor, which has twin-axis directionality; also, rotor can sometimes slightly reduce co-channel shortwave interference below about 4 MHz or occasionally even 5 MHz. Very nearly the best signal-to-noise ratio among active models tested, including reduced pickup of thunderstorm static. Balanced loop design inherently helps reduce pickup of local electrical noise. Low-noise/low-static pickup characteristic most noticeable below 8 MHz during summer, when it sometimes outperforms sophisticated outdoor wire antennas. Slightly more gain than sibling ALA 330S within little-used 2.3–2.5 MHz (120 meter) tropical world band segment. Superior build quality, including rigorous weatherproofing (see Con). Supplied AC adaptor, properly bypassed and regulated, is among the best tested for not causing hum or buzzing. Although any large loop's amplifier is inherently susceptible to inductive pickup of local thunderstorm static, during our tests the antenna's amp never suffered static damage during storms; indeed, even nearby one kilowatt shortwave transmissions did no damage to the antenna amplifier. Protected circuitry, using an easily replaced 315 mA slow-blow fuse. Superior factory support.

Con: Extended frequency range can result in mediumwave AM signals surfacing within the shortwave spectrum, degrading reception—usually a more significant issue in urban and suburban North America than elsewhere (even an unsophisticated rotor can help by turning the antenna perpendicular to an offending mediumwave AM signal's axis); this tends to be less of a problem at night because of reduced local transmitting powers, and is less of a problem in our latest unit. Prone to overloading some receivers in locations rich with strong mediumwave AM signals; this also tends to be less of a problem at night because of reduced local transmitting powers. Only moderate gain, slightly less than sibling ALA 330S, for reception within such modest-signal areas as Western Hemisphere, Asia and Australasia. Balanced loop receiving element, about one meter across, not easy to mount and is large and cumbersome to ship. Mounting mast and optional rotor add to cost and complexity of erection. BNC connector at the receiving element's base is open to the weather and thus needs to be user-sealed with Coax Seal, electrical putty or similar. Encapsulated amplifier makes repair impossible. Manufacturer cautions against allowing high winds to stress mounting flange or sunlight to damage head amplifier; however, after a summer of wind and sun at one outdoor test location, nothing untoward has materialized. Adaptor supplied for 117V AC runs hot after being plugged in for a few hours, while amplifier tends to run slightly warm. No coaxial cable supplied. Available for purchase or export only two cumbersome ways: via Sterling cheque or International Money Order through the English manufacturer (www.wellbrook.uk.com), or with credit card via an English dealer's unsecured email address (sales@shortwave.co.uk).

☞ An antenna tuner may improve signal level by as much as 6 dB.

☞ Mediumwave AM and longwave performance directionality may suffer if the '1530 is not mounted well away from other antennas.

BADMINTON ANTENNA

Listeners facing antenna restrictions have concocted a dog's breakfast of hidden and camouflaged outdoor wire antennas. Some look like a clothesline or part of a badminton net. Yet others are tucked underneath awnings or canopies.

Some play to urban apathy by hanging thin-wire antennas out in the open, then waiting to see what happens. One creative Australian even told a curious neighbor that his loop antenna was an "art sculpture"—it worked!

Trompe d'oeil antennas can perform surprisingly well when mated to the MFJ-1020C, around $80. Just remove its telescopic antenna and—voilà—it becomes a Grade A tunable active preselector.

Deep pockets? If you want something James Bondish, the SGC Stealth Antenna Kit (not tested) from wsplc.com is £407.17 in the United Kingdom, £280.81 plus shipping overseas.

☞ The '1530 is the sibling of the former ALA 330, not the newer ALA 330S.

☞ The "P" version, not tested, uses a semi-rigid plastic loop rather than aluminum and is for indoor use.

Verdict: Interested in distant broadcast goodies below the shortwave spectrum, as well as world band? If so, the Wellbrook ALA 1530 is hard to beat—so long as you don't live near local mediumwave AM transmission facilities. A rotor is *de rigeur* for nulling co-channel interference below 1.7 MHz, and also may help a skosh with tropical world band stations. As with all Wellbrook loop antennas the '1530 excels at rejecting noise and static, particularly below 8 MHz.

✪✪✪½ *Passport's Choice*
RF Systems DX-One Professional Mark II

Outdoor-indoor "eggbeater." Active, remote, broadband, 0.02–60 MHz.

Price: *DX-One Pro antenna:* $669.95 in the United States. £359.95 in the United Kingdom. €498.00 in Germany.

Pro: Outstanding dynamic range. Very low noise. Outputs for two receivers. Comes standard with switchable band rejection filter to reduce the chances of mediumwave AM signals ghosting into the shortwave spectrum. Receiving element has outstanding build quality. Coaxial connector at head amplifier is completely shielded from the weather by a clever mechanical design. Superior low noise, high gain performance on mediumwave AM.

Con: Unbalanced design makes antenna susceptible to importing buzz at some locations; this is especially noticeable because of otherwise-excellent performance. AC power supply not bypassed as well as it could be, causing slight hum on some signals. More likely than most antennas to exacerbate fading, even though design nominally reduces fading effects. No coaxial cable supplied. Output position for 10 dB gain measures +6 dB. Warranty only six months.

The RF Systems DX-One Professional Mark II. Mark II costs as much as some receivers, but offers superior dynamic range and low noise.   R. Sherwood

Verdict: The pricey RF Systems DX-One Professional Mark II is a superior performer. As with any antenna having a small capture area and an unbalanced design, at some locations it is prone to picking up local electrical noise. Made in the Netherlands.

New for 2006
✪✪✪½
DX Engineering DXE-ARAH-1P

Outdoor-indoor dipole. Active, remote, broadband 0.06–30 MHz.

Price: *DXE-ARAH-1P:* $259.00 (about $300 with shipping) in the United States. *Aftermarket coaxial cable and plugs (required):* Usually $15–45 in the United States.

Pro: Unusual capture length helps produce superior signal-to-noise ratio. Feedline does not act as involuntary antenna. Worthy gain above about 9 MHz, rising to peak at 27 MHz. Excellent freedom from mediumwave AM "ghosting" when set up appropriately.

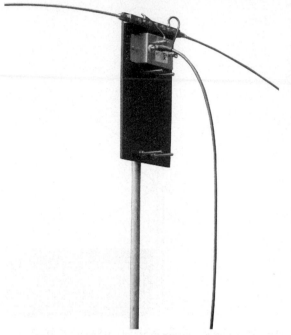

The new DX Engineering DXE-ARAH-1P gets high marks for performance. Reasonably priced, too, but its receiving elements are unusually long.   R. Sherwood

Very good mediumwave AM and longwave performance when set up appropriately. Excellent build quality. Circuit board not potted, facilitating repair.

Con: Takes up much more space than usual for a compact antenna. Wide design limits mounting options if rotatability desired. Mediumwave AM and longwave gain drops sharply when amplifier set up to avoid intermodulation within shortwave spectrum. Amplifier box not weatherproof without obtaining and applying sealant. No coaxial cables or printed owner's manual.

Verdict: Ours was one of the very first units produced, and already there were two resistors tack soldered onto the amplifier's circuit board. Too, we were able to get it working properly only just before presstime.

We'll look at this model in depth after its "shakedown cruise," but in the meantime it appears to be a well-made performer that's more active than compact. It acquits itself well, but similar performance can be had for less, while better performance isn't much costlier.

Evaluation of New Model: The DX Engineering DXE-ARAH-1P uses two end-to-end CB whips to form an 18-foot (5.5 meter) horizontal dipole having a head amplifier in the center. Although they stick out horizontally, droop makes the antenna more like an inverted-V.

The coaxial cable feedline is decoupled from the receiving elements, so it can't cause elevated pickup or overload by acting as an involuntary antenna. Recommended mounting height is 20 feet (six meters) or more, well away from transmitting antennas.

Included is an AC adaptor that produces occasional minor hum at some locations. No coaxial cables are provided, and one cable has to be fitted with a PL-259 plug and an RCA plug—an unlikely off-the-shelf combo, so an adaptor or soldering is also called for. Our unit came with no printed documentation, but an owner's manual can be downloaded at www.dxengineering. com/pdf/ARA.pdf.

The dipole's head amplifier is linear with a variety of receivers, although on a test Icom IC-R71A it became unstable at some frequencies. The amp's factory default is for locations free from powerful mediumwave AM signals, which allows for full gain throughout the longwave, mediumwave and shortwave spectra. However, at suburban and urban sites this also produces intermodulation from mediumwave AM stations. These "ghosts" can exceed a whopping S9 within tropical world band segments, petering out only around 18 MHz.

Solution: Reset the amp's internal jumpers. This drops mediumwave AM reception by 30 dB, which at all but the toughest locations banishes the problem on shortwave.

For world band the antenna has about the same gain as Wellbrook's 1530 loop, which is about 10 dB less than the top-rated Wellbrook 330S. Gain also improves as the shortwave frequency increases, especially above 10 MHz and as the dipole's resonant frequency of 27 MHz is approached.

At times the dipole's lower gain results in a superior signal-to-noise ratio on weak signals. Otherwise, the 330S wins out.

With jumpers at "rural" default, gain is worthy throughout the mediumwave AM band—longwave, too. It even does nicely on WWVB at 60 kHz—40 kHz below the nominal lower cutoff frequency.

Overall, build quality is excellent and the circuit board is not potted, so it's repairable. However, the head amplifier is inside an aluminum box that isn't fully weatherproofed. The manual recommends sealing the box's top edges, but leaving the bottom open so moisture can escape.

DX Engineering also offers the $229 DXE-ARAV-1P vertical whip, not tested; it mounts at ground level above a separately purchased ground system. Another, also not tested, is the DXE-ARAV-4P—a four-vertical phased array. It's a gilt-edged $796.

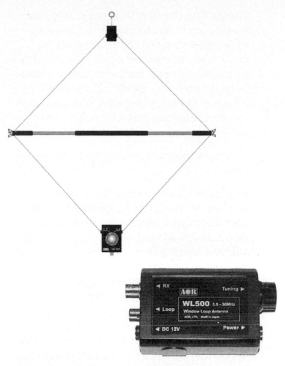

AOR's WL500 portable loop, tops in its class, was abruptly discontinued in late 2005.

❂❂❂¼ *Passport's Choice*
AOR WL500

Indoor-portable loop. Active, remote, manual preselection, 0.155–1.71 MHz + 3.1–30 MHz.

Price: *WL500, 3.1–30 MHz:* $198.95 in the United States. *Optional 500LM, 0.155–1.71 MHz:* $89.95 in the United States.

Pro: Very good for use with portables; also works well with portatop and tabletop models. Can be easily assembled and disassembled during airline and other travel, although its transportability is not so clever as that of the Sony AN-LP1 (the '500 uses zip cord held in place by a two-piece wooden rod with wing nuts on the ends); except for the two rod parts, which could be sharpened and used as weapons, it is handy for hospital, prison or other institutional use where an antenna must be stashed away periodically. Excellent gain. As compared to proximate antennas and most other indoor-remote antennas, somewhat lower pickup of local electrical noise. Modest battery consumption (16 mA) allows for use without an AC adaptor; this prevents added hum and noise (*see* Con). Screw configuration to access battery cavity unlikely to be stripped with use (*see* Con).

Con: Indoors only—can't be mounted outdoors during inclement weather. Possible sensitivity to static charges (*see first* ☞, below). Some birdies and tweets, possibly from incipient spurious oscillation. Two rod parts could be thought of by airport security as potential weapons, so should be stowed as checked luggage. Performs only marginally within little-used 2 MHz (120 meter) tropical world band segment. Requires manual peaking when significantly changing received frequency, although not as often as some other models thanks to fairly low circuit "Q." Changing 9V battery calls for unscrewing six annoyingly tiny screws to remove protective plate. AC adaptor not available from AOR for continuous-use applications, although manufacturer states that one eventually will be offered in certain as-yet-unspecified markets (alternatively, an outboard rechargeable battery can be used).

Comes with only a BNC connector for the receiver; user has to modify the antenna-to-receiver cable or obtain adaptors for other types of receiver inputs. Comes with two wing nuts that are easily lost on trips; frequent travelers should obtain spares in advance. Optional longwave/mediumwave receiving element performs poorly, not recommended.

☞ Discontinued, but sometimes still found new.

☞ Our first sample ceased functioning in a low-humidity environment when the operator's hand apparently discharged static electricity onto the connector to the antenna range switch. This happened as he reached to adjust it from high to low range, damaging circuitry within the control box at the opposite end of the cable. However, those who sell the antenna indicate that there have been no other known failures of this sort, but this is a new model so it's not yet certain whether the '500's interface unit is genuinely sensitive to static charges.

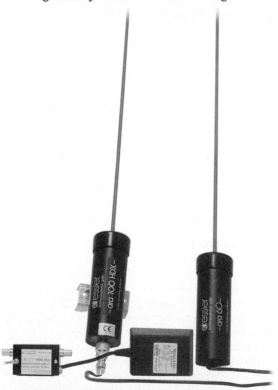

Dressler's ARA 100 HDX and ARA 60S.   R. Sherwood

☞ Although the lower tuning parameter of the WL500 is nominally 3.5 MHz, tests show that performance remains equally good down to just below 3.1 MHz.

Verdict: For the traveling listener or DXer focused on reception quality, the new AOR WL500 is a welcome but relatively costly alternative to the Sony AN-LP1. Overall, it slightly outperforms the Sony, but it lacks the Sony's spit and polish for mounting and packing on trips. Both are made in Japan.

✪✪✪
Dressler ARA 100 HDX

Outdoor-indoor rod. Active, remote, broadband, 0.04–40 MHz.

Price: $549.95 in the United States. £349.95 in the United Kingdom.

Pro: Superior build quality, with fiberglass whip and foam-encapsulated head amplifier to resist the weather (*see* Con). Very good gain below 20 MHz (*see* Con). Superior signal-to-noise ratio. Handy detachable "N" connector on bottom. AC adaptor with properly bypassed and regulated DC output is better than most.

Con: Even though it has an amplifier with superior dynamic range, tends to overload in urban/suburban environments awash in powerful mediumwave AM signals unless antenna element mounted close to the ground; this tends to be less of a problem at night because of reduced local transmitting powers. Encapsulated design makes most repairs impossible. Above 20 MHz gain begins to fall off slightly. Body of antenna runs slightly warm. "N" connector at the head amplifier/receiving element exposed to weather, needs to be sealed with Coax Seal, electrical putty or similar by user. Gain control cumbersome to adjust; fortunately, in practice it is rarely needed. Reader reports suggest that ordering direct from the factory can be a frustrating experience.

☞ Star rating applies only when used where there is not significant ambient mediumwave RF, as the Dressler ARA 100 HDX, unless mounted close to the ground, is prone to overloading at locations rich with strong mediumwave AM signals or low-band VHF-TV stations. At some locations, even mounting the antenna on the ground does not eliminate overloading.

Verdict: The robust Dressler ARA 100 HDX, made in Germany, is an excellent but costly low-noise antenna for locations not near one or more powerful mediumwave AM or low-band VHF-TV transmitters.

✪✪✪ ❷ *Passport's Choice*
MFJ-1020C (with short wire element)

Outdoor-indoor wire. Active, remote, manual preselection, 0.3–40 MHz.

Price: *MFJ-1020C (without antenna wire or insulators):* $79.95 in the United States. $125.00CAD in Canada. £89.95 in the United Kingdom. *MFJ-1312D 120V AC adaptor:* $14.95 in the United States. *Radio Shack 278-758 "Outdoor Antenna Kit":* $9.99 in the United States.

Pro: Superior dynamic range, so functions effectively with an outboard wire receiving element, preferably mounted outdoors, in lieu of built-in telescopic antenna element. Sharp preselector peak unusually effective in preventing overloading. Works best off battery (*see* Con). Choice of PL-259 or RCA connections. 30-day money-back guarantee if purchased from manufacturer.

Con: Preselector complicates operation; tune control needs adjustment even with modest frequency changes, especially within the mediumwave AM band. Knobs small and touchy to adjust. High current draw (measures 30 mA), so battery runs down quickly. Removing sheet-metal screws often to change battery should eventually result in stripping unless great care is taken. AC adaptor, optional, causes significant hum on many received signals.

☞ The '1020C serves little or no useful purpose as a tunable preselector for *long* inverted-L or other normally passive wire antennas. It cannot be used as an unamplified preselector; e.g., to improve front-end selectivity with significant wire antennas.

The **MFJ-1020C** is only so-so as a proximate antenna. Yet, remove its telescopic element and—*voilà!*— it becomes an active preselector for a remote antenna element. R. Sherwood

Trying to do something similar by using the amplified unit at reduced gain does not improve the signal-to-noise ratio, nor does it improve dynamic range (reduce potential to overload), as the gain potentiometer is only an output pad (with a measured 40 dB range).

☞ Two manufacturing flaws found on one of our "B" version units tested in the past, but this year's "C" unit had no defects. The owner's manual warns of possible "taking off" if the gain is set too high, but during our tests using a variety of receivers we encountered oscillation with only one model.

Verdict: The '1020C has a little secret: it's only okay the way the manufacturer sells it as a proximate active antenna, but as a preselector with an outdoor random-length wire antenna it is a worthy low-cost performer—better, in fact, than MFJ's designated shortwave preselector. Simply collapse (or, better, remove) the built-in telescopic antenna, then connect an outboard wire antenna to the '1020C's external antenna input. For this, Radio Shack's "Outdoor Antenna Kit" or equivalent works fine with the receiving element cut down to a convenient length.

Alas, the optional AC adaptor introduces hum much of the time, battery drain is considerable, and changing the built-in battery is inconvenient and relies on wear-prone sheet-metal screws. Best bet, unless you're into experimenting with power supplies: Skip the adaptor and use a large outboard rechargeable battery.

Peso for peso, the MFJ-1020C fed by a remote wire receiving element is the best buy among active antennas. The rub is that the use of several yards or meters of wire, preferably outdoors, makes it something of a hybrid requiring more space than other active antennas. But for many row houses, townhouses, ground-floor and rooftop apartments with a patch of outdoor space it can be a godsend. If visibility is an issue, use ultra-thin wire for the receiving element.

✪✪✪

Dressler ARA 60 S

Outdoor-indoor rod. Active, remote, broadband, 0.04–60/100 MHz.

Price: $349.95 in the United States. £189.95 in the United Kingdom. €209.00 in Germany.

Unlike other compact antennas, the RF Systems GMDSS-1 uses no electronic amplification. This limits signal boost, but provides other advantages. D. Zantow

Pro: Superior build quality, with fiberglass whip and foam-encapsulated head amplifier to resist weather (*see* Con). Very good and consistent gain, even above 20 MHz. AC adaptor with properly bypassed and regulated DC output is better than most.

Con: Encapsulated design makes most repairs impossible. RG-58 coaxial cable permanently attached on antenna end, making user replacement impossible. Gain control cumbersome to adjust; fortunately, in practice it is rarely needed. Reader reports suggest that ordering direct from the factory can be a frustrating experience.

☞ Comments about overloading in the above review of the ARA 100 HDX likely apply to the '60 S, as well.

Verdict: Very similar to the ARA 100 HDX—even its dynamic range and overloading performance are virtually identical. This makes the German-made ARA 60 S an excellent lower-cost alternative to the ARA 100 HDX.

✪✪⅞

RF Systems GMDSS-1

Outdoor vertical rod. Passive, remote, broadband, 0.1–25 MHz.

Price: *Antenna:* $204.95 in the United States. €158.00 in the Netherlands. *AK-1 mounting bracket kit:* $22.95 in the United States. *AK-2 mounting bracket kit:* $34.95 in the United States. €35.00 in the Netherlands.

Pro: Superior signal-to-noise ratio for a compact antenna except within 21 MHz segment. Superior rejection of local electrical noise. Passive (unamplified) design avoids hum, buzz and other shortcomings often inherent with active antennas (*see* Con). No amplification required; yet, from about 9 MHz through 12 MHz this short antenna (6.5 feet, two meters) produces signals almost comparable to those from a lengthy outdoor wire antenna (*see* Con). Passive design allows it to function in emergency situations where electricity is not assured. Vertical configuration unusually appropriate for certain locations; can be further camouflaged with non-metallic paint. Superior build quality, using stainless steel and heavy UV resistant PVC; also, internal helical receiving element is rigorously sealed (*see* Con). No radials required, unusual for a vertical antenna. Worthy mediumwave AM reception for a nondirectional antenna.

Con: Except for approximately 9 MHz through 12 MHz, weak-signal performance varies from fair to poor, depending on the tuned frequency. A mounting kit is required and is extra. The AK-1 mounting bracket kit, sold in North America, not stainless. Connecting cable between antenna and radio not included.

☞ A slightly less costly variant of the GMDSS-1 is the RF Systems MTA-1, which nominally operates to full specification from 0.5–30 MHz.

Verdict: Although unamplified and scarcely taller than most men, the RF Systems GMDSS-1 vertical performs surprisingly well. However, pedestrian signal oomph in many world band segments limits its attraction except with a high-sensitivity receiver or an active preselector. Some portables also benefit from the modest signal input.

Made in the Netherlands, it is constructed like a tank. Between this and its complete independence from electricity, it is unusually appropriate for emergencies, civil disorders and hostile climates.

❶❶¾ @ *Passport's Choice*
Sony AN-LP1

Indoor-portable loop. Active, remote, manual preselection, 3.9–4.3/4.7–25 MHz.

Price: $94.95 in the United States. €99.95 in Germany.

Pro: Excellent for use with portables. Very good overall performance, including generally superior gain (*see* Con), especially within world band segments—yet surprisingly free from side effects. Battery operation, so no internally caused hum or noise (*see* Con). Clever compact folding design for airline and other travel; also handy for institutional

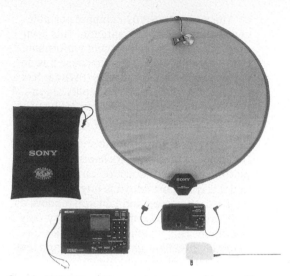

Sony's AN-LP1 has become legendary with portable radios. Handy to use and priced to move, with good performance. R. Sherwood

use where antenna must be stashed periodically. Can be used even with portables that have no antenna input jack (*see* Con). Plug-in filter to reduce local electrical noise (*see* Con). Low battery consumption (*see* Con).

Con: Indoors only—can't be mounted outdoors during inclement weather. Functions acceptably on shortwave only 3.9-4.3 MHz and 4.7-25 MHz, with no mediumwave AM or longwave coverage. Gain varies markedly throughout the shortwave spectrum, in large part because the preselector's step-tuned resonances lack variable peaking. Preselector bandswitching complicates operation slightly. Operates only from batteries (two "AA," not included)—no AC adaptor provided, not even a socket for one. Consumer-grade plastic construction with no shielding. When clipped onto a telescopic antenna instead of fed through an antenna jack, the lack of a ground connection reduces performance. Plug-in noise filter unit reduces signal strength by several decibels.

☞ Sony recommends that the AN-LP1 not be used with the Sony ICF-SW77 receiver. However, our tests indicate that so long as the control box and loop receiving element are kept reasonably away from the radio, the antenna performs well.

☞ The Sony ICF-SW07 compact portable comes with an AN-LP2 antenna. This is virtually identical in concept and performance to the AN-LP1, except that because it is designed solely for use with the 'SW07 it has automatic preselection to simplify operation. At present the AN-LP2 cannot be used with other radios, even those from Sony.

Verdict: A real winner if the shoe fits. This is the handiest model for travelers wanting superior world band reception on portables—and it is truly portable. It is often a worthy choice for portatop and tabletop models, as well, provided you don't mind battery-only operation. This Japanese-made device has generally excellent gain, low noise and few side effects. Priced right, too.

There is limited frequency coverage—90/120 meter DXers should look elsewhere—and the loop receiving element cannot be mounted permanently outdoors. Too, the lack of variable preselector peaking causes gain to vary greatly by frequency. Otherwise, the Sony AN-LP1 is nothing short of a bargain.

AOR's LA-350, with an underwhelming cost-to-performance ratio, was replaced in late 2005 by a similarly priced model. R. Sherwood

✪✪¾
AOR LA-350

Indoor loop. Active, proximate, manual preselection, 0.2–1.6 MHz/2.5–33 MHz.

Price: *LA-350 antenna, with two shortwave elements:* $330.00 in the United States. £199.00 in the United Kingdom. €349.00 in Germany. *350L longwave element, 350M mediumwave AM element:* $72.95 each in the United States. £49.00 in the United Kingdom. €79.95 in Germany.

Pro: Above-average gain. Some directivity below 10 MHz, directionally nulling local electrical noise and static. Sometimes, rotatability can also slightly reduce co-channel shortwave interference; as is the norm with loop antennas, this modest nulling of co-channel skywave interference is best at frequencies below 5 MHz. Rotatability can also improve reception by directionally nulling local electrical noise. Small, easy to rotate. Antenna elements easy to swap (*see* Con). Relatively easy to peak by ear or signal-strength indicator (*see* Con).

Con: Proximate model, so receiving element has to be placed near receiver. Unbalanced design results in local electrical noise being passed into receiver at some locations; owner's manual says a better AC adaptor can reduce this, but a $300 product should come equipped with the proper adaptor. Requires change of antenna elements when going from 3–9 MHz range to 9–33 MHz range or *vice versa*; separate (optional) elements for mediumwave AM and longwave also require shuffling. Reduced performance within 2 MHz (120 meter) world band segment. Requires manual peaking when significantly changing received frequency. Phone plug, which connects antenna elements to the head amplifier, lacks lock washer and thus may loosen; easily remedied with Loctite. User has to supply BNC female-to-PL239 male adaptor, needed to connect antenna to many models of tabletop receivers. Owner's manual says BNC-to-BNC cable comes with antenna, but was not packed with our unit.

☞ The LA-350 has been superceded by the kindred LA-380, which uses a single loop to cover 10 kHz to 500 MHz.

Verdict: The '350's unbalanced design makes it more susceptible to local electrical noise pickup than either Wellbrook model, and the supplied AC adaptor doesn't help. It also requires manual swapping of loop heads and circuit peaking. This having been said, where local electrical noise doesn't intrude the '350's superior gain, handy size and ease of rotation make it an effective choice for use indoors.

★★½ Ⓒ
Ameco TPA

Indoor rod. Active, proximate, manual preselection, 0.22–30 MHz.

Price: $76.95 in the United States $99.95CAD in Canada.

Pro: Highest recovered signal with the longest supplied antenna of the four proximate models tested. Most pleasant unit to tune to proper frequency. Superior ergonomics, including easy-to-read front panel with good-sized metal knobs (see Con). Superior gain below 10 MHz.

Con: Proximate model, so receiving element has to be placed near receiver. Above 15 MHz gain slips to slightly below average. Overloads with external antenna; because gain potentiometer is in the first stage, decreasing gain may increase overloading as current drops through the FET. Preselector complicates operation, compromising otherwise-superior ergonomics. No rubber feet, slides around in use; user-remediable. No AC adaptor. Consumer-grade plastic construction with no shielding. Comes with no printed information on warranty; however, manufacturer states by telephone that it is the customary one year.

Verdict: Back in the heyday of Hammarlund, Hallicrafters and National, there also was Ameco with its CW learning kits and the like. While most other American radio firms were crushed by the advance of technology, Ameco stayed light on its feet and survived. Well, sort of. Since 2004 Ameco has been associated with a new firm, Milestone Technologies of Colorado.

Ameco's TPA active antenna remains one of the best proximate models tested for

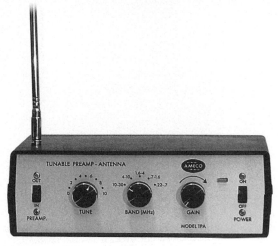

The Ameco TPA is one of the best proximate antennas tested. R. Sherwood

bringing in usable signals with a telescopic antenna, and signal recovery is excellent. However, when connected to an external antenna it overloads badly, and reducing gain doesn't help.

★★½
McKay Dymek DA100E, McKay Dymek DA100EM, Stoner Dymek DA100E, Stoner Dymek DA100EM

Indoor-outdoor-marine rod. Active, remote, broadband, 0.05–30 MHz.

Price: *DA100E:* $179.95 in the United States. *DA100EM (marine version, not tested):* $199.95 in the United States.

Pro: Respectable gain and noise. Generally good build quality, with worthy coaxial cable and an effectively sealed receiving element; marine version (not tested) appears to be even better yet for resisting weather. Jack for second antenna when turned off. Minor gain rolloff at higher shortwave frequencies. *DA100EM (not tested):* Weather-resistant fiberglass whip and brass fittings help ensure continued optimum performance.

Con: Slightly higher noise floor compared to other models. Some controls may confuse initially. Dynamic range among the lowest of any model tested; for many applications

Dymek DA100E units are warhorses which have evolved over many years.   R. Sherwood

in the Americas this is adequate, but for use near local transmitters, or in Europe and other strong-signal parts of the world, the antenna is best purchased on a returnable basis. *DA100E:* Telescopic antenna allows moisture and avian waste penetration between segments, and thus potential resis-

The MFJ 1024 provides good gain and low noise, but suffers from hum and limited dynamic range.
R. Sherwood

tance and/or spurious signals; user should seal these gaps with Coax Seal, electrical putty or similar. Telescopic antenna could, in principle, be de-telescoped by birds, ice and the like, although we did not actually encounter this. Warranty only 30 days.

Verdict: The DA100E is a proven "out of the box" choice, with generally excellent weatherproofing and coaxial cable. Because its dynamic range is relatively modest, it is more prone than some other models to overload, especially in an urban environment or other high-signal-strength location. In principle the extra twenty bucks for the marine version should be a good investment, provided its fiberglass whip is not too visible for your location.

✪✪¼
MFJ-1024

Indoor-outdoor rod. Active, remote, broadband, 0.05–30 MHz.

Price: $139.95 in the United States. $220.00CAD in Canada. £149.95 in the United Kingdom.

Pro: Overall good gain and low noise. A/B selector for quick connection to another receiver. "Aux" input for passive antenna. 30-day money-back guarantee if purchased from manufacturer.

Con: Significant hum with supplied AC adaptor; remedied when we substituted a suitable aftermarket adaptor. Non-standard power socket complicates substitution of AC adaptor; also, adaptor's sub-mini plug can spark when inserted while the adaptor is plugged in; adaptor should be unplugged beforehand. Dynamic range among the lowest of any model tested; for many applications in the Americas it is adequate, but for use near local transmitters, or in Europe and other strong-signal parts of the world, antenna is best purchased on a returnable basis. Slightly increased noise floor compared to other models. Telescopic antenna allows moisture and avian waste penetration between segments, and thus potential resistance and/or spurious signals; user should seal these gaps with Coax Seal, electrical putty or similar. Telescopic antenna could, in principle, be de-telescoped by birds, ice and the like after installation, although we did not actually encounter this. Control box/amplifier has no external weather sealing to protect from moisture, although the printed circuit board nominally comes with a water-resistant coating. Coaxial cable to receiver not provided. Mediocre coaxial cable provided between control box and receiving element. On our unit, a coaxial connector came poorly soldered from the factory.

Verdict: The MFJ-1024, made in America, performs almost identically to the Stoner Dymek DA100E, but sells for $40 less. However, that gap lessens if you factor in the cost of a worthy AC adaptor—assuming you can find or alter one to fit the unusual power jack—and the quality of the 1024's coaxial cable is not in Dymek's league.

With its built-in telescopic antenna element, the MFJ-1020C offers so-so performance with plenty of knob twiddling. R. Sherwood

★★¼
MFJ-1020C

Indoor rod. Active, proximate, manual preselection, 0.3–40 MHz.

Price: *MFJ-1020C:* $79.95 in the United States. $125.00CAD in Canada. £89.95 in the United Kingdom. *MFJ-1312D 120V AC adaptor:* $14.95 in the United States.

Pro: Rating rises to three stars if converted from a proximate to a remote model by connecting a wire to the external antenna input; see separate review, above. Superior dynamic range, and sharp preselector peak unusually effective in preventing overloading. Works best off battery (*see* Con). Choice of PL-259 or RCA connections. 30-day money-back guarantee if purchased from manufacturer.

Con: Proximate model, so receiving element has to be placed near receiver (can be converted, *see* Pro). Preselector complicates operation; tune control needs adjustment even with modest frequency changes, especially within the mediumwave AM band. Knobs small and touchy to adjust. High

current draw (measures 30 mA), so battery runs down quickly. Removing sheet-metal screws often to change battery should eventually result in stripping unless great care is taken. AC adaptor, optional, causes significant hum on many received signals.

☞ Two manufacturing flaws found on one of our "B" version units tested in the past, but this year's "C" unit had no defects. The owner's manual warns of possible "taking off" if the gain is set too high, but during our tests using a variety of receivers we encountered oscillation with only one model.

Verdict: The MFJ-1020C, made in the United States, is okay as a proximate antenna with its own telescopic antenna. However, it works much better when coupled to a random-length wire in lieu of the built-in telescopic antenna; see the separate review earlier in this article.

Alas, the optional AC adaptor introduces hum much of the time, battery drain is considerable, and changing the built-in battery is inconvenient and relies on wear-prone sheet-metal screws. Best bet, unless you're into experimenting with power supplies: Skip the adaptor and use a large outboard rechargeable battery.

New for portable radios: The Kaito KA31, also sold as the Degen DE31, provides respectable performance at an exceptionally low price.

New for 2006

★★ ◎

Degen DE31, Kaito KA31

Indoor-portable loop. Active, remote, manual preselection, 3.9–22 MHz

Price: $39.99 in the United States.

Pro: Appropriate for use with portables. Meaningful gain, especially above 9 MHz. Very good dynamic range. Low noise and absence of spurious signals. Battery operation, so no internally caused hum or noise (*see* Con). Compact collapsible design for airline and other travel; also handy for institutional use where antenna must be stashed periodically. Long cable (*see* Con) allows loop to be placed relatively far from radio. Adaptor sometimes allows for connection to a receiver lacking 1/8-inch antenna jack (*see* Con). Fairly low current draw (*see* Con).

Con: Indoors only—can't be mounted outdoors during inclement weather. Tunes only 3.9–22 MHz, so no mediumwave AM or longwave coverage. Touchy tuning control. Operates only from batteries (two "AAA," not included) and has no AC adaptor or socket. Battery consumption, although low, nearly twice manufacturer's specification, so replacement rises accordingly. Consumer-grade plastic construction with no shielding. When clipped onto radio's telescopic antenna instead of fed through an antenna jack, the lack of a ground connection on the radio greatly reduces performance. Rotation for local-noise reduction impeded by limp-rope design. Small suction cup fails if it and glass surface not exceptionally clean. Affixed suction cup not easy to remove. No carrying pouch to keep parts together. No reel to keep main cable from being tangled. *North America:* Available only as gray market import or via eBay. *Outside North America and China:* Available only via eBay. *Outside China:* No manufacturer's warranty.

Verdict: Respectable performance, minimal investment.

Evaluation of New Model: The thrifty new Degen DE31 antenna, made in China and sold in North America as the Kaito KA31, uses a thin rope-like material encompassing an antenna wire. A spreader gives it a diamond shape to create an effective and portable receiving loop.

A long cable allows this loop to be placed well away from the radio—an obvious convenience. A small suction cup holds the loop to a window, but its and the cup must be whistle clean or the antenna falls. Better is to attach the included micro clip to, say, a curtain.

There's an adaptor for radios without a 1/8-inch external antenna jack, but the radio needs a ground connecter for decent performance. If your portable has no external antenna jack or ground connection, look elsewhere.

Coverage is 3.9–22 MHz using a small thumbwheel to enhance front-end selectivity. It needs tweaking for major frequency changes, but is touchy to tune.

Gain is decent, especially above 9 MHz. There is no audible hiss or other untoward noise—worthy dynamic range, too. Like most loops the DE31 provides some rejection of local noise when rotated, although the limp-rope configuration makes it clumsy to adjust.

An LED indicates when the antenna is on and acts as a rudimentary guide to battery condition. The antenna's packaging specifies current draw as being six milliamps, but it is actually almost double that—11. There is no jack for an AC adaptor, so only batteries can be used.

Unlike the Sony AN-LP1, there is no travel bag for the odd bits that come with the antenna. Also, the long cable has no reel to keep it from getting tangled, as often happened during tests.

The Degen DE31 definitely improves reception with most portables and is eminently affordable.

 Vectronics AT-100

Indoor rod. Active, proximate, manual preselection, 0.3–30 MHz.

Price: $79.95 in the United States. $109.00CAD in Canada. £79.95 in the United Kingdom.

Pro: Good—sometimes excellent—gain (*see* Con), especially in the mediumwave AM band. Good dynamic range. Most knobs are commendably large.

Con: Proximate model, so receiving element has to be placed near receiver. No AC power; although it accepts an AC adaptor, the lack of polarity markings complicates adaptor choice (it is center-pin positive). Preselector complicates operation, especially as it is stiff to tune and thus awkward to peak. Our unit oscillated badly with some receivers, limiting usable gain—although it was more stable with other receivers, and thus appears to be a function of the load presented by a given receiver.

Verdict: If ever there were a product that needs to be purchased on a returnable basis, this is it. With one receiver, this American-made model gives welcome gain and worthy performance; with another, it goes into oscillation nearly at the drop of a hat.

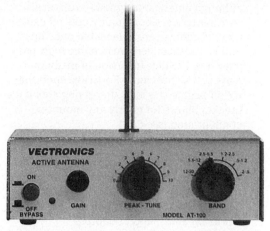

How well the Vectronics AT-100 snares signals depends in large part upon the receiver. With some it's fine, but with others it goes into oscillation.   R. Sherwood

✪¾ **Sony AN-1**

Indoor-outdoor rod. Remote, broadband, 0.15–30 MHz.

Price (as available): €119.00 in Germany.

Pro: Connects easily to any portable or other receiver, using supplied cables and inductive coupler. Unusually appropriate for low-cost portables lacking an outboard antenna input. Only portable-oriented model tested with weather resistant remote receiving element. Unlike Sony AN-LP1, it covers entire shortwave spectrum, plus mediumwave AM and longwave. AC adaptor jack,

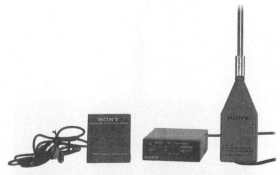

The Sony AN-1 couldn't compete with sibling AN-LP1, so it was dropped in 2005. New units have become scarce.   R. Sherwood

although antenna designed to run on six "AA" batteries. Good quality coaxial cable. Coaxial cable user-replaceable once head unit is disassembled. Switchable high-pass filter helps reduce intrusion of medium-wave AM signals into shortwave spectrum; rolloff begins at 3 MHz. Receiving element's bracket allows for nearly any mounting configuration (*see* Con).

Con: Poor gain, with pronounced reduction as frequency increases. Mediocre medium-wave AM performance. Clumsy but versatile mounting bracket makes installation tedious. No AC adaptor included, although works off aftermarket adaptors.

Verdict: The Japanese-made Sony AN-1 has feeble gain, rendering it practically useless on higher frequencies and little better below. However, for mounting outdoors and reception on lower frequencies it provides passable performance.

The AN-1 was discontinued in the second half of 2005, so it is increasingly difficult to find at retail. If nothing else works, try exporter thieCom.de.

✪¾
Palstar AA30/AA30A/AA30P/AM-30

Indoor rod. Active, proximate, manual preselection, 0.3–30 MHz.

Price: *AA30/AA30A:* $99.95 in the United States. £69.95 in the United Kingdom. *AA30P (not tested):* €96.50 in Germany. *AM-30 (not tested):* £69.95 in the United Kingdom.

The Palstar AA30 suffered from oscillation in our tests, but showed reasonable gain.   R. Sherwood

Pro: Moderate-to-good gain. Tuning control easily peaked. Can be powered directly by the Palstar R30/R30C and Lowe HF-350 tabletop receivers, an internal battery or an AC adaptor.

Con: Spurious oscillation throughout 14–30 MHz range. Overloads with external antenna. Proximate model, so receiving element has to be placed near receiver. Preselector complicates operation. No AC adaptor.

☞ At present, the AA30A's cabinets are silk screened simply as "AA30," although the accompanying owner's manual refers to the "AA30A."

☞ The Palstar AM-30, not tested, is sometimes sold in Europe. It appears to be comparable to the AA30A.

Verdict: Oscillation makes this a dubious choice except for reception below 14 MHz. Manufactured in the United States.

✪¾ *ⓒ*
MFJ-1022

Indoor rod. Active, proximate, broadband, 0.3–200 MHz.

Price: *MFJ-1022:* $49.95 in the United States. £55.95 in the United Kingdom. *MFJ-1312D 120V AC adaptor:* $14.95 in the United States.

Pro: Unusually broadband coverage reaches well into VHF spectrum. Considerable gain, peaking at 22.5 MHz, audibly helps signals that do not suffer from intermodulation. Idiot-proof to operate. Works best off battery (*see* Con). 30-day money-back guarantee if purchased from manufacturer.

Con: Proximate model, so receiving element has to be placed near receiver. Broadband design results in local mediumwave AM stations ghosting up to 2.7 MHz, and to a lesser degree up through the 3 MHz (90 meter) tropical world band segment at many locations; this often drops at night because of reduced local transmitting powers. Broadband design and high gain not infrequently results in intermodulation products/spurious signals and hiss between reasonable-level signals, and sometimes mixing with weaker signals. Within tropical world band segments, modest-level static from nearby thunderstorms, when coupled with overloading from local mediumwave AM signals, sometimes cause odd background sounds that are not heard with other antennas. High current draw (measures 35 mA), so battery runs down quickly. Removing sheet-metal screws often to change battery should eventually result in stripping unless great care is taken. AC adaptor, optional, causes significant hum on many received signals.

Verdict: Priced to move and offering broadband coverage, this compact antenna from MFJ couldn't be simpler to operate—one button, that's it. For helping to improve the listening quality of modest-strength international broadcasting signals, it works quite nicely. But don't expect to do much DXing, especially of the tropical world band segments unless you live well away from any mediumwave AM stations and maybe not

The MFJ-1022 is unusually affordable. Simple to operate, too, but performance is far from stellar.
R. Sherwood

even then. Forget the AC adaptor and stick to batteries.

Prepared by Robert Sherwood, with George Heidelman, Chuck Rippel and David Zantow; also, Lawrence Magne, with Carl Silberman, as well as Lawrence Bulk and David Crystal.

WHERE TO FIND IT: INDEX TO TESTED ANTENNAS

PASSPORT REPORTS evaluates the most relevant antennas on the market. Here's where to find the reviews, with models that are new, revised or retested shown in **bold**.

A comprehensive PASSPORT® Radio Database International White Paper®, *PASSPORT Evaluation of Popular Outdoor Antennas*, is available for $6.95 in North America, $9.95 airmail elsewhere, including shipping. It contains virtually all our panel's findings and comments during testing, along with details for proper installation and instructions for inverted-L construction. This unabridged report is available from key world band dealers, or you can contact our 24-hour VISA/MC order channels (www.passband.com, autovoice +1 215/598-9018, fax +1 215/598 3794), or write us at PASSPORT RDI White Papers, Box 300, Penn's Park, PA 18943 USA.

What's On Tonight?

PASSPORT's Hour-by-Hour Guide to World Band Shows

World band's voices offer news and entertainment rarely found elsewhere. While some shows are excellent, not everything is worth your ear. So, here is PASSPORT's hour-by-hour selection of qualified English-language programs, with icons to highlight standout choices:

■ Station superior, with several excellent shows
● Show worth hearing

Some stations provide operating schedules, others don't. Even when they do, the information can be incomplete, outdated or simply incorrect. To resolve this, PASSPORT tracks, firsthand, the real-life activity of stations around the world to detail schedule activity throughout the year. Additionally, to be as useful as possible, PASSPORT's schedules consist not just of observed activity, but also that which we have creatively opined will appear well into the year ahead. This predictive material is based on decades of experience, and is original from us. Although this is inherently less exact than real-time data, it has proven to be useful over the years.

Primary frequencies are given for North America, western Europe, East Asia and Australasia, plus the Middle East, southern Africa and Southeast Asia. If you want secondary and seasonal channels, or frequencies for other parts of the world, check out "Worldwide Broadcasts in English" and the Blue Pages.

To eliminate confusion, World Time (UTC) and World Day are used—both are explained in "Compleat Idiot's Guide to Getting Started" and the glossary. Seasons are those in the Northern Hemisphere ("summer" July, etc.; "winter" January, etc.).

Whether in Boston or, as here, Beijing, World Time (UTC) applies. This greatly demystifies foreign broadcast schedules.   M. Guha

00:00–05:59
North America—Evening Prime Time
Europe & Mideast—Early Morning
Australasia & East Asia—Midday and Afternoon

00:00

■**BBC World Service for the Caribbean.** Tuesday through Saturday winter (weekday evenings in the Americas), opens with five minutes of *news*. This is followed by the long-running *Outlook* and the 15-minute ●*Off the Shelf* (readings from world literature). Weekend fare is very much a mixed bag. Summer programming starts with *News*, then it's a variety of features (several of which are music programs). Outstanding at this hour is ●*Charlie Gillett* (world music, 0032 Thursday). Continuous programming on 5975 kHz.

■**Radio Netherlands.** Tuesday through Saturday (weekday evenings in North America) there's ●*Newsline* (current events) followed by a 30-minute feature: ●*Research File* (Tuesday), ●*EuroQuest* (Wednesday), ●*Documentary* (Thursday), *Dutch Horizons* (Friday), and *A Good Life* (Saturday). Sun-

day's combo is *Saturday Connection* and *Vox Humana*, replaced Monday by a short news summary and *Amsterdam Forum*. Fifty-seven minutes to eastern North America winter on 6165 kHz, and summer on 9845 kHz.

Radio Bulgaria. Winter only at this time. Tuesday through Saturday (weekday evenings in North America), *News* is followed by *Events and Developments*, replaced Sunday and Monday by *Views Behind the News*. The remaining time is taken up by regular programs such as *Keyword Bulgaria* and *Time Out for Music*, and weekly features like ●*Folk Studio* (Monday), *Sports* (Tuesday), *Magazine Economy* (Wednesday), *The Way We Live* (Thursday), *History Club* (Friday), *DX Programme* (Saturday) and *Answering Your Letters*, a listener-response show, on Sunday. Sixty minutes to eastern North America and Central America on 7400 and 9700 kHz. One hour earlier in summer.

00:00–00:00

Upbeat Harold Sellers helps the Ontario DX Association educate North Americans about world band radio.

J.M. Brinker

Radio Canada International. The start of a two-hour broadcast. Tuesday through Saturday (weekday evenings in North America), opens with ●*The World at Six* and continues with *As It Happens*, a combination of international stories, Canadian news and general human interest features. On the remaining days it's ●*The World This Weekend* and either Sunday's comedy show or Monday's *Maple Leaf Mailbag*. To North America and the Caribbean on 9755 and (summer) 13710 kHz. For a separate broadcast to Asia, see the next item.

Radio Canada International. Tuesday through Saturday, it's ●*The World At Six*; and a shortened version of ●*As It Happens*, both news-oriented programs. These are replaced Sunday by *The Vinyl Café*, and Monday by *Tapestry*. One hour to Southeast Asia winter on 9880 kHz, and summer on 9690 kHz. Also heard in parts of East Asia, especially during summer.

Radio Japan. *News*, then Tuesday through Saturday (weekday evenings local American date) it's *A Song for Everyone* followed by *Japan and the World 44 Minutes* (an in-depth look at current trends and events in Japan and elsewhere). This is replaced Sunday by *Hello from Tokyo*, and Monday by *Weekend Japanology* and *Japan Music Scene*. One hour to eastern North America on 6145 kHz via the powerful relay facilities of Radio Canada International in Sackville, New Brunswick. A separate 15-minute news bulletin for Southeast Asia is aired on 13650 and 17810 kHz.

Radio Exterior de España ("Spanish National Radio"). Tuesday through Saturday (local weekday evenings in the Americas), there's Spanish and international *news*, commentary, Spanish pop music, a review of the Spanish press, and a general interest feature. Weekends, it's all features, including rebroadcasts of some of the weekday programs. Sixty minutes to eastern North America winter on 6055 kHz, and summer on 15385 kHz. Popular with many listeners.

China Radio International. Starts with *News*, followed Monday through Friday (Sunday through Thursday evenings in the Americas) by special reports—current events, sports, business, culture, science and technology and press clippings. The rest of the broadcast is devoted to features. Regulars include ●*People in the Know* (Monday), *Biz China* (Tuesday), *China Horizons* (Wednesday), ●*Voices from Other Lands* (Thursday), and *Life in China* on Friday. Weekends, the news is followed by a shorter series of reports (current events and sport) and two features. Saturday there's *Cutting Edge*, and *Listeners' Garden* (listener mail, Chinese folk music, a preview of the next week's programs, and a Chinese language lesson); replaced Sunday by *Reports on Developing Countries* and *In the Spotlight*, a series of mini-features: *Cultural Carousel*, *In Vogue*, *Writings from China*, *China Melody* and *Talking Point*. To Europe winter on 7345 kHz, and summer on 13600 kHz; and to North America year-round on 6020 and 9570 kHz.

Radio Ukraine International. Summer only at this time. Ample coverage of local issues, including news, sports, politics and culture. Worth hearing is ●*Music from Ukraine*, which fills most of the Monday (Sunday evening in the Americas) broadcast. Sixty minutes to eastern North America on 7440 kHz. One hour later in winter. Budget and technical limitations have reduced audibility of this station to only a fraction of what it used to be.

Radio Australia. Part of a 24-hour service to Asia and the Pacific. Monday through Friday, continues with *In the Loop*, a mix of talk and music for listeners in the Pacific. Saturday, there's *Pacific Review*, *Asia Pacific Business* and *Hit Mix Lite*; and Sunday's feature is *Background Briefing*. On 9660, 12080, 13630, 15240, 15415 (from 0030), 17715, 17750 (from 0030), 17775 and 17795 kHz. In North America (best during summer) try 17715 and 17795 kHz; and in East Asia tune to 13630 kHz. For Southeast Asia there's 15415, 17750 and 17775 kHz.

Radio Prague, Czech Republic. Summer only at this time. *News*, then Tuesday through Saturday (weekday evenings in the Americas) there's *Current Affairs* and one or more features: *Talking Point* (Tuesday); *Czech Science* and *One on One* (Wednesday); *Czechs in History*, *Czechs Today* or *Spotlight* (Thursday); *Panorama* (Friday); and *Business Briefs* and *The Arts* on Saturday. The Sunday lineup is *Magazine*, *ABC of Czech* and *One on One*; replaced Monday by *Mailbox* and *Letter from Prague* followed by *Encore* (classical music), *Magic Carpet* (Czech world music) or *Czech Books*. Thirty minutes to North America and the Caribbean on 7345 and 9440 kHz. One hour later in winter.

Radio Austria International. Winter only at this time. Tuesday through Saturday (weekday evenings in the Americas), the 15-minute *Report from Austria* is aired at 0015. Sunday and Monday, it's ●*Report from Austria—The Week in Review* at 0005. The remainder of the half-hour broadcast is in German. To Central America on 7325 kHz. One hour later in summer.

Radio Thailand. *Newshour*. Thirty minutes to eastern and southern Africa, winter on 9680 kHz and summer on 9570 kHz.

All India Radio. The final 45 minutes of a much larger block of programming targeted at East and Southeast Asia, and heard well beyond. To East Asia on 9950, 11620 and 13605 kHz; and to Southeast Asia on 9705, 11620 and 13605 kHz.

■**Deutsche Welle,** Germany. *News*, then Tuesday through Saturday it's the comprehensive ●*NewsLink*—commentary, interviews, background reports and analysis. This is followed by *Insight* and *Business German* (Tuesday), *World in Progress* (Wednesday), ●*Money Talks* (Thursday), *Living Planet* (Friday), and *Spectrum* (Saturday). Sunday fare is *Religion and Society*, *German by Radio*, and *Asia This Week*; replaced Monday by *Mailbag*. Sixty minutes to South Asia winter on 6030 and 7290 kHz; and summer on 7130, 9505 and 9825 kHz. Also audible in parts of North America, interference permitting.

Radio Cairo, Egypt. The final half hour of a 90-minute broadcast to eastern North America. *Arabic by Radio* can be heard on the hour, and there's a daily *news* bulletin at 0015. See 2300 for more specifics. Winter on 11895 kHz, and summer on 11885 kHz.

Radio New Zealand International. A friendly package of *news* and features sometimes replaced by live sports commentary. Part of a 24-hour broadcast for the South Pacific, but also heard in parts of North America (especially during summer) on 15720 or 17675 kHz.

Voice of America. Starts with 30 minutes of *East Asia News Now*, with Special English *news* and features filling the second half-hour. The final 60 minutes of a three-hour broadcast to East and Southeast Asia on 7215, 9890 (winter), 15185, 15290, 17740 and (summer) 17820 kHz. Heard in Australasia on 17740 kHz.

AFRTS Shortwave, USA. Network news, live sports, music and features in the upper-sideband mode from the Armed Forces Radio & Television Service. Transmitted from modestly powered U.S. Navy stations around the globe. Try 4319, 5446.5, 5765, 6350, 7590, 7811, 9980, 10320, 12133.5, 12579 and 13362 kHz.

00:30–01:00

00:30

Radio Vilnius, Lithuania. Thirty minutes of news and background reports, mainly about Lithuania. Of broader appeal is *Mailbag*, aired every other Sunday (Saturday evenings local American date). For some Lithuanian music, try the next evening, towards the end of the broadcast. To eastern North America winter on 9875 kHz and summer on 11690 kHz.

Radio Austria International. Winter only at this time. Tuesday through Saturday (weekday evenings in the Americas), there's 15 minutes of *Report from Austria* at 0045. Sunday and Monday, it's ●*Report from Austria—The Week in Review* at 0035. The remainder of the half-hour broadcast is in German. To eastern North America on 7325 kHz. One hour later in summer.

Radio Thailand. *Newshour*. Thirty minutes to central and eastern North America on 5890 kHz, via a relay in Greenville, North Carolina.

01:00

■**BBC World Service for the Caribbean.** Winter only at this hour. Starts with *News*, then it's a mixed bag of features, including a fair share of music. Top choice is ●*Charlie Gillett* (world music, 0132 Thursday). Continuous programming on 5975 kHz.

Radio Canada International. The second of two hours to North America and the Caribbean. Tuesday through Saturday (weekday evenings in North America), continues with *As It Happens*. On the remaining days, there's Sunday's ●*Global Village* and Monday's *Writers and Company*. On 9755 and (summer) on 13710 kHz.

■**Radio Netherlands.** Repeat of the 0000 broadcast; see there for specifics. Fifty-seven minutes to central North America on 6165 kHz winter, and 9845 kHz summer.

Radio Slovakia International. Tuesday through Saturday (weekday evenings in the Americas), starts with *News* and *Topical*

Issue. These are usually followed by short features, although Tuesday's *Insight Central Europe* is an exception. The Sunday news is followed by *Network Europe*, and Monday there's *Sunday Newsreel* and *Listeners' Tribune*. A friendly half hour to North America on 5930 (or 7230) kHz, and to South America on 9440 kHz.

Radio Austria International. Summer only at this time. Tuesday through Saturday (weekday evenings in the Americas), there's *Report from Austria* at 0115. Sunday and Monday, it's ●*Report from Austria—The Week in Review* at 0105. The remainder of the half-hour broadcast is in German. To Central America on 9870 kHz. One hour earlier in winter.

Radio Budapest, Hungary. Summer only at this time. *News* and features, most of which are broadcast on a non-regular basis. Thirty minutes to North America on 9590 kHz. One hour later in winter.

Radio Prague, Czech Republic. *News*, then Tuesday through Saturday (weekday evenings in the Americas) there's the in-depth *Current Affairs* and a feature or two: *Talking Point* (Tuesday), *Czech Science* and *One on One* (Wednesday), *Czechs in History*, *Czechs Today* or *Spotlight* (Thursday), *Panorama* (Friday) and *Business Briefs* and *The Arts* on Saturday. The Sunday news is followed by *Magazine*, *ABC of Czech* and a repeat of Wednesday's *One on One*; and Monday's lineup is *Mailbox* and *Letter from Prague* followed by *Encore* (classical music), *Magic Carpet* (Czech world music) or *Czech Books*. Thirty minutes to eastern and central North America and the Caribbean on 6200 and 7345 kHz.

RAI International—Radio Roma, Italy. Actually starts at 0055. *News* and Italian music make up this 20-minute broadcast to North America on 11800 kHz.

Radio Japan. *News*, then Tuesday through Saturday it's *A Song for Everyone* and *Japan and the World 44 Minutes* (an in-depth look at trends and events in Japan and beyond). This is replaced Sunday by *Pop Joins the World*, and Monday by *Hello from Tokyo*.

A World of Listening from Sangean and Universal!

SANGEAN

ATS-909

The **ATS-909** is the flagship of the Sangean line. It packs features and performance into a very compact and stylish package. Coverage includes all long wave, medium wave and shortwave frequencies. FM and FM stereo to the headphone jack is also available. Shortwave performance is enhanced with a wide-narrow bandwidth switch and excellent single side band performance. Five tuning methods are featured: keypad, auto scan, manual up-down, memory recall or tuning knob. The alphanumeric memory lets you store 306 presets. The three event clock-timer displays even when the radio is tuning and has 42 world city zones. The large backlit LCD also features a signal strength and battery bar graph. The ATS-909 will display RDS on PL, PS and CT for station name and clock time in areas where this service is available. Also features a record jack and tone switch. Includes AC adapter, carry case, stereo ear buds and Sangean ANT-60 roll-up antenna. 8½" x 5½" x 1½". Requires four AA cells (not supplied). #1909

ATS-505P

The **Sangean ATS-505P** covers long wave, AM, FM and all shortwave frequencies. The backlit display can show either the frequency or the time (12/24 format). Tune (normal or fine) via the tuning knob, Up-Down buttons, automatic tuning, keypad or from the 45 memories. The ATS-505P even has a Clarify knob on the side of the radio to smoothly tune SSB. Other features include: FM stereo to headphone jack, 9/10 kHz AM step, beep on/off, dial lock, stereo-mono switch, alarm by radio or buzzer, auto-scan, auto memory, sleep-timer, tune LED, stereo-mono switch, tilt-stand, external antenna input and 6 VDC jack. With: AC adapter, ANT-60 wind-up antenna, carry case and earphones. Titanium matte finish. 8.5"x5.3"x1.6" Requires four AA cells. #3505

ATS-818ACS

Have you been waiting for a quality digital world band radio with a built-in cassette recorder? Now you have it in the exciting **Sangean ATS-818ACS**. This no-compromise receiver has full dual-conversion shortwave coverage (1.6 - 30 MHz) plus long wave, AM and FM (stereo to headphone jack). A BFO control is included for smooth SSB/CW reception. A big LCD display with dial lamp shows: frequency (1 kHz on SW), 24 hour time, battery indicator and signal strength. The receiver features an RF gain, tone control, wide-narrow selectivity, keypad entry, external antenna jack, manual tuning knob, plus 54 memories (18 for shortwave). The monaural recorder has a built-in mic and auto-shutoff. This radio comes with an AC power adapter. Requires four D cells and three AA cells (not supplied). 11¼" x 7" x 2½". #1069

PT-80

The Sangean PT-80 *Pro-Travel* is a compact digital radio with LW, AM, FM and continuous shortwave coverage. This dual conversion receiver features: 45 memories, single sideband, backlit LCD, dial lock plus dual world time clock with alarm, snooze and sleep. Tune by: keypad, autoscan, memory recall or rotary knob. Switches are provided for: Local-DX, dial lock and stereo-mono. With external antenna jack. Includes: AC adapter, earphones, wind-up antenna and butter-soft leather pouch. Requires four AA cells. #1080

TP-633

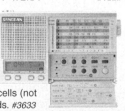

The new **TP-633** *Traveler Pro* is a compact analog AM, FM radio with 9 shortwave bands. It features a built-in dual time zone LCD 12/24 hour digital clock. Also has: LED tune and battery indicator, stereo-mono switch and power lock button. Requires 4.5 VDC or 3 AA cells (not supplied). With carry pouch and stereo ear buds. #3633

Sangean makes more than world class shortwave radios! Please visit the Universal Radio website to learn about Sangean specialty receivers.

01:00–01:45

One hour to East Asia on 17845 kHz; to South Asia on 15325 kHz; to Southeast Asia on 11860 and 17810 kHz; to Australasia on 17685 kHz; to South America on 11935 kHz; to western North America and Central America on 17825 kHz; and to the Mideast on 5960 (summer), 6030 (winter) and 17560 kHz. The broadcast on 17685 kHz has different programming after 0115.

China Radio International. Repeat of the 0000 broadcast, but with news updates. One hour to North America on 6005 (winter), 6020, 6080, 9570, 9580 and (summer) 9790 kHz, via CRI's Albanian, Cuban and Canadian relays. Also to Europe winter on 7345 kHz, and summer on 13600 kHz.

Voice of Vietnam. A relay via the facilities of Radio Canada International. Begins with *news*, then there's *Commentary* or *Weekly Review*, followed by short features and some pleasant Vietnamese music (especially at weekends). Thirty minutes to eastern North America, with reception better to the south. On 6175 kHz. Repeated at 0230 and 0330 on the same channel.

Voice of Russia World Service. Summer only at this hour, and the start of a four-hour block of programming for North America. *News*, then Tuesday through Saturday (weekday evenings in North America), there's *Commonwealth Update*. This is replaced Sunday and Monday by *Moscow Mailbag*. The second half-hour contains some interesting fare, with just about everyone's favorite being Tuesday's ●*Folk Box*. Other shows include *Kaleidoscope* (Friday), *Our Homeland* (Sunday), *Timelines* (Monday), Wednesday's ●*Jazz Show*, and Saturday's evocative ●*Christian Message from Moscow*. Best for eastern North America are 7250 and 9665 kHz (replaced by 7180 kHz in autumn). Farther west, use 15545, 15555 and 15595 kHz.

Radio Habana Cuba. The start of a two-hour cyclical broadcast to North America. Tuesday through Sunday (Monday through Saturday evenings in North America), the first half hour consists of international and Cuban *news* followed by *RHC's Viewpoint*.

The next 30 minutes consist of a *news* bulletin and the sports-oriented *Time Out* (five minutes each) plus a feature: *Caribbean Outlook* (Tuesday and Friday), *DXers Unlimited* (Wednesday and Sunday), the *Mailbag Show* (Thursday) and *Weekly Review* (Saturday). Monday, the hour is split between *Weekly Review* and *Mailbag Show*. To eastern and central North America on 6000 and 9820 kHz.

Voice of Korea, North Korea. The dinosaur of world band and the last of the old-style communist stations. One hour to East Asia on 3560, 7140, 9345 and 9730 kHz; and to Central America on 11735, 13760 and 15180 kHz.

Radio Australia. Part of a 24-hour service to Asia and the Pacific, but which can also be heard at this time in parts of North America (better to the west). Monday through Friday, it's the final half-hour of *In the Loop*, followed by *Asia Pacific* (regional current events). Weekends, it's all sport in *Grandstand*. On 9660, 12080, 13630, 15240, 15415, 17715, 17750, 17775 (till 0130) and 17795 kHz. In North America (best during summer) try 17715 and 17795 kHz; in East Asia tune to 13630 kHz; and best for Southeast Asia are 15415, 17750 and 17775 kHz.

Radio Ukraine International. Winter only at this time. Ample coverage of Ukrainian issues, including news, sports, politics and culture. Worth hearing is ●*Music from Ukraine*, which fills most of the Monday (Sunday evening in the Americas) broadcast. Sixty minutes of informative programming targeted at eastern North America. On 5910 kHz. One hour earlier in summer.

Radio Romania International. Starts with *Radio Newsreel*, a combination of news, commentary and press review. Features on Romania complete the broadcast. Regular spots include Tuesday's *Pro Memoria* (Romanian history) and *Pages of Romanian Literature* (Monday evening, local American date); Wednesday's *Business Club* and *European Horizons*; Thursday's *Society Today*, *Partners in a Changing World*, *Cultural Sur-*

vey and *Romanian Musicians*; and Friday's *Traveller's Guide, Listeners Letterbox, IT News, From Our Correspondents* and ●*The Skylark* (Romanian folk music). Saturday fare includes *Over Coffee… with Artists* and ●*The Folk Music Box*, and Sunday there's *World of Culture, Roots, Cookery Show, Radio Pictures* and *DX Mailbag*. Monday's broadcast includes *Sunday Studio* and *All That Jazz*. Fifty-five minutes to eastern North America winter on 9615, 9690 and 11970 kHz; and summer on 6040 and 9690 kHz; and to Australasia midyear on 11820 and 15430 kHz.

Radio New Zealand International. Continues with *news* and features sometimes replaced by live sports commentary. Continuous to the South Pacific, and also heard in parts of North America (especially during summer). On 15720 or 17675 kHz.

Radio Tashkent International, Uzbekistan. Monday through Saturday, opens with *News*, replaced Sunday by *Significant Events of the Week*. The remaining fare consists mainly of features, with Monday's broadcast largely devoted to exotic Uzbek music. On the remaining days there's *Economic Commentary* (Tuesday), a program for women (Wednesday and Sunday), *Echo of History* (Wednesday), *Uzbekistan and the World* and *Man and Society* (Thursday) and a program for shortwave listeners on Friday. The week ends with a Saturday sports program followed by *In the World of Literature*. Thirty minutes to West and South Asia, and occasionally heard in North America. Winter on 6165 and 11905 kHz; and summer on 7190 and 9715 kHz.

AFRTS Shortwave, USA. Network news, live sports, music and features in the upper-sideband mode from the Armed Forces Radio & Television Service. Transmitted from modestly powered U.S. Navy stations around the globe. Try 4319, 5446.5, 5765, 6350, 7590, 7811, 9980, 10320, 12133.5, 12579 and 13362 kHz.

01:30

Radio Sweden. *News* and features concentrating heavily on Scandinavian topics.

Some of the features rotate from week to week, but some are fixtures. Tuesday's *Culture* is replaced Wednesday by *Knowledge*, and Thursday by *Real Life*. The Friday feature is *Lifestyle*, with *Debate* filling the Saturday slot. The Sunday rotation is *Headset, Sweden Today, In Touch* (a listener-response program) and *Studio 49*; while Monday's offering is *Network Europe*. Thirty minutes to South Asia winter on 11550 kHz, and summer on 9435 kHz. Also to North America, summer only, on 6010 kHz. The broadcast to North America is one hour later during winter.

Radio Austria International. Summer only at this time. Tuesday through Saturday (weekday evenings in the Americas), there's 15 minutes of *Report from Austria* at 0145. Sunday and Monday, it's ●*Report from Austria – The Week in Review* at 0135. The remainder of the half-hour broadcast is in German. To eastern North America on 9870 kHz. One hour earlier in winter.

Radio Vilnius, Lithuania. Winter only at this time. Thirty minutes of mostly *news* and background reports about events in Lithuania. A listener-response program, *Mailbag*, is aired every other Sunday. For a little Lithuanian music, try the second half of Monday's broadcast. To eastern North America on 7325 kHz. One hour earlier in summer.

Voice of the Islamic Republic of Iran. Unlike the broadcasts to other parts of the world, the programs at this time are from the separate "Voice of Justice" service. One hour to North America winter on 6120 and 9665 kHz, and summer on 9495 and 11875 kHz.

01:45

Radio Tirana, Albania. Tuesday through Sunday (Monday through Saturday evenings in North America) and summer only at this time. Approximately 15 minutes of *news* and commentary from this small Balkan country. To North America on 6115 and 7160 kHz. One hour later in winter.

02:00–02:00

The National Public Broadcasting Archives and the Library of American Broadcasting are co-located at the University of Maryland in College Park. Visiting is a treasured pilgrimage for American radio history buffs.   T. Ohtake

02:00

Radio Cairo, Egypt. Repeat of the 2300 broadcast, and the first hour of a 90-minute potpourri of *news* and features about Egypt and the Arab world. To North America on winter on 7270 kHz, and summer on 7260 kHz.

Radio Argentina al Exterior—RAE Tuesday through Saturday only (local weekday evenings in the Americas). A freewheeling presentation of news, press review, short features and local Argentinian music. Not the easiest station to tune, but popular with many of those who can hear it. Fifty-five minutes nominally to North America on 11710 kHz, but tends to be best heard in the southern U.S. and the Caribbean. Sometimes pre-empted by live soccer commentary in Spanish.

Radio Budapest, Hungary. Winter only at this time. *News* and features, most of which are broadcast on a non-regular basis. Thirty minutes to North America on 9515 kHz. One hour earlier in summer.

Radio Bulgaria. Summer only at this time. Starts with *News*, then Tuesday through Saturday (weekday evenings in North America) there's *Events and Developments*, replaced Sunday and Monday by *Views Behind the News*. The remaining time is split between regular programs like *Keyword*

Bulgaria and *Time Out for Music*, and weekly features like ●*Folk Studio* (Monday), *Sports* (Tuesday), *Magazine Economy* (Wednesday), *The Way We Live* (Thursday), *History Club* (Friday), *DX Programme* (for radio enthusiasts, Saturday) and *Answering Your Letters*, a listener-response show, on Sunday. Sixty minutes to eastern North America and Central America on 9700 and 11700 kHz. One hour later in winter.

Radio Prague, Czech Republic. Winter only at this time. *News*, then Tuesday through Saturday (weekday evenings in the Americas) it's a combination of *Current Affairs* and one or more features: *Talking Point* (Tuesday), *Czech Science* and *One on One* (Wednesday), *Czechs in History*, *Czechs Today* or *Spotlight* (Thursday), *Panorama* (Friday), and *Business Briefs* and *The Arts* on Saturday. The Sunday lineup is *Magazine*, *ABC of Czech* and *One on One*; replaced Monday by *Mailbox* and *Letter from Prague* followed by *Encore* (classical music), *Magic Carpet* (Czech world music) or *Czech Books*. A half hour to North America on 6200 and 7345 kHz. One hour earlier in summer.

Radio Taiwan International. Ten minutes of *News*, followed by features. Monday (Sunday evening in North America) there's *The Undiscovered Country*, *Asia Pacific* (produced by Radio Australia) and *Let's Learn Chinese*. These are replaced on successive days by *Made in Taiwan* and *We've Got Mail* (Tuesday); *Strait Talk* and ●*Jade Bells and Bamboo Pipes* (Wednesday); *Trends, People* and *Instant Noodles* (Thursday); *Ilha Formosa* and *New Music Lounge* (Friday); *Bookworm* and *Groove Zone* (Saturday); and *News Talk, Taipei Magazine* and *Stage, Screen and Studio* (Sunday). One hour to eastern and central North America on 5950 and 9680 kHz, to East Asia on 15465 kHz, and to Southeast Asia on 11875 kHz.

Voice of Russia World Service. Winter, the start of a four-hour block of programming to North America; summer, it's the beginning of the second hour. *News*, features and music to suit all tastes. Winter fare includes *Commonwealth Update* (0211 Tuesday through Saturday), replaced Sunday and Monday by *Moscow Mailbag*. The second half-hour includes ●*Folk Box* (Tuesday), ●*Jazz Show* (Wednesday), *Kaleidoscope* (Friday), ●*Christian Message from Moscow* (Saturday), ●*Our Homeland* (Sunday) and *Timelines* (Monday). In summer, *News and Views* replaces *Commonwealth Update* and Sunday's *Moscow Mailbag*, with *Sunday Panorama* and *Russia: People and Events* filling the Monday slots. There's a news summary on the half-hour, then *The VOR Treasure Store* (Saturday), *Songs from Russia* (Sunday), *Russian by Radio* (Monday and Friday), *Kaleidoscope* (Tuesday), *Musical Tales* and *Russia: People and Events* (Wednesday) and *Our Homeland* (Thursday). Note that these days are World Time; locally in North America it will be the previous evening. For eastern North America winter, tune to 7180 and 7250 kHz; summer, it's 9665 and 9860 kHz. Listeners in western states should go for 15425, 15475 and 15595 kHz in winter; and 15455, 15555 and 15595 kHz in summer.

Radio Habana Cuba. The second half of a two-hour broadcast to eastern and central North America. Tuesday through Sunday (Monday through Saturday evenings in North America), opens with 10 minutes of international *news*. Next comes *Spotlight on the Americas* (Tuesday through Saturday) or Sunday's *The World of Stamps*. The final 30 minutes consists of news-oriented pro-

gramming. The Monday slots are *From Havana* and ●*The Jazz Place* or *Breakthrough* (science). On 6000 and 9820 kHz.

Radio Belarus. Monday, Tuesday, Wednesday, Friday and Saturday, summer only at this time. See 0300 for details. Thirty minutes to Europe on 5970, 6170 and 7210 kHz. One hour later in winter. Sometimes audible in eastern North America.

Radio Australia. Continuous programming to Asia and the Pacific, but well heard in parts of North America (especially to the west). Begins with *World News*, then Monday through Friday it's *The World Today* (comprehensive coverage of world events). Weekends, it's all sport in *Grandstand*. On 9660, 12080, 13630, 15240, 15415, 15515, 17750 and 21725 kHz. Best heard in North America (especially during summer) on 15515 kHz; in East Asia on 13630 and 21725 kHz; and in Southeast Asia on 15415 and 17750 kHz.

KBS World Radio, South Korea. Opens with 10 minutes of *news*, then Tuesday through Saturday (weekday evenings in the Americas), a commentary. This is followed by 30 minutes of *Seoul Calling* and a 15-minute feature: *Shaping Korea, Made in Korea, Cultural Promenade, Korea Today and Tomorrow* and *Seoul Report*, respectively. Sunday, the news is followed by *Worldwide Friendship* (a listener-response program), and Monday by *Korean Pop Interactive*. Sixty minutes to North America on 9560 and 15575 kHz, and to South America (and often heard in Japan) on 11810 kHz.

Voice of Korea, North Korea. Repeat of the 0100 broadcast. One hour to South East Asia on 13650 and 15100 kHz. Also audible in parts of East Asia on 4405 kHz.

AFRTS Shortwave, USA. Network news, live sports, music and features in the upper-sideband mode from the Armed Forces Radio & Television Service. Transmitted from modestly powered U.S. Navy stations around the globe. Try 4319, 5446.5, 5765, 6350, 7590, 7811, 9980, 10320, 12133.5, 12579 and 13362 kHz.

02:15

Voice of Croatia. Summer only at this time. Nominally 15 minutes of news, reports and interviews. Actual length varies. To North America and South America on 9925 kHz. One hour later in winter.

02:30

Radio Sweden. *News* and features concentrating heavily on Scandinavian topics. Some of the features rotate from week to week, but some are fixtures. Tuesday's *Culture* is replaced Wednesday by *Knowledge*, and Thursday by *Real Life*. Friday's feature is *Lifestyle*, with *Debate* filling the Saturday slot. The Sunday rotation is *Headset*, *Sweden Today*, *In Touch* (a listener-response program) and *Studio 49*; while Monday's offering is *Network Europe*. Thirty minutes to North America on 6010 kHz.

Radio Tirana, Albania. Tuesday through Sunday (Monday through Saturday evenings in North America) and summer only at this time. Thirty minutes of Balkan news and music to North America on 6115 and 7160 kHz. One hour later during winter.

Radio Budapest, Hungary. Summer only at this time. *News* and features, only a few of which are broadcast on a regular basis. Thirty minutes to North America on 9795 kHz. One hour later in winter.

Radio Belarus. Summer Sundays only at this time. Thirty minutes of local *news* and interviews, plus some Belarusian music. To Europe on 5970, 6170 and 7210 kHz. One hour later in winter. Sometimes audible in eastern North America.

Voice of Vietnam. Repeat of the 0100 broadcast; see there for specifics. A relay to eastern North America via the facilities of Radio Canada International on 6175 kHz. Reception is better to the south.

02:45

Radio Tirana, Albania. Tuesday through Sunday (Monday through Saturday local

American date) and winter only at this time. Approximately 15 minutes of *news* and commentary from one of Europe's least known countries. To North America on 6115 and 7455 kHz. One hour earlier in summer.

Vatican Radio. Actually starts at 0250. Concentrates heavily, but not exclusively, on issues affecting Catholics around the world. Thirty minutes to eastern North America on 7305 and 9605 kHz.

03:00

■**BBC World Service for the Caribbean.** Sixty minutes of predominantly news programming on 5975 kHz.

Radio Taiwan International. Repeat of the 0200 broadcast; see there for specifics. One hour to western North America on 5950 kHz, to South America on 15215 kHz, and to Southeast Asia on 15320 kHz.

China Radio International. Starts with *News*, followed Monday through Friday (Sunday through Thursday evenings in the Americas) by special reports—current events, sports, business, culture, science and technology and press clippings. The rest of the broadcast is devoted to features. Regulars include ●*People in the Know* (Monday), *Biz China* (Tuesday), *China Horizons* (Wednesday), ●*Voices from Other Lands* (Thursday), and *Life in China* on Friday. Weekends, the news is followed by a shorter series of reports (current events and sport) and two features. Saturday there's *Cutting Edge*, and *Listeners' Garden* (listener mail, Chinese folk music, a preview of the next week's programs, and a Chinese language lesson); replaced Sunday by *Reports on Developing Countries* and *In the Spotlight*, a series of mini-features: *Cultural Carousel*, *In Vogue*, *Writings from China*, *China Melody* and *Talking Point*. One hour to North America on 9690 and 9790 kHz.

Radio Ukraine International. Summer only at this time. Ample coverage of all things Ukrainian, including news, sports, politics and culture. For some enjoyable listening tune to ●*Music from Ukraine*, which fills most of the Monday (Sunday evening in the Americas) broadcast. Sixty minutes to eastern North America on 7440 kHz. One hour later in winter.

Voice of Russia World Service. Continuous programming to North America at this hour. *News*, then winter it's *News and Views*—except Monday (Sunday evening in North America) when *Sunday Panorama* and *Russia: People and Events* are aired instead. Features during the second half-hour include *The VOR Treasure Store* (Saturday), *Songs from Russia* and *Russia: People and Events* (Sunday), *Russian by Radio* (Monday and Friday), *Kaleidoscope* (Tuesday), *Musical Tales* and *Russia: People and Events* (Wednesday) and *Our Homeland* (Thursday). In summer, the news is followed by a feature: *This is Russia* (Monday), *Musical Tales* (Tuesday), *Moscow Mailbag* (Wednesday and Saturday), *Science Plus* (Thursday) and *Newmarket*(business) on Friday. More features follow a brief news summary on the half-hour: *Our Homeland* (Monday), *The Whims of Fate* (Tuesday, Thursday and Saturday), *Guest Speaker* and *People of Uncommon Destiny* (Wednesday) and ●*Russia—1,000 Years of Music* on Friday. Pride of place at this hour goes to Sunday's 45-minute ●*Music and Musicians*. In eastern North America, choose between 7180 and 7350 kHz in winter, and 9665, 9860 and 9880 (or 5900) kHz in summer. For western North America, there's 15425, 15475 and 15595 kHz in winter; and 15455, 15555 and 15595 kHz in summer.

Radio Belarus. Monday, Tuesday, Wednesday, Friday and Saturday, winter only at this time. Thirty minutes of local *news* and interviews, plus a little Belarusian music. All transmissions at this hour are repeats of broadcasts originally aired Tuesday or Thursday evenings. To Europe on 5970, 6155 and 7210 kHz, and one hour earlier in summer. Sometimes heard in eastern North America.

Radio Australia. *World News*, then Monday through Friday there's *Sport* and a 15-minute feature: *In Conversation* (Monday), ●*Ockham's Razor* (Tuesday), *Lingua Franca*

(Wednesday), *The Ark* (Thursday) and *Talking Point* on Friday. Except for Friday's *Sports Factor*, the second half-hour features a series of reports: *Health* (Monday), *Law* (Tuesday), *Religion* (Wednesday) and *Media* (Thursday). Weekends, there's live sports coverage in *Grandstand*. Continuous to Asia and the Pacific on 9660, 12080, 13630, 15240, 15415, 15515, 17750 and 21725 kHz. Also heard in North America (best in summer) on 15515 kHz. In East Asia, tune to 13630 and 21725 kHz; for Southeast Asia, there's 15415 and 17750 kHz.

Radio Habana Cuba. Repeat of the 0100 broadcast. To eastern and central North America on 6000 and 9820 kHz.

Radio Thailand. *News Magazine*. Thirty minutes to western North America on 5890 kHz, via a relay in Delano, California.

Radio Prague, Czech Republic. Summer only at this hour; see 0400 for program specifics. A half hour to North America on 7345 and 9870 kHz. This is by far the best opportunity for listeners in western states. One hour later in winter.

Radio Cairo, Egypt. The final half-hour of a 90-minute broadcast to North America winter on 7270 kHz, and summer on 7260 kHz.

Radio Bulgaria. Winter only at this time, and a repeat of the 0000 broadcast; see there for specifics. A distinctly Bulgarian potpourri of news, commentary, features and music. Not to be missed is Monday's ●*Folk Studio* (Sunday evening local American date). Sixty minutes to eastern North America and Central America on 7400 and 9700 kHz. One hour earlier in summer.

Radio Japan. *News*, then weekdays it's *A Song for Everyone* and *Asian Top News*. These are followed by a 35-minute feature: *Japan Musicscape* (Monday), Japanese language lessons (Tuesday and Thursday), *Japan Music Archives* (Wednesday), and *Music Beat* (Japanese popular music) on Friday. *Weekend Japanology* and *Japan Music Scene* fill the Saturday slots, and *Hello from Tokyo* is aired Sunday. Sixty minutes to Australasia on 21610 kHz.

03:00–04:00

Young Buddhist men routinely serve internships at monasteries, much as young Mormons undertake missionary work.   Guha

Radio New Zealand International. Continues with *news* and features targeted at a regional audience. Part of a 24-hour transmission for the South Pacific, but also heard in parts of North America (especially during summer). On 15720 or 17675 kHz. Often carries commentaries of local sporting events. Popular with many listeners.

Voice of Korea, North Korea. Abysmal programs from the last of the old-style communist stations. Worth a listen just to hear how bad they are. One hour to East Asia on 3560, 7140, 9345 and 9730 kHz.

Voice of Turkey. Summer only at this time. *News*, followed by *Review of the Turkish Press* and features (some of them exotic and unusual). Selections of Turkish popular and classical music complete the program. Fifty minutes to Europe and North America on 6140 kHz, and to the Mideast on 7270 kHz. One hour later during winter.

Voice of America. The start of six hours of continuous programming to Africa. Monday through Friday, *Daybreak Africa* fills the first half hour, and is followed by *Africa News Now*. Weekends, it's *Africa News Now* followed by Saturday's *World of Music* or Sunday's *On the Line*. On 4930, 6035 (winter), 6080, 7290, 7340 (till 0330), 9985 and (summer) 12080 and 17895 kHz. Best for southern Africa is 4930 kHz.

AFRTS Shortwave, USA. Network news, live sports, music and features in the upper-sideband mode from the Armed Forces Radio & Television Service. Transmitted from modestly powered U.S. Navy stations around the globe. Try 4319, 5446.5, 5765, 6350, 7590, 7811, 9980, 10320, 12133.5, 12579 and 13362 kHz.

03:15

Voice of Croatia. Winter only at this time. Nominally 15 minutes of news, reports and interviews. Actual length varies. To North America and South America on 7285 kHz. One hour earlier in summer.

03:30

Radio Sweden. Winter only at this time. *News* and features concentrating heavily on Scandinavian topics. Some of the features rotate from week to week, but some are fixtures. Tuesday's *Culture* is replaced Wednesday by *Knowledge*, and Thursday by *Real Life*. Friday's feature is *Lifestyle*, with *Debate* filling the Saturday slot. The Sunday rotation is *Headset*, *Sweden Today*, *In Touch* (a listener-response program) and *Studio 49*; while Monday's offering is *Network Europe*. Thirty minutes to western North America on 6010 kHz, and one hour earlier in summer.

Radio Prague, Czech Republic. Summer only at this time. See the 0400 winter broadcast for North America for program specifics. Thirty minutes to the Mideast and South Asia on 9445 and 11600 kHz. One hour later in winter.

Kol Israel. Summer only at this time. *News* for 15 minutes from Israel Radio's domestic network. To Europe and eastern North America on 7545 (or 11605) and 9435 kHz, and to Central America and Australasia on 17600 kHz. One hour later in winter.

Radio Budapest, Hungary. This time winter only. *News* and features, most of which are broadcast on a non-regular basis. Thirty minutes to North America on 9775 kHz. One hour earlier in summer.

Radio Belarus. Winter Sundays only at this time. Thirty minutes of local *news*, reports and interviews, plus some Belarusian music. To Europe on 5970, 6155 and 7210 kHz. One hour earlier in summer. Sometimes audible in eastern North America.

Voice of Vietnam. A relay via the facilities of Radio Canada International. Begins with *news*, then there's *Commentary* or *Weekly Review*, followed by short features and some pleasant Vietnamese music (particularly at weekends). A half hour to eastern North America on 6175 kHz.

Radio Tirana, Albania. Tuesday through Monday (Monday through Saturday evenings local American date) and winter only at this time. *News*, features and lively Albanian music. Thirty minutes to North America on 6115 and 7455 kHz. One hour earlier in summer.

04:00

■Radio Netherlands. Summer only at this time. Tuesday through Saturday (weekday evenings in North America), opens with ●*Newsline* (current events). The remaining half hour is filled by a feature: ●*Research File* (Tuesday), ●*EuroQuest* (Wednesday), ●*Documentary* (Thursday), *Dutch Horizons* (Friday), and *A Good Life* (Saturday). On Sunday, there's *Saturday Connection* and *Vox Humana*, replaced Monday by a short news summary and *Amsterdam Forum*. Fifty-seven minutes to western North America on 6165 and 9590 kHz. One hour later in winter.

Radio Habana Cuba. Repeat of the 0200 broadcast. To eastern and central North America on 6000 and 9820 kHz.

Radio Prague, Czech Republic. Winter only at this time. *News*, then Tuesday through Saturday (weekday evenings in the Americas) there's the in-depth *Current Affairs* and a feature or two: *Talking Point* (Tuesday), *Czech Science* and *One on One* (Wednesday), *Czechs in History*, *Czechs Today* or *Spotlight* (Thursday), *Panorama* (Friday) and *Business Briefs* and *The Arts* on Saturday. The Sunday news is followed by *Magazine*, *ABC of Czech* and a repeat of Wednesday's *One on One*; and Monday's lineup is *Mailbox* and *Letter from Prague* followed by *Encore* (classical music), *Magic Carpet* (Czech world music) or *Czech Books*. Thirty minutes to North America on 6200 and 7345 kHz. By far the best opportunity for western states. One hour earlier in summer.

■Radio France Internationale. Weekdays only at this time. Starts with a bulletin of African *news* and an international newsflash. Next, there's a review of the French dailies, an in-depth look at events in Africa, the main news event of the day in France, and sports. Thirty information-packed minutes to East Africa winter on 7315, 9555 or 11995 kHz, and summer on 7315 or 9805 kHz. Heard well beyond the intended target area.

Radio Ukraine International. Winter only at this time, and a repeat of the 0100 broadcast. Ample coverage of local issues, including news, sports, politics and culture. Well worth a listen is ●*Music from Ukraine*, which fills most of the Monday (Sunday evening in the Americas) broadcast. Sixty minutes to eastern North America on 5910 kHz. One hour earlier in summer.

Radio Australia. *World News*, then Monday through Friday, one or more feature: *Big Ideas* (Monday), ●*The Science Show* (Tuesday), *Smart Societies* and *Innovations* (Wednesday), *Background Briefing* (Thursday) and *Keys to the Music* on Friday. Weekends, it's all sport in *Grandstand*. Continuous to Asia and the Pacific on 9660, 12080, 13630, 15240, 15415 (from 0430),

04:00–05:00

15515, 17750 and 21725 kHz. Should also be audible in parts of North America (best during summer) on 15515 kHz. In East Asia, go for 13630 and 21725 kHz; for Southeast Asia, there's 15415 and 17750 kHz.

■**Deutsche Welle,** Germany. *News*, followed Tuesday through Saturday by the comprehensive and well produced ●*News-Link*—commentary, interviews, background reports and analysis. On the half-hour there's *Insight* and *Business German* (Tuesday), *World in Progress* (Wednesday), ●*Money Talks* (Thursday), *Living Planet* (Friday) and *Spectrum* (Saturday). Sunday brings ●*Inside Europe*, replaced Monday by *Mailbag*. Sixty minutes to East and Central Africa winter on 6180, 9710 and 15445 kHz; and summer on 7170, 9630 and 11945 kHz. Audible in southern Africa winter on 9710 kHz, and midyear on 11945 kHz.

Radio Romania International. Starts with *Radio Newsreel*, a combination of news, commentary and press review. Features on Romania complete the broadcast. Regular spots include Tuesday's *Pro Memoria* (Romanian history) and *Pages of Romanian Literature* (Monday evening, local American date); Wednesday's *Business Club* and *European Horizons*; Thursday's *Society Today*, *Partners in a Changing World*, *Cultural Survey* and *Romanian Musicians*; and Friday's *Traveller's Guide*, *Listeners Letterbox*, *IT News*, *From Our Correspondents* and ●*The Skylark* (Romanian folk music). Saturday fare includes *Over Coffee... with Artists* and ●*The Folk Music Box*, and Sunday there's *World of Culture*, *Roots*, *Cookery Show*, *Radio Pictures* and *DX Mailbag*. Monday's broadcast includes *Sunday Studio* and *All That Jazz*. Fifty-five minutes to western North America winter on 6125 and 9515 kHz, and summer on 9780 and 11820 kHz; and to South Asia winter on 9690 and 11895 kHz, and summer on 15140 and 17860 kHz.

Voice of Turkey. Winter only at this time. See 0300 for specifics. Fifty minutes to Europe and North America on 6020 kHz, and to the Mideast on 7240 kHz. One hour earlier in summer.

China Radio International. Repeat of the 0300 broadcast (see there for specif-

ics); one hour to western North America on 6090 (summer), 6190 (winter), 9560 (summer) and 9755 kHz.

Radio New Zealand International. Continuous programming for the South Pacific. Part of a much longer broadcast, which is also heard in parts of North America (especially during summer). On 13690, 15720 or 17675 kHz. Sometimes carries commentaries of local sports events.

Voice of Russia World Service. Continues to North America at this hour. Opens with *News*, then a feature. Winter, there's *This is Russia* (Monday), *Musical Tales* (Tuesday), *Moscow Mailbag* (Wednesday and Saturday), *Science Plus* (Thursday) and *Newmarket* (business) on Friday. More features follow a brief news summary on the half-hour: *Our Homeland* (Monday), *The Whims of Fate* (Tuesday, Thursday and Saturday), *Guest Speaker* and *People of Uncommon Destiny* (Wednesday) and ●*Russia—1,000 Years of Music* on Friday. Not to be missed at this hour is Sunday's 45-minute ●*Music and Musicians*. The summer schedule has plenty of variety, and includes *Musical Tales* and *The VOR Treasure Store* (Monday), *Moscow Mailbag*, ●*Music Around Us* and ●*Music at Your Request* (Tuesday), *Science Plus* and *Our Homeland* (Wednesday), the business oriented *Newmarket* and ●*Folk Box* (Thursday), *Moscow Mailbag* and *The VOR Treasure Store* (Friday), *This is Russia* and *Timelines* (Saturday), and *Musical Tales* and *Kaleidoscope* (Sunday). Note that these days are World Time; locally in North America it will be the previous evening. In eastern North America, choose from 7180, 7150 and 7350 kHz in winter, and 9665 and 9880 (or 5900) kHz in summer. Best winter bets for the West Coast are 12010, 15425, 15475 and 15595 kHz; and summer there's 15455, 15555 and 15595 kHz.

Voice of America. Continuous programming to Africa. Monday through Friday, starts with *News* and a feature, then *Focus* and an editorial; *Daybreak Africa* follows on the half-hour. Weekends, it's *Africa News Now* followed by Saturday's *Music Time Africa* or Sunday's *Talking History*. On 4930,

4960, 6080, 7290, 9575 and 9775 kHz; also winter on 9775 and (till 0430) 9885 kHz, and summer on 11835, 12080 and 17895 kHz. Best for southern Africa is 4930 kHz; and heard in North America on 9575 kHz.

AFRTS Shortwave, USA. Network news, live sports, music and features in the upper-sideband mode from the Armed Forces Radio & Television Service. Transmitted from modestly powered U.S. Navy stations around the globe. Try 4319, 5446.5, 5765, 6350, 7590, 7811, 9980, 10320, 12133.5, 12579 and 13362 kHz.

04:30

Radio Prague, Czech Republic. Winter only at this time. See the 0400 broadcast to North America for program specifics. Thirty minutes to the Mideast and South Asia on 9885 and 11600 kHz. One hour earlier in summer.

Kol Israel. Winter only at this time. *News* for 15 minutes from Israel Radio's domestic network. To Europe and eastern North America on 6280 kHz, and to Central America and Australasia on 15640 or 17600 kHz. One hour earlier in summer.

04:45

RAI International—Radio Roma, Italy. *News* and Italian music make up this 15-minute broadcast to southern Europe and North Africa. Winter on 5965, 6120 and 7170 kHz; and summer on 6110, 7235 and 9800 kHz.

05:00

■**Radio Netherlands.** Winter only at this time; see 0400 for specifics. Fifty-seven minutes to western North America on 6165 kHz, and one hour earlier in summer. Also available to Australasia on 11710 kHz.

■**Deutsche Welle,** Germany. *News*, then Tuesday through Saturday it's ●*News-Link*—commentary, interviews, background reports and analysis. The second half-hour

05:00–05:30

Lawyers are forcing London to phase out double-decker buses. Not so in Hong Kong, where split-level trolleys roll happily along as people movers and tourist magnets. M. Guha

features ●*A World of Music* (Tuesday), *Arts on the Air* (Wednesday), ●*Living in Germany* and *At Home in Europe* (Thursday), *Cool* (a well produced youth show, Friday) and ●*Focus on Folk* (Saturday). On Sunday there's *Religion and Society, German by Radio* and *Africa This Week*; and Monday's fare is *Religion and Society, Inspired Minds* and *Hits in Germany*. Sixty minutes to East, Central and southern Africa, winter on 7285, 9565, 12035 and 15410 kHz; and summer on 9630, 9700, 15410 and 17800 kHz. Best for southern Africa are 12035 kHz in winter (summer in the Southern Hemisphere) and 9630 kHz midyear.

■**Radio France Internationale.** Monday through Friday only at this time. Similar to the 0400 broadcast, but without the international newsflash. Thirty minutes to East Africa (and heard well beyond) on any two channels from 9825, 11850, 11995, 13680, 15155 and 15160 kHz.

Vatican Radio. Summer only at this time. Twenty minutes of programming oriented to Catholics. To Europe on 4005, 5885 and 7250 kHz. One hour later in winter.

Radio Japan. *News*, then Monday through Friday there's *Japan and the World 44*

Minutes (an in-depth look at current trends and events). This is replaced Saturday by *Hello from Tokyo* and Sunday by *Pop Joins the World*. One hour to Europe on 5975 and 7230 kHz; to East Asia on 15195 kHz; to Southeast Asia on 17810 kHz; to Australasia on 21755 kHz; and to western North America on 6110 kHz.

China Radio International. Starts with *News*, followed Monday through Friday (Sunday through Thursday evenings in the Americas) by special reports—current events, sports, business, culture, science and technology and press clippings. The rest of the broadcast is devoted to features. Regulars include ●*People in the Know* (Monday), *Biz China* (Tuesday), *China Horizons* (Wednesday), ●*Voices from Other Lands* (Thursday), and *Life in China* on Friday. Weekends, the news is followed by a shorter series of reports (current events and sport) and two features. Saturday there's *Cutting Edge*, and *Listeners' Garden* (listener mail, Chinese folk music, a preview of the next week's programs, and a Chinese language lesson); replaced Sunday by *Reports on Developing Countries* and *In the Spotlight*, a series of mini-features: *Cultural Carousel, In Vogue, Writings from China, China Melody* and *Talking Point*. One hour to western North America on 5960 (winter), 6090 (summer), 6190 and (summer) 9560 kHz via CRI's Canadian relay.

Radio Habana Cuba. The start of a two-hour broadcast for North America and Central America. Tuesday through Sunday (Monday through Saturday evenings in North America), the first half hour consists of international and Cuban news followed by *RHC's Viewpoint*. The next 30 minutes consist of a news bulletin and the sports-oriented *Time Out* (five minutes each) plus a feature: *Caribbean Outlook* (Tuesday and Friday), *DXers Unlimited* (Wednesday and Sunday), the *Mailbag Show* (Thursday) and *Weekly Review* (Saturday). Monday, the hour is split between *Weekly Review* and *Mailbag Show*. On 6000, 6060, 9550 and 11760 (or 9820) kHz.

Radio Austria International. Summer Sundays only, and actually starts at 0505. See 0600 for more details. To the Mideast on 17870 kHz, and one hour later in winter.

Radio New Zealand International. Continues with regional programming for the South Pacific. Part of a 24-hour broadcast, which is also heard in parts of North America (especially during summer). On 9615, 11820 or 13690 kHz.

Radio Australia. *World News*, then Monday through Friday there's *Pacific Beat* (background reporting on events in the Pacific)—look for a sports bulletin at 0530, followed by *On the Mat*. Weekends, it's all sport in *Grandstand*. Continuous to Asia and the Pacific on 9660, 12080, 13630, 15160, 15240, 15415 (from 0530), 15515 and 17750 kHz. In North America (best during summer) try 15160 and 15515 kHz. Best for East Asia is 13630 kHz; in Southeast Asia use 15415 or 17750 kHz.

Voice of Russia World Service. Winter, the final 60 minutes of a four-hour block of programming to North America; summer, the first of four hours to Australasia. Opens with *News*, followed winter by features: *Musical Tales* and *The VOR Treasure Store* (Monday), *Moscow Mailbag*, ●*Music Around Us* and ●*Music at Your Request* (Tuesday), *Science Plus* and *Our Homeland* (Wednesday), the business-oriented *Newmarket* and ●*Folk Box* (Thursday), *Moscow Mailbag* and *The VOR Treasure Store* (Friday), *This is Russia* and *Timelines* (Saturday), and *Musical Tales* and *Kaleidoscope* (Sunday). Note that these days are World Time; locally in North America it will be the previous evening. Tuesday through Saturday summer, there's *Focus on Asia and the Pacific*, replaced Sunday by *This is Russia* and Monday by *Moscow Mailbag*. On the half-hour, look for ●*Music Around Us* and ●*Music at Your Request* (Friday), *The VOR Treasure Store* (Sunday), *Our Homeland* (Thursday), ●*Christian Message from Moscow* (Saturday), *Russian by Radio* (Monday and Wednesday) and *Kaleidoscope* on Tuesday. Winter only to eastern North America on 7150 and 7180 kHz, and to western parts on 12010, 15425, 15475 and 15595 kHz. Summer (winter in the Southern Hemisphere) to Australasia on 21790 kHz.

Voice of America. Continuous programming to Africa. Opens with *News*, then it's music: *American Gold* (Monday), *Roots and Branches* (Tuesday), *Classic Rock* (Wednesday), *Top Twenty* (Thursday), *Country Hits* (Friday) and *Jazz America* at the weekend. Winter on 4930, 6035, 6105, 7295 and 13710 kHz; and summer on 4930, 6080, 6180, 7290, 12080 and 13645 kHz. Best for southern Africa is 4930 kHz. Heard winter in parts of North America on 6035 kHz.

AFRTS Shortwave, USA. Network news, live sports, music and features in the upper-sideband mode from the Armed Forces Radio & Television Service. Transmitted from modestly powered U.S. Navy stations around the globe. Try 4319, 5446.5, 5765, 6350, 7590, 7811, 9980, 10320, 12133.5, 12579 and 13362 kHz.

05:30

Radio Thailand. Thirty minutes of *news* and short features relayed from one of the station's domestic services. To Europe winter on 13770 kHz, and summer on 21795 kHz.

06:00–11:59
Australasia & East Asia—Evening Prime Time
Western North America—Late Evening
Europe & Mideast—Morning and Midday

06:00

■**Deutsche Welle,** Germany. *News*, then Tuesday through Saturday it's ●*News-Link*—commentary, interviews, background reports and analysis. This is followed by *Insight* and *Business German* (Tuesday), *World in Progress* (Wednesday), ●*Money Talks* (Thursday), *Living Planet* (Friday), and *Spectrum* (Saturday). Sunday fare is ●*Inside Europe*, replaced Monday by *Mailbag*. Sixty minutes to West Africa winter on 7225, 11785 and 15410 kHz; and summer on 7170, 15275 and 17860 kHz. Also year round to Europe on 6140 kHz.

Radio Habana Cuba. The second half of a two-hour broadcast. Tuesday through Sunday (Monday through Saturday evenings in North America), opens with 10 minutes of international news. Next comes *Spotlight on the Americas* (Tuesday through Saturday) or Sunday's *The World of Stamps*. The final 30 minutes consists of news-oriented programming. The Monday slots are *From Havana* and ●*The Jazz Place* or *Breakthrough* (science). To North and Central America on 6000, 6060, 9550 and 11760 (or 9820) kHz.

China Radio International. Starts with *News*, followed Monday through Friday by special reports—current events, sports, business, culture, science and technology and press clippings. The rest of the broadcast is devoted to features. Regulars include ●*People in the Know* (Monday), *Biz China* (Tuesday), *China Horizons* (Wednesday), ●*Voices from Other Lands* (Thursday), and *Life in China* on Friday. Weekends, the news is followed by a shorter series of reports (current events and sport) and two features. Saturday there's *Cutting Edge*, and *Listeners' Garden* (listener mail, Chinese folk music, a preview of the next week's programs, and a Chinese language lesson); replaced Sunday by *Reports on Developing Countries* and *In the Spotlight*, a series of mini-features: *Cultural Carousel*, *In Vogue*, *Writings from China*, *China Melody* and *Talking Point*. One hour summer to Europe on 17490 kHz; and winter to western North America on 6115 kHz. Note that these days are World Time; locally in western North America it will be the previous evening.

Radio Japan. *News*, then weekdays it's *A Song for Everyone* and *Asian Top News*. This is followed by a 35-minute feature: *Japan Musicscape* (Monday), Japanese language lessons (Tuesday and Thursday), *Japan Music Archives* (Wednesday), and *Music Beat* (Japanese popular music) on Friday. On the remaining days, *Pop Joins the World* fills the Saturday slot and *Weekend Japanology* and *Japan Music Scene* are aired on Sunday. One hour to Europe on 7230 kHz; to East Asia on 11715, 11760 and 15195 kHz; to Southeast Asia on 11740 kHz; to Australasia on 21755 kHz; and to Hawaii on 17870 kHz (this channel has different programming after 0615). Also to western North America winter on 11690 kHz, and summer on 13630 kHz.

Radio Austria International. Winter Sundays only. The 25-minute ●*Report from Austria—The Week in Review* is aired at 0605, and then repeated at 0635. The remainder of the one-hour broadcast is in German. To the Mideast on 17870 kHz, and one hour earlier in summer.

■**Radio France Internationale.** Weekdays only at this time. Similar to the 0400 broadcast (see there for specifics), but includes a report on the day's main international story. Thirty minutes to East and West Africa winter on 9865 and 17800 kHz; and summer on 11665 and 15160 kHz. Heard well beyond.

Radio Australia. Monday through Friday, there's *News*, *Regional Sports*, *Talking Point* and a relay of Radio New Zealand International's *Dateline Pacific*. These are replaced weekends by live sports coverage in *Grandstand*. Continuous to Asia and the Pacific on 9660, 12080, 13630, 15160, 15240, 15415, 15515 and 17750 kHz. Listeners in North America should try 15160 and 15515 kHz. In East Asia, tune to 13630 kHz; for Southeast Asia, use 15415 or 17750 kHz.

Radio New Zealand International. Continues with regional programming for the South Pacific, which is also heard in parts of North America (especially during summer). On 9615, 11820 or 13690 kHz.

Voice of Russia World Service. *News*, then winter it's *Focus on Asia and the Pacific* (Tuesday through Saturday), *This is Russia* (Sunday) and *Moscow Mailbag* (Monday). On the half-hour, look for ●*Music Around Us* and ●*Music at Your Request* (Friday), *The VOR Treasure Store* (Sunday), *Our Homeland* (Thursday), ●*Christian Message from Moscow* (Saturday), *Russian by Radio* (Monday and Wednesday) and *Kaleidoscope* on Tuesday. In summer, the news is followed by *Science Plus* (Monday), *This is Russia* (Tuesday and Friday), the business-oriented *Newmarket* (Wednesday), *Musical Tales* (Saturday) and *Moscow Mailbag*, on the remaining days. The second half-hour offers plenty of variety: *Kaleidoscope* (Monday and Friday), *Russian by Radio* (Tuesday), *Jazz Show* (Wednesday), *The VOR Treasure Store* (Thursday), ●*Folk Box* (Saturday) and *Timelines* on Sunday. Continuous programming to Australasia on 17665 (winter) and 21790 kHz.

Vatican Radio. Winter only at this time. Twenty minutes with a heavy Catholic slant. To Europe on 4005, 5885 and 7250 kHz. One hour earlier in summer.

Voice of Malaysia. *News*, followed Monday, Wednesday, Friday and Sunday by a two-minute Malayan language lesson (replaced by a local pop hit on Tuesday). The next 33 minutes are given over to *Hits All the Way*. Saturday, it's the 35-minute

Mailbag. The hour is rounded off with a feature: *New Horizon* (Monday), *ASEAN Focus* (Tuesday), *Malaysia in Perspective* (Wednesday), *Personality* (Thursday), *News and Views* (Friday), and *Weekly Roundup* and *Current Affairs* on the weekend. The first hour of a 150-minute broadcast to Southeast Asia and Australasia on 6175, 9750 and 15295 kHz.

AFRTS Shortwave, USA. Network news, live sports, music and features in the upper-sideband mode from the Armed Forces Radio & Television Service. Transmitted from modestly powered U.S. Navy stations around the globe. Try 4319, 5446.5, 5765, 6350, 7690, 7811, 9980, 10320, 12133.5, 12579 and 13362 kHz.

06:30

Radio Bulgaria. Summer only at this time. *News*, followed by *Answering Your Letters* (Monday), ●*Folk Studio* (Tuesday) and *Keyword Bulgaria* on the remaining days. Thirty minutes to Europe on 11600 and 13600 kHz. One hour later in winter.

Radio Romania International. *News* and commentary followed by short features on Romania. Twenty-five minutes to western Europe winter on 7180 and 9690 kHz, and summer on 9655 and 11830 kHz. Also available to Australasia winter (summer in the Southern Hemisphere) on 15135 and 17780 kHz.

07:00

■**Deutsche Welle, Germany.** *News*, followed weekdays by the excellent ●*News-Link* —commentary, interviews, background reports and analysis. The second half-hour features *Spectrum* (Monday), ●*A World of Music* (Tuesday), *Arts on the Air* (Wednesday), ●*Living in Germany* and *At Home in Europe* (Thursday) and *Cool* (a youth show, Friday). Weekend fare consists of Saturday's ●*Inside Europe* and Sunday's *Sports Report*, *Inspired Minds* and *Hits in Germany*. Sixty minutes to Europe on 6140 kHz.

07:00–08:00

Vienna's Schönbrunn Palace, although finally completed by 1780, was preceded by two centuries of construction, war damage and reconstruction.   T. Ohtake

■**Radio France Internationale.** Starts with a bulletin of African *news*. Next, there's a review of the French dailies, an in-depth look at events in Africa, the main news event of the day in France, and sports. The broadcast ends with a 25-minute feature—*French Lesson*, *Crossroads*, *Voices*, *Rendez-Vous*, *World Tracks*, *Weekend* or *Club 9516* (a listener-response program). One hour to West Africa winter on 11725 kHz, and summer on 15605 kHz. These frequencies are via RFI's Gabon relay, and are also audible in parts of North America.

Radio Prague, Czech Republic. Summer only at this time. See 0800 for specifics. Thirty minutes to Europe on 9880 and 11600 kHz. One hour later in winter.

China Radio International. Starts with *News*, followed weekdays by special reports—current events, sports, business, culture, science and technology and press clippings. The rest of the broadcast is devoted to features. Regulars include ●*People in the Know* (Monday), *Biz China* (Tuesday), *China Horizons* (Wednesday), ●*Voices from Other Lands* (Thursday), and *Life in China* on Friday. Weekends, the news is followed by a shorter series of reports (current events and sport) and two features. Saturday there's *Cutting Edge*, and *Listeners' Garden* (listener mail, Chinese folk music, a preview of the next week's programs, and a Chinese language lesson); replaced Sunday by *Reports*

on *Developing Countries* and *In the Spotlight*, a series of mini-features: *Cultural Carousel*, *In Vogue*, *Writings from China*, *China Melody* and *Talking Point*. One hour to Europe winter on 11855 kHz, and summer on 13710 and 17490 kHz.

Radio Slovakia International. Monday through Friday, starts with *News* and *Topical Issue*, then features—all with a local or regional flavor. *Insight Central Europe* (Monday) is a joint production with stations in neighboring countries. Saturday's news is followed by *Network Europe*; and Sunday's lineup is *Sunday Newsreel* and *Listeners' Tribune*. Thirty minutes to Australasia on 9440 (midyear), 13715 (winter) and 15460 kHz.

Radio Australia. *World News*, then Monday through Friday it's *Pacific Beat* (background reporting on events in the Pacific, including the latest sports news and *On the Mat*). Weekends, there's a roundup of the latest sports action in *Grandstand Wrap*, then Saturday's *Hit Mix* or Sunday's *Innovations*. Continuous to Asia and the Pacific on 9660, 12080, 13630, 15160, 15240, 15415 and 17750 kHz. Listeners in North America can try 13630 (West Coast) and 15160 kHz (best during summer), while East Asia is served by 13630 kHz. For Southeast Asia, there's 15415 and 17750 kHz.

Voice of Malaysia. Starts weekdays with 45 minutes of *Fascinating Malaysia*, replaced Saturday by *Malaysia Rama* and *Malaysia in Perspective*, and Sunday by *ASEAN Melody* and *Destination Malaysia*. Not much doubt about where the broadcast originates! The hour ends with a 15-minute feature. Continuous to Southeast Asia and Australasia on 6175, 9750 and 15295 kHz.

Voice of Russia World Service. Continuous programming to Southeast Asia and Australasia. Opens with *News*, then features: *Science Plus* (Monday), *This is Russia* (Tuesday and Friday), *Newmarket* (Wednesday), *Musical Tales* (Saturday) and *Moscow Mailbag*, on the remaining days. For the second half-hour there's *Kaleidoscope* (Monday and Friday), *Russian by Radio* (Tuesday), *Jazz Show* (Wednesday), *The VOR Treasure Store* (Thursday), ●*Folk Box* (Saturday) and *Timelines* on Sunday. Summer, the news is followed by the informative *Update* on Tuesday, Thursday and Saturday. Other offerings include *This is Russia* (Wednesday), *Moscow Mailbag* (Friday) and *Newmarket* (Sunday). Class act of the week is Monday's masterpiece, ●*Music and Musicians*. On the half-hour there's a summary of the latest news, then more features: ●*Folk Box* (Tuesday), *Our Homeland* (Wednesday and Friday), ●*Jazz Show* (Thursday), *Kaleidoscope* (Saturday) and *Songs from Russia* and *Russia: People and Events* on Sunday. Well heard in Southeast Asia summer on 17495 and 17525 kHz (there's nothing available in winter). For Australasia winter (local summer) there's 17665 and 21790 kHz; and midyear, 17495, 17525, 17635 and 21790 kHz.

Radio New Zealand International. Continues with regional programming for the South Pacific, which is also heard in parts of North America (especially during summer). On 9885 or 15720 kHz.

Radio Taiwan International. Ten minutes of *News*, followed by features. Monday (Sunday evening in North America) there's *The Undiscovered Country*, *Asia Pacific* (produced by Radio Australia) and *Let's Learn Chinese*. These are replaced on other days by *Made in Taiwan* and *We've Got Mail* (Tuesday); *Strait Talk* and ●*Jade Bells*

and Bamboo Pipes (Wednesday); *Trends*, *People* and *Instant Noodles* (Thursday); *Ilha Formosa* and *New Music Lounge* (Friday); *Bookworm* and *Groove Zone* (Saturday); and *News Talk*, *Taipei Magazine* and *Stage, Screen and Studio* (Sunday). One hour to western North America on 5950 kHz.

AFRTS Shortwave, USA. Network news, live sports, music and features in the upper-sideband mode from the Armed Forces Radio & Television Service. Transmitted from modestly powered U.S. Navy stations around the globe. Try 4319, 5446.5, 5765, 6350, 7590, 7811, 9980, 10320, 12133.5, 12579 and 13362 kHz.

07:30

Radio Bulgaria. This time winter only. *News*, followed by *Answering Your Letters* (Monday), ●*Folk Studio* (Tuesday) and *Keyword Bulgaria* on the remaining days. Thirty minutes to Europe on 9500 and 11500 kHz, and hour earlier in summer.

08:00

■**Deutsche Welle,** Germany. *News*, then Monday through Friday there's commentary, interviews, background reports and analysis in ●*NewsLink*. On the half-hour, look for ●*Focus on Folk* (Monday), *Insight* and *Business German* (Tuesday), *World in Progress* (Wednesday), ●*Money Talks* (Thursday) and *Living Planet* (Friday). Saturday's lineup is *Religion and Society*, *German by Radio* and ●*Network Europe*, replaced Sunday by *Mailbag*. Sixty minutes to Europe on 6140 kHz.

Voice of Malaysia. *News* and commentary, then *Golden Oldies*. The final half hour of a much longer transmission targeted at Southeast Asia and Australasia on 6175, 9750 and 15295 kHz.

Radio Prague, Czech Republic. Winter only at this time. *News*, then Monday through Friday it's the in-depth *Current Affairs* and one or more features: *Talking Point* (Monday), *Czech Science* and *One on*

08:00–09:00

One (Tuesday), *Czechs in History Czechs Today* or *Spotlight* (Wednesday), *Panorama* (Thursday), and *Business Briefs* and *The Arts* (Friday). Weekends, the news is followed by Saturday's *Insight Central Europe* or Sunday's *Mailbox* and *Letter from Prague* followed by *Encore* (classical music), *Magic Carpet* (Czech world music) or *Czech Books*. Thirty minutes to Europe on 7345 and 9860 kHz. One hour earlier in summer.

Radio Australia. Part of a 24-hour service to Asia and the Pacific, but which can also be heard at this time throughout much of North America. Begins with a bulletin of *World News*, then Monday through Friday there's an in-depth look at current events in *PM*. Weekend fare consists of Saturday's *Asia Pacific Review* and *Jazz Notes*, and Sunday's *Correspondents' Report* and *Smart Societies*. On 5995, 9580, 9590, 9710, 12080, 13630, 15240, 15415 (the first half hour is weekends only) and 17750 kHz. Audible in parts of North America on 9580, 9590 and 13630 kHz. Best for East Asia is 15240 kHz, with 15415 and 17750 kHz the channels for Southeast Asia.

Voice of Russia World Service. Continuous programming to Southeast Asia and Australasia. Winter, *News* is followed by the informative *Update* on Tuesday, Thursday and Saturday. Other offerings include *This is Russia* (Wednesday), *Moscow Mailbag* (Friday) and *Newmarket* (Sunday). Highlight of the week is Monday's ●*Music and Musicians*. On the half-hour there's a summary of the latest news, then more features: ●*Folk Box* (Tuesday), *Our Homeland* (Wednesday and Friday), ●*Jazz Show* (Thursday), *Kaleidoscope* (Saturday) and *Songs from Russia* and *Russia: People and Events* on Sunday. In summer, the news is followed Tuesday through Sunday by *News and Views*, and Monday by *This is Russia*. On the half-hour there's a summary of news and a feature: *Our Homeland* (Monday), *Kaleidoscope* (Tuesday), *The VOR Treasure Store* (Wednesday), ●*Folk Box* (Thursday), ●*Jazz Show* (Friday), ●*Christian Message from Moscow* (Saturday) and *Timelines* on Sunday. In Southeast Asia, choose from

17495, 17525 and (winter) 17570 kHz. These frequencies are also available for Australasia, as well as 17635 (midyear), 17665 (winter) and 21790 kHz.

Radio Taiwan International. Ten minutes of *News*, followed by features. Monday, there's *The Undiscovered Country*, Radio Australia's *Asia Pacific* and *Let's Learn Chinese*. These are replaced on the following days by *Made in Taiwan* and *We've Got Mail* (Tuesday); *Strait Talk* and ●*Jade Bells and Bamboo Pipes* (Wednesday); *Trends, People* and *Instant Noodles* (Thursday); *Ilha Formosa* and *New Music Lounge* (Friday); *Bookworm* and *Groove Zone* (Saturday); and *News Talk, Taipei Magazine* and *Stage, Screen and Studio* (Sunday). One hour to Australasia on 9610 kHz.

Radio New Zealand International. Continues with regional programming for the South Pacific. Part of a 24-hour broadcast which is also heard in parts of North America (especially during summer). On 9885 kHz.

China Radio International. Repeat of the 0700 broadcast, but with news updates. One hour to Europe on 11855 (winter), 13710 (summer) and 17490 kHz.

KBS World Radio, South Korea. Opens with 10 minutes of *news*, then Monday through Friday, a commentary. This is followed by 30 minutes of *Seoul Calling* and a 15-minute feature: *Shaping Korea, Made in Korea, Cultural Promenade, Korea Today and Tomorrow* and *Seoul Report*, respectively. Saturday's news is followed by *Worldwide Friendship* (a listener-response show), and Sunday by *Korean Pop Interactive*. Sixty minutes to Europe on 9640 kHz, and to Southeast Asia on 9570 kHz.

AFRTS Shortwave, USA. Network news, live sports, music and features in the upper-sideband mode from the Armed Forces Radio & Television Service. Transmitted from modestly powered U.S. Navy stations around the globe. Try 4319, 5446.5, 5765, 6350, 7590, 7811, 9980, 10320, 12133.5, 12579 and 13362 kHz.

08:00–09:00

08:30

Radio Vilnius, Lithuania. Summer only at this time. Thirty minutes of mostly *news* and background reports about events in Lithuania. Of broader appeal is *Mailbag,* aired every other Sunday. For a little Lithuanian music, try the second half of Monday's broadcast. To western Europe on 9710 kHz. One hour later in winter.

09:00

■**Deutsche Welle,** Germany. *News,* then Monday through Friday it's the excellent ●*NewsLink* —commentary, interviews, background reports and analysis. The second half-hour features *Spectrum* (Monday), ●*A World of Music* (Tuesday), *Arts on the Air* (Wednesday), ●*Living in Germany* and *At Home in Europe* (Thursday) and *Cool* (a well produced youth show, Friday). Weekend features are Saturday's ●*Inside Europe*

and Sunday's *Religion and Society, Inspired Minds* and *Hits in Germany.* Sixty minutes to Europe on 6140 kHz.

China Radio International. Starts with *News,* followed Monday through Friday by special reports—current events, sports, business, culture, science and technology and press clippings. The rest of the broadcast is devoted to features. Regulars include ●*People in the Know* (Monday), *Biz China* (Tuesday), *China Horizons* (Wednesday), ●*Voices from Other Lands* (Thursday), and *Life in China* on Friday. Weekends, the news is followed by a shorter series of reports (current events and sport) and two features. Saturday there's *Cutting Edge,* and *Listeners' Garden* (listener mail, Chinese folk music, a preview of the next week's programs, and a Chinese language lesson); replaced Sunday by *Reports on Developing Countries* and *In the Spotlight,* a series of mini-features: *Cultural Carousel, In Vogue, Writings*

09:00–10:30

from China, *China Melody* and *Talking Point*. One hour to Europe on 17490 kHz, and to Australasia on 15210 and 17690 kHz.

Radio New Zealand International. Continuous programming for the islands of the South Pacific, on 9885 kHz. Audible in much of North America, especially in summer.

Voice of Russia World Service. Winter only at this time. Tuesday through Sunday, *News* is followed by *News and Views*, replaced Monday by *This is Russia*. On the half-hour there's a news summary and a feature: *Our Homeland* (Monday), *Kaleidoscope* (Tuesday), *The VOR Treasure Store* (Wednesday), ●*Folk Box* (Thursday), ●*Jazz Show* (Friday), ●*Christian Message from Moscow* (Saturday) and *Timelines* on Sunday. To Southeast Asia on 17495, 17525 and 17570 kHz; and to Australasia on 17495, 17525 and 17665 kHz.

Radio Prague, Czech Republic. Summer only at this time. See 1000 for specifics. Thirty minutes to South Asia and West Africa on 21745 kHz, and heard well beyond. One hour later in winter.

Radio Australia. *World News*, then Monday through Friday it's *Australia Talks Back* (a call-in show), replaced weekends by Saturday's *Margaret Throsby* and Sunday's *The Music Show*. Continuous to Asia and the Pacific on 9580, 9590, 11880, 15240 and 15415 kHz; and heard in North America on 9580 and 9590 kHz. Best for East Asia is 15240 kHz; and for Southeast Asia, 11880 and 15415 kHz.

Voice of America. The first 60 minutes of a three-hour block of programming to the Mideast. Starts with *News*, then it's the weekday *Talk to America* or the weekend *On the Line* followed by Saturday's *Press Conference USA* or Sunday's *Encounter*. Winter on 15615 and 17555 kHz, and summer on 9520, 15205 and 17745 kHz.

AFRTS Shortwave, USA. Network news, live sports, music and features in the upper-sideband mode from the Armed Forces Radio & Television Service. Transmitted from modestly powered U.S. Navy stations around the globe. Try 4319, 5446.5, 5765, 6350, 7590, 7811, 9980, 10320, 12133.5, 12579 and 13362 kHz.

09:30

Radio Vilnius, Lithuania. Winter only at this time. Thirty minutes of mostly *news* and background reports about events in Lithuania. A listener-response program, *Mailbag*, is aired every other Sunday. For a little Lithuanian music, try the second half of Monday's broadcast. To western Europe on 9710 kHz. One hour earlier in summer.

Kol Israel. Summer only at this time. *News* for 15 minutes from Israel Radio's domestic network. To Europe and eastern North America on 15640 and 17535 kHz. One hour later in winter.

10:00

■**BBC World Service for the Caribbean.** Monday through Friday, opens with a half hour of news and current events, followed by summer's ●*World Business Report* or winter's *Analysis* (except Thursday, when there's ●*From Our Own Correspondent*). Best of the weekend fare is Saturday's *Assignment* (1006). *Sports Roundup* or *Football Extra* completes the hour. The first of four hours of continuous programming to the region. On 6195 kHz, and audible in much of the southern United States. Listeners farther west can tune to the Asian stream on 9740 kHz.

■**Radio Netherlands.** Monday through Friday it's ●*Newsline*, then a feature: ●*Research File* (Monday), ●*EuroQuest* (Tuesday), ●*Documentary* (Wednesday), *Dutch Horizons* (Thursday) and *A Good Life* (Friday). The weekend lineup consists of *Saturday Connection* followed by *Vox Humana*, and Sunday's *Amsterdam Forum*. Fifty-seven minutes to East and Southeast Asia on 7315 (winter), 9795 (winter), 12065, and (summer) 13710 and 13820 kHz. Also available midyear to Australasia on 9785 kHz.

Radio Australia. Monday through Friday, there's *World News*, *Asia Pacific* and a feature: *Health Report* (Monday), *Law Report* (Tuesday), *Religious Report* (Wednesday), *Media Report* (Thursday) and *Sports Factor* (Friday). The Saturday slots are taken by *Asia Pacific Business*, *Talking Point* and *Pacific Review*; Sunday, it's the second part of *The Music Show*. Continuous to Asia and the Pacific on 9580, 9590, 11880, 15240 and 15415 kHz; and heard in North America on 9580 and 9590 kHz. Listeners in East Asia should tune to 15240 kHz; and Southeast Asia has 11880 and 15415 kHz.

Radio Prague, Czech Republic. Winter only at this time. *News*, then Monday through Friday there's *Current Affairs* and a feature or two: *Talking Point* (Monday), *Czech Science* and *One on One* (Tuesday), *Czechs in History*, *Czechs Today* or *Spotlight* (Wednesday), *Panorama* (Thursday) and *Business Briefs* and *The Arts* (Friday). On Saturday the news is followed by *Magazine*, *ABC of Czech* and a repeat of Tuesday's *One on One*. Sunday's lineup is *Mailbox* and *Letter from Prague* followed by *Encore* (classical music), *Magic Carpet* (Czech world music) or *Czech Books*. Thirty minutes to South Asia and West Africa on 21745 kHz, but audible well beyond. One hour earlier in summer.

Radio Japan. *News*, then Monday through Friday it's *A Song for Everyone* and *Japan and the World 44 Minutes* (an in-depth look at current trends and events). This is replaced Saturday by *Hello from Tokyo*, and Sunday by *Weekend Japanology* and *Japan Music Scene*. One hour to East Asia on 11730 kHz, to Southeast Asia on 9695 kHz, to Europe on 17585 kHz, to the Mideast on 17720 kHz, to eastern North America on 6120 kHz, and to Australasia on 21755 kHz.

Voice of Mongolia. Original programming is aired on Monday, Wednesday and Friday, and is repeated on the following day. Starts with *News*, and then it's either a listener-response program (Monday) or reports and interviews. The entire Sunday broadcast is devoted to exotic Mongolian music. Thirty minutes to Southeast Asia and Australasia on 12085 (or 12015) kHz. Often well heard

in parts of the United States during March and September.

China Radio International. News, commentary, reports and interviews in the weekday ●*RealTime Beijing*. Weekends, there's Saturday's *China Roots* (folk music) and Sunday's *China Beat* (popular music). One hour to Europe on 17490 kHz, and to Australasia on 15210 and 17690 kHz.

All India Radio. *News*, then a composite program of commentary, press review and features, interspersed with exotic Indian music. One hour to East Asia on 13710, 15235 (or 15020) and 17800 kHz, and to Australasia on 13710, 17510 and 17895 kHz. Also beamed to Sri Lanka on 15260 kHz.

Voice of Korea, North Korea. Mind-numbing programs on themes such as the application of socialist thinking to steel production are basic fare for this world band curiosity. Worth the occasional listen just to hear how bad it is. One hour to Central America on 6285 (or 15180) and 9335 (or 11710) kHz; and to Southeast Asia on 6185 (or 11735) and 9850 (or 13650) kHz. Also audible in parts of East Asia on 3560 kHz.

Voice of America. Continuous programming to the Mideast. Opens with *News*, then it's music: *American Gold* (Monday), *Roots and Branches* (Tuesday), *Classic Rock* (Wednesday), *Top Twenty* (Thursday), *Country Hits* (Friday) and *Jazz America* at the weekend. Winter on 15615 and 17555 kHz, and summer on 9520, 15205 and 17745 kHz.

AFRTS Shortwave, USA. Network news, live sports, music and features in the upper-sideband mode from the Armed Forces Radio & Television Service. Transmitted from modestly powered U.S. Navy stations around the globe. Try 4319, 5446.5, 5765, 6350, 7590, 7811, 9980, 10320, 12133.5, 12579 and 13362 kHz.

10:30

Radio Prague, Czech Republic. This time summer only. Repeat of the 0700 broadcast but with different programming on Saturday: *Magazine*, *ABC of Czech* and *One on*

10:30–11:30

One replace *Insight Central Europe*. Thirty minutes to northern Europe on 9880 and 11615 kHz. One hour later during winter.

Kol Israel. Winter only at this time. *News* for 15 minutes from Israel Radio's domestic network. To Europe and eastern North America on 15640 and 17535 kHz. One hour earlier in summer.

Voice of the Islamic Republic of Iran. News, commentary and features, and a little Iranian music. Strongly reflects an Islamic point of view. One hour to South Asia, and widely heard elsewhere. Winter on 15460 and 15480 kHz, and summer on 15600 and 17660 kHz.

11:00

■**BBC World Service for the Caribbean.** Saturday and Sunday, opens with *news*, then backup reports. These are replaced weekdays by special programming for the Caribbean. Ends most days with the 15-minute *Sports Roundup*. The remaining programs change according to season. Continuous programming to the region, and heard on 11865 kHz at this hour. Also audible in the southern United States. Listeners in western North America should tune to the Asian stream on 9740 kHz.

■**Radio Netherlands.** Summer only at this time; see 1200 for specifics. Fifty-seven minutes to eastern North America on 11675 kHz, and one hour later in winter.

China Radio International. News, commentary, reports and interviews in the weekday ●*RealTime Beijing*. Weekends, there's Saturday's *China Roots* (folk music) and Sunday's *China Beat* (popular music). One hour to Europe on 17490 kHz; and to eastern North America winter on 5960 kHz, and summer on 6040 kHz.

Radio Taiwan International. Ten minutes of *News*, followed by features: *Made in Taiwan* and Radio Australia's *Asia Pacific* (Monday); *Strait Talk* and *We've Got Mail* (Tuesday); *Trends* and ●*Jade Bells and Bamboo Pipes* (Wednesday); *Ilha Formosa*, *People* and *Instant Noodles* (Thursday);

Bookworm and *New Music Lounge* (Friday); *News Talk* and *Groove Zone* (Saturday); and *The Undiscovered Country*, *Taipei Magazine* and *Stage, Screen and Studio* (Sunday). Sixty minutes to Southeast Asia on 7445 kHz.

Radio Australia. *World News*, then a mixed bag of features: *The National Interest* (Monday), *Awaye* and *Perspective* (Tuesday), *Smart Societies* and *All in the Mind* (Wednesday), *The Europeans* and *Arts on RA* (Thursday), *Movie Time* and *Books and Writing* (Friday), *Asia Pacific Review* and *All in the Mind* (Saturday), and *Sunday Profile* and *Speaking Out* on Sunday. Continuous to East Asia and the Pacific on 5995, 6020, 9475, 9560, 9580, 9590, 11880, 12080 and (till 1130) 15240 kHz; and heard in much of North America on 6020, 9580 and 9590 kHz. Listeners in Southeast Asia should tune to 9475 and 11880 kHz. For East Asia there's 9560 and (till 1130) 15240 kHz.

Radio Ukraine International. Summer only at this time. An hour's ample coverage of just about all things Ukrainian, including news, sports, politics and culture. A popular feature is ●*Music from Ukraine*, which fills most of the Sunday broadcast. Sixty minutes to western Europe on 15675 kHz. One hour later in winter.

HCJB—Voice of the Andes, Ecuador. The first hour of a religious broadcast to the Americas on 12005 kHz.

Radio Japan. *News*, then weekdays it's *A Song for Everyone* and *Asian Top News*. These are followed by a 35-minute feature: *Japan Musicscape* (Monday), Japanese language lessons (Tuesday and Thursday), *Japan Music Archives* (Wednesday), and *Music Beat* (Japanese popular music) on Friday. *Pop Joins the World* fills the Saturday slot, and is replaced Sunday by *Hello from Tokyo*. One hour to eastern North America on 6120 kHz; to East Asia on 11730 kHz; and to Southeast Asia on 9695 kHz.

Radio Singapore International. A three-hour package for Southeast Asia, and widely heard in Australasia. Starts with ten minutes of *news* (five at weekends), then Monday through Friday there's *Business and Market*

10:30–11:30

Report, replaced Saturday by *Business Ideas*, and Sunday by *Connections*. These are followed by several mini-features, including a daily news and weather bulletin on the half-hour. Monday's lineup is *Undertones*, *Discovering Singapore*, *The Write Stuff* and *E-Z Beat*; and is replaced Tuesday by *A World of Our Own*, *Young Expressions*, *The Business Feature*, *Assignment* and a shorter edition of *E-Z Beat*; Wednesday offers *Perspective*, *Traveller's Tales*, *Eco-Watch*, *The Business Feature* and *Classic Gold*; Thursday has *Frontiers*, *Eco-Watch*, *The Business Feature*, *Potluck* and *Love Songs*; and Friday brings *Asian Journal*, *Arts Arena*, *The Business Feature*, *Indonesian Media Watch* and *Classic Gold*. Saturday's list includes *Regional Press Review* and *Frontiers* and Sunday there's *Comment*, *Discovering Singapore* and *Science and Technology*. On 6080 and 6150 kHz.

Voice of Vietnam. Begins with *news*, then there's *Commentary* or *Weekly Review* followed by short features and pleasant Vietnamese music (especially at weekends). A half hour to Southeast Asia on 7285 kHz.

Voice of America. The final 60 minutes of a three-hour block of programming to the Mideast. Starts with *News*, then Monday through Friday there's *Talk to America*. Weekends, it's *Our World* followed by Saturday's *Talking History* or Sunday's *Issues in the News*. Winter on 15615 and 17555 kHz, and summer on 9520, 15205 and 17745 kHz.

AFRTS Shortwave, USA. Network news, live sports, music and features in the upper-sideband mode from the Armed Forces Radio & Television Service. Transmitted from modestly powered U.S. Navy stations around the globe. Try 4319, 5446.5, 5765, 6350, 7590, 7811, 9980, 10320, 12133.5, 12579 and 13362 kHz.

Macao continues to have a vibrant nightlife to tempt tourists and local *bons vivants*.   M. Guha

11:30

Radio Bulgaria. Summer only at this time. *News*, followed by *DX Programme* (for radio enthusiasts, Sunday), *Answering Your Letters* (a listener-response show, Monday), ●*Folk Studio* (Bulgarian folk music, Tuesday), and

Keyword Bulgaria on the remaining days. Thirty minutes to Europe on 11700 and 15700 kHz, and one hour later in winter.

Radio Prague, Czech Republic. Winter only at this time. *News*, then Monday through Friday it's *Current Affairs* plus one or more features: *Talking Point* (Monday), *Czech Science* and *One on One* (Tuesday), *Czechs in History*, *Czechs Today* or *Spotlight* (Wednesday), *Panorama* (Thursday) and *Business Briefs* and *The Arts* on Friday. The Saturday news is followed by *Magazine*, *ABC of Czech* and a repeat of Tuesday's *One on One*. Sunday's lineup is *Mailbox* and *Letter from Prague* followed by *Encore* (classical music), *Magic Carpet* (Czech world music) or *Czech Books*. Thirty minutes to northern Europe on 11640 kHz, and to East Africa on 21745 kHz. The latter channel is also audible in parts of the Mideast. The European broadcast is one hour earlier in summer, but there is no corresponding transmission for East Africa.

12:00–12:00

12:00–17:59
Western Australia & East Asia—Evening Prime Time
North America—Morning and Lunchtime
Europe & Mideast—Afternoon and Early Evening

12:00

■**BBC World Service for the Caribbean.**
A full hour of news and current events in
Newshour, except for the first 30 minutes
Monday through Friday, when there's alternative programming for the Caribbean. The
third of four hours of continuous programming to the region, and also heard in the
southern United States. On 9605 and 11865
kHz. The same programming, but without
the alternative programs, is also on 15190
kHz to South America. Listeners in western
North America may get a better signal from
the Asian stream on 9740 kHz.

Radio Canada International. Summer
weekdays only at this time. The Canadian
Broadcasting Corporation's *The Current*.
To eastern North America and the Caribbean on 9515, 13655 and 17800 kHz. For a
separate year-round service to Asia, see the
next item.

Radio Canada International. *News*, then
one or more features: *Writers and Company* (Monday), *Spotlight* and *Best of the
World* (Tuesday), *C'est la Vie* and *Wire Tap*
(Wednesday), ●*Global Village* (Thursday),
Routes Montreal (Friday), *The Circuit* (Saturday) and ●*Quirks and Quarks* (an irreverent
look at science) on Sunday. One hour to
East and Southeast Asia winter on 7105,
9665 and 11730 kHz, and summer on 9660
and 15170 kHz.

■**Radio Netherlands.** Winter only at this
time. Monday through Friday, opens with
●*Newsline* (current events) and closes with
a feature: ●*Research File* (science, Monday), ●*EuroQuest* (Tuesday), ●*Documentary*
(Wednesday), *Dutch Horizons* (Thursday)
and *A Good Life* on Friday. *Saturday Connection*, *Vox Humana* and Sunday's *Amsterdam
Forum* complete the weekend lineup. Fifty-

seven minutes to eastern North America on
9890 kHz, and one hour earlier in summer.

KBS World Radio, South Korea. Summer
only at this time. Opens with 10 minutes
of *news*, then Monday through Friday, a
commentary. This is followed by 30 minutes
of *Seoul Calling* and a 15-minute feature:
Shaping Korea, *Made in Korea*, *Cultural
Promenade*, *Korea Today and Tomorrow*
and *Seoul Report*, respectively. Saturday's
news is followed by *Worldwide Friendship* (a
listener-response show), and Sunday by *Korean Pop Interactive*. Sixty minutes to eastern North America on 9650 kHz via their
Canadian relay. One hour later in winter.

Radio Tashkent International, Uzbekistan. Monday through Saturday, opens with
News, replaced Sunday by *Significant Events
of the Week*. Other programs include *Uzbekistan and the World* (Monday), *Life in the
Village* and *Political Commentary* (Thursday),
a listener-response show (Saturday) and
Traditions and Values on Sunday. Programs
of Uzbek music are aired on Tuesday,
Wednesday and Friday. Thirty minutes to
South Asia, and also heard in parts of Europe and Australia. Winter on 5060, 5975,
6025 and 11850 kHz; and summer on 5060,
9715 and 11905 kHz.

■**Radio France Internationale.** Opens
with a *news* bulletin, then there's a 25-min-
ute feature— *French Lesson*, *Crossroads*,
Voices, *Rendez-Vous*, *World Tracks*, *Weekend*
or *Club 9516* (a listener-response program).
Thirty minutes to West Africa winter on
15275 kHz, and summer on 17815 kHz, and
to East Africa year-round on 21620 kHz.

Radio Polonia, Poland. This time summer
only. Sixty minutes of news, commentary, features and music—all with a Polish
accent. Weekdays, starts with *News from
Poland*—a potpourri of news, reports, in-

terviews and press review. This is followed Monday by *Focus* (an arts program) and *Chart Show* (a look at Polish pop music); Tuesday by *A Day in the Life* (interviews) and *Request Show*; Wednesday by *Around Poland* and *The Best of Polish Radio* (or *Bookworm*); Thursday by *Letter from Poland* and *Multimedia Show*; and Friday by *Business Week* and *High Note* (or an alternative classical music feature). The Saturday broadcast begins with *From the Weeklies*, and is followed by *Insight Central Europe* (a joint-production with other stations of the region) and *Soundcheck* (new Polish music releases). The Sunday lineup includes *Europe East* (correspondents' reports) and *In Touch*, a listener-response program. To western Europe on 9525 and 11850 kHz. One hour later in winter.

Radio Austria International. Summer only at this time. Weekdays, there's the 15-minute *Report from Austria* at 1205. Saturday and Sunday, ●*Report from Austria—The Week in Review* airs at 1205 and 1235. The remainder of the one-hour broadcast is in German. To Europe on 6155 and 13730 kHz, and to Asia and Australasia on 17715 kHz. One hour later in winter.

Radio Australia. *World News*, then Monday through Thursday it's *Late Night Live* (round-table discussion). On the remaining days there's Friday's *Best of Late Night Live*, Saturday's *Correspondents' Notebook* and *Saturday Night Country*, and Sunday's *The Spirit of Things*. Continuous to Asia and the Pacific on 5995, 6020, 9475, 9560, 9580, 9590 and 11880 kHz; and well heard in much of North America on 6020, 9580 and 9590 kHz. Listeners in East Asia can tune to 9460 kHz; and in Southeast Asia to 9475 and 11880 kHz.

Radio Ukraine International. Winter only at this time. Wide coverage of Ukrainian issues, including news, sports, politics and culture. For some enjoyable listening try ●*Music from Ukraine*, which fills most of the Monday (Sunday evening in the Americas) broadcast. Sixty minutes to Europe on 9925 kHz. One hour earlier in summer.

HCJB—Voice of the Andes, Ecuador. The second hour of a religious broadcast to the Americas on 12005 kHz.

Radio Singapore International. The second of three hours of continuous programming to Southeast Asia and beyond. Starts with five minutes of *news*, followed weekdays by *Newsline*. Most of the remaining time is devoted to short features. There's a weekday *Business and Market Report* on the half-hour, replaced weekends by a *news* bulletin. Monday's lineup includes *Perspective, Indonesian Media Watch, Frontiers, Eco-Watch* and *Young Expressions*; Tuesday, there's *Asian Journal, Undertones, Discovering Singapore* and *Film Talk*; replaced Wednesday by *Call from America, The Write Stuff, Snapshots* and *A World of Our Own*; Thursday offers, among others, *Connections, Comment, Assignment* and *Arts Arena*; and Friday has *Regional Press Review, Business Ideas* and *Limelight*. Saturday's *Connections, Perspective, Indonesian Media Watch, Young Expressions* and *Comment* are replaced Sunday by *Regional Press Review, Business Ideas, Call from America, Undertones* and *Potluck*. On 6080 and 6150 kHz.

Radio Taiwan International. Repeat of the 1100 broadcast; see there for specifics. One hour to East Asia on 7130 kHz.

Voice of America. Starts with 30 minutes of *East Asia News Now*, followed weekdays on the half-hour by a summary of *news*, a feature, *Focus* and *Opinion Roundup*. Weekend fare consists of Saturday's *Press Conference USA*, and Sunday's *On the Line* and editorial. The first of four hours of continuous programming to East and Southeast Asia winter on 6110, 9645, 9760, 11705, 11715 and 15665 kHz; and summer on 6160, 9645, 9760 and 15240 kHz. For Australasia there's 9645 kHz.

China Radio International. Starts with *News*, followed Monday through Friday by special reports—current events, sports, business, culture, science and technology and press clippings. The rest of the broadcast is devoted to features. Regulars include ●*People in the Know* (Monday), *Biz China*

12:00–13:00

(Tuesday), *China Horizons* (Wednesday), ●*Voices from Other Lands* (Thursday), and *Life in China* on Friday. Weekends, the news is followed by a shorter series of reports (current events and sport) and two features. Saturday there's *Cutting Edge*, and *Listeners' Garden* (listener mail, Chinese folk music, a preview of the next week's programs, and a Chinese language lesson); replaced Sunday by *Reports on Developing Countries* and *In the Spotlight*, a series of mini-features: *Cultural Carousel*, *In Vogue*, *Writings from China*, *China Melody* and *Talking Point*. One hour to Europe on 17490 kHz; to Southeast Asia on 9730 and 11980 kHz, and to Australasia on 11760 and 15415 (or 9760) kHz.

AFRTS Shortwave, USA. Network news, live sports, music and features in the upper-sideband mode from the Armed Forces Radio & Television Service. Transmitted from modestly powered U.S. Navy stations around the globe. Try 4319, 5446.5, 5765, 6350, 7590, 7811, 9980, 10320, 12133.5, 12579 and 13362 kHz.

12:15

Radio Cairo, Egypt. The start of a 75-minute package of news, religion, culture and entertainment, much of it devoted to Arab and Islamic themes. The initial quarter hour consists of virtually anything, from quizzes to Islamic religious talks, then there's *news* and commentary, followed by political and cultural items. To South and Southeast Asia on 17835 kHz.

12:30

Radio Bulgaria. Winter only at this time. *News*, then *DX Programme* (for radio enthusiasts, Sunday), *Answering Your Letters* (a listener-response show, Monday), ●*Folk Studio* (Bulgarian folk music, Tuesday), and *Keyword Bulgaria* on the remaining days. Thirty minutes to Europe on 11700 and 15700 kHz and one hour earlier in summer.

Bangladesh Betar. *News*, followed by Islamic and general interest features and pleasant Bengali music. Thirty minutes to

Southeast Asia, also heard in Europe, on 7185 kHz.

Voice of Vietnam. Repeat of the 1100 transmission; see there for specifics. A half hour to Southeast Asia on 9840 and 12020 kHz. Frequencies may vary slightly.

Radio Thailand. Thirty minutes of *news* and short features to Southeast Asia and Australasia, winter on 9810 kHz and summer on 9600 kHz.

Voice of Turkey. This time summer only. Fifty-five minutes of *news*, features and Turkish music. To Europe on 15225 kHz, and to Southeast Asia and Australasia on 15535 kHz. One hour later in winter.

Radio Sweden. Summer only at this time. *News* and features concentrating heavily on Scandinavian topics. Some of the features rotate from week to week, but some are fixtures. Monday's *Culture* is replaced Tuesday by *Knowledge*, Wednesday by *Real Life*, Thursday by *Lifestyle*, and Friday by *Debate*. The Saturday rotation is *Headset*, *Sweden Today*, *In Touch* (a listener-response program) and *Studio 49*; while Sunday's offering is *Network Europe*. Thirty minutes to North America on 15240 kHz; and to Asia and Australasia on 13580 and 15735 kHz. One hour later in winter.

13:00

■**BBC World Service for the Caribbean.** Weekdays, a five-minute *news* bulletin is followed by the long-running *Outlook* and ●*Off the Shelf* (readings from world literature), or *Newshour*, depending on the season. Best of the weekend fare can be found on Sunday. The last of four hours of continuous programming to the region, and heard at this hour on 15190 kHz. Also audible in the southern United States. The Asian stream on 9740 kHz is likely to provide better reception for western North America.

Radio Canada International. Monday through Friday winter, and daily in summer. Winter, it's the Canadian Broadcasting

Corporation's *The Current*. Summer weekdays there's *Sounds Like Canada*, replaced Saturday by *The House* (a look at Canadian politics) and Sunday by the first 60 minutes of *The Sunday Edition*. To eastern North America and the Caribbean winter weekdays on 9515, 13655 and 17820 kHz; and summer on 9515, 13655 and 17800 kHz.

China Radio International. Repeat of the 1200 broadcast; see there for specifics. One hour to Southeast Asia on 11980 kHz; to Australasia on 11760 and 11900 kHz; to eastern North America on 9570, 15230 (winter) and (summer) 9650 and 15260 kHz; and to western North America winter on 11885 kHz.

■**Deutsche Welle,** Germany. *News*, then weekdays it's ●*NewsLink* —commentary, interviews, background reports and analysis. Next, on the half-hour, there's *Spectrum* (Monday), *Insight* and *Business German*

(Tuesday), *World in Progress* (Wednesday), ●*Money Talks* (Thursday) and *Living Planet* (Friday). Saturday's feature is the 55-minute ●*Concert Hour*, replaced Sunday by *Mailbag*. Sixty minutes to Europe on 6140 kHz.

Radio Polonia, Poland. This time winter only. *News*, commentary, music and a variety of features. See 1200 for specifics. Sixty minutes to Europe on 9525 and 11820 kHz. One hour earlier in summer.

Radio Prague, Czech Republic. Summer only at this hour. *News*, then Monday through Friday it's *Current Affairs* plus one or more features: *Talking Point* (Monday), *Czech Science* and *One on One* (Tuesday), *Czechs in History*, *Czechs Today* or *Spotlight* (Wednesday), *Panorama* (Thursday) and *Business Briefs* and *The Arts* on Friday. The Saturday news is followed by *Insight Central Europe*, and Sunday's lineup is *Mailbox* and *Letter from Prague* followed by *Encore*

13:00–13:30

(classical music), *Magic Carpet* (Czech world music) or *Czech Books*. Thirty minutes to northern Europe on 13580 kHz, and to East Africa on 21745 kHz.

Radio Romania International. Starts with *Radio Newsreel*, a combination of news, commentary and press review. Features on Romania complete the broadcast. Regular spots include Monday's *Pro Memoria* (Romanian history) and *Pages of Romanian Literature*; Tuesday's *Business Club* and *European Horizons*; Wednesday's *Society Today*, *Partners in a Changing World*, *Cultural Survey* and *Romanian Musicians*; and Thursday's *Traveller's Guide*, *Listeners Letterbox*, *IT News*, *From Our Correspondents* and ●*The Skylark* (Romanian folk music). Friday fare includes *Over Coffee… with Artists* and ●*The Folk Music Box*, and Saturday there's *World of Culture*, *Roots*, *Cookery Show*, *Radio Pictures* and *DX Mailbag*. Sunday's broadcast includes *Sunday Studio* and *All That Jazz*. Fifty-five minutes to Europe winter on 15105 and 17745 kHz; and summer on 11830 and 15105 kHz.

Radio Jordan. Summer only at this time. The first hour of a partial relay of the station's domestic broadcasts, beamed to Europe on 11690 kHz. Continuous till 1630 (1730 in winter).

KBS World Radio, South Korea. Opens with 10 minutes of *news*, then Monday through Friday, a commentary. This is followed by 30 minutes of *Seoul Calling* and a 15-minute feature: *Shaping Korea*, *Made in Korea*, *Cultural Promenade*, *Korea Today and Tomorrow* and *Seoul Report*, respectively. Saturday's news is followed by *Worldwide Friendship* (a listener-response show), and Sunday by *Korean Pop Interactive*. Sixty minutes to Southeast Asia on 9570 and 9770 kHz, and winter only to eastern North America on 9650 kHz.

Radio Austria International. Winter only at this time. Weekdays, there's 15 minutes of *Report from Austria* at 1205. Saturday and Sunday, ●*Report from Austria—The Week in Review* airs at 1205 and 1235. The remainder of the one-hour broadcast is in

German. To Europe on 6155 and 13730 kHz, and to Asia and Australasia on 17855 kHz. One hour earlier in summer.

HCJB—Voice of the Andes, Ecuador. The final half hour of a 150-minute religious broadcast to the Americas on 12005 kHz.

Radio Canada International. Starts with *News*, then features: *Spotlight* (Monday and Thursday), *Media Zone* (Tuesday), *The Maple Leaf Mailbag* (Wednesday), *Spotlight* (Thursday), *Business Sense* (Friday and Sunday) and *Sci-Tech File* on Friday. Thirty minutes to East and Southeast Asia winter on 9665, 9725 and 11730 kHz; and summer on 9660 and 15170 kHz.

Radio Cairo, Egypt. The final half-hour of the 1215 broadcast, consisting of listener participation programs, Arabic language lessons and a summary of the latest news. To South and Southeast Asia on 17835 kHz.

Radio Australia. Monday through Friday, *News* is followed by *Asia Pacific* and a feature: *Innovations* (Monday), *Australian Express* (Tuesday), *Rural Reporter* (Wednesday), *Smart Societies* (Thursday) and *Arts on RA* (Friday). Saturday, it's a continuation of *Saturday Night Country*, and Sunday there's *Encounter*. Continuous programming to Asia and the Pacific on 5995, 6020, 9560, 9580 and 9590 kHz; and easily audible in much of North America on 6020 (West Coast), 9580 and 9590 kHz. In East Asia, try 9560 kHz.

Radio Singapore International. The third and final hour of a daily broadcast to Southeast Asia and beyond. Starts with a five-minute bulletin of the latest *news*, then most days it's music: *Singapop* (local talent, Monday and Thursday); *Rhythm in the Sun* (Latin sounds, Tuesday and Sunday); *Spin the Globe* (world music, Wednesday and Saturday); and *Hot Trax* (new releases, Friday). There's another news bulletin on the half-hour, then a short feature. Monday's offering is *Traveller's Tales*, replaced Tuesday by *The Write Stuff*. Wednesday's feature is *Potluck*; Thursday has *Call from America*; and Friday it's *Snapshots*. These are followed by the 15-minute *Newsline*. Weekend fare is made up of Saturday's *Assignment*, *Film Talk* and *Arts Arena*; and Sunday's *A World of Our Own* and *Limelight*. The broadcast ends with yet another five-minute news update. On 6080 and 6150 kHz.

Voice of Korea, North Korea. Abysmal programs from the last of the old-time communist stations. Socialist thinking coexists with choral tributes to the Great Leader. One hour to Europe on 7570 (or 13760) and 12015 (or 15245) kHz; and to North America on 9335 and 11710 kHz. Also heard in parts of East Asia on 4405 kHz.

Voice of America. Weekdays, it's 30 minutes of *East Asia News Now* followed by a repeat of the 1230 programs (see 1200 for specifics). Saturday's opening *news* bulletin is followed by 55 minutes of *Jazz America*, and Sunday fare is equally split between *East Asia News Now* and *Issues in the News*. Continuous programming to East and Southeast Asia winter on 6110, 9645, 9760 and 11705 kHz; and summer on 9645 kHz. In Australasia tune to 9645 kHz.

AFRTS Shortwave, USA. Network news, live sports, music and features in the upper-sideband mode from the Armed Forces Radio & Television Service. Transmitted from modestly powered U.S. Navy stations around the globe. Try 4319, 5446.5, 5765, 6350, 7590, 7811, 9980, 10320, 12133.5, 12579 and 13362 kHz.

Oliver Sablic of Croatia's RIZ Transmitters. Its DRM-ready shortwave senders are from 1 kW to 500 kW.

13:30

Voice of Turkey. This time winter only. *News*, then *Review of the Turkish Press* and some unusual features with a strong local flavor. Selections of Turkish popular and classical music complete the program. Fifty-five minutes to Europe on 15155 kHz, and to South and Southeast Asia and Australasia on 11735 kHz. One hour earlier in summer.

Radio Sweden. *News* and features concentrating heavily on Scandinavian topics. Some of the features rotate from week to week, but some are fixtures. Monday's *Culture* is replaced Tuesday by *Knowledge*,

Wednesday by *Real Life*, Thursday by *Lifestyle*, and Friday by *Debate*. The Saturday rotation is *Headset*, *Sweden Today*, *In Touch* (a listener-response program) and *Studio 49*; while Sunday's offering is *Network Europe*. Thirty minutes to North America on 15240 kHz; and to Asia and Australasia winter on 7420 and 11550 kHz, and summer on 15735 kHz.

All India Radio. The first half hour of a 90-minute block of regional and international *news*, commentary, exotic Indian music, and a variety of talks and features of general interest. To Southeast Asia and beyond on 9690, 11620 and 13710 kHz.

Radio Tashkent International, Uzbekistan. Monday through Saturday, opens with *News*, replaced Sunday by *Significant Events of the Week*. Other programs include *Nature and Us* and *Cooperation* (Monday), *Political Commentary* and *Youth Program* (Wednesday), a feature for women (Thursday), *Parliamentary Herald* (Friday) a show for shortwave listeners (Saturday) and *Interest-*

ing Meetings on Sunday. Programs of Uzbek music are aired on Tuesday, Friday and Saturday, and a competition with prizes on Thursday and Saturday. To South Asia, and also heard in parts of Europe and Australia. Thirty minutes winter on 5060, 5975, 6025 and 11850 kHz; and summer on 5060, 9715 and 11905 kHz.

14:00

Radio Japan. *News*, then Monday through Friday it's *Japan and the World 44 Minutes* (an in-depth look at current trends and events). On the remaining days there's Saturday's *Weekend Japanology* and *Japan Music Scene*, and Sunday's *Pop Joins the World*. One hour to Southeast Asia on 7200 kHz; to Australasia on 11840 kHz; and to South Asia winter on 9875 kHz, and summer on 11730 kHz.

■Radio France Internationale. Weekdays, opens with international and Asian *news*, then in-depth reports, a look at the main news event of the day in France, and sports. *Asia-Pacific*, replaces the international report on Saturday, and Sunday fare includes a weekly report on cultural events in France and a phone-in feature. These are followed on the half-hour by a 25-minute feature— *French Lesson, Crossroads, Voices, Rendez-Vous, World Tracks, Weekend* or *Club 9516* (a listener-response program). An hour of interesting and well-produced programming to the Mideast and beyond, winter on 17515 kHz and summer on 15615 or 17515 kHz. Also to South Asia on 7180 or 9580 kHz.

■Deutsche Welle, Germany. *News*, then Monday through Friday there's ●*NewsLink*. This is followed on the half-hour by ●*Focus on Folk* (Monday), ●*A World of Music* (Tuesday), *Arts on the Air* (Wednesday), ●*Living in Germany* and *At Home in Europe* (Thursday) and the youth-oriented *Cool* (Friday). Weekends, the Saturday news is followed by ●*Inside Europe*; and Sunday by *Religion and Society, Inspired Minds* and *Hits in Germany*. Sixty minutes to Europe on 6140 kHz.

Voice of Russia World Service. Summer only at this time. Eleven minutes of

News, followed Monday through Saturday by much of the same in *News and Views*. Completing the lineup is *Sunday Panorama* and *Russia: People and Events*. The second half-hour includes some of the station's better entertainment features: ●*Folk Box* (Monday), ●*Music Around Us* and ●*Music at Your Request* (Tuesday and Thursday), ●*Jazz Show* (Wednesday), *Our Homeland* (Friday), *Timelines* (Saturday) and *Kaleidoscope* on Sunday. To Southeast Asia on 7390 kHz.

■Radio Netherlands. The first 60 minutes of an approximately two-hour block of programming for South Asia. Monday through Friday, opens with ●*Newsline* (current events), then a feature: ●*Research File* (Monday), ●*EuroQuest* (Tuesday), ●*Documentary* (Wednesday), *Dutch Horizons* (Thursday) and *A Good Life* (Friday). The weekend opens with *Saturday Connection* and *Vox Humana*; and Sunday there's a repeat of *Vox Humana* followed by ●*Documentary*. Winter on 9345, 12080 and 15595 kHz; and summer on 9345, 9890 and 11835 kHz. Heard well beyond the target area.

Radio Australia. Weekdays, *World News* is followed by *PM* and *Perspective*. At the same time Saturday it's a continuation of *Saturday Night Country*, and Sunday there's ●*The Science Show* and *Perspective*. Continuous to Asia and the Pacific on 5995, 6080, 7240, 9475 (from 1430), 9590, 9625 (summer), 11660 (from 1430) and (winter) 11750 kHz (5995, 7240 and 9590 kHz are audible in North America, especially to the west). In Southeast Asia, use 6080, 9475, 11660 and 9625 (or 11750) kHz.

Radio Prague, Czech Republic. Winter only at this time. *News*, then Monday through Friday it's *Current Affairs* plus one or more features: *Talking Point* (Monday), *Czech Science* and *One on One* (Tuesday), *Czechs in History, Czechs Today* or *Spotlight* (Wednesday), *Panorama* (Thursday) and *Business Briefs* and *The Arts* on Friday. The Saturday news is followed by *Insight Central Europe*, and Sunday's lineup is *Mailbox* and *Letter from Prague* followed by *Encore* (classical music), *Magic Carpet* (Czech world music) or *Czech Books*. A friendly half hour to eastern North America on 21745 kHz, and to South Asia on 11600 kHz.

Radio Taiwan International. Ten minutes of *News*, followed by features: *Made in Taiwan* and Radio Australia's *Asia Pacific* (Monday); *Strait Talk* and *We've Got Mail* (Tuesday); *Trends* and ●*Jade Bells and Bamboo Pipes* (Wednesday); *Ilha Formosa*, *People* and *Instant Noodles* (Thursday); *Bookworm* and *New Music Lounge* (Friday); *News Talk* and *Groove Zone* (Saturday); and *The Undiscovered Country*, *Taipei Magazine* and *Stage, Screen and Studio* (Sunday). Sixty minutes to Southeast Asia on 15265 kHz.

China Radio International. Starts with *News*, followed Monday through Friday by special reports—current events, sports, business, culture, science and technology and press clippings. The rest of the broadcast is devoted to features. Regulars include ●*People in the Know* (Monday), *Biz China* (Tuesday), *China Horizons* (Wednesday), ●*Voices from Other Lands* (Thursday), and *Life in China* on Friday. Weekends, the news is followed by a shorter series of reports (current events and sport) and two features. Saturday there's *Cutting Edge*, and *Listeners' Garden* (listener mail, Chinese folk music, a preview of the next week's programs, and a Chinese language lesson); replaced Sunday by *Reports on Developing Countries* and *In the Spotlight*, a series of mini- features: *Cultural Carousel*, *In Vogue*, *Writings from China*, *China Melody* and *Talking Point*. One hour to western North America on 13675 (winter) and 13740 kHz; to South Asia on 9700, 11675 and 11765 kHz; to East Africa on 13685 and 17630 kHz; and to Europe on 13610 (winter), 13790 and (summer) 17490 kHz.

All India Radio. The final hour of a 90-minute composite program of commentary, press review, features and exotic Indian music. To Southeast Asia and beyond on 9690, 11620 and 13710 kHz.

Radio Canada International. Winter weekdays it's *Sounds Like Canada*, replaced summer by *Outfront* (except for Friday's *C'est la Vie*). Winter Saturdays, there's a look at Canadian politics in *The House*; and

summer it's the entertaining ●*Vinyl Café*. On Sunday there's 60 minutes of the three-hour show, *The Sunday Edition*. To eastern North America and the Caribbean winter on 9515, 13655 and 17820 kHz; and summer on 9515, 13655 and 17800 kHz.

Radio Jordan. Winter, starts at this time; summer, it's the second hour of a partial relay of the station's domestic broadcasts, and continuous till 1630 (1730 in winter). Aimed at European listeners but also audible in parts of eastern North America, especially during winter. On 11690 kHz.

Voice of America. Continuous programming to East and Southeast Asia. Starts with 30 minutes of *East Asia News Now*, followed by a repeat of the 1230 programming (see 1200 for specifics). Winter on 6110, 9645, 9760, 11705 and 15425 kHz; and summer on 6160 and 15185 kHz. Heard in Australasia winter on 9645 kHz, and midyear on 15185 kHz.

Radio Thailand. Thirty minutes of tourist features for Southeast Asia and Australasia. Winter on 9725 kHz, and summer on 9830 kHz.

AFRTS Shortwave, USA. Network news, live sports, music and features in the upper-sideband mode from the Armed Forces Radio & Television Service. Transmitted from modestly powered U.S. Navy stations around the globe. Try 4319, 5446.5, 5765, 6350, 7590, 7811, 9980, 10320, 12133.5, 12579 and 13362 kHz.

14:30

Radio Sweden. Winter only at this time. *News* and features concentrating heavily on Scandinavian topics. Some of the features rotate from week to week, but some are fixtures. Monday's *Culture* is replaced Tuesday by *Knowledge*, Wednesday by *Real Life*, Thursday by *Lifestyle*, and Friday by *Debate*. The Saturday rotation is *Headset*, *Sweden Today*, *In Touch* (a listener-response program) and *Studio 49*; while Sunday's offering is *Network Europe*. Thirty minutes to North America on 15240 kHz, and to Asia and Australasia on 11550 kHz.

14:00–15:00

Road markers are common on some Tibetan roads, although largely absent on others. They are handy for keeping track of distance traveled.
M. Guha

15:00

China Radio International. See 1400 for program details. Sixty minutes to western North America on 13675 (winter) and 13740 kHz; to South Asia on 7160 and 9785 kHz; to East Africa on 13685 and 17630 kHz; and to Europe winter on 9435 and 9525 kHz, and summer on 13790, 17490 and 17650 kHz.

Radio Austria International. Summer only at this time. Monday, the 15-minute *Report from Austria* airs at 1505 and 1545; Tuesday through Friday, the times are 1515 and 1545. Saturday and Sunday, there's ●*News from Austria—The Week in Review* at 1505 and 1535. The remainder of the broadcast is in German To western North America on 13775 kHz, and one hour later in winter.

■**Radio Netherlands.** The final 57 minutes of an approximately two-hour broadcast targeted at South Asia. Monday through Friday, starts with a feature and ends with ●*Newsline* (current events). The features are repeats of programs aired during the previous six days, and are all worthy of a second hearing: ●*EuroQuest* (Monday), *A Good Life* (Tuesday), *Dutch Horizons*

(Wednesday) ●*Research File* (science, Thursday) and ●*Documentary* (winner of several prestigious awards) on Friday. Weekend fare consists of Saturday's *Dutch Horizons* and *Saturday Connection*; and Sunday's *Amsterdam Forum*. Winter on 9345, 12080 and 15595 kHz; and summer on 9345, 9890 and 11835 kHz. Heard well beyond the target area.

Radio Australia. *World News*, then weekdays there's *Asia Pacific* and a feature on the half-hour: *Health Report* (Monday), *Law Report* (Tuesday), *Religion Report* (Wednesday), *Smart Societies* (Thursday) and *The Sports Factor* on Friday. These are replaced Saturday by the final hour of *Saturday Night Country*, and Sunday by *National Interest* and *Perspective*. Continuous programming to the Pacific (and well heard in western North America) on 5995, 7240 and 9590 kHz. Additionally available to Southeast Asia on 6080, 9475, 9625 (summer), 11660 and (winter) 11750 kHz.

■**Deutsche Welle,** Germany. *News*, then weekdays it's ●*NewsLink* —commentary, interviews, background reports and analysis. Next, on the half-hour, there's *Spectrum* (Monday), *Insight* and *Business German* (Tuesday), *World in Progress* (Wednesday),

●*Money Talks* (Thursday) and *Living Planet* (Friday). Saturday's features are *Religion and Society*, *German by Radio* and ●*Network Europe*; and the 55-minute ●*Concert Hour* fills the Sunday slot. Sixty minutes to Europe on 6140 kHz.

Voice of America. Continuous programming for East and Southeast Asia. The weekday lineup is five minutes of *news* followed by 55 minutes of music in *Border Crossings*. Weekends, there's a half hour of *East Asia News Now*, followed by Saturday's *Our World* and an editorial, or Sunday's *Talking History*. Winter on 9645 (also available to Australasia), 11780 and 13735 kHz; and summer on 13690 and 15105 kHz. The same programming is available to the Mideast, winter on 9685, 11835 and 15255 kHz; and summer on 9825, 15195 and 15445 kHz.

Radio Canada International. Daily in winter, but weekends only in summer. Winter weekdays there's *Outfront* (except for Friday's *C'est la Vie*), replaced Saturday by the unique ●*Vinyl Café* (readings and music). Summer, the Saturday slot goes to ●*Quirks and Quarks* (a science show with a difference). On the remaining day it's *The Sunday Edition* both winter and summer. To North America and the Caribbean, winter on 9515, 13655 and 17820 kHz; and summer on 9515, 13655 and 17800 kHz. For a separate broadcast to South Asia, see the next item.

Radio Canada International. *News*, then Monday through Friday it's *Canada Today*, replaced Saturday by *Business Sense* and Sunday by *Maple Leaf Mailbag* (a listener-response show). On the half-hour there's *Spotlight* (Wednesday and Sunday), *Media Zone* (Monday), *The Maple Leaf Mailbag* (repeat, Tuesday), *Business Sense* (Thursday) and *Sci-Tech File* on Friday and Saturday. Sixty minutes to South Asia winter on 9635 and 11975 kHz, and summer on 11675, 15360 and 17720 kHz. Heard well beyond the intended target area, especially to the west.

Radio Japan. *News*, then weekdays it's *A Song for Everyone* and *Asian Top News*. A 35-minute feature completes the broadcast: *Japan Musicscape* (Monday), Japanese language lessons (Tuesday and Thursday), *Japan Music Archives* (Wednesday), and *Music Beat* (Japanese popular music) on Friday. *Pop Joins the World* is aired Saturday, and *Hello from Tokyo* fills the Sunday slot. One hour to East Asia on 6190 kHz; to South Asia winter on 9875 kHz, and summer on 11730 kHz; to Southeast Asia on 7200 kHz; and to western North America and Central America on 9505 kHz.

Voice of Russia World Service. Winter, *News* is followed Monday through Saturday by *News and Views*, with *Sunday Panorama* and *Russia: People and Events* on the remaining day. The second half-hour is all features: ●*Folk Box* (Monday), ●*Music Around Us* and ●*Music at Your Request* (Tuesday and Thursday), ●*Jazz Show* (Wednesday), *Our Homeland* (Friday), *Timelines* (Saturday) and *Kaleidoscope* on Sunday. Summer weekdays, the news is followed by more of the same in *Focus on Asia and the Pacific*, replaced Saturday by *This is Russia* and Sunday by *Moscow Mailbag*. The features that follow include some of the station's best: ●*Jazz Show* (Monday), *Our Homeland* (Tuesday), *The VOR Treasure Store* (Wednesday), ●*Folk Box* (Thursday), *Songs from Russia* and *Russia: People and Events* (Friday), ●*Christian Message from Moscow* (Saturday) and *Russian by Radio* on Sunday. To Southeast Asia on 6205 (winter), 7390 (summer) and 11500 kHz. Also available summer to the Mideast (one hour later in winter) on 7325 and 11985 kHz.

Voice of Mongolia. Original programming is aired on Monday, Wednesday and Friday, and is repeated on the following day. Starts with *News*, and then it's either a listener-response program (Monday) or reports and interviews. The entire Sunday broadcast is devoted to exotic Mongolian music. Thirty minutes to West and Central Asia on 9720 kHz, and sometimes heard in Europe.

Radio Jordan. A partial relay of the station's domestic broadcasts, beamed to Europe on 11690 kHz. Continuous till 1630 (1730 in winter). Audible in parts of eastern North America, especially during winter.

15:00–16:00

Voice of Korea, North Korea. Repeat of the 1300 broadcast. One hour to Europe on 7570 (or 13760) and 12015 (or 15245) kHz; and to North America on 9335 and 11710 kHz. Also heard in parts of East Asia on 4405 kHz.

Voice of Vietnam. Repeat of the 1100 transmission; see there for specifics. A half hour to Southeast Asia on 7285, 9840 and 12020 kHz. Frequencies may vary slightly.

AFRTS Shortwave, USA. Network news, live sports, music and features in the upper-sideband mode from the Armed Forces Radio & Television Service. Transmitted from modestly powered U.S. Navy stations around the globe. Try 4319, 5446.5, 5765, 6350, 7590, 7811, 9980, 10320, 12133.5, 12579 and 13362 kHz.

15:30

Voice of the Islamic Republic of Iran. News, commentary and features, strongly reflecting an Islamic point of view. One hour to South and Southeast Asia (also heard in parts of Australasia), winter on 7330 and 9940 kHz, and summer on 9635 and 11650 kHz.

16:00

■Radio France Internationale. The first half hour includes *news* and reports from across Africa, international newsflashes and news about France. Next is a 25-minute feature— *French Lesson*, *Crossroads*, *Voices*, *Rendez-Vous*, *World Tracks*, *Weekend* or *Club 9516* (a listener-response program). A fast-moving hour to Africa and the Mideast on any four frequencies from 7170, 9730, 11615, 15160, 15365, 15605, 17605 and 17850 kHz. Best for the Mideast is 11615 kHz in winter, and 15605 kHz in summer. In southern Africa, tune to 9730 or 17850 kHz.

Radio Austria International. Winter only at this time; see 1500 for specifics. To western North America on 13675 kHz, and one hour earlier in summer.

■Deutsche Welle, Germany. *News*, then Monday through Friday, ●*NewsLink*. The final 30 minutes consist of *Insight* and *At Home in Europe* (Monday), *World in Progress* (Tuesday), ●*Money Talks* (Wednesday), *Living Planet* (Thursday) and *Asia This Week* (Friday). Weekends, the Saturday news is followed by ●*Inside Europe* and the youth-oriented *Cool*; and Sunday by *Mailbag*. Sixty minutes to South Asia on 6170, 7225, 9795 (winter), 11695 (winter) and (summer) 17595 kHz.

KBS World Radio, South Korea. Opens with 10 minutes of *news*, then Monday through Friday, a commentary. This is followed by 30 minutes of *Seoul Calling* and a 15-minute feature: *Shaping Korea*, *Made in Korea*, *Cultural Promenade*, *Korea Today and Tomorrow* and *Seoul Report*, respectively. Saturday's news is followed by *Worldwide Friendship* (a listener-response show), and Sunday by *Korean Pop Interactive*. One hour to East Asia on 5975 kHz, and to the Mideast and parts of Africa on 9870 kHz.

Radio Taiwan International. Ten minutes of *News*, followed by features: *Made in Taiwan* and Radio Australia's *Asia Pacific* (Monday); *Strait Talk* and *We've Got Mail* (Tuesday); *Trends* and ●*Jade Bells and Bamboo Pipes* (Wednesday); *Ilha Formosa*, *People* and *Instant Noodles* (Thursday); *Bookworm* and *New Music Lounge* (Friday); *News Talk* and *Groove Zone* (Saturday); and *The Undiscovered Country*, *Taipei Magazine* and *Stage, Screen and Studio* on Sunday. Sixty minutes to South Asia and southern China on 11815 kHz, and heard well beyond.

Voice of Korea, North Korea. Not quite the old-time communist station it was, but the "Beloved Leader" and "Unrivaled Great Man" continue to feature prominently, as does socialist thinking. One hour to the Mideast and Africa on 9975 (or 9990) and 11535 (or 11545) kHz. Also audible in parts of East Asia on 3560 kHz.

Radio Prague, Czech Republic. Summer only at this time. *News*, then Monday through Friday it's *Current Affairs* plus one or more features: *Talking Point* (Monday), *Czech Science* and *One on One* (Tuesday), *Czechs in History*, *Czechs Today* or *Spotlight* (Wednesday), *Panorama* (Thursday) and *Business Briefs* and *The Arts* on Friday. The Saturday news is followed by *Magazine*, *ABC of Czech* and a repeat of Tuesday's *One on One*. Sunday's lineup is *Mailbox* and *Letter from Prague* followed by *Encore* (classical music), *Magic Carpet* (Czech world music) or *Czech Books*. A half hour to Europe on 5930 kHz, and to East Africa on 17485 kHz. The transmission for Europe is one hour later in winter, but there is no corresponding broadcast for East Africa.

Voice of Vietnam. *News*, then *Commentary* or *Weekly Review* followed by short features and pleasant Vietnamese music (especially at weekends). A half hour to Europe on 7280 and 9730 kHz. Also available to West and Central Africa on 7220 and 9550 kHz.

Radio Australia. Continuous programming to Asia and the Pacific. Monday through Friday, *World News* is followed by *Australia Talks Back*, and weekends by *Margaret Throsby*. Beamed to the Pacific on 5995, 7240 and 9710 kHz; and to Southeast Asia on 6080, 9475 and 11660 kHz. Also well heard in western North America on 5995 and 7240 kHz.

Radio Ethiopia. An hour-long broadcast divided into two parts by the 1630 *news* bulletin. Regular weekday features include *Kaleidoscope* and *Women's Forum* (Monday), *Press Review* and *Africa in Focus* (Tuesday), *Guest of the Week* and *Ethiopia Today* (Wednesday), *Ethiopian Music* and *Spotlight* (Thursday) and *Press Review* and *Introducing Ethiopia* on Friday. For weekend listening, there's *Contact* and *Ethiopia This Week* (Saturday), or Sunday's *Listeners' Choice* and *Commentary*. Best heard in parts of Africa and the Mideast, but sometimes audible in Europe. On 7165, 9560 and 11800 kHz.

Radio Jordan. A partial relay of the station's domestic broadcasts, beamed to Europe on 11690 kHz. The final half-hour in summer, but a full 60 minutes in winter.

Sometimes audible in parts of eastern North America, especially during winter.

Voice of Russia World Service. Continuous programming to the Mideast and West Asia at this hour. *News*, then very much a mixed bag, depending on the day and season. Winter weekdays, there's *Focus on Asia and the Pacific*, with Saturday's *This is Russia* and Sunday's *Moscow Mailbag* making up the week. On the half-hour, choose from: ●*Jazz Show* (Monday), *Our Homeland* (Tuesday), *The VOR Treasure Store* (Wednesday), ●*Folk Box* (Thursday), *Songs from Russia* and *Russia: People and Events* (Friday), ●*Christian Message from Moscow* (Saturday) and *Russian by Radio* (Sunday). Summer, the news is followed by *Science Plus* (Monday and Wednesday), *Moscow Mailbag* (Tuesday and Friday), the business-oriented *Newmarket* (Thursday), *Musical Tales* (Saturday) and *This is Russia* on Sunday. More features follow a news summary on the half-hour: *The Whims of Fate* (Monday, Wednesday and Friday), *Guest Speaker* and *People of Uncommon Destiny* (Tuesday), ●*Russia—1,000 Years of Music* (Thursday), *The VOR Treasure Store* (Saturday) and *Timelines* on Sunday. Audible in the Mideast winter on 6005 and 9830 kHz, and summer on 11985 and 15540 kHz.

Radio Canada International. Winter weekends only at this hour. Saturday there's ●*Quirks and Quarks* (science), and Sunday it's the final hour of *The Sunday Edition*. To North America and the Caribbean on 9515, 13655 and 17820 kHz.

China Radio International. Starts with *News*, followed Monday through Friday by special reports—current events, sports, business, culture, science and technology and press clippings. The rest of the broadcast is devoted to features. Regulars include ●*People in the Know* (Monday), *Biz China* (Tuesday), *China Horizons* (Wednesday), ●*Voices from Other Lands* (Thursday), and *Life in China* (Friday). Weekends, the news is followed by a shorter series of reports (current events and sport) and two features. Saturday there's *Cutting Edge*, and *Listeners' Garden* (listener mail, Chinese folk music, a preview of the next week's programs, and a Chinese language lesson); replaced Sunday by *Reports on Developing Countries* and *In the Spotlight*, a series of mini-features: *Cultural Carousel*, *In Vogue*, *Writings from China*, *China Melody* and *Talking Point*. One hour to Europe winter on 7255, 9435 and 9525 kHz; and summer on 11940, 11965, 13760 and 17490 kHz. Also to southern Africa on 6100, 9570 and 11900 kHz.

Voice of America. The second of two hours to the Mideast. Monday through Friday, there's *News*, *Talk to America* and *Opinion Roundup*; weekends, it's *Nightline Africa*. Winter on 9685, 11835 and 15255 kHz; and summer on 9700, 9825, 15195 and 15445 kHz. The weekday programs are also available to East and Southeast Asia on 6160, 9645 (winter) ans 9760 kHz. For a separate service to Africa, see the next item.

Voice of America. Continuous programming for Africa. Monday through Friday, similar to the service for the Mideast (see previous item) except for Thursday's *Shaka Ssali hosts*. Weekends, there's *Nightline Africa* and an editorial. Winter on 4930, 15240, 17715 and 17895 kHz; and summer on 4930, 9850, 15410 and 15580 kHz. Best for southern Africa is 4930 kHz.

AFRTS Shortwave, USA. Network news, live sports, music and features in the upper-sideband mode from the Armed Forces Radio & Television Service. Transmitted from modestly powered U.S. Navy stations around the globe. Try 4319, 5446.5, 5765, 6350, 7590, 7811, 9980, 10320, 12133.5, 12579 and 13362 kHz.

16:30

Radio Slovakia International. Summer only at this time; see 1730 for specifics. Thirty minutes of friendly programming to western Europe on 5920 and 7345 kHz. One hour later in winter.

Xizang [Tibet] People's Broadcasting Station, China. *Holy Tibet*, a 20-minute package of information and local (mostly popular) music. Sometimes acknowledges

listeners' reception reports during the program. Well heard in East Asia, and sometimes provides fair reception in Europe. On 4905, 4920, 5240, 6110, 6130, 6200 and 7385 kHz.

Radio Cairo, Egypt. The first 30 minutes of a two-hour mix of Arab music and features on Egyptian and Islamic themes, with *news*, commentary, quizzes, mailbag shows, and answers to listeners' questions. To southern Africa winter on 11785 kHz, and midyear on 11880 kHz.

17:00

Radio Prague, Czech Republic. See 1800 for program specifics. Thirty minutes winter to West Africa on 15710 kHz, and summer to Central Africa on 17485 kHz. Also year round to Europe on 5930 kHz.

Radio Australia. Continuous programming to Asia and the Pacific. Starts with *World News*, then a feature: *Innovations* (Monday), *Australian Express* (Tuesday), *Rural Reporter* (Wednesday), *Smart Societies* (Thursday), *Big Ideas* (Friday), *Best of Late Night Live* (Saturday) and *In the Loop (Rewind)* and *The Sports Factor* on Sunday. Weekdays, the second half-hour is also given over to *In the Loop (Rewind)*. Beamed to the Pacific on 5995, 9580, 9710 and 11880 kHz; and to Southeast Asia on 6080 and 9475 kHz. Also audible in parts of western North America on 5995 and 11880 kHz.

Radio Polonia, Poland. This time summer only. Monday through Friday, opens with *News from Poland*—a compendium of news, reports and interviews. A couple of features complete the broadcast. Monday's combo is *Around Poland* and *The Best of Polish Radio* (or *Bookworm*); Tuesday, it's *Letter from Poland* and *Multimedia Show*; Wednesday, *A Day in the Life* (interviews) and *High Note* (or an alternative classical music program); Thursday, *Focus* (the arts in Poland) and *Soundcheck* (new Polish music releases); and Friday, *Business Week* and *In Touch*, a listener-response show. The Saturday broadcast begins with *Europe East* (correspondents' reports), and is followed by *From The Weeklies* and *Chart Show*. Sundays, it's five minutes of *news* followed by *Insight Central Europe* (a joint-production with other stations of the region) and *Request Show*. Sixty minutes to western Europe on 5965 and 7285 kHz. One hour later during winter.

Radio Jordan. Winter only at this time. The final 30 minutes of a partial relay of the station's domestic broadcasts. To Europe on 11690 kHz.

Voice of Russia World Service. Winter, *News* is followed by *Science Plus* (Monday and Wednesday), *Moscow Mailbag* (Tuesday and Friday), the business-oriented *Newmarket* (Thursday), *Musical Tales* (Saturday) and *This is Russia* on Sunday. More features follow a news summary on the half-hour: *The Whims of Fate* (Monday, Wednesday and Friday), *Guest Speaker* and *People of Uncommon Destiny* (Tuesday), ●*Russia—1,000 Years of Music* (Thursday), *The VOR Treasure Store* (Saturday) and *Timelines* on Sunday. In summer, the news is followed by *Moscow Mailbag* (Monday and Thursday), *Newmarket* (Tuesday), *Science Plus* (Wednesday) and *This is Russia* on Friday. Weekends, it's the excellent ●*Music and Musicians*. On the half-hour, the lineup includes *Kaleidoscope* (Monday), ●*Music Around Us* and ●*Music at Your Request* (Tuesday), *Our Homeland* (Wednesday), *Musical Tales* and *Russia: People and Events* (Thursday) and ●*Folk Box* on Friday. Summer only to Europe on 9890 kHz, plus weekends on 9480 and 11675 kHz. For the Mideast, tune to 9830 kHz in winter, and 11985 kHz in summer. In Southern Africa, try 11510 kHz midyear.

Radio Japan. *News*, then weekdays it's *A Song for Everyone* and *Japan and the World 44 Minutes* (in-depth reporting). Saturday's feature is *Hello From Tokyo*, replaced Sunday by *Pop Joins the World*. One hour to Europe on 11970 kHz; to southern Africa on 15355 kHz; and to western North America and Central America on 9535 kHz.

China Radio International. News, commentary, reports and interviews in the weekday ●*RealTime Beijing*. Weekends, there's Saturday's *China Roots* (folk music) and Sunday's *China Beat* (popular music). One hour to eastern and southern Africa on 6100, 9570 and 11900 kHz.

Voice of Vietnam. Summer only at this time. Thirty minutes to western Europe via an Austrian relay on 9725 kHz. See 1800 for specifics. One hour later in winter.

Voice of America. Continues with programs for Africa. Monday through Friday, it's *Africa World Tonight*, replaced Saturday by *News*, *On the Line* and *Press Conference USA*; and Sunday by *Africa News Now* and *Music Time in Africa*. Audible well beyond where it is targeted. Winter on 13710, 15240 and 15445 kHz; and summer on 9850, 15410 and 15580 kHz. In southern Africa, tune to 15240 kHz in winter, and 15410 kHz midyear.

■**Radio France Internationale.** An additional half-hour (see 1600) of predominantly African fare. Monday through Friday,

Discover Something New At C.CRANE

MiniCCRadio.com

17:00–18:00

Cars, capitalism and cachet mock China's communist ideology. Today's Beijing is little more than a caricature of its dour Maoist past.

M. Guha

focuses on *news* from the eastern part of Africa. Weekends, there's *Spotlight on Africa*, health issues, features on French culture, sports, media in Africa, and a phone-in feature, *On-Line*. To the Mideast winter on 11615 kHz, and summer on 15605 kHz; and to East Africa winter on 15605 kHz, and summer on 17605 kHz.

Radio Cairo, Egypt. See 1630 for specifics. Continues with a broadcast to southern Africa, winter on 11785 kHz, and summer on 11880 kHz.

AFRTS Shortwave, USA. Network news, live sports, music and features in the upper-sideband mode from the Armed Forces Radio & Television Service. Transmitted from modestly powered U.S. Navy stations around the globe. Try 4319, 5446.5, 5765, 6350, 7590, 7811, 9980, 10320, 12133.5, 12579 and 13362 kHz.

17:30

Radio Slovakia International. Winter only at this time. Monday through Friday, starts with *News* and *Topical Issue*, then features focusing on local and regional topics. Saturday's news is followed by *Network Europe*, and the Sunday lineup is *Sunday Newsreel* and *Listeners' Tribune*. A friendly half-hour to western Europe on 5915 and 7345 kHz. One hour earlier in summer.

Radio Bulgaria. Summer only at this time. *News*, followed weekdays by *Events and Developments*, and Saturday and Sunday by *Views Behind the News*. Thirty minutes to Europe on 9500 and 11500 kHz, and one hour later in winter.

Kol Israel. Summer only at this time. *News* for 15 minutes from Israel Radio's domestic network. To Europe and eastern North America on 9345 and 15640 kHz. One hour later in winter.

Radio Sweden. Summer only at this hour; see 1830 for program details. Thirty minutes of Scandinavian fare for Europe, Monday through Saturday, on 6065 kHz. One hour later in winter.

17:45

All India Radio. The first 15 minutes of a two-hour broadcast to Europe, Africa and the Mideast, consisting of regional and international *news*, commentary, a variety of talks and features, press review and exotic Indian music. Continuous till 1945. To Europe on 7410, 9950 and 11620 kHz; to West Africa on 9445, 13605 and 15155 kHz; and to East Africa on 11935, 15075 and 17670 kHz.

Bangladesh Betar. *Voice of Islam*, a 30-minute broadcast focusing on Islamic themes. To Europe on 7185 kHz.

18:00–23:59
Europe & Mideast—Evening Prime Time
East Asia—Early Morning
Australasia—Morning
Eastern North America—Afternoon and Suppertime
Western North America—Midday

18:00

■**Radio Netherlands.** The first 60 minutes of an approximately three-hour broadcast targeted at Africa, and heard well beyond. Monday through Friday, the initial 27 minutes are taken up by ●*Newsline* (current events), with a feature occupying the next half hour: ●*Research File* (Monday), ●*Euro-Quest* (Tuesday), ●*Documentary* (Wednesday), *Dutch Horizons* (Thursday) and *A Good Life* on Friday. *Saturday Connection* and *Vox Humana* fill the Saturday slots, and are replaced Sunday by a short news summary and *Amsterdam Forum* To West, Central and East Africa on 9895 and 11655 kHz; and to southern Africa on 6020 kHz.

Voice of Vietnam. Begins with *news*, which is followed by *Commentary* or *Weekly Review*, short features and some pleasant Vietnamese music (especially at weekends). A half hour to Europe on 5955 (winter), 7280 and 9730 kHz. The 5955 kHz channel is via an Austrian relay, and should provide good reception.

All India Radio. Continuation of the transmission to Europe, Africa and the Mideast (see 1745). *News* and commentary, followed by programming of a more general nature. To Europe on 7410, 9950 and 11620 kHz; to West Africa on 9445, 13605 and 15155 kHz; and to East Africa on 11935, 15075 and 17670 kHz.

Radio Prague, Czech Republic. Winter only at this time. *News*, then Monday through Friday there's *Current Affairs* and one or more features: *Talking Point* (Monday), *Czech Science* and *One on One* (Tuesday), *Czechs in History*, *Czechs Today* or *Spotlight* (Wednesday), *Panorama* (Thursday) and *Business Briefs* and *The Arts* (Friday). On

Saturday the news is followed by *Insight Central Europe*, and Sunday fare is *Mailbox* and *Letter from Prague* followed by *Encore* (classical music), *Magic Carpet* (Czech world music) or *Czech Books*. Thirty minutes to Europe on 5930 kHz, and to Australasia on 9400 kHz. Europe's broadcast is one hour earlier in summer, but for Australasia it's two hours later.

Radio Romania International. Starts with *Radio Newsreel*, a combination of news, commentary and press review. Features on Romania complete the broadcast. Regular spots include Monday's *Pro Memoria* (Romanian history) and *Pages of Romanian Literature*; Tuesday's *Business Club* and *European Horizons*; Wednesday's *Society Today*, *Partners in a Changing World*, *Cultural Survey* and *Romanian Musicians*; and Thursday's *Traveller's Guide*, *Listeners Letterbox*, *IT News*, *From Our Correspondents* and ●*The Skylark* (Romanian folk music). Friday fare includes *Over Coffee…with Artists* and ●*The Folk Music Box*, and Saturday there's *World of Culture*, *Roots*, *Cookery Show*, *Radio Pictures* and *DX Mailbag*. Sunday's broadcast includes *Sunday Studio* and *All That Jazz*. Fifty-five minutes to Europe winter on 7120 and 9640 kHz, and summer on 9635 and 11830 kHz.

Radio Australia. Sunday through Thursday, *World News* is followed by *Pacific Beat* (news and current events). The Friday slots are *Pacific Review* and *Australian Express*, replaced Saturday by *Correspondents' Report* and the first half-hour of *Australia All Over*. Part of a continuous 24-hour service, and at this hour beamed to the Pacific on 6080, 7240, 9580, 9710 and 11880 kHz; to East Asia on 6080 kHz; and to Southeast Asia on 9475 kHz. In western North America, try 11880 kHz.

18:00–19:00

Neuschwanstein, built relatively recently in the 19th century, is Bavarian King Ludwig's most elaborate castle. Alpsee lake is in the background.   Corbis

Radio Polonia, Poland. This time winter only. See 1700 for program specifics. *News*, features and music reflecting Polish life and culture. Sixty minutes to Europe on 5995 and 7170 kHz. One hour earlier in summer.

Voice of Russia World Service. Continuous programming to Europe and beyond. Predominantly news-related fare during the initial half hour in summer, but the winter schedule offers a more varied diet. Winter, *News* is followed by a *Moscow Mailbag* (Monday and Thursday), *Newmarket* (Tuesday), *Science Plus* (Wednesday) and *This is Russia* on Friday. Saturday and Sunday, it's the excellent ●*Music and Musicians*. On the half-hour, the lineup includes *Kaleidoscope* (Monday), ●*Music Around Us* and ●*Music at Your Request* (Tuesday), *Our Homeland* (Wednesday), *Musical Tales* and *Russia: People and Events* (Thursday) and ●*Folk Box* on Friday. Summer weekdays, the first half-

hour consists of *news* followed by *Update*. The Saturday slot is filled by *Newmarket*, replaced Sunday by *Musical Tales*. More features complete the hour: *The Whims of Fate* (Monday, Wednesday and Friday), *Guest Speaker* and *People of Uncommon Destiny* (Tuesday), ●*Russia—1,000 Years of Music* (Thursday), *Kaleidoscope* (Saturday) and ●*Christian Message from Moscow* on Sunday. Best winter bets for Europe are 5950 and 6175 (weekends), and 7290 kHz; summer, try 9480, 9890 and 11630 kHz. Also available winter only to the Mideast on 9830 kHz. In southern Africa, tune to 11510 kHz.

China Radio International. See 1900 for program details. Sixty minutes to Europe winter on 6160 kHz, and summer on 9695, 11940 and 13760 kHz.

Radio Argentina al Exterior—R.A.E. Monday through Friday only. *News*, press review and short features on Argentina, plus folk music and tangos. Fifty-five minutes to Europe on 9690 and 15345 kHz.

Voice of America. Continues with programs for Africa. Saturday through Thursday, starts with 30 minutes of *Africa News Now*, replaced Friday by *Sonny Side of Sports*. On the half-hour, it's Wednesday's *Straight Talk Africa*, Sunday's *Encounter*, or *World of Music*. Winter on 4930, 6035, 11975, 13710, 15240 and 17895 kHz; and summer on 4930, 9850, 11975, 15410, 15580 and 17895 kHz. Best for southern Africa is 4930 kHz.

Radio Cairo, Egypt. See 1630 for specifics. The final 30 minutes of a two-hour broadcast to southern Africa winter on 11785 kHz, and summer on 11880 kHz.

Radio Taiwan International. Ten minutes of *News*, followed by features: *Made in Taiwan* and Radio Australia's *Asia Pacific* (Monday); *Strait Talk* and *We've Got Mail* (Tuesday); *Trends* and ●*Jade Bells and Bamboo Pipes* (Wednesday); *Ilha Formosa*, *People* and *Instant Noodles* (Thursday); *Bookworm* and *New Music Lounge* (Friday); *News Talk* and *Groove Zone* (Saturday); and *The Undiscovered Country*, *Taipei Magazine* and *Stage, Screen and Studio* on Sunday. One hour to western Europe on 3965 kHz.

Radio Canada International. *News*, then Monday through Friday it's *Canada Today*, replaced Saturday by *Business Sense* and Sunday by *Maple Leaf Mailbag* (a listener-response show). On the half-hour there's *Spotlight* (Wednesday and Sunday), *Media Zone* (Monday), *The Maple Leaf Mailbag* (repeat, Tuesday), *Business Sense* (Thursday) and *Sci-Tech File* on Friday and Saturday. One hour to Africa winter on 5850, 7185, 9770, 11875 and 17740 kHz, and summer on 9530, 9780, 13730, 15255 and 15420 kHz. Best for southern Africa is 17740 kHz in winter (summer in the Southern Hemisphere), and 13730 and 15420 kHz midyear. Heard well beyond the African continent.

AFRTS Shortwave, USA. Network news, live sports, music and features in the upper-sideband mode from the Armed Forces Radio & Television Service. Transmitted from modestly powered U.S. Navy stations around the globe. Try 4319, 5446.5, 5765, 6350, 7590, 7811, 9980, 10320, 12133.5, 12579 and 13362 kHz.

18:15

Bangladesh Betar. *News*, followed by Islamic and general interest features; some nice Bengali music, too. Thirty minutes to Europe on 7185 kHz.

18:30

Radio Bulgaria. This time winter only. *News*, then *Events and Developments* (weekdays) or *Views Behind the News* (Saturday and Sunday). Thirty minutes to Europe on 5800 and 7500 kHz, and one hour earlier in summer.

Radio Slovakia International. Summer only at this time; see 1930 for program specifics. Thirty minutes of *news* and features with a strong Slovak flavor. To western Europe on 5920 and 6055 kHz. One hour later in winter.

Voice of Turkey. This time summer only. *News*, then *Review of the Turkish Press* followed by features on Turkish history, culture and international relations. Some enjoyable Turkish music, too. Fifty minutes to western Europe on 9785 kHz. One hour later in winter.

Kol Israel. Winter only at this time. *News* for 15 minutes from Israel Radio's domestic network. To Europe and eastern North America on 11585 and 11605 kHz. One hour earlier in summer.

Voice of Armenia. Actually starts at 1825, and summer only at this time. Twenty minutes of Armenian *news* and culture to Europe on 9775 (or 9965) kHz, and to the Mideast on 4810 kHz. One hour later in winter.

International Radio of Serbia and Montenegro. Summer only at this time. News, commentary and reports from the former Yugoslavia. Thirty minutes to Europe on 6100 kHz, and one hour later in winter.

Radio Sweden. *News* and features concentrating heavily on Scandinavian topics. Some of the features rotate from week to week, but some are fixtures. Monday's *Culture* is replaced Tuesday by *Knowledge*, Wednesday by *Real Life*, Thursday by *Lifestyle*, and Friday by *Debate*. The Saturday rotation is *Headset*, *Sweden Today*, *In Touch* (a listener-response program) and *Studio 49*. Thirty minutes to Europe, Monday through Saturday, on 6065 kHz. One hour earlier in summer.

18:45

Radio Tirana, Albania. Monday through Saturday, and summer only at this time. Approximately 15 minutes of *news* and commentary from this small Balkan country. To Europe on 6115 kHz. One hour later in winter.

19:00

■**Radio Netherlands.** The second hour of an approximately three-hour block of

19:00–19:30

programming for Africa. Monday through Friday, starts with a feature and ends with ●*Newsline* (current events). The features are repeats of programs aired during the previous six days, and are well worth a second hearing: ●*EuroQuest* (Monday), *A Good Life* (Tuesday), *Dutch Horizons* (Wednesday) ●*Research File* (science, Thursday) and the award-winning ●*Documentary* on Friday. Weekends, there's Saturday's *Dutch Horizons* and *Saturday Connection*, and Sunday's *Vox Humana* and ●*Documentary*. On 7120, 9895, 11655 and 17810 kHz. In southern Africa, tune to 7120 kHz. The weekend broadcasts are also available to North America, winter on 15315, 15525 and 17725 kHz; and summer on 15315, 17660 and 17735 kHz. On other days, listeners in the United States should try 17810 kHz, which is via a relay in the Netherlands Antilles.

Radio Australia. Begins with *World News*, then Sunday through Thursday it's the second hour of *Pacific Beat* (in-depth reporting on the region). Friday's slots go to *Asia Pacific Review* and *Rural Reporter*, and Saturday there's a continuation of *Australia All Over*. Continuous to Asia and the Pacific on 6080, 7240, 9500, 9580, 9710 and 11880 kHz. Listeners in western North America should try 11880 kHz, and best for East Asia is 6080 kHz. For Southeast Asia there's 9500 kHz.

Kol Israel. Summer only at this time. Twenty-five minutes of even-handed and comprehensive news reporting from and about Israel. To Europe and North America on 11590 and 15640 kHz; and to Africa and South America on 15615 kHz. One hour later in winter.

All India Radio. The final 45 minutes of a two-hour broadcast to Europe, Africa and the Mideast (see 1745). Starts off with *news*, then continues with a mixed bag of features and Indian music. To Europe on 7410, 9950 and 11620 kHz; to West Africa on 9445, 13605 and 15155 kHz; and to East Africa on 11935, 15075 and 17670 kHz.

Radio Budapest, Hungary. Summer only at this time. *News* and features, few of which are broadcast on a regular basis. Thirty minutes to Europe on 3975 and 6025 kHz. One hour later in winter.

■**Deutsche Welle,** Germany. *News*, then Monday through Friday there's ●*NewsLink*. The second half-hour consists of ●*A World Music* (Monday), *Arts on the Air* (Tuesday), ●*Living in Germany* and *At Home in Europe* (Wednesday), the youth-oriented *Cool* (Thursday) and ●*Focus on Folk* (Friday). Weekends, the Saturday news is followed by *Sports Report*, *German by Radio* and *Africa This Week*; and Sunday by *Sports Report*, *Inspired Minds* and *Hits in Germany*. One hour to Central and East Africa winter on 11865, 12025 and 15470 kHz; and summer on 13780, 15520 and 17770 kHz.

Voice of Russia World Service. Continuous programming to Europe at this hour. Winter, the first half-hour consists of *news* followed by *Update* (news and reports from and about the CIS), replaced Saturday by *Newmarket*, and Sunday by *Musical Tales*. A series of features complete the hour: *The Whims of Fate* (Monday, Wednesday and Friday), *Guest Speaker* and *People of Uncommon Destiny* (Tuesday), ●*Russia—1,000 Years of Music* (Thursday), *Kaleidoscope* (Saturday) and ●*Christian Message from Moscow* on Sunday. Monday through Saturday summer, it's *News and Views*; Sunday, there's *Sunday Panorama* and *Russia: People and Events*. On the half-hour, a news summary is followed by features: *Our Homeland* (Sunday, Monday and Friday), *Russian by Radio* (Tuesday), ●*Jazz Show* (Wednesday) and ●*Christian Message from Moscow* on Saturday. On 6175, 6235, 7290 and 7400 kHz in winter; and 7380, 9890 and 12070 (or 7310) kHz.

China Radio International. Starts with *News*, followed Monday through Friday by special reports—current events, sports, business, culture, science and technology and press clippings. The rest of the broadcast is devoted to features. Regulars include ●*People in the Know* (Monday), *Biz China* (Tuesday), *China Horizons* (Wednesday), ●*Voices from Other Lands* (Thursday), and *Life in China* (Friday). Weekends, the news is followed by a shorter series of reports (current events and sport) and two features. Saturday there's *Cutting Edge*, and *Listeners' Garden* (listener mail, Chinese folk music, a preview of the next week's programs, and a Chinese language lesson); replaced Sunday by *Reports on Developing Countries* and *In the Spotlight*, a series of mini-features: *Cultural Carousel, In Vogue, Writings from China, China Melody* and *Talking Point*. One hour to the Mideast and North Africa on 7295 and 9440 kHz.

Radio Thailand. A 60-minute package of *news*, features and (if you're lucky) enjoyable Thai music. To Northern Europe winter on 9805 kHz, and summer on 7155 kHz.

Voice of Korea, North Korea. For now, of curiosity value only. An hour of old-style communist programming to Europe on 7570 (or 13760) and 12015 (or 15245) kHz. Also heard in parts of East Asia on 4405 kHz.

Voice of Vietnam. Repeat of the 1800 transmission (see there for specifics). A half hour to Europe on 7280 and 9730 kHz.

Voice of America. Continuous programming for Africa. Weekday fare is heavily news oriented, but is replaced Saturday by *Hip Hop Connection*, and Sunday by *Africa News Now* and *Music Time in Africa*. Winter on 4930, 4940, 6035, 11975, 13710, 15240, 15580 and 17895 kHz; and summer on 4930, 4940, 9850, 11975, 13670, 15410, 15445, 15580 and 17895 kHz. Best for southern Africa is 4930 kHz. In North America, try 15580 kHz in winter, and 15445 kHz in summer.

KBS World Radio, South Korea. Opens with 10 minutes of *news*, then Monday through Friday, a commentary. This is followed by 30 minutes of *Seoul Calling* and a 15-minute feature: *Shaping Korea, Made in Korea, Cultural Promenade, Korea Today and Tomorrow* and *Seoul Report*, respectively. Saturday's news is followed by *Worldwide Friendship* (a listener-response show), and Sunday by *Korean Pop Interactive*. Sixty minutes to East Asia on 5975 kHz, and to Europe on 7275 kHz.

Voice of Korea, North Korea. Repeat of the 1800 broadcast. The last of the old-time communist stations. One hour to the Mideast on 9975 kHz; and to southern Africa on 7100 and 11710 (or 11910) kHz. Also heard in parts of East Asia on 4405 kHz.

AFRTS Shortwave, USA. Network news, live sports, music and features in the upper-sideband mode from the Armed Forces Radio & Television Service. Transmitted from modestly powered U.S. Navy stations around the globe. Try 4319, 5446.5, 5765, 6350, 7590, 7811, 9980, 10320, 12133.5, 12579 and 13362 kHz.

19:30

Radio Slovakia International. Winter only at this time. Monday through Friday, starts with *News* and *Topical Issue*. These are followed by features focusing on local and regional topics. The Saturday news is followed by *Network Europe*, and Sunday's features are *Sunday Newsreel* and *Listeners' Tribune*. Thirty minutes to western Europe on 5915 and 7345 kHz. One hour earlier in summer.

Voice of Turkey. Winter only at this time. See 1830 for program details. Some unusual programs and friendly presentation make for entertaining listening. Fifty minutes to western Europe on 6055 kHz. One hour earlier in summer.

International Radio of Serbia and Montenegro. Winter only at this time. News, commentary and reports from the former Yugoslavia. Thirty minutes to Europe on 6100 kHz, and one hour earlier in summer.

Voice of the Islamic Republic of Iran. A one-hour broadcast of news, commentary and features reflecting Islamic values. To Europe winter on 6010 and 7320 kHz, and summer on 7205 and 11860 kHz. Also available to southern Africa winter on 9855 and 11695 kHz, and midyear on 9800 and 9925 kHz.

Radio Sweden. Summer only at this time. *News* and features concentrating heavily on

19:30–20:00

Scandinavian topics. Some of the features rotate from week to week, but some are fixtures. Monday's *Culture* is replaced Tuesday by *Knowledge*, Wednesday by *Real Life*, Thursday by *Lifestyle*, and Friday by *Debate*. The Saturday rotation is *Headset*, *Sweden Today*, *In Touch* (a listener-response program) and *Studio 49*; while Sunday's offering is *Network Europe*. Thirty minutes to Europe on 6065 kHz, and one hour later in winter.

RAI International—Radio Roma, Italy. Actually starts at 1935. Approximately 12 minutes of *news*, then some Italian music. Twenty minutes to western Europe winter on 6035 and 9760 kHz, and summer on 5960 and 9845 kHz.

Voice of Armenia. Winter only at this time, and actually starts at 1925. Twenty minutes of Armenian *news* and culture to Europe on 9965 kHz, and to the Mideast on 4910 kHz. One hour earlier in summer.

Radio Belarus. Monday, Tuesday, Thursday and Friday, summer only at this time. See 2030 for specifics. Thirty minutes to Europe on 7105, 7280 and 7290 kHz. One hour later in winter.

19:45

Radio Tirana, Albania. Monday through Saturday, and winter only at this time. Approximately 15 minutes of *news* and commentary from this small Balkan country. To Europe on 7180 and/or 7210 kHz. One hour earlier in summer.

Vatican Radio. Summer only at this time, and actually starts at 1950. Twenty minutes of programming oriented to Catholics. To Europe on 4005, 5885 and 7250 kHz. One hour later in winter.

20:00

■Deutsche Welle, Germany. *News*, then Monday through Friday there's the in-depth ●*NewsLink*. The second half-hour consists of features: *Insight* and *Business German* (Monday), *World in Progress* (Tuesday), ●*Money Talks* (Wednesday), *Living Planet*

(Thursday) and *Spectrum* (Friday). Weekends, there's Saturday's ●*Inside Europe* and Sunday's *Mailbag*. One hour to East, Central and southern Africa, winter on 6145, 9735, 9830 12025 and 15410 kHz; and summer on 7130, 11895, 13780 and 15205 kHz. Best for southern Africa is 12025 kHz in winter, and 7130 kHz midyear.

Radio Canada International. Summer only at this time. *News*, then Monday through Friday it's *Canada Today*, replaced Saturday by *Business Sense* and Sunday by *Maple Leaf Mailbag* (a listener-response show). On the half-hour there's *Spotlight* (Wednesday and Sunday), *Media Zone* (Monday), *The Maple Leaf Mailbag* (repeat, Tuesday), *Business Sense* (Thursday) and *Sci-Tech File* on Friday and Saturday. Sixty minutes to Europe, North Africa and the Mideast on 5850, 11765 and 15325 kHz. One hour later during winter.

■Radio Netherlands. The final 57 minutes of an approximately three-hour broadcast targeted at Africa. Monday through Friday, opens with a feature: ●*Research File* (Monday), ●*EuroQuest* (Tuesday), ●*Documentary* (Wednesday), *Dutch Horizons* (Thursday) and *A Good Life* (Friday). ●*Newsline* (current events) completes the broadcast. Weekend fare consists of Saturday's *Vox Humana* and *Saturday Connection*, and Sunday's *Amsterdam Forum*. To southern Africa on 7120 kHz; and to West and Central Africa on 9895, 11655 and 17810 kHz. The weekend broadcasts are also available to North America, winter on 15315, 15525 and 17725 kHz; and summer on 15315, 17660 and 17735 kHz. On other days, listeners in the United States can try 17810 kHz, which is via a relay in the Netherlands Antilles.

Radio Damascus, Syria. Actually starts at 2005. *News*, a daily press review, and different features for each day of the week. These can be heard at approximately 2030 and 2045, and include a mix of political commentary, Islamic philosophy and Arab and Syrian culture. Most of the transmission, however, is given over to Syrian and some western popular music. One hour to Europe, occasionally audible in eastern

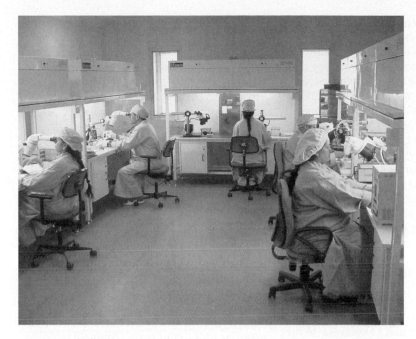

Etón makes use of space-grade components in its new testing laboratory.

Etón

North America, on 12085 (frequently off the air) and 9330 or 13610 kHz. Low audio level is often a problem.

Radio Australia. Starts with *World News*, then Sunday through Thursday it's the final hour of *Pacific Beat* (in-depth reporting). Friday fare consists of *Correspondents' Notebook*, *Saturday AM* and *Saturday Breakfast*; and Saturday there's a continuation of *Australia All Over* (a popular show from the Radio National domestic service). Continuous programming to the Pacific on 6080 and 7240 (Friday and Saturday only), 9580, 11650, 11660, 11880 and 12080 kHz; and to Southeast Asia on 9500 kHz. In western North America, try 11650, 11660 and 11880 kHz.

Voice of Russia World Service. Continuous programming to Europe at this hour. Monday through Saturday winter, there's *News and Views*, replaced Sunday by *Sunday Panorama* and *Russia: People and Events*. On the half-hour, there's a news summary and features: *Our Homeland* (Sunday, Monday and Friday), *Russian by Radio* (Tuesday), ●*Jazz Show* (Wednesday) and ●*Christian Message from Moscow* on Saturday. Monday through Saturday summer, *News* is followed

by features: *Science Plus* (Monday), *Moscow Mailbag* (Tuesday and Friday), *Newmarket* (Wednesday and Saturday) and *This is Russia* on Thursday. Pick of the features during the second half-hour are: *Songs from Russia* (Monday), ●*Music Around Us* (Tuesday), *Musical Tales* (Wednesday), ●*Folk Box* (Thursday) and ●*Jazz Show* on Friday. Highlight of the week is ●*Music and Musicians* which follows the news on Sunday. Winter on 6145, 6175, 6235, 7290 and 7330 kHz; and summer on 9890, 12070 (or 7310) and 15455 (or 7330) kHz. Some channels are audible in eastern North America.

Radio Exterior de España ("Spanish National Radio"). Weekdays only at this time. Spanish and international *news*, commentary, Spanish pop music, a review of the Spanish press, and a general interest feature. Sixty minutes to Europe winter on 9690 kHz, and summer on 15290 kHz; and to North and West Africa winter on 9595 kHz, and summer on 9570 kHz.

Radio Budapest, Hungary. Winter only at this time. *News* and features, most of which are broadcast on a non-regular basis. Thirty minutes to Europe on 3975 and 6025 kHz. One hour earlier in summer.

20:00–20:45

China Radio International. Starts with *News*, followed weekdays by special reports—current events, sports, business, culture, science and technology and press clippings. The rest of the broadcast is devoted to features. Regulars include ●*People in the Know* (Monday), *Biz China* (Tuesday), *China Horizons* (Wednesday), ●*Voices from Other Lands* (Thursday), and *Life in China* (Friday). Weekends, the news is followed by a shorter series of reports (current events and sport) and two features. Saturday there's *Cutting Edge*, and *Listeners' Garden* (listener mail, Chinese folk music, a preview of the next week's programs, and a Chinese language lesson); replaced Sunday by *Reports on Developing Countries* and *In the Spotlight*, a series of mini-features: *Cultural Carousel, In Vogue, Writings from China, China Melody* and *Talking Point*. One hour to Europe on 5960, 7190, 7285, 9600 and (summer) 9800 and 11790 kHz; to the Mideast and North Africa on 7295 and 9440 kHz; and to eastern and southern Africa on 11640 and 13630 kHz.

Under Chinese rule, modern buildings in Lhasa have only a touch of local aesthetic.   M. Guha

Kol Israel. Winter only at this time. Twenty-five minutes of *news* and in-depth reporting from and about Israel. To Europe and North America on any three channels from 6280, 7520, 9435 and 11605 kHz; and to southern Africa and South America on 15640 kHz. One hour earlier in summer.

Voice of Vietnam. *News*, then it's either *Commentary* or *Weekly Review*, which in turn is followed by short features. Look for some pleasant Vietnamese music towards the end of the broadcast (more at weekends). A half hour to Europe on 7280 and 9730 kHz.

Radio Prague, Czech Republic. Summer only at this time. *News*, then Monday through Friday it's *Current Affairs* plus one or more features: *Talking Point* (Monday), *Czech Science* and *One on One* (Tuesday), *Czechs in History, Czechs Today* or *Spotlight* (Wednesday), *Panorama* (Thursday) and *Business Briefs* and *The Arts* on Friday. The Saturday news is followed by *Magazine, ABC of Czech* and a repeat of Tuesday's *One on One*. Sunday's lineup is *Mailbox* and *Letter from Prague* followed by *Encore* (classical music), *Magic Carpet* (Czech world music) or *Czech Books*. Thirty minutes to western Europe on 5930 kHz, and to Southeast Asia and Australasia on 11600 kHz. One hour later in winter.

Voice of America. Continuous programming for Africa. Monday through Friday, it's *Africa World Tonight*; and weekends, *Nightline Africa*. Winter on 4930, 4940, 6035, 11975, 13710, 15240 and 15580 kHz; and summer on 4930, 4940, 11975, 13670, 15410 and 15445 kHz. Best for southern Africa is 4930 kHz. In North America, try 15580 kHz in winter, and 15445 kHz in summer.

AFRTS Shortwave, USA. Network news, live sports, music and features in the upper-sideband mode from the Armed Forces Radio & Television Service. Transmitted from modestly powered U.S. Navy stations around the globe. Try 4319, 5446.5, 5765, 6350, 7590, 7811, 9980, 10320, 12133.5, 12579 and 13362 kHz.

20:30

Radio Sweden. Winter only at this time. *News* and features concentrating heavily on Scandinavian topics. Monday's *Culture* is replaced Tuesday by *Knowledge*, Wednesday by *Real Life*, Thursday by *Lifestyle*, and Friday by *Debate*. The Saturday rotation is *Headset*, *Sweden Today*, *In Touch* (a listener-response program) and *Studio 49*; while Sunday's offering is *Network Europe*. Thirty minutes to Europe (one hour earlier in summer) on 6065 kHz, and to Asia and Australasia (one hour later in summer) on 7420 kHz.

Radio Thailand. Fifteen minutes of *news* targeted at Europe. Winter on 9535 kHz, and summer on 9680 kHz.

Voice of Turkey. This time summer only. *News*, followed by *Review of the Turkish Press* and features with a strong local flavor. Selections of Turkish popular and classical music complete the program. Fifty minutes to Southeast Asia and Australasia on 7170 kHz. One hour later during winter.

Radio Belarus. Monday, Tuesday, Thursday and Friday, winter only at this time. Thirty minutes of local *news* and interviews, plus some Belarusian music. To Europe on 7105, 7340 and 7440 kHz. Occasionally heard in eastern North America.

Radio Habana Cuba. The first half of a 60-minute broadcast. Monday through Saturday, there's international and Cuban news followed by *RHC's Viewpoint*. This is replaced Sunday by *Weekly Review*. To eastern North America on 11760 kHz, and heard in parts of Europe.

Radio Tashkent International, Uzbekistan. Monday through Saturday, opens with *News*, replaced Sunday by *Significant Events of the Week*. Other programs include *Uzbekistan and the World* (Monday), *Life in the Village* and *Political Commentary* (Thursday), a listener-response show (Saturday) and *Traditions and Values* on Sunday. Programs of Uzbek music are aired on Tuesday, Wednesday and Friday. Thirty minutes to Europe winter on 5025, 7185 and 11905 kHz; and summer on 5025 and 11905 kHz.

CEO Esmail Hozour finds environmentally friendly transportation to plop in at Etón's Bangalore facility.
E.A. Hozour

Voice of Vietnam. *News*, then it's either *Commentary* or *Weekly Review*, which in turn is followed by short features. Look for some pleasant Vietnamese music, especially at weekends. A half hour to West and Central Africa on 7220 and 9550 kHz, and heard far beyond.

RAI International—Radio Roma, Italy. Actually starts at 2025. Twenty minutes of *news* and Italian music to the Mideast. Winter on 6020 kHz; and summer on 6050 and 11875 kHz.

20:45

All India Radio. The first 15 minutes of a much longer broadcast, consisting of a press review, Indian music, regional and international *news*, commentary, and a variety of talks and features of general interest. Continuous till 2230. To Western Europe on 7410, 9445, 9950 and 11620 kHz; and to Australasia on 9575, 9910, 11620 and 11715 kHz. Early risers in Southeast Asia can try the channels for Australasia.

Vatican Radio. Winter only at this time, and actually starts at 2050. Twenty minutes of predominantly Catholic fare. To Europe on 4005, 5885 and 7250 kHz. One hour earlier in summer.

21:00

■**BBC World Service for the Caribbean.** Summer, starts with five minutes of *news*, then features, including some of the BBC's better offerings. The lineup includes ●*Health Matters* (Monday), *Go Digital* and *Everywoman* (Tuesday), *Discovery* (science, Wednesday), ●*One Planet* (Thursday) and *Science in Action* (Friday). Winter programming is heavily oriented to news. Winter on 11675 kHz, and summer on 15390 kHz. Separate regional programming for the Caribbean can be heard at 2100-2130 weekdays, winter on 15390 kHz, and summer on 11675 kHz.

Radio Exterior de España ("Spanish National Radio"). Summer weekends only at this time. Features, including rebroadcasts of programs aired earlier in the week. One hour to Europe on 9840 kHz, and to North and West Africa on 9570 kHz. One hour later in winter.

Radio Ukraine International. Summer only at this time. *News*, commentary, reports and interviews, providing ample coverage of Ukrainian life. A listener-response program is aired Saturday, and most of Sunday's broadcast is a showpiece for Ukrainian music. Sixty minutes to western Europe on 7490 (or 7420) kHz. One hour later in winter. Should be easily heard despite the station's technical limitations.

Radio Canada International. Winter only at this time. See 2000 for program specifics. Sixty minutes to western Europe and North Africa on 5850 and 9770 kHz. One hour earlier in summer.

Radio Prague, Czech Republic. Winter only at this time. See 2000 for program details. *News* and features on Czech life and culture. A half hour to western Europe (and easily audible in parts of eastern North America) on 5930 kHz, and to Southeast Asia and Australasia on 9430 kHz. One hour earlier in summer.

Radio Bulgaria. This time summer only. Starts with *News*, then Monday through Friday there's *Events and Developments,*

replaced weekends by *Views Behind the News*. The remaining time is taken up by regular programs such as *Keyword Bulgaria* and *Time Out for Music*, and weekly features like *Sports* (Monday), *Magazine Economy* (Tuesday), *The Way We Live* (Wednesday), *History Club* (Thursday), *DX Programme* (for radio enthusiasts, Friday) and *Answering Your Letters* (a listener-response show, Saturday). The week's highlight is Sunday's ●*Folk Studio* (Bulgarian folk music). Sixty minutes to Europe on 5800 and 7500 kHz. One hour later during winter.

China Radio International. Repeat of the 2000 transmission; see there for specifics. One hour to Europe on 5960, 7190, 7285, 9600 and (summer) 9800 and 11790 kHz. A 30-minute reduced version is also available for eastern and southern Africa on 11640 and 13630 kHz.

Voice of Russia World Service. Winter only at this time. *News*, then *Science Plus* (Monday), *Moscow Mailbag* (Tuesday and Friday), the business-oriented *Newmarket* (Wednesday and Saturday), *This is Russia* (Thursday) and the excellent ●*Music and Musicians* on Sunday. Pick of the features during the second half-hour are: *Songs from Russia* (Monday), ●*Music Around Us* (Tuesday), *Musical Tales* (Wednesday), ●*Folk Box* (Thursday) and ●*Jazz Show* on Friday. One hour earlier in summer. To Europe on 6235, 7290, 7300 and 7330 kHz. Some channels are audible in eastern North America.

Radio Budapest, Hungary. Summer only at this time. *News* and features, few of which are broadcast on a regular basis. Thirty minutes to Europe on 6025 kHz, and to southern Africa on 9525 kHz. One hour later in winter.

Radio Belarus. Summer Sundays only at this time. Thirty minutes of local *news*, reports and interviews, plus some Belarusian music. To Europe on 7105, 7280 and 7290 kHz. One hour later in winter.

Radio Japan. *News*, then Monday through Friday (Tuesday through Saturday local date in Australasia) it's *A Song for Everyone* and *Asian Top News*. A 35-minute feature com-

21:00–21:00

Beijing rushes to modernize. This has given birth to soulless high rise apartments in place of bulldozed ancient homes and tight-knit neighborhood alleyways.
M. Guha

pletes the hour: *Japan Musicscape* (Monday), Japanese language lessons (Tuesday and Thursday), *Japan Music Archives* (Wednesday), and *Music Beat* (Japanese popular music) on Friday. *Weekend Japanology* and *Japan Music Scene* fill the Saturday slots, and *Pop Joins the World* is aired Sunday. Sixty minutes to Europe on 6055 (summer), 6090 (winter) and 6180 kHz; to Australasia on 6035 kHz; to western North America on 17825 kHz; to Hawaii on 21670 kHz; and to Central Africa on 11855 kHz. The broadcast on 17825 kHz has different programming after 2115.

Radio Australia. *World News*, then Sunday through Thursday there's a look at current events in *AM*, followed by a relay of Radio New Zealand International's *Dateline Pacific*. Friday, there's a continuation of *Saturday Breakfast*, and Saturday it's the final hour of *Australia All Over*. Continuous to the Pacific on 9660, 11650, 11660, 12080, 13630 and 15515 kHz; and to Southeast Asia (till 2130) on 9500 an 11695 kHz. Listeners in western North America should try 11650 and 11660 kHz.

■**Deutsche Welle,** Germany. *News*, then weekdays there's ●*NewsLink*. On the half-hour you can listen to ●*A World of Music* (Monday), *Arts on the Air* (Tuesday),

●*Living in Germany* and *At Home in Europe* (Wednesday), the youth-oriented *Cool* (Thursday) and ●*Focus on Folk* (Friday). Weekends, the Saturday news is followed by *Sports Report*, *German by Radio* and *Africa This Week*; and Sunday by *Religion and Society*, *Inspired Minds* and *Hits in Germany*. One hour to West Africa, and audible in much of eastern and southern North America. Winter on 7280, 9615 and 11690 kHz; and summer on 9440, 11865 and 15205 kHz. In North America, try 9615 and 11690 kHz in winter, and 11865 and 15205 kHz in summer.

KBS World Radio, South Korea. Summer only at this time. Opens with 10 minutes of *news*, then Monday through Friday, a commentary. This is followed by a 15-minute feature: *Shaping Korea*, *Made in Korea*, *Cultural Promenade*, *Korea Today and Tomorrow* and *Seoul Report*, respectively. Saturday's news is followed by *Worldwide Friendship* (a listener-response show), and Sunday by *Korean Pop Interactive*. Thirty minutes to Europe on 3955 kHz.

Voice of Korea, North Korea. Repeat of the 1800 broadcast. The last of the old-time communist stations. One hour to Europe on 7570 (or 13760) and 12015 (or 15245) kHz.

21:00–22:00

Also heard in parts of East Asia on 4405 kHz.

Radio Habana Cuba. The final 30 minutes of a one-hour broadcast. Monday through Saturday, there's a *news* bulletin and the sports-oriented *Time Out* (five minutes each), then a feature: *Caribbean Outlook* (Monday and Thursday), *DXers Unlimited* (Tuesday and Saturday), the *Mailbag Show* (Wednesday) and *Weekly Review* (Friday). These are replaced Sunday by a longer edition of *Mailbag Show*. To eastern North America on 11760 kHz, and also heard in parts of Europe.

Voice of America. Opens with *news*, then it's music: *American Gold* (Monday), *Roots and Branches* (Tuesday), *Classic Rock* (Wednesday), *Top Twenty* (Thursday), *Country Hits* (Friday) and jazz at the weekend. The final 60 minutes of seven hours of programming for Africa; winter on 4930, 6035, 11975, 13710, 15240 and 15580 kHz; and summer on 4930, 11975, 13670, 15410 and 15445 kHz. Best for southern Africa is 4930 kHz. In North America, try 15580 kHz in winter, and 15445 kHz in summer.

All India Radio. Continues to Western Europe on 7410, 9445, 9950 and 11620 kHz; and to Australasia on 9575, 9910, 11620 and 11715 kHz. Look for some authentic Indian music from 2115 onwards. The European frequencies are audible in parts of eastern North America, while those for Australasia are also heard in Southeast Asia.

21:15

Radio Damascus, Syria. Actually starts at 2110. *News*, a daily press review, and different features for each day of the week. These include a mix of political commentary, Islamic themes and Arab and Syrian culture. The transmission also contains Syrian and some western popular music. Sixty minutes to North America and Australasia on 12085 (frequently off the air) and 9330 or 13610 kHz. Audio level is often very low.

Radio Cairo, Egypt. The start of a 90-minute broadcast highlighting Arab and Egyptian themes. The initial quarter-hour of general programming is followed by *news*, commentary and political items. This in turn is followed by a cultural program until 2215, when the station again reverts to more general fare. A big signal to Europe on 9990 kHz.

AFRTS Shortwave, USA. Network news, live sports, music and features in the upper-sideband mode from the Armed Forces Radio & Television Service. Transmitted from modestly powered U.S. Navy stations around the globe. Try 4319, 5446.5, 5765, 6350, 7590, 7811, 9980, 10320, 12133.5, 12579 and 13362 kHz.

21:30

Radio Romania International. *News* and commentary followed by short features on Romania. Twenty-five minutes to Europe winter on 7145 and 9650 kHz, and summer on 7165 and 9535 kHz; and to eastern North America winter on 9755 and 11940 kHz, and summer on 9645 and 11940 kHz.

Radio Prague, Czech Republic. Summer only at this time; see 2230 for program specifics. Thirty minutes to North America on 11600 kHz, and to West Africa on 9800 kHz. The broadcast for North America is one hour later in winter, but there is no corresponding broadcast for West Africa.

Radio Tashkent International, Uzbekistan. Monday through Saturday, opens with *News*, replaced Sunday by *Significant Events of the Week*. Other programs include *Nature and Us* and *Cooperation* (Monday), *Political Commentary* and *Youth Program* (Wednesday), a feature for women (Thursday), *Parliamentary Herald* (Friday) a show for shortwave listeners (Saturday) and *Interesting Meetings* on Sunday. Programs of Uzbek music are aired on Tuesday, Friday and Saturday, and a competition with prizes on Thursday and Saturday. Thirty minutes to Europe winter on 5025, 7185 and 11905 kHz; and summer on 5025 and 11905 kHz.

Radio Tirana, Albania. Monday through Saturday, summer only at this time. *News*, short features and some lively Albanian music. Thirty minutes to Europe on 7120 kHz. One hour later in winter.

Voice of Turkey. This time winter only. *News*, followed by *Review of the Turkish Press* and features, some of them unusual. Exotic Turkish music, too. Fifty minutes to Southeast Asia and Australasia on 9525 kHz. One hour earlier in summer.

Radio Sweden. Summer only at this time. Thirty minutes of predominantly Scandinavian fare (see 2230 for specifics). To Europe on 6065 kHz, and to Australasia on 7420 kHz.

22:00

■**BBC World Service for the Caribbean.** Winter, starts with five minutes of *news*, then features, including some of the BBC's better offerings. The lineup includes ●*Health Matters* (Monday), *Go Digital* and *Everywoman* (Tuesday), *Discovery* (science, Wednesday), ●*One Planet* (Thursday) and *Science in Action* (Friday). Summer, it's mostly *The World Today*, but don't miss the excellent ●*Reporting Religion* at 2232 Saturday. Continuous programming on 5975 kHz.

■**Deutsche Welle,** Germany. *News*, then Monday through Friday (Tuesday through Saturday local date in the target area) it's ●*NewsLink*—commentary, interviews, background reports and analysis. The second half-hour consists of features: *Insight* and *Business German* (Monday), *World in Progress* (Tuesday), ●*Money Talks* (Wednesday), *Living Planet* (Thursday) and *Spectrum* (Friday). Weekends, there's Saturday's ●*Inside Europe* and *Asia This Week*, and Sunday's *Mailbag*. One hour to East Asia winter on 6180 kHz, and summer on 7115 and 9720 kHz.

Radio Bulgaria. This time winter only. Opens with *News*, then Monday through Friday there's *Events and Developments*, replaced weekends by *Views Behind the News*. The remaining time is taken up by regular programs such as *Keyword Bulgaria*

and *Time Out for Music*, and weekly features like *Sports* (Monday), *Magazine Economy* (Tuesday), *The Way We Live* (Wednesday), *History Club* (Thursday), *DX Programme* (for radio enthusiasts, Friday) and *Answering Your Letters* (a listener-response show, Saturday). The week's highlight is Sunday's ●*Folk Studio* (Bulgarian folk music). Sixty minutes to Europe, also heard in parts of eastern North America, on 5800 and 7500 kHz. One hour earlier in summer.

Radio Cairo, Egypt. The second half of a 90-minute broadcast to Europe on 9990 kHz; see 2115 for program details.

Radio Exterior de España ("Spanish National Radio"). Winter weekends only at this time. Features, including repeats of programs aired earlier in the week. One hour to Europe on 9680 kHz, and to North and West Africa on 9595 kHz. One hour earlier in summer.

China Radio International. Starts with *News*, followed weekdays by special reports—current events, sports, business, culture, science and technology and press clippings. The rest of the broadcast is devoted to features. Regulars include ●*People in the Know* (Monday), *Biz China* (Tuesday), *China Horizons* (Wednesday), ●*Voices from Other Lands* (Thursday), and *Life in China* (Friday). Weekends, the news is followed by a shorter series of reports (current events and sport) and two features. Saturday there's *Cutting Edge*, and *Listeners' Garden* (listener mail, Chinese folk music, a preview of the next week's programs, and a Chinese language lesson); replaced Sunday by *Reports on Developing Countries* and *In the Spotlight*, a series of mini-features: *Cultural Carousel*, *In Vogue*, *Writings from China*, *China Melody* and *Talking Point*. One hour to Europe winter on 7170 kHz, and summer on 7175 kHz, via CRI's Moscow relay.

Voice of America. The first of three hours to East and Southeast Asia and the Pacific. Starts with 30 minutes of *East Asia News Now*, then weekdays (Tuesday through Saturday in the target area) there's a summary of *news*, a 14-minute feature, *Focus* and an

22:00–23:00

China Radio International's English newsroom is increasingly "ground central" for China's overseas influence.   M. Guha

editorial. Weekend fare consists of *Global College Forum*, *Wordmaster* and an editorial. To East and Southeast Asia on 7215, 9890 (winter), 15185, 15290, 15305, 17740 and (summer) 17820 kHz; and to Australasia on 17740 kHz.

RAI International—Radio Roma, Italy. Actually starts at 2205. Twenty-five minutes of *news* and Italian music to East Asia winter on 6000 (or 6090) kHz, and summer on 11895 kHz.

Radio Australia. *News*, followed Sunday through Thursday by *AM* (current events), *Talking Point* and *Perspective*. Friday, it's a continuation of *Saturday Breakfast*, and Saturday there's *Spirit of Things* and *Heywire*. Continuous programming to the Pacific on 13630, 15230, 15515 and 17785 (or 21740) kHz; to East Asia on 15240 kHz; and to Southeast Asia on 13620 kHz. In North America, try 17785 (or 21740) kHz, especially during summer.

Radio Taiwan International. Ten minutes of *News*, followed by features: *Made in Taiwan* and Radio Australia's *Asia Pacific* (Monday); *Strait Talk* and *We've Got Mail* (Tuesday); *Trends* and ●*Jade Bells and Bamboo Pipes* (Wednesday); *Ilha Formosa*, *People* and *Instant Noodles* (Thursday); *Bookworm* and *New Music Lounge* (Friday);

News Talk and *Groove Zone* (Saturday); and *The Undiscovered Country*, *Taipei Magazine* and *Stage, Screen and Studio* (Sunday). One hour to Europe via RTI's North American relay, winter on 9355 kHz, and summer on 15600 kHz.

Radio Belarus. Winter Sundays only at this time. *News*, reports and interviews, plus some Belarusian music. Thirty minutes to Europe on 7105, 7280 and 7290 kHz. One hour earlier in summer. Sometimes audible in eastern North America

Radio Budapest, Hungary. Winter only at this time. *News* and features, most of which are broadcast on a non-regular basis. Thirty minutes to Europe on 6025 kHz, and to southern Africa on 9735 kHz. One hour earlier in summer.

Voice of Turkey. Summer only at this time. *News*, then *Review of the Turkish Press* and features on Turkish history and culture. Selections of Turkish popular and classical music complete the program. Fifty minutes to western Europe and eastern North America on 9830 (or 7300) kHz. One hour later during winter.

Radio Ukraine International. Winter only at this time. A potpourri of things Ukrainian, with the Sunday broadcast often featuring some excellent music. Sixty minutes to

Europe and beyond on 5840 kHz. One hour earlier in summer.

All India Radio. The final half-hour of a transmission to Western Europe and Australasia, consisting mainly of news-related fare. To Western Europe on 7410, 9445, 9950 and 11620 kHz; and to Australasia on 9575, 9910, 11620 and 11715 kHz. Frequencies for Europe are audible in parts of eastern North America, while those for Australasia are also heard in Southeast Asia.

AFRTS Shortwave, USA. Network news, live sports, music and features in the upper-sideband mode from the Armed Forces Radio & Television Service. Transmitted from modestly powered U.S. Navy stations around the globe. Try 4319, 5446.5, 5765, 6350, 7590, 7811, 9980, 10320, 12133.5, 12579 and 13362 kHz.

22:30

Radio Sweden. Winter only at this time. *News* and features concentrating heavily on Scandinavian topics. Some of the features rotate from week to week, but some are fixtures. Monday's *Culture* is replaced Tuesday by *Knowledge*, Wednesday by *Real Life*, Thursday by *Lifestyle*, and Friday by *Debate*. The Saturday rotation is *Headset*, *Sweden Today*, *In Touch* (a listener-response program) and *Studio 49*; while Sunday's offering is *Network Europe*. Thirty minutes to Europe on 6065 kHz, and one hour earlier in summer.

Radio Prague, Czech Republic. *News*, then Monday through Friday there's *Current Affairs* followed by a feature or two. Monday's *Talking Point* is replaced Tuesday by *Czech Science* and *One on One* (interviews); Wednesday's slot is *Czechs in History*; *Czechs Today* or *Spotlight*; Thursday's feature is *Panorama*; and Friday brings *Business Briefs* and *The Arts*. Saturday's *Insight Central Europe* is replaced Sunday by *Mailbox* and *Letter from Prague* followed by *Encore* (classical music), *Magic Carpet* (Czech world music) or *Czech Books*. A half hour to North America winter on 5930 and 7345 kHz, and summer on 7345 and 9415 kHz.

Radio Tirana, Albania. Monday through Saturday, winter only at this time. Thirty minutes of news, short features and Albanian music. To Europe on 7110 kHz. One hour earlier in summer.

Radio Canada International. *News* and a feature: *Media Zone* (Monday and Saturday), *The Maple Leaf Mailbag* (listener mail, Sunday and Tuesday), *Spotlight* (Wednesday), *Business Sense* (Thursday) and *Sci-Tech File* on Friday. Thirty minutes to East and Southeast Asia winter on 6160, 7195 and 9730 kHz; and summer on 9525, 9870 and 12035 kHz.

22:45

All India Radio. The first 15 minutes of a much longer broadcast, consisting of Indian music, regional and international *news*, commentary, and a variety of talks and features of general interest. Continuous till 0045. To East Asia on 9950, 11620 and 13605 kHz; and to Southeast Asia on 9705, 11620 and 13605 kHz.

23:00

■**BBC World Service for the Caribbean.** Winter, it's mostly *The World Today*, but don't miss the excellent ●*Reporting Religion* at 2332 Saturday. Summer weekdays, opens with five minutes of *news*. Next comes the long-running *Outlook*, and the hour is rounded off with ●*Off the Shelf* (readings from world literature). Continuous programming on 5975 kHz.

Voice of Turkey. Winter only at this hour; see 2200 for specifics. Fifty minutes to western Europe and eastern North America on 5960 kHz. One hour earlier in summer.

■**Deutsche Welle,** Germany. *News*, then Monday through Friday (Tuesday through Saturday local date in the target area), it's ●*NewsLink*. The lineup for the second half-hour is ●*A World of Music* (Monday), *Arts on the Air* (Tuesday), ●*Living in Germany* and *At Home in Europe* (Wednesday), *Cool* (a youth show, Thursday) and ●*Focus on*

23:00–23:30

Folk (Friday). Weekends, Saturday's news is followed by *Sports Report*, *German by Radio* and *Asia This Week*; and Sunday there's *Sports Report*, *Inspired Minds* and *Hits in Germany*. Sixty minutes to Southeast Asia winter on 6070, 9555 and 9815 kHz; and summer on 5955, 9890 and 15135 kHz.

Radio Australia. *World News*, followed Sunday through Thursday by *Asia Pacific* and the first half-hour of *In the Loop* (regional current events). These are replaced Friday by *Asia Pacific Review* and *Australian Express*, and Saturday by *Correspondents' Report* and *Innovations*. Continuous to the Pacific on 9660, 12080, 13630, 15230, 17785 (or 21740) and 17795 kHz; to East Asia on 13630 and (till 2330) 15240 kHz; and to Southeast Asia on 13620 and (from 2330) 15415 and 17750 kHz. Listeners in North America should try 17785 (or 21740) and 17795 kHz, especially during summer.

China Radio International. Starts with *News*, followed Sunday through Thursday by special reports—current events, sports, business, culture, science and technology and press clippings. The rest of the broadcast is devoted to features. Regulars include ●*People in the Know* (Sunday), *Biz China* (Monday), *China Horizons* (Tuesday), ●*Voices from Other Lands* (Wednesday), and *Life in China* on Thursday. On Friday and Saturday the news is followed by a shorter series of reports (current events and sport) and two features. Friday brings *Cutting Edge*, and *Listeners' Garden* (listener mail, Chinese folk music, a preview of the next week's programs, and a Chinese language lesson); replaced Saturday by *Reports on Developing Countries* and *In the Spotlight*, a series of mini-features: *Cultural Carousel*, *In Vogue*, *Writings from China*, *China Melody* and *Talking Point*. One hour to the United States and Caribbean via CRI's Cuban and Canadian relays, winter on 5990, 6040 and 11970 kHz; and summer on 5990, 6145 and 13680 kHz.

Radio Cairo, Egypt. The first hour of a 90-minute broadcast to eastern North America. A ten-minute *news* bulletin is aired at 2315, with the remaining time taken up by short

features on Egypt, the Middle East and Islam. For the intellectual listener there's *Literary Readings* at 2345 Monday, and *Modern Arabic Poetry* at the same time Friday. More general fare is available in *Listener's Mail* at 2325 Thursday and Saturday. Winter on 11895 kHz, and summer on 11885 kHz.

Radio Romania International. Starts with *Radio Newsreel*, a combination of news, commentary and press review. Features on Romania complete the broadcast. Regular spots include Monday's *Pro Memoria* (Romanian history) and *Pages of Romanian Literature*; Tuesday's *Business Club* and *European Horizons*; Wednesday's *Society Today*, *Partners in a Changing World*, *Cultural Survey* and *Romanian Musicians*; and Thursday's *Traveller's Guide*, *Listeners Letterbox*, *IT News*, *From Our Correspondents* and ●*The Skylark* (Romanian folk music). Friday fare includes *Over Coffee... with Artists* and ●*The Folk Music Box*, and Saturday there's *World of Culture*, *Roots*, *Cookery Show*, *Radio Pictures* and *DX Mailbag*. Sunday's broadcast includes *Sunday Studio* and *All That Jazz*. Fifty-five minutes to western Europe winter on 7105 and 9640 kHz, and summer on 6140 and 7265 kHz. Also to eastern North America winter on 9610, 9640 and 11730 kHz; and summer on 9645 and 11940 kHz.

Radio Bulgaria. Summer only at this time. Starts with *News*, then Monday through Friday there's *Events and Developments*, replaced weekends by *Views Behind the News*. The remaining time is taken up by regular programs such as *Keyword Bulgaria* and *Time Out for Music*, and weekly features like *Sports* (Monday), *Magazine Economy* (Tuesday), *The Way We Live* (Wednesday), *History Club* (Thursday), *DX Programme* (for radio enthusiasts, Friday) and *Answering Your Letters* (a listener-response show, Saturday). Highlight of the week is Sunday's ●*Folk Studio* (Bulgarian folk music) Sixty minutes to eastern North America on 9700 and 11700 kHz. One hour later during winter.

Voice of America. Continuous programming to East and Southeast Asia and the Pacific. Opens with *News*, then it's music:

23:00–23:30

St. Mark's basilica is one of Venice's most prominent sites. It dates back to 1096 and holds the remains of St. Mark.
Corbis

American Gold (Monday), *Roots and Branches* (Tuesday), *Classic Rock* (Wednesday), *Top Twenty* (Thursday), *Country Hits* (Friday) and *Jazz America* at the weekend. To East and Southeast Asia on 7215, 9890 (winter), 15185, 15290, 15305, 17740 and (summer) 17820 kHz; and to Australasia on 17740 kHz.

AFRTS Shortwave, USA. Network news, live sports, music and features in the upper-sideband mode from the Armed Forces Radio & Television Service. Transmitted from modestly powered U.S. Navy stations around the globe. Try 4319, 5446.5, 5765, 6350, 7590, 7811, 9980, 10320, 12133.5, 12579 and 13362 kHz.

23:30

Radio Prague, Czech Republic. Winter only at this time. *News*, then Monday through Friday there's *Current Affairs* and one or more features: *Talking Point* (Monday), *Czech Science* and *One on One* (Tuesday), *Czechs in History*, *Czechs Today* or *Spotlight* (Wednesday), *Panorama* (Thursday) and *Business Briefs* and *The Arts* (Friday). On Saturday the news is followed by *Insight Central Europe*, and Sunday's lineup is *Mailbox* and *Letter from Prague* followed by *Encore* (classical music), *Magic Carpet*

(Czech world music) or *Czech Books*. Thirty minutes to eastern North America on 5930 and 7345 kHz, and one hour earlier in summer.

Radio Vilnius, Lithuania. Thirty minutes of mostly *news* and background reports about events in Lithuania. Of broader appeal is *Mailbag*, aired every other Saturday. For some Lithuanian music, try the second half of Sunday's broadcast. To eastern North America winter on 7325 kHz, and summer on 9875 kHz.

All India Radio. Continuous programming to East and Southeast Asia. A potpourri of *news*, commentary, features and exotic Indian music. To East Asia on 9950, 11620 and 13605 kHz; and to Southeast Asia on 9705, 11620 and 13605 kHz.

Voice of Vietnam. *News*, then *Commentary* or *Weekly Review*. These are followed by short features and some pleasant Vietnamese music (especially at the weekend). A half hour to Southeast Asia on 9840 and 12020 kHz. Frequencies may vary slightly.

Prepared by Tony Jones and the staff of PASSPORT TO WORLD BAND RADIO.

www.passband.com

Addresses PLUS—2006

Station Postal and Email Addresses . . . PLUS Webcasts, Websites, Who's Who, Phones, Faxes, Bureaus, Future Plans, Items for Sale, Giveaways . . . PLUS Summer and Winter Times in Each Country!

PASSPORT shows how stations reach out to you, but Addresses PLUS also shows how you can reach out to stations. This details, country by country, how broadcasters go beyond world band radio to keep in touch, inform and entertain.

"Applause" Replies

When radio broadcasting was in its infancy, listeners sent in "applause" cards to let stations how well they were being received. To say "thanks," stations would reply with a letter or illustrated card verifying ("QSLing" in Morse code) that the station the listener heard was, in fact, theirs. While they were at it, some would throw in a free souvenir—station calendar, pennant or sticker.

The tradition continues to this day, although obtaining QSLs is tougher than it used to be. You can learn how to provide feedback to stations by looking under "Verification" in PASSPORT's "Worldly Words" glossary. Some stations also sell goods—radios, CDs, publications, clothing, tote bags, caps, watches, clocks, pens, knives, letter openers, lighters, refrigerator magnets and keyrings.

Paying Postfolk

Most stations reply to listener correspondence—even email—through the postal system. That way, they can send out printed schedules, verification cards and other "hands-on" souvenirs. Major stations usually do this for free, but smaller ones often seek reimbursement for postage.

Most effective, especially for Latin American and Indonesian stations, is to enclose some unused (mint) stamps from the station's country. These are available from Plum's Airmail Postage, 12 Glenn Road, Flemington NJ 08822 USA, plumdx@msn.com, phone +1 (908) 788-1020, fax +1 (908) 782 2612. One way to help ensure your return-postage stamps are properly used is to stick them onto a pre-addressed return airmail envelope—self-addressed stamped envelope, or SASE.

You can also prompt reluctant stations by donating one paper U.S. dollar, preferably hidden from prying eyes by a piece of foil-covered carbon paper or the like. Registration often helps, as cash tends to get stolen. In some countries, though, registered mail is a prime target for would-be thieves, especially in parts of Latin America. International Reply Coupons (IRCs), which recipients may exchange locally for air or surface stamps, are available at a number of post offices worldwide, particularly in large cities. Thing is, they're increasingly hard to find, relatively costly, not fully effective, and aren't accepted by postal authorities in some countries.

Stamp Out Crime

Mail theft is still a problem in several countries. We identify these and offer proven countermeasures, but start by using common sense. For example, some postal employees are stamp collectors and steal mail with unusual stamps, so use everyday stamps. A postal meter, PC-generated postage or an aerogram are other options.

> **Icons show stations offering audio on the Internet.**

¿Que Hora Es?

World Time, explained in "Setting Your World Time Clock," is essential if you want to find out when your favorite station is on. But if you want to know what time it is in any given country, World Time and "Addresses PLUS" work together to provide a solution.

Here's how. So that you don't have to wrestle with seasonal changes in your own time, "Addresses PLUS" gives local times for each country in terms of hours' difference from World Time (which stays constant year-round). For example, if you look below under "Albania," you'll see that country is World Time +1; that is, one hour ahead of World Time. So, if World Time is 12:00, the local time in Albania is 13:00 (1:00 PM). On the other hand, México City is World Time –6; that is, six hours behind World Time. If World Time is 12:00, in México City it's 6:00 AM.

Local times shown in parentheses are for the middle of the year—roughly April-October; specific dates of seasonal-time changeovers for individual countries can be obtained at www.timeanddate.com/world-clock.

Spotted Something New?

Has something changed since we went to press? A missing detail? Please let us know! Your update information, especially photocopies of material received from stations, is highly valued. Contact the IBS Editorial Office, Box 300, Penn's Park, PA 18943 USA, fax +1 (215) 598 3794, email addresses@passband.com.

Muchas gracias to the kindly folks and helpful organizations mentioned at the end of this chapter for their tireless cooperation in the preparation of this section. Without you, none of this would have been possible.

Using PASSPORT's Addresses PLUS Section

Stations included: All stations are listed if known to reply, however erratically. Also, new stations which possibly may reply to correspondence from listeners.

Leased-time programs: Private organizations/NGOs that lease program time, but which possess no world band transmitters of their own, are usually not listed. However, they can usually be reached at the stations over which they are heard.

Postal addresses are given. These sometimes differ from transmitter locations in the Blue Pages.

Phone and fax numbers. To help avoid confusion, telephone numbers have hyphens, fax numbers don't. All are configured for international dialing once you add your country's International access code (011 in the United States and Canada, 010 in the United Kingdom, and so on). For domestic dialing within countries outside the United States, Canada and the Caribbean, replace the country code (1-3 digits preceded by a "+") by a zero.

Giveaways. If you want freebies, say so politely in your correspondence. These are usually available until supplies run out.

Webcasting. World band stations which simulcast and/or provide archived programming over the Internet are indicated by 📑.

Unless otherwise indicated, stations:

- Reply regularly within six months or so to most listeners' correspondence in English.
- Provide, upon request, free station schedules and verification ("QSL") postcards or letters (see "Verification" in the glossary). When other items are available for free or for purchase, it is specified.
- Do not require compensation for postage costs incurred in replying to you. Where compensation is required, details are provided.

Local times. These are given in difference from World Time. For example, "World Time –5" means that if you subtract five hours from World Time, you'll get the local time in that country. So, if it were 11:00 World Time, it would be 06:00 local time in that country. Times in (parentheses) are for the middle of the year—roughly April-October. For exact changeover dates, see the explanatory paragraph under "¿Que Hora Es?" earlier in this introduction.

AFGHANISTAN World Time +4:30

Internews Radio (when operating), c/o Internews Afghanistan, Baharistan, Karti-parwan, Next to Haji Mir Ahmad Mosque, Kabul, Afghanistan. Email: (Internews Afghanistan parent organization) afghanmedia@internews.org; (Trilling) david.trilling@internews.org. Web: www.internews.org/regions/afghanistan/afghan_radioreport_2004-08.htm. Contact: David Trilling, Country Director. No longer verifies reception reports due to lack of resources. Funded by the U.S. Agency for International Development/Office of Transitional Initiatives. Operates on shortwave as funding allows. Airs via transmitters in Europe or the Mideast, although programming originates from Afghanistan.
Salaam Watandar—the national program of Internews Radio (*see*, above).

ALBANIA World Time +1 (+2 midyear)

Radio Tirana, External Service, Rruga Ismail Qemali Nr. 11, Tirana, Albania. Phone/Fax: +355 (4) 223-650. Fax: (technical directorate) +355 (4) 226-203. Email: (reception reports) dcico@icc.al.eu.org. Web: http://www.rtsh.com.al. Contact: Astrit Ibro, Director of External Services; Adriana Bislea, English Department; Clara Ceska; Marjeta Thoma; Pandi Skaka, Producer; or Diana Koci; (technical directorate) Arben Mehilli, Technical Director ARTV; (frequency management) Mrs. Drita Cico, Head of RTV Monitoring Center. May send free stickers and postcards.

ANGOLA World Time +1

Rádio Ecclésia (if reactivated), Rua Comandante Bula 118, São Paulo, Luanda, Angola; or Caixa Postal 3579, Luanda, Angola. Phone: (general) +244 (2) 443-041; (studios) +244 (2) 445-484. Fax: +244 (2) 443 093. Email: ecclesia@snet.co.ao. Web: http://recclesia.org. Contact: Fr. Antônio Jaca, General Manager. A Catholic station founded in 1954 and which broadcast continuously from March 1955 until closed by presidential decree in 1978. Reestablished in March 1997, when it was granted a permit to operate on FM. Experimented with shortwave transmissions via Radio Nederland facilities during July 2000, but these were terminated for technical reasons. Restarted transmissions in April 2001 via facilities of Germany's T-Systems International (*see*) and switched to a South African relay in May 2002. Although these transmissions were also terminated, the station hopes to resume shortwave broadcasts via its own transmitter sometime in the future, if and when the current tight regulations in Angola are relaxed. According to press reports, the shortwave equipment has already been purchased by the Episcopal Conference of Portugal.
Rádio Nacional de Angola, Caixa Postal 1329, Luanda, Angola. Fax: +244 (2) 391 234. Email: (general, including reception reports) diop@rna.ao; (Magalhães) josela30@hotmail.com; (technical) rochapinto@rna.ao; (reception reports only) departamento133@hotmail.com. Web: (includes streaming audio) www.rna.ao; if the audio link doesn't work, try www.netangola.com/p/default.htm. Contact: Júlio Mendonça, Diretor dos Serviços de Programas; [Ms.] Josefa Canzuela Magalhães, Departamento de Intercâmbio e Opinião Pública; or Manuel Rabelais, Diretor Geral; (technical) Cândido Rocha Pinto, Diretor dos Serviços Técnicos. Replies irregularly. Best is to correspond in Portuguese and include $1, return postage or 2 IRCs.

Antarctica isn't just icebergs—it hosts a low-power world band station heard continents away. They usually reply to listeners' letters. Corbis

ANTARCTICA World Time –3 Base Antárctica Esperanza

Radio Nacional Arcángel San Gabriel—LRA36, Base Esperanza, V9411XAD Antártida Argentina, Argentina. Phone/Fax: +54 (2964) 421 519. Email: lra36@infovia.com.ar. Return postage required. Replies to correspondence in Spanish, and sometimes to correspondence in English or French, depending on who is at the station (the staff changes each year, usually around February). If no reply, try sending your correspondence (but don't write the station's name on the envelope) and 2 IRCs via the helpful Gabriel Iván Barrera, Casilla 2868, C1000WBC Buenos Aires, Argentina.

ANGUILLA World Time –4

Caribbean Beacon, Box 690, Anguilla, British West Indies. Phone: +1 (264) 497- 4340. Fax: +1 (264) 497 4311. Contact: Monsell Hazell, Chief Engineer. $2 or return postage helpful. Relays University Network—*see* USA.

ARGENTINA World Time –3

Radio Baluarte (when operating), Casilla de Correo 45, 3370 Puerto Iguazú, Provincia de Misiones, Argentina. Phone: +54 (3737) 422-557. Email: icnfuturo@hotmail.com. Contact: Hugo Eidinger, Director. Free tourist literature. Return postage helpful. The same programs are aired on 1610 kHz (Radio Maranatha) and 101.7 MHz (Radio Futuro), and all three outlets are believed to be unlicensed. However, given the current radio licensing situation in the country, this is not unusual.
Radiodifusión Argentina al Exterior—RAE, Casilla de Correos 555, C1000WBC Buenos Aires, Argentina. Phone/Fax: +54 (11) 4325-6368; (technical) +54 (11) 4325-5270. Email: (general) rae@radionacional.gov.ar; (technical) operativa@radionacional.gov.ar; (Marcela Campos) camposrae@fibertel.com.ar (this address is to be phased out). Web: www.radionacional.gov.ar/rae/rae.asp. Contact: (general) John Anthony Middleton, Head of English Team; María Dolores López, Spanish Team; (admin-

istration) Marcela G. R. Campos, Directora; (technical) Gabriel Iván Barrera, DX Editor. Return postage (3 IRCs) appreciated. The station asks listeners not to send currency notes, as it's a breach of local postal regulations. Reports covering at least 20-30 minutes of reception are appreciated.

Radio Nacional Buenos Aires, Maipú 555, C1006ACE Buenos Aires, Argentina. Phone: +54 (11) 4325-9100. Fax: (management—Gerencia General) +54 (11) 4325 9433; (Director) +54 (11) 4325-4590, +54 (11) 4322-4313; (technical—Gerencia Operativa) +54 (11) 4325-5270. Email: (general) info@radionacional.gov.ar, or buenosaires@radionacional.gov.ar; (Director) direccion@radionacional.gov.ar, or mariogiorgi@uol.com.ar; (technical) operativa@radionacional.gov.ar. Web: (includes streaming audio) www.radionacional.gov.ar. Contact: (general) Mario Giorgi, Director; (technical) Alberto Enríquez. Return postage (3 IRCs) helpful. Prefers correspondence in Spanish, and usually replies via RAE (*see* above). If no reply, try sending your correspondence (but don't write the station's name on your envelope) and 3 IRCs via the helpful Gabriel Iván Barrera, Casilla 2868, C1000WBC Buenos Aires, Argentina.

ARMENIA   World Time +4 (+5 midyear)

🕮**Public Radio of Armenia/Voice of Armenia**, Radio Agency, Alek Manoukyan Street 5, 375025 Yerevan, Armenia. Phone: +374 (1) 551-143. Fax: +374 (1) 554 600. Email: (general director) president@mediaconcern.am; (foreign broadcasts department, reception reports and comments on programs) pr@armradio.am. Web: (includes streaming audio) www.armradio.am. Contact: Armen Amiryan, General Director. Free postcards and stamps. Requests 2 IRCs for postal reply. Replies slowly.

ASCENSION   World Time exactly

BBC World Service—Atlantic Relay Station, English Bay, Ascension (South Atlantic Ocean). Fax: +247 6117. Contact: (technical) Jeff Cant, Staff Manager; M.R. Watkins, A/Assistant Resident Engineer; or Mrs. Nicola Nicholls, Transmitter Engineer. Nontechnical correspondence should be sent to the BBC World Service in London (*see*).

AUSTRALIA   World Time +11 (+10 midyear) Victoria (VIC), New South Wales (NSW), Australian Capital Territory (ACT) and Tasmania (TAS); +10:30 (+9:30 midyear) South Australia (SA); +10 Queensland (QLD); +9:30 Northern Territory (NT); +8 Western Australia (WA)

Australian Broadcasting Corporation Northern Territory HF Service—ABC Radio 8DDD Darwin, Administrative Center for the Northern Territory Shortwave Service, ABC, Box 9994, GPO Darwin NT 0801, Australia; (street address) 1 Cavenagh Street, Darwin NT 0800, Australia. Phone: +61 (8) 8943-3222; (engineering) +61 (8) 8943-3209. Fax: +61 (8) 8943 3235 or +61 (8) 8943 3208. Contact: (general) Tony Bowden, Branch Manager; (administration) Barbra Lilliebridge, Administration Officer; (technical) Peter Camilleri or Yvonne Corby. Free stickers and postcards. "Traveller's Guide to ABC Radio" for $1. T-shirts US$20. Three IRCs or return postage helpful.

BBC World Service via Radio Australia—For verification direct from the Australian transmitters, contact John Westland, Director of English Programs at Radio Australia (*see*). Nontechnical correspondence should be sent to the BBC World Service in London (*see*).

🕮**Christian Vision Communications (CVC)**, PO Box 6361, Maroochydore, QLD 4558, Australia. Phone: + 61-7-5477-1555. Fax: + 61-7-5477-1727. Email: online forms; ("Mailbag" program) mailbag@cvc.tv. Web: (includes on-demand and streaming audio) www.cvc.tv. Contact: (general) Mike Edmiston, Director; Raymond Moti, Station Manager; or Richard Daniel, Corporate Relations Manager. May send T-shirt, baseball cap, key ring or other small gifts. Formerly Voice International Limited, and before that, Christian Voice International Australia.
HONG KONG ADDRESS (CHINESE SERVICE): Liu Sheng, Flat 1b, 67 Ha Heung Road, Kowloon, Hong Kong, China.
INDIA ADDRESS (HINDI SERVICE): CVC, P.O. Box 1, Kangra, Pin Code 176001, Himachal, India.
INDONESIA ADDRESS (INDONESIAN SERVICE): CVC, P.O. Box 2634, Jakarta Pusat, 10026 Indonesia. Phone: +62 (21) 390-0039.
INTERNATIONAL TOLL-FREE NUMBERS: (Indonesia only) 001-803-61-555; (India only) 000-800-610-1019.
TRANSMITTER SITE: CVC, PMB 5777, Darwin NT 0801, Australia. Phone: (general) +61 (8) 8981-6591 or (operations manager) +61 (8) 8981-8822. Fax: +61 (8) 8981 2846. Contact: Mrs. Lorna Manning, Site Administrator; or Robert Egoroff, Operations Manager.

🕮**Community Development Radio Service—CDRS**, ARDS, Box 1671, Nhulunbuy NT 0881, Australia; or (street address) 19 Pera Circuit, Nhulunbuy NT 0880, Australia. Phone: +61 (8) 8987-3910. Fax: +61 (8) 8987 3912. Email: (general) nhulun@ards.com.au, mediaservices@ards.com.au; (technical) dale@ards.com.au. Web: (includes on-demand audio) http://www.ards.com.au/broadcast.htm. Contact: Dale Chesson, Radio Service Manager.

CVC—*see* Christian Vision Communications.

EDXP News Report, 404 Mont Albert Road, Mont Albert, Victoria 3127, Australia. Phone/Fax: +61 (3) 9898-2906. Email: info@edxp.org. Web: http://edxp.org. Contact: Bob Padula. " EDXP News Report" is compiled by the "Electronic DX Press" and airs over several world band stations. Focuses on shortwave broadcasters beaming to, or located in Asia and the Pacific. Currently heard on Adventist World Radio, HCJB-Australia, HCJB-Ecuador, WINB, WWCR, World Harvest Radio and KBS World Radio. Verifies postal reports with full-detail "EDXP" QSL cards showing Australian fauna, flora, and scenery. Return postage required; four 50c stamps within Australia, and one IRC or US dollar elsewhere. Email reports welcome, and are confirmed with animated Web-delivered QSLs. Does not verify reports on Internet broadcasts.

HCJB Australia, P.O. Box 291, Kilsyth VIC 3137, Australia. Phone: +61 (3) 9761-4844. Fax: +61 (3) 9761 4061. Email: office@hcjb.org.au. Contact: Derek Kickbush, Director of Broadcasting; Dennis Adams; or David Yetman, Frequency Manager.
VERIFICATION OF RECEPTION REPORTS: Voice of the Great Southland, GPO Box 691, Melbourne VIC 3001, Australia. Email: english@hcjb.org.au; or (Yetman) dyetman@hcjb.org.au. One IRC required for postal reply.
NEW DELHI OFFICE: Radio GMTA, P.O. Box 4960, New Delhi 110 029 India.

🕮**Radio Australia**, GPO Box 428G, Melbourne VIC 3001, Australia. Phone: ("Openline" voice mail for listeners' messages and requests) +61 (3) 9626-1825; (switchboard) +61 (3) 9626-1800; (English programs) +61 (3) 9626-1922; (marketing manager) +61 (3) 9626 1723. Fax: (general) +61 (3) 9626 1899. Email: (general) english@ra.abc.net.au; (marketing manager) marketing@radioaustralia.net.au. (Web: (includes on-demand and streaming audio) www.radioaustralia.net. au. Contact: (general) Brendon Telfer, Head of English Language Programming; Tony Hastings, Director of Programs; Mark Hemetsberger, Marketing & Communications Manager; or Jean-Gabriel Manguy, General Manager; (technical) Nigel Holmes, Chief Engineer, Transmission Management Unit. All reception reports received by Radio Australia are forwarded to the Australian Radio DX Club for assessment and checking. ARDXC will forward completed QSLs to Radio Australia for mailing. For further information, contact Brendon Telfer, Director of English Programs at radio Australia (Email: telfer. brendon@abc.net.au).

SAN FRANCISCO OFFICE, SCHEDULES: 2654 17th Avenue, San Francisco CA 94116 USA. Phone: +1 (415) 564-9968. Email: GPoppin@aol.com. Contact: George Poppin. This address, a volunteer office, only provides Radio Australia schedules to listeners. All other correspondence should be sent directly to the main office in Melbourne.

AUSTRIA   World Time +1 (+2 midyear)

Radio Austria International, Listener Service, Argentinier strasse 30a, A-1040 Vienna, Austria. Phone: +43 (1) 50101-16060. Fax: +43 (1) 50101 16066. Email: (frequency schedules, comments, reception reports) roi.service@orf.at. Web: (includes online reception report form) http://oe1.orf.at/service/international_en; (on-demand and streaming audio from ÖE1, which makes up most of Radio Austria International's European service) http://oe1.orf.at. Contact: (general) Vera Bock, Listener Service; (English Department) David Ward.

FREQUENCY MANAGEMENT: ORF Sendetechnik, Attn. Ernst Vranka, Würzburggasse 30, A-1136 Vienna, Austria. Phone: +43 (1) 87878-12629. Fax: +43 (1) 87878 12773. Email: ernst.vranka@orf.at. Contact: Ing. Ernst Vranka, Frequency Manager.

Trans World Radio—*see* USA.

AZERBAIJAN   World Time +4 (+5 midyear)

Radio Dada Gorgud/Voice of Azerbaijan (when operating), Medhi Hüseyin küçäsi 1, 370011 Baku, Azerbaijan. Phone: +994 (12) 398 585. Fax: +994 (12) 395 452. Contact: Mrs. Tamam Bayatli-Öner, Director; Kamil Mamedov, Director of Division of International Relations; or Arzu Abdullayev. Free postcards, and occasionally, books. $1 or return postage helpful. Replies irregularly to correspondence in English.

BAHRAIN   World Time +3

Coalition Maritime Forces (CMF) Radio One—*see* International Waters.

Radio Bahrain (when operating), Broadcasting and Television, Ministry of Information, P.O. Box 194, Al Manāmah, Bahrain. Phone: (Arabic Service) +973 781-888; (English Service) +973 629-085. Fax: (Arabic Service) +973 681 544; (English Service) +973 780 911. Web: www.gna.gov.bh/brtc/radio.html. Contact: A. Suliman (for Director of Broadcasting). $1 or IRC required. Replies irregularly.

BANGLADESH   World Time +6

Bangladesh Betar
NONTECHNICAL: External Services, Bangladesh Betar, Shah Bagh Post Box No. 2204, Dhaka 1000, Bangladesh; (street address) Betar Bhaban Sher-e-Bangla Nagar, Agargaon Road, Dhaka 1207, Bangladesh. Phone: (director general) +880 (2) 8615-294; (Rahman Khan) +880 (2) 8613-949; (external services) +880 (2) 8618-119. Fax:(director general) +880 (2) 8612 021. Email: (Office of Director General) dgbetar@bd.drik.net; dgbetar@bttb.net.bd; (external services) ts-betar@bdonline. com. Web: (includes on-demand audio) www.betar.org.bd. Contact: M.A. Basher Khan, Director - External Services; Ashfaque-ur Rahman Khan, Director - Programmes.

TECHNICAL: Research and Receiving Centre, National Broadcasting Authority, 121 Kazi Nazrul Islam Avenue, Shah Bagh, Dhaka-1000, Bangladesh. Phone: +880 (2) 8625-904. Fax: +880 (2) 8612 021. Email: rrc@dhaka.net. Contact: Md. Kamal Uddin, or Ahmed Quamruzzaman, Station Engineer. Sometimes verifies reception reports.

BELARUS   World Time +2 (+3 midyear)

Belarusian Radio—*see* Radio Station Belarus, below, for details.

Radio Hrodna—contact via Radio Station Belarus, below.

Radio Mahiliou—contact via Radio Station Belarus, below.

Radio Station Belarus, 4, Krasnaya St., Minsk 220807, Belarus. Phone: (domestic Belarusian Radio) +375 (17) 239-5810; (external services, general) +375 (17) 239-5852; +375 (17) 239 5831; (English and German Departments) +375 (17) 239-5875. Fax: (all services) +375 (17) 284 8574. Email: (domestic Belarusian Radio) tvr@tvr.by; (external services) radio-minsk@tvr.by. Web: (includes on-demand and streaming audio) www.tvr.by. Contact: Naum Galperovich, Director External Service; Vyacheslav Laktjuishin, Head of English Service; Grigori Mityushnikov, Editor, English Service; Elena Khoroshevich, Head of German Service; or Jürgen Eberhardt, German Program Editor. Free Belarus stamps.

BELGIUM   World Time +1 (+2 midyear)

Maeva 6015, Postbus 550, B-1000 Brussels, Belgium. Phone: +32 (9) 227-0487. Email: maevaradio@hotmail.com. Web: (includes streaming audio) www.maeva6015.com, or www.maevaradio.be. Contact: Eric Hofman. Via T-Systems International facilities in Jülich, Germany (*see*).

RTBF-International, local 3P09, 52 bd Reyers, B-1044 Brussels, Belgium. Phone: +32 (2) 737-4014. Fax: +32 (2) 737 3032. Email: relint.r@rtbf.be, or rtbfi@rtbf.be. Web: (includes on-demand and streaming audio) www.rtbf.be. Contact: Jean-Pol Hecq, Directeur des Relations Internationales (or "Head, International Service" if writing in English). Broadcasts are essentially a relay of programs from the domestic service "La Première" of RTBF (Radio-Télévision Belge de la Communauté Française) via a transmitter in Wavre and facilities of Germany's T-Systems International (*see*). The Wavre transmitter sometimes airs RTBF's "Vivacité" in place of "La Première." Return postage not required. Accepts email reception reports.

Radio Traumland, P.O. Box 15, B-4730 Raeren, Belgium. Phone: +31 87 301-722. Email: radiotraumland@skynet.be. Email reports can only be confirmed with electronic QSLs; for a postal reply include 1 IRC, $1, 1 Euro or mint Belgian/German stamps. Transmits via T-Systems International facilities in Jülich, Germany (see).

Radio Vlaanderen Internationaal (RVI), B-1043 Brussels, Belgium. Phone: +32 (2) 741-5611, +32 (2) 741-3806/7, +32 (2) 741-3802. Fax: +32 (2) 741-4689. Email: info@rvi.be. Web: (includes on-demand and streaming audio) www.rvi.be.

Contact: (station manager) Wim Jansen; (listener mail) Tine De Bruycker, or Rita Penne.

Transmitter Documentation Project (TDP), P.O. Box 1, B-2310 Rijkevorsel, Belgium. Phone: +32 (3) 314-7800. Fax: +32 (3) 314 1212. Email: info@transmitter.org. Web: www. broadcast.be; (shortwave schedule) www.airtime.be/schedule. html. Contact: Ludo Maes, Managing Director. A free online publication by Belgian Dxer Ludo Maes. TDP lists current and past shortwave transmitters used worldwide in country order with station name, transmitter site & geographical coordinates, transmitter type, power and year of installation etc. Also brokers leased airtime over world band transmitters, and verifies reception reports for client stations.

☞Zwart of Wit, Vlaams Belang, Madouplein 8 bus 9, B-1210 Brussels, Belgium. Phone: +32 (2) 219-6009. Fax +32 (2) 219 5047. Email: info@vlaamsbelang.org. Web: (includes on-demand audio) www.vlaamsbelang.org. Broadcasts are produced by the Vlaams Belang ("Flemish Republic") political organization and aired over transmitters outside Belgium.

BENIN   World Time +1

Office de Radiodiffusion et Télévision du Benin, Boite Postale 366, Cotonou, Benin. Phone/Fax: +229 302-184. Contact: Fidèle Ayikoue, Directeur Generale; (technical) Anastase Adjoko, Chef du Service Technique. Return postage, $1 or IRC required. Replies irregularly and slowly to correspondence in French.
PARAKOU REGIONAL STATION: ORTB-Parakou, Boite Postale 128, Parakou, Benin. Phone: +229 610-773, +229 611-096, +229 611080. Fax: +229 610 881. Contact: (general) J. de Matha, Le Chef de la Station; (technical) Léon Donou, Chef des Services Techniques. Return postage required. Replies tend to be extremely irregular, and a safer option is to send correspondence to the Cotonou address.

BHUTAN   World Time +6

☞Bhutan Broadcasting Service
STATION: Department of Information and Broadcasting, Ministry of Communications, P.O. Box 101, Thimphu, Bhutan. Phone: +975 (2) 323-071/72. Fax: +975 (2) 323 073. Email: (general) webmaster@bbs.com.bt; (News and Current Affairs) news@bbs.com.bt; (Thinley Tobgay Dorji) thinley@bbs.com.bt; (Sonam Tobgay) toby@bbs.com.bt. Web: (includes on-demand audio) www.bbs.com.bt. Contact: (general) Thinley Tobgay Dorji, News Coordinator; Ms. Sherpem Sherpa, Web Editor & Presenter "Bhutan this Week" & "Internet on the Radio"; or Kinga Singye, Executive Director; (technical) Dorji Wangchuk, Station Engineer. Two IRCs, return postage or $1 required. Replies irregularly; correspondence to the U.N. Mission (*see* following) may be more fruitful.
UNITED NATIONS MISSION: Permanent Mission of the Kingdom of Bhutan to the United Nations, Two United Nations Plaza, 27th Floor, New York NY 10017 USA. Fax: +1 (212) 826 2998. Contact: Mrs. Kunzang C. Namgyel, Third Secretary; Mrs. Sonam Yangchen, Attaché; Ms. Leki Wangmo, Second Secretary; or Hari K. Chhetri, Second Secretary. Free newspapers and booklet on the history of Bhutan.

BOLIVIA   World Time –4

NOTE ON STATION IDENTIFICATIONS: Many Bolivian stations listed as "Radio..." may also announce as "Radio Emisora..." or "Radiodifusora..."
Paititi Radiodifusión—*see* Radio Paitití, below.

Radio Animas (if reactivated), Chocaya, Animas, Potosí, Bolivia. Contact: Julio Acosta Campos, Director. Return postage or $1 required. Replies irregularly to correspondence in Spanish.
Radio Camargo—*see* Radio Emisoras Camargo, below.
Radio Centenario "La Nueva"
MAIN OFFICE: Casilla 818, Santa Cruz de la Sierra, Bolivia. Phone: +591 (3) 352-9265. Fax: +591 (3) 352 4747. Email: mision.eplabol@scbbs-bo.com. Contact: Napoleón Ardaya B., Director. May send a calendar. Free stickers. Return postage or $1 required. Audio cassettes of contemporary Christian music and Bolivian folk music $10, including postage; CDs of Christian folk music $15, including postage. Replies to correspondence in English or Spanish.
U.S. BRANCH OFFICE: LATCOM, 1218 Croton Avenue, New Castle PA 16101 USA. Phone: +1 (412) 652-0101. Fax: +1 (412) 652 4654. Contact: Hope Cummins.
Radio Chicha, Tocla, Provincia Nor-Chichas, Departamento de Potosí, Bolivia.
Radio Eco
MAIN ADDRESS: Correo Central, Reyes, Ballivián, Beni, Bolivia. Contact: Gonzalo Espinoza Cortés, Director. Free station literature. $1 or return postage required. Replies to correspondence in Spanish.
ALTERNATIVE ADDRESS: Rolmán Medina Méndez, Correo Central, Reyes, Ballivián, Bolivia.
Radio Emisoras Ballivián (when operating), Correo Central, San Borja, Beni, Bolivia. Replies to correspondence in Spanish, and sometimes sends pennant.
Radio Emisoras Camargo, Casilla Postal 9, Camargo, Provincia Nor-Cinti, Chuquisaca, Bolivia. Email: jlgarpas@hotmail. com. Contact: Pablo García B., Gerente Propietario; or José Luís García. Return postage or $1 required. Replies slowly to correspondence in Spanish.
Radio Emisoras Minería—*see* Radiodifusoras Minería.
Radio Estambul, Avenida Primero de Mayo esq. Loreto, Guayaramerín, Beni, Bolivia. Phone: +591 (3) 855-4145. Email: ninafelima@hotmail.com Contact: Sra. Felima Bruno de Yamal, Propietaria, who welcomes postcards, pennants or small flags from foreign listeners.
☞Radio Fides, Casilla 9143, La Paz, Bolivia. Fax: +591 (2) 237 9030. Email: rafides@fidesbolivia.com (if that fails, try: sistemas@radiofides.com). Web: (includes on-demand and streaming audio) http://fidesbolivia.com. Contact: R.P. Eduardo Pérez Iribarne, S.J., Director. Replies occasionally to correspondence in Spanish.
Radio Guanay (when operating), calle Boston de Guanay 123, Guanay, La Paz, Bolivia; or Casilla de Correo 15012, La Paz, Bolivia. Replies irregularly to correspondence in Spanish.
Radio Illimani, Casilla 1042, La Paz, Bolivia. Phone: +591 (2) 237-6364. Fax: +591 (2) 235 9275. Email: illimani@communica. gov.bo. Contact: José Luis Almanza, Director. $1 required, and registered mail recommended. Replies irregularly to friendly correspondence in Spanish.
Radio Juan XXIII [Veintitrés], Avenida Santa Cruz al frente de la plaza principal, San Ignacio de Velasco, Santa Cruz, Bolivia. Phone: +591 (3962) 2087. Phone/Fax: +591 (3962) 2188. Contact: Pbro. Elías Cortezón, Director; or María Elffy Gutiérrez Méndez, Encargada de la Discoteca. Return postage or $1 required. Replies occasionally to correspondence in Spanish.
☞Radio La Cruz del Sur, Casilla 1408, La Paz, Bolivia. Phone: +591 (2) 222-0541. Fax: +591 (2) 224 3337. Email: cruzdelsur@zuper.net. Contact: Carlos Montesinos, Director. $1 or return postage required. Replies slowly to correspondence in Spanish.

Radio La Palabra (if reactivated), Parroquia de Santa Ana de Yacuma, Beni, Bolivia. Phone: +591 (3848) 2117. Contact: Padre Yosu Arketa, Director. Return postage necessary. Replies to correspondence in Spanish.

Radio Mallku, Casilla No. 16, Uyuni, Provincia Antonio Quijarro, Departamento de Potosí, Bolivia. Phone: +591 (2693) 2145. Email: (FRUTCAS parent organization) frutcas@hotmail. es. Contact: Freddy Juárez Huarachi, Director; Erwin Freddy Mamani Machaca, Jefe de Prensa y Programación. Spanish preferred. Return postage in the form of two U.S. dollars appreciated, as the station depends on donations for its existence. Station owned by La Federación Unica de Trabajadores Campesinos del Altiplano Sud (FRUTCAS) and formerly known as Radio A.N.D.E.S.

Radio Minería—*see* Radiodifusoras Minería.

Radio Mosoj Chaski, Casilla 4493, Cochabamba, Bolivia; (street address) Calle Abaroa 254, Cochabamba, Bolivia. Phone: +591 (4) 422-0641 or +591 (4) 422-0644. Fax: +591 (44) 251 041. Email: chaski@bo.net. Contact: Paul G. Pittman, Administrator; Ann Matthews, Director. Replies to correspondence in Spanish or English. Return postage helpful.
NORTH AMERICAN OFFICE: Quechuan Radio, c/o SIM USA, P.O. Box 7900, Charlotte NC 28241 USA.

Radio Movima (if reactivated), Calle Baptista No. 24, Santa Ana de Yacuma, Beni, Bolivia. Contact: Rubén Serrano López, Director; Javier Roca Díaz, Director Gerente; or Mavis Serrano, Directora. Return postage or $1 required. Replies irregularly to correspondence in Spanish.

TIPS FOR EFFECTIVE CORRESPONDENCE

Golden Rule: Write unto others as you would have them write unto you. The milk of human kindness is mighty skim these days, so a considerate message stands out.

Be interesting and helpful from the recipient's point of view, yet friendly without being chummy. Comments on specific programs are almost always appreciated, even if you are sending in what is basically a technical report.

Incorporate language courtesies. Using the broadcaster's tongue is always a plus— Addresses PLUS indicates when it is a requirement—but English is usually the next-best bet. When writing in any language to Spanish-speaking countries, remember that what gringos think of as the "last name" is actually written as the penultimate name. Thus, Juan Antonio Vargas García, which can also be written as Juan Antonio Vargas G., refers to Sr. Vargas; so your salutation should read, *Estimado Sr. Vargas*.

What's that "García" doing there, then? That's *mamita's* father's family name. Latinos more or less solved the problem of gender fairness in names long before Anglos.

But, wait—what about Portuguese, used by all those stations in Brazil? Same concept, but in reverse. *Mamá's* father's family name is penultimate, and the "real" last name is where English-speakers are used to it, at the end.

In Chinese, the "last" name comes first. However, when writing in English, Chinese names are often reversed for the benefit of *weiguoren*—foreigners. For example, "Li" is a common Chinese last name, so if you see "Li Dan," it's "Mr. Li." But if it's "Dan Li"—and certainly if it's been Westernized into "Dan Lee"—he's already one step ahead of you, and it's still "Mr. Li" (or Lee). Less widely known is that the same can also occur in Hungarian. For example, "Bartók Béla" for Béla Bartók.

If in doubt, fall back on the ever-safe "Dear Sir" or "Dear Madam"—"Hi" is still not appropriate with most letters—or use email, where salutations are not expected. Avoid first names, too, especially for recipients outside the United States. However, if you know the recipient is an amateur radio operator ("ham"), it is safe to use the first name if you include ham call letters in the address; e.g. Norman Gorman, WA3CRN, Station Engineer.

Be patient, as replies by post take weeks, sometimes months. Slow responders, those that tend to take beaucoup months to reply, are cited in Addresses PLUS, as are erratic repliers.

Radio Municipal, Correo Central, Caranavi, Departamento de La Paz, Bolivia.

Radio Nacional de Huanuni, Casilla 681, Oruro, Bolivia. Contact: Rafael Linneo Morales, Director General; or Alfredo Murillo, Director. Return postage or $1 required. Replies irregularly to correspondence in Spanish.

Radio Nueva Esperanza (when operating), Raúl Salmón 92 entre calles 4 y 5, Zona 12 de Octubre, El Alto, La Paz, Bolivia.

Radio Paitití, Casilla 172, Guayaramerín, Beni, Bolivia. Contact: Armando Mollinedo Bacarreza, Director; Luis Carlos Santa Cruz Cuéllar, Director Gerente; or Ancir Vaca Cuéllar, Gerente-Propietario. Free pennants. Return postage or $3 required. Replies irregularly to correspondence in Spanish.

Radio Panamericana, Casilla 5263, La Paz, Bolivia; (street address) Av. 16 de Julio, Edif. 16 de Julio, Of. 902, El Prado, La Paz, Bolivia. Phone: +591 (2) 231-2644, +591 (2) 231-1383, +591 (2) 231-3980. Fax: +591 (2) 233-4271. Email: pana@panamericanabolivia.com. Web: (includes streaming audio) www.panamericanabolivia.com. Contact: Daniel Sánchez Rocha, Director. Replies irregularly, with correspondence in Spanish preferred. $1 or 2 IRCs helpful.

Radio Perla del Acre (when operating), Casilla 7, Cobija, Departamento de Pando, Bolivia. Return postage or $1 required. Replies irregularly to correspondence in Spanish.

Radio Pío XII [Doce], Casilla 434, Oruro, Bolivia. Phone: +591 (258) 20-250. Fax: +591 (258) 20 544. Email: rpiodoce@entelnet.bo. Web: www.radiopio12.org. Contact: Pbro. Roberto Durette, OMI, Director General; or José Blanco. Return postage necessary.

Radio San Gabriel, Casilla 4792, La Paz, Bolivia. Phone: +591 (2) 241-4371. Phone/Fax: +591 (2) 241-1174. Email: rsg@fundayni.rds.org.bo; (technical, including reception reports) remoc@entelnet.bo. Contact: (general) Hno. [Brother] José Canut Saurat, Director General; or Sra. Martha Portugal, Dpto. de Publicidad; (technical) Rómulo Copaja Alcón, Director Técnico. $1 or return postage helpful. Free book on station, Aymara calendars and *La Voz del Pueblo Aymara* magazine. Replies fairly regularly to correspondence in Spanish. Station of the Hermanos de la Salle Catholic religious order.

Radio San Miguel, Casilla 102, Riberalta, Beni, Bolivia. Phone: +591 (385) 8268 or +591 (385) 8363. Fax: +591 (385) 8268. Contact: Félix Alberto Rada Q., Director; or Gerin Pardo Molina, Director. Free stickers and pennants; has a different pennant each year. Return postage or $1 required. Replies irregularly to correspondence in Spanish.

Radio Santa Ana, Calle Sucre No. 250, Santa Ana de Yacuma, Beni, Bolivia. Contact: Mario Roberto Suárez, Director; or Mariano Verdugo. Return postage or $1 required. Replies irregularly to correspondence in Spanish.

Radio Santa Cruz, Emisora del Instituto Radiofónico Fé y Alegría (IRFA), Casilla 672, Santa Cruz, Bolivia. Phone: +591 (3) 353-1817. Fax: +591 (3) 353 2257. Email: irfacruz@entelnet.bo. Contact: Padre Francisco Flores, S.J., Director General; Srta. María Yolanda Marcó Escobar, Secretaria de Dirección; Señora Mirian Suárez, Productor, "Protagonista Ud."; or Lic. Silvia Nava S. Free pamphlets, stickers and pennants. Welcomes correspondence in English, French and Spanish, but return postage required for a reply.

Radio Tacana (when operating), Tumupasa, Provincia Iturralde, Departamento de La Paz, Bolivia.

Radio Uncia (if reactivated), Plaza 6 de Agosto y calle Villazón, Uncia, Departamento de Potosí, Bolivia.

Radio Virgen de los Remedios, Casilla 198, Tupiza, Departamento de Potosí, Bolivia; or (physical address) Parroquia Nuestra Señora de la Candelaria, Tupiza, Departamento de Potosí, Bolivia. Phone: +591 (269) 44-662. Email: radiovirgende remedios@hotmail.com. Contact: Padre Estanislao Odroniec.

Radio Yura (La Voz de los Ayllus), Casilla 326, Yura, Provincia Quijarro, Departamento de Potosí, Bolivia. Phone: +591 (281) 36-216. Email: radioyura@hotmail.com. Contact: Rolando Cueto F., Director.

Radiodifusoras Minería, Casilla de Correo 247, Oruro, Bolivia. Phone: +591 (252) 77-736. Contact: Dr. José Carlos Gómez Espinoza, Gerente Propietario; or Srta. Costa Colque Flores, Responsable del programa "Minería Cultural." Free pennants. Replies to correspondence in Spanish.

Radiodifusoras Trópico, Casilla 60, Trinidad, Beni, Bolivia. Contact: Eduardo Avila Alberdi, Director. Replies slowly to correspondence in Spanish. Return postage required for reply.

BOTSWANA   World Time +2

IBB Botswana Transmitting Station
TRANSMITTER SITE: Voice of America, Botswana Relay Station, Moepeng Hill, Selebi-Phikwe, Botswana; or VOA-Botswana Transmitting Station, Private Bag 38, Selebi-Phikwe, Botswana. Phone: +267 810-932. Fax: +267 261 0185. Email: manager_botswana@bot.ibb.gov. Contact: Station Manager or Transmitting Plant Supervisor. This address for specialized technical correspondence only, although reception reports may occasionally be verified. All other correspondence should be directed to the regular VOA or IBB addresses (*see* USA).

Radio Botswana, (when operating) Private Bag 0060, Gaborone, Botswana. Phone: +267 352-541 or +267 352-861. Fax: +267 357 138. Contact: (general) Ted Makgekgenene, Director; or Monica Mphusu, Producer, "Maokaneng/Pleasure Mix"; (technical) Kingsley Reetsang, Principal Broadcasting Engineer. Free stickers, pennants and pins. Return postage, $1 or 2 IRCs required. Replies slowly and irregularly.

BRAZIL   World Time –1 (–2 midyear) Atlantic Islands; –2 (–3 midyear) Eastern, including Brasília and Rio de Janeiro; –3 (–4 midyear) Western; –4 Northwestern; –5 Acre. There are often slight variations from one year to the next. Information regarding Daylight Saving Time can be found at http://pcdsh01.on.br.

NOTE: Postal authorities recommend that, because of the level of theft in the Brazilian postal system, correspondence to Brazil be sent only via registered mail.

CBN Anhanguera—*see* Rádio Anhanguera (Goiânia).

Emissora Rural A Voz do São Francisco, Caixa Postal 8, 56300-000 Petrolina PE, Brazil. Email: emissorarural@silcons.com.br. Contact: Maria Letecia de Andrade Nunes. Return postage necessary. Replies to correspondence in Portuguese.

Nossa Rádio—*see* Rádio Relógio.

Rádio Nossa Voz, Rua Nadir Dias de Figueiredo 1329, 02110-000 São Paulo SP, Brazil. Phone: (listener feedback) +55 (11) 3016-1764/5.

Rádio Alvorada (Londrina), Rua Dom Bosco 145, Bairro Iguaçu, 86060-340 Londrina PR, Brazil. Phone: +55 (43) 3347-0606. Fax: +55 (43) 3347 0303. Email: alvorada@radioalvorada.am.br. Web: www.radioalvorada.am.br. $1 or return postage. Replies to correspondence in Portuguese.

Rádio Alvorada (Parintins), Rua Governador Leopoldo Neves 516, 69151-460 Parintins AM, Brazil. Phone: +55 (92) 3533-2002, +55 (92) 3533-3097. Fax: +55 (92) 3533 2004. Email: alvorada@parintinsnet.com, or alvorada@jurupari.com.br.

Contact: Raimunda Ribeiro da Silva. Return postage required. Replies occasionally to correspondence in Portuguese.

Rádio Alvorada (Rio Branco), Avenida Ceará 2150, Jardim Nazle, 69900-460 Rio Branco AC, Brazil. Phone: +55 (68) 3226-2301. Email: seve@jornalatribuna.com.br. Contact: José Severiano, Diretor. Occasionally replies to correspondence in Portuguese.

Rádio Araguaia—FM sister-station to Rádio Anhanguera (see next entry) and sometimes relayed via the latter's shortwave outlet. Usually identifies as "Araguaia FM."

Rádio Anhanguera (Araguaína), BR-157 Km. 1103, Zona Rural, 77804-970 Araguaína TO, Brazil. Return postage required. Occasionally replies to correspondence in Portuguese. Sometimes airs programming from sister-station Rádio Araguaia, 97.1 FM (see previous item).

Rádio Anhanguera (Goiânia), Rua Thomas Edison, Quadra 7, Setor Serrinha, 74835-130 Goiânia GO, Brazil; or Caixa Postal 13, 74823-000 Goiânia GO, Brazil. Email: anhanguera@radioexecutiva.com.br. Web: (streaming audio only) http://goiasnet.globo.com/tv_radio. Contact: Fábio de Campos Roriz, Diretor; or Eng. Domingo Vicente Tinoco. Return postage required. Replies to correspondence in Portuguese, often slowly. Although—like its namesake in Araguaína (see, above)—a member of the Sistema de Rádio da Organização Jaime Câmara, this station is also an affiliate of the CBN network and often identifies as "CBN Anhanguera," especially when airing news programming.

Rádio Aparecida, Avenida Getúlio Vargas 186, Centro, 12570-000 Aparecida SP, Brazil; or Caixa Postal 2, 12570-970 Aparecida SP, Brazil. Phone/Fax: +55 (12) 3104-4400. Fax: +55 (12) 3104-4427. Email: (nontechnical) radioaparecida@radioaparecida.com.br; (Macedo) cassianomac@yahoo.com. Web: www.radioaparecida.com.br. Contact: Savio Trevisan, Departamento Técnico; Cassiano Alves Macedo, Producer, "Encontro DX" (aired 2200 Saturday; one hour earlier when Brazil on DST); Ana Cristina Carvalho, Secretária da Direção; João Climaco, Diretor Geral. Return postage or $1 required. Replies to correspondence in Portuguese.

Rádio Bandeirantes, Rua Radiantes 13, Bairro Morumbi, 05699-900 São Paulo SP, Brazil. Phone: +55 (11) 3745-7552; (listener feedback) +55 (11) 3743-8040. Fax: +55 (11) 3743 5391. Email: (general) rbradio@band.com.br or rbnoar@band. com.br; (Huertas) ahuertas@band.com.br; (Dorin) ldorin@band. com.br. Web: (includes streaming audio) www.radiobandeirantes.com.br. Contact: Augusto Huertas, Coordenador Técnico; or Luciano Dorin, Apresentador. Free stickers, pennants and canceled Brazilian stamps. $1 or return postage required.

Rádio Baré Ondas Tropicais, Av. Tefé 3025, Japiim, 69078-000 Manaus AM, Brazil. Phone: +55 (92) 3231-1299; +55 (92) 3231-1379. Fax: +55 (92) 3614 5555. Email: sbomfin@radiobare.com.br. Web: www.radiobare.com.br. Contact: Rosivaldo Ferreira, Diretor da programação. A service for listeners in the interior of the state of Amazonas, produced and managed by PROCLIP, a local advertising agency. Replies to correspondence in Portuguese.

Rádio Boa Vontade, Av. São Paulo 722, 3º andar, 90230-160 Porto Alegre RS, Brazil. Phone: +55 (51) 3325-7019 or +55 (51) 3374-0203. Email: rbv1300am@hotmail.com. Web: (includes streaming audio) www.redeboavontade.com.br. Contact: José Joaquim Martins Rodrigues, Gerente Administrativo.

Rádio Brasil, Av. Benjamin Constant, 1214, 5º andar, 13010-141 Campinas SP, Brazil. Email: radio@brasilcampinas.com. Web: www.brasilcampinas.com. Contact: Adilson Gasparini, Diretor Comercial e Artístico. Email reports accepted. Free stickers. Replies to correspondence in Portuguese.

Rádio Brasil Central, Caixa Postal 330, 74001-970 Goiânia GO, Brazil; (street address) Rua SC-1 No. 299, Parque Santa Cruz, 74860-270 Goiânia GO, Brazil. Phone: +55 (62) 201-7600. Email: rbc@agecom.go.gov.br. Web: www.agecom.go.gov.br/AM. Contact: Sílvio José da Silva, Gerente Executivo; Ney Raymundo Fernández, Diretor Administrativo; Sergio Rubens da Silva; or Arizio Pedro Soárez, Diretor Gerente. Free stickers. $1 or return postage required. Replies to correspondence in Portuguese, and sometimes to correspondence in English.

Rádio Brasil Tropical (if reactivated), Caixa Postal 405, 78005-970 Cuiabá MT, Brazil; (street address) Rua Joaquim Murtinho 1456, Bairro Porto, 78020-830 Cuiabá MT, Brazil. Phone: +55 (65) 321-6198, +55 (65) 321-6882, +55 (65) 321-6226. Fax: +55 (65) 624 3455. Email: rcultura@terra.com.br. Contact: Klécius Antônio dos Santos, Diretor Comercial; or Roberto Ferreira, Gerente Comercial. Free stickers. $1 required. Replies to correspondence in Portuguese. Shortwave sister-station to Rádio Cultura de Cuiabá (see).

Rádio Cacique (when operating), Rua Saldanha da Gama 168, Centro, 18035-040, Sorocaba SP, Brazil. Phone: (listener feedback) +55 (15) 223-2922 or +55 (15) 231-3712. Email: online form. Web: www.radiocacique.com.br. Contact: Edir Correa.

Rádio Caiari, Rua das Crianças 4646, Bairro Areal da Floresta, 78912-210 Porto Velho RO, Brazil. Phone: (studio) +55 (69) 3227-2277 or +55 (69) 3216-0707; Phone/Fax: (Commercial Dept.) +55 (69) 3210-3621. Email: caiari@radiocaiari.com. br. Web: www.radiocaiari.com. Contact: Alisângela Lima, Gerente Operacional. Free stickers. Return postage helpful. Replies irregularly to correspondence in Portuguese.

Rádio Canção Nova, Caixa Postal 57, 12630-000 Cachoeira Paulista SP, Brazil; (street address) Rua João Paulo II s/n, Alto da Bela Vista, 12630-000 Cachoeira Paulista SP, Brazil. Phone: (studio) +55 (12) 3186-2046. Fax: (general) +55 (12) 3186 2022 Email: (general) online form (radio@cancaonova.com.br may also work); (reception reports) dx@cancaonova.com. Web: (includes streaming audio) www.cancaonova.com/portal/canais/radio. Free stickers, pennants and station brochure sometimes sent on request. May send magazines. $1 helpful.

Rádio Capixaba (when operating), Caixa Postal 509, 29000-000 Vitória ES, Brazil; (street address) Av. Santo Antônio 366, 29025-000 Vitória ES, Brazil. Email: radiocap@terra.com.br. Contact: Jairo Gouvea Maia, Diretor; or Sr. Sardinha, Técnico. Replies occasionally to correspondence in Portuguese.

Rádio Clube de Dourados (if reactivated), Rua Ciro Mello 2045, Dourados MS, Brazil. Replies irregularly to correspondence in Portuguese.

Rádio Clube de Varginha (when operating), Caixa Postal 102, 37000-000 Varginha MG, Brazil. Email: sistemaclube@varginha.com.br. Contact: Mariela Silva Gómez. Return postage required. Replies to correspondence in Spanish and Portuguese.

Rádio Clube do Pará, Av. Almirante Barroso 2190 - 3º andar, Marco, 66093-020 Belém PA, Brazil. Phone: +55 (91) 3084-0100. Fax: +55 (91) 3296 2848. Email: clubedamanha@expert.com.br, or timaocampeao@expert.com.br. Web: (includes streaming audio) www.radioclubedopara.com.br. Contact: Camilo Centeno, Diretor Geral. Replies to correspondence in Portuguese or English, and verifies reception reports. Free stickers, postcards and occasional T-shirt.

Radio Clube Paranaense, Rua Rockefeller 1311, Prado Velho, 80230-130 Curitiba PR, Brazil. Phone: +55 (41) 332-2772. Fax: +55 (41) 332-2398. Email: (commercial department.) clubcoml@rla13.pucpr.br. Web: (includes streaming audio) www.clubeb2.com.br. Contact: Vicente Mickosz, Superintendente; Marisa Ap. Zanon, Gerente Administrativa.

Rádio Congonhas, Praça da Basílica 130, 36404-000 Congonhas MG, Brazil. Replies to correspondence in Portuguese.

⬛**Rádio Cultura Araraquara**, Avenida Bento de Abreu 789, Bairro Fonte Luminosa, 14802-396 Araraquara SP, Brazil. Phone: +55 (16) 3303-7799. Fax: +55 (16) 3303 7792. Email: (administration) cultura@radiocultura.net; (listener feedback) ouvintes@radiocultura.net; (Wagner Luiz) wagner@radiocultura.net. Web: (includes streaming audio) www.radiocultura.net. Contact: Wagner Luiz, Diretor Artístico. Return postage required. Replies slowly to correspondence in Portuguese.

Rádio Cultura de Cuiabá—AM sister-station of Rádio Brasil Tropical (*see*) and whose programming is partly relayed by RBT. Email: rcultura@terra.com.br. Web: www.grupocultura.com.br.

Rádio Cultura Filadélfia, Avenida Brasil 531, Sala 74, 85851-000 Foz do Iguaçu PR, Brazil. Phone: +55 (45) 523-2930. Replies irregularly to correspondence in Portuguese.

Rádio Cultura Ondas Tropicais, Rua Barcelos s/n, Praça 14 de Janeiro, 69020-200 Manaus AM, Brazil. Phone: +55 (92) 2101-4967, +55 (92) 2101-4953. Fax: +55 (92) 2101 4950. Email: radiocultura@hotmail.com. Contact: Maria Jerusalem dos Santos (also known as Jerusa Santos), Chefa da Divisão de Rádio. Replies to correspondence in Portuguese. Return postage appreciated. Station is part of the FUNTEC (Fundação Televisão e Rádio Cultura do Amazonas) network.

⬛**Rádio Cultura São Paulo**, Rua Vladimir Herzog 75, Água Branca, 05036-900 São Paulo SP, Brazil; or Caixa Postal 11544, 05049-970 São Paulo SP, Brazil. Phone: (general) +55 (11) 3874-3122; (Cultura AM) +55 (11) 3874-3081; (Cultura FM) +55 (11) 3874-3092. Fax: +55 (11) 3611 2014. Email: (Cultura AM, relayed on 9615 and 17815 kHz) falecom@radiocultura.am.br; (Cultura FM, relayed on 6170 kHz) falecom@radioculturasp.fm.br. Web: (includes streaming audio) www.tvcultura.com.br. Contact: Eduardo Weber, Coordenador de Produção Cultura AM. $1 or return postage required. Replies slowly to postal correspondence in Portuguese.

Rádio Difusora Acreana, Rua Benjamin Constant 1232, Centro, 69900-161 Rio Branco AC, Brazil. Phone: +55 (68) 3223-9696. Fax: +55 (68) 3223 8610. Email: comercial.difusora@ac.gov.br. Contact: Antônio Washington de Aquino Sobrinho, Gerente Geral. Replies irregularly to correspondence in Portuguese.

Rádio Difusora Cáceres, Caixa Postal 297, 78200-000 Cáceres MT, Brazil; (street address) Rua Tiradentes 979, Centro, 78200-000 Cáceres MT, Brazil. Phone: +55 (65) 223-3830. Fax: +55 (65) 223-5986. Contact: Sra. Maridalva Amaral Vignard. $1 or return postage required. Replies occasionally to correspondence in Portuguese.

Rádio Difusora de Aquidauana (if reactivated), Caixa Postal 18, 79200-000 Aquidauana MS, Brazil. Phone: +55 (67) 241-3956 or +55 (67) 241-3957. Contact: Joel Severino da Silva, Diretor Geral. Free tourist literature and used Brazilian stamps. $1 or return postage required. This station sometimes identifies during the program day as "Nova Difusora," but its sign-off announcement gives the official name as "Rádio Difusora, Aquidauana."

Rádio Difusora de Londrina, Caixa Postal 916, 86000-000 Londrina PR, Brazil; (street address) Rua Sergipe, 843 - Sala 05, 86010-360 Londrina PR, Brazil. Phone: +55 (43) 3322-1105; Phone/fax: +55 (43) 3324-7369. Email: radiodifusora690@aol.com. Web: www.radiodifusoradelondrina.com.br. Contact: Oscar Simões, Diretor. Free tourist brochure, which sometimes seconds as a verification. $1 or return postage helpful. Replies irregularly to correspondence in Portuguese.

Rádio Difusora de Macapá, Rua Cândido Mendes 525, Centro, 68900-100 Macapá AP, Brazil. Phone: +55 (96) 212-1120. Fax: +55 (96) 212 1116. Email:difusoramcp@yahoo.com.br. Contact: Carlos Luiz Pereira Marques. $1 or return postage required. Replies irregularly to correspondence in Portuguese or English. Sometimes sends stickers, key rings and—on rare occasions—T-shirts.

Rádio Difusora de Poços de Caldas, Rua Rio Grande do Sul 631- 1º andar, Centro, 37701-001 Poços de Caldas MG, Brazil. Phone/Fax: +55 (35) 3722-1530. Email: difusora@difusorapocos.com.br. Web: www.difusorapocos.com.br. Contact: (general) Orlando Cioffi, Diretor Geral; (technical) Ronaldo Cioffi, Diretor Técnico. $1 or return postage required. Replies to correspondence in Portuguese.

⬛**Rádio Difusora do Amazonas**, Av. Eduardo Ribeiro 639 - 20º andar, Centro, 69010-001 Manaus AM, Brazil. Phone: +55 (92) 3633-1009. Fax: +55 (92) 3234 3750. Email: (Fesinha de Souza Anzoatégui) fesinha@uol.com.br; (Commercial Dept.) sac@difusoramanaus.com.br; (Josué Filho) josuefilhocomun icando@bol.com.br. Web: (includes streaming audio) www.difusoramanaus.com.br. Contact: Josué Filho; or Fesinha de Souza Anzoatégui. Replies to correspondence in Portuguese. $1 or return postage helpful.

Rádio Difusora Roraima, Avenida Capitão Ene Garcez 860, São Francisco, 69301-160 Boa Vista RR, Brazil. Phone/Fax: +55 (95) 623-2259. Email: radioadm@technet.com.br, or radio.adm@uol.com.br. Web: www.radiororaima.com.br. Contact: Francisco Geraldo de França. Return postage required. Replies occasionally to correspondence in Portuguese.

Rádio Difusora São Luís (if reactivated), Av.Camboa do Mato 120, Camboa, 65020-260 São Luís MA, Brazil. Phone: +55 98 3214-3000. Fax: +55 98 3214 3094. Web: www.sistemadifusora.com.br/radioam.php. Contact: Paula Lobão. Inactive on shortwave for several years, but projected to return sometime in 2006. Programming likely to be a relay of 680 kHz mediumwave AM, currently leased to the Igreja Universal do Reino de Deus religious organization.

Rádio Difusora Taubaté (when operating), Rua Dr. Sousa Alves 960, 12020-030 Taubaté SP, Brazil. Contact: Emilio Amadei Beringhs Neto, Diretor Superintendente. May send free stickers, pens, keychains and T-shirts. Return postage or $1 helpful.

Rádio Educação Rural (Campo Grande), Avenida Mato Grosso 530, Centro, 79002-906 Campo Grande MS, Brazil. Phone: +55 (67) 384-3164, +55 (67) 382-2238 or +55 (67) 384-3345. Contact: Ângelo Jayme Venturelli, Diretor. $1 or return postage required. Replies to correspondence in Portuguese.

Rádio Educação Rural (Coari), Praça São Sebastião 228, 69460-000 Coari AM, Brazil. Phone: +55 (97) 3561-2474. Fax: +55 (97) 3561 2633. Email: radiocoari@portalcoari.com.br. Contact: Sidomar Alfaia. $1 or return postage helpful. Replies irregularly to correspondence in Portuguese.

Rádio Educação Rural de Tefé, Caixa Postal 21, 69470-000 Tefé AM, Brazil. Phone: +55 (97) 3343-3017. Fax: +55 (97) 3343-2663. Email: rert@osite.com.br, or fjoaquim@mandic.com.br. Contact: Thomas Schwamborn, Diretor Administrativo.

Rádio Educadora 6 de Agosto, Rua Coronel Brandão s/n, Bairro Aeroporto, 69930-000 Xapuri AC, Brazil. Phone: +55 (68) 3542-3063. Fax: +55 (68) 3452 2367 (mark to the attention of the station, for forwarding, as this number belongs to the local town council). Contact: Raimare Sombra Cardoso. Replies to correspondence in Portuguese.

Rádio Educativa 6 de Agosto—*see* Rádio Educadora 6 de Agosto, above.

Rádio Educadora (Bragança), Praça das Bandeiras s/n, 68600-000 Bragança PA, Brazil. Phone: +55 (91) 3425-1295. Fax: +55 (91) 3425 1702. Email: fundacaoeducadora@uol.com.br. Contact: Padre Maurício de Souza. $1 or return postage required. Replies to correspondence in Portuguese.

Rádio Educadora (Guajará Mirim), Praça Mário Corrêa No.90, 78957-000 Guajará Mirim RO, Brazil. Phone: +55 (69) 3541-2274. Fax: +55 (69) 3541 6333. Email: radioeducadora@uol.com.br. Contact: Edimilson da Silva. Return postage helpful. Replies to correspondence in Portuguese.

Rádio Educadora (Limeira), Caixa Postal 105, 13480-970 Limeira SP, Brazil; (street address) Rua Prof. Maria Aparecida Martinelli Faveri 988, Jardim Elisa Fumagalli, 13485-316 Limeira SP, Brazil. Email: (Bortolan) bab@zaz.com.br. Web: (streaming audio only) www.educadoraam.com.br. Contact: Bruno Arcaro Bortolan, Gerente; Rosemary Ap. Giratto, Secretária Administrativa. Free stickers.

Rádio Gaúcha, Avenida Ipiranga 1075 - 3º andar, Bairro Azenha, 90160-093 Porto Alegre RS, Brazil. Phone: +55 (51) 3218-6600. Fax: +55 (51) 3218 6680. Email: (listener feedback) reportagem@rdgaucha.com.br; (technical) caio.klein@rdgaucha.com.br. Web: (includes on-demand and streaming audio) www.rdgaucha.com.br. Contact: Caio Klein, Gerente Técnico. Replies to correspondence, preferably in Portuguese. Reception reports should be sent to the attention of "Eng. Caio Klein" at the station address above.

Rádio Gazeta, Avenida Paulista 900, Cerqueira César, 01310-940 São Paulo SP, Brazil. Phone: +55 (11) 3170-5757. Fax: +55 (11) 3170 5630. Email: (Fundação Cásper Líbero parent organization) fcl@fcl.com.br. Web: (Fundação Cásper Líbero parent organization) www.fcl.com.br. Contact: Shakespeare Ettinger, Supervisor Geral de Operação; Bernardo Leite da Costa; José Roberto Mignone Chcibub, Gerente Geral; or Ing. Aníbal Horta Figueiredo. Free stickers. $1 or return postage necessary. Replies to correspondence in Portuguese.

Rádio Globo (Rio de Janeiro), Rua do Russel 434, Glória, 22210-210 Rio de Janeiro RJ, Brazil. Phone: +55 (21) 2555-8282. Fax: +55 (21) 2558 6385. Email: (administration) gerenciaamrio@radioglobo.com.br. Web: (includes streaming audio) http://radioclick.globo.com/globobrasil. Contact: Marcos Libretti, Diretor Geral. Replies irregularly to correspondence in Portuguese. Return postage helpful.

Rádio Globo (São Paulo), Rua das Palmeiras 315, Santa Cecilia, 01226-901 São Paulo SP, Brazil. Phone: +55 (11) 3824-3217. Fax: +55 (11) 3824 3210. Email: (Rapussi) margarete@radioglobo.com.br. Web: (includes streaming audio) http://radioclick.globo.com/globobrasil. Contact: Ademar Dutra, Locutor, "Programa Ademar Dutra"; Margarete Rapussi; Guilherme Viterbo; or José Marques. Replies to correspondence, preferably in Portuguese.

Rádio Guaíba, Rua Caldas Júnior 219 - 2º Andar, 90019-900 Porto Alegre RS, Brazil. Phone: +55 (51) 3215-6222. Email: (administration) diretor@radioguaiba.com.br; (technical) centr altecnica@radioguaiba.com.br. Web: (includes streaming audio) www.radioguaiba.com.br. Contact: Ademar J. Dallanora, Gerente Administrativo. Return postage helpful. Free stickers.

Rádio Guarujá (Florianópolis), Caixa Postal 45, 88000-000 Florianópolis SC, Brazil. Email: guaruja@radioguaruja.com.br. Web: www.radioguaruja.com.br. Contact: Mario Silva, Diretor; Joana Sempre Bom Braz, Assessora de Marketing e Comunicação; or Rosa Michels de Souza. Return postage required. Replies irregularly to correspondence in Portuguese.

NEW YORK OFFICE: 45 West 46 Street, 5th Floor, Manhattan, NY 10036 USA.

Rádio Guarujá (Guarujá SP), Rua José Vaz Porto 175, Vila Santa Rosa, 11431-190 Guarujá SP, Brazil; (technical, including reception reports) A/C Orivaldo Rampazzo, Rua Montenegro 196, Bairro Villa Maia, 11410-040 Guarujá SP, Brazil. Phone: +55 (13) 3386-6092; (listener feedback) +55 (13) 3386-6965. Email: atendimento@radioguaruaam.com.br. Web: www.radioguaruaam.com.br. Contact: Orivaldo Rampazzo, Diretor. Replies to correspondence in Portuguese. Free stickers and station brochure. Operates on 1550 kHz AM, and relayed on shortwave via facilities of former world band stations in the state of São Paulo, which are fed via the Internet.

Rádio Guarujá Paulista—*see* Rádio Guarujá (Guarujá SP), above.

Rádio Inconfidência, Avenida Raja Gabáglia 1666, Luxemburgo, 30350-540 Belo Horizonte MG, Brazil. Phone: +55 (31) 3297-7344. Fax: +55 (31) 3297 7348. Phone/Fax: (Commercial Dept.) +55 (31) 3297-7343. Email: inconfidencia@inconfidencia.com.br. Web: (includes streaming audio) www.inconfidencia.com.br. Contact: Isaias Lansky, Diretor; Manuel Emilio de Lima Torres, Diretor Superintendente, Jairo Antolio Lima, Diretor Artístico; or Eugenio Silva. Free stickers and postcards. May send CD of Brazilian music. $1 or return postage helpful.

Rádio Integração (when operating), Rua de Alagoas 270, Bairro Escola Técnica, 69980-000 Cruzeiro do Sul AC, Brazil. Phone: +55 (68) 3322-4637. Fax: +55 (68) 3322 6511. Email: rtvi@omegasul.com.br. Contact: Albelia Bezerra da Cunha. Return postage helpful.

Rádio Itatiaia, Rua Itatiaia 117, 31210-170 Belo Horizonte MG, Brazil. Fax: +55 (31) 446 2900. Email: itatiaia@itatiaia. com.br. Web: (includes on-demand and streaming audio) www. itatiaia.com.br/am/index.html. Contact: Lúcia Araújo Bessa, Assistente da Diretória; or Claudio Carneiro.

Rádio Jornal "A Crítica" (when operating), Av. André Araujo 1024A, Aleixo, 69060-001 Manaus AM, Brazil. Phone/Fax: +55 (92) 2123-1000. Email: getulio@acritica.com.br. Contact: Getúlio Cetraro.

Rádio Liberal (if reactivated), Av. Nazaré, 319 Nazaré, 66035-170 Belém PA, Brazil. Phone: +55 (91) 3213-1500. Fax: +55 (91) 3224 5240. Email: dirgel@radioliberal.com.br, or radio@radioliberal.com.br. Web: (includes streaming audio) www.radioliberal.com.br. Contact: Hilbert Nascimento.

Rádio Marumby (Curitiba)—see Rádio Novas de Paz.

Rádio Marumby (Florianópolis), Caixa Postal 296, 88010-970 Florianópolis SC, Brazil; (street address) Rua Angelo Laporta 841, 88020-600 Florianópolis SC, Brazil. Web: (includes on-demand audio) www.gmuh.com.br/radio/radio. htm. Contact: Davi Campos, Diretor Artístico; Dr. Cesino Bernardino, Presidente, GMUH; or Jair Albano, Diretor. $1 or return postage required. Free diploma and stickers. Replies to correspondence in Portuguese.

GMUH MISSIONARY PARENT ORGANIZATION: Gideões Missionários da Última Hora—GMUH, Rua Joaquim Nunes 244, 88340-000 Camboriú SC, Brazil; (postal address) Caixa Postal 2004, 88340-000 Camboriú SC, Brazil. Phone: +55 (47) 261-3232. Email: gmuh@gmuh.com.br. Web: www.gmuh.com.br.

Rádio Meteorologia Paulista, Rua Capitão João Marques 89, Jardim Centenário, 14940-000 Ibitinga, São Paulo SP, Brazil; or Caixa Postal 91, 14940-000 Ibitinga SP, Brazil. Phone: +55 (16) 242-6378/79/80. Fax: +55 (16) 242 5056. Email: radioibitinga@radioibitinga.com.br. Web: (includes streaming audio from Ternura FM, relayed several hours each day by Rádio Meteorologia Paulista) www.radioibitinga.com.br/meteorologia. Contact: Roque de Rosa, Diretor. Replies to correspondence in Portuguese. $1 or return postage required.

Rádio Missões da Amazônia, Travessa Dr. Lauro Sodré 299, 68250-000 Óbidos PA, Brazil. Phone: +55 (93) 3547-2827. Fax: +55 (93) 3547-1699. Contact: Ronald Santos, Diretor. Part of the Rede Boas Novas network (www.rbn.org.br). Return postage required. Replies occasionally to correspondence in Portuguese.

Rádio Morimoto (if reactivated), Rua Costa e Silva 1297, Vila Jotão, 78964-140 Ji-Paraná RO, Brazil. Phone/Fax: +55 69 3421-0054. Email: radiojiparana@bol.com.br. Contact: Joel Nogueira.

Rádio Mundial, Av. Paulista 2198-Térreo, Cerqueira César, 01310-300 São Paulo SP, Brazil. Phone: +55 (11) 3016 5999. Email: (general) radiomundial@radiomundial.com; (administration) administrativo@radiomundial.com. Web: (includes streaming audio) www.radiomundial.com.br. Contact: (non-technical) Luci Rothschild de Abreu, Diretora Presidente.

REDE CBS PARENT ORGANIZATION: Rede CBS, Av. Paulista, 2200 - 14° andar, Cerqueira César, 01310-300 São Paulo SP, Brazil. Phone: +55 (11) 3016 5999. Fax: +55 (11) 3016 5980. Email: comercial@redecbs.com.br. Web: www.redecbs.com.br.

Rádio Municipal, Avenida Álvaro Maia s/n, 69750-000 São Gabriel da Cachoeira AM, Brazil. Phone/Fax: +55 (97) 3471-1768. Email: rmunicipalsgc@yahoo.com.br. Contact: Oscar de Jesus Rodrigues. Return postage necessary. Replies to correspondence in Portuguese. Formerly Rádio Nacional de São Gabriel da Cachoeira, prior to the station's transfer from Radiobrás to the local municipality.

Rádio Nacional da Amazônia, Caixa Postal 258, 70359-970 Brasília-DF, Brazil; or SCRN 702/703 - Edif. Radiobrás - Subsolo, 70710-750 Brasília-DF, Brazil. Phone: +55 (61) 327-1981. Email: nacionaloc@radiobras.gov.br. Web: (includes streaming audio) www.radiobras.gov.br (click on "Rádio Nacional"). Contact: (technical) Taís Ladeira de Madeiros, Chefe da Divisão de Ondas Curtas da Radiobrás. Free stickers. Will occasionally verify reception reports if a prepared card is included.

Rádio Nacional de Tabatinga (if reactivated), A/C Prefeitura Municipal de Tabatinga, 69640-000 Tabatinga AM, Brazil. Phone: +55 (97) 3412-4078. Contact: Rui Pacifico Barbosa.

Rádio Nacional do Brasil—Radiobrás (External Service), Caixa Postal 08840, 70912-970 Brasília-DF, Brazil. Phone: +55 (61) 327-4124. Fax: +55 (61) 327 1377. Email: radiona cionaldobrasil@radiobras.gov.br. Web: (includes on-demand audio) www.radiobras.gov.br (click on "Rádio Nacional"). Replies to correspondence in Portuguese, and verifies reception reports. Returned to the air in August 2003 after several years off the air.

Rádio Novas de Paz, Avenida Paraná 1896, 82510-000 Curitiba PR, Brazil; or Caixa Postal 22, 80000-000 Curitiba PR, Brazil. Phone: +55 (41) 257-4109. Contact: João Falavinha Ienzen, Gerente. $1 or return postage required. Replies irregularly to correspondence in Portuguese.

Rádio Novo Tempo, Caixa Postal 146, 79002-970 Campo Grande MS, Brazil; (street address) Rua Amando de Oliveira 135, Bairro Amambaí, 79005-370 Campo Grande MS, Brazil. Email: novotempo.ms@usb.org.br; (Ramos) ellen.ramos@usb. org.br. Web: www.asm.org.br (click on "Rádio Novo Tempo"). Contact: Ellen Ramos, Locutora; or Pastor Paulo Melo. Return postage required. Replies to correspondence in Portuguese. A station of the Seventh Day Adventists.

Rádio Pioneira de Teresina, Rua 24 de Janeiro 150 sul, 64001-230 Teresina PI, Brazil. Phone: +55 (86) 3221-8121. Fax: +55 (86) 3221 8122. Email: (general) pioneira@radiopioneira. am.br; (management) gerencia@radiopioneira.am.br; (comments on programs) programacao@radiopioneira.am.br. Web: www.radiopioneira.am.br. Contact: Rosemiro Robinson da Costa. $1 or return postage required. Replies slowly to correspondence in Portuguese.

Rádio Record, Caixa Postal 7920, 04084-002 São Paulo SP, Brazil. Email: radiorecord@rederecord.com.br. Web: (includes streaming audio) www.rederecord.com.br/radiorecord. Contact: Mário Luíz Catto, Diretor Geral. Free stickers. Return postage or $1 required. Replies occasionally to correspondence in Portuguese.

Rádio Relógio, Rua Paramopama 131, Ribeira, Ilha do Governador, 21930-110 Rio de Janeiro RJ, Brazil. Phone: +55 (21) 2467-0201. Fax: +55 (21) 2467 4656. Email: radiorelogio@ig. com.br. Contact: Olindo Coutinho, Diretor Geral; or Renato Castro. Replies occasionally to correspondence in Portuguese. Relays FM station Nossa Rádio.

NOSSA RÁDIO: Web: (includes program schedule) http://nossaradio.ongrace.com/rj; (streaming audio) http://streaming. ongrace.com.br/radiorj.

Rádio Ribeirão Preto (if reactivated), Avenida Jerônimo Gonçalves 640, 14010-040 Ribeirão Preto SP, Brazil. Replies to correspondence in Portuguese.

Rádio Rio Mar, Rua José Clemente 500, Centro, 69010-070 Manaus AM, Brazil. Phone: +55 (92) 3633-2295. Fax: +55 (92) 3232 5020. Email: decom@click21.com.br. Contact: Martin James Lauman. Replies to correspondence in Portuguese. $1 or return postage helpful.

Rádio Roraima—see Rádio Difusora Roraima.

Rádio Rural, Avenida São Sebastião 622 - Bloco A, 68005-090 Santarém PA, Brazil. Phone: +55 (93) 3523-1006. Fax: +55 (93) 3523 2685. Email: comrural@netsan.com.br, or edilrural@icabo.com.br. Contact: Padre Edilberto Moura Sena, Diretor Executivo. Replies slowly to correspondence in Portuguese. Free stickers. Return postage or $1 required.

Rádio Senado, Caixa Postal 070-747, 70359-970 Brasília DF, Brazil; (physical address) Praça dos Três Poderes, Anexo II - Bloco B - Térreo, 70165-900 Brasília DF, Brazil. Phone: (general) +55 (61) 311-4691, +55 (61) 311-1257; (technical) +55 (61) 311-1285; (shortwave department) +55 (61) 311-1238. Fax: (general) +55 (61) 311 4238. Email: radio@senado.gov.br; (Fabiano) max@senado.gov.br. Web: www.senado.gov.br/radio/ondascurtas.asp; (streaming audio from FM Service, partly relayed on shortwave) mms://bombadil.senado.gov.br/wmtencoder/radio.wmv. Contact: Max Fabiano, Diretor; (technical) José Carlos Sigmaringa, Coordenador do Núcleo de Ondas Curtas.

Rádio Timbira (if reactivated), Avenida Jerônimo de Albuquerque 73, Cohafuma, 65071-750 São Luís MA, Brazil. Phone: +55 98 3236-9419, Fax: +55 98 3226 8896. Email: timbira.raimundofilho@bol.com.br. Contact: Raimundo Nonato R. Filho. Inactive on shortwave for several years, but projected to return sometime in 2006.

Rádio Trans Mundial, Caixa Postal 18300, 04626 970 São Paulo SP, Brazil; (street address) Rua Épiro 110, 04635-030 São Paulo SP, Brazil. Phone/Fax: +55 (11) 5031-3533. Email: (general) rtm@transmundial.com.br; (technical) tecnica@transmundial.com.br; ("Amigos do Rádio" DX-program) amigosdoradio@transmundial.com.br. Web: (includes streaming audio) www.transmundial.com.br. Contact: José Carlos de Santos, Diretor; or Rudolf Grimm, programa "Amigos do Rádio." Free stickers, postcards, bookmarkers or other small gifts. Sells religious books and CDs of religious music (from hymns to bossa nova). Prices, in local currency, can be found at the Website (click on "Publicações"). Programming comes from São Paulo, but transmitter site is located in Santa Maria, Rio Grande do Sul.

Rádio Tupi, Rua João Negrão 595, Centro, 80010-200, Curitiba PR, Brazil. Phone: +55 (41) 323-1353. Contact: (technical) Eng.Latuf Aurani (who is based in São Paulo). Relays "Voz de Libertação" (see). Rarely replies, and only to correspondence in Portuguese.

Rádio Vale do Rio Madeira (if activated), Rua Júlio de Oliveira 1323, São Pedro, 69800-000 Humaitá AM, Brazil. Phone/Fax: +55 (97) 373-2073. Email: radiovrm@dnknet.com.br. Contact: Izael Feitoza. Although assigned a shortwave frequency years ago, the station never used it. Now, the station is again proposing to operate on shortwave, but only if it is granted a new frequency, for which it has already applied. In the meantime, broadcasts continue on 670 kHz AM.

Rádio Vale do Xingu, Rua Primeira de Janeiro 1359, Catedral, 68371-020 Altamira PA, Brazil. Phone/Fax: +55 (93) 3515-1182, +55 (93) 3515-4899, +55 (93) 3515-4411. Email: radioetv@valedoxingu.com.br. Contact: Miguel Ceccin.

Rádio Verdes Florestas, Fundação Verdes Florestas, Rua Mário Lobão 81, 69980-000 Cruzeiro do Sul AC, Brazil; (transmitter location) Estrado do Aeroporto, km 02, Bairro Nossa Senhora das Graças, Cruzeiro do Sul AC, Brazil. Phone/Fax: +55 (68) 3322-3309, +55 (68) 3322-2634. Email: verdesflorestas@yahoo.com.br. Contact: José Graci Soares Rezende. Return postage required. Replies occasionally to correspondence in Portuguese.

Rádio Voz do Coração Imaculado (when operating), Caixa Postal 354, 75001-970 Anápolis GO, Brazil; (street address) Rua Barão de Cotegipe s/n, Centro, 75001-970 Anápolis GO, Brazil. Email: radioimaculada@immacolata.com. Web: (includes streaming audio) www.immacolata.com/radiovoz. Contact: P. Domingos M. Esposito A religious station which started shortwave operation in 1999 with the transmitter formerly used by Rádio Carajá. Operation tends to be irregular, as the station is funded entirely from donations.

Super Rádio Alvorada —see Rádio Alvorada (Rio Branco).

Voz de Libertação. Ubiquitous programming originating from the "Deus é Amor" Pentecostal church's Rádio Universo (1300 kHz) in São Bernardo do Campo, São Paulo, and aired over several shortwave stations, especially Rádio Tupi, Curitiba (see). Streaming audio is available at the "Deus é Amor" Website, www.ipda.org.br.

Voz do Coração Imaculado—see Rádio Voz do Coração Imaculado.

BULGARIA   World Time +2 (+3 midyear)

Radio Bulgaria

NONTECHNICAL AND TECHNICAL: P.O. Box 900, BG-1000, Sofia, Bulgaria; or (street address) 4 Dragan Tsankov Blvd., 1040 Sofia, Bulgaria. Phone: (general) +359 (2) 985-241; (Managing Director) +359 (2) 854-604. Fax: (general, usually weekdays only) +359 (2) 871 060, +359 (2) 871 061 or +359 (2) 650 560; (Managing Director) +359 (2) 946 1576; +359 (2) 988 5103; (Frequency Manager) +359 (2) 963 4464. Email: (English program and schedule information) english@bnr.bg (same format for other languages, e.g. french@...; spanish@...). Web: (includes on-demand audio, plus streaming audio from domestice services not aired on shortwave) www.bnr.bg. Contact: (general) Mrs. Iva Delcheva, English Section; Svilen Stoicheff, Head of English Section; (administration and technical) Anguel H. Nedyalkov, Managing Director; (technical) Atanas Tzenov, Director. Replies regularly, but sometimes slowly. Return postage helpful. Verifies email reports with QSL cards. For concerns about frequency usage, contact BTC, below, with copies to Messrs. Nedyalkov and Tzenov of Radio Bulgaria.

FREQUENCY MANAGEMENT AND TRANSMISSION OPERATIONS: Bulgarian Telecommunications Company (BTC), Ltd., 8 Totleben Blvd., 1606 Sofia, Bulgaria. Phone: +359 (2) 88-00-75. Fax: +359 (2) 87 58 85 or +359 (2) 80 25 80. Contact: Roumen Petkov, Frequency Manager; or Mrs. Margarita Krasteva, Radio Regulatory Department.

Radio Varna, 22 Primorski blvd, 9000 Varna, Bulgaria. Phone: +359 (52) 602-802. Fax: +359 (52) 664 411. Email: bnr@radiovarna.com. Web: (includes streaming audio from the domestic service, not aired on shortwave) www.radiovarna.com. Contact: (technical) Kostadin Kovachev, Chief Engineer.

BURKINA FASO   World Time exactly

Radiodiffusion-Télévision Burkina, B.P. 7029, Ouagadougou, Burkina Faso. Phone: +226 310-441. Contact: Tahéré Ouedraogo, Le Chef des Programmes. Replies irregularly to correspondence in French. IRC or return postage helpful.

BURMA—see MYANMAR.

BURUNDI   World Time +2

La Voix de la Révolution, B.P. 1900, Bujumbura, Burundi. Phone: +257 22-37-42. Fax: +257 22 65 47 or +257 22 66 13.

Email: rtnb@cbinf.com. Contact: (general) Grégoire Baram-pumba, Head of News Section; or Frederic Havugiyaremye, Journaliste; (administration) Gérard Mfuranzima, Le Directeur de la Radio; or Didace Baranderetse, Directeur Général de la Radio; (technical) Abraham Makuza, Directeur Technique. $1 required.

CAMBODIA   World Time +7

National Radio of Cambodia (when operating)
STATION ADDRESS: 106 Preah Kossamak Street, Monivong Boulevard, Phnom Penh, Cambodia. Phone: +855 (23) 423-369 or +855 (23) 422-869. Fax: + 855 (23) 427 319. Email: vocri@vocri.org. Web: www.vocri.org. Contact: (general) Miss Hem Bory, English Announcer; Kem Yan, Chief of External Relations; or Touch Chhatha, Producer, Art Department; (administration) In Chhay, Chief of Overseas Service; Som Sarun, Chief of Home Service; Van Sunheng, Deputy Director General, Cambodian National Radio and Television; or Ieng Muli, Minister of Information; (technical) Oum Phin, Chief of Technical Department. Free program schedule. Replies irregularly and slowly. Do not include stamps, currency, IRCs or dutiable items in envelope. Registered letters stand a much better chance of getting through. Has been increasingly off the air in recent years.

CANADA   World Time –3:30 (–2:30 midyear) Newfoundland; –4 (–3 midyear) Atlantic; –5 (–4 midyear) Eastern, including Québec and Ontario; –6 (–5 midyear) Central; except Saskatchewan; –6 Saskatchewan; –7 (–6 midyear) Mountain; –8 (–7 midyear) Pacific, including Yukon.

Canadian Broadcasting Corporation (CBC)—English Programs, P.O. Box 500, Station A, Toronto, Ontario, M5W 1E6, Canada. Phone: (toll-free, Canada only) +1 (866) 306-4636; (Audience Relations) +1 (416) 205-3700. Email: cbcinput@toronto.cbc.ca. Web: (includes on-demand and streaming audio) www.radio.cbc.ca. CBC prepares some of the programs heard over Radio Canada International (*see*).
LONDON NEWS BUREAU: CBC, 43-51 Great Titchfield Street, London W1P 8DD, United Kingdom. Phone: +44 (20) 7412-9200. Fax: +44 (20) 7631 3095.
PARIS NEWS BUREAU: CBC, 17 avenue Matignon, F-75008 Paris, France. Phone: +33 (1) 4421-1515. Fax: +33 (1) 4421 1514.
WASHINGTON NEWS BUREAU: CBC, National Press Building, Suite 500, 529 14th Street NW, Washington DC 20045 USA. Phone: +1 (202) 383-2900. Contact: Jean-Louis Arcand, David Hall or Susan Murray.
Canadian Broadcasting Corporation (CBC)—French Programs, Société Radio-Canada, C.P. 6000, succ. centre-ville, Montréal, Québec, H3C 3A8, Canada. Phone: (Audience Relations) +1 (514) 597-6000. Web: (includes on-demand and streaming audio) www.radio-canada.ca. Welcomes correspondence, but may not reply due to shortage of staff. CBC prepares some of the programs heard over Radio Canada International (*see*).
CBC Northern Québec Shortwave Service—*see* Radio Canada International, below.
CFRX-CFRB
MAIN ADDRESS: 2 St. Clair Avenue West, Toronto, Ontario, M4V 1L6, Canada. Phone:(main switchboard) +1 (416) 924-5711; (talk shows switchboard) +1 (416) 872-1010; (news centre) +1 (416) 924-6717. Fax: (main fax line) +1 (416) 872 8683; (CFRB news fax line) +1 (416) 323 6816. Email: (comments on pro-grams) cfrbcomments@cfrb.com; (News Director) news@cfrb.com; (general, nontechnical) info@cfrb.com; or opsmngr@cfrb.com. Web: (includes on-demand and streaming audio) www.cfrb.com. Contact: (nontechnical) Carlo Massaro, Information Officer; or Steve Kowch, Operations Manager. Reception reports should be sent to the verification address, below.
VERIFICATION ADDRESS: Ontario DX Association, 155 Main St. N., Apt. 313, Newmarket, Ontario, L3Y 8C2, Canada. Email: odxa@rogers.com. Web: www.odxa.on.ca. Contact: Steve Canney, VA3SC.
CFVP-CKMX, AM 1060, Standard Broadcasting, P.O. Box 2750, Station 'M', Calgary, Alberta, T2P 4P8, Canada. Phone: (general) +1 (403) 240-5800; (news) +1 (403) 240-5844; (technical) +1 (403) 240-5867. Fax: (general and technical) +1 (403) 240 5801; (news) +1 (403) 246 7099. Contact: (general) Gary Russell, General Manager; or Beverley Van Tighem, Executive Assistant; (technical) Ken Pasolli, Technical Director.
CHU. Radio Station CHU, National Research Council of Canada, 1200 Montreal Road, Bldg M-36, Ottawa, Ontario, K1A 0R6, Canada. Phone: +1 (613) 993-5186. Fax: +1 (613) 952 1394. Email: radio.chu@nrc.ca. Web: http://inms-ienm.nrc-cnrc.gc.ca/time_services/shortwave_broadcasts_e.html. Contact: Dr. Rob Douglas; Dr. Jean-Simon Boulanger, Group Leader; or Ray Pelletier, Technical Officer. Official standard frequency and World Time station for Canada on 3330, 7335 and 14670 kHz. Brochure available upon request. Those with a personal computer, Bell 103 compatible modem and appropriate software can get the exact time, from CHU's cesium clock, via the telephone; details available upon request, or direct from the Website. Verifies reception reports with a QSL card.
CKZN, CBC Newfoundland and Labrador, P.O. Box 12010, Station 'A', St. John's, Newfoundland, A1B 3T8, Canada. Phone: +1 (709) 576-5155. Fax: +1 (709) 576 5099. Email: (administration) radiomgt@stjohns.cbc.ca; (engineer) keith_durnford@cbc.ca. Web: (includes on-demand audio) www.stjohns.cbc.ca; (streaming audio) www.cbc.ca/listen/index.html# (click on "St. John's"). Contact: (general) Heather Elliott, Communications Officer; (technical) Shawn R. Williams, Manager, Transmission and Distribution; Keith Durnford, Supervisor, Transmission Operations; Terry Brett, Transmitter Department; or Rosemary Sampson. Free CBC sticker and verification card with the history of Newfoundland included. Don't enclose money, stamps or IRCs with correspondence, as they will only have to be returned. Relays CBN (St. John's, 640 kHz) except at 1000-1330 World Time (one hour earlier in summer) when programming comes from CFGB Goose Bay.
CFGB ADDRESS: CBC Radio, Box 1029 Station C, Happy Valley, Goose Bay, Labrador, Newfoundland A0P 1C0, Canada. Email: (program relayed via CKZN) labmorns@cbc.ca.
CKZU-CBU, CBC, P.O. Box 4600, Vancouver, British Columbia, V6B 4A2, Canada—for verification of reception reports, mark the envelope, "Attention: Engineering." Phone: (general) +1 (604) 662-6000; (toll-free, U.S. and Canada only) 1-800-961-6161; (engineering) +1 (604) 662-6060. Fax: +1 (604) 662 6350. Email: (general) webmaster@vancouver.cbc.ca; (Newbury) newburyd@vancouver.cbc.ca. Web: (includes on-demand audio) www.vancouver.cbc.ca; (streaming audio) www.cbc.ca/listen/index.html# (click on "Vancouver"). Contact: (general) Public Relations; (technical) Dave Newbury, Transmission Engineer.
Église du Christ, 2500-2510 rue Charland, Montréal, Québec, H1Z 1C5, Canada. Phone: +1 (514) 387-6163. Fax: +1 (514) 387-1153. Web: www3.sympatico.ca/micdan. Broadcasts via a transmitter in the United Kingdom.

High Adventure Gospel Communication Ministries—*see* Bible Voice Broadcasting, United Kingdom.

🔲**Radio Canada International**
NOTE: (CBC Northern Québec Service) The following P. O Box 6000 postal address and street address are also valid for the Northern Québec Service, provided that you mention the name of the service and "17ᵗʰ Floor" on the envelope. RCI does not issue technical verifications for Northern Québec Service transmissions.
MAIN OFFICE: P.O. Box 6000, Montréal, Québec, H3C 3A8, Canada; or (street address) 1400 boulevard René-Lévesque Est, Montréal, Québec, H2L 2M2, Canada. Phone: (general) +1 (514) 597-7500; (Audience Relations, Bill Westenhaver) +1 (514) 597-5899. Fax: (Audience Relations) +1 (514) 597 7760. Email: info@rcinet.ca. Web: (includes streaming and on-demand audio) www.rcinet.ca. Contact: (general and technical verifications) Bill Westenhaver, Audience Relations; Stéphane Parent, Producer/Host "Le courrier mondial"; or Ian Jones, Producer/Host "The Maple Leaf Mailbag"; (administration) Jean Larin, Director. Free stickers, antenna booklet & lapel pins on request
TRANSMISSION OFFICE, INTERNATIONAL SERVICES, CBC TRANSMISSION: Room: B52-70, 1400 boulevard René-Lévesque Est, Montréal, Québec, H2L 2M2, Canada. Phone: +1 (514) 597-7618/19. Fax: +1 (514) 284 2052. Email: (Théorêt) gerald theoret@radio-canada.ca; (Bouliane) jacques_bouliane@radio-canada.ca. Contact: (general) Gérald Théorêt, Frequency Manager, CBC Transmission Management; or Ms. Nicole Vincent, Frequency Management; (administration) Jacques Bouliane, Senior Manager, International Services. This office only for informing about transmitter-related problems (interference, modulation quality, etc.), especially by fax. Verifications not given out at this office; requests for verification should be sent to the main office, above.
TRANSMITTER SITE: CBC, P.O. Box 6131, Sackville New Brunswick, E4L 1G6, Canada. Phone: +1 (506) 536-2690/1. Fax: +1 (506) 536 2342. Contact: Raymond Bristol, Sackville Plant Manager, CBC Transmission. All correspondence not concerned with transmitting equipment should be directed to the appropriate address in Montréal, above. Free tours given during normal working hours.
MONITORING STATION: P.O. Box 460, Station Main Stittsville, Ontario, K2S 1A6, Canada. Phone: +1 (613) 831-4802. Fax: +1 (613) 831 0343. Email: derek.williams@cbc.ca. Contact: Derek Williams, Manager of Monitoring.
Shortwave Classroom, R. Tait McKenzie Public School, 175 Paterson Street, Almonte, Ontario, K0A 1A0, Canada. Phone: +1 (613) 256-8248. Fax: +1 (613) 256 4791. Email: neil.carletonn@ucdsb.on.ca. Contact: Neil Carleton, VE3NCE, Editor & Publisher. *The Shortwave Classroom* newsletter was published three times per year as a nonprofit volunteer project for teachers around the world that use shortwave listening in the classroom, or as a club activity, to teach about global perspectives, media studies, world geography, languages, social studies and other subjects. Although no longer published, a set of back issues with articles and classroom tips from teachers around the globe is available for $10.

CENTRAL AFRICAN REPUBLIC   World Time +1

Radio Centrafrique (when operating), Radiodiffusion-Télévision Centrafricaine, B.P. 940, Bangui, Central African Republic. Contact: (technical) Directeur des Services Techniques. Replies

on rare occasions to correspondence in French. Return postage required.
🔲**Radio Ndeke Luka** (when operating), PNUD, B.P. 872, Bangui, Central African Republic. Email: (including reception reports) ndekeluka@hotmail.com. Contact: Cédrine Beney, Chargée de projet. Replies to correspondence in French, and may reply in French to correspondence in English. The station is managed by the Fondation Hirondelle, based in Switzerland, and operates under the aegis of the United Nations, in partnership with the UNDP (United Nations Development Programme). The main studio is located in Bangui. Broadcasts domestically on FM, and produces a program aired irregularly via shortwave facilities in the United Kingdom or the United Arab Emirates.
FONDATION HIRONDELLE: 3 Rue Traversière, CH 1018-Lausanne, Switzerland. Phone: +41 (21) 647-2805. Fax: +41 (21) 647 4469. Email info@hirondelle.org. Web: (includes on-demand news bulletins from Radio Ndeke Luka) www.hirondelle.org. Verifies reception reports.

CHAD   World Time +1

Radiodiffusion Nationale Tchadienne—N'djamena, B.P. 892, N'Djamena, Chad. Contact: Djimadoum Ngoka Kilamian; or Ousmane Mahamat. Two IRCs or return postage required. Replies slowly to correspondence in French.

CHILE   World Time –3 (–4 midyear)

Radio Esperanza
OFFICE: Casilla 830, Temuco, Chile. Phone: +56 (45) 213 790. Phone/Fax: +56 (45) 367-070. Email: esperanza@telsur.cl. Contact: (general) Juanita Cárcamo, Departmento de Programación; Eleazar Jara, Dpto. de Programación; Ramón P. Woerner K., Publicidad; or Alberto Higueras Martínez, Locutor; (verifications) Rodolfo Campos, Director; Juanita Carmaco M., Dpto. de Programación; (technical) Juan Luis Puentes, Dpto. Técnico. Free pennants, stickers, bookmarks and tourist information. Two IRCs, $1 or 2 U.S. stamps appreciated. Replies, often slowly, to correspondence in Spanish or English.
STUDIO: Calle Luis Durand 03057, Temuco, Chile. Phone/Fax: +56 (45) 240-161.
Radio Parinacota, Casilla 82, Arica, Chile. Phone: +56 (58) 245-889. Phone/Fax: +56 (58) 245 986. Email: rparinacota@latinmail.com. Contact: Tomislav Simunovich Gran, Director.
🔲**Radio Voz Cristiana**
TRANSMISSION FACILITIES: Casilla 395, Talagante, Santiago, Chile. Phone: (engineering) +56 (2) 855-7046. Fax: +56 (2) 855 7053. Email: (Chief Engineer) antonio@vozcristiana.cl; (Frequency Manager) andrewflynn@christianvision.com; (administration) admin@vozcristiana.cl. Contact: Antonio Reyes, Chief Engineer; Gisela Vergara, Senior Transmission Engineer. Free program and frequency schedules. Sometimes sends small souvenirs. All QSL requests should be sent to the Miami address, below.
PROGRAM PRODUCTION: P.O. Box 2889, Miami FL 33144 USA; (street address) 15485 Eagle Nest Lane, Suite 220, Miami Lakes FL 33014 USA. Phone: +1 (305) 231-7704; (Portuguese Service) +1 (305) 231-7742. Email: (Gallardo) info@vozcristiana.com; (listener feedback) comentarios@vozcristiana.com. Web: (includes streaming audio) www.vozcristiana.com. Contact: (administration) Juan Mark Gallardo, Gerente de Programación. Verifies reception reports.
ENGINEERING DEPARTMENT: Ryder Street, West Bromwich, West Midlands B70 0EJ, United Kingdom. Phone: +44 (121)

522-6087. Fax: +44 (121) 522 6083. Email: andrewflynn@christ ianvision.com. Contact: Andrew Flynn, Head of Engineering.

CHINA   World Time +8; still nominally +6 ("Urümqi Time") in the Xinjiang Uighur Autonomous Region, but in practice +8 is observed there, as well.

NOTE: If a Chinese regional station does not respond to your correspondence within four months, send your reception reports to China Radio International (*see*) which will verify them. CRI apparently no longer forwards correspondence to regional stations, as it sometimes did in the past.

Central People's Broadcasting Station (CPBS)—China National Radio (Zhongyang Renmin Guangbo Diantai), P.O. Box 4501, Beijing 100866, China. Phone: +86 (10) 6851-2435 or +86 (10) 6851-5522. Fax: +86 (10) 6851 6630. Email: cn@cnradio.com; (services for Taiwan) cnrtw@cnrtw.com. Web: (includes on-demand and streaming audio) www.cnradio. com; (services for Taiwan) www.nihaotw.com. Contact: Wang Changquan, Audience Department, China National Radio. Tape recordings of music and news $5 plus postage. CPBS T-shirts $10 plus postage; also sells ties and other items with CPBS logo. No credit cards. Free stickers, pennants and other small souvenirs. Return postage helpful. Responds regularly to correspondence in English or Standard Chinese (Mandarin). Although in recent years this station has officially been called "China National Radio" in English-language documents, all on-air identifications in Standard Chinese continue to be "Zhongyang Renmin Guangbo Diantai" (Central People's Broadcasting Station). To quote from the Website of China's State Administration of Radio, Film and TV: "The station moved to Beijing on March 25, 1949. It was renamed the Central People's Broadcasting Station (it [sic] English name was changed to China National Radio later on)..."

China Business Radio—the Second Program of Central People's Broadcasting Station (see).

China Huayi Broadcasting Company—*see* China Huayi Broadcasting Corporation, below.

China Huayi Broadcasting Corporation, P.O. Box 251, Fu-zhou, Fujian 350001, China. Email: (station) hanyu@chbcnews. com; (Yuan Jia) chrisyuanjia@sohu.com; Web: (includes streaming audio) www.chbcnews.com. Contact: Lin Hai Chun, Announcer; Yuan Jia, Program Manager; or Wu Gehong. Replies to correspondence in English or Chinese. Although the station refers to itself in English as China Huayi Broadcasting Company, the correct translation of the Chinese name is China Huayi Broadcasting Corporation.

VERIFICATION OF RECEPTION REPORTS: Although verifications are sometimes received direct from the station, reception reports are best sent to the QSL Manager: Qiao Xiaoli, Feng Jing Xin Cun 3-4-304, Changshu, Jiangsu 215500, China. Recordings accepted, and return postage (IRC) required for a QSL card. Email: 2883752@163.com, dxswl@21cn.com.

China National Radio—*see* Central People's Broadcasting Station (CPBS), above.

China Radio International

MAIN OFFICE, NON-CHINESE LANGUAGES SERVICE: 16A Shi-jingshan Street, Beijing 100040, China; or P.O. Box 4216, CRI-2 Beijing 100040 China. Phone: (Director's office) +86 (10) 6889-1625; (Audience Relations.) +86 (10) 6889-1617 or +86 (10) 6889-1652; (English newsroom/current affairs) +86 (10) 6889-1619; (Technical Director) +86 (10) 6609-2577. Fax: (Director's office) +86 (10) 6889 1582; (English Service) +86 (10) 6889 1378 or +86 (10) 6889 1379; (audience relations) +86 (10) 6889

3175; (administration) +86 (10) 6851 3174; (German Service) +86 (10) 6889 2053; (Spanish Service) +86 (10) 6889 1909. Email: (English) crieng@cri.com.cn, yinglian@cri.com.cn, or garden@cri.com.cn; (Listener's Liason) gaohuiying@crifm.com; (English, technical, including reception reports) crieng@crifm. com; (Chinese) chn@cri.com.cn; (French) crifra@cri.com.cn; (German) ger@cri.com.cn (*see* also the entry for the Berlin Bureau, below); (Japanese) jap@cri.com.cn; (Portuguese) cripor@cri.com.cn; (Spanish) spa@cri.com.cn. Web: (includes on-demand and streaming audio) www.chinabroadcast.cn; (English, official) http://en.chinabroadcast.cn; (English, unofficial, but regularly updated) http://pw2.netcom.com/~jleq/cri1. htm. Contact: Yang Lei, Director, English Service; Ms. Wang Anjing, Director of Audience Relations, English Service; Ying Lian, English Service; Gao Huiying, Editor, Listener's Liason; Shang Chunyan, "Listener's Garden"; Yu Meng, Editor; (administration) Li Dan, President, China Radio International; Xia Jixuan, Vice President; Wang Gengnian Director General; Xia Jixuan, Chen Minyi, Chao Tieqi and Wang Dongmei, Deputy Directors, China Radio International; Xin Liancai, Director International Relations, China Radio International. Free bi-monthly *Messenger* newsletter for loyal listeners, pennants, stickers, desk calendars, pins and handmade papercuts. Every year, China Radio International holds contests and quizzes, with the overall winner getting a free trip to China. T-shirts for $8. Two-volume, 820-page set of *Day-to-Day Chinese* language-lesson books $15, including postage worldwide; a 155-page book, *Learn to Speak Chinese: Sentence by Sentence*, plus two cassettes for $15. Two Chinese music tapes for $15. Various other books (on arts, medicine, Chinese idioms etc.) in English available from Audience Relations Department, English Service, China Radio International, 100040 Beijing, China. Payment by postal money order to Mr. Li Yi. Every year, the Audience Relations Department will renew the mailing list of the *Messenger* newsletter. CRI is also relayed via shortwave transmitters in Canada, Cuba, France, French Guiana, Mali, Russia and Spain.

ARLINGTON NEWS BUREAU: 2000 South Eads Street APT#712, Arlington VA 22202 USA. Phone: +1 (703) 521-8689. Contact: Mr. Yongjing Li.

BERLIN BUREAU: Berliner Büro, Gürtelstr. 32 B, D-10247 Berlin, Germany. Phone: +49 (30) 2966-8998. Fax: +49 (30) 2966 8997. Email: deyubu@hotmail.com. Correspondence to CRI's German Service can be sent to this office.

CHINA (HONG KONG) NEWS BUREAU: 387 Queen's Road East, Room 1503, Hong Kong, China. Phone: +852 2834-0384. Contact: Ms. He Jincao.

JERUSALEM NEWS BUREAU: Flat 16, Hagdud Ha'ivri 12, Je-rusalem 92345, Israel. Phone: +972 (2) 566-6084. Contact: Ms. Liu Suyun.

LONDON NEWS BUREAU: 13B Clifton Gardens, Golders Green, London NW11 7ER, United Kingdom. Phone: +44 (20) 8458-6943. Contact: Ms. Wu Manling.

NEW YORK NEWS BUREAU: 630 First Avenue #35K, New York NY 10016 USA. Fax: +1 (212) 889 2076. Contact: Mr Qian Jun.

SYDNEY NEWS BUREAU: Unit 53, Block A15 Herbert Street, St. Leonards NSW 2065, Australia. Phone: +61 (2) 9436-1493. Contact: Mr. Yang Binyuan.

WASHINGTON BUREAU: 1600 South Eads Street, # 1005N, Arlington VA 22202 USA. Phone: +1 (703) 486-0330. Fax: +1 (703) 521 8689. Email: crius@comcast.net. Contact: Qinduo Xu, Chief Correspondent.

SAN FRANCISCO OFFICE, SCHEDULES: 2654 17th Avenue, San Francisco CA 94116 USA. Phone: +1 (415) 564-9968. Email: GPoppin@aol.com. Contact: George Poppin. This address,

China's vast expanse includes rugged mountain crags, including this gorge that thrives off sightseers.
M. Guha

a volunteer office, only provides CRI schedules to listeners. All other correspondence should be sent directly to the main office in Beijing.

FREQUENCY PLANNING DIVISION: Radio and Television of People's Republic of China, 2 Fuxingmenwai Street, Beijing 100866, China; or P.O. Box 2144, Beijing 100866, China. Phone: (Yang Minmin) +86 (10) 8609-2064; or (Zheng Shuguang & Pang Junhua) +86 (10) 8069-2120. Fax: +86 (10) 6609 2176. Email: (Yang Minmin) pdc@abrs.chinasartft. Contact: Ms. Yang Minmin, Manager, Frequency Coordination; Mr. Zheng Shuguang, Frequency Manager; Mrs. Ling Li Wen, Frequency Manager; or Ms. Pang Junhua, Frequency Manager.

MAIN OFFICE, CHINESE LANGUAGES SERVICE. China Radio International, Beijing 100040, China. Prefers correspondence in Chinese (Mandarin).

MONITORING CENTER: 2 Fuxingmenwai Street, Beijing 100866, China or P.O Box 4502 Beijing 100866, China. Phone: +86 (10) 8609-1745/6. Fax: +86 (10) 8609 2176 or +86 (10) 8609 3269. Email: mc@chinasarft.gov.cn or jczhxjch@public.fhnet.cn.net. Contact: Ms. Zhang Wei, Chief Engineer, Monitoring Department; Zhao Chengping, Monitoring Manager; or Ms. Xu Tao, Deputy Director of Monitoring Department.

Fujian People's Broadcasting Station, 2 Gutian Lu, Fuzhou, Fujian 350001, China. $1 or IRC helpful. Web: (includes on-demand audio) www.66163.com/fjbs. Contact: Audience Relations Section. Replies irregularly and usually slowly. Prefers correspondence in Chinese.

Gannan People's Broadcasting Station, 49 Renmin Xije, Hezuo Zhen, Xiahe, Gian Su 747000, China. Verifies reception reports written in English. Return postage not required.

Guangxi Foreign Broadcasting Station, 12 Min Zu Avenue, Nanning, Guangxi 530022, China. Phone: +86 (771) 585-4403, +86 (771) 587-4745. Email: gxfbs2003@yahoo.com.cn. Web: www.gxradio.com/index/dwgbjj.htm; (streaming audio) www.gxradio.com. Free stickers and handmade papercuts. IRC helpful. Replies irregularly. Broadcasts in Vietnamese and Cantonese to listeners in Vietnam.

Hulunbuir People's Broadcasting Station, 11 Dengli Dajie, Hailar Qu, Nei Menggu 021008 China. Replies in Chinese to correspondence in Chinese or English.

Heilongjiang People's Broadcasting Station, 181 Zhongshan Lu, Harbin, Heilongjiang 150001, China. Phone: +86 (451) 8289-3443; (Korean Service) +86 (451) 8289-8873. Fax: +86 (451) 8289 3539. Email: am621@sina.com; (Korean Service) 873k@873k. com. Web: (includes on-demand audio) www.am621.com.cn; (Korean Service) www.873k.com. Rarely replies.

Hunan People's Broadcasting Station, 167 Yuhua Lu, Changsha, Hunan 410007, China. Phone: +86 (731) 554-7202. Fax: +86 (731) 554 7220. Email: hnradio@163.com; (news channel, relayed on shortwave) hnradio.cs.hn.cn. Web: (includes on-demand and streaming audio) www.hnradio. com; (news channel, relayed on shortwave) www.hnradio. com/hnradio/weixing/weixing.htm; (streaming audio page) www.hnradio.com/ssst/index.htm. Rarely replies.

Nei Menggu (Inner Mongolia) People's Broadcasting Station, 19 Xinhua Darjie, Hohhot, Nei Menggu 010058, China. Email: nmrb@nmrb.com.cn; imbs@163.net.
Web: www.nmrb.cn. Replies irregularly, mainly to correspondence in Chinese.

Qinghai People's Broadcasting Station, 96 Kunlun Lu, Xining, Qinghai 810001, China. Email: qhradio@sina.com. Web: (includes streaming audio) www.qhradio.com. Contact: Technical Department. Verifies reception reports written in English. $1 helpful.

Radio Television Hong Kong, C.P.O Box 70200, Kowloon, Hong Kong, China. Provides weather reports for the South China Sea Yacht Race (*see* www.rhkyc.org.hk./chinacoastraceweek.htm) on 3940 kHz.

CAPE D'AGUILAR HF STATION: P.O. Box 9896, GPO Hong Kong, China. Phone:
+852 2888-1128; (station manager) +852 2888-1122; (assistant engineer) +852 2888-1130. Fax: +852 2809 2434. Contact: K.C. Liu, Station Manager; (technical) Lam Chi Keung, Assistant Engineer. Provides transmission facilities for weather reports to the South China Sea Yacht Race (*see*, above).

Shaanxi People's Broadcasting Station, 336 Chang'an Nanlu, Xi'an, Shaanxi 710061, China. Web: www.sxradio.com. cn. Replies irregularly to correspondence in Chinese.

Voice of China (Zhonghua shi Sheng). The First Program of Central People's Broadcasting Station—China National Radio (*see*).

☞**Voice of Jinling** (Jinling zhi Sheng), P.O. Box 268, Nanjing, Jiangsu 210002, China. Fax: +86 (25) 413 235. Web: (streaming audio, and on-demand until the next transmission) mms://vod.jsgd.com.cn/audio0. Free stickers and calendars, plus Chinese-language color station brochure. Replies to correspondence in Chinese and to simple correspondence in English. $1 or 1 IRC required for return postage. Voice of Jinling is the Taiwan Service of Jiangsu People's Broadcasting Station.

Voice of Pujiang (Pujiang zhi Sheng), P.O. Box 3064, Shanghai 200002, China. Phone: +86 (21) 6208-2797. Fax: +86 (21) 6208 2850. Replies irregularly to correspondence in Chinese or English.

☞**Voice of the Straits (Haixia zhi Sheng)**, P.O. Box 187, Fuzhou, Fujian 350012, China. Email: (English) vos@am666.net. Web: (includes streaming audio) www.vos.com.cn. Replies irregularly to correspondence in Chinese or English.

"FOCUS ON CHINA" ENGLISH PROGRAM: Box 308, Hong Kong, China. Email: (host "Jacqueline") hua_diao@hotmail.com.

☞**Xinjiang People's Broadcasting Station**, 84 Tuanjie Lu, Urümqi, Xinjiang 830044, China. Phone: +86 (991) 256-0089. Email: mw738@21cn.com. Web: (includes on-demand and streaming audio) www.xjbs.com.cn. Contact: Ms. Zhao Donglan, Editorial Office. Free tourist booklet, postcards and used Chinese stamps. Replies in Chinese to correspondence in Chinese or English. Verifies reception reports. $1 or 1 IRC helpful.

Xizang People's Broadcasting Station, 180 Beijing Zhonglu, Lhasa, Xizang 850000, China. Phone: (director) +86 (891) 681-9516; (technical division) +86 (891) 681-9521; (technical manager) +86 (891) 681-9525; (chief engineer) +86 (891) 681-9529. Phone/Fax: (general) +86 (891) 682-7910. Email: xzzbs2003@yahoo.com.cn. Web: www.tibetradio.cn. Contact: Mo Shu-ji, Director; (technical) Tuo Bao-shen, Technical Manager; Wang Yong (Chief Engineer). Chinese or Tibetan preferred, since correspondence in English is processed by freelance translators hired only when accumulated mail reaches a critical mass. Return postage required. Sometimes announces itself in English as "China Tibet Broadcasting Company" or "Tibet China Broadcasting Station."

"HOLY TIBET" ENGLISH PROGRAM: Foreign Affairs Office, China Tibet People's Broadcasting Company, 41 Beijing Middle Road, Lhasa, Xizang 850000, China. Phone: +86 (891) 681-9541. Contact: Ms.Tse Ring Dekye, Producer/Announcer. Two IRCs requested. Verifies reception reports.

Yunnan Broadcasting Station, 73 Renmin Xilu, Kunming, Yunnan 650031, China. Broadcasts in Chinese and Vietnamese to Vietnam.

CHINA (TAIWAN)   World Time +8

China Radio, 53 Min Chuan West Road 9th Floor, Taipei 10418, Taiwan, Republic of China. Phone: +886 (2) 2598-1009. Fax: +886 (2) 2598 8348. Email: (Adams) readams@usa.net. Contact: Richard E. Adams, Station Director. Verifies reception reports. A religious broadcaster, sometimes referred to as "True Light Station," transmitting via leased facilities in Petropavlovsk-Kamchatskiy, Russia.

☞**Fu Hsing Broadcasting Station**, 5 Lane 280, Section 5, Chungshan North Road, Taipei 111, Taiwan, Republic of China. Email: fushinge@ms63.hinet.net. Web: (includes streaming audio) www.fhbs.com.tw. Contact: Xieyi Zhao, Station Manager. Free key rings and other small souvenirs. Replies to correspondence in Chinese or English and verifies reception reports. Return postage not required.

☞**Radio Taiwan International (RTI)**, P.O. Box 24-38 (or P.O. Box 24-777), Taipei 10651, Taiwan, Republic of China; (street address) 55 Pei-An Road, Taipei 104, Taiwan, Republic of China. Phone: +886 (2) 2885-6168, X-752 or 753; (English) X-385 or 387; (French) X-386; (German) X-382; (Japanese) X-328; (Spanish) X-384. Fax: +886 (2) 2885 0023; (European languages) +886 (2) 2886 7088; (Japanese) +886 (2) 2885 2254. Email: (general) rti@rti.org.tw; (English) prog@rti.org.tw; (French) fren@rti.org.tw; (German) deutsch@rti.org.tw; (Japanese) jpn@rti.org.tw. Web: (includes on-demand and streaming audio) www.rti.org.tw. Contact: (general) Wayne Wang Tao-Fang, Chief of International Affairs Section; (administration) Lin Feng-Jeng, Chairman; (technical) Peter Lee, Manager, Engineering Department. Free stickers. May send publications and an occasional surprise gift. Broadcasts to the Americas are relayed via WYFR's Okeechobee site in the USA. Also uses relay facilities in France, Germany and the United Kingdom.

BANGKOK OFFICE: P.O. Box 44 PorNorFor Trairat Bangkhen Bangkok 10223 Thailand.

BERLIN OFFICE: Postfach 30 92 43, D-10760 Berlin, Germany.

DAKAR OFFICE: B.P. 6867, Dakar, Senegal.

HANOI OFFICE: G.P.O. Box 104 Hanoi, Vietnam.

MOSCOW OFFICE: 24/2Tverskaya St., Korpus 1, gate 4, 3rd Fl, 103050 Moscow, Russia. Contact: Chang Yu-tang.

NEW DELHI OFFICE: P.O. Box 4914, Safdarjung Enclave, New Delhi, 110 029 India.

SURABAYA OFFICE: P.O. Box 1024, Surabaya, 60008 Indonesia.

☞**Trans World Broadcasting Ministry**, 467 Chih Sien 1st Road 7/F, Kaohsiung 800, Taiwan, Republic of China. Phone: +886 (7) 235-9223/4. Fax: +886 (7) 235 9220. Email: youth@twbm.com. Web: (includes on-demand audio) www.twbm.com. Contact: Naishang Kuo, Manager; or Daosheng Yao, Recording Engineer. Broadcasts via facilities of Radio Taiwan International (see).

NORTH AMERICAN OFFICE: 1 Spruce Street, Millbrae CA 94030 USA. Phone: +1 (925) 283-0210; (toll-free outside San Francisco Bay area) 1-866-235-224. Fax: +1 (415) 337 1846. Email: contact@twbm.

☞**Voice of Han**, B Building 5F, 3 Hsin-Yi Road, Sec.1, Taipei, Taiwan, Republic of China. Phone: +886 (2) 2321-5053. Fax: +886 (2) 2393 0970. Email: tony257@ms55.hinet.net. Web: (includes streaming audio) www.voh.com.tw. Contact: Tony Tu.

Voice of Kuanghua—the Mainland Service of Voice of Han (see).

CLANDESTINE

Clandestine broadcasts are often subject to abrupt change or termination. Being operated by anti-establishment political and/or military organizations, these groups tend to be suspicious of outsiders' motives. Thus, they are more likely to reply to contacts from those who communicate in the station's native tongue, and who are perceived to be at least somewhat favorably disposed to their cause. Most will provide, upon request, printed matter on their cause, though not necessarily in English. For detailed information on clandestine stations, refer to one of the following Internet sites:

ClandestineRadio.com (www.ClandestineRadio.com) specializes in background information on these stations and is organized by region and target country.

Clandestine Radio Watch (www.schoechi.de) contains clandestine radio information plus a twice monthly report on the latest news and developments affecting the study of clandestine radio.

"Al Mustaqbal"—*see* USA.

"Coalition Maritime Forces (CMF) Radio One"—*see* International Waters.

"Degar Radio," Montagnard Foundation, Inc., P.O. Box 171114, Spartanburg SC 29301 USA. Phone: +1 (864) 576-0698. Fax: +1 (864) 595 1940. Email: degar@montagnard-foundation.org; (Kok Sor) kksor@montagnard-foundation.org, or ksorpo@yahoo. com. Web: (Montagnard Foundation parent organization) www. montagnard-foundation.org. Contact: Kok Sor, President, Montagnard Foundation. Mint stamps or $1 helpful.

📻**"Dejen Radio,"** Liberty Bell Communications, Inc., P.O. Box 792, Indianapolis IN 46206-0792 USA. Email: dejen@e thiopiancommentator.com. Web: (on-demand audio) www. ethiopiancommentator.com/dejenradio.

📻**"Democratic Voice of Burma"** ("Democratic Myanmar a-Than"), P.O. Box 6720, St. Olavs Plass, N-0130 Oslo, Norway. Phone: (Director/Chief Editor) +47 (22) 868-486; (Aministration) +47 (22) 868-472. Email: (general) comment@dvb.no; (Director) director@dvb.no; (technical problems) comments@dvb. no. Web: (includes on-demand audio) www.dvb.no. Contact: (general) Dr. Anng Kin, Listener Liaison; Aye Chan Naing, Daily Editor; or Thida, host for "Songs Request Program"; (administration) Harn Yawnghwe, Director; or Daw Khin Pyone, Manager; (technical) Saw Neslon Ku, Studio Technician; Petter Bernsten; or Technical Dept. Norwegian kroner requested for a reply, but presumably Norwegian mint stamps would also suffice. Programs produced by Burmese democratic movements, as well as professional and independent radio journalists, to provide informational and educational services for the democracy movement inside and outside Burma. Opposes the current Myanmar government. Transmitted originally via facilities in Norway, but more recently has broadcast from sites in Germany, Madagascar and Central Asia.

📻**"Hmong Lao Radio,"** P.O. Box 6426, St. Paul MN 55106 USA. Phone: +1 (651) 292-0774. Fax: +1 (651) 292 0795. Email: (Lor) blor@hmonglaoradio.org; (Vang) cvang@hmonglaoradio. org. Web: (includes on-demand audio) www.hmonglaoradio. org. Contact: Bee Lor; or Cha Vang. Verifies reception reports. Transmits via facilities in Taiwan, and also carried by World Harvest Radio (*see* USA).

"Information Radio" (when operating), 193rd Special Operations Wing, 81 Constellation Court, Middletown PA 17057 USA. Email: (Public Affairs Officer) pa.193sow@paharr.ang.af.mil. Web: (193rd Special Operation Wing parent organization) www.paharr.ang.af.mil. Contact: Public Affairs Officer. Psy-ops station operated by the 193rd Special Operations Wing of the Pennsylvania Air National Guard.

📻**"IOTM Radio"** (when operating), Iran of Tomorrow Movement, 17328 Ventura Blvd. #209, Encino CA 91316 USA. Phone: +1 818-986-0200. Fax: +1 818-474-7229. Email: radio@sosiran. com. Web: (includes on-demand audio) www.sosiran.com.

📻**"Minivan Radio,"** 15 Fowler's Road, Salisbury, SP1 2QP, United Kingdom. Phone: +44 (1722) 332-874. Email: minivanradio@gmail.com. Web: (on-demand audio) http://radio.minivannews.com. Contact: Monica Michie. Return postage helpful. Promotes human rights in the Maldives and is opposed to the present government. Via facilities of Germany's T-Systems International (*see*).

FRIENDS OF MALDIVES SPONSORING ORGANIZATION: 64 Milford Street, Salisbury SP1 2BP, United Kingdom. Phone: +44 (1722) 504-330. Email: admin@friendsofmaldives.co.uk. Web: www.friendsofmaldives.co.uk. Contact: David Hardingham.

"National Radio of the Democratic Saharan Arab Republic"—*see* Radio Nacional de la República Arabe Saharaui Democrática, Western Sahara.

"Quê Hu'o'ng Radio"—*see* USA.

📻**"Radio Anternacional,"** BM Box 1499, London WC1N 3XX, United Kingdom. Phone: +44 (20) 8962-2707. Fax: +44 (20) 8346 2203. Email: radio7520@yahoo.com; (Majedi) azarmajedi@yahoo.com. Web: (includes on-demand audio) www.radio-international.org. Contact: Ms. Azar Majedi. Broadcasts via a transmitter in Moldova. Has ties to the Worker-Communist Party of Iran.

"Radio Azadi, Voice of the Communist Party of Iraqi Kurdistan" ("Era ezgay azadiya, dengi hizbi shuyu'i kurdistani iraqa") (when operating).

COMMUNIST PARTY OF IRAQI KURDISTAN PARENT ORGANIZATION: Email:info@kurdistancp.org. Web: www.kurdistancp. org.

"Radio Free Afghanistan"—*see* USA.

"Radio Freedom, Voice of the Ogadeni People"—*see* "Radio Xoriyo"

📻**"Radio Horyaal,"** P.O. Box 51045, Scarborough, Ontario, Canada. Email: radio@horyaal.net. Web: (includes on-demand audio) www.horyaal.net. Broadcasts via a transmitter in western Russia.

"Radio International"—*see* "Radio Anternacional."

📻**"Radio Komala"** (when operating), c/o Representation of Komala Abroad, Postfach 800272, D-51002 Köln, Germany; or by fax to: +1 (561) 760 5814. Email: komala radio@hotmail. com. Web: (includes on-demand audio) http://radio.komala. org. Replies to correspondence in English. Komala, one of the founder members of the Communist Party of Iran in 1982, left that organization in 2000.

"Radio Nacional de la República Arabe Saharaui Democrática"—*see* Western Sahara.

📻**"Radio Payam-e Dost"** (Bahá'í Radio International), P.O. Box 765, Great Falls VA 22066 USA. Phone: +1 (703) 671-8888. Fax: +1 (301) 292 6947. Email: payam@bahairadio.org. Web: (includes on-demand audio) www.bahairadio.org. Does not verify reception reports.

"Radio Quê Me" (Radio Homeland), B.P. 63, 94472 Boissy Saint Léger Cedex, France. Phone: +33 (1) 4598-3085. Fax: +33 (1) 4598 3261. Email: queme@free.fr. Web: (Quê Me parent organization) www.queme.net. Contact: Penelope Faulkner, Vice-President of Vietnam Committee on Human Rights.

📻**"Radio Rhino International - Africa,"** (when operating) c/o Allerweltshaus e.V., Koernerstr. 77 - 79, D - 50823 Köln, Germany. Phone: +49 (221) 356-1754/5/6. Fax: +49 (221) 3561 8080, +49 (221) 3561 7539. Email: mail@radiorhino. org, radiorhino01@intertech.de. Web: (includes on-demand audio) www.radiorhino.org. Contact: Godfrey Ayoo, Director. Opposed to the Uganda government. Via the Jülich facilities of Germany's T-Systems International (*see*).

"Radio Seda-ye Iran"—*see* KRSI, USA.

"Radio Nile"—*see* Netherlands.

"Radio Voice of ENUF," c/o Ethiopian National United Front (ENUF), P. O. Box 2206, Washington DC 20013-2206 USA. Opposed to the current Ethiopian government.

ENUF PARENT ORGANIZATION: Phone: +1 (214) 594-2102. Fax: +1 (909) 985 7741. Email: info@enuffforethiopia.org. Web: www.enufforethiopia.org.

📻**"Radio Voice of Oromo Liberation"** ("Raadiyoo Sagalee Qabsoo Bilisummaa Oromoo"). Email: rsqbo@yahoo.com. Web: (includes on-demand audio) http://www.oromia.org/rsqbo/ rsqbo.htm. Broadcasts via a transmitter in western Russia.

Reception reports can be verified via the broker, TDP (*see* Transmitter Documentation Project, Belgium).

"Radio Voice of the People"—*see* Zimbabwe

"Radio Voice of the Iranian Nation" ("Radio Seda-ye Mellat-e Iran"). Email: radiomelate@yahoo.com. Opposed to the Iranian government.

"Radio VOP"—*see* Zimbabwe.

📻**"Radio Xoriyo,"** ("Halkani wa Radio Xoriyo, Codkii Ummadda Odageniya"). Email: radioxoriyo@ogaden.com; or ogaden@yahoo.com (some verifications received from these addresses). If these fail, try webmaster@ogaden.com. Web: (archived audio of most recent broadcast; click on "Radio Xoriyo") www.ogaden.com. Broadcasts are supportive of the Ogadenia National Liberation Front, and hostile to the Ethiopian government. Via facilities of Germany's T-Systems International (*see*).

"Radio Waaberi." Email: info@radiowaaberi.org. Web: (includes on-demand audio) www.radiowaaberi.org. Contact: Ali Gulaid, President. A Somali broadcast to East Africa via Germany's T-Systems International (*see*).

"Salama Radio"—*see* Nigeria.

"Sudan Radio Service"—*see* USA.

📻**"SW Radio Africa"** (when operating), P.O. Box 243, Borehamwood, Herts., WD6 4WA, United Kingdom. Phone: +44 (20) 8387-1441. Email: (general) views@swradioafrica.com, or mail@swradioafrica.com; (technical) tech@swradioafrica.com; (Jackson) gerry@swradioafrica.com. Web: (includes on-demand and streaming audio) www.swradioafrica.com. Contact: [Ms.] Gerry Jackson, Station Manager; (technical) Keith Farquharson, Technical Manager. Return postage helpful. Run by exiled Zimbabweans in the United Kingdom, and opposes the Mugabe government.

📻**"Tensae Ethiopia Voice of Unity,"** P.O.Box 2945, Washington DC 20013 USA. Phone: +1 (202) 276 1645, +1 678 437 5597. Email: ethiopia44@yahoo.com. Web: (includes on-demand audio) www.tensae.com. Broadcasts via a transmitter in western Russia. Reception reports can be verified via the broker, TDP (*see* Transmitter Documentation Project, Belgium). *EUROPEAN OFFICE (GERMANY):* Phone: +49 (69) 6640-3923. Fax: +49 (69) 6636 6672, +49 (69) 3399 8632, or +49 (69) 6636 6674. Email: tensae.ethiopia@gmail.com. Some reception reports to this address have been verified by email.

📻**"Voice of Biafra International,"** 733 15th Street NW, Suite 700, Washington DC 20005 USA. Phone: +1 (202) 347-2983. Email: biafrafoundation@yahoo.com; (Nkwocha) oguchi@pacbell.net; oguchi@mbay.net. Web: (includes on-demand audio) www.biafraland.com/vobi.htm. Contact: Oguchi Nkwocha, M.D.; or Chima Osondu. A project of the Biafra Foundation and the Biafra Actualization Forum.

"Voice of Delina" ("Dimtsi Delina"), Tesfa Delina Foundation, Inc., 17326 Edwards Road, Suite A-230, Cerritos CA 90703 USA. Email: tesfa@delina.org, info@delina.org. Web: (includes sample broadcast) http://dmsi.delina.org. Opposed to the current Eritrean government.

📻**"Voice of Democratic Eritrea International"** ("Sawt Eritrea al-Dimuqratiya-Sawtu Jabhat al-Tahrir al-Eritrea") (when operating), Postfach 1946, D-65409 Rüsselsheim, Germany. Phone: +49 (228) 356-181. Email: (ELF-RC parent organization) elfrc@nharnet.com. Web: (includes on-demand audio) www.nharnet.com/Radio/radiopage.htm. Contact: Seyoum O. Michael, Member of Executive Committee, ELF-RC; or Neguse Tseggon. Station of the Eritrean Liberation Front-Revolutionary Council, hostile to the government of Eritrea. Via facilities of T-Systems International (*see*), in Germany.

📻**"Voice of Ethiopian Medhin,"** P.O. Box 13875, Silver Spring MD 20911 USA Phone: +1 (202) 234-1035. Fax: +1 (202) 234 4747. Web: (includes on-demand audio) www.medhininfo.com/radio/radioeng.htm. Broadcast produced by overseas members of the Ethiopian Medhin Democratic Party, a broad-based coalition of Ethiopians aiming to democratize their country, and recognized by the Ethiopian government in 2004 as an official opposition party.

MEDHIN OFFICE IN GERMANY: Medhin Dimts, Postfach 110744, D-76057 Karlsruhe, Germany.

"Voice of Ethiopian Salvation"—*see* "Voice of Ethiopian Medhin"

"Voice of Ethiopian Unity"—*see* "Voice of the Democratic Path of Ethiopian Unity.

"Voice of Iranian Kurdistan" ("Seda-ye Kordestan-e Iran"). Fax: +1 (270) 682 4654. Email: info@rdki.com; rdk_iran@yahoo.com. Web: (includes on-demand audio) www.rdki.com. For further contact, try one of the PDKI (Democratic Party of Iranian Kurdistan parent organization) offices, below.

PDKI INTERNATIONAL BUREAU: AFK, Boite Postale 102, F-75623 Paris Cedex 13, France. Phone: +33 (1) 4585-6431. Fax: +33 (1) 4585 2093. Email: pdkiran@club-internet.fr. Web: www.pdk-iran.org.

PDKI CANADA BUREAU: P.O. Box 29010, London, Ontario N6K 4L9, Canada. Phone/Fax: +1 (519) 680-7784. Email: pdkicanada@pdki.org. Web: www.pdki.org.

"Voice of Iraqi Kurdistan"—*see* Iraq.

"Voice of Jammu Kashmir Freedom" ("Sada-i Hurriyat-i Jammu Kashmir"), P.O. Box 102, Muzaffarabad, Azad Kashmir, via Pakistan. Contact: Programme Manager. Pro-Moslem and favors Azad Kashmiri independence from India. Believed to transmit via facilities in Pakistan. Return postage not required, and replies to correspondence in English.

📻**"Voice of Komalah"** ("Seda-ye Komalah") (when operating). Station of the Kurdish branch of the Communist Party of Iran.

KOMALAH PARENT ORGANIZATION (KURDISTAN): Email: komalah@hotmail.com.

SWEDISH OFFICE: P.O. Box 750 26, Uppsala, Sweden. Phone/Fax: +46 (18) 468-493. Email: komala@cpiran.org.

"Voice of Kurdistan Toilers" ("Aira dengi zahmatkishan-e kurdistana") (when operating).

KURDISTAN TOILERS PARTY PARENT ORGANIZATION: Email: info@ktp.nu. Web: www.ktp.nu.

📻**"Voice of Liberty"** ("Dimtsi Harnet Ertra"). Email: vol@selfi-democracy.com. Web: (includes on-demand audio) http://selfi-democracy.com. Reception reports can be verified via the broker, TDP (*see* Transmitter Documentation Project, Belgium). Supports the opposition-in-exile Eritrean Democratic Party. Broadcasts via a transmitter in western Russia.

ERITREAN DEMOCRATIC PARTY PARENT ORGANIZATION: P.O. Box 93982, Atlanta GA 30377-0982 USA. Email: northamerica@selfi-democracy.com; (European office) europe@selfi-democracy.com.

"Voice of Mesopotamia" ("Dengê Mezopotamya")
Phone: +32 (53) 648-827/29. Fax: +32 (53) 680 779. Email: info@denge-mezopotamya.com. Web: www.denge-mezopotamya.com. Contact: Ahmed Dicle, Director.

KURDISTAN WORKERS PARTY (PKK, also known as Kongra-Gel, KGK) SPONSORING ORGANIZATION: Email: info@kongra-gel.com. Web: www.kongra-gel.com.

ADDRESS FOR RECEPTION REPORTS: TDP, P.O. Box 1, B-2310 Rijkevorsel, Belgium (return postage required).

📻**"Voice of Oromiyaa"** (if reactivated), P.O. Box 17662, Atlanta GA 30316

USA. Email: sagaloromo@aol.com. Web: (includes on-demand audio) www.voiceoforomiyaa.com.

📻**"Voice of Oromo Liberation"** ("Sagalee Bilisummaa Oromoo"), Postfach 510610, D-13366 Berlin, Germany; or SBO, Prinzenallee 81, D-13357 Berlin, Germany. Phone/Fax: +49 (30) 494 3372. Email: sbo13366@aol.com. Web: (includes on-demand audio) www.oromoliberationfront.org/sbo.html. Contact: Taye Teferah, European Coordinator. Occasionally replies to correspondence in English or German. Return postage required. Station of the Oromo Liberation Front of Ethiopia, an Oromo nationalist organization. Via Germany's T-Systems International (*see*).

OROMO LIBERATION FRONT USA OFFICE: P.O. Box 73247, Washington DC 20056 USA. Phone: +1 (202) 462-5477. Fax: +1 (202) 332 7011.

"Voice of the Communist Party of Iran" ("Seda-ye Hezb-e Komunist-e Iran")

COMMUNIST PARTY OF IRAN SPONSORING ORGANIZATION: C.D.C.R.I., Box 704 45, S-107 25 Stockholm, Sweden. Phone/Fax: +46 (8) 786-8054. Email: cpi@cpiran.org. Web: www.cpiran.org.

"Voice of the Communist Party of Iraqi Kurdistan"—*see* "Radio Azadi"

"Voice of the Democratic Alliance"
Web: (Democratic Alliance parent organization) http://www.erit-alliance.org. Airs via the facilities of Radio Ethiopia, and is opposed to the Eritrean government.

📻**"Voice of the Democratic Path of Ethiopian Unity,"** Finote Democracy, P.O. Box 88675, Los Angeles CA 90009 USA. Email: efdpu@finote.org. Web: (Includes on-demand audio) www.finote.org. Via Germany's T-Systems International (*see*).

EUROPEAN ADDRESS: Finote Democracy, Postbus 10573, 1001 EN, Amsterdam, Netherlands.

📻**"Voice of the Iraqi People, Voice of the Iraqi Communist Party"** (when operating)
IRAQI COMMUNIST PARTY PARENT ORGANIZATION: BM Al-Tariq, London WC1N 3XX, United Kingdom. Phone/Fax: +44 (207) 419-2552. Email: iraq@iraqcp.org. Web: www.iraqcp.org.

"Voice of the Iranian Nation"—*see* Radio Voice of the Iranian Nation.

"Voice of the Kurdistan People"—*see* Iraq.

📻**"Voice of the Worker"** ("Seda-ye Kargar") (when operating)
WORKER-COMMUNIST PARTY OF IRAN (WPI) PARENT ORGANIZATION: Email: wpi@wpiran.org. Web: www.wpiran.org.

WPI INTERNATIONAL OFFICE: WPI, Office of International Relations, Suite 730, 28 Old Brompton Road, South Kensington, London SW7 3SS, United Kingdom. Phone: +44 (77) 7989-8968. Fax: +44 (87) 0136 2182. Email: wpi.international.office@ukonline.co.uk, or markazi@ukonline.co.uk.

📻**"Voice of Tibet"**
ADMINISTRATIVE OFFICE: Voice of Tibet Foundation, St. Olavsgate 24, N-0166 Oslo, Norway. Phone: (administration) +47 2211-2700. Fax: +47 2211 5474. Email: voti@online.no; (Norbu) votibet@online.no. Web: (includes on-demand audio) www.vot.org. Contact: Øystein Alme, Project Manager [sometimes referred to as "Director"]; or Chophel Norbu, Project Coordinator.

MAIN EDITORIAL OFFICE: Voice of Tibet, Narthang Building, Gangchen, Kyishong, Dharamsala-176 215 H.P., India. Phone: +91 (1892) 228-179/222 or +91 (1892) 222 384. Fax: +91 (1892) 224 957. Email: (general) vot1@gov.tibet.net or (editor-in-chief) voteditor@gov.tibet.net. Contact: Karma Yeshi Nazee,

Editor-in-Chief; Tenzin Peldon, Assistant Editor. A joint venture of the Norwegian Human Rights House, Norwegian Tibet Committee and World-View International. Programs focus on Tibetan culture, education, human rights and news from Tibet. Opposed to Chinese control of Tibet. A colorful QSL card is issued from the office in Dharamsala. Return postage helpful. Verifications have been received from both addresses. Broadcasts via transmitters in the former Soviet Union.

"Voices from the Diaspora"—a broadcast produced by Save the Gambia Democracy Project, and aired via the facilities of T-Systems International (*see*) in Germany.

SAVE THE GAMBIA DEMOCRACY PROJECT PARENT ORGANIZATION: Email: stgdp@sunugambia.com. Web: www.sunugambia.com.

VERIFICATIONS: If no reply is received direct from the STGDP, send your report to Jeff White at WRMI (*see* USA) who brokers the transmissions, or to Walter Brodowsky at Germany's T-Systems International (*see*).

"Voz de la Resistencia"
Email: (FARC-EP parent organization) elbarcino@laneta.apc.org (updated transmission schedules and QSLs available from this address, but correspond in Spanish). Contact: Olga Lucía Marín, Comisión Internacional de las FARC-EP. Station of the Fuerzas Armadas Revolucionarias de Colombia - Ejercito del Pueblo.

"Zwart of Wit"—*see* Belgium.

COLOMBIA   World Time –5

NOTE: Colombia, the country, is always spelled with two o's. It should never be written as "Columbia."

Alcaravan Radio   *see* La Voz de Tu Conciencia.

Caracol Villavicencio—*see* La Voz de los Centauros.

Ecos del Atrato (if reactivated), Apartado Aéreo 196, Quibdó, Chocó, Colombia. Phone: +57 (49) 711-450. Contact: Absalón Palacios Agualimpia, Administrador. Free pennants. Replies to correspondence in Spanish.

La Voz de Tu Conciencia, Colombia para Cristo, Apartado Aéreo 95300, Santafé de Bogotá, D.C., Colombia; or (street address) Colombia para Cristo, Calle 44 No. 13-67, Santafé de Bogotá, D.C., Colombia. Phone: +57 (1) 338-4716. Email: info@fuerzadepaz.com, contacto@fuerzadepaz.com, or libreria@fuerzadepaz.com; (Stendal, specialized technical correspondence only) martinstendal@etb.net.co. Web: www.fuerzadepaz.com/emisoras.asp. Contact: Russel Martín Stendal, Administrador. Station is actually located in Puerto Lleras, in the guerrilla "combat zone." Sometimes carries programming from sister stations Alcaravan Radio (1530 kHz) or Marfil Estéreo (88.8 MHz). Replies to correspondence in English or Spanish. Return postage helpful. Free stickers.

La Voz de los Centauros (Caracol Villavicencio) (when operating), Cra. 31 No. 37-71 Of. 1001, Villavicencio, Meta, Colombia. Phone: +57 (986) 214-995; (technical) +57 (986) 662-3666. Fax: +57 (986) 623 954. Contact: Carlos Torres Leyva, Gerencia; or Olga Arenas, Administradora. Replies to correspondence in Spanish.

La Voz del Guaviare, Carrera 22 con Calle 9, San José del Guaviare, Colombia. Phone: +57 (986) 840-153/4. Fax: +57 (986) 840 102. Email: mercorio@col3.telecom.com.co. Contact: Luis Fernando Román Robayo, Director General. Replies slowly to correspondence in Spanish.

La Voz del Llano (when operating), Calle 41B No. 30-11, Barrio La Grama, Villavicencio, Meta, Colombia; or (postal address in Bogotá) Apartado Aéreo 67751, Santafé de Bogotá, Colombia. Phone: +57 (986) 624-102. Fax: +57 (986) 625 045. Contact:

Not only Radio Prague, but also RFE-RL have made their home in Prague. T. Ohtake

Luis F. Rivero, Director. Replies occasionally to correspondence in Spanish. $1 or return postage necessary.

Marfil Estéreo—*see* La Voz de Tu Conciencia.

Ondas del Orteguaza (when operating), Calle 16, No. 12-48, piso 2, Florencia, Caquetá, Colombia. Phone: +57 (88) 352-558. Contact: Sandra Liliana Vásquez, Secretaria; Señora Elisa Viuda de Santos; or Henry Valencia Vásquez. Free stickers. IRC, return postage or $1 required. Replies occasionally to correspondence in Spanish.

Radio Líder (when operating), Apartado Aéreo 19823, Santafé de Bogotá, Colombia; (street address) Calle 45 No. 13-70, Santafé de Bogotá, Colombia. Phone: +57 (1) 323- 1500. Fax: +57 (1) 288 4020. Email: radiolider@cadenamelodia.com. Web: www.cadenamelodia.com. A station of the Cadena Melodía network.

CONGO (DEMOCRATIC REPUBLIC)   World Time
+1 Western, including Kinshasa; +2 Eastern

Radio Bukavu (when operating), B.P. 475, Bukavu, Democratic Republic of the Congo. $1 or return postage required. Replies slowly. Correspondence in French preferred.

Radio CANDIP, B.P. 373, Bunia, Democratic Republic of Congo. Letters should preferably be sent via registered mail. $1 or return postage required. Correspondence in French preferred.

Radio Kahuzi, c/o AIMServe, Box 53435 (BUKAVU), Nairobi, Kenya. Email: radiokahuzi@kivu-online.com, or besi@alltel. net. Web: www.besi.org. Contact: Richard & Kathy McDonald. Verifies reception reports by email.

HOME OFFICE: Believers Express Service, Inc. (BESI), P.O. Box 189, Eastanollee, GA 30538 USA. Phone: +1 (706) 282-0495. Fax: +1 (706) 886 0658. Email: besi@besi.org. Contact: Barbara Smith, Home Office Secretary. Verifies reception reports.

Radio Lubumbashi (when operating), B.P. 7296, Lubumbashi, Democratic Republic of the Congo. Letters should be sent via registered mail. $1 or 3 IRCs helpful. Correspondence in French preferred.

Radio Okapi, 12 Av. des Aviateurs, Kinshasa, Gombe, Democratic Republic of the Congo. Email: online form. Web: (includes on-demand and streaming audio) www.radiookapi. net. A joint project involving the United Nations Mission in the Democratic Republic of the Congo (MONUC) and the Swiss-based Fondation Hirondelle.

MONUC:
(USA) P.O. Box 4653, Grand Central Station, New York NY 10163-4653 USA. Phone: +1 (212) 963-0103. Fax: +1 (212) 963 0205. Email: info@monuc.org. Web: www.monuc.org. Verifies reception reports.

(Congo) 12 Av. des Aviateurs, Kinshasa, Gombe, Democratic Republic of the Congo; or B.P. 8811, Kinshasa 1, Democratic Republic of the Congo. Phone: +243 81- 890-6000. Fax: +243 890 56208. Contact: Georges Schleger, VE2EK, Communications Officer & Head of Technical Services.

FONDATION HIRONDELLE: 3 Rue Traversière, CH 1018-Lausanne, Switzerland. Phone: +41 (21) 647-2805. Fax: +41 (21) 647 4469. Email info@hirondelle.org. Web: www.hirondelle. org. Verifies reception reports.

Radio-Télévision Nationale Congolaise (when operating), B.P. 3171, Kinshasa-Gombe, Democratic Republic of the Congo. Letters should be sent via registered mail. $1 or 3 IRCs helpful. Correspondence in French preferred.

CONGO (REPUBLIC)   World Time +1

Radiodiffusion Nationale Congolaise (also announces as "Radio Nationale" or "Radio Congo"), Telediffusion du Congo, B.P. 2912, Brazzaville, Congo. Email: (technical) actu_rtnc@hotmail.com. Contact: Félix Lossombo, Le Directeur Administratif et Financier; or Roger Olingou. Return postage required, but smallest denomination currency notes (e.g. $1US or 1 euro) reportedly cannot be changed into local currency. Replies irregularly to letters in French (and sometimes English) sent via registered mail.

COSTA RICA   World Time –6

Faro del Caribe—TIFC, Apartado 2710, 1000 San José, Costa Rica. Phone: +506 226-4358, +506 227-5048, +506 286-1755. Fax: +506 227-1725. Email: radio@farodelcaribe.org; (technical) tecnico@farodelcaribe.org. Web: (includes streaming audio) www.farodelcaribe.org. Contact: Carlos A. Rozotto Piedrasanta, Director Administrativo; or Mauricio Ramires; (technical) Minor Enrique, Station Engineer. Free stickers, pennants, books and bibles. $1 or IRCs helpful.

U.S. OFFICE, NONTECHNICAL: Misión Latinoamericana, P.O. Box 620485, Orlando FL 32862 USA.

Radio Exterior de España—Cariari Relay Station, Cariari de Pococí, Costa Rica. Phone: +506 767-7308 or +506 767-7311. Fax: +506 225 2938.

Radio Universidad de Costa Rica (when operating), Apartado 1-06, 2060 Universidad de Costa Rica, San Pedro de Montes de Oca, San José, Costa Rica. Phone: (general) +506 207-4727; (studio) +506 225-3936. Fax: +506 207 5459. Email: radioucr@cariari.ucr.ac.cr. Web: http://cariari.ucr.ac.cr/ ~radioucr/radioucr. Contact: Marco González Muñoz; Henry Jones, Locutor de Planta; or Nora Garita B., Directora. Marco González is a radio amateur, call-sign TI3AGM. Free postcards, station brochure and stickers. Replies slowly to correspondence in Spanish or English. $1 or return postage required.

University Network—*see* USA.

CROATIA   World Time +1 (+2 midyear)

Croatian Radio-Television (Hrvatska Radio-Televizija, HRT)

MAIN OFFICE: Hrvatska Radio-Televizija (HRT), Prisavlje 3, HR-10000 Zagreb, Croatia. Phone: (operator) +385 (1) 634-3366;

(Managing Director) +385 (1) 634-3308; (Technical Director) +385 (1) 634-3663. Fax: (Technical Director) +385 (1) 634 3636. Email: (Managing Director) i.lucev@hrt.hr; (Technical Director) nikola.percin@hrt.hr; (technical, including reception reports) z.klasan@hrt.hr. Web: (includes on-demand and streaming audio) www.hrt.hr. Contact: (general) Ivanka Lucev, Managing Director; (Technical Director) Nikola Percin.

TRANSMITTING STATION DEANOVEC: P.O Box 3, 10313 Graberje Ivaanicko, Croatia. Phone: +385 (1) 283-0533. Fax: +385 (1) 283 0534. Email: dane.pavlic@oiv.hr. Contact: Dane Pavlic, Head of Station.

TRANSMISSION AUTHORITY: Odasiljaci i Veze D.O.O., Vlaska 106, HR-10000 Zagreb, Croatia. Phone: +385 (1) 464-6160. Fax: +385 (1) 464 6161. Email: Zelimir.Klasan@hrt.hr. Contact: Zelimir Klasan. This independent state-owned company replaces the former Transmitters and Communications Department of HRT.

Voice of Croatia (Glas Hrvatske)—same address as "Hrvatska Radio," above. Phone: (Editor-in-Chief) +385 (1) 634-2602; (Shortwave Technical Coordinator) +385 (1) 634-3428; (Shortwave Technical Coordinator, mobile) +385 9857-7565. Fax: (Editor-in-Chief) +385 (1) 634 3305; (Shortwave Technical Coordinator) +385 (1) 634 3347. Email: glas.hrvatske@hrt.hr; (Editor-in-Chief) ivana.jadresic@hrt.hr; (Shortwave Technical Coordinator) z.klasan@hrt.hr. Web: (includes streaming audio) www.hrt.hr/hr/glashrvatske/index.htm. Contact: (Editor-in-Chief) Ivana Jadresic; (Shortwave Technical Coordinator, domestic & external) Zelimir Klasan.

Croatian Radio operates two services on world band: the domestic (first) national radio program, transmitted via HRT's Deanovec shortwave station for listeners in Europe and the Mediterranean; and a special service in Croatian, with news segments in English and Spanish for Croatian expatriates, which airs via T-Systems International (*see*) in Jülich, Germany and is sponsored by the Croatian Heritage Organization. The previous Croatian external broadcasting service known as "Radio Hrvatska" and produced by the Croatian Information Center (Hrvatski Informativni Centar, HIC) was discontinued on October 1st 2000. The external service resumed its transmissions on April 18th 2001 as Glas Hrvatske (Voice of Croatia) under the authority of HRT.

WASHINGTON NEWS BUREAU: Croatian-American Association, 2020 Pennsylvania Avenue NW, Suite 287, Washington DC 20006 USA. Phone: +1 (202) 429-5543. Fax: +1 (202) 429 5545. Email: 73150.3552@compuserve.com. Web: www.hrnet.org/CAA. Contact: Frank Brozovich, President.

CUBA   World Time –5 (–4 midyear)

Radio Habana Cuba, Apartado Postal 6240, 10600 La Habana, Cuba. Phone: (general) +53 (7) 878-4954; (English Department) +53 (7) 877-6628. Fax: +53 (7) 870 5810. Email: radiohc@enet.cu; (Arnie Coro) arnie@rhc.cu, or coro@enet.cu. Web: (includes on-demand and streaming audio) www.radiohc.cu. Contact: (general) Lourdes López, Head of Correspondence Department; Isabel García, Director of English Department; (administration) Luis López López, General Director; (technical) Arnaldo Coro Antich, ("Arnie Coro"), Producer, "DXers Unlimited"; or Arturo González, Head of Technical Department. Free pennants, stickers, keychains, pins and other small souvenirs. DX Listeners' Club. Free sample *Granma International* newspaper. Contests with various prizes, including trips to Cuba.

Radio Rebelde, Departamento de Relaciones Públicas, Apartado Postal 6277, 10600 La Habana 6, Cuba; or (street address) Calle 23 No. 258 entre L y M, El Vedado, 10600 La Habana, Cuba. For technical correspondence (including reception reports), substitute "Servicio de Onda Corta" in place of "Departamento de Relaciones Públicas." Reception reports can also be emailed to Radio Habana Cuba's Arnie Coro (arnie@radiohc.cu) for forwarding to Radio Rebelde. Phone: +53 (7) 831-3514. Fax: +53 (7) 334 270. Email: (nontechnical) webrebelde@rrebelde.icrt.cu; (technical and nontechnical): relapubli@rrebelde.icrt.cu. Web (includes on-demand and streaming audio): www.radiorebelde.com.cu. Contact: Daimelis Monzón; Noemí Cairo Marín; Iberlise González Padua; or Marisel Ramos Soca (all from "Relaciones Públicas"); or Jorge L. Martín, Jefe de Relaciones Públicas. Replies slowly, with correspondence in Spanish preferred.

CYPRUS   World Time +2 (+3 midyear)

Bayrak Radio International (when operating), BRTK Campus, Dr. Fazil Küçük Boulevard, P.O. Box 417, Lefkosa T.R.N.C., via Mersin 10, Turkey. Phone: +90 (392) 225-5555. Fax: (general) +90 (392) 225 4581. Email: (general) brt@cc.emu.edu.tr; (technical, including reception reports) tosun@cc.emu.edu.tr. Web: (includes streaming audio) www.brt.gov.nc.tr. Contact: Mustafa Tosun, Head of Transmission Department; Halil Balbaz, Transmitter Manager; Ülfet Kortmaz, Head of Bayrak International; Bertil Wedin, Producer of "Magazine North."

BBC World Service—East Mediterranean Relay Station, P.O. Box 209, Limassol, Cyprus. Contact: Steve Welch. This address for technical matters only. Other correspondence should be sent to the BBC World Service in London (*see*).

Cyprus Broadcasting Corporation, Broadcasting House, P.O. Box 4824, Nicosia 1397, Cyprus; or (street address) RIK Street, Athalassa, Nicosia 2120, Cyprus. Phone: +357 (2) 286-2000. Fax: +357 (2) 231 4050. Email: rik@cybc.com.cy. Web: (includes streaming audio from domestic services not on shortwave) www.cybc.com.cy. Contact: (general) Pavlos Soteriades, Director General; or Evangella Gregoriou, Head of Public and International Relations; (technical) Andreas Michaelides, Director of Technical Services. Free stickers. Replies irregularly, sometimes slowly. IRC or $1 helpful.

CZECH REPUBLIC   World Time +1 (+2 midyear)

Radio Prague, Czech Radio, Vinohradská 12, 12099 Prague 2, Czech Republic. Phone: +420 (2) 2155-2900; (Czech Department) +420 (2) 2155-2922; (English Department) +420 (2) 2155-2930; (German Department) +420 (2) 2155-2941; (French Department) +420 (2) 2155-2911; (Spanish Department) +420 (2) 2155-2950; (Russian Department) +420 (2) 2155-2964. Phone/Fax: (Oldrich Čip, technical) +420 (2) 2271-5005. Fax: (all languages) +420 (2) 2155 2903. Email: (general) cr@radio.cz; (Director) Miroslav.Krupicka@radio.cz; (English Department) english@radio.cz; (German Department) deutsch@radio.cz; (French Department) francais@radio.cz; (Spanish Department) espanol@radio.cz; (Russian Department) rusky@radio.cz; (Program Director) David.Vaughan@radio.cz; (free news texts) robot@radio.cz, writing "Subscribe English" (or other desired language) within the subject line; (technical, chief engineer) cip@radio.cz. Web: (includes on-demand and live audio) www.radio.cz. Contact: (general) Marie Pittnerova; or David Vaughan, Editor-in-Chief; (administration) Miroslav Krupička, Director; (technical) Oldrich Čip, Chief Engineer. Free

stickers; also key chains, pens, bookmarks, mouse pads and other souvenirs when available.
RFE-RL—*see* USA.

DENMARK   World Time +1 (+2 midyear)

World Music Radio (when operating), P. O. Box 112, DK-8900 Randers, Denmark. Phone: (Monday through Friday, 0800-1400 World Time) +45 70 222 222. Fax: +45 70 222 888. E-mail: wmr@wmr.dk. URL: www.wmr.dk. Contact: Stig Hartvig Nielsen. Return postage required. An independent station, WMR first went on the air in 1967 from the Netherlands, from where broadcasting continued until August 1973. Later, programs were aired via the facilities of Radio Andorra (in 1976 and 1980), Radio Milano International (1982-1983) and Radio Dublin (1983-1989). In 1997, WMR returned to the air between May 31 and August 24 from a new HQ in Denmark, leasing airtime over powerful transmitters in South Africa. These broadcasts ceased due to lack of commercial advertising. Has been operating irregularly with its own transmitter since 2003.

DJIBOUTI   World Time +3

☞Radio Télévision de Djibouti, Boite Postale 97, Djibouti, Djibouti; (street address) Avenue Saint Laurent du Var, Djibouti, Djibouti. Phone: +253 352-294. Fax: +253 356 502. Email: (general) rtd@intnet.dj; (information) rtd-information@intnet.dj; (technical) rtdtech@intnet.dj. Web: (includes on-demand audio) www.rtd.dj. Contact: (general) Abdi Atteyeh Abdi, Directeur Général; (technical) Yahya Moussed, Chef du Service Technique. Return postage helpful. Transmission facilities are located at Dorale, about 10 km west of Djibouti City.

DOMINICAN REPUBLIC   World Time –4

☞Radio Amanecer Internacional, Apartado Postal 1500, Santo Domingo, Dominican Republic; (street address) Juan Sánchez Ramírez #40, Santo Domingo, Dominican Republic. Phone: +1 (809) 688-5600, +1 (809) 688-5609. Fax: +1 (809) 227 1869. Email: cabina@radioamanecer.org, or online form. Web: (includes streaming audio) www.radioamanecer.org. Contact: (general) Lic. Germán Lorenzo, Director; (technical) Ing. Sócrates Domínguez. $1 or return postage required. Replies slowly to correspondence in Spanish.
Radio Barahona (when operating), Apartado 201, Barahona, Dominican Republic; or Gustavo Mejía Ricart No. 293, Apto. 2-B, Ensanche Quisqueya, Santo Domingo, Dominican Republic. Phone: +1 (809) 524-4040. Fax: +1 (809) 524 5461. Contact: (general) Rodolfo Z. Lama Jaar, Administrador; (technical) Ing. Roberto Lama Sajour, Administrador General. Free stickers. Letters should be sent via registered mail. $1 or return postage helpful. Replies to correspondence in Spanish.
EMPRESAS RADIOFÓNICAS PARENT ORGANIZATION: Empresas Radiofónicas S.A., Apartado Postal 20339, Santo Domingo, Dominican Republic. Phone: +1 (809) 567-9698. Fax: +1 (809) 472-3313. Web: www.suprafm.com.
Radio Cima Cien (when operating), Apartado 804, Santo Domingo, Dominican Republic. Fax: +1 (809) 541 1088. Contact: Roberto Vargas, Director. Free pennants, postcards, coins and taped music. Roberto likes collecting stamps and coins.
Radio Cristal Internacional (if reactivated), Apartado Postal 894, Santo Domingo, Dominican Republic; or (street address) Calle Pepillo Salcedo No. 18, Altos, Santo Domingo, Dominican

Republic. Phone: +1 (809) 565-1460 or +1 (809) 566-5411. Fax: +1 (809) 567 9107. Contact: (general) Fernando Hermón Gross, Director de Programas; or Margarita Reyes, Secretaria; (administration) Darío Badía, Director General; or Héctor Badía, Director de Administración. Seeks reception reports. Return postage of $2 appreciated.

ECUADOR   World Time –5 (–4 sometimes, in times of drought); –6 Galapagos

NOTE: According to HCJB's "DX Party Line," during periods of drought, such as caused by "El Niño," electricity rationing causes periods in which transmitters cannot operate because of inadequate hydroelectric power, as well as spikes which occasionally damage transmitters. Accordingly, many Ecuadorian stations tend to be irregular, or even entirely off the air, during drought conditions. IRCs are exchangeable only in the cities of Quito and Guayaquil, so enclosing $2 for return postage may be helpful when writing to stations in other locations.
Escuelas Radiofónicas Populares del Ecuador, Juan de Velasco 4755 y Guayaquil, Casilla Postal 06-01-341, Riobamba, Chimborazo, Ecuador. Phone: +593 (3) 961-608, +593 (3) 960-247. Fax: +593 (3) 961 625. Email: admin@esrapoec.ecuanex.net.ec. Web: www.ded.org.ec/essapa01.htm. Contact: Juan Pérez Sarmiento, Director Ejecutivo; or María Ercilia López, Secretaria. Free pennants and key rings. "Chimborazo" cassette of Ecuadorian music for 10,000 sucres plus postage; T-shirts for 12,000 sucres plus postage; and caps with station logo for 8,000 sucres plus postage. Return postage helpful. Replies to correspondence in Spanish.
☞HCJB World Radio, The Voice of the Andes
STATION: Casilla 17-17-691, Quito, Ecuador. Phone: (general) +593 (2) 226-6808 (X-4441, 1300-2200 World Time Monday through Friday, for the English Dept.); (Frequency management) +593 (2) 226-6808 (X-4627); (*DX Partyline* English program, toll-free, U.S. only, for reception reports, loggings and other correspondence) +1 866 343-0791. Fax: (general) +593 (2) 226 7263; (Frequency Manager) +593 (2) 226 4765. Email: (Graham) agraham@hcjb.org.ec; (Frequency management) irops@hcjb.org.ec or dweber@hcjb.org.ec; (language sections) format is language@hcjb.org.ec; so to reach, say, the Spanish Department, it would be spanish@hcjb.org.ec. Web: (English, includes on-demand audio and online reception report form) www.hcjb.org; (Spanish, includes on-demand and streaming audio) www.vozandes.org. Contact: (general) English [or other language] Department; (administration) Jim Estes, Director of Broadcasting; Alex Saks, Station Manager; Curt Cole, Programme Director, or Allen Graham, Ecuador National Director; (technical) Douglas Weber, Frequency Manager. Free religious brochures, calendars, stickers and pennants. IRC or $1 required.
INTERNATIONAL HEADQUARTERS: HCJB World Radio, P.O. Box 39800, Colorado Springs CO 80949-9800 USA. Phone: +1 (719) 590-9800. Fax: +1 (719) 590 9801. Email: info@hcjb.org. Contact: Andrew Braio, Public Information; (administration) Richard D. Jacquin, Director, International Operations. Various items sold via U.S. address—catalog available. This address is not a mail drop, so listeners' correspondence, except those concerned with purchasing HCJB items, should be directed to the usual Quito address.
ENGINEERING CENTER: HCJBWorld Engineering Center, 2830 South 17th Street, Elkhart IN 46517 USA. Phone: +1 (574) 970 4252. Fax: +1 (574) 293 9910. Email: info@hcjbeng.org. Web: www.hcjbeng.org. Contact: Dave Pasechnik, Project Manager; or Bob Moore, Engineering. This address only for those

professionally concerned with the design and manufacture of transmitter and antenna equipment. Listeners' correspondence should be directed to the usual Quito address.

REGIONAL OFFICES: Although HCJB has over 20 regional offices throughout the world, the station wishes that all listener correspondence be directed to the station in Quito, as the regional offices do not serve as mail drops for the station.

HD2IOA, Instituto Oceanográfico de la Armada, Avenida de la Marina, via Puerto Marítimo, Código Postal 5940, Guayaquil, Ecuador. Operating on 3810 kHz, HD2IOA is a time signal station operated by Eduador's Naval Oceanographic Institute. Replies to correspondence in Spanish and verifies reception reports.

La Voz de Saquisilí—Radio Libertador (when operating), Calle 24 de Mayo, Saquisilí, Cotopaxi, Ecuador. Phone: +593 (3) 721-035. Contact: Arturo Mena Herrera, Gerente-Propietario. Reception reports actively solicited. Return postage, in the form of $2 or mint Ecuadorian stamps, appreciated; IRCs difficult to exchange. Spanish strongly preferred.

La Voz del Napo, Misión Josefina, Tena, Napo, Ecuador. Phone: +593 (6) 886-356. Email: coljav20@yahoo.es. Contact: Padre Humberto Dorigatti, Director. Free pennants and stickers. $2 or return postage required. Replies irregularly to correspondence in Spanish or Italian.

La Voz del Upano

STATION: Vicariato Apostólico de Méndez, Misión Salesiana, 10 de Agosto s/n, Macas, Provincia de Morona Santiago, Ecuador. Phone: +593 (7) 505-247. Email: radioupano@easynet.net.cc. Contact: Sra. Leonor Guzmán, Directora. Free pennants and calendars. On one occasion, not necessarily to be repeated, sent tape of Ecuadorian folk music for $2. Otherwise, $2 required. Replies to correspondence in Spanish.

QUITO OFFICE: Procura Salesiana, Equinoccio 623 y Queseras del Medio, Quito, Ecuador. Phone: +593 (2) 255-1012.

Radio Buen Pastor—*see* Radio El Buen Pastor.

Radio Centinela del Sur (C.D.S. Internacional), Casilla 11-01-106, Loja, Ecuador; or (studios) Olmedo 11-56 y Mercadillo, Loja, Ecuador. Phone: +593 (7) 561-166 or +593 (7) 570-211. Fax: +593 (7) 562 270. Contact: (general) Marcos G. Coronel V., Director de Programas; or José A. Coronel V., Director del programa "Ovación"; (technical) José A. Coronel Illescas, Gerente General. Return postage required. Replies occasionally to correspondence in Spanish.

Radio Centro, Casilla 18-01-574, Ambato, Ecuador. Phone: +593 (3) 822-240 or +593 (3) 841-126. Fax: +593 (3) 829 824. Contact: Luis Alberto Gamboa Tello, Director Gerente; or Lic. María Elena de López. Free stickers. Return postage appreciated. Replies to correspondence in Spanish.

Radio Chaskis, Jirón Roldos Aguilera y Panamericana Norte, Otavalo, Imbabura, Ecuador; (offices) Calle Bolívar 805 y Juan Montalvo, Otavalo, Imbabura, Ecuador. Phone: +593 (62) 920-922, +593 (62) 920-256. Email: radiochaskis@hotmail.com. Contact: Luis Enrique Cachiguango Cotacachi, Propietario. Welcomes correspondence in Spanish, but replies are irregular because of limited resources.

Radiodifusora Cultural Católica La Voz del Upano—*see* La Voz del Upano, above.

Radiodifusora Cultural, La Voz del Napo—*see* La Voz del Napo, above.

Radio El Buen Pastor, Asociación Cristiana de Indígenas Saraguros (ACIS), Reino de Quito y Azuay, Correo Central, Saraguro, Loja, Ecuador. Phone: +593 (2) 00-146. Contact: (general) Dean Pablo Davis, Sub-director; Segundo Poma, Director; Mark Vogan, OMS Missionary; Mike Schrode, OMS Ecuador Field Director; Juana Guamán, Secretaria; or Zoila Vacacela, Secretaria; (technical) Miguel Kelly. $2 or return postage in the form of mint Ecuadorian stamps required, as IRCs are difficult to exchange in Ecuador. Station is keen to receive reception reports; may respond to English, but correspondence in Spanish preferred. $10 required for QSL card and pennant.

Radio Federación Shuar, Casilla 17-01-1422, Quito, Ecuador. Phone/Fax: +593 (2) 250-4264. Contact: Manuel Jesús Vinza Chacucuy, Director; Yurank Tsapak Rubén Gerardo, Director; or Prof. Albino M. Utitiaj P., Director de Medios. Return postage or $2 required. Replies irregularly to correspondence in Spanish.

📻**Radio María,** Baquerizo Moreno 281 y Leonidas Plaza, Quito, Ecuador. Phone: +593 (2) 256-4714. Web: (includes streaming audio) www.radiomariaecuador.org. A Catholic radio network currently leasing airtime over La Voz del Napo (*see*), but which is looking into the possiblity of setting up its own shortwave station.

Radio Oriental, Casilla 260, Tena, Napo, Ecuador. Phone: +593 (6) 886-033 or +593 (6) 886-388. Contact: Luis Enrique Espín Espinosa, Gerente General. $2 or return postage helpful. Reception reports welcome.

📻**Radio Quito,** Casilla 17-21-1971, Quito, Ecuador. Phone/Fax: +593 (2) 250 8301. Email: radioquito@ecuadoradio.com. Web: (includes streaming audio) www.elcomercio.com/secciones.asp?seid=329. Contact: Xavier Almeida, Gerente General; or José Almeida, Subgerente. Free stickers. Return postage normally required, but occasionally verifies email reports. Replies slowly, but regularly.

EGYPT   World Time +2 (+3 midyear)

WARNING: MAIL THEFT. Feedback from Passport readership indicates that money is sometimes stolen from envelopes sent to Radio Cairo.

Egyptian Radio, P.O. Box 1186, 11511 Cairo, Egypt. Email: ertu@ertu.gov.cg. Web: www.ertu.gov.eg. For additional details, *see* Radio Cairo, below.

Radio Cairo

NONTECHNICAL: P.O. Box 566, Cairo 11511, Egypt. Phone: +20 (2) 677-8945. Fax: +20 (2) 575 9553. Email: (English Service) egyptianoverseas_english@hotmail.com; (Spanish Service) radioelcairoespa@yahoo.com; (Brazilian Service) brazilian_prog@egyptradio.tv. Web: www.freewebs.com/overseas-radio. Contact: Mrs. Amal Badr, Head of English Programme; Mrs. Sahar Kalil, Director of English Service to North America and Producer, "Questions and Answers"; or Mrs. Magda Hamman, Secretary. Free stickers, postcards, stamps, maps, papyrus souvenirs, calendars and *External Services of Radio Cairo* book. Free booklet and individually tutored Arabic-language lessons with loaned textbooks from Kamila Abdullah, Director General, Arabic by Radio, Radio Cairo, P.O. Box 325, Cairo, Egypt. Arabic-language religious, cultural and language-learning audio and video tapes from the Egyptian Radio and Television Union sold via Sono Cairo Audio-Video, P.O. Box 2017, Cairo, Egypt; when ordering video tapes, inquire to ensure they function on the television standard (NTSC, PAL or SECAM) in your country. Once replied regularly, if slowly, but recently replies have been increasingly scarce. Comments welcomed about audio quality—*see* TECHNICAL, below. Avoid enclosing money (*see* WARNING, above).

TECHNICAL: Broadcast Engineering Department, 24th Floor—TV Building (Maspiro), Egyptian Radio and Television

Union, P.O. Box 1186, 11511 Cairo, Egypt. Phone/Fax: +20 (2) 574-6840. Email: (general) freqmeg@yahoo.com; (Lawrence) niveenl@hotmail.com. Contact: Hamdy Emara, Chairman of Engineering Sector; Mrs. Rokaya M. Kamel, Head of Engineering & Training; Mrs.Laila Hamdalla, Director of Monitoring & Frequency Management; or Mrs. Niveen W. Lawrence, Director of Shortwave Department. Comments and suggestions on audio quality and level especially welcomed. One Passport reader reported that his letter to this address was returned by the Egyptian postal authorities, but we have not received any other reports of returned mail.

EL SALVADOR   World Time –6

Radio Imperial (when operating), Apartado 56, Sonsonante, El Salvador. Fax: +503 450-0189. Contact: (general) Nubia Ericka García, Directora; Pastor Pedro Mendoza; (technical) Moisés B. Cruz G., Ingeniero. Replies to correspondence in English or Spanish, and verifies reception reports by fax, if number provided. $1 helpful.

ENGLAND—*see* UNITED KINGDOM.

EQUATORIAL GUINEA   World Time +1

Radio Africa, P.O. Box 851, Malabo, Equatorial Guinea. Email: radioafrica@myway.com.
U.S. ADDRESS FOR CORRESPONDENCE AND VERIFICATIONS: Pan American Broadcasting, 2021 The Alameda, Suite 240, San Jose CA 95126-1145 USA. Phone: +1 (408) 996-2033; (toll-free, U.S. only) 1-800-726-2620. Fax: +1 (408) 252 6855. Email: info@panambc.com; (Bernald) gbernald@panambc.com; (Jung) cjung@panambc.com. Web: www.panambc.com. Contact: (listener correspondence) Terry Kraemer; (general) Carmen Jung, Office and Sales Administrator; or Gene Bernald, President. $1, mint U.S. stamps or 2 IRCs required for reply.
Radio East Africa—same details as "Radio Africa," above.
Radio Nacional de Guinea Ecuatorial—Bata ("Radio Bata"), Apartado 749, Bata, Río Muni, Equatorial Guinea. Phone: +240 (8) 2592. Fax: +240 (8) 2093. Contact: José Mba Obama, Director. Not known to reply to correspondence.
Radio Nacional de Guinea Ecuatorial—Malabo ("Radio Malabo"), Apartado 195, Malabo, Isla Bioko, Equatorial Guinea. Phone: +240 (9) 2260. Fax: (general) +240 (9) 2097; (technical) +240 (9) 3122. Contact: (general) Román Manuel Mané-Abaga, Jefe de Programación; Ciprano Somon Suakin; or Manuel Sobede, Inspector de Servicios de Radio y TV; (technical) Hermenegildo Moliko Chele, Jefe Servicios Técnicos de Radio y Televisión. $1 or return postage required. Replies irregularly to correspondence in Spanish.

ERITREA   World Time +3

Radio UNMEE—*see* United Nations.
📻**Voice of the Broad Masses of Eritrea** (Dimtsi Hafash), Ministry of Information, Radio Division, P.O. Box 872, Asmara, Eritrea; or Ministry of Information, Technical Branch, P.O. Box 242, Asmara, Eritrea. Phone: +291 (1) 116-084 or +291 (1) 120-497. Fax: +291 (1) 126 747. Email: nesredin@tse.com.er. Web: (includes on-demand audio) www.shabait.com (click on "Dimtsi Hafash"). Contact: Ghebreab Ghebremedhin; or Berhane Gerzgiher, Director, Engineering Division. Return postage or $1 helpful. Free information on history of the station and about Eritrea.

ETHIOPIA   World Time +3

Radio Ethiopia: (external service) P.O. Box 654; (domestic service) P.O. Box 1020—both in Addis Ababa, Ethiopia (address your correspondence to "Audience Relations"). Phone: (main office) +251 (1) 116-427 or +251 (1) 551-011; (engineering) +251 (1) 200-948. Fax: +251 (1) 552 263. Web: www.angelfire.com/biz/radioethiopia. Contact: (external service, general) Kahsai Tewoldemedhin, Program Director; Ms. Woinshet Woldeyes, Secretary, Audience Relations; Ms. Ellene Mocria, Head of Audience Relations; or Yohaness Ruphael, Producer, "Contact"; (administration) Kasa Miliko, Head of Station; (technical) Terefe Ghebre Medhin or Zegeye Solomon. Free stickers and tourist brochures. Poor replier.
📻**Radio Fana** (Radio Torch), P.O. Box 30702, Addis Ababa, Ethiopia. Phone: +251 (1) 516-777. Fax: +251 (1) 515 039. Email: rfana@telecom.net.et. Web: (includes on-demand audio) www.radiofana.com. Contact: Woldu Yemessel, General Manager; Mesfin Alemayehu, Head, External Relations; or Girma Lema, Head, Planning and Research Department. Station is autonomous and receives its income from non-governmental educational sponsorship.
Voice of the Tigray Revolution, P.O. Box 450, Mek'ele, Tigray, Ethiopia. Contact: Fre Tesfamichael, Director. $1 helpful.

FINLAND   World Time +2 (+3 midyear)

📻**YLE Radio Finland**
MAIN OFFICE: Box 78, FIN-00024 Yleisradio, Finland. Phone: (general, 24-hour English speaking switchboard for both Radio Finland and Yleisradio Oy) +358 (9) 14801; (international information) +358 (9) 1480-3729; (administration) +358 (9) 1480-4320 or +358 (9) 1480-4316; (Technical Customer Service) +358 (9) 1480-3213; (comments on programs) +358 (9) 1480-5490. Fax: (general) +358 (9) 148 1169; (international information) +358 (9) 1480 3391; (Technical Affairs) +358 (9) 1480 3588. Email: (general) rfinland@yle.fi, or rfinland@aol.com; (comments on programs) christina.rockstroh@yle.fi; (Yleisradio Oy parent organization) fbc@yle.fi; (reception reports) raimoe.makela@yle.fi. To contact individuals, the format is firstname.lastname@yle.fi; so to reach, say, Pertti Seppä, it would be pertti.seppa@yle.fi. Web: (includes on-demand and streaming audio) www.yle.fi/rfinland. Contact—Radio Finland: (administration) Juhani Niinistö, Head of International Radio; (comments on programs) Mrs. Christina Rockstroh, Managing Editor, foreign language radio. Contact—Yleisradio Oy parent organization: (general) Marja Salusjärvi, Head of International PR; (administration) Arne Wessberg, Managing Director; or Tapio Siikala, Director for Domestic and International Radio. Sometimes provides free stickers and small souvenirs, as well as tourist and other magazines. For a free color catalog of souvenirs, clothes, toys, timepieces, binoculars, CDs, tapes and other merchandise, contact the YLE Shop, Yleisradio, Pl 77, FIN-00003 Helsinki, Finland. Phone: +358 (9) 1480-3555. Fax: +358 (9) 1480 3466 or go to www.yle.fi/yleshop. Replies to correspondence. For verification of reception reports, *see* Transmission Facility, below. YLE Radio Finland external broadcasting is a part of YLE and not a separate administrative unit. Radio Finland itself is not a legal entity. *NUNTII LATINI (Program in Latin):* P.O. Box 99, FIN- 00024 Yleisradio, Finland. Fax: +358 (9) 1480 3391. Email: nuntii.latini@yle.fi. Web: www.yle.fi/fbc/nuntii.html. Six years of Nuntii Latini now available in books I to III at US$30 each from: Bookstore Tiedekirja, Kirkkokatu 14, FIN-00170 Helsinki, Finland; Fax: +358 (9) 635 017. VISA/MC/EURO.

SHORTWAVE PLANNING: Digita, Site Management and Operations, P.O. Box 135, FIN-00521 Helsinki, Finland. Phone: (Huuhka) +358 (20) 411-7287; (Hautala) +358 (20) 411-7282. Fax: +358 (9) 148 5260. Email: esko.huuhka@digita.fi or kari.hautala@digita.fi. Contact: Kari Hautala, Frequency Manager; or Esko Huuhka, Head of Broadcast Planning.

TRANSMISSION FACILITY: Digita Shortwave Centre, Makholmantie 79, FIN-28660 Pori; or (verifications) Pori SW Base, Preiviikki, FIN-28660 Pori, Finland—Attention: Raimo Mäkelä. (Email: raimo.makela@yle.fi). Web: (Digita Oy) www.digita.fi; www.yle.fi/sataradio/preiviiki.html. Contact: Kalevi Vahtera, Station Manager; or Raimo Mäkelä (QSL-verifications). Issues full-data verification cards for good reception reports, and provides free illustrated booklets about the transmitting station.

NORTH AMERICAN OFFICE—LISTENER and MEDIA LIAISON: P.O. Box 462, Windsor CT 06095 USA. Phone: +1 (860) 688-5540 or +1 (860) 688-5098. Phone/Fax: (24-hour toll-free within U.S. and Canada for recorded schedule and voice mail) 1-800-221-9539. Fax: +1 (860) 688 0113. Email: yleus@aol.com. Contact: John Berky, YLE Finland Transcriptions. Free *YLE North America* newsletter. This office does not verify reception reports.

Scandinavian Weekend Radio (international service), P.O. Box 99, FIN-34801, Virrat, Finland. Phone: (live when on air and SMS service) +358 (400) 995-559. Fax: (when on air) +358 (3) 475 5776. Email: (general) info@swradio.net; (technical) esa.saunamaki@swradio.net; (reception reports) online report form at the station's Website: www.swradio.net. Contact: Alpo Heinonen, Informant; Esa Saunamäki, Chief editor; or Teemu Lehtimäki, QSL Manager. $2 or 2 euros required for verification card via mail. Web reports also verified via the internet.

FRANCE   World Time +1 (+2 midyear)

Le Héraut de la Christian Science, B.P. 80014, F-95601 Eaubonne Cedex, France.
Email: (Flamand) jflamand@club-internet.fr. Web: www.cs2paris.org/radios.html. Contact: Josette Flamand. Broadcasts via the Jülich facilities of Germany's T-Systems International (see).
SCHEDULES AND RELIGIOUS PUBLICATIONS: Le Héraut, P.O. Box 1524, Boston MA 02117-1524 USA. Email: heraut@csps.com. Web: www.tfccs.com/gv/csps/herald/french/radio.jhtml.

Radio France Internationale (RFI)
MAIN OFFICE: B.P. 9516, F-75016 Paris Cedex 16, France; (street address) 116, avenue du président Kennedy, F-75016 Paris, France. Phone: (general) +33 (1) 5640-1212; (International Affairs and Program Placement) +33 (1) 4430-8932 or +33 (1) 4430-8949; (Service de la communication) +33 (1) 4230-2951; (Audience Relations) +33 (1) 4430-8969/70/71; (Media Relations) +33 (1) 4230-2985; (Développement et de la communication) +33 (1) 4430-8921; *(Fréquence Monde)* +33 (1) 4230-1086; (English Service) +33 (1) 5640-3062; (Spanish Department) +33 (1) 4230-3048. Fax: (general) +33 (1) 5640 4759; (International Affairs and Program Placement) +33 (1) 4430 8920; (Audience Relations) +33 (1) 4430 8999; (other nontechnical) +33 (1) 4230 4481; (English Service) +33 (1) 5640 2674; (Spanish Department) +33 (1) 4230 4669. Email: (Audience Relations) courrier.auditeurs@rfi.fr; (English Service) english.service@rfi.fr; (Maguire) john.maguire@rfi.fr; (Spanish Service) america.latina@rfi.fr. Web: (includes on-demand and streaming audio) www.rfi.fr. Contact: John Maguire, Editor, English Language Service; J.P. Charbonnier, Producer, "Lettres des Auditeurs"; Joël Amar, International Affairs/Program Place-

ment Department; Arnaud Littardi, Directeur du développement et de la communication; Nicolas Levkov, Rédactions en Langues Etrangères; Daniel Franco, Rédaction en français; Mme. Anne Toulouse, Rédacteur en chef du Service Mondiale en français; Christine Berbudeau, Rédacteur en chef, *Fréquence* **Monde**; or Marc Verney, Attaché de Presse; (administration) Jean-Paul Cluzel, Président-Directeur Général; (technical) M. Raymond Pincon, Producer, "Le Courrier Technique." Free *Fréquence* **Monde** bi-monthly magazine in French upon request. Free souvenir keychains, pins, lighters, pencils, T-shirts and stickers have been received by some—especially when visiting the headquarters at 116 avenue du Président Kennedy, in the 16th Arrondissement. Can provide supplementary materials for "Dites-moi tout" French-language course; write to the attention of Mme. Chantal de Grandpre, "Dites-moi tout." "Le Club des Auditeurs" French-language listener's club ("Club 9516" for English-language listeners); applicants must provide name, address and two passport-type photos, whereupon they will receive a membership card and the club bulletin. RFI exists primarily to defend and promote Francophone culture, but also provides meaningful information and cultural perspectives in non-French languages.

TRANSMISSION OFFICE, TECHNICAL: TéléDiffusion de France, Direction de la Production et des Méthodes, Service ondes courtes, 10 rue d'Oradour sur Glane, 75732 Paris Cedex 15, France. Phone: (Gruson) +33 (1) 5595 1553; (Meunier) +33 (1) 5595-1161. Fax: +33 (1) 5595 2137. Email: (Gruson) jacques.gruson@tdf.fr; (Meunier) a_meunier@compuserve.com or (Penneroux) michel.penneroux@tdf.fr. Contact: Jacques Gruson; Alain Meunier; Michel Penneroux, Business Development Manager AM-HF; Mme Annick Daronian or Mme Sylvie Greuillet (short wave service). This office is for informing about transmitter-related problems (interference, modulation quality), and also for reception reports and verifications.

UNITED STATES PROMOTIONAL, SCHOOL LIAISON, PROGRAM PLACEMENT AND CULTURAL EXCHANGE OFFICES:

NEW ORLEANS: Services Culturels, Suite 2105, Ambassade de France, 300 Poydras Street, New Orleans LA 70130 USA. Phone: +1 (504) 523-5394. Phone/Fax: +1 (504) 529-7502. Contact: Adam-Anthony Steg, Attaché Audiovisuel. This office promotes RFI, especially to language teachers and others in the educational community within the southern United States, and arranges for bi-national cultural exchanges. It also sets up RFI feeds to local radio stations within the southern United States.

NEW YORK: Audiovisual Bureau, Radio France Internationale, 972 Fifth Avenue, New York NY 10021 USA. Phone: +1 (212) 439-1452. Fax: +1 (212) 439 1455. Contact: Gérard Blondel or Julien Vin. This office promotes RFI, especially to language teachers and others within the educational community outside the southern United States, and arranges for bi-national cultural exchanges. It also sets up RFI feeds to local radio stations within much of the United States.

NEW YORK NEWS BUREAU: 1290 Avenue of the Americas, New York NY 10019 USA. Phone: +1 (212) 581-1771. Fax: +1 (212) 541 4309. Contact: Ms. Auberi Edler, Reporter; or Bruno Albin, Reporter.

WASHINGTON NEWS BUREAU: 529 14th Street NW, Suite 1126, Washington DC 20045 USA. Phone: +1 (202) 879-6706. Contact: Pierre J. Cayrol.

SAN FRANCISCO OFFICE, SCHEDULES: 2654 17th Avenue, San Francisco CA 94116 USA. Phone: +1 (415) 564-9968. Email: GPoppin@aol.com. Contact: George Poppin. This address, a volunteer office, only provides RFI schedules to listeners. All other correspondence should be sent directly to the main office in Paris.

📻Radio Monte Carlo-Middle East

MAIN OFFICE: Radio Monte Carlo-Moyen Orient, 116 avenue du président Kennedy, F-75116 Paris, France; or B.P. 371, Paris 16, France. Email: contact@rmc-mo.com. Web: (includes on-demand and streaming audio) www.rmc-mo.com. A station of the RFI group whose programs are produced in Paris and aired via a mediumwave AM transmitter in Cyprus; also via FM in France and parts of the Middle East. Provides programs for RFI's Arabic service. A daily Arabic program is also broadcast on shortwave to North America via Radio Canada International's Sackville facililities.

CYPRUS ADDRESS: P.O. Box 2026, Nicosia, Cyprus. Contact: M. Pavlides, Chef de Station. Reception reports have sometimes been verified via this address.

Voice of Orthodoxy—*see* Voix de l'Orthodoxie, below.

Voix de l'Orthodoxie, B.P. 416-08, F-75366 Paris Cedex 08, France. Phone: +33 (1) 4977-0366. Fax: +33 (1) 4353 4066. Email: voix.orthodoxie@wanadoo.fr. Web: www.russie.net/orthodoxie/vo. Contact: Michel Solovieff, General Secretary. Broadcasts religious programming to Russia via a shortwave transmitter in Kazakstan. Verifies reception reports, including those written in English.

ADDRESS IN RUSSIA: Golos Pravoslavia, 39 Nab. Leyt. Schmidta, 199034 St. Petersburg, Russia. Phone/Fax: +7 (812) 323-2867.

FRENCH GUIANA   World Time –3

Radio France Internationale Guyane Relay Station, Télédiffusion de France S.A., Délégation Territoriale de Guyane, B.P. 7024, 97307 Cayenne Cedex, French Guiana. Phone: Tel: +594 350-550. Fax: +594 350 555. Contact: (technical) Le Responsable pour Groupe Maintenance. All correspondence concerning non-technical matters should be sent directly to the main addresses (*see*) for Radio France Internationale in France. Can consider replies only to technical correspondence in French. Occasionally verifies reception reports, albeit slowly.

GABON   World Time +1

Afrique Numéro Un, B.P. 1, Libreville, Gabon. Fax: +241 742 133. Email: online form. Web: (includes streaming audio) www.africa1.com. Contact: (general) Gaston Didace Singangoye; or Jean Félix Ngawin Ndong; (technical) Mme. Marguerite Bayimbi, Le Directeur [sic] Technique. Free calendars and bumper stickers. $1, 2 IRCs or return postage helpful. Replies very slowly.

RTV Gabonaise (when operating), B.P. 10150, Libreville, Gabon. Contact: André Ranaud-Renombo, Le Directeur Technique, Adjoint Radio. Free stickers. $1 required. Replies occasionally, but slowly, to correspondence in French.

GEORGIA   World Time +3 (+4 midyear)

📻Georgian Radio, TV-Radio Tbilisi, ul. M. Kostava 68, Tbilisi 380071, Republic of Georgia. Phone: (external service) +995 (32) 360-063. Fax: +995 (32) 955 137. Email: foraf@geotvr.ge; (Shonova) dodo.shonava@geotvr.ge; (Mumladze) lia_mumladse@yahoo.ge. Web: (includes streaming audio from domestic service not on shortwave) www.geotvr.ge. Contact: Mrs. Dodo Shonava, General Director; Mrs. Lia Mumladse, German Section. Replies erratically and slowly, in part due to financial restrictions. Return postage or $1 helpful.

Radio Hara, Rustaveli Ave. 52, II Floor, Apt. 211-212, Tbilisi, Georgia. Email: league@geoconst.org.ge. Contact: Nino Berdznishvili, Program Manager; or Zourab Shengelia. Programs are produced by the Georgian-Abkhazian Relations Institute.

Republic of Abkhazia Radio, Abkhaz State Radio and TV Co., Aidgylara Street 34, Sukhum 384900, Republic of Abkhazia; or Zvanba Street 8, Sukhum 384900, Republic of Abkhazia. However, given the problems in getting mail to Abkhazia, the station requests that reception reports be sent to the following address: National Library of Abkhazia, Krasnodar District, P.O. Box 964, 354000 Sochi, Russia. Phone: +995 (881) 24-867 or +995 (881) 25-321. Fax: +995 (881) 21 144. Contact: Zurab Argun, Director. A 1992 uprising in northwestern Georgia drove the majority of ethnic Georgians from the region. This area remains virtually autonomous from Georgia.

GERMANY   World Time +1 (+2 midyear)

Christliche Wissenschaft (Christian Science), Radiosendungen, E. Bethmann, Postfach 7330, D-22832 Norderstedt, Germany; or CS-Radiosendungen, Alexanderplatz 2, D-20099 Hamburg, Germany. Contact: Erich Bethmann. Replies to correspondence in German and verifies reception reports. Return postage helpful. Via the Jülich facilities of T-Systems International (*see*).

T-Systems International. *See* "Shortwave Radio Station Jülich—T-Systems International AG."

📻Deutsche Welle

MAIN OFFICE: Kurt-Schumacher-Str. 3, D-53113 Bonn, Germany; or (postal address) DW, D-53110, Bonn, Germany. Phone: +49 (228) 429-0; (English Service) +49 (228) 429-4144. Fax: +1 (228) 429 3000; (English Service) +49 (228) 429 2860. Email: online@dw-world.de; (English Service) feedback.english@dw-world.de. To reach specific individuals by email at Deutsche Welle the format is: firstname.lastname@dw-world.de. For language courses: feedback.radio@dw-world.de. Web: (includes on-demand and streaming audio) www.dw-world.de. Contact: Erik Bettermann, Director General; or Uta Thofern, Head of English Service. Broadcasts via transmitters in Germany, Canada, Madagascar, Netherlands Antilles, Portugal, Russia, Rwanda, Singapore, Sri Lanka and Taiwan.

TECHNICAL ADVISORY SERVICE: Phone: +49 (228) 429-3208. Fax: +49 (228) 429 3220. Email: tb@dw-world.de. All technical mail and QSL-reports should be sent to the Technical Advisory Service.

U.S./CANADIAN LISTENER CONTACT OFFICE: 2000 M Street, NW, Suite 335, Washington DC 20036 USA. Phone: +1 (202) 785-5730. Fax: +1 (202) 785 5735.

📻Deutschlandfunk, Raderberggürtel 40, D-50968 Köln, Germany. Phone: +49 (221) 345-0. Fax: +49 (221) 345 4802. Email: (program information) deutschlandfunk@dradio.de. Web: (includes on-demand and streaming audio) www.dradio.de/dlf. Verifies reception reports in German or English.

📻DeutschlandRadio-Berlin, Hans-Rosenthal-Platz, D-10825 Berlin Schönberg, Germany. Phone: +49 (30) 8503-0. Fax: +49 (30) 8503 6168. Email: (program information) dkultur@dradio. de Web: (includes on-demand and streaming audio) www. dradio.de/dkultur. Contact: Dr. Karl-Heinz Stamm; or Ulrich Reuter. Verifies reception reports in German or English. Sometimes sends stickers, pens, magazines and other souvenirs.

Evangeliums-Radio-Hamburg, Postfach 920741, D-21137 Hamburg, Germany. Phone: +49 (40) 702-7025. Email: evangeliums-radio-hamburg@t-online.de. Web: www.evr-hamburg.de.

Verifies reception reports in German or English. Via T-Systems International's Jülich facilities, and locally on FM and cable.

Freie Volksmission Krefeld.(Free People's Mission Krefeld), Postfach 100707, D-47707 Krefeld, Germany; (street address) Freie Volksmission, Am Herbertzhof 15, D-47809 Krefeld, Germany; (English correspondence) Mission Center, P.O. Box 100707, D-47707 Krefeld, Germany. Phone: +49 (2151) 545-151. Email: postmaster@freie-volksmission.de. Web: (includes on-demand and streaming audio) www.freie-volksmission.de. Replies to correspondence in English or German. Via T-Systems International (*see*).

Hamburger Lokalradio
STUDIO ADDRESS: Kulturzentrum Lola, Lohbrügger, Landstrasse 8, D-21031 Hamburg, Germany. Phone: +49 (40) 7269-2422. Fax: +49 (40) 7269 2423. Web: www.hamburger-lokalradio. de, or www.hhlr.de.
EDITORIAL ADDRESS: Michael Kittner, Hamburger Lokalradio, Max-Eichholz-Ring 18, D-21031 Hamburg, Germany. Phone/Fax: +49 (40) 738-2417. Email: m.kittner@freenet.de. Contact: Michael Kittner.
Broadcasts regularly on FM and cable, and intermittently on world band via the Jülich facilities of T-Systems International (*see*) and a Latvian transmitter. Replies to correspondence in German or English. Return postage required for postal reply.

Missionswerk Friedensstimme, Postfach 100638, D-51606 Gummersbach, Germany; or (street address) Gimborner Str. 20, D-51709 Marienheide, Germany. Phone: +49 (2261) 24717. Fax: +49 (2261) 60170. Contact: N. Berg. Replies to correspondence and verifies reception reports in German or Russian. Broadcasts to Russia via T-Systems International (*see*).

Missionswerk Werner Heukelbach, D-51702 Bergneustadt 2, Germany. Contact: Manfred Paul. Religious broadcaster heard via the Voice of Russia, and formerly via the Jülich facilities of T-Systems International (*see*). Replies to correspondence in German or English and verifies reception reports. IRC helpful.

MV Baltic Radio, R&R Medienservice, Roland Rohde, Seestrasse 17, D-19089 Göhren, Germany. Phone: +49 (3861) 301 380. Fax: +49 (3861) 302 9720. Email: info@rrms.de, info@mvbalticradio.de. Web: www.mvbalticradio.de. Contact: Roland Rohde. Replies to correspondence in German or English, and verifies reception reports. IRC or $1 required for postal reply. A monthly broadcast produced in Göhren (Mecklenburg-Vorpommern) and aired via the Jülich facilities of T-Systems International (*see*). Prior to April 2005, operated as Stör-Sender via a Latvian transmitter.

Radio Multikulti, Rundfunk Berlin-Brandenburg, D-14046 Berlin, Germany; (street address) Rundfunk Berlin-Brandenburg, Masurenallee 8-14, D-14057 Berlin, Germany.
Phone: +49 (30) 3031-1655. Email: multikulti@rbb-online.de. Web: (includes on-demand and streaming audio) www.multikulti.de. Provides programming for the Romany transmissions of Deutsche Welle (*see*) and verifies reception reports on those broadcasts. Accepts email reports, which are verified with QSL cards.

Radio Santec, Marienstrasse 1, D-97070 Würzburg, Germany. Phone: (0800-1600 Central European Time, Monday through Friday) +49 (931) 3903-264. Fax: +49 (931) 3903 195. Email: info@radio-santec.com. Web: (includes on-demand and streaming audio) www.radio-santec.com. Reception reports verified with QSL cards only if requested. Radio Santec, constituted as a separate legal entity in 1999, is the radio branch of Universelles Leben (Universal Life).

Shortwave Radio Station Jülich—T-Systems International
Rundfunksendestelle Jülich, Merscher Höehe D-52428 Jülich, Germany. Phone: (head of station) +49 (2461) 697-310; (Technical Engineer) +49 (2461) 697-330; (Brodowsky, Sales and Marketing) +49 (2461) 937-164; (Ralf Weyl, back office) +49 (2461) 697-340. Fax: (all offices) +49 (2461) 937 165. Email: (Hirte) guenter.hirte@t-systems.com; (Goslawski) roman. goslawski@t-systems.com; (Brodowsky) walter.brodowsky@t-systems.com; (Weyl) ralf.weyl@t-systems.com. Contact: Günter Hirte, Head of Shortwave Radio Station Jülich; Roman Goslawski, Deputy Head of Shortwave Radio Station Jülich; Horst Tobias, Frequency Manager; Walter Brodowsky, Sales and Marketing Manager for Shortwave Broadcasts; or Ralf Weyl, Customer Services. Reception reports accepted by mail or fax, and should be clearly marked to the attention of Walter Brodowsky. T-Systems International operates transmitters on German soil used by Deutsche Welle, as well as those leased to various international world band stations.

Stimme des Evangeliums, Evangelische Missions-Gemeinden, Jahnstrasse 9, D-89182 Bernstadt, Germany. Phone: +49 (7348) 948-026. Fax: +49 (7348) 948-027. Contact: Pastor Albert Giessler. Verifies reception reports in German or English. A broadcast of the Evangelical Missions Congregations in Germany, and aired via T-Systems International (*see*) in Jülich.

T-Systems International—see Shortwave Radio Station Jülich—T-Systems International.

GHANA   World Time exactly

WARNING—CONFIDENCE ARTISTS: Attempted correspondence with Radio Ghana may result in requests, perhaps resulting from mail theft, from skilled confidence artists for money, free electronic or other products, publications or immigration sponsorship. To help avoid this, correspondence to Radio Ghana should be sent via registered mail.

Ghana Broadcasting Corporation, Broadcasting House, P.O. Box 1633, Accra, Ghana. Phone: +233 (21) 221-161. Fax: +233 (21) 221 153 or +233 (21) 773 227. Contact: (general) Director of Corporate Affairs; (administration) Director of Radio; (technical) Director of Engineering, or Propagation Department. Replies tend to be erratic, and reception reports are best sent to the attention of the Propagation Engineer, GBC Monitoring Station. Enclosing an IRC, return postage or $1 and registering your letter should improve the chances of a reply.

GREECE   World Time +2 (+3 midyear)

Foni tis Helladas (Voice of Greece)
NONTECHNICAL: Hellenic Radio-Television, ERA-5, The Voice of Greece, 432 Mesogion Av., 15342 Athens, Greece; or P.O. Box 60019, 15310 Aghia Paraskevi, Athens, Greece. Phone: +30 210-606-6310. Fax: +30 210 606 6309. Email: era5@ert. gr; (Foreign Language News Department) interprogram@ert. gr. Web: (includes streaming audio) www.voiceofgreece.gr. Contact: Angeliki Barka, Head of Programmes; or Gina Vogiatzoglou, Managing Director. Free tourist literature.
TECHNICAL: Elliniki Radiophonia—ERA-5, General Technical Directorate, ERT/ERA Hellenic Radio Television SA, Mesogion 402, 15342 Athens, Greece. Phone: (Charalambopoulos) +30 210-606-6257; (Vorgias) +30 210-606-6256 or +30 210-606-6263. Fax: +30 210 606 6243. Email: (reception reports) era5@ert.gr; (Vorgias) svorgias@ert.gr; (Charalambopoulos) bcharalabopoulos@ert.gr. Contact: Charalambos Charalambopoulos or Sotiris Vorgias, Planning Engineer; (administration) Th. Kokossis, General Director; or Nicolas Yannakakis, Director. Technical reception reports may be sent via mail, fax or email. Taped reports not accepted.

☞**Radiophonikos Stathmos Makedonias**, Subdirection of Technical Support, P.O. Box 11312, 54110 Thessaloniki, Greece (this address for technical correspondence only); or Angelaki 14, 54636 Thessaloniki, Greece. Phone: +30 2310-299-400. Fax: +30 2310 299 550. Email: eupro@ert3.gr. Web: (includes streaming audio) www.ert3.gr. Contact: (general) Mrs. Tatiana Tsioli, Program Director; or Lefty Kongalides, Head of International Relations; (technical) Dimitrios Keramidas, Engineer. Free booklets, stickers and other small souvenirs.

GUAM   World Time +10

Adventist World Radio—KSDA
OPERATIONS AND ENGINEERING: P.O. Box 8990, Agat, GU 96928 USA. Phone: +1 (671) 565-2289. Fax: +1 (671) 565 2983. Email: brook@awr.org. Contact: Brook Powers. This address for specialized technical correspondence only. For further information, see AWR listing under USA.

Trans World Radio—KTWR
MAIN OFFICE, ENGINEERING INQUIRIES & FREQUENCY COORDINATION ONLY: P.O. Box 8780, Agat, GU 96928 USA. Phone: +1 (671) 828-8637. Fax: +1 (671) 828 8636. Email: (White) cwhite@guam.twr.org; (Ross) ktwrfcd@guam.twr.org. Contact: Chuck White, Chief Engineer/Station Manager; or George Ross, Frequency Coordination Manager. This office will also verify email reports with a QSL card. Requests reports covering 15-30 minutes of programming. All English listener mail of a nontechnical nature should be sent to the Australian office (*see* next entry). Addresses for listener mail in other languages are given in the broadcasts. Also, *see* Trans World Radio, USA.
ENGLISH LISTENER MAIL, NONTECHNICAL: Trans World Radio, P.O. Box 390, Box Hill, Victoria 3128, Australia. Phone: +61 (3) 9899 3800. Fax: +61 (3) 9899 3900. Email: infoaus@twr.org. Web: http://twraustralia.org. Contact: John Reeder, National Director.

GUATEMALA   World Time –6

Radio Amistad (when operating), Iglesia Bautista Getsemani, San Pedro La Laguna, Solola, Guatemala.
ADDRESS FOR RECEPTION REPORTS: David Daniell, Asesor de Comunicaciones, Apartado Postal 25, Bulevares MX, 53140 Mexico. Phone/Fax: +52 (55) 5572-9633. Email: dpdaniell@aol.com. Replies to correspondence in English or Spanish.
Radio Buenas Nuevas, 13020 San Sebastián, Huehuetenango, Guatemala. Contact: Israel G. Rodas Mérida, Gerente. $1 or return postage helpful. Free religious and station information in Spanish. Sometimes includes a small pennant. Replies to correspondence in Spanish.
Radio Coatán—*see* Radio Cultural Coatán.
☞**Radio Cultural—TGNA**, Apartado 601, 01901 Guatemala City, Guatemala; (studios) 4Av. 30-09 Zona 3, Guatemala City, Guatemala. Phone: +502 2472-1745, +502 2471-4378, +502 2440-0260. Fax: +502 2440-0260. Email: tgn@radiocultural.com; tgna@guate.net. Web: (includes streaming audio) www.radiocultural.com. Contact: Wayne Berger, Chief Engineer; or [Ms.] Yojhana Ajsivinac, Secretary. Free religious printed matter, tourist information and pennant (when available). Return postage or $1 appreciated.
Radio Cultural Coatán—TGCT, San Sebastián Coatán 13035, Huehuetenango, Guatemala. Phone: +502 7758-3491, +502 7758-5494. Contact: Diego Sebastián Miguel, Locutor. $1 or return postage required. Often announces as just "Radio Coatán."

Radio K'ekchi—TGVC, 3ra Calle 7-15, Zona 1, 16015 Fray Bartolomé de las Casas, Alta Verapaz, Guatemala; (Media Consultant) David Daniell, Asesor de Comunicaciones, Apartado Postal 25, Bulevares MX, 53140 Mexico. Phone: (station) +502 7950-0299; (Daniell, Phone/Fax) +52 (55) 5572-9633. Fax: (station) +502 7950 0398. Email: dpdaniell@aol.com. Contact: (general) Gilberto Sun Xicol, Gerente; Ancelmo Cuc Chub, Director; or Mateo Botzoc, Director de Programas; (technical) Larry Baysinger, Ingeniero Jefe. Free paper pennant. $1 or return postage required. Replies to correspondence in Spanish.
Radio Maya de Barillas—TGBA (when operating), 13026 Villa de Barillas, Huehuetenango, Guatemala. Contact: José Castañeda, Pastor Evangélico y Gerente. Free pennants and pins. Station is very interested in receiving reception reports. $1 or return postage required. Replies occasionally to correspondence in Spanish.
Radio Verdad, Apartado Postal 5, Chiquimula, Guatemala. Email: radioverdad@chiquimula.zzn.com. Contact: Dr. Édgar Amílcar Madrid Morales, Gerente. May send free pennants & calendars. Replies to correspondence in Spanish or English; return postage appreciated. An evangelical and educational station.

GUINEA   World Time exactly

Radiodiffusion-Télévision Guinéenne, B.P. 391, Conakry, Guinea. If no reply is forthcoming from this address, try sending your letter to: D.G.R./P.T.T., B.P. 3322, Conakry, Guinea. Phone/Fax: +224 451-408. Email: (Issa Conde, Directeur) issaconde@yahoo.fr. Contact: (general) Yaoussou Diaby, Journaliste Sportif; Boubacar Yacine Diallo, Directeur Général/ORTG; Issa Conde, Directeur; or Seny Camara; (administration) Momo Toure, Chef Services Administratifs; (technical, studio) Mbaye Gagne, Chef de Studio; (technical, overall) Direction des Services Techniques. Return postage or $1 required. Replies very irregularly to correspondence in French.

GUYANA   World Time –3

Voice of Guyana, Guyana Broadcasting Corporation, Broadcasting House, P.O. Box 10760, Georgetown, Guyana; or Operations Centre, 44 High Street, Werk-en-Rust, Georgetown, Guyana. Phone: +592 (2) 258-734, +592 (2) 258-083 or +592 (2) 262-691. Fax: +592 (2) 258 756, but persist as the fax machine appears to be switched off much of the time. Contact: (general) Indira Anandjit, Personnel Assistant; or M. Phillips; (technical) Roy Marshall, Senior Technician; or Shiroxley Goodman, Chief Engineer. $1 or IRC helpful. Sending a spare sticker from another station helps assure a reply. Note that when the station's mediumwave AM transmitter is down because of a component fault, parts of the shortwave unit are sometimes 'borrowed' until spares become available. As a result, the station is sometimes off shortwave for several weeks at a time.

HOLLAND—*see* NETHERLANDS

HONDURAS   World Time –6

La Voz de la Mosquitia (if reactivated)
STATION: Barrio El Centro, Puerto Lempira, Dpto. Gracias a Dios, Honduras. Contact: Sammy Simpson, Director; or Larry Sexton. Free pennants.
U.S. OFFICE: Global Outreach, Box 1, Tupelo MS 38802 USA. Phone: +1 (601) 842-4615. Another U.S. contact is Larry

Hooker, who occasionally visits the station, and who can be reached at +1 (334) 694-7976.

La Voz Evangélica—HRVC

MAIN OFFICE: Apartado Postal 3252, Tegucigalpa, M.D.C., Honduras. Phone: +504 234-3468/69/70. Fax: +504 233 3933. Email: programas@hrvc.org. Web (includes streaming audio): www.hrvc.org. Contact: (general) Srta. Orfa Esther Durón Mendoza, Secretaria; Tereso Ramos, Director de Programación; Alan Maradiaga; or Modesto Palma, Jefe, Depto. Tráfico; (technical) Carlos Paguada, Director del Dpto. Técnico; (administration) Venancio Mejía, Gerente; or Nelson Perdomo, Director. Free calendars. Three IRCs or $1 required. Replies to correspondence in English, Spanish, Portuguese or German.

REGIONAL OFFICE, SAN PEDRO SULA: Apartado 2336, San Pedro Sula, Honduras. Phone: +504 557-5030. Contact: Hernán Miranda, Director.

REGIONAL OFFICE, LA CEIBA: Apartado 164, La Ceiba, Honduras. Phone: +504 443-2390. Contact: José Banegas, Director.

Radio HRMI, Radio Misiones Internacionales

STATION: Apartado Postal 20583, Comayagüela, M.D.C., Honduras. Phone: +504 233 9029, +504 238-4933. Contact: Wayne Downs, Director. $1 or return postage helpful.

U.S. OFFICE: IMF World Missions, P.O. Box 6321, San Bernardino CA 92412, USA. Phone +1 (909) 370-4515. Fax: +1 (909) 370 4862. Email: jkpimf@msn.com. Contact: Dr. James K. Planck, President; or Gustavo Roa, Coordinator.

Radio Luz y Vida—HRPC, Apartado 303, San Pedro Sula, Honduras; (reception reports in English) HRPC Radio, P. O. Box 303, San Pedro Sula, Honduras. Phone: +504 654-1221. Fax: +504 557 0394. Email: efmhonduras@globalnet.hn. Contact: Donald R. Moore, Station Director; or, to have your letter read over the air, "English Friendship Program." Return postage or $1 appreciated.

HUNGARY   World Time +1 (+2 midyear)

Kossuth Rádió, Bródy Sándor utca 5-7, H-1800 Budapest, Hungary. Phone: +36 (1) 328-7945. Web: (includes on-demand and streaming audio) www.radio.hu/index.php?rovat_id=76; (English) www.english.radio.hu/rovat/1056.

Radio Budapest, Bródy Sándor utca 5-7, H-1800 Budapest, Hungary. Phone: (general) +36 (1) 328-7224, +36 (1) 328-8328, +36 (1) 328-7357 +36 (1) 328-8588, +36 (1) 328-7710 or +36 (1) 328-7723; (voice mail, English) +36 (1) 328-8320; (voice mail, German) +36 (1) 328-7325; (administration) +36 (1) 328-7503 or +36 (1) 328-8415; (technical) +36 (1) 328-7226 or +36 (1) 328-8923. Fax: (general) +36 (1) 328 8517; (administration) +36 (1) 328 8838; (technical) +36 (1) 328 7105. Email: (English) english@kaf.radio.hu; (German) nemet1@kaf. radio.hu; (Spanish) espanol@kaf.radio.hu; (technical) (Füszfás) fuszfasla@muszak.radio.hu. Web: www.english.radio.hu/index. php?rovat_id=1059; (on-demand audio) http://real1.radio. hu/nemzeti.htm. Contact: (English Language Service) Ágnes Kevi, Correspondence; Louis Horváth, DX Editor; or Sándor Laczkó, Editor; (administration) László Krassó, Director, Foreign Broadcasting; Dr. Zsuzsa Mészáros, Vice-Director, Foreign Broadcasting; (technical) László Füszfás, Deputy Technical Director, Magyar Rádió.

TRANSMISSION AUTHORITY: Ministry of Transport, Communications and Water Management, P.O. Box 87, H-1400 Budapest, Hungary. Phone: +36 (1) 461-3390. Fax: +36 (1) 461 3392. Email: (Horváth) horvathf@cms.khvm.hu. Contact: Ferenc Horváth, Frequency Manager, Radio Communications Engineering Services.

ICELAND   World Time exactly

AFRTS-American Forces Radio and Television Service (Shortwave). Email: keflavik@mediacen.navy.mil. Contact: Officer-in-Charge. Replies irregularly, usually via email, and sometimes verifies reception reports.

Ríkisútvarpid, International Relations Department, Efstaleiti 1, IS-150 Reykjavík, Iceland. Phone: +354 515-3000. Fax: +354 515 3010. Email: isradio@ruv.is. Web: (includes streaming audio) www.ruv.is. Contact: Dóra Ingvadóttir, Head of International Relations; or Markús Öern Antonsson, Director.

INDIA   World Time +5:30

WARNING—MAIL THEFT: Passport readers report that letters to India containing IRCs and other valuables have disappeared en route when not registered. Best is either to register your letter or to send correspondence in an unsealed envelope, and without enclosures.

VERIFICATION OF REGIONAL STATIONS. All Indian regional stations can be verified via New Delhi (*see* All India Radio External Services Division for contact details), but some listeners prefer contacting each station individually, in the hope of receiving a direct QSL. Well-known Indian DXer Jose Jacob makes the following suggestions: address your report to the station engineer of the respective station; specify the time of reception in both World Time (UTC) and Indian Standard Time (IST); instead of using the SINPO code, write a brief summary of reception quality; and if possible, report on local programs rather than relays of national programming from New Delhi. Jose adds that reports should be written in English, and return postage is not required. Enclosing currency notes is against the law.

Akashvani—All India Radio

ADMINISTRATION/ENGINEERING: Directorate General of All India Radio, Akashvani Bhawan, 1 Sansad Marg, New Delhi-110 001, India. Phone: +91 (11) 2342-1006 or +91 (11) 2371-5413; (Director General) +91 (11) 2371-0300 Ext. 102; (Engineer-in-Chief) +91 (11) 2342-1058 or (Phone/Fax) +91 (11) 2342-1459; (Director, Spectrum Management) +91 (11) 2342-1062 or +91 (11) 2342-1145. Fax: +91 (11) 2371 11956; (Director General) +91 (11) 2342 1956. Email: airlive@air.org. in; (Director General) dgair@air.org.in; (Engineer-in-Chief) einc@air.org.in; (Director, Spectrum Management) faair@nda. vsnl.net.in. Web: (includes live audio) www.allindiaradio.org. Contact: (technical) K.M. Paul, Engineer-in-Chief; Y.K. Sharma, Director, Spectrum Management; or Devendra Singh, Deputy Director, Spectrum Management.

AUDIENCE RESEARCH: Audience Research Unit, All India Radio, Press Trust of India Building, 2nd floor, Sansad Marg, New Delhi-110 001, India. Phone: (general) +91 (11) 2371-0033 or +91 (11) 2371-9215; (Director) +91 (11) 2338-6506. Contact: Ramesh Chandra, Director.

CENTRAL MONITORING STATION: All India Radio, Ayanagar, New Delhi-110 047, India. Phone: +91 (11) 2650-2955 or +91 (11) 2650 1763. Contact: Y.K. Sharma, Director.

COMMERCIAL SERVICE: Vividh Bharati Service, AIR, P.O. Box 11497, 101 M.K. Road, Mumbai-400 020, India. Phone: +91 (22) 2203-7193.

INTERNATIONAL MONITORING STATION—MAIN OFFICE: International Monitoring Station, All India Radio, Dr. K.S. Krishnan Road, Todapur, New Delhi-110 097, India. Phone: +91 (11) 2584-2939. Contact: B.L. Kasturiya, Deputy Director; D.P. Chhabra or R.K. Malviya, Assistant Research Engineers—Frequency Planning.

NATIONAL CHANNEL: AIR, Gate 22, Jawaharlal Nehru Stadium, Lodhi Road, New Delhi-110 003. Phone: +91 (11) 2584-3825; (station engineer) +91 (11) 2584-3207. Contact: J.K. Das, Director; or V.D. Sharma, Station Engineer.

NEWS SERVICES DIVISION: News Services Division, Broadcasting House, 1 Sansad Marg, New Delhi-110 001, India. Phone: (newsroom) +91 (11) 2342-1006 or +91 (11) 2371-5413; (Special Director General—News) +91 (11) 2371-0084 or +91 (11) 2373-1510; (News on phone in English) +91 (11) 2332-4343; (News on phone in Hindi) +91 (11) 2332-4242. Fax: +91 (11) 2371 1196. Email: nsdair@giasdl01.vsnl.net.in. Contact: B.I. Saini, Special Director General—News.

PROGRAMMING: Broadcasting House, 1 Sansad Marg, New Delhi-110 001 India. Phone: (general) +91 (11) 2371-5411.

RESEARCH AND DEVELOPMENT: Office of the Chief Engineer R&D, All India Radio, 14-B Ring Road, Indraprastha Estate, New Delhi-110 002, India. Phone: (general) +91 (11) 2337-8211/12; (Chief Engineer) +91 (11) 2337 9255 or +91 (11) 2337-9329. Fax: +91 (11) 2331 8329 or +91 (11) 2331 6674. Email: rdair@nda.vsnl.net.in. Web: www.air.kode.net. Contact: B.L. Mathur, Chief Engineer.

TRANSCRIPTION AND PROGRAM EXCHANGE SERVICES: Akashvani Bhawan, 1 Sansad Marg, New Delhi-110 001, India. Phone: (Director, Transcription & Program Exchange Services: V.A. Magazine) +91 (11) 2342-1927. Contact: D.P. Jadav, Director.

All India Radio—Aizawl, Radio Tila, Tuikhuahtlang, Aizawl-796 001, Mizoram, India. Phone: (engineering) +91 (389) 2322-415. Fax: +91 (389) 2322 114. Email: aizawl@air.org.in. Contact: (technical) S. Nellai Nayagam, Station Engineer.

All India Radio—Aligarh, Anoopshahar Road, Aligarh-202 001, Uttar Pradesh, India. Phone: (engineering) +91 (571) 2700-972. Email: aligarh@air.org.in.

All India Radio—Bangalore Shortwave Transmitting Centre

HEADQUARTERS: see All India Radio—External Services Division.

AIR OFFICE NEAR TRANSMITTERS: Superintending Engineer, Super Power Transmitters, All India Radio, Yelahanka New Town, Bangalore-560 065, Karnataka, India. Phone: +91 (80) 2226-1243. Email: bangalore.spt@air.org.in. Contact: (technical) Suresh Naik, Superintending Engineer; or T. Rajendiran, Station Engineer.

All India Radio—Bhopal, Akashvani Bhawan, Shyamla Hills, Bhopal-462 002, Madhya Pradesh, India. Phone: (engineering) +91 (755) 2661-241. Email: bhopal@air.org.in. Contact: (technical) S.K. Gaur, Station Engineer.

All India Radio—Chennai

EXTERNAL SERVICES: see All India Radio—External Services Division.

DOMESTIC SERVICE: Avadi, Chennai-600 002, Tamil Nadu, India. Phone: (engineering) +91 (44) 2638-3204. Email: chennai.avadi@air.org.in.

All India Radio—External Services Division

MAIN ADDRESS: Broadcasting House, 1 Sansad Marg, P.O. Box 500, New Delhi-110 001, India. Phone: (engineering) +91 (11) 2371-5411. Contact: (general) P.P. Setia, Director of External Services; or S.C. Panda, Audience Relations Officer. Email (Research Dept.): rdair@giasdl01.vsnl.net.in. Web: www.allindiaradio.org. Free monthly *India Calling* magazine and stickers. Replies are somewhat erratic.

VERIFICATION ADDRESS: Spectrum Management, All India Radio, Room 204, Akashani Bhavan, New Delhi-110 001, India; or P.O. Box 500, New Delhi-110 001, India. Fax: +91 (11) 2342 1062 or +91 (11) 2342 1145. Email: spectrum-manager@air.

org.in. Contact: Y. K. Sharma, Director, Spectrum Management & Synergy.

All India Radio—Gangtok, Old M.L.A. Hostel, Gangtok-737 101, Sikkim, India. Phone: (engineering) +91 (3592) 202-636. Email: gangtok@air.org.in. Contact: (general) Y.P. Yolmo, Station Director; (technical) A.K. Sarkar, Assistant Engineer.

All India Radio—Gorakhpur

NEPALESE EXTERNAL SERVICE: see All India Radio—External Services Division.

DOMESTIC SERVICE: Town Hall, Post Bag 26, Gorakhpur-273 001, Uttar Pradesh, India. Phone/Fax: (engineering) +91 (551) 2337-401. Email: gorakhpur@air.org.in. Contact: (technical) Dr. S.M. Pradhan, Superintending Engineer; or P.P. Shukle, Station Engineer.

All India Radio—Guwahati, P.O. Box 28, Chandmari, Guwahati-781 003, Assam, India. Phone: (engineering) +91 (361) 2660-235. Email: guwahati@air.org.in. Contact: (technical) P.C. Sanghi, Superintending Engineer; or H.S. Dhillon, Station Engineer.

All India Radio—Hyderabad, Rocklands, Saifabad, Hyderabad-500 004, Andhra Pradesh, India. Phone: (engineering) +91 (40) 2323-4904. Fax: +91 (40) 2323 2239 or +91 (40) 2323 4282. Email: hyderabad@air.org.in. Contact: (technical) P. Vishwanathan, Superintending Engineer.

All India Radio—Imphal, Palau Road, Imphal-795 001, Manipur, India. Phone: (engineering) +91 (385) 220-534. Email: imphal@air.org.in. Contact: (technical) M. Jayaraman, Superintending Engineer.

All India Radio—Itanagar, Naharlagun, Itanagar-791 111, Arunachal Pradesh, India. Phone: (engineering) +91 (360) 2212-881. Fax: +91 (360) 2213 008 or +91 (360) 2212 933. Email: itanagar@air.org.in. Contact: J.T. Jirdoh, Station Director; P.K. Bez Baruah, Assistant Station Engineer; or P. Sanghi, Superintending Engineer. Verifications direct from station are difficult, as engineering is done by staff visiting from the Regional Engineering Headquarters at AIR—Guwahati (*see*); that address might be worth contacting if all else fails.

All India Radio—Jaipur, 5 Park House, Mirza Ismail Road, Jaipur-302 001, Rajasthan, India. Phone: +91 (141) 2366-263. Fax: +91 (141) 2363 196. Email: jaipur@air.org.in. Contact: (technical) S.C. Sharma, Station Engineer; or C.L. Goel, Assistant Station Engineer.

All India Radio—Jammu—*see* Radio Kashmir—Jammu.

All India Radio—Jeypore, Jeypore-764 005, Orissa, India. Phone: (engineering) +91 (6854) 232-524. Email: jeypore@air.org.in. Contact: K. Naryan Das, Assistant Station Engineer.

All India Radio—Kohima, P.O. Box 42, Kohima-797 001, Nagaland, India. Phone: (engineering) +91 (370) 2245-556. Email: kohima@air.org.in. Contact: (technical) M. Tyagi, Superintending Engineer; K.K Jose, Assistant Engineer; or K. Morang, Assistant Station Engineer. Return postage, $1 or IRC helpful.

All India Radio—Kolkata, G.P.O. Box 696, Kolkata—700 001, West Bengal, India. Phone: (engineering) +91 (33) 2248-1705. Email: kolkata@air.org.in. Contact: (technical) S.K. Pal, Superintending Engineer.

All India Radio—Kurseong, Mehta Club Building, Kurseong-734 203, Darjeeling District, West Bengal, India. Phone: (engineering) +91 (354) 2344-350. Email: kurseong@air.org.in. Contact: (general) George Kuruvilla, Assistant Director; (technical) R.K. Sinha, Chief Engineer; or B.K. Behara, Station Engineer.

All India Radio—Leh, Leh-194 101, Ladakh District, Jammu and Kashmir, India. Phone: (engineering) +91 (1982) 252-080.

Email: leh@air.org.in. Contact: (technical) L.K. Gandotar, Station Engineer; T.S. Sreekumar, Assistant Station Engineer.

All India Radio—Lucknow, 18 Vidhan Sabha Marg, Lucknow-226 001, Uttar Pradesh, India. Phone: (engineering) +91 (522) 2237-601. Email: lucknow@air.org.in. Contact: Dr. S.M. Pradhan, Superintending Engineer. This station now appears to be replying via the External Services Division, New Delhi.

All India Radio—Mumbai

EXTERNAL SERVICES: see All India Radio—External Services Division.

COMMERCIAL SERVICE (VIVIDH BHARATI): All India Radio, P.O. Box 19705, 101 M K Road, Mumbai-400 091, Maharashtra, India. Phone: (director) +91 (22) 2869-2698; (engineering) +91 (22) 2868-7351. Email: vbs@vsnl.com. Contact: Vijayalakshmi Sinha, Director; or (technical) Superintending Engineer.

DOMESTIC SERVICE: Broadcasting House, Backbay Reclamation, Mumbai-400 020, Maharashtra, India. Phone: (engineering) +91 (22) 2202-9853. Email: mumbai.malad@air.org.in.

All India Radio—New Delhi, Broadcasting House, New Delhi-110 011, India. Phone: (engineering) +91 (11) 2371 0113. Email: delhi.bh@air.org.in. Contact: (technical) V. Chaudhry, Superintending Engineer.

All India Radio—Panaji Shortwave Transmitting Centre

HEADQUARTERS: see All India Radio—External Services Division, above.

AIR OFFICE NEAR TRANSMITTERS: P.O. Box 220, Altinho, Panaji-403 001, Goa, India. Phone: (engineering) +91 (832) 2230-696. Email: panaji.spt@air.org.in. Contact: (technical) S. Jayaraman, Superintending Engineer.

All India Radio—Port Blair, Haddo Post, Dilanipur, Port Blair-744 102, South Andaman, Andaman and Nicobar Islands, Union Territory, India. Phone: (engineering) +91 (3192) 30-682. Fax: +91 (3192) 230 260. Email: portblair@air.org.in. Contact: V.M. Ratnaprasad, Station Engineer. Registering letters appears to be useful.

All India Radio—Ranchi, 6 Ratu Road, Ranchi-834 001, Jharkhand, India. Phone: (engineering) +91 (651) 2283-310. Email: ranchi@air.org.in. Contact: (technical) H.K. Sinha, Superintending Engineer.

All India Radio—Shillong, P.O. Box 14, Shillong-793 001, Meghalaya, India. Phone: (engineering) +91 (364) 2222-272. Email: shillong.nes@air.org.in. Contact: (general) C. Lalsaronga, Director NEIS; (technical) R. Venugopal, Superintending Engineer; or H. Diengdoh, Station Engineer. Free booklet on station's history. Replies tend to be rare, due to a shortage of staff.

All India Radio—Shimla, Choura Maidan, Shimla-171 004, Himachal Pradesh, India. Phone: (engineering) +91 (177) 2811-355. Email: shimla@air.org.in. Contact: (technical) V.K. Upadhayay, Superintending Engineer; or Krishna Murari, Assistant Engineer. Return postage helpful.

All India Radio—Srinagar—*see* Radio Kashmir—Srinagar.

All India Radio—Thiruvananthapuram, P.O. Box 403, Bhakti Vilas, Vazuthacaud, Thiruvananthapuram-695 014, Kerala, India. Phone: (engineering) +91 (471) 2325-009. Fax: +91 (471) 2324 406 or +91 (471) 2324 982. Email: thiruvananthapuram@air.org.in. Contact: KV. Ramachandran, Station Engineer.

Radio Kashmir—Jammu, Palace Road, Jammu-188 001, Jammu and Kashmir, India. Phone: (engineering) +91 (191) 2544-411. Email: jammu@air.org.in.

Radio Kashmir—Srinagar, Sherwani Road, Srinagar-190 001, Jammu and Kashmir, India. Phone: (engineering) +91 (194) 2452-100/177. Email: srinagar@air.org.in. Contact: G.H. Zia, Station Director; or V.P. Singh, Superintending Engineer.

INDONESIA
World Time +7 Western: Waktu Indonesia Bagian Barat (Jawa, Sumatera); +8 Central: Waktu Indonesia Bagian Tengal (Bali, Kalimantan, Sulawesi, Nusa Tenggara); +9 Eastern: Waktu Indonesia Bagian Timur (Papua, Maluku)

NOTE: Except where otherwise indicated, Indonesian stations, especially those of the Radio Republik Indonesia (RRI) network, will reply to at least some correspondence in English. However, correspondence in Indonesian is more likely to ensure a reply.

Kang Guru Radio English, Indonesia Australia Language Foundation, P.O. Box 3095, Denpasar 80030, Bali, Indonesia. Phone: +62 (361) 225-243. Fax: +62 (361) 263 509. Email: kangguru@ialf.edu; (Pearson) rpearson@ialf.edu. Web: www.kangguru.org. Contact: Kevin Dalton, Kang Guru Project Manager; Rachel Pearson, ELT Media and Training Specialist; or Ms. Ogi Yutarini, Project Coordinating Officer. Free "Kang Guru" magazine. This program is aired over various RRI outlets, including Jakarta and Sorong.

Radio Pemerintah Daerah Kabupaten TK II—RPDK Manggarai, Ruteng, Flores, Nusa Tenggara Timur, Indonesia. Contact: Simon Saleh, B.A. Return postage required.

Radio Pemerintah Daerah Kabupaten Daerah TK II—RSPK Ngada, Jalan Soekarno-Hatta, Bjawa, Flores, Nusa Tenggara Tengah, Indonesia. Phone: +62 (384) 21-142. Contact: Drs. Petrus Tena, Kepala Studio.

Radio Republik Indonesia — RRI Ambon (when operating), Jalan Jendral Akhmad Yani 1, Ambon 97124, Maluku, Indonesia. Phone: +62 (911) 52-740, +62 (911) 53-261 or +62 (911) 53-263. Fax: +62 (911) 53 262. Contact: Drs. H. Ali Amran or Pirla C. Noija, Kepala Seksi Siaran. A very poor replier to correspondence in recent years. Correspondence in Indonesian and return postage essential.

Radio Republik Indonesia—RRI Banda Aceh (when operating), Kotak Pos 112, Banda Aceh 23243, Aceh, Indonesia. Phone: +62 (651) 22-116/156. Contact: Parmono Prawira, Technical Director; or S.H. Rosa Kim. Return postage helpful.

Radio Republik Indonesia Bandar Lampung, *see* RRI Tanjung Karang listing below.

Radio Republik Indonesia—RRI Bandung (when operating), Stasiun Regional 1, Kotak Pos 1055, Bandung 40122, Jawa Barat, Indonesia. Email: rribandung@yahoo.com. Web: www.kangguru.org/rristationprofiles.htm. Contact: Drs. Idrus Alkaf, Kepala Stasiun; Mrs. Ati Kusmiati; or Eem Suhaemi, Kepala Seksi Siaran. Return postage or IRC helpful.

Radio Republik Indonesia—RRI Banjarmasin (when operating), Stasiun Nusantara 111, Kotak Pos 117, Banjarmasin 70234, Kalimantan Selatan, Indonesia. Phone: +62 (511) 268-601 or +62 (511) 261-562. Fax: +62 (511) 252 238. Contact: Jul Chaidir, Stasiun Kepala; or Harmyn Husein. Free stickers. Return postage or IRCs helpful.

Radio Republik Indonesia—RRI Bengkulu, Stasiun Regional 1, Kotak Pos 13 Kawat, Kotamadya Bengkulu 38227, Indonesia. Phone: +62 (736) 350-811. Fax: +62 (736) 350 927. Contact: Drs. Drs. Jasran Abubakar, Kepala Stasiun. Free picture postcards, decals and tourist literature. Return postage or 2 IRCs helpful.

Radio Republik Indonesia—RRI Biak (when operating), Kotak Pos 505, Biak 98117, Papua, Indonesia. Phone: +62 (981) 21-211 or +62 (981) 21-197. Fax: +62 (981) 21 905. Contact: Butje Latuperissa, Kepala Seksi Siaran; or Drs. D.A. Siahainenia, Kepala Stasiun. Correspondence in Indonesian preferred.

Radio Republik Indonesia—RRI Bukittinggi (when operating), Stasiun Regional 1 Bukittinggi, Jalan Prof. Muhammad

Yamin 199, Aurkuning, Bukittinggi 26131, Propinsi Sumatera Barat, Indonesia. Phone: +62 (752) 21-319 or +62 (752) 21-320. Fax: +62 (752) 367 132. Contact: Mr. Effendi, Sekretaris; Zul Arifin Mukhtar, SH; or Samirwan Sarjana Hukum, Producer, "Phone in Program." Replies to correspondence in Indonesian or English. Return postage helpful.

Radio Republik Indonesia—RRI Denpasar (when operating), Kotak Pos 3031, Denpasar 80233, Bali, Indonesia. Phone: +62 (361) 222-161 or +62 (361) 223-087. Fax: +62 (361) 227 312. Contact: I Gusti Ngurah Oka, Kepala Stasiun. Replies slowly to correspondence in Indonesian. Return postage or IRCs helpful.

Radio Republik Indonesia—RRI Dili (when operating), Stasiun Regional 1 Dili, Jalan Kaikoli, Kotak Pos 103, Díli 88000, Timor-Timur, Indonesia. Contact: Harry A. Silalahi, Kepala Stasiun; Arnoldus Klau; or Paul J. Amalo, BA. Return postage or $1 helpful. Replies occasionally to correspondence in Indonesian.

Radio Republik Indonesia—RRI Fak Fak, Jalan Kapten P. Tendean, Kotak Pos 54, Fak-Fak 98612, Papua, Indonesia. Phone: +62 (956) 22-519 or +62 (956) 22-521. Contact: Bahrun Siregar, Kepala Stasiun; Aloys Ngotra, Kepala Seksi Siaran; Drs. Tukiran Erlantoko; or Richart Tan, Kepala Sub Seksi Siaran Kata. Station plans to upgrade its transmitting facilities with the help of the Japanese government. Return postage required. Replies occasionally.

Radio Republik Indonesia—RRI Gorontalo, Jalan Jendral Sudirman 30, Gorontalo 96115, Sulawesi Utara, Indonesia. Fax: +62 (435) 821 590/91. Contact: Drs. Bagus Edi Asmoro; Drs. Muhammad. Assad, Kepala Stasiun; or Saleh S. Thalib, Technical Manager. Return postage helpful. Replies occasionally, preferably to correspondence in Indonesian.

Radio Republik Indonesia—RRI Jakarta
STATION: Stasiun Nasional Jakarta, Kotak Pos 356, Jakarta 10110, Daerah Khusus Jakarta Raya, Indonesia; or (street address) Jalan Medan Merdeka Barat 4-5, Jakarta 10110, Indonesia. Phone: +62 (21) 345-9091 or +62 (21) 384-6817. Fax: +62 (21) 345 7132 or +62 (21) 345 7134. Email: rri@rri-online.com. Web: (includes on-demand audio) www.rri-online.com. Contact: Drs. Beni Koesbani, Kepala Stasiun; or Drs. Nuryudi, MM. Return postage helpful. Replies irregularly.
"DATELINE" ENGLISH PROGRAM: see Kang Guru Radio English.
TRANSMITTERS DIVISION: Jalan Merdeka Barat 4-5, Jakarta 10110 Indonesia. Phone/Fax: +62 (21) 385-7831. Email: sruslan@yahoo.com or sruslan@msn.com. Contact: Sunarya Ruslan, Head of Transmitters Division.

Radio Republik Indonesia—RRI Jambi (when operating), Jalan Jendral A. Yani 5, Telanaipura, Jambi 36122, Propinsi Jambi, Indonesia. Contact: M. Yazid, Kepala Siaran; H. Asmuni Lubis, BA; or Byamsuri, Acting Station Manager. Return postage helpful.

Radio Republik Indonesia—RRI Jayapura, Kotak Pos 1077, Jayapura 99200, Papua, Indonesia. Phone: +62 (967) 33-339. Fax: +62 (967) 33 439. Contact: Harry Liborang, Direktorat Radio; Hartono, Bidang Teknik; or Dr. David Alex Siahainenia, Kepala. Return postage of $1 helpful. Replies to correspondence in Indonesian or English.

Radio Republik Indonesia—RRI Kendari, Kotak Pos 7, Kendari 93111, Sulawesi Tenggara, Indonesia. Phone: +62 (401) 21-464. Fax: +62 (401) 21 730. Contact: H. Sjahbuddin, BA; Muniruddin Amin, Programmer; or Drs. Supandi. Return postage required. Replies slowly to correspondence in Indonesian.

Radio Republik Indonesia—RRI Kupang (Regional I) (when operating), Jalan Tompello 8, Kupang 85225, Timor, Indonesia. Phone: +62 (380) 821-437 or +62 (380) 825-444. Fax: +62 (380) 833 149. Contact: Drs. P.M. Tisera, Kepala Stasiun; Qustigap Bagang, Kepala Seksi Siaran; or Said Rasyid, Kepala Studio. Return postage helpful. Correspondence in Indonesian preferred. Replies occasionally.

Radio Republik Indonesia—RRI Madiun (when operating), Jalan Mayjend Panjaitan 10, Madiun 63133, Jawa Timur, Indonesia. Phone: +62 (351) 464-419, +62 (351) 459-198, +62 (351) 462-726 or +62 (351) 459-495. Fax: +62 (351) 464 964. Web: www.kangguru.org/rristationprofiles.htm. Contact: Sri Lestari, SS; or Imam Soeprapto, Kepala Seksi Siaran. Replies to correspondence in Indonesian or English. Return postage helpful.

Radio Republik Indonesia—RRI Makassar, Jalan Riburane 3, Makassar, 90111, Sulawesi Selatan, Indonesia. Phone: +62 (411) 321-853. Contact: Dra. Rasdimanbudi B, Senior Manajer Bagian Adm. & Keuangan. Replies to correspondence in Indonesian or English. Return postage, $1 or IRCs helpful.

Radio Republik Indonesia—RRI Malang (when operating), Kotak Pos 78, Malang 65140, Jawa Timur, Indonesia; or Jalan Candi Panggung No. 58, Mojolangu, Malang 65142, Indonesia. Email: makobu@mlg.globalxtrem.net. Contact: Drs.Tjutju Tjuar Na Adikorya, Kepala Stasiun; Ml. Mawahib, Kepala Seksi Siaran; or Dra Hartati Soekemi, Mengetahui. Return postage required. Free history and other booklets. Replies irregularly to correspondence in Indonesian.

Radio Republik Indonesia—RRI Manado (when operating), Kotak Pos 1110, Manado 95124 Propinsi Sulawesi Utara, Indonesia. Phone: +62 (431) 863-392. Fax: +62 (431) 863 492. Contact: Costher H. Gulton, Kepala Stasiun; or Untung Santoso, Kepala Seksi Teknik. Free stickers and postcards. Return postage or $1 required. Replies occasionally to correspondence in Indonesian.

Radio Republik Indonesia—RRI Manokwari (when operating), Regional II, Jalan Merdeka 68, Manokwari 98311, Papua, Indonesia. Phone: +62 (962) 21-343. Contact: Eddy Kusbandi, Manager; or Nurdin Mokogintu. Return postage helpful.

Radio Republik Indonesia—RRI Mataram (when operating), Stasiun Regional I Mataram, Jalan Langko 83 Ampenan, Mataram 83114, Nusa Tenggara Barat, Indonesia. Phone: +62 (370) 23-713 or +62 (370) 21-355. Contact: Drs. Hamid Djasman, Kepala; or Bochri Rachman, Ketua Dewan Pimpinan Harian. Free stickers. Return postage required. With sufficient return postage or small token gift, sometimes sends tourist information and Batik print. Replies to correspondence in Indonesian.

Radio Republik Indonesia—RRI Medan (when operating), Jalan Letkol Martinus Lubis 5, Medan 20232, Sumatera, Indonesia. Phone: +62 (61) 324-222/441. Fax: +62 (61) 512 161. Contact: Kepala Stasiun, Ujamalul Abidin Ass; Drs. S. Parlin Tobing, SH, Produsennya, "Kontak Pendengar"; Drs. H. Suryanta Saleh; or Suprato. Free stickers. Return postage required. Replies to correspondence in Indonesian.

Radio Republik Indonesia—RRI Merauke, Stasiun Regional 1, Kotak Pos 11, Merauke 99611, Papua, Indonesia. Phone: +62 (971) 21-396 or +62 (971) 21-376. Contact: (general) Drs. Buang Akhir, Direktor; Achmad Ruskaya B.A., Kepala Stasiun, Drs.Tuanakotta Semuel, Kepala Seksi Siaran; or John Manuputty, Kepala Subseksi Pemancar; (technical) Daf'an Kubangun, Kepala Seksi Tehnik. Return postage helpful.

Radio Republik Indonesia—RRI Nabire (when operating), Kotak Pos 110, Jalan Merdeka 74 Nabire 98811, Papua, Indonesia. Phone: +62 (984) 21-013. Contact: Muchtar Yushaputra, Kepala

Stasiun. Free stickers and occasional free picture postcards. Return postage or IRCs helpful.

Radio Republik Indonesia—RRI Padang, Kotak Pos 77, Padang 25111, Sumatera Barat, Indonesia. Phone: +61 (751) 28-363, +62 (751) 21-030 or +62 (751) 27-482. Contact: H. Hutabarat, Kepala Stasiun; or Amir Hasan, Kepala Seksi Siaran. Return postage helpful.

Radio Republik Indonesia—RRI Palangkaraya (when operating), Jalan M. Husni Thamrin 1, Palangkaraya 73111, Kalimantan Tengah, Indonesia. Phone: +62 (536) 21-779. Fax: +62 (536) 21 778. Contact: Andy Sunandar; Drs.Amiruddin; S. Polin; A.F. Herry Purwanto; Meyiwati SH; Supardal Djojosubrojo, Sarjana Hukum; Dr. S. Parlin Tobing, Station Manager; Murniaty Oesin, Transmission Department Engineer; Gumer Kamis; or Ricky D. Wader, Kepala Stasiun. Return postage helpful. Will respond to correspondence in Indonesian or English.

Radio Republik Indonesia—RRI Palembang (when operating), Jalan Radio 2, Km. 4, Palembang 30128, Sumatera Selatan, Indonesia. Phone: +62 (711) 350-811, +62 (711) 309-977 or +62 (711) 350-927. Contact: Drs. H. Mursjid Noor, Kepala Stasiun; H.Ahmad Syukri Ahkab, Kepala Seksi Siaran; or H.Iskandar Suradilaga. Return postage helpful. Replies slowly and occasionally.

Radio Republik Indonesia—RRI Palu, Jalan R.A. Kartini 39, Palu 94112, Sulawesi Tengah, Indonesia. Phone: +62 (451) 21 621 or +62 (451) 94-112. Contact: Akson Boole; Nyonyah Netty Ch. Soriton, Kepala Seksi Siaran; Gugun Santoso; Untung Santoso, Kepala Seksi Teknik; or M. Hasjim, Head of Programming. Return postage required. Replies slowly to correspondence in Indonesian.

Radio Republik Indonesia—RRI Pekanbaru (when operating), Kotak Pos 51, Pekanbaru 28113, Kepulauan Riau, Indonesia. Phone: +62 (761) 22-081, +62 (761) 23-606 or +62 (761) 25-111. Fax: +62 (761) 23 605. Contact: (general) Hendri Yunis, ST, Kepala Stasiun, Ketua DPH; Arisun Agus, Kepala Seksi Siaran; Drs. H. Syamsidi, Kepala Supag Tata Usaha; or Zainal Abbas. Return postage helpful.

Radio Republik Indonesia—RRI Pontianak, Kotak Pos 1005, Pontianak 78117, Kalimantan Barat, Indonesia. Phone: +62 (561) 734 987. Fax: +62 (561) 734 659. Contact: Ruddy Banding, Kepala Seksi Siaran; Achmad Ruskaya, BA; Drs. Effendi Afati, Producer, "Dalam Acara Kantong Surat"; Subagio, Kepala Sub Bagian Tata Usaha; Augustwus Campek; Rahayu Widati; Suryadharma, Kepala Sub Seksi Programa; or Muchlis Marzuki B.A. Return postage or $1 helpful. Replies some of the time to correspondence in Indonesian (preferred) or English.

Radio Republik Indonesia—RRI Samarinda, Kotak Pos 45, Samarinda, Kalimantan Timur 75110, Indonesia. Phone: +62 (541) 743-495. Fax: +62 (541) 741 693. Contact: Siti Thomah, Kepala Seksi Siaran; Tyranus Lenjau, English Announcer; S. Yati; Marthin Tapparan; or Sunendra, Kepala Stasiun. May send tourist brochures and maps. Return postage helpful. Replies to correspondence in Indonesian.

Radio Republik Indonesia—RRI Semarang (when operating), Kotak Pos 1073, Semarang 50241, Jawa Tengah, Indonesia. Phone: +62 (24) 831-6686, +62 (24) 831-6661 or +62 (24) 831-6330. (Phone/Fax, marketing) +62 (24) 831-6330. Web: www.kangguru.org/rristationprofiles.htm. Contact: Djarwanto, SH; Drs. Sabeni, Doktorandus; Drs. Purwadi, Program Director; Dra. Endang Widiastuti, Kepala Sub Seksi Periklanan Jasa dan Hak Cipta; H. Sutakno, Kepala Stasiun; or Mardanon, Kepala Teknik. Return postage helpful.

Radio Republik Indonesia—RRI Serui, Jalan Pattimura Kotak Pos 19, Serui 98213, Papua, Indonesia. Phone: +62 (983) 31-150 or +62 (983) 31-121. Contact: Agus Raunsai, Kepala Stasiun; J. Lolouan, BA, Kepala Studio; Ketua Tim Pimpinan Harian, Kepala Seksi Siaran; Yance Yebi-Yebi; Natalis Edowai; Albertus Corputty; or Drs. Jasran Abubakar. Replies occasionally to correspondence in Indonesian. IRC or return postage helpful.

Radio Republik Indonesia—RRI Sibolga (when operating), Jalan Ade Irma Suryani, Nasution No. 11, Sibolga 22513, Sumatera Utara, Indonesia. Phone: +61 (631) 21-183, +62 (631) 22-506 or +62 (631) 22-947. Contact: Mrs. Laiya, Mrs. S. Sitoupul or B.A. Tanjung. Return postage required. Replies occasionally to correspondence in Indonesian.

Radio Republik Indonesia—RRI Sorong
STATION: Kotak Pos 146, Sorong 98414, Papua, Indonesia. Phone: +62 (951) 21-003, +62 (951) 22-111, or +62 (951) 22-611. Contact: Drs. Sallomo Hamid; Tetty Rumbay S., Kasubsi Siaran Kata; Mrs. Tien Widarsanto, Resa Kasi Siaran; Ressa Molle; Mughpar Yushaputra, Kepala Stasiun; Umar Solle, Station Manager; or Linda Rumbay. Return postage helpful. Replies to correspondence in English.

"DATELINE" ENGLISH PROGRAM: See Kang Guru Radio English.

Radio Republik Indonesia—RRI Sumenep (when operating), Jalan Urip Sumoharjo 26, Sumenep 69411, Madura, Jawa Timur, Indonesia. Phone: +62 (328) 62-317, +62 (328) 21 811, +62 (328) 21-317 or +62 (328) 66-768. Contact: Dian Irianto, Kepala Stasiun. Return postage helpful.

Radio Republik Indonesia—RRI Surabaya, (when operating) Stasiun Regional 1, Kotak Pos 239, Surabaya 60271, Jawa Timur, Indonesia. Phone: +62 (31) 534-1327, +62 (31) 534-2327, +62 (31) 534-1327, +62 (31) 534-5474, +62 (31) 534-0478 or +62 (31) 547-3610. Fax: +62 (31) 534 2351. Contact: Zainal Abbas, Kepala Stasiun; Usmany Johozua, Kepala Seksi Siaran; Drs. E. Agus Widjaja, MM, Kasi Siaran; Pardjingat, Kepala Seksi Teknik; or Ny Koen Tarjadi. Return postage or IRCs helpful.

Radio Republik Indonesia—RRI Surakarta (when operating), Kotak Pos 40, Surakarta 57133, Jawa Tengah, Indonesia. Phone: +62 (271) 634-004/05, +62 (271) 638-145, +62 (271) 654-399 or +62 (271) 641-178. Fax: +62 (271) 642 208. Contact: H. Tomo, B.A., Head of Broadcasting; or Titiek Sudartik, S.H., Kepala. Return postage helpful.

Radio Republik Indonesia—RRI Tanjungkarang, Kotak Pos 24, Bandar Lampung 35213, Indonesia. Phone: +62 (721) 555-2280 or +62 (721) 569-720. Fax: +62 (721) 562 767. Contact: M. Nasir Agun, Kepala Stasiun; Hi Hanafie Umar; Djarot Nursinggih, Tech. Transmission; Drs. Doewadji, Kepala Seksi Siaran; Drs. Zulhaqqi Hafiz, Kepala Sub Seksi Periklanan; or Asmara Haidar Manaf. Return postage helpful. Also identifies as RRI Bandar Lampung. Replies in Indonesian to correspondence in Indonesian or English.

Radio Republik Indonesia—RRI Tanjungpinang, Stasiun RRI Regional II Tanjungpinang, Kotak Pos 8, Tanjungpinang 29123, Kepulauan Riau, Indonesia. Phone: +62 (771) 21-278, +62 (771) 21-540, +62 (771) 21-916 or +62 (771) 29-123. Contact: M. Yazid, Kepala Stasiun; Wan Suhardi, Produsennya, "Siaran Bahasa Melayu"; or Rosakim, Sarjana Hukum. Return postage helpful. Replies occasionally to correspondence in Indonesian or English.

Radio Republik Indonesia—RRI Ternate (when operating), Jalan Sultan Khairun, Kedaton, Ternate 97720 (Ternate), Maluku Utara, Indonesia. Phone: +62 (921) 21-582, +62 (921) 21-762 or +62 (921) 25-525. Contact: (general) Abd. Latief Kamarudin, Kepala Stasiun; (technical) Rusdy Bachmid, Head

The Voice of America's Hong Kong office is to expand its news gathering activities, replacing staff in Washington.   M. Guha

of Engineering; or Abubakar Alhadar. Return postage helpful.

Radio Republik Indonesia Tual (when operating), Watden, Pulau Kai, Tual 97661 Maluku, Indonesia.

Radio Republik Indonesia—RRI Wamena (when operating), RRI Regional II, Kotak Pos 10, Wamena, Papua 99511, Indonesia. Phone: +62 (969) 31-380. Fax: +62 (969) 31 299. Contact: Yoswa Kumurawak, Penjab Subseksi Pemancar. Return postage helpful.

Radio Republik Indonesia—RRI Yogyakarta (when operating), Jalan Amat Jazuli 4, Kotak Pos 18, Yogyakarta 55224, Jawa Tengah, Indonesia. Fax: +62 (274) 2784. Phone: +62 (274) 512-783/85 or +62 (274) 580-333. Email: rri-yk@yogya.wasantara.net.id. Contact: Phoenix Sudomo Sudaryo; Tris Mulyanti, Seksi Programa Siaran; Martono, ub. Kabid Penyelenggaraan Siaran; Mr. Kadis, Technical Department; or Drs. H. Hamdan Sjahbeni, Kepala Stasiun. IRC, return postage or $1 helpful. Replies occasionally to correspondence in Indonesian or English.

Radio Siaran Pemerintah Daerah TK II—RSPD Halmahera Tengah, Soasio, Jalan A. Malawat, Soasio, Maluku Tengah 97812, Indonesia. Contact: Drs. S. Chalid A. Latif, Kepala Badan Pengelola.

Voice of Indonesia, Kotak Pos 1157, Jakarta 10001, Daerah Khusus Jakarta Raya, Indonesia; (street address) Jalan Medan Merdeka Barat No. 4-5, Jakarta 10110 Indonesia. Phone: +62 (21) 345-6811. Fax: +62 (21) 350 0990. Email: voi@rri-online.com. Web: www.rri-online.com. Contact: Anastasia Yasmine, Head of Foreign Affairs Section; or Amy Aisha, Presenter, "Listeners Mailbag." Free stickers and calendars. Correspondence is best addressed to the individual language sections. Be careful when addressing your letters to the station as mail sent to the Voice of Indonesia, Japanese Section, has sometimes been incorrectly delivered to NHK's Jakarta Bureau. Very slow in replying but enclosing 4 IRCs may help speed things up.

INTERNATIONAL WATERS

Coalition Maritime Forces (CMF) Radio One, MARLO, P.O. Box 116 (NSA-MARLO), Manama, Bahrain. Email: (including reception reports) marlo@nsa.bahrain.navy.mil. Web: (MARLO Bahrain parent organization) www.me.navy.mil/MARLO. Station of the Maritime Liaison Office (MARLO) of the United States Navy. Broadcasts via low power transmitters on ships in the Persian Gulf and nearby waters. Verifies reception reports.

IRAN   World Time +3:30 (+4:30 midyear)

▣Voice of the Islamic Republic of Iran
MAIN OFFICE: IRIB External Services, P.O. Box 19395-6767, Tehran, Iran. Phone: +98 (21) 204-2808; (English Service) +98 (21) 201-3720, +98 (21) 216-2895, +98 (21) 216-2734. Fax: +98 (21) 205 1635, +98 (21) 204 1097 or + 98 (21) 291 095; (English Service) +98 (21) 201 3770; (technical) +98 (21) 654 841. Email: (all technical matters other than reception reports) sw@irib.ir or tech@irib.ir; (English Service) englishradio@irib.ir (same format for German and Spanish, e.g. spanishradio@irib.ir); (French Service) radio_fr@irib.ir. Web: (includes streaming audio) www.irib.ir/worldservice. Contact: Mohammad B. Khoshnevisan, IRIB English Radio. Free books on Islam, magazines, calendars, bookmarkers, tourist literature and postcards. Verifications require a minimum of two days' reception data on two or more separate broadcasts, plus return postage. Is currently asking listeners to send their telephone numbers so that they can be called by the station. You can send your phone number to the postal address above, or fax it to: + 98 (21) 205 1635.
SIRJAN TRANSMITTING STATION: P.O. Box 369, Sirjan, Iran. Contact: Aliasghar Shakoori Moghaddam, Head of Sirjan Station.

Mashhad Regional Radio, P.O. Box 555, Mashhad Center, Jomhoriye Eslame, Iran. Contact: J. Ghanbari, General Director.

IRAQ   World Time +3 (+4 midyear)

▣Voice of Iraqi Kurdistan ("Aira dangi Kurdestana Iraqiyah"). Web: (includes streaming audio) http://kdp.nu (click on "KDP's Media," then on "KDP info"). Station of the Kurdistan Democratic Party-Iraq (KDP), led by Masoud Barzani. Broadcasts from its own transmitting facilities, located in the Kurdish section of Iraq. To contact the station or to obtain verification of reception reports, try going via one of the following KDP offices:

KDP INTERNATIONAL RELATIONS BUREAU (U.K.): Phone: +44 (207) 498-2664. Fax: +44 (207) 498 2531. Email: kdpinternational@yahoo.com.
KDP REPRESENTATION IN WASHINGTON: 17115 Leesburg Pike #110, Falls Church VA 22043 USA. Phone: +1 (703) 533-5882. Fax: +1 (703) 599 5886. Email: pdk7usa@aol.com.
KDP-SWEDEN OFFICE: Email: party@kdp.se. Web: (includes streaming audio) www.kdp.se. Contact: Alex Atroushi. Reception reports to this address have sometimes been verified by email.
Voice of Kurdistan—*see* Voice of Iraqi Kurdistan, above.
Voice of the People of Kurdistan ("Aira dangi gelli kurdistana"). Email: said@aha.ru; or puk@puk.org. Web: www.aha.ru/~said/dang.htm; (PUK parent organization) www.puk.org. Official radio station of the Patriotic Union of Kurdistan (PUK) led by Jalal Talabani. Originally called "Voice of the Iraqi Revolution."
PUK GERMAN OFFICE: Patriotische Union Kurdistans (PUK), Postfach 21 0231, D-10502 Berlin, Germany. Phone: +49 (30) 3409-7850. Fax: +49 (30) 3409 7849. Email: pukoffice@pukg.de. Contact: Ahmad Berwari. Replies to correspondence in English or German, and verifies reception reports.

ISRAEL World Time +2 (+3 midyear)

Bezeq—Israel Telecommunication Corp. Ltd., Engineering and Planning Division, Radio and T.V. Broadcasting Section, P.O. Box 62081, Tel-Aviv 61620, Israel. Phone: +972 (3) 626-4562 or +972 (3) 626-4500. Fax: +972 (3) 626 4559. Email: (Oren) mosheor@bezeq.com; or rms2@bezeqint.net. Web: www.bezeq.co.il. Contact: Moshe Oren, Frequency Manager. Bezeq is responsible for transmitting the programs of the Israel Broadcasting Authority (IBA), which *inter alia* parents Kol Israel. This address only for pointing out transmitter related problems (interference, modulation quality, network mixups, etc.), especially by fax, of transmitters based in Israel. Does not verify reception reports.
Galei Zahal (Israel Defence Forces Radio), Zahal, Military Mail No. 01005, Israel. Phone: +972 (3) 512-6666. Fax: +972 (3) 512 6760. Email: glz@galatz.co.il. Web: (includes on-demand and streaming audio) www.glz.msn.co.il.
Kol Israel (Israel Radio International), P.O. Box 1082, Jerusalem 91010, Israel. Phone: (general) +972 (2) 530-2222; (Engineering Dept.) +972 (2) 501-3453; (Hebrew voice mail for Reshet Bet program "The Israel Connection") +972 (3) 765-1929. Fax: (English Service) +972 (2) 530 2424. Email: (general) ask@israel-info.gov.il; (English Service) englishradio@iba.org.il; (correspondence relating to reception problems, only) engineering@israelradio.org; (Reshet Bet program for Israelis abroad) kesherisraeli@yahoo.com. Web: (includes on-demand and streaming audio) www.israelradio.org; (on-demand and streaming audio) www.iba.org.il. Contact: Edmond Sehayeq, Head of Programming, Arabic, Persian and Yemenite broadcasts; Yishai Eldar, Reporter, English News Department; Steve Linde, Head of English News Department; or Sara Gabbai, Head of Western Broadcasting Department; (administration) Yonni Ben-Menachem, Director of External Broadcasting; (technical, frequency management) Raphael Kochanowski, Director of Liaison and Coordination, Engineering Dept. No verifications or freebies, due to limited budget.
SAN FRANCISCO OFFICE, SCHEDULES: 2654 17th Avenue, San Francisco CA 94116 USA. Phone: +1 (415) 564-9968. Email: GPoppin@aol.com. Contact: George Poppin. This address, a volunteer office, only provides KOL Israel schedules to listen-

ers. All other correspondence should be sent directly to the main office in Jerusalem.

ITALY World Time +1 (+2 midyear)

Italian Radio Relay Service, IRRS-Shortwave, Nexus-IBA, P.O. Box 11028, 20110 Milano, Italy; (reception reports) P.O. Box 10980, 20110 Milano, Italy. Phone: +39 (02) 266-6971. Fax: +39 (02) 7063 8151. Email: (general) info@nexus.org; (reception reports) reports@nexus.org; (Cotroneo) alfredo@nexus.org; (Norton) ron@nexus.org. Web: www.nexus.org/radio.htm; (streaming audio) http://mp3.nexus.org; (International Public Access Radio) www.nexus.org/IPAR; (European Gospel Radio) www.egradio.org. Contact: (general) Vanessa Dickinson; Anna S. Boschetti, President; Alfredo E. Cotroneo, CEO; (technical) Ron Norton, Verification Manager. Correspondence and reception reports by email are answered promptly and at no charge, but for budget reasons the station may be unable to reply to all postal correspondence. Two IRCs or $1 helpful.
Radio Roma-RAI International (external service)
MAIN OFFICE. (street address) External Service, Centro RAI, Saxa Rubra, 00188 Rome, Italy; (postal address, including reception reports) P.O. Box 320, Correspondence Sector, 00100 Rome, Italy. Phone: +39 (06) 33-17-2360. Fax: +39 (06) 33 17 18 95 or +39 (06) 322 6070. Email: raiinternational@rai.it. Web: (includes streaming audio) www.raiinternational.rai.it/radio. Contact: (general) Rosaria Vassallo, Correspondence Sector; or Augusto Milana, Editor in-Chief, Shortwave Programs in Foreign Languages; Esther Casas, Servicio Español; (administration) Angela Buttiglione, Managing Director; or Gabriella Tambroni, Assistant Director. Free stickers, banners, calendars and *RAI Calling from Rome* magazine. Can provide supplementary materials, including on VHS and CD-ROM, for Italian-language video course, "Viva l' italiano," with an audio equivalent soon to be offered, as well. Is constructing "a new, more powerful and sophisticated shortwave transmitting center" in Tuscany, when this is activated, RAI International plans to expand news, cultural items and music in Italian and various other language services—including Spanish & Portuguese, plus new services in Chinese and Japanese. Responses can be very slow. Pictures of RAI's Shortwave Center at Prato Smeraldo can be found at www.mediasuk.org/archive.
SHORTWAVE FREQUENCY MONITORING OFFICE: RaiWay Monitoring Centre, Centro di Controllo, Via Mirabellino 1, 20052 Monza (MI), Italy. Phone: +39 (039) 388-389. Fax: +39 (02) 3199 6245, +39 (039) 386-222. Email: raiway.hfmonitoring@rai.it or cqmonza@rai.it. Contact: Mrs. Lucia Luisa La Franceschina; or Mario Ballabio.
ENGINEERING OFFICE, ROME: Via Teulada 66, 00195 Rome, Italy. Phone: +39 (06) 331-70721. Fax: +39 (06) 331 75142 or +39 (06) 372 3376. Email: isola@rai.it. Contact: Clara Isola.
ENGINEERING OFFICE, TURIN: Via Cernaia 33, 10121 Turin, Italy. Phone: +39 (011) 810-2293. Fax: +39 (011) 575 9610. Email: allamano@rai.it. Contact: Giuseppe Allamano, HF Frequency Planning.
NEW YORK OFFICE, NONTECHNICAL: 1350 Avenue of the Americas—21st floor, New York NY 10019 USA. Phone: +1 (212) 468-2500. Fax: +1 (212) 765 1956. Contact: Umberto Bonetti, Deputy Director of Radio Division. RAI caps, aprons and tote bags for sale at Boutique RAI, c/o the aforementioned New York address.
SAN FRANCISCO OFFICE, SCHEDULES: 2654 17th Avenue, San Francisco CA 94116 USA. Phone: +1 (415) 564-9968. Email: GPoppin@aol.com. Contact: George Poppin. This address,

a volunteer office, only provides RAI schedules to listeners. All other correspondence should be sent directly to the main office in Rome.

RTV Italiana-RAI (domestic service), Centro RAI, Saxa Rubra, 00188 Rome, Italy. Fax: +39 (06) 322 6070. Email: grr@rai.it. Web: www.rai.it.

JAPAN   World Time +9

🖥**Radio Japan/NHK World** (external service)

MAIN OFFICE: NHK World, Nippon Hoso Kyokai, Tokyo 150-8001, Japan. Phone: +81 (3) 3465-1111. Fax: (general) +81 (3) 3481 1350; ("Hello from Tokyo" and Production Center) +81 (3) 3465 0966. Email: (general) nhkworld@nhk.jp; ("Hello from Tokyo" program) hello@intl.nhk.or.jp; (Spanish Section) rj-espa@intl.nhk.or.jp. Web: (English, includes on-demand and streaming audio) www.nhk.or.jp/english or (Japanese, includes on-demand and streaming audio) www.nhk.or.jp/nhkworld. Contact: (administration) Saburo Eguchi, Deputy Director General; Shuichiro Sunohara, Deputy Director International Planning & Programming; Tadao Sakomizu, Director, English Service; Ms. Kyoko Hirotani, Planning & Programming Division.

ENGINEERING ADMINISTRATION DEPARTMENT: Nippon Hoso Kyokai, Tokyo 150-8001, Japan. Phone: +81 (3) 5455-5395, +81 (3) 5455-5384, +81 (3) 5455-5376 or +81 (3) 5455-2288. Fax: +81 (3) 3485 0952 or + 81 (3) 3481 4985. Email: (general) rj-freq@eng.nhk.or.jp; yoshimi@eng.nhk.or.jp or kurasima@eng.nhk.or.jp. Contact: Fujimoto Hiroki, Frequency Manager; Akira Mizuguchi, Transmissions Manager; Tetsuya Itsuk or Toshiki Kurashima.

MONITORING DIVISION: NHK World/Radio Japan. Fax: +81 (3) 3481 1877.

HONG KONG BUREAU: Phone: +852 2509-0238.

EUROPEAN (LONDON) BUREAU: Phone: +44 (20) 7393-8100.

LOS ANGELES OFFICE: Phone: +1 (310) 586-1600.

USA (NEW YORK) BUREAU: Phone: +1 (212) 704-9898.

🖥**Radio Nikkei**, Nikkei Radio Broadcasting Corporation, 9-15 Akasaka 1-chome, Minato-ku, Tokyo 107-8373, Japan. Fax: +81 (3) 3583 9062. Web: (includes on-demand and streaming audio) www.radionikkei.jp. Contact: H. Nagao, Public Relations; M. Teshima; Ms. Terumi Onoda; or H. Ono. Sending a reception report may help with a reply. Free stickers and Japanese stamps. $1 or 2 IRCs helpful.

JORDAN   World Time +2 (+3 midyear)

🖥**Radio Jordan**, P.O. Box 909, Amman, Jordan; or P.O. Box 1041, Amman, Jordan. Phone: (general) +962 (6) 477-4111; (International Relations) +962 (6) 477-8578; (English Service) +962 (6) 475-7410 or +962 (6) 477-3111; (Arabic Service) +962 (6) 463-6454; (Saleh) +962 (6) 474-8048; or (Al-Arini) +962 (6) 474-9161. Fax: (general) +962 (6) 478 8115; (English Service) +962 (6) 420 7862; (Al-Arini) +962 (6) 474 9190. Email: (general) general@jrtv.gov.jo, or online form; (programs) rj@jrtv.gov.jo; (schedule) feedback@jrtv.gov.jo; (technical) eng@jrtv.gov.jo; (Director of Radio TV Engineering) arini@jrtv.gov.jo. Web: (includes streaming audio) www.jrtv.jo/rj. Contact: (general) Jawad Zada, Director of Foreign Service; Mrs. Firyal Zamakhshari, Director of Arabic Programs; or Qasral Mushatta; (administrative) Abdul Hamid Al Majali, Director of Radio; Mrs. Fatima Massri, Director of International Relations; or Muwaffaq al-Rahayifah, Director of Shortwave Services; (technical) Youssef Al-Arini, Director of Radio TV Engineering. Free stickers. Replies irregularly and slowly. Enclosing $1 helps.

KENYA   World Time

Kenya Broadcasting Corporation, P.O. Box 30456, Harry Thuku Road, Nairobi, Kenya. Phone: +254 (20) 334-567. Fax: +254 (20) 220 675. Email: (general) kbc@swiftkenya.com; (management) mdkbc@swiftkenya.com; (technical services) kbctechnical@swiftkenya.com. Web: www.kbc.co.ke. Contact: (general) Henry Makokha, Liaison Office; (administration) Joe Matano Khamisi, Managing Director; (technical) Nathan Lamu, Senior Principal Technical Officer; Augustine Kenyanjier Gochui; Lawrence Holnati, Engineering Division; or Daniel Githua, Assistant Manager Technical Services (Radio). IRC required. Replies irregularly. If all you want is verfication of your reception report(s), you may have better luck sending your letter to: Engineer in Charge, Maralal Radio Station, P.O. Box 38, Maralal, Kenya.

KIRIBATI   World Time +12

Radio Kiribati (if reactivated), Broadcasting & Publications Authority, P.O. Box 78, Bairiki, Tarawa, Republic of Kiribati. Phone: +686 21187. Fax: +686 21096. Email: bpa@tskl.net.ki. Contact: (general) Atiota Bauro, Programme Organiser; Mrs. Otiri Laboia; Batiri Bataua, News Editor; or Moia Tetoa, Radio Manager; (technical) Tooto Kabwebwenibeia, Broadcast Engineer; Martin Ouma Ojwach, Senior Superintendent of Electronics; Kautabuki Rubeiarki, Senior Technician; or T. Fakaofo, Technical Staff. Cassettes of local songs available for purchase. $1 or return postage required for a reply (IRCs not accepted). Currently off the air due to transmitter problems.

KOREA (DPR)   World Time +9

Korean Central Broadcasting Station, Chongsung-dong, Moranbong District, Pyongyang, Democratic People's Republic of Korea. If you don't speak Korean, try sending your correspondence via the Voice of Korea (*see*).

Regional KCBS stations—Not known to reply, but a long-shot possibility is to try corresponding in Korean to the Pyongyang address, above.

Pyongyang Broadcasting Station—Correspondence should be sent to the Voice of Korea, which sometimes verifies reception reports on PBS broadcasts.

Voice of Korea, External Service, Korean Central Broadcasting Station, Pyongyang, Democratic People's Republic of Korea (*not* "North Korea"). Phone: +850 (2) 381-6035. Fax: +850 (2) 381 4416. Phone and fax numbers valid only in those countries with direct telephone service to North Korea. Free publications, pennants, calendars, newspapers, artistic prints and pins. Do not include dutiable items in your envelope. Replies are irregular, as mail from countries not having diplomatic relations with North Korea is sent via circuitous routes and apparently does not always arrive. Indeed, some Passport readers continue to report that mail to the station results in their receiving anti-communist literature from *South* Korea, which indicates that mail interdiction has not ceased. One way around the problem is to add "VIA BEIJING, CHINA" to the address, but replies via this route tend to be slow in coming. According to some listeners sending your letters via the English Section of China Radio International in a separate envelope addressed to the Voice of Korea asking them to forward your letter on to Pyongyang. Explain the mail situation to the good folks in Beijing and you may have success. Another gambit is to send your correspondence to an associate in a country—such as China, Ukraine or India having reasonable relations with North Korea, and ask that it be forwarded. If you don't know anyone in these countries, try using the good offices of the following person: Willi Passman, Oberhausener Str. 100, D-45476, Mülheim, Germany. Send correspondence in a sealed envelope without any address on the back. That should be sent inside another envelope. Include 2 IRCs to cover the cost of forwarding.

KOREA (REPUBLIC) World Time +9.

📻**KBS World Radio** (formerly Radio Korea International)
MAIN OFFICE, INTERNATIONAL BROADCASTING DEPARTMENT: KBS World Radio, Global Center, Korean Broadcasting System, Yoido-dong 18, Youngdeungpo-gu, Seoul, Republic of Korea 150-790. Phone: (general) +82 (2) 781-3650/60/70; (English Section) +82 (2) 781-3674/5/6; (Korean Section) +82 (2) 781-3669/71/72/73; (German Section) +82 (2) 781-3682/3/9; (Japanese Section) +82 (2) 781-3654/5/6 (Spanish Section) +82 (2) 781-3679/81/97. Fax: (general) +82 (2) 781 3694/5/6. Email: (English) english@kbs.co.kr; (German) german@kbs.co.kr; (Japanese) japanese@kbs.co.kr; (Spanish) spanish@kbs.co.kr; (other language sections use the same format, except for Vietnamese: vietnam@kbs.co.kr); (Executive Director) hheejoo@kbs.co.kr. Web: (includes streaming audio) http://world.kbs.co.kr. Contact: Ms. Hee Joo Han, Executive Director, KBS World-External Radio & TV; or Park Young-seok, Chief; (administration) Sang Myung Kim; (English Section) Chae Hong-Pyo, Manager; Ms. Seung Joo ("Sophia") Hong, Producer; Mr. Chun Hye-Jin, DX Editor, *Seoul Calling*; (Korean Section) Hae Ok Lee, Producer; (Japanese Section) Ms. Hye Young Kim, Producer; (Spanish Section) Ms. Sujin Cho, Producer; (German Section) Chung Soon Wan, Manager; Lee Bum Suk, Producer; Sabastian Ratzer, Journalist. Free stickers, calendars, *Let's Learn Korean* book and a wide variety of other small souvenirs. *History of Korea* is available on CD-ROM (upon request) and via the station's Website.
ENGINEERING DEPARTMENT: IBC, Center, Korean Broadcasting System, Yoido-dong 18, Youngdeungpo-Gu, Seoul, Republic of Korea 150-790. Phone: (general) +82 (2) 781-5141/5137; (Radio Transmission Division) +82 (2) 781-5663. Fax: +82 (2) 781 5159. Email: (Radio Transmission Division) poeto@hanmail.net; (Frequency Manager) kdhy@kbs.co.kr; (Planning Engineer) pulo5@kbs.co.kr. Contact: Mr. Oh Daesik, Radio Transmission

Thanks to superb structural design, only two pagodas in Japan have collapsed during earthquakes over the past 1,400 years. T. Ohtake

Division; Mr. Dae-hyun Kim, Frequency Manager; or Mr. Chun-soo Lee, Planning Engineer.
📻**Korean Broadcasting System (KBS)**, 18 Yoido-dong, Youngdeungpo-gu, Seoul, Republic of Korea 150-790. Phone: +82 (2) 781-1000; (duty officer) +82 (2) 781-1711/1792; (news desk) +82 (2) 781-4444; (overseas assistance) +82 (2) 781-1473/1497. Fax: +82 (2) 781 1698 or +82 (2) 781 2399. Email: pr@kbs.co.kr. Web: (includes streaming audio) http://kbs.co.kr.

KUWAIT World Time +3

IBB Kuwait Transmitting Station, c/o American Embassy-Bayan, P.O.Box 77, Safat, 13001 Kuwait, Kuwait. Contact: Supervisor. This address for specialized technical correspondence only, although reception reports may occasionally be verified. All other correspondence should be directed to the regular VOA or IBB addresses (*see* USA).
📻**Radio Kuwait**, P.O. Box 397, 13004 Safat, Kuwait; (technical) Department of Frequency Management, P.O. Box 967, 13010 Safat, Kuwait. Phone: (general) 965 242-3774; (technical) +965 241-0301. Fax: (general) +965 245 6660; (technical) +965 241 5946. Email: (technical) kwtfreq@hotmail.com; (general) radiokuwait@radiokuwait.org, info@mointo.gov.kw. Web: (on-demand news audio) www.radiokuwait.org; (streaming audio) www.media.gov.kw. Contact: (general) Manager, External Service; (technical) Wessam Najaf. Sometimes gives away stickers, desk calendars, pens or key chains.
TRANSMISSION AND FREQUENCY MANAGEMENT OFFICE: Ministry of Information, P.O. Box 967 13010 Safat, Kuwait. Phone: +965 241-3590 or +965 241- 7830. Fax: +965 241 5498. Email: kwtfreq@yahoo.com. Contact: Ahmed J. Alawdhi, Head of Frequency Section; Abdel Amir Mohamed Ali, Head of Frequency Planning; Nasser Al-Saffar, Frequency Manager; or Muhamad Abdullah, Director of Transmitting Stations.

KYRGYZSTAN World Time +6

Kyrgyz Radio, Kyrgyz TV and Radio Center, 59 Jash Gvardiya Boulevard, 720010 Bishkek, Kyrgyzstan. Phone: (general) +996 (312) 253-404 or +996 (312) 255-741; (Director) +996 (312) 255-700 or +996 (312) 255-709; (Assemov) +996 (312) 650-7341 or +996 (312) 255-703; (Atakanova) +996 (312) 251-927;

(technical) +996 (312) 257-771. Fax: +996 (312) 257 952. Note that from a few countries, the dialing code is still the old +7 (3312). Email: trk@kyrnet.kg. Web: www.ktr.kg. Contact: (administration), Myrzakul Mambetaliev, Vice-Chairman - Kyrgyz Radio; or Eraly Ayilchiyev, Director; (general) Talant Assemov, Editor - Kyrgyz/Russian/German news; Gulnara Abdulaeva, Announcer - Kyrgyz/Russian/German news; (technical) Mirbek Uursabekov, Technical Director. Kyrgyz and Russian preferred, but correspondence in English or German can also be processed. For quick processing of reception reports, use email in German to Talant Assemov.

TRANSMISSION FACILITIES: Ministry of Transport and Communications, 42 Issanova Street, 720000 Bishkek, Kyrgyzstan. Phone: +996 (312) 216-672. Fax: +996 (312) 213 667. Contact: Jantoro Satybaldiyev, Minister. The shortwave transmitting station is located at Krasnaya-Rechka (Red River), a military encampment in the Issk-Ata region, about 40 km south of Bishkek.

LAO PEOPLE'S DEMOCRATIC REPUBLIC World Time +7

NOTE: Although universally known as Laos, the official name of the country is "Lao People's Democratic Republic." English has now replaced French as the preferred foreign language.

Houa Phanh Provincial Radio Station, Sam Neua, Houa Phanh Province, Lao P.D.R. Phone: +856 (64) 312-008. Fax: +856 (21) 312 017. Contact: Mr. Veeyang, Hmong Announcer, and the only person who speaks English at the station; Ms. Nouan Thong, Lao Announcer; Mr. Vilaphone Bounsouvanh, Director; or Mr. Khong Kam, Engineer.

Lao National Radio

PROGRAM OFFICE AND NATIONAL STUDIOS: Lao National Radio, Phaynam Road, Vientiane, Lao P.D.R; (postal address) P.O. Box 310, Vientiane, Lao P.D.R. Phone: +856 (21) 212-097/428/429/431/432; (Head of English service & External Relations) +856 (21) 252-863. Fax: +856 (21) 212 430. Email: laonatradio@lnr.org.la. (Head of English Service) inpanhs@hotmail.com. Web: (includes on-demand audio in Lao and English) www.lnr.org.la. Contact: Mr. Bounthan Inthaxay, Director General; Mr. Inpanh Satchaphansy, Head of English Service & External relations; Mr. Vorasak Pravongviengkham, Head of French Service; Ms. Mativarn Simanithone, Deputy Head, English Section; Ms Chanthery Vichitsavanh, Announcer, English Section. Sometimes includes a program schedule and Laotian stamps when replying.

HF TRANSMITTER SITE: Transmitting Station KM6, Phone Tong Road, Ban Chommany Neuk, Vientiane Province, Lao P.D.R. Phone: +856 (21) 710-181. Contact: Mr. Sysamone Phommaxay, Station Engineer.

TECHNICAL OFFICE: Mass Media Department, Ministry of Information & Culture, 01000 Thanon Setthathirath, Vientiane, Lao P.D.R; or P.O. Box 122, Vientiane, Lao P.D.R. Phone/Fax: +856 (21) 212-424. Email: dy_sisombath@yahoo.com. Contact: Mr. Dy Sisombath, Deputy Director General & Manager, Technical Network Expansion Planning.

LATVIA World Time +2 (+3 midyear)
KREBS TV, P.O. Box 371, LV-1010 Riga, Latvia. Email: tesug@parks.lv. This company holds the license, and brokers airtime, for the shortwave transmitter formerly used by Latvian Radio and which now operates on 9290 kHz. Reception reports on Radio Tatras International can be verified from this address, but reports on other broadcasts should be sent to the individual program producers or stations which hire airtime over the transmitter.

LEBANON World Time +2 (+3 midyear)

Radio Voice of Charity, Rue Fouad Chéhab, Jounieh, Lebanon; or B.P. 850, Jounieh, Lebanon. Phone: +961 (9) 918-090, +961 (9) 917-917, +961 (9) 636-344. Fax: +961 (9) 930 272. Email: mahaba@radiocharity.org.lb. Web: (includes streaming audio from domestic service) www.radiocharity.org. Contact: Father Fadi Tabet, General Director. Operates domestically on FM, and airs a 30-minute daily Arabic broadcast via the shortwave facilities of Vatican Radio. Replies to correspondence in English, French or Arabic, and verifies reception reports. Return postage helpful.

LESOTHO World Time +2

Radio Lesotho (if reactivated), P.O. Box 552, Maseru 100, Lesotho. Phone/Fax: +266 323-371. Email: online form. Web: www.radioles.co.ls. Contact: (general) Mamonyane Matsaba, Acting Programming Director; or Sekhonyana Motlohi, Producer, "What Do Listeners Say?"; (administration) Ms. Mpine Tente, Principal Secretary, Ministry of Information and Broadcasting; (technical) Lebohang Monnapula, Chief Engineer; Emmanuel Rametse, Transmitter Engineer; or Motlatsi Monyane, Studio Engineer. Return postage necessary, but do not include currency notes—local currency exchange laws are very strict.

LIBERIA World Time exactly

Radio ELWA, Box 192, Monrovia, Liberia. Phone: +231 (6) 515-511. Email: radio.staff@radioelwa.org; (Nyantee) moses.nyantee@radioelwa.org. Web: www.elwaministries.org/radio.htm. Contact: Moses T. Nyantee, Station Manager.

Radio Veritas, P.O. Box 3569, Monrovia, Liberia. Phone: +231 221-658. Email: radioveritas@hotmail.com. Contact: Ledgerhood Rennie, Station Manager.

Star Radio, P.O. Box 3081, 1000 Monrovia 10, Liberia. Phone: +231 (6) 518-572. Email: starradio_liberia@yahoo.com. Web: www.starradio.org.lr. Contact: James Morlu, Station Manager. An independent station supported by the Swiss-based Fondation Hirondelle. Transmits round the clock on 104 FM in Monrovia, and airs morning and evening broadcasts on world band via a leased transmitter on Ascension Island.

FONDATION HIRONDELLE: 3 Rue Traversière, CH 1018-Lausanne, Switzerland. Phone: +41 (21) 647-2805. Fax: +41 (21) 647 4469. Email info@hirondelle.org. Web: www.hirondelle.org. Verifies reception reports.

LIBYA World Time +2

Libyan Jamahiriyah Broadcasting Corporation, P.O. Box 9333, Tripoli, Libya. Phone: +218 (21) 361-4508. Fax: +218 (21) 489 4240. Email: info@ljbc.net. Web: (includes streaming audio) www.ljbc.net. Contact: Youssef Aimoujrab.

Voice of Africa, P.O. Box 4677 (or 4396 or 2009), Tripoli, Libya. Phone: +218 (21) 444-0112, +218 (21) 444-9106. Fax: +218 (21) 444 9875. Email: africavoice@hotmail.com. The external service of the Libyan Jamahiriyah Broadcasting Corporation. Replies slowly and irregularly.

MALTA OFFICE: P.O. Box 17, Hamrun, Malta. Replies tend to be more forthcoming from this address than direct from Libya.

LITHUANIA World Time +2 (+3 midyear)

Radio Vilnius, Lietuvos Radijas, Konarskio 49, LT-2600 Vilnius, Lithuania. Phone: +370 (5) 236-3079. Email:

radiovilnius@lrt.lt. Web: (includes on-demand audio) www. lrt.lt (click on "English"). Contact: Ms. Ilona Rukiene, Head of English Department. Free stickers, pennants, Lithuanian stamps and other souvenirs.

MADAGASCAR   World Time +3

Radio Feon'ny Filazantsara. A broadcast produced by the Lutheran Church of Madagascar (Fiangonana Loterana Malagasy) and aired via the Madagascar relay of Radio Nederland (see). *LUTHERAN CHURCH OF MADAGASCAR:* Fiangonana Loterana Malagasy. P.O. Box 741, 101 Antananarivo, Madagascar. Phone: +261 321-2107, +261 2022-21001. Fax: +261 2022 33767. Email: flm@wanadoo.mg.

Radio Madagasikara, B.P. 442 - Anosy, 101 Antananarivo, Madagascar. Phone: +261 2022-21745. Fax: +261 2022 32715. Email: (Director's Office) mmdir@dts.mg; (Editorial Dept.) mminfo@dts.mg; (Program Dept.) mmprog@dts.mg; (Webmaster) radmad@dts.mg. Web: http://takelaka.dts.mg/radmad. Contact: Mlle. Rakotonirina Soa Herimanitia, Secrétaire de Direction, a young lady who collects stamps; Mamy Rafenomanantsoa, Directeur; or J.J. Rakotonirina, who has been known to request hi-fi catalogs. $1 required, and enclosing used stamps from various countries may help. Tape recordings accepted. Replies slowly and somewhat irregularly, usually to correspondence in French.

Radio Nederland Wereldomroep—Madagascar Relay, B.P. 404, Antananarivo, Madagascar. Contact: (technical) Rahamefy Eddy, Technische Dienst; or J.A. Ratobimiarana, Chief Engineer. Nontechnical correspondence should be sent to Radio Nederland Wereldomroep in the Netherlands (see).

MALAWI   World Time +2

Malawi Broadcasting Corporation (when operating), P.O. Box 30133, Chichiri, Blantyre 3, Malawi. Phone: (general) +265 671-222; (transmitting station) +265 694-208. Fax: +265 671 257 or +265 671 353. Email: dgmbc@malawi.net. Contact: (general) Wilson Bankuku, Director General; J.O. Mndeke; or T.J. Sinela; (technical) Abraham E. Nsapato, Controller of Transmitters; Phillip Chinseu, Engineering Consultant; or Joseph Chikagwa, Director of Engineering. Tends to be irregular due to lack of transmitter spares. Return postage or $1 helpful, as the station is underfunded.

MALAYSIA   World Time +8

Asia-Pacific Broadcasting Union (ABU), P.O. Box 1164, 59700 Kuala Lumpur, Malaysia; or (street address) 2nd Floor, Bangunan IPTAR, Angkasapuri, 50614 Kuala Lumpur, Malaysia. Phone: (general) +60 (3) 2282-3592; (Programme Department) +60 (3) 2282-2480; (Technical Department) +60 (3) 2282-3108. Fax: +60 (3) 2282 5292. Email: (Office of Secretary-General) sg@abu.org.my; (Programme Department) prog@abu.org.my; (Technical Department) tech@abu.org.my. Web: www.abu.org.my. Contact: (administration) David Astley, Secretary-General; (technical) Sharad Sadhu and Rukmin Wijemanne, Senior Engineers, Technical Department.

Radio Malaysia Kota Kinabalu, RTM Sabah, 2.4 km Jalan Tuaran, 88614 Kota Kinabalu, Sabah, Malaysia. Phone: +60 (88) 213-444, +60 (88) 212-086. Fax: +60 (88) 223 493. Email: rtmkk@rtm.net.my. Web: www.p.sabah.gov.my/rtm. Contact: Benedict Janil, Director of Broadcasting; Hasbullah Latiff; or Mrs. Angrick Saguman. Registering your letter may help. $1 or return postage required.

⊠Radio Malaysia, Kuala Lumpur

MAIN OFFICE: RTM, Angkasapuri, Bukit Putra, 50614 Kuala Lumpur, Malaysia; (postal address) RTM, P.O. Box 11272, 50740 Kuala Lumpur, Malaysia. Phone: +60 (3) 2282-5333, +60 (3) 2282-4976; (Radio 1, Malay) +60 (3) 2288-7841, +60 (3) 2288-7261; (Radio 4, English) +60 (3) 2288-7282/3/4/5, +60 (3) 2288-7663. Fax: +60 (3) 2282 4735, +60 (3) 2282 5103, +60 (3) 2282 5859; (Radio 1) +60 (3) 2284 7593; (Radio 4) +60 (3) 2284 5750. Email: sabariah@rtm.net.my or helpdesk@rtm.net.my; (Radio 1) komit@radio1.com.my; (Radio 4) radio4@rtm.net.my. Web: (includes streaming audio) www.rtm.net.my. Contact: (general) Madzhi Johari, Director of Radio; (technical) Ms. Aminah Din, Deputy Director Engineering (Radio); Abdullah Bin Shahadan, Engineer, Transmission and Monitoring; or Ong Poh, Chief Engineer. May sell T-shirts and key chains. Return postage required.

ENGINEERING DIVISION: 3rd Floor, Angkasapum, 50616 Kuala Lumpur, Malaysia. Phone: +60 (3) 2285-7544. Fax: +60 (3) 2283 2446. Email: zulrahim@rtm.net.my. Contact: Zulkifli Ab Rahim.

TRANSMISSION OFFICE: Controller of Engineering, Department of Broadcasting (RTM), 43000 Kajang, Selangor Darul Ehsan, Malaysia. Phone: +60 (3) 8736-1530 or +60 (3) 8736-1530/1863. Fax: +60 (3) 8736 1226/7. Email: rtmkjg@rtm.net.my. Contact: Jeffrey Looi; or Ab Wahid Bin Hamid, Supervisor, Transmission Engineering.

Radio Malaysia Sarawak (Kuching), RTM Sarawak, Jalan Satok, 93614 Kuching, Sarawak, Malaysia. Phone: +60 (82) 248-422. Fax: +60 (82) 241 914. Email: rtmkuc@rtm.net.my. Contact: (general) Yusof Ally, Director of Broadcasting; Mohd Hulman Abdollah; Wilson Eddie Gaong, Head of Secretariat for Director of Broadcasting; or Human Resources Development; (technical, but also nontechnical) Colin A. Minoi, Technical Correspondence; (technical) Kho Kwang Khoon, Deputy Director of Engineering. Return postage helpful.

Radio Malaysia Sarawak (Miri), RTM Miri, Bangunan Penyiaran, 98000 Miri, Sarawak, Malaysia. Phone: +60 (85) 422-524 or +60 (85) 423-645. Fax: +60 (85) 411 430. Contact: Clement Stia. $1 or return postage helpful.

Radio Malaysia Sarawak (Sibu), RTM Sibu, Bangunan Penyiaran, 96009 Sibu, Sarawak, Malaysia. Phone: +60 (84) 323-566. Fax: +60 (84) 321 717. Contact: Clement Stia, Divisional Controller, Broadcasting Department. $1 or return postage required. Replies irregularly and slowly.

Voice of Islam—Program of the Voice of Malaysia (see, below).

Voice of Malaysia, Suara Malaysia, Wisma Radio Angkasapuri, P.O. Box 11272, 50740 Kuala Lumpur, Malaysia. Phone: (general) +60 (3) 2288-7824; (English Service) +60 (3) 2282-7826. Fax: +60 (3) 2284 7594. Email: vom@rtm.net.my; (technical, Kajang transmitter site) rtmkjg@po.jaring.my. Web: http://202.190.233.9/vom/utama.htm. Contact: (general) Mrs. Mahani bte Ujang, Supervisor, English Service; Hajjah Wan Chuk Othman, English Service; (administration) Santokh Singh Gill, Director; or Mrs. Adilan bte Omar, Assistant Director; (technical) Lin Chew, Director of Engineering; (Kajang transmitter site) Kok Yoon Yeen, Technical Assistant. Free calendars, stickers or other small souvenirs. Two IRCs or return postage helpful. Replies slowly and irregularly.

MALI   World Time exactly

Office de Radiodiffusion Télévision du Mali, B.P. 171, Bamako, Mali. Phone: +223 212-019 or +223 212-474. Fax:

+223 214 205. Email: (general) ortm@ortm.net; (Traore) cotraore@sotelma.ml. Web: www.ortm.net. Contact: Karamoko Issiaka Daman, Directeur des Programmes; (administration) Abdoulaye Sidibe, Directeur General; (Technical) Nouhoum Traore. $1 or IRC helpful. Replies slowly and irregularly to correspondence in French (preferred) or English.

MAURITANIA   World Time exactly

Radio Mauritanie, B.P. 200, Nouakchott, Mauritania. Phone: +222 525-2101. Fax: +222 525 1264. Email: rm@mauritania. mr. Contact: Madame Amir Feu; Lemrabott Boukhary; Madame Fatimetou Fall Dite Ami, Secretaire de Direction; Mr. El Hadj Diagne; or Mr. Hane Abou. Return postage or $1 required. Rarely replies.

MEXICO   World Time −6 (−5 midyear) Central, South and Eastern, including D.F.; −7 (−6 midyear) Mountain; −7 Sonora; −8 (−7 midyear) Pacific

Candela FM—see RASA Onda Corta.

☞Radio Educación Onda Corta—XEPPM, Apartado Postal 21-465, 04021 - México, D.F., Mexico; (street address) Angel Urraza No. 622, 03100 - Col. del Valle, México D.F., Mexico. Phone: (switchboard) +52 (55) 1500-1050; (director's office) +52 (55) 1500-1051; (transmission plant) +52 (55) 5745-7282. Email: (general) informes@radioeducacion.edu.mx; (Lidia Camacho) direccion@radioeducacion.edu.mx; (Nicolás Hernández) nhem@radioeducacion.edu.mx. Web:(includes on-demand and streaming audio) www.radioeducacion.edu.mx. Contact: (general) Lic. María Del Carmen Limón Celorio, Directora de Producción y Planeación; (administration) Lic. Lidia Camacho Camacho, Directora General; (technical) Ing. Jesús Aguilera Jiménez, Subdirector de Desarrollo Técnico; Nicolás Hernández Menchaca, Jefe del Departamento de Planta Transmisora. Free stickers, calendars and station photo. Return postage or $1 required. Replies, sometimes slowly, to correspondence in English, Spanish, Italian or French.

Radio Huayacocotla—XEJN, Apartado Postal 13, 92601 - Huayacocotla, VER, Mexico; (street address) "Radio Huaya," Gutiérrez Najera s/n, 92600 - Huayacocotla, VER, Mexico. Phone: +52 (774) 758-0067. Contact: Pedro Ruperto Albino, Coordinador. Return postage or $1 helpful. Replies irregularly to correspondence in Spanish.

Radio Mil Onda Corta—XEOI, Prol. Paseo de la Reforma No. 115, Col. Paseo de las Lomas, 01330 - México, D.F., Mexico; or Apartado Postal 21-1000, 04021-México, D.F., Mexico (this address for reception reports and listeners' correspondence on the station's shortwave broadcasts, and mark the envelope to the attention of Dr. Julián Santiago Díez de Bonilla). Phone: (studios) +52 (55) 5258-1351; (NRM Comunicaciones parent organization) +52 (55) 5258-1200. Email: radiomil@nrm.com. mx; (reception reports) ingenieria@nrm.com.mx. Web: www. nrm.com.mx/estaciones/radiomil. Contact: (administration) Lic. Gustavo Alvite Martínez, Director de Radio Mil; or Edilberto Huesca P., Vicepresidente Ejecutivo de NRM Comunicaciones; (technical) Juan Iturria, Ingeniero Jefe; (shortwave service) Dr. Julián Santiago Díez de Bonilla. Free stickers. $1 or return postage required.

☞Radio Transcontinental—XERTA, Plaza San Juan 5, 1er piso - Despacho 2, Centro Histórico, 06070 - México D.F., Mexico. Phone: +52 (55) 5518-4938. Email: charlaxerta@yahoo.com. mx; xerta@radiodifusion.com. Web: (includes streaming audio) www.misionradio.com. Contact: Verónica Coria Miranda,

Representante Ejecutiva; or Lic. Rubén Castañeda Espíndola, Director General.

☞Radio UNAM [Universidad Nacional Autónoma de México]—XEYU (when operating), Adolfo Prieto 133, Colonia del Valle, 03100 - México D.F., Mexico. Phone: +52 (55) 5623-3250, +52 (55) 5623-3251, +52 (55) 5687-3989; (listener feedback) +52 (55) 5536-8989; (toll-free within Mexico) 01-800-505-2688. Fax: +52 (55) 5543 6852. Email: radiounam@www.unam. mx; (Fernando Álvarez) Álvarez. Web: (includes on-demand and streaming audio) www.unam.mx/radiounam. Contact: Mtro. Fernando Álvarez del Castillo A., Director General. Free tourist literature and stickers. $1 or return postage required. Replies irregularly to correspondence in Spanish.

Radio Universidad—XEXQ Onda Corta, Apartado Postal 456, 78001 - San Luis Potosí, SLP, Mexico; (street address) Gral. Mariano Arista 245, Centro Histórico, 78000 - San Luis Potosí, SLP, Mexico. Phone: +52 (444) 826-1345; (studio) +52 (444) 826-1347. Fax: +52 (444) 826 1388. Contact: Lic. Leticia Zavala Pérez, Coordinadora; Lizbeth Deyanira Tapia Hernández, Radio Operadora.

RASA Onda Corta—XEQM (when operating), Apartado Postal 217, 97001 - Mérida, YUC, Mexico. Phone: +52 (999) 236-155. Fax: +52 (999) 280 680. Contact: Lic. Bernardo Laris Rodríguez, Director General del Grupo RASA Mérida. Replies irregularly to correspondence in Spanish.

MOLDOVA   World Time +2 (+3 midyear)

Radio DMR, Rose Luxembourg Street 10, Tiraspol 3300, Republic of Moldova. Email: radiopmr@inbox.ru. Web: www. president-pmr.org. Contact: Arkady D Shablienko, Director; Ms. Antonina N. Voronkova, Editor-in-Chief; Ernest A. Vardanean, Editor and Translator; Vadim A. Rudomiotov, Announcer; Vlad Butuk, Technician Engineer. Replies to correspondence in Russian or English. Return postage helpful. Broadcasts from the separatist, pro-Russian, "Dniester Moldavian Republic" (also known as "Trans-Dniester Moldavian Republic").

MONGOLIA   World Time +8 (+9 midyear)

Mongolian Radio—same postal and email addresses as Voice of Mongolia, below. Phone: (administration) +976 (11) 323-520 or +976 (11) 328-978; (editorial) +976 (11) 329-766; (MRTV parent organization) +976 (11) 326-663. Fax: +976 (11) 327 234. Email: mr@mongol.net. Contact: A. Buidakhmet, Director.

Voice of Mongolia, C.P.O. Box 365, Ulaanbaatar 13, Mongolia. Phone: +976 (1) 321-624; (English Section) +976 (11) 327-900. Fax: +976 (11) 323 096; (English Section) +976 (11) 327 234. Email: mr@mongol.net; (Densmaa) densmaa9@yahoo.com. Contact: (general) Mrs. Narantuya, Chief of Foreign Service; Z. Densmaa, Mail Editor; Mrs. Oyunchimeg Alagsai, Head of English Department; or Ms. Tsegmid Burmaa, Japanese Department; (administration) Ch. Surenjav, Director; (technical) Ing. Ganhuu, Chief of Technical Department. Correpondence should be directed to the relevant language section and 2 IRCs or 1$ appreciated. Sometimes very slow in replying. Accepts taped reception reports, preferably containing five-minute excerpts of the broadcast(s) reported, but cassettes cannot be returned. Free pennants, postcards, newspapers, Mongolian stamps, and occasionally, CDs of Mongolian music.

TECHNICAL DEPARTMENT: C.P.O Box 1126, Ulaanbaatar Mongolia. Phone: +976 (11) 363-584. Fax: +976 (11) 327 900. Email: aem@mongol.net. Contact: Mr. Tumurbaatar Gantumur, Director of Technical Department; or Ms. Buyanbaatar Unur, Engineer, Technical Center of Transmission System.

MOROCCO World Time exactly

IBB Morocco Transmitting Station, Briech. Phone: (office) +212 (9) 93-24-81. Fax: +212 (9) 93 55 71. Contact: Station Manager. These numbers for urgent technical matters only. Otherwise, does not welcome direct correspondence; *see* USA for acceptable VOA and IBB Washington addresses and related information.

Radio Medi Un
MAIN OFFICE: B.P. 2055, Tanger, Morocco; (street address) 3, rue Emsallah, 90000 Tanger, Morocco. Phone: +212 3993-6363. Fax: +212 3993 5755. Email: (general) medi1@medi1. com; (technical) technique@medi1.com; or multi-contact online form. Web: (includes on-demand and streaming audio) www.medi1.com (or www.medi1.co.ma). Contact: J. Dryk, Responsable Haute Fréquence. Two IRCs helpful. Free stickers. Correspondence in French preferred.
PARIS BUREAU, NONTECHNICAL: 78 Avenue Raymond Poincaré, F-75016 Paris, France. Phone: +33 (1) 45-01-53-30. Correspondence in French preferred.

Radio Mediterranée Internationale—*see* Radio Medi Un.
Radiodiffusion-Télévision Marocaine, 1 rue El Brihi, Rabat, Morocco. Phone: +212 (7) 766 881/83/85, +212 (7) 701-740 or +212 (7) 201-404. Fax: +212 (7) 722 047, or +212 (7) 703 208. Email: rtm@rtm.gov.ma; (technical) hammouda@rtm.gov. ma.Contact: (nontechnical and technical) Ms. Naaman Khadija, Ingénieur d'Etat en Télécommunication; Abed Bendalh; or Rahal Sabir; (technical) Tanone Mohammed Jamaledine, Technical Director; Hammouda Mohammed, Engineer; or N. Read. Correspondence welcomed in English, French, Arabic or Berber.

MYANMAR (BURMA) World Time +6:30

Defense Forces Broadcasting Unit, Taunggi, Shan State, Myanmar. Email: sny@mandalay.net.mm. Occasionally replies to correspondence in English.
Radio Myanmar
STATION: GPO Box 1432, Yangon 11181, Myanmar; or (street address) 426, Pyay Road, Yangon-11041, Myanmar. Phone: +95 (1) 531-850. Fax. +95 (1) 525 428. Email: mrtv@mptmail. net.mm. Web: www.myanmar.com/RADIO_TV.HTM. Contact: Ko Ko Htway, Director (Broadcasting).

NAGORNO-KARABAGH World Time +4 (+5 midyear)

Voice of Justice, Tigranmetz Street 23a, Stepanakert, Nagorno-Karabagh. Contact: Mikael Hajyan, Station Manager. Replies to correspondence in Armenian, Azeri, Russian or German.

NAMIBIA World Time +2 (+1 midyear)

Radio Namibia/Namibian Broadcasting Corporation, P.O. Box 321, Windhoek 9000, Namibia. Phone: (general) +264 (61) 291-3111; (National Radio—English Service) +264 (61) 291-2440; (German Service) +264 (61) 291-2330; (Schachtschneider) +264 (61) 291-2188. Fax: (general) +264 (61) 217 760; (German Service) +264 (61) 291 2291; (Duwe, technical) +264 (61) 231 881. Email: (general) webmaster@nbc.com.na; (German Service) gssecretary@nbc.com.na. To contact individuals, the format is initiallastname@nbc.com.na; so to reach, say, Peter Schachtschneider, it would be pschachtschneider@nbc. com.na. Web: www.nbc.com.na. Contact: (general) Corry Tjaveondja, Manager, National Radio; (technical) Peter Schachtschneider, Manager, Transmitter Maintenance; Joe Duwe, Chief Technician. Free stickers.

NEPAL World Time +5:45

Radio Nepal, G.P.O. Box 634, Singha Durbar, Kathmandu, Nepal. Phone: (general) +977 (1) 424-3569, +977 (1) 423-1803/4; (executive director) +977 (1) 422-3910; (programme section) +977 (1) 424-2569; (engineering) +977 (1) 424-1923; (chief engineer) +977 (1) 422-5467. Fax: (executive director) +977 (1) 422 1952; (news division) +977 (1) 422 8652. Email: (director) radio@rne.wlink.com.np; (technical) radio@engg. wlink.com.np. Web: (includes on-demand audio) www.radionepal.org. Contact: (general) Tapanath Shukla, Executive Director; Ram Sharan Karki, Deputy Executive Director; P. Shivakoti, Director; Pandav Sunuwar, Chief of Programme Section; (technical) Ramesh Jung Kharkee, Chief Engineer - Transmission; Bishnu Prasad Shivakoti, Chief Engineer - Studios and Planning. 3 IRCs necessary, but station urges that neither mint stamps nor cash be enclosed, as this invites theft by Nepalese postal employees. Replies irregularly.
KHUMALTAR SHORTWAVE STATION: Phone: +977 1 552-1221 or +977 (1) 554-3480. Fax: +977 1 554 3481. Email: radio@txs. wlink.com.np. Contact: Padma Jyoti Dhakhwa, Chief Technical Officer; Madhu Sudan Thapa, Deputy Chief Technical Officer.

NETHERLANDS World Time +1 (+2 midyear)

Radio Nederland Wereldomroep (Radio Netherlands)
MAIN OFFICE: P.O. Box 222, 1200 JG Hilversum, The Netherlands. Phone: (general) +31 (35) 672-4211; (English Language Service) +31 (35) 672-4242; (24-hour listener Answerline) +31 (35) 672 4222. Fax: (general) +31 (35) 672 4207, but indicate destination department on fax cover sheet; (English Language Service) +31 (35) 672 4239. Email: (English Service) letters@rnw.nl; (Spanish Service): cartas@rnw.nl; ("Media Network") media@rnw.nl. Web: (includes on-demand and streaming audio) www.rnw.nl. Contact: (management) Ian Hoek, Director General; Joop Dalmeijer, Editor-in-Chief; Mike Shaw, Head of English Language Service. Semi-annual *On Target* newsletter free upon request, as are stickers and booklets. Other language departments have their own newsletters. The Radio Netherlands Music Department produces concerts heard on many NPR stations in North America, as well as a line of CDs, mainly of classical, jazz, world music and the Euro Hit 40. Most of the productions are only for rebroadcasting on other stations, but recordings on the NM Classics label are for sale. More details available at www.rnmusic. nl. Visitors welcome, but must call in advance.
PROGRAMME DISTRIBUTION, NETWORK AND FREQUENCY PLANNING: P.O. Box 222, 1200 JG Hilversum, The Netherlands. Phone: +31 (35) 672-4422. Fax: +31 (35) 672 4429. Contact: Leo van der Woude, Frequency Manager; or Jan Willem Drexhage, Head of Programme Distribution.
Radio Nile, Plot No. 15, Komi Crescent, Lusira, 338829 Kampala, Uganda. Phone: +256 (41) 220-334. Return postage requested. Programs are produced by the New Sudan Council of Churches (NSCC) at studios in the Netherlands and Uganda. Transmits via the Radio Nederland relay station in Madagascar, and is a project sponsored by the Dutch public broadcaster NCRV and supported by Pax Christi and the Interchurch Organization for Development Corporation.
KENYA ADDRESS: P.O. Box 66168, Nairobi, Kenya. Phone: +254 (20) 446-966 or +254 (20) 448-141/2. Fax: +254 (20) 447 015. Email: nscc-nbo@maf.org.

NETHERLANDS ANTILLES   World Time –4

Radio Nederland Wereldomroep—Bonaire Relay, P.O. Box 45, Kralendijk, Netherlands Antilles. Contact: Leo Kool, Manager. This address for specialized technical correspondence only. All other correspondence should be sent to Radio Nederland Wereldomroep in the Netherlands (*see*).

NEW ZEALAND   World Time +13 (+12 midyear)

📻**Radio New Zealand International (Te Reo Irirangi O Aotearoa, O Te Moana-nui-a-kiwa)**, P.O. Box 123, Wellington, New Zealand. Phone: +64 (4) 474-1437. Fax: +64 (4) 474 1433 or +64 (4) 474 1886. Email: info@rnzi.com. Web: (includes on-demand and streaming audio and online reception report form) www.rnzi.com. Contact: Florence de Ruiter, Listener Mail; Myra Oh, Producer, "Mailbox"; or Walter Zweifel, News Editor; (administration) Ms. Linden Clark, Manager; (technical) Adrian Sainsbury, Technical Manager. Free stickers, schedule/ flyer about station, map of New Zealand and tourist literature available. English/Maori T-shirts for US$20; sweatshirts $40; interesting variety of CDs, as well as music cassettes and spoken programs, in Domestic "Replay Radio" catalog (VISA/MC). Two IRCs or $2 for QSL card, one IRC for schedule/catalog. Email reports verified by email only.
Radio Reading Service—ZLXA, P.O. Box 360, Levin 5500, New Zealand. Phone: (general) +64 (6) 368-2229; (engineering) +64 (25) 985-360. Fax: +64 (6) 368 7290. Email: (general, including reception reports) info@radioreading.org; (Bell) abell@radioreading.org; (Stokoe) bstokoe@radioreading.org. Web: www.radioreading.org. Contact: (general) Ash Bell, Manager/Station Director; (technical, including reception reports) Brian Stokoe. Operated by volunteers 24 hours a day, seven days a week. Station is owned by the "New Zealand Radio for the Print Disabled Inc." Free brochure, postcards and stickers. $1, return postage or 3 IRCs appreciated.

NICARAGUA   World Time –6 (–7 midyear)

NOTE: Nicaragua introduced Daylight Saving Time for summer 2005 as an energy conservation measure. It is not known if the same will occur in 2006 and beyond.
Radio Miskut (when operating), Barrio Pancasan, Puerto Cabezas, R.A.A.N., Nicaragua. Phone: +505 (282) 2443. Fax: +505 (267) 3032. Contact: Evaristo Mercado Pérez, Director de Operación y de Programas; or Abigail Zúñiga Fagoth. Replies slowly and irregularly to correspondence in English or Spanish. $2 helpful, as is registering your letter.

NIGER   World Time +1

La Voix du Sahel, O.R.T.N., B.P. 361, Niamey, Niger. Fax: +227 72 35 48. Contact: (general) Adamou Oumarou; Issaka Mamadou; Zakari Saley; Souley Boubacou; or Mounkaïla Inazadan, Producer, "Inter-Jeunes Variétés"; (administration) Oumar Tiello, Directeur; (technical) Afo Sourou Victor. $1 helpful. Correspondence in French preferred. Correspondence by males with this station may result in requests for certain unusual types of magazines and photographs.

NIGERIA   World Time +1

WARNING—MAIL THEFT: For the time being, correspondence from abroad to Nigerian addresses has a relatively high probability of being stolen.

WARNING—CONFIDENCE ARTISTS: For years, now, correspondence with Nigerian stations has sometimes resulted in letters from highly skilled "pen pal" confidence artists. These typically offer to send you large sums of money, if you will provide details of your bank account or similar information (after which they clean out your account). Other scams are disguised as tempting business proposals; or requests for money, free electronic or other products, publications or immigration sponsorship. Persons thus approached should contact their country's diplomatic offices. For example, Americans should contact the Diplomatic Security Section of the Department of State [phone +1 (202) 647-4000], or an American embassy or consulate.
Radio Nigeria—Abuja (when operating), Broadcasting House, P.M.B. 71, Garki, Abuja, Federal Capital Territory, Nigeria. Phone: +234 (9) 882-1040. Two IRCs, return postage or $1 required. Replies slowly.
Radio Nigeria—Enugu (when operating), P.M.B. 1051, Enugu, Enugu State, Nigeria. Phone: +234 (42) 254-400. Fax: +234 (42) 254 173. Two IRCs, return postage or $1 required. Replies slowly.
Radio Nigeria—Ibadan, Broadcasting House, P.M.B. 5003, Ibadan, Oyo State, Nigeria. Phone: +234 (22) 241-4093 or +234 (22) 241-4106. Fax: +234 (22) 241 3930. $1 or return postage required. Replies slowly.
Radio Nigeria—Kaduna, P.O. Box 250, Kaduna (Kaduna), Nigeria. Contact: Shehu Muhammad, Chief Technical Officer. $1 or return postage required. Replies slowly.
Radio Nigeria—Lagos, Broadcasting House, P.M.B. 12504, Ikoyi, Lagos, Nigeria. Phone: +234 (1) 269-0301. Fax: +234 (1) 269 0073. Two IRCs or return postage helpful. Replies slowly and irregularly.
Salama Radio, PO Box 6316, Jos, Plateau State, Nigeria. Phone: +234 (803) 703-2530. Contact: Dr. Jacob Abdalla. Broadcasts via a transmitter in the United Kingdom.
Voice of Nigeria
ABUJA OFFICE: 6th Floor, Radio House Herbert Macaulay, Garki, Abuja, Federal Capital Territory, Nigeria. Phone: +234 (9) 234-6973, +234 (9) 234-4017. Fax: +234 (9) 234 6970. Email: (general) dgovon@nigol.net.ng, vonabuja@rosecom.net; (Idowu) tidowu@yahoo.com. Web: www.voiceofnigeria.org. Contact: Ayodele Suleiman, Director of Programming; Tope Idowu, Editor "Voice Of Nigeria Airwaves" program magazine & Special Assistant to the Director General; Frank Iloye, Station Manager; (technical) Timothy Gyang, Deputy Director, Engineering.
LAGOS OFFICE: P.M.B. 40003, Falomo, Lagos, Nigeria. Phone: +234 (1) 269-3075 or +234 (1) 269-3078. Fax: +234 (1) 269 3078, +234 (9) 269 1944. Email: vonlagos@fiberia.com.
Replies from the station tend to be erratic, but continue to generate unsolicited correspondence from supposed "pen pals" (*see WARNING—CONFIDENCE ARTISTS,* above); faxes, which are much less likely to be intercepted, may be more fruitful. Two IRCs or return postage helpful.

NORTHERN MARIANA ISLANDS   World Time +10

Far East Broadcasting Company—Radio Station KFBS, P.O. Box 500209, Saipan, Mariana Islands MP 96950 USA. Phone: +1 (670) 322-3841. Fax: +1 (670) 322 3060. Email: saipan@febc. org. Web: www.febi.org. Contact: Robert Springer, Director; or Irene Gabbie, QSL Secretary. Replies sometimes take months. Also, *see* FEBC Radio International, USA.

NORWAY World Time +1 (+2 midyear).

UKEsenderen,d Elgesetergate 1, N-7030 Trondheim, Norway. Email: uka@uka.no. Web: www.uka.no. A student station which operates on 7215 kHz for approximately three weeks (mid-October to early November) in odd-numbered years.

OMAN World Time +4

BBC World Service—A'Seela Relay Station
Resident Engineer, VT Merlin Communications & Partners LLC, BBC Relay Station, P.O. Box 40, Al Ashkarah, Post Code 422, Oman. Email: rebers@omantel.net.com. Contact: Dave Battey, Resident Engineer; or Afrah Al Orimi. Nontechnical correspondence should be sent to the BBC World Service in London (see).
📻**Radio Sultanate of Oman**, Ministry of Information, P.O. Box 600, Muscat, Post Code 113, Sultanate of Oman. Phone: +968 2460-2127, +968 2460-4577, +968 2460-3222, +968 2460-3888; (frequency managment) +968 2460-2494; (engineering) +968 2460-1538. Fax: (general) +968 2469 3770; (frequency management) +968 2460 4629, +968 2460 7239. Email: (general) feedback_rd@oman_radio.gov.om; (frequency management) molfreqs@omantel.net.om, or abulukman@hotmail.com. Web: (includes streaming audio) www.oman-radio.gov.om. Contact: (Directorate General of Technical Affairs) Mohamed Al Marhoubi, Director General of Engineering; or Salim Al-Nomani, Director of Frequency Management. Verifies reception reports. $1, mint stamps or 3 IRCs helpful.

PAKISTAN World Time +5 (+6 midyear)

Azad Kashmir Radio, Muzaffarabad, Azad Kashmir, Pakistan. Contact: (technical) M. Sajjad Ali Siddiqui, Director of Engineering; or Liaquatullah Khan, Engineering Manager. Registered mail helpful. Rarely replies to correspondence.
📻**Pakistan Broadcasting Corporation**—same address, fax and contact details as Radio Pakistan, below. Web: (includes on-demand and streaming audio) www.radio.gov.pk
Radio Pakistan, P.O. Box 1393, Islamabad 44000, Pakistan. Phone: +92 (51) 921-6942 or +92 (51) 921-7321. Fax: +92 (51) 920 1861, +92 (51) 920 1118 or +92 (51) 922 3877. Email: (general) cnoradio@isb.comsats.net.pk; (technical) cfmpbchq@isb.comsats.net.pk (reception reports to this address have been verified with QSL cards). Web: www.radio.gov.pk/exter.html. Contact: (technical) Ahmed Nawaz, Senior Broadcast Engineer, Room No. 324, Frequency Management Cell; Iftikhar Malik, Senior Broadcast Engineer & Frequency Manager, Frequency Management Cell; Ajmal Kokhar, Controller, Frequency Management; Syed Asmat Ali Shah, Senior Broadcasting Engineer; Zulfiqar Ahmad, Director of Engineering; or Nasirahmad Bajwa, Frequency Management. Free stickers, pennants and *Pakistan Calling* magazine. May also send pocket calendar. Replies irregularly to postal correspondence; better is to use email if you can. Plans to replace two 50 kW transmitters with 500 kW units if and when funding is forthcoming.

PALAU World Time +9

Radio Station T8BZ (formerly KHBN and name still used), P.O. Box 66, Koror, Palau PW 96940. Phone: +680 488-2162, +680 544-1050. Fax: (main office) +680 488 2163; (engineering) +680 544 1008. Email:(general) hamadmin@palaunet.com or highadventure@fastmail.fm; (technical) cacciatore@lineone.net. Contact: (technical) Ben Chen, Engineering Manager. IRC requested.

PAPUA NEW GUINEA World Time +10

NOTE: Regional stations are sometimes off the air due to financial or technical problems which can take weeks or months to resolve.
Catholic Radio Network
STATION: Web: www.catholicpng.org.pg.
RECEPTION REPORTS: Email: wwilson@tepng.com. Contact: Wayne Wilson, Construction Manager, TE(PNG).
National Broadcasting Corporation of Papua New Guinea, P.O. Box 1359, Boroko 111, NCD, Papua New Guinea. Phone: +675 325-5233, + 675 325-5949 or +675 325-6779. Fax: +675 323 0404, +675 325 0796 or +675 325 6296. Email: pom@nbc.com.pg. Web: www.nbc.com.pg. Contact: (general) Renagi R. Lohia, CBE, Managing Director and C.E.O.; or Ephraim Tammy, Director, Radio Services; (technical) Bob Kabewa, Sr. Technical Officer; or F. Maredey, Chief Engineer. Two IRCs or return postage helpful. Replies irregularly.
Radio Bougainville, P.O. Box 35, Buka, NSP, Papua New Guinea. Contact: Ivo Tsika, Station Manager; Aloysius Rumina, Provincial Programme Manager; Ms. Christine Talei, Assistant Provincial Manager; or Aloysius Laukai, Senior Programme Officer. Replies irregularly.
Radio Central (when operating), P.O. Box 1359, Boroko, NCD, Papua New Guinea. Contact: Steven Gamini, Station Manager; Lahui Lovai, Provincial Programme Manager; or Amos Langit, Technician. $1, 2 IRCs or return postage helpful. Replies irregularly.

Radio Eastern Highlands (when operating), P.O. Box 311, Goroka, EHP, Papua New Guinea. Phone: +675 732-1533, +675 732-1733. Contact: Tony Mill, Station Manager; Tonko Nonao, Program Manager; Ignas Yanam, Technical Officer; or Kiri Nige, Engineering Division. $1 or return postage required. Replies irregularly.

Radio East New Britain (when operating), P.O. Box 393, Rabaul, ENBP, Papua New Guinea. Contact: Esekia Mael, Station Manager; or Oemas Kumaina, Provincial Program Manager. Return postage required. Replies slowly.

Radio East Sepik, P.O. Box 65, Wewak, ESP, Papua New Guinea. Contact: Elias Albert, Assistant Provincial Program Manager; or Luke Umbo, Station Manager.

Radio Enga (if reactivated), P.O. Box 300, Wabag, Enga Province, Papua New Guinea. Phone: +675 547-1213. Contact: (general) John Lyein Kur, Station Manager; or Robert Papuvo, (technical) Gabriel Paiao, Station Technician.

Radio Gulf (when operating), P.O. Box 36, Kerema, Gulf, Papua New Guinea. Contact: Tmothy Akia, Station Manager; or Timothy Akia, Provincial Program Manager.

Radio Madang, P.O. Box 2138, Madang, Papua New Guinea. Phone: +675 852-2415. Fax: +675 852 2360. Email: (Gedabing) geo@daltron.com.pg. Contact: Geo Gedabing, Provincial Programme Manager. Return postage helpful.

Radio Manus, P.O. Box 505, Lorengau, Manus, Papua New Guinea. Phone: +675 470-9029. Fax: +675 470 9079. Contact: (technical and nontechnical) John P. Mandrakamu, Provincial Program Manager. Station is seeking the help of DXers and broadcasting professionals in obtaining a second hand, but still usable broadcasting quality CD player that could be donated to Radio Manus. Replies regularly. Return postage appreciated.

Radio Milne Bay (when operating), P.O. Box 111, Alotau, Milne Bay, Papua New Guinea. Contact: (general) Trevor Webumo, Assistant Manager; Simon Muraga, Station Manager; or Raka Petuely, Program Officer; (technical) Philip Maik, Technician. Return postage in the form of mint stamps helpful.

Radio Morobe, P.O. Box 1262, Lae, Morobe, Papua New Guinea. Fax: +675 472 6423. Contact: Ken L. Tropu, Assistant Program Manager; Peter W. Manua, Program Manager; Kekalem M. Meruk, Assistant Provincial Program Manager; or Aloysius R. Nase, Station Manager.

Radio New Ireland (when operating), P.O. Box 140, Kavieng, New Ireland, Papua New Guinea. Contact: Otto A. Malatana, Station Manager; or Ruben Bale, Provincial Program Manager. Currently off air due to a shortage of transmitter spares. Return postage or $1 helpful.

Radio Northern (when operating), Voice of Oro, P.O. Box 137, Popondetta, Oro, Papua New Guinea. Contact: Roma Tererembo, Assistant Provincial Programme Manager; or Misael Pendaia, Station Manager. Return postage required.

Radio Sandaun, P.O. Box 37, Vanimo, Sandaun Province, Papua New Guinea. Contact: (nontechnical) Gabriel Deckwalen, Station Manager; Zacharias Nauot, Acting Assistant Manager; Celina Korei, Station Journalist; Elias Rathley, Provincial Programme Manager; Mrs. Maria Nauot, Secretary; (technical) Paia Ottawa, Technician. $1 helpful.

Radio Simbu, P.O. Box 228, Kundiawa, Chimbu, Papua New Guinea. Phone: +675 735-1038 or +675 735-1082. Fax: +675 735 1012. Contact: (general) John Bare, Manager; Tony Mill Waine, Provincial Programme Manager; Felix Tsiki; or Thomas Ghiyandiule, Producer, "Pasikam Long ol Pipel." Cassette recordings $5. Free two-Kina banknotes.

Radio Southern Highlands (when operating), P.O. Box 104, Mendi, SHP, Papua New Guinea. Contact: (general) Andrew Me-les, Provincial Programme Manager; Miriam Piapo, Programme Officer; Benard Kagaro, Programme Officer; Lucy Aluy, Programme Officer; Jacob Mambi, Shift Officer; or Nicholas Sambu, Producer, "Questions and Answers"; (technical) Ronald Helori, Station Technician. $1 or return postage helpful; or donate a wall poster of a rock band, singer or American landscape.

Radio Western, P.O. Box 23, Daru, Western Province, Papua New Guinea. Contact: Robin Wainetti, Manager; (technical) Samson Tobel, Technician. $1 or return postage required. Replies irregularly.

Radio Western Highlands (when operating), P.O. Box 311, Mount Hagen, WHP, Papua New Guinea. Contact: (general) Anna Pundia, Station Manager; (technical) Esau Okole, Technician. $1 or return postage helpful. Replies occasionally. Often off the air because of theft, armed robbery or inadequate security for the station's staff.

Radio West New Britain, P.O. Box 412, Kimbe, WNBP, Papua New Guinea. Fax: +675 983 5600. Contact: Valuka Lowa, Provincial Station Manager; Darius Gilime, Provincial Program Manager; Lemeck Kuam, Producer, "Questions and Answers"; or Esekial Mael. Return postage required.

Wantok Radio Light, P.O. Box 1273, Attn: Chief Engineer, Port Moresby, NCD, Papua New Guinea. Email: (general) online form; (Olson, technical) david@heart-to-serve.com. Web: www.wantokradio.net. Contact: David Olson. Return postage (3 IRCs) required for postal reply. Verifies reception reports. Wantok Radio Light is the shortwave station of the PNG Christian Broadcasting Network, and is a joint project involving Life Radio Ministries, HCJB World Radio and others.
U.S. SPONSORING ORGANIZATION: Life Radio Ministries, Inc., Joe Emert, P.O. Box 2020, Griffin GA 30223 USA. Phone: +1 (770) 229-9267, +1 (770) 229-2020. Fax: +1 (770) 229 4820. Email: jemert@wmvv.com. Web: www.wmvv.com/intmin.htm. Contact: Joseph C. Emert, President, Life Radio Ministries, Inc.

PARAGUAY   World Time –3 (–4 midyear)

Radio América (when operating), Casilla de Correo 2220, Asunción, Paraguay. Fax: +595 (21) 963-149. Email: radioamerica@lycos.com, ramerica@rieder.net.py. Contact: Adán Mur, Asesor Técnico. Replies to correspondence in Spanish or English. Operates on legally assigned 1480 kHz on mediumwave AM, but is believed to be unlicensed on shortwave.

Radio Nacional del Paraguay, Blas Garay 241 entre Yegros e Iturbe, Asunción, Paraguay. Phone: +595 (21) 390-375. Fax: +595 (21) 390 376. Email: info@rnpy.com. Web: www.rnpy.com. Free tourist brochure. $1 or return postage required. Replies, sometimes slowly, to correspondence in Spanish.

PERU   World Time-5

NOTE: Obtaining replies from Peruvian stations calls for creativity, tact, patience—and the proper use of Spanish, not form letters and the like.

Frecuencia Líder (Radio Bambamarca), Jirón Jorge Chávez 416, Bambamarca, Hualgayoc, Cajamarca, Peru. Phone: (office) +51 (74) 713-260; (studio) +51 (74) 713-249. Contact: (general) Valentín Peralta Díaz, Gerente; Irma Peralta Rojas; or Carlos Antonio Peralta Rojas; (technical) Oscar Lino Peralta Rojas. Free station photos. *La Historia de Bambamarca* book for 5 Soles; cassettes of Peruvian and Latin American folk music for 4 Soles each; T-shirts for 10 Soles each (sending US$1 per Sol should suffice and cover foreign postage costs, as well).

Replies occasionally to correspondence in Spanish. Considering replacing their transmitter to improve reception.

Frecuencia San Ignacio (when operating), Jirón Villanueva Pinillos 330, San Ignacio, Cajamarca, Peru. Contact: Franklin R. Hoyos Cóndor, Director Gerente; or Ignacio Gómez Torres, Técnico de Sonido. Replies to correspondence in Spanish. $1 or return postage necessary.

Frecuencia VH—*see* Radio Frecuencia VH.

La Voz de la Selva—*see* Radio La Voz de la Selva.

La Voz del Campesino—*see* Radio La Voz del Campesino.

Ondas del Suroriente—*see* Radio Ondas del Suroriente.

Radio Altura, Casilla de Correo 140, Cerro de Pasco, Pasco, Peru. Phone: +51 (64) 721-875, +51 (64) 722-398. Contact: Oswaldo de la Cruz Vásquez, Gerente General. Replies to correspondence in Spanish.

Radio Altura, Antonio Raymondi 3ra Cuadra, Distrito de Huarmaca, Provincia de Huancabamba, Piura, Peru.

Radio Amistad, Manzana I-11, Lote 6, Calle 22, Urbanización Mariscal Cáceres, San Juan de Lurigancho, Lima, Peru. Phone: +51 (1) 392-3640. Email: radioamistad@peru.com. Contact: Manuel Mejía Barboza. Accepts email reception reports.

Radio Ancash, Casilla de Correo 221, Huaraz, Peru. Phone: +51 (44) 721-381,+51 (44) 721-359, +51 (44) 721-487, +51 (44) 722-512. Fax: +51 (44) 722 992. Contact: Armando Moreno Romero, Gerente General. Replies to correspondence in Spanish.

Radio Andahuaylas, Jr. Ayacucho No. 248, Andahuaylas, Apurímac, Peru. Contact: Sr. Daniel Andréu C., Gerente. $1 required. Replies irregularly to correspondence in Spanish.

Radio Andina, Real 175, Huancayo, Junín, Peru. Phone: +51 (64) 231-123. Replies infrequently to correspondence in Spanish.

Radio Atlántida
STATION: Jirón Arica 441, Iquitos, Loreto, Peru. Phone: +51 (94) 234-452, +51 (94) 234-962. Contact: Pablo Rojas Bardales.
LISTENER CORRESPONDENCE: Sra. Carmela López Paredes, Directora del prgrama "Trocha Turística," Jirón Arica 1083, Iquitos, Loreto, Peru. Free pennants and tourist information. $1 or return postage required. Replies to most correspondence in Spanish, the preferred language, and some correspondence in English.

Radio Bambamarca—*see* Frecuencia Líder, above.

Radio Bethel—*see* Radio Bethel Arequipa, below.

Radio Bethel Arequipa, Avenida Unión 215, 3er piso, Distrito Miraflores, Arequipa, Peru. Contact: Josué Ascarruz Pacheco. Usually announces as "Radio Bethel" and belongs to the "Movimiento Misionero Mundial" evangelistic organization.

Radio Cajamarca, Jirón La Mar 675, Cajamarca, Peru. Phone: +51 (44) 921-014. Contact: Porfirio Cruz Potosí.

Radio Chaski, Baptist Mid-Missions, Apartado Postal 368, Cusco, Peru; or Alameda Pachacútec s/n B-5, Cusco, Peru. Phone: +51 (84) 225-052. Contact: Andrés Tuttle H., Gerente; or Felipe S. Velarde Hinojosa M., Representante Legal.

Radio Chincheros, Jirón Apurímac s/n, Chincheros, Departamento de Apurímac, Peru.

Radio Chota, Jirón Anaximandro Vega 690, Apartado Postal 3, Chota, Cajamarca, Peru. Phone: +51 (44) 771-240. Contact: Aladino Gavidia Huamán, Administrador. $1 or return postage required. Replies slowly to correspondence in Spanish.

Radio Comas (if reactivated), Avenida Estados Unidos 327, Urbanización Huaquillay, km 10 de la Avenida Túpac Amaru, Distrito de Comas, Lima, Peru. Phone: +51 (1) 525-0859. Fax: +51 (1) 525 0094. Email: rtcomas@terra.com.pe. Web: (includes streaming audio) www.radiocomas.com. Contact:

Edgar Saldaña R.; Juan Rafael Saldaña Reátegui (Relaciones Públicas) or Gamaniel Francisco Chahua, Productor-Programador General.

Radio Cultural Amauta, Apartado Postal 24, Huanta, Ayacucho, Peru; (street address) Jr. Cahuide 278, Huanta, Ayacucho, Peru. Phone/Fax: +51 (64) 832-153. Email: arca@terra.com.pe; (Montes Sinforoso) montessd@terra.com.pe. Web: (includes streaming audio) www.rca.es.vg. Contact: Demetria Montes Sinforoso (Administradora); or Vicente Saico Tinco.

Radio Cusco, Apartado Postal 251, Cusco, Peru. Phone: (general)+51 (84) 225-851; (management) +51 (84) 232-457. Fax: +51 (84) 223 308. Contact: Sra. Juana Huamán Yépez, Administradora; or Raúl Siú Almonte, Gerente General; (technical) Benjamín Yábar Alvarez. Free pennants, postcards and key rings. Audio cassettes of Peruvian music $10 plus postage. $1 or return postage required. Replies irregularly to correspondence in Spanish or English. Station is looking for folk music recordings from around the world to use in their programs.

Radio del Pacífico, Apartado Postal 4236, Lima 1, Peru. Phone: +51 (1) 433-3275. Fax: +51 (1) 433 3276. Contact: J. Petronio Allauca, Secretario, Departamento de Relaciones Públicas; or Julio Villarreal. $1 or return postage required. Replies occasionally to correspondence in Spanish.

Radio El Sol de los Andes, Jirón 2 de Mayo 257, Juliaca, Peru. Phone: +51 (54) 321-115. Fax: +51 (54) 322 981. Contact: Armando Alarcón Velarde.

Radio Frecuencia VH ("La Voz de Celendín"; "RVC"), Jirón José Gálvez 1030, Celendín, Cajamarca, Peru. Contact: Fernando Vásquez Castro, Propietario.

Radio Frecuencia San Ignacio—*see* Frecuencia San Ignacio.

Radio Horizonte, Apartado Postal 69 (or Jirón Amazonas 1177), Chachapoyas, Amazonas, Peru. Phone: +51 (74) 757-793. Fax: +51 (74) 757 004. Contact: Sra. Rocío García Rubio, Ing. Electrónico, Directora; Percy Chuquizuta Alvarado, Locutor; María Montaldo Echaiz, Locutora; Marcelo Mozambite Chavarry, Locutor; Ing. María Dolores Gutiérrez Atienza, Administradora; Juan Nancy Ruíz de Valdez, Secretaria; Yoel Toro Morales, Técnico de Transmisión; or María Soledad Sánchez Castro, Administradora. Replies to correspondence in English, French, German and Spanish. $1 required.

Radio Horizonte, Jirón Incanato 387 Altos, Distrito José Leonardo Ortiz, Chiclayo, Lambayeque, Peru. Phone: +51 (74) 252-917. Contact: Enrique Becerra Rojas, Owner and General Manager. Return postage required.

Radio Huanta 2000, Jirón Gervacio Santillana 455, Huanta, Peru. Phone: +51 (64) 932-105. Fax: +51 (64) 832 105. Contact: Ronaldo Sapaico Maravi, Departmento Técnico; or Sra. Lucila Orellana de Paz, Administradora. Free photo of staff. Return postage or $1 appreciated. Replies to correspondence in Spanish.

Radio Huarmaca, Av. Grau 454 (detrás de Inversiones La Loretana), Distrito de Huarmaca, Provincia de Huancabamba, Región Grau, Peru. Contact: Simón Zavaleta Pérez. Return postage helpful.

Radio Ilucán, Jirón Lima 290, Cutervo, Región Nororiental del Marañón, Peru. Phone: +51 (44) 737-010 or +51 (44) 737-231. Email: radioilucan@hotmail.com. Contact: José Gálvez Salazar, Gerente Administrativo. $1 required. Replies occasionally to correspondence in Spanish.

Radio Imperio, Av. Pedro Ruíz 1250, Urbanización San Juan, Chiclayo, Departamento de Lambayeque, Peru.

Radio La Hora, Av. Garcilaso 180, Cusco, Peru. Phone: +51 (84) 225-615 or +51 (84) 231-371. Contact: (general) Edmundo Montesinos Gallo, Gerente General; (reception reports) Carlos

Gamarra Moscoso, who is also a DXer. Free stickers, pins, pennants and postcards of Cusco. Return postage required. Replies to correspondence in Spanish. Reception reports are best sent direct to Carlos Gamarra's home address: Av. Garcilaso 411, Wanchaq, Cusco, Peru.

Radio Lajas, Jirón Rosendo Mendívil 589, Lajas, Chota, Cajamarca, Nor Oriental del Marañón, Peru. Contact: Alfonso Medina Burga, Gerente Propietario.

Radio La Oroya (when operating), Calle Lima 190, Tercer Piso Of. 3, Apartado Postal 88, La Oroya, Provincia de Yauli, Departamento de Junín, Peru. Phone: +51 (64) 391-401. Fax: +51 (64) 391 440. Email: rlofigu@net.cosapidata.com.pe. Contact: Jacinto Manuel Figueroa Yauri, Gerente-Propietario. Free pennants. $1 or return postage necessary. Replies to correspondence in Spanish.

Radio La Voz, Andahuaylas, Apurímac, Peru. Contact: Lucio Fuentes, Director Gerente.

Radio La Voz de Bolívar, Jirón Cáceres s/n, Bolívar, Provincia de Bolívar, Departamento de La Libertad, Peru. Phone: +51 4423-0277 Contact: Julio Dávila Echevarría, Gerente. May send free pennant. Return postage helpful.

Radio La Voz de Chiriaco (when operating), Jirón Ricardo Palma s/n, Chiriaco, Distrito de Imaza, Provincia de Bagua, Departamento de Amazonas, Peru. Contact: Hildebrando López Pintado, Director; Santos Castañeda Cubas, Director Gerente; or Fidel Huamuro Curinambe, Técnico de Mantenimiento. $1 or return postage helpful.

Radio La Voz de la Selva, Jirón Abtao 255, Casilla de Correo 207, Iquitos, Loreto, Peru. Phone: +51 (94) 265-245. Fax: +51 (94) 264 531. Email: lvsradio@terra.com.pe. Contact: Julia Jáuregui Rengifo, Directora; Marcelino Esteban Benito, Director; Pedro Sandoval Guzmán, Announcer; or Mery Blas Rojas. Replies to correspondence in Spanish.

Radio La Voz de las Huarinjas, Barrio El Altillo s/n, Huancabamba, Piura, Peru. Phone: +51 (74) 473-126 or +51 (74) 473-259. Contact: Alfonso García Silva, Gerente Director (also the owner of the station); or Bill Yeltsin, Administrador. Replies to correspondence in Spanish.

Radio La Voz del Campesino, Av. Ramón Castilla s/n en la salida a Chiclayo, Huarmaca, Provincia de Huancabamba, Piura, Peru. Contact: Fermín Santos. Replies slowly and irregularly to correspondence in Spanish.

Radio Libertad de Junín, Cerro de Pasco 528, Apartado Postal 2, Junín, Peru. Phone: +51 (64) 344-026. Contact: Mauro Chaccha G., Director Gerente. Replies slowly to correspondence in Spanish. Return postage necessary.

Radio Luz y Sonido, Apartado Postal 280, Huánuco, Peru; or (street address) Jirón Dos de Mayo 1286, Oficina 205, Huánuco, Peru. Phone: +51 (64) 512-394 or +51 (64) 518-500. Fax: +51 (64) 511 985. Contact: (technical) Jorge Benavides Moreno; (nontechnical) Pedro Martínez Tineo, Director Ejecutivo; Lic. Orlando Bravo Jesús; or Seydel Saavedra Cabrera, Operador/Locutor. Return postage or $2 required. Replies to correspondence in Spanish, Italian and Portuguese. Sells video cassettes of local folk dances and religious and tourist themes.

Radio Macedonia (when operating), Seminario Bautista Macedonia, Casilla 1677, Arequipa, Peru. Phone/Fax: +51 (54) 444-376. Email: (W.A. Gardner) gardner@world-evangelism. com. Contact: W. Austin Gardner; or Chris Gardner. Replies to correspondence in Spanish or English.

U.S. PARENT ORGANIZATION: Macedonia World Baptist Missions Inc., P.O. Box 519, Braselton GA 30517 USA. Phone: +1 (706) 654-2818. Fax: +1 (706) 654 2816. Email: mwbm@mwbm. org. Web: http://mwbm.org.

Radio Madre de Dios, Daniel Alcides Carrión 385, Apartado Postal 37, Puerto Maldonado, Madre de Dios, Peru. Phone: +51 (84) 571-050. Fax: +51 (84) 571 018 or +51 (84) 573 542. Contact: (administration) Padre Rufino Lobo Alonso, Director; (general) Alcides Arguedas Márquez, Director del programa "Un Festival de Música Internacional," heard Mondays 0100 to 0200 World Time. Sr. Arguedas is interested in feedback for this letterbox program. Replies to correspondence in Spanish. $1 or return postage appreciated.

Radio Marañón, Apartado Postal 50, Jaén, Cajamarca, Peru; or (street address) Francisco de Orellana 343, Jaén, Cajamarca, Peru. Phone: +51 (44) 731-147 or +51 (44) 732-168. Fax: +51 (44) 732 580. Email: (general) correo@radiomaranon.org.pe; (director) pmaguiro@radiomaranon.org.pe. Web: www.radiomaranon. org.pe. Contact: Francisco Muguiro Ibarra S.J., Director. Return postage necessary. May send free pennant. Replies slowly to correspondence in Spanish and (sometimes) English.

Radio Melodía, San Camilo 501-A, Cercado, Arequipa, Peru. Phone: +51 (54) 205-811, +51 (54) 223-661. Fax: +51 (54) 204 420. Contact: Elba Alvarez Delgado, Gerente. Replies to correspondence in Spanish.

Radio Municipal, Jirón Tacna 385, Panao, Pachitea, Huánuco, Peru. Email: dalsmop1@hotmail.com. Contact: Pablo Alfredo Albornoz Rojas, Gerente Técnico, who collects station stickers and pennants. Replies to correspondence in Spanish.

Radio Naylamp (when operating), Avenida Andrés Avelino Cáceres 800, Lambayeque, Peru. Phone: +51 (74) 283-353. Contact: Dr. Juan José Grández Vargas, Director Gerente; or Delicia Coronel Muñoz, who is interested in receiving postcards and the like. Free stickers, pennants and calendars. Return postage necessary.

Radio Ondas del Huallaga, Jirón Leoncio Prado 723, Apartado Postal 343, Huánuco, Peru. Phone: +51 (64) 511-525 or +51 (64) 512-428. Contact: Flaviano Llanos Malpartida, Representante Legal. $1 or return postage required. Replies to correspondence in Spanish.

Radio Ondas del Río Mayo (if reactivated), Jirón Huallaga 348, Nueva Cajamarca, San Martín, Peru. Phone: +51 (94) 556-006. Contact: Edilberto Lucío Peralta Lozada, Gerente; or Víctor Huaras Rojas, Locutor. Free pennants. Return postage helpful. Replies slowly to correspondence in Spanish.

Radio Ondas del Suroriente (when operating), Jirón Ricardo Palma 510, Quillabamba, La Convención, Cusco, Peru.

Radio Oriente, Vicariato Apostólico, Avenida Progreso 114, Yurimaguas, Loreto, Peru. Phone: +51 (94) 352-156. Fax: +51 (94) 352 128. Email: rovay@qnet.co.pe. Web: www.dxing.info/radio/oriente. Contact: (general) Sra. Elisa Cancino Hidalgo; or Juan Antonio López-Manzanares M., Director; (technical) Pedro Capo Moragues, Gerente Técnico. $1 or return postage required. Replies occasionally to correspondence in English, French, Spanish and Catalan.

Radio Paucartambo, Plaza de Armas 124, Paucartambo, Departamento de Cusco, Peru.

Radio Quillabamba, Jirón Ricardo Palma 432, Apartado Postal 76, Quillabamba, La Convención, Cusco, Peru. Phone: +51 (84) 281-002. Fax: +51 (84) 281 771. Contact: Padre Francisco Javier Panera, Director. Replies very irregularly to correspondence in Spanish.

Radio Reina de la Selva, Jirón Ayacucho 944, Plaza de Armas, Chachapoyas, Región Nor Oriental del Marañón, Peru. Phone: +51 (74) 757-203. Contact: José David Reina Noriega, Gerente General; or Jorge Oscar Reina Noriega, Director General. Replies irregularly to correspondence in Spanish. Return postage necessary.

Radio San Andrés, La Municipalidad, Distrito de San Andrés, Provincia de Cutervo, Departamento de Cajamarca, Peru. Email: (Meza): leoncio_ meza@hotmail.com. Contact: Leoncio Samane Meza.

Radio San Antonio (Callalli), Parroquia San Antonio de Padua, Plaza Principal s/n, Callalli, Departamento de Arequipa, Peru. Contact: Hermano [Brother] Rolando.

Radio San Antonio (Villa Atalaya), Jirón Iquitos s/n, Villa Atalaya, Departamento de Ucayali, Peru. Email: (Zerdin) zerdin@terra.com.pe. Contact: Gerardo Zerdin.

Radio San Miguel, Av. Huayna Cápac 146, Huánchac, Cusco, Peru. Contact: Sra. Catalina Pérez de Alencastre, Gerente General; or Margarita Mercado. Replies to correspondence in Spanish.

Radio San Miguel de El Faique (if reactivated), Distrito de El Faique, Provincia de Huancabamba, Departamento de Piura, Peru.

Radio San Nicolás, Jirón Amazonas 114, Rodríguez de Mendoza, Peru. Contact: Juan José Grández Santillán, Gerente; or Violeta Grández Vargas, Administradora. Return postage necessary.

Radio Santa Mónica, Urbanización Marcavalle P-20, Cusco, Peru. Phone:+ 51 (84) 225-357.

Radio Santa Rosa, Jirón Camaná 170, Casilla 4451, Lima 01, Peru. Phone: +51 (1) 427-7488. Fax: +51 (1) 426 9219. Email: radiosantarosa@terra.com.pe. Web: http://barrioperu.terra.com.pe/radiosantarosa. Contact: Padre Juan Sokolich Alvarado, Director; or Lucy Palma Barreda. Free stickers and pennants. $1 or return postage necessary. Replies to correspondence in Spanish or English.

Radio Sicuani, Jirón 2 de Mayo 212, Sicuani, Canchis, Cusco, Peru; or Apartado Postal 45, Sicuani, Peru. Phone: +51 (84) 351-136 or +51 (84) 351-698. Fax: +51 (84) 351 697. Email: cecosda@mail.cosapidata.com.pe. Contact: Mario Ochoa Vargas, Director.

Radio Sudamérica (when operating), Jirón Ramón Castilla 491, tercer nivel, Plaza de Armas, Cutervo, Cajamarca, Peru. Phone: +51 (74) 736-090 or +51 (74) 737-443. Contact: Jorge Luis Paredes Guerra, Administrador; or Amadeo Mario Muñoz Guivar, Propietario.

Radio Tacna, Aniceto Ibarra 436, Casilla de Correo 370, Tacna, Peru. Phone: +51 (54) 714-871. Fax: +51 (54) 723 745. Email: scaceres@viabcp.com. Contact: (nontechnical and technical) Ing. Alfonso Cáceres Contreras, Gerente de Operaciones; (administration) Yolanda Vda. de Cáceres C., Directora Gerente. Free stickers and samples of *Correo* local newspaper. $1 or return postage helpful. Audio cassettes of Peruvian and other music $2 plus postage. Replies irregularly to correspondence in Spanish or English.

Radio Tawantinsuyo, Av. Sol 806, Cusco, Peru. Phone: +51 (84) 226-955 or +51 (84) 228-411. Contact: Ing. Raul Montesinos Espejo, Director Gerente. Has a very attractive QSL card, but only replies occasionally to correspondence, which should be in Spanish.

Radio Tarma, Jirón Molino del Amo 167, Apartado Postal 167, Tarma, Peru. Phone/Fax: +51 (64) 321-167 or +51 (64) 321-510. Contact: Mario Monteverde Pomareda, Gerente General. Sometimes sends 100 Inti banknote in return when $1 enclosed. Free stickers. $1 or return postage required. Replies irregularly to correspondence in Spanish.

Radio Tayacaja (when operating), Correo Central, Distrito de Pampas, Tayacaja, Huancavelica, Peru. Phone: +51 (64) 220-217, Anexo 238. Contact: (general) J. Jorge Flores Cárdenas; (technical) Ing. Larry Guido Flores Lezama. Free stickers and pennants. Replies to correspondence in Spanish. Hopes to replace transmitter.

Radio Unión, Apartado Postal 833, Lima 27, Peru; or (street address) Avenida Central 717 - Piso 12, San Isidro, Lima 27, Peru. Phone: +51 (1) 221-3158/9, +51 (1) 440-1785. Fax: +51 (1) 221 0888. Contact: Raúl Rubbeck Jiménez, Director Gerente; Juan Zubiaga Santiváñez, Gerente; Natividad Albizuri Salinas, Secretaria; or Juan Carlos Sologuren, Dpto. de Administración, who collects stamps. Free satin pennants and stickers. IRC required, and enclosing used or new stamps from various countries is especially appreciated. Replies irregularly to correspondence and tape recordings, with Spanish preferred.

Radio Victoria, Jr.Reynel 320, Mirones Bajo, Lima 1, Peru. Phone: +51 (1) 336-5448. Fax: +51 (1) 427 1195. Email: (Ramos) silvioramos777@hotmail.com. Contact: Henrique Silvio Ramos, Administrador. This station is owned by the Brazilian-run Pentecostal Church "Dios Es Amor," with local headquarters at Av. Arica 248, Lima; Phone: +51 (1) 330-8023. Their program "La Voz de la Liberación" is produced locally and aired over numerous Peruvian shortwave stations.

Radio Virgen del Carmen ("RVC"), Jirón Virrey Toledo 466, Huancavelica, Peru. Phone: +51 (64) 752-740. Contact: Rvdo. Samuel Morán Cárdenas, Gerente.

Radiodifusoras Huancabamba, Calle Unión 409, Huancabamba, Piura, Peru. Phone: +51 (74) 473-233. Contact: Federico Ibáñez Maticorena, Director.

Radiodifusoras Paratón, Jirón Alfonso Ugarte 1090, contiguo al Parque Leoncio Prado, Huarmaca, Provincia de Huancabamba, Piura, Peru. Contact: Prof. Hernando Huancas Huancas, Gerente General; or Prof. Rómulo Chincay Huamán, Gerente Administrativo.

PHILIPPINES   World Time +8

NOTE: Philippine stations sometimes send publications with lists of Philippine young ladies seeking "pen pal" courtships.

Far East Broadcasting Company—FEBC Radio International (External Service)

MAIN OFFICE: P.O. Box 1, Valenzuela, Metro Manila, Philippines 0560. Phone: (general) +63 (2) 292-5603, +63 (2) 292-9403 or +63 (2) 292-5790; (International Broadcast Manager) +63 (2) 292-5603 ext. 158. Fax: +63 (2) 292 9430, +63 (2) 292-5603, +63 (2) 291 4982; (International Broadcast Manager) +63 (2) 292 9724, but lacks funds to provide faxed replies. Email: febcomphil@febc.org.ph; info@febc.org.ph (reception reports to this address are sometimes verified with a QSL card); (Peter McIntyre) pm@febc.jfm.org.ph; (Larry Podmore) lpodmore@febc.jmf.org.ph; (Chris Cooper) ccooper@febc.org.ph. Web: www.febi.org. Contact: (general) Peter McIntyre, Manager, International Operations Division; (administration) Carlos Peña, Managing Director; Chris Cooper, International Broadcast Manager; (engineering) Ing. Renato Valentin, Frequency Manager; Larry Podmore, IBG Chief Engineer. Free stickers and calendar cards. Three IRCs appreciated for airmail reply. Plans to add a new 100 kW shortwave transmitter.

INTERNATIONAL SCHEDULLING OFFICE: FEBC, 20 Ayer Rajah Crescent, Technopreneur Center, #09-22, Singapore 139964, Singapore. Phone: +65 6773-9017. Fax: +65 6773 9018. Email: phsu@febc.org. Contact: Peter C. Hsu, International Schedule Manager.

NEW DELHI BUREAU, NONTECHNICAL: c/o FEBC, Box 6, New Delhi-110 001, India.

IBB Philippines Transmitting Station

MAIN ADDRESS: International Broadcasting Bureau, Philippines Transmitting Station, c/o US Embassy, 1201 Roxas Boulevard, Ermita 1000, Manila, Philippines.

ALTERNATIVE ADDRESS: IBB/PTS, PSC 500 Box 28, FPO AP 96515-1000.

These addresses for specialized technical correspondence only, although reception reports may occasionally be verified. All other correspondence should be directed to the regular VOA or IBB addresses (*see* USA).

Philippine Broadcasting Service—DUR2 (when operating), Bureau of Broadcasting Services, Media Center, Bohol Avenue, Quezon City, Philippines. Relays DZRB Radio ng Bayan and DZRM Radio Manila. Web: (Radio ng Bayan streaming audio) www.pbs.gov.ph.

Radyo Pilipinas, the Voice of Democracy, Philippine Broadcasting Service, 4th Floor, PIA Building, Visayas Avenue, Quezon City 1100, Metro Manila, Philippines. Phone: (general) +63 (2) 924-2620; +63 (2) 920-3963; or +63 (2) 924-2548; (engineering, Phone/Fax) +63 (2) 924-2268. Email: (general) radyo_pilipinas_overseas@yahoo.com (if this fails, try: pbs.pao@pbs.gov.ph); (Mike Pangilinan, technical) mpangilinan@pbs.ops.gov.ph. Web: www.pbs.gov.ph/DZRP_page.htm. Contact: (nontechnical) Joy Montero; Evelyn Salvador Agato, Officer-in-Charge; Mercy Lumba; Leo Romano, Producer, "Listeners and Friends"; Tanny V. Rodriguez, Station Manager; or Richard G. Lorenzo, Production Coordinator; (technical) Danilo Alberto, Supervisor; or Miguelito ("Mike") Pangilinan, Chief Engineer. Free postcards and stickers.

Radio Veritas Asia

STUDIOS AND ADMINISTRATIVE HEADQUARTERS: P.O. Box 2642, Quezon City, 1166 Philippines. Phone: +63 (2) 939-0011 to 14, +63 (2) 939-4692; (technical director) +63 (2) 938-1940. Fax: (general) +63 (2) 938 1940; (frequency manager) +63 (2) 939 7556. Email: (general) rveritas-asia@rveritas-asia.org; (Program Dept.) rvaprogram@rveritas-asia.org; (Audience Research) rva-ars@rveritas-asia.org; (technical) technical@rveritas-asia.org. Web: (includes on-demand and streaming audio) www.rveritas-asia.org. Contact: (administration) Ms. Erlinda G. So, Manager; (general) Ms. Cleofe R. Labindao, Audience Relations Officer; Mrs. Regie de Juan Galindez; or Msgr. Pietro Nguyen Van Tai, Program Director; (technical) Honorio L. Llavore, Technical Director; Alex M. Movilla, Assistant Technical Director; or Alfonso L. Macaranas, Frequency and Monitoring. Free caps, T-shirts, stickers, pennants, rulers, pens, postcards and calendars. Free bi-monthly newsletter *UPLINK*. Return postage appreciated.

TRANSMITTER SITE: Radio Veritas Asia, Palauig, Zambales, Philippines. Contact: Fr. Hugo Delbaere, CICM, Technical Consultant.

BRUSSELS BUREAUS AND MAIL DROPS: Catholic Radio and Television Network, 32-34 Rue de l' Association, B-1000 Brussels, Belgium; or UNDA, 12 Rue de l'Orme, B-1040 Brussels, Belgium.

PIRATE

Pirate radio stations are usually one-person operations airing home-brew entertainment and/or iconoclastic viewpoints. In order to avoid detection by the authorities, they tend to appear irregularly, with little concern for the niceties of conventional program scheduling. Most are found in Europe chiefly on weekends and holidays, often just above 6200 and 7375 kHz; and in North America mainly during evenings, just below 7000 kHz (usually 6925 plus or minus 10 kHz). These *sub rosa* stations and their addresses are subject to unusually abrupt change or termination, sometimes as a result of forays by radio authorities.

A worthy source of current addresses and other information on American pirate radio activity is: A*C*E, P.O. Box 1, Belfast NY 14711-0001 USA (email: acehdq@localnet.com; Web: www.frn.net/ace), a club which publishes a monthly newsletter ($22/year U.S., US$27 Canada, US$40 airmail elsewhere) for serious pirate radio enthusiasts. A popular Internet source of information is the Free Radio Network (www.frn.net).

For Europirate DX news, try:

Swedish Report Service: SRS, Ostra Porten 29, SE-442 54 Ytterby, Sweden. Web: www.srs.pp.se.

Free Radio Service Holland: FRSH, P.O. Box 2727, NL-6049 ZG Herten, Netherlands. Email: freak55@gironet.nl, or peter.verbruggen@tip.nl. Web: www.gironet.nl/home/freak55/nl.htm. Publishes the quarterly "FRS Newsletter."

FRC-Finland, P.O. Box 82, FIN-40101 Jyvaskyla, Finland.

A good list of pirate links can be found at: www.alfalima.net/links-links.htm.

For up-to-date listener discussions and other pirate-radio information on the Internet, the usenet URLs are: alt.radio.pirate and rec.radio.pirate.

POLAND   World Time +1 (+2 midyear)

Bible Christian Association (BCA). Email (English and Polish) kontakt@radio.zapraszamy.pl. Web: (includes on-demand audio) www.radio.zapraszamy.pl. Rarely replies. Reception reports are best sent to Walter Brodowsky at Germany's T-Systems International (*see*) from where the broadcasts are transmitted.

Radio Polonia, P.O. Box 46, PL-00-977 Warsaw, Poland; (street address) al. Niepodległości 77/85, 00-977 Warsaw, Poland. Phone: (general) +48 (22) 645-9305; (English Section) +48 (22) 645-9262; (German Section) +48 (22) 645-9333; (placement liaison) +48 (2) 645-9002. Fax: (general and administration) +48 (22) 645 5917. Email: (general): radio.polonia@radio.com.pl; (Polish Section) polonia@radio.com.pl; (English Section) english.section@radio.com.pl; (German Section) deutsche.redaktion@radio.com.pl; (Esperanto Section) esperanto.redakcio@radio.com.pl. Web: (includes on-demand and streaming audio) www.polskieradio.pl/polonia. Contact: (general) Rafał Kiepuszewski, Head, English Section and Producer, "Postbag"; Peter Gentle, Presenter, "Postbag"; or Ann Flapan, Corresponding Secretary; (administration) Jerzy M. Nowakowski, Managing Director; Wanda Samborska, Managing Director; Bogumiła Berdychowska, Deputy Managing Director; or Maciej Lętowski, Executive Manager. On-air Polish language course with free printed material. Free stickers, pens, key rings and possibly T-shirts depending on financial cutbacks. DX Listeners' Club.

TRANSMISSION AUTHORITY: PAR (National Radiocommunication Agency), ul. Kasprzaka 18/20, PL-01-211 Warsaw, Poland. Phone: +48 (22) 608-8139/40, +48 (22) 608-8174 or +48 (22) 608-8191. Fax: +48 (22) 608 8195. Email: the format is initial.last name@par.gov.pl, so to reach, say, Filomena Grodzicka, it would be f.grodzicka@par.gov.pl. Contact: Mrs. Filomena Grodzicka, Head of BC Section; Lukasz Trzos; Mrs. Katalin Jaros; Ms. Urszula Rzepa or Jan Kondej. Responsible for coordinating Radio Polonia's frequencies.

PORTUGAL   World Time exactly (+1 midyear); Azores World Time –1 (World Time midyear)

RDP Internacional—Rádio Portugal, Av. Marechal Gomes da Costa nº 37, 1849-030 Lisboa, Portugal. Phone:

St. Basil's Cathedral, near Red Square in Moscow. This architectural gem commemorates Ivan the Terrible's victory over Tartar Mongols in 1552.

Corbis

(general) +351 (21) 382-0000. Fax: (general) +351 (21) 382 0165. Email: (general) rdpinternacional@rdp.pt; (reception reports and listener correspondence) isabelsaraiva@rdp.pt, or christianchaupt@rdp.pt. Web: (includes streaming audio and bilingual English-Portuguese online reception report form) http://programas.rtp.pt/EPG/radio. Contact: Isabel Saraiva or Christiane Haupt, Listener's Service Department. Free stickers. May also send literature from the Portuguese National Tourist Office.

DIRECÇÃO TÉCNICA-GRUPO REDES DE EMISSORES: Av. Marechal Gomes da Costa, 37, Bloco B 2º 1849 030 Lisbon Portugal. Phone: +351 (21) 382-0228. Fax: +351 (21) 382 0098. Email: teresaabreu@rdp.pt or paulacarvalho@rdp.pt. Contact: Mrs. Teresa Beatriz Abreu, Frequency Manager; or Ms. Paula Carvalho.

Radio Trans Europe (transmission facilities), 6º esq. Rua Braamcamp 84, 1200 Lisbon, Portugal. Transmitters located at Sines, and used by RDP Internacional and Germany's Deutsche Welle (*see*).

ROMANIA   World Time +2 (+3 midyear)

📻**Radio România International**, 60-62 Berthelot St., RO-70747 Bucharest, Romania; or P.O. Box 111, RO-70756 Bucharest, Romania. Phone: (general) +40 (21) 222-2556, +40 (21) 303-1172, +40 (21) 303-1488, +40 (21) 312-3645; (English Department) +40 (21) 303-1357, +40 (21) 303-1465; (engineering) +40 (21) 303-1193. Fax: (general) +40 (21) 223 2613 [if no connection, try via the office of the Director General of Radio România, but mark fax "Pentru RRI"; that fax is +40 (21) 222 5641]; (Engineering Services) +40 (21) 312 1056/7 or +40 (21) 615 6992. Email: (general) rri@rri.ro; (English Service) engl@rri.ro; (Nisipeanu) mnisipeanu@radio.rornet.ro; (Ianculescu) rianculescu@rri.ro. Web: (includes streaming audio) www.rri.ro; (on-demand audio) www.wrn.org/listeners/stations/station.php?StationID=106. Contact: (communications in English or Romanian) Dan Balamat, "Listeners' Letterbox"; Lacramioara Simion & Iulian Muresan, Producers "Listener's Day"; or Ioana Masariu, Head of the English Service; (radio enthusiasts' issues, English only) "DX Mailbag," English Department; (communications in French or Romanian) Doru Vasile Ionescu, Deputy General Director; (listeners' letters) or

Dan Dumitrescu; (technical) Sorin Floricu, Head of Broadcasting Department; Radu Ianculescu, HF Planning & Monitoring; or Marius Nisipeanu, Director, Production & Broadcasting. Listeners' Club. Annual contests. Concerns about frequency management should be directed to the PTT (*see* below), with copies to the Romanian Autonomous Company (*see* farther below) and to a suitable official at RRI.

TRANSMISSION AND FREQUENCY MANAGEMENT, PTT: General Directorate of Regulations, Ministry of Communications, 14a Al. Libertatii, R-70060 Bucharest, Romania. Phone: +40 (21) 400 1312 or +40 (21) 400 177. Fax: +40 (21) 400 1230. Email: marian@snr.ro. Contact: Mrs. Elena Danila, Head of Frequency Management Department.

TRANSMISSION AND FREQUENCY MANAGEMENT, AUTONO-MOUS COMPANY: Romanian Autonomous Company for Radio Communications, 14a Al. Libertatii, R-70060 Bucharest, Romania. Phone: +40 (21) 400-1072. Fax: +40 (21) 400 1228 or +40 (1) 335 5965. Email: marian@snr.ro. Contact: Mr. Marian Ionitá, Executive Director of Operations.

RUSSIA   Times given for republics, oblasts and krays):

- World Time +2 (+3 midyear) Kaliningradskaya;
- World Time +3 (+4 midyear) Adygeya, Arkhangelskaya, Astrakhanskaya, Belgorodskaya, Bryanskaya, Chechnya, Chuvashiya, Dagestan, Ingushetiya, Kabardino-Balkariya, Kalmykiya, Kaluzhskaya, Karachayevo-Cherkesiya, Ivanovskaya, Karelia, Kirovskaya, Komi, Kostromskaya, Krasnodarskiy, Kurskaya, Leningradskaya (including St. Petersburg), Lipetskaya, Mariy-El, Mordoviya, Moskovskaya (including the capital, Moscow), Murmanskaya, Nenetskiy, Nizhegorodskaya, Novgorodskaya, Severnaya Osetiya, Orlovskaya, Penzenskaya, Pskovskaya, Rostovskaya, Ryazanskaya, Saratovskaya, Smolenskaya, Stavropolskiy, Tambovskaya, Tatarstan, Tulskaya, Tverskaya, Ulyanovskaya, Vladimirskaya, Volgogradskaya, Vologodskaya, Voronezhskaya, Yaroslavskaya;
- World Time +4 (+5 midyear) Samarskaya, Udmurtiya;
- World Time +5 (+6 midyear) Bashkortostan, Chelyabinskaya, Khanty-Mansiyskiy, Komi-Permyatskiy, Kurganskaya, Orenburgskaya, Permskaya, Sverdlovskaya, Tyumenskaya, Yamalo-Nenetskiy;

- World Time +6 (+7 midyear) Altayskiy, Novosibirskaya, Omskaya, Tomskaya;
- World Time +7 (+8 midyear) Evenkiyskiy, Kemerovskaya, Khakasiya, Krasnoyarskiy, Taymyrskiy, Tyva;
- World Time +8 (+9 midyear) Buryatiya, Irkutskaya, Ust-Ordynskiy;
- World Time +9 (+10 midyear) Aginskiy-Buryatskiy, Amurskaya, Chitinskaya, Sakha;
- World Time +10 (+11 midyear) Khabarovskiy, Primorskiy, Yevreyskaya;
- World Time +11 (+12 midyear) Magadanskaya, Sakhalinskaya;
- World Time +12 (+13 midyear) Chukotskiy, Kamchatskaya, Koryakskiy.

C.I.S. FREQUENCY MANAGEMENT ENGINEERING OFFICE: General Radio Frequency Center, 25 Pyatnitskaya Str., 113326 Moscow, Russia. Phone: +7 (095) 950-6022; Phone/Fax: +7 (095) 789-3587. Email: (Titov) a_titov@vor.ru. Web: (General Radio Frequency Center parent organization) www.grfc.ru. Contact: (general) Mrs. Nina Bykova, Monitoring Coordinator; (administration) Anatoliy T. Titov, Chief of Division for SW and MW Frequency Broadcasting Schedules. This office is responsible for the operation of radio broadcasting in the Russian Federation, as well as for frequency usage of transmitters throughout much of the C.I.S. Correspondence should be concerned only with significant technical observations or engineering suggestions concerning frequency management improvement—not regular requests for verifications. Correspondence in Russian preferred, but English accepted.

Adygey Radio—*see* Maykop Radio.

Amur Radio—*see* Blagoveschensk Radio.

Arkhangel'sk Radio, GTRK "Pomorye," ul. Popova 2, 163061 Arkhangel'sk, Arkhangel'skaya Oblast, Russia; or U1PR, Valentin G. Kalasnikov, ul. Suvorov 2, kv. 16, Arkhangel'sk, Arkhangel'skaya Oblast, Russia. Replies irregularly to correspondence in Russian.

Blagoveschensk Radio, GTRK "Amur," per Svyatitelya Innokentiya 15, 675000 Blagoveschensk, Russia. Contact: V.I. Kal'chenko, Chief Engineer.

Buryat Radio—*see* Ulan-Ude Radio.

Kabardino-Balkar Radio—*see* Nalchik Radio.

Kamchatka Rybatskaya—a special service for fishermen off the coasts of China, Japan and western North America; *see* Petropavlovsk-Kamchatskiy Radio for contact details.

Khanty-Mansiysk Radio, GTRK "Yugoriya," ul. Mira 7, 626200 Khanty-Mansiysk, Russia. Contact: (technical) Vladimir Sokolov, Engineer.

Krasnoyarsk Radio, Krasnoyarskaya GTRK, "Tsentr Rossii," ul. Mechnikova 44A, 660028 Krasnoyarsk, Krasnoyarsky Kray, Russia. Email: postmaster@telegid.krasnoyarsk.su. Contact: Valeriy Korotchenko; or Anatoliy A. Potehin, RAØAKE. Free local information booklets in English/Russian. Replies in Russian to correspondence in Russian or English. Return postage helpful.

Kyzyl Radio, GTRK "Tyva," ul. Gornaya 31, 667003 Kyzyl, Respublika Tyva, Russia. Email: tv@tuva.ru. Replies to correspondence in Russian.

Magadan Radio, GTRK "Magadan," ul. Kommuny 8/12, 685024 Magadan, Magadanskaya Oblast, Russia. Contact: Viktor Loktionov or V.G. Kuznetsov. Return postage helpful. Occasionally replies to correspondence in Russian.

Mariy Radio—*see* Yoshkar-Ola Radio.

Mayak—*see* Radiostantsiya Mayak.

Maykop Radio, GTRK "Adygeya," ul. Zhukovskogo 24, 385000 Maykop, Republic of Adygeya, Russia. Contact: A.T. Kerashev,

Chairman. English accepted but Russian preferred. Return postage helpful.

Murmansk Radio, GTRK "Murman," per. Rusanova 7, 183032 Murmansk, Murmanskaya Oblast, Russia. Phone: +7 (8152) 472-327. Email: radio@tvmurman.com. Web: http://sampo.ru/~tvmurman/index_ie.html. Contact: D. Perederi (chairman).

Nalchik Radio, GTRK "Kabbalk Teleradio," pr. Lenina 3, 360000 Nalchik, Republic of Kabardino-Balkariya, Russia. Contact: Kamal Makitov, Vice-Chairman. Replies to correspondence in Russian.

Palana Radio (if reactivated), Koryakskaya GTRK "Palana," ul. Obukhova 4, 684620 Palana, Koryakskiy avt. Okrug, Russia.

Perm Radio, Permskaya GTRK "T-7," ul. Tekhnicheskaya 7, 614070 Perm, Permskaya Oblast, Russia. Contact: M. Levin, Senior Editor; or A. Losev, Acting Chief Editor.

Petropavlovsk-Kamchatskiy Radio, GTRK "Kamchatka," ul. Sovetskaya 62, 683000 Petropavlovsk-Kamchatskiy, Kamchatskaya Oblast, Russia. Contact: A.F. Borodin, Head of GTRK "Kamchatka." Email: gtrkbuh@mail.iks.ru. $1 required for postal reply. Replies in Russian to correspondence in Russian or English. Currently inactive on shortwave, apart from a special program for fishermen—*see* Kamchatka Rybatskaya.

Radio Gardarika (when operating), Radio Studio Dom Radio, Ligovsky Prospekt 174, 197002 St. Petersburg, Russia. Email: studiosw@metroclub.ru. Contact: Suvorov Alexey, Shortwave Project Manager. Replies to correspondence in Russian or English. Return postage helpful.

Radio Nalchik—*see* Nalchik Radio, above.

Radio Radonezh—*see* Radiostantsiya Radonezh

⏂**Radio Rossii** (Russia's Radio), GRK "Radio Rossii," Yamskogo Polya 5-YA ul. 19/21, 125040 Moscow, Russia. Phone: +7 (095) 213-1054, +7 (095) 250-0511 or +7 (095) 251-4050. Fax: +7 (095) 250 0105, +7 (095) 233 6449 or +7 (095) 214 4767. Email: mail@radiorus.ru; direction@radiorus.ru Web: (includes on-demand and streaming audio) www.radiorus.ru. Contact: Sergei Yerofeyev, Director of International Operations [sic]; or Sergei Davidov, Director. Free English-language information sheet.

Radio Studio—*see* Radio Gardarika.

⏂**Radiostantsiya Radonezh**, ul. Pyatnitskaya 25, Moscow 115326, Russia. Phone: +7 (095) 959-5939. Phone/Fax: +7 (095) 950-6356. Email: radonezh@radonezh.ru. Web: (includes on-demand and streaming audio) www.radonezh.ru/radio. Replies to correspondence in Russian or English.

⏂**Radiostantsiya Tikhiy Okean** ("Radio Station Pacific Ocean"), GTRK "Vladivostok," ul. Uborevicha 20-A, 690950 Vladivostok, Primorskiy Kray, Russia. Email: ptr@ptr-vlad.ru. Web: (includes streaming audio) www.ptr-vlad.ru/tv&radio. Contact: (technical) Alexey Giryuk, Engineer, Technical Department. $2 return postage helpful. Replies to correspondence in Russian or English. A program for mariners produced by Primorye Radio and aired on 810 kHz mediumwave AM and shortwave.

Russian International Radio (Russkoye Mezhdunarodnoye Radio)—a service of the Voice of Russia (*see*) in cooperation with the domestic Russkoye Radio.

Sakhalin Radio, GTRK "Sakhalin," ul. Komsomolskaya 209, 693000 Yuzhno-Sakhalinsk, Sakhalinskaya Oblast, Russia. Phone: (Director of Radio) +7 (42422) 729-349. Phone/Fax: (GTRK parent company) +7 (42422) 35286. Email: gtrk@sakhalin.ru; (Romanov) romanov@gtrk.sakhalin.su. Web: www.gtrk.ru/Company/o_radio.html. Contact: S. Romanov, Director of Radio.

⏂**Special Radio** (Spezialnoye Radio), Office 417, Efremova st. 10, 113092 Moscow, Russia. Email: admin@specialradio.ru; (Anikeeva) anikmay@specialradio.ru. Web: (includes streaming audio) www.specialradio.ru Contact: Maria Anikeeva, Press Secretary/PR Manager. An Internet broadcaster which describes itself as "an international corporate Internet project of musicians and contemporary art activists." The shortwave broadcast, "Actual music from Russia," is via a hired Russian transmitter.

Tatarstan Wave ("Tatarstan Dulkynda"), GTRK "Tatarstan," ul. Gor'kogo 15, 420015 Kazan, Tatarstan, Russia. Phone: (general) +7 (8432) 384-846; (editorial) +7 (8432) 367-493. Fax: +7 (8432) 361 283. Email: root@gtrkrt.kazan.su; postmaster@stvcrt.kazan.su. Contact: Hania Hazipovna Galinova. Formerly known as Voice of Tatarstan.
ADDRESS FOR RECEPTION REPORTS: QSL Manager, P.O. Box 134, 420136 Kazan, Tatarstan, Russia. Contact: Ildus Ibatullin, QSL Manager. Offers an honorary diploma in return for 12 correct reports in a given year. The diploma costs 2 IRCs for Russia and 4 IRCs elsewhere. Accepts reports in Russian or English. Return postage helpful.

Tura Radio (if reactivated), Evenkiyskaya GTRK "Kheglen," ul. 50 Let Oktyabrya 28, 663370 Tura, Russia.

Ufa Radio (if reactivated), GTRK "Bashkortostan," ul. Gafuri 9/1, 450076 Ufa, Respublika Bashkortostan, Russia. Email: gtrk@bashinform.ru. Replies to correspondence in Russian.

Ulan-Ude Radio, Buryatskaya GTRK, ul. Erbanova 7, 670000 Ulan-Ude, Republic of Buryatia, Russia. Contact: Z.A. Telin; Mrs. M.V. Urbaeva, 1st Vice-Chairman; or L.S. Shikhanova.

Voice of Russia, GRK "Golos Rossii," ul. Pyatnitskaya 25, 115326 Moscow, Russia. Phone: (Chairman) +7 (095) 950-6331; (International Relations Department) +7 (095) 950-6440; (Technical Department) +7 (095) 950-6115. Fax: (Chairman & World Service in English) +7 (095) 230 2828; Email: letters@vor.ru; (Spanish) cartas@vor.ru. Web: (includes on-demand and streaming audio) www.vor.ru. Contact: (Letters Department, World Service in English) Elena Osipova or Elena Frolovskaya; (Chairman) Armen Oganesyan; (International Relations Department) Victor Kopytin, Director; (Technical Department) Ms. Rachel Staviskaya, Director; (World Service in English) Vladimir Zhamkin, Director. For language services other than English contact the International Relations Department.
SAN FRANCISCO OFFICE, SCHEDULES: 2654 17th Avenue, San Francisco CA 94116 USA. Phone: +1 (415) 564-9968. Email: GPoppin@aol.com. Contact: George Poppin. This address, a volunteer office, only provides Voice of Russia schedules to listeners. All other correspondence should be sent directly to the Voice of Russia in Moscow.

Yakutsk Radio, NVK "Sakha," ul. Ordzhonikidze 48, 677007 Yakutsk, Respublika Sakha, Russia. Contact: (general) Alexandra Borisova; Lia Sharoborina, Advertising Editor; or Albina Danilova, Producer, "Your Letters"; (technical) Sergei Bobnev, Technical Director. Russian books $15; audio cassettes $10. Free station stickers and original Yakutian souvenirs. Replies to correspondence in English.

RWANDA   World Time +2

Deutsche Welle—Relay Station Kigali—Correspondence should be directed to the main offices in Bonn, Germany *(see)*.
Radio Rwanda, B.P. 83, Kigali, Rwanda. Phone: +250 76180. Fax: +250 76185. Contact: Marcel Singirankabo. $1 required. Occasionally replies, with correspondence in French preferred.

SAO TOME E PRINCIPE   World Time exactly

Voice of America/IBB—São Tomé Relay Station, P.O. Box 522, São Tomé, São Tomé e Príncipe. Contact: Charles L. Lewis,

Transmitting Station Manager. This address for specialized technical correspondence only. All other correspondence, including reception reports, should be sent to the usual VOA or IBB addresses in Washington (*see* USA).

SAUDI ARABIA   World Time +3

Broadcasting Service of the Kingdom of Saudi Arabia, P.O. Box 61718, Riyadh-11575, Saudi Arabia. Phone: (general) +966 (1) 404-2795; (administration) +966 (1) 442-5493; (engineering) +966 (1) 442-5170; (frequency management) +966 (1) 442-5127. Fax: (general) +966 (1) 402 8177; (engineering and frequency management) +966 (1) 404 1692. Email: (frequency management) freq.mgt@saudinform.org; (Al-Samnan) alsamnan@yahoo.com. Web: (streaming audio) www.saudiradio.net. Contact: (general) Mutlaq A. Albegami; (technical) Suleiman Al-Samnan, Director of Engineering; Youssef Dhim, Frequency Management. Free travel information and book on Saudi history.

SENEGAL   World Time exactly

West Africa Democracy Radio (WADR), P.O. Box 16650, Dakar-Fann, Senegal. Phone: +221 869-1569. Fax: +221 864 7090. Email: wadr@wadr.org. Web: (includes on demand audio) www.wadr.org. Broadcasts via leased facilities in the United Kingdom.

SERBIA AND MONTENEGRO   World Time +1 (+2 midyear)

International Radio of Serbia and Montenegro—*see* Radio Srbija i Crna Gora.
Radio Beograd—a service of Radio-Televizija Srbije (*see*).
Radio Srbija i Crna Gora, Hilendarska 2, P.O. Box 200, 11000 Beograd, Serbia and Montenegro. Phone: +381 (11) 324-4455. Fax: +381 (11) 323 2014. Email: radioyu@bltsyu.net. Web: (includes on-demand audio) www.radioyu.org. Contact: (general) Milena Jokich, Director & Editor-in-Chief; Aleksandar Georgiev; Aleksandar Popovic, Head of Public Relations; Pance Zafirovski, Head of Programs; or Slobodan Topovi_, Producer, "Post Office Box 200/Radio Hams' Corner"; (technical) B. Miletic, Operations Manager of HF Broadcasting; Technical Department; or Rodoljub Medan, Chief Engineer. Free pennants, stickers, pins and tourist information. $1 helpful. Formerly known as Radio Yugoslavia.
Radio-Televizija Srbije, Takovska 10, 11000 Beograd, Serbia and Montenegro. Phone: +381 (11) 321-2000. Email: rtstv@rts.co.yu. Web: (includes streaming audio) www.rts.co.yu.

SEYCHELLES   World Time +4

BBC World Service—Indian Ocean Relay Station, P.O. Box 448, Victoria, Mahé, Seychelles. Phone: +248 78-496. Fax: +248 78 500. Contact: (technical) Albert Quatre, Senior Engineer. Nontechnical correspondence should be sent to the BBC World Service in London (*see*).

SIERRA LEONE   World Time exactly

Radio UNAMSIL (when operating), Mammy Yoko Hotel, P.O. Box 5, Freetown, Sierra Leone. Email: info@unamsil.org; or patrickcoker@unamsil.org. Web: (UNAMSIL parent organization) www.unamsil.org. Contact: Patrick Coker or Sheila Dallas, Station Manager & Executive Producer. Station of the United Nations Mission in Sierra Leone.

Sierra Leone Broadcasting Service (if reactivated), New England, Freetown, Sierra Leone. Phone: +232 (22) 240-123; +232 (22) 240-173; +232 (22) 240-497 or 232 (22) 241-919. Fax: +232 (22) 240 922. Contact: Cyril Juxon-Smith, Officer in Charge; or Henry Goodaig Hjax, Assistant Engineer.

SINGAPORE   World Time +8

BBC World Service—Far Eastern Relay Station, VT Merlin Communications, 51 Turut Track, Singapore 718930, Singapore. Phone: + 65 6793-7511/3. Fax: +65 6793 7834. Email: (Wui Pin Yong) wuipin@singnet.com.sg. Contact: (technical) Mr. Wui Pin Yong, Operations Manager; or Far East Resident Engineer. Nontechnical correspondence should be sent to the BBC World Service in London (see).

MediaCorp Radio, Farrer Road, P.O. Box 968, Singapore 912899, Singapore; (street address) Caldecott Broadcast Centre, Caldecott Hill, Andrew Road, Singapore 299939, Singapore. Phone: (general) +65 6333-3888; (transmitting station) +65 6793-7651. Fax: +65 6251 5628. Web: (includes streaming audio) www.mediacorpradio.com.sg. Free regular and Post-It stickers, pens, umbrellas, mugs, towels, wallets and lapel pins. Do not include currency in envelope. Successor to the former Radio Corporation of Singapore.

Radio Singapore International, Farrer Road, P.O. Box 5300, Singapore 912899, Singapore; (street address) Caldecott Broadcast Centre, Annex Building Level 1, Andrew Road, Singapore 299939, Singapore. Phone: (general) + 65 6359-7663; (English Service) + 65 6359-7671. Fax: (general) +65 6259 1357. Email: info@rsi.sg; (English Service) english@rsi.sg (if these don't work, try the online email form). Web: (includes on-demand audio) www.rsi.sg. Contact: (general) Sakuntala Gupta, Programme Director, English Service; Augustine Anthuvan, Assistant Programme Director, English Service; (technical) Lim Wing Kee, RSI Engineering. Free souvenir T-shirts and key chains to selected listeners. Do not include currency in envelope.

SLOVAKIA   World Time +1 (+2 midyear)

Radio Slovakia International, M_tna 1, P.O. Box 55, 817 55 Bratislava 15, Slovakia. Phone: (Editor-in-Chief) +421 (2) 5727-3730; (English Service) +421 (2) 5727-3736 or +421 (2) 5727-2737; (technical) +421 (2) 5727-3251. Fax: +421 (2) 5249 6282 or +421 (2) 5249 8247; (technical) +421 (2) 5249 7659. Email: (English Section) englishsection @slovakradio.sk; for other language sections, the format is rsi_language@slovakradio.sk, where the language is written in English (e.g. rsi_spanish@slovakradio.sk); (Frequency Manager) chocholata@slovakradio.sk. Web: (includes on-demand audio and online reception report form) www.rsi.sk. Contact: Martina Grenova, Director of English Broadcasting; (administration) PhDr. Karol Palkovič, Head of External Broadcasting; or Dr. Slavomira Kubickova, Head of International Relations; (technical) Ms. Edita Chocholatá, Frequency Manager.

SOLOMON ISLANDS   World Time +11

Solomon Islands Broadcasting Corporation (Radio Happy Isles), P.O. Box 654, Honiara, Solomon Islands. Phone: +677 20051. Fax: +677 23159 or +677 25652. Email: sibcnews@solomon.com.sb. Web: www.sibconline.com.sb.

Contact: (general) David Palapu, Manager Broadcast Operations; Julian Maka'a, Producer, "Listeners From Far Away"; Walter Nalangu, News & Current Affairs; Rachel Rahi'i, Commercial/Advertising; or Bart Basi, Programmes; (administration) Grace Ngatulu; Johnson Honimae, General Manager; (technical) Cornelius Rathamana, Technical Division. IRC or $1 helpful. Problems with the domestic mail system may cause delays. Plans to reactivate shortwave frequency 9545 kHz.

SOMALIA   World Time +3

Radio Banaadir—see Radio Banadir, below.
Radio Banadir (when operating), Tahlil Warsame Building, KM 4, Maka Al Mukarama Rd., Mogadishu, Somalia. Phone: +252 (5) 944-176 or +252 (5) 960-368. Email: radiobanadir@ somalinternet.com. Web: (includes on-demand audio) www. radiobanadir.com.

Radio Galkayo (when operating), 2 Griffith Avenue, Roseville NSW 2069, Australia. Phone/Fax: +61 (2) 9417-1066. Email: svoron@hotmail.com. Contact: Sam Voron, VK2BVS, 6O0A, Australian Director. Replies to email correspondence at no charge, but $5, AUS$5 or 5 IRCs required for postal replies. A community radio station in the Mudug region, Puntland State, northern Somalia and supported by local and overseas volunteers. Seeks volunteers, donations of radio equipment and airline tickets, and is setting up a Radio Galkayo Amateur Radio Club station.

Radio Hargeysa—see SOMALILAND.
Radio Shabelle, Global Building, 3rd Floor, Mogadishu, Somalia. Phone: +252 (1) 659-699, +252 (1) 227-733 or +252 (5) 933-111. Fax: +252 (1) 659 699. Email: radio@shabelle.net; info@shabelle.net; (Malik) maalik@shabelle.net. Web: (includes on-demand audio) www.shabelle.net. Contact:Abdi Malik Yusuf Mahmuud, Chairman.

SOMALILAND   World Time +3

NOTE: "Somaliland," claimed as an independent nation, is diplomatically recognized only as part of Somalia.
Radio Hargeysa, P.O. Box 14, Hargeysa, Somaliland, Somalia. Email: radiohargeysa@yahoo.com. Web: (on-demand audio) www.radiosomaliland.com/radiohargeisa.html. Contact: Muhammad Said Muhummad, Manager.

SOUTH AFRICA   World Time +2

BBC World Service via South Africa—For verification direct from the South African transmitters, contact Sentech (see below). Nontechnical correspondence should be sent to the BBC World Service in London (see).
Channel Africa, P.O. Box 91313, Auckland Park 2006, South Africa. Phone: (executive editor) +27 (11) 714-2255; (technical) +27 (11) 714-2537. Fax: (technical) +27 (11) 714 2072. Email: (general) africancan@channelafrica.org; (M. Mate, technical) matemm@channelafrica.org. Web: (includes on-demand and streaming audio) www.channelafrica.org. Contact: (general) Thami Ntenteni, Executive Editor; (technical) Maurice M. Mate, Web & Technical Senior Manager. Reception reports are best directed to Sentech (see), which operates the transmission facilities.
Radio Veritas (when operating), P.O. Box 53687, Troyeville 2139, South Africa; or (street address) 36 Beelaerts Street, Troyeville 2094, South Africa. Phone: +27 (11) 624-2516; (studio) +27 (11) 614-6225. Fax: +27 (11) 614 7711. Email:

info@radioveritas.co.za; (Fr. Blaser) eblaser@iafrica.com. Web: www.radioveritas.co.za. Contact: Fr. Emil Blaser OP, Director. Return postage helpful. Reception reports can also be directed to Sentech (*see*), which operates the transmission facilities.

Radiosondergrense (Radio Without Boundaries), Posbus 91312, Auckland Park 2006, South Africa. Phone: +27 (11) 714-2702. Fax: +27 (11) 714 3472. Email: info@rsg.co.za. Web: (includes streaming audio) www.rsg.co.za. Reception reports are best directed to Sentech (*see*, below), which operates the shortwave transmission facilities. A domestic service of the South African Broadcasting Corporation, and formerly known as Afrikaans Stereo. The shortwave operation is scheduled to be eventually replaced by a satellite and FM network.

Sentech Ltd., Transmission Planning, Private Bag X06, Honeydew 2040, South Africa. Phone: (general) +27 (11) 471-4400 or +27 (11) 691-7000; (shortwave) +27 (11) 471-4658. Fax: (shortwave) +27 (11) 471 4754. Email: (Kathy Otto) ottok@sentech.co.za. Web: (schedules & frequencies) www.sentech.co.za. Contact: Kathy Otto, HF Coverage Planner. Sentech verifies reception reports on transmissions from the Meyerton shortwave facilities.

South African Radio League—Amateur Radio Mirror International, P.O. Box 90438, Garsfontein 0042, South Africa. Email: armi@sarl.org.za. Web: www.sarl.org.za/public/ARMI/ARMI.asp; (on-demand audio) www.amsatsa.org.za. Accepts email reception reports. Amateur Radio Mirror International is a weekly broadcast aired via Sentech's Meyerton facilities.

Trans World Radio Africa
NONTECHNICAL CORRESPONDENCE: Trans World Radio Africa, P.O. Box 4232, Kempton Park 1620, South Africa. Phone: +27 (11) 974-2885. Fax: +27 (11) 974 9960. Email: online form. Web: www.twrafrica.org.
TECHNICAL CORRESPONDENCE: Reception reports and other technical correspondence are best directed to Sentech (*see*, above) or to TWR's Swaziland office (*see*). Also, *see* USA.

SPAIN   World Time +1 (+2 midyear)

Radio Exterior de España (Spanish National Radio, World Service)
MAIN OFFICE: Apartado de Correos 156.202, E-28080 Madrid, Spain. Phone: (general) +34 (91) 346-1081/1083; (Audience Relations) +34 (91) 346-1149. Fax: +34 (91) 346 1815. Email: (Director) dir_ree.rne@rtve.es; (Spanish programming, listener feedback) audiencia_ree.rne@rtve.es, or radioexterior.espana@rtve.es. Web: (includes on-demand and streaming audio) www.ree.rne.es. Contact: (Audience Relations) Pilar Salvador M.; (Assistant Director) Pedro Fernández Céspedes; (Director) Francisco Fernández Oria. Free stickers and tourist information. Verification of reception reports is temporarily suspended due to "staffing and budget constraints." Listeners are requested not to send cash or IRCs, since the limited services which still exist are free. An alternative, for those who understand Spanish, is to send a reception report on the program "Españoles en la Mar" which is produced in the Canary Islands by Mary Cortés. Times and frequencies can be found at the REE Website. Reports should be sent to: Programa "Españoles en la Mar," Apartado Postal 1233, Santa Cruz de Tenerife, Islas Canarias, Spain. Magazines and small souvenirs are sometimes included with verifications from this address. Correspondence in Spanish preferred, but English also accepted.
TRANSCRIPTION SERVICE: Radio Nacional de España, Servicio de Transcripciones, Apartado 156.200, Casa de la Radio (Prado del Rey), E-28223 Madrid, Spain.

HF FREQUENCY PLANNING OFFICE: Prado del Rey. Pozuelo de Alarcom, E-28223 Madrid, Spain. Phone: (Huerta) +34 (91) 346-1276; (Arlanzón) +34 (91) 346-1639; or (Almarza) +34 (91) 346-1978. Fax: (Huerta & Almarza) +34 (91) 346 1402 or (Alanzón) +34 (91) 346 1275. Email: (Almarza) planif_red2.rne@rtve.es; or (Huerta & Arlanzón) plan_red.rne@rtve.es. Contact: Fernando Almarza, Frequency Planning; Salvador Arlanzón, HF Frequency Manager; or José Maria Huerta, Technical Director.
NOBLEJAS TRANSMITTER SITE: Centro Emisor de RNE en Onda Corta, Ctra. Dos Barrios s/n, E-45350 Noblejas-Toledo, Spain.
COSTA RICA RELAY FACILITY—see Costa Rica.

SRI LANKA   World Time +6:00

Deutsche Welle—Relay Station Sri Lanka, 92/1 D.S. Senanayake Mawatha, Colombo 08, Sri Lanka. Phone: +94 (11) 2464-483. Fax: +94 (11) 2699 450. Contact: R. Groschkus, Resident Engineer. This address for specialized technical correspondence only. All other correspondence should be sent to Deutsche Welle in Germany (*see*).
Radio Japan/NHK—All correspondence should be sent to the Radio Japan address in Tokyo (*see* Japan).
Sri Lanka Broadcasting Corporation (also announces as "Radio Sri Lanka" in the external service), P.O. Box 574, Independence Square, Colombo 7, Sri Lanka. Phone: +94 (11) 2697-491. Fax: (general) +94 (11) 2691 568; (Director General) +94 (11) 2695 488. Email: slbc@sri.lanka.net. Web: (includes streaming audio) www.slbc.lk.
Voice of America/IBB—Iranawila Relay Station.
ADDRESS: Station Manager, IBB Sri Lanka Transmitting Station, c/o U.S. Embassy, 210 Galle Road, Colombo 3, Sri Lanka. Contact: Walter Patterson, Station Manager. This address for specialized technical correspondence only, although some reception reports may be verified, depending on who is at the site. All other correspondence should be directed to the regular VOA or IBB addresses (*see* USA).

SUDAN   World Time +3

Radio Peace
ADDRESS FOR RECEPTION REPORTS: pete@edmedia.org. Contact: Peter Stover, who requests that audio attachments not be sent with reception reports.
Sudan National Radio Corporation, P.O. Box 1111 (P.O. Box 572 may also work), Omdurman, Sudan. Phone/Fax: +249 (187) 999-999. Email: (general) snrc@sudanmail.net; has2000@hotmail.com; (technical) salihb@maktoob.com. Web: www.srtc.info. Contact: (general) Mohammed Elfatih El Sumoal; (technical) Abbas Sidig, Director General, Engineering and Technical Affairs; Mohammed Elmahdi Khalil, Administrator, Engineering and Technical Affairs; Saleh Al-Hay; Bachir Saleh, Deputy Director of Engineering; or Adil Didahammed, Engineering Department. Replies irregularly. Return postage necessary.

SURINAME   World Time –3

Radio Apintie, Postbus 595, Paramaribo, Suriname; (street address) verl. Gemenelandsweg 37, Paramaribo, Suriname. Phone: (studio) +597 400-500, (office) +597 400-450. Fax: +597 400 684. Email: apintie@sr.net. Web: (includes streaming audio) www.apintie.sr. Contact: Charles E. Vervuurt, Director. Free pennant. Return postage or $1 required. Email reception reports preferred, since local mail service is unreliable.

SWAZILAND   World Time +2

Trans World Radio, P.O. Box 64, Manzini, Swaziland. Phone: +268 505-2781/2/3. Fax: +268 505 5333. Email: (Chief Engineer) sstavrop@twr.org; (Mrs. Stavropoulos) lstavrop@twr.org; (Greg Shaw) gshaw@twr.org. Web: (transmission schedule) www.twrafrica.org/programmes/index.asp. Contact: (general) Greg Shaw, Follow-up Department; G.J. Alary, Station Director; or Joseph Ndzinisa, Program Manager; (technical) Mrs. L. Stavropoulos, DX Secretary. Free stickers, postcards and calendars. A free Bible Study course is available. May swap canceled stamps. $1, return postage or 3 IRCs required. Also, *see* USA.

SWEDEN   World Time +1 (+2 midyear)

IBRA Radio, SE-141 99 Stockholm, Sweden. Phone: +46 (8) 608-9680. Fax: +46 (8) 608 9650. Email: ibra@ibra.se. Web: (Swedish) www.ibra.se; (English) www.ibra.org. Contact: Mikael Stjernberg, Public Relations Manager; or Helene Hasslof. Free pennants and stickers. IBRA Radio's programs are aired over various world band stations, including Trans World Radio and FEBA Radio; and also broadcast independently via transmitters in Germany and Russia. Accepts email reception reports.
Radio Sweden, SE-105 10 Stockholm, Sweden. Phone: (general) +46 (8) 784-7207/8; (listener voice mail) +46 (8) 784-7238; (technical department) +46 (8) 784-7282/6. Fax: (general) +46 (8) 667 6283; (listener service) +46 8 660 2990. Email: (general) radiosweden@sr.se; (English Service) mark.cummins@sr.se; or george.wood@sr.se; (PR & Information) victoria.padin@sr.se or frida.sjolander@sr.se; (technical) anders.backlin@sr.se. Web: (includes on-demand and streaming audio) www.sr.se/rs or (shortcut to the English web page) www.radiosweden.org. Contact: (administration) Anne Sseruwagi, Director General, SR International; or Gundula Adolfsson, Head of Radio Sweden; (English Service) Mark Cummins, Head of English Service; Gabby Katz, Producer; Bill Schiller, Producer; George Wood, Webmaster; (public relations and information) Victoria Padin; or Frida Sjolander; (technical department) Anders Backlin.
TRANSMISSION AUTHORITY: TERACOM, Svensk Rundradio AB, P.O. Box 17666, SE-118 92 Stockholm, Sweden. Phone: (general) +46 (8) 555-420-00; (Wiberg) +46 (8) 555-420-66. Fax: (general) +46 (8) 555 420 01; (Wiberg) +46 (8) 555 20 60. Email: (general) info@teracom.se; (Wiberg) magnus.wiberg@teracom.se. Web: www.teracom.se. Contact: (Frequency Planning Dept.—Head Office): Magnus Wiberg; (Engineering) Hakan Widenstedt, Chief Engineer. Free stickers; sometimes free T-shirts to those monitoring during special test transmissions. Seeks monitoring feedback for new frequency usages.

SWITZERLAND   World Time +1 (+2 midyear)

European Broadcasting Union, 17A Ancienne Route, CH-1218 Grand-Saconnex, Geneva, Switzerland; or Case Postal 67, CH-1218 Grand-Saconnex, Geneva, Switzerland. Phone: +41 (22) 717-2111. Fax: +41 (22) 747 2010. Email: ebu@ebu.ch. Web: www.ebu.ch. Contact: Mr. Jean Réveillon, Secretary-General. Umbrella organization for broadcasters in 49 European and Mediterranean countries.
International Telecommunication Union, Place des Nations, CH-1211 Geneva 20, Switzerland. Phone: (switchboard) +41 (22) 730-5111; (Broadcasting Services Division) +41 (22) 730-5933 or +41 (22) 730-6136; (Terrestrial Services Department)

+41 (22) 730-5514. Fax: (general) +41 (22) 733 7256; (Broadcasting Services Division) +41 (22) 730 5785. Email: (general) itumail@itu.int; (schedules and reference tables) brmail@itu.int. The ITU is the world's official regulatory body for all telecommunication activities, including world band radio. Offers a wide range of official multilingual telecommunication publications in print and/or digital formats.
Radio Réveil, Paroles, Les Chapons 4, CH-2022 Bevaix, Switzerland. Phone: +41 (32) 846-1655. Fax: +41 (32) 846 2547. Email: contact@paroles.ch. Web (includes on-demand audio): www.paroles.ch. An evangelical radio ministry, part of the larger Radio Réveil Paroles de Vie organization, which apart from broadcasting to much of Europe on longwave, mediumwave AM and FM, also targets an African audience via the shortwave facilities of Germany's T-Systems International (*see*). Replies to correspondence in French or English, and verifies reception reports.
Stimme des Trostes, Missionswerk Arche, CH-9642 Ebnat-Kappel, Switzerland. Replies to correspondence in German or English, and verifies reception reports.Via Germany's T-Systems International (*see*).

SYRIA   World Time +2 (+3 midyear)

Radio Damascus, Syrian Radio and Television, P.O. Box 4702, Damascus, Syria. Phone: +963 (11) 221-7653. Fax: +963 (11) 222 2692. Email: tv-radio@net.sy; mostafab@scs-net.org; (Riad Sharaf Al-Din) riadsharafaldin@yahoo.com; (Marian Galindo, comments and reception reports in Spanish) mmhrez@shuf.com. Web: (includes on-demand audio) www.rtv.gov.sy. Contact: Adnan Salhab; Farid Shalash; Mohamed Hamida; (Spanish Section) Riad Sharaf Al-Din, Supervisor de Programas; Marian Galindo, Locutora; (technical) Mazen Al-Achhab, Head of Frequency Department. Free stickers, pennants and occasionally books and newspapers. Replies can be highly erratic, and sometimes slow. Members of the Spanish Section have suggested listeners use email, because of letters going astray.

TAIWAN—*see* CHINA (TAIWAN)

TAJIKISTAN   World Time +5

Radio Tajikistan, Chapaev Street 31, 734025 Dushanbe, Tajikistan; or English Service, International Service, Radio Tajikistan, P.O. Box 108, 734025 Dushanbe, Tajikistan. Phone: (Director) +992 (372) 210-877 or +992 (372) 277-417; (English Department) +992 (372) 277-417; (Ramazonov) +992 (372) 277-667 or +992 (372) 277-347. Fax: +992 (372) 211 198. Email: treng@td.silk.org. Web: http://radio.tojikiston.com. Contact: (administration) Mansur Sultanov, Director - Tajik Radio; Nasrullo Ramazonov, Foreign Relations Department. Correspondence in Russian or Tajik preferred. There is no official policy for verification of listeners' reports, so try sending reception reports and correspondence in English to the attention of Mr. Ramazonov, who is currently the sole English speaker at the station. Caution should be exercised when contacting him via email, as it is his personal account and he is charged for both incoming and outgoing mail. In addition, all email is routinely monitored and censored. Return postage (IRCs) helpful.
Tajik Radio, ul. Chapaeva 31, 734025 Dushanbe, Tajikistan. Contact information as for Radio Tajikistan, above.

TANZANIA World Time +3

Radio Tanzania, Nyerere Road, P.O. Box 9191, Dar es Salaam, Tanzania. Phone: +255 (51) 860-760. Fax: +255 (51) 865 577. Email: radiotanzania@raha.com. Contact: (general) Abdul Ngarawa, Director of Broadcasting; Mrs. Edda Sanga, Controller of Programs; N. Nyamwocha; Ms. Penzi Nyamungumi, Head of English Service and International Relations Unit; or Ahmed Jongo, Producer, "Your Answer"; (technical) Taha Usi, Chief Engineer; or Emmanuel Mangula, Deputy Chief Engineer. Replies to correspondence in English.

Voice of Tanzania—Zanzibar, Department of Broadcasting, Radio Tanzania Zanzibar, P.O. Box 1178, Zanzibar, Tanzania—if this address brings no reply, try P.O. Box 2503. Phone: +255 (54) 231-088. Fax: + 255 (54) 257 207. $1 return postage helpful.

THAILAND World Time +7

BBC World Service—Asia Relay Station, P.O. Box 20, Muang, Nakhon Sawan 60000, Thailand; (physical address) Mu 1, Tambon Ban Kaeng, Muang District, Nakhon Sawan 6000, Thailand. Phone: +66 5622-7275/6. Fax: +66 (56) 227 277. Contact: Ms. Jaruwan Meesaurtong, Executive Secretary; or Ms. Sukontha Saisaengthong, Senior Engineer. Nontechnical correspondence should be sent to the BBC World Service in London (see UK).

IBB Thailand Transmitting Station, P.O. Box 99, Ampur Muang, Udon Thani 41000, Thailand. Email: thai@voa.gov. This address for specialized technical correspondence only, although some reception reports may be verified. All other correspondence should be directed to the regular VOA or IBB addresses (see USA).

Radio Thailand World Service, 236 Vibhavadi Rangsit Road, Huai Khwang, Bangkok 10320, Thailand. Phone: + 66 (2) 277-4022. Fax: +66 (2) 274 9298/9 or +66 (2) 277 1840. Email: (general) radiothailandbkk@yahoo.com. Web: www.hsk9.com. Contact: Mrs. Chantima Choeysanguan, Executive Director; Ms. Porntip Utogapach, Director; Ms. Suweraya Lohavicharn, Producer; (technical) Mr. Boontharm Ratanasang, Director; or Mr. Weerasac Cherngchow, Assistant Director. Free pennants. Replies irregularly, especially to those who persist.

TRANSMITTER SITE: Rang-sit, Tumbol Klong haa, Amphur Klong laung, Pathumthani Province 12120, Thailand. Phone: +62 (30) 27-523. Contact: Mano Tamkal, Technician.

TOGO World Time exactly

▣Radio Lomé (when operating), B.P. 434, Lomé, Togo. Phone: +228 221-2492/3. Fax: +228 221 3673. E-mail: radiolome@radiolome.tg. Web: (includes streaming audio) www.radiolome.tg. Return postage, $1 or 2 IRCs helpful. French preferred, but English accepted.

TUNISIA World Time +1 (+2 midyear)

NOTE: Tunisia introduced Daylight Saving Time for summer 2005 as an energy conservation measure. It is not known if the same will occur in 2006 and beyond.

Arab States Broadcasting Union, 6, rue des Enterpreneurs, Z.I. Ariana Cedex, TN-1080 Tunis, Tunisia. Phone: +216 (71) 703-855. Fax: +216 (71) 704 203. Email: a.suleiman@asbu. intl.tn. Contact: Abdelrahim Suleiman, Director, Technical Department; or Bassil Ahmad Zoubi, Head of Transmission Department.

▣Radiodiffusion Télévision Tunisienne, 71 Avenue de la Liberté, TN-1070 Tunis, Tunisia. Phone: +216 (1) 801-177. Fax:

+216 (1) 781 927. Email: info@radiotunis.com. Web: (includes on-demand and streaming audio) www.radiotunis.com/news. html. Contact: Mongai Caffai, Director General; Mohamed Abdelkafi, Director; Kamel Cherif, Directeur; Masmoudi Mahmoud; Mr. Bechir Betteib, Director of Operations; or Smaoui Sadok, Le Sous-Directeur Technique. Replies irregularly and slowly to correspondence in French or Arabic. $1 helpful. For reception reports try: Le Chef de Service du Controle de la Récepcion de l'Office National de la Télediffusion, O.N.T, Cité Ennassim I, Bourjel, B.P. 399, TN-1080 Tunis, Tunisia. Phone: +216 (1) 801-177. Fax: +216 (1) 781 927. Email: ont.@ati.tn. Contact: Abdesselem Slim.

TURKEY World Time +2 (+3 midyear)

Meteoroloji Sesi Radyosu (Voice of Meteorology), T.C. Tarim Bakanliği, Devlet Meteoroloji İşleri, Genel Müdürlüğü, P.K. 401, Ankara, Turkey. Phone: +90 (312) 359-7545, X-281. Fax: +90 (312) 314 1196. Email: info@meteor.gov.tr; e-mail@meteor.gov. tr. Contact: Prof. Atila Dorum. Free tourist literature. Return postage helpful.

▣Voice of Turkey (Turkish Radio-Television Corporation External Service)

MAIN OFFICE, NONTECHNICAL: TRT External Services Department, TRT Sitesi, Turan Güneş Blv., Or-An Çankaya, 06450 Ankara, Turkey; or P.K. 333, Yenişehir, 06443 Ankara, Turkey. Phone: (general) +90 (312) 490-9800/9801; (English desk) +90 (312) 490-9842. Fax: (English desk) +90 (312) 490 9846. Email: (English desk) englishdesk@trt.net.tr; (Spanish Service) espanol@trt.net.tr. Web: (includes streaming audio) www. trt.net.tr; (transmission schedule) www.trt.net.tr/wwwtrt/ frekanstsr.aspx. Contact: (English and non-technical) Mr. Osman Erkan, Chief, English desk; or Michael Daventry, English Announcer. Technical correspondence, such as on reception quality should be directed to: Ms. Sedef Somaltin (see next entry below). On-air language courses offered in Arabic and German, but no printed course material. Free stickers, pennants, and tourist literature.

MAIN OFFICE, TECHNICAL (FOR EMIRLER AND ÇAKIRLAR TRANSMITTER SITES AND FOR FREQUENCY MANAGEMENT): TRT Teknik Yardimcilik, TRT Sitesi, Kat: 5/C, 06109 ORAN, Ankara, Turkey. Phone: +90 (312) 490-1732. Fax: +90 (312) 490 1733. Email: sedef.somaltin@trt.net.tr or kiymet.erdal@trt. net.tr. Contact: Mr. Haluk Buran, TRT Deputy Director General (Head of Engineering); Ms. Sedef Somaltin, Engineer & Frequency Manager; or Ms. Kiymet Erdal, Engineer & Frequency Manager. The HFBC seasonal schedules can be reached directly from: www.trt.net.tr/duyurufiles/vot.htm.

SAN FRANCISCO OFFICE, SCHEDULES: 2654 17th Avenue, San Francisco CA 94116 USA. Phone: +1 (415) 564-9968. Email: GPoppin@aol.com. Contact: George Poppin. This address, a volunteer office, only provides TRT schedules to listeners. All other correspondence should be sent directly to Ankara.

TURKMENISTAN World Time +5

Radio Turkmenistan, National TV and Radio Broadcasting Company, Mollanepes St. 3, 744000 Ashgabat, Turkmenistan. Phone: +993 (12) 251-515. Fax: +993 (12) 251 421. Contact: (administration) Yu M. Pashaev, Deputy Chairman of State Television and Radio Company; (technical) G. Khanmamedov; Kakali Karayev, Chief of Technical Department; or A.A Armanklichev, Deputy Chief, Technical Department. This country is currently under strict censorship and media people are

Begun in 1499, Bath Abbey is England's lone surviving great medieval church. It was restored after Henry VIII forced it into ruin. M. Wright

closely watched. A lot of foreign mail addressed to a particular person may attract the attention of the security services. Best is not to address your mail to particular individuals but to the station itself.

UGANDA   World Time +3

Radio Uganda
GENERAL OFFICE: P.O. Box 7142, Kampala, Uganda. Phone: +256 (41) 257-256. Fax: +256 (41) 257 252. Email: ugabro@infocom.co.ug. Contact: (general) Charles Byekwaso, Controller of Programmes; Machel Rachel Makibuuka; or Mrs. Florence Sewanyana, Head of Public Relations. $1 or return postage required. Replies infrequently and slowly. Correspondence to this address has sometimes been returned with the annotation "storage period overdue"—presumably because the mail is not collected on a regular basis.
ENGINEERING DIVISION: P.O. Box 2038, Kampala, Uganda. Phone: +256 (41) 256-647. Contact: Leopold B. Lubega, Principal Broadcasting Engineer; or Rachel Nakibuuka, Secretary. Four IRCs or $2 required. Enclosing a self addressed envelope may also help to get a reply.

UKRAINE   World Time +2 (+3 midyear)

Radio Ukraine International, Kreshchatyk Str. 26, 01001 Kyiv, Ukraine. Phone: (Ukrainian Service) +380 (44) 279-1757; (English Service) + 380 (44) 279-5484; (German Service) +380 (44) 279-3134. Fax: (Ukrainian Service) +380 (44) 279 7894; (English section) +380 (44) 279 7356; (Technical Department) +380 (44) 239-6029. Email: (Ukrainian Service) marinenko@nrcu.gov.ua; (English Service) vsru@nrcu.gov.ua; (German Service) rui@nrcu.gov.ua; (technical, including reception reports) egorov@nrcu.gov.ua. Web: (includes streaming audio) www.nrcu.gov.ua. Contact: Olexander Dykyi, Director; Inna Chichinadze, Deputy-Director; Mykola Marynenko, Editor-in-Chief, Ukrainian Section; Volodymyr Perpadia, Editor-in-Chief, German Section; Zhanna Mescherska, Editor-in-Chief, English Section; (technical) Alexander Yegorov, Head of Technical Department. Free stickers, calendars and Ukrainian stamps.

UNITED ARAB EMIRATES   World Time +4

Emirates Radio (if reactivated), P.O. Box 1695, Dubai, United Arab Emirates. Phone: +971 (4) 370-255. Fax: +971 (4) 374 111, +971 (4) 370 283 or +971 (4) 371 079. Email: radio@dubaitv. gov.ae; radio@dubaidd.org.ae. Web: www.dubaitv.gov.ae. Contact: Ms. Khulud Halaby; or Sameer Aga, Producer, "Cassette Club Cinarabic"; (technical) K.F. Fenner, Chief Engineer—Radio; or Ahmed Al Muhaideb, Assistant Controller, Engineering. Free pennants. Replies irregularly.

UNITED KINGDOM   World Time exactly (+1 midyear)

BBC Monitoring, Caversham Park, Reading, Berkshire RG4 8TZ, United Kingdom. Phone: (switchboard) +44 (118) 948-6000; (Media Services) +44 (118) 948-6261; Marketing Department) +44 (118) 948-6289. Fax: (Media Services) +44 (118) 946 1993; (Marketing Department) +44 (118) 946 3823. Email: (marketing department/publications and real time services) marketing@mon.bbc.co.uk; (media services) mediaservices@mon.bbc.co.uk. Web: www.monitor.bbc.co.uk. Contact: Chris Wescott, Director of Monitoring; (all enquiries and publication sales) Marketing. BBC Monitoring produces a daily email service on the world's media covering political, economic, legal, organisational, programming and technical developments. Reports are based on material from radio and TV stations, news agencies, websites, publications and from other relevant bodies. Information is also obtained by BBC Monitoring's own observations of the media. Available on yearly subscription from £600.00. Payment by check, bankers draft or credit card (VISA/MC/AMEX).

BBC World Service
MAIN OFFICE, NONTECHNICAL: Bush House, Strand, London WC2B 4PH, United Kingdom. Phone: (general) +44 (20) 7240-3456; (Press Office) +44 (20) 7557-2947/1; (International Marketing) +44 (20) 7557-1143. Fax: (Audience Relations) +44 (20) 7557 1258; ("Write On" listeners' letters program) +44 (20) 7436 2800; (Audience and Market Research) +44 (20) 7557 1254; (International Marketing) +44 (20) 7557 1254. Email: (general listener correspondence) worldservice. letters@bbc.co.uk; ("Write On") writeon@bbc.co.uk. Web: (includes on-demand and streaming audio) www.bbc.co.uk/ worldservice. Also, *see* Ascension, Oman, Seychelles, Singapore and Thailand. Does not verify reception reports due to budget limitations.
SAN FRANCISCO OFFICE, SCHEDULES: 2654 17th Avenue, San Francisco CA 94116 USA. Phone: +1 (415) 564-9968. Email: GPoppin@aol.com. Contact: George Poppin. This address, a volunteer office, only provides BBC World Service schedules to listeners. All other correspondence should be sent directly to the main office in London.

TECHNICAL: See VT Merlin Communications.

BFBS—British Forces Broadcasting Service (when operating), Services Sound and Vision, Chalfont Grove, Narcot Lane, Chalfont St. Peter, Gerrards Cross, Buckinghamshire SL9 8TN, United Kingdom; or BFBS Worldwide, P.O. Box 903, Gerrards Cross, Buckinghamshire SL9 8TN, United Kingdom. Email: (general) adminofficer@bfbs.com. Web: (includes on-demand and streaming audio) www.ssvc.com/bfbs. Normally only on satellite and FM, but hires additional shortwave facilities when British troops are fighting overseas.

Bible Voice Broadcasting

EUROPEAN OFFICE: P. O. Box 220, Leeds LS26 0WW, United Kingdom. Phone: +44 (1900) 827-355. Email: mail@biblevoice.org.
Web: www.biblevoice.org. Contact: Martin and Liz Thompson.
NORTH AMERICAN OFFICE: High Adventure Gospel Communication Ministries, P.O. Box 425, Station E, Toronto, ON M6H 4E3, Canada.
Phone: +1 (905) 898-5447; (toll-free, U.S. and Canada only) 1-800-550-4670. Email: highadventure@sympatico.ca. Contact: Mrs. Marty McLaughlin.
Bible Voice Broadcasting is a partnership between Bible Voice (U.K.) and High Adventure Gospel Communication Ministries (Canada).

Commonwealth Broadcasting Association, CBA Secretariat, 17 Fleet Street, London EC4Y 1AA, United Kingdom. Phone: +44 (20) 7583-5550. Fax: +44 (20) 7583 5549. Email: cba@cba.org.uk. Web: www.cba.org.uk. Publishes the annual *Commonwealth Broadcaster Directory* and the quarterly *Commonwealth Broadcaster* (online subscription form available).

FEBA Radio, Ivy Arch Road, Worthing, West Sussex BN14 8BX, United Kingdom. Phone: +44 (1903) 237-281. Fax: +44 (1903) 205 294. Email: (general) info@feba.org.uk; (Whittington) rwhittington@feba.org.uk. Web: www.feba.org.uk. Contact: (nontechnical) Angela Brooke, Supporter Relations; (technical) Richard Whittington, Schedule Engineer. Does not verify reception reports. Try sending reports to individual program producers (addresses are usually given over the air).

IBC-Tamil, 3 College Fields, Prince George's Road, Colliers Wood, London SW19 2PT, United Kingdom. Phone: +44 (20) 8100-0012. Fax: +44 (20) 8100 0003. Email: radio@ibctamil.co.uk. Web: (includes on-demand and streaming audio) www.ibctamil.co.uk. Contact: A.C. Tarcisius, Managing Director; S. Shivaranjith, Manager; K. Pillai; or Public Relations Officer.

Radio Ezra (when operating), P.O. Box 674, Stockton on Tees, TS18 3WR, United Kingdom. Fax: +44 (1642) 887 546. Email: info@radioezra.com. Web: www.radioezra.com. Contact: John D. Hill, Station Owner. Broadcasts irregularly via transmitters in the former Sovet Union. Welcomes reception reports via post, fax or email, and verifies with a QSL certificate. $1 or 1 IRC for return postage appreciated. Describes itself as a "countermissionary station." Supports the World Karaite movement and broadcasts when funding becomes available.

VT Merlin Communications, 20 Lincoln's Inn Fields, London WC2A 3ED, United Kingdom. Phone: +44 (20) 7969-0000. Fax: +44 (20) 7396 6223. Email: marketing@merlincommunications.com. Web: www.vtplc.com/communications. Contact: Fiona Lowry, Chief Executive; Rory Maclachlan, Director of International Communications & Digital Services; Ciaran Fitzgerald, Head of Engineering & Operations; Richard Hurd, Head of Transmission Sales; Laura Jelf, Marketing Manager; or Anna Foakes, Marketing Department. Formerly known as Merlin Communications International. Does not verify reception reports.

Wales Radio International (if reactivated), Preseli Radio Productions, Pros Kairon, Crymych, Pembrokeshire, SA41 3QE, Wales, United Kingdom. Phone: +44 (1437) 563-361. Fax: +44 (1239) 831 390. Email: jenny@wri.cymru.net. Web: (includes on-demand audio) http://wri.cymru.net. Contact: Jenny O'Brien. A weekly broadcast via the facilities of VT Merlin Communications (*see*, above). Suspended transmissions late March 2005.

WRN, P.O. Box 1212, London SW8 2ZF, United Kingdom. Phone: +44 (20) 7896-9000. Fax: + 44 (20) 7896 9007. Email: (general) email@wrn.org; (Ayris) tim.ayris@wrn.org. Web: (includes on-demand and streaming audio) www.wrn.org. Contact: Tim Ayris, Broadcast Sales Manager for WRN's networks. Provides Webcasts and program placements for international broadcasters.

UNITED NATIONS   World Time –5 (–4 midyear)

Radio UNMEE
Web: (includes on-demand audio) www.un.org/Depts/dpko/unmee/radio.htm.
NEW YORK OFFICE: Same contact details as United Nations Radio, below.
ERITREA OFFICE: P.O. Box 5805, Asmara, Eritrea. Phone: +291 (1) 151 908. Email: kellyb@un.org.
ETHIOPIA OFFICE: ECA Building, P.O. Box 3001, Addis Ababa, Ethiopia. Phone: +251 (1) 443-396. Email: walkera@un.org. Radio service of the United Nations Mission in Eritrea and Ethiopia (UNMEE). Aired via facilities in the United Arab Emirates, and also relayed over Eritrea's national radio, Voice of the Broad Masses of Eritrea.

United Nations Radio, Secretariat Building, Room S-850A, United Nations, New York NY 10017 USA, or write to the station over which UN Radio was heard. Phone: +1 (917) 367-5007. Fax: +1 (212) 963 6869. Email: (general) unradio@un.org; (comments on programs) audio-visual@un.org; (reception reports) smithd@un.org; or (Villanueva) villanueva1@un.org. Web: (includes on-demand audio) www.un.org/radio; (on-demand audio) www.wrn.org/ondemand/unitednations.html. Contact: (general) Sylvester E. Rowe, Chief, Radio and Video Service; or Ayman El-Amir, Chief, Radio Section, Department of Public Information; (reception reports) David Smith; or Trixie Villanueva; (technical and nontechnical) Sandra Guy, Secretary. Free stamps and *UN Frequency* publication. Reception reports (including those sent by email) are verified with a QSL card.
GENEVA OFFICE: Room G209, Palais des Nations, CH-1211 Geneva 10, Switzerland. Phone: +41 (22) 917-4222. Fax: +41 (22) 917 0123.

URUGUAY   World Time –3 (sometimes –2, to save electricity)

Banda Oriental—*see* Radio Sarandí del Yí.
Emisora Ciudad de Montevideo, Canelones 2061, 11200 Montevideo, Uruguay. Phone: +598 (2) 402-0142 or +598 (2) 402-4242. Fax: +598 (2) 402 0700. Email: online form. Web: (includes streaming audio) www.emisoraciudaddemontevideo.com.uy. Contact: Aramazd Yizmeyian, Director General. Free stickers. Return postage helpful.
Radiodifusion Nacional—*see* S.O.D.R.E.
Radio Oriental (when operating), Cerrito 475, 11000 Montevideo, Uruguay. Phone/Fax: +598 (2) 916-1130. Email: (Management) director@oriental.com.uy; (general) info@oriental.com.uy or secretaria@oriental.com.uy. Web:

(includes streaming audio) www.oriental.com.uy. Contact: Presbítero Jorge Techera, Director; (technical) José A. Porro, Technician. Correspondence in Spanish preferred. Formerly a private station, Radio Oriental was purchased by the Uruguayan Catholic Church in 2003.

Radio Sarandí del Yí (when operating), Sarandí 328, 97100 Sarandí del Yí, Uruguay. Phone/Fax: +598 (367) 9155. Email: (owner) norasan@adinet.com.uy. Contact: Nora San Martín de Porro, Propietaria.

Radio Universo (when activated), Ferrer 1265, 27000 Castillos, Dpto. de Rocha, Uruguay. Email: am1480@adinet.com.uy. Contact: Juan Héber Brañas, Propietario. Currently only on 1480 kHz mediumwave AM, but has been granted a license to operate on shortwave.

S.O.D.R.E., Radiodifusión Nacional, Casilla 1412, 11000 Montevideo, Uruguay. Phone: +598 (2) 916-1933; (technical) +598 (2) 915-7865. Email: dirradio@sodre.gub.uy. Web: (includes streaming audio) www.sodre.gub.uy. Contact: (management) Sergio Sacomani, Director de Radiodifusión Nacional; (technical) José Cuello, División Técnica Radio.

USA
World Time –4 Atlantic, including Puerto Rico and Virgin Islands; –5 (–4 midyear) Eastern, including southeast Indiana; –5 Indiana, except northwest, southwest and southeast portions; –6 (–5 midyear) Central, including northwest and southwest Indiana; –7 (–6 midyear) Mountain, except Arizona; –7 Arizona; –8 (–7 midyear) Pacific; –9 (–8 midyear) Alaska, except Aleutian Islands; –10 (–9 midyear) Aleutian Islands; –10 Hawaii; –11 Samoa.

Adventist World Radio
HEADQUARTERS: 12501 Old Columbia Pike, Silver Spring MD 20904 USA. Phone: +1 (301) 680-6304; (toll-free, U.S. only) 1-800-337-4297. Fax: +1 (301) 680 6303. Email: info@awr.org. Web: (includes on-demand audio) www.awr.org.
NONTECHNICAL LISTENER CORRESPONDENCE: E-mail: letters@awr.org.
RECEPTION REPORTS:
LISTENERS IN AFRICA, AMERICAS AND EUROPE: P.O. Box 29235, Indianapolis IN 46229 USA. Phone/Fax: +1 (317) 891-8540. Email: adrian@awr.org. Contact: Dr. Adrian M. Peterson. Provides technical information and processes reception reports and issues QSL cards.
LISTENERS IN ASIA AND THE PACIFIC: Adventist World Radio—Asia/Pacific, 798 Thompson Road, Singapore 298186, Singapore. Email: aproffice@awr.org. Contact: Akinori Kaibe.
OPERATIONS AND ENGINEERING: See AWR entry Guam.
AWR EUROPE FREQUENCY MANAGEMENT OFFICE: Postfach 100252, D-64202 Darmstadt, Germany. Phone: (Dedio) +49 (6151) 953-151; (Crillo) +49 (6151) 953-153. Fax: +61 (6151) 953 152. Email: (Dedio) dedio@awr.org; (Cirillo) pino@awr.org. Contact: Claudius Dedio, Frequency Coordinator; or Giuseppe Cirillo, Monitoring Engineer.

Al Mustaqbal (when operating), EDC, 1000 Potomac Street NW - Suite 350, Washington DC 20007 USA. Phone: +1 (202) 572-3700. Fax: +1 (202) 223-4059. Email: (Houssein) ahoussein@edc.org. Web: http://main.edc.org/international/region.asp?region=Africa&country=ETHIOPIA. Contact: Abdoulkhader Houssein. A project of Education Development Center, Inc., funded by the U.S. Agency for International Development (USAID), and targeted at Somali-speaking children in Ethiopia. Broadcast via a transmitter in the United Arab Emirates. Off the air during school vacations.

AFRTS-American Forces Radio and Television Service (Shortwave), Naval Media Center, NDW Anacostia Annex, 2713 Mitscher Road SW, Washington DC 20373-5819 USA. For verification of reception, be sure to mark the envelope, "Attn: Short Wave Reception Reports." Email: (verifications) qsl@mediacen.navy.mil, although this service appears to have been suspended. Web: http://myafn.dodmedia.osd.mil/radio/shortwave; (AFRTS parent organization) www.afrts.osd.mil; (2-minute on-demand audio news clips): www.defenselink.mil/news/radio; (Naval Media Center) www.mediacen.navy.mil. The Naval Media Center is responsible for all AFRTS broadcasts aired on shortwave.
FLORIDA ADDRESS: NCTS-Jacksonville-Detachment Key West, Building A 1004, Naval Air Station Boca Chica, Key West, FL 33040 USA.
Also, *see* Iceland.

Aurora Communications (under construction), Mile 129, Sterling Highway, Ninilchik, Alaska, USA. Plans to commence broadcasts to Russia when circumstances allow.

Broadcasting Board of Governors (BBG), 330 Independence Avenue SW, Room 3360, Washington DC 20237 USA. Phone: +1 (202) 619-2538. Fax: +1 (202) 619 1241. Email: pubaff@ibb.gov. Web: www.bbg.gov. Contact: Kathleen Harrington, Public Relations. The BBG, created in 1994 and headed by nine members nominated by the President, is the overseeing agency for all official non-military United States international broadcasting operations, including the VOA, RFE-RL, Radio Martí and Radio Free Asia.

Eternal Good News, International Radio Broadcasts, Wilshire Church of Christ, Oklahoma City OK USA; or P.O.Box 5333, Edmond OK 73083, USA. Phone: +1 (405) 359-1235, +1 (405) 340-0877. Email: eternalgoodnews@sbcglobal.net. Web: (includes on-demand audio) www.oldpaths.net/Works/Radio/Wilshire/index.html. Contact: Germaine Charles Lockwood, Evangelist; or Sandra Lockwood, Secretary. Programs are aired via world band transmitters in Germany, Russia and United Arab Emirates, as well as U.S. station World Harvest Radio.

Family Radio Worldwide
NONTECHNICAL: Family Stations, Inc., 290 Hegenberger Road, Oakland CA 94621-1436 USA. Phone: (general) +1 (510) 568-6200; (toll-free, U.S. only) 1-800-543-1495; (engineering) +1 (510) 568-6200 ext. 242. Fax: (main office) +1 (510) 568 6200. Email: (general) famradio@familyradio.com; (international department, shortwave program schedules) international@familyradio.com. Web: (includes streaming audio) www.familyradio.com. Contact: (general) Harold Camping, General Manager; or David Hoff, Manager of International Department. Free gospel tracts (50 languages), books, booklets, quarterly *Family Radio News* magazine and frequency schedule. Free CD containing domestic and international program schedules plus audio lessons in MP 3 format and bible study materials. 2 IRCs helpful.
TECHNICAL: WYFR—Family Radio, 10400 NW 240th Street, Okeechobee FL 34972 USA. Phone: +1 (863) 763-0281. Fax: +1 (863) 763 8867. Email: (technical) fsiyfr@okeechobee.com; (frequency schedule) wyfr@okeechobee.com. Contact: Dan Elyea, Engineering Manager; or Edward F. Dearborn, Chief Operator; (frequency schedule) Evelyn Marcy.

FEBC Radio International
INTERNATIONAL HEADQUARTERS: Far East Broadcasting Company, Inc., P.O. Box 1, La Mirada CA 90637 USA. Phone: +1 (310) 947-4651. Fax: +1 (310) 943 0160. Email: febc@febc.org. Web: www.febi.org. Operates world band stations in the Philippines and Northern Mariana Islands (*see*). Does not verify reception reports from this address.

Federal Communications Commission, 445 12th Street SW, Washington DC 20554 USA. Phone: +1 (202) 418-0190;

In February, 2005 "The Gates" by Christo and Jeanne-Claude were displayed as artwork in New York's Central Park. They stayed up for 16 days before being recycled. M. Wright

(toll-free, U.S. only) 1-888-225-5322. Fax: +1 (202) 418 0232. Email: tpolzin@fcc.gov. Web: (general) www.fcc.gov; (high frequency operating schedules) http://ftp.fcc.gov/ib/sand/neg/hf_web/seasons.html. Contact: (International Bureau, technical) Thomas E. Polzin.

Fundamental Broadcasting Network, Grace Missionary Baptist Church, 520 Roberts Road, Newport NC 28570 USA. Phone: +1 (252) 223-6088; (toll-free, U.S. only) 1-800-245-9685; (Robinson) +1 (252) 223-4600. Email: (general) fbn@clis.com; (technical, David Robinson) davidwr@clis.com. Web: (includes streaming audio) www.fbnradio.com. Contact: Pastor Clyde Eborn; (technical) David Robinson, Chief Engineer. Verifies reception reports if an IRC or (within the USA) an SASE is included. Accepts email reports. Free stickers. A religious and educational non-commercial broadcasting network which operates sister stations WBOH and WTJC.

Gospel for Asia, 1800 Golden Trail Court, Carrollton TX 75010 USA. Phone: +1 (972) 300-7777; (toll-free, U.S. only) 1-800-946-2742. Email: info@gfa.org. Web: www.gfa.org. Transmits via facilities in Jülich, Germany, and Dhabayya, U.A.E.

CALIFORNIA OFFICE: P.O. Box 1210 Somis, California 93066 USA. Email: gfaradio@mygfa.org. Contact: Rhonda Penland, Coordinator.

CANADIAN OFFICE: 245 King Street E., Stoney Creek, ON L8G 1L9, Canada. Phone: +1 (905) 662-2101. Email: infocanada@gfa.org.

UNITED KINGDOM OFFICE: P.O. Box 166, York YO10 5WA, United Kingdom. Phone: +44 (1904) 643-233. Email: infouk@gfa.org.

International Broadcasting Bureau (IBB)—Reports to the Broadcasting Board of Governors (*see*), and includes, among others, the Voice of America, RFE-RL, Radio Martí and Radio Free Asia. IBB Engineering (Office of Engineering and Technical Operations) provides broadcast services for these stations. Contact: (administration) Brian Conniff, Director; or Joseph O'Connell, Director of External Affairs. Web: www.ibb.gov/ibbpage.html.

FREQUENCY AND MONITORING OFFICE, TECHNICAL: IBB/EOF: Spectrum Management Division, International Broadcasting Bureau (IBB), Room 4611 Cohen Bldg., 330 Independence Avenue SW, Washington DC 20237 USA. Phone: +1 (202) 619-1669. Fax: +1 (202) 619 1680. Email: (scheduling) dlferguson@ibb.gov; (monitoring) bw@his.com. Web: (general) http://monitor.ibb.gov; (email reception report form) http://monitor.ibb.gov/now_you_try_it.html. Contact: Dan Ferguson (dferguson@ibb.gov); or Bill Whitacre (bw@his.com).

KAIJ

ADMINISTRATION OFFICE: Two-if-by-Sea Broadcasting Co., 22720 SE 410th St., Enumclaw WA 89022 USA. Phone/Fax: (Mike Parker, California) +1 (818) 606-1254; (Washington State office, if and when operating) +1 (206) 825 4517. Email: (Parker) mparker@kaij.org. Web: www.kaij.org. Contact: Mike Parker (mark envelope, "please forward"). Replies occasionally.

TRANSMITTER SITE: RR#3 Box 120, Frisco TX 75034 USA; or Highway 380 West, Prosper TX 75078 USA (physical location: Highway 380, 3.6 miles west of State Rt. 289, near Denton TX; transmitters and antennas located on Belt Line Road along the lake in Coppell TX). Phone: +1 (972) 346-2758. Contact: Walt Green or Fred Bithell. Station encourages mail to be sent to the administration office, which seldom replies.

KJES—King Jesus Eternal Savior

STATION: The Lord's Ranch, 230 High Valley Road, Vado NM 88072 USA. Phone: +1 (505) 233-2090. Fax: +1 (505) 233 3019. Email: kjes@aol.com. Contact: Michael Reuter, Manager. $1 or return postage appreciated.

SPONSORING ORGANIZATION: Our Lady's Youth Center, P.O. Box 1422, El Paso TX 79948 USA. Phone: +1 (915) 533-9122.

KNLS—New Life Station

OPERATIONS CENTER: World Christian Broadcasting, 605 Bradley Ct., Franklin TN 37067 USA (letters sent to the Alaska transmitter site are usually forwarded to Franklin). Phone: +1 (615) 371-8707 ext.140. Fax: +1 (615) 371 8791. Email: knls@aol.com. Web: (includes on-demand audio of sample programs) www.

knls.org. Contact: (general) Dale R. Ward, Executive Producer; L. Wesley Jones, Director of Follow-Up Teaching; or Rob Scobey, Senior Producer, English Language Service; (technical) F.M. Perry, Frequency Coordinator. Free *Alaska Calling!* newsletter and station pennants. Free spiritual literature and bibles in Russian, Mandarin or English. Free Alaska books, tapes, postcards and cloth patches. Two free DX books for beginners. Special, individually numbered, limited edition, verification cards issued for each new transmission period to the first 200 listeners providing confirmed reception reports. Stamp and postcard exchange. Return postage appreciated. *TRANSMITTER SITE:* P.O. Box 473, Anchor Point AK 99556 USA. Phone: +1 (907) 235-8262. Fax: +1 (907) 235 2326. Contact: (technical) Kevin Chambers, Chief Engineer.

KRSI—Radio Sedaye Iran (when operating), Suite 207, 9744 Wilshire Boulevard, Beverly Hills CA 90212-1812 USA. Phone: +1 (310) 888-2818. Fax: +1 (310) 859 8444. Web: (includes streaming audio and online email form) www.krsi.net. Operates via a closed broadcasting system and the Internet. Transmits irregularly on shortwave, and via different countries.

KTBN—Trinity Broadcasting Network:
GENERAL CORRESPONDENCE: P.O. Box A, Santa Ana CA 92711 USA. Phone: +1 (714) 832-2950. Fax: +1 (714) 730 0661. Email: comments@tbn.org. Web: (Trinity Broadcasting Network, includes streaming audio) www.tbn.org. Contact: Dr. Paul F. Crouch, Managing Director. Monthly TBN newsletter. Free booklets, stickers and small souvenirs sometimes available. *TECHNICAL CORRESPONDENCE:* Engineering/QSL Department, 2442 Michelle Drive, Tustin CA 92780-7015 USA. Phone: +1 (714) 665-2145. Fax: +1 (714) 730 0661. Email: cgilroy@tbn.org. Contact: Cheryl Gilroy, QSL Manager; or Ben Miller, Vice President, Engineering. Responds to reception reports; write to: Trinity Broadcasting Network, Attention: Superpower KTBN Radio QSL Manager Cheryl Gilroy, 2442 Michelle Drive, Tustin CA 92780 USA. Return postage (IRC or SASE) helpful. Although a California operation, KTBN's shortwave transmitter is located at Salt Lake City, Utah.

KVOH—La Voz de Restauración, 4409 W. Adams Blvd., Los Angeles CA 90016 USA. Phone: +1 (323) 766-2454. Fax: +1 (323) 766-2458. Email: comentarios@kvoh.org. Web: (includes streaming audio) www.restauracion.com/radio.html.

KWHR-World Harvest Radio:
ADMINISTRATION OFFICE: See World Harvest Radio.
TRANSMITTER: Although located 6 1/2 miles southwest of Naalehu, 8 miles north of South Cape, and 2000 feet west of South Point (Ka La) Road (the antennas are easily visible from this road) on Big Island, Hawaii, the operators of this rural transmitter site maintain no post office box in or near Naalehu, and their telephone number is unlisted, Best bet is to contact them via their administration office (*see* World Harvest Radio), or to drive in unannounced (it's just off South Point Road) the next time you vacation on Big Island.

Leading The Way, P.O. Box 20100, Atlanta GA 30325 USA. Phone: +1 (404) 841-0100. Email: (Wattenbarger) adam@leadingtheway.org; (reception reports) qsl@leadingtheway.org. Web: www.leadingtheway.org; (includes on-demand audio) www.oneplace.com/ministries/leading_the_way. Contact: Adam Wattenbarger, Senior Producer for Radio. Airs via U.K. facilities of VT Merlin Communications (*see*) and various world band religious broadcasters.

Leinwoll (Stanley)—Telecommunication Consultant, 305 E. 86th Street, Suite 21S-W, New York NY 10028 USA. Phone: +1 (212) 987-0456. Fax: +1 (212) 987 3532. Email: stanL00011@aol.com. Contact: Stanley Leinwoll, President.

This firm provides frequency management and other engineering services for some private U.S. world band stations, but does not correspond with the general public.

Little Saigon Radio, 15781 Brookhurst St. - Suite 101, Westminster CA 92683 USA. Phone: +1 (714) 918-4444. Web: (includes streaming audio from domestic service) www.littlesaigonradio.com. Contact: Joe Dinh, Technical Director. A Californian mediumwave AM station which airs a special broadcast for Vietnam via leased facilities in Taiwan.

National Association of Shortwave Broadcasters, 10400 NW 240th Street, Okeechobee, FL 34972 USA; P.O. Box 8700, Cary NC 27512 USA. Phone: +1 (863) 763-0281. Fax: +1 (863) 763 8867. Email: nasbmem@rocketmail.com. Web: www.shortwave.org. Contact: Dan Elyea, Secretary-Treasurer. Association of most private U.S. world band stations, as well as a group of other international broadcasters, equipment manufacturers and organizations related to shortwave broadcasting. Includes committees on various subjects, such as digital shortwave radio. Interfaces with the Federal Communications Commission's International Bureau and other broadcasting-related organizations to advance the interests of its members. Publishes *NASB Newsletter* for members and associates and is available for free via their website. Annual one-day convention held in Washington DC early each spring; non-members wishing to attend should contact the Secretary-Treasurer in advance; convention fee typically $50 per person.

Overcomer Ministry ("Voice of the Last Day Prophet of God"), P.O. Box 691, Walterboro SC 29488 USA. Phone: (0900-1700 local time, Sunday through Friday) +1 (803) 538-3892. Fax: +1 (843) 628 4131. Email: brotherstair@overcomerministry.org. Web: (includes on-demand and streaming audio) www.overcomerministry.org. Contact: Brother R.G. Stair. Sample "Overcomer" newsletter and various pamphlets free upon request. Via Germany's T-Systems International (*see*) and various U.S. stations.

Pan American Broadcasting, 2021 The Alameda, Suite 240, San Jose CA 95126-1145 USA. Phone: +1 (408) 996-2033; (toll-free, U.S. only) 1-800-726-2620. Fax: +1 (408) 252 6855. Email: info@panambc.com; (Bernald) gbernald@panambc.com; (Jung) cjung@panambc.com. Web: www.panambc.com. Contact: (listener correspondence) Terry Kraemer; (general) Carmen Jung, Office and Sales Administrator; or Gene Bernald, President. $1, mint U.S. stamps or 2 IRCs required for reply. Operates transmitters in Equatorial Guinea (*see*) and hires airtime over a number of world band stations, plus T-Systems International facilities in Germany.

Quê H_ng Radio, 2670 South White Road, Suite 165, San Jose CA 95148 USA. Phone: +1 (408) 223-3130. Fax: +1 (408) 223 3131. Email: qhradio@aol.com. Web: (includes on-demand audio) www.quehuongmedia.com. Contact: Nguyen Khoi, Manager. A Californian Vietnamese station operating on mediumwave AM, and which broadcasts to Vietnam via a transmitter in Central Asia.

Radio Farda—a joint venture between Radio Free Europe-Radio Liberty (*see*) and the Voice of America (*see*). Email: radiofarda@rferl.com. Web: (includes on-demand and streaming audio) www.radiofarda.com. Broadcasts a mix of news, information and popular Iranian and western music to younger audiences in Iran.

Radio Free Afghanistan—the Afghan service of Radio Free Europe-Radio Liberty (*see*). Web: (includes on-demand and streaming audio) www.azadiradio.org.

Radio Free Asia, Suite 300, 2025 M Street NW, Washington DC 20036 USA (for reports on reception, add "Reception Reports" before "Radio Free Asia"). You can also submit reception reports at: www.techweb.rfa.org (click on the QSL REPORTS link) or send them via email to: QSL@rfa.org. Phone: (general) +1 (202) 530-4900; (president) +1 (202) 457-4901;(vice president of editorial) +1 (202) 530-4907; (vice-president of administration) +1 (202) 530-4902; (chief technology officer) +1 (202) 530-4958; (director of production support) +1 (202) 530-4943. Fax: +1 (202) 530 7794 or +1 (202) 721 7468. Email: (individuals) the format is lastnameinitial@rfa.org; so to reach, say the CTO, David Baden, it would be badend@rfa.org; (language sections) the format is language@rfa.org; so to contact, say, the Vietnamese section, address your message to vietnamese@rfa.org; (general) communications@rfa.org; (reception reports) qsl@rfa.org. Web: (includes on-demand audio) www.rfa.org; (automated reception report system) www.techweb.rfa.org. Contact: (administration) Daniel Southerland, Vice President of Editorial; Libby Liu, Vice-President of Administration; (technical) David M. Baden, Chief Technology Officer; A. J. Janitschek, Manager of Production Support; Sam Stevens, Director of Technical Support. RFA, originally created in 1996 as the Asia Pacific Network, is funded as a private nonprofit U.S. corporation by a grant from the US Congress to the Broadcasting Board of Governors (see).

HONG KONG OFFICE: Room 904, Mass Mutal Tower, 38 Gloucester Road, Wanchai, Hong Kong, China.

THAILAND OFFICE: Maxim House, 112 Witthayu Road, Pathomwan, Bangkok 10330, Thailand.

Radio Free Europe-Radio Liberty/RFE-RL

PRAGUE HEADQUARTERS: Vinohradská 1, 110 00 Prague 1, Czech Republic. Phone: +420 (2) 2112-1111; (outreach coordinator) +420 (2) 2112-2407; (president) +420 (2) 2112-3000; (news desk) +420 (2) 2112-3629; (public relations) +420 (2) 2112-3012; (technical operations) +420 (2) 2112-3700; (broadcast operations) +420 (2) 2112-3550; (affiliate relations). +420 (2) 2112-2539. Fax: +420 (2) 2112 3013; (president) +420 (2) 2112 3002; (news desk) +420 (2) 2112 3613, (public relations) +420 (2) 2112 2995; (technical operations) +420 (2) 2112 3702; (broadcast operations) +420 (2) 2112 3540; (affiliate operations) +420 (2) 2112 4563. Email: the format is lastnameinitial@rferl.org; so to reach, say, Luke Springer, it would be springerl@rferl.org; (reception reports) lukaso@rferl.org. Web: (includes on-demand and streaming audio) www.rferl.org. Contact: Kestutis Girnius, Managing Editor, News and Current Affairs; Luke Springer, Deputy Director, Technology; Jana Horakova, Public Relations Coordinator; Uldis Grava, Marketing Director; Christopher Carzoli, Broadcast Operations Director; Ondrej Lukas, Outreach Coordinator.

WASHINGTON OFFICE: 1201 Connecticut Avenue NW, Washington DC 20036 USA. Phone: +1 (202) 457-6900; (Director of Communications) +1 202) 457-6947; (newsdesk) +1 (202) 457-6950; (technical) +1 (202) 457-6963. Fax: +1 (202) 457 6992; (news desk) +1 (202) 457 6997; (technical) +1 (202) 457 6913. Email and Web: *see* above. Contact: Don Jensen, Director of Communications. A private non-profit corporation funded by a grant from the Broadcasting Board of Governors, RFE/RL broadcasts in 21 languages (but not English) from transmission facilities now part of the International Broadcasting Bureau (IBB), *see.*

Radio Martí, Office of Cuba Broadcasting, 4201 N.W. 77th Avenue, Miami FL 33166 USA. Phone: +1 (305) 437-7000; (Director) +1 (305) 437-7117; (Technical Operations) +1 (305) 437-7051. Fax: +1 (305) 437 7016. Email: infomarti@ocb.ibb.gov. Web: (includes on-demand and streaming audio) www.martinoticias.com/radio.asp. Contact: (technical) Michael Pal-

lone, Director, Engineering and Technical Operations; or Tom Warden, Chief of Radio Operations.

Sound of Hope Radio Network, 2520 Wyandotte Street - Suite A, Mountain View CA 94043 USA. Phone: +1 (866) 432-7764. Fax: +1 (415) 276 5861. Email: (general) englishfeedback@soundofhope.org; (reception reports) 9ping@soundofhope.org. Web: (includes on-demand audio) www.soundofhope.org. Transmits via facilities in Taiwan.

Sudan Radio Service, Education Development Center, 1000 Potomac Street NW, Suite 350, Washington DC 20007 USA. Phone: +1 (202) 572-3700. Fax: +1 (202) 223 4059. Email: srs@edc.org; (Groce) jgroce@edc.org or jgroce@sudanradio.org. (Laflin) mlaflin@edc.org. Web: (includes on-demand audio) www.sudanradio.org; (EDC parent organization) www.edc.org. Contact: Jeremy Groce, Radio Programming Advisor, EDC; or Mike Laflin, Director, EDC.

PRODUCTION STUDIOS, KENYA: c/o EDC, P.O. Box 4392, 00100 Nairobi, Kenya. Phone: +254 (20) 570-906, +254 (20) 572-269. Fax: +254 (20) 576 520. Email: srs@sudanradio.org. Contact: Mike Kuenzli.

Trans World Radio

INTERNATIONAL HEADQUARTERS: P.O. Box 8700, Cary NC 27512-8700 USA. Phone: +1 (919) 460-3700; (toll-free, U.S. only) 1-800-456-7897. Fax: +1 (919) 460 3702. Email: info2@twr.org. Web: (includes on-demand audio) www.gospelcom.net/twr. Contact: (general) Jon Vaught, Public Relations; Richard Greene, Director, Public Relations; Joe Fort, Director, Broadcaster Relations; or Bill Danick; (technical) Glenn W. Sink, Assistant Vice President, International Operations. Free "Towers to Eternity" publication for those living in the U.S. This address for nontechnical correspondence only.

TRANS WORLD RADIO EUROPE (TECHNICAL): Trans World Radio, Postfach 141, A-1235 Vienna, Austria. Phone: +43 (1) 863-12-0. Fax: +43 (1) 863 1220, +43 (1) 862 1257. Email: eurofreq@twr-europe.at. Contact: Bernhard Schraut, Deputy Technical Director; Kalman Dobos, Frequency Coordinator; or Anna Marie Dobos. Verifies reception reports.

TRANS WORLD RADIO EUROPE (NONTECHNICAL): Trans World Radio Europe, Communications Department, P.O. Box 12, 820 02 Bratislava 22, Slovakia. Fax: +421 (2) 4329 3729. Web: www.twreurope.org.

Also, *see* Guam, South Africa and Swaziland.

Truth for the World, P.O. Box 5048, Duluth GA 30096-0065 USA. Email: tftworld@aol.com; (Grubb) jmgrubb@tftw.org. Web: www.tftw.org. Contact: John Grubb, Chinese Missions. Airs Chinese programming via a transmitter in Taiwan, and English programs via world band stations in Equatorial Guinea, Sri Lanka, U.S.A. and elsewhere.

University Network, P.O. Box 1, Los Angeles CA 90053 USA. Phone: +1 (818) 240-8151; (toll-free, U.S. and Canada only) 1-800-338-3030. Web: (includes streaming audio) www.drgenescott.com. Transmits over KAIJ and WWCR (USA); Caribbean Beacon (Anguilla, West Indies) and the former AWR facilities in Cahuita, Costa Rica. Does not verify reception reports.

Voice of America—All Transmitter Locations

(Main Office) 330 Independence Avenue SW, Washington DC 20237 USA; (listener feedback) Voice of America, Audience Mail, Room 4409, 330 Independence Ave SW,Washington DC 20237 USA. If contacting the VOA directly is impractical, write c/o the American Embassy in your country. Phone: (Office of Public Affairs) +1 (202) 401-7000; (Audience Mail Division) +1 (202) 619-2770; (Africa Division) +1 (202) 619-1666 or +1 (202) 619-2879; (Office of Research) +1 (202) 619-4965; (administration) +1 (202) 619-1088. Fax: (Office of Public Affairs) +1 (202)

619 1241; (Africa Division) +1 (202) 619 1664; (Audience Mail Division and Office of Research) +1 (202) 619 0211. Email: (general business) publicaffairs@voa.gov; (reception reports and schedule requests) letters@voa.gov; (listener feedback) letters@voanews.com; (VOA Special English) special@voanews.com. Web: (includes on-demand and streaming audio) www.voa.gov. Contact: Mrs. Betty Lacy Thompson, Chief, Audience Mail Division, B/K. G759A Cohen; Larry James, Director, English Programs Division; Leo Sarkisian; Rita Rochelle, Africa Division; George Mackenzie, Audience Research Officer; (reception reports) Mrs. Irene Greene, QSL Desk, Audience Mail Division, Room G-759-C. May send free stickers, fridge magnets pens and calendars. Also, *see* Botswana, Greece, Morocco, Philippines, São Tomé e Príncipe, Sri Lanka and Thailand.

VOA ASIA NEWS CENTER: 17th Floor Asia Orient Tower, 33 Lockhart Road, Wanchai, Hong Kong, China. Phone: +852 2526-9809. Fax: +852 2877 8805. Email: jenjano@voanews.com. Contact: Jennifer A. Janin, Director.

Voice of America/IBB—Delano Relay Station, Rt. 1, Box 1350, Delano CA 93215 USA; (physical address) 11015 Melcher Road, Delano CA 93215 USA. Phone: +1 (805) 725-0150. Fax: +1 (805) 725 6511. Email: (Vodenik) jvodenik@del.ibb.gov, k9hsp@juno.com. Contact: (technical) John Vodenik, Engineer. Photos of this facility can be seen at the following Website: www.hawkins.pair.com/voadelano.shtml. Nontechnical correspondence should be sent to the VOA address in Washington.

Voice of America/IBB—Greenville Relay Station, P.O. Box 1826, Greenville NC 27834 USA. Phone: (site A) +1 (252) 752-7115 or (site B) +1 (252) 752-7181. Fax: (site A) +1 (252) 758 8742 or (site B) +1 (252) 752 5959. Contact: (technical) Bruce Hunter, Manager; or Glenn Ruckleson. Nontechnical correspondence should be sent to the VOA address in Washington.

WBCQ—"The Planet," 274 Britton Road, Monticello ME 04760 3110 USA. Phone: +1 (207) 985-7547; (transmitter site, urgent technical matters only) +1 (207) 538-9180. Email: wbcq@gwi.net. Web: (includes on-demand audio) http://theplanet.wbcq.net. Contact: Allan H. Weiner, Owner; or Elayne Star, Assistant Manager. Verifies reception reports if 1 IRC or (within USA) an SASE is included. Does not verify email reports.

WBOH—*see* Fundamental Broadcasting Network.

WEWN—EWTN Global Catholic Radio, 5817 Old Leeds Rd., Birmingham AL 35210 USA. Phone: +1 (205) 271-2900. Fax: +1 (205) 271 2926. Email: (general) wewn@ewtn.com; (technical) radio@ewtn.com; (Spanish) rcm@ewtn.com. To contact individuals, the format is initiallastname@ewtn.com; so to reach, say, Thom Price, it would be tprice@ewtn.com. Web: (includes on-demand and streaming audio and online reception report form) www.ewtn.com/radio. Contact: (general) Thom Price, Director of English Programming; Doug Archer, Director of Spanish Programming; (marketing) John Pepe, Radio Marketing Manager; (administration) Michael Warsaw, President; Doug Keck, Sr. Vice-President, Programming & Production; Scott Hults, Vice President, Communications; Frank Leurck, Station Manager; (technical) Terry Borders, Vice President Engineering; Glen Tapley, Frequency Manager. Listener correspondence welcome. IRC or return postage appreciated for correspondence. Although a Catholic entity, WEWN is not an official station of the Vatican, which operates its own Vatican Radio (*see*).

WHRA-World Harvest Radio:
ADMINISTRATION OFFICE: See World Harvest Radio.
TRANSMITTERS: Located in Greenbush, Maine. Technical and other correspondence should be sent to the main office of World Harvest Radio (*see*).

WHRI-World Harvest Radio:
ADMINISTRATION OFFICE: See World Harvest Radio.
TRANSMITTERS: Located in Cypress Creek, South Carolina. Technical and other correspondence should be sent to the main office of World Harvest Radio (*see*).

WINB—World International Broadcasters, 2900 Windsor Road, P.O. Box 88, Red Lion PA 17356 USA. Phone: (all departments) +1 (717) 244-5360. Fax: +1 (717) 246 0363. Email: (general) info@winb.com; (reception reports) winb40th@yahoo.com. Web: www.winb.com. Contact: (general) Mrs. Sally Spyker, Manager; (Sales & Frequency Manager) Hans Johnson; (technical) Fred W. Wise, Technical Director; or John H. Norris, Owner. Return postage helpful outside United States. No giveaways or items for sale.

WJIE Shortwave, P.O. Box 197309, Louisville KY 40259 USA. Phone: +1 (502) 968-1220. Fax: +1 (502) 964 3304. Email: wjiesw@hotmail.com; (Rumsey) doug@wjie.org (put "WJIE International Shortwave" in the Subject line); (Freeman, technical) morgan@wjie.org. Web: (includes streaming audio) www.wjiesw.com. Contact: Morgan Freeman; or Doug Rumsey.

WMLK—Assemblies of Yahweh, 190 Frantz Road, P.O. Box C, Bethel PA 19507 USA. Phone: +1 (717) 933-4518, +1 (717) 933-4880; (toll-free, U.S. only) 1-800-523-3827. Email: (general) aoy@wmlkradio.net; (technical) technician@wmlkradio.net; (Elder Meyer) jacobmeyer@wmlkradio.net; (McAvin) garymcavin@wmlkradio.net. Web: http://wmlkradio.net. Contact: (general) Elder Jacob O. Meyer, Manager and Producer of "The Open Door to the Living World"; (technical) Gary McAvin, Operating Engineer. Free stickers, *The Sacred Name Broadcaster* monthly magazine, and other religious material. Bibles, audio and video (VHS) tapes and religious paperback books offered. Enclosing return postage ($1 or IRCs) helps speed things up.

World Harvest Radio, LeSEA Broadcasting, 61300 Ironwood Road, South Bend IN 46614 USA. Phone: +1 (219) 291-8200. Fax: +1 (219) 291 9043. Email: (general) whr@lesea.com; (Sarkisian) lsarkisian@lesea.com. Web: (includes streaming audio and online reception report form) www.whr.org; (LeSEA Broadcasting parent organization, includes streaming audio) www.lesea.com. Contact: (technical) Lori Sarkisian. World Harvest Radio T-shirts available. Return postage appreciated.
ENGINEERING DEPARTMENT: P.O. Box 50450, Indianapolis, IN 46250 USA.

WRMI—Radio Miami International, 175 Fontainebleau Blvd., Suite 1N4, Miami FL 33172 USA. Phone: +1 (305) 559-9764. Fax: +1 (305) 559 8186. Email: info@wrmi.net. Web: (includes streaming audio) www.wrmi.net. Contact: (technical and nontechnical) Jeff White, General Manager/Sales Manager. Free station stickers and tourist brochures. Sells "public access" airtime to nearly anyone to say virtually anything for $1 per minute.

WRNO WORLDWIDE (when operating)
TRANSMITTER SITE: 4539 I-10 Service Road North, Metairie LA 70006 USA. Web: www.wrnoworldwide.org.
GOOD NEWS WORLDWIDE, PARENT ORGANIZATION: P.O. Box 895, Fort Worth TX 76101 USA. Phone: +1 (817) 850-9990. Fax: +1 (817) 850 9994. Email: hope@goodnewsworld.org. Web: www.goodnewsworld.org.

WTJC—*see* Fundamental Broadcasting Network.

WWBS (if reactivated), P.O. Box 18174. Macon GA 31209 USA. Phone: +1 (912) 477-3433. Email: wwbsradio@aol.com. Contact: Joanne Josey. Return postage required for postal reply.

WWCR—World Wide Christian Radio, F.W. Robbert Broadcasting Co., 1300 WWCR Avenue, Nashville TN 37218 USA. Phone: (general) +1 (615) 255-1300. Fax: +1 (615) 255 1311.

Email: (general) wwcr@wwcr.com; ("Ask WWCR" program) askwwcr@wwcr.com. Web: www.wwcr.com. Contact: (administration) George McClintock, K4BTY, General Manager; Adam W. Lock, Sr., WA2JAL, Head of Operations; or Dawn Keen, Program Director; (technical) William Hair, Chief Engineer. Free program guides, updated monthly. Return postage helpful. For items sold on the air and tapes of programs, contact the producers of the programs, and *not* WWCR. Replies as time permits. Carries programs from various political organizations, which may be contacted directly.

WWRB—World Wide Religious Broadcasters, c/o Airline Transport Communications, Box 7, Manchester TN 37349-0007 USA. Phone/Fax: +1 (931) 841-0492. Email: (general) online form; (Dave Frantz) dfrantz@tennessee.com. Web: www.wwrb. org. Contact: Dave Frantz, Chief Engineer; or Angela Frantz. Verifies reception reports with a large certificate and automatic membership of the WWRB Shortwave Listener's Club. Does not accept email reports.

WWV/WWVB (official time and frequency stations): NIST Radio Station WWV, 2000 East County Road #58, Ft. Collins CO 80524 USA. Phone: +1 (303) 497-3914. Fax: +1 (303) 497 4063. Email: (general) nist.radio@boulder.nist.gov; (Deutch) deutch@boulder.nist.gov. Web: http://tf.nist.gov/timefreq/ stations/wwv.html. Contact: Matthew J. ("Matt") Deutch, Engineer-In-Charge. Along with branch sister station WWVH in Hawaii (*see* below), WWV and WWVB are the official time and frequency stations of the United States, operating over longwave (WWVB) on 60 kHz, and over shortwave (WWV) on 2500, 5000, 10000, 15000 and 20000 kHz.

PARENT ORGANIZATION: National Institute of Standards and Technology, Time and Frequency Division, 325 Broadway, Boulder CO 80305-3328 USA. Phone: +1 (303) 497-5453. Fax: +1 303-497-6461. Email: (Lowe) lowe@boulder.nist.gov. Contact: John P. Lowe, Group Leader.

WWVH (official time and frequency station): NIST Radio Station WWVH, P.O. Box 417, Kekaha, Kauai HI 96752 USA. Phone: +1 (808) 335-4361; (live audio) +1 (808) 335 4363; (Automated Computer Time Service) +1 (808) 335 4721. Fax: +1 (808) 335 4747. Email: (general) wwvh@boulder.nist.gov; (Okayama) okayama@boulder.nist.gov. Web: http://tf.nist.gov/stations/ wwvh.htm. Contact: Dean T. Okayama, Engineer-in-Charge. Along with sister stations WWV and WWVB (*see* preceding), WWVH is the official time and frequency station of the United States, operating on 2500, 5000, 10000 and 15000 kHz.

WYFR—Family Radio—*see* Family Radio Worldwide.

UZBEKISTAN   World Time +5

Radio Tashkent International, Khorazm Street 49, Tashkent 700047, Uzbekistan. Phone: +998 (71) 133-3894, +998 (71) 113-3038; (Chief Editor, English and German Services) +998 (71) 113-3133; (Head of English Department) +998 (71) 113-3185; (Head of German Department) +998 (71) 113-3184. Fax: +998 (71) 133 6068. Email: ino@uzpak.uz. Web: http://ino. uzpak.uz. Contact: Sherzod Guliamov, Director; Mirtuichi Agzamov, Head of English Department; Erkin Holboyev, Head of German Department; Ms. Nargiza Kamilova, Chief Editor, English and German Services; Mrs Gulya Bosacova, Correspondence Section. Correspondence is welcomed in English, German, Russian, Uzbek and nine other languages broadcast by the station. Reception reports are verified with colorful QSL cards. Free pennants, badges, wallet calendars and postcards. Has quizzes from time to time with prizes and souvenirs. Books in English by Uzbek writers are sometimes available for pur-

chase. Station offers free membership to the "Salum Aleikum Listeners' Club" for regular listeners.

VANUATU   World Time +12 (+11 midyear)

Radio Vanuatu, Information and Public Relations, Private Mail Bag 049, Port Vila, Vanuatu. Phone: +678 22999 or +678 23026. Fax: +678 22026. Contact: Maxwell E. Maltok, General Manager; Ambong Thompson, Head of Programmes; or Allan Kalfabun, Sales and Marketing Consultant, who is interested in exchanging letters and souvenirs from other countries; (technical) K.J. Page, Principal Engineer; or Willie Daniel, Technician.

VATICAN CITY STATE   World Time +1 (+2 midyear)

☞**Radio Vaticana (Vatican Radio)**

MAIN AND PROMOTION OFFICES: 00120 Città del Vaticano, Vatican City State. Phone: (general) +39 (06) 6988-3551; (Director General) +39 (06) 6988-3945; (Programme Director) +39 (06) 6988-3996; (Publicity and Promotion Department) +39 (06) 6988-3045; (technical, general) +39 (06) 6988-4897; (frequency management) +39 (06) 6988-5258. Fax: (general) +39 (06) 6988 4565; (frequency management) +39 (06) 6988 5062. Email: sedoc@vatiradio.va; (Director General) dirgen@vatiradio.va; (frequency management) mc6790@mclink. it; or gestfreq@vatiradio.va; (technical direction, general) sectec@vatiradio.va; (Programme Director) dirpro@vatiradio. va; (Publicity and Promotion Department) promo@vatiradio. va; (English Section) englishpr@vatiradio.va; (French Section) magfra@vatiradio.va; (German Section) deutsch@vatiradio. va; (Japanese Section) japan@vatiradio.va. Web: (includes on-demand and streaming audio) www.vatican.va/news ser-vices/radio; (includes on-demand and streaming audio) www. vaticanradio.org. Contact: (general) Elisabetta Vitalini Sacconi, Promotion Office and schedules; Eileen O'Neill, Head of Program Development, English Service; Fr. Lech Rynkiewicz S.J., Head of Promotion Office; Fr. Federico Lombardi, S.J., Program Director; Dr. Giacomo Ghisani, Head of International Relations; Sean Patrick Lovett, Head of English Service; or Veronica Sca-risbrick, Producer, "On the Air;" (administration) Fr. Pasquale Borgomeo, S.J., Director General; (technical) Sergio Salvatori, Assistant Frequency Manager, Direzione Tecnica; Dr. Alberto Gasbarri, Technical Director; or Giovanni Serra, Frequency Management Department. Correspondence sought on religious and programming matters, rather than the technical minutiae of radio. Free station stickers and paper pennants.

INDIA OFFICE: Loyola College, P.B. No 3301, Chennai-600 03, India. Fax: +91 (44) 2825 7340. Email: (Tamil) tamil@vatiradio. va; (Hindi) hindi@vatiradio.va; (English) india@vatiradio.va.

REGIONAL OFFICE, INDIA: Pastoral Orientation Centre, P.B. No 2251, Palarivattom, India. Fax: +91 (484) 2336 227. Email: (Malayalam) malayalam@vatiradio.va.

JAPAN OFFICE: 2-10-10 Shiomi, Koto-ku, Tokyo 135, Japan. Fax: +81 (3) 5632 4457.

VENEZUELA   World Time −4

Ecos del Torbes (if reactivated), Apartado 152, San Cristóbal 5001-A, Táchira, Venezuela. Phone: (general) +58 (276) 341-4189. Contact: (general) Lic. Dinorah González Zerpa, Gerente; Simón Zaidman Krenter; (technical) Ing. Iván Escobar S., Jefe Técnico.

Observatorio Cagigal—YVTO (when operating), Apartado 6745, Armada 84-DHN, Caracas 103, Venezuela. Phone: +58

In Binh Hien, Vietnam, weaving is done in the traditional manner—right down to the use of shuttles. M. Richer

(212) 481-2761. Email: armdhn@ven.net. Contact: Jesús Alberto Escalona, Director Técnico; or Gregorio Pérez Moreno, Director. $1 or return postage helpful.

Radio Amazonas, Av. Simón Bolívar 4, Puerto Ayacucho 7101, Amazonas, Venezuela. Contact: Angel María Pérez, Propietario.

ADDRESS FOR RECEPTION REPORTS: Sr. Jorge García Rangel, Radio Amazonas QSL Manager, Calle Roma, Qta: Costa Rica No. A-16, Urbanización Alto Barinas, Barinas 5201, Venezuela. Two IRC's or $2 required.

Radio Nacional de Venezuela - Antena Internacional, Final Calle Las Marías, El Pedregal de Chapellín, 1050 Caracas, Venezuela. If this fails, try: Director de la Onda Corta, Apartado Postal 3979, Caracas 1010-A, Venezuela. Phone: +58 (212) 730-6022, +58 (212) 730-6666. Fax: +58 (212) 731 1457 Email: ondacortavenezuela@hotmail.com. Web: (includes streaming audio from domestic services not on shortwave) www.rnv.gov.ve. Contact: Ali Méndez Martínez, periodista y representativo de onda corta; or José Luis Noguera, Director. Currently broadcasts via the transmission facilities of Radio Habana Cuba. "Antena Internacional" is also aired at 0600-0700 World Time on mediumwave AM via Radio Nacional's domestic "Canal Informativo," available in streaming audio at the RNV Website.

Radio Táchira (when operating), Apartado 152, San Cristóbal 5001-A, Táchira, Venezuela. Phone: +58 (276) 356-7444, +58 (276) 355-0560. Contact: Desirée González Zerpa, Directora; Sra. Albertina, Secretaria; or Eleázar Silva Malavé, Gerente.

Radio Valera (if reactivated), Av. 10 No. 9-31, Valera 3102, Trujillo, Venezuela. Phone: +58 (271) 225-3978. Contact: Gladys Barroeta; or Mariela Leal. Replies to correspondence in Spanish. Return postage required.

VIETNAM   World Time +7

NOTE: Reception reports on Vietnamese regional stations should be sent to the Voice of Vietnam Overseas Service *(see)*.

Voice of Vietnam—Domestic Service (Đài Tiếng Nói Việt Nam, TNVN)—Addresses and contact numbers as for all sections of Voice of Vietnam—Overseas Service, below. Contact: Phan Quang, Director General.

Voice of Vietnam—Overseas Service

TRANSMISSION FACILITY (MAIN ADDRESS FOR NONTECHNICAL CORRESPONDENCE AND GENERAL VERIFICATIONS): 58 Quán Sú, Hànôi, Vietnam. Phone: +84 (4) 824-0044. Fax: +84 (4) 826 1122. Email: qhqt.vov@hn.vnn.vn; rtc.vov@hn.vnn.vn or ktpt@hn.vnn.vn. Web: (English text) www.vov.org.vn/docs1/ english; (Vietnamese text and on-demand and streaming audio in English and Vietnamese) www.vov.org.vn. Contact: Ms. Hoang Minh Nguyet, Director of International Relations.

STUDIOS (NONTECHNICAL CORRESPONDENCE AND GENERAL VERIFICATIONS): 45 Ba Trieu Street, Hànôi, Vietnam. Phone: (director) +84 (4) 825-7870; (English service) +84 (4) 934-2456 or +84 (4) 825-4482; (newsroom) +84 (4) 825-5761 or +84 (4) 825-5862. Fax: (English service) +84 (4) 826 6707. Email: btdn.vov@hn.vnn.vn; (Spanish Service contact) tieng-noi_vietnam2004@yahoo.es. Contact: Ms. Nguyen Thi Hue, Director, Overseas Service. Voice of Vietnam Overseas Service broadcasts in 11 foreign languages, namely English, French, Japanese, Russian, Spanish, Mandarin, Cantonese, Indonesian, Lao, Thai, Khmer and Vietnamese for overseas Vietnamese.

TECHNICAL CORRESPONDENCE: Office of Radio Reception Quality, Central Department of Radio and Television Broadcast Engineering, Vietnam General Corporation of Posts and Telecommunications, Hànôi, Vietnam.

WESTERN SAHARA   World Time exactly

Radio Nacional de la República Arabe Saharaui Democrática, c/o Directeur d'Information, Frente Polisario, B.P. 10, El-Mouradia, 16000 Algiers, Algeria. Email: rasdradio@yahoo.es. Web: (includes recording made in the station's studios) http://web.jet.es/rasd/amateur4.htm. Email correspondence recommended, as postal service is unreliable. Pro-Polisario Front, and supported by the Algerian government. Operates from Rabuni, near Tindouf, on the Algerian side of the border with Western Sahara.

YEMEN   World Time +3

📻**Republic of Yemen Radio**, Ministry of Information, P.O. Box 2182, Sana'a-al Hasbah, Yemen; (alternative address, technical) Technical Department, P. O. Box 2371, Sana'a, Yemen. Phone: (general) +967 (1) 282-005; (Technical Department) +967 (1) 282-060/1. Fax: (general) +967 (1) 230 761; (Technical Department) +967 (1) 282 053. Email: yradio@y.net.ye, or hussein3itu@y.net.ye. Web: (includes on-demand audio) www.yradio.gov.ye. Contact: (general) English Service; (administration) Mohammed Dahwan, General Director of Sana'a Radio; (technical) Eng. Altashi Ali Ahmed, Technical Department Director.

ZAMBIA   World Time +2

📻**The Voice Africa**

STATION: Private Bag E606, Lusaka, Zambia. Phone: +260 (1) 274-251. Fax: +260 (1) 274 526. Email: cvoice@zamnet.zm. Web: (includes streaming audio) www.voiceafrica.net. Contact: Philip Haggar, Station Manager; Beatrice Phiri; or Lenganji Nanyangwe, Assistant to Station Manager. Free calendars and stickers; pens, as available. Free religious books and items under selected circumstances. Sells T-shirts and sundry other items. $1 or 2 IRCs appreciated for reply. Verifies reception reports. Broadcasts Christian teachings and music, as well as news and programs on farming, sport, education, health, business and children's affairs. Formerly known as Radio Christian Voice.

U. K. OFFICE: The Voice, P.O. Box 3040, West Bromwich, West Midlands, B70 0EJ, United Kingdom. Phone:+44 (121) 224-1614. Fax: +44 (121) 224 1613. Email: feedback@voiceafrica.net; (Joynes) sandra@voiceafrica.net. Contact: Sandra Joynes, Office Administrator.

Radio Zambia, Mass Media Complex, Alick Nkhata Road, P.O. Box 50015, Lusaka 10101, Zambia. Phone: (general) +260 (1) 254-989, +260 (1) 253-301 or +260 (1) 252-005; (Public Relations) +260 (1) 254-989, X-216; (engineering) +260 (1) 250-380. Fax: +260 (1) 254 317 or +260 (1) 254 013. Email: (general, including reception reports) znbc@microlink.zm. Web: www.znbc.co.zm; (streaming audio) www.coppernct.zm/home.html. Contact: (general) Keith M. Nalumango, Director of Programmes; or Lawson Chishimba, Public Relations Manager; (administration) Duncan H. Mbazima, Director-General; (technical) James M. Phiri, Director of Engineering. Free *Zamwaves* newsletter. Sometimes gives away stickers, postcards and small publications. $1 required, and postal correspondence should be sent via registered mail. Tours given of the station Tuesdays to Fridays between 9:00 AM and noon local time; inquire in advance. Used to reply slowly and irregularly, but seems to be better now.

ZIMBABWE   World Time +2

Radio Voice of the People, P.O. Box 5750, Harare, Zimbabwe. Phone: +263 (4) 707-123, +263 (91) 913-560. Email: voxpopzim@yahoo.co.uk, or voxpop@ecoweb.co.zw. Web: www.vopradio.co.zw. Contact: John Masuku, Executive Director. Airs via Radio Nederland facilities in Madagascar.

Radio VOP—*see* Radio Voice of the People, above.

📻**Zimbabwe Broadcasting Corporation**, Broadcasting Center, Pockets Hill, P.O. Box HG444, Highlands, Harare, Zimbabwe. Phone: +263 (4) 498-610, +263 (4) 498-630; (Guinea Fowl Shortwave Transmitting Station) +263 (54) 22-104. Fax: +263 (4) 498 613. Email: zbc@zbc.co.zw; (general enquiries) pr@zbc.co.zw; (engineering) hbt@zbc.co.zw. Web: (includes streaming audio) www.zbc.co.zw. Contact: (general) Rugare Sangomoyo; or Lydia Muzenda; (administration) Alum Mpofu, Chief Executive Officer; (news details) Munyaradzi Hwengwere; (Broadcasting Technology, Engineering) Craig Matambo. $1 helpful.

CREDITS: Craig Tyson (Australia), Editor, with Tony Jones (Paraguay). Special thanks to Gabriel Iván Barrera (Argentina), Dino Bloise (USA), Héctor García Bojorge (Mexico). David Crystal (Israel), Graeme Dixon (New Zealand), Jose Jacob (India), Marie Lamb (USA), Grant Murray (Canada), Gary Neal (USA), Fotios Padazopulos (USA), George Poppin (USA), T.R. Rajeesh (India), Paulo Roberto e Souza (Brazil) and Célio Romais (Brazil); also the following organizations for their support and cooperation: Conexión Digital and RUS-DX/Anatoly Klepov (Russia).

Worldwide Broadcasts in English— 2006

Country-by-Country Guide to Best-Heard Stations

Dozens of countries reach out in English, and here are the times and frequencies to hear them. If you want to know which shows are on hour-by-hour, check out "What's On Tonight."

•**When and where:** "Best Times and Frequencies," earlier in this edition, pinpoints where each world band segment is found and gives tuning tips. Best is late afternoon and evening, when most programs are beamed your way. Tune world band segments within the 5730-10000 kHz range in winter, 5730-15800 kHz during summer. Around breakfast, you can also explore segments within the 5730-17900 kHz range for fewer but intriguing catches.

•**Strongest (and weakest) frequencies:** Frequencies shown in italics—

say, *5965* kHz—tend to be best, as they are from relay transmitters that may be located near you. However, other frequencies beamed your way might do almost as well. Some signals not beamed to you can also be heard, especially when they are targeted to nearby parts of the world. Frequencies with no target zones are typically for domestic coverage, so they are unlikely to be heard unless you're in or near that country.

Program Times

Times and days of the week are in World Time, explained in "Setting Your World Time Clock" and PASSPORT's glossary; for local times in each country, see "Addresses PLUS." Midyear, some stations are an hour earlier (▣) or later (▣) because of daylight saving/summer time. Those used only seasonally are labeled ▣ for summer (midyear, typically the last Sunday in March until the last Sunday in October) and ▣ for winter. Stations may also extend their hours of transmission, or air special programs, for national holidays, emergencies or sports events.

> **Signals not beamed to you can also be heard.**

Indigenous Music

Broadcasts in other than English? Turn to the next section, "Voices from Home," or the Blue Pages. Keep in mind that stations for kinsfolk abroad sometimes carry delightful chunks of native music. They make for enjoyable listening, regardless of language.

Schedules for Entire Year

To be as useful as possible over the months to come, PASSPORT's schedules consist not just of observed activity, but also that which we have creatively opined will take place during the forthcoming year. This predictive material is based on decades of experience and is original from us. Although inherently not as exact as real-time data, over the years it's been of tangible value to PASSPORT readers.

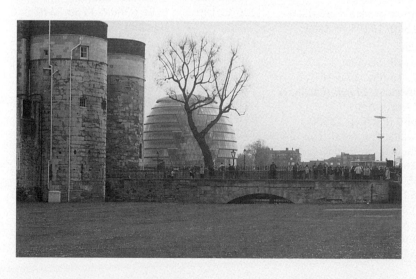

Two silos and a beehive? Holy Henry's hatchet!— it's the Tower of London and City Hall. M. Wright

ALBANIA

RADIO TIRANA
0245-0300 &	
0330-0400 ▣	Tu-Su 6115 & Tu-Su 7455/7160 (E North Am)
1845-1900	🅂 M-Sa 6115 (W Europe)
1945-2000 ▣	M-Sa 7210 (W Europe)
1945-2000	🅆 M-Sa 7180 (W Europe)
2130-2200	🅂 M-Sa 7120 (W Europe)
2230-2300	🅆 M-Sa 7110 (W Europe)

ARGENTINA

RADIO ARGENTINA AL EXTERIOR-RAE
0200-0300	Tu-Sa 11710 (Americas)
1800-1900	M-F 9690 (Europe & N Africa), M-F 15345 (Europe)

ARMENIA

VOICE OF ARMENIA
1825-1845	🅂 9775 (Europe)
1925-1945 ▣	M-Sa 4810 (E Europe, Mideast & W Asia)
1925-1945	🅆 9965 (Europe)

AUSTRALIA

Christian Vision Communications
0100-0300	*7355* (S Asia)
0300-0600	*13685* (S Asia)
0515-1545	*9555* (S Africa)
0600-0900	15335 (S Asia & SE Asia)
0900-1100	11955 (SE Asia)
1000-1400	13685 (E Asia)
1100-1800	13635 (S Asia & SE Asia)
1400-1800	11840/15205 (E Asia)

RADIO AUSTRALIA
0000-0130	17775 (SE Asia)
0000-0200	17715 (Pacific & N America), 17795 (Pacific & W North Am)
0000-0800	9660 (Pacific), 13630 (Pacific & E Asia), 15240 (Pacific)
0000-0900	12080 (S Pacific), 17750 (SE Asia)
0030-0400	15415 (SE Asia)
0200-0500	21725 (E Asia)
0200-0700	15515 (Pacific & N America)
0430-0500	15415 (SE Asia)
0500-0800	15160 (Pacific & N America)
0530-0800	15415 (SE Asia)
0700-0900	13630 (Pacific & W North Am)
0800-0830	Sa/Su *11550* & Sa/Su 15415 (SE Asia)
0800-0900	5995 & 9710 (Pacific)
0800-1130	*15240* (E Asia)
0800-1400	9580 (Pacific & N America)
0800-1600	9590 (Pacific & W North Am)
0830-0900	15415 (SE Asia)
0900-0930	Sa/Su *11550* & Sa/Su 15415 (SE Asia)
0900-1300	11880 (SE Asia)
0930-1100	15415 (SE Asia)
1100-1200	12080 (S Pacific)
1100-1300	9475 (SE Asia)
1100-1400	5995 (Pacific), 6020 (Pacific & W North Am), 9560 (E Asia & Pacific)
1400-1600	🅂 9625 & 🅆 11750 (SE Asia)
1400-1700	7240 (Pacific & W North Am)
1400-1800	5995 (Pacific & W North Am), 6080 (SE Asia)
1430-1700	11660 (SE Asia)
1430-1900	9475 (SE Asia)
1600-2000	9710 (Pacific)
1700-2100	9580 (Pacific), 11880 (Pacific & W North Am)
1800-2000	6080 (Pacific & E Asia), 7240 (Pacific)
1900-2130	9500 (SE Asia)
2000-2100	F/Sa 6080 & F/Sa 7240 (Pacific)
2000-2200	11650 & 11660 (Pacific & W North Am), 12080 (S Pacific)
2100-2130	11695 (SE Asia)
2100-2200	9660 (Pacific)
2100-2300	13630 & 15515 (Pacific)
2200-2330	*15240* (E Asia)
2200-2400	13620 (SE Asia), 15230 (Pacific), 17785/21740 (Pacific & N America)
2300-2400	9660 (Pacific), 12080 (S Pacific), 13630 (Pacific & E Asia), 17795 (Pacific & W North Am)
2330-2400	15415 & 17750 (SE Asia)

ORF-Funkhaus, global headquarters for Austrian Radio in Vienna.

T. Ohtake

AUSTRIA

RADIO AUSTRIA INTERNATIONAL
0005-0015	■ Su/M 7325 (C America)
0015-0030	■ 7325 (C America)
0035-0045	■ Su/M 7325 (E North Am)
0045-0100	■ 7325 (E North Am)
0105-0115	■ Su/M 9870 (C America)
0115-0130	■ 9870 (C America)
0135-0145	■ Su/M 9870 (E North Am)
0145-0200	■ 9870 (E North Am)
0605-0630 &	
0635-0700 ■	Su 17870 (Mideast)
1205-1220	■ M 17715 (S Asia, SE Asia & Australasia)
1205-1230 &	
1235-1300	■ Sa/Su 17715 (S Asia, SE Asia & Australasia)
1245-1300	■ Tu-F 17715 (S Asia, SE Asia & Australasia)
1305-1320 ■	M 6155 & M 13730 (Europe)
1305-1320	■ M 17855 (S Asia, SE Asia & Australasia)
1305-1330 ■	Sa/Su 6155 & Sa/Su 13730 (Europe)
1315-1330 ■	Tu-F 6155 & Tu-F 13730 (Europe)
1315-1330	■ Tu-F 17855 (S Asia, SE Asia & Australasia)
1335-1345	■ Sa/Su 17855 (S Asia, SE Asia & Australasia)
1335-1355 ■	Sa/Su 6155 (Europe)
1335-1400 ■	Sa/Su 13730 (Europe)
1345-1400 ■	M-F 6155 & M-F 13730 (Europe)
1345-1400	■ 17855 (S Asia, SE Asia & Australasia)
1505-1520	■ *13775* (W North Am)
1520-1530 &	
1535-1545	■ Sa/Su *13775* (W North Am)
1545-1600	■ M-F *13775* (W North Am)
1605-1620	■ *13675* (W North Am)
1620-1630 &	
1635-1645	■ Sa/Su *13675* (W North Am)
1645-1700	■ *13675* (W North Am)
2335-2345 ■	Sa/Su 9870 (S America)
2345-2400	9870 (S America)

BANGLADESH

BANGLADESH BETAR
1230-1300	7185 (SE Asia)
1745-1815 &	
1815-1900	7185 (Europe)

BELARUS

RADIO BELARUS—(W Europe)
0200-0230	■ M-W/F/Sa 6170
0230-0300	■ Su 6170
0300-0330 ■	M-W/F/Sa 5970 & M-W/F/Sa 7210

0300-0330	W M-W/F/Sa 6155
0330-0400 ▣	Su 5970 & Su 7210
0330-0400	W Su 6155
1930-2000	S M/Tu/Th/F 7280 & S M/Tu/Th/F 7290
2030-2100 ▣	M/Tu/Th/F 7105
2030-2100	W M/Tu/Th/F 7340 & W M/Tu/Th/F 7440
2100-2130	S Su 7280 & S Su 7290
2200-2230 ▣	Su 7105
2200-2230	W Su 7340 & W Su 7440

BULGARIA
RADIO BULGARIA

0000-0100	W 7400 & W 9700 (E North Am)
0200-0300	S 9700 & S 11700 (E North Am)
0300-0400	W 7400 & W 9700 (E North Am)
0630-0700	S 11600 & S 13600 (W Europe)
0730-0800	W 9500 & W 11500 (W Europe)
1230-1300 ▣	11700 & 15700 (W Europe)
1730-1800	S 9500 & S 11500 (W Europe)
1830-1900	W 5800 & W 7500 (W Europe)
2200-2300 ▣	5800 & 7500 (W Europe)
2300-2400	S 9700 & S 11700 (E North Am)

CANADA
CANADIAN BROADCASTING CORP—(E North Am)

0000-0300 ▣	Su 9625
0200-0300 ▣	Tu-Sa 9625
0300-0310 &	
0330-0609 ▣	M 9625
0400-0609 ▣	Su 9625
0500-0609 ▣	Tu-Sa 9625
1200-1255 ▣	M-F 9625
1200-1505 ▣	Sa 9625
1200-1700 ▣	Su 9625
1600-1615 &	
1700-1805 ▣	Sa 9625
1800-2400 ▣	Su 9625
1945-2015,	
2200-2225 &	
2240-2330 ▣	M-F 9625

CFRX-CFRB, Toronto—(E North Am)

24 Hr	6070

CKZN, Newfoundland—(E North Am)

24 Hr	6160

CKZU-CBU, Vancouver—(W North Am)

24 Hr	6160

RADIO CANADA INTERNATIONAL

0000-0100	S 9690 (E Asia & SE Asia), W 9880 (SE Asia)
0000-0200	S 13710 (W North Am)
0030-0200	S 11990 (S America)
1200-1300	W 7105 (E Asia)
1200-1330	S 9660 (E Asia), W 9665 (SE Asia), S 15170 (E Asia & SE Asia)
1300-1330	W 9725 (E Asia)
1300-1600	S 17800 (C America)
1400-1700 ▣	9515 & 13655 (E North Am & C America)
1400-1700	W 17820 (C America)
1500-1600	W 9635, S 11675, W 11975, S 15360 & S 17720 (S Asia)
1800-1900	W 5850, W 7185, S 9530, W 9770 & S 9780 (E Africa), W 11875 (C Africa & E Africa), S 13730 (C Africa & S Africa), S 15255 (W Africa), S 15420 (E Africa & S Africa), W 17740 (W Africa & C Africa)
1900-2200	S 17765 (C America)
2000-2100	S 11765 (Europe & Mideast), S 15325 (W Europe)
2000-2300	W 15180 (C America)
2100-2200 ▣	5850 (W Europe)
2100-2200	W 9770 (W Europe)
2230-2300	W 6160 (E Asia), W 7195, S 9525 & W 9730 (E Asia & SE Asia), S 9870 (E Asia), S 12035 (E Asia & SE Asia)
2300-2400	W 6100 (E North Am & C America)

CHINA
CHINA RADIO INTERNATIONAL

0000-0100	W 5975, 7180 & S 9515 (S Asia)
0000-0200	6020 (N America), W 7345 (Europe), 9570 (N America), S 13600 (Europe)

0000-0400	**S** 5915 (S Asia)
0100-0200	**W** 6005 (W North Am), 6080 (N America), 9580 (E North Am), **S** 9790 (W North Am), **S** 13640 (S Asia)
0100-0400	**S** 11870 (S Asia)
0200-0300	13640 (S Asia)
0200-0400	**W** 11770 (S Asia)
0300-0400	9690 (N America & C America), 9790 (W North Am), 15110 (S Asia)
0400-0500	**W** 6190 & 9755 (W North Am)
0400-0600	**S** 6090 & **S** 9560 (W North Am)
0500-0600	**W** 5960 (N America), 6190 (W North Am), **W** 7220 (N Africa)
0500-0700	**S** 9590 & **S** 11710 (N Africa), 17505 (N Africa & W Africa)
0500-0900	**W** 11880, 15350, 15465 & 17540 (S Asia)
0600-0700	**W** 6115 (W North Am), **W** 11750 (N Africa), **S** 11870 & **S** 13620 (S Asia)
0600-0800	**S** 17490 (Europe)
0700-0900	**W** 11855 & **S** 13710 (W Europe)
0800-1300	17490 (Europe)
0900-1100	15210 & 17690 (Australasia)
1000-1200	**S** 6040 (E North Am)
1100-1200	**W** 5960 (E North Am), **S** 11750 (W North Am)
1100-1300	**S** 13650 & **W** 13665 (W Europe)
1200-1300	9730 (SE Asia), **S** 9760 & **W** 15415 (Australasia)
1200-1400	11760 (Australasia), 11980 (SE Asia), 13790 (Europe)
1300-1400	9570 (E North Am), **S** 9650 (E North Am & C America), **W** 11885 (W North Am), 11900 (Australasia), **S** 15260 (E North Am & C America), 17625 (S America)
1300-1500	**W** 13610 (Europe), **W** 15230 (E North Am & C America)
1300-1700	**S** 17490 (W Europe)
1400-1500	9560 (SE Asia), **S** 9560 (S Asia), **W** 9700 & **W** 9795 (Europe), 11675 & 11765 (S Asia), **W** 13675 (W North Am), **S** 13790 & **S** 17650 (Europe)
1400-1600	11775 (S Asia), 13685 (E Africa), 13740 (W North Am), 17630 (C Africa)
1500-1600	**W** 7160 & 9785 (S Asia), **S** 13640 (Europe), **W** 13675 (W North Am)
1500-1700	**W** 9435, **W** 9525 & **S** 11965 (Europe)
1500-1800	6100 (S Africa)
1600-1800	**W** 7255 (Europe), 9570 (E Africa & S Africa), 11900 (S Africa)
1600-1900	**S** 13760 (Europe)
1600-2000	**S** 11940 (Europe)
1700-1800	**W** 6100 (Europe)
1700-1900	**S** 9695 (Europe)
1800-2000	**W** 6160 (Europe)
1900-2100	7295 (Mideast & N Africa), 9440 (Mideast, W Africa & C Africa)
2000-2130	11640 (E Africa & S Africa), 13630 (E Africa)
2000-2200	5960 (W Europe), 7190 (Europe), 7285 (W Europe), 9600 (Europe), **S** 9800 (W Europe), **S** 11790 (Europe)
2200-2300	**W** 7170 & **S** 7175 (N Europe)
2300-2400	**S** 5915 & **W** 5975 (S Asia), 5990 (C America), **W** 6040 & **S** 6145 (E North Am), 7180 (S Asia), **W** 11970 & **S** 13680 (W North Am)

CHINA (TAIWAN)
RADIO TAIWAN INTERNATIONAL

0200-0300	5950 (E North Am), 9680 (N America), 11875 (SE Asia), 15465 (E Asia)
0300-0400	5950 (W North Am), 15215 (S America), 15320 (SE Asia)
0700-0800	5950 (W North Am)
0800-0900	9610 (SE Asia & Australasia)
1100-1200	7445 (SE Asia)
1200-1300	7130 (E Asia)
1400-1500	15265 (SE Asia)

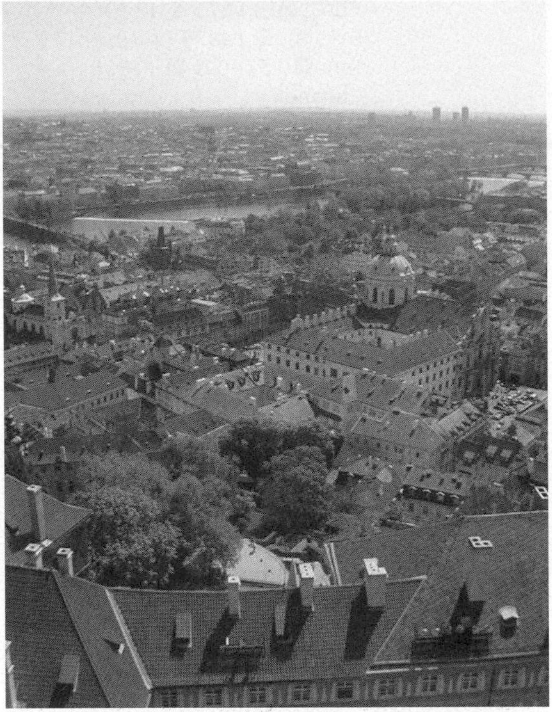

Prague's traditional architecture and plentiful trees endear visitors and residents. T. Ohtake

1600-1700	11815 (E Asia & S Asia)
1800-1900	*3965* (W Europe)
2200-2300	[W] *9355* & [S] *15600* (Europe)

CROATIA

VOICE OF CROATIA

0200-0215	[S] *9925* (N America & S America)
0300-0315	[W] *7285* (N America & S America)
2215-2230	[S] *9925* (S America)
2315-2330	[W] *7285* (S America)

CUBA

RADIO HABANA CUBA

0000-0100	9550 (C America)
0100-0500	6000 (E North Am), 9820 (N America)
0500-0700	6000 (E North Am), 6060 (C America), 9550 (W North Am), 11760 (Americas)
2030-2130	11760 (E North Am)
2300-2400	9550 (C America)

CZECH REPUBLIC

RADIO PRAGUE

0000-0030	[S] 7345 (E North Am & C America), [S] 9440 (N America & C America)
0100-0130	6200 & 7345 (N America & C America)
0200-0230	[W] 6200 & [W] 7345 (N America & C America)
0300-0330	[S] 7345 (N America & C America), [S] 9870 (W North Am & C America)
0330-0400	[S] 9445 (Mideast & E Africa), [S] 11600 (Mideast & S Asia)
0400-0430	[W] 6200 (W North Am & C America), [W] 7345 (N America & C America)
0430-0500	[W] 9885 (Mideast), [W] 11600 (Mideast & S Asia)
0700-0730	[S] 9880 & [S] 11600 (W Europe)
0800-0830	[W] 7345 & [W] 9860 (W Europe)
0900-0930	[S] 21745 (S Asia & W Africa)
1000-1030	[W] 21745 (S Asia & W Africa)
1030-1100	[S] 9880 & [S] 11615 (N Europe)
1130-1200	[W] 11640 (N Europe), [W] 21745 (E Africa & Mideast)
1300-1330	[S] 13580 (N Europe), [S] 21745 (E Africa)
1400-1430	[W] 11600 (S Asia), [W] 21745 (N America)
1600-1630	[S] 17485 (E Africa)
1700-1730 ⬅	5930 (W Europe)
1700-1730	[W] 15710 (W Africa & C Africa), [S] 17485 (C Africa)
1800-1830 ⬅	5930 (W Europe)
1800-1830	[W] 9400 (Asia & Australasia)
2000-2030	[S] 11600 (SE Asia & Australasia)
2100-2130 ⬅	5930 (W Europe)
2100-2130	[W] 9430 (SE Asia & Australasia)
2130-2200	[S] 9800 (W Africa & C Africa), [S] 11600 (N America)
2230-2300	[W] 5930 (N America), 7345 (E North Am & C America), [S] 9415 (N America)

2330-2400	◼W 5930 (N America), ◼W 7345 (E North Am & C America)

ECUADOR
HCJB-VOICE OF THE ANDES
1100-1330	12005 (Americas), 21455 USB (Europe & Australasia)

EGYPT
RADIO CAIRO
0000-0030	◼S 11885 & ◼W 11895 (N America)
0200-0330	7270/7260 (N America)
1215-1330	17835 (S Asia & SE Asia)
1630-1830	◼W 11785 & ◼S 11880 (S Africa)
2030-2200	15375 (W Africa)
2115-2245	9990 (Europe)
2300-2400	◼S 11885 & ◼W 11895 (N America)

ETHIOPIA
RADIO ETHIOPIA
1030-1100	M-F 5990, M-F 7110, M-F 9704
1600-1700	7165 & 9560 (E Africa)

FRANCE
RADIO FRANCE INTERNATIONALE
0400-0430	◼W M-F 7315, ◼W M-F 9555/11995 & ◼S M-F 9805/7315 (E Africa)
0500-0530	◼S M-F 9825, ◼W M-F 11850, ◼W M-F 11995/15155, ◼S M-F 11995 & ◼S M-F 15160/13680 (E Africa)
0600-0630	◼W M-F 9865 & ◼S M-F 11665 (W Africa), ◼W M-F 15155, ◼S M-F 15160 & M-F 17800 (E Africa)
0700-0800	◼W 11725 & ◼S 15605 (W Africa)
1200-1230	◼W 15275 & ◼S 17815 (W Africa), 21620 (E Africa)
1400-1500	7180/9580 (S Asia), ◼S 15615 & ◼W 17515 (Mideast)
1600-1700	◼S 7170 & ◼W 9730 (E Africa & S Africa), 11615 (N Africa), 15160 (W Africa & C Africa), ◼W 15365/17850 & ◼S 17850 (C Africa & S Africa)
1600-1730	◼W 11615 & ◼S 15605 (Mideast), ◼W 15605 & ◼S 17605 (E Africa)

GERMANY
DEUTSCHE WELLE
0000-0100	◼W 6030, ◼S 7130, ◼W 7290, ◼S 9505 & ◼S 9825 (S Asia)
0400-0500	◼W 6180 (E Africa), ◼S 7170 (C Africa), ◼S 9630 (E Africa), ◼W 9710 (C Africa), ◼S 11945 (E Africa), 15445 (C Africa & E Africa)
0500-0600	◼W 7285 (C Africa & S Africa), ◼W 9565 (C Africa & E Africa), ◼S 9630 (C Africa & S Africa), ◼S 9700 & ◼W 12035 (S Africa), ◼S 15410 (C Africa & E Africa), ◼W 15410 (E Africa, C Africa & S Africa), ◼S 17800 (E Africa & S Africa)
0600-0700	◼S 7170 & ◼W 7225 (W Africa), ◼W 11785 (W Africa & C Africa), ◼S 15275 (W Africa), ◼W 15440 & ◼S 17860 (W Africa & C Africa)
0600-1000 & 1300-1600	6140 (W Europe)
1600-1700	6170, ◼S 7225 & ◼W 9795 (S Asia), ◼W 11695 (S Asia, SE Asia & Australasia), ◼S 17595 (S Asia)
1900-2000	◼W 11865 & ◼W 12025 (C Africa & E Africa), ◼S 13780 (Mideast & E Africa), ◼W 15470, ◼S 15520 & ◼S 17770 (C Africa & E Africa)
2000-2100	◼W 6145 (C Africa & E Africa), ◼S 7130 (S Africa), ◼W 9735 (C Africa & E Africa), ◼W 9830 (W Africa & C Africa), ◼S 11895, ◼W 12025, ◼S 13780 & ◼S 15205 (C Africa & S Africa), ◼W 15410 (C Africa & E Africa)
2100-2200	◼W 7280 & ◼S 9440 (W Africa), ◼W 9615 (W Africa &

C Africa), ▪W *11690*, ▪S *11865* & ▪S *15205* (W Africa)
2200-2300	▪W *6180*, ▪S *7115* & ▪S *9720* (E Asia & SE Asia)
2300-2400	▪S *5955*, ▪W *6070*, ▪W *9555*, ▪W *9815*, ▪S *9890* & ▪S *15135* (SE Asia)

HUNGARY
RADIO BUDAPEST
0100-0130	▪S 9590 (N America)
0200-0230	▪W 9515 (N America)
0230-0300	▪S 9795 (N America)
0330-0400	▪W 9775 (N America)
1500-1530	▪S Su 9655 (N Europe)
1600-1630 ▪	Su 6025 (Europe)
1600-1630	▪W Su 9565 (N Europe)
2000-2030 ▪	3975 & 6025 (Europe)
2100-2130	▪S 9525 (S Africa)
2200-2230 ▪	6025 (Europe)
2200-2230	▪W 9735 (S Africa)

INDIA
ALL INDIA RADIO
0000-0045	9705 (SE Asia), 9950 (E Asia), 11620 (East & SE Asia), 11645 (E Asia), 13605 (E Asia & SE Asia 11830, 15135
1000-1100	13695/13710 (E Asia & Australasia), 15020 (E Asia), 15260 (S Asia), 15410/15235 (E Asia), 17510 (Australasia), 17800 (E Asia), 17895 (Australasia)
1330-1500	9690, 11620 & 13710 (SE Asia)
1745-1945	7410 (Europe), 9445 (W Africa), 9950 & 11620 (Europe), 11935 (E Africa), 13605 (W Africa), 15075 (E Africa), 15155 (W Africa), 17670 (E Africa)
2045-2230	7410 & 9445 (Europe), 9910 (Australasia), 9950 (Europe), 11620 & 11715 (Australasia)
2245-2400	9705 (SE Asia), 9950 (E Asia), 11620 (E & SE Asia), 11645 (E Asia), 13605 (E Asia & SE Asia)

IRAN
VOICE OF THE ISLAMIC REPUBLIC
0130-0230	▪W 6120, ▪S 9495, ▪W 9665 & ▪S 11875 (N America)
1030-1130	▪W 15460, ▪W 15480, ▪S 15600 & ▪S 17660 (S Asia)
1530-1630	▪W 7330, ▪S 9635, ▪W 9940 & ▪S 11650 (S Asia & SE Asia)
1930-2030	▪W 6010, ▪S 7205 & ▪W 7320 (Europe), ▪S 9800, ▪W 9855, ▪S 9925 & ▪W 11695 (S Africa), ▪S 11860 (Europe)

ISRAEL
KOL ISRAEL
0330-0345	▪S 9435 & ▪S 11590 (W Europe & E North Am)
0430-0445 ▪	17600/15640 (Australasia)
0430-0445	▪W 6280 & ▪W 7545 (W Europe & E North Am)
1030-1045 ▪	15640 (W Europe & E North Am), 17535 (W Europe & N America)
1730-1745	▪S 9345 (Europe), ▪S 15640 (W Europe & E North Am)
1830-1845	▪W 11585 & ▪W 11605 (W Europe & E North Am)
1900-1925	▪S 11590 (W Europe & E North Am), ▪S 15615 (S Africa), ▪S 15640 (W Europe & E North Am)
2000-2025	▪W 6280, ▪W 7520 & ▪W 9435 (W Europe & E North Am), ▪W 15640 (S Africa)

ITALY
RAI INTERNATIONAL
0055-0115	11800 (N America)
0445-0500	▪W 5965 (S Europe & N Africa), ▪S 6110 & ▪W 6120 (N Africa), ▪W 7170, ▪S 7235 & ▪S 9800 (S Europe & N Africa)
1935-1955	▪S 5960, ▪W 6035, ▪W 9760 & ▪S 9845 (W Europe)
2025-2045	▪W 6020, ▪S 6050 & 11875 (Mideast)
2205-2230	▪W 6000/6090 & ▪S 11895 (E Asia)

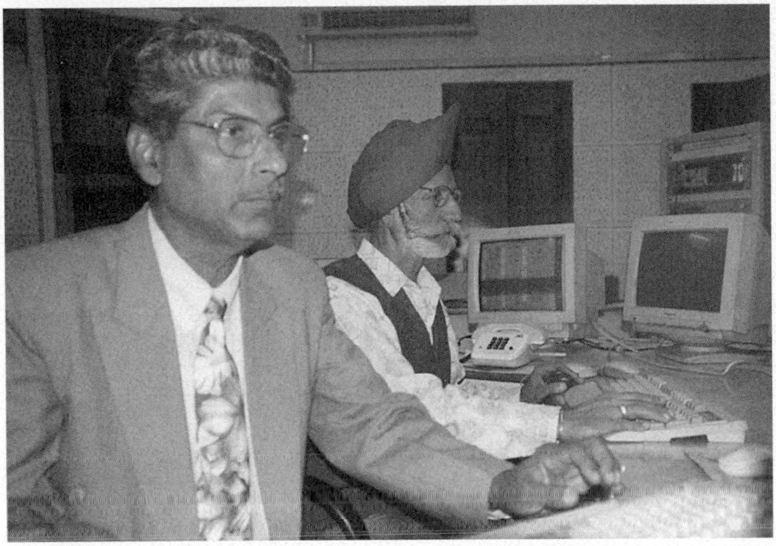

Experienced technicians help maintain All India Radio technical standards.

M. Guha

JAPAN

RADIO JAPAN

0000-0015	13650 & 17810 (SE Asia)
0000-0100	*6145* (E North Am)
0100-0200	[S] *5960* & [W] *6030* (Mideast), *11860* (SE Asia), *11935* (S America), 15325 (S Asia), 17560 (Mideast), 17685 (Australasia), 17810 (SE Asia), 17825 (W North Am & C America), 17845 (E Asia)
0300-0400	21610 (Australasia)
0500-0600	*5975* (W Europe), *6110* (W North Am), 17810 (SE Asia)
0500-0700	*7230* (Europe), 15195 (E Asia), 21755 (Australasia)
0600-0700	[W] 11690 (W North Am & C America), 11715 (E Asia), *11740* (SE Asia), 11760 (E Asia), [S] 13630 (W North Am & C America), 17870 (Pacific)
1000-1100	*17585* (Europe), *17720* (Mideast), 21755 (Australasia)
1000-1200	*6120* (E North Am), 9695 (SE Asia), 11730 (E Asia)
1400-1500	*11840* (Australasia)
1400-1600	7200 (SE Asia), [W] 9875 & [S] 11730 (S Asia)
1500-1600	6190 (E Asia), 9505 (W North Am & C America)
1700-1800	9535 (W North Am & C America), 11970 (Europe), *15355* (S Africa)
2100-2200	*6035* (Australasia), [S] *6055* & [W] *6090* (W Europe), *6180* (Europe), *11855* (C Africa), 17825 (W North Am & C America), 21670 (Pacific)

JORDAN

RADIO JORDAN—(W Europe & E North Am)

1400-1730 ⇦	11690

KOREA (DPR)

VOICE OF KOREA

0100-0200	3560, 7140, 9345 & 9730 (E Asia), 11735, 13760 & 15180 (C America)
0200-0300	4405 (E Asia), 13650 & 15100 (SE Asia)
0300-0400	3560, 7140, 9345 & 9730 (E Asia)
1000-1100	3560 (E Asia), [W] 6185 (SE Asia), [W] 6285 & [W] 9335 (C America), [W] 9850 (SE Asia), [S] 11710 (C America), [S] 11735 & [S] 13650 (SE Asia), [S] 15180 (C America)
1300-1400 & 1500-1600	4405 (E Asia), [W] 7570 (W Europe), 9335 & 11710

(N America), **W** 12015,
S 13760 & **S** 15245 (W
Europe)

1600-1700   3560 (E Asia), 9975/9990
& 11535/11545 (Mideast
& N Africa)

1800-1900   4405 (E Asia), **W** 7570, **W**
12015, **S** 13760 & **S** 15245
(W Europe)

1900-2000   3560 (E Asia), 7100 (S
Africa), 9975 (Mideast &
N Africa), 11710/11910 (S
Africa)

2100-2200   4405 (E Asia), **W** 7570, **W**
12015, **S** 13760 & **S** 15245
(W Europe)

KOREA (REPUBLIC)
KBS WORLD RADIO
0200-0300   *9560* (W North Am), 11810
(S America), 15575 (N
America)

0800-0900   9570 (SE Asia), 9640
(Europe)

1200-1300   **S** *9650* (E North Am)

1300-1400   9570 (SE Asia), **W** *9650* (E
North Am), 9770 (SE Asia)

1600-1700   5975 (E Asia), 9870
(Mideast)

1900-2000   5975 (E Asia), 7275
(Europe)

2100-2130   *3955* (W Europe)

LITHUANIA
RADIO VILNIUS
0030-0100 ▣   9875 (E North Am)
0030-0100 **S**   11690 (E North Am)
0130-0200 **W**   7325 (E North Am)
0930-1000 ▣   9710 (W Europe)
2330-2400 **W**   7325 (E North Am)

MALAYSIA
VOICE OF MALAYSIA
0300-0600 &
0600-0825   6175 & 9750 (SE Asia),
15295 (Australasia)

MOLDOVA
RADIO DMR—(Europe)
1700-1720 ▣   M-F 5960/5910

MONGOLIA
VOICE OF MONGOLIA
1000-1030   12085/12015 (E Asia, SE
Asia & Australasia)

1500-1530   9720/12015 (C Asia)

2000-2030   9720/12015 (E Europe &
W Asia)

NETHERLANDS
RADIO NETHERLANDS
0000-0100   **W** *6165* & **S** *9845* (E North
Am)

0100-0200   **W** *6165* & **S** *9845* (N
America)

0400-0500   **S** *6165* (N America), **S**
9590 (W North Am)

0500-0600   **W** *6165* (W North Am), **W**
11710 (Australasia)

1000-1100   **W** *7315* (E Asia), **S** *9790*
(Australasia), **W** *9795* (E
Asia & SE Asia), **S** *12065*
(E Asia), **W** *12065* (E Asia,
SE Asia & Australasia), **S**
13710 & **S** *13820* (E Asia &
SE Asia)

1100-1200   **S** *11675* (E North Am)

1200-1300   **W** *9890* (E North Am)

1400-1600   *9345*, **S** *9890*, **S** *11835*, **W**
12080 & **W** *15595* (S Asia)

1800-1900   *6020* (S Africa)

1800-2000   **W** *9895* & **S** *11655* (E
Africa)

1800-2100   **S** *9895* (W Africa, C Africa
& E Africa), **W** *11655* (W
Africa & C Africa)

1900-2100   *7120* (C Africa & S Africa),
Sa/Su *15315* (N America),
W Sa/Su *15525* (E North
Am), **S** Sa/Su *17660* & **W**
Sa/Su *17725* (W North Am),
S Sa/Su *17735* (E North
Am), *17810* (W Africa)

2000-2100   **W** 9895 & **S** 11655 (W
Africa)

NEW ZEALAND
RADIO NEW ZEALAND
INTERNATIONAL—(Pacific)
0000-0400   **W** 15720/17675
0000-0500   **S** 13730/15720
0400-0800   **W** 13690/15720

0500-0705	[S] 9615/11820
0706-0800	[S] 9885/7145
0800-1100	9885/9815/7145
1100-1300	[S] 9885 & [W] 15530
1300-1750	[W] 7230/9870
1300-1850	[S] 6095/7145
1750-1950	[W] 11610/11980
1851-1950	[S] 6095/7145
1921-2050	[S] 11675/11725
1950-2238	[W] 13595
2051-2400	[S] 15720
2236-2400	[W] 15720/17675

PHILIPPINES

RADYO PILIPINAS—(S Asia & Mideast)

0200-0330	[S] 11885, [W] 12015, 15120/17665 & 15270

POLAND

RADIO POLONIA

1300-1400 ⬅	9525 & 11820 (W Europe)
1700-1800	[S] 7285 (N Europe)
1800-1900 ⬅	5995 (W Europe)
1800-1900	[W] 7170 (N Europe)

ROMANIA

RADIO ROMANIA INTERNATIONAL

0100-0200	[S] 6040, [W] 9615 & 9690 (E North Am), [S] 11820 (Australasia), [W] 11970 (E North Am), [S] 15430 (Australasia)
0400-0500	[W] 6125 & [W] 9515 (W North Am), [W] 9690 (S Asia), [S] 9780 & [S] 11820 (W North Am), [W] 11895, [S] 15140 & [S] 17860 (S Asia)
0630-0700	[W] 7180, [S] 9655, [W] 9690 & [S] 11830 (W Europe), [W] 15135 & [W] 17780 (Australasia)
1300-1400	[S] 11830, 15105 & [W] 17745 (W Europe)
1800-1900	[W] 7120, [S] 9635, [W] 9640 & [S] 11830 (W Europe)
2130-2200	[W] 7145, [S] 7165 & [S] 9535 (W Europe), [S] 9645 (E North Am), [W] 9650 (W Europe), [W] 9755 & 11940 (E North Am)
2300-2400	[S] 6140, [W] 7105 & [S] 7265 (W Europe), [W] 9610 (E North Am), [W] 9640 (W Europe), [S] 9645, [W] 11730 & [S] 11940 (E North Am)

RUSSIA

VOICE OF RUSSIA

0100-0500	[S] *9665/7180* (E North Am), [S] 15455 & 15555 (W North Am)
0200-0400	[S] *9860* (E North Am)
0200-0600 ⬅	15595 (W North Am)
0200-0600	[W] *7180* (E North Am), [W] 15425 & 15475 (W North Am)
0300-0500	[W] *7350* & [S] 9880/7300 (E North Am)
0400-0600	[W] 7150 (E North Am), [W] 12010 (W North Am)
0600-0900	21790 (Australasia)
0700-0900	[S] 17635 (Australasia)
0800-1000 ⬅	*17495* & *17525* (SE Asia & Australasia)
0800-1000	[W] 17665 (Australasia), [W] 17570 (SE Asia)
1400-1500	[S] 9745 (S Asia), [S] 12055 (SE Asia), [S] 15605 (S Asia), [S] 17645 (S Asia & SE Asia)
1400-1600	[S] 7390 (E Asia & SE Asia)
1500-1600	[W] 6205 (SE Asia), [W] 7315 (W Asia & S Asia), [S] 7325 (Mideast), [W] 7350 (S Asia), *11500* (SE Asia)
1500-1800	[S] 11985 (Mideast & E Africa)
1600-1700 ⬅	*4940*, *4965* & *4975* (W Asia & S Asia)
1600-1700	[W] 6005 (Mideast), [S] 12055 (W Asia & S Asia)
1600-1800	[S] 9405 (S Asia)
1600-1900	[W] 9830 (Mideast, E Africa & S Africa)
1700-1800 ⬅	5945 (S Asia)
1700-1800	[S] Sa/Su 9480/9820 & [S] Sa/Su 11675/7350 (N Europe)
1700-1900	[W] 5910 (S Asia)
1700-2100	[S] 9890 (Europe)
1800-1900	[W] Sa/Su 5950, [W] Sa/Su 6175 & [S] 9480/9820 (N Europe), [S] 9745 (E Africa), [S] 11630/9480 (Europe)

1800-2000 ▫	*11510* (E Africa & S Africa)	0330-0338	Sa/Su 5020
1800-2200	Ⓦ 7290 (N Europe)	0338-0430	5020
1900-2000	Ⓦ 7360 & Ⓢ 7380 (Europe)	0430-0438	Sa/Su 5020
1900-2100	Ⓢ 12070/7310 (Europe)	0438-0545	5020
1900-2200	Ⓦ 6175 (N Europe), Ⓦ 6235	0545-0600	Sa/Su 5020
	(W Europe)	0600-0648	5020
2000-2100	Ⓦ 6145 & Ⓢ 15455	0648-0700	Sa/Su 5020
	(Europe)	0700-0800	5020
2000-2200	Ⓦ 7330 (Europe)	0800-0830	Sa/Su 5020
2100-2200	Ⓦ 7300 (Europe)	0830-0945	5020

SERBIA AND MONTENEGRO

INTERNATIONAL RADIO OF SERBIA & MONTENEGRO
1930-2000 ▫   *6100* (Europe)

SINGAPORE

MEDIACORP RADIO
1400-1600 &
2300-1100   6150

RADIO SINGAPORE INTERNATIONAL—
(SE Asia)
1100-1400   6080 & 6150

0945-1000	Su-F 5020
1000-1010	5020
1010-1030	Sa/Su 5020
1030-1100,	
1100-1900,	
1900-1930 &	
1945-2030	5020
2030-2045	F/Sa 5020
2045-2130	5020
2130-2138	F/Sa 5020
2138-2230	5020
2230-2238	F/Sa 5020
2238-2330	5020
2330-2345	F/Sa 5020
2345-2400	5020

SLOVAKIA

RADIO SLOVAKIA INTERNATIONAL
0100-0130	Ⓢ 5930 & Ⓦ 7230 (E North Am & C America), 9440 (S America)
0700-0730	Ⓢ 9440, Ⓦ 13715 & 15460 (Australasia)
1630-1700	Ⓢ 5920 & Ⓢ 7345 (W Europe)
1730-1800	Ⓦ 5915 & Ⓦ 7345/6055 (W Europe)
1830-1900	Ⓢ 5920 & Ⓢ 6055 (W Europe)
1930-2000	Ⓦ 5915 & Ⓦ 7345 (W Europe)

SOLOMON ISLANDS

SOLOMON ISLANDS BROADCASTING
0000-0030	5020
0030-0038	Sa/Su 5020
0038-0130	5020
0130-0145	Sa/Su 5020
0145-0230	5020
0230-0245	Sa/Su 5020
0240-0330	5020

SOUTH AFRICA

CHANNEL AFRICA
0300-0355	Ⓢ 6160 & Ⓦ 7390 (E Africa)
0300-0500	3345 (S Africa)
0500-0555	Ⓢ 9685 & Ⓦ 11875 (C Africa)
0500-0700	7240 (S Africa)
0600-0655	Ⓦ 15165/15255 & Ⓢ 15440 (W Africa)
0700-0800	Ⓢ 7240 & Ⓦ 11825 (S Africa)
1000-1200 &	
1400-1600	11825 (S Africa)
1500-1555	17770 (C Africa & E Africa)
1700-1755	Ⓢ 15235 & Ⓦ 15285 (W Africa)
1900-2200	3345 (S Africa)

SPAIN

RADIO EXTERIOR DE ESPAÑA
0000-0100	Ⓦ 6055 (N America), Ⓢ 15385 (N America & C America)
2000-2100	Ⓢ M-F 9570 & Ⓦ M-F 9595 (N Africa & W Africa), Ⓦ

	M-F 9680 & 🅂 M-F 15290 (Europe)
2100-2200	🅂 Sa/Su 9570 (N Africa & W Africa), 🅂 Sa/Su 9840 (Europe)
2200-2300	🆆 Sa/Su 9595 (N Africa & W Africa), 🆆 Sa/Su 9680 (Europe)

SWEDEN

RADIO SWEDEN

0130-0200	🅂 *9435* & 🆆 *11550* (S Asia)
0230-0300 🔲	*6010* (E North Am)
0330-0400 🔲	*6010* (N America)
1230-1300	🅂 13580 (E Asia & Australasia), 🅂 15735 (Asia & Australasia)
1330-1400 🔲	15240 (N America)
1330-1400	🆆 7420 (E Asia & Australasia), 🆆 11550 (SE Asia & Australasia), 🅂 15735 (Mideast, SE Asia & Australasia)
1430-1500 🔲	*15240* (N America)
1430-1500	🆆 11550 (Asia & Australasia)
1830-1900 🔲	M-Sa 6065 (Europe)
2030-2100 🔲	6065 (Europe)
2030-2100 ➡	*7420* (SE Asia & Australasia)
2230-2300 🔲	6065 (Europe)

SYRIA

RADIO DAMASCUS

2005-2105	9330/13610 (Europe), 12085 (W Europe)
2110-2210	9330/13610 (Australasia), 12085 (N America)

THAILAND

RADIO THAILAND

0000-0030	🅂 9570 & 🆆 9680 (E Africa & S Africa)
0030-0100	*5890* (E North Am)
0300-0330	*5890* (W North Am)
0530-0600	🆆 13780 & 🅂 21795 (Europe)
1230-1300	🅂 9600 & 🆆 9810 (SE Asia & Australasia)
1400-1430	🆆 9725 & 🅂 9830 (SE Asia & Australasia)

The Macau Tower looms fully 732 feet (220 m) above the surrounding landscape.   M. Guha

1900-2000	🅂 7155 & 🆆 9840 (N Europe)
2030-2045	🆆 9535 & 🅂 9680 (Europe)

TURKEY

VOICE OF TURKEY

0300-0350	🅂 6140 (Europe & N America), 🅂 7270 (Mideast)
0400-0450	🆆 6020 (Europe & N America), 🆆 7240 (Mideast)
1230-1325	🅂 15225 (Europe), 🅂 15535 (S Asia, SE Asia & Australasia)
1330-1425	🆆 11735 (S Asia, SE Asia & Australasia), 🆆 15155 (W Europe)
1830-1920	🅂 9785 (W Europe)
1930-2020	🆆 6055 (W Europe)
2030-2120	🅂 7170 (S Asia, SE Asia & Australasia)

2130-2220	☒ 9525 (S Asia, SE Asia & Australasia)
2200-2250	☒ 9830/7300 (W Europe & E North Am)
2300-2350	☒ 5960 (W Europe & E North Am)

UKRAINE

RADIO UKRAINE

0000-0100	☒ 7440 (E North Am)
0100-0200	☒ 7440/5910 (E North Am)
0300-0400	☒ 7440 (E North Am)
0400-0500	☒ 7440/5910 (E North Am)
1200-1300	◨ 15675 (W Europe)
2100-2200	☒ 7420/7490 (W Europe)
2200-2300	☒ 5840 (W Europe)

UNITED KINGDOM

BBC WORLD SERVICE

0000-0030	*3915* (SE Asia), *11945* (E Asia)
0000-0100	*5970* (S Asia), *5975* (C America), *9740* (SE Asia), *11955* (S Asia), *17615* & ☒ *17655* (E Asia)
0000-0200	*6195* (SE Asia), *9410* (W Asia)
0000-0300	*15310* (S Asia), *15360* (SE Asia), *17790* (S Asia)
0000-0530	*15280* (E Asia)
0030-0100	☒ *9580* (S Asia)
0100-0300	*11955* (S Asia)
0200-0300	*5975* (C America), *9750* (E Africa), *9825* & *12095* (S America)
0200-0400	☒ *6195* (W Asia)
0200-0500	☒ *11760* (Mideast & W Asia)
0300-0400	*5975* (C America & W North Am), *6005* (S Africa), ☒ *9410* (Europe), *9750* (E Africa), ☒ *11760* (Mideast & W Asia), *12035* (E Africa)
0300-0500	*3255* (S Africa), ☒ *7120* & ☒ *11765* (W Africa & C Africa), *15360* (SE Asia), *17760* (E Asia)
0300-0600	☒ *6195* (Europe), *7160* (W Africa & C Africa), *15310* (S Asia)
0300-0700	*17790* (S Asia)
0300-1030	*21660* (E Asia)
0300-2200	*6190* (S Africa)
0330-0600	*15420* (E Africa)
0400-0500	☒ *7130* (Europe), *12035* (E Africa)
0400-0600	◨ *15575* (Mideast & W Asia)
0400-0600	☒ *11760* (Mideast & W Asia), ☒ *12095* (E Europe)
0400-0700	☒ *6195* (Europe & Mideast)
0400-0720	*6005* (W Africa)
0430-0445	☒ *9815* (E Europe & Mideast)
0500-0530	◨ Sa/Su *6010* (E Europe & Mideast)
0500-0530	☒ Sa/Su *7130* (E Europe & Mideast), *17885* (E Africa)
0500-0600	☒ *11760* (Mideast & W Asia), ☒ *11940* (S Africa), ☒ *12095* (E Europe), ☒ *15575* (W Asia)
0500-0700	◨ *9410* (Europe & Mideast)
0500-0700	*11765* (W Africa & C Africa), *17640* (E Africa)
0500-0800	*11955* (SE Asia), *15360* (E Asia, SE Asia & Australasia)
0500-1000	*17760* (E Asia & SE Asia)
0530-0545	☒ *7130* (E Europe & Mideast), ☒ Sa/Su *9875* (E Europe)
0530-0600	M-F *17885* (E Africa)
0600-0700	*7160* (W Europe), *12095* (E Europe)
0600-0730	*15575* (W Asia)
0600-0800	◨ *15565* (E Europe)
0600-0800	Sa/Su *17885* (E Africa)
0600-1600	*11940* (S Africa)
0600-1800	*15310* (S Asia)
0630-0700	*15400* (W Africa & C Africa)
0700-0800	◨ *9410* (W Europe & N Africa)
0700-0800	☒ *6195* (W Europe & N Africa), *11765* (W Africa), ☒ *12095* (E Europe), *17830* (N Africa)
0700-1000	*15400* (W Africa)
0700-1400	*11760* (Mideast)
0700-1500	*17640* (E Europe & Mideast)
0700-1600	*17790* (S Asia)
0700-1700	*15485* (W Europe & N Africa)

Hong Kong is East Asia's Monaco, only more crowded. M. Guha

0730-0900	Sa/Su *15575* (W Asia)
0800-0900	ⓦ 6195 (SE Asia), ⓦ *9740* (SE Asia & Australasia), ⓢ *11955* (SE Asia), ⓢ *15360* (E Asia, SE Asia & Australasia)
0800-1000	*17830* (W Africa & C Africa)
0800-1030	ⓦ *15280* (E Asia)
0800-1300	*21470* (S Africa)
0800-1400	*17885* (E Africa)
0900-1030	ⓢ *15360* (E Asia)
0900-1100	6195 (SE Asia), *9605* (E Asia)
0900-1500	*15575* (W Asia)
0900-1600	*9740* (SE Asia & Australasia)
1000-1030	ⓦ *11945* (E Asia)
1000-1100	*6195* (C America), Sa/Su *17830* (W Africa & C Africa)
1000-1130	Sa/Su *15400* (W Africa)
1000-1400	ⓢ *17760* (E Asia)
1100-1300	ⓦ *11855* & ⓢ *11865* (C America)
1100-1700	*6195* (SE Asia)
1100-2100	*17830* (W Africa & C Africa)
1200-1300	*9605* (C America), *15190* (S America)
1300-1400	ⓢ *12095* (Mideast), *15190* (C America), *15420* (E Africa), ⓢ 15565 (E Europe), ⓢ 17640 (E Europe & W Asia)
1300-1900	*21470* (S Africa)
1400-1600	ⓦ *5970* & ⓢ *11750* (E Asia), 17640 (E Europe & W Asia)
1400-1700	15565 (E Europe), *21660* (E Africa)
1400-1800	*12095* (Mideast)
1500-1530	ⓢ *9695*, ⓢ *11690*, ⓦ *11860*, *15420*, 21490 & ⓦ *21490* (E Africa)
1500-1600	*5975* (S Asia)
1500-2300	*15400* (W Africa)
1530-1545	ⓢ *15540* (S Asia)
1600-1700	ⓦ *11940* (S Africa), ⓢ 17790 (W Asia), ⓦ 17820 (N Africa)
1600-1800	*3915* (S Asia & SE Asia), *7160* (SE Asia), ⓢ 15105 (W Europe & N Africa)
1600-1830	*5975*, ⓢ *9510* & ⓦ *9740* (S Asia)
1600-1900	ⓦ 12095 (E Europe)
1615-1700	ⓢ Sa/Su 9695, ⓢ Sa/Su *11690*, ⓦ Sa/Su *11860*, Sa/Su *15420* & ⓦ Sa/Su *21490* (E Africa)
1700-1745	*6005* & *9630* (E Africa)
1700-1800	ⓢ 15565 (E Europe), ⓦ 17820 (N Africa)

1700-1900	▫ 9410 (E Europe & W Asia), ▪ 11945 (E Africa), ▫ 15420 (C Africa & E Africa)
1700-2100	6195 (Europe)
1700-2200 ▭	9410 (Europe)
1700-2200	3255 (S Africa)
1800-1900	▪ 12095 (Mideast)
1800-2000	▫ 13700 (N Africa), ▪ 17795 (W Europe & N Africa)
1830-2000	▫ 5975, ▫ 9740 & ▪ 12045 (S Asia)
1830-2100	6005 & 9630 (E Africa)
1900-2100	12095 (S Africa)
2100-2130	▪ M-F 11675 & ▫ M-F 15390 (C America)
2100-2200	3915 (S Asia & SE Asia), 6005 (S Africa), ▫ 6110 (E Asia), 6195 (SE Asia), ▫ 6195 (W Europe), ▪ 11675 (C America & W North Am), ▪ 11945 (E Asia), ▫ 15390 (C America & W North Am)
2100-2300	▫ 9605 & ▪ 9860 (W Africa)
2100-2400	5965 (E Asia)
2130-2145	▫ Tu/F 11680 & ▪ Tu/F 11720 (Atlantic & S America)
2200-2300	▫ 5955 & ▪ 5990 (E Asia & SE Asia), 7105 & 9660 (SE Asia), 12080 (S Pacific)
2200-2400	5975 (C America), 6195 & 9740 (SE Asia)
2300-2400	3915 (SE Asia), ▫ 9605 & 11945 (E Asia), 11955 (SE Asia), ▪ 15280 (E Asia)

UNITED NATIONS

UNITED NATIONS RADIO

| 1730-1745 | ▪ M-F 7150 & ▫ M-F 7170 (S Africa), ▫ M-F 9565 & ▪ M-F 15495 (Mideast), M-F 17810 (W Africa & C Africa) |

USA

ADVENTIST WORLD RADIO

0200-0230	▫ 5965 & ▪ 9895 (S Asia)
1000-1030	▫ 11870 & ▪ 11930 (SE Asia)
1200-1230	▫ 15110 & ▪ 15135 (S Asia)

1330-1400	11980 (E Asia), ▪ M/Tu/Th-Sa 15275 & ▫ M/Tu/Th-Sa 15660 (S Asia)
1530-1600	▫ 11695 & ▪ 15225 (S Asia)
1600-1630	▫ 9585, ▪ 11640, ▪ 11680 & ▫ 12065 (S Asia)
1630-1700	▪ 11975 & ▫ 11980 (S Asia)
1730-1800	▪ 9385 & ▫ 9980 (Mideast)
1800-1830	3215 & 3345 (S Africa), ▫ W/F 9530 & ▪ W/F 15280 (C Africa)
1800-1900	▪ 9590 & ▫ 11925 (E Africa)
2000-2030	▪ 7175 & ▫ 9655 (C Africa)
2100-2200	▪ 9715 & ▫ 9830 (W Africa)
2230-2300	▫ 11655, 11850 & ▪ 15320 (SE Asia)

AFRTS-AMERICAN FORCES RADIO & TV SERVICE

| 24 Hr | 4319/12579 USB (S Asia), 5447 USB (C America), 5765/13362 USB & 6350/10320 USB (Pacific), 7590 USB (Atlantic), 7811 USB (Americas), 9980 USB (Atlantic), 12134 USB (Americas) |

FAMILY RADIO

0000-0045	▪ 17805 (S America)
0000-0100	▪ 6065 & ▫ 6085 (E North Am), ▫ 11720 (S America), ▪ 11835 (W North Am)
0000-0445	9505 (N America)
0100-0200	15195 (S Asia)
0100-0445	6065 (E North Am)
0200-0245	▪ 11835 (W North Am)
0200-0300	5985 (C America), ▫ 9525 (W North Am), 11855 (C America)
0300-0400	▫ 9985 (S America), 11740 (C America), ▪ 15255 (S America)
0400-0500	7355 (Europe), 9715 (W North Am)
0400-0600	6855 (E North Am)
0500-0600	▫ 7520 & ▪ 9355 (Europe)
0600-0700	▫ 5745 & ▪ 5810 (C America), 9680 (N America), ▪ 11530 (C Africa & S Africa), ▫ 11530 & ▪ 11580 (Europe), ▫ 11580 (C Africa & S Africa)

0600-0745	7355 (Europe)
0700-0800	◩9495 & ◪9505 (C America), 9715 (W North Am)
0700-0845	◪9930 & ◩9985 (W Africa)
0700-1045	◩7455 (N America)
0700-1100	6855 (E North Am)
0700-1245	◪5985 (N America)
0800-0845	5950 (W North Am)
0845-1145	◩5950 (W North Am)
0900-1100	9450 (E Asia)
0900-1145	◪9755 (W North Am)
1000-1245	◪5950 & ◩6890 (E North Am)
1100-1145	◩5810 & ◪9550 (S America)
1100-1200	◪7355 (C America), ◪9625 (S America), ◩11725 (C America), ◩11830 (S America)
1100-1345	◩7355 (N America)
1200-1300	◩11530 & ◪17505 (S America)
1200-1345	◩11970 (W North Am)
1200-1645	◪17750 (W North Am)
1300-1400	11830 & ◪11865 (N America)
1300-1500	7580 & 11560 (S Asia)
1300-1600	◩11855 & ◪11910 (E North Am)
1400-1500	11520 (SE Asia), 13695 (E North Am)
1400-1645	◩11565 & ◪11830 (N America), ◩17760 (W North Am)
1500-1545	◩15210 & ◪15770 (S America)
1500-1600	6280 & 15520 (S Asia)
1600-1645	◩11830 & ◪11865 (N America)
1600-1700	6085 (C America), ◩12010 & ◪15520 (S Asia), ◩17690 (C Africa), ◪21525 (C Africa & S Africa)
1600-1800	21455 (Europe)
1600-1945	13695 (E North Am), 18980 (Europe)
1700-1800	➡ 3955 (W Europe)
1700-1800	21680 (C Africa & E Africa)
1700-2145	◩17510 & ◪17795 (W North Am)
1800-1845	◪17535 (W Africa)
1800-1900	◩7240 (Mideast & W Asia), ◪13780 (Mideast)
1800-2100	◩15115 (W Africa)
1800-2145	◪13800 & ◩17535 (N America)
1900-1945	6085 (C America), ◩15565 (Europe)
1900-2000	◪18930 (Europe)
1900-2100	3230 (S Africa), 6020 (E Africa & S Africa)
1900-2200	◪17845 (W Africa)
1945-2000	◪13695 (E North Am)
1945-2145	◪18980 (Europe)
2000-2045	◪17750 (Europe)
2000-2100	15195 (C Africa)
2000-2200	◩5810 & ◩6855 (Europe), ◩7360 (W Europe), ◩17575 & ◪17725 (S America)
2100-2200	◪11565 (Europe), ◩15565 (W Africa)
2200-2245	◪15770 & ◩21525 (C Africa & S Africa)
2200-2300	◩9690 (S America)
2200-2345	11740 (N America)
2300-2400	◩15170, ◪15255, ◩15400 & ◪17750 (S America)

KAIJ—(N America)

0000-0200	5755/13815
0200-0700	5755
1400-2400	13815

KJES

0200-0300	▭ 7555 (W North Am)
0300-0330	▭ 7555 (N America)
1400-1500	▭ 11715 (E North Am)
1500-1600	▭ 11715 (W North Am)
1900-2000	15385 (Australasia)

KTBN—(E North Am)

0000-0100	◩7505 & ◪15590
0100-1500	7505
1500-1600	◩7505 & ◪15590
1600-2400	15590

TRANS WORLD RADIO

0430-0500	◪M-F 3200, M-F 4775 & ◩M-F 6120 (S Africa)
0500-0630	◪4775 & 6120 (S Africa)
0500-0900	◩7205 (S Africa), 9500 (S Africa & E Africa)
0600-0635	M-Sa 11640 (W Africa)

Nothing has been compromised at China Radio International's headquarters. Even the English Service hallways feature attractive artwork and creative lighting.

M. Guha

0630-0900	**S** *6120* (S Africa)
0730-0740	Sa/Su *15225* (SE Asia)
0740-0900	*15225* (SE Asia)
0745-0755 ▣	Sa/Su *9870* & *11865* (W Europe)
0755-0850 ▣	*9870* & *11865* (W Europe)
0815-0930	*11840* (Australasia & S Pacific)
0850-0920 ▣	Su-F *9870* & *11865* (W Europe)
1315-1330	▥ Sa *7560* (S Asia)
1500-1630	*12105* (S Asia)
1630-1715	*6130* (S Africa)
1710-1725 ▣	*5855* (W Asia & C Asia)
1715-2045	*3200* (S Africa)
1730-1900	*9500* (E Africa)

VOA-VOICE OF AMERICA

0000-0030	▥ *11760* (SE Asia & Australasia), *12140* (W Asia & S Asia), ▥ *17740* (E Asia & Australasia)
0000-0100	▥ *7120*, **S** *7215*, ▥ *9890* & *15185* (SE Asia), *15290* & *17820* (E Asia)
0030-0100	▥ *7130*, ▥ *9620*, **S** *9715*, **S** *9780*, **S** *11760*, ▥ *11805*, **S** *15115* & *15205* (SE Asia), *17740* (E Asia & Australasia)
0100-0200	**S** *7115*, ▥ *7200*, **S** *9885*, *11705*, **S** *11725*, ▥ *11820* & ▥ *17740* (S Asia)

0130-0200	Tu-Sa 7405, Tu-Sa 9775 & Tu-Sa 13740 (C America & S America)
0200-0300	**S** M-F *7115*, ▥ M-F *7200*, **S** M-F *9885*, M-F 11705, **S** M-F *11725*, ▥ M-F *11820* & ▥ M-F *17740* (S Asia)
0300-0330	▥ 7340 (E Africa & S Africa)
0300-0400	▥ *6035* (E Africa & S Africa), ▥ *6045* (W Africa & C Africa)
0300-0430	*9885* (C Africa)
0300-0500	▥ *7290* & **S** *17895* (C Africa & E Africa)
0300-0600	*4930* (S Africa), **S** *7290* (C Africa & S Africa)
0300-0700	**S** *12080* (E Africa & S Africa)
0300-0900	*6080* (C Africa & S Africa)
0400-0500	*4960* & *9575* (W Africa & C Africa), ▥ *9775* (C Africa & E Africa), **S** *11835* (Africa)
0500-0600	▥ *9700* (W Africa)
0500-0630	▥ *6035* & ▥ *6105* (W Africa & C Africa), ▥ *13710* (E Africa & S Africa)
0500-0700	**S** *6180* (W Africa), ▥ *7295* (W Africa & C Africa)
0500-0900	**S** *13645* (Africa)
0600-0630	▥ *4930* (S Africa), ▥ *11995* (C Africa & E Africa)

0600-0700	[W] *11835* (C Africa & S Africa)
0600-0900	[S] *7290* (W Africa & C Africa)
0700-0900	[W] *11655* (W Africa & C Africa)
0900-1200	[S] *9520*, [W] *13865*, [S] *15205*, [W] *15615*, [W] *17555* & [S] *17745* (Mideast)
1200-1300	[W] *6110* & [S] *6160* (SE Asia), [W] *11715* (Australasia), [S] *15240* & [W] *15665* (SE Asia)
1200-1400	*9645* (SE Asia & Australasia), *9760* (E Asia, S Asia & SE Asia)
1200-1500	[W] *11705* (E Asia)
1300-1600	[W] *6110* (S Asia & SE Asia)
1400-1500	[W] *9645* (S Asia & SE Asia), [S] *9760* (E Asia, S Asia & SE Asia), [W] *9760* (S Asia & SE Asia), [S] *15185* (SE Asia), *15425* (SE Asia & Pacific)
1400-1600	[S] *6160* (S Asia & SE Asia), *7125* (S Asia)
1500-1600	[W] *7175* (E Asia), [S] *9580* (S Asia), [S] *9590* (S Asia & SE Asia), [W] *9645* (S Asia), [W] *9760* (E Asia, S Asia & SE Asia), [W] *9795* & [S] *9845* (E Asia), [W] *11895* (E Asia & SE Asia), [S] *12040* (E Asia), [W] *13600* (C Africa & E Africa), [S] *13690* (S Asia), [W] *13735* (E Asia & SE Asia), [S] *13795* (C Africa & E Africa), [W] *13865* (E Africa), [S] *15105* (S Asia), [W] *15460* (SE Asia), [S] *15550* (SE Asia & Australasia), [S] *17715* (C Africa), [W] *17715* (C Africa & E Africa)
1500-1700	[W] *9685*, [S] *9825* & [W] *11835* (Mideast), [S] *15195* (Mideast & C Asia), [W] *15255* (Mideast), [S] *15445* (Mideast & C Asia), [W] *17895* (C Africa)
1500-2100	[S] *9850* (C Africa & S Africa)
1530-1600	[W] *9865* (C Asia)
1600-1700	*4930* (S Africa), M-F *6160* (S Asia & SE Asia), M-F *7125* & [W] M-F *9645* (S Asia), [S] *9700* (Mideast & C Asia), M-F *9760* (S Asia & SE Asia), [S] *12080* (C Africa & S Africa), [S] *13600* (SE Asia & Australasia), [W] *13600* (S Africa), [S] *15410* & [W] *15445* (C Africa & E Africa), [W] *17640* (E Africa), [W] *17715* (C Africa), [S] *17895* (C Africa & S Africa)
1600-2000	[S] *15580* (Africa)
1600-2200	[W] *15240* (Africa)
1700-1800	[W] *15445* (C Africa & E Africa)
1700-2000	[W] *13710* (E Africa & S Africa)
1700-2200	[S] *15410* (Africa)
1740-1800	*4930*, *11975* & *17895* (S Africa)
1800-1830	[S] *17895* (C Africa & S Africa)
1800-2000	[W] *17895* (C Africa)
1800-2200	*4930* (S Africa), [W] *6035* (W Africa), *11975* (C Africa & E Africa)
1830-2000	[S] *17895* (W Africa)
1900-2000	[W] *9785*, [W] *12015* & [W] *13640* (Mideast)
1900-2030	*4940* (W Africa & C Africa)
1900-2100	[S] *6040*, [S] *9670* & [S] *13635* (Mideast)
1900-2200	[S] *13670* (E Africa), [S] *15445* (W Africa), [W] *15580* (W Africa & C Africa)
2000-2200	[W] *13710* (W Africa & C Africa)
2030-2100	Sa/Su *4940* (W Africa & C Africa)
2030-2230	[W] *11835* (W Asia & S Asia)
2030-2330	[S] *12140* (W Asia & S Asia)
2200-2400	[W] *7120*, [S] *7215*, [W] *9890*, [W] *11760* & *15185* (SE Asia), *15290* (E Asia), *15305* (SE Asia), *17740* (E Asia & Australasia), *17820* (E Asia)
2230-2300	[W] *7230* & *13755* (E Asia)
2230-2400	[S] *9570*, [W] *9780* & [S] *15145* (E Asia)
2300-2400	[W] *6180*, [W] *7205*, [W] *11655*, [S] *13755* & [W] *15150* (E Asia)
2330-2400	[S] *7260* (SE Asia), *12140* (W Asia & S Asia), [W] *13640* & [S] *13725* (SE Asia)

Traditional costumes hold sway at Vietnam's Sapa Market.   Global Spectrum

WBCQ-"THE PLANET"—(N America)

0000-0100 🔲	5105
0000-0230 🔲	9330/13610 LSB
0000-0530 🔲	7415
0100-0500 🔲	M/Sa 5105
0230-0500 🔲	Tu-Su 9330/13610 LSB
0530-0600 🔲	Su/M 7415
0600-0800 🔲	Su 7415
1700-2030 🔲	M-F 17495
1945-2100 🔲	M-F 7415 & M-F 9330/13610 LSB
2030-2200 🔲	M-Sa 17495
2100-2200 🔲	M-Sa 7415
2100-2400 🔲	M-F 5105 & 9330/13610 LSB
2200-2400 🔲	7415 & M-F 17495

WBOH—(C America)

0200-1105 &	
1200-0100 🔲	5920

WEWN

0000-0500	5810 (N America)
0500-1300	5850 (N America)
0600-0900 🔲	7570 (Europe)
1300-1400	🅂 5850 & 🅆 9955 (N America)
1400-1600	9955 (N America)
1600-2000	🅂 15685 & 🅆 15695 (Europe)
1600-2200	13615 (N America)
2000-2200	17595 (W Africa)
2200-2400	9975 (N America), 🅆 11565 (Europe), 🅂 15745 (W Africa)

WINB-WORLD INTERNATIONAL BROADCASTERS—(C America & W North Am)

1200-1300 🔲	Sa/Su 9320
1300-2300 🔲	9740/13570
2300-0500 🔲	9320

WJIE SHORTWAVE

0600-2200	7490 (E North Am & C America)

WMLK—(Europe & N America)

1600-2100	Su-F 9265

WRMI-RADIO MIAMI INTERNATIONAL

0000-0300 🔲	Tu-Sa 7385 (N America)
0300-0330 🔲	M-Sa 7385 (N America)
0330-1000 🔲	7385 (N America)
1000-1045 🔲	Su-F 9955 (C America)
1045-1100 🔲	9955 (C America)
1100-1200 🔲	Su 9955 (C America)
1200-1230 🔲	Sa 9955 (C America)
1230-1300 🔲	Sa/Su 9955 (C America)
1300-2300 🔲	7385 (N America)
2300-2400 🔲	M-F 7385 (N America)

WTJC—(E North Am)

0400-0300 🔲	9370

WWCR

0000-0100	3210 (E North Am)
0000-0200	5935/13845 & 🅆 7465 (E North Am)
0000-1200	5070 (E North Am)
0100-0900	3210 (E North Am)
0200-0400	5765/7465 (E North Am)
0200-1200	5935 (E North Am)
0400-1000	5765 (E North Am)
0900-1000	🅆 3210 & 🅂 9985 (E North Am)
1000-1100	🅆 9985 & 🅂 Su-F 15825 (E North Am)

1000-1300	5765/7465 (E North Am)
1100-1130	**S** Sa/Su 15825 (E North Am)
1100-1200	**W** Su-F 15825 (E North Am)
1130-1200	**S** 15825 (E North Am)
1200-1230	**S** 15825 & **W** Sa/Su 15825 (E North Am)
1200-1300	**W** 5070 (E North Am)
1200-1400	5935/13845 (E North Am)
1230-2100	15825 (E North Am)
1300-1500	7465 (E North Am)
1300-1600	▭ 9985 (E North Am)
1400-2400	13845 (E North Am)
1500-1600	**W** 7465 (E North Am), **S** 12160 (E North Am & Europe)
1600-2200	9975/9985 (E North Am), 12160 (E North Am & Europe)
2100-2145	**S** Sa/Su 15825 (E North Am)
2100-2200	**W** 15825 (Irr) (E North Am)
2145-2200	**S** 15825 (E North Am)
2200-2245	**W** Sa/Su 9985 (E North Am)
2200-2400	5070/12160 (E North Am & Europe), **W** 7465 (E North Am)
2300-2400	**W** 3210/9985 (E North Am)

UZBEKISTAN

RADIO TASHKENT INTERNATIONAL

0100-0130	**W** 5975 & **W** 6165 (W Asia & S Asia), **W** 7160 (S Asia), **S** 7190 & **S** 9715 (W Asia & S Asia), **W** 11905 (S Asia)
1200-1230 & 1330-1400	5060, **W** 5975, **W** 6025, **S** 7285 & **S** 9715 (S Asia), **W** 11850 (W Asia & S Asia), **S** 11905 (S Asia)
2030-2100 & 2130-2200	5025, **W** 7185 & 11905 (Europe)

VATICAN STATE

VATICAN RADIO

0250-0320	7305 (E North Am), 9605 (E North Am & C America)
0600-0620 ▭	4005 (Europe), 5885 (W Europe)
0620-0700 ▭	5885 (W Europe)
0730-0745 ▭	M-Sa 4005 (Europe), M-Sa 5885 (W Europe), M-Sa 7250 (Europe)
1120-1130 ▭	M-Sa 7250 (Europe), M-Sa 11740 (W Europe), M-Sa 15210 (Mideast)
1715-1730 ▭	4005 (Europe), 5885 & 9645 (W Europe)
1715-1730	**W** 7250 (Mideast)
2050-2110 ▭	4005 & 5885 (Europe)

VIETNAM

VOICE OF VIETNAM

0100-0130, 0230-0300 & 0330-0400	*6175* (E North Am & C America)
1100-1130	7285 (SE Asia)
1230-1300	9840 & 12020 (SE Asia)
1500-1530	7285, 9840 & 12020 (SE Asia)
1600-1630	7220 (W Africa & C Africa), 7280 (Europe), 9550 (W Africa & C Africa), 9730 (Europe)
1700-1730	**S** *9725* (W Europe)
1800-1830	**W** *5955* (W Europe), 7280 & 9730 (Europe)
1900-1930 & 2000-2030	7280 & 9730 (Europe)
2030-2100	7220 & 9550 (W Africa & C Africa)
2330-2400	9840 & 12020 (SE Asia)

YEMEN

REPUBLIC OF YEMEN RADIO—(Mideast)

1800-1900	9780

M. Guha

Voices from Home—2006

Country-by-Country Guide to Native Broadcasts

For some, English offerings are merely icing on the cake. Their real interest is in eavesdropping on broadcasts for *nativos*—the home folks. These can be enjoyable regardless of language, especially when they offer traditional music.

Some you'll hear, many you won't, depending on your location and equipment. Keep in mind that native-language broadcasts are sometimes weaker than those in English, so you may need more patience and better hardware. PASSPORT REPORTS shows which radios and antennas work best.

When to Tune

Some broadcasts come in better during the day within world band segments from 9300 to 21850 kHz. However, signals from Latin

America and Africa peak near or during darkness, especially from 4700 to 5100 kHz. See "Best Times and Frequencies" for specifics.

Times and days of the week are in World Time, explained in "Setting Your World Time Clock" and Passport's glossary; for local times in each country, see "Addresses PLUS." Midyear, some stations are an hour earlier (⬛) or later (⬛) because of daylight saving/summer time. Those used only seasonally are labeled **S** for summer (midyear, typically the last Sunday in March until the last Sunday in October) and **W** for winter. Stations may also extend their hours for holidays, emergencies or sports events.

Frequencies in *italics* may be best, as they come from relay transmitters that could be near you, although other frequencies beamed your way might do almost as well. Some signals not beamed to you can also be heard, especially when they are for audiences in nearby parts of the world. Frequencies with no target zones are usually for domestic coverage, so they are the least likely to be heard unless you're in or near that country.

> **Even non-speakers enjoy native music.**

Schedules for Entire Year

To be as useful as possible over the months to come, Passport's schedules consist not just of observed activity, but also that which we have creatively opined will take place during the forthcoming year. This predictive material is based on decades of experience and is original from us. Although inherently not as exact as real-time data, over the years it's been of tangible value to Passport readers.

Before the Second World War much of Germany looked like this. Now, visitors flock to Prague for urban serenity instead of high rise sterility.

T. Ohtake

ALBANIA—Albanian
RADIO TIRANA
0000-0130 ▣ 7455/6115 (E North Am)
0730-1000 ▣ 7105 (Europe)
2130-2300 ▣ 6205 (Europe)

ARGENTINA—Spanish
RADIO ARGENTINA AL EXTERIOR-RAE
1200-1400   M-F 11710 (S America)
2200-2400   M-F 6060 (C America &
             S America), M-F 11710
             (Europe & N Africa), M-F
             15345 (Europe)

RADIO NACIONAL
0000-0100   M 11710 (S America)
0000-0230   Su/M 6060 (C America &
             S America), Su/M 15345
             (Americas)
0230-0300   M 6060 (C America &
             S America), M 15345
             (Americas)
0900-1200   6060 (S America)
1800-2000   Su 6060 & Su 11710
             (S America), Su 15345
             (Europe)
2000-2200   Sa/Su 11710 (S America)
2000-2400   Sa/Su 6060 (S America),
             Sa/Su 15345 (Europe)
2200-2400   Su 11710 (S America)

ARMENIA—Armenian
VOICE OF ARMENIA
0300-0330 ▣ 4810 (E Europe, Mideast &
             W Asia), 9965 (S America)
0400-0430 ▣ 9965 (Irr) (S America)
1715-1745 🆂 9775 (Europe)
1815-1845 ▣ M-Sa 4810 (E Europe,
             Mideast & W Asia)
1815-1845 🆆 9965 (Europe)
2000-2100 ▣ M-Sa 4810 (E Europe,
             Mideast & W Asia)

AUSTRIA—German
RADIO AUSTRIA INTERNATIONAL
0005-0015   🆆 Tu-Sa 7325 (C America)
0035-0045   🆆 Tu-Sa 7325 (E North Am)
0105-0115   🆂 Tu-Sa 9870 (C America)
0135-0145   🆂 Tu-Sa 9870 (E North Am)
0500-1305 ▣ 6155 & 13730 (Europe)
0600-0700 ▣ M-Sa 17870 (Mideast)

1200-1215   🆂 Tu-F 17715 (SE Asia &
             Australasia)
1220-1300   🆂 M 17715 (SE Asia &
             Australasia)
1230-1245   🆂 M-F 17715 (SE Asia &
             Australasia)
1300-1315   🆆 Tu-F 17855 (SE Asia &
             Australasia)
1305-1345 ▣ Tu-F 6155 & Tu-F 13730
             (Europe)
1320-1400 ▣ M 6155 & M 13730
             (Europe)
1320-1400   🆆 M 17855 (SE Asia &
             Australasia)
1330-1345   🆆 M-F 17855 (SE Asia &
             Australasia)
1400-1830 ▣ 13730 (Europe)
1400-2308 ▣ 6155 (Europe)
1500-1515   🆂 Tu-F *13775* (W North Am)
1520-1530   🆂 M *13775* (W North Am)
1530-1545   🆂 M-F *13775* (W North Am)
1600-1615   🆆 Tu-F *13675* (W North Am)
1620-1630   🆆 M *13675* (W North Am)
1630-1645   🆆 M-F *13675* (W North Am)
1830-2308 ▣ 5945 (Europe, N Africa &
             Mideast)
2335-2345 ➡ M-F 9870 (S America)

BANGLADESH—Bangla
BANGLADESH BETAR
1630-1730   7185 (Mideast)
1915-2000   7185 (Europe)

BRAZIL—Portuguese
RADIO BANDEIRANTES
24 Hr   6090, 9645, 11925

RADIO BRASIL CENTRAL
0000-0330 ➡ 4985, 11815
0330-0600 ➡ 4985 (Irr), 11815 (Irr)
0600-2400 ➡ 4985, 11815

RADIO CULTURA
0000-0200 ➡ 6170, 9615, 17815
0700-2400 ➡ 9615, 17815
0800-2400 ➡ 6170

RADIO GUAIBA
0700-0300 ➡ 6000, 11785

RADIO NACIONAL DA AMAZONIA
0000-0050   6185
0000-0230 ➡ 11780
0230-0650 ➡ Su 11780

0650-2400 [→] 11780
0650-0750 [W] 6185
0750-1850 &
2055-2400 6185

RADIO NACIONAL DO BRASIL—(Africa)
0500-0650 &
1900-2050 9665

BULGARIA—Bulgarian
RADIO BULGARIA
0000-0100 [S] 9700 & [S] 11700 (E North Am)
0100-0200 [→] 9500 & 11600/11500 (S America)
0100-0200 [W] 7400 & [W] 9700 (E North Am)
0400-0430 [S] Sa/Su 7200 (S Europe), [S] Sa/Su 11500 (W Europe)
0430-0500 [S] 7200 (S Europe), [S] 11500 (W Europe)
0500-0530 [→] Sa/Su 7500 & Sa/Su 9400 (E Europe), Sa/Su 9500 (W Europe)
0500-0530 [W] Sa/Su 5800 (W Europe), [W] Sa/Su 5900 (S Europe)
0530-0600 [→] 7500 & 9400 (E Europe), 9500 (W Europe)
0530-0600 [W] 5800 (W Europe), [W] 5900 (S Europe)
1100-1130 [→] 7200 (S Europe), 11600 (E Europe), 11700 (W Europe), 13600 (E Europe), 15700 (W Europe)
1300-1500 [→] 11700 & 15700 (W Europe)
1500-1600 [S] 7200 (S Europe), [S] 9400 (E Europe), [S] 15700 (Mideast)
1600-1700 [→] 7500 (E Europe), 17500 (S Africa)
1600-1700 [W] 5800 (E Europe), [W] 5900 (S Europe), [W] 9400 (Mideast)
1900-2000 [→] 5900 (S Europe)
1900-2100 [→] 7200 (W Europe), 7400 (Mideast)

CANADA—French
CANADIAN BROADCASTING CORP—(E North Am)
0100-0300 [→] M 9625
0300-0400 [→] Su 9625 & Tu-Sa 9625

1300-1310 &
1500-1555 [→] M-F 9625
1700-1715 [→] Su 9625
1900-1945 [→] M-F 9625
1900-2310 [→] Sa 9625

RADIO CANADA INTERNATIONAL
0000-0100 [W] 6100 (E North Am & C America)
1100-1300 [S] 11945 (E North Am & C America)
1200-1400 [W] 6120 (E North Am & C America)
1430-1500 [S] 9540, [W] 9780 & [S] 11935 (E Asia)
1600-1900 [S] 17765 (C America)
1700-2000 [W] 17835 (C America)
1800-1900 [W] 13650 (W Europe)
1900-2000 [S] 11765 (Europe & Mideast), [W] 11845 (C Africa), [W] 13650 & [S] 15255 (W Africa), [S] 15325 (W Europe), [W] 17740 (W Africa & C Africa)
1900-2100 [S] 7235 (N Africa), [S] 13700 (W Africa & C Africa)
2000-2100 [S] 15255 (N Africa & W Africa)
2100-2200 [W] 7235, [W] 9805 & [W] 11845 (N Africa)
2200-2300 [S] 9390 (W Africa), [S] 11755 (W Africa & C Africa), [S] 15180 (C America)
2300-2400 [W] 15180 (C America)

CHINA
CHINA RADIO INTERNATIONAL
Chinese
0000-0100 [S] 5960 & [W] 6040 (E North Am), [S] 9765 (E Africa), [W] 9790 & [S] 11930 (W North Am)
0200-0300 9580 (E North Am), 9690 (N America & C America), [S] 9815 & [W] 11695 (S America)
0200-0400 6020 & 9570 (N America)
0300-0400 [W] 9590 (Europe), 9720 (W North Am), [S] 13600 (Europe)
0400-0500 15350 & 17540 (S Asia)
0600-0900 17650 (Europe)

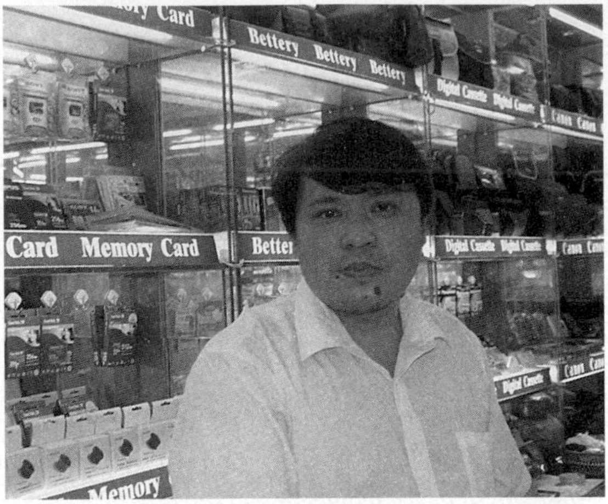

Beijing has replaced Tokyo as the Holy See of electronics—here, you can even buy a "bettery."

M. Guha

0700-0900	*11785* (W Europe)
0900-1000	9665 (E Asia), 15440 & 17670 (Australasia)
0900-1100	11980, 15250 & 15340 (SE Asia)
1000-1200	17650 (Europe)
1200-1300	*9570* (E North Am), *17625* (S America)
1200-1400	7160 & 9855 (SE Asia)
1500-1600	[S] 9560 (S Asia), [W] 9700 & [S] 17650 (Europe)
1600-1700	[W] *17735* (W North Am)
1700-1800	[W] 6150 & [W] 7120 (Europe), 7160 & [W] 7315 (Mideast), [S] 9685 (Europe), 9745 (Mideast), [S] 11660 (Europe), [S] 11835 (Mideast & N Africa)
1730-1830	9645 (W Africa & C Africa)
1800-1900	*6100* (S Africa)
2000-2100	7120 (Europe), 7245 (Mideast & N Africa), [W] 7335 & [S] 9770 (Europe), 9865 (Mideast)
2200-2300	[W] 5975 (Mideast), 6140 (SE Asia), [W] 7180 (E Asia), [S] 7190 (E Africa & S Africa), 7220/7215 (SE Asia), 7265 (Mideast & W Asia), 7325 & 9460 (SE Asia), [S] 9695 (E Asia)
2230-2300	*15505* (W Africa, C Africa & E Africa)
2230-2400	*11975* (N Africa)
2300-2400	*7170* (W Africa), [S] 9765 (E Africa)

Cantonese

0400-0500	*9790* (W North Am)
1000-1100	15440 & 17670 (Australasia)
1100-1200	9590 (SE Asia)
1200-1300	[W] *9560* & [S] *11855* (E North Am & C America)
1700-1800	[W] 7185, 9770 & [S] 11750 (E Africa & S Africa)
1900-2000	[W] 7255, 9770 & [S] 11895 (Europe)
2300-2400	6140, 7325, 9460, [W] 9860, 11945 & [S] 15100 (SE Asia)

CHINA (TAIWAN)

RADIO TAIWAN INTERNATIONAL

Amoy

0000-0100	*15440* (W North Am)
0000-0200	11875 (SE Asia)
0500-0700	15580 (SE Asia)
0900-1100	15465 (SE Asia)
1000-1100	11605 (E Asia)
1200-1300	11715 (SE Asia)
1300-1400	11635 & 15465 (SE Asia)
2100-2200	[W] *5950* & [S] *13695* (E North Am)

Chinese

0000-0300	9660 (E Asia)
0000-0400	15245 (E Asia)
0000-0500	11640 & 11885 (E Asia)
0100-0200	[W] *11825*, *15215* & [S] *17845* (S America)
0200-0500	15290 (SE Asia)
0400-0500	*5950* (W North Am), *9680* (N America), 15320 (SE Asia)
0400-0600	15270 (SE Asia)
0500-0600	[W] *9495* & [S] *9505* (C America)
0600-1000	11795 (E Asia)
0900-1000	11605 (E Asia), 11635 (SE Asia), 11715 (Australasia), 11940 & 15525 (SE Asia)
0900-1100	9415 (E Asia)
0900-1400	11640 (E Asia)
0900-1500	6085 (E Asia)
0900-1800	7185 & 11665 (E Asia)

1100-1200	11715 (Australasia)
1100-1500	9780 & 11780 (E Asia)
1100-1800	9680 (E Asia)
1200-1300	11605 (E Asia), 15465 (SE Asia)
1300-1400	15265 (SE Asia)
1300-1500	7445 (SE Asia)
1400-1800	6145 & 7130 (E Asia)
1900-2000	9955, [S] *17750* & [W] *17760* (Europe)
2200-2300	*3965* (W Europe)
2200-2400	*5950* (E North Am), 6150 (E Asia), 11635 (SE Asia), 11710 & 11885 (E Asia), *15440* (W North Am)
2300-2400	9660 (E Asia), 9785/9780 (SE Asia), 15245 (E Asia)

VOICE OF HAN—(E Asia)
Chinese

0655-0105	9745

CROATIA—Croatian

CROATIAN RADIO

0400-1000	[S] 13830 (Europe)
0500-1000	[W] 7365 (Europe & Mideast)
0500-1800 ⬅	9830 (Europe & Mideast)
0500-2400 ⬅	6165 (Europe)
1000-2200	13830 (Europe & Mideast)
2200-2300	[S] 13830 (Europe)

VOICE OF CROATIA

0000-0100	[S] *9925* (E North Am & S America)
0000-0300	[W] *7285* (E North Am & S America)
0100-0200 0215-0230 & 0250-0300	[S] *9925* (N America & S America)
0300-0500	[S] *9925* (W North Am)
0315-0330 & 0350-0400	[W] *7285* (N America & S America)
0400-0600	[W] *7285* (W North Am)
0500-0800 ⬅	*9470* (Australasia)
0600-1000	*13820/12110* (Australasia)
2200-2215 & 2250-2300	[S] *9925* (S America)
2300-2315	[W] *7285* (S America)
2300-2400	[S] *9925* (E North Am & S America)
2350-2400	[W] *7285* (S America)

CUBA—Spanish

RADIO HABANA CUBA

0000-0100 ⬅	Tu-Sa 6000 (E North Am)
0000-0100	9820 (N America)
0000-0500	5965 (C America & W North Am), 6060 (E North Am), 9505 (C America), 9600 (S America), 11760 (Americas), 11875 & 15230 (S America)
0200-0500	9550 (C America)
1100-1400	6000 (C America)
1100-1500	9550 (C America), 11760 (Americas), 11800 (C America & S America), 12000 (E North Am), 15230 (S America)
2100-2300	9550 (C America), [S] 15120 (S Europe & N Africa), 15230 (S America)
2200-2400	11875 (S America)
2300-2400 ⬅	M-F 6000 (E North Am)

RADIO REBELDE

24 Hr	5025
0300-0400	6120 (C America)
1100-1300 ⬅	6140/9505 (C America)
1100-1300	9600 (C America)
1700-1800	11655 & 15570 (C America)

CZECH REPUBLIC—Czech

RADIO PRAGUE

0030-0100	[W] 5930 (S America), [W] 7345 (N America & C America)
0130-0200	[S] 6200 (N America & C America), [S] 7345 (S America)
0230-0300	[W] 6200 & [S] 7345 (N America & C America), [W] 7345 (S America), [S] 9870 (W North Am & C America)
0330-0400	[W] 6200 (W North Am & C America), [W] 7345 (N America & C America)
0830-0900	[S] 15710 (E Africa & Mideast)
0930-1000 ⬅	11600 (W Europe & N Africa)
0930-1000	[S] 21745 (S Asia & W Africa), [W] 21745 (E Africa & Mideast)

1030-1100	▣ 21745 (S Asia & W Africa)
1100-1130	▣ 11615 (N Europe), ▣ 15710 (S Asia)
1200-1230	▣ 11640 (N Europe), ▣ 21745 (S Asia, SE Asia & Australasia)
1330-1400 ▣	6055 (Europe), 7345 (W Europe)
1330-1400	▣ 13580 (N Europe), ▣ 21745 (E Africa)
1430-1500	▣ 11600 (S Asia), ▣ 21745 (N America)
1530-1600	▣ 17485 (E Africa)
1630-1700 ▣	5930 (W Europe)
1630-1700	▣ 15710 (W Africa & C Africa)
1730-1800	▣ 5930 (E Europe, Asia & Australasia), ▣ 17485 (C Africa)
1830-1900	▣ 5930 (W Europe), ▣ 9400 (Asia & Australasia)
1930-2000	▣ 11600 (SE Asia & Australasia)
2030-2100 ▣	5930 (W Europe)
2030-2100	▣ 9430 (SE Asia & Australasia)
2100-2130	▣ 9800 (W Africa & C Africa), ▣ 11600 (W Europe & N Africa)
2200-2230	▣ 5930 (W Europe), ▣ 9435 (W Europe & S America)
2330-2400	▣ 7345 (S America), ▣ 9440 (N America & C America)

EGYPT—Arabic

EGYPTIAN RADIO

0000-0030 ▣	11665 (E Africa)
0000-0400 ▣	12050 (Europe & E North Am)
0700-1100 ▣	15115 (W Africa)
1200-2400 ▣	12050 (Europe & E North Am)
1900-2400 ▣	11665 (E Africa)

RADIO CAIRO

0000-0045	9735 & 11755 (S America)
0030-0430	▣ 11885 & ▣ 11895 (N America)
1015-1215	17775 (Mideast)
1300-1600	15365 (C Africa)
2000-2200	7270 (Australasia)
2330-2400	9735 & 11755 (S America)

FINLAND—Finnish & Swedish

YLE RADIO FINLAND

0250-0330	▣ 7185 (E Europe & Mideast), ▣ 9625 (C Africa & E Africa)
0350-0430	▣ 6130 (E Europe & Mideast), ▣ 9815 (E Africa & S Africa)
0400-0500	▣ 6120 (W Europe), ▣ 9740 (Mideast), ▣ 11995 (E Africa & S Africa)
0500-0600	▣ 9815 (E Africa), ▣ 11755 (Europe), ▣ 11865 (E Africa & S Africa)
0500-0700 ▣	6120 (E Europe & Mideast)
0500-2100	6120 (Europe)
0600-0800	▣ 15135 (W Europe & Australasia)
0600-1900	11755 (Europe)
0630-0800	▣ Sa/Su 17715 (SE Asia & Australasia)
0700-0900 ▣	9560 (W Europe & Australasia)
0730-0900	▣ Sa/Su 17780 (SE Asia & Australasia)
0830-0945	▣ 17655 (E Asia)
0930-1100	▣ 15490 (E Asia, SE Asia & Australasia)
0945-1000	▣ 17810 (C Asia & E Asia)
1000-1100	▣ 17695 (S America), ▣ 17710 (SE Asia & Australasia)
1100-1200	▣ Su 13710 (E Asia, SE Asia & Australasia), ▣ 15330 (SE Asia & Australasia), ▣ 21800 (S America)
1200-1300 ▣	21800 (E Africa & S Africa)
1200-1300	▣ Su 13695 (E Asia, SE Asia & Australasia)
1300-1400 ▣	13715 (N America)
1300-1500 ▣	15400 (N America)
1300-1500	▣ 9705 (E Europe)
1345-1400 ▣	9595 (E Europe)
1400-1600	▣ 7195 (E Europe)
1400-1800 ▣	9630 (W Europe)
1500-1600	▣ 9705 (W Asia & S Asia), ▣ 13665 (W North Am), ▣ 17730 (S America)
1600-1700	▣ 11920 (W North Am), ▣ 13645 (W Asia & S Asia), ▣ 17730 (S America)

1700-1800	[W] 9610 & [S] 15165 (E Africa & S Africa)
1800-1850	[S] 15335 (E Africa & S Africa)
1900-2000	[W] 7175 (E Europe & Mideast)
1900-2100	[S] 11755 (Europe)
2100-2130	[S] 9760 (S America)
2100-2300	[S] 6120 (Europe)
2200-2230	[W] 5970 (Europe)
2200-2300	[S] 9715 (S America)

FRANCE—French

RADIO FRANCE INTERNATIONALE

0000-0030	[W] *17710* (SE Asia)
0000-0200	*15415* (SE Asia)
0100-0200	[W] *11970/13690* & [S] *13690* (S Asia)
0130-0200	[W] *5995/9800* (C America)
0300-0400	[S] 5925 (C Africa & E Africa), [W] 5945 (C Africa), [W] *7135* (C Africa & E Africa), [W] 7315 (Mideast), [S] 9790 (C Africa)
0300-0500	7135 (C Africa)
0400-0430	[W] Sa/Su 9555/11995 (E Africa)
0400-0500	[S] *3965/5925* & [W] 3965 (N Africa), [S] *7150* (C Africa & S Africa), [W] *7270* (S Africa), [W] 7315/9555 (Mideast)
0400-0600	*4890* & 9790 (C Africa), *15210* (E Africa)
0430-0445	[S] 6045 (E Europe)
0430-0500	[W] 9555/11995 (E Africa)
0500-0530	[W] Sa/Su 11995/15155 & [S] Sa/Su 15160/13680 (E Africa)
0500-0600	[W] 7135 & [S] 7280 (N Africa), [W] 9555/11685 (Mideast), [W] 9790 (N Africa & W Africa), 11700 & [S] 15300 (C Africa & S Africa)
0530-0545	[W] 5990 (E Europe)
0530-0600	[W] 11995/15155 & [S] 15160/13680 (E Africa)
0600-0630	[W] Sa/Su *9865* & [S] Sa/Su *11665* (W Africa), [W] Sa/Su 15155, [S] Sa/Su 15160 & Sa/Su 17800 (E Africa)
0600-0700	[W] 5925 (N Africa), 9790/13680 & 11700 (N Africa & W Africa), [W] 11700 (C Africa & S Africa), [S] 13695 (W Africa), 15300 (C Africa & S Africa), [S] 15315 (W Africa), *17770* (C Africa), [S] 17850 (C Africa & S Africa)
0600-0800	[W] 7135 (N Africa)
0630-0700	[W] *9865* & [S] *11665* (W Africa), 17800 (E Africa)
0700-0800	[W] 9790 & 11700 (N Africa & W Africa), *15170* (C Africa), [S] 15300 (N Africa & W Africa), [S] 17620 (W Africa), 17850 & [S] 21580 (C Africa & S Africa)
0700-1000	15315 (W Africa)
0800-1000	15300 (N Africa & W Africa)
0800-1600	11845 (N Africa), 21580 (C Africa & S Africa)
0800-1700	17620 (W Africa)
1000-1100	15300 & [S] 15315 (W Africa), 17850 (C Africa & S Africa)
1000-1200	[W] 21685 (W Africa)
1030-1200	[W] *7140* & [S] *9830* (E Asia), [W] *9830* & [S] *11890* (SE Asia)
1100-1200	6175 (W Europe & Atlantic), *11600* (SE Asia), [W] *11670* & *13640* (C America), [S] 17570 (E North Am & C America), *17850* (C Africa)
1100-1400	15300 (N Africa & W Africa)
1130-1200	[S] 15365/21645 (C America), [W] 15515 (E North Am & C America), [W] 17610, [S] 17800 & [W] 21645 (C America)
1200-1400	[S] 15300 (N Africa & W Africa), *17850* (C Africa)
1200-1500	21685 (W Africa)
1230-1300	*15515* (C America), 21620 (E Africa), *21760* (W Africa & C Africa)
1300-1330	[S] *15515* & [W] *17860* (C America)
1330-1400	[S] M-Sa *15515* & [W] M-Sa *17860* (C America)
1400-1600	15300 (W Africa)

1500-1600	15605 (W Africa), 17850 (C Africa & S Africa)
1600-1700	*6090* (SE Asia), 🆂 15300 (W Africa), 🆆 15300 (Africa), 🆂 21580 (C Africa & S Africa)
1700-1800	🆂 11700 (N Africa), 15300 (Africa), 🆂 17620 (W Africa)
1700-2000	🆆 11965 (W Africa)
1800-1900	9790 (N Africa & W Africa), 🆂 15300 (Africa), 🆂 15605 (W Africa)
1800-2000	🆆 7315 (N Africa), *11995* (W Africa)
1800-2200	11705 (C Africa & S Africa)
1900-2000	🆆 6175 & 🆂 9790 (N Africa), 🆆 9790 (Africa), 🆂 15300 (C Africa & S Africa), 🆂 15605 (W Africa)
1900-2100	🆂 11615 (W Africa)
1900-2200	*7160* (C Africa)
2000-2100	🆂 9485 (W Africa)
2000-2200	6175 (N Africa), 7315 (N Africa & W Africa), 🆂 9790 (Africa), 🆆 9790 (C Africa & S Africa), 🆆 *9790* & 🆂 *11995* (W Africa), 🆆 13720 (N Africa & W Africa)
2100-2200	🆆 3965 (N Africa), 9485 (W Africa)
2300-2330	🆂 *15445* (SE Asia)
2300-2400	🆆 *11890*, 🆆 *12075*, *15415* & 🆂 *15595* (SE Asia)

GABON—French

AFRIQUE NUMERO UN

0500-2315	9580 (C Africa)
0700-0800	17630 (Irr) (W Africa)
0800-1600	17630 (W Africa)
1600-1700	15475 (W Africa & E North Am)
1700-1900	15475 (Irr) (W Africa & E North Am)

GERMANY—German

DEUTSCHE WELLE

0000-0200	🆆 *6135* (E North Am & C America), 🆆 *7430* & 🆆 *9540* (S Asia), 🆂 9545 (E North Am), 🆂 *9640* (S America), 🆆 *9655* (C America), 🆆 *9830* (E North Am), 🆆 *11690* & 🆂 *11865* (S America), 🆂 *11955* (E North Am), 🆂 *12040* (S America)
0000-0400 24 Hr	🆂 *6100* (N America) 6075 (Europe)
0200-0400	🆆 6075 (Mideast), 🆆 *6100* (N America), 🆆 6145 (E North Am), 🆆 *9875* (C America)
0200-0600	🆂 *9735* (W North Am)
0400-0600	🆆 7150 (C Africa & E Africa), 🆂 *12025* (C America), 🆆 *13780* (C Africa & E Africa), 🆆 *17800* (E Africa & S Africa)
0600-0700	🆆 *11865* (C Africa & S Africa)
0600-0800	🆆 7210 (N Europe), 🆆 9545 (S Europe & Mideast), 9735 (Australasia), 🆆 12045 (E Europe), 🆂 13780 (Mideast), 🆆 13780 (W Africa)
0600-2000	9545 (S Europe & Atlantic)
0700-0800	🆆 17710 (C Africa & S Africa)
0800-1000	🆆 7175 (N Europe), 🆆 9545 (S Europe & N Africa), 13780 (Australasia), 🆂 *17715* & 🆆 *21640* (SE Asia & Australasia)
0800-1400	13780 (Mideast)
1000-1200	🆆 *5905* (C America), 🆆 *11510* (SE Asia & Australasia), 🆆 *15110* (Australasia), 🆆 17770 (S America), 🆂 21840 (E Asia), 🆆 21840 (SE Asia & Australasia)
1000-1400	🆆 *5910* (E Asia), 🆆 *7400* (E Asia & SE Asia), 🆂 *7430* (E Asia), 🆂 9900, 🆂 *17635* & 🆂 *17845* (E Asia & SE Asia)
1200-1400	🆆 *9395* (SE Asia), 🆆 *12035* & 🆆 15320 (E North Am), 🆆 *15610* (C Asia), 🆆 17630 (S Asia & SE Asia), 🆆 *17710* (E North Am), 🆂 17820 (C Asia & SE Asia)
1400-1500	🆆 *15445* (W North Am)
1400-1600	🆂 15275 (Mideast & E Africa), 🆆 *15275* (Mideast & W Asia), 🆆 15335 (Mideast)

1400-1800	🅂 *9655* (S Asia & C Asia), 🅂 13780 (Mideast), 🅆 *13780* (Mideast & N Africa), 🅂 15275 (S Asia & SE Asia), 🅂 *17860* (Mideast & C Asia)
1500-1600	🅆 *15445* (W North Am)
1600-1800	🅆 6075 (Mideast), 🅆 *9535* (S Africa), 🅂 15275 (C Africa & E Africa)
1800-2000	🅂 6075 (Mideast), 🅆 6075 (N Africa), 🅆 *7170* (S Africa), 🅆 9735 (W Africa), 🅂 11795 (Africa), 🅆 *15275* (E Africa)
1800-2200	🅂 *7185* (S Africa), 🅂 *9545* (Europe), 🅂 9735 (C Africa & S Africa)
2000-2100	🅆 *11935* (Australasia)
2000-2200	🅂 *7330* (Australasia), 9545 (Atlantic & S America), 🅂 11795 (N Africa & W Africa)
2000-2400	🅆 *5895* (E Asia), 🅂 15275 (C America)
2100-2200	🅆 *11935* (Australasia)
2200-2400	🅆 *6225* (E Asia), 🅂 7105 (W Africa), 🅆 *7395* (E Asia & SE Asia), 9545 (S America), 🅂 *11690* (E North Am & C America), 🅆 *11690*, 🅂 *11840* & *11865* (S America), 🅂 *15410* (E North Am)

DEUTSCHLANDRADIO—(Europe)
24 Hr   6005

HUNGARY—Hungarian

RADIO BUDAPEST

0000-0100	🅆 M 9580 (S America), 🅂 9770 (N America), 🅆 M 12010 (S America)
0100-0200	🅆 9870 (N America)
0130-0230	🅂 9820 (N America)
0230-0330	🅆 9855 (N America)
1200-1300	▭ 21590 (Australasia)
1400-1500	▭ Su 6025 (Europe)
1700-1800	🅂 15335 (S Africa)
1800-1900	🅂 11990 (Australasia)
1900-2000	▭ 3975 & 6025 (Europe)
1900-2000	🅆 11675 (Australasia)
2000-2100	🅂 11695 (N America), 🅆 11785 (S Africa)
2100-2200	🅂 3975 (Europe)
2200-2300	🅆 9825 (N America), 🅂 9850 & 🅂 12030 (S America)
2300-2400	▭ 6025 (Europe)
2300-2400	🅆 9580, 🅂 Su 9850, 🅆 12010 & 🅂 Su 12030 (S America)

RADIO KOSSUTH—(Europe)
0500-1300 ▭ 6025
1300-1700 ▭ M-Sa 6025

ISRAEL

GALEI ZAHAL—(Europe)
Hebrew
24 Hr   6973/15785

KOL ISRAEL
Arabic
0345-2210 ▭ 5915 (Mideast)
Hebrew

0000-0330	11585 (W Europe & E North Am)
0000-0430	🅆 7545 (W Europe & E North Am)
0000-0500	🅆 9345 (W Europe & E North Am)
0330-0600	🅆 11585 (W Europe & E North Am)
0400-0500	🅂 11590 (W Europe & E North Am)
0500-0600	🅆 7545 (W Europe & E North Am)
0500-1900	▭ 15760 (W Europe & E North Am)
0600-1030 & 1115-1500	▭ 17535 (W Europe & N America)
1700-2355	🅆 9390 (Europe & E North Am)
1800-1830	🅂 11585 (W Europe & E North Am)
1800-2400	🅆 9345 (W Europe & E North Am)
1830-2400	11585 (W Europe & E North Am)
2000-2400	🅂 13635 (W Europe & N America)
2025-2400	🅆 6280 (W Europe & E North Am)

Yiddish
1600-1625   🅂 11605 (Europe), 🅂 11590

Etón's new E1 receiver is assembled at its BEL partner's Bangalore facility. Etón

	& ⓢ 15640 (W Europe & E North Am)	1500-1525	M-Sa 9670 (S Europe & N Africa), ⓢ M-Sa 11795 (N Africa & Mideast), ⓦ M-Sa 11800 & ⓢ M-Sa 11855 (S Europe & N Africa), ⓦ M-Sa 11900 (N Africa & Mideast)
1700-1725	ⓦ 9390 (Europe), ⓦ 11605 & ⓦ 17535 (W Europe & E North Am)		
		1555-1625	ⓦ M-Sa 5985, ⓦ M-Sa 9570, ⓢ M-Sa 9670, ⓦ M-Sa 11680 & ⓢ M-Sa 11855 (W Europe)

ITALY—Italian

RAI INTERNATIONAL

0000-0055	9840 (S America), 11800 (N America)	1700-1800	ⓦ M-Sa 6140 (Mideast), ⓢ 9670 & ⓦ M-Sa 9755 (S Europe & N Africa), ⓢ 11670 (E Africa), ⓢ 11725 (S Europe & N Africa), ⓦ 11875 (E Africa), ⓦ 11895 (S Europe & N Africa), ⓦ 15250 (C Africa), *15320* & ⓢ 17800 (C Africa & S Africa)
0130-0230	*9670* (S America), *11765* (C America)		
0130-0315	9840 (S America), 11800 (N America)		
0435-0445	ⓦ 5965 (S Europe & N Africa), ⓦ 6000 & ⓢ 6110 (N Africa), ⓦ 7230, ⓢ 7235 & ⓢ 9875 (S Europe & N Africa)		
0455-0530	ⓢ 11900 & ⓦ 11985 (E Africa)	1830-1905	ⓦ 11800, ⓦ 15250, ⓢ 17780 & ⓢ 21520 (N America)
0630-1300	ⓢ 9670 & ⓦ 11800 (E Europe)	2240-2400	9840 (S America), 11800 (N America)
1000-1100	*11920* (Australasia)		
1250-1630	ⓢ Su 11775 (E Africa), ⓢ Su 17780 (N America), ⓢ Su 21535 (S America)		

RAI-RADIOTELEVISIONE ITALIANA—
(Europe, Mideast & N Africa)

1350-1730 ▭	Su 9670 (W Europe), Su 21710 (C Africa & S Africa)	0000-0003, 0012-0103, 0112-0203, 0212-0303, 0312-0403, 0412-0500 & 2300-2400 ▭ 6060	
1350-1730	ⓦ Su 21520 (N America), ⓦ Su 21550 (S America)		
1400-1425	M-Sa 17780 (N America)		
1400-1430	M-Sa 21520 (N America)		

JAPAN—Japanese

RADIO JAPAN

0200-0300	*11860* (SE Asia), *11935* (S America), 17845 (E Asia)
0200-0500	*5960* (E North Am), 15195 (E Asia), 15325 (S Asia), 17810 (SE Asia)
0300-0400	*9660* (S America)
0300-0500	17560 (Mideast), 17685 (Australasia), 17825 (W North Am & C America)
0700-0800	6145, 6165 & 15195 (E Asia), 17870 (Pacific)
0700-0900	17860 (SE Asia)
0700-1000	*11740* (SE Asia), *11920* & 21755 (Australasia)
0800-1000	*9530* (S America), *9540* (W North Am & C America), 9825 (Pacific & S America), *11710* (Europe), 15590 (S Asia), *17650* (W Africa), *17720* (Mideast)
0800-1700	9750 (E Asia)
0900-1600	11815 (SE Asia)
1300-1500	*11705* (E North Am)
1500-1700	9535 (W North Am & C America), *12045* (S Asia), *21630* (C Africa)
1600-1900	6035 (E Asia), 7200 (SE Asia)
1700-1800	*9750* (N Europe), *11865* & [W] *12045* (S Asia), *21600* (S America)
1700-1900	*6175* (W Europe), 7140 (Australasia), [W] *9575* (Mideast & N Africa), 9835 (Pacific & S America), [S] *13740* (Mideast & N Africa)
1800-1900	*15355* (S Africa)
1900-2100	*6035* (Australasia)
2000-2100	6165 (E Asia), 11970 (Europe)
2000-2200	[W] 7225 & 11665 (SE Asia)
2000-2400	11910 (E Asia), [S] 13680 (SE Asia)
2100-2200	9560 (E Asia)
2200-2300	*6115* (W Europe), [W] *7115* & [S] *9650* (Mideast), *11770* (Australasia), *11895* (C America), *15220* (S America), 17825 (W North Am & C America)
2200-2400	[W] 11665 (SE Asia)
2300-2400	*17605* (S America)

RADIO NIKKEI

0000-0800	3925, Sa/Su 9760
0000-0900	Sa/Su 3945, Sa/Su 6115
0000-1400	6055, 9595
0800-1400 & 2030-2300	3925
2030-2400	6055, 9595
2300-2400	3925, F/Sa 3945, F/Sa 6115, F/Sa 9760

JORDAN—Arabic

RADIO JORDAN

0500-0810 ⬅	11810 (Mideast, S Asia & Australasia)
0600-0815 ⬅	11960 (E Europe)
1130-1300 ⬅	15290 (N Africa & C America)
1200-1600 ⬅	11810 (Mideast, S Asia & Australasia)
1845-2100 ⬅	9830 (W Europe)
1845-2300 ⬅	11810 (Mideast, S Asia & Australasia)
2100-2300 ⬅	15435 (S America)

KOREA (DPR)—Korean

KOREAN CENTRAL BS

0000-0630	6100
0000-0930	9665
0000-1800	2850, 11680
0900-0950	4405, 7140 & 9345 (E Asia)
1200-1250	3560 (E Asia), [W] 6185 (SE Asia), [W] 6285 & [W] 9335 (C America), [W] 9850 (SE Asia), [S] 11710 (C America), [S] 11735, [S] 13650 & [S] 15180 (SE Asia)
1400-1450	3560 (E Asia), [W] 6185, [W] 9850, [S] 11735 & [S] 13650 (SE Asia)
1500-1800	6100
1700-1750	4405 (E Asia), [W] 7570 (W Europe), 9335 & 11710 (N America), [W] 12015, [S] 13760 & [S] 15245 (W Europe)
2000-2050	3560 (E Asia), [W] 6285 (Europe), 7100 (S Africa),

	9325 (Europe), 9975 & 11535 (Mideast & N Africa), 11710/11910 (S Africa), [S] 12015 (Europe)
2000-2400	2850, 6100, 9665, 11680
2300-2350	3560, 4405 & 7140/7180 (E Asia), [W] 7570 (W Europe), 9345, 9975 & 11535 (E Asia), [W] 12015, [S] 13760 & [S] 15245 (W Europe)

PYONGYANG BROADCASTING STATION

0000-0050	3560, 7140 & 9345 (E Asia)
0000-0100	9730 (E Asia)
0000-0925	6248 (E Asia)
0000-1800	6398 (E Asia)
0000-1900	3320 (E Asia)
0200-0630	3250 (E Asia)
0700-0750	4405, 7140 & 9345 (E Asia)
0900-0950	3560, 9975 & 11735 (E Asia), 13760 & 15245 (E Europe)
1000-1050 & 1200-1250	4405, 7140 & 9345 (E Asia)
1300-1350	[W] 6285, 9325 & [S] 12015 (Europe)
1500-1900	6248 (E Asia)
1500-2030	3250 (E Asia)
2100-2400	3320, 6248 & 6398 (E Asia)

KOREA (REPUBLIC)—Korean

KBS WORLD RADIO

0100-0200	15575 (N America)
0300-0400	11810 (S America)
0700-0800	*9535* (Europe)
0900-1000	15210 (Europe)
0900-1100	5975 & 7275 (E Asia), 9570 (SE Asia), 9640 (Europe)
1000-1100	[S] *9650* (E North Am)
1200-1300	7275 (E Asia), [W] *9650* (E North Am)
1600-1800	7275 (Europe), 15575 (Mideast & Africa)
1700-1900	5975 (E Asia), 7150 (Mideast), 9515 (Europe)
1800-2000	9870 (Mideast)
2100-2300	5975 (E Asia)

KUWAIT—Arabic

RADIO KUWAIT

0200-0500	6055 (Mideast & W Asia)
0200-0530	11675 (W North Am)
0200-1305	15495 (N Africa)
0400-0740	15505 (E Europe & W Asia)
0800-0925	15110 (S Asia & SE Asia)
0900-1305	6055 (Mideast & W Asia)
1015-1740	15505 (W Africa & C Africa)
1200-1505	17885 (E Asia & Australasia)
1300-1605	13620/11990 (Europe & E North Am)
1315-1600	15110 (S Asia)
1615-1800	11990 (Europe & E North Am)
1730-2130	9880 (N Africa)
1745-2130	15505 (Europe & E North Am)
1800-2400	15495 (W Africa & C Africa)
1815-2400	9855 (Europe & E North Am)

LITHUANIA—Lithuanian

RADIO VILNIUS

0000-0030 ⇦	9875 (E North Am)
0000-0030	[S] 11690 (E North Am)
0100-0130	[W] 7325 (E North Am)
0900-0930 ⇦	9710 (W Europe)
2300-2330	[W] 7325 (E North Am)

MEXICO—Spanish

RADIO EDUCACION

0000-1200 ⇦	6185

MOROCCO

RADIO MEDI UN—(Europe & N Africa)
Arabic & French

0500-0400	9575

RTV MAROCAINE
Arabic

0000-0500	[W] 5980 & [S] 11920 (N Africa & Mideast)
0900-2200	15345 (N Africa & Mideast)
1100-1500	15335 (Europe)
2200-2400	7135 (Europe)

NETHERLANDS—Dutch

RADIO NEDERLAND

0300-0400	[S] *6165* (N America), [S] *9590* (C America)
0400-0500	[W] *5975* (C America), [W] *6165* (N America)
0500-0600	[S] *6165* (N America), [S] 7125 (Europe)
0500-0700	[S] 6015 (S Europe)
0600-0700 ⇦	5955 (Europe)
0600-0700	[W] *6015* (W Europe), [W] *6165* (W North Am), [S] *9625* & [W] *9895* (Australasia), [S] *11655* (N Europe)
0600-0800	[W] 7125 (Europe)
0700-0800	[W] *6015* (W Europe), [W] 6035 (S Europe), [S] *9610* (N Europe), *9625* (Australasia)
0700-0900 ⇦	9895 (S Europe)
0700-1800 ⇦	5955 (W Europe)
0800-0900 ⇦	11935 (S Europe)
0900-1100	[W] *6035* (Europe)
0900-1600 ⇦	Sa/Su 9895 & Sa/Su 13700 (S Europe)
0930-1015	M-Sa *6020* (C America)
1100-1200	[S] *9895* (E North Am)
1200-1300	[W] *15565* (E Asia)
1300-1400	[W] *5885*, [S] *7400* & [W] *9940* (E Asia & SE Asia), [S] *12065* (SE Asia), [W] *12070* (S Asia), [S] *13695*, [S] *13735* & [S] *15640* (SE Asia), [W] *17580* & [S] *17585* (S Asia), [W] *17815* (SE Asia)
1600-1700 ⇦	9895 (S Europe)
1600-1700	[W] 7175 & [S] 9895 (S Europe), [W] *11655* (E Africa & Europe), [W] *13700* (Africa), *13840* (Mideast), [S] *15335* (Europe, Mideast & N Africa)
1600-1800	[S] 13700 (S Europe & Mideast)
1700-1800	[W] 6010 (S Europe), *6020* (S Africa), [W] 7105 (S Europe), [W] *9895* (E Africa & Europe), [S] *11655* (E Africa), [W] *11655* (E Africa & Europe)
2100-2200	[S] 6015 (S Europe), *7120* (C Africa), *15315* (S America), *17810* (W Africa), *17895* (S America)
2200-2300	[W] *6015* (Europe), *15315* (S America)
2300-2400	[W] *6165* (E North Am), *9525* (C America & S America)

OMAN—Arabic

RADIO SULTANATE OF OMAN

0000-0200	9760 (Irr) (Europe & Mideast)
0200-0300	15355 (Irr) (E Africa)
0200-0400	6085 (Mideast)
0400-0600	9515 (Mideast), 17590 (Irr) (E Africa)
0600-1000	17630 (Irr) (Europe & Mideast)
0600-1400	13640 (Mideast)
1400-1800	15375 (E Africa)
1500-1800	15140 (Irr) (Europe & Mideast)
1800-2000	6190 & 15355 (Irr) (E Africa)
2000-2200	6085 (E Africa), 13640/15355 (Irr) (Europe & Mideast)
2300-2400	9760 (Irr) (Europe & Mideast)

PARAGUAY—Spanish

RADIO NACIONAL—(S America)

24 Hr	9737

POLAND—Polish

RADIO POLONIA

1130-1200 ⇦	7285 (E Europe)
1130-1200	[W] 5965 (Europe)
1530-1630	[S] 5965 (W Europe)
1630-1730	[W] 6035 (W Europe)
2100-2200	[S] 7265 (W Europe)
2200-2300 ⇦	6050 (E Europe)
2200-2300	[W] 7285 (W Europe)

PORTUGAL—Portuguese

RDP INTERNATIONAL

0000-0200	[S] Tu-Sa 11630 (W North Am), [S] Tu-Sa 13660 & [S] Tu-Sa 15295 (S America)
0000-0300 ⇦	Tu-Sa 9715 (E North Am), Tu-Sa 13700 (C America)
0000-0300	[W] Tu-Sa 9410 (W North Am), [W] Tu-Sa 11980 & [W] Tu-Sa 13770 (S America)

0500-0700	[S] M-F 7240 (W Europe)
0500-0755	[S] M-F 9840 (Europe)
0600-0855	[W] M-F 9755 (Europe)
0600-1300	[W] M-F 9815 (Europe)
0645-0800	[S] M-F 11850 (Europe)
0700-0755	[S] M-F 9815 (Europe)
0700-0800	[S] Sa/Su 12020 (Europe)
0700-0955	[S] Sa/Su 12000 (W Africa & S America)
0700-1000	[S] Sa/Su 15160 (E Africa & S Africa)
0745-0900	[W] M-F 11660 (Europe)
0800-0900	[W] Sa/Su 11875 (Europe)
0800-1055	[W] Sa/Su 17710 (W Africa & S America)
0800-1100	[W] Sa/Su 21830 (E Africa & S Africa)
0800-1200	[S] 12020 (Europe)
0800-1455	[W] Sa/Su 15575 (Europe)
0830-1000	[S] Sa/Su 11995 (Europe)
0900-1055	[W] 11875 (Europe)
0930-1100	[W] Sa/Su 9815 (Europe)
1000-1200	[S] M-F 15575 (W Africa & S America)
1055-1455	[W] Sa/Su 11875 (Europe)
1100-1300 ⇦	Sa/Su 21655 (W Africa & S America), 21830 (E Africa & S Africa)
1100-1300	[W] M-F 15140 (Europe), [W] M-F 21655 (W Africa & S America)
1200-1355	[S] Sa/Su 12020 (Europe)
1200-2000	[S] Sa/Su/Holidays 15560 (N America), [S] Sa/Su/Holidays 17615 (C America)
1300-1500	[S] M-F 15770 (Mideast & S Asia)
1300-1655 ⇦	Sa/Su 21830 (E Africa & S Africa)
1300-1700 ⇦	Sa/Su 21655 (W Africa & S America)
1300-1700	[W] Sa/Su/Holidays 15575 (E North Am)
1300-1800	[W] Sa/Su/Holidays 17745 (C America)
1400-1600	[W] M-F 15690 (Mideast & S Asia)
1400-2000	[S] Sa/Su 13590 & [S] Sa/Su 15555 (Europe)
1500-1755	[W] Sa/Su 11635 (Europe)
1500-1800	[W] Sa/Su 11960 (Europe)
1600-1900	[S] M-F 13590 & [S] M-F 15555 (Europe)
1700-1900	[S] M-F 15555 (Irr) (C America), [W] Sa/Su/Holidays 17825 & [W] M-F 17825 (Irr) (E North Am)
1700-2000 ⇦	17680 (E Africa & S Africa), 21655 (W Africa & S America)
1700-2000	[W] M-F 11630 (Europe)
1800-2100	[W] Sa/Su 11630 (Europe), [W] Sa/Su/Holidays 15535 (C America)
1900-2100	[W] Sa/Su 15540 & [W] M-F 15540 (Irr) (E North Am)
1900-2300	[S] 11945 (Irr) (S Africa), [S] 13720 (Irr) (Europe), [S] 15555 (Irr) (C America)
2000-2100 ⇦	Sa/Su 21655 (W Africa & S America)
2000-2300	[S] Sa/Su 9820 (Irr) (Europe), [S] M-F 15295 (Irr) (S America), [S] 15560 (Irr) (E North Am)
2000-2400	[W] 9615 (Irr) & [W] 9795 (Irr) (Europe), [W] 11825 (Irr) (E Africa & S Africa), [W] 15555 (Irr) (W Africa & S America)
2100-2400	[W] 11635 (Irr) (C America), [W] 15540 (Irr) (E North Am)
2300-2400	[S] M-F 11630 (W North Am), [S] M-F 13660 & [S] M-F 15295 (S America)

ROMANIA—Romanian

RADIO ROMANIA

0800-0900	[S] Su 11970 (Mideast), [S] Su 15270 (W Asia & S Asia), Su 15370 (Mideast), [W] Su 15430, [W] Su 17775 & [S] Su 17805 (W Asia & S Asia), [W] Su 17810 (Mideast)
0900-1000	[W] Su 15380 (N Africa & Mideast), Su 15430 (Mideast), [S] Su 15450, [W] Su 17745 & [S] Su 17770 (N Africa & Mideast), [W] Su 17775 & [S] Su 17860 (Mideast)
1000-1100	[S] Su 11830, [S] Su 15250 & [W] Su 15260 (W Europe), Su 15380, [W] Su 17735 & [S]

Su 17740 (N Africa), 🇼 Su 17825 (W Europe)

RADIO ROMANIA INTERNATIONAL

0100-0200	🇼 11960 (E North Am)
0200-0300	🇼 9640 & 🇼 11950 (E North Am)
1200-1300	🇸 9750 & 🇸 11920 (W Europe)
1300-1400	🇼 7120 (S Europe), 🇼 15170 & 🇼 17825 (W Europe)
1400-1500	🇸 9760 & 🇸 11965 (W Europe)
1500-1600	🇼 9595 & 🇼 11970 (W Europe)
1600-1700	🇸 9690 & 🇸 11960 (Mideast)
1700-1800	🇼 7195 (Mideast), 🇸 9765 (W Europe), 🇼 9790 (Mideast), 🇸 11865 (W Europe)
1800-1900	🇼 7140, 🇸 9625, 🇼 9625 & 🇸 11765 (W Europe)
1900-2000	🇼 7125 & 🇼 9640 (W Europe)
2000-2100	🇸 9515 & 🇸 11925 (W Europe)

SAUDI ARABIA—Arabic

BROADCASTING SERVICE OF THE KINGDOM

0300-0600	9580 (Mideast & E Africa), 15170 (E Europe & W Asia)
0300-0800	17895 (C Asia & E Asia)
0300-0900	9675 (Mideast)
0600-0900	15380 (Mideast), 17730 (N Africa), 17740 (W Europe)
0600-1700	11855 (Mideast & E Africa)
0900-1200	11935 (Mideast), 17615 (S Asia & SE Asia), 17805 (N Africa), 21495 (E Asia & SE Asia), 21705 (W Europe)
0900-1600	9675 (Mideast)
1200-1400	15380 (Mideast), 21600 (SE Asia)
1200-1500	17895 & 21505 (N Africa), 21640 (W Europe)
1300-1600	21460 (E Africa)
1500-1800	13710 & 15315 (N Africa), 15435 (W Europe)
1600-1800	15205 (W Europe), 17560 (C Africa & W Africa)
1700-2200	9580 (Mideast & E Africa)
1800-2300	9555 (N Africa), 9870 (W Europe), 11740 (C Africa & W Africa), 11820 (W Europe), 11915 (N Africa)

SINGAPORE—Chinese

MEDIACORP RADIO

1400-1600 & 2300-1100	6000

RADIO SINGAPORE INTERNATIONAL—(SE Asia)

1100-1400	6000 & 6185

SLOVAKIA—Slovak

RADIO SLOVAKIA INTERNATIONAL

0130-0200	🇸 5930 & 🇼 7230 (E North Am & C America), 9440 (S America)
0730-0800	🇸 9440, 🇼 13715 & 15460 (Australasia)
1530-1600	🇸 5920 & 🇸 7345 (W Europe)
1630-1700	🇼 5915 & 🇼 7345/6055 (W Europe)
1900-1930	🇸 5920 & 🇸 6055 (W Europe)
2000-2030	🇼 5915 & 🇼 7345 (W Europe)

SPAIN

RADIO EXTERIOR DE ESPAÑA
Galician, Catalan & Basque

1240-1255	🇸 M-F *9765* (C America), 🇸 M-F *11815* (C America & S America), 🇸 M-F 13720 (W Europe), 🇸 M-F *15170* (W North Am), 🇸 M-F 15585 (Europe), 🇸 M-F 21540 (C Africa & S Africa), 🇸 M-F 21570 (S America), 🇸 M-F 21610 (Mideast), 🇸 M-F 21700 (N America & C America)
1340-1355	🇼 M-F *5970* (C America), 🇼 M-F *15170* (W North Am), 🇼 M-F 15585 (Europe), 🇼 M-F 17595 (N America), 🇼 M-F 21540 (C Africa & S Africa), 🇼 M-F 21570 (S

America), ⓦ M-F 21610 (Mideast)

Spanish

Time	Details
0000-0200	Ⓢ 11680 & ⓦ 11945 (S America)
0000-0400	Ⓢ 6020 & ⓦ *11815* (C America & S America)
0000-0500	Ⓢ 9535 & ⓦ 9540 (N America & C America), 9620 (S America), 15160 (C America & S America)
0100-0600	6055 (N America)
0200-0600	Ⓢ *3350* & ⓦ *6040* (C America), Ⓢ *6125* & ⓦ *11880* (N America)
0500-0600	Ⓢ 12035 (Europe)
0500-0700	11890 (Mideast)
0600-0700	ⓦ 13720 (W Europe)
0600-0800	ⓦ Sa/Su 5985 (W Europe), ⓦ Sa/Su 9710 (Europe)
0600-0900	12035 (Europe)
0700-0900	17770 & Sa/Su 21610 (Australasia)
0700-1240	13720 (W Europe)
0800-1000	M-F 21570 (S America)
0900-1240	15585 (Europe), 21540 (C Africa & S Africa), 21610 (Mideast)
1000-1200	*9660* (E Asia), M-F *11815* (C America & S America)
1000-1240	21570 (S America), Ⓢ M-F 21700 (N America & C America)
1000-1300	ⓦ M-F 17595 (N America & C America)
1100-1200	ⓦ M-F *5970* (C America)
1100-1240	Ⓢ M-F *9765* (C America), M-F *15170* (W North Am)
1200-1240	Ⓢ M-F *11815* (C America & S America)
1200-1300	ⓦ M-Sa *5970* (C America)
1200-1400	Ⓢ Su *9765* (C America), *11910* (SE Asia)
1200-1500	Su *15170* (W North Am & C America), Sa/Su 21700 (C America & S America)
1200-1600	Ⓢ Su *11815* & ⓦ Su *15125* (C America & S America)
1240-1255	ⓦ 13720 (W Europe), ⓦ M-F *15170* (W North Am), Ⓢ Sa/Su 15585 & ⓦ 15585 (Europe), Ⓢ Sa/Su 21540 & ⓦ 21540 (C Africa & S Africa), Ⓢ Sa/Su 21570 & ⓦ 21570 (S America), Ⓢ Sa/Su 21610 & ⓦ 21610 (Mideast)
1240-1300	Ⓢ Sa/Su 13720 (W Europe)
1255-1340	M-F *15170* (W North Am), 15585 (Europe), 21540 (C Africa & S Africa), 21570 (S America), 21610 (Mideast)
1255-1400	Ⓢ M-F *9765* (C America)
1300-1340	ⓦ M-F *5970* (C America), ⓦ M-F 17595 (N America)
1300-1400	Sa/Su 13720 (W Europe)
1300-1500	ⓦ Su *5970* (C America), Ⓢ 17595 (N America)
1340-1355	Ⓢ M-F *15170* (W North Am), Ⓢ 15585 & ⓦ Sa/Su 15585 (Europe), Ⓢ 21540 & ⓦ Sa/Su 21540 (C Africa & S Africa), Ⓢ 21570 & ⓦ Sa/Su 21570 (S America), Ⓢ 21610 & ⓦ Sa/Su 21610 (Mideast)
1355-1500	M-F 17595 (N America), 21610 (Mideast)
1355-1700	15585 (Europe), 21570 (S America)
1400-1500	Ⓢ Sa 15385 (W Africa & C Africa), Ⓢ 17755 & ⓦ 21540 (C Africa & S Africa)
1500-1600	Su *9765* (C America), Su *17850* (W North Am)
1500-1700	M-Sa 15385 (W Africa & C Africa), 21610 (Mideast)
1500-1800	21700 (C America & S America)
1500-1900	17755 (C Africa & S Africa)
1600-1800	Sa/Su *9765* (C America), Ⓢ Sa/Su *11815* & ⓦ Sa/Su *15125* (C America & S America), Sa/Su *17850* (W North Am)
1700-1900	17715 (S America)
1700-2000	Sa/Su 9665 (Europe)
1700-2300	7275 (Europe)
1800-2000	*9765* (C America), Ⓢ *11815* & ⓦ *15125* (C America & S America), *17850* (W North Am)
1800-2100	Sa/Su 21700 (C America & S America)
1800-2230	M-F 21700 (Irr) (C America & S America)

1900-2100	Su 17755 (C Africa & S Africa)
1900-2300	15110 (N America & C America)
2000-2100	⬛ Sa 9665 & ◰ Sa/Su 9665 (Europe)
2000-2230	M-F *9765* (Irr) (C America), ⬛ M-F *11815* (Irr) & ◰ M-F *15125* (Irr) (C America & S America), M-F *17850* (Irr) (W North Am)
2000-2300	Sa/Su *9765* (C America), ⬛ Sa/Su *11815* & ◰ Sa/Su *15125* (C America & S America), Sa/Su *17850* (W North Am)
2100-2200	◰ Sa 9665 (Europe), ◰ M-F 11625 (C Africa)
2100-2300	◰ Sa/Su 21700 (C America & S America)
2200-2300	7270 (N Africa & W Africa), ◰ Sa 11625 (C Africa)
2300-2400	⬛ 9535 & ◰ 9540 (N America & C America), 9620, ⬛ 11680 & ◰ 11945 (S America), ◰ Su *15125* (Irr) & 15160 (C America & S America), Su *17850* (Irr) (W North Am)

SWEDEN—Swedish

RADIO SWEDEN

0000-0030	*9490* (S America)
0100-0130	⬛ *9435* (S Asia), ◰ *9490* (S America), ◰ *11550* (S Asia)
0200-0230 ▭	*6010* (E North Am)
0300-0330 ▭	*6010* (N America)
0300-0330	⬛ *9490* (S America)
0330-0500	⬛ M-F 9435 (Mideast & E Africa)
0430-0500	⬛ M-F 6065 & ◰ M-F 7465 (E Europe & Mideast)
0430-0600	◰ M-F 9490 (Mideast & E Africa)
0500-0700 ▭	M-F 6065 (Europe & N Africa)
0600-0700 ▭	M-F 9490 (W Europe & W Africa)
0600-0800	⬛ Sa 13580 (Mideast)
0700-0800 ▭	M-Sa 9490 (Europe & N Africa)
0700-0900	◰ Sa 6065 (Europe & N Africa), ⬛ Su 13580 (Mideast), ◰ Sa 17505 (Africa)
0800-0900 ▭	Sa/Su 9490 (Europe & N Africa)
0800-1000	◰ Su 6065 (Europe & N Africa), ◰ Su 17505 (Africa)
0900-1000 ▭	Su 9490 (Europe & N Africa)
1000-1010	⬛ 15735 (Asia & Australasia)
1010-1030	⬛ Sa/Su 15735 (Asia & Australasia)
1030-1040	⬛ 15735 (E Asia & Australasia)
1040-1100	⬛ Sa/Su 15735 (E Asia & Australasia)
1100-1110 ▭	9490 (Europe & N Africa)
1100-1110	◰ 7420 (E Asia & Australasia)
1110-1130 ▭	Sa/Su 9490 (Europe & N Africa)
1110-1130	◰ Sa/Su 7420 (E Asia & Australasia)
1130-1140 ▭	21810 (Africa)
1130-1140	◰ *9485* (C America & Australasia), ◰ 11610 (Asia & Australasia)
1140-1200 ▭	Sa/Su 21810 (Africa)
1140-1200	◰ Sa/Su *9485* (C America & Australasia), ◰ Sa/Su 11610 (Asia & Australasia)
1200-1210 ▭	15240 (E North Am)
1200-1215	⬛ 15735 (Asia & Australasia)
1210-1230 ▭	Sa/Su 15240 (E North Am)
1215-1230	⬛ M-F 15735 (E Asia & Australasia), ⬛ Sa/Su 15735 (Asia & Australasia)
1300-1315 ▭	15240 (E North Am)
1300-1315	◰ 7420 & ⬛ 15735 (E Asia & Australasia)
1315-1330 ▭	M-F 15240 (N America), Sa/Su 15240 (E North Am)
1315-1330	◰ Sa/Su 7420 (E Asia & Australasia), ◰ M-F 11550 & ⬛ M-F 15735 (SE Asia & Australasia), ⬛ Sa/Su 15735 (E Asia & Australasia)
1400-1415	◰ 11550 (SE Asia & Australasia)

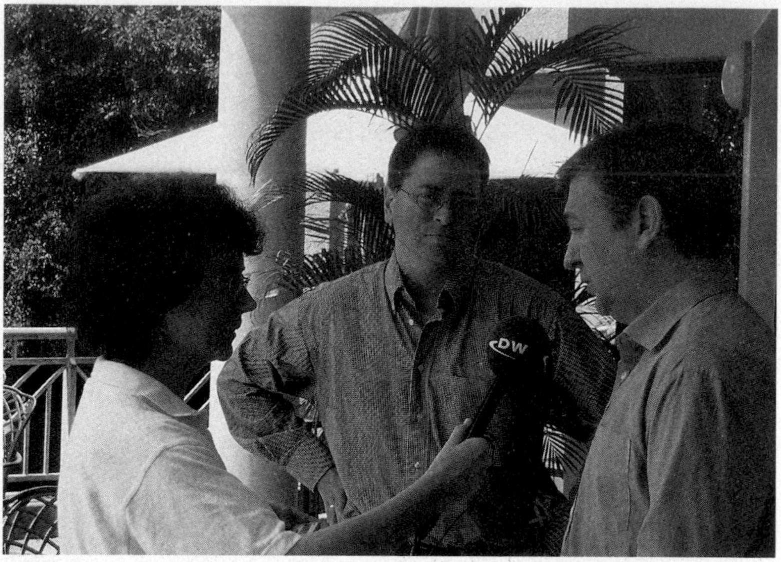

Veteran reporter Irene Quaile conducts an alfresco interview for Deutsche Welle.

DW

1400-1430 ⇦	*15240* (N America)
1400-1430	[S] 15735 (Mideast, SE Asia & Australasia)
1415-1430	[W] M-F 7420 (E Asia & Australasia), [W] Sa/Su 11550 (SE Asia & Australasia), [W] M-F 11560 (E Asia & Australasia)
1500-1530 ⇦	15240 (N America)
1500-1530	[S] 9410 (E Europe & Mideast), [W] 11550 (Mideast, Asia & Australasia)
1545-1600 ⇦	15240 (N America)
1545-1600	[S] 13580 (Mideast & W Africa), [S] 15735 (W Europe & W Africa)
1545-1700 ⇦	6065 (Europe)
1600-1615	[S] M-F 13580 (Mideast & W Africa), [S] M-F 15735 (W Europe & W Africa)
1600-1630	[W] 5850 (E Europe & Mideast)
1645-1700	[W] 7420 (Mideast), [W] 13580 (W Europe & W Africa)
1700-1715	[W] M-F 6065 (Europe), [W] M-F 7420 (Mideast), [W] M-F 13580 (W Europe & W Africa)
1730-1800 ⇦	6065 (Europe)
1800-1830	[S] 9390 & [S] 13710 (Mideast)
1800-1900 ⇦	Su 6065 (Europe)
1900-1930 ⇦	6065 (Europe)
1900-1930	[W] 7530 (N Africa & Mideast), [W] 9375 (W Europe & W Africa), [S] 11605 (Africa), [W] 13580 (Mideast)
2000-2030 ⇨	*7420* (SE Asia & Australasia)
2000-2100	[S] 9390 (W Africa & S America)
2100-2200	[W] 9510 (W Africa & S America)
2100-2230 ⇦	6065 (Europe)

SYRIA—Arabic

RADIO DAMASCUS—(S America)

2330-0030	9330/13610 & 12085

SYRIAN BROADCASTING SERVICE

1100-1400 ⇦	12085

THAILAND—Thai

RADIO THAILAND

0100-0200	*5890* (E North Am)
0330-0430	*5890* (W North Am)
1000-1100	[W] 7285 & [S] 11870 (SE Asia & Australasia)
1330-1400	[W] 7160 & [S] 11685 (E Asia)
1800-1900	[S] 9695 & [W] 11855 (Mideast)
2045-2115	[W] 9535 & [S] 9680 (Europe)

TUNISIA—Arabic
RTV TUNISIENNE
0200-0500	◨	9720 & 12005 (N Africa & Mideast)
0400-0700	◨	7190 (N Africa), 7275 (W Europe)
1200-1600	◨	15450 & 17735 (N Africa & Mideast)
1400-1600	◨	11730 (W Europe)
1400-1700	◨	11950 (N Africa)
1600-2100	◨	9720 & 12005 (N Africa & Mideast)
1600-2300	◨	7225 (W Europe)
1700-2300	◨	7190 (N Africa)

TURKEY—Turkish
VOICE OF TURKEY
0000-0200	▥ 7300 (W Europe & N America)
0000-0700	▤ 9460/7300 (Europe & E North Am)
0400-0700	▤ 15225 (W Asia & C Asia)
0400-0900	▤ 11750 (Mideast)
0500-0800	▥ 9460 (Europe & E North Am), ▥ 17690 (W Asia & C Asia)
0500-1000	▥ 11925 (Mideast)
0700-0800	▤ 15350 (Europe)
0800-1500	15350 (Europe)
0800-1700	◨ 11955 (N Africa & Mideast)
0900-1200	▤ 17605 & ▥ 17720 (Australasia)
1000-1500	▤ F 17705 (N Africa)
1100-1600	▥ F 17860 (N Africa)
1500-1600	▤ 15350 (Europe)
1500-2300	▥ 5980 (Europe)
1600-2100	▤ 9460/7300 (Europe)
1600-2200	▤ 5960 (Mideast)
1700-2200	▤ 7215 (N Africa & W Africa)
1700-2300	▥ 6120 (N Africa & Mideast)
1800-2300	▥ 9840 (N Africa & W Africa)
2300-2400	▥ 7300 (W Europe & N America), ▤ 9460/7300 (Europe & E North Am)

UKRAINE—Ukrainian
RADIO UKRAINE
0000-0100	▥ 7440/5910 (E North Am)

0000-0500	▤	7485 (W Asia)
0100-0300	▤	7440 (E North Am)
0100-0600	▥	7420 (W Asia)
0200-0400	▥	7440/5910 (E North Am)
0500-0800	▤	9945 (W Europe)
0600-0900	▥	7490 (W Europe)
0900-1200 &		
1300-1400	◨	15675 (W Europe)
1300-1700	▤	7530 (W Asia)
1400-1800	▥	7400 (W Asia)
1800-2000	▤	7490 (W Europe)
1900-2100	▥	7555 (W Europe)
2200-2300	▤	7420/7490 (W Europe)
2300-2400	▥	5840 (W Europe), ▤ 7440 (E North Am)

VIETNAM—Vietnamese
VOICE OF VIETNAM
0000-0100	7285 (SE Asia)
0130-0230	*6175* (E North Am & C America)
0430-0530	*6175* (N America & C America)
1330-1430	7285 (SE Asia)
1500-1600	7220 & 9550 (W Africa & C Africa)
1700-1800	7280 & 9730 (Europe)
1730-1830	▤ *9725* (W Europe)
1830-1930	▥ *5955* (W Europe)
1930-2030	▤ *9725* (S Europe)
2030-2130	▥ *5970* (S Europe)

YEMEN—Arabic
REPUBLIC OF YEMEN RADIO—(Mideast)
0300-0650	9780
0300-1500	5950 & 6135
1700-1800 &	
1900-2208	9780

M. Guha

Worldly Words

PASSPORT's Definitive Glossary of World Band Terms and Abbreviations

ABCDEFGHIJKLMNOPQ

A variety of terms and abbreviations are used in world band parlance. Many are specialized and benefit from explanation; some are foreign words that need translation; while others are simply adaptations of everyday usage.

Here, then, is PASSPORT's A–Z guide to world band words and what they mean to your listening. For a thorough understanding of the specialized terms and lab tests used in evaluating world band radios, read the Radio Database International White Paper, *How to Interpret Receiver Lab Tests and Measurements*.

A. Summer schedule season for world band stations. *See* ◨. *See* HFCC. *Cf.* B.

Absorption. Reduction in signal strength during bounces (refraction) off the earth's ionosphere (*see* Propagation) or the earth itself.

AC. Alternating ("household" or "mains") Current, 120V throughout North America, 100V in Japan and usually 220–240V elsewhere in the world.

Active Antenna. An antenna that electronically amplifies signals. Active, or amplified, antennas are typically mounted indoors, but some weatherproofed models can also be erected outdoors. Active antennas take up relatively little space, but their amplification circuits may introduce certain problems that can result in unwanted sounds being heard (*see Dynamic Range*). *Cf.* Passive Antenna. *See* Feedline.

Adjacent-Channel Interference. *See* Interference.

Adjacent-Channel Rejection. *See* Selectivity.

A. Summer schedule season for world band stations. *See* ◨. *See* HFCC. *Cf.* B.

Absorption. Reduction in signal strength during bounces (refraction) off the earth's ionosphere (*see* Propagation) or the earth itself.

AC. Alternating ("household" or "mains") Current, 120V throughout North America, 100V in Japan and usually 220–240V elsewhere in the world.

Active Antenna. An antenna that electronically amplifies signals. Active, or amplified, antennas are typically mounted indoors, but some weatherproofed models can also be erected outdoors. Active antennas take up relatively little space, but their amplification circuits may introduce certain problems that can result in unwanted sounds being heard (*see Dynamic Range*). *Cf.* Passive Antenna. *See* Feedline.

Adjacent-Channel Interference. *See* Interference.

Adjacent-Channel Rejection. *See* Selectivity.

AGC. *See* Automatic Gain Control.

AGC Threshold. The threshold at which the automatic gain control (AGC, *see*) chooses to act relates to both listening pleasure and audible sensitivity. If the threshold is too low, the AGC will tend to act on internal receiver noise and minor static, desensitizing the receiver. However, if the threshold is too high, variations in loudness will be uncomfortable to the ear, forcing the listener to manually twiddle with the volume control to do, in effect, what the AGC should be doing automatically. Measured in μV (microvolts).

Alt. Freq. Alternative frequency or channel. Frequency or channel which may be used in place of that which is regularly scheduled.

Amateur Radio. *See* Hams.

AM Band. The 520-1705 kHz radio broadcast band that lies within the 0.3-3.0 MHz (300-3,000 kHz) mediumwave (MW) or Medium Frequency (MF) portion of the radio spectrum. Outside North America it is usually called the mediumwave (MW) band. However, in parts of Latin America it is sometimes called, by the general public and a few stations, *onda larga*—longwave band (*see*)—strictly speaking, a misnomer. In the United States, travelers information stations (TIS) and other public information services are sometimes also found on 1710 kHz, making 1715 kHz the *de facto* upper limit of the American AM band.

AM Equivalent (AME). *See* Single Sideband (second paragraph).

AM Mode. *See* Mode.

Amplified Antenna. *See* Active Antenna.

Analog Frequency Readout. This type of received-frequency indication is used on radios having needle-and-dial or "slide-rule" tuning. This is much less accurate and handy than digital frequency readout. *See* Synthesizer. *Cf.* Digital Frequency Display.

Antenna. *See* Active Antenna, Feedline, Passive Antenna.

Antennae. The accepted spelling for feelers protruding from insects. In electronics, the preferred plural for "antenna" is "antennas."

Antenna Polarization. *See* Polarization.

Arrestor. *See* MOV.

Attenuator. A circuit, typically switched with one or more levels, to desensitize a receiver by reducing the strength of incoming signals. *See* RF Gain.

Audio Quality. At Passport, audio quality refers to what in computer testing is called "benchmark" quality. This means, primarily, the freedom from distortion of a signal fed through a receiver's entire circuitry—*not* just the audio stage—from the antenna input through to the speaker terminals. A lesser characteristic of audio quality is the audio bandwidth needed for pleasant world band reception of music. Also, *see* Enhanced Fidelity.

Automatic Gain Control (AGC). Smooths out fluctuations in signal strength brought about by fading (*see*), a regular occurrence with world band signals, so a receiver's audio level tends to stay relatively constant. This is accomplished by AGC attack, then AGC hang, and finally AGC decay. Each of these three actions involved in smoothing a fade has a micro-time preset at the factory for optimum performance. Top-end receivers often provide for user control of at least the decay timing—a few rarified models also allow for user control over one or both of the other two actions. *See* AGC Threshold.

AV. A Voz—Portuguese for "The Voice." In Passport, this term is also used to represent "The Voice of."

B. Winter schedule season for world band stations, typically valid from the last Sunday in October until the last Sunday in March. *See* ◨. *See* HFCC. *Cf.* A.

Balun. BALanced-to-UNbalanced device to match the two. Typically, a balun is placed between an unbalanced antenna feedline and a balanced antenna input, or *vice versa*.

Bands, Shortwave Broadcasting. *See* World Band Segments.

Bandwidth. A key variable that determines selectivity (*see*), bandwidth is the amount of radio signal, at –6 dB (–3 dB with *i.a.* professional gear), a radio's circuitry will let pass, and thus be heard. With world band channel spacing standardized at 5 kHz, the best single bandwidths are usually in the vicinity of 3 to 6 kHz. Better radios offer two or more selectable bandwidths: at least one of 5 to 9 kHz or so for when a station is in the clear, and one or more others between 2 to 6 kHz for when a station is hemmed in by other signals next to it; with synchronous selectable sideband (*see* Synchronous Detector), these bandwidths can safely be at the upper ends of these ranges to provide enhanced fidelity. Proper selectivity is a key determinant of the aural quality of what you hear, and some newer models of tabletop receivers have dozens of bandwidths.

Bandscanning. Hunting around for stations by continuously tuning up and/or down a given world band segment (*see*), such as in concert with Passport's Blue Pages.

Baud. Measurement of the speed by which radioteletype (*see*), radiofax (*see*) and other digital data are transmitted. Baud is properly written entirely in lower case, and thus is abbreviated as b (baud), kb (kilobaud) or Mb (Megabaud). Baud rate standards are usually set by the international CCITT regulatory body.

BC. Broadcaster, Broadcasters, Broadcasting, Broadcasting Company, Broadcasting Corporation.

BCB (Broadcast Band). *See* AM Band.

BFO (beat-frequency oscillator). Carrier generated within a receiver. *Inter alia*, this replaces a received signal's full or vestigial transmitted carrier when a receiver is in the single-sideband mode (*see*) or synchronous selectable mode (*see*).

Birdie. A silent spurious signal, similar to a station's open carrier, created by circuit interaction within a receiver. The fewer and weaker the birdies within a receiver's tuning range, the better, although in reality birdies rarely degrade reception.

Tibetan exile gives the news at the "Voice of Tibet's" studios in India. M. Guha

Blocking. The ability of a receiver to avoid being desensitized by powerful adjacent signals or signals from other nearby frequencies. Measured in dB (decibels) at 100 kHz signal spacing.

Boat Anchor. Radio argot for a classic or vintage tube-type communications receiver. These large, heavy biceps builders—Jackie Gleason called them "real radios"—were manufactured mainly from before World War II through the mid-1970s, although a few continued to be available up to a decade later. The definitive reference for collectors of elder receivers is *Shortwave Receivers Past & Present* by Universal Radio.

BPL. Broadband over Power Lines. Emerging technology to allow Internet and other digital communication via AC (mains) power grids. Thus far it has seen only limited use, offering throughput faster than that of dial-up but slower than that of broadband. A major side effect is noise *(see)* radiation, which seriously disrupts traditional and DRM *(see)* world band radio reception. From the perspective of enhanced government oversight this is a positive tradeoff, as it blots out relatively unfettered world band information and replaces it with controllable Internet links.

Broadcast. A radio or television transmission meant for the general public. *Cf.* Utility Stations, Hams.

BS. Broadcasting Station, Broadcasting Service.

Buzz. Noise typically generated by digital electronic circuitry. *See* Noise.

Carrier. *See* Mode.

Cd. Ciudad—Spanish for "City."

Cellular Telephone Bands. In the United States, the cellular telephone bands are 824-849 and 869-894 MHz. Years ago, when analog cell transmissions were the norm, a powerful senator was overheard engaged in an awkward conversation. Shortly thereafter, receivers which could tune cellular frequencies were made illegal in the United States. As a practical matter, eavesdropping on these bands yields nothing intelligible because of the encrypted nature of digital cellular transmissions that by now have all but replaced analog. Receivers tuning these "forbidden" ranges are readily acquired in Canada and nearly every other part of the world except North Korea.

Channel. An everyday term to indicate where a station is supposed to be located on the dial. World band channels are standardized at 5 kHz spacing. Stations operating outside this norm are "off-channel" (for these, PASSPORT provides resolution to better than 1 kHz to aid in station identification).

Chuffing, Chugging. The sound made by some synthesized tuning systems when the tuning knob is turned. Called "chugging" or "chuffing," as it is suggestive of the rhythmic "chuf, chuf" sound of steam locomotives or "chugalug" gulping of beverages.

Cl. Club, Clube.

Co-Channel Interference. *See* Interference.

Coordinated Universal Time. *See* UTC, World Time.

Cult. Cultura, Cultural.

Curtain Antennas. Often used for long-distance world band transmitting, these consist of horizontal dipole arrays interconnected and typically strung between a pair of masts or towers that are usually fixed, but which sometimes can be rotated. Curtains produce excellent forward gain, reasonable directivity and a low takeoff angle that is desirable for successful long-distance broadcasts. *See* Polarization.

CW. Continuous wave, or telegraph-type ("Morse code," etc.) communication by telegraph key that opens and closes an unmodulated signal to create variations of long and short bursts that on a radio with a BFO *(see)* sound like dih-dah "beeps." Used mainly by hams *(see)*, occasionally by utility stations *(see)*.

DAB. Digital audio broadcasting. *See* Digital Radio Mondiale.

DC. Direct current, such as emanates from batteries. *Cf.* AC.

DC-to-Daylight. Hyperbolic slang for an exceptionally wide frequency tuning range. For example, some wideband receivers will tune from under 10 kHz to over 3 GHz *(see)*. However, in the United States it is illegal to sell new radios to the public that tune the cellular telephone bands *(see)*.

Default. The setting at which a control of a digitally operated electronic device, including many world band radios, normally operates, and to which it will eventually return (e.g., when the radio is next switched on).

Digital Frequency Display, Digital Frequency Readout. Indicates that a receiver displays the tuned frequency digitally, usually in kilohertz *(see)*. Because this is so much handier than an analog frequency readout, all models included in PASSPORT REPORTS have digital frequency readout. Most models with digital frequency display are synthesizer *(see)* tuned, but some low-cost models are analog tuned.

Digital Radio Mondiale (DRM). International organization (www.drm.org) seeking to convert world band and other transmissions from traditional analog mode to DRM digital mode, which is moving from its test phase to limited regular use. DRM transmissions—unlike the conventional analog variety—are easily jammed. *See* Mode, Interference.

Digital Signal Processing (DSP). Where digital circuitry and software are used to perform radio circuit functions traditionally done using analog circuits. Used on certain world band receivers; also, available as an add-on accessory for audio processing only.

Dipole Antenna. *See* Passive Antenna.

Distortion. *See* Overall Distortion.

Domestic Service. *See* DS.

Double Conversion a/k/a **Dual Conversion.** *See* IF.

DRM. *See* Digital Radio Mondiale.

DS. Domestic Service—Broadcasting intended primarily for audiences in the broadcaster's home country. However, some domestic programs are beamed on world band to expatriates and other kinfolk abroad, as well as interested foreigners. *Cf.* ES.

DSP. *See* Digital Signal Processing.

Dual Conversion a/k/a/ **Double Conversion.** *See* IF.

DX, DXers, DXing. From an old telegraph abbreviation for distance (D) unknown (X); thus, to DX is to communicate over a great distance. DXers are those who specialize in finding distant or exotic stations that are considered to be rare catches. Few world band listeners are considered to be regular DXers, but many others seek out DX stations every now and then—usually by bandscanning, which is facilitated by PASSPORT's Blue Pages.

DXpedition. Typically, a gathering of DXers who camp out in a remote location favorable to catching the toughest of stations. These DX bases are usually far away from electrically noisy AC power and cable TV lines.

Dynamic Range. The ability of, *i.a.*, a receiver or active antenna *(see)* to handle weak signals in the presence of strong competing signals within or near the same world band segment *(see* World Band Spectrum). Devices with inferior dynamic range sometimes "overload," especially with external antennas, causing a mishmash of false signals up and down—and even beyond—the segment being received. Dynamic range is closely related to the third-order intercept point, or IP3. Where possible, PASSPORT measures dynamic range and IP3 at the traditional 20 kHz and more challenging 5 kHz signal-separation points.

Earliest Heard (or Latest Heard). See key at the bottom of each Blue Page. If the PASSPORT monitoring team cannot establish the definite sign-on (or sign-off) time of a station, the earliest (or latest) time that the station could be traced is indicated by a left-facing or right-facing "arrowhead flag." This means that the station almost certainly operates beyond the time shown by that "flag." It also means that, unless you live relatively close to the station, you're unlikely to be able to hear it beyond that "flagged" time.

EBS. Economic Broadcasting Station, a type of broadcast operation in China.

ECSS (Exalted-Carrier Selectable Sideband). Manual tuning of a conventional AM-mode signal, using a receiver's single-sideband circuitry to zero-beat *(see)* the receiver's BFO with the transmitted signal's carrier. The better-sounding of the signal's sidebands is then selected by the listener. As ECSS is manual, there is a degree, however slight, of phase mismatch between the fade-prone transmitted carrier and the stable synthetic replacement carrier generated within the receiver. *Cf.* Synchronous Selectable Sideband, Synchronous Detector.

Ed, Educ. Educational, Educação, Educadora.

Electrical Noise. See Noise.

Elevation Panel, Elevation Rod. Plastic panel or metal rod which flips out from a radio's back or bottom panel to place the radio at a comfortable operating angle.

Elevation Tab. Plastic tab, typically affixed to a portable radio's carrying strap, which when inserted into the radio's back panel places the radio at a comfortable operating angle.

Em. Emissora, Emisora, Emissor, Emetteur—in effect, "station" in various languages.

Enhanced Fidelity. Radios with good audio performance and certain types of high-tech circuitry can improve the fidelity of world band signals. Among the newer fidelity-enhancing techniques is synchronous detection *(see* Synchronous Detector), especially when coupled with selectable sideband. Another technological means to improve fidelity is digital world band transmission, which is currently being implemented *(see* Digital Radio Mondiale).

EP. Emissor Provincial—Portuguese for "Provincial Station."

ER. Emissor Regional—Portuguese for "Regional Station."

Ergonomics. How handy and comfortable—intuitive—a set is to operate, especially hour after hour.

ES. External Service—Broadcasting intended primarily for audiences abroad. *Cf.* DS.

Exalted-Carrier Selectable Sideband. See ECSS.

External Service. See ES.

F. Friday.

Fading. Signals which scatter off the ionosphere *(see* Propagation) are subject to some degree of phase mismatch as the scattered bits of signal arrive at a receiver at minutely varying times. This causes fading, where signal strength varies anywhere from a few times per minute to many times per second, the latter being known as "flutter fading" and often caused by disruption by the earth's geomagnetic field *(see* Great Circle Path). "Selective fading" is a special type that is audible on shortwave and mediumwave AM when a fade momentarily sweeps across a signal's three components (lower sideband, carrier, upper sideband), attenuating the carrier more than the sidebands; with the carrier thus attenuated, the result is "selective-fading distortion." See Automatic Gain Control, Propagation, Synchronous Detection.

Fax. See Radiofax.

Feeder, Shortwave. A utility *(see)* shortwave transmission from the broadcaster's home country to a shortwave or other relay site or local placement facility *(see)* some distance away. Although these specialized transmissions carry world band programs, they are not intended to be received by the general public. Many world band radios can process these quasi-broadcasts anyway. Shortwave feeders operate in lower sideband (LSB), upper sideband (USB) or independent sideband (termed ISL if heard on the lower side, ISU if heard on the upper side) modes. Feeders are now via satellites and Internet audio, but a few stations keep shortwave feeders in reserve should their satellite/Internet feeders fail. See Single Sideband, Utility Stations, NBFM.

Feedline. The wire or cable that runs between an antenna's receiving element(s) and a receiver. For sophisticated antennas, twin-lead ribbon feedlines are unusually efficient, and can reject much nearby electrical noise via phasing. However, coaxial cable feedlines are generally superior in high-local-electrical-noise environments. See Balun.

First IF Rejection. A relatively uncommon source of false signals occurs when powerful transmitters operate on the same frequency as a receiver's first intermediate frequency (IF). The ability of receiving circuitry to avoid such transmitters' causing reception problems is called "IF rejection."

Flutter Fading. See Fading.

FM. The FM broadcast band is now standardized at 87.5-108 MHz worldwide except in Japan (76-90 MHz) and parts of Eastern Europe (66-74 MHz). Also, for communications there is a special FM mode *(see* NBFM).

Frequency. The standard term to indicate where a station is located within the radio spectrum—regardless of whether it is "on-channel" or "off-channel" *(see* Channel). Below 30 MHz this is customarily expressed in kilohertz (kHz, *see*), but some receivers display in Megahertz (MHz, *see*). These differ only in the placement of a decimal; e.g., 5970 kHz is the same as 5.97 MHz. Either measurement is equally valid, but to minimize confusion PASSPORT and most stations designate frequencies only in kHz. *Cf.* Meters.

Frequency Synthesizer. See Synthesizer, Frequency.

Front-End Selectivity. The ability of the initial stage of receiving circuitry to admit only limited frequency ranges into succeeding stages of circuitry. Good front-end selectivity keeps signals from other, powerful bands or segments from being superimposed upon the frequency range you're tuning. For example, a receiver with good front-end selectivity will receive only shortwave signals within the range 3200-3400 kHz. However, a receiver with mediocre front-end selectivity might allow powerful local mediumwave AM stations from 520-1700 kHz to be heard "ghosting in" between 3200 and 3400 kHz, along with the desired shortwave signals. Obviously, mediumwave AM signals don't belong on shortwave. Receivers with inadequate front-end selectivity can benefit from the addition of a preselector *(see)* or a high-pass filter.

GHz. Gigahertz, equivalent to 1,000 MHz *(see)*.

GMT. Greenwich Mean Time. See World Time.

Great Circle Path. The shortest route a signal takes to arrive at a receiving location, following the circumference of the earth. Normal printed maps are too distorted for this purpose, but an ideal solution is to take a globe and run a string from a station's transmitter site *(see* PASSPORT's Blue Pages) to your location. Among other things, the closer a signal's path is to the geomagnetic North Pole, the greater the chance of its being disrupted by flutter fading *(see* Fading) during geomagnetic propagational disturbances *(see* Propagation). An Internet search can turn up several software programs to generate great circle maps centered at your location, but for most a globe and string are more visually intuitive.

Hams. Government-licensed amateur radio hobbyists who *transmit* to each other by radio, often by voice using single sideband *(see)*, within special amateur bands. Many of these bands are within the shortwave spectrum *(see)*. This spectrum is also used by world band radio, but world band radio and ham radio, which laymen sometimes confuse with each other, are two very separate entities. The easiest way is to think of hams as making something like phone calls, whereas world band stations are like long-distance versions of ordinary mediumwave AM stations.

Harmonic, Harmonic Radiation, Harmonic Signal. Usually, an unwanted weak spurious repeat of a signal in multiple(s) of the fundamental, or "real," frequency. Thus, the third harmonic of a mediumwave AM station on 1120 kHz might be heard faintly on 4480 kHz within the world band spectrum. Stations almost always try to minimize harmonic radiation, as it wastes energy and spectrum space. However, in rare cases stations have been known to amplify a harmonic signal so they can operate inexpensively on a second frequency. Also, *see* Subharmonic.

Hash. Electrical buzzing noise. *See* Noise.

Hertz. *See* Hz.

Heterodyne. A whistle equal in pitch to the separation between two carriers. Thus, two world band stations 5 kHz apart will generate a 5000 Hz whistle unless receiver circuitry (e.g., *see* Notch Filter) keeps this from being audible.

High Fidelity. *See* Enhanced Fidelity.

High-Pass Filter. A filter which lets frequencies pass unattenuated only if they are above a designated frequency. For world band receivers and antennas, 2 MHz or thereabouts is the norm for high-pass filters, as this keeps out mediumwave AM and longwave signals.

HF (High Frequency). Shortwave. *See* Shortwave Spectrum.

HFCC (High Frequency Co-ordination Conference). Founded in 1990 and headquartered in Prague, the HFCC (www.hfcc.org) helps coordinate frequency usage by dozens of broadcasting organizations from numerous countries. These represent a solid majority of the global output for international shortwave broadcasting. Coordination meetings take place twice yearly: once for the "A" (summer) schedule season from the last Sunday in March until the last Sunday in October, another for "B" (winter), and these gatherings have been a great help in preventing frequency conflicts.

Hz. Hertz, a unit of frequency measurement formerly known as cycles per second (c/s). A thousand Hertz is equivalent to 1 kHz *(see)*. Also, *see* Frequency, Meters, MHz.

IBS. International Broadcasting Services, Ltd., publishers of PASSPORT TO WORLD BAND RADIO.

IF (Intermediate Frequency). Virtually all world band receivers use the "superheterodyne" principle, where tuned radio frequencies are converted to a single intermediate frequency to facilitate reception, then amplified and detected to produce audio. In virtually all world band portables and most tabletop models, this frequency is either 455 kHz or 450 kHz. If this is not complemented by a second and higher intermediate frequency (double conversion), "images" readily occur at twice the IF; i.e., 910 kHz or 900 kHz. *See* Image.

IF Shift. *See* Passband Offset.

Image. A common type of spurious signal found on low-cost "single conversion" (single IF) radios where a strong signal appears at reduced strength, usually on a frequency 910 kHz or 900 kHz lower down. For example, the BBC on 5875 kHz might repeat on 4965 kHz, its "image frequency." Double-conversion (two IF) receivers have little problem with images, but the additional IF circuitry adds to manufacturing cost. *See* IF, Spurious-Signal Rejection.

Impedance. Opposition, expressed in ohms, to the flow of alternating current. Components work best when impedance is comparable from one to another; so, for example, a receiver with a 75-ohm antenna socket will work best with antennas having a similar feedline impedance. Antenna tuning units can resolve this, albeit at the cost of added operational complexity.

Independent Sideband. *See* Single Sideband.

Interference. Sounds from other signals, notably on the same frequency ("co-channel interference"), or on an adjacent or other nearby channel(s) ("adjacent-channel interference"), that disturb the station you are trying to hear; DRM *(see)* signals cause interference over a wider frequency range than do conventional analog signals. Worthy radios reduce interference by having good selectivity *(see)* and synchronous selectable sideband *(see* Synchronous Detector). Nearby television sets and cable television wiring may also generate a special type of radio interference called TVI, a "growl," typically from a television horizontal oscillator, heard every 15 kHz or so. Sometimes referred to as QRM, a term based on Morse-code shorthand.

Intermediate Frequency. *See* IF.

International Reply Coupon (IRC). Sold by selected post offices in most parts of the world, IRCs amount to official international "scrip" that may be exchanged for postage in most countries of the world. Because they amount to an international form of postage repayment, over many decades they have been handy for listeners trying to encourage foreign stations to write them back. However, IRCs are very costly for the amount in stamps that is provided in return. Too, an increasing number of countries are not forthcoming about "cashing in" IRCs, which are fading from general use. Specifics on this and related matters are provided in the Addresses PLUS section of this PASSPORT.

International Telecommunication Union (ITU). The regulatory body, headquartered in Geneva, for all international telecommunications, including world band radio. Sometimes incorrectly referred to as the "International Telecommunications Union." In recent years, the ITU has become increasingly ineffective as a regulatory body for world band radio, with much of its former role having been taken up by the HFCC *(see)*.

Internet Radio. *See* Web radio.

Inverted-L Antenna. *See* Passive Antenna.

Ionosphere. *See* Propagation.

IP3. Third-order intercept point. *See* Dynamic Range.

IRC. *See* International Reply Coupon.

Irr. Irregular operation or hours of operation; i.e., schedule tends to be unpredictable.

ISB. Independent sideband. *See* Single Sideband.

ISL. Independent sideband, lower. *See* Feeder.

ISU. Independent sideband, upper. *See* Feeder.

ITU. *See* International Telecommunication Union.

Jamming. Deliberate interference to a transmission with the intent of discouraging listening. However, analog shortwave broadcasts, when properly transmitted, are uniquely resistant to jamming. This ability to avoid "gatekeeping" is a major reason why traditional shortwave continues to be the workhorse for international broadcasting. Jamming is practiced now much less than it was during the Cold War. The main exception is China, where superpower transmitters and rotatable curtain antennas from France are increasingly being used to disrupt world band broadcasts.

Keypad. On a world band radio, like a cell phone, a keypad can be used to control many variables. Radio keypads are used primarily so you can enter a station's frequency for reception, and the best keypads have real keys (not a membrane) in the standard telephone format of 3x4 with "zero" under the "8" key. Many keypads are also used for presets, but this means you have to remember code numbers for stations (e.g., BBC 5975 kHz is "07"); handier radios have separate keys for presets, while some others use LCD-displayed "pages" to access presets.

kHz. Kilohertz, the most common unit of frequency for measuring where a station is located on the world band dial if it is below 30,000 kHz. Formerly known as "kilocycles per second," or kc/s. 1,000 kilohertz equals one Megahertz. *See* Frequency. *Cf.* MHz, Meters.

kilohertz. *See* kHz. The "k" in "kilo" is not properly capitalized, although the computer modem industry got it wrong years back and most modem firms have as yet to correct the error.

kilowatt. *See* kW.

kW. A kilowatt(s), the most common unit of measurement for transmitter power (*see* Power).

LCD. Liquid-crystal display. LCDs, if properly designed, are fairly easily seen in bright light, but require illumination under darker conditions. LCDs—typically monochrome and gray on gray—also tend to have mediocre contrast, and sometimes can be read from only a certain angle or angles, but they consume nearly no battery power.

LED. Light-emitting diode. LEDs have a long life and are very easily read in the dark or in normal room light, but consume more battery power than LCDs and are hard to read in bright ambient light.

Lightning Arrestor. *See* MOV.

Line Output. Fixed-level audio output typically used to feed a recorder or outboard audio amplifier-speaker system.

Location. Physical location. In the case of a radio station, the transmitter location, which is what is cited in PASSPORT's Blue Pages, may be different from that of the studio location. Transmitter location is useful as a guide to reception quality. For example, if you're in eastern North America and wish to listen to the Voice of Russia, a transmitter located in St. Petersburg will almost certainly provide better reception than, say, one located in Siberia.

Longwave (LW) Band. The 148.5–283.5 kHz portion of the low-frequency (LF) radio spectrum used for domestic broadcasting in Europe, the Near East, North Africa, Russia and Mongolia. As a practical matter, these longwave signals, which have nothing to do with world band or other shortwave signals, are not readily audible in other parts of the world.

Longwire Antenna. *See* Passive Antenna.

Loop Antenna. Round (like a hula hoop) or square-ish antenna often used for reception of longwave, mediumwave AM and even shortwave signals. These can be highly directive below around 2 MHz, and can even show some directivity up to 5 MHz or 6 MHz. For this reason, most such antennas can be rotated and even tilted manually—or by an antenna rotor. "Barefoot" loops tend to have low gain, and thus need electrical amplification in order to reach their potential. When properly mounted, top-caliber amplified loops can produce superior signal-to-noise ratios that help with weak-signal (DX) reception.

Strictly speaking, ferrite-rod antennas, found inside nearly every mediumwave AM radio as well as some specialty outboard antennas, are not loops. However, in everyday parlance these tiny antennas are often referred to as "loops" or "loopsticks."

Low-Pass Filter. A filter which lets frequencies pass unattenuated only if they are below a designated frequency. For world band receivers and antennas, 30 MHz or thereabouts is the norm for low-pass filters, as this keeps out VHF/UHF signals.

LSB. Lower Sideband. *See* Mode, Single Sideband, Feeder.

LV. La Voix, La Voz—French and Spanish for "The Voice." In PASSPORT, this term is also used to represent "The Voice of."

LW. *See* Longwave (LW) Band.

M. Monday.

Mains. *See* AC.

Manual Selectable Sideband. *See* ECSS.

Mediumwave Band, Mediumwave AM Band, Mediumwave Spectrum. *See* AM Band.

Megahertz. *See* MHz.

Memory, Memories. *See* Preset.

Meters (Wavelength). An elder unit of measurement used

i.a. for individual world band segments of the shortwave spectrum. The frequency range covered by a given meters designation—also known as "wavelength"—can be gleaned from the following formula: *frequency (kHz) = 299,792 ÷ meters*. Thus, 49 meters comes out to a frequency of 6118 kHz—well within the range of frequencies included in that segment (*see* World Band Spectrum). Inversely, wavelength in meters can be derived from the following: *wavelength (meters) = 299,792 ÷ frequency (kHz)*.

The figure 299,792 is based on the speed of light (299,792,458 m/s) as agreed upon by the International Committee on Weights and Measurements in 1983. However, in practice this fumbling figure is rounded to 300,000 for computational purposes. Thus, in everyday practice the two formulas are: *frequency (kHz) = 300,000 ÷ meters*; *wavelength (meters) = 300,000 ÷ frequency (kHz)*.

MHz. Megahertz, a common unit of frequency *(see)* to measure where a station is located on the dial, especially above 30 MHz, although in the purest sense all measurements above 3 MHz are supposed to be in MHz. In earlier days of radio this was known as "Megacycles per second," or Mc/s. One Megahertz equals 1,000 kilohertz. *See* Frequency. *Cf.* kHz, Meters.

Mode. Method of transmission of radio signals. World band radio broadcasts are almost always in the analog AM (amplitude modulation) mode, the same mode used in the mediumwave AM band *(see)*. The AM mode consists of three components: two "sidebands," plus one "carrier" that resides between the two sidebands. Each sideband contains the same programming as the other, and the carrier carries no programming, so a few stations have experimented with the single-sideband (SSB, *see*) mode. SSB contains only one sideband, either the lower sideband (LSB) or upper sideband (USB), and a reduced carrier. It requires special radio circuitry to be demodulated, or made intelligible, which is the main reason SSB is unlikely to be widely adopted as a world band mode. However, major efforts are currently underway to implement digital-mode world band transmissions (*see* Digital Radio Mondiale).

There are yet other modes used on shortwave, but not for world band. These include CW (Morse-type code, *see*), radiofax *(see)* and RTTY (radioteletype, *see*) used by utility *(see)* and ham *(see)* stations. A variant FM mode, narrow-band FM (NBFM, *see*), is also used by utility and ham operations; however, it is not for music or within the FM broadcast bands (*see* FM).

Modulation. The sounds contained within a radio signal.

MOV. Often used in power-line and antenna surge arrestors (a/k/a lightning arrestors) to shunt line-power surges to ground. MOVs perform well and are inexpensive, but tend to lose effectiveness with use; costlier alternatives are thus sometimes worth considering. On rare occasion they also appear to have been implicated in starting fires, so a UL or other recognized certification is helpful. For both these reasons MOV-based arrestors should be replaced at least once every decade that they are in service. *See* Surge Arrestor.

MW. Mediumwave AM band; *see* AM Band. Also, Megawatt, which equals 1,000 kW; *cf.* kilowatt; *see* Power.

N. New, Nueva, Nuevo, Nouvelle, Nacional, National, Nationale.

Nac. Nacional. Spanish and Portuguese for "National."

Narrow-band FM. *See* NBFM, Mode.

Nat, Natl, Nat'l. National, Nationale.

NB. *See* Noise Blanker.

NBFM. Narrow-band FM, used within the shortwave spectrum by some "utility" stations, including (between 25-30 MHz) point-to-point broadcast station remote links. *See* Mode.

Noise. Static, buzzes, pops and the like caused by the earth's atmosphere (typically lightning), and to a lesser extent by galactic noise. Also, electrical noise emanating from such man-made sources as electric blankets, fish-tank heaters, heating pads, electrical and gasoline motors, light dimmers, flickering light bulbs, non-incandescent lights, computers and computer peripherals, office machines, electric fences, and electric utility wiring—especially with BPL *(see)*—and related components. Sometimes referred to as QRN, a term based on Morse-code shorthand.

Noise Blanker. Receiver circuit, often found on costly tabletop and profession models, that reduces the impact of pulse-type electrical noises (nearby light dimmers, etc.) or certain unusual types of pulse transmissions. In practice, these circuits use long-established designs which act only on pulses which are greater in strength than the received signal, although designs without this limitation exist on paper.

Noise Floor. *See* Sensitivity.

Notch Filter, Tunable. A feature found on some tabletop and professional receivers for reducing or rejecting annoying heterodyne *(see)* interference—the whistles, howls and squeals for which shortwave has traditionally been notorious. Some notch filters operate within the IF *(see)* stage, whereas others operate as audio filters. IF notch filters tend to respond exceptionally well where there is fading, whereas audio filters usually have more capacity to attack higher-pitched heterodynes.

Other. Programs are in a language other than one of the world's primary languages.

Overall Distortion. Nothing makes listening quite so tiring as distortion. PASSPORT has devised techniques to measure overall cumulative distortion from signal input through audio output—not just distortion within the audio stage. This level of distortion is thus equal to what is heard by the ear.

Overloading. *See* Dynamic Range.

Passband Offset. Continuously variable control that can be user-adjusted such that only the best-sounding portion of a given sideband is heard when the receiver is in either the single-sideband mode *(see)* or the synchronous selectable sideband mode *(see)*. This allows for a finer degree of control over adjacent-channel interference and tonal response than does a simple LSB or USB switch associated with a fixed BFO *(see)*. Also known as Passband Tuning, Passband Shift and IF Shift. The same nomenclature is sometimes used to describe variable-bandwidth circuitry.

Passband Shift. *See* Passband Offset.

Passband Tuning. *See* Passband Offset.

Passive Antenna. Not electronically amplified. Typically, such antennas are mounted outdoors, although the "tape-measure" type that comes as an accessory with some portables is usually strung indoors. For world band reception, virtually all outboard models for consumers are made from wire, rather than rods or tubular elements. The two most common designs are the inverted-L (so-called "longwire") and trapped dipole (mounted either horizontally or as a "sloper"). These antennas are usually preferable to active antennas *(cf.)*, and are reviewed at length, along with construction and erection instructions, in the Radio Database International White Paper, PASSPORT *Evaluation of Popular Outdoor Antennas (Unamplified)*. *See* Feedline.

PBS. In China, People's Broadcasting Station.

Phase Cancellation. In synchronous selectable sideband *(see)*, two identical wave patterns (lower and upper sidebands) are brought together 180 degrees out of phase so as to cancel out the unwanted sideband. This is a less costly way of sideband attenuation than through the use of discrete IF filtering.

Phase Noise. Synthesizers and other circuits can create a "rushing" noise that is usually noticed only when the receiver is tuned alongside the edge of a powerful broadcast or other carrier. In effect, the signal becomes "modulated" by the noise. Phase noise is a useful measurement if you tune weak signals alongside powerful signals. Measured in dBc (decibels below carrier).

Pirate. Illegal radio station operated by enthusiast(s) with little if any political purpose other than to defy radio laws. Programs typically consist of music, satire or comments relevant to pirate colleagues.

Placement Facility. Typically a local FM or mediumwave AM station which leases airtime for one or more programs or program segments from an international broadcaster. These programs are usually supplied by feeders *(see)*, although some placement facilities pick up programs via regular world band radio.

PLL (Phase-Locked Loop). With world band receivers, a PLL circuit means that the radio can be tuned digitally, often using a number of handy tuning techniques, such as a keypad *(see)* and presets *(see)*.

Polarization. Radio and other over-the-air signals tend to be either horizontally or vertically polarized. Unsurprisingly, stations which transmit using vertical antennas produce vertically polarized signals, and so on. Long-haul world band transmissions are almost always horizontally polarized *(see* Curtain Antennas), so most outdoor receiving antennas are also horizontal. However, the scattering effects of the ionosphere turn the single horizontal transmitted signal, like a bread slicer, into numerous bits *(see* Fading). Some continue on as horizontal while others morph into vertical, but most fall somewhere in between. As a result, the angle of receiving antenna elements tends to be noncritical for reception of long-distance shortwave signals.

Power. Transmitter power *before* antenna gain, expressed in kilowatts (kW). The present range of world band powers is virtually always 0.01 to 1,000 kW.

Power Lock. *See* Travel Power Lock.

PR. People's Republic.

Preamplifier. An inboard or outboard broadband amplifier to increase the strength of signals fed into a receiver's circuitry. Active antennas *(see)* incorporate a preamplifier or an amplified preselector *(see)*.

Preselector. A circuit—outboard as an accessory, or inboard as part of the receiver—that effectively limits the range of frequencies which can enter a receiver's circuitry or the circuitry of an active antenna *(see)*; that is, which improves front-end selectivity *(see)*. For example, a preselector may let in the range 15000-16000 kHz, thus helping ensure that your receiver or active antenna will not encounter problems within that range caused by signals from, say, 5730-6250 kHz or local mediumwave AM signals (520-1705 kHz). This range usually can be varied, manually or automatically, according to the frequency to which the receiver is being tuned. A preselector may be passive (unamplified) or active (amplified).

Preset. Allows you to select a station pre-stored in a radio's memory. The handiest presets require only one push of a button, as on a car radio.

Propagation. World band signals travel, like a basketball, up and down from the station to your radio. The "floor" below is the earth's surface, whereas the "player's hand" on high is the *ionosphere*, a gaseous layer that envelops the planet. While the earth's surface remains pretty much the same from day to day, the ionosphere—nature's own passive "satellite"—varies in how it propagates radio signals, depending on how much sunlight hits the "bounce points."

Thus, some world band segments do well mainly by day, whereas others are best by night. During winter there's less sunlight, so the "night bands" become unusually active, whereas the "day bands" become correspondingly less useful *(see* World Band Spectrum). Day-to-day changes in the sun's weather also cause short-term changes in world band radio reception; this explains why some days you can hear rare signals.

Additionally, the 11-year sunspot cycle has a long term effect on propagation, with sunspot maximum greatly enhancing reception on higher world band segments. The last maximum was in late 2000, while the next minimum is occurring around now.

These bounce, or refraction, points are not absolutely efficient. Some loss comes about from absorption *(see)*, and signal scattering brings about fading *(see)*.

Propagation, like the weather, varies considerably, which adds to the intrigue of world band radio. The accepted standard for propagation prediction is WWV (and sometimes WWVH) on 2500, 5000, 10000, 15000 and 20000 kHz. An explanation of prediction measurements is at www.boulder.nist.gov/timefreq/stations/iform.html#geo. Also, view www.sunspotcycle.com.

PS. Provincial Station, Pangsong.

Pto. Puerto, Porto.

QRM. *See* Interference.

QRN. *See* Noise.

QSL. *See* Verification.

R. Radio, Radiodiffusion, Radiodifusora, Radiodifusão, Radiophonikos, Radiostantsiya, Radyo, Radyosu, and so forth.

Radiofax, Radio Facsimile. Like ordinary telefax (facsimile by telephone lines), but by radio.

Radioteletype (RTTY). Characters, but not illustrations, transmitted by radio. *See* Baud.

RDI. Radio Database International®, a registered trademark of International Broadcasting Services, Ltd.

Receiver. Synonym for "radio," but sometimes—especially when called a "communications receiver" implying a radio with superior tough-signal or utility-signal performance.

Reception Report. *See* Verification.

Reduced Carrier. *See* Single Sideband.

Reg. Regional.

Relay. A retransmission facility, often highlighted in "Worldwide Broadcasts in English" and "Voices from Home" in PASSPORT's WorldScan® section. Relay facilities are generally considered to be located outside the broadcaster's country. Being closer to the target audience, they usually provide superior reception. *See* Feeder.

Rep. Republic, République, República.

RF Gain. A variable control to reduce the gain of a receiver's earliest amplification, in the RF stage. However, modern receivers often function better without an RF stage, in which case an RF gain control usually acts simply as a variable attenuator *(see)*.

RN. *See* R and N.

RS. Radio Station, Radiostantsiya, Radiostudiya, Radiophonikos Stathmos.

RT, RTV. Radiodiffusion Télévision, Radio Télévision, and so forth.

RTTY. *See* Radioteletype.

◨ Transmission aired summer (midyear) only, typically from the last Sunday in March until the last Sunday in October; *see* "HFCC." *Cf.* ◨

S. San, Santa, Santo, São, Saint, Sainte. Also, South.

Sa. Saturday.

SASE. Self-addressed, stamped envelope. *See* introduction to Addresses PLUS in this PASSPORT.

Scan, Scanning. Circuitry within a radio that allows it to bandscan or memory scan automatically.

Season, Schedule Season. *See* HFCC.

Segments. *See* Shortwave Spectrum.

Selectivity. The ability of a radio to reject interference *(see)* from signals on adjacent channels. Thus, also known as adjacent-channel rejection, a key variable in radio quality. *See* Bandwidth. *See* Shape Factor. *See* Ultimate Rejection. *See* Synchronous Detector.

Sensitivity. The ability of a radio to receive weak signals; thus, also known as weak-signal sensitivity. Of special importance if you are listening during the day or tuning domestic tropical band broadcasts—or if you are located in such parts of the world as Western North America, Hawaii or Australasia, where signals tend to be relatively weak. The best measurement of sensitivity is the noise floor.

Shape Factor. Skirt selectivity helps reduce interference and increase audio fidelity. It is important if you will be tuning

stations that are weaker than adjacent-channel signals. Skirt selectivity is measured by the shape factor, the ratio between the bandwidth at –6 dB (adjacent signal at about the same strength as the received station) and –60 dB (adjacent signal relatively much stronger), although with some professional receivers and in certain labs –3 dB is used in lieu of –6 dB. A good shape factor provides the best defense against adjacent powerful signals' muscling their way in to disturb reception of the desired signal.

SHF. Super high frequency, 3-30 GHz.

Shortwave Spectrum. The shortwave spectrum—also known as the High Frequency (HF) spectrum—is that portion of the radio spectrum from 3 MHz through 30 MHz (3,000-30,000 kHz). The shortwave spectrum is occupied not only by world band radio (*see* World Band Segments), but also hams *(see)* and utility stations *(see)*.

Sideband. *See* Mode.

Signal Polarization. *See* Polarization.

Signal-to-Noise Ratio. A common form of noise comes from a radio's (and/or active antenna's) electronic circuitry and usually sounds like "hiss." Depending upon its antenna's location, a receiver may also pick up and reproduce noise *(see)* from nearby electrical and electronic sources, such as power and cable TV lines, light dimmers and digital electronic products. A third type of noise, galactic, is rarely a problem, and even then can be heard only above 20 MHz. Thus, a key part of enjoyable radio reception is to have a worthy signal-to-noise ratio; that is, where the received radio signal is strong enough relative to the various noises that it drowns out those noises.

Single Sideband, Independent Sideband. Spectrum and power-conserving modes of transmission commonly used by utility stations *(see)* and hams *(see)*. Single-sideband transmitted signals usually consist of one full sideband (lower sideband, LSB; or, more typically, upper sideband, USB) and a reduced or suppressed carrier, but no second sideband. Very few broadcasters (e.g., the popular American AFRTS) use, or are expected ever to use, the single-sideband mode. Many world band radios are already capable of demodulating single-sideband transmissions, and some can even process independent-sideband signals.

Independent-sideband (ISB) signals are like single-sideband signals, but with both sidebands. Content is usually different in the two sidebands—for stereo, as in the original Kahn AM-stereo system where the left channel can be LSB, right channel USB. More typically, entirely different programming may be carried by each sideband, such as in a shortwave feed to a relay facility that retransmits two entirely different programs. *See* Feeder, Mode.

Certain world band broadcasters and time-standard stations emit single-sideband transmissions which have virtually no carrier reduction, or a minimum of reduction; say, 3 or 6 dB. These "AM equivalent" (AME) signals can be listened to, with slightly added distortion, on ordinary radios not equipped to demodulate pure single sideband signals. Properly designed synchronous detectors *(see)* help reduce distortion with AME transmissions. A variety of AME signals, called "compatible AM," include a minor FM component to help improve reception fidelity. This concept was experimented with decades ago by inventor Leonard Kahn and the VOA, but was not found to offer any meaningful improvement over ordinary AME transmission.

Site. *See* Location.

Skirt Selectivity. *See* Shape Factor.

Slew Controls. Up/down controls, usually buttons, to tune a radio. On many radios with synthesized tuning, slewing is used in lieu of tuning by knob. Better is when slew controls are complemented by a genuine tuning knob, which is more versatile for bandscanning.

Sloper Antenna. *See* Passive Antenna.

Solar Cycle. Synonym for "sunspot cycle." *See* Propagation.

SPR. Spurious (false) extra signal from a transmitter actually operating on another frequency. One such type is harmonic *(see)*.

Spur. *See* SPR.

Spurious Signal. *See* SPR.

Spurious-Signal Rejection. The ability of a radio receiver to avoid producing false signals, such as images *(see)* and birdies *(see)*, that might otherwise interfere with the clarity of the station you're trying to hear.

Squelch. A circuit which mutes a receiver until the received signal's strength exceeds a specified threshold, which is usually user-adjustable.

SSB. *See* Single Sideband.

St, Sta, Sto. Abbreviations for words that mean "Saint."

Stability. The ability of a receiver to rest exactly the tuned frequency without drifting.

Static. *See* Noise.

Static Arrestor. *See* Surge Arrestor.

Su. Sunday.

Subharmonic. A harmonic heard at 1.5 or 0.5 times the operating frequency. This anomaly is caused by the way signals are generated within vintage-model transmitters, and thus cannot take place with modern transmitters. For example, the subharmonic of a station on 3360 kHz might be heard faintly on 5040 or 1680 kHz. Also, *see* Harmonic.

Sunspot Cycle. *See* Propagation.

Superheterodyne. *See* IF.

Surge Arrestor. Protective device to eliminate the harmful impact of voltage spikes, which enter electronic equipment via AC (mains) power lines, telephone lines and radio/TV antennas. *See* MOV, although some premium arrestors (e.g., ZeroSurge) use non-MOV technologies.

SW. *See* Shortwave Spectrum.

SWL. Shortwave listener. The overwhelming preponderance of shortwave listening is to world band stations, but some radio enthusiasts also enjoy eavesdropping on utility stations *(see)* and hams *(see)*.

Synchronous Detector, Synchronous Detection. Some world band radios are equipped with this high-tech circuit that greatly reduces fading distortion; unlike ECSS *(see)* it automatically steers clear of received *vs.* internally generated carrier phase mismatch. Better synchronous detectors also allow for synchronous selectable sideband *(see)*; that is, the ability to select the less-interfered of the two sidebands of a world band or other AM-mode signal. *See* Mode, Phase Cancellation.

Synchronous Selectable Sideband. Derived from synchronous detection *(see)* circuitry, this function greatly reduces the impact of adjacent-channel interference *(see)* on listening.

Synthesizer, Frequency. Better world band receivers utilize a digital frequency synthesizer to tune signals. Among other things, such synthesizers allow for pushbutton tuning and presets, and display the exact frequency digitally—pluses that make tuning to the world considerably easier. Virtually a "must" feature. *See* Analog Frequency Readout, Digital Frequency Display.

Target. The part of the world where a transmission is beamed, a/k/a target zone.

Th. Thursday.

Third Order Intercept Point. *See* Dynamic Range.

Travel Power Lock. Control which disables the on/off switch to prevent a radio from switching on accidentally.

Transmitter Power. *See* Power.

Trap Dipole Antenna, Trapped Dipole Antenna. Dipole antenna with several coil "traps" that allow for optimum reception on several world band or other segments or bands. *See* Passive Antenna.

Tropical Band Segments. *See* World Band Segments.

Tu. Tuesday.

UHF. Ultra High Frequency, 300 MHz through 3 GHz.

Ultimate Rejection, Ultimate Selectivity. The point at which a receiver is no longer able to reject adjacent-channel interference. Ultimate rejection is important if you listen to signals that are markedly weaker than are adjacent signals. *See* Selectivity.

Universal Day. *See* World Time.

Universal Time. *See* World Time.

URL. Universal Resource Locator; i.e., the Internet address for a given webpage.

USB. Upper Sideband. *See* Mode, Single Sideband, Feeder.

UTC. Coordinated Universal Time. The occasional variation "Universal Time Coordinated" is not correct, although for everyday use it's okay to refer simply to "Universal Time." *See* World Time.

Utility Stations. Most signals within the shortwave spectrum are not world band stations. Rather, they are utility stations—radio telephones, ships at sea, aircraft, ionospheric sounders, over-the-horizon radar and the like—that transmit strange sounds (growls, gurgles, dih-dah sounds, etc.). Although these can be picked up on many receivers, they are rarely intended to be utilized by the general public. *Cf.* Broadcast, Feeders, Hams and Mode.

v. Variable frequency; i.e., one that is unstable or drifting because of a transmitter malfunction or, less often, to avoid jamming or other interference.

Verification. A "QSL" card or letter from a station verifying that a listener indeed heard that particular station. In order to stand a chance of qualifying for a verification card or letter, you should respond with a reception report shortly after having heard the transmission. You need to provide the station heard with, at a minimum, the following information in a three-number "SIO" code, in which "SIO 555" is best and "SIO 111" is worst:

• **S**ignal strength, with 5 being of excellent quality, comparable to that of a local mediumwave AM station, and 1 being inaudible or at least so weak as to be virtually unintelligible, 2 (faint, but somewhat intelligible), 3 (moderate strength) and 4 (good strength) represent the signal-strength levels usually encountered with world band stations.

• **I**nterference from other stations, with 5 indicating no interference whatsoever, and 1 indicating such extreme interference that the desired signal is virtually drowned out. Ratings of 2 (heavy interference), 3 (moderate interference) and 4 (slight interference) represent the differing degrees of interference more typically encountered with world band signals. If possible, indicate the names of the interfering station(s) and the channel(s) they are on. Otherwise, at least describe what the interference sounds like.

• **O**verall quality of the signal, with 5 being best, 1 worst.

• In addition to providing SIO findings, you should indicate which programs you've heard, as well as comments on how you liked or disliked those programs. Refer to the Addresses PLUS section of this edition for information on where and to whom your report should be sent, and whether return postage should be included.

• Expanded versions of the SIO reporting code are the SINPO and SINFO codes, where "N" refers to atmospheric noise, "F" to fading and "P" to propagation conditions on the same 1-5 scale. As atmospheric noise is rarely audible below 20 MHz and propagation conditions are highly subjective, SIO tends to provide more accurate feedback. Fading, however, is not hard for an experienced monitor to rate, but the SIFO code has never caught on.

• Few stations wish to receive unsolicited recordings of their transmissions. However, a few stations' websites actively seek MP3, RealAudio or other Internet-sent files or mailed CD recordings of certain transmissions.

VHF. Very high frequency spectrum, 30-300 MHz, which starts just above the shortwave spectrum *(see)* and ends at the UHF spectrum. *See* FM, which operates within the VHF spectrum. Somewhat confusingly, in German VHF is known as UKW (Ultra Short Wave), which is different from UHF (Ultra High Frequency).

Vo. Voice of.

◩ Transmission aired winter only, typically from the last Sunday in October until the last Sunday in March; *see* HFCC. *Cf.* ◪

W. Wednesday.

Wavelength. *See* Meters.

Weak-Signal Sensitivity. *See* Sensitivity.

Webcasting. *See* Web Radio.

Web Radio, Webcasts. Broadcasts aired over the Internet. These thousands of stations worldwide include simulcast FM, mediumwave AM and world band stations, as well as Internet-only stations. Although webcasting was originally unfettered, it has increasingly been subjected to official gatekeeping (censorship), as well as uniquely steep copyright and union royalties and rules that have hobbled web simulcasting by AM/FM stations in the United States. This PASSPORT lists URL information for all world band stations which webcast live or on-demand.

World Band Radio. Broadcasts (news, music, sports and the like) transmitted within and just below the shortwave spectrum *(see)*. Virtually all are found within 14 discrete world band segments *(see)*. These broadcasting stations are similar to regular mediumwave AM band and FM band broadcasters, except that world band stations can be heard over enormous distances. As a result, they often carry programs created especially for audiences abroad. Traditional analog world band transmissions—with properly located, configured and operated facilities—are also uniquely difficult to "jam" (*see* Jamming), making world band the most effective vehicle for outflanking official censorship. Some world band stations have regular audiences in the tens of millions, and even over 100 million, including many who listen for extended periods. Although world band lacks the glamour of new broadcasting technologies, making it an easy target for tech-hungry officials, around 600 million people worldwide continue to listen.

World Band Segments. Fourteen slices within the shortwave spectrum *(see)* and upper reaches of the mediumwave spectrum (*see* AM Band) that are used almost exclusively for world band broadcasts. Those below 5.1 MHz are called "Tropical Band Segments." *See* "Best Times and Frequencies" sidebar elsewhere within this PASSPORT.

World Band Spectrum. *See* World Band Segments.

World Day. *See* World Time.

World Time. Also known as Coordinated Universal Time (UTC), Greenwich Mean Time (GMT), Zulu time (Z) and "military time." With over 150 countries on world band radio, if each announced its own local time you would need a calculator to figure it all out. To get around this, a single international time—World Time—is used. The differences between World Time and local time are detailed in the Addresses PLUS and Setting Your World Time Clock sections of this edition. World Time can also be determined simply by listening to time announcements given on the hour by world band stations—or minute by minute by WWV in the United States on 2500, 5000, 10000, 15000 and 20000 kHz; WWVH in Hawaii on 2500, 5000, 10000 and 15000 kHz; and CHU in Canada on 3330, 7335 and 14670 kHz. A 24-hour clock format is used, so "1800 World Time" means 6:00 PM World Time. If you're in, say, North America, Eastern Time is five hours behind World Time winters and four hours behind World Time summers, so 1800 World Time would be 1:00 PM EST or 2:00 PM EDT. The easiest solution is to use a 24-hour digital clock set to World Time. Many radios already have these built in, and World Time clocks are also available as accessories. World Time also applies to the days of the week. So if it's 9:00 PM (21:00) Wednesday in New York during the winter, it's 0200 *Thursday* World Time.

WS. World Service.

X-Band. The mediumwave AM band segment from 1605-1705 kHz in the Western Hemisphere, Australia and ultimately beyond. In the United States, travelers information stations (TIS) and other public information services are sometimes also found on 1710 kHz.

Zero beat. When tuning a world band or other AM-mode signal in the single-sideband mode, there is a whistle, or "beat," whose pitch is the result of the difference in frequency between the receiver's internally generated carrier (BFO, or beat-frequency oscillator) and the station's transmitted carrier. By tuning carefully, the listener can reduce the difference between these two carriers to the point where the whistle is deeper and deeper, to the point where it no longer audible. This silent sweet spot is known as "zero beat." *See* ECSS.

Zulu Time. *See* World Time.

Printed in Canada

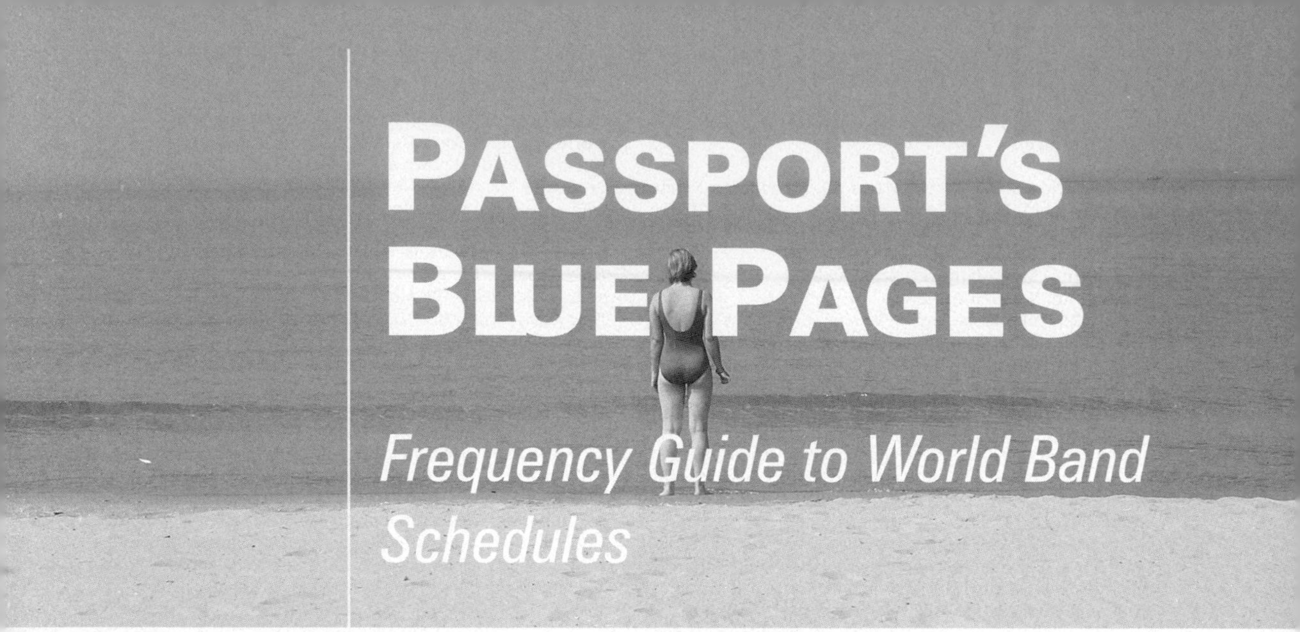

PASSPORT'S BLUE PAGES

Frequency Guide to World Band Schedules

If you scan the world band airwaves, you'll find much more than what is aimed your way. That's because shortwave signals are scattered by the heavens, allowing stations not targeted to your area to be heard.

Blue Pages Identify Stations

But bandscanning can be frustrating if you don't have a "map"—PASSPORT's Blue Pages. Let's say you've stumbled across something Asian-sounding on 7410 kHz at 2035 World Time. The Blue Pages show All India Radio beamed to Western Europe, with 250 kW of power from Delhi. These suggest this is probably what you're hearing, even if you're not in Europe. You can also see that English from India will begin on that same channel in about ten minutes.

Schedules for Entire Year

Times and days of the week are in World Time, explained in "Setting Your World Time Clock" and PASSPORT's glossary; for local times in each country, see "Addresses PLUS." Midyear, some stations are an hour earlier (⬅) or later (➡) because of daylight saving/summer time. Frequencies used only seasonally are labeled [S] for summer (midyear, typically the last Sunday in March until the last Sunday in October) and [W] for winter. Stations may also extend hours of transmission, or air special programs, for national holidays, emergencies or sports events.

To be as useful as possible over the months to come, PASSPORT's schedules consist not just of observed activity, but also that which we have creatively opined will take place during the forthcoming year. This predictive material is based on decades of experience and is original from us. Although inherently not as exact as real-time data, over the years it has been of tangible value to PASSPORT readers.

Guide to Blue Pages Format

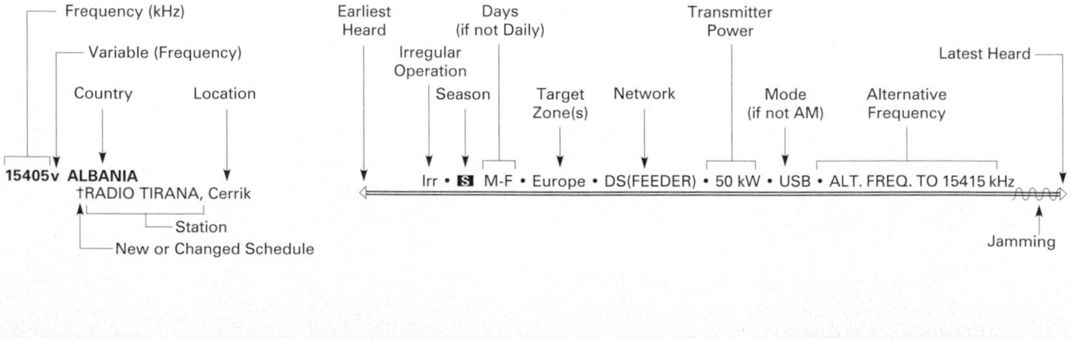

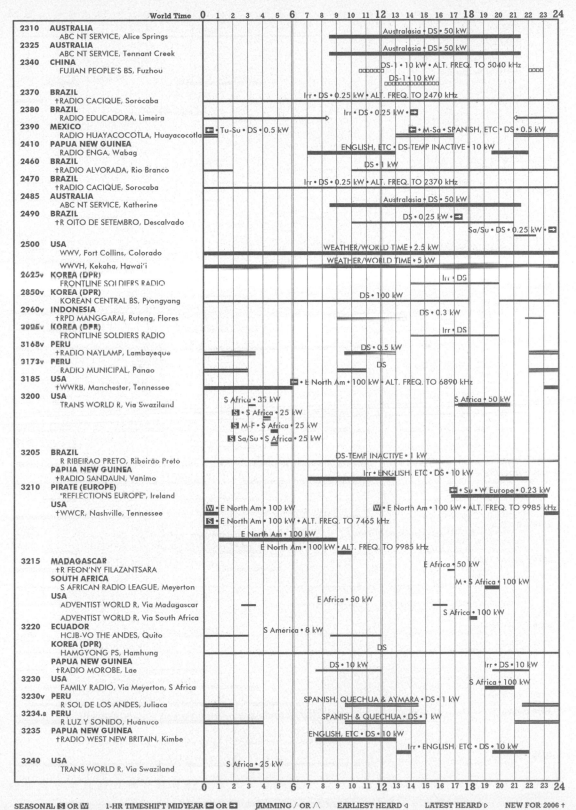

Freq	Country / Station	World Time 0–24
2310	**AUSTRALIA** ABC NT SERVICE, Alice Springs	Australasia • DS • 50 kW
2325	**AUSTRALIA** ABC NT SERVICE, Tennant Creek	Australasia • DS • 50 kW
2340	**CHINA** FUJIAN PEOPLE'S BS, Fuzhou	DS-1 • 10 kW • ALT. FREQ. TO 5040 kHz / DS-1 • 10 kW
2370	**BRAZIL** †RADIO CACIQUE, Sorocaba	Irr • DS • 0.25 kW • ALT. FREQ. TO 2470 kHz
2380	**BRAZIL** RADIO EDUCADORA, Limeira	Irr • DS • 0.25 kW •
2390	**MEXICO** RADIO HUAYACOCOTLA, Huayacocotla	Tu–Su • DS • 0.5 kW / M–Sa • SPANISH, ETC • DS • 0.5 kW
2410	**PAPUA NEW GUINEA** RADIO ENGA, Wabag	ENGLISH, ETC • DS-TEMP INACTIVE • 10 kW
2460	**BRAZIL** †RADIO ALVORADA, Rio Branco	DS • 1 kW
2470	**BRAZIL** †RADIO CACIQUE, Sorocaba	Irr • DS • 0.25 kW • ALT. FREQ. TO 2370 kHz
2485	**AUSTRALIA** ABC NT SERVICE, Katherine	Australasia • DS • 50 kW
2490	**BRAZIL** †R OITO DE SETEMBRO, Descalvado	DS • 0.25 kW • / Sa/Su • DS • 0.25 kW •
2500	**USA** WWV, Fort Collins, Colorado	WEATHER/WORLD TIME • 2.5 kW
	WWVH, Kekaha, Hawai'i	WEATHER/WORLD TIME • 5 kW
2625v	**KOREA (DPR)** FRONTLINE SOLDIERS RADIO	Irr • DS
2850v	**KOREA (DPR)** KOREAN CENTRAL BS, Pyongyang	DS • 100 kW
2960v	**INDONESIA** †RPD MANGGARAI, Ruteng, Flores	DS • 0.3 kW
3025v	**KOREA (DPR)** FRONTLINE SOLDIERS RADIO	Irr • DS
3168v	**PERU** †RADIO NAYLAMP, Lambayeque	DS • 0.5 kW
3173v	**PERU** RADIO MUNICIPAL, Panao	DS
3185	**USA** †WWRB, Manchester, Tennessee	E North Am • 100 kW • ALT. FREQ. TO 6890 kHz
3200	**USA** TRANS WORLD R, Via Swaziland	S Africa • 35 kW / S Africa • 50 kW / S • S Africa • 25 kW / M-F • S Africa • 25 kW / S • Sa/Su • S Africa • 25 kW
3205	**BRAZIL** R RIBEIRAO PRETO, Ribeirão Preto	DS-TEMP INACTIVE • 1 kW
	PAPUA NEW GUINEA †RADIO SANDAUN, Vanimo	Irr • ENGLISH, ETC • DS • 10 kW
3210	**PIRATE (EUROPE)** "REFLECTIONS EUROPE", Ireland	Su • W Europe • 0.23 kW
	USA †WWCR, Nashville, Tennessee	W • E North Am • 100 kW / W • E North Am • 100 kW • ALT. FREQ. TO 9985 kHz / S • E North Am • 100 kW • ALT. FREQ. TO 7465 kHz / E North Am • 100 kW / E North Am • 100 kW • ALT. FREQ. TO 9985 kHz
3215	**MADAGASCAR** †R FEON'NY FILAZANTSARA	E Africa • 50 kW
	SOUTH AFRICA S AFRICAN RADIO LEAGUE, Meyerton	M • S Africa • 100 kW
	USA ADVENTIST WORLD R, Via Madagascar	E Africa • 50 kW
	ADVENTIST WORLD R, Via South Africa	S Africa • 100 kW
3220	**ECUADOR** HCJB-VO THE ANDES, Quito	S America • 8 kW
	KOREA (DPR) HAMGYONG PS, Hamhung	DS
	PAPUA NEW GUINEA †RADIO MOROBE, Lae	DS • 10 kW / Irr • DS • 10 kW
3230	**USA** FAMILY RADIO, Via Meyerton, S Africa	S Africa • 100 kW
3230v	**PERU** R SOL DE LOS ANDES, Juliaca	SPANISH, QUECHUA & AYMARA • DS • 1 kW
3234.8	**PERU** R LUZ Y SONIDO, Huánuco	SPANISH & QUECHUA • DS • 1 kW
3235	**PAPUA NEW GUINEA** †RADIO WEST NEW BRITAIN, Kimbe	ENGLISH, ETC • DS • 10 kW / Irr • ENGLISH, ETC • DS • 10 kW
3240	**USA** TRANS WORLD R, Via Swaziland	S Africa • 25 kW

SEASONAL ⑤ OR Ⓦ   1-HR TIMESHIFT MIDYEAR ⏴ OR ⏵   JAMMING / OR ∧   EARLIEST HEARD ◁   LATEST HEARD ▷   NEW FOR 2006 †

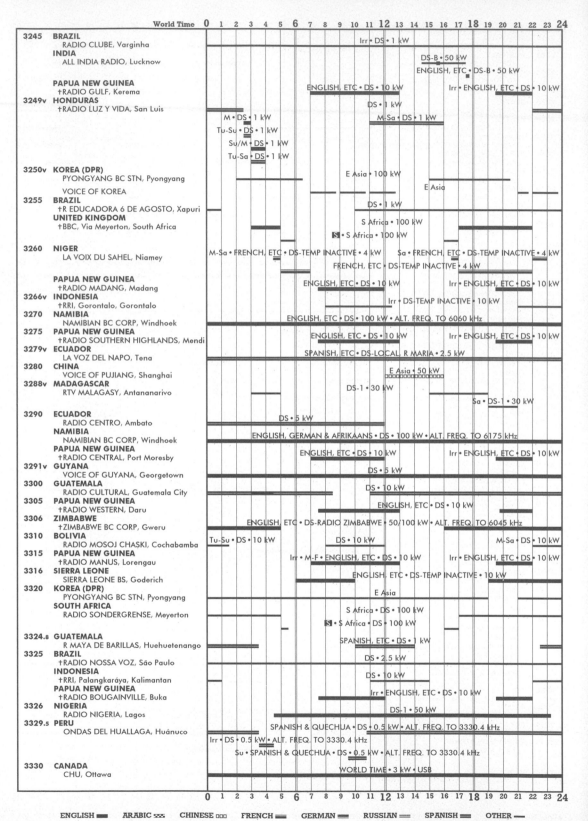

World Time 0 1 2 3 4 5 6 7 8 9 10 11 12 13 14 15 16 17 18 19 20 21 22 23 24

Freq	Country / Station	Schedule Notes
3245	**BRAZIL** — RADIO CLUBE, Varginha	Irr • DS • 1 kW
	INDIA — ALL INDIA RADIO, Lucknow	DS-B • 50 kW / ENGLISH, ETC • DS-B • 50 kW
	PAPUA NEW GUINEA — †RADIO GULF, Kerema	ENGLISH, ETC • DS • 10 kW / Irr • ENGLISH, ETC • DS • 10 kW
3249v	**HONDURAS** — †RADIO LUZ Y VIDA, San Luis	DS • 1 kW / M • DS • 1 kW / M-Sa • DS • 1 kW / Tu-Su • DS • 1 kW / Su/M • DS • 1 kW / Tu-Sa • DS • 1 kW
3250v	**KOREA (DPR)** — PYONGYANG BC STN, Pyongyang	E Asia • 100 kW
	VOICE OF KOREA	E Asia
3255	**BRAZIL** — †R EDUCADORA 6 DE AGOSTO, Xapuri	DS • 1 kW
	UNITED KINGDOM — †BBC, Via Meyerton, South Africa	S Africa • 100 kW / [S] • S Africa • 100 kW
3260	**NIGER** — LA VOIX DU SAHEL, Niamey	M-Sa • FRENCH, ETC • DS-TEMP INACTIVE • 4 kW / Sa • FRENCH, ETC • DS-TEMP INACTIVE • 4 kW / FRENCH, ETC • DS-TEMP INACTIVE • 4 kW
	PAPUA NEW GUINEA — †RADIO MADANG, Madang	ENGLISH, ETC • DS • 10 kW / Irr • ENGLISH, ETC • DS • 10 kW
3266v	**INDONESIA** — †RRI, Gorontalo, Gorontalo	Irr • DS-TEMP INACTIVE • 10 kW
3270	**NAMIBIA** — NAMIBIAN BC CORP, Windhoek	ENGLISH, ETC • DS • 100 kW • ALT. FREQ. TO 6060 kHz
3275	**PAPUA NEW GUINEA** — †RADIO SOUTHERN HIGHLANDS, Mendi	ENGLISH, ETC • DS • 10 kW / Irr • ENGLISH, ETC • DS • 10 kW
3279v	**ECUADOR** — LA VOZ DEL NAPO, Tena	SPANISH, ETC • DS-LOCAL R MARIA • 2.5 kW
3280	**CHINA** — VOICE OF PUJIANG, Shanghai	E Asia • 50 kW
3288v	**MADAGASCAR** — RTV MALAGASY, Antananarivo	DS-1 • 30 kW / Sa • DS-1 • 30 kW
3290	**ECUADOR** — RADIO CENTRO, Ambato	DS • 5 kW
	NAMIBIA — NAMIBIAN BC CORP, Windhoek	ENGLISH, GERMAN & AFRIKAANS • DS • 100 kW • ALT. FREQ. TO 6175 kHz
	PAPUA NEW GUINEA — †RADIO CENTRAL, Port Moresby	ENGLISH, ETC • DS • 10 kW / Irr • ENGLISH, ETC • DS • 10 kW
3291v	**GUYANA** — VOICE OF GUYANA, Georgetown	DS • 5 kW
3300	**GUATEMALA** — RADIO CULTURAL, Guatemala City	DS • 10 kW
3305	**PAPUA NEW GUINEA** — †RADIO WESTERN, Daru	ENGLISH, ETC • DS • 10 kW
3306	**ZIMBABWE** — †ZIMBABWE BC CORP, Gweru	ENGLISH, ETC • DS-RADIO ZIMBABWE • 50/100 kW • ALT. FREQ. TO 6045 kHz
3310	**BOLIVIA** — RADIO MOSOJ CHASKI, Cochabamba	Tu-Su • DS • 10 kW / DS • 10 kW / M-Sa • DS • 10 kW
3315	**PAPUA NEW GUINEA** — †RADIO MANUS, Lorengau	Irr • M-F • ENGLISH, ETC • DS • 10 kW / Irr • ENGLISH, ETC • DS • 10 kW
3316	**SIERRA LEONE** — SIERRA LEONE BS, Goderich	ENGLISH, ETC • DS-TEMP INACTIVE • 10 kW
3320	**KOREA (DPR)** — PYONGYANG BC STN, Pyongyang	E Asia
	SOUTH AFRICA — RADIO SONDERGRENSE, Meyerton	S Africa • DS • 100 kW / [S] • S Africa • DS • 100 kW
3324.8	**GUATEMALA** — R MAYA DE BARILLAS, Huehuetenango	SPANISH, ETC • DS • 1 kW
3325	**BRAZIL** — †RADIO NOSSA VOZ, São Paulo	DS • 2.5 kW
	INDONESIA — †RRI, Palangkaráya, Kalimantan	DS • 10 kW
	PAPUA NEW GUINEA — †RADIO BOUGAINVILLE, Buka	Irr • ENGLISH, ETC • DS • 10 kW
3326	**NIGERIA** — RADIO NIGERIA, Lagos	DS-1 • 50 kW
3329.5	**PERU** — ONDAS DEL HUALLAGA, Huánuco	SPANISH & QUECHUA • DS • 0.5 kW • ALT. FREQ. TO 3330.4 kHz / Irr • DS • 0.5 kW • ALT. FREQ. TO 3330.4 kHz / Su • SPANISH & QUECHUA • DS • 0.5 kW • ALT. FREQ. TO 3330.4 kHz
3330	**CANADA** — CHU, Ottawa	WORLD TIME • 3 kW • USB

0 1 2 3 4 5 6 7 8 9 10 11 12 13 14 15 16 17 18 19 20 21 22 23 24

ENGLISH ▬ ARABIC ▨▨▨ CHINESE □□□ FRENCH ══ GERMAN ▬▬ RUSSIAN ═══ SPANISH ▬▬ OTHER —

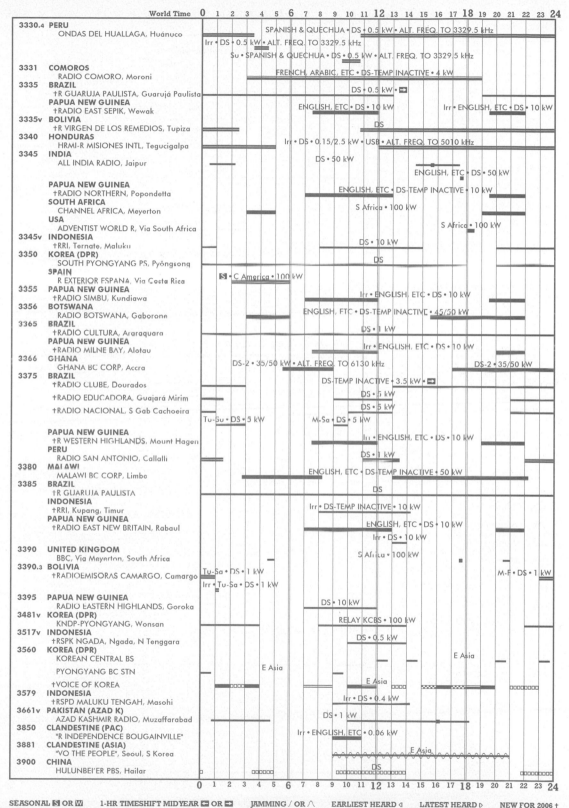

World Time 0 1 2 3 4 5 6 7 8 9 10 11 12 13 14 15 16 17 18 19 20 21 22 23 24

3330.4 PERU
ONDAS DEL HUALLAGA, Huánuco
SPANISH & QUECHUA • DS • 0.5 kW • ALT. FREQ. TO 3329.5 kHz
Irr • DS • 0.5 kW • ALT. FREQ. TO 3329.5 kHz
Su • SPANISH & QUECHUA • DS • 0.5 kW • ALT. FREQ. TO 3329.5 kHz

3331 COMOROS
RADIO COMORO, Moroni
FRENCH, ARABIC, ETC • DS-TEMP INACTIVE • 4 kW

3335 BRAZIL
†R GUARUJA PAULISTA, Guarujá Paulista
DS • 0.5 kW • ➡

PAPUA NEW GUINEA
†RADIO EAST SEPIK, Wewak
ENGLISH, ETC • DS • 10 kW　　Irr • ENGLISH, ETC • DS • 10 kW

3335v BOLIVIA
†R VIRGEN DE LOS REMEDIOS, Tupiza
DS

3340 HONDURAS
HRMI-R MISIONES INTL, Tegucigalpa
Irr • DS • 0.15/2.5 kW • USB • ALT. FREQ. TO 5010 kHz

3345 INDIA
ALL INDIA RADIO, Jaipur
DS • 50 kW
ENGLISH, ETC • DS • 50 kW

PAPUA NEW GUINEA
†RADIO NORTHERN, Popondetta
ENGLISH, ETC • DS-TEMP INACTIVE • 10 kW
SOUTH AFRICA
CHANNEL AFRICA, Meyerton
S Africa • 100 kW
USA
ADVENTIST WORLD R, Via South Africa
S Africa • 100 kW

3345v INDONESIA
†RRI, Ternate, Maluku
DS • 10 kW

3350 KOREA (DPR)
SOUTH PYONGYANG PS, Pyŏngsong
DS
SPAIN
R EXTERIOR ESPANA, Via Costa Rica
S • C America • 100 kW

3355 PAPUA NEW GUINEA
†RADIO SIMBU, Kundiawa
Irr • ENGLISH, ETC • DS • 10 kW

3356 BOTSWANA
RADIO BOTSWANA, Gaborone
ENGLISH, ETC • DS-TEMP INACTIVE • 45/50 kW

3365 BRAZIL
†RADIO CULTURA, Araraquara
DS • 1 kW
PAPUA NEW GUINEA
†RADIO MILNE BAY, Alotau
Irr • ENGLISH, ETC • DS • 10 kW

3366 GHANA
GHANA BC CORP, Accra
DS-2 • 35/50 kW • ALT. FREQ. TO 6130 kHz　　DS-2 • 35/50 kW

3375 BRAZIL
†RADIO CLUBE, Dourados
DS-TEMP INACTIVE • 3.5 kW • ➡
†RADIO EDUCADORA, Guajará Mirim
DS • 5 kW
†RADIO NACIONAL, S Gab Cachoeira
DS • 5 kW
Tu-Su • DS • 5 kW　　M-Sa • DS • 5 kW

PAPUA NEW GUINEA
†R WESTERN HIGHLANDS, Mount Hagen
Irr • ENGLISH, ETC • DS • 10 kW
PERU
RADIO SAN ANTONIO, Callalli
DS • 1 kW

3380 MALAWI
MALAWI BC CORP, Limbe
ENGLISH, ETC • DS-TEMP INACTIVE • 50 kW

3385 BRAZIL
†R GUARUJA PAULISTA
DS
INDONESIA
†RRI, Kupang, Timur
Irr • DS-TEMP INACTIVE • 10 kW
PAPUA NEW GUINEA
†RADIO EAST NEW BRITAIN, Rabaul
ENGLISH, ETC • DS • 10 kW
Irr • DS • 10 kW

3390 UNITED KINGDOM
BBC, Via Meyerton, South Africa
S Africa • 100 kW
3390.3 BOLIVIA
†RADIOEMISORAS CAMARGO, Camargo
Tu-Sa • DS • 1 kW　　M-F • DS • 1 kW
Irr • Tu-Sa • DS • 1 kW

3395 PAPUA NEW GUINEA
RADIO EASTERN HIGHLANDS, Goroka
DS • 10 kW
3481v KOREA (DPR)
KNDP-PYONGYANG, Wonsan
RELAY KCBS • 100 kW
3517v INDONESIA
†RSPK NGADA, Ngada, N Tenggara
DS • 0.5 kW
3560 KOREA (DPR)
KOREAN CENTRAL BS
E Asia
PYONGYANG BC STN
E Asia
†VOICE OF KOREA
E Asia
3579 INDONESIA
†RSPD MALUKU TENGAH, Masohi
Irr • DS • 0.4 kW
3661v PAKISTAN (AZAD K)
AZAD KASHMIR RADIO, Muzaffarabad
DS • 1 kW
3850 CLANDESTINE (PAC)
"R INDEPENDENCE BOUGAINVILLE"
Irr • ENGLISH, ETC • 0.06 kW
3881 CLANDESTINE (ASIA)
"VO THE PEOPLE", Seoul, S Korea
E Asia
3900 CHINA
HULUNBEI'ER PBS, Hailar
DS

0 1 2 3 4 5 6 7 8 9 10 11 12 13 14 15 16 17 18 19 20 21 22 23 24

SEASONAL ⑤ OR Ⓦ　　1-HR TIMESHIFT MIDYEAR ⬅ OR ➡　　JAMMING / OR ∧　　EARLIEST HEARD ◁　　LATEST HEARD ▷　　NEW FOR 2006 †

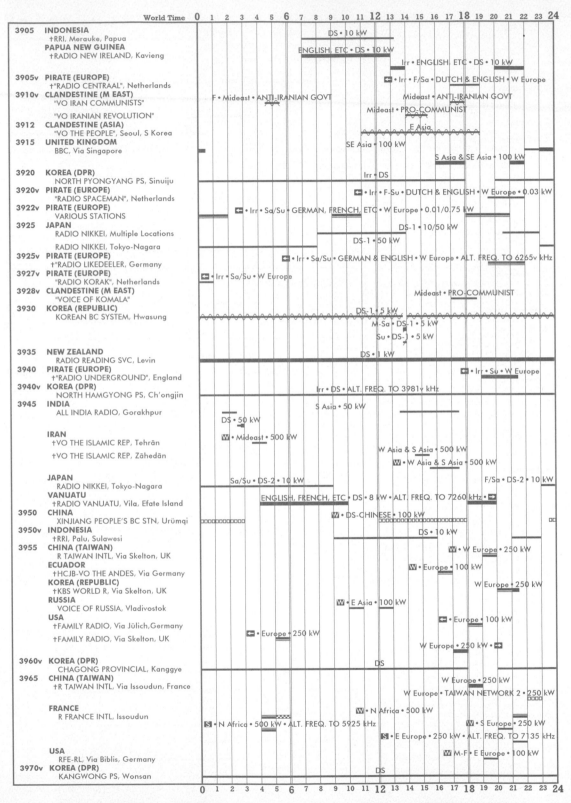

| | World Time | 0 | 1 | 2 | 3 | 4 | 5 | 6 | 7 | 8 | 9 | 10 | 11 | 12 | 13 | 14 | 15 | 16 | 17 | 18 | 19 | 20 | 21 | 22 | 23 | 24 |

3905 INDONESIA
†RRI, Merauke, Papua — DS • 10 kW

PAPUA NEW GUINEA
†RADIO NEW IRELAND, Kavieng — ENGLISH, ETC • DS • 10 kW / Irr • ENGLISH, ETC • DS • 10 kW

3905v PIRATE (EUROPE)
†"RADIO CENTRAAL", Netherlands — Irr • F/Sa • DUTCH & ENGLISH • W Europe

3910v CLANDESTINE (M EAST)
"VO IRAN COMMUNISTS" — F • Mideast • ANTI-IRANIAN GOVT / Mideast • ANTI-IRANIAN GOVT

"VO IRANIAN REVOLUTION" — Mideast • PRO-COMMUNIST

3912 CLANDESTINE (ASIA)
"VO THE PEOPLE", Seoul, S Korea — E Asia

3915 UNITED KINGDOM
BBC, Via Singapore — SE Asia • 100 kW / S Asia & SE Asia • 100 kW

3920 KOREA (DPR)
NORTH PYONGYANG PS, Sinuiju — Irr • DS

3920v PIRATE (EUROPE)
"RADIO SPACEMAN", Netherlands — Irr • F-Su • DUTCH & ENGLISH • W Europe • 0.03 kW

3922v PIRATE (EUROPE)
VARIOUS STATIONS — Irr • Sa/Su • GERMAN, FRENCH, ETC • W Europe • 0.01/0.75 kW

3925 JAPAN
RADIO NIKKEI, Multiple Locations — DS-1 • 10/50 kW

RADIO NIKKEI, Tokyo-Nagara — DS-1 • 50 kW

3925v PIRATE (EUROPE)
†"RADIO LIKEDEELER", Germany — Irr • Sa/Su • GERMAN & ENGLISH • W Europe • ALT. FREQ. TO 6265v kHz

3927v PIRATE (EUROPE)
"RADIO KORAK", Netherlands — Irr • Sa/Su • W Europe

3928v CLANDESTINE (M EAST)
"VOICE OF KOMALA" — Mideast • PRO-COMMUNIST

3930 KOREA (REPUBLIC)
KOREAN BC SYSTEM, Hwasung — DS-1 • 5 kW / M-Sa • DS-1 • 5 kW / Su • DS-1 • 5 kW

3935 NEW ZEALAND
RADIO READING SVC, Levin — DS • 1 kW

3940 PIRATE (EUROPE)
†"RADIO UNDERGROUND", England — Irr • Su • W Europe

3940v KOREA (DPR)
NORTH HAMGYONG PS, Ch'ongjin — Irr • DS • ALT. FREQ. TO 3981v kHz

3945 INDIA
ALL INDIA RADIO, Gorakhpur — S Asia • 50 kW / DS • 50 kW

IRAN
†VO THE ISLAMIC REP, Tehrān — W • Mideast • 500 kW

†VO THE ISLAMIC REP, Zāhedān — W Asia & S Asia • 500 kW / W • W Asia & S Asia • 500 kW

JAPAN
RADIO NIKKEI, Tokyo-Nagara — Sa/Su • DS-2 • 10 kW / F/Sa • DS-2 • 10 kW

VANUATU
†RADIO VANUATU, Vila, Efate Island — ENGLISH, FRENCH, ETC • DS • 8 kW • ALT. FREQ. TO 7260 kHz

3950 CHINA
XINJIANG PEOPLE'S BC STN, Urümqi — W • DS-CHINESE • 100 kW

3950v INDONESIA
†RRI, Palu, Sulawesi — DS • 10 kW

3955 CHINA (TAIWAN)
R TAIWAN INTL, Via Skelton, UK — W • W Europe • 250 kW

ECUADOR
†HCJB-VO THE ANDES, Via Germany — W • Europe • 100 kW

KOREA (REPUBLIC)
†KBS WORLD R, Via Skelton, UK — W Europe • 250 kW

RUSSIA
VOICE OF RUSSIA, Vladivostok — W • E Asia • 100 kW

USA
†FAMILY RADIO, Via Jülich, Germany — Europe • 100 kW

†FAMILY RADIO, Via Skelton, UK — Europe • 250 kW / W Europe • 250 kW

3960v KOREA (DPR)
CHAGONG PROVINCIAL, Kanggye — DS

3965 CHINA (TAIWAN)
†R TAIWAN INTL, Via Issoudun, France — W Europe • 250 kW / W Europe • TAIWAN NETWORK 2 • 250 kW

FRANCE
R FRANCE INTL, Issoudun — W • N Africa • 500 kW / S • N Africa • 500 kW • ALT. FREQ. TO 5925 kHz / S • E Europe • 250 kW • ALT. FREQ. TO 7135 kHz / W • S Europe • 250 kW

USA
RFE-RL, Via Biblis, Germany — W M-F • E Europe • 100 kW

3970v KOREA (DPR)
KANGWONG PS, Wonsan — DS

| | 0 | 1 | 2 | 3 | 4 | 5 | 6 | 7 | 8 | 9 | 10 | 11 | 12 | 13 | 14 | 15 | 16 | 17 | 18 | 19 | 20 | 21 | 22 | 23 | 24 |

ENGLISH ▬ ARABIC ⌇⌇⌇ CHINESE ▯▯▯ FRENCH ═ GERMAN ▬ RUSSIAN ═ SPANISH ═ OTHER ▬

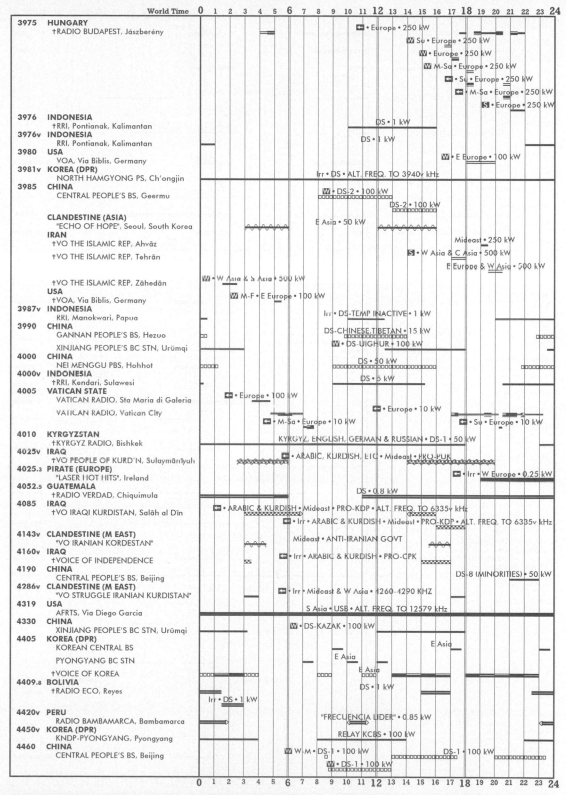

World Time   0 1 2 3 4 5 6 7 8 9 10 11 12 13 14 15 16 17 18 19 20 21 22 23 24

3975 HUNGARY
†RADIO BUDAPEST, Jászberény
• Europe • 250 kW
W Su • Europe • 250 kW
W • Europe • 250 kW
W M-Sa • Europe • 250 kW
• Su • Europe • 250 kW
• M-Sa • Europe • 250 kW
S • Europe • 250 kW

3976 INDONESIA
†RRI, Pontianak, Kalimantan — DS • 1 kW
3976v INDONESIA
RRI, Pontianak, Kalimantan — DS • 1 kW
3980 USA
VOA, Via Biblis, Germany — W • E Europe • 100 kW
3981v KOREA (DPR)
NORTH HAMGYONG PS, Ch'ongjin — Irr • DS • ALT. FREQ. TO 3940v kHz
3985 CHINA
CENTRAL PEOPLE'S BS, Geermu — W • DS-2 • 100 kW
DS-2 • 100 kW

CLANDESTINE (ASIA)
"ECHO OF HOPE", Seoul, South Korea — E Asia • 50 kW
IRAN
†VO THE ISLAMIC REP, Ahvāz — Mideast • 250 kW
†VO THE ISLAMIC REP, Tehrān — S • W Asia & C Asia • 500 kW
E Europe & W Asia • 500 kW

†VO THE ISLAMIC REP, Zāhedān — W • W Asia & S Asia • 500 kW
USA
†VOA, Via Biblis, Germany — W M-F • E Europe • 100 kW
3987v INDONESIA
RRI, Manokwari, Papua — Irr • DS-TEMP INACTIVE • 1 kW
3990 CHINA
GANNAN PEOPLE'S BS, Hezuo — DS-CHINESE TIBETAN • 15 kW
XINJIANG PEOPLE'S BC STN, Urümqi — W • DS-UIGHUR • 100 kW
4000 CHINA
NEI MENGGU PBS, Hohhot — DS • 50 kW
4000v INDONESIA
†RRI, Kendari, Sulawesi — DS • 5 kW
4005 VATICAN STATE
VATICAN RADIO, Sta Maria di Galeria — • Europe • 100 kW
VATICAN RADIO, Vatican City — • Europe • 10 kW
• M-Sa • Europe • 10 kW
• Su • Europe • 10 kW
4010 KYRGYZSTAN
†KYRGYZ RADIO, Bishkek — KYRGYZ, ENGLISH, GERMAN & RUSSIAN • DS-1 • 50 kW
4025v IRAQ
†VO PEOPLE OF KURD'N, Sulaymānīyuh — • ARABIC, KURDISH, ETC • Mideast • PRO-PUK
4025.3 PIRATE (EUROPE)
"LASER HOT HITS", Ireland — • Irr • W Europe • 0.25 kW
4052.5 GUATEMALA
†RADIO VERDAD, Chiquimula — DS • 0.8 kW
4085 IRAQ
†VO IRAQI KURDISTAN, Salāh al Dīn — • ARABIC & KURDISH • Mideast • PRO-KDP • ALT. FREQ. TO 6335v kHz
• Irr • ARABIC & KURDISH • Mideast • PRO-KDP • ALT. FREQ. TO 6335v kHz

4143v CLANDESTINE (M EAST)
"VO IRANIAN KORDESTAN" — Mideast • ANTI-IRANIAN GOVT
4160v IRAQ
†VOICE OF INDEPENDENCE — • Irr • ARABIC & KURDISH • PRO-CPK
4190 CHINA
CENTRAL PEOPLE'S BS, Beijing — DS-8 (MINORITIES) • 50 kW
4286v CLANDESTINE (M EAST)
"VO STRUGGLE IRANIAN KURDISTAN" — • Irr • Mideast & W Asia • 4260-4290 KHZ
4319 USA
AFRTS, Via Diego Garcia — S Asia • USB • ALT. FREQ. TO 12579 kHz
4330 CHINA
XINJIANG PEOPLE'S BC STN, Urümqi — W • DS-KAZAK • 100 kW
4405 KOREA (DPR)
KOREAN CENTRAL BS — E Asia
PYONGYANG BC STN — E Asia
†VOICE OF KOREA — E Asia
4409.8 BOLIVIA
†RADIO ECO, Reyes — DS • 1 kW
Irr • DS • 1 kW
4420v PERU
RADIO BAMBAMARCA, Bambamarca — "FRECUENCIA LIDER" • 0.85 kW
4450v KOREA (DPR)
KNDP-PYONGYANG, Pyongyang — RELAY KCBS • 100 kW
4460 CHINA
CENTRAL PEOPLE'S BS, Beijing — W W-M • DS-1 • 100 kW
DS-1 • 100 kW
W • DS-1 • 100 kW

0 1 2 3 4 5 6 7 8 9 10 11 12 13 14 15 16 17 18 19 20 21 22 23 24

SEASONAL S OR W   1-HR TIMESHIFT MIDYEAR ⊡ OR ⊡   JAMMING / OR ∧   EARLIEST HEARD ◁   LATEST HEARD ▷   NEW FOR 2006 †

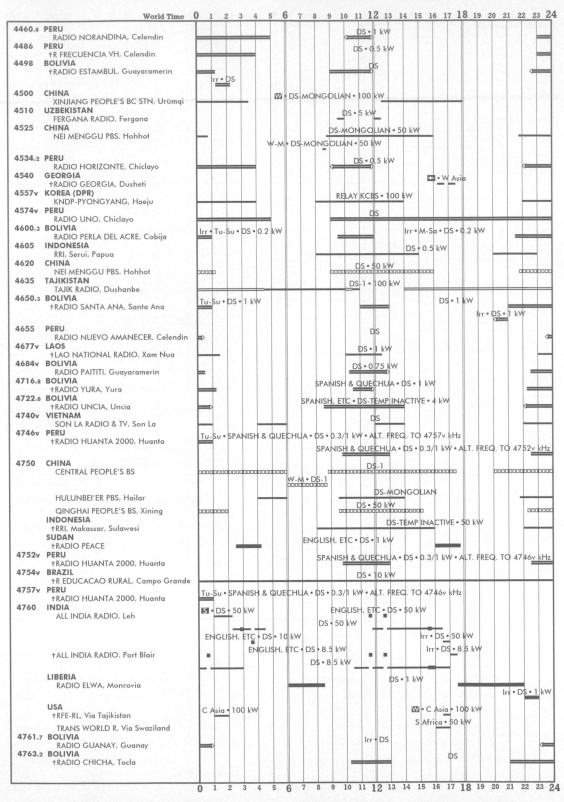

World Time 0 1 2 3 4 5 6 7 8 9 10 11 12 13 14 15 16 17 18 19 20 21 22 23 24

Freq	Country / Station	Notes
4460.8	**PERU** — RADIO NORANDINA, Celendin	DS • 1 kW
4486	**PERU** — †R FRECUENCIA VH, Celendin	DS • 0.5 kW
4498	**BOLIVIA** — †RADIO ESTAMBUL, Guayaramerin	DS / Irr • DS
4500	**CHINA** — XINJIANG PEOPLE'S BC STN, Urümqi	W • DS-MONGOLIAN • 100 kW
4510	**UZBEKISTAN** — FERGANA RADIO, Fergana	DS • 5 kW
4525	**CHINA** — NEI MENGGU PBS, Hohhot	DS-MONGOLIAN • 50 kW / W-M • DS-MONGOLIAN • 50 kW
4534.2	**PERU** — RADIO HORIZONTE, Chiclayo	DS • 0.5 kW
4540	**GEORGIA** — †RADIO GEORGIA, Dusheti	• W Asia
4557v	**KOREA (DPR)** — KNDP-PYONGYANG, Haeju	RELAY KCBS • 100 kW
4574v	**PERU** — RADIO UNO, Chiclayo	DS
4600.3	**BOLIVIA** — RADIO PERLA DEL ACRE, Cobija	Irr • Tu-Su • DS • 0.2 kW / Irr • M-Sa • DS • 0.2 kW
4605	**INDONESIA** — RRI, Serui, Papua	DS • 0.5 kW
4620	**CHINA** — NEI MENGGU PBS, Hohhot	DS • 50 kW
4635	**TAJIKISTAN** — TAJIK RADIO, Dushanbe	DS-1 • 100 kW
4650.3	**BOLIVIA** — †RADIO SANTA ANA, Santa Ana	Tu-Su • DS • 1 kW / DS • 1 kW / Irr • DS • 1 kW
4655	**PERU** — RADIO NUEVO AMANECER, Celendin	DS
4677v	**LAOS** — †LAO NATIONAL RADIO, Xam Nua	DS • 1 kW
4684v	**BOLIVIA** — RADIO PAITITI, Guayaramerin	DS • 0.75 kW
4716.8	**BOLIVIA** — †RADIO YURA, Yura	SPANISH & QUECHUA • DS • 1 kW
4722.8	**BOLIVIA** — †RADIO UNCIA, Uncia	SPANISH, ETC • DS-TEMP INACTIVE • 4 kW
4740v	**VIETNAM** — SON LA RADIO & TV, Son La	DS
4746v	**PERU** — †RADIO HUANTA 2000, Huanta	Tu-Su • SPANISH & QUECHUA • DS • 0.3/1 kW • ALT. FREQ. TO 4757v kHz / SPANISH & QUECHUA • DS • 0.3/1 kW • ALT. FREQ. TO 4752v kHz
4750	**CHINA** — CENTRAL PEOPLE'S BS	DS-1 / W-M • DS-1
	HULUNBEI'ER PBS, Hailar	DS-MONGOLIAN
	QINGHAI PEOPLE'S BS, Xining	DS • 50 kW
	INDONESIA — †RRI, Makassar, Sulawesi	DS-TEMP INACTIVE • 50 kW
	SUDAN — †RADIO PEACE	ENGLISH, ETC • DS • 1 kW
4752v	**PERU** — †RADIO HUANTA 2000, Huanta	SPANISH & QUECHUA • DS • 0.3/1 kW • ALT. FREQ. TO 4746v kHz
4754v	**BRAZIL** — †R EDUCACAO RURAL, Campo Grande	DS • 10 kW
4757v	**PERU** — †RADIO HUANTA 2000, Huanta	Tu-Su • SPANISH & QUECHUA • DS • 0.3/1 kW • ALT. FREQ. TO 4746v kHz
4760	**INDIA** — ALL INDIA RADIO, Leh	S • DS • 50 kW / ENGLISH, ETC • DS • 50 kW / DS • 50 kW
		ENGLISH, ETC • DS • 10 kW / Irr • DS • 50 kW
	†ALL INDIA RADIO, Port Blair	ENGLISH, ETC • DS • 8.5 kW / Irr • DS • 8.5 kW / DS • 8.5 kW
	LIBERIA — RADIO ELWA, Monrovia	DS • 1 kW / Irr • DS • 1 kW
	USA — †RFE-RL, Via Tajikistan	C Asia • 100 kW / W • C Asia • 100 kW
	TRANS WORLD R, Via Swaziland	S Africa • 50 kW
4761.7	**BOLIVIA** — RADIO GUANAY, Guanay	Irr • DS
4763.2	**BOLIVIA** — †RADIO CHICHA, Tocla	DS

0 1 2 3 4 5 6 7 8 9 10 11 12 13 14 15 16 17 18 19 20 21 22 23 24

ENGLISH ▬   ARABIC ≋   CHINESE ▫▫▫   FRENCH ▬   GERMAN ▬   RUSSIAN ═   SPANISH ▬   OTHER ▬

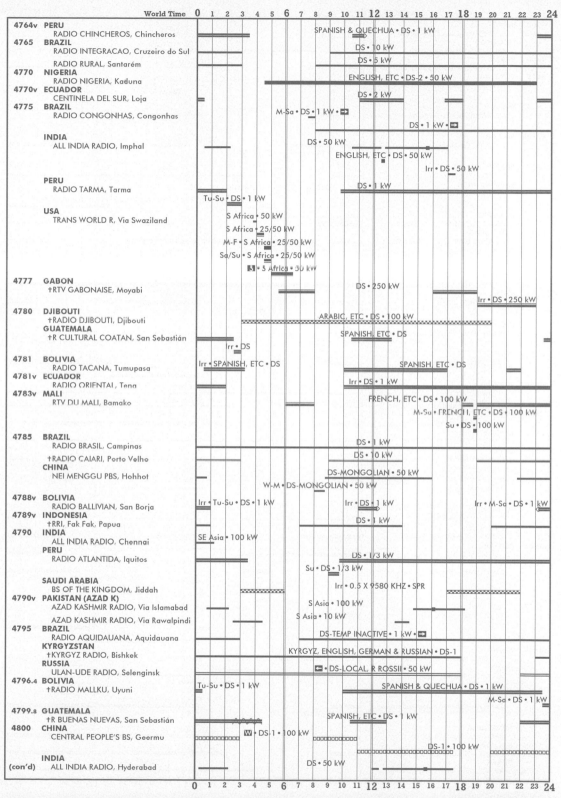

World Time 0 1 2 3 4 5 6 7 8 9 10 11 12 13 14 15 16 17 18 19 20 21 22 23 24

kHz	Country	Station	Details
4764v	PERU	RADIO CHINCHEROS, Chincheros	SPANISH & QUECHUA • DS • 1 kW
4765	BRAZIL	RADIO INTEGRACAO, Cruzeiro do Sul	DS • 10 kW
		RADIO RURAL, Santarém	DS • 5 kW
4770	NIGERIA	RADIO NIGERIA, Kaduna	ENGLISH, ETC • DS-2 • 50 kW
4770v	ECUADOR	CENTINELA DEL SUR, Loja	DS • 2 kW
4775	BRAZIL	RADIO CONGONHAS, Congonhas	M-Sa • DS • 1 kW • ➡; DS • 1 kW • ➡
	INDIA	ALL INDIA RADIO, Imphal	DS • 50 kW; ENGLISH, ETC • DS • 50 kW; Irr • DS • 50 kW
	PERU	RADIO TARMA, Tarma	DS • 1 kW; Tu-Su • DS • 1 kW
	USA	TRANS WORLD R, Via Swaziland	S Africa • 50 kW; S Africa • 25/50 kW; M-F • S Africa • 25/50 kW; Sa/Su • S Africa • 25/50 kW; [S] • S Africa • 30 kW
4777	GABON	†RTV GABONAISE, Moyabi	DS • 250 kW; Irr • DS • 250 kW
4780	DJIBOUTI	†RADIO DJIBOUTI, Djibouti	ARABIC, ETC • DS • 100 kW
	GUATEMALA	†R CULTURAL COATAN, San Sebastián	SPANISH, ETC • DS; Irr • DS
4781	BOLIVIA	RADIO TACANA, Tumupasa	Irr • SPANISH, ETC • DS; SPANISH, ETC • DS
4781v	ECUADOR	RADIO ORIENTAL, Tena	Irr • DS • 1 kW
4783v	MALI	RTV DU MALI, Bamako	FRENCH, ETC • DS • 100 kW; M-Sa • FRENCH, ETC • DS • 100 kW; Su • DS • 100 kW
4785	BRAZIL	RADIO BRASIL, Campinas	DS • 1 kW
		†RADIO CAIARI, Porto Velho	DS • 10 kW
	CHINA	NEI MENGGU PBS, Hohhot	DS-MONGOLIAN • 50 kW; W-M • DS-MONGOLIAN • 50 kW
4788v	BOLIVIA	RADIO BALLIVIAN, San Borja	Irr • Tu-Su • DS • 1 kW; Irr • DS • 1 kW; Irr • M-Sa • DS • 1 kW
4789v	INDONESIA	†RRI, Fak Fak, Papua	DS • 1 kW
4790	INDIA	ALL INDIA RADIO, Chennai	SE Asia • 100 kW
	PERU	RADIO ATLANTIDA, Iquitos	DS • 1/3 kW; Su • DS • 1/3 kW
	SAUDI ARABIA	BS OF THE KINGDOM, Jiddah	Irr • 0.5 X 9580 KHZ • SPR
4790v	PAKISTAN (AZAD K)	AZAD KASHMIR RADIO, Via Islamabad	S Asia • 100 kW
		AZAD KASHMIR RADIO, Via Rawalpindi	S Asia • 10 kW
4795	BRAZIL	RADIO AQUIDAUANA, Aquidauana	DS-TEMP INACTIVE • 1 kW • ➡
	KYRGYZSTAN	†KYRGYZ RADIO, Bishkek	KYRGYZ, ENGLISH, GERMAN & RUSSIAN • DS-1
	RUSSIA	ULAN-UDE RADIO, Selenginsk	⬅ • DS-LOCAL, R ROSSII • 50 kW
4796.4	BOLIVIA	†RADIO MALLKU, Uyuni	Tu-Su • DS • 1 kW; SPANISH & QUECHUA • DS • 1 kW; M-Sa • DS • 1 kW
4799.8	GUATEMALA	†R BUENAS NUEVAS, San Sebastián	SPANISH, ETC • DS • 1 kW
4800	CHINA	CENTRAL PEOPLE'S BS, Geermu	[W] • DS-1 • 100 kW; DS-1 • 100 kW
(con'd)	INDIA	ALL INDIA RADIO, Hyderabad	DS • 50 kW

0 1 2 3 4 5 6 7 8 9 10 11 12 13 14 15 16 17 18 19 20 21 22 23 24

SEASONAL [S] OR [W] 1-HR TIMESHIFT MIDYEAR ⬅ OR ➡ JAMMING / OR /\ EARLIEST HEARD ◁ LATEST HEARD ▷ NEW FOR 2006 †

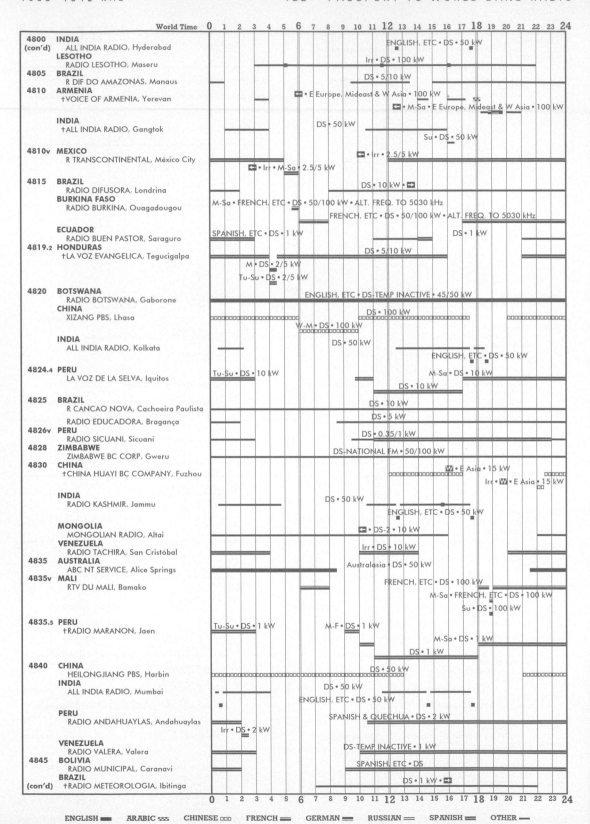

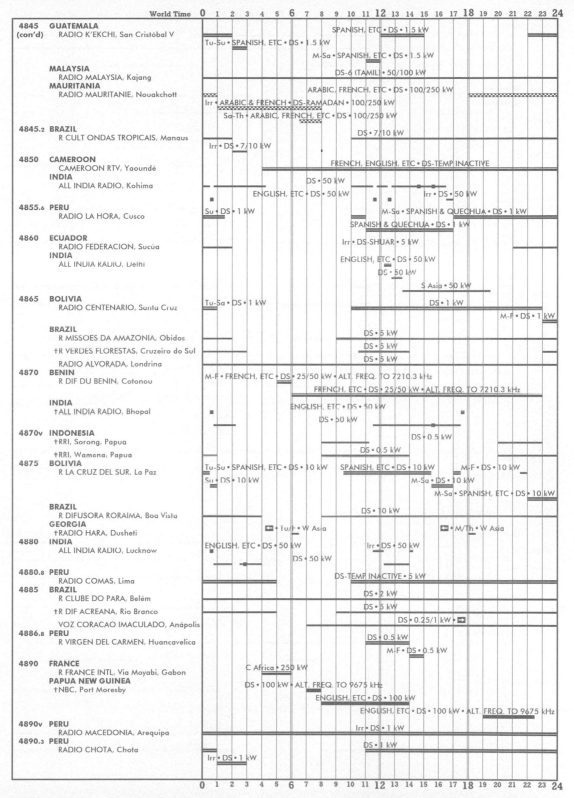

World Time   0 1 2 3 4 5 6 7 8 9 10 11 12 13 14 15 16 17 18 19 20 21 22 23 24

4845 GUATEMALA
(con'd) RADIO K'EKCHI, San Cristóbal V
- SPANISH, ETC • DS • 1.5 kW
- Tu-Su • SPANISH, ETC • DS • 1.5 kW
- M-Sa • SPANISH, ETC • DS • 1.5 kW

MALAYSIA
RADIO MALAYSIA, Kajang
- DS-6 (TAMIL) • 50/100 kW

MAURITANIA
RADIO MAURITANIE, Nouakchott
- ARABIC, FRENCH, ETC • DS • 100/250 kW
- Irr • ARABIC & FRENCH • DS-RAMADAN • 100/250 kW
- Sa-Th • ARABIC, FRENCH, ETC • DS • 100/250 kW

4845.2 BRAZIL
R CULT ONDAS TROPICAIS, Manaus
- DS • 7/10 kW
- Irr • DS • 7/10 kW

4850 CAMEROON
CAMEROON RTV, Yaoundé
- FRENCH, ENGLISH, ETC • DS-TEMP INACTIVE

INDIA
ALL INDIA RADIO, Kohima
- DS • 50 kW
- ENGLISH, ETC • DS • 50 kW
- Irr • DS • 50 kW

4855.6 PERU
RADIO LA HORA, Cusco
- Su • DS • 1 kW
- M-Sa • SPANISH & QUECHUA • DS • 1 kW
- SPANISH & QUECHUA • DS • 1 kW

4860 ECUADOR
RADIO FEDERACION, Sucúa
- Irr • DS-SHUAR • 5 kW

INDIA
ALL INDIA RADIO, Delhi
- ENGLISH, ETC • DS • 50 kW
- DS • 50 kW
- S Asia • 50 kW

4865 BOLIVIA
RADIO CENTENARIO, Santa Cruz
- Tu-Sa • DS • 1 kW
- DS • 1 kW
- M-F • DS • 1 kW

BRAZIL
R MISSOES DA AMAZONIA, Obidos
- DS • 5 kW
†R VERDES FLORESTAS, Cruzeiro do Sul
- DS • 5 kW
RADIO ALVORADA, Londrina
- DS • 5 kW

4870 BENIN
R DIF DU BENIN, Cotonou
- M-F • FRENCH, ETC • DS • 25/50 kW • ALT. FREQ. TO 7210.3 kHz
- FRENCH, ETC • DS • 25/50 kW • ALT. FREQ. TO 7210.3 kHz

INDIA
†ALL INDIA RADIO, Bhopal
- ENGLISH, ETC • DS • 50 kW
- DS • 50 kW

4870v INDONESIA
†RRI, Sorong, Papua
- DS • 0.5 kW
†RRI, Wamena, Papua
- DS • 0.5 kW

4875 BOLIVIA
R LA CRUZ DEL SUR, La Paz
- Tu-Su • SPANISH, ETC • DS • 10 kW
- SPANISH, ETC • DS • 10 kW
- M-F • DS • 10 kW
- Su • DS • 10 kW
- M-Sa • DS • 10 kW
- M-Sa • SPANISH, ETC • DS • 10 kW

BRAZIL
R DIFUSORA RORAIMA, Boa Vista
- DS • 10 kW

GEORGIA
†RADIO HARA, Dusheti
- Tu/F • W Asia
- M/Th • W Asia

4880 INDIA
ALL INDIA RADIO, Lucknow
- ENGLISH, ETC • DS • 50 kW
- Irr • DS • 50 kW
- DS • 50 kW

4880.8 PERU
RADIO COMAS, Lima
- DS-TEMP INACTIVE • 5 kW

4885 BRAZIL
R CLUBE DO PARA, Belém
- DS • 2 kW
†R DIF ACREANA, Rio Branco
- DS • 5 kW
VOZ CORACAO IMACULADO, Anápolis
- DS • 0.25/1 kW

4886.8 PERU
R VIRGEN DEL CARMEN, Huancavelica
- DS • 0.5 kW
- M-F • DS • 0.5 kW

4890 FRANCE
R FRANCE INTL, Via Moyabi, Gabon
- C Africa • 250 kW

PAPUA NEW GUINEA
†NBC, Port Moresby
- DS • 100 kW • ALT. FREQ. TO 9675 kHz
- ENGLISH, ETC • DS • 100 kW
- ENGLISH, ETC • DS • 100 kW • ALT. FREQ. TO 9675 kHz

4890v PERU
RADIO MACEDONIA, Arequipa
- Irr • DS • 1 kW

4890.3 PERU
RADIO CHOTA, Chota
- DS • 1 kW
- Irr • DS • 1 kW

World Time   0 1 2 3 4 5 6 7 8 9 10 11 12 13 14 15 16 17 18 19 20 21 22 23 24

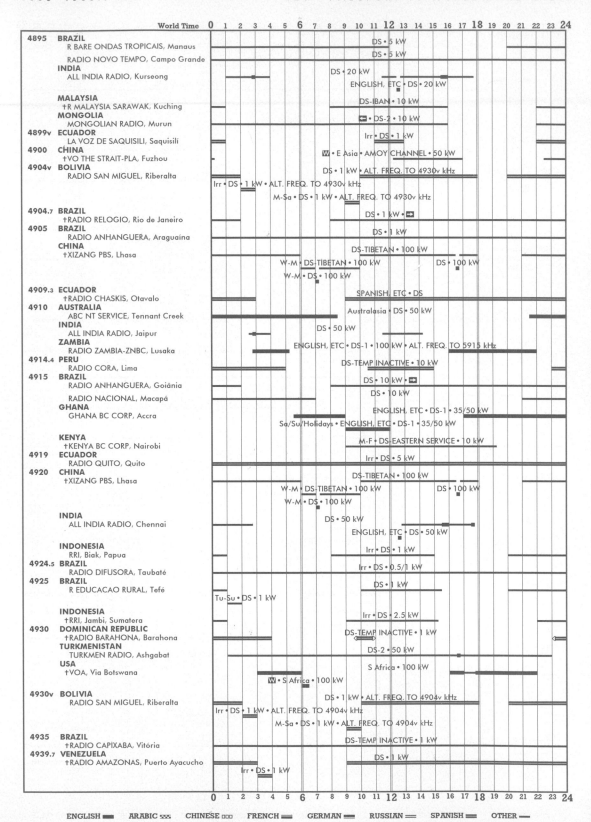

World Time	4895	BRAZIL
		R BARE ONDAS TROPICAIS, Manaus — DS • 5 kW
		RADIO NOVO TEMPO, Campo Grande — DS • 5 kW
	INDIA	ALL INDIA RADIO, Kurseong — DS • 20 kW / ENGLISH, ETC • DS • 20 kW
	MALAYSIA	†R MALAYSIA SARAWAK, Kuching — DS-IBAN • 10 kW
	MONGOLIA	MONGOLIAN RADIO, Murun — DS-2 • 10 kW
4899v	ECUADOR	LA VOZ DE SAQUISILI, Saquisili — Irr • DS • 1 kW
4900	CHINA	†VO THE STRAIT-PLA, Fuzhou — W • E Asia • AMOY CHANNEL • 50 kW
4904v	BOLIVIA	RADIO SAN MIGUEL, Riberalta — DS • 1 kW • ALT. FREQ. TO 4930v kHz / Irr • DS • 1 kW • ALT. FREQ. TO 4930v kHz / M-Sa • DS • 1 kW • ALT. FREQ. TO 4930v kHz
4904.7	BRAZIL	†RADIO RELOGIO, Rio de Janeiro — DS • 1 kW
4905	BRAZIL	RADIO ANHANGUERA, Araguaína — DS • 1 kW
	CHINA	†XIZANG PBS, Lhasa — DS-TIBETAN • 100 kW / W-M • DS-TIBETAN • 100 kW / DS • 100 kW / W-M • DS • 100 kW
4909.3	ECUADOR	†RADIO CHASKIS, Otavalo — SPANISH, ETC • DS
4910	AUSTRALIA	ABC NT SERVICE, Tennant Creek — Australasia • DS • 50 kW
	INDIA	ALL INDIA RADIO, Jaipur — DS • 50 kW
	ZAMBIA	RADIO ZAMBIA-ZNBC, Lusaka — ENGLISH, ETC • DS-1 • 100 kW • ALT. FREQ. TO 5915 kHz
4914.4	PERU	RADIO CORA, Lima — DS-TEMP INACTIVE • 10 kW
4915	BRAZIL	RADIO ANHANGUERA, Goiânia — DS • 10 kW / RADIO NACIONAL, Macapá — DS • 10 kW
	GHANA	GHANA BC CORP, Accra — ENGLISH, ETC • DS-1 • 35/50 kW / Sa/Su/Holidays • ENGLISH, ETC • DS-1 • 35/50 kW
	KENYA	†KENYA BC CORP, Nairobi — M-F • DS-EASTERN SERVICE • 10 kW
4919	ECUADOR	RADIO QUITO, Quito — Irr • DS • 5 kW
4920	CHINA	†XIZANG PBS, Lhasa — DS-TIBETAN • 100 kW / W-M • DS-TIBETAN • 100 kW / DS • 100 kW / W-M • DS • 100 kW
	INDIA	ALL INDIA RADIO, Chennai — DS • 50 kW / ENGLISH, ETC • DS • 50 kW
	INDONESIA	RRI, Biak, Papua — Irr • DS • 1 kW
4924.5	BRAZIL	RADIO DIFUSORA, Taubaté — Irr • DS • 0.5/1 kW
4925	BRAZIL	R EDUCACAO RURAL, Tefé — DS • 1 kW / Tu-Su • DS • 1 kW
	INDONESIA	†RRI, Jambi, Sumatera — Irr • DS • 2.5 kW
4930	DOMINICAN REPUBLIC	†RADIO BARAHONA, Barahona — DS-TEMP INACTIVE • 1 kW
	TURKMENISTAN	TURKMEN RADIO, Ashgabat — DS-2 • 50 kW
	USA	†VOA, Via Botswana — S Africa • 100 kW / W • S Africa • 100 kW
4930v	BOLIVIA	RADIO SAN MIGUEL, Riberalta — DS • 1 kW • ALT. FREQ. TO 4904v kHz / Irr • DS • 1 kW • ALT. FREQ. TO 4904v kHz / M-Sa • DS • 1 kW • ALT. FREQ. TO 4904v kHz
4935	BRAZIL	†RADIO CAPIXABA, Vitória — DS-TEMP INACTIVE • 1 kW
4939.7	VENEZUELA	†RADIO AMAZONAS, Puerto Ayacucho — DS • 1 kW / Irr • DS • 1 kW

ENGLISH ▬ ARABIC ⋙ CHINESE ▭▭▭ FRENCH ▬ GERMAN ▬ RUSSIAN ═ SPANISH ▬ OTHER ▬

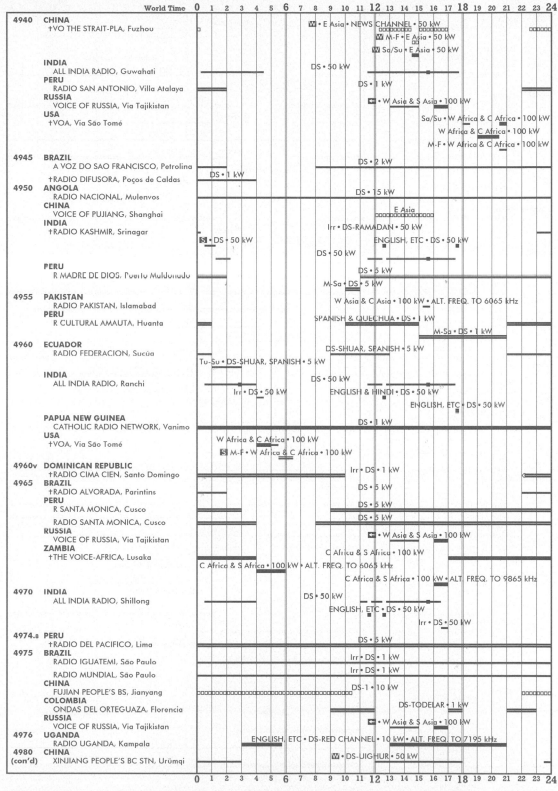

| | | World Time | 0 | 1 | 2 | 3 | 4 | 5 | 6 | 7 | 8 | 9 | 10 | 11 | 12 | 13 | 14 | 15 | 16 | 17 | 18 | 19 | 20 | 21 | 22 | 23 | 24 |

4940 CHINA
†VO THE STRAIT-PLA, Fuzhou — W • E Asia • NEWS CHANNEL • 50 kW
W M-F • E Asia • 50 kW
W Sa/Su • E Asia • 50 kW

INDIA
ALL INDIA RADIO, Guwahati — DS • 50 kW

PERU
RADIO SAN ANTONIO, Villa Atalaya — DS • 1 kW

RUSSIA
VOICE OF RUSSIA, Via Tajikistan — • W Asia & S Asia • 100 kW

USA
†VOA, Via São Tomé — Sa/Su • W Africa & C Africa • 100 kW
W Africa & C Africa • 100 kW
M-F • W Africa & C Africa • 100 kW

4945 BRAZIL
A VOZ DO SAO FRANCISCO, Petrolina — DS • 2 kW
†RADIO DIFUSORA, Poços de Caldas — DS • 1 kW

4950 ANGOLA
RADIO NACIONAL, Mulenvos — DS • 15 kW

CHINA
VOICE OF PUJIANG, Shanghai — E Asia

INDIA
†RADIO KASHMIR, Srinagar — Irr • DS-RAMADAN • 50 kW
ENGLISH, ETC • DS • 50 kW
S • DS • 50 kW
DS • 50 kW

PERU
R MADRE DE DIOS, Puerto Maldonado — DS • 5 kW
M-Sa • DS • 5 kW

4955 PAKISTAN
RADIO PAKISTAN, Islamabad — W Asia & C Asia • 100 kW • ALT. FREQ. TO 6065 kHz

PERU
R CULTURAL AMAUTA, Huanta — SPANISH & QUECHUA • DS • 1 kW
M-Sa • DS • 1 kW

4960 ECUADOR
RADIO FEDERACION, Sucúa — DS-SHUAR, SPANISH • 5 kW
Tu-Su • DS-SHUAR, SPANISH • 5 kW

INDIA
ALL INDIA RADIO, Ranchi — DS • 50 kW
Irr • DS • 50 kW
ENGLISH & HINDI • DS • 50 kW
ENGLISH, ETC • DS • 50 kW

PAPUA NEW GUINEA
CATHOLIC RADIO NETWORK, Vanimo — DS • 1 kW

USA
†VOA, Via São Tomé — W Africa & C Africa • 100 kW
S M-F • W Africa & C Africa • 100 kW

4960v DOMINICAN REPUBLIC
†RADIO CIMA CIEN, Santo Domingo — Irr • DS • 1 kW

4965 BRAZIL
†RADIO ALVORADA, Parintins — DS • 5 kW

PERU
R SANTA MONICA, Cusco — DS • 5 kW
RADIO SANTA MONICA, Cusco — DS • 5 kW

RUSSIA
VOICE OF RUSSIA, Via Tajikistan — • W Asia & S Asia • 100 kW

ZAMBIA
†THE VOICE-AFRICA, Lusaka — C Africa & S Africa • 100 kW
C Africa & S Africa • 100 kW • ALT. FREQ. TO 6065 kHz
C Africa & S Africa • 100 kW • ALT. FREQ. TO 9865 kHz

4970 INDIA
ALL INDIA RADIO, Shillong — DS • 50 kW
ENGLISH, ETC • DS • 50 kW
Irr • DS • 50 kW

4974.8 PERU
†RADIO DEL PACIFICO, Lima — DS • 5 kW

4975 BRAZIL
RADIO IGUATEMI, São Paulo — Irr • DS • 1 kW
RADIO MUNDIAL, São Paulo — Irr • DS • 1 kW

CHINA
FUJIAN PEOPLE'S BS, Jianyang — DS-1 • 10 kW

COLOMBIA
ONDAS DEL ORTEGUAZA, Florencia — DS-TODELAR • 1 kW

RUSSIA
VOICE OF RUSSIA, Via Tajikistan — • W Asia & S Asia • 100 kW

4976 UGANDA
RADIO UGANDA, Kampala — ENGLISH, ETC • DS-RED CHANNEL • 10 kW • ALT. FREQ. TO 7195 kHz

4980 CHINA
(con'd) XINJIANG PEOPLE'S BC STN, Urümqi — W • DS-UIGHUR • 50 kW

| | World Time | 0 | 1 | 2 | 3 | 4 | 5 | 6 | 7 | 8 | 9 | 10 | 11 | 12 | 13 | 14 | 15 | 16 | 17 | 18 | 19 | 20 | 21 | 22 | 23 | 24 |

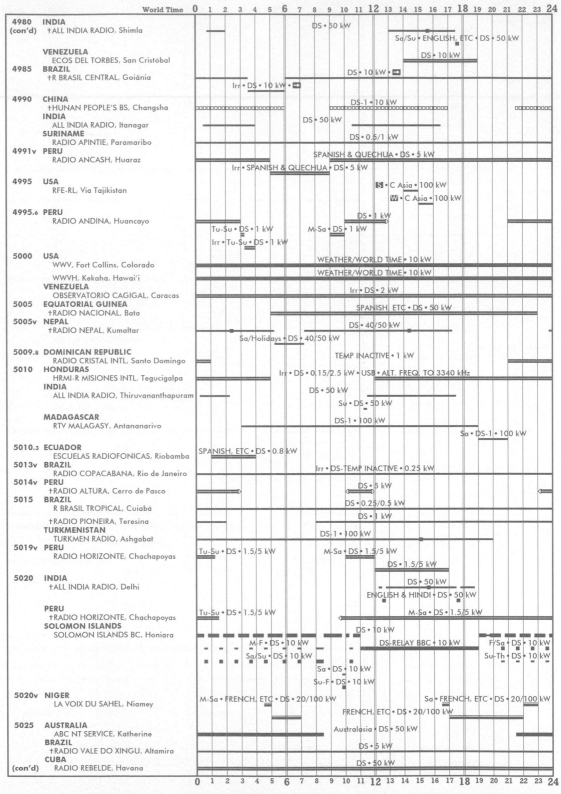

ENGLISH ▬ ARABIC ▨ CHINESE ▢▢▢ FRENCH ▬ GERMAN ▬ RUSSIAN ═ SPANISH ▬ OTHER ▬

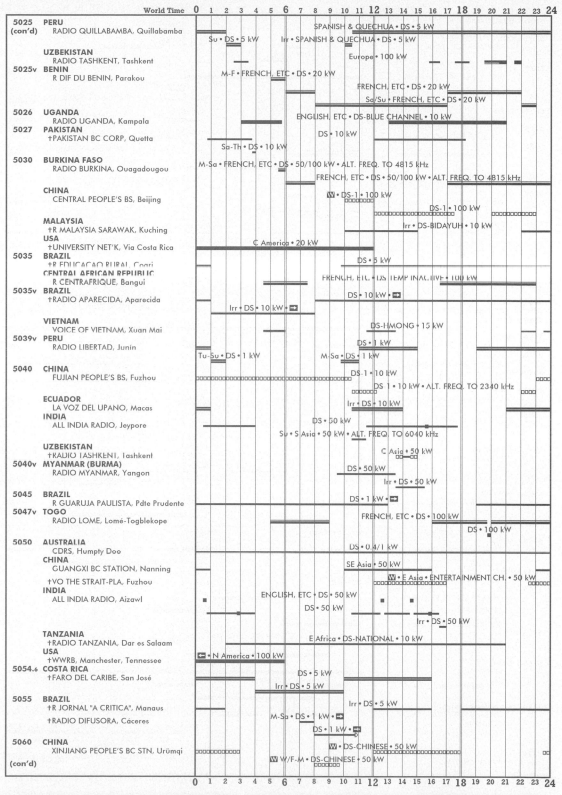

World Time

5025	PERU	
(con'd)	RADIO QUILLABAMBA, Quillabamba	SPANISH & QUECHUA • DS • 5 kW
		Su • DS • 5 kW Irr • SPANISH & QUECHUA • DS • 5 kW
	UZBEKISTAN	
	RADIO TASHKENT, Tashkent	Europe • 100 kW
5025v	BENIN	
	R DIF DU BENIN, Parakou	M-F • FRENCH, ETC • DS • 20 kW
		FRENCH, ETC • DS • 20 kW
		Sa/Su • FRENCH, ETC • DS • 20 kW
5026	UGANDA	
	RADIO UGANDA, Kampala	ENGLISH, ETC • DS-BLUE CHANNEL • 10 kW
5027	PAKISTAN	
	†PAKISTAN BC CORP, Quetta	DS • 10 kW
		Sa-Th • DS • 10 kW
5030	BURKINA FASO	
	RADIO BURKINA, Ouagadougou	M-Sa • FRENCH, ETC • DS • 50/100 kW • ALT. FREQ. TO 4815 kHz
		FRENCH, ETC • DS • 50/100 kW • ALT. FREQ. TO 4815 kHz
	CHINA	
	CENTRAL PEOPLE'S BS, Beijing	W • DS-1 • 100 kW
		DS-1 • 100 kW
	MALAYSIA	
	†R MALAYSIA SARAWAK, Kuching	Irr • DS-BIDAYUH • 10 kW
	USA	
	†UNIVERSITY NET'K, Via Costa Rica	C America • 20 kW
5035	BRAZIL	
	†R EDUCACAO RURAL, Coari	DS • 5 kW
	CENTRAL AFRICAN REPUBLIC	
	R CENTRAFRIQUE, Bangui	FRENCH, ETC • DS TEMP INACTIVE • 100 kW
5035v	BRAZIL	
	†RADIO APARECIDA, Aparecida	DS • 10 kW • ⊡
		Irr • DS • 10 kW • ⊡
	VIETNAM	
	VOICE OF VIETNAM, Xuan Mai	DS-HMONG • 15 kW
5039v	PERU	
	RADIO LIBERTAD, Junín	DS • 1 kW
		Tu-Su • DS • 1 kW M-Sa • DS • 1 kW
5040	CHINA	
	FUJIAN PEOPLE'S BS, Fuzhou	DS-1 • 10 kW
		DS-1 • 10 kW • ALT. FREQ. TO 2340 kHz
	ECUADOR	
	LA VOZ DEL UPANO, Macas	Irr • DS • 10 kW
	INDIA	
	ALL INDIA RADIO, Jeypore	DS • 50 kW
		Su • S Asia • 50 kW • ALT. FREQ. TO 6040 kHz
	UZBEKISTAN	
	†RADIO TASHKENT, Tashkent	C Asia • 50 kW
5040v	MYANMAR (BURMA)	
	RADIO MYANMAR, Yangon	DS • 50 kW
		Irr • DS • 50 kW
5045	BRAZIL	
	R GUARUJA PAULISTA, Pdte Prudente	DS • 1 kW • ⊡
5047v	TOGO	
	RADIO LOME, Lomé-Togblekope	FRENCH, ETC • DS • 100 kW
		DS • 100 kW
5050	AUSTRALIA	
	CDRS, Humpty Doo	DS • 0.4/1 kW
	CHINA	
	GUANGXI BC STATION, Nanning	SE Asia • 50 kW
	†VO THE STRAIT-PLA, Fuzhou	W • E Asia • ENTERTAINMENT CH. • 50 kW
	INDIA	
	ALL INDIA RADIO, Aizawl	ENGLISH, ETC • DS • 50 kW
		DS • 50 kW
		Irr • DS • 50 kW
	TANZANIA	
	†RADIO TANZANIA, Dar es Salaam	E Africa • DS-NATIONAL • 10 kW
	USA	
	†WWRB, Manchester, Tennessee	⊡ • N America • 100 kW
5054.6	COSTA RICA	
	†FARO DEL CARIBE, San José	DS • 5 kW
		Irr • DS • 5 kW
5055	BRAZIL	
	†R JORNAL "A CRITICA", Manaus	Irr • DS • 5 kW
	†RADIO DIFUSORA, Cáceres	M-Sa • DS • 1 kW • ⊡
		DS • 1 kW • ⊡
5060	CHINA	
	XINJIANG PEOPLE'S BC STN, Urümqi	W • DS-CHINESE • 50 kW
(con'd)		W W/F-M • DS-CHINESE • 50 kW

SEASONAL ⑤ OR Ⓦ   1-HR TIMESHIFT MIDYEAR ⊡ OR ⊡   JAMMING / OR /\   EARLIEST HEARD ◁   LATEST HEARD ▷   NEW FOR 2006 †

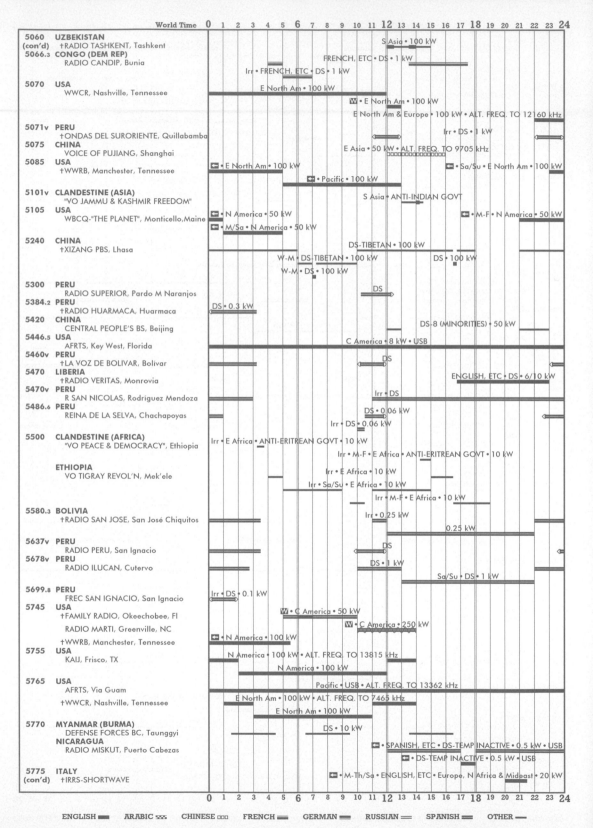

| World Time | 0 | 1 | 2 | 3 | 4 | 5 | 6 | 7 | 8 | 9 | 10 | 11 | 12 | 13 | 14 | 15 | 16 | 17 | 18 | 19 | 20 | 21 | 22 | 23 | 24 |

5060 UZBEKISTAN
(con'd) †RADIO TASHKENT, Tashkent — S Asia • 100 kW

5066.3 CONGO (DEM REP)
RADIO CANDIP, Bunia — FRENCH, ETC • DS • 1 kW; Irr • FRENCH, ETC • DS • 1 kW

5070 USA
WWCR, Nashville, Tennessee — E North Am • 100 kW; ⓦ • E North Am • 100 kW; E North Am & Europe • 100 kW • ALT. FREQ. TO 12160 kHz

5071v PERU
†ONDAS DEL SURORIENTE, Quillabamba — Irr • DS • 1 kW

5075 CHINA
VOICE OF PUJIANG, Shanghai — E Asia • 50 kW • ALT. FREQ. TO 9705 kHz

5085 USA
†WWRB, Manchester, Tennessee — • E North Am • 100 kW; Sa/Su • E North Am • 100 kW; • Pacific • 100 kW

5101v CLANDESTINE (ASIA)
"VO JAMMU & KASHMIR FREEDOM" — S Asia • ANTI-INDIAN GOVT

5105 USA
WBCQ-"THE PLANET", Monticello, Maine — • N America • 50 kW; M-F • N America • 50 kW; • M/Sa • N America • 50 kW

5240 CHINA
†XIZANG PBS, Lhasa — DS-TIBETAN • 100 kW; W-M • DS-TIBETAN • 100 kW; DS • 100 kW; W-M • DS • 100 kW

5300 PERU
RADIO SUPERIOR, Pardo M Naranjos — DS

5384.2 PERU
†RADIO HUARMACA, Huarmaca — DS • 0.3 kW

5420 CHINA
CENTRAL PEOPLE'S BS, Beijing — DS-8 (MINORITIES) • 50 kW

5446.5 USA
AFRTS, Key West, Florida — C America • 8 kW • USB

5460v PERU
†LA VOZ DE BOLIVAR, Bolivar — DS

5470 LIBERIA
†RADIO VERITAS, Monrovia — ENGLISH, ETC • DS • 6/10 kW

5470v PERU
R SAN NICOLAS, Rodriguez Mendoza — Irr • DS

5486.6 PERU
REINA DE LA SELVA, Chachapoyas — DS • 0.06 kW; Irr • DS • 0.06 kW

5500 CLANDESTINE (AFRICA)
"VO PEACE & DEMOCRACY", Ethiopia — Irr • E Africa • ANTI-ERITREAN GOVT • 10 kW; Irr • M-F • E Africa • ANTI-ERITREAN GOVT • 10 kW

ETHIOPIA
VO TIGRAY REVOL'N, Mek'ele — Irr • E Africa • 10 kW; Irr • Sa/Su • E Africa • 10 kW; Irr • M-F • E Africa • 10 kW

5580.3 BOLIVIA
†RADIO SAN JOSE, San José Chiquitos — Irr • 0.25 kW; 0.25 kW

5637v PERU
RADIO PERU, San Ignacio — DS

5678v PERU
RADIO ILUCAN, Cutervo — DS • 1 kW; Sa/Su • DS • 1 kW

5699.8 PERU
FREC SAN IGNACIO, San Ignacio — Irr • DS • 0.1 kW

5745 USA
†FAMILY RADIO, Okeechobee, Fl — ⓦ • C America • 50 kW
RADIO MARTI, Greenville, NC — ⓦ • C America • 250 kW
†WWRB, Manchester, Tennessee — • N America • 100 kW

5755 USA
KAIJ, Frisco, TX — N America • 100 kW • ALT. FREQ. TO 13815 kHz; N America • 100 kW

5765 USA
AFRTS, Via Guam — Pacific • USB • ALT. FREQ. TO 13362 kHz
†WWCR, Nashville, Tennessee — E North Am • 100 kW • ALT. FREQ. TO 7465 kHz; E North Am • 100 kW

5770 MYANMAR (BURMA)
DEFENSE FORCES BC, Taunggyi — DS • 10 kW

NICARAGUA
RADIO MISKUT, Puerto Cabezas — • SPANISH, ETC • DS-TEMP INACTIVE • 0.5 kW • USB; • DS-TEMP INACTIVE • 0.5 kW • USB

5775 ITALY
(con'd) †IRRS-SHORTWAVE — • M-Th/Sa • ENGLISH, ETC • Europe, N Africa & Mideast • 20 kW

| 0 | 1 | 2 | 3 | 4 | 5 | 6 | 7 | 8 | 9 | 10 | 11 | 12 | 13 | 14 | 15 | 16 | 17 | 18 | 19 | 20 | 21 | 22 | 23 | 24 |

ENGLISH ▬ ARABIC ░ CHINESE ▫▫▫ FRENCH ▬▬ GERMAN ▬▬ RUSSIAN ══ SPANISH ▬▬ OTHER ──

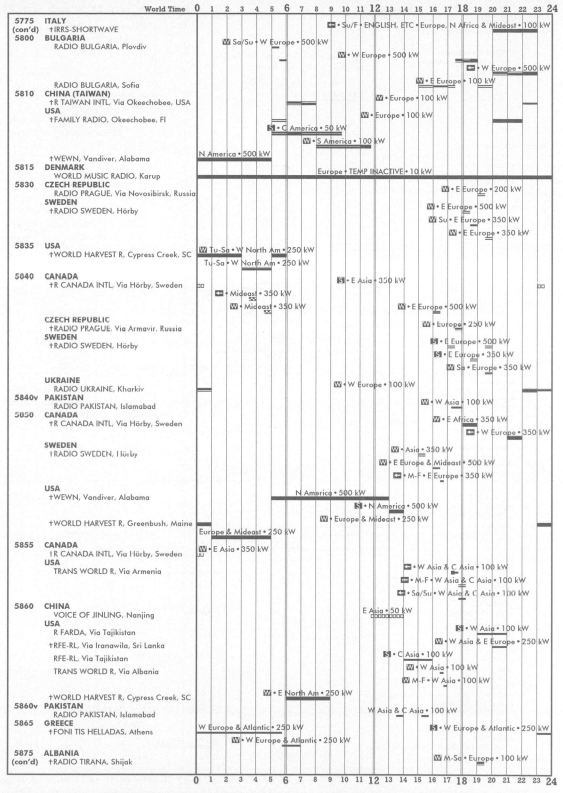

		World Time
5775 (con'd)	ITALY †IRRS-SHORTWAVE	◁•Su/F•ENGLISH, ETC•Europe, N Africa & Mideast•100 kW
5800	BULGARIA RADIO BULGARIA, Plovdiv	W Sa/Su•W Europe•500 kW
		W•W Europe•500 kW
		◁•W Europe•500 kW
	RADIO BULGARIA, Sofia	W•E Europe•100 kW
5810	CHINA (TAIWAN) †R TAIWAN INTL, Via Okeechobee, USA	W•Europe•100 kW
	USA †FAMILY RADIO, Okeechobee, Fl	W•Europe•100 kW
		◁•C America•50 kW
		W•S America•100 kW
	†WEWN, Vandiver, Alabama	N America•500 kW
5815	DENMARK WORLD MUSIC RADIO, Karup	Europe•TEMP INACTIVE•10 kW
5830	CZECH REPUBLIC RADIO PRAGUE, Via Novosibirsk, Russia	W•E Europe•200 kW
	SWEDEN †RADIO SWEDEN, Hörby	W•E Europe•500 kW
		W Su•E Europe•350 kW
		W•E Europe•350 kW
5835	USA †WORLD HARVEST R, Cypress Creek, SC	W Tu-Sa•W North Am•250 kW
		Tu-Sa•W North Am•250 kW
5040	CANADA †R CANADA INTL, Via Hörby, Sweden	S•E Asia•350 kW
		◁•Mideast•350 kW
		W•Mideast•350 kW
	CZECH REPUBLIC †RADIO PRAGUE, Via Armavir, Russia	W•E Europe•500 kW
	SWEDEN †RADIO SWEDEN, Hörby	W•Europe•250 kW
		S•E Europe•500 kW
		S•E Europe•350 kW
		W Sa•Europe•350 kW
	UKRAINE RADIO UKRAINE, Kharkiv	W•W Europe•100 kW
5840v	PAKISTAN RADIO PAKISTAN, Islamabad	W•W Asia•100 kW
5050	CANADA †R CANADA INTL, Via Hörby, Sweden	W•E Africa•350 kW
		◁•W Europe•350 kW
	SWEDEN †RADIO SWEDEN, Hörby	W•Asia•350 kW
		W•E Europe & Mideast•500 kW
		◁•M-F•E Europe•350 kW
	USA †WEWN, Vandiver, Alabama	N America•500 kW
		S•N America•500 kW
	†WORLD HARVEST R, Greenbush, Maine	W•Europe & Mideast•250 kW
		Europe & Mideast•250 kW
5855	CANADA †R CANADA INTL, Via Hörby, Sweden	W•E Asia•350 kW
	USA TRANS WORLD R, Via Armenia	◁•W Asia & C Asia•100 kW
		◁•M-F•W Asia & C Asia•100 kW
		◁•Sa/Su•W Asia & C Asia•100 kW
5860	CHINA VOICE OF JINLING, Nanjing	E Asia•50 kW
	USA R FARDA, Via Tajikistan	S•W Asia•100 kW
	†RFE-RL, Via Iranawila, Sri Lanka	W•W Asia & E Europe•250 kW
	RFE-RL, Via Tajikistan	S•C Asia•100 kW
	TRANS WORLD R, Via Albania	W•W Asia•100 kW
		W M-F•W Asia•100 kW
	†WORLD HARVEST R, Cypress Creek, SC	W•E North Am•250 kW
5860v	PAKISTAN RADIO PAKISTAN, Islamabad	W Asia & C Asia•100 kW
5865	GREECE †FONI TIS HELLADAS, Athens	W Europe & Atlantic•250 kW
		S•W Europe & Atlantic•250 kW
		W•W Europe & Atlantic•250 kW
5875 (con'd)	ALBANIA †RADIO TIRANA, Shijak	W M-Sa•Europe•100 kW

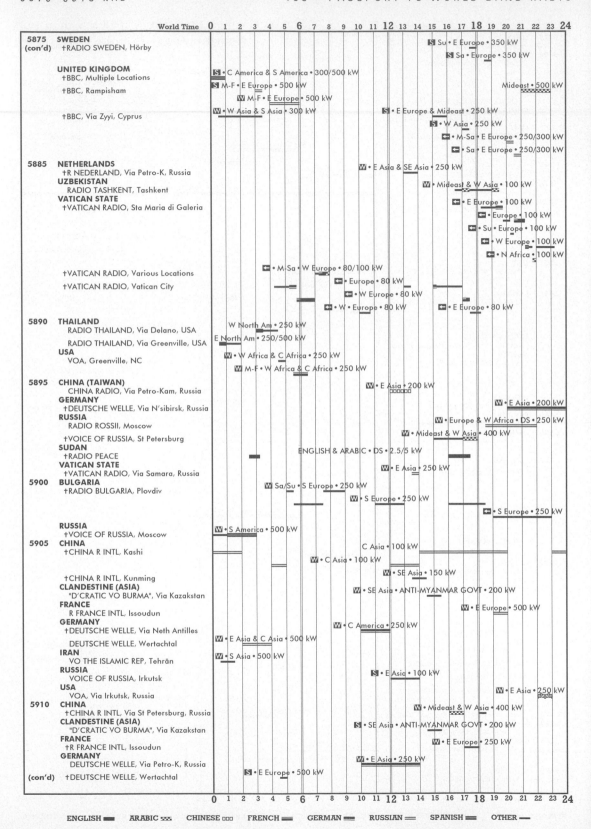

World Time 0 1 2 3 4 5 6 7 8 9 10 11 12 13 14 15 16 17 18 19 20 21 22 23 24

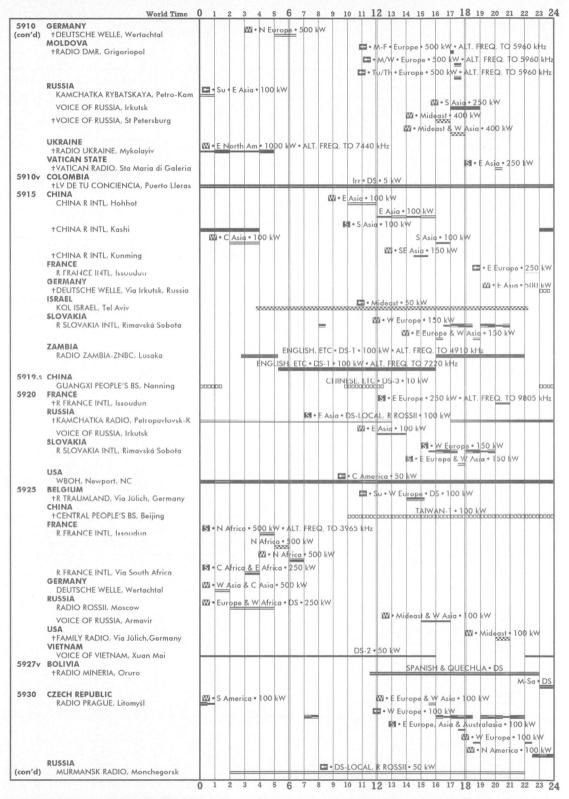

5910 **GERMANY**	
(con'd) †DEUTSCHE WELLE, Wertachtal	W • N Europe • 500 kW
MOLDOVA	
†RADIO DMR, Grigoriopol	⮂ • M-F • Europe • 500 kW • ALT. FREQ. TO 5960 kHz
	⮂ • M/W • Europe • 500 kW • ALT. FREQ. TO 5960 kHz
	⮂ • Tu/Th • Europe • 500 kW • ALT. FREQ. TO 5960 kHz
RUSSIA	
KAMCHATKA RYBATSKAYA, Petro-Kam	⮂ • Su • E Asia • 100 kW
VOICE OF RUSSIA, Irkutsk	W • S Asia • 250 kW
†VOICE OF RUSSIA, St Petersburg	W • Mideast • 400 kW
	W • Mideast & W Asia • 400 kW
UKRAINE	
†RADIO UKRAINE, Mykolayiv	W • E North Am • 1000 kW • ALT. FREQ. TO 7440 kHz
VATICAN STATE	
†VATICAN RADIO, Sta Maria di Galeria	S • E Asia • 250 kW
5910v COLOMBIA	
†LV DE TU CONCIENCIA, Puerto Lleras	Irr • DS • 5 kW
5915 CHINA	
CHINA R INTL, Hohhot	W • E Asia • 100 kW
	E Asia • 100 kW
†CHINA R INTL, Kashi	S • S Asia • 100 kW
	W • C Asia • 100 kW S Asia • 100 kW
†CHINA R INTL, Kunming	W • SE Asia • 150 kW
FRANCE	
R FRANCE INTL, Issoudun	⮂ • E Europe • 250 kW
GERMANY	
†DEUTSCHE WELLE, Via Irkutsk, Russia	W • E Asia • 500 kW
ISRAEL	
KOL ISRAEL, Tel Aviv	⮂ • Mideast • 50 kW
SLOVAKIA	
R SLOVAKIA INTL, Rimavská Sobota	W • W Europe • 150 kW
	W • E Europe & W Asia • 150 kW
ZAMBIA	
RADIO ZAMBIA-ZNBC, Lusaka	ENGLISH, ETC • DS-1 • 100 kW • ALT. FREQ. TO 4910 kHz
	ENGLISH, ETC • DS-1 • 100 kW • ALT. FREQ. TO 7220 kHz
5919.5 CHINA	
GUANGXI PEOPLE'S BS, Nanning	CHINESE, ETC • DS-3 • 10 kW
5920 FRANCE	
†R FRANCE INTL, Issoudun	S • E Europe • 250 kW • ALT. FREQ. TO 9805 kHz
RUSSIA	
†KAMCHATKA RADIO, Petropavlovsk-K	S • E Asia • DS-LOCAL, R ROSSII • 100 kW
VOICE OF RUSSIA, Irkutsk	W • E Asia • 100 kW
SLOVAKIA	
R SLOVAKIA INTL, Rimavská Sobota	S • W Europe • 150 kW
	S • E Europe & W Asia • 150 kW
USA	
WBOH, Newport, NC	⮂ • C America • 50 kW
5925 BELGIUM	
†R TRAUMLAND, Via Jülich, Germany	⮂ • Su • W Europe • DS • 100 kW
CHINA	
†CENTRAL PEOPLE'S BS, Beijing	TAIWAN-1 • 100 kW
FRANCE	
R FRANCE INTL, Issoudun	S • N Africa • 500 kW • ALT. FREQ. TO 3965 kHz
	N Africa • 500 kW
	W • N Africa • 500 kW
R FRANCE INTL, Via South Africa	S • C Africa & E Africa • 250 kW
GERMANY	
DEUTSCHE WELLE, Wertachtal	W • W Asia & C Asia • 500 kW
RUSSIA	
RADIO ROSSII, Moscow	W • Europe & W Africa • DS • 250 kW
VOICE OF RUSSIA, Armavir	W • Mideast & W Asia • 100 kW
USA	
†FAMILY RADIO, Via Jülich, Germany	W • Mideast • 100 kW
VIETNAM	
VOICE OF VIETNAM, Xuan Mai	DS-2 • 50 kW
5927v BOLIVIA	
†RADIO MINERIA, Oruro	SPANISH & QUECHUA • DS
	M-Sa • DS
5930 CZECH REPUBLIC	
RADIO PRAGUE, Litomyšl	W • S America • 100 kW
	W • E Europe & W Asia • 100 kW
	⮂ • W Europe • 100 kW
	S • E Europe, Asia & Australasia • 100 kW
	W • W Europe • 100 kW
	W • N America • 100 kW
RUSSIA	
(con'd) MURMANSK RADIO, Monchegorsk	⮂ • DS-LOCAL, R ROSSII • 50 kW

0 1 2 3 4 5 6 7 8 9 10 11 12 13 14 15 16 17 18 19 20 21 22 23 24

SEASONAL S OR W 1-HR TIMESHIFT MIDYEAR ⮂ OR ⮂ JAMMING / OR /\ EARLIEST HEARD ◁ LATEST HEARD ▷ NEW FOR 2006 †

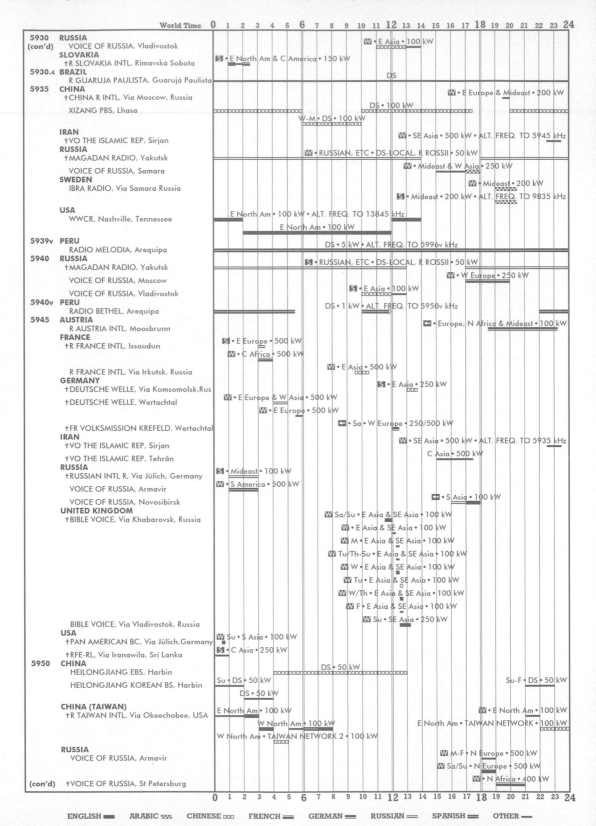

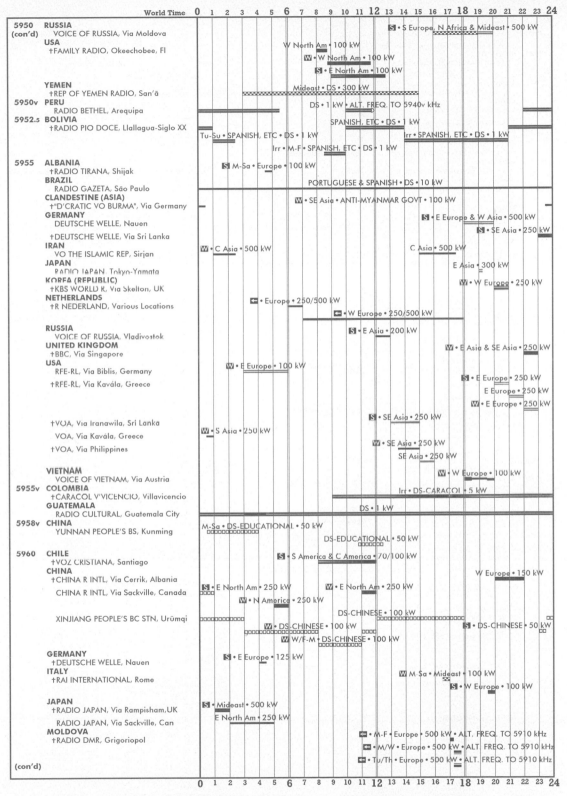

	World Time	0 1 2 3 4 5 6 7 8 9 10 11 12 13 14 15 16 17 18 19 20 21 22 23 24

5950
(con'd) RUSSIA
　VOICE OF RUSSIA, Via Moldova — S · S Europe, N Africa & Mideast · 500 kW
　USA
　†FAMILY RADIO, Okeechobee, Fl — W North Am · 100 kW / W · W North Am · 100 kW / S · E North Am · 100 kW
　YEMEN
　†REP OF YEMEN RADIO, San'ā — Mideast · DS · 300 kW
5950v PERU
　RADIO BETHEL, Arequipa — DS · 1 kW · ALT. FREQ. TO 5940v kHz
5952.5 BOLIVIA
　†RADIO PIO DOCE, Llallagua-Siglo XX — SPANISH, ETC · DS · 1 kW / Tu-Su · SPANISH, ETC · DS · 1 kW / Irr · SPANISH, ETC · DS · 1 kW / Irr · M-F · SPANISH, ETC · DS · 1 kW
5955 ALBANIA
　†RADIO TIRANA, Shijak — S · M-Sa · Europe · 100 kW
　BRAZIL
　RADIO GAZETA, São Paulo — PORTUGUESE & SPANISH · DS · 10 kW
　CLANDESTINE (ASIA)
　†"D'CRATIC VO BURMA", Via Germany — W · SE Asia · ANTI-MYANMAR GOVT · 100 kW
　GERMANY
　DEUTSCHE WELLE, Nauen — S · E Europe & W Asia · 500 kW / S · SE Asia · 250 kW
　IRAN
　VO THE ISLAMIC REP, Sirjan — W · C Asia · 500 kW / C Asia · 500 kW
　JAPAN
　RADIO JAPAN, Tokyo-Yamata — E Asia · 300 kW
　KOREA (REPUBLIC)
　†KBS WORLD R, Via Skelton, UK — W · W Europe · 250 kW
　NETHERLANDS
　†R NEDERLAND, Various Locations — ⬌ · Europe · 250/500 kW / ⬌ · W Europe · 250/500 kW
　RUSSIA
　VOICE OF RUSSIA, Vladivostok — S · E Asia · 200 kW
　UNITED KINGDOM
　†BBC, Via Singapore — W · E Asia & SE Asia · 250 kW
　USA
　RFE-RL, Via Biblis, Germany — W · E Europe · 100 kW
　†RFE-RL, Via Kavála, Greece — S · E Europe · 250 kW / E Europe · 250 kW / W · E Europe · 250 kW
　†VOA, Via Iranawila, Sri Lanka — S · SE Asia · 250 kW
　VOA, Via Kavála, Greece — W · S Asia · 250 kW
　†VOA, Via Philippines — W · SE Asia · 250 kW / SE Asia · 250 kW
　VIETNAM
　VOICE OF VIETNAM, Via Austria — W · W Europe · 100 kW
5955v COLOMBIA
　†CARACOL V'VICENCIO, Villavicencio — Irr · DS-CARACOL · 5 kW
　GUATEMALA
　RADIO CULTURAL, Guatemala City — DS · 1 kW
5958v CHINA
　YUNNAN PEOPLE'S BS, Kunming — M-Sa · DS-EDUCATIONAL · 50 kW / DS-EDUCATIONAL · 50 kW
5960 CHILE
　†VOZ CRISTIANA, Santiago — S · S America & C America · 70/100 kW
　CHINA
　†CHINA R INTL, Via Cerrik, Albania — W Europe · 150 kW
　CHINA R INTL, Via Sackville, Canada — S · E North Am · 250 kW / W · E North Am · 250 kW / W · N America · 250 kW
　XINJIANG PEOPLE'S BC STN, Urümqi — DS-CHINESE · 100 kW / W · DS-CHINESE · 100 kW / S · DS-CHINESE · 50 kW / W/F-M · DS-CHINESE · 100 kW
　GERMANY
　†DEUTSCHE WELLE, Nauen — S · E Europe · 125 kW
　ITALY
　†RAI INTERNATIONAL, Rome — W · M-Sa · Mideast · 100 kW / S · W Europe · 100 kW
　JAPAN
　†RADIO JAPAN, Via Rampisham, UK — S · Mideast · 500 kW
　RADIO JAPAN, Via Sackville, Can — E North Am · 250 kW
　MOLDOVA
　†RADIO DMR, Grigoriopol — ⬌ · M-F · Europe · 500 kW · ALT. FREQ. TO 5910 kHz / ⬌ · M/W · Europe · 500 kW · ALT. FREQ. TO 5910 kHz / ⬌ · Tu/Th · Europe · 500 kW · ALT. FREQ. TO 5910 kHz

(con'd)

	World Time	0 1 2 3 4 5 6 7 8 9 10 11 12 13 14 15 16 17 18 19 20 21 22 23 24

SEASONAL S OR W   1-HR TIMESHIFT MIDYEAR ⬅ OR ➡   JAMMING / OR ∧   EARLIEST HEARD ◁   LATEST HEARD ▷   NEW FOR 2006 †

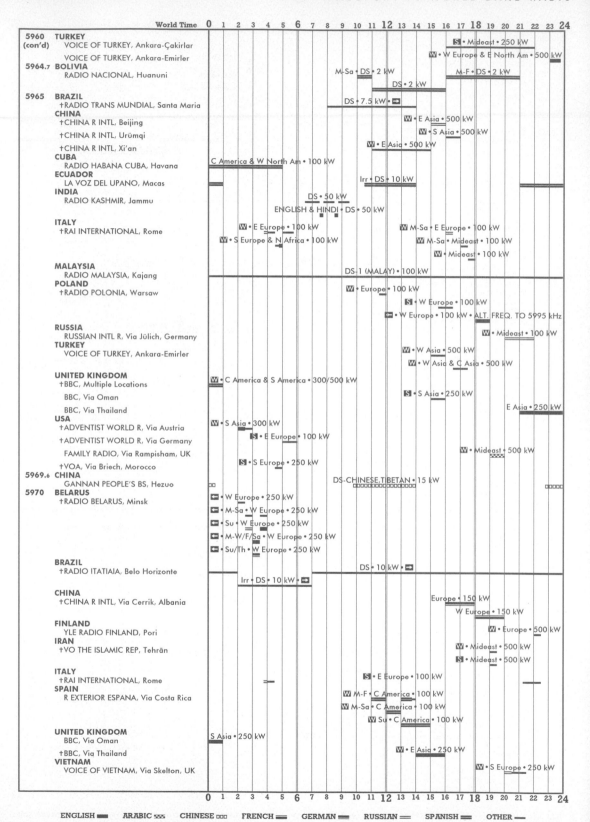

World Time scale: 0 1 2 3 4 5 6 7 8 9 10 11 12 13 14 15 16 17 18 19 20 21 22 23 24

Freq	Country / Station	Schedule
5960 (con'd)	**TURKEY** VOICE OF TURKEY, Ankara-Çakirlar	S • Mideast • 250 kW
	VOICE OF TURKEY, Ankara-Emirler	W • W Europe & E North Am • 500 kW
5964.7	**BOLIVIA** RADIO NACIONAL, Huanuni	M-Sa • DS • 2 kW / M-F • DS • 2 kW / DS • 2 kW
5965	**BRAZIL** †RADIO TRANS MUNDIAL, Santa Maria	DS • 7.5 kW • ➡
	CHINA †CHINA R INTL, Beijing	W • E Asia • 500 kW
	†CHINA R INTL, Urümqi	W • S Asia • 500 kW
	†CHINA R INTL, Xi'an	W • E Asia • 500 kW
	CUBA RADIO HABANA CUBA, Havana	C America & W North Am • 100 kW
	ECUADOR LA VOZ DEL UPANO, Macas	Irr • DS • 10 kW
	INDIA RADIO KASHMIR, Jammu	DS • 50 kW / ENGLISH & HINDI • DS • 50 kW
	ITALY †RAI INTERNATIONAL, Rome	W • E Europe • 100 kW / W M-Sa • E Europe • 100 kW
		W • S Europe & N Africa • 100 kW / W M-Sa • Mideast • 100 kW
		W • Mideast • 100 kW
	MALAYSIA RADIO MALAYSIA, Kajang	DS-1 (MALAY) • 100 kW
	POLAND †RADIO POLONIA, Warsaw	W • Europe • 100 kW
		S • W Europe • 100 kW
		➡ • W Europe • 100 kW • ALT. FREQ. TO 5995 kHz
	RUSSIA RUSSIAN INTL R, Via Jülich, Germany	W • Mideast • 100 kW
	TURKEY VOICE OF TURKEY, Ankara-Emirler	W • W Asia • 500 kW
		W • W Asia & C Asia • 500 kW
	UNITED KINGDOM †BBC, Multiple Locations	W • C America & S America • 300/500 kW
	BBC, Via Oman	S • S Asia • 250 kW
	BBC, Via Thailand	E Asia • 250 kW
	USA †ADVENTIST WORLD R, Via Austria	W • S Asia • 300 kW
	†ADVENTIST WORLD R, Via Germany	S • E Europe • 100 kW
	FAMILY RADIO, Via Rampisham, UK	W • Mideast • 500 kW
	†VOA, Via Briech, Morocco	S • S Europe • 250 kW
5969.6	**CHINA** GANNAN PEOPLE'S BS, Hezuo	DS-CHINESE, TIBETAN • 15 kW
5970	**BELARUS** †RADIO BELARUS, Minsk	➡ • W Europe • 250 kW
		➡ • M-Sa • W Europe • 250 kW
		➡ • Su • W Europe • 250 kW
		➡ • M-W/F/Sa • W Europe • 250 kW
		➡ • Su/Th • W Europe • 250 kW
	BRAZIL †RADIO ITATIAIA, Belo Horizonte	DS • 10 kW • ➡
		Irr • DS • 10 kW • ➡
	CHINA †CHINA R INTL, Via Cerrik, Albania	Europe • 150 kW
		W Europe • 150 kW
	FINLAND YLE RADIO FINLAND, Pori	W • Europe • 500 kW
	IRAN †VO THE ISLAMIC REP, Tehrān	W • Mideast • 500 kW
		S • Mideast • 500 kW
	ITALY †RAI INTERNATIONAL, Rome	S • E Europe • 100 kW
	SPAIN R EXTERIOR ESPANA, Via Costa Rica	W M-F • C America • 100 kW
		W M-Sa • C America • 100 kW
		W Su • C America • 100 kW
	UNITED KINGDOM BBC, Via Oman	S Asia • 250 kW
	†BBC, Via Thailand	W • E Asia • 250 kW
	VIETNAM VOICE OF VIETNAM, Via Skelton, UK	W • S Europe • 250 kW

ENGLISH ▬ ARABIC ⧓⧓⧓ CHINESE ▯▯▯ FRENCH ▭▭ GERMAN ▬▬ RUSSIAN ══ SPANISH ▭▭ OTHER ▬

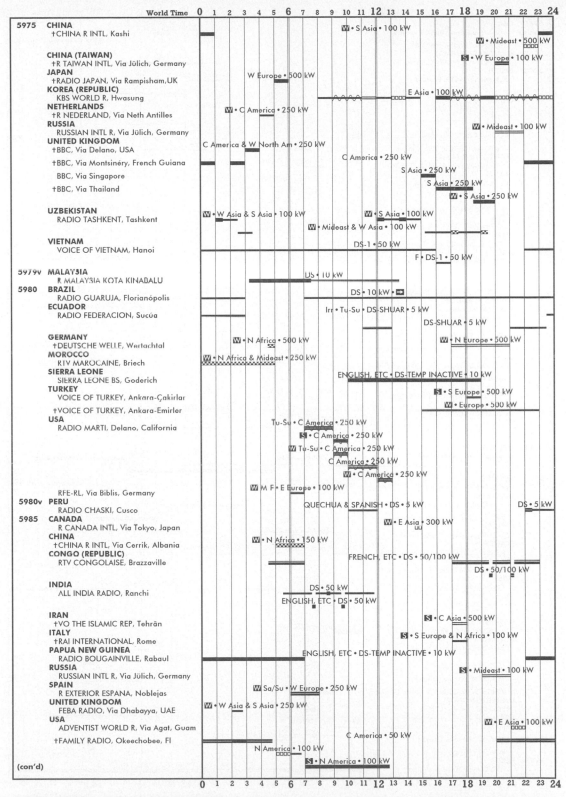

World Time | 0 1 2 3 4 5 6 7 8 9 10 11 12 13 14 15 16 17 18 19 20 21 22 23 24

5975 CHINA
†CHINA R INTL, Kashi
W • S Asia • 100 kW
W • Mideast • 500 kW

CHINA (TAIWAN)
†R TAIWAN INTL, Via Jülich, Germany
S • W Europe • 100 kW

JAPAN
†RADIO JAPAN, Via Rampisham, UK
W Europe • 500 kW

KOREA (REPUBLIC)
KBS WORLD R, Hwasung
E Asia • 100 kW

NETHERLANDS
†R NEDERLAND, Via Neth Antilles
W • C America • 250 kW

RUSSIA
RUSSIAN INTL R, Via Jülich, Germany
W • Mideast • 100 kW

UNITED KINGDOM
†BBC, Via Delano, USA
C America & W North Am • 250 kW

†BBC, Via Montsinéry, French Guiana
C America • 250 kW

BBC, Via Singapore
S Asia • 250 kW

†BBC, Via Thailand
S Asia • 250 kW
W • S Asia • 250 kW

UZBEKISTAN
RADIO TASHKENT, Tashkent
W • W Asia & S Asia • 100 kW
W • S Asia • 100 kW
W • Mideast & W Asia • 100 kW

VIETNAM
VOICE OF VIETNAM, Hanoi
DS-1 • 50 kW
F • DS-1 • 50 kW

5979v MALAYSIA
R MALAYSIA KOTA KINABALU
DS • 10 kW

5980 BRAZIL
RADIO GUARUJA, Florianópolis
DS • 10 kW • ⇨

ECUADOR
RADIO FEDERACION, Sucúa
Irr • Tu-Su • DS-SHUAR • 5 kW
DS-SHUAR • 5 kW

GERMANY
†DEUTSCHE WELLE, Wertachtal
W • N Africa • 500 kW
W • N Europe • 500 kW

MOROCCO
RTV MAROCAINE, Briech
W • N Africa & Mideast • 250 kW

SIERRA LEONE
SIERRA LEONE BS, Goderich
ENGLISH, ETC • DS-TEMP INACTIVE • 10 kW

TURKEY
VOICE OF TURKEY, Ankara-Çakirlar
S • S Europe • 500 kW

†VOICE OF TURKEY, Ankara-Emirler
W • Europe • 500 kW

USA
RADIO MARTI, Delano, California
Tu-Su • C America • 250 kW
S • C America • 250 kW
W • Tu-Su • C America • 250 kW
C America • 250 kW
W • C America • 250 kW

RFE-RL, Via Biblis, Germany
W • M F • E Europe • 100 kW

5980v PERU
RADIO CHASKI, Cusco
QUECHUA & SPANISH • DS • 5 kW
DS • 5 kW

5985 CANADA
R CANADA INTL, Via Tokyo, Japan
W • E Asia • 300 kW

CHINA
†CHINA R INTL, Via Cerrik, Albania
W • N Africa • 150 kW

CONGO (REPUBLIC)
RTV CONGOLAISE, Brazzaville
FRENCH, ETC • DS • 50/100 kW
DS • 50/100 kW

INDIA
ALL INDIA RADIO, Ranchi
DS • 50 kW
ENGLISH, ETC • DS • 50 kW

IRAN
†VO THE ISLAMIC REP, Tehrān
S • C Asia • 500 kW

ITALY
†RAI INTERNATIONAL, Rome
S • S Europe & N Africa • 100 kW

PAPUA NEW GUINEA
RADIO BOUGAINVILLE, Rabaul
ENGLISH, ETC • DS-TEMP INACTIVE • 10 kW

RUSSIA
RUSSIAN INTL R, Via Jülich, Germany
S • Mideast • 100 kW

SPAIN
R EXTERIOR ESPANA, Noblejas
W • Sa/Su • W Europe • 250 kW

UNITED KINGDOM
FEBA RADIO, Via Dhabayya, UAE
W • W Asia & S Asia • 250 kW

USA
ADVENTIST WORLD R, Via Agat, Guam
W • E Asia • 100 kW

†FAMILY RADIO, Okeechobee, Fl
C America • 50 kW
N America • 100 kW
S • N America • 100 kW

(con'd)

World Time | 0 1 2 3 4 5 6 7 8 9 10 11 12 13 14 15 16 17 18 19 20 21 22 23 24

SEASONAL S OR W   1-HR TIMESHIFT MIDYEAR ⇦ OR ⇨   JAMMING / OR ∧   EARLIEST HEARD ◁   LATEST HEARD ▷   NEW FOR 2006 †

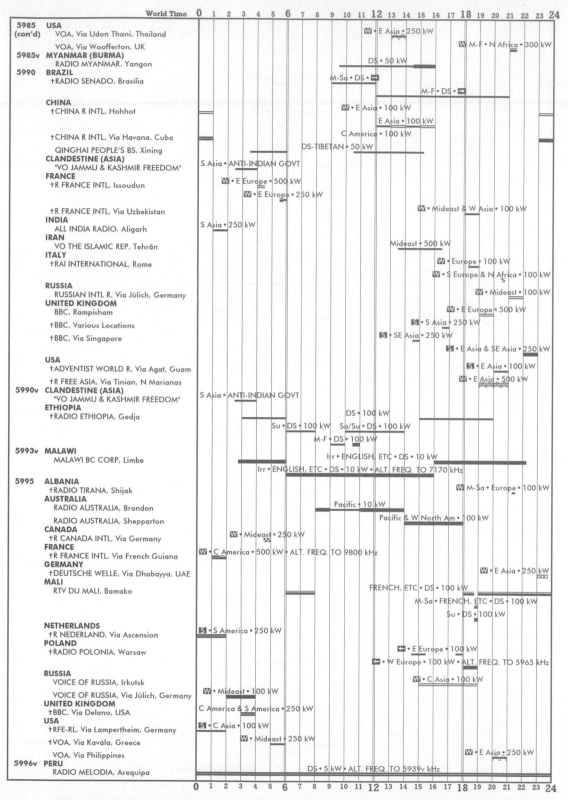

World Time   0 1 2 3 4 5 6 7 8 9 10 11 12 13 14 15 16 17 18 19 20 21 22 23 24

5985
(con'd)
    USA
        VOA, Via Udon Thani, Thailand   W • E Asia • 250 kW
        VOA, Via Woofferton, UK   W • M-F • N Africa • 300 kW
5985v MYANMAR (BURMA)
        RADIO MYANMAR, Yangon   DS • 50 kW
5990 BRAZIL
        †RADIO SENADO, Brasilia   M-Sa • DS • ▭
                                                                    M-F • DS • ▭
    CHINA
        †CHINA R INTL, Hohhot   W • E Asia • 100 kW
                                                             E Asia • 100 kW
        †CHINA R INTL, Via Havana, Cuba   C America • 100 kW
        QINGHAI PEOPLE'S BS, Xining   DS-TIBETAN • 50 kW
    CLANDESTINE (ASIA)
        "VO JAMMU & KASHMIR FREEDOM"   S Asia • ANTI-INDIAN GOVT
    FRANCE
        †R FRANCE INTL, Issoudun   W • E Europe • 500 kW
                                          W • E Europe • 250 kW
        †R FRANCE INTL, Via Uzbekistan   W • Mideast & W Asia • 100 kW
    INDIA
        ALL INDIA RADIO, Aligarh   S Asia • 250 kW
    IRAN
        VO THE ISLAMIC REP, Tehrān   Mideast • 500 kW
    ITALY
        †RAI INTERNATIONAL, Rome   W • Europe • 100 kW
                                                                     W • S Europe & N Africa • 100 kW
    RUSSIA
        RUSSIAN INTL R, Via Jülich, Germany   W • Mideast • 100 kW
    UNITED KINGDOM
        BBC, Rampisham   W • E Europe • 500 kW
        †BBC, Various Locations   S • S Asia • 250 kW
        †BBC, Via Singapore   S • SE Asia • 250 kW
                                                             S • E Asia & SE Asia • 250 kW
    USA
        †ADVENTIST WORLD R, Via Agat, Guam   S • E Asia • 100 kW
        †R FREE ASIA, Via Tinian, N Marianas   W • E Asia • 500 kW
5990v CLANDESTINE (ASIA)
        "VO JAMMU & KASHMIR FREEDOM"   S Asia • ANTI-INDIAN GOVT
    ETHIOPIA
        †RADIO ETHIOPIA, Gedja   DS • 100 kW
                                                 Su • DS • 100 kW   Sa/Su • DS • 100 kW
                                                    M-F • DS • 100 kW
5993v MALAWI
        MALAWI BC CORP, Limbe   Irr • ENGLISH, ETC • DS • 10 kW
                                          Irr • ENGLISH, ETC • DS • 10 kW • ALT. FREQ. TO 7170 kHz
5995 ALBANIA
        †RADIO TIRANA, Shijak   W • M-Sa • Europe • 100 kW
    AUSTRALIA
        RADIO AUSTRALIA, Brandon   Pacific • 10 kW
        RADIO AUSTRALIA, Shepparton   Pacific & W North Am • 100 kW
    CANADA
        †R CANADA INTL, Via Germany   W • Mideast • 250 kW
    FRANCE
        †R FRANCE INTL, Via French Guiana W • C America • 500 kW • ALT. FREQ. TO 9800 kHz
    GERMANY
        †DEUTSCHE WELLE, Via Dhabayya, UAE   W • E Asia • 250 kW
    MALI
        RTV DU MALI, Bamako   FRENCH, ETC • DS • 100 kW
                                                                     M-Sa • FRENCH, ETC • DS • 100 kW
                                                                     Su • DS • 100 kW
    NETHERLANDS
        †R NEDERLAND, Via Ascension   S • S America • 250 kW
    POLAND
        †RADIO POLONIA, Warsaw   ▭ • E Europe • 100 kW
                                                             ▭ • W Europe • 100 kW • ALT. FREQ. TO 5965 kHz
    RUSSIA
        VOICE OF RUSSIA, Irkutsk   W • C Asia • 100 kW
        VOICE OF RUSSIA, Via Jülich, Germany W • Mideast • 100 kW
    UNITED KINGDOM
        †BBC, Via Delano, USA   C America & S America • 250 kW
    USA
        †RFE-RL, Via Lampertheim, Germany S • C Asia • 100 kW
        †VOA, Via Kavála, Greece   W • Mideast • 250 kW
        VOA, Via Philippines   W • E Asia • 250 kW
5996v PERU
        RADIO MELODIA, Arequipa   DS • 5 kW • ALT. FREQ. TO 5939v kHz

0 1 2 3 4 5 6 7 8 9 10 11 12 13 14 15 16 17 18 19 20 21 22 23 24

ENGLISH ▬▬   ARABIC ▨▨   CHINESE ▫▫▫   FRENCH ══   GERMAN ▬▬   RUSSIAN ══   SPANISH ▬▬   OTHER ──

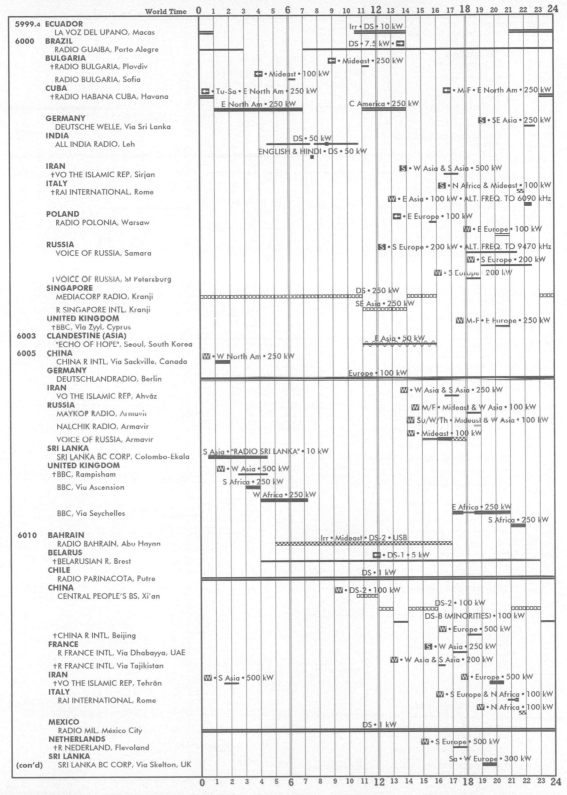

World Time 0 1 2 3 4 5 6 7 8 9 10 11 12 13 14 15 16 17 18 19 20 21 22 23 24

Freq	Country / Station	Details
5999.4	ECUADOR LA VOZ DEL UPANO, Macas	Irr • DS • 10 kW
6000	BRAZIL RADIO GUAIBA, Porto Alegre	DS • 7.5 kW
	BULGARIA †RADIO BULGARIA, Plovdiv	Mideast • 250 kW
	RADIO BULGARIA, Sofia	Mideast • 100 kW
	CUBA †RADIO HABANA CUBA, Havana	Tu-Sa • E North Am • 250 kW / M-F • E North Am • 250 kW E North Am • 250 kW / C America • 250 kW
	GERMANY DEUTSCHE WELLE, Via Sri Lanka	S • SE Asia • 250 kW
	INDIA ALL INDIA RADIO, Leh	DS • 50 kW ENGLISH & HINDI • DS • 50 kW
	IRAN †VO THE ISLAMIC REP, Sirjan	S • W Asia & S Asia • 500 kW
	ITALY †RAI INTERNATIONAL, Rome	S • N Africa & Mideast • 100 kW W • E Asia • 100 kW • ALT. FREQ. TO 6090 kHz
	POLAND RADIO POLONIA, Warsaw	E Europe • 100 kW W • E Europe • 100 kW
	RUSSIA VOICE OF RUSSIA, Samara	S • S Europe • 200 kW • ALT. FREQ. TO 9470 kHz W • S Europe • 200 kW
	†VOICE OF RUSSIA, St Petersburg	W • S Europe • 200 kW
	SINGAPORE MEDIACORP RADIO, Kranji	DS • 250 kW
	R SINGAPORE INTL, Kranji	SE Asia • 250 kW
	UNITED KINGDOM †BBC, Via Zyyl, Cyprus	W • M-F • E Europe • 250 kW
6003	CLANDESTINE (ASIA) "ECHO OF HOPE", Seoul, South Korea	E Asia • 50 kW
6005	CHINA CHINA R INTL, Via Sackville, Canada	W • W North Am • 250 kW
	GERMANY DEUTSCHLANDRADIO, Berlin	Europe • 100 kW
	IRAN VO THE ISLAMIC REP, Ahvāz	W • W Asia & S Asia • 250 kW
	RUSSIA MAYKOP RADIO, Armavir	W • M/F • Mideast & W Asia • 100 kW
	NALCHIK RADIO, Armavir	W • Su/W/Th • Mideast & W Asia • 100 kW
	VOICE OF RUSSIA, Armavir	W • Mideast • 100 kW
	SRI LANKA SRI LANKA BC CORP, Colombo-Ekala	S Asia • "RADIO SRI LANKA" • 10 kW
	UNITED KINGDOM †BBC, Rampisham	W • W Asia • 500 kW
	BBC, Via Ascension	S Africa • 250 kW W Africa • 250 kW
	BBC, Via Seychelles	E Africa • 250 kW S Africa • 250 kW
6010	BAHRAIN RADIO BAHRAIN, Abu Hayan	Irr • Mideast • DS-2 • USB
	BELARUS †BELARUSIAN R, Brest	DS-1 • 5 kW
	CHILE RADIO PARINACOTA, Putre	DS • 1 kW
	CHINA CENTRAL PEOPLE'S BS, Xi'an	W • DS-2 • 100 kW DS-2 • 100 kW DS-8 (MINORITIES) • 100 kW
	†CHINA R INTL, Beijing	W • Europe • 500 kW
	FRANCE R FRANCE INTL, Via Dhabayya, UAE	S • W Asia • 250 kW
	†R FRANCE INTL, Via Tajikistan	W • W Asia & S Asia • 200 kW
	IRAN †VO THE ISLAMIC REP, Tehrān	W • S Asia • 500 kW W • Europe • 500 kW
	ITALY RAI INTERNATIONAL, Rome	W • S Europe & N Africa • 100 kW W • N Africa • 100 kW
	MEXICO RADIO MIL, México City	DS • 1 kW
	NETHERLANDS †R NEDERLAND, Flevoland	W • S Europe • 500 kW
(con'd)	SRI LANKA SRI LANKA BC CORP, Via Skelton, UK	Sa • W Europe • 300 kW

World Time 0 1 2 3 4 5 6 7 8 9 10 11 12 13 14 15 16 17 18 19 20 21 22 23 24

SEASONAL S OR W   1-HR TIMESHIFT MIDYEAR ⇦ OR ⇨   JAMMING / OR ∧   EARLIEST HEARD ◁   LATEST HEARD ▷   NEW FOR 2006 †

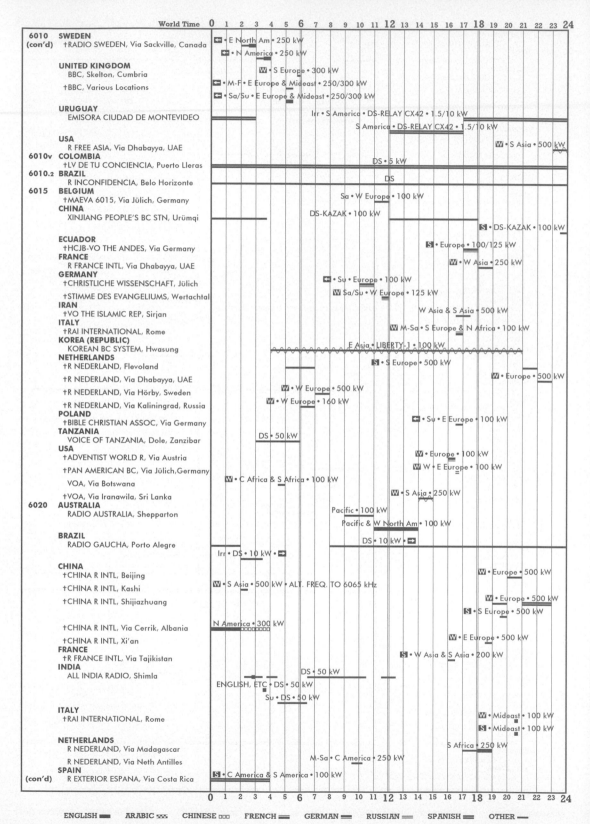

World Time 0 1 2 3 4 5 6 7 8 9 10 11 12 13 14 15 16 17 18 19 20 21 22 23 24

Frequency / Country / Station	Schedule
6010 SWEDEN	
(con'd) †RADIO SWEDEN, Via Sackville, Canada	E North Am • 250 kW / N America • 250 kW
UNITED KINGDOM	
BBC, Skelton, Cumbria	W • S Europe • 300 kW
†BBC, Various Locations	• M-F • E Europe & Mideast • 250/300 kW / Sa/Su • E Europe & Mideast • 250/300 kW
URUGUAY	
EMISORA CIUDAD DE MONTEVIDEO	Irr • S America • DS-RELAY CX42 • 1.5/10 kW / S America • DS-RELAY CX42 • 1.5/10 kW
USA	
R FREE ASIA, Via Dhabayya, UAE	W • S Asia • 500 kW
6010v COLOMBIA	
†LV DE TU CONCIENCIA, Puerto Lleras	DS • 5 kW
6010.2 BRAZIL	
R INCONFIDENCIA, Belo Horizonte	DS
6015 BELGIUM	
†MAEVA 6015, Via Jülich, Germany	Sa • W Europe • 100 kW
CHINA	
XINJIANG PEOPLE'S BC STN, Urümqi	DS-KAZAK • 100 kW / S • DS-KAZAK • 100 kW
ECUADOR	
†HCJB-VO THE ANDES, Via Germany	S • Europe • 100/125 kW
FRANCE	
R FRANCE INTL, Via Dhabayya, UAE	W • W Asia • 250 kW
GERMANY	
†CHRISTLICHE WISSENSCHAFT, Jülich	• Su • Europe • 100 kW
†STIMME DES EVANGELIUMS, Wertachtal	W Sa/Su • W Europe • 125 kW
IRAN	
†VO THE ISLAMIC REP, Sirjan	W Asia & S Asia • 500 kW
ITALY	
†RAI INTERNATIONAL, Rome	W M-Sa • S Europe & N Africa • 100 kW
KOREA (REPUBLIC)	
KOREAN BC SYSTEM, Hwasung	E Asia • LIBERTY-1 • 100 kW
NETHERLANDS	
†R NEDERLAND, Flevoland	S • S Europe • 500 kW
†R NEDERLAND, Via Dhabayya, UAE	W • Europe • 500 kW
†R NEDERLAND, Via Hörby, Sweden	W • W Europe • 500 kW
†R NEDERLAND, Via Kaliningrad, Russia	W • W Europe • 160 kW
POLAND	
†BIBLE CHRISTIAN ASSOC, Via Germany	• Su • E Europe • 100 kW
TANZANIA	
VOICE OF TANZANIA, Dole, Zanzibar	DS • 50 kW
USA	
†ADVENTIST WORLD R, Via Austria	W • Europe • 100 kW
†PAN AMERICAN BC, Via Jülich, Germany	W • E Europe • 100 kW
VOA, Via Botswana	W • C Africa & S Africa • 100 kW
†VOA, Via Iranawila, Sri Lanka	W • S Asia • 250 kW
6020 AUSTRALIA	
RADIO AUSTRALIA, Shepparton	Pacific • 100 kW / Pacific & W North Am • 100 kW
BRAZIL	
RADIO GAUCHA, Porto Alegre	DS • 10 kW • / Irr • DS • 10 kW •
CHINA	
†CHINA R INTL, Beijing	W • Europe • 500 kW
†CHINA R INTL, Kashi	W • S Asia • 500 kW • ALT. FREQ. TO 6065 kHz
†CHINA R INTL, Shijiazhuang	W • Europe • 500 kW / S • S Europe • 500 kW
†CHINA R INTL, Via Cerrik, Albania	N America • 300 kW
†CHINA R INTL, Xi'an	W • E Europe • 500 kW
FRANCE	
†R FRANCE INTL, Via Tajikistan	S • W Asia & S Asia • 200 kW
INDIA	
ALL INDIA RADIO, Shimla	DS • 50 kW / ENGLISH, ETC • DS • 50 kW / Su • DS • 50 kW
ITALY	
†RAI INTERNATIONAL, Rome	W • Mideast • 100 kW / S • Mideast • 100 kW
NETHERLANDS	
R NEDERLAND, Via Madagascar	S Africa • 250 kW
R NEDERLAND, Via Neth Antilles	M-Sa • C America • 250 kW
SPAIN	
(con'd) R EXTERIOR ESPANA, Via Costa Rica	S • C America & S America • 100 kW

World Time 0 1 2 3 4 5 6 7 8 9 10 11 12 13 14 15 16 17 18 19 20 21 22 23 24

ENGLISH ▬ ARABIC ⌇⌇⌇ CHINESE ▫▫▫ FRENCH ═ GERMAN ▬ RUSSIAN ═ SPANISH ═ OTHER ▬

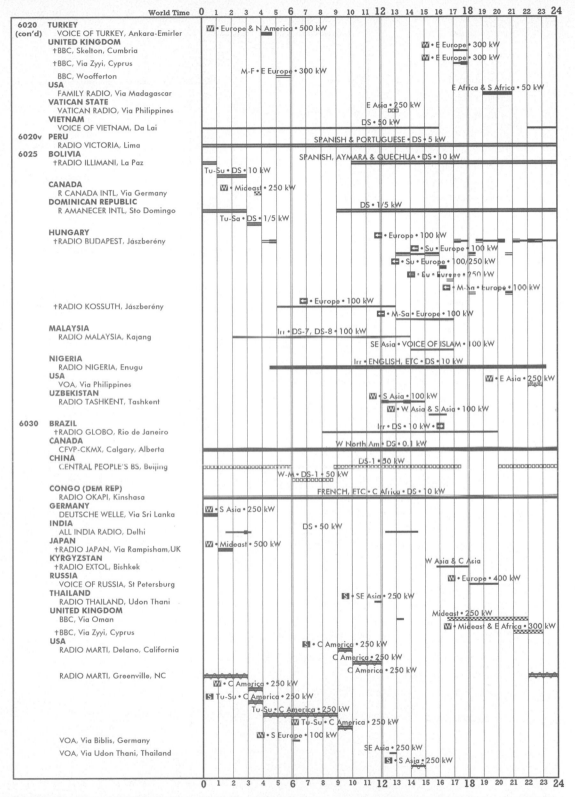

World Time

6020	**TURKEY** (con'd)
	VOICE OF TURKEY, Ankara-Emirler — W • Europe & N America • 500 kW
	UNITED KINGDOM
	†BBC, Skelton, Cumbria — W • E Europe • 300 kW
	†BBC, Via Zyyi, Cyprus — W • E Europe • 300 kW
	BBC, Woofferton — M-F • E Europe • 300 kW
	USA
	FAMILY RADIO, Via Madagascar — E Africa & S Africa • 50 kW
	VATICAN STATE
	VATICAN RADIO, Via Philippines — E Asia • 250 kW
	VIETNAM
	VOICE OF VIETNAM, Da Lai — DS • 50 kW
6020v	**PERU**
	RADIO VICTORIA, Lima — SPANISH & PORTUGUESE • DS • 5 kW
6025	**BOLIVIA**
	†RADIO ILLIMANI, La Paz — SPANISH, AYMARA & QUECHUA • DS • 10 kW / Tu-Su • DS • 10 kW
	CANADA
	R CANADA INTL, Via Germany — W • Mideast • 250 kW
	DOMINICAN REPUBLIC
	R AMANECER INTL, Sto Domingo — DS • 1/5 kW / Tu-Sa • DS • 1/5 kW
	HUNGARY
	†RADIO BUDAPEST, Jászberény — Europe • 100 kW / Su • Europe • 100 kW / Su • Europe • 100/250 kW / Su • Europe • 250 kW / M-Sa • Europe • 100 kW
	†RADIO KOSSUTH, Jászberény — Europe • 100 kW / M-Sa • Europe • 100 kW
	MALAYSIA
	RADIO MALAYSIA, Kajang — Irr • DS-7, DS-8 • 100 kW / SE Asia • VOICE OF ISLAM • 100 kW
	NIGERIA
	RADIO NIGERIA, Enugu — Irr • ENGLISH, ETC • DS • 10 kW
	USA
	VOA, Via Philippines — W • E Asia • 250 kW
	UZBEKISTAN
	RADIO TASHKENT, Tashkent — W • S Asia • 100 kW / W • W Asia & S Asia • 100 kW
6030	**BRAZIL**
	†RADIO GLOBO, Rio de Janeiro — Irr • DS • 10 kW
	CANADA
	CFVP-CKMX, Calgary, Alberta — W North Am • DS • 0.1 kW
	CHINA
	CENTRAL PEOPLE'S BS, Beijing — DS-1 • 50 kW / W-M • DS-1 • 50 kW
	CONGO (DEM REP)
	RADIO OKAPI, Kinshasa — FRENCH, ETC • C Africa • DS • 10 kW
	GERMANY
	DEUTSCHE WELLE, Via Sri Lanka — W • S Asia • 250 kW
	INDIA
	ALL INDIA RADIO, Delhi — DS • 50 kW
	JAPAN
	†RADIO JAPAN, Via Rampisham, UK — W • Mideast • 500 kW
	KYRGYZSTAN
	†RADIO EXTOL, Bishkek — W Asia & C Asia
	RUSSIA
	VOICE OF RUSSIA, St Petersburg — W • Europe • 400 kW
	THAILAND
	RADIO THAILAND, Udon Thani — S • SE Asia • 250 kW
	UNITED KINGDOM
	BBC, Via Oman — Mideast • 250 kW / W • Mideast & E Africa • 300 kW
	†BBC, Via Zyyi, Cyprus
	USA
	RADIO MARTI, Delano, California — S • C America • 250 kW / C America • 250 kW / C America • 250 kW
	RADIO MARTI, Greenville, NC — W • C America • 250 kW / S • Tu-Su • C America • 250 kW / Tu-Su • C America • 250 kW / W Tu-Su • C America • 250 kW
	VOA, Via Biblis, Germany — W • S Europe • 100 kW
	VOA, Via Udon Thani, Thailand — SE Asia • 250 kW / S • S Asia • 250 kW

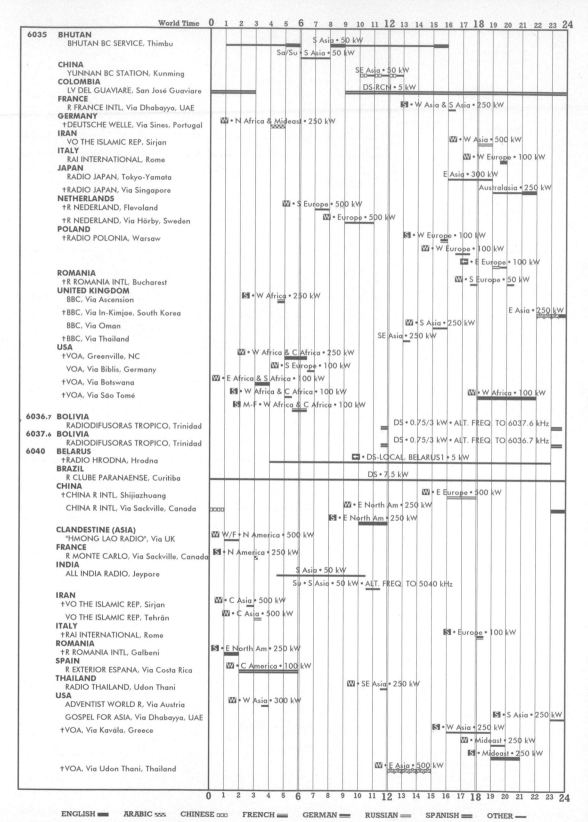

World Time   0 1 2 3 4 5 6 7 8 9 10 11 12 13 14 15 16 17 18 19 20 21 22 23 24

6035 BHUTAN
  BHUTAN BC SERVICE, Thimbu — S Asia • 50 kW
  — Sa/Su • S Asia • 50 kW
  CHINA
  YUNNAN BC STATION, Kunming — SE Asia • 50 kW
  COLOMBIA
  LV DEL GUAVIARE, San José Guaviare — DS-RCN • 5 kW
  FRANCE
  R FRANCE INTL, Via Dhabayya, UAE — S • W Asia & S Asia • 250 kW
  GERMANY
  †DEUTSCHE WELLE, Via Sines, Portugal — W • N Africa & Mideast • 250 kW
  IRAN
  VO THE ISLAMIC REP, Sirjan — W • W Asia • 500 kW
  ITALY
  RAI INTERNATIONAL, Rome — W • W Europe • 100 kW
  JAPAN
  RADIO JAPAN, Tokyo-Yamata — E Asia • 300 kW
  †RADIO JAPAN, Via Singapore — Australasia • 250 kW
  NETHERLANDS
  †R NEDERLAND, Flevoland — W • S Europe • 500 kW
  †R NEDERLAND, Via Hörby, Sweden — W • Europe • 500 kW
  POLAND
  †RADIO POLONIA, Warsaw — S • W Europe • 100 kW
  — W • W Europe • 100 kW
  — C • E Europe • 100 kW
  ROMANIA
  †R ROMANIA INTL, Bucharest — W • S Europe • 50 kW
  UNITED KINGDOM
  BBC, Via Ascension — S • W Africa • 250 kW
  †BBC, Via In-Kimjae, South Korea — E Asia • 250 kW
  BBC, Via Oman — W • S Asia • 250 kW
  †BBC, Via Thailand — SE Asia • 250 kW
  USA
  †VOA, Greenville, NC — W • W Africa & C Africa • 250 kW
  VOA, Via Biblis, Germany — W • S Europe • 100 kW
  †VOA, Via Botswana — W • E Africa & S Africa • 100 kW
  †VOA, Via São Tomé — S • W Africa & C Africa • 100 kW
  — S • M-F • W Africa & C Africa • 100 kW
  — W • W Africa • 100 kW

6036.7 BOLIVIA
  RADIODIFUSORAS TROPICO, Trinidad — DS • 0.75/3 kW • ALT. FREQ. TO 6037.6 kHz
6037.6 BOLIVIA
  RADIODIFUSORAS TROPICO, Trinidad — DS • 0.75/3 kW • ALT. FREQ. TO 6036.7 kHz
6040 BELARUS
  †RADIO HRODNA, Hrodna — C • DS-LOCAL, BELARUS1 • 5 kW
  BRAZIL
  R CLUBE PARANAENSE, Curitiba — DS • 7.5 kW
  CHINA
  †CHINA R INTL, Shijiazhuang — W • E Europe • 500 kW
  CHINA R INTL, Via Sackville, Canada — W • E North Am • 250 kW
  — S • E North Am • 250 kW
  CLANDESTINE (ASIA)
  "HMONG LAO RADIO", Via UK — W • W/F • N America • 500 kW
  FRANCE
  R MONTE CARLO, Via Sackville, Canada — S • N America • 250 kW
  INDIA
  ALL INDIA RADIO, Jeypore — S Asia • 50 kW
  — Su • S Asia • 50 kW • ALT. FREQ. TO 5040 kHz
  IRAN
  †VO THE ISLAMIC REP, Sirjan — W • C Asia • 500 kW
  VO THE ISLAMIC REP, Tehrān — W • C Asia • 500 kW
  ITALY
  †RAI INTERNATIONAL, Rome — S • Europe • 100 kW
  ROMANIA
  †R ROMANIA INTL, Galbeni — S • E North Am • 250 kW
  SPAIN
  R EXTERIOR ESPANA, Via Costa Rica — W • C America • 100 kW
  THAILAND
  RADIO THAILAND, Udon Thani — W • SE Asia • 250 kW
  USA
  ADVENTIST WORLD R, Via Austria — W • W Asia • 300 kW
  GOSPEL FOR ASIA, Via Dhabayya, UAE — S • S Asia • 250 kW
  †VOA, Via Kavála, Greece — S • W Asia • 250 kW
  — W • Mideast • 250 kW
  — S • Mideast • 250 kW
  †VOA, Via Udon Thani, Thailand — W • E Asia • 500 kW

0 1 2 3 4 5 6 7 8 9 10 11 12 13 14 15 16 17 18 19 20 21 22 23 24

ENGLISH ▬   ARABIC ⧀⧀⧀   CHINESE □□□   FRENCH ═══   GERMAN ▬▬   RUSSIAN ═══   SPANISH ═══   OTHER ▬

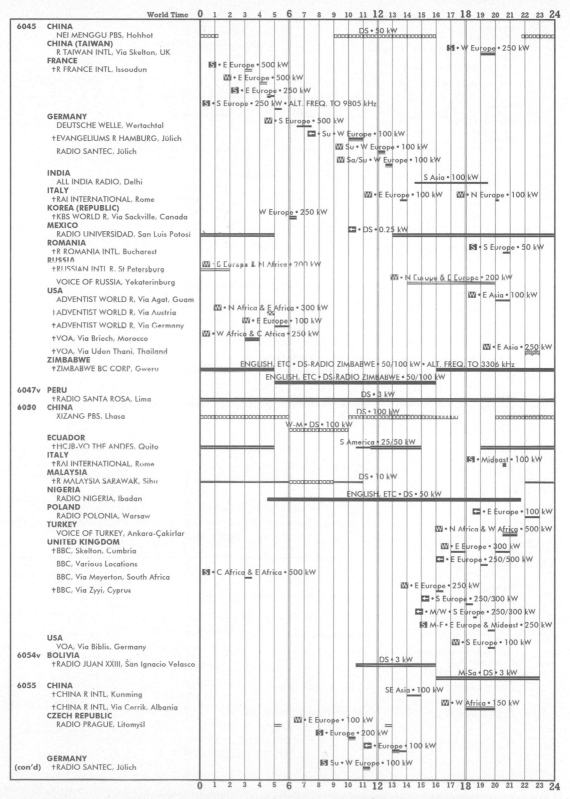

World Time | 0 1 2 3 4 5 6 7 8 9 10 11 12 13 14 15 16 17 18 19 20 21 22 23 24

6045 CHINA
NEI MENGGU PBS, Hohhot — DS • 50 kW

CHINA (TAIWAN)
R TAIWAN INTL, Via Skelton, UK — W • W Europe • 250 kW

FRANCE
†R FRANCE INTL, Issoudun
- S • E Europe • 500 kW
- W • E Europe • 500 kW
- S • E Europe • 250 kW
- S • S Europe • 250 kW • ALT. FREQ. TO 9805 kHz

GERMANY
DEUTSCHE WELLE, Wertachtal — W • S Europe • 500 kW

†EVANGELIUMS R HAMBURG, Jülich — Su • W Europe • 100 kW

RADIO SANTEC, Jülich
- W Su • W Europe • 100 kW
- W Sa/Su • W Europe • 100 kW

INDIA
ALL INDIA RADIO, Delhi — S Asia • 100 kW

ITALY
†RAI INTERNATIONAL, Rome
- W • E Europe • 100 kW
- W • N Europe • 100 kW

KOREA (REPUBLIC)
†KBS WORLD R, Via Sackville, Canada — W Europe • 250 kW

MEXICO
RADIO UNIVERSIDAD, San Luis Potosí — DS • 0.25 kW

ROMANIA
†R ROMANIA INTL, Bucharest — S • S Europe • 50 kW

RUSSIA
†RUSSIAN INTL R, St Petersburg — W • C Europe & N Africa • 200 kW

VOICE OF RUSSIA, Yekaterinburg
- W • N Europe & C Europe • 200 kW
- W • E Asia • 100 kW

USA
ADVENTIST WORLD R, Via Agat, Guam — W • N Africa & E Africa • 300 kW

†ADVENTIST WORLD R, Via Austria — W • E Europe • 100 kW

†ADVENTIST WORLD R, Via Germany — W • W Africa & C Africa • 250 kW

†VOA, Via Briech, Morocco

†VOA, Via Udon Thani, Thailand — W • E Asia • 250 kW

ZIMBABWE
†ZIMBABWE BC CORP, Gweru
- ENGLISH, ETC • DS-RADIO ZIMBABWE • 50/100 kW • ALT. FREQ. TO 3306 kHz
- ENGLISH, ETC • DS-RADIO ZIMBABWE • 50/100 kW

6047v PERU
†RADIO SANTA ROSA, Lima — DS • 3 kW

6050 CHINA
XIZANG PBS, Lhasa
- DS • 100 kW
- W-M • DS • 100 kW

ECUADOR
†HCJB-VO THE ANDES, Quito — S America • 25/50 kW

ITALY
†RAI INTERNATIONAL, Rome — S • Mideast • 100 kW

MALAYSIA
†R MALAYSIA SARAWAK, Sibu — DS • 10 kW

NIGERIA
RADIO NIGERIA, Ibadan — ENGLISH, ETC • DS • 50 kW

POLAND
RADIO POLONIA, Warsaw — • E Europe • 100 kW

TURKEY
VOICE OF TURKEY, Ankara-Çakirlar — W • N Africa & W Africa • 500 kW

UNITED KINGDOM
†BBC, Skelton, Cumbria — W • E Europe • 300 kW

BBC, Various Locations — • E Europe • 250/500 kW

BBC, Via Meyerton, South Africa — S • C Africa & E Africa • 500 kW

†BBC, Via Zyyi, Cyprus
- W • E Europe • 250 kW
- • S Europe • 250/300 kW
- M/W • S Europe • 250/300 kW
- S M-F • E Europe & Mideast • 250 kW

USA
VOA, Via Biblis, Germany — W • S Europe • 100 kW

6054v BOLIVIA
†RADIO JUAN XXIII, San Ignacio Velasco
- DS • 3 kW
- M-Sa • DS • 3 kW

6055 CHINA
†CHINA R INTL, Kunming — SE Asia • 100 kW

†CHINA R INTL, Via Cerrik, Albania — W • W Africa • 150 kW

CZECH REPUBLIC
RADIO PRAGUE, Litomyšl
- W • E Europe • 100 kW
- S • Europe • 200 kW
- • Europe • 100 kW

GERMANY
(con'd) †RADIO SANTEC, Jülich — S Su • W Europe • 100 kW

World Time | 0 1 2 3 4 5 6 7 8 9 10 11 12 13 14 15 16 17 18 19 20 21 22 23 24

SEASONAL S OR W   1-HR TIMESHIFT MIDYEAR ⇦ OR ⇨   JAMMING / OR ∧   EARLIEST HEARD ◁   LATEST HEARD ▷   NEW FOR 2006 †

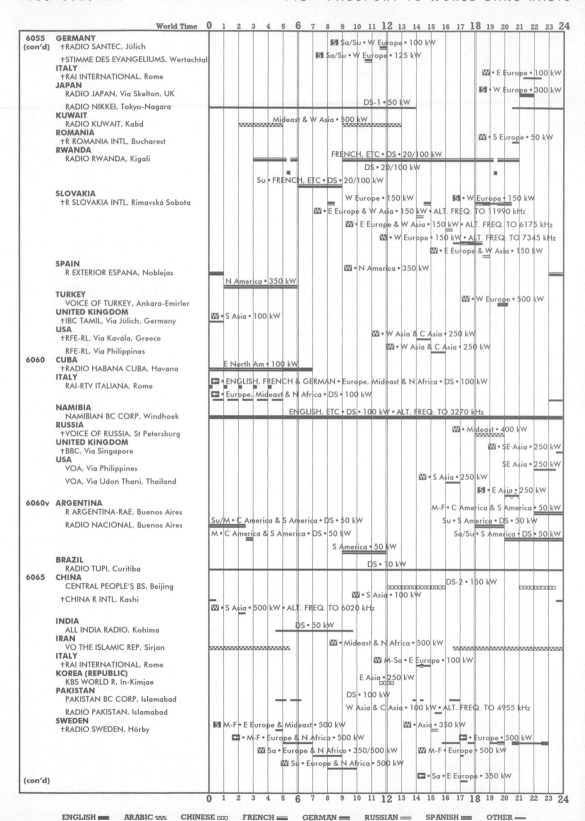

World Time 0 1 2 3 4 5 6 7 8 9 10 11 12 13 14 15 16 17 18 19 20 21 22 23 24

6055
(con'd)   GERMANY
         †RADIO SANTEC, Jülich   S Sa/Su • W Europe • 100 kW
         †STIMME DES EVANGELIUMS, Wertachtal   S Sa/Su • W Europe • 125 kW
ITALY
         †RAI INTERNATIONAL, Rome   W • E Europe • 100 kW
JAPAN
         RADIO JAPAN, Via Skelton, UK   S • W Europe • 300 kW
         RADIO NIKKEI, Tokyo-Nagara   DS-1 • 50 kW
KUWAIT
         RADIO KUWAIT, Kabd   Mideast & W Asia • 500 kW
ROMANIA
         †R ROMANIA INTL, Bucharest   W • S Europe • 50 kW
RWANDA
         RADIO RWANDA, Kigali   FRENCH, ETC • DS • 20/100 kW
                                                    DS • 20/100 kW
                                          Su • FRENCH, ETC • DS • 20/100 kW
SLOVAKIA
         †R SLOVAKIA INTL, Rimavská Sobota   W Europe • 150 kW   S • W Europe • 150 kW
                                          W • E Europe & W Asia • 150 kW • ALT. FREQ. TO 11990 kHz
                                           W • E Europe & W Asia • 150 kW • ALT. FREQ. TO 6175 kHz
                                             W • W Europe • 150 kW • ALT. FREQ. TO 7345 kHz
                                              W • E Europe & W Asia • 150 kW
SPAIN
         R EXTERIOR ESPANA, Noblejas   W • N America • 350 kW
                                          N America • 350 kW
TURKEY
         VOICE OF TURKEY, Ankara-Emirler   W • W Europe • 500 kW
UNITED KINGDOM
         †IBC TAMIL, Via Jülich, Germany   W • S Asia • 100 kW
USA
         †RFE-RL, Via Kavála, Greece   W • W Asia & C Asia • 250 kW
         RFE-RL, Via Philippines   W • W Asia & C Asia • 250 kW
6060   CUBA
         †RADIO HABANA CUBA, Havana   E North Am • 100 kW
ITALY
         RAI-RTV ITALIANA, Rome   ⇦ ENGLISH, FRENCH & GERMAN • Europe, Mideast & N Africa • DS • 100 kW
                                      ⇦ Europe, Mideast & N Africa • DS • 100 kW
NAMIBIA
         NAMIBIAN BC CORP, Windhoek   ENGLISH, ETC • DS • 100 kW • ALT. FREQ. TO 3270 kHz
RUSSIA
         †VOICE OF RUSSIA, St Petersburg   W • Mideast • 400 kW
UNITED KINGDOM
         †BBC, Via Singapore   W • SE Asia • 250 kW
USA
         VOA, Via Philippines   SE Asia • 250 kW
         VOA, Via Udon Thani, Thailand   W • S Asia • 250 kW
                                                    S • E Asia • 250 kW
6060v ARGENTINA
         R ARGENTINA-RAE, Buenos Aires   M-F • C America & S America • 50 kW
         RADIO NACIONAL, Buenos Aires   Su/M • C America & S America • DS • 50 kW   Su • S America • DS • 50 kW
                                         M • C America & S America • DS • 50 kW   Sa/Su • S America • DS • 50 kW
                                                   S America • 50 kW
BRAZIL
         RADIO TUPI, Curitiba   DS • 10 kW
6065   CHINA
         CENTRAL PEOPLE'S BS, Beijing   DS-2 • 150 kW
         †CHINA R INTL, Kashi   W • S Asia • 100 kW
                                          W • S Asia • 500 kW • ALT. FREQ. TO 6020 kHz
INDIA
         ALL INDIA RADIO, Kohima   DS • 50 kW
IRAN
         VO THE ISLAMIC REP, Sirjan   W • Mideast & N Africa • 500 kW
ITALY
         †RAI INTERNATIONAL, Rome   W M-Sa • E Europe • 100 kW
KOREA (REPUBLIC)
         KBS WORLD R, In-Kimjae   E Asia • 250 kW
PAKISTAN
         PAKISTAN BC CORP, Islamabad   DS • 100 kW
         RADIO PAKISTAN, Islamabad   W Asia & C Asia • 100 kW • ALT. FREQ. TO 4955 kHz
SWEDEN
         †RADIO SWEDEN, Hörby   S M-F • E Europe & Mideast • 500 kW   W • Asia • 350 kW
                                  ⇦ • M-F • Europe & N Africa • 500 kW   ⇦ • Europe • 500 kW
                                   W Sa • Europe & N Africa • 350/500 kW   W M-F • Europe • 500 kW
                                    W Su • Europe & N Africa • 500 kW
                                                    ⇦ • Sa • E Europe • 350 kW
(con'd)

0 1 2 3 4 5 6 7 8 9 10 11 12 13 14 15 16 17 18 19 20 21 22 23 24

ENGLISH ▬▬   ARABIC ⋙   CHINESE ▫▫▫   FRENCH ══   GERMAN ▬▬   RUSSIAN ══   SPANISH ══   OTHER ──

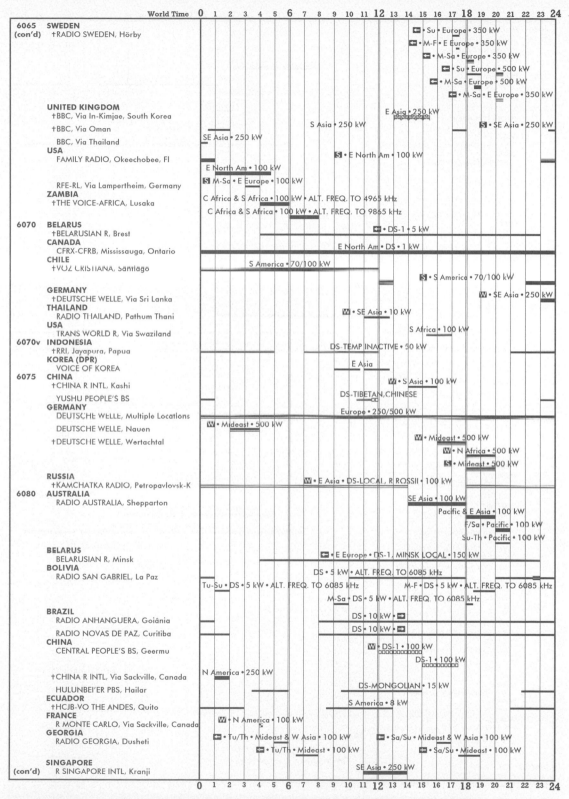

World Time

6065
(con'd) **SWEDEN**
†RADIO SWEDEN, Hörby
- ⬅ • Su • Europe • 350 kW
- ⬅ • M-F • E Europe • 350 kW
- ⬅ • M-Sa • Europe • 350 kW
- ⬅ • Su • Europe • 500 kW
- ⬅ • M-Sa • Europe • 500 kW
- ⬅ • M-Sa • E Europe • 350 kW

UNITED KINGDOM
†BBC, Via In-Kimjae, South Korea — E Asia • 250 kW
†BBC, Via Oman — S Asia • 250 kW — S • SE Asia • 250 kW
BBC, Via Thailand — SE Asia • 250 kW
USA
FAMILY RADIO, Okeechobee, Fl — S • E North Am • 100 kW
— E North Am • 100 kW
RFE-RL, Via Lampertheim, Germany — S • M-Sa • E Europe • 100 kW
ZAMBIA
†THE VOICE-AFRICA, Lusaka — C Africa & S Africa • 100 kW • ALT. FREQ. TO 4965 kHz
— C Africa & S Africa • 100 kW • ALT. FREQ. TO 9865 kHz

6070 **BELARUS**
†BELARUSIAN R, Brest — ⬅ • DS-1 • 5 kW
CANADA
CFRX-CFRB, Mississauga, Ontario — E North Am • DS • 1 kW
CHILE
†VOZ CRISTIANA, Santiago — S America • 70/100 kW
— S • S America • 70/100 kW

GERMANY
†DEUTSCHE WELLE, Via Sri Lanka — W • SE Asia • 250 kW
THAILAND
RADIO THAILAND, Pathum Thani — W • SE Asia • 10 kW
USA
TRANS WORLD R, Via Swaziland — S Africa • 100 kW
6070v **INDONESIA**
†RRI, Jayapura, Papua — DS-TEMP INACTIVE • 50 kW
KOREA (DPR)
VOICE OF KOREA — E Asia
6075 **CHINA**
†CHINA R INTL, Kashi — W • S Asia • 100 kW
YUSHU PEOPLE'S BS — DS-TIBETAN, CHINESE
GERMANY
DEUTSCHE WELLE, Multiple Locations — Europe • 250/500 kW
DEUTSCHE WELLE, Nauen — W • Mideast • 500 kW
†DEUTSCHE WELLE, Wertachtal — W • Mideast • 500 kW
— W • N Africa • 500 kW
— S • Mideast • 500 kW
RUSSIA
†KAMCHATKA RADIO, Petropavlovsk-K — W • E Asia • DS-LOCAL, R ROSSII • 100 kW
6080 **AUSTRALIA**
RADIO AUSTRALIA, Shepparton — SE Asia • 100 kW
— Pacific & E Asia • 100 kW
— F/Sa • Pacific • 100 kW
— Su-Th • Pacific • 100 kW

BELARUS
BELARUSIAN R, Minsk — ⬅ • E Europe • DS-1, MINSK LOCAL • 150 kW
BOLIVIA
RADIO SAN GABRIEL, La Paz — DS • 5 kW • ALT. FREQ. TO 6085 kHz
— Tu-Su • DS • 5 kW • ALT. FREQ. TO 6085 kHz — M-F • DS • 5 kW • ALT. FREQ. TO 6085 kHz
— M-Sa • DS • 5 kW • ALT. FREQ. TO 6085 kHz
BRAZIL
RADIO ANHANGUERA, Goiânia — DS • 10 kW • ⮕
RADIO NOVAS DE PAZ, Curitiba — DS • 10 kW • ⮕
CHINA
CENTRAL PEOPLE'S BS, Geermu — W • DS-1 • 100 kW
— DS-1 • 100 kW
†CHINA R INTL, Via Sackville, Canada — N America • 250 kW
HULUNBEI'ER PBS, Hailar — DS-MONGOLIAN • 15 kW
ECUADOR
†HCJB-VO THE ANDES, Quito — S America • 8 kW
FRANCE
R MONTE CARLO, Via Sackville, Canada — W • N America • 100 kW
GEORGIA
RADIO GEORGIA, Dusheti — ⬅ • Tu/Th • Mideast & W Asia • 100 kW — ⬅ • Sa/Su • Mideast & W Asia • 100 kW
— ⬅ • Tu/Th • Mideast • 100 kW — ⬅ • Sa/Su • Mideast • 100 kW
SINGAPORE
(con'd) R SINGAPORE INTL, Kranji — SE Asia • 250 kW

0 1 2 3 4 5 6 7 8 9 10 11 12 13 14 15 16 17 18 19 20 21 22 23 24

SEASONAL S OR W   1-HR TIMESHIFT MIDYEAR ⬅ OR ⮕   JAMMING / OR /\   EARLIEST HEARD ◁   LATEST HEARD ▷   NEW FOR 2006 †

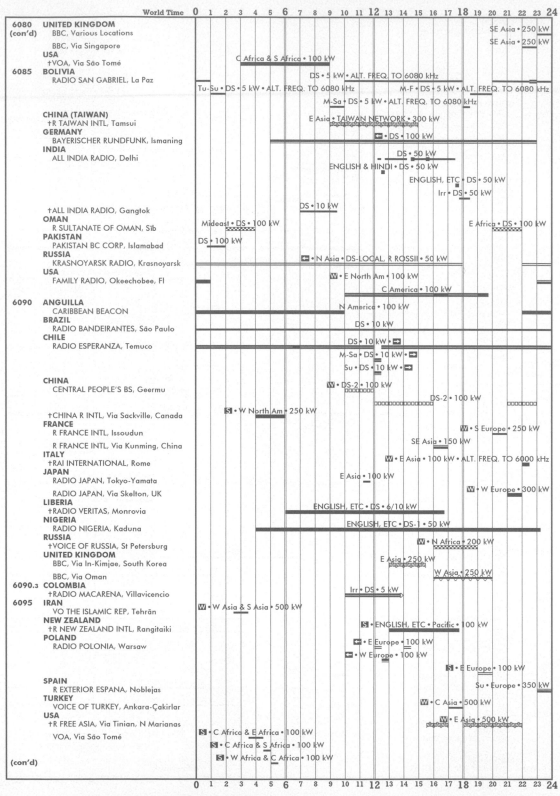

World Time 0 1 2 3 4 5 6 7 8 9 10 11 12 13 14 15 16 17 18 19 20 21 22 23 24

6080 **UNITED KINGDOM**
(con'd)   BBC, Various Locations — SE Asia • 250 kW
           BBC, Via Singapore — SE Asia • 250 kW
         USA
           †VOA, Via São Tomé — C Africa & S Africa • 100 kW
6085 **BOLIVIA**
           RADIO SAN GABRIEL, La Paz — DS • 5 kW • ALT. FREQ. TO 6080 kHz
              Tu-Su • DS • 5 kW • ALT. FREQ. TO 6080 kHz   M-F • DS • 5 kW • ALT. FREQ. TO 6080 kHz
              M-Sa • DS • 5 kW • ALT. FREQ. TO 6080 kHz

         CHINA (TAIWAN)
           †R TAIWAN INTL, Tamsui — E Asia • TAIWAN NETWORK • 300 kW
         GERMANY
           BAYERISCHER RUNDFUNK, Ismaning — ▭ • DS • 100 kW
         INDIA
           ALL INDIA RADIO, Delhi — DS • 50 kW
              ENGLISH & HINDI • DS • 50 kW
              ENGLISH, ETC • DS • 50 kW
              Irr • DS • 50 kW

           †ALL INDIA RADIO, Gangtok — DS • 10 kW
         OMAN
           R SULTANATE OF OMAN, Sīb — Mideast • DS • 100 kW   E Africa • DS • 100 kW
         PAKISTAN
           PAKISTAN BC CORP, Islamabad — DS • 100 kW
         RUSSIA
           KRASNOYARSK RADIO, Krasnoyarsk — ⬅ • N Asia • DS-LOCAL, R ROSSII • 50 kW
         USA
           FAMILY RADIO, Okeechobee, Fl — W • E North Am • 100 kW
              C America • 100 kW

6090 **ANGUILLA**
           CARIBBEAN BEACON — N America • 100 kW
         BRAZIL
           RADIO BANDEIRANTES, São Paulo — DS • 10 kW
         CHILE
           RADIO ESPERANZA, Temuco — DS • 10 kW • ➡
              M-Sa • DS • 10 kW • ➡
              Su • DS • 10 kW • ➡

         CHINA
           CENTRAL PEOPLE'S BS, Geermu — W • DS-2 • 100 kW
              DS-2 • 100 kW

           †CHINA R INTL, Via Sackville, Canada — S • W North Am • 250 kW
         FRANCE
           R FRANCE INTL, Issoudun — W • S Europe • 250 kW
           R FRANCE INTL, Via Kunming, China — SE Asia • 150 kW
         ITALY
           †RAI INTERNATIONAL, Rome — W • E Asia • 100 kW • ALT. FREQ. TO 6000 kHz
         JAPAN
           RADIO JAPAN, Tokyo-Yamata — E Asia • 100 kW
           RADIO JAPAN, Via Skelton, UK — W • W Europe • 300 kW
         LIBERIA
           †RADIO VERITAS, Monrovia — ENGLISH, ETC • DS • 6/10 kW
         NIGERIA
           RADIO NIGERIA, Kaduna — ENGLISH, ETC • DS-1 • 50 kW
         RUSSIA
           †VOICE OF RUSSIA, St Petersburg — W • N Africa • 200 kW
         UNITED KINGDOM
           BBC, Via In-Kimjae, South Korea — E Asia • 250 kW
           BBC, Via Oman — W Asia • 250 kW
6090.3 COLOMBIA
           †RADIO MACARENA, Villavicencio — Irr • DS • 5 kW ➡
6095 **IRAN**
           VO THE ISLAMIC REP, Tehrān — W • W Asia & S Asia • 500 kW
         NEW ZEALAND
           †R NEW ZEALAND INTL, Rangitaiki — S • ENGLISH, ETC • Pacific • 100 kW
         POLAND
           RADIO POLONIA, Warsaw — ⬅ • E Europe • 100 kW
              ⬅ • W Europe • 100 kW
              S • E Europe • 100 kW

         SPAIN
           R EXTERIOR ESPANA, Noblejas — Su • Europe • 350 kW
         TURKEY
           VOICE OF TURKEY, Ankara-Çakirlar — W • C Asia • 500 kW
         USA
           †R FREE ASIA, Via Tinian, N Marianas — W • E Asia • 500 kW
           VOA, Via São Tomé — S • C Africa & E Africa • 100 kW
              S • C Africa & S Africa • 100 kW
              S • W Africa & C Africa • 100 kW

(con'd)

0 1 2 3 4 5 6 7 8 9 10 11 12 13 14 15 16 17 18 19 20 21 22 23 24

ENGLISH ▬▬   ARABIC ⬚⬚⬚   CHINESE ᐧᐧᐧ   FRENCH ▬▬   GERMAN ▬▬   RUSSIAN ══   SPANISH ▬▬   OTHER ▬▬

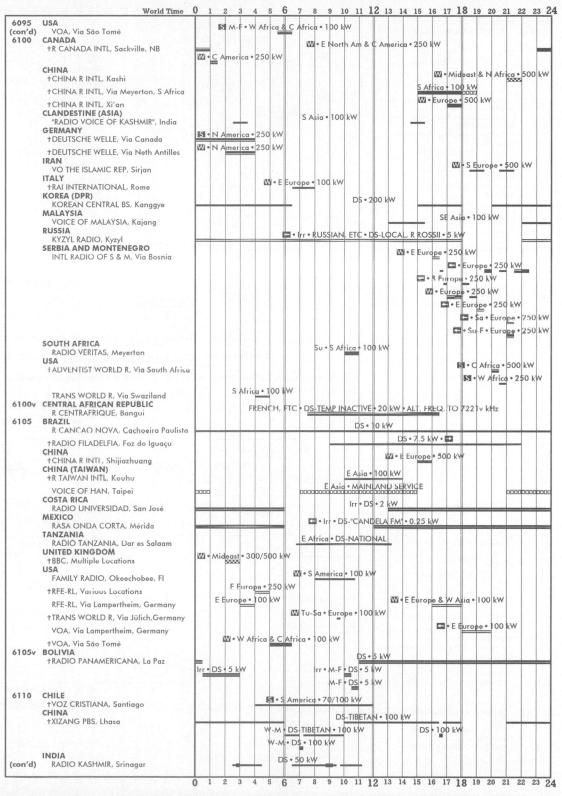

		World Time	0 1 2 3 4 5 6 7 8 9 10 11 12 13 14 15 16 17 18 19 20 21 22 23 24

6095 **USA**
(con'd)   VOA, Via São Tomé — Ⓢ M-F • W Africa & C Africa • 100 kW

6100 **CANADA**
   †R CANADA INTL, Sackville, NB — Ⓦ • E North Am & C America • 250 kW
   Ⓦ • C America • 250 kW

CHINA
   †CHINA R INTL, Kashi — Ⓦ • Mideast & N Africa • 500 kW
   †CHINA R INTL, Via Meyerton, S Africa — S Africa • 100 kW
   †CHINA R INTL, Xi'an — Ⓦ • Europe • 500 kW

CLANDESTINE (ASIA)
   "RADIO VOICE OF KASHMIR", India — S Asia • 100 kW

GERMANY
   †DEUTSCHE WELLE, Via Canada — Ⓢ • N America • 250 kW
   †DEUTSCHE WELLE, Via Neth Antilles — Ⓦ • N America • 250 kW

IRAN
   VO THE ISLAMIC REP, Sirjan — Ⓦ • S Europe • 500 kW

ITALY
   †RAI INTERNATIONAL, Rome — Ⓦ • E Europe • 100 kW

KOREA (DPR)
   KOREAN CENTRAL BS, Kanggye — DS • 200 kW

MALAYSIA
   VOICE OF MALAYSIA, Kajang — SE Asia • 100 kW

RUSSIA
   KYZYL RADIO, Kyzyl — ⇦ Irr • RUSSIAN, ETC • DS-LOCAL, R ROSSII • 5 kW

SERBIA AND MONTENEGRO
   INTL RADIO OF S & M, Via Bosnia — Ⓦ • E Europe • 250 kW
   ⇦ • Europe • 250 kW
   ⇦ • R Europe • 250 kW
   Ⓦ • Europe • 250 kW
   ⇦ • E Europe • 250 kW
   ⇦ • Sa • Europe • 250 kW
   ⇦ • Su-F • Europe • 250 kW

SOUTH AFRICA
   RADIO VERITAS, Meyerton — Su • S Africa • 100 kW

USA
   †ADVENTIST WORLD R, Via South Africa — Ⓢ • C Africa • 500 kW
   Ⓢ • W Africa • 250 kW
   TRANS WORLD R, Via Swaziland — S Africa • 100 kW

6100v **CENTRAL AFRICAN REPUBLIC**
   R CENTRAFRIQUE, Bangui — FRENCH, ETC • DS-TEMP INACTIVE • 20 kW • ALT. FREQ. TO 7221v kHz

6105 **BRAZIL**
   R CANÇAO NOVA, Cachoeira Paulista — DS • 10 kW
   †RADIO FILADELFIA, Foz do Iguaçu — DS • 7.5 kW • ⇦

CHINA
   †CHINA R INTL, Shijiazhuang — Ⓦ • E Europe • 500 kW

CHINA (TAIWAN)
   †R TAIWAN INTL, Kouhu — E Asia • 100 kW
   VOICE OF HAN, Taipei — E Asia • MAINLAND SERVICE

COSTA RICA
   RADIO UNIVERSIDAD, San José — Irr • DS • 2 kW

MEXICO
   RASA ONDA CORTA, Mérida — ⇦ • Irr • DS-"CANDELA FM" • 0.25 kW

TANZANIA
   RADIO TANZANIA, Dar es Salaam — E Africa • DS-NATIONAL

UNITED KINGDOM
   †BBC, Multiple Locations — Ⓦ • Mideast • 300/500 kW

USA
   FAMILY RADIO, Okeechobee, Fl — Ⓦ • S America • 100 kW
   †RFE-RL, Various Locations — E Europe • 250 kW
   RFE-RL, Via Lampertheim, Germany — E Europe • 100 kW
   Ⓦ • E Europe & W Asia • 100 kW
   †TRANS WORLD R, Via Jülich, Germany — Ⓦ • Tu-Sa • Europe • 100 kW
   VOA, Via Lampertheim, Germany — ⇦ • E Europe • 100 kW
   †VOA, Via São Tomé — Ⓦ • W Africa & C Africa • 100 kW

6105v **BOLIVIA**
   †RADIO PANAMERICANA, La Paz — DS • 5 kW
   Irr • DS • 5 kW
   Irr • M-F • DS • 5 kW
   M-F • DS • 5 kW

6110 **CHILE**
   †VOZ CRISTIANA, Santiago — Ⓢ • S America • 70/100 kW

CHINA
   †XIZANG PBS, Lhasa — DS-TIBETAN • 100 kW
   W-M • DS-TIBETAN • 100 kW
   DS • 100 kW
   W-M • DS • 100 kW

INDIA
(con'd)   RADIO KASHMIR, Srinagar — DS • 50 kW

	0 1 2 3 4 5 6 7 8 9 10 11 12 13 14 15 16 17 18 19 20 21 22 23 24

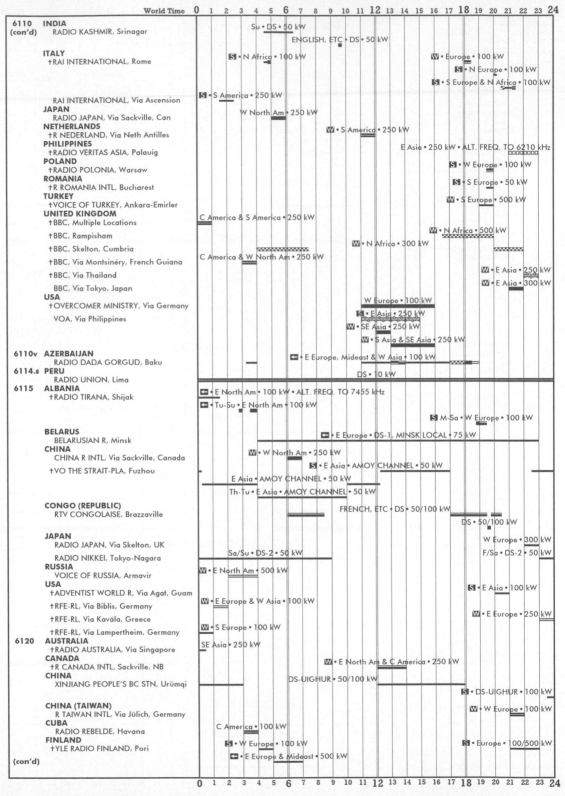

| | | | World Time | 0 | 1 | 2 | 3 | 4 | 5 | 6 | 7 | 8 | 9 | 10 | 11 | 12 | 13 | 14 | 15 | 16 | 17 | 18 | 19 | 20 | 21 | 22 | 23 | 24 |

6110 (con'd)

INDIA
RADIO KASHMIR, Srinagar — Su • DS • 50 kW — ENGLISH, ETC • DS • 50 kW

ITALY
†RAI INTERNATIONAL, Rome — S • N Africa • 100 kW — W • Europe • 100 kW — S • N Europe • 100 kW — S • S Europe & N Africa • 100 kW

RAI INTERNATIONAL, Via Ascension — S • S America • 250 kW

JAPAN
RADIO JAPAN, Via Sackville, Can — W North Am • 250 kW

NETHERLANDS
†R NEDERLAND, Via Neth Antilles — W • S America • 250 kW

PHILIPPINES
†RADIO VERITAS ASIA, Palauig — E Asia • 250 kW • ALT. FREQ. TO 6210 kHz

POLAND
†RADIO POLONIA, Warsaw — S • W Europe • 100 kW

ROMANIA
†R ROMANIA INTL, Bucharest — S • S Europe • 50 kW

TURKEY
†VOICE OF TURKEY, Ankara-Emirler — W • S Europe • 500 kW

UNITED KINGDOM
†BBC, Multiple Locations — C America & S America • 250 kW

†BBC, Rampisham — W • N Africa • 500 kW

†BBC, Skelton, Cumbria — W • N Africa • 300 kW

†BBC, Via Montsinéry, French Guiana — C America & W North Am • 250 kW

†BBC, Via Thailand — W • E Asia • 250 kW

BBC, Via Tokyo, Japan — W • E Asia • 300 kW

USA
†OVERCOMER MINISTRY, Via Germany — W Europe • 100 kW

VOA, Via Philippines — S • E Asia • 250 kW — W • SE Asia • 250 kW — W • S Asia & SE Asia • 250 kW

6110v AZERBAIJAN
RADIO DADA GORGUD, Baku — E Europe, Mideast & W Asia • 100 kW

6114.8 PERU
RADIO UNION, Lima — DS • 10 kW

6115 ALBANIA
†RADIO TIRANA, Shijak — E North Am • 100 kW • ALT. FREQ. TO 7455 kHz — Tu-Su • E North Am • 100 kW — S • M-Sa • W Europe • 100 kW

BELARUS
BELARUSIAN R, Minsk — E Europe • DS-1, MINSK LOCAL • 75 kW

CHINA
CHINA R INTL, Via Sackville, Canada — W • W North Am • 250 kW — S • E Asia • AMOY CHANNEL • 50 kW

†VO THE STRAIT-PLA, Fuzhou — E Asia • AMOY CHANNEL • 50 kW — Th-Tu • E Asia • AMOY CHANNEL • 50 kW

CONGO (REPUBLIC)
RTV CONGOLAISE, Brazzaville — FRENCH, ETC • DS • 50/100 kW — DS • 50/100 kW

JAPAN
RADIO JAPAN, Via Skelton, UK — W Europe • 300 kW

RADIO NIKKEI, Tokyo-Nagara — Sa/Su • DS-2 • 50 kW — F/Sa • DS-2 • 50 kW

RUSSIA
VOICE OF RUSSIA, Armavir — W • E North Am • 500 kW

USA
†ADVENTIST WORLD R, Via Agat, Guam — S • E Asia • 100 kW

†RFE-RL, Via Biblis, Germany — W • E Europe & W Asia • 100 kW — W • E Europe • 250 kW

†RFE-RL, Via Kavála, Greece

†RFE-RL, Via Lampertheim, Germany — W • S Europe • 100 kW

6120 AUSTRALIA
†RADIO AUSTRALIA, Via Singapore — SE Asia • 250 kW

CANADA
†R CANADA INTL, Sackville, NB — W • E North Am & C America • 250 kW

CHINA
XINJIANG PEOPLE'S BC STN, Urümqi — DS-UIGHUR • 50/100 kW — S • DS-UIGHUR • 100 kW

CHINA (TAIWAN)
R TAIWAN INTL, Via Jülich, Germany — W • W Europe • 100 kW

CUBA
RADIO REBELDE, Havana — C America • 100 kW

FINLAND
†YLE RADIO FINLAND, Pori — S • W Europe • 100 kW — S • Europe • 100/500 kW — E Europe & Mideast • 500 kW

(con'd)

| | 0 | 1 | 2 | 3 | 4 | 5 | 6 | 7 | 8 | 9 | 10 | 11 | 12 | 13 | 14 | 15 | 16 | 17 | 18 | 19 | 20 | 21 | 22 | 23 | 24 |

ENGLISH ▬▬ ARABIC ⋙ CHINESE □□□ FRENCH ▬▬ GERMAN ▬▬ RUSSIAN ══ SPANISH ▬▬ OTHER ──

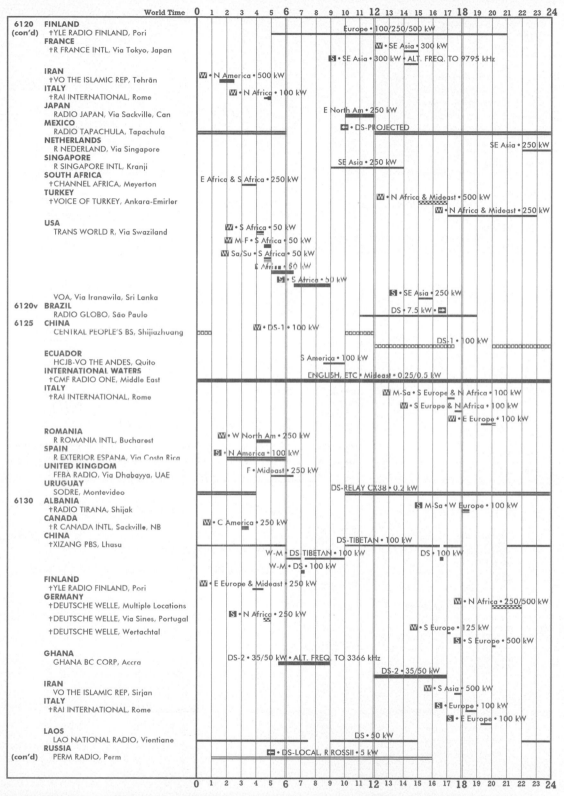

World Time 0 1 2 3 4 5 6 7 8 9 10 11 12 13 14 15 16 17 18 19 20 21 22 23 24

6120 **FINLAND**
(con'd) †YLE RADIO FINLAND, Pori — Europe • 100/250/500 kW
FRANCE
†R FRANCE INTL, Via Tokyo, Japan — W • SE Asia • 300 kW
— S • SE Asia • 300 kW • ALT. FREQ. TO 9795 kHz
IRAN
†VO THE ISLAMIC REP, Tehrān — W • N America • 500 kW
ITALY
†RAI INTERNATIONAL, Rome — W • N Africa • 100 kW
JAPAN
RADIO JAPAN, Via Sackville, Can — E North Am • 250 kW
MEXICO
RADIO TAPACHULA, Tapachula — DS-PROJECTED
NETHERLANDS
R NEDERLAND, Via Singapore — SE Asia • 250 kW
SINGAPORE
R SINGAPORE INTL, Kranji — SE Asia • 250 kW
SOUTH AFRICA
†CHANNEL AFRICA, Meyerton — E Africa & S Africa • 250 kW
TURKEY
†VOICE OF TURKEY, Ankara-Emirler — W • N Africa & Mideast • 500 kW
— W • N Africa & Mideast • 250 kW

USA
TRANS WORLD R, Via Swaziland — W • S Africa • 50 kW
— W M-F • S Africa • 50 kW
— W Sa/Su • S Africa • 50 kW
— S Africa • 50 kW
— S • S Africa • 50 kW

VOA, Via Iranawila, Sri Lanka — S • SE Asia • 250 kW
6120v **BRAZIL**
RADIO GLOBO, São Paulo — DS • 7.5 kW
6125 **CHINA**
CENTRAL PEOPLE'S BS, Shijiazhuang — W • DS-1 • 100 kW — DS-1 • 100 kW

ECUADOR
HCJB-VO THE ANDES, Quito — S America • 100 kW
INTERNATIONAL WATERS
†CMF RADIO ONE, Middle East — ENGLISH, ETC • Mideast • 0.25/0.5 kW
ITALY
†RAI INTERNATIONAL, Rome — W M-Sa • S Europe & N Africa • 100 kW
— W • S Europe & N Africa • 100 kW
— W • E Europe • 100 kW

ROMANIA
R ROMANIA INTL, Bucharest — W • W North Am • 250 kW
SPAIN
R EXTERIOR ESPANA, Via Costa Rica — S • N America • 100 kW
UNITED KINGDOM
FEBA RADIO, Via Dhabayya, UAE — F • Mideast • 250 kW
URUGUAY
SODRE, Montevideo — DS-RELAY CX38 • 0.2 kW
6130 **ALBANIA**
†RADIO TIRANA, Shijak — S M-Sa • W Europe • 100 kW
CANADA
†R CANADA INTL, Sackville, NB — W • C America • 250 kW
CHINA
†XIZANG PBS, Lhasa — DS-TIBETAN • 100 kW
— W-M • DS TIBETAN • 100 kW — DS • 100 kW
— W-M • DS • 100 kW

FINLAND
†YLE RADIO FINLAND, Pori — W • E Europe & Mideast • 250 kW
GERMANY
†DEUTSCHE WELLE, Multiple Locations — W • N Africa • 250/500 kW

†DEUTSCHE WELLE, Via Sines, Portugal — S • N Africa • 250 kW

†DEUTSCHE WELLE, Wertachtal — W • S Europe • 125 kW
— S • S Europe • 500 kW

GHANA
GHANA BC CORP, Accra — DS-2 • 35/50 kW • ALT. FREQ. TO 3366 kHz
— DS-2 • 35/50 kW

IRAN
VO THE ISLAMIC REP, Sirjan — W • S Asia • 500 kW
ITALY
†RAI INTERNATIONAL, Rome — S • Europe • 100 kW
— S • E Europe • 100 kW

LAOS
LAO NATIONAL RADIO, Vientiane — DS • 50 kW
RUSSIA
(con'd) PERM RADIO, Perm — DS-LOCAL, R ROSSII • 5 kW

0 1 2 3 4 5 6 7 8 9 10 11 12 13 14 15 16 17 18 19 20 21 22 23 24

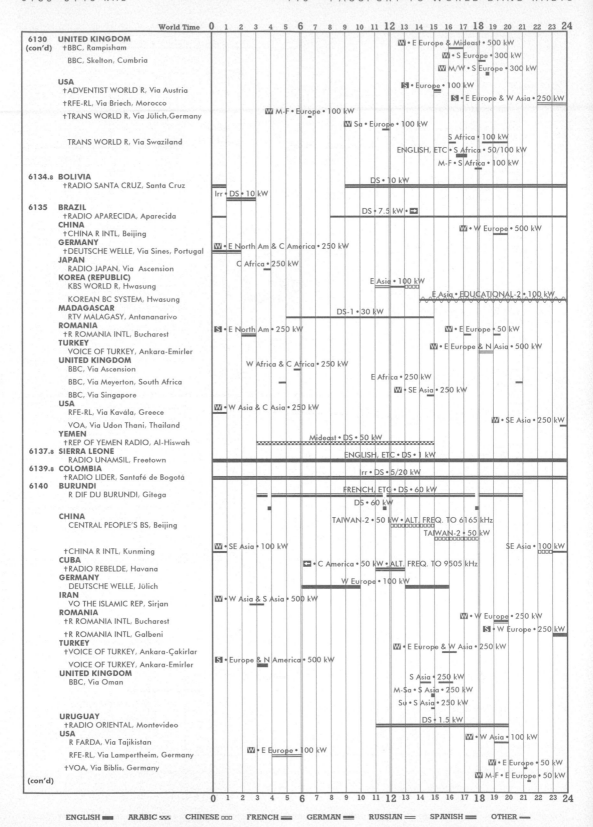

World Time 0 1 2 3 4 5 6 7 8 9 10 11 12 13 14 15 16 17 18 19 20 21 22 23 24

6130
(con'd)   UNITED KINGDOM
            †BBC, Rampisham — W • E Europe & Mideast • 500 kW

            BBC, Skelton, Cumbria — W • S Europe • 300 kW
                                     W M/W • S Europe • 300 kW

USA
            †ADVENTIST WORLD R, Via Austria — S • Europe • 100 kW
            †RFE-RL, Via Briech, Morocco — S • E Europe & W Asia • 250 kW
            †TRANS WORLD R, Via Jülich, Germany — W M-F • Europe • 100 kW
                                                   W Sa • Europe • 100 kW

            TRANS WORLD R, Via Swaziland — S Africa • 100 kW
                                            ENGLISH, ETC • S Africa • 50/100 kW
                                            M-F • S Africa • 100 kW

6134.8 BOLIVIA
            †RADIO SANTA CRUZ, Santa Cruz — DS • 10 kW
                                             Irr • DS • 10 kW

6135   BRAZIL
            †RADIO APARECIDA, Aparecida — DS • 7.5 kW •
CHINA
            †CHINA R INTL, Beijing — W • W Europe • 500 kW
GERMANY
            †DEUTSCHE WELLE, Via Sines, Portugal — W • E North Am & C America • 250 kW
JAPAN
            RADIO JAPAN, Via Ascension — C Africa • 250 kW
KOREA (REPUBLIC)
            KBS WORLD R, Hwasung — E Asia • 100 kW

            KOREAN BC SYSTEM, Hwasung — E Asia • EDUCATIONAL-2 • 100 kW
MADAGASCAR
            RTV MALAGASY, Antananarivo — DS-1 • 30 kW
ROMANIA
            †R ROMANIA INTL, Bucharest — S • E North Am • 250 kW
                                          W • E Europe • 50 kW
TURKEY
            VOICE OF TURKEY, Ankara-Emirler — W • E Europe & N Asia • 500 kW
UNITED KINGDOM
            BBC, Via Ascension — W Africa & C Africa • 250 kW

            BBC, Via Meyerton, South Africa — E Africa • 250 kW

            BBC, Via Singapore — W • SE Asia • 250 kW
USA
            RFE-RL, Via Kavála, Greece — W • W Asia & C Asia • 250 kW

            VOA, Via Udon Thani, Thailand — W • SE Asia • 250 kW
YEMEN
            †REP OF YEMEN RADIO, Al-Hiswah — Mideast • DS • 50 kW
6137.8 SIERRA LEONE
            RADIO UNAMSIL, Freetown — ENGLISH, ETC • DS • 1 kW
6139.8 COLOMBIA
            †RADIO LIDER, Santafé de Bogotá — Irr • DS • 5/20 kW
6140   BURUNDI
            R DIF DU BURUNDI, Gitega — FRENCH, ETC • DS • 60 kW
                                        DS • 60 kW

CHINA
            CENTRAL PEOPLE'S BS, Beijing — TAIWAN-2 • 50 kW • ALT. FREQ. TO 6165 kHz
                                            TAIWAN-2 • 50 kW

            †CHINA R INTL, Kunming — W • SE Asia • 100 kW
                                      SE Asia • 100 kW
CUBA
            †RADIO REBELDE, Havana — C America • 50 kW • ALT. FREQ. TO 9505 kHz
GERMANY
            DEUTSCHE WELLE, Jülich — W Europe • 100 kW
IRAN
            VO THE ISLAMIC REP, Sirjan — W • W Asia & S Asia • 500 kW
ROMANIA
            †R ROMANIA INTL, Bucharest — W • W Europe • 250 kW
                                          S • W Europe • 250 kW
            †R ROMANIA INTL, Galbeni — W • E Europe & W Asia • 250 kW
TURKEY
            †VOICE OF TURKEY, Ankara-Çakirlar — S • Europe & N America • 500 kW

            VOICE OF TURKEY, Ankara-Emirler — S Asia • 250 kW
UNITED KINGDOM
            BBC, Via Oman — M-Sa • S Asia • 250 kW
                            Su • S Asia • 250 kW

URUGUAY
            †RADIO ORIENTAL, Montevideo — DS • 1.5 kW
USA
            R FARDA, Via Tajikistan — W • W Asia • 100 kW

            RFE-RL, Via Lampertheim, Germany — W • E Europe • 100 kW

            †VOA, Via Biblis, Germany — W • E Europe • 50 kW
                                         W M-F • E Europe • 50 kW
(con'd)

World Time 0 1 2 3 4 5 6 7 8 9 10 11 12 13 14 15 16 17 18 19 20 21 22 23 24

ENGLISH ▬   ARABIC ▨   CHINESE ▫▫▫   FRENCH ═══   GERMAN ▬▬   RUSSIAN ══   SPANISH ══   OTHER ─

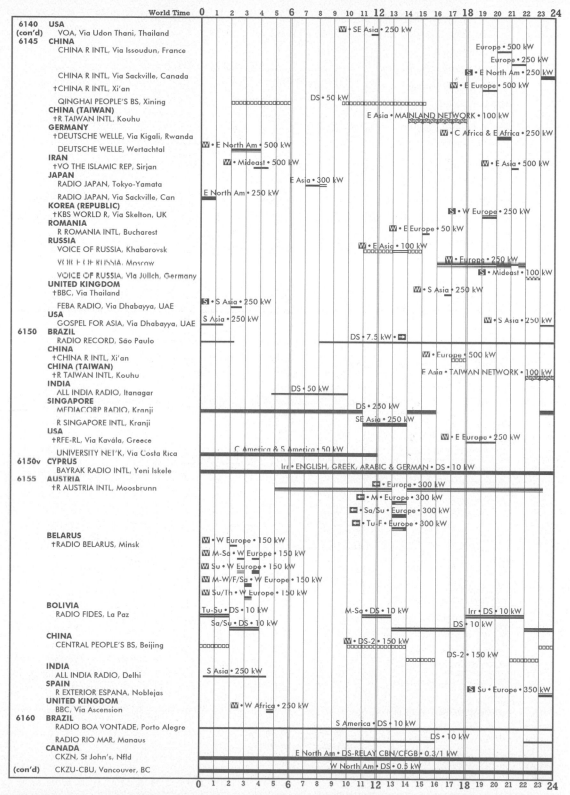

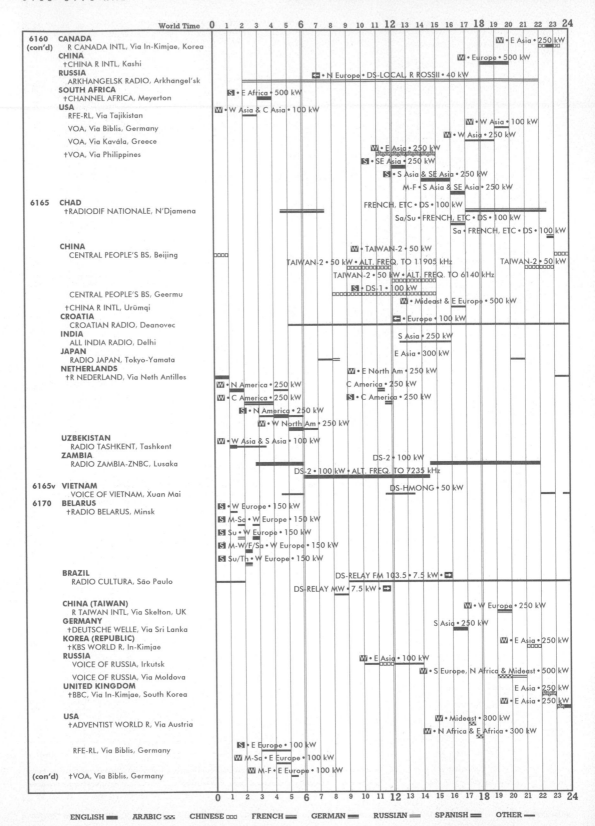

		World Time	0 1 2 3 4 5 6 7 8 9 10 11 12 13 14 15 16 17 18 19 20 21 22 23 24

6160
(con'd) **CANADA**
  R CANADA INTL, Via In-Kimjae, Korea — W • E Asia • 250 kW
CHINA
  †CHINA R INTL, Kashi — W • Europe • 500 kW
RUSSIA
  ARKHANGELSK RADIO, Arkhangel'sk — N Europe • DS-LOCAL, R ROSSII • 40 kW
SOUTH AFRICA
  †CHANNEL AFRICA, Meyerton — S • E Africa • 500 kW
USA
  RFE-RL, Via Tajikistan — W • W Asia & C Asia • 100 kW
  VOA, Via Biblis, Germany — W • W Asia • 100 kW
  VOA, Via Kavála, Greece — W • W Asia • 250 kW
  †VOA, Via Philippines — W • E Asia • 250 kW; S • SE Asia • 250 kW; S • S Asia & SE Asia • 250 kW; M-F • S Asia & SE Asia • 250 kW

6165 **CHAD**
  †RADIODIF NATIONALE, N'Djamena — FRENCH, ETC • DS • 100 kW; Sa/Su • FRENCH, ETC • DS • 100 kW; Sa • FRENCH, ETC • DS • 100 kW

CHINA
  CENTRAL PEOPLE'S BS, Beijing — W • TAIWAN-2 • 50 kW; TAIWAN-2 • 50 kW • ALT. FREQ. TO 11905 kHz; TAIWAN-2 • 50 kW • ALT. FREQ. TO 6140 kHz; TAIWAN-2 • 50 kW
  CENTRAL PEOPLE'S BS, Geermu — S • DS-1 • 100 kW
  †CHINA R INTL, Urümqi — W • Mideast & E Europe • 500 kW
CROATIA
  CROATIAN RADIO, Deanovec — Europe • 100 kW
INDIA
  ALL INDIA RADIO, Delhi — S Asia • 250 kW
JAPAN
  RADIO JAPAN, Tokyo-Yamata — E Asia • 300 kW
NETHERLANDS
  †R NEDERLAND, Via Neth Antilles — W • E North Am • 250 kW; W • N America • 250 kW; C America • 250 kW; W • C America • 250 kW; S • C America • 250 kW; S • N America • 250 kW; W • W North Am • 250 kW
UZBEKISTAN
  RADIO TASHKENT, Tashkent — W • W Asia & S Asia • 100 kW
ZAMBIA
  RADIO ZAMBIA-ZNBC, Lusaka — DS-2 • 100 kW; DS-2 • 100 kW • ALT. FREQ. TO 7235 kHz

6165v **VIETNAM**
  VOICE OF VIETNAM, Xuan Mai — DS-HMONG • 50 kW
6170 **BELARUS**
  †RADIO BELARUS, Minsk — S • W Europe • 150 kW; S • M-Sa • W Europe • 150 kW; S • Su • W Europe • 150 kW; S • M-W/F/Sa • W Europe • 150 kW; S • Su/Th • W Europe • 150 kW

BRAZIL
  RADIO CULTURA, São Paulo — DS-RELAY FM 103.5 • 7.5 kW; DS-RELAY MW • 7.5 kW

CHINA (TAIWAN)
  R TAIWAN INTL, Via Skelton, UK — W • W Europe • 250 kW
GERMANY
  †DEUTSCHE WELLE, Via Sri Lanka — S Asia • 250 kW
KOREA (REPUBLIC)
  †KBS WORLD R, In-Kimjae — W • E Asia • 250 kW
RUSSIA
  VOICE OF RUSSIA, Irkutsk — W • E Asia • 100 kW
  VOICE OF RUSSIA, Via Moldova — W • S Europe, N Africa & Mideast • 500 kW
UNITED KINGDOM
  †BBC, Via In-Kimjae, South Korea — E Asia • 250 kW; W • E Asia • 250 kW

USA
  †ADVENTIST WORLD R, Via Austria — W • Mideast • 300 kW; W • N Africa & E Africa • 300 kW
  RFE-RL, Via Biblis, Germany — S • E Europe • 100 kW; W • M-Sa • E Europe • 100 kW
(con'd) †VOA, Via Biblis, Germany — W • M-F • E Europe • 100 kW

		0 1 2 3 4 5 6 7 8 9 10 11 12 13 14 15 16 17 18 19 20 21 22 23 24

ENGLISH ▬   ARABIC ▨▨   CHINESE ▢▢▢   FRENCH ▬   GERMAN ▬   RUSSIAN ═   SPANISH ▬   OTHER ▬

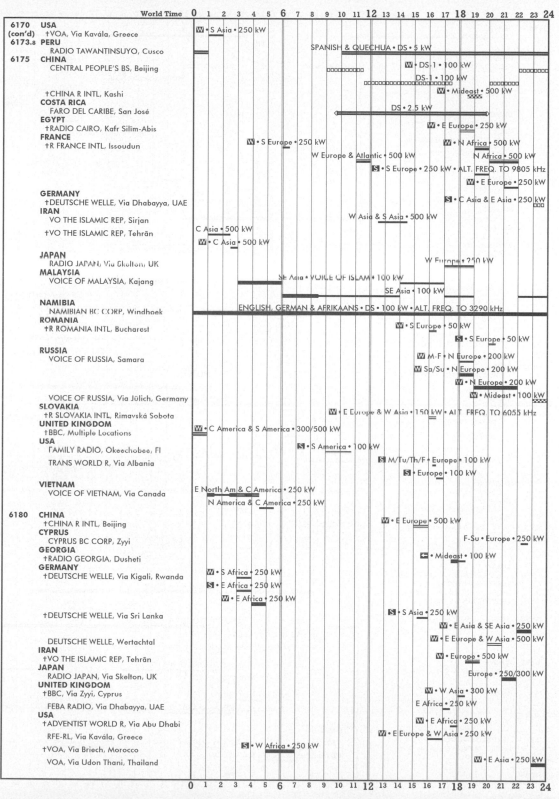

	World Time	0 1 2 3 4 5 6 7 8 9 10 11 12 13 14 15 16 17 18 19 20 21 22 23 24
6170 (con'd)	**USA** †VOA, Via Kavála, Greece	W • S Asia • 250 kW
6173.8	**PERU** RADIO TAWANTINSUYO, Cusco	SPANISH & QUECHUA • DS • 5 kW
6175	**CHINA** CENTRAL PEOPLE'S BS, Beijing	W • DS-1 • 100 kW DS-1 • 100 kW
	†CHINA R INTL, Kashi	W • Mideast • 500 kW
	COSTA RICA FARO DEL CARIBE, San José	DS • 2.5 kW
	EGYPT †RADIO CAIRO, Kafr Silīm-Abis	W • E Europe • 250 kW
	FRANCE †R FRANCE INTL, Issoudun	W • S Europe • 250 kW W • N Africa • 500 kW W Europe & Atlantic • 500 kW N Africa • 500 kW S • S Europe • 250 kW • ALT. FREQ. TO 9805 kHz W • E Europe • 250 kW
	GERMANY †DEUTSCHE WELLE, Via Dhabayya, UAE	S • C Asia & E Asia • 250 kW
	IRAN VO THE ISLAMIC REP, Sirjan	W Asia & S Asia • 500 kW
	†VO THE ISLAMIC REP, Tehrān	C Asia • 500 kW W • C Asia • 500 kW
	JAPAN RADIO JAPAN, Via Skelton, UK	W Europe • 250 kW
	MALAYSIA VOICE OF MALAYSIA, Kajang	SE Asia • VOICE OF ISLAM • 100 kW SE Asia • 100 kW
	NAMIBIA NAMIBIAN BC CORP, Windhoek	ENGLISH, GERMAN & AFRIKAANS • DS • 100 kW • ALT. FREQ. TO 3290 kHz
	ROMANIA †R ROMANIA INTL, Bucharest	W • S Europe • 50 kW S • S Europe • 50 kW
	RUSSIA VOICE OF RUSSIA, Samara	W • M-F • N Europe • 200 kW W • Sa/Su • N Europe • 200 kW W • N Europe • 200 kW
	VOICE OF RUSSIA, Via Jülich, Germany	W • Mideast • 100 kW
	SLOVAKIA †R SLOVAKIA INTL, Rimavská Sobota	W • E Europe & W Asia • 150 kW • ALT. FREQ. TO 6055 kHz
	UNITED KINGDOM †BBC, Multiple Locations	W • C America & S America • 300/500 kW
	USA FAMILY RADIO, Okeechobee, Fl	S • S America • 100 kW
	TRANS WORLD R, Via Albania	S • M/Tu/Th/F • Europe • 100 kW S • Europe • 100 kW
	VIETNAM VOICE OF VIETNAM, Via Canada	E North Am & C America • 250 kW N America & C America • 250 kW
6180	**CHINA** †CHINA R INTL, Beijing	W • E Europe • 500 kW
	CYPRUS CYPRUS BC CORP, Zyyi	F-Su • Europe • 250 kW
	GEORGIA †RADIO GEORGIA, Dusheti	← • Mideast • 100 kW
	GERMANY †DEUTSCHE WELLE, Via Kigali, Rwanda	W • S Africa • 250 kW S • E Africa • 250 kW W • E Africa • 250 kW
	†DEUTSCHE WELLE, Via Sri Lanka	S • S Asia • 250 kW
	DEUTSCHE WELLE, Wertachtal	W • E Asia & SE Asia • 250 kW W • E Europe & W Asia • 500 kW
	IRAN †VO THE ISLAMIC REP, Tehrān	W • Europe • 500 kW
	JAPAN RADIO JAPAN, Via Skelton, UK	Europe • 250/300 kW
	UNITED KINGDOM †BBC, Via Zyyi, Cyprus	W • W Asia • 300 kW
	FEBA RADIO, Via Dhabayya, UAE	E Africa • 250 kW
	USA †ADVENTIST WORLD R, Via Abu Dhabi	W • E Africa • 250 kW
	RFE-RL, Via Kavála, Greece	W • E Europe & W Asia • 250 kW
	†VOA, Via Briech, Morocco	S • W Africa • 250 kW
	VOA, Via Udon Thani, Thailand	W • E Asia • 250 kW

| | 0 1 2 3 4 5 6 7 8 9 10 11 12 13 14 15 16 17 18 19 20 21 22 23 24 |

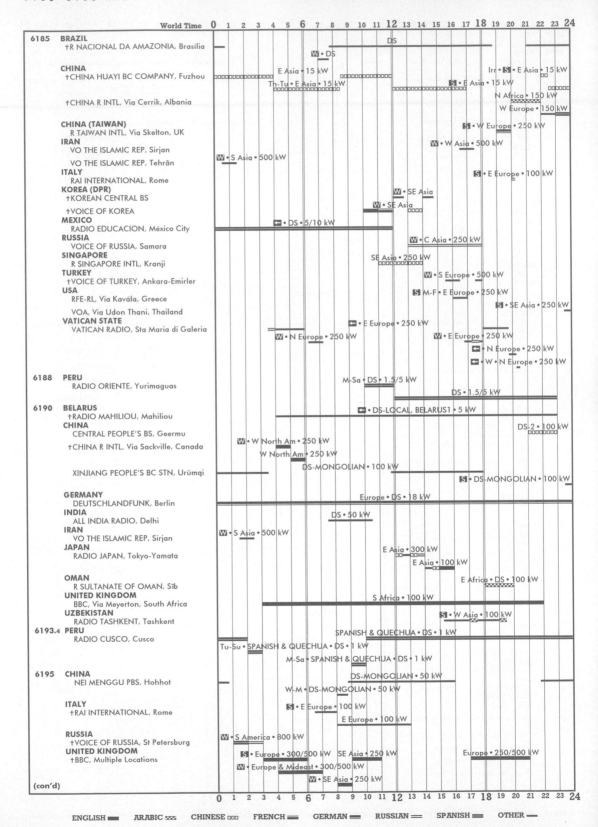

World Time 0 1 2 3 4 5 6 7 8 9 10 11 12 13 14 15 16 17 18 19 20 21 22 23 24

6185 BRAZIL
  †R NACIONAL DA AMAZONIA, Brasilia

CHINA
  †CHINA HUAYI BC COMPANY, Fuzhou

  †CHINA R INTL, Via Cerrik, Albania

CHINA (TAIWAN)
  R TAIWAN INTL, Via Skelton, UK
IRAN
  VO THE ISLAMIC REP, Sirjan

  VO THE ISLAMIC REP, Tehrān
ITALY
  RAI INTERNATIONAL, Rome
KOREA (DPR)
  †KOREAN CENTRAL BS

  †VOICE OF KOREA
MEXICO
  RADIO EDUCACION, México City
RUSSIA
  VOICE OF RUSSIA, Samara
SINGAPORE
  R SINGAPORE INTL, Kranji
TURKEY
  †VOICE OF TURKEY, Ankara-Emirler
USA
  RFE-RL, Via Kavála, Greece

  VOA, Via Udon Thani, Thailand
VATICAN STATE
  VATICAN RADIO, Sta Maria di Galeria

6188 PERU
  RADIO ORIENTE, Yurimaguas

6190 BELARUS
  †RADIO MAHILIOU, Mahiliou
CHINA
  CENTRAL PEOPLE'S BS, Geermu

  †CHINA R INTL, Via Sackville, Canada

  XINJIANG PEOPLE'S BC STN, Urümqi

GERMANY
  DEUTSCHLANDFUNK, Berlin
INDIA
  ALL INDIA RADIO, Delhi
IRAN
  VO THE ISLAMIC REP, Sirjan
JAPAN
  RADIO JAPAN, Tokyo-Yamata

OMAN
  R SULTANATE OF OMAN, Sīb
UNITED KINGDOM
  BBC, Via Meyerton, South Africa
UZBEKISTAN
  RADIO TASHKENT, Tashkent
6193.4 PERU
  RADIO CUSCO, Cusco

6195 CHINA
  NEI MENGGU PBS, Hohhot

ITALY
  †RAI INTERNATIONAL, Rome

RUSSIA
  †VOICE OF RUSSIA, St Petersburg
UNITED KINGDOM
  †BBC, Multiple Locations

(con'd)

0 1 2 3 4 5 6 7 8 9 10 11 12 13 14 15 16 17 18 19 20 21 22 23 24

ENGLISH ▬ ARABIC ⧉ CHINESE ⌷⌷⌷ FRENCH ▬ GERMAN ▬ RUSSIAN ══ SPANISH ══ OTHER ▬

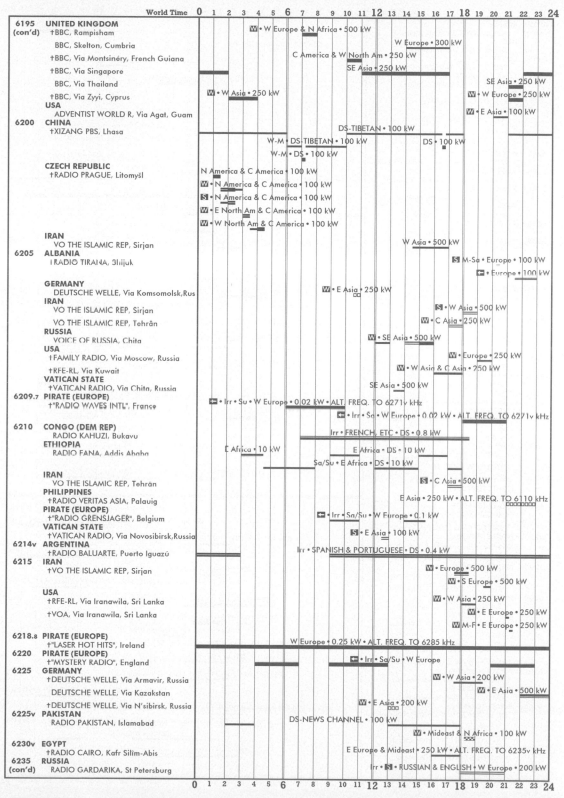

World Time 0 1 2 3 4 5 6 7 8 9 10 11 12 13 14 15 16 17 18 19 20 21 22 23 24

6195 UNITED KINGDOM
(con'd) †BBC, Rampisham — W • W Europe & N Africa • 500 kW

BBC, Skelton, Cumbria — W Europe • 300 kW

†BBC, Via Montsinéry, French Guiana — C America & W North Am • 250 kW

†BBC, Via Singapore — SE Asia • 250 kW

BBC, Via Thailand — SE Asia • 250 kW

†BBC, Via Zyyi, Cyprus — W • W Asia • 250 kW   W • W Europe • 250 kW

USA
ADVENTIST WORLD R, Via Agat, Guam — W • E Asia • 100 kW

6200 CHINA
†XIZANG PBS, Lhasa — DS-TIBETAN • 100 kW
— W-M • DS-TIBETAN • 100 kW   DS • 100 kW
— W-M • DS • 100 kW

CZECH REPUBLIC
†RADIO PRAGUE, Litomyšl — N America & C America • 100 kW
— W • N America & C America • 100 kW
— S • N America & C America • 100 kW
— W • E North Am & C America • 100 kW
— W • W North Am & C America • 100 kW

IRAN
VO THE ISLAMIC REP, Sirjan — W Asia • 500 kW

6205 ALBANIA
†RADIO TIRANA, Shijak — S • M-Sa • Europe • 100 kW
— • Europe • 100 kW

GERMANY
DEUTSCHE WELLE, Via Komsomolsk, Rus — W • E Asia • 250 kW

IRAN
VO THE ISLAMIC REP, Sirjan — S • W Asia • 500 kW

VO THE ISLAMIC REP, Tehrän — W • C Asia • 250 kW

RUSSIA
VOICE OF RUSSIA, Chita — W • SE Asia • 500 kW

USA
†FAMILY RADIO, Via Moscow, Russia — W • Europe • 250 kW

†RFE-RL, Via Kuwait — W • W Asia & C Asia • 250 kW

VATICAN STATE
†VATICAN RADIO, Via Chita, Russia — SE Asia • 500 kW

6209.7 PIRATE (EUROPE)
†"RADIO WAVES INTL", France — • Irr • Su • W Europe • 0.02 kW • ALT. FREQ. TO 6271v kHz
— • Irr • Sa • W Europe • 0.02 kW • ALT. FREQ. TO 6271v kHz

6210 CONGO (DEM REP)
RADIO KAHUZI, Bukavu — Irr • FRENCH, ETC • DS • 0.8 kW

ETHIOPIA
RADIO FANA, Addis Ababa — E Africa • 10 kW
— E Africa • DS • 10 kW
— Sa/Su • E Africa • DS • 10 kW

IRAN
VO THE ISLAMIC REP, Tehrän — S • C Asia • 500 kW

PHILIPPINES
†RADIO VERITAS ASIA, Palauig — E Asia • 250 kW • ALT. FREQ. TO 6110 kHz

PIRATE (EUROPE)
†"RADIO GRENSJAGER", Belgium — • Irr • Sa/Su • W Europe • 0.1 kW

VATICAN STATE
†VATICAN RADIO, Via Novosibirsk, Russia — S • E Asia • 100 kW

6214v ARGENTINA
†RADIO BALUARTE, Puerto Iguazú — Irr • SPANISH & PORTUGUESE • DS • 0.4 kW

6215 IRAN
†VO THE ISLAMIC REP, Sirjan — W • Europe • 500 kW
— W • S Europe • 500 kW

USA
†RFE-RL, Via Iranawila, Sri Lanka — W • W Asia • 250 kW

†VOA, Via Iranawila, Sri Lanka — W • E Europe • 250 kW
— W • M-F • E Europe • 250 kW

6218.8 PIRATE (EUROPE)
†"LASER HOT HITS", Ireland — W Europe • 0.25 kW • ALT. FREQ. TO 6285 kHz

6220 PIRATE (EUROPE)
†"MYSTERY RADIO", England — • Irr • Sa/Su • W Europe

6225 GERMANY
†DEUTSCHE WELLE, Via Armavir, Russia — W • W Asia • 200 kW

DEUTSCHE WELLE, Via Kazakstan — W • E Asia • 500 kW

†DEUTSCHE WELLE, Via N'sibirsk, Russia — W • E Asia • 200 kW

6225v PAKISTAN
RADIO PAKISTAN, Islamabad — DS-NEWS CHANNEL • 100 kW
— W • Mideast & N Africa • 100 kW

6230v EGYPT
†RADIO CAIRO, Kafr Silïm-Abis — E Europe & Mideast • 250 kW • ALT. FREQ. TO 6235v kHz

6235 RUSSIA
(con'd) RADIO GARDARIKA, St Petersburg — Irr • S • RUSSIAN & ENGLISH • W Europe • 200 kW

0 1 2 3 4 5 6 7 8 9 10 11 12 13 14 15 16 17 18 19 20 21 22 23 24

SEASONAL S OR W   1-HR TIMESHIFT MIDYEAR ⊏ OR ⊐   JAMMING / OR ∧   EARLIEST HEARD ◁   LATEST HEARD ▷   NEW FOR 2006 †

World Time: 0 1 2 3 4 5 6 7 8 9 10 11 12 13 14 15 16 17 18 19 20 21 22 23 24

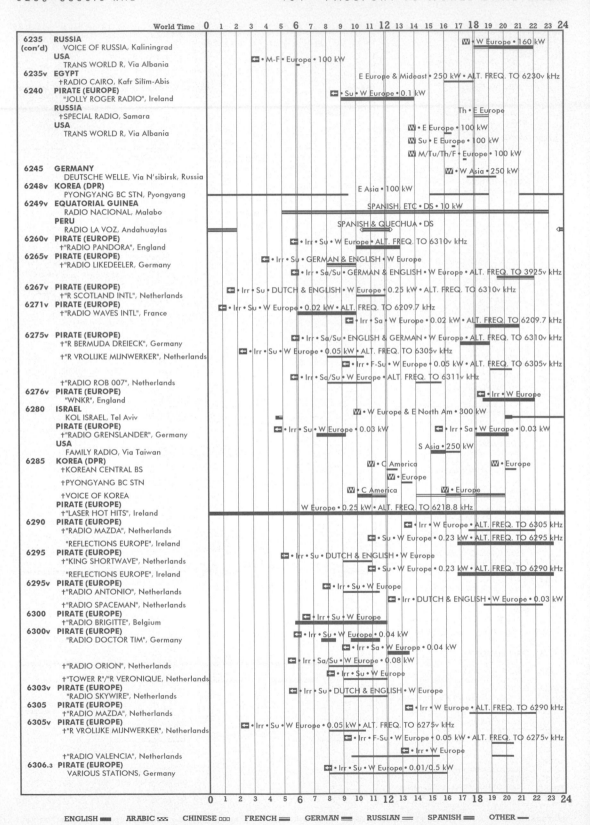

- **6235 (con'd) RUSSIA** — VOICE OF RUSSIA, Kaliningrad — W • W Europe • 160 kW
- **USA** — TRANS WORLD R, Via Albania — M-F • Europe • 100 kW
- **6235v EGYPT** — †RADIO CAIRO, Kafr Silim-Abis — E Europe & Mideast • 250 kW • ALT. FREQ. TO 6230v kHz
- **6240 PIRATE (EUROPE)** — "JOLLY ROGER RADIO", Ireland — Su • W Europe • 0.1 kW
- **RUSSIA** — †SPECIAL RADIO, Samara — Th • E Europe
- **USA** — TRANS WORLD R, Via Albania — W • E Europe • 100 kW / W Su • E Europe • 100 kW / W M/Tu/Th/F • Europe • 100 kW
- **6245 GERMANY** — DEUTSCHE WELLE, Via N'sibirsk, Russia — W • W Asia • 250 kW
- **6248v KOREA (DPR)** — PYONGYANG BC STN, Pyongyang — E Asia • 100 kW
- **6249v EQUATORIAL GUINEA** — RADIO NACIONAL, Malabo — SPANISH, ETC • DS • 10 kW
- **PERU** — RADIO LA VOZ, Andahuaylas — SPANISH & QUECHUA • DS
- **6260v PIRATE (EUROPE)** — †"RADIO PANDORA", England — Irr • Su • W Europe • ALT. FREQ. TO 6310v kHz
- **6265v PIRATE (EUROPE)** — †"RADIO LIKEDEELER", Germany — Irr • Su • GERMAN & ENGLISH • W Europe / Irr • Sa/Su • GERMAN & ENGLISH • W Europe • ALT. FREQ. TO 3925v kHz
- **6267v PIRATE (EUROPE)** — †"R SCOTLAND INTL", Netherlands — Irr • Su • DUTCH & ENGLISH • W Europe • 0.25 kW • ALT. FREQ. TO 6310v kHz
- **6271v PIRATE (EUROPE)** — †"RADIO WAVES INTL", France — Irr • Su • W Europe • 0.02 kW • ALT. FREQ. TO 6209.7 kHz / Irr • Sa • W Europe • 0.02 kW • ALT. FREQ. TO 6209.7 kHz
- **6275v PIRATE (EUROPE)** — †"R BERMUDA DREIECK", Germany — Irr • Sa/Su • ENGLISH & GERMAN • W Europe • ALT. FREQ. TO 6310v kHz
- †"R VROLIJKE MIJNWERKER", Netherlands — Irr • Su • W Europe • 0.05 kW • ALT. FREQ. TO 6305v kHz / Irr • F-Su • W Europe • 0.05 kW • ALT. FREQ. TO 6305v kHz
- †"RADIO ROB 007", Netherlands — Irr • Sa/Su • W Europe • ALT. FREQ. TO 6311v kHz
- **6276v PIRATE (EUROPE)** — "WNKR", England — Irr • W Europe
- **6280 ISRAEL** — KOL ISRAEL, Tel Aviv — W • W Europe & E North Am • 300 kW
- **PIRATE (EUROPE)** — †"RADIO GRENSLANDER", Germany — Irr • Su • W Europe • 0.03 kW / Irr • Sa • W Europe • 0.03 kW
- **USA** — FAMILY RADIO, Via Taiwan — S Asia • 250 kW
- **6285 KOREA (DPR)** — †KOREAN CENTRAL BS — W • C America / W • Europe
- †PYONGYANG BC STN — W • Europe
- †VOICE OF KOREA — W • C America / W • Europe
- **PIRATE (EUROPE)** — †"LASER HOT HITS", Ireland — W Europe • 0.25 kW • ALT. FREQ. TO 6218.8 kHz
- **6290 PIRATE (EUROPE)** — †"RADIO MAZDA", Netherlands — Irr • W Europe • ALT. FREQ. TO 6305 kHz
- "REFLECTIONS EUROPE", Ireland — Su • W Europe • 0.23 kW • ALT. FREQ. TO 6295 kHz
- **6295 PIRATE (EUROPE)** — †"KING SHORTWAVE", Netherlands — Irr • Su • DUTCH & ENGLISH • W Europe
- "REFLECTIONS EUROPE", Ireland — Su • W Europe • 0.23 kW • ALT. FREQ. TO 6290 kHz
- **6295v PIRATE (EUROPE)** — †"RADIO ANTONIO", Netherlands — Irr • Su • W Europe
- †"RADIO SPACEMAN", Netherlands — Irr • DUTCH & ENGLISH • W Europe • 0.03 kW
- **6300 PIRATE (EUROPE)** — †"RADIO BRIGITTE", Belgium — Irr • Su • Europe
- **6300v PIRATE (EUROPE)** — "RADIO DOCTOR TIM", Germany — Irr • Su • W Europe • 0.04 kW / Irr • Sa • W Europe • 0.04 kW
- †"RADIO ORION", Netherlands — Irr • Sa/Su • W Europe • 0.08 kW
- †"TOWER R"/"R VERONIQUE, Netherlands — Irr • Su • W Europe
- **6303v PIRATE (EUROPE)** — "RADIO SKYWIRE", Netherlands — Irr • Su • DUTCH & ENGLISH • W Europe
- **6305 PIRATE (EUROPE)** — †"RADIO MAZDA", Netherlands — Irr • W Europe • ALT. FREQ. TO 6290 kHz
- **6305v PIRATE (EUROPE)** — †"R VROLIJKE MIJNWERKER", Netherlands — Irr • Su • W Europe • 0.05 kW • ALT. FREQ. TO 6275v kHz / Irr • F-Su • W Europe • 0.05 kW • ALT. FREQ. TO 6275v kHz
- †"RADIO VALENCIA", Netherlands — Irr • W Europe
- **6306.3 PIRATE (EUROPE)** — VARIOUS STATIONS, Germany — Irr • Su • W Europe • 0.01/0.5 kW

ENGLISH ▬ ARABIC ▨ CHINESE ▭▭▭ FRENCH ▬▬ GERMAN ▬ RUSSIAN ══ SPANISH ═ OTHER ▬

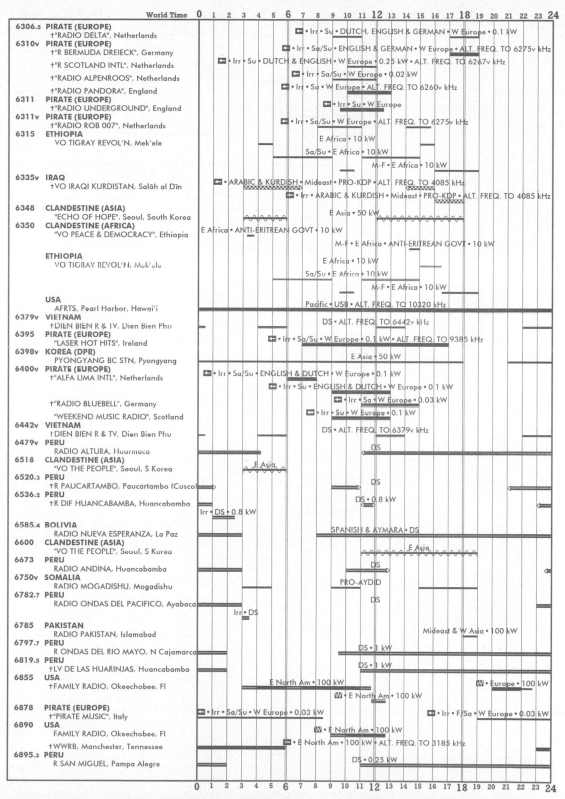

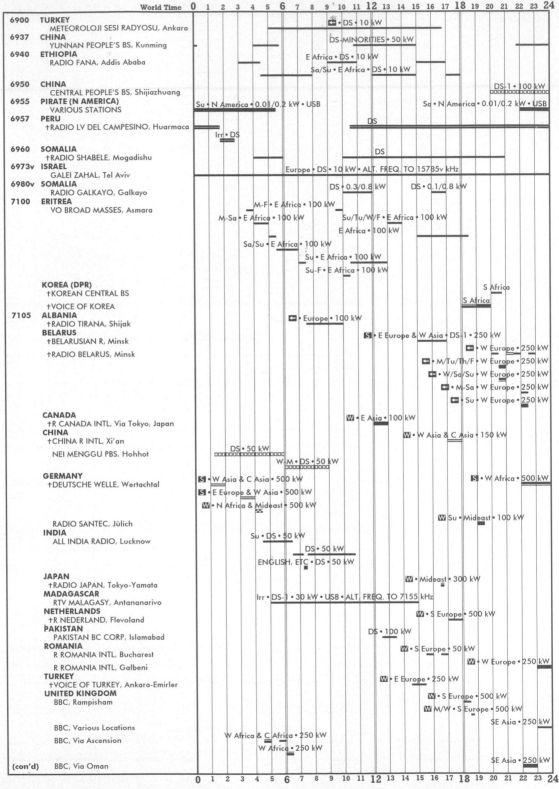

World Time			
6900	**TURKEY**	METEOROLOJI SESI RADYOSU, Ankara	DS • 10 kW
6937	**CHINA**	YUNNAN PEOPLE'S BS, Kunming	DS-MINORITIES • 50 kW
6940	**ETHIOPIA**	RADIO FANA, Addis Ababa	E Africa • DS • 10 kW / Sa/Su • E Africa • DS • 10 kW
6950	**CHINA**	CENTRAL PEOPLE'S BS, Shijiazhuang	DS-1 • 100 kW
6955	**PIRATE (N AMERICA)**	VARIOUS STATIONS	Su • N America • 0.01/0.2 kW • USB / Sa • N America • 0.01/0.2 kW • USB
6957	**PERU**	†RADIO LV DEL CAMPESINO, Huarmaca	DS / Irr • DS
6960	**SOMALIA**	†RADIO SHABELE, Mogadishu	DS
6973v	**ISRAEL**	GALEI ZAHAL, Tel Aviv	Europe • DS • 10 kW • ALT. FREQ. TO 15785v kHz
6980v	**SOMALIA**	RADIO GALKAYO, Galkayo	DS • 0.3/0.8 kW / DS • 0.1/0.8 kW
7100	**ERITREA**	VO BROAD MASSES, Asmara	M-F • E Africa • 100 kW / M-Sa • E Africa • 100 kW / Su/Tu/W/F • E Africa • 100 kW / E Africa • 100 kW / Sa/Su • E Africa • 100 kW / Su • E Africa • 100 kW / Su-F • E Africa • 100 kW
	KOREA (DPR)	†KOREAN CENTRAL BS	
		†VOICE OF KOREA	S Africa / S Africa
7105	**ALBANIA**	†RADIO TIRANA, Shijak	• Europe • 100 kW
	BELARUS	†BELARUSIAN R, Minsk	• E Europe & W Asia • DS-1 • 250 kW
		†RADIO BELARUS, Minsk	• W Europe • 250 kW / • M/Tu/Th/F • W Europe • 250 kW / • W/Sa/Su • W Europe • 250 kW / • M-Sa • W Europe • 250 kW / • Su • W Europe • 250 kW
	CANADA	†R CANADA INTL, Via Tokyo, Japan	W • E Asia • 100 kW
	CHINA	†CHINA R INTL, Xi'an	W • W Asia & C Asia • 150 kW
		NEI MENGGU PBS, Hohhot	DS • 50 kW / W-M • DS • 50 kW
	GERMANY	†DEUTSCHE WELLE, Wertachtal	S • W Asia & C Asia • 500 kW / S • E Europe & W Asia • 500 kW / W • N Africa & Mideast • 500 kW / S • W Africa • 500 kW / W Su • Mideast • 100 kW
		RADIO SANTEC, Jülich	
	INDIA	ALL INDIA RADIO, Lucknow	Su • DS • 50 kW / DS • 50 kW / ENGLISH, ETC • DS • 50 kW
	JAPAN	†RADIO JAPAN, Tokyo-Yamata	W • Mideast • 300 kW
	MADAGASCAR	RTV MALAGASY, Antananarivo	Irr • DS-1 • 30 kW • USB • ALT. FREQ. TO 7155 kHz
	NETHERLANDS	†R NEDERLAND, Flevoland	W • S Europe • 500 kW
	PAKISTAN	PAKISTAN BC CORP, Islamabad	DS • 100 kW
	ROMANIA	R ROMANIA INTL, Bucharest	W • S Europe • 50 kW
		R ROMANIA INTL, Galbeni	W • W Europe • 250 kW
	TURKEY	†VOICE OF TURKEY, Ankara-Emirler	W • E Europe • 250 kW
	UNITED KINGDOM	BBC, Rampisham	W • S Europe • 500 kW / W M/W • S Europe • 500 kW / SE Asia • 250 kW
		BBC, Various Locations	W Africa & C Africa • 250 kW
		BBC, Via Ascension	W Africa • 250 kW
(con'd)		BBC, Via Oman	SE Asia • 250 kW

ENGLISH ▬   ARABIC ⠶⠶⠶   CHINESE ▫▫▫   FRENCH ═══   GERMAN ▬▬   RUSSIAN ══   SPANISH ═══   OTHER ▬

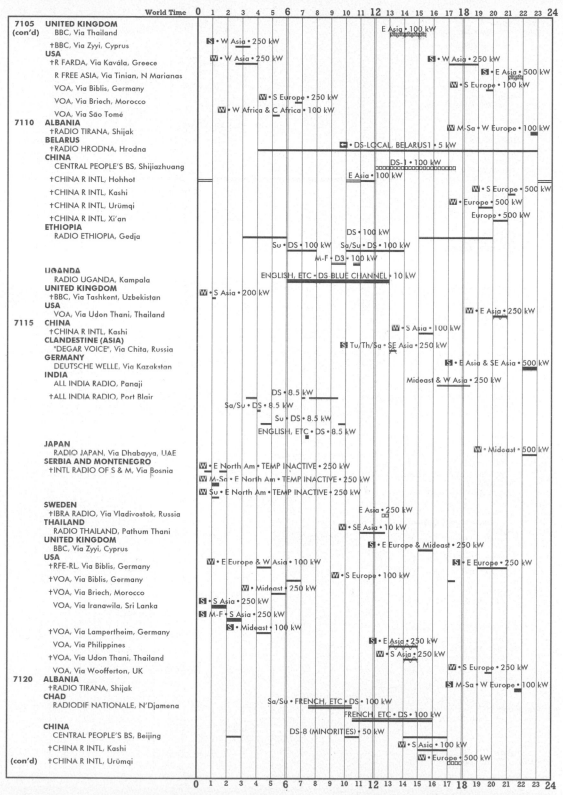

World Time

7105 UNITED KINGDOM (con'd)
BBC, Via Thailand — E Asia • 100 kW
†BBC, Via Zyyi, Cyprus — S • W Asia • 250 kW
USA
†R FARDA, Via Kavála, Greece — W • W Asia • 250 kW ; S • W Asia • 250 kW
R FREE ASIA, Via Tinian, N Marianas — S • E Asia • 500 kW
VOA, Via Biblis, Germany — W • S Europe • 100 kW
VOA, Via Briech, Morocco — W • S Europe • 250 kW
VOA, Via São Tomé — W • W Africa & C Africa • 100 kW

7110 ALBANIA
†RADIO TIRANA, Shijak — W M-Sa • W Europe • 100 kW
BELARUS
†RADIO HRODNA, Hrodna — DS-LOCAL, BELARUS1 • 5 kW
CHINA
CENTRAL PEOPLE'S BS, Shijiazhuang — DS-1 • 100 kW
†CHINA R INTL, Hohhot — E Asia • 100 kW
†CHINA R INTL, Kashi — W • S Europe • 500 kW
†CHINA R INTL, Urümqi — W • Europe • 500 kW
†CHINA R INTL, Xi'an — Europe • 500 kW
ETHIOPIA
RADIO ETHIOPIA, Gedja — DS • 100 kW ; Su • DS • 100 kW ; Sa/Su • DS • 100 kW ; M-F • D3 • 100 kW
UGANDA
RADIO UGANDA, Kampala — ENGLISH, ETC • DS-BLUE CHANNEL • 10 kW
UNITED KINGDOM
†BBC, Via Tashkent, Uzbekistan — W • S Asia • 200 kW
USA
VOA, Via Udon Thani, Thailand — W • E Asia • 250 kW

7115 CHINA
†CHINA R INTL, Kashi — W • S Asia • 100 kW
CLANDESTINE (ASIA)
"DEGAR VOICE", Via Chita, Russia — S Tu/Th/Sa • SE Asia • 250 kW
GERMANY
DEUTSCHE WELLE, Via Kazakstan — S • E Asia & SE Asia • 500 kW
INDIA
ALL INDIA RADIO, Panaji — Mideast & W Asia • 250 kW
†ALL INDIA RADIO, Port Blair — DS • 8.5 kW ; Sa/Su • DS • 8.5 kW ; Su • DS • 8.5 kW ; ENGLISH, ETC • DS • 8.5 kW
JAPAN
RADIO JAPAN, Via Dhabayya, UAE — W • Mideast • 500 kW
SERBIA AND MONTENEGRO
†INTL RADIO OF S & M, Via Bosnia — W • E North Am • TEMP INACTIVE • 250 kW ; W M-Sa • E North Am • TEMP INACTIVE • 250 kW ; W Su • E North Am • TEMP INACTIVE • 250 kW
SWEDEN
†IBRA RADIO, Via Vladivostok, Russia — E Asia • 250 kW
THAILAND
RADIO THAILAND, Pathum Thani — W • SE Asia • 10 kW
UNITED KINGDOM
BBC, Via Zyyi, Cyprus — S • E Europe & Mideast • 250 kW
USA
†RFE-RL, Via Biblis, Germany — W • E Europe & W Asia • 100 kW ; S • E Europe • 250 kW
†VOA, Via Biblis, Germany — W • S Europe • 100 kW
†VOA, Via Briech, Morocco — W • Mideast • 250 kW
VOA, Via Iranawila, Sri Lanka — S • S Asia • 250 kW ; S M-F • S Asia • 250 kW
†VOA, Via Lampertheim, Germany — S • Mideast • 100 kW
VOA, Via Philippines — S • E Asia • 250 kW
†VOA, Via Udon Thani, Thailand — W • S Asia • 250 kW
VOA, Via Woofferton, UK — W • S Europe • 250 kW

7120 ALBANIA
†RADIO TIRANA, Shijak — S M-Sa • W Europe • 100 kW
CHAD
RADIODIF NATIONALE, N'Djamena — Sa/Su • FRENCH, ETC • DS • 100 kW ; FRENCH, ETC • DS • 100 kW
CHINA
CENTRAL PEOPLE'S BS, Beijing — DS-8 (MINORITIES) • 50 kW
†CHINA R INTL, Kashi — W • S Asia • 100 kW
(con'd) †CHINA R INTL, Urümqi — W • Europe • 500 kW

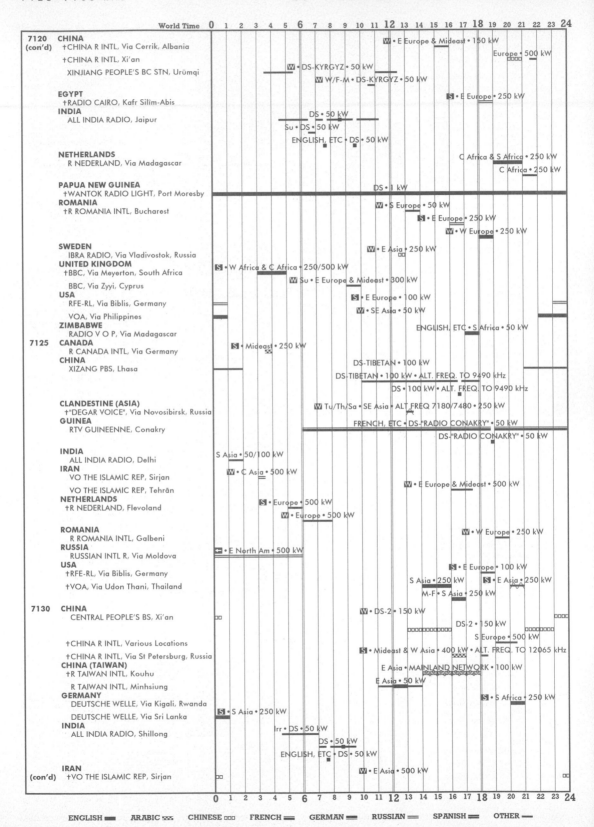

	World Time	0 1 2 3 4 5 6 7 8 9 10 11 12 13 14 15 16 17 18 19 20 21 22 23 24

7120 (con'd) CHINA
†CHINA R INTL, Via Cerrik, Albania — W • E Europe & Mideast • 150 kW
†CHINA R INTL, Xi'an — Europe • 500 kW
XINJIANG PEOPLE'S BC STN, Urümqi — W • DS-KYRGYZ • 50 kW / W W/F-M • DS-KYRGYZ • 50 kW

EGYPT
†RADIO CAIRO, Kafr Silîm-Abis — S • E Europe • 250 kW

INDIA
ALL INDIA RADIO, Jaipur — DS • 50 kW / Su • DS • 50 kW / ENGLISH, ETC • DS • 50 kW

NETHERLANDS
R NEDERLAND, Via Madagascar — C Africa & S Africa • 250 kW / C Africa • 250 kW

PAPUA NEW GUINEA
†WANTOK RADIO LIGHT, Port Moresby — DS • 1 kW

ROMANIA
†R ROMANIA INTL, Bucharest — W • S Europe • 50 kW / S • E Europe • 250 kW / W • W Europe • 250 kW

SWEDEN
IBRA RADIO, Via Vladivostok, Russia — W • E Asia • 250 kW

UNITED KINGDOM
†BBC, Via Meyerton, South Africa — S • W Africa & C Africa • 250/500 kW
BBC, Via Zyyi, Cyprus — W Su • E Europe & Mideast • 300 kW

USA
RFE-RL, Via Biblis, Germany — S • E Europe • 100 kW
VOA, Via Philippines — W • SE Asia • 50 kW

ZIMBABWE
RADIO V O P, Via Madagascar — ENGLISH, ETC • S Africa • 50 kW

7125 CANADA
R CANADA INTL, Via Germany — S • Mideast • 250 kW

CHINA
XIZANG PBS, Lhasa — DS-TIBETAN • 100 kW / DS-TIBETAN • 100 kW • ALT. FREQ. TO 9490 kHz / DS • 100 kW • ALT. FREQ. TO 9490 kHz

CLANDESTINE (ASIA)
†"DEGAR VOICE", Via Novosibirsk, Russia — W Tu/Th/Sa • SE Asia • ALT FREQ 7180/7480 • 250 kW

GUINEA
RTV GUINEENNE, Conakry — FRENCH, ETC • DS-"RADIO CONAKRY" • 50 kW / DS-"RADIO CONAKRY" • 50 kW

INDIA
ALL INDIA RADIO, Delhi — S Asia • 50/100 kW

IRAN
VO THE ISLAMIC REP, Sirjan — W • C Asia • 500 kW
VO THE ISLAMIC REP, Tehrãn — W • E Europe & Mideast • 500 kW

NETHERLANDS
†R NEDERLAND, Flevoland — S • Europe • 500 kW / W • Europe • 500 kW

ROMANIA
R ROMANIA INTL, Galbeni — W • W Europe • 250 kW

RUSSIA
RUSSIAN INTL R, Via Moldova — S • E North Am • 500 kW

USA
†RFE-RL, Via Biblis, Germany — S • E Europe • 100 kW
†VOA, Via Udon Thani, Thailand — S Asia • 250 kW / S • E Asia • 250 kW / M-F • S Asia • 250 kW

7130 CHINA
CENTRAL PEOPLE'S BS, Xi'an — W • DS-2 • 150 kW / DS-2 • 150 kW / S Europe • 500 kW
†CHINA R INTL, Various Locations — S • Mideast & W Asia • 400 kW • ALT. FREQ. TO 12065 kHz
†CHINA R INTL, Via St Petersburg, Russia

CHINA (TAIWAN)
†R TAIWAN INTL, Kouhu — E Asia • MAINLAND NETWORK • 100 kW
R TAIWAN INTL, Minhsiung — E Asia • 50 kW

GERMANY
DEUTSCHE WELLE, Via Kigali, Rwanda — S • S Africa • 250 kW
DEUTSCHE WELLE, Via Sri Lanka — S • S Asia • 250 kW

INDIA
ALL INDIA RADIO, Shillong — Irr • DS • 50 kW / DS • 50 kW / ENGLISH, ETC • DS • 50 kW

(con'd) IRAN
†VO THE ISLAMIC REP, Sirjan — W • E Asia • 500 kW

	0 1 2 3 4 5 6 7 8 9 10 11 12 13 14 15 16 17 18 19 20 21 22 23 24

ENGLISH ▬   ARABIC ▨   CHINESE ▯▯▯   FRENCH ▬   GERMAN ▬   RUSSIAN ═   SPANISH ═   OTHER ▬

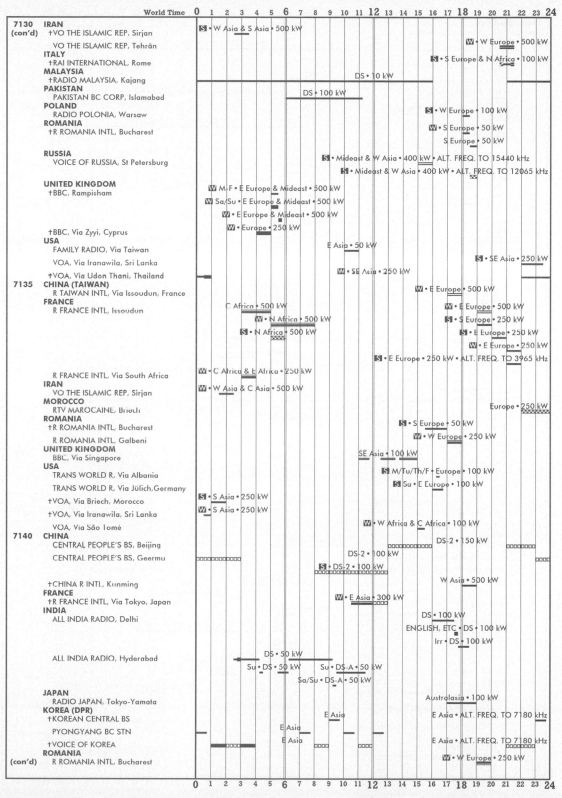

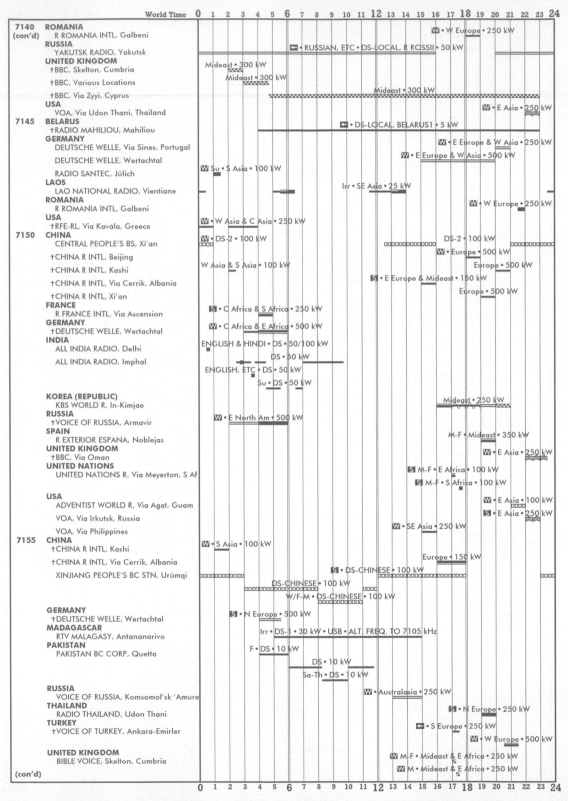

World Time 0 1 2 3 4 5 6 7 8 9 10 11 12 13 14 15 16 17 18 19 20 21 22 23 24

7140 **ROMANIA**
(con'd) R ROMANIA INTL, Galbeni — W • W Europe • 250 kW
RUSSIA
YAKUTSK RADIO, Yakutsk — RUSSIAN, ETC • DS-LOCAL, R ROSSII • 50 kW
UNITED KINGDOM
†BBC, Skelton, Cumbria — Mideast • 300 kW
†BBC, Various Locations — Mideast • 300 kW
†BBC, Via Zyyi, Cyprus — Mideast • 300 kW
USA
VOA, Via Udon Thani, Thailand — W • E Asia • 250 kW

7145 **BELARUS**
†RADIO MAHILIOU, Mahiliou — DS-LOCAL, BELARUS1 • 5 kW
GERMANY
DEUTSCHE WELLE, Via Sines, Portugal — W • E Europe & W Asia • 250 kW
DEUTSCHE WELLE, Wertachtal — W • E Europe & W Asia • 500 kW
RADIO SANTEC, Jülich — W Su • S Asia • 100 kW
LAOS
LAO NATIONAL RADIO, Vientiane — Irr • SE Asia • 25 kW
ROMANIA
R ROMANIA INTL, Galbeni — W • W Europe • 250 kW
USA
†RFE-RL, Via Kavála, Greece — W • W Asia & C Asia • 250 kW

7150 **CHINA**
CENTRAL PEOPLE'S BS, Xi'an — W • DS-2 • 100 kW / DS-2 • 100 kW
†CHINA R INTL, Beijing — W • Europe • 500 kW
†CHINA R INTL, Kashi — W Asia & S Asia • 100 kW / Europe • 500 kW
†CHINA R INTL, Via Cerrik, Albania — S • E Europe & Mideast • 150 kW
†CHINA R INTL, Xi'an — Europe • 500 kW
FRANCE
R FRANCE INTL, Via Ascension — S • C Africa & S Africa • 250 kW
GERMANY
†DEUTSCHE WELLE, Wertachtal — W • C Africa & E Africa • 500 kW
INDIA
ALL INDIA RADIO, Delhi — ENGLISH & HINDI • DS • 50/100 kW
ALL INDIA RADIO, Imphal — DS • 50 kW / ENGLISH, ETC • DS • 50 kW / Su • DS • 50 kW
KOREA (REPUBLIC)
KBS WORLD R, In-Kimjae — Mideast • 250 kW
RUSSIA
†VOICE OF RUSSIA, Armavir — W • E North Am • 500 kW
SPAIN
R EXTERIOR ESPANA, Noblejas — M-F • Mideast • 350 kW
UNITED KINGDOM
†BBC, Via Oman — W • E Asia • 250 kW
UNITED NATIONS
UNITED NATIONS R, Via Meyerton, S Af — S M-F • E Africa • 100 kW / S M-F • S Africa • 100 kW
USA
ADVENTIST WORLD R, Via Agat, Guam — W • E Asia • 100 kW
VOA, Via Irkutsk, Russia — S • E Asia • 250 kW
VOA, Via Philippines — W • SE Asia • 250 kW

7155 **CHINA**
†CHINA R INTL, Kashi — W • S Asia • 100 kW
†CHINA R INTL, Via Cerrik, Albania — Europe • 150 kW
XINJIANG PEOPLE'S BC STN, Urümqi — S • DS-CHINESE • 100 kW / DS-CHINESE • 100 kW / W/F-M • DS-CHINESE • 100 kW
GERMANY
†DEUTSCHE WELLE, Wertachtal — S • N Europe • 500 kW
MADAGASCAR
RTV MALAGASY, Antananarivo — Irr • DS-1 • 30 kW • USB • ALT. FREQ. TO 7105 kHz
PAKISTAN
PAKISTAN BC CORP, Quetta — F • DS • 10 kW / DS • 10 kW / Sa-Th • DS • 10 kW
RUSSIA
VOICE OF RUSSIA, Komsomol'sk 'Amure — W • Australasia • 250 kW
THAILAND
RADIO THAILAND, Udon Thani — S • N Europe • 250 kW
TURKEY
†VOICE OF TURKEY, Ankara-Emirler — S Europe • 250 kW / W • W Europe • 500 kW
UNITED KINGDOM
BIBLE VOICE, Skelton, Cumbria — W M-F • Mideast & E Africa • 250 kW / W M • Mideast & E Africa • 250 kW

(con'd)

0 1 2 3 4 5 6 7 8 9 10 11 12 13 14 15 16 17 18 19 20 21 22 23 24

ENGLISH ▬ ARABIC ⋙ CHINESE □□□ FRENCH ▬ GERMAN ▬ RUSSIAN ═ SPANISH ▬ OTHER ▬

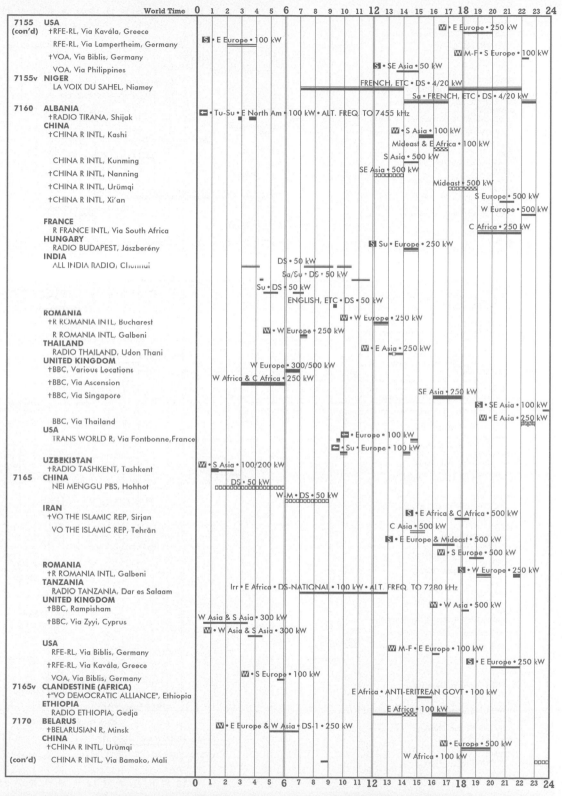

| | World Time | 0 | 1 | 2 | 3 | 4 | 5 | 6 | 7 | 8 | 9 | 10 | 11 | 12 | 13 | 14 | 15 | 16 | 17 | 18 | 19 | 20 | 21 | 22 | 23 | 24 |

7155 USA
(con'd) †RFE-RL, Via Kavála, Greece — W • E Europe • 250 kW
RFE-RL, Via Lampertheim, Germany — S • E Europe • 100 kW
†VOA, Via Biblis, Germany — W M-F • S Europe • 100 kW
VOA, Via Philippines — S • SE Asia • 50 kW

7155v NIGER
LA VOIX DU SAHEL, Niamey — FRENCH, ETC • DS • 4/20 kW
Sa • FRENCH, ETC • DS • 4/20 kW

7160 ALBANIA
†RADIO TIRANA, Shijak — Tu-Su • E North Am • 100 kW • ALT. FREQ. TO 7455 kHz
CHINA
†CHINA R INTL, Kashi — W • S Asia • 100 kW
Mideast & E Africa • 100 kW
CHINA R INTL, Kunming — S Asia • 500 kW
†CHINA R INTL, Nanning — SE Asia • 500 kW
†CHINA R INTL, Urümqi — Mideast • 500 kW
†CHINA R INTL, Xi'an — S Europe • 500 kW
W Europe • 500 kW

FRANCE
R FRANCE INTL, Via South Africa — C Africa • 250 kW
HUNGARY
RADIO BUDAPEST, Jászberény — S Su • Europe • 250 kW
INDIA
ALL INDIA RADIO, Chennai — DS • 50 kW
Sa/Su • DS • 50 kW
Su • DS • 50 kW
ENGLISH, ETC • DS • 50 kW

ROMANIA
†R ROMANIA INTL, Bucharest — W • W Europe • 250 kW
R ROMANIA INTL, Galbeni — W • W Europe • 250 kW
THAILAND
RADIO THAILAND, Udon Thani — W • E Asia • 250 kW
UNITED KINGDOM
†BBC, Various Locations — W Europe • 300/500 kW
†BBC, Via Ascension — W Africa & C Africa • 250 kW
†BBC, Via Singapore — SE Asia • 250 kW
S • SE Asia • 100 kW
W • E Asia • 250 kW
BBC, Via Thailand
USA
TRANS WORLD R, Via Fontbonne, France — • Europe • 100 kW
• Su • Europe • 100 kW

UZBEKISTAN
†RADIO TASHKENT, Tashkent — W • S Asia • 100/200 kW
7165 CHINA
NEI MENGGU PBS, Hohhot — DS • 50 kW
W, M • DS • 50 kW

IRAN
†VO THE ISLAMIC REP, Sirjan — S • E Africa & C Africa • 500 kW
VO THE ISLAMIC REP, Tehrān — C Asia • 500 kW
S • E Europe & Mideast • 500 kW
W • S Europe • 500 kW

ROMANIA
†R ROMANIA INTL, Galbeni — S • W Europe • 250 kW
TANZANIA
RADIO TANZANIA, Dar es Salaam — Irr • E Africa • DS-NATIONAL • 100 kW • ALT FREQ TO 7280 kHz
UNITED KINGDOM
†BBC, Rampisham — W • W Asia • 500 kW
†BBC, Via Zyyi, Cyprus — W Asia & S Asia • 300 kW
W • W Asia & S Asia • 300 kW
USA
RFE-RL, Via Biblis, Germany — W M-F • E Europe • 100 kW
†RFE-RL, Via Kavála, Greece — S • E Europe • 250 kW
†VOA, Via Biblis, Germany — W • S Europe • 100 kW
7165v CLANDESTINE (AFRICA)
†"VO DEMOCRATIC ALLIANCE", Ethiopia — E Africa • ANTI-ERITREAN GOVT • 100 kW
ETHIOPIA
RADIO ETHIOPIA, Gedja — E Africa • 100 kW
7170 BELARUS
†BELARUSIAN R, Minsk — W • E Europe & W Asia • DS-1 • 250 kW
CHINA
†CHINA R INTL, Urümqi — W • Europe • 500 kW
(con'd) CHINA R INTL, Via Bamako, Mali — W Africa • 100 kW

| | 0 | 1 | 2 | 3 | 4 | 5 | 6 | 7 | 8 | 9 | 10 | 11 | 12 | 13 | 14 | 15 | 16 | 17 | 18 | 19 | 20 | 21 | 22 | 23 | 24 |

SEASONAL S OR W   1-HR TIMESHIFT MIDYEAR ⊡ OR ⊟   JAMMING / OR ∧   EARLIEST HEARD ◁   LATEST HEARD ▷   NEW FOR 2006 †

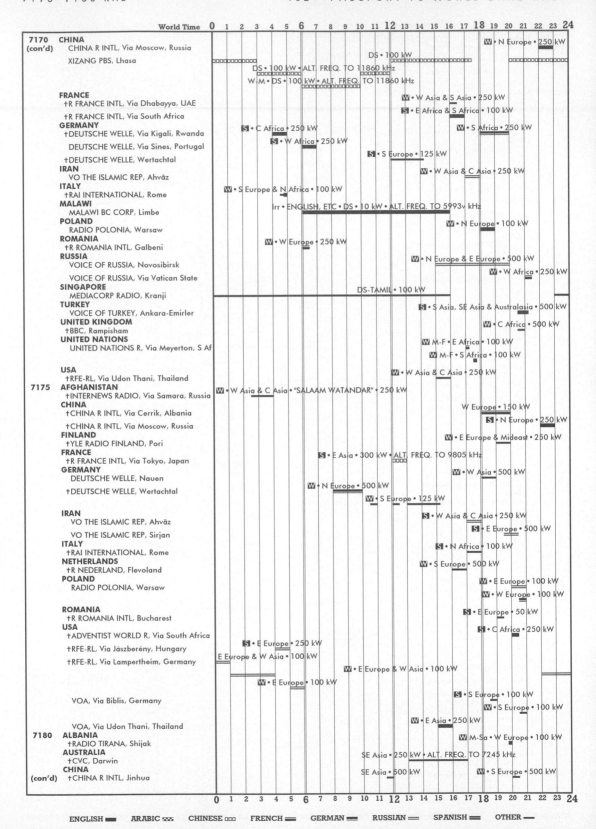

World Time 0 1 2 3 4 5 6 7 8 9 10 11 12 13 14 15 16 17 18 19 20 21 22 23 24

7170 **CHINA**
(con'd) CHINA R INTL, Via Moscow, Russia — W • N Europe • 250 kW
     XIZANG PBS, Lhasa — DS • 100 kW / DS • 100 kW • ALT. FREQ. TO 11860 kHz / W-M • DS • 100 kW • ALT. FREQ. TO 11860 kHz

FRANCE
†R FRANCE INTL, Via Dhabayya, UAE — W • W Asia & S Asia • 250 kW / S • E Africa & S Africa • 100 kW
†R FRANCE INTL, Via South Africa
GERMANY
†DEUTSCHE WELLE, Via Kigali, Rwanda — S • C Africa • 250 kW / W • S Africa • 250 kW
DEUTSCHE WELLE, Via Sines, Portugal — S • W Africa • 250 kW
†DEUTSCHE WELLE, Wertachtal — S • S Europe • 125 kW
IRAN
VO THE ISLAMIC REP, Ahvāz — W • W Asia & C Asia • 250 kW
ITALY
†RAI INTERNATIONAL, Rome — W • S Europe & N Africa • 100 kW
MALAWI
MALAWI BC CORP, Limbe — Irr • ENGLISH, ETC • DS • 10 kW • ALT. FREQ. TO 5993v kHz
POLAND
RADIO POLONIA, Warsaw — W • N Europe • 100 kW
ROMANIA
†R ROMANIA INTL, Galbeni — W • W Europe • 250 kW
RUSSIA
VOICE OF RUSSIA, Novosibirsk — W • N Europe & E Europe • 500 kW
VOICE OF RUSSIA, Via Vatican State — W • W Africa • 250 kW
SINGAPORE
MEDIACORP RADIO, Kranji — DS-TAMIL • 100 kW
TURKEY
VOICE OF TURKEY, Ankara-Emirler — S • S Asia, SE Asia & Australasia • 500 kW
UNITED KINGDOM
†BBC, Rampisham — W • C Africa • 500 kW
UNITED NATIONS
UNITED NATIONS R, Via Meyerton, S Af — W M-F • E Africa • 100 kW / W M-F • S Africa • 100 kW
USA
†RFE-RL, Via Udon Thani, Thailand — W • W Asia & C Asia • 250 kW

7175 **AFGHANISTAN**
†INTERNEWS RADIO, Via Samara, Russia — W • W Asia & C Asia • "SALAAM WATANDAR" • 250 kW
CHINA
†CHINA R INTL, Via Cerrik, Albania — W Europe • 150 kW
†CHINA R INTL, Via Moscow, Russia — S • N Europe • 250 kW
FINLAND
†YLE RADIO FINLAND, Pori — W • E Europe & Mideast • 250 kW
FRANCE
†R FRANCE INTL, Via Tokyo, Japan — S • E Asia • 300 kW • ALT. FREQ. TO 9805 kHz
GERMANY
DEUTSCHE WELLE, Nauen — W • W Asia • 500 kW
†DEUTSCHE WELLE, Wertachtal — W • N Europe • 500 kW / W • S Europe • 125 kW
IRAN
VO THE ISLAMIC REP, Ahvāz — S • W Asia & C Asia • 250 kW
VO THE ISLAMIC REP, Sirjan — S • E Europe • 500 kW
ITALY
†RAI INTERNATIONAL, Rome — S • N Africa • 100 kW
NETHERLANDS
†R NEDERLAND, Flevoland — W • S Europe • 500 kW
POLAND
RADIO POLONIA, Warsaw — W • E Europe • 100 kW / W • W Europe • 100 kW
ROMANIA
†R ROMANIA INTL, Bucharest — S • E Europe • 50 kW
USA
†ADVENTIST WORLD R, Via South Africa — S • C Africa • 250 kW
†RFE-RL, Via Jászberény, Hungary — S • E Europe • 250 kW
†RFE-RL, Via Lampertheim, Germany — E Europe & W Asia • 100 kW / W • E Europe & W Asia • 100 kW / W • E Europe • 100 kW
VOA, Via Biblis, Germany — S • S Europe • 100 kW / W • S Europe • 100 kW
VOA, Via Udon Thani, Thailand — W • E Asia • 250 kW

7180 **ALBANIA**
†RADIO TIRANA, Shijak — W M-Sa • W Europe • 100 kW
AUSTRALIA
†CVC, Darwin — SE Asia • 250 kW • ALT. FREQ. TO 7245 kHz
CHINA
(con'd) †CHINA R INTL, Jinhua — SE Asia • 500 kW / W • S Europe • 500 kW

0 1 2 3 4 5 6 7 8 9 10 11 12 13 14 15 16 17 18 19 20 21 22 23 24

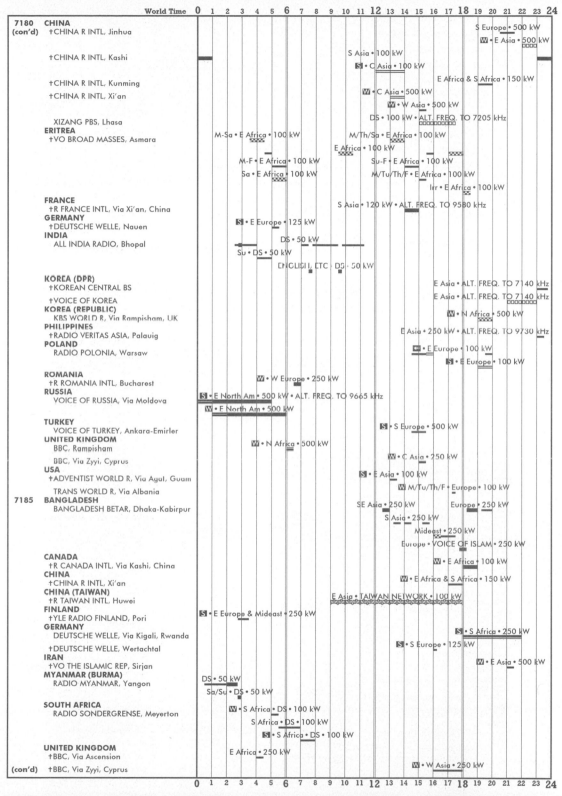

World Time 0 1 2 3 4 5 6 7 8 9 10 11 12 13 14 15 16 17 18 19 20 21 22 23 24

7180   **CHINA**
(con'd)   †CHINA R INTL, Jinhua — S Europe • 500 kW / W • E Asia • 500 kW

†CHINA R INTL, Kashi — S Asia • 100 kW / S • C Asia • 100 kW

†CHINA R INTL, Kunming — E Africa & S Africa • 150 kW

†CHINA R INTL, Xi'an — W • C Asia • 500 kW / W • W Asia • 500 kW

XIZANG PBS, Lhasa — DS • 100 kW • ALT. FREQ. TO 7205 kHz
ERITREA
†VO BROAD MASSES, Asmara — M-Sa • E Africa • 100 kW / M/Th/Sa • E Africa • 100 kW / E Africa • 100 kW / M-F • E Africa • 100 kW / Su-F • E Africa • 100 kW / Sa • E Africa • 100 kW / M/Tu/Th/F • E Africa • 100 kW / Irr • E Africa • 100 kW

FRANCE
†R FRANCE INTL, Via Xi'an, China — S Asia • 120 kW • ALT. FREQ. TO 9580 kHz
GERMANY
†DEUTSCHE WELLE, Nauen — S • E Europe • 125 kW
INDIA
ALL INDIA RADIO, Bhopal — DS • 50 kW / Su • DS • 50 kW / ENGLISH, ETC • DS • 50 kW

KOREA (DPR)
†KOREAN CENTRAL BS — E Asia • ALT. FREQ. TO 7140 kHz

†VOICE OF KOREA — E Asia • ALT. FREQ. TO 7140 kHz
KOREA (REPUBLIC)
KBS WORLD R, Via Rampisham, UK — W • N Africa • 500 kW
PHILIPPINES
†RADIO VERITAS ASIA, Palauig — E Asia • 250 kW • ALT. FREQ. TO 9730 kHz
POLAND
RADIO POLONIA, Warsaw — E Europe • 100 kW / S • E Europe • 100 kW

ROMANIA
†R ROMANIA INTL, Bucharest — W • W Europe • 250 kW
RUSSIA
VOICE OF RUSSIA, Via Moldova — S • E North Am • 500 kW • ALT. FREQ. TO 9665 kHz / W • E North Am • 500 kW

TURKEY
VOICE OF TURKEY, Ankara-Emirler — S • S Europe • 500 kW
UNITED KINGDOM
BBC, Rampisham — W • N Africa • 500 kW

BBC, Via Zyyi, Cyprus — W • C Asia • 250 kW
USA
†ADVENTIST WORLD R, Via Agat, Guam — S • E Asia • 100 kW

TRANS WORLD R, Via Albania — W M/Tu/Th/F • Europe • 100 kW
7185   **BANGLADESH**
BANGLADESH BETAR, Dhaka-Kabirpur — SE Asia • 250 kW / Europe • 250 kW / S Asia • 250 kW / Mideast • 250 kW / Europe • VOICE OF ISLAM • 250 kW

CANADA
†R CANADA INTL, Via Kashi, China — W • E Africa • 100 kW
CHINA
†CHINA R INTL, Xi'an — W • E Africa & S Africa • 150 kW
CHINA (TAIWAN)
†R TAIWAN INTL, Huwei — E Asia • TAIWAN NETWORK • 100 kW
FINLAND
†YLE RADIO FINLAND, Pori — S • E Europe & Mideast • 250 kW
GERMANY
DEUTSCHE WELLE, Via Kigali, Rwanda — S • S Africa • 250 kW

†DEUTSCHE WELLE, Wertachtal — S • S Europe • 125 kW
IRAN
†VO THE ISLAMIC REP, Sirjan — W • E Asia • 500 kW
MYANMAR (BURMA)
RADIO MYANMAR, Yangon — DS • 50 kW / Sa/Su • DS • 50 kW

SOUTH AFRICA
RADIO SONDERGRENSE, Meyerton — W • S Africa • DS • 100 kW / S Africa • DS • 100 kW / S • S Africa • DS • 100 kW

UNITED KINGDOM
†BBC, Via Ascension — E Africa • 250 kW
(con'd)   †BBC, Via Zyyi, Cyprus — W • W Asia • 250 kW

0 1 2 3 4 5 6 7 8 9 10 11 12 13 14 15 16 17 18 19 20 21 22 23 24

SEASONAL **S** OR **W**   1-HR TIMESHIFT MIDYEAR ⇦ OR ⇨   JAMMING / OR ∧   EARLIEST HEARD ◁   LATEST HEARD ▷   NEW FOR 2006 †

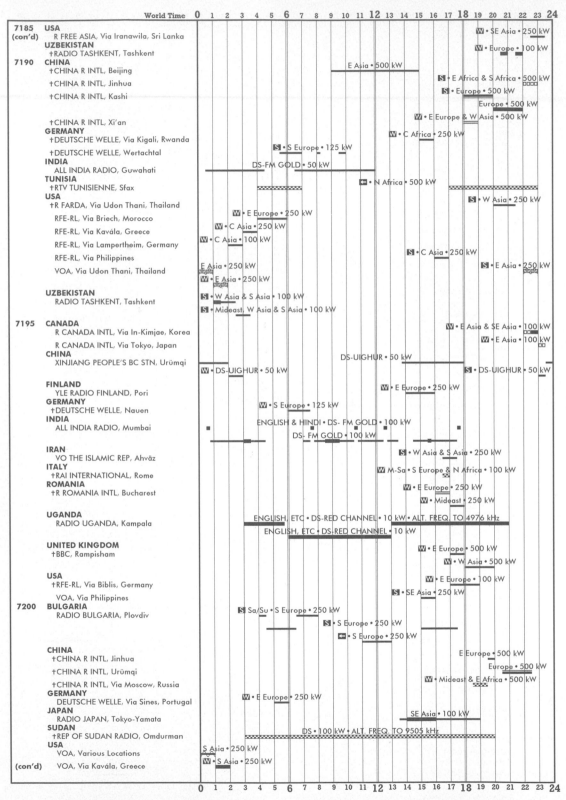

ENGLISH ▬ ARABIC ⌇⌇⌇ CHINESE □□□ FRENCH ▬ GERMAN ▬ RUSSIAN ═ SPANISH ▭ OTHER ▬

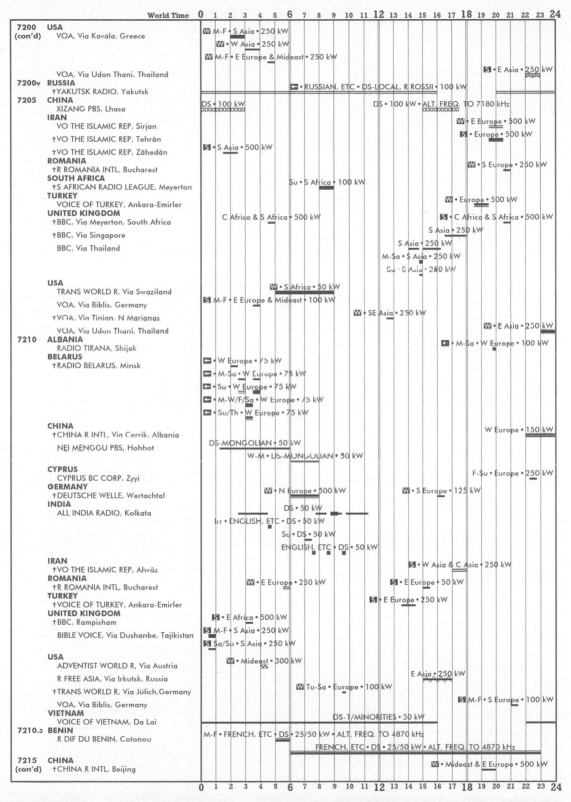

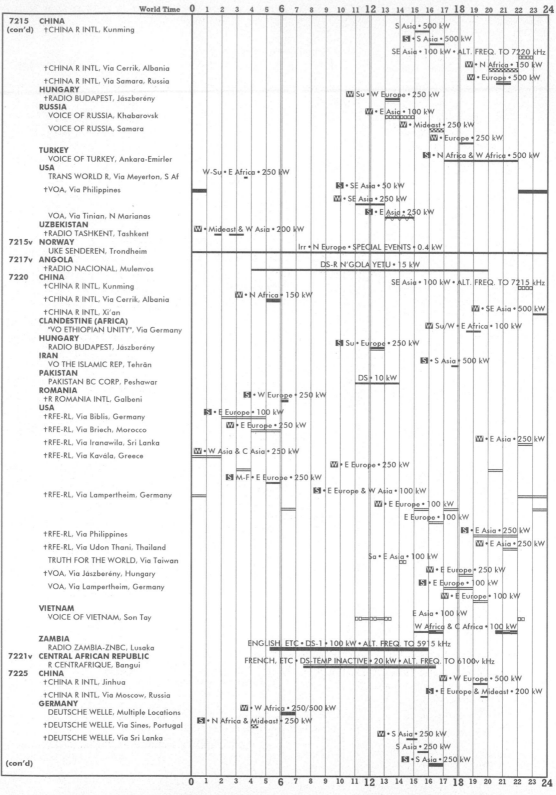

World Time	0 1 2 3 4 5 6 7 8 9 10 11 12 13 14 15 16 17 18 19 20 21 22 23 24
7215 **CHINA**	
(con'd) †CHINA R INTL, Kunming	S Asia • 500 kW
	S • S Asia • 500 kW
	SE Asia • 100 kW • ALT. FREQ. TO 7220 kHz
†CHINA R INTL, Via Cerrik, Albania	W • N Africa • 150 kW
†CHINA R INTL, Via Samara, Russia	W • Europe • 500 kW
HUNGARY	
†RADIO BUDAPEST, Jászberény	W Su • W Europe • 250 kW
RUSSIA	
VOICE OF RUSSIA, Khabarovsk	W • E Asia • 100 kW
VOICE OF RUSSIA, Samara	W • Mideast • 250 kW
	W • Europe • 250 kW
TURKEY	
VOICE OF TURKEY, Ankara-Emirler	S • N Africa & W Africa • 500 kW
USA	
TRANS WORLD R, Via Meyerton, S Af	W-Su • E Africa • 250 kW
†VOA, Via Philippines	S • SE Asia • 50 kW
	W • SE Asia • 250 kW
VOA, Via Tinian, N Marianas	S • E Asia • 250 kW
UZBEKISTAN	
†RADIO TASHKENT, Tashkent	W • Mideast & W Asia • 200 kW
7215v NORWAY	
UKE SENDEREN, Trondheim	Irr • N Europe • SPECIAL EVENTS • 0.4 kW
7217v ANGOLA	
†RADIO NACIONAL, Mulenvos	DS-R N'GOLA YETU • 15 kW
7220 CHINA	
†CHINA R INTL, Kunming	SE Asia • 100 kW • ALT. FREQ. TO 7215 kHz
†CHINA R INTL, Via Cerrik, Albania	W • N Africa • 150 kW
†CHINA R INTL, Xi'an	W • SE Asia • 500 kW
CLANDESTINE (AFRICA)	
"VO ETHIOPIAN UNITY", Via Germany	W Su/W • E Africa • 100 kW
HUNGARY	
RADIO BUDAPEST, Jászberény	S Su • Europe • 250 kW
IRAN	
VO THE ISLAMIC REP, Tehrān	S • S Asia • 500 kW
PAKISTAN	
PAKISTAN BC CORP, Peshawar	DS • 10 kW
ROMANIA	
†R ROMANIA INTL, Galbeni	S • W Europe • 250 kW
USA	
†RFE-RL, Via Biblis, Germany	S • E Europe • 100 kW
†RFE-RL, Via Briech, Morocco	W • E Europe • 250 kW
†RFE-RL, Via Iranawila, Sri Lanka	W • E Asia • 250 kW
†RFE-RL, Via Kavála, Greece	W • W Asia & C Asia • 250 kW
	W • E Europe • 250 kW
†RFE-RL, Via Lampertheim, Germany	S M-F • E Europe • 250 kW
	S • E Europe & W Asia • 100 kW
	W • E Europe • 100 kW
	E Europe • 100 kW
†RFE-RL, Via Philippines	S • E Asia • 250 kW
†RFE-RL, Via Udon Thani, Thailand	W • E Asia • 250 kW
TRUTH FOR THE WORLD, Via Taiwan	Sa • E Asia • 100 kW
†VOA, Via Jászberény, Hungary	W • E Europe • 250 kW
VOA, Via Lampertheim, Germany	S • E Europe • 100 kW
	W • E Europe • 100 kW
VIETNAM	
VOICE OF VIETNAM, Son Tay	E Asia • 100 kW
	W Africa & C Africa • 100 kW
ZAMBIA	
RADIO ZAMBIA-ZNBC, Lusaka	ENGLISH, ETC • DS-1 • 100 kW • ALT. FREQ. TO 5915 kHz
7221v CENTRAL AFRICAN REPUBLIC	
R CENTRAFRIQUE, Bangui	FRENCH, ETC • DS-TEMP INACTIVE • 20 kW • ALT. FREQ. TO 6100v kHz
7225 CHINA	
†CHINA R INTL, Jinhua	W • W Europe • 500 kW
†CHINA R INTL, Via Moscow, Russia	S • E Europe & Mideast • 200 kW
GERMANY	
DEUTSCHE WELLE, Multiple Locations	W • W Africa • 250/500 kW
†DEUTSCHE WELLE, Via Sines, Portugal	S • N Africa & Mideast • 250 kW
†DEUTSCHE WELLE, Via Sri Lanka	W • S Asia • 250 kW
	S Asia • 250 kW
	S • S Asia • 250 kW
(con'd)	

	0 1 2 3 4 5 6 7 8 9 10 11 12 13 14 15 16 17 18 19 20 21 22 23 24

ENGLISH ▬   ARABIC ▨   CHINESE ▢▢▢   FRENCH ▬   GERMAN ▬   RUSSIAN ═   SPANISH ▬   OTHER ▬

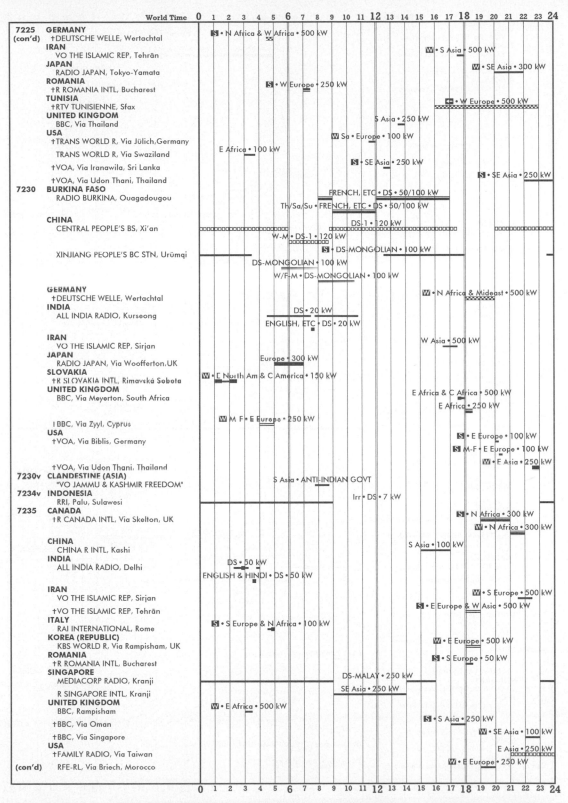

World Time 0 1 2 3 4 5 6 7 8 9 10 11 12 13 14 15 16 17 18 19 20 21 22 23 24

7225 **GERMANY**
(con'd) †DEUTSCHE WELLE, Wertachtal — S • N Africa & W Africa • 500 kW
    IRAN
      VO THE ISLAMIC REP, Tehrān — W • S Asia • 500 kW
    JAPAN
      RADIO JAPAN, Tokyo-Yamata — W • SE Asia • 300 kW
    ROMANIA
      †R ROMANIA INTL, Bucharest — S • W Europe • 250 kW
    TUNISIA
      †RTV TUNISIENNE, Sfax — ⇔ • W Europe • 500 kW
    UNITED KINGDOM
      BBC, Via Thailand — S Asia • 250 kW
    USA
      †TRANS WORLD R, Via Jülich, Germany — W • Sa • Europe • 100 kW
      TRANS WORLD R, Via Swaziland — E Africa • 100 kW
      †VOA, Via Iranawila, Sri Lanka — S • SE Asia • 250 kW
      †VOA, Via Udon Thani, Thailand — S • SE Asia • 250 kW

7230 **BURKINA FASO**
    RADIO BURKINA, Ouagadougou — FRENCH, ETC • DS • 50/100 kW
       Th/Sa/Su • FRENCH, ETC • DS • 50/100 kW
    CHINA
      CENTRAL PEOPLE'S BS, Xi'an — DS-1 • 120 kW
       W-M • DS-1 • 120 kW
      XINJIANG PEOPLE'S BC STN, Urümqi — S • DS-MONGOLIAN • 100 kW
       DS-MONGOLIAN • 100 kW
       W/F-M • DS-MONGOLIAN • 100 kW
    GERMANY
      †DEUTSCHE WELLE, Wertachtal — W • N Africa & Mideast • 500 kW
    INDIA
      ALL INDIA RADIO, Kurseong — DS • 20 kW
       ENGLISH, ETC • DS • 20 kW
    IRAN
      VO THE ISLAMIC REP, Sirjan — W Asia • 500 kW
    JAPAN
      RADIO JAPAN, Via Woofferton, UK — Europe • 300 kW
    SLOVAKIA
      †R SLOVAKIA INTL, Rimavská Sobota — W • E North Am & C America • 150 kW
    UNITED KINGDOM
      BBC, Via Meyerton, South Africa — E Africa & C Africa • 500 kW
       E Africa • 250 kW
       BBC, Via Zyyl, Cyprus — W M F • E Europe • 250 kW
    USA
      †VOA, Via Biblis, Germany — S • E Europe • 100 kW
       S • M-F • E Europe • 100 kW
       W • E Asia • 250 kW
      †VOA, Via Udon Thani, Thailand

7230v **CLANDESTINE (ASIA)**
    "VO JAMMU & KASHMIR FREEDOM" — S Asia • ANTI-INDIAN GOVT

7234v **INDONESIA**
    RRI, Palu, Sulawesi — Irr • DS • 7 kW

7235 **CANADA**
    †R CANADA INTL, Via Skelton, UK — S • N Africa • 300 kW
       W • N Africa • 300 kW
    CHINA
      CHINA R INTL, Kashi — S Asia • 100 kW
    INDIA
      ALL INDIA RADIO, Delhi — DS • 50 kW
       ENGLISH & HINDI • DS • 50 kW
    IRAN
      VO THE ISLAMIC REP, Sirjan — W • S Europe • 500 kW
      †VO THE ISLAMIC REP, Tehrān — S • E Europe & W Asia • 500 kW
    ITALY
      RAI INTERNATIONAL, Rome — S • S Europe & N Africa • 100 kW
    KOREA (REPUBLIC)
      KBS WORLD R, Via Rampisham, UK — W • E Europe • 500 kW
    ROMANIA
      †R ROMANIA INTL, Bucharest — S • S Europe • 50 kW
    SINGAPORE
      MEDIACORP RADIO, Kranji — DS-MALAY • 250 kW
      R SINGAPORE INTL, Kranji — SE Asia • 250 kW
    UNITED KINGDOM
      BBC, Rampisham — W • E Africa • 500 kW
      †BBC, Via Oman — S • S Asia • 250 kW
      †BBC, Via Singapore — W • SE Asia • 100 kW
    USA
      †FAMILY RADIO, Via Taiwan — E Asia • 250 kW
(con'd) RFE-RL, Via Briech, Morocco — W • E Europe • 250 kW

0 1 2 3 4 5 6 7 8 9 10 11 12 13 14 15 16 17 18 19 20 21 22 23 24

SEASONAL S OR W   1-HR TIMESHIFT MIDYEAR ⇔ OR ⇒   JAMMING / OR ∧   EARLIEST HEARD ◁   LATEST HEARD ▷   NEW FOR 2006 †

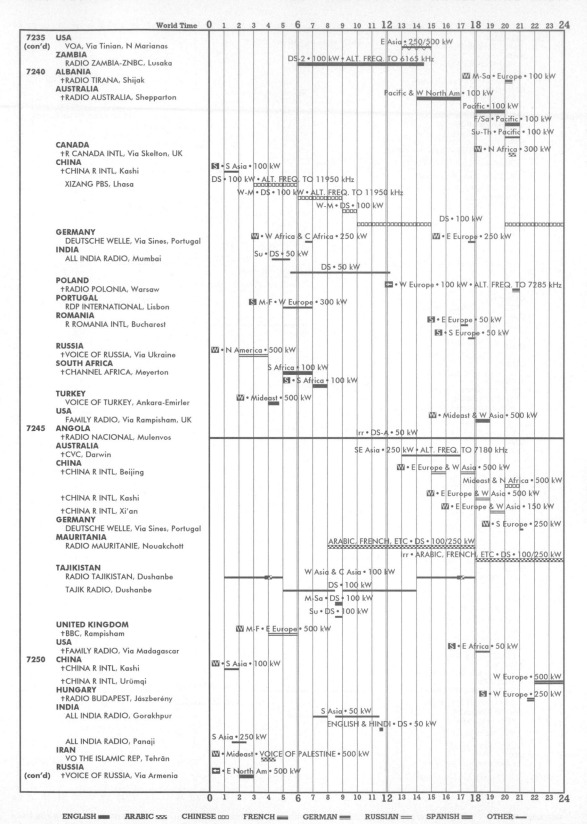

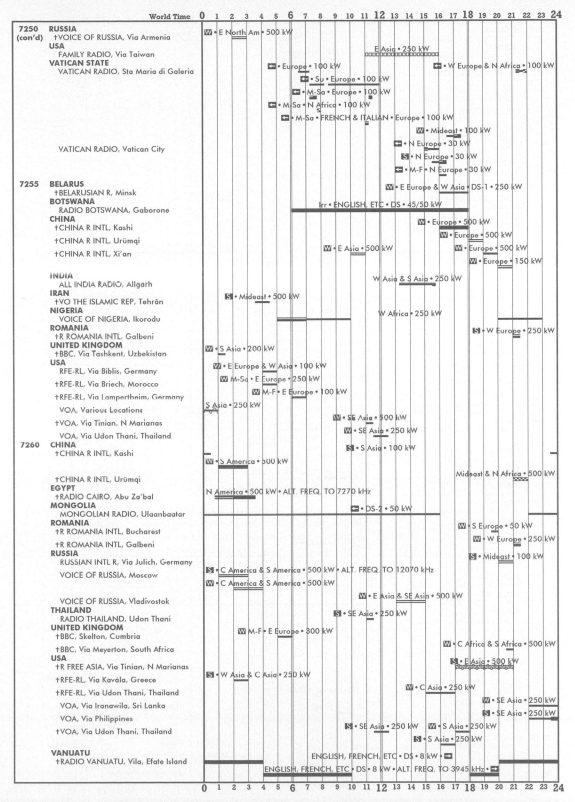

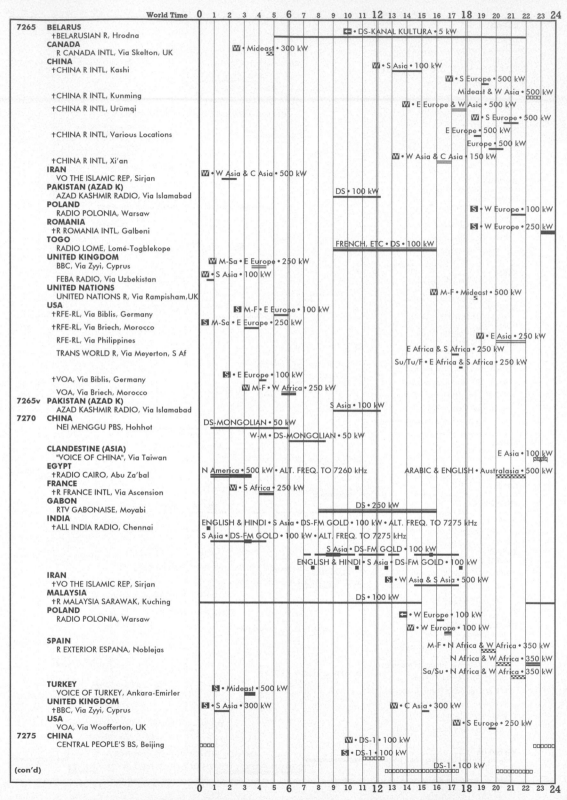

World Time 0 1 2 3 4 5 6 7 8 9 10 11 12 13 14 15 16 17 18 19 20 21 22 23 24

7265 BELARUS
†BELARUSIAN R, Hrodna — DS-KANAL KULTURA • 5 kW
CANADA
R CANADA INTL, Via Skelton, UK — W • Mideast • 300 kW
CHINA
†CHINA R INTL, Kashi — W • S Asia • 100 kW
W • S Europe • 500 kW
Mideast & W Asia • 500 kW
†CHINA R INTL, Kunming — W • E Europe & W Asia • 500 kW
†CHINA R INTL, Urümqi — W • S Europe • 500 kW
E Europe • 500 kW
†CHINA R INTL, Various Locations — Europe • 500 kW
†CHINA R INTL, Xi'an — W • W Asia & C Asia • 150 kW
IRAN
VO THE ISLAMIC REP, Sirjan — W • W Asia & C Asia • 500 kW
PAKISTAN (AZAD K)
AZAD KASHMIR RADIO, Via Islamabad — DS • 100 kW
POLAND
RADIO POLONIA, Warsaw — S • W Europe • 100 kW
ROMANIA
†R ROMANIA INTL, Galbeni — S • W Europe • 250 kW
TOGO
RADIO LOME, Lomé-Togblekope — FRENCH, ETC • DS • 100 kW
UNITED KINGDOM
BBC, Via Zyyi, Cyprus — W M-Sa • E Europe • 250 kW
FEBA RADIO, Via Uzbekistan — W • S Asia • 100 kW
UNITED NATIONS
UNITED NATIONS R, Via Rampisham, UK — W M-F • Mideast • 500 kW
USA
†RFE-RL, Via Biblis, Germany — S M-F • E Europe • 100 kW
†RFE-RL, Via Briech, Morocco — S M-Sa • E Europe • 250 kW
RFE-RL, Via Philippines — W • E Asia • 250 kW
TRANS WORLD R, Via Meyerton, S Af — E Africa & S Africa • 250 kW
Su/Tu/F • E Africa & S Africa • 250 kW
†VOA, Via Biblis, Germany — S • E Europe • 100 kW
VOA, Via Briech, Morocco — W M-F • W Africa • 250 kW
7265v PAKISTAN (AZAD K)
AZAD KASHMIR RADIO, Via Islamabad — S Asia • 100 kW
7270 CHINA
NEI MENGGU PBS, Hohhot — DS-MONGOLIAN • 50 kW
W-M • DS-MONGOLIAN • 50 kW
CLANDESTINE (ASIA)
"VOICE OF CHINA", Via Taiwan — E Asia • 100 kW
EGYPT
†RADIO CAIRO, Abu Za'bal — N America • 500 kW • ALT. FREQ. TO 7260 kHz
ARABIC & ENGLISH • Australasia • 500 kW
FRANCE
†R FRANCE INTL, Via Ascension — W • S Africa • 250 kW
GABON
RTV GABONAISE, Moyabi — DS • 250 kW
INDIA
†ALL INDIA RADIO, Chennai — ENGLISH & HINDI • S Asia • DS-FM GOLD • 100 kW • ALT. FREQ. TO 7275 kHz
S Asia • DS-FM GOLD • 100 kW • ALT. FREQ. TO 7275 kHz
S Asia • DS-FM GOLD • 100 kW
ENGLISH & HINDI • S Asia • DS-FM GOLD • 100 kW
IRAN
†VO THE ISLAMIC REP, Sirjan — S • W Asia & S Asia • 500 kW
MALAYSIA
†R MALAYSIA SARAWAK, Kuching — DS • 100 kW
POLAND
RADIO POLONIA, Warsaw — W Europe • 100 kW
W • W Europe • 100 kW
SPAIN
R EXTERIOR ESPANA, Noblejas — M-F • N Africa & W Africa • 350 kW
N Africa & W Africa • 350 kW
Sa/Su • N Africa & W Africa • 350 kW
TURKEY
VOICE OF TURKEY, Ankara-Emirler — S • Mideast • 500 kW
UNITED KINGDOM
†BBC, Via Zyyi, Cyprus — S • S Asia • 300 kW
W • C Asia • 300 kW
USA
VOA, Via Woofferton, UK — W • S Europe • 250 kW
7275 CHINA
CENTRAL PEOPLE'S BS, Beijing — W • DS-1 • 100 kW
S • DS-1 • 100 kW
DS-1 • 100 kW

(con'd)

0 1 2 3 4 5 6 7 8 9 10 11 12 13 14 15 16 17 18 19 20 21 22 23 24

ENGLISH ▬   ARABIC ░   CHINESE □□□   FRENCH ═   GERMAN ▬   RUSSIAN ═   SPANISH ▬   OTHER ─

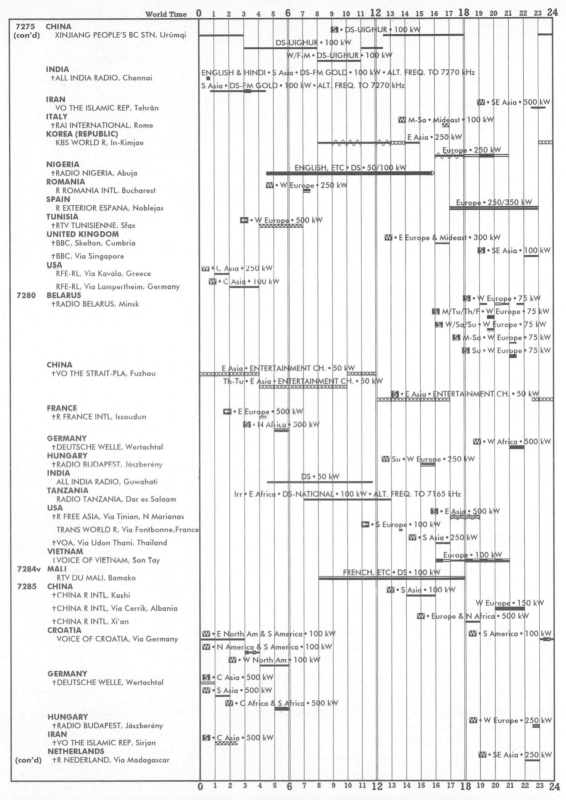

World Time 0 1 2 3 4 5 6 7 8 9 10 11 12 13 14 15 16 17 18 19 20 21 22 23 24

7275 (con'd) CHINA
XINJIANG PEOPLE'S BC STN, Urümqi
- [S] • DS-UIGHUR • 100 kW
- DS-UIGHUR • 100 kW
- W/F-M • DS-UIGHUR • 100 kW

INDIA
†ALL INDIA RADIO, Chennai
- ENGLISH & HINDI • S Asia • DS-FM GOLD • 100 kW • ALT. FREQ. TO 7270 kHz
- S Asia • DS-FM GOLD • 100 kW • ALT. FREQ. TO 7270 kHz

IRAN
VO THE ISLAMIC REP, Tehrān
- [W] • SE Asia • 500 kW

ITALY
†RAI INTERNATIONAL, Rome
- [W] M-Sa • Mideast • 100 kW

KOREA (REPUBLIC)
KBS WORLD R, In-Kimjae
- E Asia • 250 kW
- Europe • 250 kW

NIGERIA
†RADIO NIGERIA, Abuja
- ENGLISH, ETC • DS • 50/100 kW

ROMANIA
R ROMANIA INTL, Bucharest
- [W] • W Europe • 250 kW

SPAIN
R EXTERIOR ESPANA, Noblejas
- Europe • 250/350 kW

TUNISIA
†RTV TUNISIENNE, Sfax
- ⇐ • W Europe • 500 kW

UNITED KINGDOM
†BBC, Skelton, Cumbria
- [W] • E Europe & Mideast • 300 kW

†BBC, Via Singapore
- [S] • SE Asia • 100 kW

USA
RFE-RL, Via Kavála, Greece
- [W] • C Asia • 250 kW

RFE-RL, Via Lampertheim, Germany
- [W] • C Asia • 100 kW

7280 BELARUS
†RADIO BELARUS, Minsk
- [S] • W Europe • 75 kW
- [S] M/Tu/Th/F • W Europe • 75 kW
- [S] W/Sa/Su • W Europe • 75 kW
- [S] M-Sa • W Europe • 75 kW
- [S] Su • W Europe • 75 kW

CHINA
†VO THE STRAIT-PLA, Fuzhou
- E Asia • ENTERTAINMENT CH. • 50 kW
- Th-Tu • E Asia • ENTERTAINMENT CH. • 50 kW
- [S] • E Asia • ENTERTAINMENT CH. • 50 kW

FRANCE
†R FRANCE INTL, Issoudun
- ⇐ • E Europe • 500 kW
- [S] • N Africa • 500 kW

GERMANY
†DEUTSCHE WELLE, Wertachtal
- [W] • W Africa • 500 kW

HUNGARY
†RADIO BUDAPEST, Jászberény
- [W] Su • W Europe • 250 kW

INDIA
ALL INDIA RADIO, Guwahati
- DS • 50 kW

TANZANIA
RADIO TANZANIA, Dar es Salaam
- Irr • E Africa • DS-NATIONAL • 100 kW • ALT. FREQ. TO 7165 kHz

USA
†R FREE ASIA, Via Tinian, N Marianas
- [S] • E Asia • 500 kW

TRANS WORLD R, Via Fontbonne, France
- ⇐ • S Europe • 100 kW

†VOA, Via Udon Thani, Thailand
- [W] • S Asia • 250 kW

VIETNAM
†VOICE OF VIETNAM, Sơn Tay
- Europe • 100 kW

7284v MALI
RTV DU MALI, Bamako
- FRENCH, ETC • DS • 100 kW

7285 CHINA
†CHINA R INTL, Kashi
- [W] • S Asia • 100 kW

†CHINA R INTL, Via Cerrik, Albania
- W Europe • 150 kW

†CHINA R INTL, Xi'an
- [W] • Europe & N Africa • 500 kW

CROATIA
VOICE OF CROATIA, Via Germany
- [W] • E North Am & S America • 100 kW
- [W] • S America • 100 kW
- [W] • N America & S America • 100 kW
- [W] • W North Am • 100 kW

GERMANY
†DEUTSCHE WELLE, Wertachtal
- [S] • C Asia • 500 kW
- [W] • S Asia • 500 kW
- [W] • C Africa & S Africa • 500 kW

HUNGARY
†RADIO BUDAPEST, Jászberény
- [W] • W Europe • 250 kW

IRAN
†VO THE ISLAMIC REP, Sirjan
- [S] • C Asia • 500 kW

NETHERLANDS (con'd)
†R NEDERLAND, Via Madagascar
- [W] • SE Asia • 250 kW

0 1 2 3 4 5 6 7 8 9 10 11 12 13 14 15 16 17 18 19 20 21 22 23 24

SEASONAL [S] OR [W] 1-HR TIMESHIFT MIDYEAR ⇐ OR ⇒ JAMMING / OR ∧ EARLIEST HEARD ◁ LATEST HEARD ▷ NEW FOR 2006 †

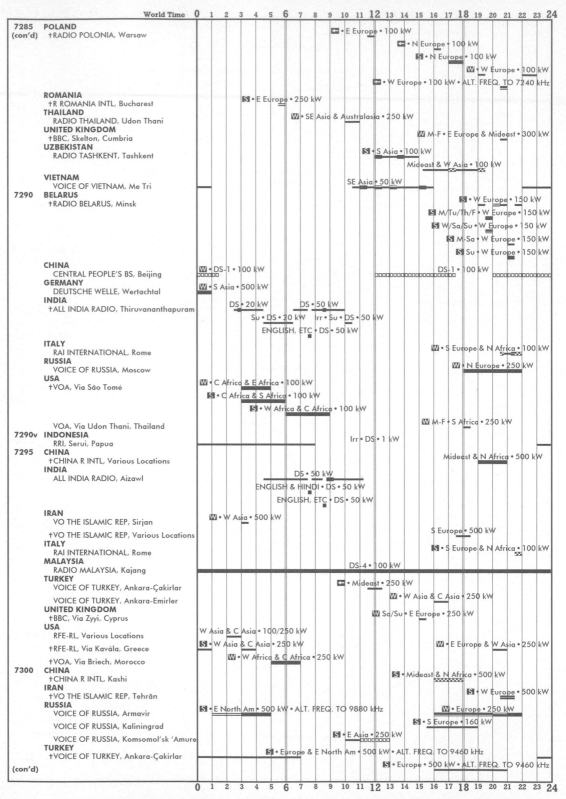

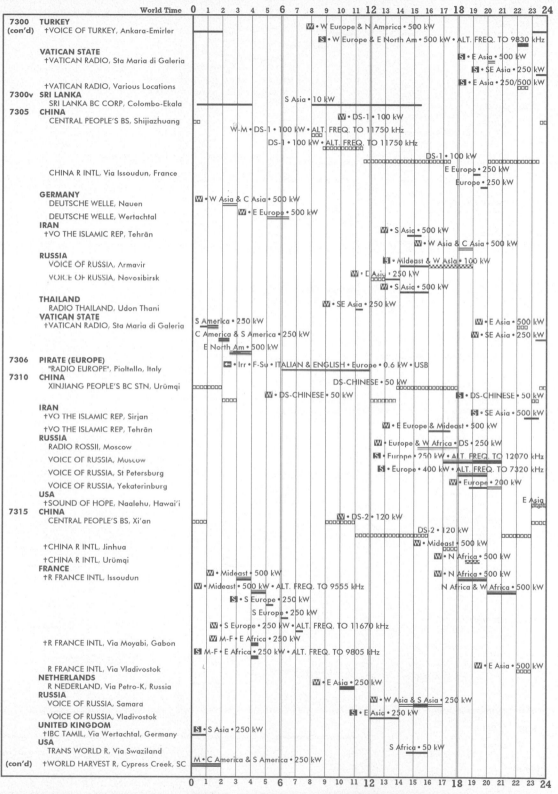

World Time 0 1 2 3 4 5 6 7 8 9 10 11 12 13 14 15 16 17 18 19 20 21 22 23 24

7300 TURKEY
(con'd) †VOICE OF TURKEY, Ankara-Emirler
- W • W Europe & N America • 500 kW
- S • W Europe & E North Am • 500 kW • ALT. FREQ. TO 9830 kHz

VATICAN STATE
†VATICAN RADIO, Sta Maria di Galeria
- S • E Asia • 500 kW
- S • SE Asia • 250 kW

†VATICAN RADIO, Various Locations
- S • E Asia • 250/500 kW

7300v SRI LANKA
SRI LANKA BC CORP, Colombo-Ekala
- S Asia • 10 kW

7305 CHINA
CENTRAL PEOPLE'S BS, Shijiazhuang
- W • DS-1 • 100 kW
- W-M • DS-1 • 100 kW • ALT. FREQ. TO 11750 kHz
- DS-1 • 100 kW • ALT. FREQ. TO 11750 kHz
- DS-1 • 100 kW

CHINA R INTL, Via Issoudun, France
- E Europe • 250 kW
- Europe • 250 kW

GERMANY
DEUTSCHE WELLE, Nauen
- W • W Asia & C Asia • 500 kW

DEUTSCHE WELLE, Wertachtal
- W • E Europe • 500 kW

IRAN
†VO THE ISLAMIC REP, Tehrān
- W • S Asia • 500 kW
- W • W Asia & C Asia • 500 kW

RUSSIA
VOICE OF RUSSIA, Armavir
- S • Mideast & W Asia • 100 kW

VOICE OF RUSSIA, Novosibirsk
- W • E Asia • 250 kW
- W • S Asia • 500 kW

THAILAND
RADIO THAILAND, Udon Thani
- W • SE Asia • 250 kW

VATICAN STATE
†VATICAN RADIO, Sta Maria di Galeria
- S America • 250 kW
- C America & S America • 250 kW
- E North Am • 500 kW
- W • E Asia • 500 kW
- W • SE Asia • 250 kW

7306 PIRATE (EUROPE)
"RADIO EUROPE", Pioltello, Italy
- Irr • F-Su • ITALIAN & ENGLISH • Europe • 0.6 kW • USB

7310 CHINA
XINJIANG PEOPLE'S BC STN, Urümqi
- DS-CHINESE • 50 kW
- W • DS-CHINESE • 50 kW
- S • DS-CHINESE • 50 kW

IRAN
†VO THE ISLAMIC REP, Sirjan
- S • SE Asia • 500 kW

†VO THE ISLAMIC REP, Tehrān
- W • E Europe & Mideast • 500 kW

RUSSIA
RADIO ROSSII, Moscow
- W • Europe & W Africa • DS • 250 kW

VOICE OF RUSSIA, Moscow
- S • Europe • 250 kW • ALT. FREQ. TO 12070 kHz

VOICE OF RUSSIA, St Petersburg
- S • Europe • 400 kW • ALT. FREQ. TO 7320 kHz

VOICE OF RUSSIA, Yekaterinburg
- W • Europe • 200 kW

USA
†SOUND OF HOPE, Naalehu, Hawai'i
- E Asia

7315 CHINA
CENTRAL PEOPLE'S BS, Xi'an
- W • DS-2 • 120 kW
- DS-2 • 120 kW
- W • Mideast • 500 kW

†CHINA R INTL, Jinhua
- W • N Africa • 500 kW

†CHINA R INTL, Urümqi
- W • Mideast • 500 kW

FRANCE
†R FRANCE INTL, Issoudun
- W • Mideast • 500 kW • ALT. FREQ. TO 9555 kHz
- W • N Africa • 500 kW
- N Africa & W Africa • 500 kW
- S • S Europe • 250 kW
- S Europe • 250 kW
- W • S Europe • 250 kW • ALT. FREQ. TO 11670 kHz
- W M-F • E Africa • 250 kW
- S M-F • E Africa • 250 kW • ALT. FREQ. TO 9805 kHz

†R FRANCE INTL, Via Moyabi, Gabon

R FRANCE INTL, Via Vladivostok
- W • E Asia • 500 kW

NETHERLANDS
R NEDERLAND, Via Petro-K, Russia
- W • E Asia • 250 kW

RUSSIA
VOICE OF RUSSIA, Samara
- W • W Asia & S Asia • 250 kW

VOICE OF RUSSIA, Vladivostok
- S • E Asia • 250 kW

UNITED KINGDOM
†IBC TAMIL, Via Wertachtal, Germany
- S • S Asia • 250 kW

USA
TRANS WORLD R, Via Swaziland
- S Africa • 50 kW

(con'd) †WORLD HARVEST R, Cypress Creek, SC
- M • C America & S America • 250 kW

0 1 2 3 4 5 6 7 8 9 10 11 12 13 14 15 16 17 18 19 20 21 22 23 24

SEASONAL S OR W   1-HR TIMESHIFT MIDYEAR ⇇ OR ⇉   JAMMING / OR ∧   EARLIEST HEARD ◁   LATEST HEARD ▷   NEW FOR 2006 †

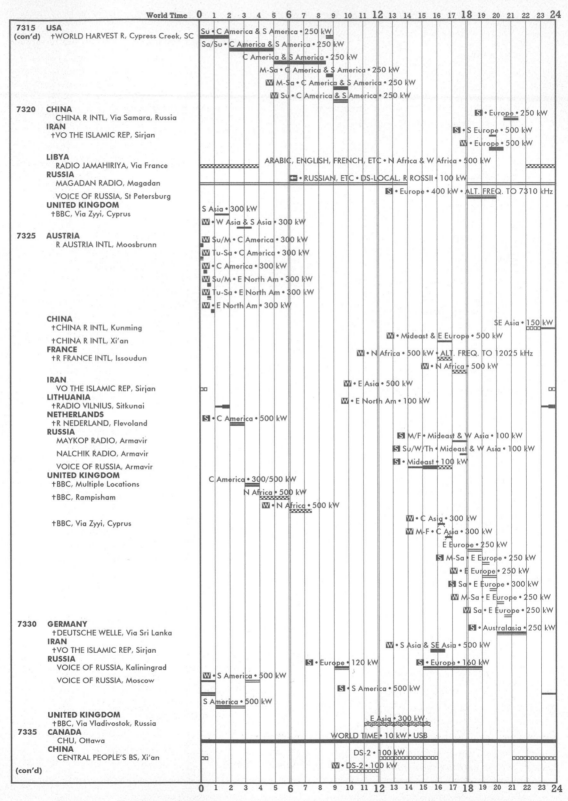

| | | World Time | 0 | 1 | 2 | 3 | 4 | 5 | 6 | 7 | 8 | 9 | 10 | 11 | 12 | 13 | 14 | 15 | 16 | 17 | 18 | 19 | 20 | 21 | 22 | 23 | 24 |

7315 **USA**
(con'd) †WORLD HARVEST R, Cypress Creek, SC
- Su • C America & S America • 250 kW
- Sa/Su • C America & S America • 250 kW
- C America & S America • 250 kW
- M-Sa • C America & S America • 250 kW
- W • M-Sa • C America & S America • 250 kW
- W Su • C America & S America • 250 kW

7320 **CHINA**
CHINA R INTL, Via Samara, Russia
- S • Europe • 250 kW

IRAN
†VO THE ISLAMIC REP, Sirjan
- S • S Europe • 500 kW
- W • Europe • 500 kW

LIBYA
RADIO JAMAHIRIYA, Via France
- ARABIC, ENGLISH, FRENCH, ETC • N Africa & W Africa • 500 kW

RUSSIA
MAGADAN RADIO, Magadan
- RUSSIAN, ETC • DS-LOCAL, R ROSSII • 100 kW

VOICE OF RUSSIA, St Petersburg
- S • Europe • 400 kW • ALT. FREQ. TO 7310 kHz

UNITED KINGDOM
†BBC, Via Zyyi, Cyprus
- S Asia • 300 kW
- W • W Asia & S Asia • 300 kW

7325 **AUSTRIA**
R AUSTRIA INTL, Moosbrunn
- W Su/M • C America • 300 kW
- W Tu-Sa • C America • 300 kW
- W • C America • 300 kW
- W Su/M • E North Am • 300 kW
- W Tu-Sa • E North Am • 300 kW
- W • E North Am • 300 kW

CHINA
†CHINA R INTL, Kunming
- SE Asia • 150 kW
†CHINA R INTL, Xi'an
- W • Mideast & E Europe • 500 kW

FRANCE
†R FRANCE INTL, Issoudun
- W • N Africa • 500 kW • ALT. FREQ. TO 12025 kHz
- W • N Africa • 500 kW

IRAN
VO THE ISLAMIC REP, Sirjan
- W • E Asia • 500 kW

LITHUANIA
†RADIO VILNIUS, Sitkunai
- W • E North Am • 100 kW

NETHERLANDS
†R NEDERLAND, Flevoland
- S • C America • 500 kW

RUSSIA
MAYKOP RADIO, Armavir
- S M/F • Mideast & W Asia • 100 kW
NALCHIK RADIO, Armavir
- S Su/W/Th • Mideast & W Asia • 100 kW
VOICE OF RUSSIA, Armavir
- S • Mideast • 100 kW

UNITED KINGDOM
†BBC, Multiple Locations
- C America • 300/500 kW
†BBC, Rampisham
- N Africa • 500 kW
- W • N Africa • 500 kW

†BBC, Via Zyyi, Cyprus
- W • C Asia • 300 kW
- W M-F • C Asia • 300 kW
- E Europe • 250 kW
- S M-Sa • E Europe • 250 kW
- W • E Europe • 250 kW
- S Sa • E Europe • 300 kW
- W M-Sa • E Europe • 250 kW
- W Sa • E Europe • 250 kW

7330 **GERMANY**
†DEUTSCHE WELLE, Via Sri Lanka
- S • Australasia • 250 kW

IRAN
†VO THE ISLAMIC REP, Sirjan
- W • S Asia & SE Asia • 500 kW

RUSSIA
VOICE OF RUSSIA, Kaliningrad
- S • Europe • 120 kW
- S • Europe • 160 kW
VOICE OF RUSSIA, Moscow
- W • S America • 500 kW
- S • S America • 500 kW
- S America • 500 kW

UNITED KINGDOM
†BBC, Via Vladivostok, Russia
- E Asia • 300 kW

7335 **CANADA**
CHU, Ottawa
- WORLD TIME • 10 kW • USB

CHINA
CENTRAL PEOPLE'S BS, Xi'an
- DS-2 • 100 kW
- W • DS-2 • 100 kW

(con'd)

| 0 | 1 | 2 | 3 | 4 | 5 | 6 | 7 | 8 | 9 | 10 | 11 | 12 | 13 | 14 | 15 | 16 | 17 | 18 | 19 | 20 | 21 | 22 | 23 | 24 |

ENGLISH ▬   ARABIC ▧   CHINESE ▫▫▫   FRENCH ▭   GERMAN ▬   RUSSIAN ═   SPANISH ▬   OTHER ▬

World Time 0 1 2 3 4 5 6 7 8 9 10 11 12 13 14 15 16 17 18 19 20 21 22 23 24

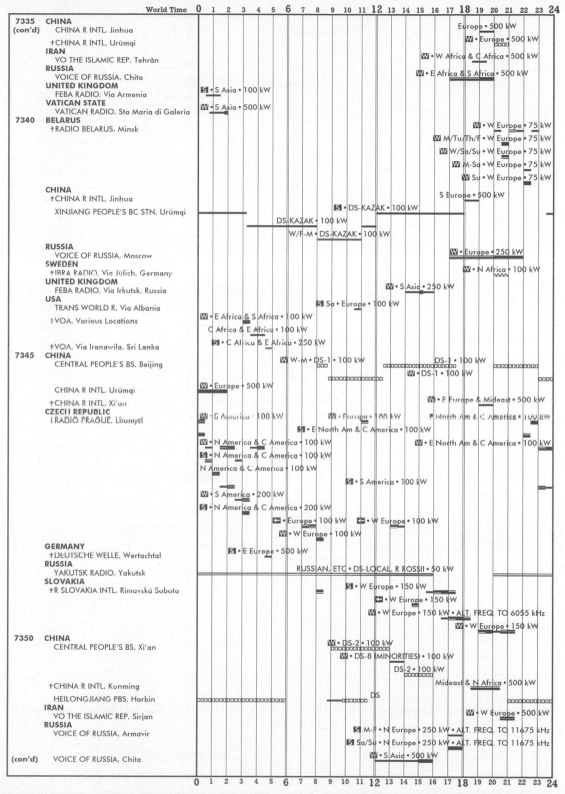

7335 **CHINA**
(con'd)   CHINA R INTL, Jinhua — Europe • 500 kW
      †CHINA R INTL, Urümqi — W • Europe • 500 kW
    IRAN
      VO THE ISLAMIC REP, Tehrān — W • W Africa & C Africa • 500 kW
    RUSSIA
      VOICE OF RUSSIA, Chita — W • E Africa & S Africa • 500 kW
    UNITED KINGDOM
      FEBA RADIO, Via Armenia — S • S Asia • 100 kW
    VATICAN STATE
      VATICAN RADIO, Sta Maria di Galeria — W • S Asia • 500 kW
7340 **BELARUS**
      †RADIO BELARUS, Minsk — W • W Europe • 75 kW
                                       W M/Tu/Th/F • W Europe • 75 kW
                                       W W/Sa/Su • W Europe • 75 kW
                                       W M-Sa • W Europe • 75 kW
                                       W Su • W Europe • 75 kW
    CHINA
      †CHINA R INTL, Jinhua — S Europe • 500 kW
      XINJIANG PEOPLE'S BC STN, Urümqi — S • DS-KAZAK • 100 kW
                                       DS-KAZAK • 100 kW
                                       W/F-M • DS-KAZAK • 100 kW
    RUSSIA
      VOICE OF RUSSIA, Moscow — W • Europe • 250 kW
    SWEDEN
      †IBRA RADIO, Via Jülich, Germany — W • N Africa • 100 kW
    UNITED KINGDOM
      FEBA RADIO, Via Irkutsk, Russia — W • S Asia • 250 kW
    USA
      TRANS WORLD R, Via Albania — S • Sa • Europe • 100 kW
      †VOA, Various Locations — W • E Africa & S Africa • 100 kW
                                C Africa & E Africa • 100 kW
                                S • C Africa & E Africa • 250 kW
      †VOA, Via Iranawila, Sri Lanka
7345 **CHINA**
      CENTRAL PEOPLE'S BS, Beijing — W W-M • DS-1 • 100 kW   DS-1 • 100 kW
                                       W • DS-1 • 100 kW
      CHINA R INTL, Urümqi — W • Europe • 500 kW
      †CHINA R INTL, Xi'an — W • E Europe & Mideast • 500 kW
    CZECH REPUBLIC
      †RADIO PRAGUE, Litomyšl — W • C America • 100 kW   W • Europe • 100 kW   E North Am & C America • 100 kW
                                S • E North Am & C America • 100 kW
                                W • N America & C America • 100 kW   W • E North Am & C America • 100 kW
                                S • N America & C America • 100 kW
                                N America & C America • 100 kW
                                S • S America • 100 kW
                                W • S America • 200 kW
                                S • N America & C America • 200 kW
                                ← • Europe • 100 kW   ← • W Europe • 100 kW
                                W • W Europe • 100 kW
    GERMANY
      †DEUTSCHE WELLE, Wertachtal — S • E Europe • 500 kW
    RUSSIA
      YAKUTSK RADIO, Yakutsk — RUSSIAN, ETC • DS-LOCAL, R ROSSII • 50 kW
    SLOVAKIA
      †R SLOVAKIA INTL, Rimavská Sobota — S • W Europe • 150 kW
                                ← • W Europe • 150 kW
                                W • W Europe • 150 kW • ALT. FREQ. TO 6055 kHz
                                W • W Europe • 150 kW
7350 **CHINA**
      CENTRAL PEOPLE'S BS, Xi'an — W • DS-2 • 100 kW
                                W • DS-8 (MINORITIES) • 100 kW
                                DS-2 • 100 kW
      †CHINA R INTL, Kunming — Mideast & N Africa • 500 kW
      HEILONGJIANG PBS, Harbin — DS
    IRAN
      VO THE ISLAMIC REP, Sirjan — W • W Europe • 500 kW
    RUSSIA
      VOICE OF RUSSIA, Armavir — S M-F • N Europe • 250 kW • ALT. FREQ. TO 11675 kHz
                                S Sa/Su • N Europe • 250 kW • ALT. FREQ. TO 11675 kHz
(con'd)   VOICE OF RUSSIA, Chita — W • S Asia • 500 kW

0 1 2 3 4 5 6 7 8 9 10 11 12 13 14 15 16 17 18 19 20 21 22 23 24

SEASONAL S OR W   1-HR TIMESHIFT MIDYEAR ← OR →   JAMMING / OR ∧   EARLIEST HEARD ◁   LATEST HEARD ▷   NEW FOR 2006 †

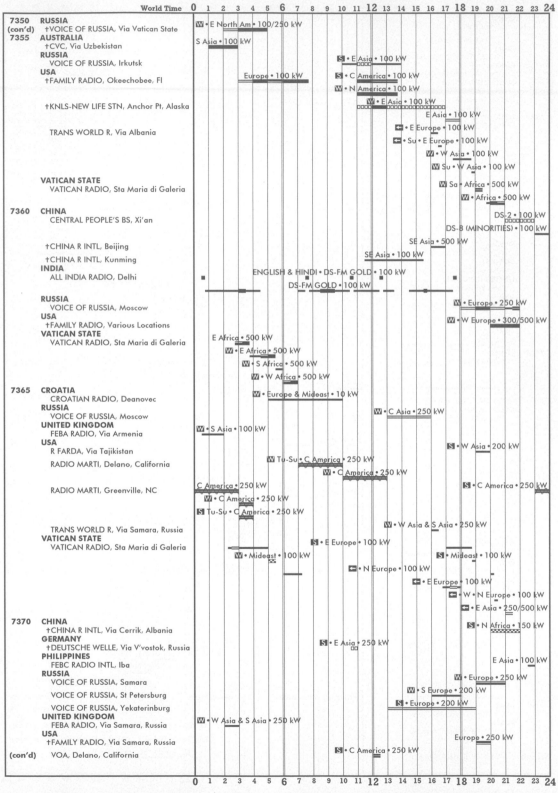

		World Time	0 1 2 3 4 5 6 7 8 9 10 11 12 13 14 15 16 17 18 19 20 21 22 23 24

7350 (con'd) **RUSSIA**
†VOICE OF RUSSIA, Via Vatican State — W • E North Am • 100/250 kW

7355 **AUSTRALIA**
†CVC, Via Uzbekistan — S Asia • 100 kW

RUSSIA
VOICE OF RUSSIA, Irkutsk — S • E Asia • 100 kW

USA
†FAMILY RADIO, Okeechobee, Fl — Europe • 100 kW / S • C America • 100 kW / W • N America • 100 kW

†KNLS-NEW LIFE STN, Anchor Pt, Alaska — W • E Asia • 100 kW / E Asia • 100 kW

TRANS WORLD R, Via Albania — ◄ • E Europe • 100 kW / ◄ • Su • E Europe • 100 kW / W • W Asia • 100 kW / W Su • W Asia • 100 kW

VATICAN STATE
VATICAN RADIO, Sta Maria di Galeria — W Sa • Africa • 500 kW / W • Africa • 500 kW

7360 **CHINA**
CENTRAL PEOPLE'S BS, Xi'an — DS-2 • 100 kW / DS-8 (MINORITIES) • 100 kW

†CHINA R INTL, Beijing — SE Asia • 500 kW

†CHINA R INTL, Kunming — SE Asia • 100 kW

INDIA
ALL INDIA RADIO, Delhi — ENGLISH & HINDI • DS-FM GOLD • 100 kW / DS-FM GOLD • 100 kW

RUSSIA
VOICE OF RUSSIA, Moscow — W • Europe • 250 kW

USA
†FAMILY RADIO, Various Locations — W • W Europe • 300/500 kW

VATICAN STATE
VATICAN RADIO, Sta Maria di Galeria — E Africa • 500 kW / W • E Africa • 500 kW / W • S Africa • 500 kW / W • W Africa • 500 kW

7365 **CROATIA**
CROATIAN RADIO, Deanovec — W • Europe & Mideast • 10 kW

RUSSIA
VOICE OF RUSSIA, Moscow — W • C Asia • 250 kW

UNITED KINGDOM
FEBA RADIO, Via Armenia — W • S Asia • 100 kW

USA
R FARDA, Via Tajikistan — S • W Asia • 200 kW

RADIO MARTI, Delano, California — W Tu-Su • C America • 250 kW / W • C America • 250 kW

RADIO MARTI, Greenville, NC — C America • 250 kW / S • C America • 250 kW / W • C America • 250 kW / S Tu-Su • C America • 250 kW

TRANS WORLD R, Via Samara, Russia — W • W Asia & S Asia • 250 kW

VATICAN STATE
VATICAN RADIO, Sta Maria di Galeria — S • E Europe • 100 kW / S • Mideast • 100 kW / W • Mideast • 100 kW / ◄ • N Europe • 100 kW / ◄ • E Europe • 100 kW / ◄ • W • N Europe • 100 kW / ◄ • E Asia • 250/500 kW

7370 **CHINA**
†CHINA R INTL, Via Cerrik, Albania — S • N Africa • 150 kW

GERMANY
†DEUTSCHE WELLE, Via V'vostok, Russia — S • E Asia • 250 kW

PHILIPPINES
FEBC RADIO INTL, Iba — E Asia • 100 kW

RUSSIA
VOICE OF RUSSIA, Samara — W • Europe • 250 kW

VOICE OF RUSSIA, St Petersburg — W • S Europe • 200 kW

VOICE OF RUSSIA, Yekaterinburg — S • Europe • 200 kW

UNITED KINGDOM
FEBA RADIO, Via Samara, Russia — W • W Asia & S Asia • 250 kW

USA
†FAMILY RADIO, Via Samara, Russia — Europe • 250 kW

(con'd) VOA, Delano, California — S • C America • 250 kW

	World Time	0 1 2 3 4 5 6 7 8 9 10 11 12 13 14 15 16 17 18 19 20 21 22 23 24

ENGLISH ▬▬ ARABIC ▨▨▨ CHINESE □□□ FRENCH ▭▭ GERMAN ▬▬ RUSSIAN ══ SPANISH ▬▬ OTHER ▬

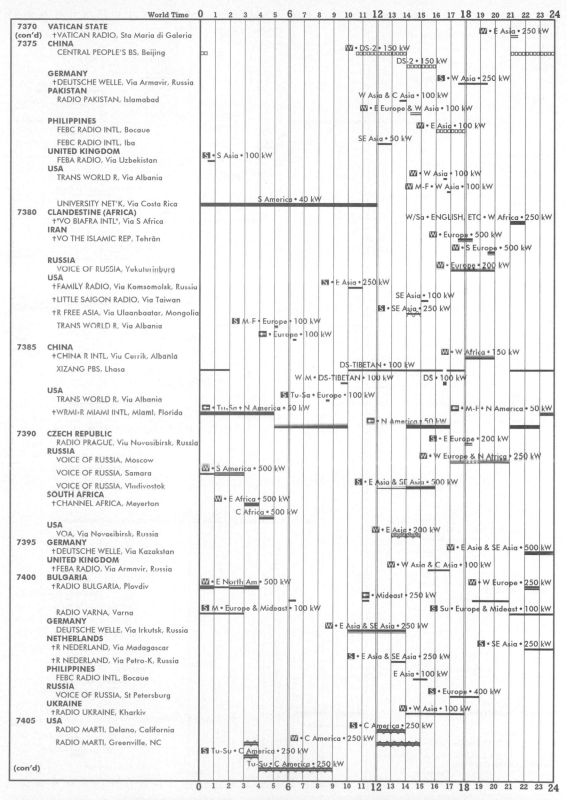

World Time   0 1 2 3 4 5 6 7 8 9 10 11 12 13 14 15 16 17 18 19 20 21 22 23 24

7370 VATICAN STATE
(con'd) †VATICAN RADIO, Sta Maria di Galeria — W • E Asia • 250 kW

7375 CHINA
CENTRAL PEOPLE'S BS, Beijing — W • DS-2 • 150 kW / DS-2 • 150 kW

GERMANY
†DEUTSCHE WELLE, Via Armavir, Russia — S • W Asia • 250 kW

PAKISTAN
RADIO PAKISTAN, Islamabad — W Asia & C Asia • 100 kW / W • E Europe & W Asia • 100 kW

PHILIPPINES
FEBC RADIO INTL, Bocaue — W • E Asia • 100 kW
FEBC RADIO INTL, Iba — SE Asia • 50 kW

UNITED KINGDOM
FEBA RADIO, Via Uzbekistan — S • S Asia • 100 kW

USA
TRANS WORLD R, Via Albania — W • W Asia • 100 kW / W M-F • W Asia • 100 kW
UNIVERSITY NET'K, Via Costa Rica — S America • 40 kW

7380 CLANDESTINE (AFRICA)
†"VO BIAFRA INTL", Via S Africa — W/Sa • ENGLISH, ETC • W Africa • 250 kW

IRAN
†VO THE ISLAMIC REP, Tehrān — W • Europe • 500 kW / W • S Europe • 500 kW

RUSSIA
VOICE OF RUSSIA, Yekaterinburg — W • Europe • 200 kW

USA
†FAMILY RADIO, Via Komsomolsk, Russia — S • E Asia • 250 kW
†LITTLE SAIGON RADIO, Via Taiwan — SE Asia • 100 kW
†R FREE ASIA, Via Ulaanbaatar, Mongolia — S • SE Asia • 250 kW
TRANS WORLD R, Via Albania — S • M-F • Europe • 100 kW / ⇆ • Europe • 100 kW

7385 CHINA
†CHINA R INTL, Via Cerrik, Albania — W • W Africa • 150 kW
XIZANG PBS, Lhasa — DS-TIBETAN • 100 kW / W M • DS-TIBETAN • 100 kW / DS • 100 kW

USA
TRANS WORLD R, Via Albania — S • Tu-Sa • Europe • 100 kW
†WRMI-R MIAMI INTL, Miami, Florida — ⇆ • Tu-Sa • N America • 50 kW / ⇆ • M-F • N America • 50 kW / ⇆ • N America • 50 kW

7390 CZECH REPUBLIC
RADIO PRAGUE, Via Novosibirsk, Russia — S • E Europe • 200 kW

RUSSIA
VOICE OF RUSSIA, Moscow — W • W Europe & N Africa • 250 kW
VOICE OF RUSSIA, Samara — W • S America • 500 kW
VOICE OF RUSSIA, Vladivostok — S • E Asia & SE Asia • 500 kW

SOUTH AFRICA
†CHANNEL AFRICA, Meyerton — W • E Africa • 500 kW / C Africa • 500 kW

USA
VOA, Via Novosibirsk, Russia — W • E Asia • 200 kW

7395 GERMANY
†DEUTSCHE WELLE, Via Kazakstan — S • E Asia & SE Asia • 500 kW

UNITED KINGDOM
†FEBA RADIO, Via Armavir, Russia — W • W Asia & C Asia • 100 kW

7400 BULGARIA
†RADIO BULGARIA, Plovdiv — W • E North Am • 500 kW / ⇆ • Mideast • 250 kW / W • W Europe • 250 kW
RADIO VARNA, Varna — S M • Europe & Mideast • 100 kW / S • Su • Europe & Mideast • 100 kW

GERMANY
DEUTSCHE WELLE, Via Irkutsk, Russia — W • E Asia & SE Asia • 250 kW

NETHERLANDS
†R NEDERLAND, Via Madagascar — S • SE Asia • 250 kW
†R NEDERLAND, Via Petro-K, Russia — S • E Asia & SE Asia • 250 kW

PHILIPPINES
FEBC RADIO INTL, Bocaue — E Asia • 100 kW

RUSSIA
VOICE OF RUSSIA, St Petersburg — S • Europe • 400 kW

UKRAINE
†RADIO UKRAINE, Kharkiv — W • W Asia • 100 kW

7405 USA
RADIO MARTI, Delano, California — S • C America • 250 kW
RADIO MARTI, Greenville, NC — W • C America • 250 kW / S Tu-Su • C America • 250 kW / Tu-Su • C America • 250 kW

(con'd)

0 1 2 3 4 5 6 7 8 9 10 11 12 13 14 15 16 17 18 19 20 21 22 23 24

SEASONAL S OR W   1-HR TIMESHIFT MIDYEAR ⇆ OR ⇄   JAMMING / OR ∧   EARLIEST HEARD ◁   LATEST HEARD ▷   NEW FOR 2006 †

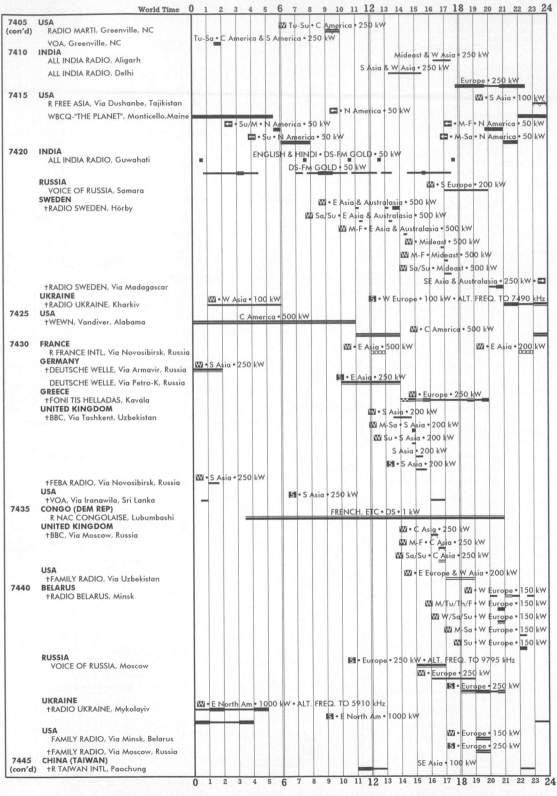

World Time 0 1 2 3 4 5 6 7 8 9 10 11 12 13 14 15 16 17 18 19 20 21 22 23 24

Freq	Country / Station	
7405 (con'd)	**USA** RADIO MARTI, Greenville, NC	W Tu-Su • C America • 250 kW
	VOA, Greenville, NC	Tu-Sa • C America & S America • 250 kW
7410	**INDIA** ALL INDIA RADIO, Aligarh	Mideast & W Asia • 250 kW
	ALL INDIA RADIO, Delhi	S Asia & W Asia • 250 kW
		Europe • 250 kW
7415	**USA** R FREE ASIA, Via Dushanbe, Tajikistan	W • S Asia • 100 kW
	WBCQ-"THE PLANET", Monticello, Maine	N America • 50 kW
		Su/M • N America • 50 kW M-F • N America • 50 kW
		Su • N America • 50 kW M-Sa • N America • 50 kW
7420	**INDIA** ALL INDIA RADIO, Guwahati	ENGLISH & HINDI • DS-FM GOLD • 50 kW
		DS-FM GOLD • 50 kW
	RUSSIA VOICE OF RUSSIA, Samara	W • S Europe • 200 kW
	SWEDEN †RADIO SWEDEN, Hörby	W • E Asia & Australasia • 500 kW
		W Sa/Su • E Asia & Australasia • 500 kW
		W M-F • E Asia & Australasia • 500 kW
		W • Mideast • 500 kW
		W M-F • Mideast • 500 kW
		W Sa/Su • Mideast • 500 kW
	†RADIO SWEDEN, Via Madagascar	SE Asia & Australasia • 250 kW
	UKRAINE †RADIO UKRAINE, Kharkiv	W • W Asia • 100 kW S • W Europe • 100 kW • ALT. FREQ. TO 7490 kHz
7425	**USA** †WEWN, Vandiver, Alabama	C America • 500 kW
		W • C America • 500 kW
7430	**FRANCE** R FRANCE INTL, Via Novosibirsk, Russia	W • E Asia • 500 kW W • E Asia • 200 kW
	GERMANY †DEUTSCHE WELLE, Via Armavir, Russia	W • S Asia • 250 kW
	DEUTSCHE WELLE, Via Petro-K, Russia	S • E Asia • 250 kW
	GREECE †FONI TIS HELLADAS, Kavála	W • Europe • 250 kW
	UNITED KINGDOM †BBC, Via Tashkent, Uzbekistan	W • S Asia • 200 kW
		W M-Sa • S Asia • 200 kW
		W Su • S Asia • 200 kW
		S Asia • 200 kW
		S • S Asia • 200 kW
	†FEBA RADIO, Via Novosibirsk, Russia	W • S Asia • 250 kW
	USA †VOA, Via Iranawila, Sri Lanka	S • S Asia • 250 kW
7435	**CONGO (DEM REP)** R NAC CONGOLAISE, Lubumbashi	FRENCH, ETC • DS • 1 kW
	UNITED KINGDOM †BBC, Via Moscow, Russia	W • C Asia • 250 kW
		W M-F • C Asia • 250 kW
		W Sa/Su • C Asia • 250 kW
	USA †FAMILY RADIO, Via Uzbekistan	W • E Europe & W Asia • 200 kW
7440	**BELARUS** †RADIO BELARUS, Minsk	W • W Europe • 150 kW
		W M/Tu/Th/F • W Europe • 150 kW
		W W/Sa/Su • W Europe • 150 kW
		W M-Sa • W Europe • 150 kW
		W Su • W Europe • 150 kW
	RUSSIA VOICE OF RUSSIA, Moscow	S • Europe • 250 kW • ALT. FREQ. TO 9795 kHz
		W • Europe • 250 kW
		S • Europe • 250 kW
	UKRAINE †RADIO UKRAINE, Mykolayiv	W • E North Am • 1000 kW • ALT. FREQ. TO 5910 kHz
		S • E North Am • 1000 kW
	USA FAMILY RADIO, Via Minsk, Belarus	W • Europe • 150 kW
	†FAMILY RADIO, Via Moscow, Russia	S • Europe • 250 kW
7445 (con'd)	**CHINA (TAIWAN)** †R TAIWAN INTL, Paochung	SE Asia • 100 kW

0 1 2 3 4 5 6 7 8 9 10 11 12 13 14 15 16 17 18 19 20 21 22 23 24

ENGLISH ▬ ARABIC ░ CHINESE ▫▫▫ FRENCH ▬ GERMAN ▬ RUSSIAN ═ SPANISH ▬ OTHER ▬

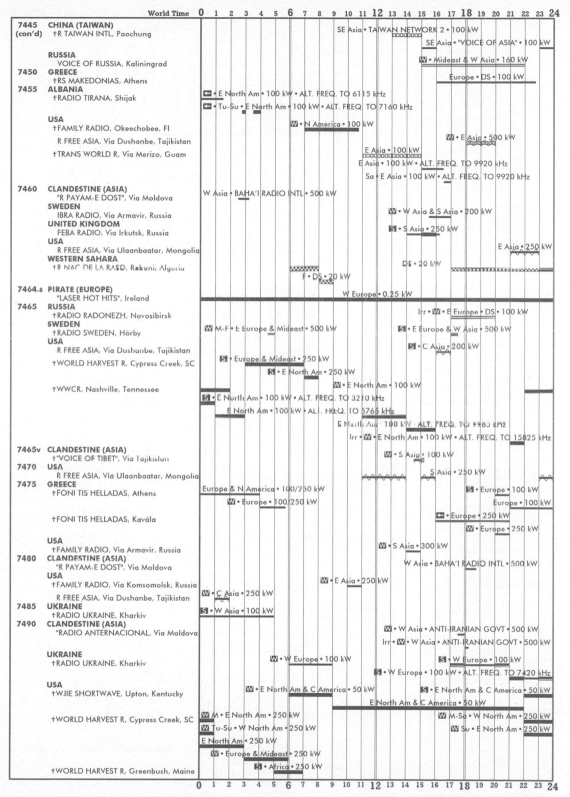

World Time | 0 1 2 3 4 5 6 7 8 9 10 11 12 13 14 15 16 17 18 19 20 21 22 23 24

Freq	Station	Schedule (chart)
7445 (con'd)	CHINA (TAIWAN) †R TAIWAN INTL, Paochung	SE Asia • TAIWAN NETWORK 2 • 100 kW
		SE Asia • "VOICE OF ASIA" • 100 kW
	RUSSIA VOICE OF RUSSIA, Kaliningrad	W • Mideast & W Asia • 160 kW
7450	GREECE †RS MAKEDONIAS, Athens	Europe • DS • 100 kW
7455	ALBANIA †RADIO TIRANA, Shijak	← • E North Am • 100 kW • ALT. FREQ. TO 6115 kHz
		← • Tu-Su • E North Am • 100 kW • ALT. FREQ. TO 7160 kHz
	USA †FAMILY RADIO, Okeechobee, Fl	W • N America • 100 kW
	R FREE ASIA, Via Dushanbe, Tajikistan	W • E Asia • 500 kW
	†TRANS WORLD R, Via Merizo, Guam	E Asia • 100 kW
		E Asia • 100 kW • ALT. FREQ. TO 9920 kHz
		Sa • E Asia • 100 kW • ALT. FREQ. TO 9920 kHz
7460	CLANDESTINE (ASIA) "R PAYAM-E DOST", Via Moldova	W Asia • BAHA'I RADIO INTL • 500 kW
	SWEDEN IBRA RADIO, Via Armavir, Russia	W • W Asia & S Asia • 200 kW
	UNITED KINGDOM FEBA RADIO, Via Irkutsk, Russia	S • S Asia • 250 kW
	USA R FREE ASIA, Via Ulaanbaatar, Mongolia	E Asia • 250 kW
	WESTERN SAHARA †R NAC DE LA RASD, Rabuni, Algeria	DS • 20 kW
		F • DS • 20 kW
7464.8	PIRATE (EUROPE) "LASER HOT HITS", Ireland	W Europe • 0.25 kW
7465	RUSSIA †RADIO RADONEZH, Novosibirsk	Irr • W • E Europe • DS • 100 kW
	SWEDEN †RADIO SWEDEN, Hörby	W • M-F • E Europe & Mideast • 500 kW
		S • E Europe & W Asia • 500 kW
	USA R FREE ASIA, Via Dushanbe, Tajikistan	S • C Asia • 200 kW
	†WORLD HARVEST R, Cypress Creek, SC	S • Europe & Mideast • 250 kW
		S • E North Am • 250 kW
	†WWCR, Nashville, Tennessee	W • E North Am • 100 kW
		S • E North Am • 100 kW • ALT. FREQ. TO 3210 kHz
		E North Am • 100 kW • ALT. FREQ. TO 5765 kHz
		E North Am • 100 kW • ALT. FREQ. TO 9985 kHz
		Irr • W • E North Am • 100 kW • ALT. FREQ. TO 15825 kHz
7465v	CLANDESTINE (ASIA) †"VOICE OF TIBET", Via Tajikistan	W • S Asia • 100 kW
7470	USA R FREE ASIA, Via Ulaanbaatar, Mongolia	S Asia • 250 kW
7475	GREECE †FONI TIS HELLADAS, Athens	Europe & N America • 100/250 kW
		S • Europe • 100 kW
		W • Europe • 100/250 kW
		Europe • 100 kW
	†FONI TIS HELLADAS, Kavála	← • Europe • 250 kW
		W • Europe • 250 kW
	USA †FAMILY RADIO, Via Armavir, Russia	W • S Asia • 300 kW
7480	CLANDESTINE (ASIA) "R PAYAM-E DOST", Via Moldova	W Asia • BAHA'I RADIO INTL • 500 kW
	USA †FAMILY RADIO, Via Komsomolsk, Russia	W • E Asia • 250 kW
	R FREE ASIA, Via Dushanbe, Tajikistan	W • C Asia • 250 kW
7485	UKRAINE †RADIO UKRAINE, Kharkiv	S • W Asia • 100 kW
7490	CLANDESTINE (ASIA) "RADIO ANTERNACIONAL, Via Moldova	W • W Asia • ANTI-IRANIAN GOVT • 500 kW
		Irr • W • W Asia • ANTI-IRANIAN GOVT • 500 kW
	UKRAINE †RADIO UKRAINE, Kharkiv	W • W Europe • 100 kW
		S • W Europe • 100 kW
		S • W Europe • 100 kW • ALT. FREQ. TO 7420 kHz
	USA †WJIE SHORTWAVE, Upton, Kentucky	W • E North Am & C America • 50 kW
		S • E North Am & C America • 50 kW
		E North Am & C America • 50 kW
	†WORLD HARVEST R, Cypress Creek, SC	W • M • E North Am • 250 kW
		W • M-Sa • W North Am • 250 kW
		W • Tu-Su • W North Am • 250 kW
		W • Su • E North Am • 250 kW
		E North Am • 250 kW
		W • Europe & Mideast • 250 kW
	†WORLD HARVEST R, Greenbush, Maine	S • Africa • 250 kW

0 1 2 3 4 5 6 7 8 9 10 11 12 13 14 15 16 17 18 19 20 21 22 23 24

SEASONAL S OR W   1-HR TIMESHIFT MIDYEAR ← OR →   JAMMING / OR /\   EARLIEST HEARD ◁   LATEST HEARD ▷   NEW FOR 2006 †

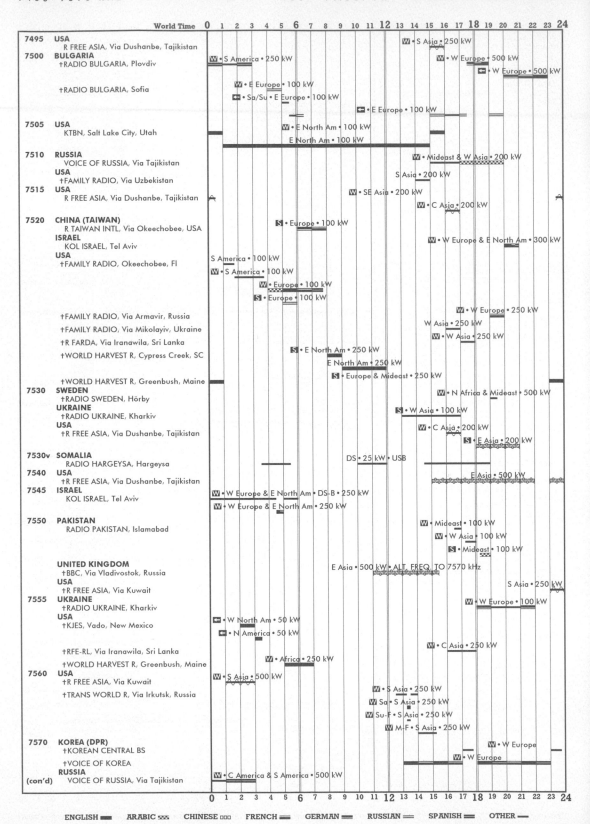

		World Time	0 1 2 3 4 5 6 7 8 9 10 11 12 13 14 15 16 17 18 19 20 21 22 23 24

7495 USA
R FREE ASIA, Via Dushanbe, Tajikistan — W • S Asia • 250 kW

7500 BULGARIA
†RADIO BULGARIA, Plovdiv — W • S America • 250 kW / W • W Europe • 500 kW / W Europe • 500 kW

†RADIO BULGARIA, Sofia — W • E Europe • 100 kW / Sa/Su • E Europe • 100 kW / E Europe • 100 kW

7505 USA
KTBN, Salt Lake City, Utah — W • E North Am • 100 kW / E North Am • 100 kW

7510 RUSSIA
VOICE OF RUSSIA, Via Tajikistan — W • Mideast & W Asia • 200 kW
USA
†FAMILY RADIO, Via Uzbekistan — S Asia • 200 kW

7515 USA
R FREE ASIA, Via Dushanbe, Tajikistan — W • SE Asia • 200 kW / W • C Asia • 200 kW

7520 CHINA (TAIWAN)
R TAIWAN INTL, Via Okeechobee, USA — S • Europe • 100 kW
ISRAEL
KOL ISRAEL, Tel Aviv — W • W Europe & E North Am • 300 kW
USA
†FAMILY RADIO, Okeechobee, Fl — S America • 100 kW / W • S America • 100 kW / W • Europe • 100 kW / S • Europe • 100 kW

†FAMILY RADIO, Via Armavir, Russia — W • W Europe • 250 kW

†FAMILY RADIO, Via Mikolayiv, Ukraine — W Asia • 250 kW

†R FARDA, Via Iranawila, Sri Lanka — W • W Asia • 250 kW

†WORLD HARVEST R, Cypress Creek, SC — S • E North Am • 250 kW / E North Am • 250 kW

†WORLD HARVEST R, Greenbush, Maine — S • Europe & Mideast • 250 kW

7530 SWEDEN
†RADIO SWEDEN, Hörby — W • N Africa & Mideast • 500 kW
UKRAINE
†RADIO UKRAINE, Kharkiv — S • W Asia • 100 kW
USA
†R FREE ASIA, Via Dushanbe, Tajikistan — W • C Asia • 200 kW / S • E Asia • 200 kW

7530v SOMALIA
RADIO HARGEYSA, Hargeysa — DS • 25 kW • USB

7540 USA
†R FREE ASIA, Via Dushanbe, Tajikistan — E Asia • 500 kW

7545 ISRAEL
KOL ISRAEL, Tel Aviv — W • W Europe & E North Am • DS-B • 250 kW / W • W Europe & E North Am • 250 kW

7550 PAKISTAN
RADIO PAKISTAN, Islamabad — W • Mideast • 100 kW / W • W Asia • 100 kW / S • Mideast • 100 kW

UNITED KINGDOM
†BBC, Via Vladivostok, Russia — E Asia • 500 kW • ALT. FREQ. TO 7570 kHz
USA
†R FREE ASIA, Via Kuwait — S Asia • 250 kW

7555 UKRAINE
†RADIO UKRAINE, Kharkiv — W • W Europe • 100 kW
USA
†KJES, Vado, New Mexico — W North Am • 50 kW / N America • 50 kW

†RFE-RL, Via Iranawila, Sri Lanka — W • C Asia • 250 kW

†WORLD HARVEST R, Greenbush, Maine — W • Africa • 250 kW

7560 USA
†R FREE ASIA, Via Kuwait — W • S Asia • 500 kW

†TRANS WORLD R, Via Irkutsk, Russia — W • S Asia • 250 kW / W Sa • S Asia • 250 kW / W Su-F • S Asia • 250 kW / W M-F • S Asia • 250 kW

7570 KOREA (DPR)
†KOREAN CENTRAL BS — W • W Europe

†VOICE OF KOREA — W • W Europe
RUSSIA
(con'd) VOICE OF RUSSIA, Via Tajikistan — W • C America & S America • 500 kW

ENGLISH ▬ ARABIC ⁞⁞⁞ CHINESE ▫▫▫ FRENCH ═ GERMAN ▬ RUSSIAN ═ SPANISH ▬ OTHER ▬

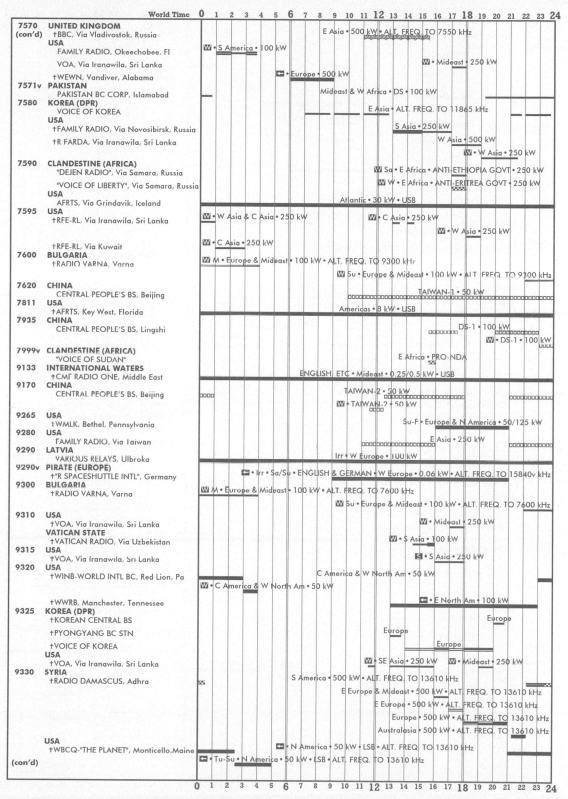

Freq	Country / Station	
7570 (con'd)	UNITED KINGDOM	†BBC, Via Vladivostok, Russia
	USA	FAMILY RADIO, Okeechobee, Fl
		VOA, Via Iranawila, Sri Lanka
		†WEWN, Vandiver, Alabama
7571v	PAKISTAN	PAKISTAN BC CORP, Islamabad
7580	KOREA (DPR)	VOICE OF KOREA
	USA	†FAMILY RADIO, Via Novosibirsk, Russia
		†R FARDA, Via Iranawila, Sri Lanka
7590	CLANDESTINE (AFRICA)	"DEJEN RADIO", Via Samara, Russia
		"VOICE OF LIBERTY", Via Samara, Russia
	USA	AFRTS, Via Grindavik, Iceland
7595	USA	†RFE-RL, Via Iranawila, Sri Lanka
		†RFE-RL, Via Kuwait
7600	BULGARIA	†RADIO VARNA, Varna
7620	CHINA	CENTRAL PEOPLE'S BS, Beijing
7811	USA	†AFRTS, Key West, Florida
7935	CHINA	CENTRAL PEOPLE'S BS, Lingshi
7999v	CLANDESTINE (AFRICA)	"VOICE OF SUDAN"
9133	INTERNATIONAL WATERS	†CMF RADIO ONE, Middle East
9170	CHINA	CENTRAL PEOPLE'S BS, Beijing
9265	USA	†WMLK, Bethel, Pennsylvania
9280	USA	FAMILY RADIO, Via Taiwan
9290	LATVIA	VARIOUS RELAYS, Ulbroka
9290v	PIRATE (EUROPE)	†"R SPACESHUTTLE INTL", Germany
9300	BULGARIA	†RADIO VARNA, Varna
9310	USA	†VOA, Via Iranawila, Sri Lanka
	VATICAN STATE	†VATICAN RADIO, Via Uzbekistan
9315	USA	†VOA, Via Iranawila, Sri Lanka
9320	USA	†WINB-WORLD INTL BC, Red Lion, Pa
		†WWRB, Manchester, Tennessee
9325	KOREA (DPR)	†KOREAN CENTRAL BS
		†PYONGYANG BC STN
		†VOICE OF KOREA
	USA	†VOA, Via Iranawila, Sri Lanka
9330	SYRIA	†RADIO DAMASCUS, Adhra
	USA	†WBCQ-"THE PLANET", Monticello, Maine
(con'd)		

Annotations on the time-grid:

- 7570 (con'd) UNITED KINGDOM †BBC: E Asia • 500 kW • ALT. FREQ. TO 7550 kHz
- USA FAMILY RADIO: W • S America • 100 kW
- VOA: W • Mideast • 250 kW
- †WEWN: ↹ • Europe • 500 kW
- 7571v PAKISTAN: Mideast & W Africa • DS • 100 kW
- 7580 VOICE OF KOREA: E Asia • ALT. FREQ. TO 11865 kHz
- †FAMILY RADIO: S Asia • 250 kW
- †R FARDA: W Asia • 500 kW / W • W Asia • 250 kW
- 7590 "DEJEN RADIO": W • Sa • E Africa • ANTI-ETHIOPIA GOVT • 250 kW
- "VOICE OF LIBERTY": W • E Africa • ANTI-ERITREA GOVT • 250 kW
- AFRTS: Atlantic • 30 kW • USB
- 7595 †RFE-RL Iranawila: W • W Asia & C Asia • 250 kW / W • C Asia • 250 kW / W • W Asia • 250 kW
- †RFE-RL Kuwait: W • C Asia • 250 kW
- 7600 †RADIO VARNA: W M • Europe & Mideast • 100 kW • ALT. FREQ. TO 9300 kHz / W Su • Europe & Mideast • 100 kW • ALT. FREQ. TO 9300 kHz
- 7620 CENTRAL PEOPLE'S BS: TAIWAN-1 • 50 kW
- 7811 †AFRTS: Americas • 8 kW • USB
- 7935 CENTRAL PEOPLE'S BS: DS-1 • 100 kW / W • DS-1 • 100 kW
- 7999v "VOICE OF SUDAN": E Africa • PRO-NDA
- 9133 †CMF RADIO ONE: ENGLISH, ETC • Mideast • 0.25/0.5 kW • USB
- 9170 CENTRAL PEOPLE'S BS: TAIWAN-2 • 50 kW / W • TAIWAN-2 • 50 kW
- 9265 †WMLK: Su-F • Europe & N America • 50/125 kW
- 9280 FAMILY RADIO: E Asia • 250 kW
- 9290 VARIOUS RELAYS: Irr • W Europe • 100 kW
- 9290v †"R SPACESHUTTLE INTL": ↹ • Irr • Sa/Su • ENGLISH & GERMAN • W Europe • 0.06 kW • ALT. FREQ. TO 15840v kHz
- 9300 †RADIO VARNA: W M • Europe & Mideast • 100 kW • ALT. FREQ. TO 7600 kHz / W Su • Europe & Mideast • 100 kW • ALT. FREQ. TO 7600 kHz
- 9310 †VOA: W • Mideast • 250 kW
- †VATICAN RADIO: W • S Asia • 100 kW
- 9315 †VOA: S • S Asia • 250 kW
- 9320 †WINB: C America & W North Am • 50 kW / W • C America & W North Am • 50 kW
- †WWRB: ↹ • E North Am • 100 kW
- 9325 †KOREAN CENTRAL BS: Europe
- †PYONGYANG BC STN: Europe
- †VOICE OF KOREA: Europe
- †VOA: W • SE Asia • 250 kW / W • Mideast • 250 kW
- 9330 †RADIO DAMASCUS: S America • 500 kW • ALT. FREQ. TO 13610 kHz / E Europe & Mideast • 500 kW • ALT. FREQ. TO 13610 kHz / E Europe • 500 kW • ALT. FREQ. TO 13610 kHz / Europe • 500 kW • ALT. FREQ. TO 13610 kHz / Australasia • 500 kW • ALT. FREQ. TO 13610 kHz
- †WBCQ-"THE PLANET": ↹ • N America • 50 kW • LSB • ALT. FREQ. TO 13610 kHz / ↹ • Tu-Su • N America • 50 kW • LSB • ALT. FREQ. TO 13610 kHz

World Time scale: 0 1 2 3 4 5 6 7 8 9 10 11 12 13 14 15 16 17 18 19 20 21 22 23 24

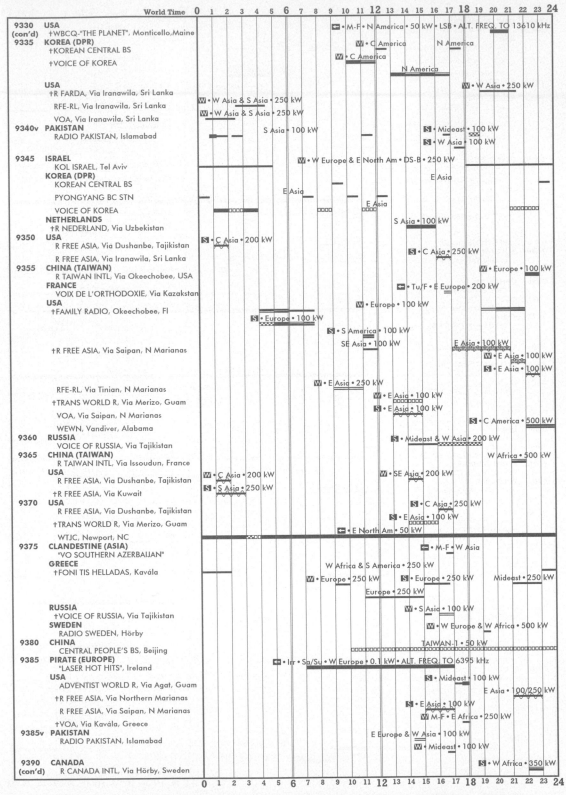

	World Time	0 1 2 3 4 5 6 7 8 9 10 11 12 13 14 15 16 17 18 19 20 21 22 23 24
9330 (con'd)	USA	
	†WBCQ-"THE PLANET", Monticello, Maine	• M-F • N America • 50 kW • LSB • ALT. FREQ. TO 13610 kHz
9335	KOREA (DPR)	
	†KOREAN CENTRAL BS	W • C America N America
	†VOICE OF KOREA	W • C America
		N America
	USA	
	†R FARDA, Via Iranawila, Sri Lanka	W • W Asia • 250 kW
	RFE-RL, Via Iranawila, Sri Lanka	S • W Asia & S Asia • 250 kW
	VOA, Via Iranawila, Sri Lanka	W • W Asia & S Asia • 250 kW
9340v	PAKISTAN	
	RADIO PAKISTAN, Islamabad	S Asia • 100 kW S • Mideast • 100 kW
		W • W Asia • 100 kW
9345	ISRAEL	
	KOL ISRAEL, Tel Aviv	W • W Europe & E North Am • DS-B • 250 kW
	KOREA (DPR)	
	KOREAN CENTRAL BS	E Asia
	PYONGYANG BC STN	E Asia
	VOICE OF KOREA	E Asia
	NETHERLANDS	
	†R NEDERLAND, Via Uzbekistan	S Asia • 100 kW
9350	USA	
	R FREE ASIA, Via Dushanbe, Tajikistan	S • C Asia • 200 kW
	R FREE ASIA, Via Iranawila, Sri Lanka	S • C Asia • 250 kW
9355	CHINA (TAIWAN)	
	R TAIWAN INTL, Via Okeechobee, USA	W • Europe • 100 kW
	FRANCE	
	VOIX DE L'ORTHODOXIE, Via Kazakstan	• Tu/F • E Europe • 200 kW
	USA	
	†FAMILY RADIO, Okeechobee, Fl	W • Europe • 100 kW
		S • Europe • 100 kW
		S • S America • 100 kW
		SE Asia • 100 kW E Asia • 100 kW
	†R FREE ASIA, Via Saipan, N Marianas	W • E Asia • 100 kW
		S • E Asia • 100 kW
	RFE-RL, Via Tinian, N Marianas	W • E Asia • 250 kW
	†TRANS WORLD R, Via Merizo, Guam	W • E Asia • 100 kW
	VOA, Via Saipan, N Marianas	S • E Asia • 100 kW
	WEWN, Vandiver, Alabama	S • C America • 500 kW
9360	RUSSIA	
	VOICE OF RUSSIA, Via Tajikistan	S • Mideast & W Asia • 200 kW
9365	CHINA (TAIWAN)	
	R TAIWAN INTL, Via Issoudun, France	W Africa • 500 kW
	USA	
	R FREE ASIA, Via Dushanbe, Tajikistan	W • C Asia • 200 kW W • SE Asia • 200 kW
	†R FREE ASIA, Via Kuwait	S • S Asia • 250 kW
9370	USA	
	R FREE ASIA, Via Dushanbe, Tajikistan	S • C Asia • 250 kW
	†TRANS WORLD R, Via Merizo, Guam	S • E Asia • 100 kW
	WTJC, Newport, NC	• E North Am • 50 kW
9375	CLANDESTINE (ASIA)	
	"VO SOUTHERN AZERBAIJAN"	• M-F • W Asia
	GREECE	
	†FONI TIS HELLADAS, Kavála	W Africa & S America • 250 kW
		W • Europe • 250 kW S • Europe • 250 kW Mideast • 250 kW
		Europe • 250 kW
	RUSSIA	
	†VOICE OF RUSSIA, Via Tajikistan	W • S Asia • 100 kW
	SWEDEN	
	RADIO SWEDEN, Hörby	W • W Europe & W Africa • 500 kW
9380	CHINA	
	CENTRAL PEOPLE'S BS, Beijing	TAIWAN-1 • 50 kW
9385	PIRATE (EUROPE)	
	"LASER HOT HITS", Ireland	• Irr • Sa/Su • W Europe • 0.1 kW • ALT. FREQ. TO 6395 kHz
	USA	
	ADVENTIST WORLD R, Via Agat, Guam	S • Mideast • 100 kW
		E Asia • 100/250 kW
	†R FREE ASIA, Via Northern Marianas	S • E Asia • 100 kW
	R FREE ASIA, Via Saipan, N Marianas	W • M-F • E Africa • 250 kW
	†VOA, Via Kavála, Greece	
9385v	PAKISTAN	
	RADIO PAKISTAN, Islamabad	E Europe & W Asia • 100 kW
		W • Mideast • 100 kW
9390 (con'd)	CANADA	
	R CANADA INTL, Via Hörby, Sweden	S • W Africa • 350 kW
		0 1 2 3 4 5 6 7 8 9 10 11 12 13 14 15 16 17 18 19 20 21 22 23 24

ENGLISH ▬   ARABIC ⋙   CHINESE ▫▫▫   FRENCH ═   GERMAN ▬   RUSSIAN ═   SPANISH ═   OTHER ▬

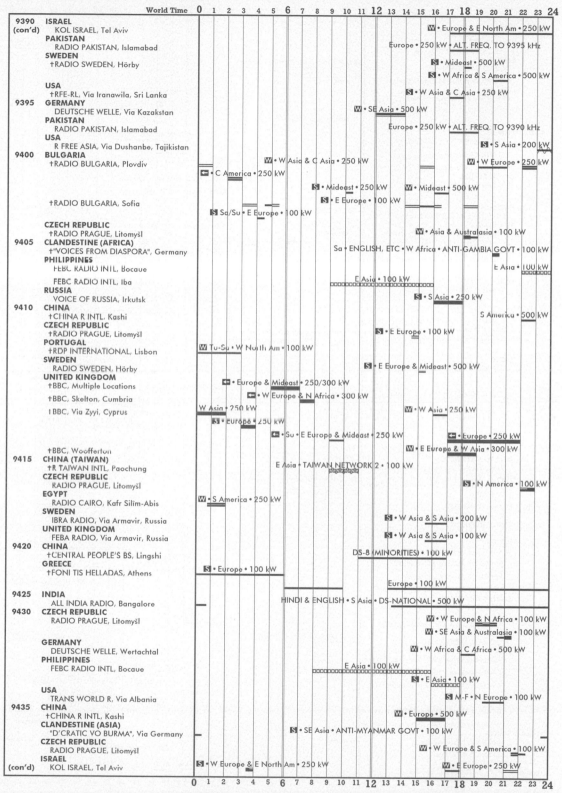

| World Time | 0 | 1 | 2 | 3 | 4 | 5 | 6 | 7 | 8 | 9 | 10 | 11 | 12 | 13 | 14 | 15 | 16 | 17 | 18 | 19 | 20 | 21 | 22 | 23 | 24 |

9390 (con'd)
ISRAEL
  KOL ISRAEL, Tel Aviv — W • Europe & E North Am • 250 kW
PAKISTAN
  RADIO PAKISTAN, Islamabad — Europe • 250 kW • ALT. FREQ. TO 9395 kHz
SWEDEN
  †RADIO SWEDEN, Hörby — S • Mideast • 500 kW
                         S • W Africa & S America • 500 kW
USA
  †RFE-RL, Via Iranawila, Sri Lanka — S • W Asia & C Asia • 250 kW

9395
GERMANY
  DEUTSCHE WELLE, Via Kazakstan — W • SE Asia • 500 kW
PAKISTAN
  RADIO PAKISTAN, Islamabad — Europe • 250 kW • ALT. FREQ. TO 9390 kHz
USA
  R FREE ASIA, Via Dushanbe, Tajikistan — S • S Asia • 200 kW

9400
BULGARIA
  †RADIO BULGARIA, Plovdiv — W • W Asia & C Asia • 250 kW
                           W • W Europe • 250 kW
                           ⇥ • C America • 250 kW
                           S • Mideast • 250 kW   W • Mideast • 500 kW
                           S • E Europe • 100 kW
  †RADIO BULGARIA, Sofia — S Sa/Su • E Europe • 100 kW

9405
CZECH REPUBLIC
  †RADIO PRAGUE, Litomyšl — W • Asia & Australasia • 100 kW
CLANDESTINE (AFRICA)
  †"VOICES FROM DIASPORA", Germany — Sa • ENGLISH, ETC • W Africa • ANTI-GAMBIA GOVT • 100 kW
PHILIPPINES
  FEBC RADIO INTL, Bocaue — E Asia • 100 kW
  FEBC RADIO INTL, Iba — E Asia • 100 kW
RUSSIA
  VOICE OF RUSSIA, Irkutsk — S • S Asia • 250 kW

9410
CHINA
  †CHINA R INTL, Kashi — S America • 500 kW
CZECH REPUBLIC
  †RADIO PRAGUE, Litomyšl — S • E Europe • 100 kW
PORTUGAL
  †RDP INTERNATIONAL, Lisbon — W Tu-Su • W North Am • 100 kW
SWEDEN
  RADIO SWEDEN, Hörby — S • E Europe & Mideast • 500 kW
UNITED KINGDOM
  †BBC, Multiple Locations — ⇥ • Europe & Mideast • 250/300 kW
                           ⇥ • W Europe & N Africa • 300 kW
  †BBC, Skelton, Cumbria — W Asia • 250 kW   W • W Asia • 250 kW
  †BBC, Via Zyyi, Cyprus — S • Europe • 250 kW
                         ⇥ • Su • E Europe & Mideast • 250 kW   ⇥ • Europe • 250 kW
  †BBC, Woofferton — W • E Europe & W Asia • 300 kW

9415
CHINA (TAIWAN)
  †R TAIWAN INTL, Paochung — E Asia • TAIWAN NETWORK 2 • 100 kW
CZECH REPUBLIC
  RADIO PRAGUE, Litomyšl — S • N America • 100 kW
EGYPT
  RADIO CAIRO, Kafr Silim-Abis — W • S America • 250 kW
SWEDEN
  IBRA RADIO, Via Armavir, Russia — S • W Asia & S Asia • 200 kW
UNITED KINGDOM
  FEBA RADIO, Via Armavir, Russia — S • W Asia & S Asia • 100 kW

9420
CHINA
  †CENTRAL PEOPLE'S BS, Lingshi — DS-8 (MINORITIES) • 100 kW
GREECE
  †FONI TIS HELLADAS, Athens — S • Europe • 100 kW
                             Europe • 100 kW

9425
INDIA
  ALL INDIA RADIO, Bangalore — HINDI & ENGLISH • S Asia • DS-NATIONAL • 500 kW

9430
CZECH REPUBLIC
  RADIO PRAGUE, Litomyšl — W • W Europe & N Africa • 100 kW
                          W • SE Asia & Australasia • 100 kW
GERMANY
  DEUTSCHE WELLE, Wertachtal — W • W Africa & C Africa • 500 kW
PHILIPPINES
  FEBC RADIO INTL, Bocaue — E Asia • 100 kW
                          S • E Asia • 100 kW
USA
  TRANS WORLD R, Via Albania — S M-F • N Europe • 100 kW

9435
CHINA
  †CHINA R INTL, Kashi — W • Europe • 500 kW
CLANDESTINE (ASIA)
  "D'CRATIC VO BURMA", Via Germany — S • SE Asia • ANTI-MYANMAR GOVT • 100 kW
CZECH REPUBLIC
  RADIO PRAGUE, Litomyšl — W • W Europe & S America • 100 kW
ISRAEL
(con'd) KOL ISRAEL, Tel Aviv — S • W Europe & E North Am • 250 kW
                                 W • E Europe • 250 kW

| | 0 | 1 | 2 | 3 | 4 | 5 | 6 | 7 | 8 | 9 | 10 | 11 | 12 | 13 | 14 | 15 | 16 | 17 | 18 | 19 | 20 | 21 | 22 | 23 | 24 |

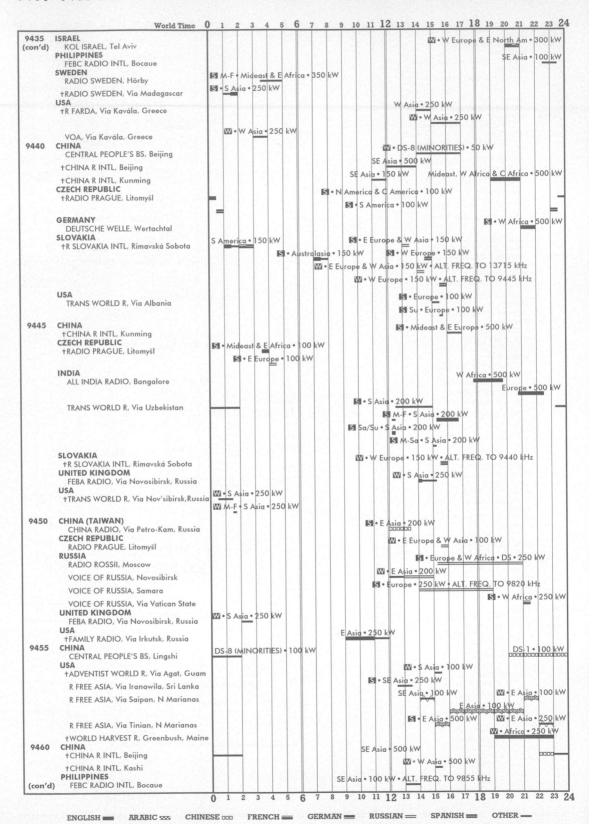

World Time 0 1 2 3 4 5 6 7 8 9 10 11 12 13 14 15 16 17 18 19 20 21 22 23 24

9435 **ISRAEL**
(con'd)   KOL ISRAEL, Tel Aviv
          PHILIPPINES
          FEBC RADIO INTL, Bocaue
          SWEDEN
          RADIO SWEDEN, Hörby
          †RADIO SWEDEN, Via Madagascar
          USA
          †R FARDA, Via Kavála, Greece

          VOA, Via Kavála, Greece
9440 **CHINA**
          CENTRAL PEOPLE'S BS, Beijing
          †CHINA R INTL, Beijing
          †CHINA R INTL, Kunming
          CZECH REPUBLIC
          †RADIO PRAGUE, Litomyšl

          GERMANY
          DEUTSCHE WELLE, Wertachtal
          SLOVAKIA
          †R SLOVAKIA INTL, Rimavská Sobota

          USA
          TRANS WORLD R, Via Albania
9445 **CHINA**
          †CHINA R INTL, Kunming
          CZECH REPUBLIC
          †RADIO PRAGUE, Litomyšl

          INDIA
          ALL INDIA RADIO, Bangalore

          TRANS WORLD R, Via Uzbekistan

          SLOVAKIA
          †R SLOVAKIA INTL, Rimavská Sobota
          UNITED KINGDOM
          FEBA RADIO, Via Novosibirsk, Russia
          USA
          †TRANS WORLD R, Via Nov'sibirsk,Russia
9450 **CHINA (TAIWAN)**
          CHINA RADIO, Via Petro-Kam, Russia
          CZECH REPUBLIC
          RADIO PRAGUE, Litomyšl
          RUSSIA
          RADIO ROSSII, Moscow
          VOICE OF RUSSIA, Novosibirsk
          VOICE OF RUSSIA, Samara
          VOICE OF RUSSIA, Via Vatican State
          UNITED KINGDOM
          FEBA RADIO, Via Novosibirsk, Russia
          USA
          †FAMILY RADIO, Via Irkutsk, Russia
9455 **CHINA**
          CENTRAL PEOPLE'S BS, Lingshi
          USA
          †ADVENTIST WORLD R, Via Agat, Guam
          R FREE ASIA, Via Iranawila, Sri Lanka
          R FREE ASIA, Via Saipan, N Marianas

          R FREE ASIA, Via Tinian, N Marianas
          †WORLD HARVEST R, Greenbush, Maine
9460 **CHINA**
          †CHINA R INTL, Beijing
          †CHINA R INTL, Kashi
          PHILIPPINES
(con'd)   FEBC RADIO INTL, Bocaue

0 1 2 3 4 5 6 7 8 9 10 11 12 13 14 15 16 17 18 19 20 21 22 23 24

ENGLISH ▬ ARABIC ⩘ CHINESE ▭▭▭ FRENCH ▬ GERMAN ▬ RUSSIAN ═ SPANISH ▬ OTHER ▬

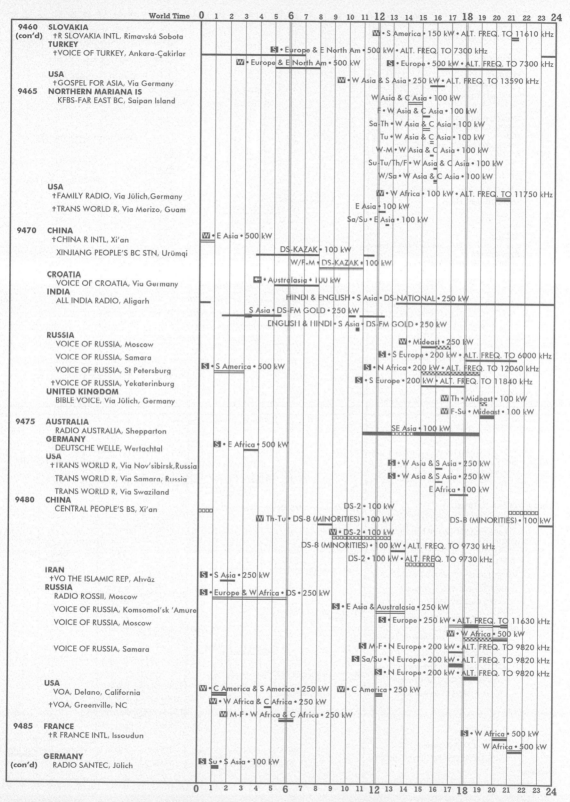

World Time: 0 1 2 3 4 5 6 7 8 9 10 11 12 13 14 15 16 17 18 19 20 21 22 23 24

9460 (con'd) SLOVAKIA
†R SLOVAKIA INTL, Rimavská Sobota — W • S America • 150 kW • ALT. FREQ. TO 11610 kHz

TURKEY
†VOICE OF TURKEY, Ankara-Çakirlar — S • Europe & E North Am • 500 kW • ALT. FREQ. TO 7300 kHz
W • Europe & E North Am • 500 kW — S • Europe • 500 kW • ALT. FREQ. TO 7300 kHz

USA
†GOSPEL FOR ASIA, Via Germany — W • W Asia & S Asia • 250 kW • ALT. FREQ. TO 13590 kHz

9465 NORTHERN MARIANA IS
KFBS-FAR EAST BC, Saipan Island — W Asia & C Asia • 100 kW
F • W Asia & C Asia • 100 kW
Sa-Th • W Asia & C Asia • 100 kW
Tu • W Asia & C Asia • 100 kW
W-M • W Asia & C Asia • 100 kW
Su-Tu/Th/F • W Asia & C Asia • 100 kW
W/Sa • W Asia & C Asia • 100 kW

USA
†FAMILY RADIO, Via Jülich, Germany — W • W Africa • 100 kW • ALT. FREQ. TO 11750 kHz
†TRANS WORLD R, Via Merizo, Guam — E Asia • 100 kW
Sa/Su • E Asia • 100 kW

9470 CHINA
†CHINA R INTL, Xi'an — W • E Asia • 500 kW
XINJIANG PEOPLE'S BC STN, Urümqi — DS-KAZAK • 100 kW
W/F-M • DS-KAZAK • 100 kW

CROATIA
VOICE OF CROATIA, Via Germany — • Australasia • 100 kW

INDIA
ALL INDIA RADIO, Aligarh — HINDI & ENGLISH • S Asia • DS-NATIONAL • 250 kW
S Asia • DS-FM GOLD • 250 kW
ENGLISH & HINDI • S Asia • DS-FM GOLD • 250 kW

RUSSIA
VOICE OF RUSSIA, Moscow — W • Mideast • 250 kW
VOICE OF RUSSIA, Samara — S • S Europe • 200 kW • ALT. FREQ. TO 6000 kHz
VOICE OF RUSSIA, St Petersburg — S • S America • 500 kW / S • N Africa • 200 kW • ALT. FREQ. TO 12060 kHz
†VOICE OF RUSSIA, Yekaterinburg — S • S Europe • 200 kW • ALT. FREQ. TO 11840 kHz

UNITED KINGDOM
BIBLE VOICE, Via Jülich, Germany — W Th • Mideast • 100 kW
W F-Su • Mideast • 100 kW

9475 AUSTRALIA
RADIO AUSTRALIA, Shepparton — SE Asia • 100 kW

GERMANY
DEUTSCHE WELLE, Wertachtal — S • E Africa • 500 kW

USA
†TRANS WORLD R, Via Nov'sibirsk, Russia — S • W Asia & S Asia • 250 kW
TRANS WORLD R, Via Samara, Russia — S • W Asia & S Asia • 250 kW
TRANS WORLD R, Via Swaziland — E Africa • 100 kW

9480 CHINA
CENTRAL PEOPLE'S BS, Xi'an — DS-2 • 100 kW
W Th-Tu • DS-8 (MINORITIES) • 100 kW — DS-8 (MINORITIES) • 100 kW
W • DS-2 • 100 kW
DS-8 (MINORITIES) • 100 kW • ALT. FREQ. TO 9730 kHz
DS-2 • 100 kW • ALT. FREQ. TO 9730 kHz

IRAN
†VO THE ISLAMIC REP, Ahvāz — S • S Asia • 250 kW

RUSSIA
RADIO ROSSII, Moscow — S • Europe & W Africa • DS • 250 kW
VOICE OF RUSSIA, Komsomol'sk 'Amure — S • E Asia & Australasia • 250 kW
VOICE OF RUSSIA, Moscow — S • Europe • 250 kW • ALT. FREQ. TO 11630 kHz
W • W Africa • 500 kW
VOICE OF RUSSIA, Samara — S M-F • N Europe • 200 kW • ALT. FREQ. TO 9820 kHz
S Sa/Su • N Europe • 200 kW • ALT. FREQ. TO 9820 kHz
S • N Europe • 200 kW • ALT. FREQ. TO 9820 kHz

USA
VOA, Delano, California — W • C America & S America • 250 kW / W • C America • 250 kW
†VOA, Greenville, NC — W • W Africa & C Africa • 250 kW
W M-F • W Africa & C Africa • 250 kW

9485 FRANCE
†R FRANCE INTL, Issoudun — S • W Africa • 500 kW
W Africa • 500 kW

(con'd) GERMANY
RADIO SANTEC, Jülich — S Su • S Asia • 100 kW

0 1 2 3 4 5 6 7 8 9 10 11 12 13 14 15 16 17 18 19 20 21 22 23 24

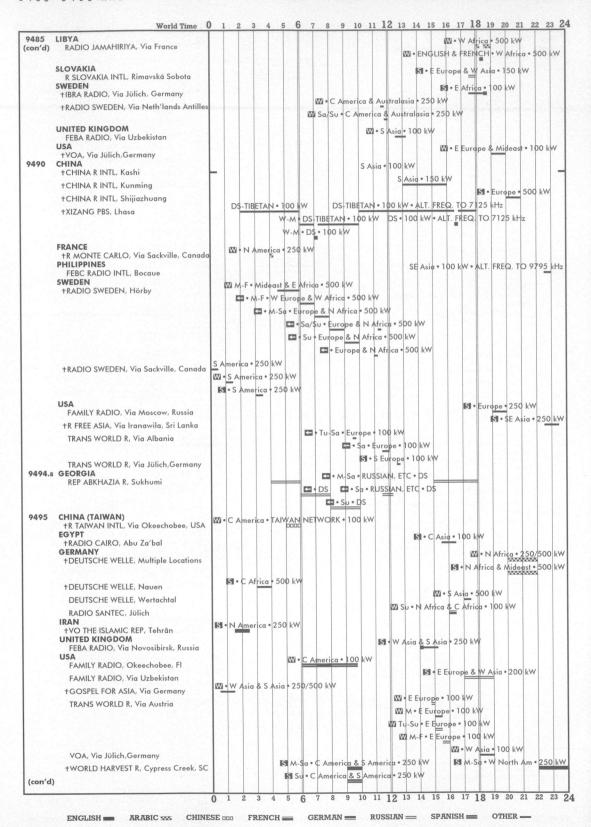

World Time 0 1 2 3 4 5 6 7 8 9 10 11 12 13 14 15 16 17 18 19 20 21 22 23 24

Station	Schedule
9485 **LIBYA**	
(con'd) RADIO JAMAHIRIYA, Via France	W • W Africa • 500 kW
	W • ENGLISH & FRENCH • W Africa • 500 kW
SLOVAKIA	
R SLOVAKIA INTL, Rimavská Sobota	S • E Europe & W Asia • 150 kW
SWEDEN	S • E Africa • 100 kW
†IBRA RADIO, Via Jülich, Germany	
†RADIO SWEDEN, Via Neth'lands Antilles	W • C America & Australasia • 250 kW
	W Sa/Su • C America & Australasia • 250 kW
UNITED KINGDOM	
FEBA RADIO, Via Uzbekistan	W • S Asia • 100 kW
USA	
†VOA, Via Jülich, Germany	W • E Europe & Mideast • 100 kW
9490 CHINA	
†CHINA R INTL, Kashi	S Asia • 100 kW
†CHINA R INTL, Kunming	S Asia • 150 kW
†CHINA R INTL, Shijiazhuang	S • Europe • 500 kW
†XIZANG PBS, Lhasa	DS-TIBETAN • 100 kW DS-TIBETAN • 100 kW • ALT. FREQ. TO 7125 kHz
	W-M • DS-TIBETAN • 100 kW DS • 100 kW • ALT. FREQ. TO 7125 kHz
	W-M • DS • 100 kW
FRANCE	
†R MONTE CARLO, Via Sackville, Canada	W • N America • 250 kW
PHILIPPINES	
FEBC RADIO INTL, Bocaue	SE Asia • 100 kW • ALT. FREQ. TO 9795 kHz
SWEDEN	
†RADIO SWEDEN, Hörby	W M-F • Mideast & E Africa • 500 kW
	M-F • W Europe & W Africa • 500 kW
	M-Sa • Europe & N Africa • 500 kW
	Sa/Su • Europe & N Africa • 500 kW
	Su • Europe & N Africa • 500 kW
	Europe & N Africa • 500 kW
†RADIO SWEDEN, Via Sackville, Canada	S America • 250 kW
	W • S America • 250 kW
	S • S America • 250 kW
USA	
FAMILY RADIO, Via Moscow, Russia	S • Europe • 250 kW
	S • SE Asia • 250 kW
†R FREE ASIA, Via Iranawila, Sri Lanka	
TRANS WORLD R, Via Albania	Tu-Sa • Europe • 100 kW
	Sa • Europe • 100 kW
TRANS WORLD R, Via Jülich, Germany	S • S Europe • 100 kW
9494.8 GEORGIA	
REP ABKHAZIA R, Sukhumi	M-Sa • RUSSIAN, ETC • DS
	DS Sa • RUSSIAN, ETC • DS
	Su • DS
9495 CHINA (TAIWAN)	
†R TAIWAN INTL, Via Okeechobee, USA	W • C America • TAIWAN NETWORK • 100 kW
EGYPT	
†RADIO CAIRO, Abu Za'bal	S • C Asia • 100 kW
GERMANY	
†DEUTSCHE WELLE, Multiple Locations	W • N Africa • 250/500 kW
	S • N Africa & Mideast • 500 kW
†DEUTSCHE WELLE, Nauen	S • C Africa • 500 kW
	W • S Asia • 500 kW
DEUTSCHE WELLE, Wertachtal	W Su • N Africa & C Africa • 100 kW
RADIO SANTEC, Jülich	
IRAN	
†VO THE ISLAMIC REP, Tehrän	S • N America • 250 kW
UNITED KINGDOM	
FEBA RADIO, Via Novosibirsk, Russia	S • W Asia & S Asia • 250 kW
USA	
FAMILY RADIO, Okeechobee, Fl	W • C America • 100 kW
FAMILY RADIO, Via Uzbekistan	S • E Europe & W Asia • 200 kW
†GOSPEL FOR ASIA, Via Germany	W • W Asia & S Asia • 250/500 kW
TRANS WORLD R, Via Austria	W • E Europe • 100 kW
	W M • E Europe • 100 kW
	W Tu-Su • E Europe • 100 kW
	W M-F • E Europe • 100 kW
	W • W Asia • 100 kW
VOA, Via Jülich, Germany	S M-Sa • C America & S America • 250 kW S M-Sa • W North Am • 250 kW
†WORLD HARVEST R, Cypress Creek, SC	S Su • C America & S America • 250 kW
(con'd)	

0 1 2 3 4 5 6 7 8 9 10 11 12 13 14 15 16 17 18 19 20 21 22 23 24

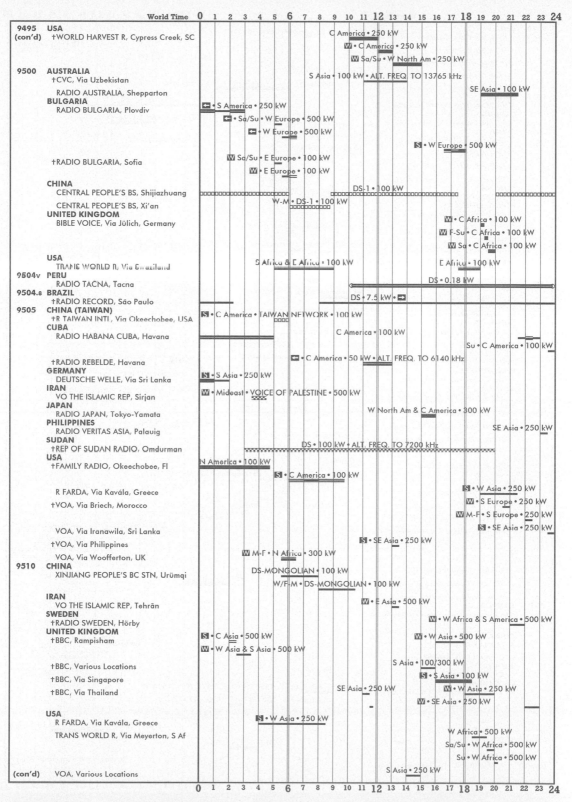

World Time 0 1 2 3 4 5 6 7 8 9 10 11 12 13 14 15 16 17 18 19 20 21 22 23 24

9495 **USA**
(con'd) †WORLD HARVEST R, Cypress Creek, SC
- C America • 250 kW
- W • C America • 250 kW
- W Sa/Su • W North Am • 250 kW

9500 **AUSTRALIA**
†CVC, Via Uzbekistan
- S Asia • 100 kW • ALT. FREQ. TO 13765 kHz
- SE Asia • 100 kW

RADIO AUSTRALIA, Shepparton
BULGARIA
RADIO BULGARIA, Plovdiv
- ⬅ • S America • 250 kW
- ⬅ • Sa/Su • W Europe • 500 kW
- ⬅ • W Europe • 500 kW
- S • W Europe • 500 kW

†RADIO BULGARIA, Sofia
- W Sa/Su • E Europe • 100 kW
- W • E Europe • 100 kW

CHINA
CENTRAL PEOPLE'S BS, Shijiazhuang
- DS-1 • 100 kW

CENTRAL PEOPLE'S BS, Xi'an
- W-M • DS-1 • 100 kW
UNITED KINGDOM
BIBLE VOICE, Via Jülich, Germany
- W • C Africa • 100 kW
- W F-Su • C Africa • 100 kW
- W Sa • C Africa • 100 kW

USA
TRANS WORLD R, Via Swaziland
- S Africa & E Africa • 100 kW
- E Africa • 100 kW
9504v **PERU**
RADIO TACNA, Tacna
- DS • 0.18 kW
9504.8 **BRAZIL**
†RADIO RECORD, São Paulo
- DS • 7.5 kW • ⬅
9505 **CHINA (TAIWAN)**
†R TAIWAN INTL, Via Okeechobee, USA
- S • C America • TAIWAN NETWORK • 100 kW
CUBA
RADIO HABANA CUBA, Havana
- C America • 100 kW
- Su • C America • 100 kW

†RADIO REBELDE, Havana
- ⬅ • C America • 50 kW • ALT. FREQ. TO 6140 kHz
GERMANY
DEUTSCHE WELLE, Via Sri Lanka
- S • S Asia • 250 kW
IRAN
VO THE ISLAMIC REP, Sirjan
- W • Mideast • VOICE OF PALESTINE • 500 kW
JAPAN
RADIO JAPAN, Tokyo-Yamata
- W North Am & C America • 300 kW
PHILIPPINES
RADIO VERITAS ASIA, Palauig
- SE Asia • 250 kW
SUDAN
†REP OF SUDAN RADIO, Omdurman
- DS • 100 kW • ALT. FREQ. TO 7200 kHz
USA
†FAMILY RADIO, Okeechobee, Fl
- N America • 100 kW
- S • C America • 100 kW

R FARDA, Via Kavála, Greece
- S • W Asia • 250 kW

†VOA, Via Briech, Morocco
- W • S Europe • 250 kW
- W M-F • S Europe • 250 kW
- S • SE Asia • 250 kW

VOA, Via Iranawila, Sri Lanka

†VOA, Via Philippines
- S • SE Asia • 250 kW

VOA, Via Woofferton, UK
- W M-F • N Africa • 300 kW
9510 **CHINA**
XINJIANG PEOPLE'S BC STN, Urümqi
- DS-MONGOLIAN • 100 kW
- W/F-M • DS-MONGOLIAN • 100 kW

IRAN
VO THE ISLAMIC REP, Tehrān
- W • E Asia • 500 kW
SWEDEN
†RADIO SWEDEN, Hörby
- W • W Africa & S America • 500 kW
UNITED KINGDOM
†BBC, Rampisham
- S • C Asia • 500 kW
- W • W Asia & S Asia • 500 kW
- W • W Asia • 500 kW

†BBC, Various Locations
- S Asia • 100/300 kW

†BBC, Via Singapore
- S • S Asia • 100 kW

†BBC, Via Thailand
- SE Asia • 250 kW
- W • W Asia • 250 kW
- W • SE Asia • 250 kW

USA
R FARDA, Via Kavála, Greece
- S • W Asia • 250 kW

TRANS WORLD R, Via Meyerton, S Af
- W Africa • 500 kW
- Sa/Su • W Africa • 500 kW
- Su • W Africa • 500 kW

(con'd) VOA, Various Locations
- S Asia • 250 kW

0 1 2 3 4 5 6 7 8 9 10 11 12 13 14 15 16 17 18 19 20 21 22 23 24

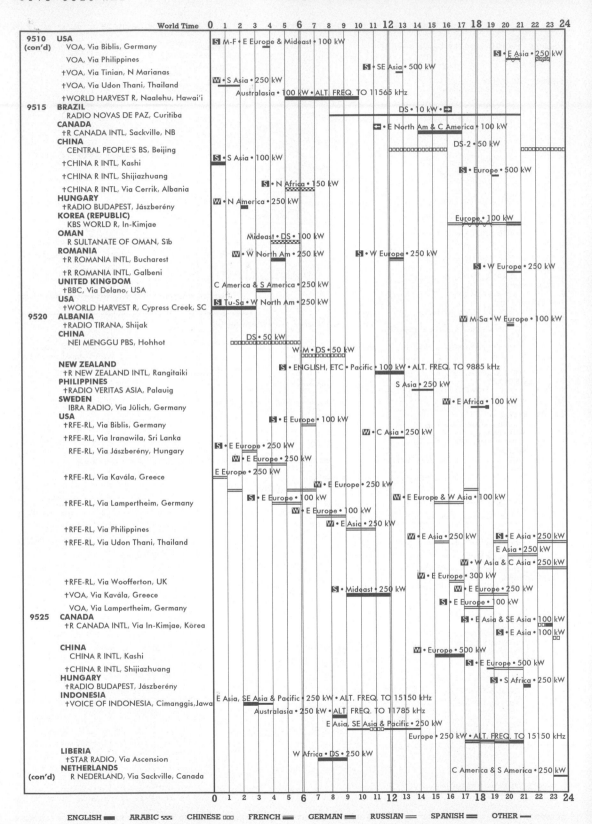

	World Time	0 1 2 3 4 5 6 7 8 9 10 11 12 13 14 15 16 17 18 19 20 21 22 23 24

9510
(con'd) **USA**
  VOA, Via Biblis, Germany — ⓈM-F•E Europe & Mideast•100 kW
  VOA, Via Philippines — Ⓢ•E Asia•250 kW
  †VOA, Via Tinian, N Marianas — Ⓢ•SE Asia•500 kW
  †VOA, Via Udon Thani, Thailand — Ⓦ•S Asia•250 kW
  †WORLD HARVEST R, Naalehu, Hawai'i — Australasia•100 kW•ALT. FREQ. TO 11565 kHz

9515 **BRAZIL**
  RADIO NOVAS DE PAZ, Curitiba — DS•10 kW•
  CANADA
  †R CANADA INTL, Sackville, NB — •E North Am & C America•100 kW
  CHINA
  CENTRAL PEOPLE'S BS, Beijing — DS-2•50 kW
  †CHINA R INTL, Kashi — Ⓢ•S Asia•100 kW
  †CHINA R INTL, Shijiazhuang — Ⓢ•Europe•500 kW
  †CHINA R INTL, Via Cerrik, Albania — Ⓢ•N Africa•150 kW
  HUNGARY
  †RADIO BUDAPEST, Jászberény — Ⓦ•N America•250 kW
  KOREA (REPUBLIC)
  KBS WORLD R, In-Kimjae — Europe•100 kW
  OMAN
  R SULTANATE OF OMAN, Sïb — Mideast•DS•100 kW
  ROMANIA
  †R ROMANIA INTL, Bucharest — Ⓦ•W North Am•250 kW   Ⓢ•W Europe•250 kW
  †R ROMANIA INTL, Galbeni — Ⓢ•W Europe•250 kW
  UNITED KINGDOM
  †BBC, Via Delano, USA — C America & S America•250 kW
  USA
  †WORLD HARVEST R, Cypress Creek, SC — ⓈTu-Sa•W North Am•250 kW

9520 **ALBANIA**
  †RADIO TIRANA, Shijak — ⓌM-Sa•W Europe•100 kW
  CHINA
  NEI MENGGU PBS, Hohhot — DS•50 kW   W,M•DS•50 kW
  NEW ZEALAND
  †R NEW ZEALAND INTL, Rangitaiki — Ⓢ•ENGLISH, ETC•Pacific•100 kW•ALT. FREQ. TO 9885 kHz
  PHILIPPINES
  †RADIO VERITAS ASIA, Palauig — S Asia•250 kW
  SWEDEN
  IBRA RADIO, Via Jülich, Germany — Ⓦ•E Africa•100 kW
  USA
  †RFE-RL, Via Biblis, Germany — Ⓢ•E Europe•100 kW
  †RFE-RL, Via Iranawila, Sri Lanka — Ⓦ•C Asia•250 kW
  RFE-RL, Via Jászberény, Hungary — Ⓢ•E Europe•250 kW   Ⓦ•E Europe•250 kW
  †RFE-RL, Via Kavála, Greece — E Europe•250 kW   Ⓦ•E Europe•250 kW
  †RFE-RL, Via Lampertheim, Germany — Ⓢ•E Europe•100 kW   Ⓦ•E Europe & W Asia•100 kW   Ⓦ•E Europe•100 kW
  †RFE-RL, Via Philippines — Ⓦ•E Asia•250 kW
  †RFE-RL, Via Udon Thani, Thailand — Ⓦ•E Asia•250 kW   Ⓢ•E Asia•250 kW   E Asia•250 kW   Ⓦ•W Asia & C Asia•250 kW
  †RFE-RL, Via Woofferton, UK — Ⓦ•E Europe•300 kW
  †VOA, Via Kavála, Greece — Ⓢ•Mideast•250 kW   Ⓦ•E Europe•250 kW
  VOA, Via Lampertheim, Germany — Ⓢ•E Europe•100 kW

9525 **CANADA**
  †R CANADA INTL, Via In-Kimjae, Korea — Ⓢ•E Asia & SE Asia•100 kW   Ⓢ•E Asia•100 kW
  CHINA
  CHINA R INTL, Kashi — Ⓦ•Europe•500 kW
  †CHINA R INTL, Shijiazhuang — Ⓢ•E Europe•500 kW
  HUNGARY
  †RADIO BUDAPEST, Jászberény — Ⓢ•S Africa•250 kW
  INDONESIA
  †VOICE OF INDONESIA, Cimanggis, Jawa — E Asia, SE Asia & Pacific•250 kW•ALT. FREQ. TO 15150 kHz
    Australasia•250 kW•ALT. FREQ. TO 11785 kHz
    E Asia, SE Asia & Pacific•250 kW
    Europe•250 kW•ALT. FREQ. TO 15150 kHz
  LIBERIA
  †STAR RADIO, Via Ascension — W Africa•DS•250 kW
  NETHERLANDS
(con'd) R NEDERLAND, Via Sackville, Canada — C America & S America•250 kW

	0 1 2 3 4 5 6 7 8 9 10 11 12 13 14 15 16 17 18 19 20 21 22 23 24

ENGLISH ▬   ARABIC ⟋⟍⟋   CHINESE ▫▫▫   FRENCH ▬▬   GERMAN ▬▬   RUSSIAN ══   SPANISH ══   OTHER ──

World Time 0 1 2 3 4 5 6 7 8 9 10 11 12 13 14 15 16 17 18 19 20 21 22 23 24

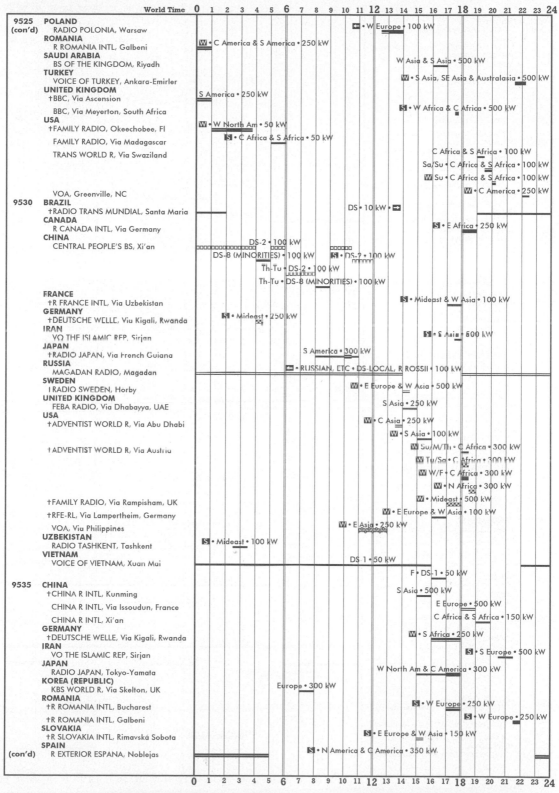

Freq	Station	
9525 (con'd)	POLAND	
	RADIO POLONIA, Warsaw	W Europe • 100 kW
	ROMANIA	
	R ROMANIA INTL, Galbeni	W • C America & S America • 250 kW
	SAUDI ARABIA	
	BS OF THE KINGDOM, Riyadh	W Asia & S Asia • 500 kW
	TURKEY	
	VOICE OF TURKEY, Ankara-Emirler	W • S Asia, SE Asia & Australasia • 500 kW
	UNITED KINGDOM	
	†BBC, Via Ascension	S America • 250 kW
	BBC, Via Meyerton, South Africa	S • W Africa & C Africa • 500 kW
	USA	
	†FAMILY RADIO, Okeechobee, Fl	W • W North Am • 50 kW
	FAMILY RADIO, Via Madagascar	S • C Africa & S Africa • 50 kW
	TRANS WORLD R, Via Swaziland	C Africa & S Africa • 100 kW
		Sa/Su • C Africa & S Africa • 100 kW
		W Su • C Africa & S Africa • 100 kW
	VOA, Greenville, NC	W • C America • 250 kW
9530	BRAZIL	
	†RADIO TRANS MUNDIAL, Santa Maria	DS • 10 kW
	CANADA	
	R CANADA INTL, Via Germany	S • E Africa • 250 kW
	CHINA	
	CENTRAL PEOPLE'S BS, Xi'an	DS-2 • 100 kW
		DS-8 (MINORITIES) • 100 kW / DS-2 • 100 kW
		Th-Tu • DS-2 • 100 kW
		Th-Tu • DS-8 (MINORITIES) • 100 kW
	FRANCE	
	†R FRANCE INTL, Via Uzbekistan	S • Mideast & W Asia • 100 kW
	GERMANY	
	†DEUTSCHE WELLE, Via Kigali, Rwanda	S • Mideast • 250 kW
	IRAN	
	VO THE ISLAMIC REP, Sirjan	S • S Asia • 500 kW
	JAPAN	
	†RADIO JAPAN, Via French Guiana	S America • 300 kW
	RUSSIA	
	MAGADAN RADIO, Magadan	RUSSIAN, ETC • DS-LOCAL, R ROSSII • 100 kW
	SWEDEN	
	I RADIO SWEDEN, Horby	W • E Europe & W Asia • 500 kW
	UNITED KINGDOM	
	FEBA RADIO, Via Dhabayya, UAE	S Asia • 250 kW
	USA	
	†ADVENTIST WORLD R, Via Abu Dhabi	W • C Asia • 250 kW
		W • S Asia • 100 kW
	†ADVENTIST WORLD R, Via Austria	W Su/M/Th • C Africa • 300 kW
		W Tu/Sa • C Africa • 300 kW
		W W/F • C Africa • 300 kW
		W • N Africa • 300 kW
	†FAMILY RADIO, Via Rampisham, UK	W • Mideast • 500 kW
	†RFE-RL, Via Lampertheim, Germany	W • E Europe & W Asia • 100 kW
	VOA, Via Philippines	W • E Asia • 250 kW
	UZBEKISTAN	
	RADIO TASHKENT, Tashkent	S • Mideast • 100 kW
	VIETNAM	
	VOICE OF VIETNAM, Xuan Mai	DS-1 • 50 kW
9535	CHINA	
	†CHINA R INTL, Kunming	F • DS-1 • 50 kW
		S Asia • 500 kW
	CHINA R INTL, Via Issoudun, France	E Europe • 500 kW
	CHINA R INTL, Xi'an	C Africa & S Africa • 150 kW
	GERMANY	
	†DEUTSCHE WELLE, Via Kigali, Rwanda	W • S Africa • 250 kW
	IRAN	
	VO THE ISLAMIC REP, Sirjan	S • S Europe • 500 kW
	JAPAN	
	RADIO JAPAN, Tokyo-Yamata	W North Am & C America • 300 kW
	KOREA (REPUBLIC)	
	KBS WORLD R, Via Skelton, UK	Europe • 300 kW
	ROMANIA	
	†R ROMANIA INTL, Bucharest	S • W Europe • 250 kW
	†R ROMANIA INTL, Galbeni	S • W Europe • 250 kW
	SLOVAKIA	
	†R SLOVAKIA INTL, Rimavská Sobota	S • E Europe & W Asia • 150 kW
	SPAIN	
(con'd)	R EXTERIOR ESPANA, Noblejas	S • N America & C America • 350 kW

0 1 2 3 4 5 6 7 8 9 10 11 12 13 14 15 16 17 18 19 20 21 22 23 24

SEASONAL S OR W   1-HR TIMESHIFT MIDYEAR ⇐ OR ⇒   JAMMING / OR /\   EARLIEST HEARD ◁   LATEST HEARD ▷   NEW FOR 2006 †

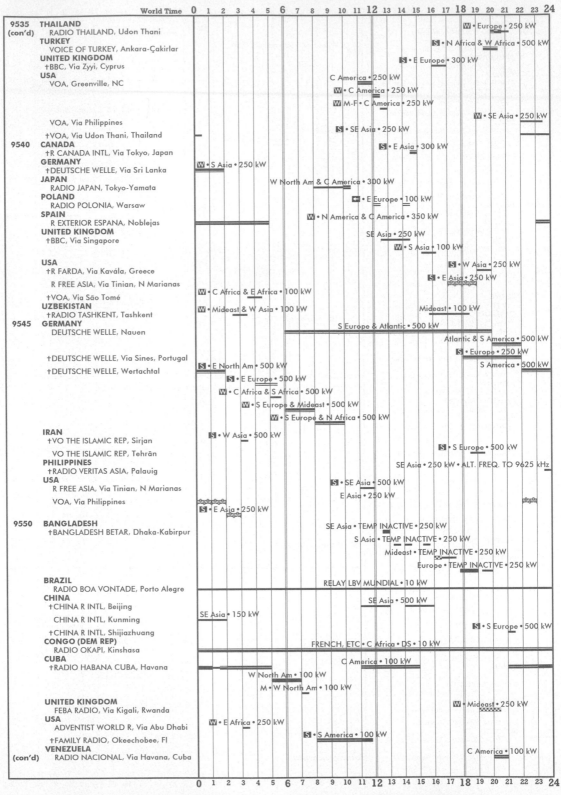

World Time   0 1 2 3 4 5 6 7 8 9 10 11 12 13 14 15 16 17 18 19 20 21 22 23 24

9535 **THAILAND**
(con'd)   RADIO THAILAND, Udon Thani
           TURKEY
               VOICE OF TURKEY, Ankara-Çakirlar
           UNITED KINGDOM
               †BBC, Via Zyyi, Cyprus
           USA
               VOA, Greenville, NC

               VOA, Via Philippines
               †VOA, Via Udon Thani, Thailand
9540   **CANADA**
               †R CANADA INTL, Via Tokyo, Japan
           GERMANY
               †DEUTSCHE WELLE, Via Sri Lanka
           JAPAN
               RADIO JAPAN, Tokyo-Yamata
           POLAND
               RADIO POLONIA, Warsaw
           SPAIN
               R EXTERIOR ESPANA, Noblejas
           UNITED KINGDOM
               †BBC, Via Singapore

           USA
               †R FARDA, Via Kavála, Greece
               R FREE ASIA, Via Tinian, N Marianas
               †VOA, Via São Tomé
           UZBEKISTAN
               †RADIO TASHKENT, Tashkent
9545   **GERMANY**
               DEUTSCHE WELLE, Nauen

               †DEUTSCHE WELLE, Via Sines, Portugal
               †DEUTSCHE WELLE, Wertachtal

           IRAN
               †VO THE ISLAMIC REP, Sirjan
               VO THE ISLAMIC REP, Tehrān
           PHILIPPINES
               †RADIO VERITAS ASIA, Palauig
           USA
               R FREE ASIA, Via Tinian, N Marianas
               VOA, Via Philippines

9550   **BANGLADESH**
               †BANGLADESH BETAR, Dhaka-Kabirpur

           BRAZIL
               RADIO BOA VONTADE, Porto Alegre
           CHINA
               †CHINA R INTL, Beijing
               CHINA R INTL, Kunming
               †CHINA R INTL, Shijiazhuang
           CONGO (DEM REP)
               RADIO OKAPI, Kinshasa
           CUBA
               †RADIO HABANA CUBA, Havana

           UNITED KINGDOM
               FEBA RADIO, Via Kigali, Rwanda
           USA
               ADVENTIST WORLD R, Via Abu Dhabi
               †FAMILY RADIO, Okeechobee, Fl
           VENEZUELA
(con'd)   RADIO NACIONAL, Via Havana, Cuba

0 1 2 3 4 5 6 7 8 9 10 11 12 13 14 15 16 17 18 19 20 21 22 23 24

ENGLISH ▬ ARABIC ▨ CHINESE ▫▫▫ FRENCH ▬ GERMAN ▬ RUSSIAN ═ SPANISH ▬ OTHER ▬

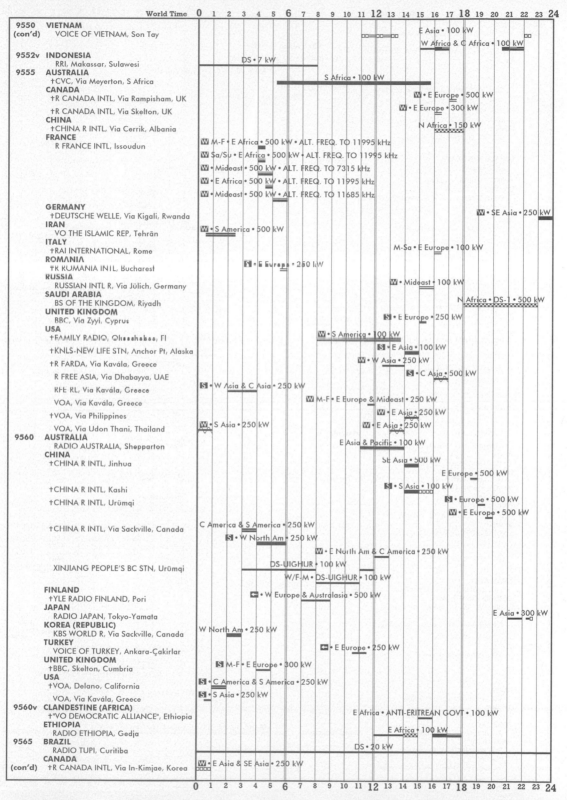

World Time 0 1 2 3 4 5 6 7 8 9 10 11 12 13 14 15 16 17 18 19 20 21 22 23 24

9550 VIETNAM
(con'd) VOICE OF VIETNAM, Son Tay — E Asia • 100 kW / W Africa & C Africa • 100 kW

9552v INDONESIA
RRI, Makassar, Sulawesi — DS • 7 kW

9555 AUSTRALIA
†CVC, Via Meyerton, S Africa — S Africa • 100 kW
CANADA
†R CANADA INTL, Via Rampisham, UK — W • E Europe • 500 kW
†R CANADA INTL, Via Skelton, UK — W • E Europe • 300 kW
CHINA
†CHINA R INTL, Via Cerrik, Albania — N Africa • 150 kW
FRANCE
R FRANCE INTL, Issoudun — W • M-F • E Africa • 500 kW • ALT. FREQ. TO 11995 kHz
— W • Sa/Su • E Africa • 500 kW • ALT. FREQ. TO 11995 kHz
— W • Mideast • 500 kW • ALT. FREQ. TO 7315 kHz
— W • E Africa • 500 kW • ALT. FREQ. TO 11995 kHz
— W • Mideast • 500 kW • ALT. FREQ. TO 11685 kHz
GERMANY
†DEUTSCHE WELLE, Via Kigali, Rwanda — W • SE Asia • 250 kW
IRAN
VO THE ISLAMIC REP, Tehrān — W • S America • 500 kW
ITALY
†RAI INTERNATIONAL, Rome — M-Sa • E Europe • 100 kW
ROMANIA
†R ROMANIA INTL, Bucharest — S • E Europe • 250 kW
RUSSIA
RUSSIAN INTL R, Via Jülich, Germany — W • Mideast • 100 kW
SAUDI ARABIA
BS OF THE KINGDOM, Riyadh — N Africa • DS-1 • 500 kW
UNITED KINGDOM
BBC, Via Zyyi, Cyprus — S • E Europe • 250 kW
USA
†FAMILY RADIO, Okeechobee, Fl — W • S America • 100 kW
†KNLS-NEW LIFE STN, Anchor Pt, Alaska — S • E Asia • 100 kW
†R FARDA, Via Kavála, Greece — W • W Asia • 250 kW
R FREE ASIA, Via Dhabayya, UAE — S • C Asia • 500 kW
RFE RL, Via Kavála, Greece — S • W Asia & C Asia • 250 kW
VOA, Via Kavála, Greece — W • M-F • E Europe & Mideast • 250 kW
†VOA, Via Philippines — W • E Asia • 250 kW
VOA, Via Udon Thani, Thailand — W • S Asia • 250 kW / W • E Asia • 250 kW

9560 AUSTRALIA
RADIO AUSTRALIA, Shepparton — E Asia & Pacific • 100 kW
CHINA
†CHINA R INTL, Jinhua — SE Asia • 500 kW / E Europe • 500 kW
†CHINA R INTL, Kashi — S • S Asia • 100 kW
†CHINA R INTL, Urümqi — S • Europe • 500 kW / W • E Europe • 500 kW
†CHINA R INTL, Via Sackville, Canada — C America & S America • 250 kW
— S • W North Am • 250 kW
— W • E North Am & C America • 250 kW
XINJIANG PEOPLE'S BC STN, Urümqi — DS-UIGHUR • 100 kW
— W/F-M • DS-UIGHUR • 100 kW
FINLAND
†YLE RADIO FINLAND, Pori — ← • W Europe & Australasia • 500 kW
JAPAN
RADIO JAPAN, Tokyo-Yamata — E Asia • 300 kW
KOREA (REPUBLIC)
KBS WORLD R, Via Sackville, Canada — W North Am • 250 kW
TURKEY
VOICE OF TURKEY, Ankara-Çakirlar — ← • E Europe • 250 kW
UNITED KINGDOM
†BBC, Skelton, Cumbria — S • M-F • E Europe • 300 kW
USA
†VOA, Delano, California — S • C America & S America • 250 kW
VOA, Via Kavála, Greece — S • S Asia • 250 kW
9560v CLANDESTINE (AFRICA)
†"VO DEMOCRATIC ALLIANCE", Ethiopia — E Africa • ANTI-ERITREAN GOVT • 100 kW
ETHIOPIA
RADIO ETHIOPIA, Gedja — E Africa • 100 kW
9565 BRAZIL
RADIO TUPI, Curitiba — DS • 20 kW
CANADA
(con'd) †R CANADA INTL, Via In-Kimjae, Korea — W • E Asia & SE Asia • 250 kW

0 1 2 3 4 5 6 7 8 9 10 11 12 13 14 15 16 17 18 19 20 21 22 23 24

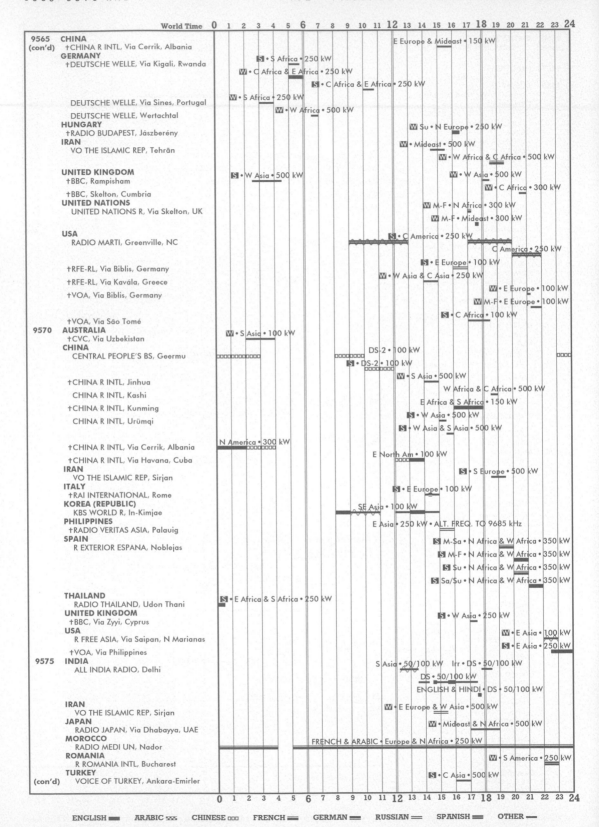

World Time 0 1 2 3 4 5 6 7 8 9 10 11 12 13 14 15 16 17 18 19 20 21 22 23 24

9565 CHINA
(con'd) †CHINA R INTL, Via Cerrik, Albania — E Europe & Mideast • 150 kW
GERMANY
  †DEUTSCHE WELLE, Via Kigali, Rwanda — S • S Africa • 250 kW
  — W • C Africa & E Africa • 250 kW
  — S • C Africa & E Africa • 250 kW
  DEUTSCHE WELLE, Via Sines, Portugal — W • S Africa • 250 kW
  DEUTSCHE WELLE, Wertachtal — W • W Africa • 500 kW
HUNGARY
  †RADIO BUDAPEST, Jászberény — W • Su • N Europe • 250 kW
IRAN
  VO THE ISLAMIC REP, Tehrãn — W • Mideast • 500 kW
  — W • W Africa & C Africa • 500 kW
UNITED KINGDOM
  †BBC, Rampisham — S • W Asia • 500 kW
  — W • W Asia • 500 kW
  †BBC, Skelton, Cumbria — W • C Africa • 300 kW
UNITED NATIONS
  UNITED NATIONS R, Via Skelton, UK — W M-F • N Africa • 300 kW
  — W M-F • Mideast • 300 kW
USA
  RADIO MARTI, Greenville, NC — S • C America • 250 kW
  — C America • 250 kW
  †RFE-RL, Via Biblis, Germany — S • E Europe • 100 kW
  †RFE-RL, Via Kavála, Greece — W • W Asia & C Asia • 250 kW
  †VOA, Via Biblis, Germany — W • E Europe • 100 kW
  — W M-F • E Europe • 100 kW
  †VOA, Via São Tomé — S • C Africa • 100 kW
9570 AUSTRALIA
  †CVC, Via Uzbekistan — W • S Asia • 100 kW
CHINA
  CENTRAL PEOPLE'S BS, Geermu — DS-2 • 100 kW
  — S • DS-2 • 100 kW
  †CHINA R INTL, Jinhua — W • S Asia • 500 kW
  CHINA R INTL, Kashi — W Africa & C Africa • 500 kW
  †CHINA R INTL, Kunming — E Africa & S Africa • 150 kW
  CHINA R INTL, Urümqi — S • W Asia • 500 kW
  — S • W Asia & S Asia • 500 kW
  †CHINA R INTL, Via Cerrik, Albania — N America • 300 kW
  †CHINA R INTL, Via Havana, Cuba — E North Am • 100 kW
IRAN
  VO THE ISLAMIC REP, Sirjan — S • S Europe • 500 kW
ITALY
  †RAI INTERNATIONAL, Rome — S • E Europe • 100 kW
KOREA (REPUBLIC)
  KBS WORLD R, In-Kimjae — SE Asia • 100 kW
PHILIPPINES
  †RADIO VERITAS ASIA, Palauig — E Asia • 250 kW • ALT. FREQ. TO 9685 kHz
SPAIN
  R EXTERIOR ESPANA, Noblejas — S M-Sa • N Africa & W Africa • 350 kW
  — S M-F • N Africa & W Africa • 350 kW
  — S Su • N Africa & W Africa • 350 kW
  — S Sa/Su • N Africa & W Africa • 350 kW
THAILAND
  RADIO THAILAND, Udon Thani — S • E Africa & S Africa • 250 kW
UNITED KINGDOM
  †BBC, Via Zyyi, Cyprus — S • W Asia • 250 kW
USA
  R FREE ASIA, Via Saipan, N Marianas — W • E Asia • 100 kW
  — S • E Asia • 250 kW
  †VOA, Via Philippines
9575 INDIA
  ALL INDIA RADIO, Delhi — S Asia • 50/100 kW   Irr • DS • 50/100 kW
  — DS • 50/100 kW
  — ENGLISH & HINDI • DS • 50/100 kW
IRAN
  VO THE ISLAMIC REP, Sirjan — W • E Europe & W Asia • 500 kW
JAPAN
  RADIO JAPAN, Via Dhabayya, UAE — W • Mideast & N Africa • 500 kW
MOROCCO
  RADIO MEDI UN, Nador — FRENCH & ARABIC • Europe & N Africa • 250 kW
ROMANIA
  R ROMANIA INTL, Bucharest — W • S America • 250 kW
TURKEY
(con'd) VOICE OF TURKEY, Ankara-Emirler — S • C Asia • 500 kW

0 1 2 3 4 5 6 7 8 9 10 11 12 13 14 15 16 17 18 19 20 21 22 23 24

ENGLISH ▬ ARABIC ▧ CHINESE ▫▫▫ FRENCH ═ GERMAN ▬ RUSSIAN ═ SPANISH ▬ OTHER ▬

World Time 0 1 2 3 4 5 6 7 8 9 10 11 12 13 14 15 16 17 18 19 20 21 22 23 24

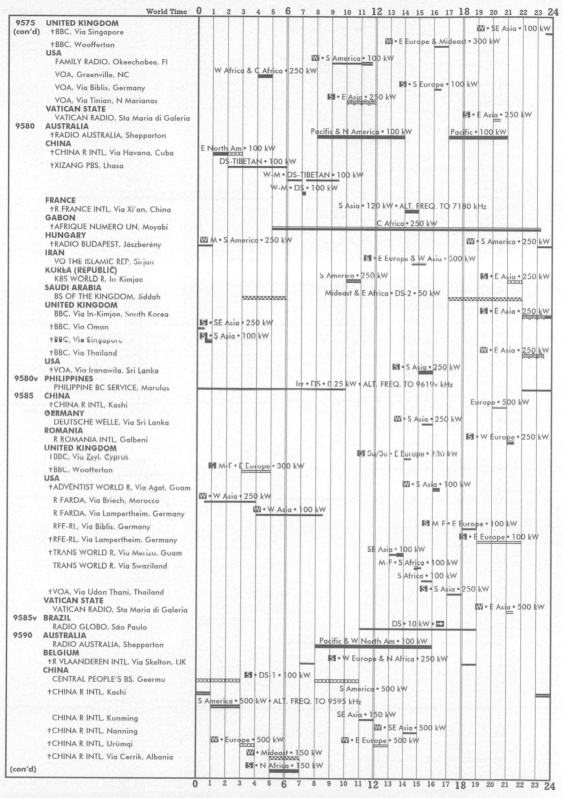

Freq	Country / Station	Details
9575 (con'd)	**UNITED KINGDOM** †BBC, Via Singapore	W • SE Asia • 100 kW
	†BBC, Woofferton	W • E Europe & Mideast • 300 kW
	USA FAMILY RADIO, Okeechobee, Fl	W • S America • 100 kW
	VOA, Greenville, NC	W Africa & C Africa • 250 kW
	VOA, Via Biblis, Germany	S • S Europe • 100 kW
	VOA, Via Tinian, N Marianas	S • E Asia • 250 kW
	VATICAN STATE VATICAN RADIO, Sta Maria di Galeria	S • E Asia • 250 kW
9580	**AUSTRALIA** †RADIO AUSTRALIA, Shepparton	Pacific & N America • 100 kW Pacific • 100 kW
	CHINA †CHINA R INTL, Via Havana, Cuba	E North Am • 100 kW
	†XIZANG PBS, Lhasa	DS-TIBETAN • 100 kW
		W-M • DS-TIBETAN • 100 kW
		W-M • DS • 100 kW
	FRANCE †R FRANCE INTL, Via Xi'an, China	S Asia • 120 kW • ALT. FREQ. TO 7180 kHz
	GABON †AFRIQUE NUMERO UN, Moyabi	C Africa • 250 kW
	HUNGARY †RADIO BUDAPEST, Jászberény	W M • S America • 250 kW W • S America • 250 kW
	IRAN VO THE ISLAMIC REP, Sirjan	S • E Europe & W Asia • 500 kW
	KOREA (REPUBLIC) KBS WORLD R, In Kimjae	S America • 250 kW S • E Asia • 250 kW
	SAUDI ARABIA BS OF THE KINGDOM, Jiddah	Mideast & E Africa • DS-2 • 50 kW
	UNITED KINGDOM BBC, Via In-Kimjae, South Korea	S • E Asia • 250 kW
	†BBC, Via Oman	S • SE Asia • 250 kW
	†BBC, Via Singapore	S • S Asia • 100 kW
	†BBC, Via Thailand	W • E Asia • 250 kW
	USA †VOA, Via Iranawila, Sri Lanka	S • S Asia • 250 kW
9580v	**PHILIPPINES** PHILIPPINE BC SERVICE, Marulas	Irr • DS • 0.25 kW • ALT. FREQ. TO 9619v kHz
9585	**CHINA** †CHINA R INTL, Kashi	Europe • 500 kW
	GERMANY DEUTSCHE WELLE, Via Sri Lanka	W • S Asia • 250 kW
	ROMANIA R ROMANIA INTL, Galbeni	S • W Europe • 250 kW
	UNITED KINGDOM †BBC, Via Zyyi, Cyprus	S • Su/Su • E Europe • 250 kW
	†BBC, Woofferton	S • M-F • E Europe • 300 kW
	USA †ADVENTIST WORLD R, Via Agat, Guam	W • S Asia • 100 kW
	R FARDA, Via Briech, Morocco	W • W Asia • 250 kW
	R FARDA, Via Lampertheim, Germany	W • W Asia • 100 kW
	RFE-RL, Via Biblis, Germany	S M F • E Europe • 100 kW
	†RFE-RL, Via Lampertheim, Germany	S • E Europe • 100 kW
	†TRANS WORLD R, Via Merizo, Guam	SE Asia • 100 kW
	TRANS WORLD R, Via Swaziland	M-F • S Africa • 100 kW S Africa • 100 kW
	†VOA, Via Udon Thani, Thailand	S • S Asia • 250 kW
	VATICAN STATE VATICAN RADIO, Sta Maria di Galeria	W • E Asia • 500 kW
9585v	**BRAZIL** RADIO GLOBO, São Paulo	DS • 10 kW • →
9590	**AUSTRALIA** RADIO AUSTRALIA, Shepparton	Pacific & W North Am • 100 kW
	BELGIUM †R VLAANDEREN INTL, Via Skelton, UK	S • W Europe & N Africa • 250 kW
	CHINA CENTRAL PEOPLE'S BS, Geermu	S • DS-1 • 100 kW
	†CHINA R INTL, Kashi	S America • 500 kW
		S America • 500 kW • ALT. FREQ. TO 9595 kHz
	†CHINA R INTL, Kunming	SE Asia • 150 kW
	†CHINA R INTL, Nanning	W • SE Asia • 500 kW
	†CHINA R INTL, Urümqi	W • Europe • 500 kW W • E Europe • 500 kW
	†CHINA R INTL, Via Cerrik, Albania	W • Mideast • 150 kW
(con'd)		S • N Africa • 150 kW

World Time 0 1 2 3 4 5 6 7 8 9 10 11 12 13 14 15 16 17 18 19 20 21 22 23 24

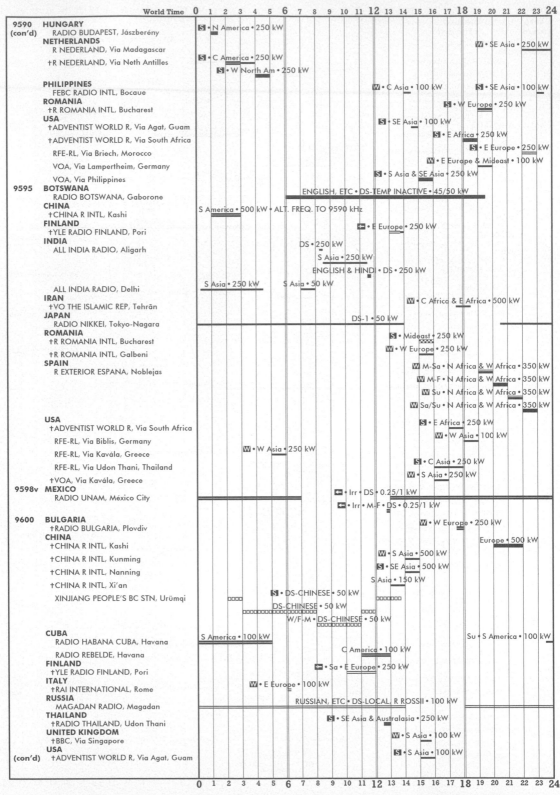

World Time: 0 1 2 3 4 5 6 7 8 9 10 11 12 13 14 15 16 17 18 19 20 21 22 23 24

9590
(con'd) HUNGARY
  RADIO BUDAPEST, Jászberény — S • N America • 250 kW
  NETHERLANDS
    R NEDERLAND, Via Madagascar — W • SE Asia • 250 kW
    †R NEDERLAND, Via Neth Antilles — S • C America • 250 kW / S • W North Am • 250 kW
  PHILIPPINES
    FEBC RADIO INTL, Bocaue — W • C Asia • 100 kW / S • SE Asia • 100 kW
  ROMANIA
    †R ROMANIA INTL, Bucharest — S • W Europe • 250 kW
  USA
    †ADVENTIST WORLD R, Via Agat, Guam — S • SE Asia • 100 kW
    †ADVENTIST WORLD R, Via South Africa — S • E Africa • 250 kW
    RFE-RL, Via Briech, Morocco — S • E Europe • 250 kW
    VOA, Via Lampertheim, Germany — W • E Europe & Mideast • 100 kW
    VOA, Via Philippines — S • S Asia & SE Asia • 250 kW

9595 BOTSWANA
  RADIO BOTSWANA, Gaborone — ENGLISH, ETC • DS-TEMP INACTIVE • 45/50 kW
  CHINA
    †CHINA R INTL, Kashi — S America • 500 kW • ALT. FREQ. TO 9590 kHz
  FINLAND
    †YLE RADIO FINLAND, Pori — ⬛ • E Europe • 250 kW
  INDIA
    ALL INDIA RADIO, Aligarh — DS • 250 kW / S Asia • 250 kW / ENGLISH & HINDI • DS • 250 kW
    ALL INDIA RADIO, Delhi — S Asia • 250 kW / S Asia • 50 kW
  IRAN
    †VO THE ISLAMIC REP, Tehrān — W • C Africa & E Africa • 500 kW
  JAPAN
    RADIO NIKKEI, Tokyo-Nagara — DS-1 • 50 kW
  ROMANIA
    †R ROMANIA INTL, Bucharest — S • Mideast • 250 kW
    †R ROMANIA INTL, Galbeni — W • W Europe • 250 kW
  SPAIN
    R EXTERIOR ESPANA, Noblejas — W • M-Sa • N Africa & W Africa • 350 kW
      W • M-F • N Africa & W Africa • 350 kW
      W • Su • N Africa & W Africa • 350 kW
      W • Sa/Su • N Africa & W Africa • 350 kW
  USA
    †ADVENTIST WORLD R, Via South Africa — S • E Africa • 250 kW
    RFE-RL, Via Biblis, Germany — W • W Asia • 100 kW
    RFE-RL, Via Kavála, Greece — W • W Asia • 250 kW
    RFE-RL, Via Udon Thani, Thailand — S • C Asia • 250 kW
    †VOA, Via Kavála, Greece — W • S Asia • 250 kW

9598v MEXICO
  RADIO UNAM, México City — ⬅ • Irr • DS • 0.25/1 kW / ⬅ • Irr • M-F • DS • 0.25/1 kW

9600 BULGARIA
    †RADIO BULGARIA, Plovdiv — W • W Europe • 250 kW
  CHINA
    †CHINA R INTL, Kashi — Europe • 500 kW
    †CHINA R INTL, Kunming — W • S Asia • 500 kW
    †CHINA R INTL, Nanning — S • SE Asia • 500 kW
    †CHINA R INTL, Xi'an — S Asia • 150 kW
    XINJIANG PEOPLE'S BC STN, Urümqi — S • DS-CHINESE • 50 kW / DS-CHINESE • 50 kW / W/F-M • DS-CHINESE • 50 kW
  CUBA
    RADIO HABANA CUBA, Havana — S America • 100 kW / Su • S America • 100 kW
    RADIO REBELDE, Havana — C America • 100 kW
  FINLAND
    †YLE RADIO FINLAND, Pori — ⬛ • Sa • E Europe • 250 kW
  ITALY
    †RAI INTERNATIONAL, Rome — W • E Europe • 100 kW
  RUSSIA
    MAGADAN RADIO, Magadan — RUSSIAN, ETC • DS-LOCAL, R ROSSII • 100 kW
  THAILAND
    †RADIO THAILAND, Udon Thani — S • SE Asia & Australasia • 250 kW
  UNITED KINGDOM
    †BBC, Via Singapore — W • S Asia • 100 kW
  USA
(con'd) †ADVENTIST WORLD R, Via Agat, Guam — S • S Asia • 100 kW

0 1 2 3 4 5 6 7 8 9 10 11 12 13 14 15 16 17 18 19 20 21 22 23 24

ENGLISH ▬ ARABIC ⸙⸙ CHINESE ▯▯▯ FRENCH ▬▬ GERMAN ▬▬ RUSSIAN ══ SPANISH ▬▬ OTHER ▬

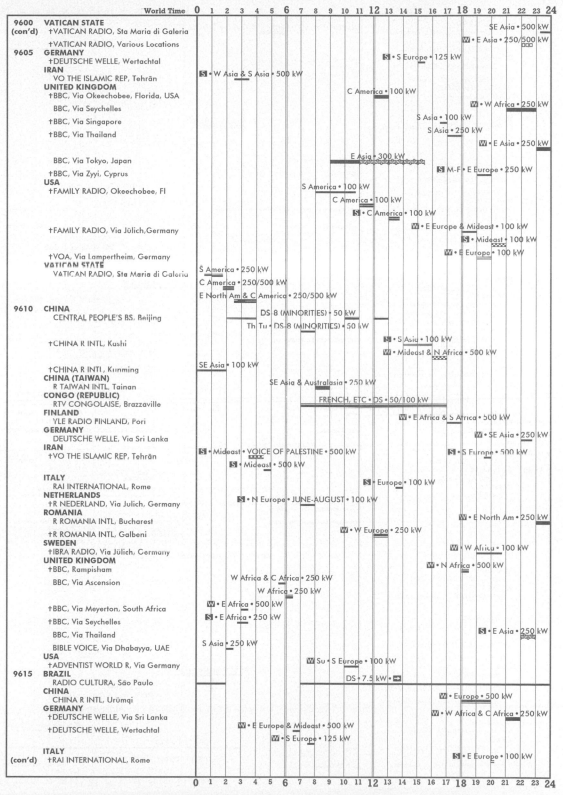

World Time — 0 1 2 3 4 5 6 7 8 9 10 11 12 13 14 15 16 17 18 19 20 21 22 23 24

9600 VATICAN STATE
(con'd) †VATICAN RADIO, Sta Maria di Galeria — SE Asia • 500 kW
†VATICAN RADIO, Various Locations — W • E Asia • 250/500 kW

9605 GERMANY
†DEUTSCHE WELLE, Wertachtal — S • S Europe • 125 kW

IRAN
VO THE ISLAMIC REP, Tehrān — S • W Asia & S Asia • 500 kW

UNITED KINGDOM
†BBC, Via Okeechobee, Florida, USA — C America • 100 kW
BBC, Via Seychelles — W • W Africa • 250 kW
†BBC, Via Singapore — S Asia • 100 kW
†BBC, Via Thailand — S Asia • 250 kW ; W • E Asia • 250 kW
BBC, Via Tokyo, Japan — E Asia • 300 kW
†BBC, Via Zyyi, Cyprus — M-F • E Europe • 250 kW

USA
†FAMILY RADIO, Okeechobee, Fl — S America • 100 kW ; C America • 100 kW ; S • C America • 100 kW
†FAMILY RADIO, Via Jülich, Germany — W • E Europe & Mideast • 100 kW ; S • Mideast • 100 kW
†VOA, Via Lampertheim, Germany — W • E Europe • 100 kW

VATICAN STATE
VATICAN RADIO, Sta Maria di Galeria — S America • 250 kW ; C America • 250/500 kW ; E North Am & C America • 250/500 kW

9610 CHINA
CENTRAL PEOPLE'S BS, Beijing — DS-8 (MINORITIES) • 50 kW ; Th Tu • DS-8 (MINORITIES) • 50 kW
†CHINA R INTL, Kashi — S • S Asia • 100 kW ; W • Mideast & N Africa • 500 kW
†CHINA R INTL, Kunming — SE Asia • 100 kW

CHINA (TAIWAN)
R TAIWAN INTL, Tainan — SE Asia & Australasia • 250 kW

CONGO (REPUBLIC)
RTV CONGOLAISE, Brazzaville — FRENCH, ETC • DS • 50/100 kW

FINLAND
YLE RADIO FINLAND, Pori — W • E Africa & S Africa • 500 kW

GERMANY
DEUTSCHE WELLE, Via Sri Lanka — W • SE Asia • 250 kW

IRAN
†VO THE ISLAMIC REP, Tehrān — S • Mideast • VOICE OF PALESTINE • 500 kW ; S • S Europe • 500 kW ; S • Mideast • 500 kW

ITALY
RAI INTERNATIONAL, Rome — S • Europe • 100 kW

NETHERLANDS
†R NEDERLAND, Via Julich, Germany — S • N Europe • JUNE-AUGUST • 100 kW

ROMANIA
R ROMANIA INTL, Bucharest — W • E North Am • 250 kW
†R ROMANIA INTL, Galbeni — W • W Europe • 250 kW

SWEDEN
†IBRA RADIO, Via Jülich, Germany — W • W Africa • 100 kW

UNITED KINGDOM
†BBC, Rampisham — W • N Africa • 500 kW
BBC, Via Ascension — W Africa & C Africa • 250 kW ; W Africa • 250 kW
†BBC, Via Meyerton, South Africa — W • E Africa • 500 kW
†BBC, Via Seychelles — S • E Africa • 250 kW
BBC, Via Thailand — S • E Asia • 250 kW
BIBLE VOICE, Via Dhabayya, UAE — S Asia • 250 kW

USA
†ADVENTIST WORLD R, Via Germany — W Su • S Europe • 100 kW

9615 BRAZIL
RADIO CULTURA, São Paulo — DS • 7.5 kW • ⇒

CHINA
CHINA R INTL, Urümqi — W • Europe • 500 kW

GERMANY
†DEUTSCHE WELLE, Via Sri Lanka — W • W Africa & C Africa • 250 kW
†DEUTSCHE WELLE, Wertachtal — W • E Europe & Mideast • 500 kW ; W • S Europe • 125 kW

ITALY
(con'd) †RAI INTERNATIONAL, Rome — S • E Europe • 100 kW

0 1 2 3 4 5 6 7 8 9 10 11 12 13 14 15 16 17 18 19 20 21 22 23 24

SEASONAL S OR W   1-HR TIMESHIFT MIDYEAR ⇐ OR ⇒   JAMMING / OR ∧   EARLIEST HEARD ◁   LATEST HEARD ▷   NEW FOR 2006 †

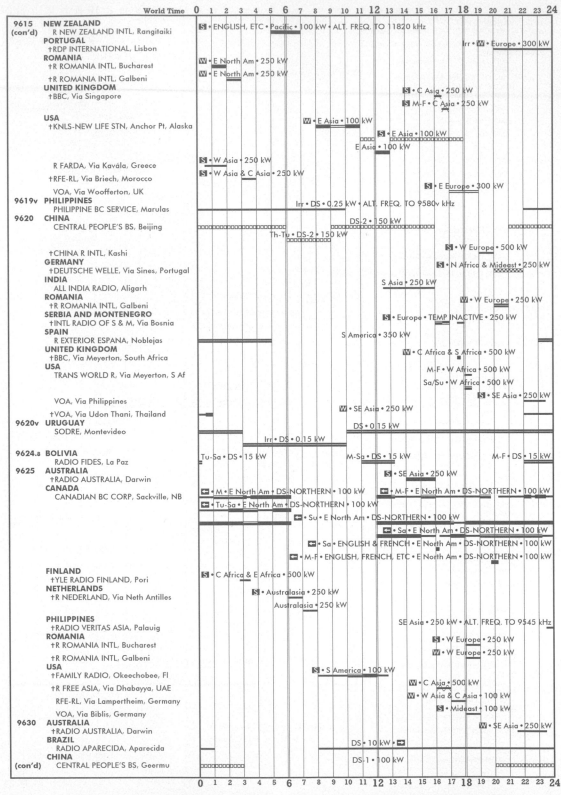

| | World Time | 0 | 1 | 2 | 3 | 4 | 5 | 6 | 7 | 8 | 9 | 10 | 11 | 12 | 13 | 14 | 15 | 16 | 17 | 18 | 19 | 20 | 21 | 22 | 23 | 24 |

9615 **NEW ZEALAND**
(con'd) R NEW ZEALAND INTL, Rangitaiki — S • ENGLISH, ETC • Pacific • 100 kW • ALT. FREQ. TO 11820 kHz
PORTUGAL
 †RDP INTERNATIONAL, Lisbon — Irr • W • Europe • 300 kW
ROMANIA
 †R ROMANIA INTL, Bucharest — W • E North Am • 250 kW
 †R ROMANIA INTL, Galbeni — W • E North Am • 250 kW
UNITED KINGDOM
 †BBC, Via Singapore — S • C Asia • 250 kW / M-F • C Asia • 250 kW

USA
 †KNLS-NEW LIFE STN, Anchor Pt, Alaska — W • E Asia • 100 kW / S • E Asia • 100 kW / E Asia • 100 kW

 R FARDA, Via Kavála, Greece — S • W Asia • 250 kW
 †RFE-RL, Via Briech, Morocco — S • W Asia & C Asia • 250 kW
 VOA, Via Woofferton, UK — S • E Europe • 300 kW
9619v **PHILIPPINES**
 PHILIPPINE BC SERVICE, Marulas — Irr • DS • 0.25 kW • ALT. FREQ. TO 9580v kHz
9620 **CHINA**
 CENTRAL PEOPLE'S BS, Beijing — DS-2 • 150 kW / Th-Tu • DS-2 • 150 kW

 †CHINA R INTL, Kashi — S • W Europe • 500 kW
GERMANY
 †DEUTSCHE WELLE, Via Sines, Portugal — S • N Africa & Mideast • 250 kW
INDIA
 ALL INDIA RADIO, Aligarh — S Asia • 250 kW
ROMANIA
 †R ROMANIA INTL, Galbeni — W • W Europe • 250 kW
SERBIA AND MONTENEGRO
 †INTL RADIO OF S & M, Via Bosnia — S • Europe • TEMP INACTIVE • 250 kW
SPAIN
 R EXTERIOR ESPANA, Noblejas — S America • 350 kW
UNITED KINGDOM
 †BBC, Via Meyerton, South Africa — W • C Africa & S Africa • 500 kW
USA
 TRANS WORLD R, Via Meyerton, S Af — M-F • W Africa • 500 kW / Sa/Su • W Africa • 500 kW

 VOA, Via Philippines — S • SE Asia • 250 kW
 †VOA, Via Udon Thani, Thailand — W • SE Asia • 250 kW
9620v **URUGUAY**
 SODRE, Montevideo — DS • 0.15 kW / Irr • DS • 0.15 kW

9624.8 **BOLIVIA**
 RADIO FIDES, La Paz — Tu-Sa • DS • 15 kW / M-Sa • DS • 15 kW / M-F • DS • 15 kW
9625 **AUSTRALIA**
 †RADIO AUSTRALIA, Darwin — S • SE Asia • 250 kW
CANADA
 CANADIAN BC CORP, Sackville, NB — M • E North Am • DS-NORTHERN • 100 kW / M-F • E North Am • DS-NORTHERN • 100 kW
  — Tu-Sa • E North Am • DS-NORTHERN • 100 kW
  — Su • E North Am • DS-NORTHERN • 100 kW
  — Sa • E North Am • DS-NORTHERN • 100 kW
  — Sa • ENGLISH & FRENCH • E North Am • DS-NORTHERN • 100 kW
  — M-F • ENGLISH, FRENCH, ETC • E North Am • DS-NORTHERN • 100 kW

FINLAND
 †YLE RADIO FINLAND, Pori — S • C Africa & E Africa • 500 kW
NETHERLANDS
 †R NEDERLAND, Via Neth Antilles — S • Australasia • 250 kW / Australasia • 250 kW

PHILIPPINES
 †RADIO VERITAS ASIA, Palauig — SE Asia • 250 kW • ALT. FREQ. TO 9545 kHz
ROMANIA
 †R ROMANIA INTL, Bucharest — S • W Europe • 250 kW
 †R ROMANIA INTL, Galbeni — W • W Europe • 250 kW
USA
 †FAMILY RADIO, Okeechobee, Fl — S • S America • 100 kW
 †R FREE ASIA, Via Dhabayya, UAE — W • C Asia • 500 kW
 RFE-RL, Via Lampertheim, Germany — W • W Asia & C Asia • 100 kW
 VOA, Via Biblis, Germany — S • Mideast • 100 kW
9630 **AUSTRALIA**
 †RADIO AUSTRALIA, Darwin — W • SE Asia • 250 kW
BRAZIL
 RADIO APARECIDA, Aparecida — DS • 10 kW
CHINA
(con'd) CENTRAL PEOPLE'S BS, Geermu — DS-1 • 100 kW

| | 0 | 1 | 2 | 3 | 4 | 5 | 6 | 7 | 8 | 9 | 10 | 11 | 12 | 13 | 14 | 15 | 16 | 17 | 18 | 19 | 20 | 21 | 22 | 23 | 24 |

ENGLISH ■■■   ARABIC ░░░   CHINESE ▫▫▫   FRENCH ▬▬   GERMAN ▬▬   RUSSIAN ══   SPANISH ══   OTHER ──

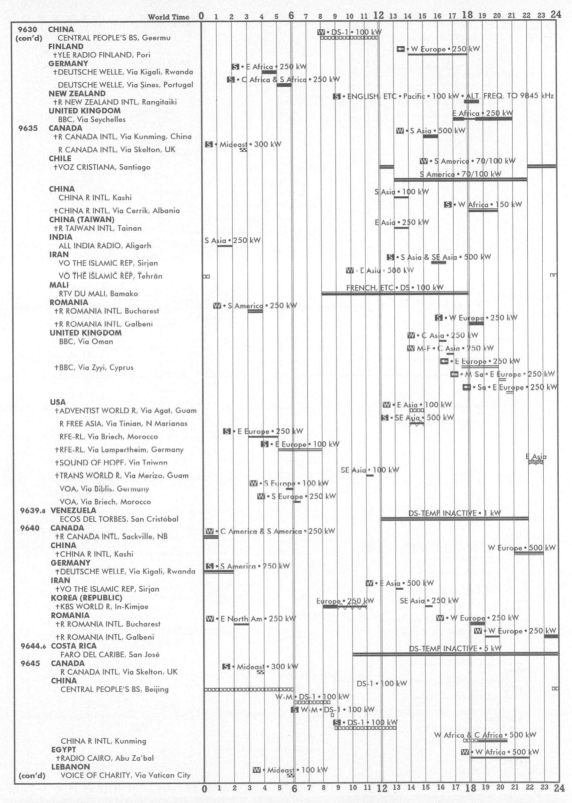

World Time 0 1 2 3 4 5 6 7 8 9 10 11 12 13 14 15 16 17 18 19 20 21 22 23 24

kHz	Country / Station	Schedule
9630 (con'd)	**CHINA**	
	CENTRAL PEOPLE'S BS, Geermu	[W] • DS-1 • 100 kW
	FINLAND	
	†YLE RADIO FINLAND, Pori	⬅ • W Europe • 250 kW
	GERMANY	
	†DEUTSCHE WELLE, Via Kigali, Rwanda	[S] • E Africa • 250 kW
	DEUTSCHE WELLE, Via Sines, Portugal	[S] • C Africa & S Africa • 250 kW
	NEW ZEALAND	
	†R NEW ZEALAND INTL, Rangitaiki	[S] • ENGLISH, ETC • Pacific • 100 kW • ALT. FREQ. TO 9845 kHz
	UNITED KINGDOM	
	BBC, Via Seychelles	E Africa • 250 kW
9635	**CANADA**	
	†R CANADA INTL, Via Kunming, China	[W] • S Asia • 500 kW
	R CANADA INTL, Via Skelton, UK	[S] • Mideast • 300 kW
	CHILE	
	†VOZ CRISTIANA, Santiago	[W] • S America • 70/100 kW; S America • 70/100 kW
	CHINA	
	CHINA R INTL, Kashi	S Asia • 100 kW
	†CHINA R INTL, Via Cerrik, Albania	[S] • W Africa • 150 kW
	CHINA (TAIWAN)	
	†R TAIWAN INTL, Tainan	E Asia • 250 kW
	INDIA	
	ALL INDIA RADIO, Aligarh	S Asia • 250 kW
	IRAN	
	VO THE ISLAMIC REP, Sirjan	[S] • S Asia & SE Asia • 500 kW
	VO THE ISLAMIC REP, Tehrān	[W] • E Asia • 500 kW
	MALI	
	RTV DU MALI, Bamako	FRENCH, ETC • DS • 100 kW
	ROMANIA	
	†R ROMANIA INTL, Bucharest	[W] • S America • 250 kW
	†R ROMANIA INTL, Galbeni	[S] • W Europe • 250 kW
	UNITED KINGDOM	
	BBC, Via Oman	[W] • C Asia • 250 kW; [W] M-F • C Asia • 250 kW
	†BBC, Via Zyyi, Cyprus	⬅ • E Europe • 250 kW; ⬅ • M Sa • E Europe • 250 kW; ⬅ • Sa • E Europe • 250 kW
	USA	
	†ADVENTIST WORLD R, Via Agat, Guam	[W] • E Asia • 100 kW
	R FREE ASIA, Via Tinian, N Marianas	[S] • SE Asia • 500 kW
	RFE-RL, Via Briech, Morocco	[S] • E Europe • 250 kW
	†RFE-RL, Via Lampertheim, Germany	[S] • E Europe • 100 kW
	†SOUND OF HOPE, Via Taiwan	E Asia
	†TRANS WORLD R, Via Merizo, Guam	SE Asia • 100 kW
	VOA, Via Biblis, Germany	[W] • S Europe • 100 kW
	VOA, Via Briech, Morocco	[W] • S Europe • 250 kW
9639.8	**VENEZUELA**	
	ECOS DEL TORBES, San Cristóbal	DS-TEMP INACTIVE • 1 kW
9640	**CANADA**	
	†R CANADA INTL, Sackville, NB	[W] • C America & S America • 250 kW
	CHINA	
	†CHINA R INTL, Kashi	W Europe • 500 kW
	GERMANY	
	†DEUTSCHE WELLE, Via Kigali, Rwanda	[S] • S America • 250 kW
	IRAN	
	†VO THE ISLAMIC REP, Sirjan	[W] • E Asia • 500 kW
	KOREA (REPUBLIC)	
	†KBS WORLD R, In-Kimjae	Europe • 250 kW; SE Asia • 250 kW
	ROMANIA	
	†R ROMANIA INTL, Bucharest	[W] • E North Am • 250 kW; [W] • W Europe • 250 kW
	†R ROMANIA INTL, Galbeni	[W] • W Europe • 250 kW
9644.6	**COSTA RICA**	
	FARO DEL CARIBE, San José	DS-TEMP INACTIVE • 5 kW
9645	**CANADA**	
	R CANADA INTL, Via Skelton, UK	[S] • Mideast • 300 kW
	CHINA	
	CENTRAL PEOPLE'S BS, Beijing	DS-1 • 100 kW; W-M • DS-1 • 100 kW; [S] W-M • DS-1 • 100 kW; [S] • DS-1 • 100 kW
	CHINA R INTL, Kunming	W Africa & C Africa • 500 kW
	EGYPT	
	†RADIO CAIRO, Abu Za'bal	[W] • W Africa • 500 kW
	LEBANON	
(con'd)	VOICE OF CHARITY, Via Vatican City	[W] • Mideast • 100 kW

0 1 2 3 4 5 6 7 8 9 10 11 12 13 14 15 16 17 18 19 20 21 22 23 24

SEASONAL [S] OR [W] 1-HR TIMESHIFT MIDYEAR ⬅ OR ➡ JAMMING / OR /\ EARLIEST HEARD ◁ LATEST HEARD ▷ NEW FOR 2006 †

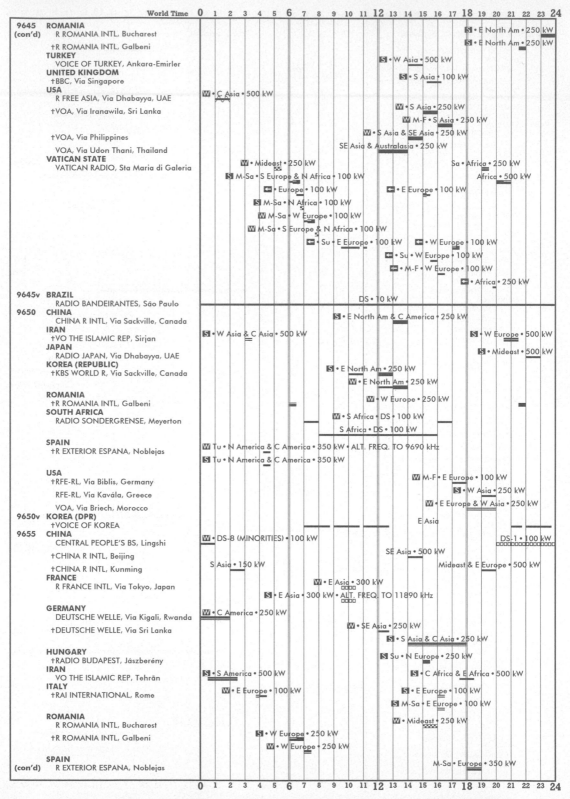

World Time 0 1 2 3 4 5 6 7 8 9 10 11 12 13 14 15 16 17 18 19 20 21 22 23 24

9645
(con'd) **ROMANIA**
  R ROMANIA INTL, Bucharest — S • E North Am • 250 kW
  †R ROMANIA INTL, Galbeni — S • E North Am • 250 kW
TURKEY
  VOICE OF TURKEY, Ankara-Emirler — S • W Asia • 500 kW
UNITED KINGDOM
  †BBC, Via Singapore — S • S Asia • 100 kW
USA
  R FREE ASIA, Via Dhabayya, UAE — W • C Asia • 500 kW
  †VOA, Via Iranawila, Sri Lanka — W • S Asia • 250 kW / W • M-F • S Asia • 250 kW
  †VOA, Via Philippines — W • S Asia & SE Asia • 250 kW
  VOA, Via Udon Thani, Thailand — SE Asia & Australasia • 250 kW
VATICAN STATE
  VATICAN RADIO, Sta Maria di Galeria — W • Mideast • 250 kW / Sa • Africa • 250 kW / Africa • 500 kW
  S M-Sa • S Europe & N Africa • 100 kW
  Europe • 100 kW / E Europe • 100 kW
  S M-Sa • N Africa • 100 kW
  W M-Sa • W Europe • 100 kW
  W M-Sa • S Europe & N Africa • 100 kW
  Su • E Europe • 100 kW / W Europe • 100 kW
  Su • W Europe • 100 kW
  M-F • W Europe • 100 kW
  Africa • 250 kW

9645v **BRAZIL**
  RADIO BANDEIRANTES, São Paulo — DS • 10 kW
9650 **CHINA**
  CHINA R INTL, Via Sackville, Canada — S • E North Am & C America • 250 kW
IRAN
  †VO THE ISLAMIC REP, Sirjan — S • W Asia & C Asia • 500 kW / S • W Europe • 500 kW
JAPAN
  RADIO JAPAN, Via Dhabayya, UAE — S • Mideast • 500 kW
KOREA (REPUBLIC)
  †KBS WORLD R, Via Sackville, Canada — S • E North Am • 250 kW / W • E North Am • 250 kW
ROMANIA
  †R ROMANIA INTL, Galbeni — W • W Europe • 250 kW
SOUTH AFRICA
  RADIO SONDERGRENSE, Meyerton — W • S Africa • DS • 100 kW / S Africa • DS • 100 kW
SPAIN
  †R EXTERIOR ESPANA, Noblejas — W Tu • N America & C America • 350 kW • ALT. FREQ. TO 9690 kHz / S Tu • N America & C America • 350 kW
USA
  †RFE-RL, Via Biblis, Germany — W M-F • E Europe • 100 kW
  RFE-RL, Via Kavála, Greece — S • W Asia • 250 kW
  VOA, Via Briech, Morocco — W • E Europe & W Asia • 250 kW
9650v **KOREA (DPR)**
  †VOICE OF KOREA — E Asia
9655 **CHINA**
  CENTRAL PEOPLE'S BS, Lingshi — W • DS-8 (MINORITIES) • 100 kW / DS-1 • 100 kW
  †CHINA R INTL, Beijing — SE Asia • 500 kW
  †CHINA R INTL, Kunming — S Asia • 150 kW / Mideast & E Europe • 500 kW
FRANCE
  R FRANCE INTL, Via Tokyo, Japan — W • E Asia • 300 kW / S • E Asia • 300 kW • ALT. FREQ. TO 11890 kHz
GERMANY
  DEUTSCHE WELLE, Via Kigali, Rwanda — W • C America • 250 kW
  †DEUTSCHE WELLE, Via Sri Lanka — W • SE Asia • 250 kW / S • S Asia & C Asia • 250 kW
HUNGARY
  †RADIO BUDAPEST, Jászberény — S Su • N Europe • 250 kW
IRAN
  VO THE ISLAMIC REP, Tehrān — S • S America • 500 kW / S • C Africa & E Africa • 500 kW
ITALY
  †RAI INTERNATIONAL, Rome — W • E Europe • 100 kW / S • E Europe • 100 kW / S M-Sa • E Europe • 100 kW
ROMANIA
  R ROMANIA INTL, Bucharest — W • Mideast • 250 kW
  †R ROMANIA INTL, Galbeni — S • W Europe • 250 kW / W • W Europe • 250 kW
SPAIN
(con'd) R EXTERIOR ESPANA, Noblejas — M-Sa • Europe • 350 kW

0 1 2 3 4 5 6 7 8 9 10 11 12 13 14 15 16 17 18 19 20 21 22 23 24

ENGLISH ▬   ARABIC ⌇⌇⌇   CHINESE ▭▭▭   FRENCH ▬▬   GERMAN ▬▬   RUSSIAN ═══   SPANISH ▭▭   OTHER ▬▬

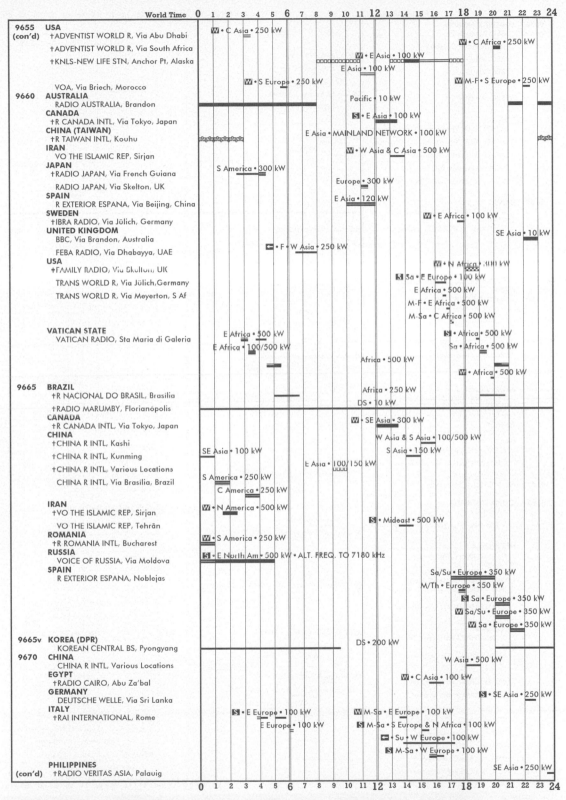

		World Time	0 1 2 3 4 5 6 7 8 9 10 11 12 13 14 15 16 17 18 19 20 21 22 23 24

9655 USA
(con'd) †ADVENTIST WORLD R, Via Abu Dhabi — W • C Asia • 250 kW
†ADVENTIST WORLD R, Via South Africa — W • C Africa • 250 kW
†KNLS-NEW LIFE STN, Anchor Pt, Alaska — W • E Asia • 100 kW / E Asia • 100 kW
VOA, Via Briech, Morocco — W • S Europe • 250 kW / W M-F • S Europe • 250 kW

9660 AUSTRALIA
RADIO AUSTRALIA, Brandon — Pacific • 10 kW
CANADA
†R CANADA INTL, Via Tokyo, Japan — S • E Asia • 100 kW
CHINA (TAIWAN)
†R TAIWAN INTL, Kouhu — E Asia • MAINLAND NETWORK • 100 kW
IRAN
VO THE ISLAMIC REP, Sirjan — W • W Asia & C Asia • 500 kW
JAPAN
†RADIO JAPAN, Via French Guiana — S America • 300 kW
RADIO JAPAN, Via Skelton, UK — Europe • 300 kW
SPAIN
R EXTERIOR ESPANA, Via Beijing, China — E Asia • 120 kW
SWEDEN
†IBRA RADIO, Via Jülich, Germany — W • E Africa • 100 kW
UNITED KINGDOM
BBC, Via Brandon, Australia — SE Asia • 10 kW
FEBA RADIO, Via Dhabayya, UAE — ⇦ • F • W Asia • 250 kW
USA
†FAMILY RADIO, Via Skelton, UK — W • N Africa • 300 kW
TRANS WORLD R, Via Jülich, Germany — S • Sa • E Europe • 100 kW
TRANS WORLD R, Via Meyerton, S Af — E Africa • 500 kW / M-F • E Africa • 500 kW / M-Sa • C Africa • 500 kW
VATICAN STATE
VATICAN RADIO, Sta Maria di Galeria — E Africa • 500 kW / S • Africa • 500 kW
E Africa • 100/500 kW / Sa • Africa • 500 kW
Africa • 500 kW / W • Africa • 500 kW

9665 BRAZIL
†R NACIONAL DO BRASIL, Brasilia — Africa • 250 kW
†RADIO MARUMBY, Florianópolis — DS • 10 kW
CANADA
†R CANADA INTL, Via Tokyo, Japan — W • SE Asia • 300 kW
CHINA
†CHINA R INTL, Kashi — W Asia & S Asia • 100/500 kW
†CHINA R INTL, Kunming — SE Asia • 100 kW / S Asia • 150 kW
†CHINA R INTL, Various Locations — E Asia • 100/150 kW
CHINA R INTL, Via Brasilia, Brazil — S America • 250 kW / C America • 250 kW
IRAN
†VO THE ISLAMIC REP, Sirjan — W • N America • 500 kW
VO THE ISLAMIC REP, Tehrān — S • Mideast • 500 kW
ROMANIA
†R ROMANIA INTL, Bucharest — W • S America • 250 kW
RUSSIA
VOICE OF RUSSIA, Via Moldova — S • E North Am • 500 kW • ALT. FREQ. TO 7180 kHz
SPAIN
R EXTERIOR ESPANA, Noblejas — Sa/Su • Europe • 350 kW / M/Th • Europe • 350 kW / S • Sa • Europe • 350 kW / W Sa/Su • Europe • 350 kW / W • Sa • Europe • 350 kW

9665v KOREA (DPR)
KOREAN CENTRAL BS, Pyongyang — DS • 200 kW
9670 CHINA
CHINA R INTL, Various Locations — W Asia • 500 kW
EGYPT
†RADIO CAIRO, Abu Za'bal — W • C Asia • 100 kW
GERMANY
DEUTSCHE WELLE, Via Sri Lanka — S • SE Asia • 250 kW
ITALY
†RAI INTERNATIONAL, Rome — S • E Europe • 100 kW / W M-Sa • E Europe • 100 kW
E Europe • 100 kW / S M-Sa • S Europe & N Africa • 100 kW
⇦ • Su • W Europe • 100 kW / S M-Sa • W Europe • 100 kW
PHILIPPINES
(con'd) †RADIO VERITAS ASIA, Palauig — SE Asia • 250 kW

	0 1 2 3 4 5 6 7 8 9 10 11 12 13 14 15 16 17 18 19 20 21 22 23 24

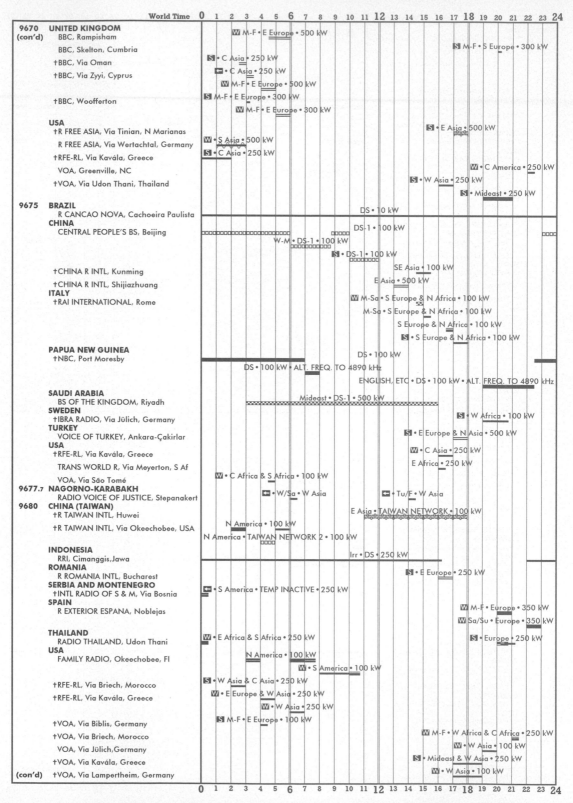

World Time 0 1 2 3 4 5 6 7 8 9 10 11 12 13 14 15 16 17 18 19 20 21 22 23 24

9670 UNITED KINGDOM
(con'd)   BBC, Rampisham — W • M-F • E Europe • 500 kW
          BBC, Skelton, Cumbria — S • M-F • S Europe • 300 kW
          †BBC, Via Oman — S • C Asia • 250 kW
          †BBC, Via Zyyi, Cyprus — C Asia • 250 kW
                                   W • M-F • E Europe • 500 kW
          †BBC, Woofferton — S • M-F • E Europe • 300 kW
                             W • M-F • E Europe • 300 kW

          USA
          †R FREE ASIA, Via Tinian, N Marianas — S • E Asia • 500 kW
          R FREE ASIA, Via Wertachtal, Germany — W • S Asia • 500 kW
          †RFE-RL, Via Kavála, Greece — S • C Asia • 250 kW
          VOA, Greenville, NC — W • C America • 250 kW
          †VOA, Via Udon Thani, Thailand — S • W Asia • 250 kW
                                           S • Mideast • 250 kW

9675 BRAZIL
          R CANCAO NOVA, Cachoeira Paulista — DS • 10 kW
          CHINA
          CENTRAL PEOPLE'S BS, Beijing — DS-1 • 100 kW
                                         W-M • DS-1 • 100 kW
                                         S • DS-1 • 100 kW
          †CHINA R INTL, Kunming — SE Asia • 100 kW
          †CHINA R INTL, Shijiazhuang — E Asia • 500 kW
          ITALY
          †RAI INTERNATIONAL, Rome — W • M-Sa • S Europe & N Africa • 100 kW
                                     M-Sa • S Europe & N Africa • 100 kW
                                     S Europe & N Africa • 100 kW
                                     S • S Europe & N Africa • 100 kW

          PAPUA NEW GUINEA
          †NBC, Port Moresby — DS • 100 kW
                               DS • 100 kW • ALT. FREQ. TO 4890 kHz
                               ENGLISH, ETC • DS • 100 kW • ALT. FREQ. TO 4890 kHz

          SAUDI ARABIA
          BS OF THE KINGDOM, Riyadh — Mideast • DS-1 • 500 kW
          SWEDEN
          †IBRA RADIO, Via Jülich, Germany — S • W Africa • 100 kW
          TURKEY
          VOICE OF TURKEY, Ankara-Çakirlar — S • E Europe & N Africa • 500 kW
          USA
          †RFE-RL, Via Kavála, Greece — W • C Asia • 250 kW
          TRANS WORLD R, Via Meyerton, S Af — E Africa • 250 kW
          VOA, Via São Tomé — W • C Africa & S Africa • 100 kW

9677.7 NAGORNO-KARABAKH
          RADIO VOICE OF JUSTICE, Stepanakert — W/Sa • W Asia   Tu/F • W Asia
9680 CHINA (TAIWAN)
          †R TAIWAN INTL, Huwei — E Asia • TAIWAN NETWORK • 100 kW
          †R TAIWAN INTL, Via Okeechobee, USA — N America • 100 kW
                                                N America • TAIWAN NETWORK 2 • 100 kW

          INDONESIA
          RRI, Cimanggis, Jawa — Irr • DS • 250 kW
          ROMANIA
          R ROMANIA INTL, Bucharest — S • E Europe • 250 kW
          SERBIA AND MONTENEGRO
          †INTL RADIO OF S & M, Via Bosnia — S America • TEMP INACTIVE • 250 kW
          SPAIN
          R EXTERIOR ESPANA, Noblejas — W • M-F • Europe • 350 kW
                                        W • Sa/Su • Europe • 350 kW

          THAILAND
          RADIO THAILAND, Udon Thani — W • E Africa & S Africa • 250 kW
                                       S • Europe • 250 kW
          USA
          FAMILY RADIO, Okeechobee, Fl — N America • 100 kW
                                         W • S America • 100 kW
          †RFE-RL, Via Briech, Morocco — S • W Asia & C Asia • 250 kW
          †RFE-RL, Via Kavála, Greece — W • E Europe & W Asia • 250 kW
                                        W • W Asia • 250 kW
          †VOA, Via Biblis, Germany — S • M-F • E Europe • 100 kW
          †VOA, Via Briech, Morocco — W • M-F • W Africa & C Africa • 250 kW
          VOA, Via Jülich, Germany — W • W Asia • 100 kW
          †VOA, Via Kavála, Greece — S • Mideast & W Asia • 250 kW
(con'd)   †VOA, Via Lampertheim, Germany — W • W Asia • 100 kW

0 1 2 3 4 5 6 7 8 9 10 11 12 13 14 15 16 17 18 19 20 21 22 23 24

ENGLISH ▬   ARABIC ⌇⌇   CHINESE □□□   FRENCH ▬▬   GERMAN ▬   RUSSIAN ═   SPANISH ▬   OTHER ▬

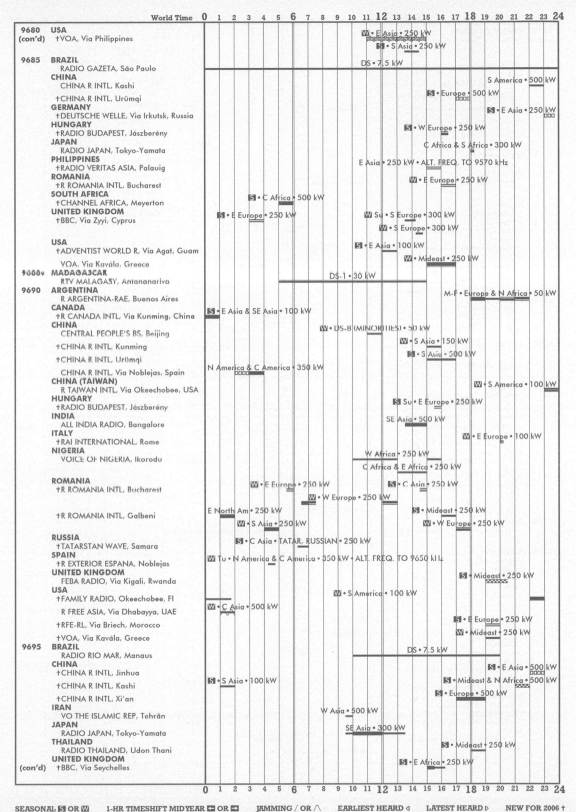

World Time		
9680 USA		
(con'd) †VOA, Via Philippines	W • E Asia • 250 kW	
	S • S Asia • 250 kW	
9685 BRAZIL		
RADIO GAZETA, São Paulo	DS • 7.5 kW	
CHINA	S America • 500 kW	
CHINA R INTL, Kashi		
†CHINA R INTL, Urümqi	S • Europe • 500 kW	
GERMANY	S • E Asia • 250 kW	
†DEUTSCHE WELLE, Via Irkutsk, Russia		
HUNGARY	S • W Europe • 250 kW	
†RADIO BUDAPEST, Jászberény		
JAPAN	C Africa & S Africa • 300 kW	
RADIO JAPAN, Tokyo-Yamata		
PHILIPPINES	E Asia • 250 kW • ALT. FREQ. TO 9570 kHz	
†RADIO VERITAS ASIA, Palauig		
ROMANIA	W • E Europe • 250 kW	
†R ROMANIA INTL, Bucharest		
SOUTH AFRICA	S • C Africa • 500 kW	
†CHANNEL AFRICA, Meyerton		
UNITED KINGDOM	S • E Europe • 250 kW	W Su • S Europe • 300 kW
†BBC, Via Zyyi, Cyprus	W • S Europe • 300 kW	
USA		
†ADVENTIST WORLD R, Via Agat, Guam	S • E Asia • 100 kW	
VOA, Via Kavála, Greece	W • Mideast • 250 kW	
9688v MADAGASCAR		
RTV MALAGASY, Antananarivo	DS-1 • 30 kW	
9690 ARGENTINA	M-F • Europe & N Africa • 50 kW	
R ARGENTINA-RAE, Buenos Aires		
CANADA	S • E Asia & SE Asia • 100 kW	
†R CANADA INTL, Via Kunming, China		
CHINA	W • DS-8 (MINORITIES) • 50 kW	
CENTRAL PEOPLE'S BS, Beijing		
†CHINA R INTL, Kunming	W • S Asia • 150 kW	
†CHINA R INTL, Urümqi	S • S Asia • 500 kW	
CHINA R INTL, Via Noblejas, Spain	N America & C America • 350 kW	
CHINA (TAIWAN)	W • S America • 100 kW	
R TAIWAN INTL, Via Okeechobee, USA		
HUNGARY	S Su • E Europe • 250 kW	
†RADIO BUDAPEST, Jászberény		
INDIA	SE Asia • 500 kW	
ALL INDIA RADIO, Bangalore		
ITALY	W • E Europe • 100 kW	
†RAI INTERNATIONAL, Rome		
NIGERIA	W Africa • 250 kW	
VOICE OF NIGERIA, Ikorodu	C Africa & E Africa • 250 kW	
ROMANIA	W • E Europe • 250 kW	S • C Asia • 250 kW
†R ROMANIA INTL, Bucharest	W • W Europe • 250 kW	
	E North Am • 250 kW	S • Mideast • 250 kW
†R ROMANIA INTL, Galbeni	W • S Asia • 250 kW	W • W Europe • 250 kW
RUSSIA	S • C Asia • TATAR, RUSSIAN • 250 kW	
†TATARSTAN WAVE, Samara		
SPAIN	W Tu • N America & C America • 350 kW • ALT. FREQ. TO 9650 kHz	
†R EXTERIOR ESPANA, Noblejas		
UNITED KINGDOM	S • Mideast • 250 kW	
FEBA RADIO, Via Kigali, Rwanda		
USA	W • S America • 100 kW	
†FAMILY RADIO, Okeechobee, Fl		
R FREE ASIA, Via Dhabayya, UAE	W • C Asia • 500 kW	
†RFE-RL, Via Briech, Morocco	S • E Europe • 250 kW	
†VOA, Via Kavála, Greece	W • Mideast • 250 kW	
9695 BRAZIL	DS • 7.5 kW	
RADIO RIO MAR, Manaus		
CHINA	S • E Asia • 500 kW	
†CHINA R INTL, Jinhua		
†CHINA R INTL, Kashi	S • S Asia • 100 kW	S • Mideast & N Africa • 500 kW
†CHINA R INTL, Xi'an	S • Europe • 500 kW	
IRAN	W Asia • 500 kW	
VO THE ISLAMIC REP, Tehrān		
JAPAN	SE Asia • 300 kW	
RADIO JAPAN, Tokyo-Yamata		
THAILAND	S • Mideast • 250 kW	
RADIO THAILAND, Udon Thani		
UNITED KINGDOM	S • E Africa • 250 kW	
(con'd) †BBC, Via Seychelles		

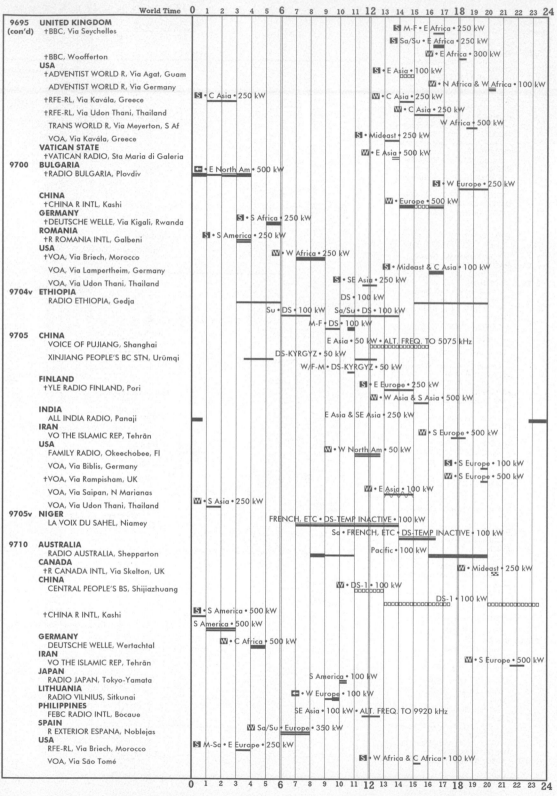

ENGLISH ▬ ARABIC ⋙ CHINESE □□□ FRENCH ▭ GERMAN ▬ RUSSIAN ═ SPANISH ▬ OTHER ▬

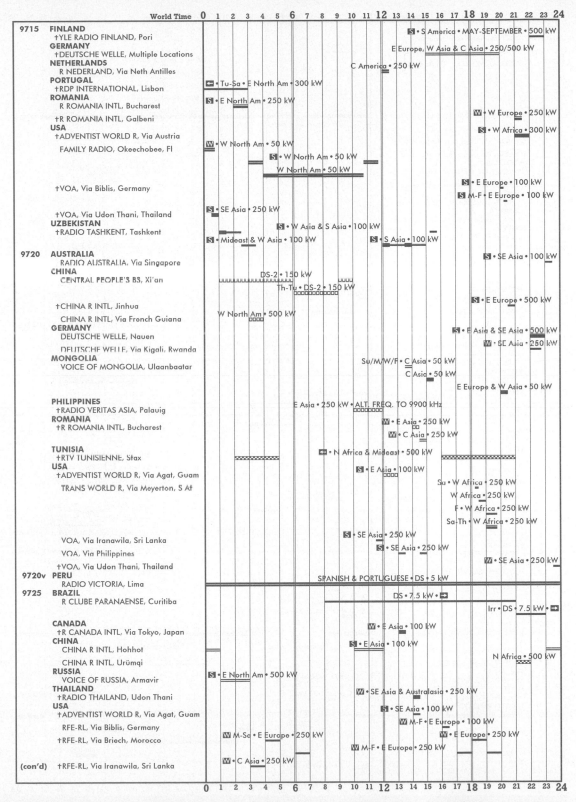

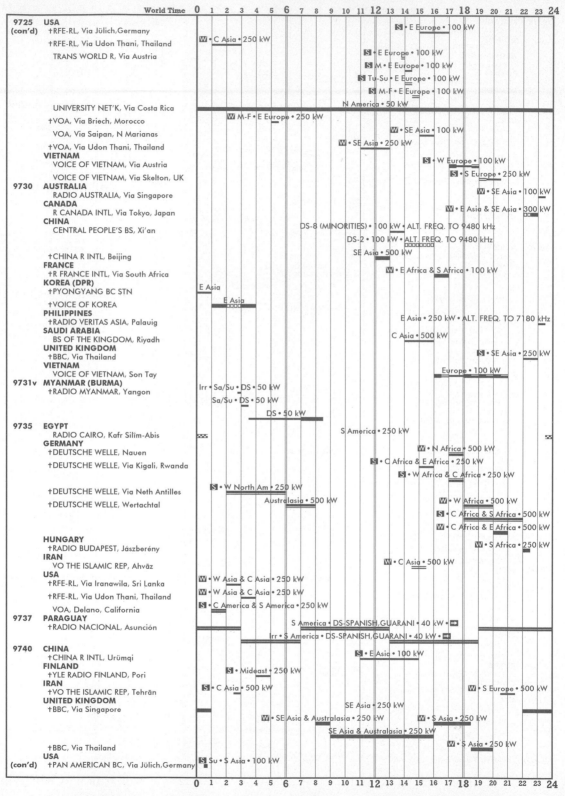

World Time 0 1 2 3 4 5 6 7 8 9 10 11 12 13 14 15 16 17 18 19 20 21 22 23 24

kHz	Country / Station	Schedule
9725 (con'd)	**USA**	
	†RFE-RL, Via Jülich,Germany	[S] • E Europe • 100 kW
	†RFE-RL, Via Udon Thani, Thailand	[W] • C Asia • 250 kW
	TRANS WORLD R, Via Austria	[S] • E Europe • 100 kW
		[S] M • E Europe • 100 kW
		[S] Tu-Su • E Europe • 100 kW
		[S] M-F • E Europe • 100 kW
	UNIVERSITY NET'K, Via Costa Rica	N America • 50 kW
	†VOA, Via Briech, Morocco	[W] M-F • E Europe • 250 kW
	VOA, Via Saipan, N Marianas	[W] • SE Asia • 100 kW
	†VOA, Via Udon Thani, Thailand	[W] • SE Asia • 250 kW
	VIETNAM	
	VOICE OF VIETNAM, Via Austria	[S] • W Europe • 100 kW
	VOICE OF VIETNAM, Via Skelton, UK	[S] • S Europe • 250 kW
9730	**AUSTRALIA**	
	RADIO AUSTRALIA, Via Singapore	[W] • SE Asia • 100 kW
	CANADA	
	R CANADA INTL, Via Tokyo, Japan	[W] • E Asia & SE Asia • 300 kW
	CHINA	
	CENTRAL PEOPLE'S BS, Xi'an	DS-8 (MINORITIES) • 100 kW • ALT. FREQ. TO 9480 kHz
		DS-2 • 100 kW • ALT. FREQ. TO 9480 kHz
	†CHINA R INTL, Beijing	SE Asia • 500 kW
	FRANCE	
	†R FRANCE INTL, Via South Africa	[W] • E Africa & S Africa • 100 kW
	KOREA (DPR)	
	†PYONGYANG BC STN	E Asia
	†VOICE OF KOREA	E Asia
	PHILIPPINES	
	†RADIO VERITAS ASIA, Palauig	E Asia • 250 kW • ALT. FREQ. TO 7180 kHz
	SAUDI ARABIA	
	BS OF THE KINGDOM, Riyadh	C Asia • 500 kW
	UNITED KINGDOM	
	†BBC, Via Thailand	[S] • SE Asia • 250 kW
	VIETNAM	
	VOICE OF VIETNAM, Son Tay	Europe • 100 kW
9731v	**MYANMAR (BURMA)**	
	†RADIO MYANMAR, Yangon	Irr • Sa/Su • DS • 50 kW
		Sa/Su • DS • 50 kW
		DS • 50 kW
9735	**EGYPT**	
	RADIO CAIRO, Kafr Silîm-Abis	S America • 250 kW
	GERMANY	
	†DEUTSCHE WELLE, Nauen	[W] • N Africa • 500 kW
	†DEUTSCHE WELLE, Via Kigali, Rwanda	[S] • C Africa & E Africa • 250 kW
		[S] • W Africa & C Africa • 250 kW
	†DEUTSCHE WELLE, Via Neth Antilles	[S] • W North Am • 250 kW
	†DEUTSCHE WELLE, Wertachtal	Australasia • 500 kW
		[W] • W Africa • 500 kW
		[S] • C Africa & S Africa • 500 kW
		[W] • C Africa & E Africa • 500 kW
	HUNGARY	
	†RADIO BUDAPEST, Jászberény	[W] • S Africa • 250 kW
	IRAN	
	VO THE ISLAMIC REP, Ahvāz	[W] • C Asia • 500 kW
	USA	
	†RFE-RL, Via Iranawila, Sri Lanka	[W] • W Asia & C Asia • 250 kW
	†RFE-RL, Via Udon Thani, Thailand	[W] • W Asia & C Asia • 250 kW
	VOA, Delano, California	[S] • C America & S America • 250 kW
9737	**PARAGUAY**	
	†RADIO NACIONAL, Asunción	S America • DS-SPANISH,GUARANI • 40 kW • →
		Irr • S America • DS-SPANISH,GUARANI • 40 kW • →
9740	**CHINA**	
	†CHINA R INTL, Urümqi	[S] • E Asia • 100 kW
	FINLAND	
	†YLE RADIO FINLAND, Pori	[S] • Mideast • 250 kW
	IRAN	
	†VO THE ISLAMIC REP, Tehrān	[S] • C Asia • 500 kW
		[W] • S Europe • 500 kW
	UNITED KINGDOM	
	†BBC, Via Singapore	SE Asia • 250 kW
		[W] • SE Asia & Australasia • 250 kW
		[W] • S Asia • 250 kW
		SE Asia & Australasia • 250 kW
	†BBC, Via Thailand	[W] • S Asia • 250 kW
	USA	
(con'd)	†PAN AMERICAN BC, Via Jülich,Germany	[S] Su • S Asia • 100 kW

0 1 2 3 4 5 6 7 8 9 10 11 12 13 14 15 16 17 18 19 20 21 22 23 24

ENGLISH ▬ ARABIC ▭ CHINESE ▭▭▭ FRENCH ▬ GERMAN ▬ RUSSIAN ═ SPANISH ▬ OTHER —

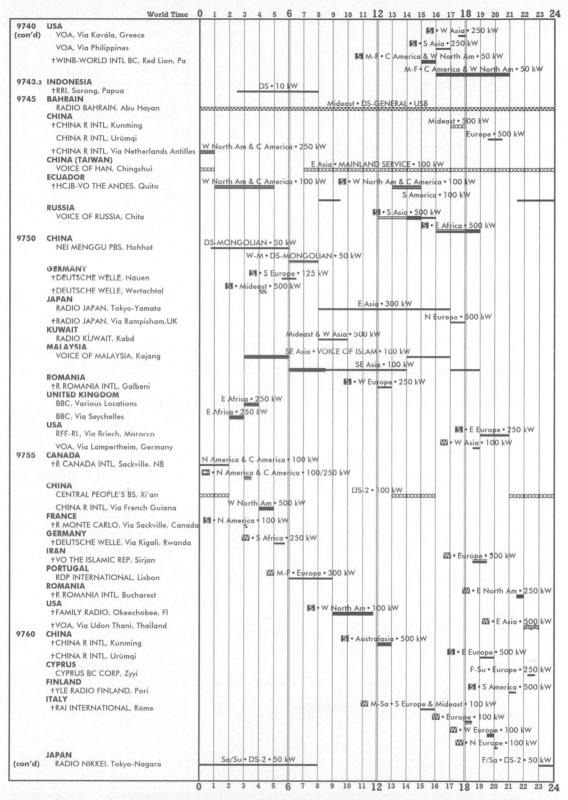

Freq	Station	
9740 (con'd)	**USA**	
	VOA, Via Kavála, Greece	S • W Asia • 250 kW
	VOA, Via Philippines	S • S Asia • 250 kW
	†WINB-WORLD INTL BC, Red Lion, Pa	S • M-F • C America & W North Am • 50 kW
		M-F • C America & W North Am • 50 kW
9743.2	**INDONESIA**	
	†RRI, Sorong, Papua	DS • 10 kW
9745	**BAHRAIN**	
	RADIO BAHRAIN, Abu Hayan	Mideast • DS-GENERAL • USB
	CHINA	
	†CHINA R INTL, Kunming	Mideast • 500 kW
	CHINA R INTL, Urümqi	Europe • 500 kW
	†CHINA R INTL, Via Netherlands Antilles	W North Am & C America • 250 kW
	CHINA (TAIWAN)	
	VOICE OF HAN, Chingshui	E Asia • MAINLAND SERVICE • 100 kW
	ECUADOR	
	†HCJB-VO THE ANDES, Quito	W North Am & C America • 100 kW / S • W North Am & C America • 100 kW
		S America • 100 kW
	RUSSIA	
	VOICE OF RUSSIA, Chita	S • S Asia • 500 kW
		S • E Africa • 500 kW
9750	**CHINA**	
	NEI MENGGU PBS, Hohhot	DS-MONGOLIAN • 50 kW
		W-M • DS-MONGOLIAN • 50 kW
	GERMANY	
	†DEUTSCHE WELLE, Nauen	S • S Europe • 125 kW
	†DEUTSCHE WELLE, Wertachtal	S • Mideast • 500 kW
	JAPAN	
	RADIO JAPAN, Tokyo-Yamata	E Asia • 300 kW
	†RADIO JAPAN, Via Rampisham, UK	N Europe • 500 kW
	KUWAIT	
	RADIO KUWAIT, Kabd	Mideast & W Asia • 500 kW
	MALAYSIA	
	VOICE OF MALAYSIA, Kajang	SE Asia • VOICE OF ISLAM • 100 kW
		SE Asia • 100 kW
	ROMANIA	
	†R ROMANIA INTL, Galbeni	S • W Europe • 250 kW
	UNITED KINGDOM	
	BBC, Various Locations	E Africa • 250 kW
	BBC, Via Seychelles	E Africa • 250 kW
	USA	
	RFE-RL, Via Briech, Morocco	S • E Europe • 250 kW
	VOA, Via Lampertheim, Germany	W • W Asia • 100 kW
9755	**CANADA**	
	†R CANADA INTL, Sackville, NB	N America & C America • 100 kW
		⇦ • N America & C America • 100/250 kW
	CHINA	
	CENTRAL PEOPLE'S BS, Xi'an	DS-2 • 100 kW
	CHINA R INTL, Via French Guiana	W North Am • 500 kW
	FRANCE	
	†R MONTE CARLO, Via Sackville, Canada	S • N America • 100 kW
	GERMANY	
	†DEUTSCHE WELLE, Via Kigali, Rwanda	W • S Africa • 250 kW
	IRAN	
	†VO THE ISLAMIC REP, Sirjan	W • Europe • 500 kW
	PORTUGAL	
	RDP INTERNATIONAL, Lisbon	W M-F • Europe • 300 kW
	ROMANIA	
	†R ROMANIA INTL, Bucharest	W • E North Am • 250 kW
	USA	
	†FAMILY RADIO, Okeechobee, Fl	S • W North Am • 100 kW
	†VOA, Via Udon Thani, Thailand	W • E Asia • 500 kW
9760	**CHINA**	
	†CHINA R INTL, Kunming	S • Australasia • 500 kW
	†CHINA R INTL, Urümqi	S • E Europe • 500 kW
	CYPRUS	
	CYPRUS BC CORP, Zyyi	F-Su • Europe • 250 kW
	FINLAND	
	†YLE RADIO FINLAND, Pori	S • S America • 500 kW
	ITALY	
	†RAI INTERNATIONAL, Rome	W M-Sa • S Europe & Mideast • 100 kW
		W • Europe • 100 kW
		W • W Europe • 100 kW
		W • N Europe • 100 kW
	JAPAN	
(con'd)	RADIO NIKKEI, Tokyo-Nagara	Sa/Su • DS-2 • 50 kW / F/Sa • DS-2 • 50 kW

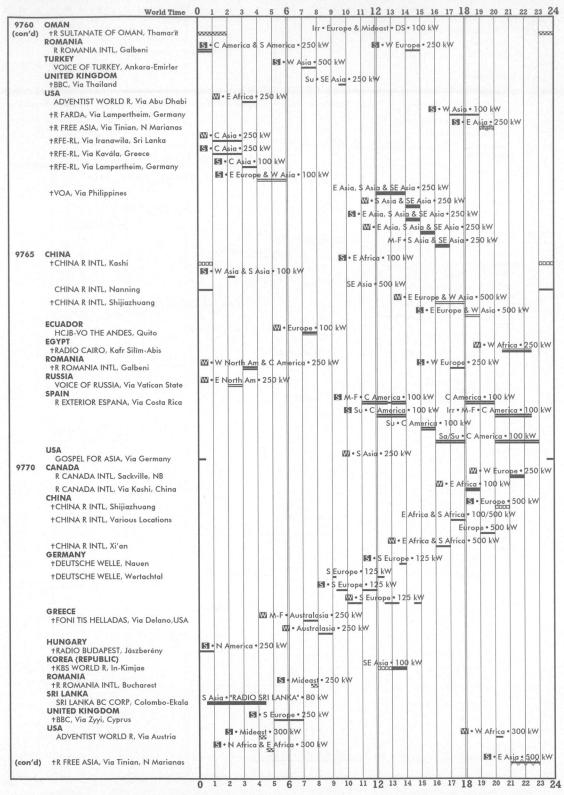

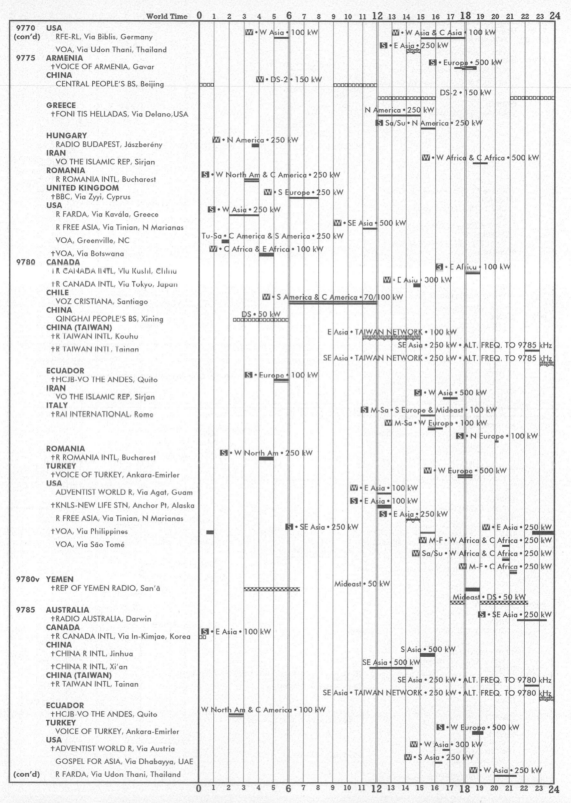

World Time   0 1 2 3 4 5 6 7 8 9 10 11 12 13 14 15 16 17 18 19 20 21 22 23 24

Freq	Country / Station	Details
9770 (con'd)	USA — RFE-RL, Via Biblis, Germany	W • W Asia • 100 kW / W • W Asia & C Asia • 100 kW
	VOA, Via Udon Thani, Thailand	S • E Asia • 250 kW
9775	ARMENIA — †VOICE OF ARMENIA, Gavar	S • Europe • 500 kW
	CHINA — CENTRAL PEOPLE'S BS, Beijing	W • DS-2 • 150 kW / DS-2 • 150 kW
	GREECE — †FONI TIS HELLADAS, Via Delano, USA	N America • 250 kW / S • Sa/Su • N America • 250 kW
	HUNGARY — RADIO BUDAPEST, Jászberény	W • N America • 250 kW
	IRAN — VO THE ISLAMIC REP, Sirjan	W • W Africa & C Africa • 500 kW
	ROMANIA — R ROMANIA INTL, Bucharest	S • W North Am & C America • 250 kW
	UNITED KINGDOM — †BBC, Via Zyyi, Cyprus	W • S Europe • 250 kW
	USA — R FARDA, Via Kavála, Greece	S • W Asia • 250 kW
	R FREE ASIA, Via Tinian, N Marianas	W • SE Asia • 500 kW
	VOA, Greenville, NC	Tu-Sa • C America & S America • 250 kW
	†VOA, Via Botswana	W • C Africa & E Africa • 100 kW
9780	CANADA — †R CANADA INTL, Via Kushi, China	S • C Africa • 100 kW
	†R CANADA INTL, Via Tokyo, Japan	W • C Asia • 300 kW
	CHILE — VOZ CRISTIANA, Santiago	W • S America & C America • 70/100 kW
	CHINA — QINGHAI PEOPLE'S BS, Xining	DS • 50 kW
	CHINA (TAIWAN) — †R TAIWAN INTL, Kouhu	E Asia • TAIWAN NETWORK • 100 kW
	†R TAIWAN INTL, Tainan	SE Asia • 250 kW • ALT. FREQ. TO 9785 kHz / SE Asia • TAIWAN NETWORK • 250 kW • ALT. FREQ. TO 9785 kHz
	ECUADOR — †HCJB-VO THE ANDES, Quito	S • Europe • 100 kW
	IRAN — VO THE ISLAMIC REP, Sirjan	S • W Asia • 500 kW
	ITALY — †RAI INTERNATIONAL, Rome	S M-Sa • S Europe & Mideast • 100 kW / W M-Sa • W Europe • 100 kW / S • N Europe • 100 kW
	ROMANIA — †R ROMANIA INTL, Bucharest	S • W North Am • 250 kW
	TURKEY — †VOICE OF TURKEY, Ankara-Emirler	W • W Europe • 500 kW
	USA — ADVENTIST WORLD R, Via Agat, Guam	W • E Asia • 100 kW
	†KNLS-NEW LIFE STN, Anchor Pt, Alaska	S • E Asia • 100 kW
	R FREE ASIA, Via Tinian, N Marianas	S • E Asia • 250 kW
	†VOA, Via Philippines	S • SE Asia • 250 kW / W • E Asia • 250 kW
	VOA, Via São Tomé	W M-F • W Africa & C Africa • 250 kW / W Sa/Su • W Africa & C Africa • 250 kW / W M-F • C Africa • 250 kW
9780v	YEMEN — †REP OF YEMEN RADIO, San'ā	Mideast • 50 kW / Mideast • DS • 50 kW
9785	AUSTRALIA — †RADIO AUSTRALIA, Darwin	S • SE Asia • 250 kW
	CANADA — †R CANADA INTL, Via In-Kimjae, Korea	S • E Asia • 100 kW
	CHINA — †CHINA R INTL, Jinhua	S Asia • 500 kW
	†CHINA R INTL, Xi'an	SE Asia • 500 kW
	CHINA (TAIWAN) — †R TAIWAN INTL, Tainan	SE Asia • 250 kW • ALT. FREQ. TO 9780 kHz / SE Asia • TAIWAN NETWORK • 250 kW • ALT. FREQ. TO 9780 kHz
	ECUADOR — †HCJB-VO THE ANDES, Quito	W North Am & C America • 100 kW
	TURKEY — VOICE OF TURKEY, Ankara-Emirler	S • W Europe • 500 kW
	USA — †ADVENTIST WORLD R, Via Austria	W • W Asia • 300 kW
	GOSPEL FOR ASIA, Via Dhabayya, UAE	W • S Asia • 250 kW
(con'd)	R FARDA, Via Udon Thani, Thailand	W • W Asia • 250 kW

0 1 2 3 4 5 6 7 8 9 10 11 12 13 14 15 16 17 18 19 20 21 22 23 24

SEASONAL 🅂 OR 🅆   1-HR TIMESHIFT MIDYEAR ⬅ OR ➡   JAMMING / OR ∧   EARLIEST HEARD ◁   LATEST HEARD ▷   NEW FOR 2006 †

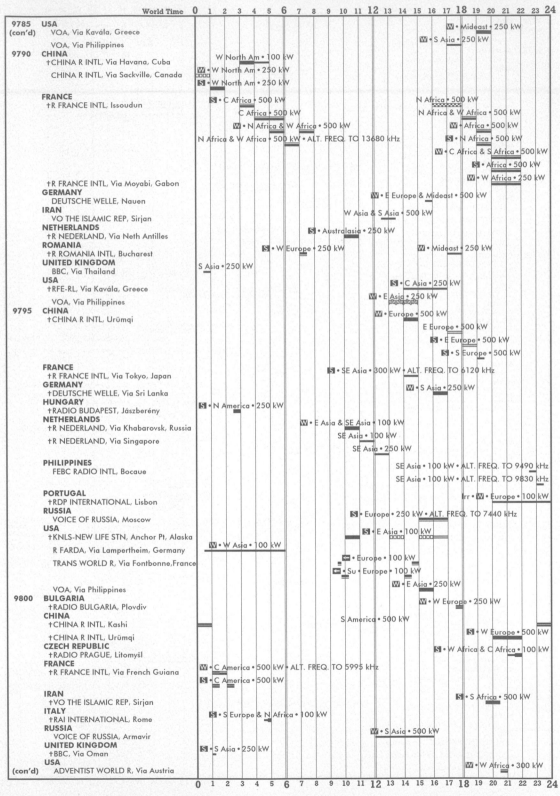

World Time 0 1 2 3 4 5 6 7 8 9 10 11 12 13 14 15 16 17 18 19 20 21 22 23 24

9785 USA
(con'd) VOA, Via Kavála, Greece — W • Mideast • 250 kW
  VOA, Via Philippines — W • S Asia • 250 kW
9790 CHINA
  †CHINA R INTL, Via Havana, Cuba — W North Am • 100 kW
  CHINA R INTL, Via Sackville, Canada — W • W North Am • 250 kW / S • W North Am • 250 kW

FRANCE
  †R FRANCE INTL, Issoudun — S • C Africa • 500 kW / C Africa • 500 kW / N Africa • 500 kW / N Africa & W Africa • 500 kW / W • N Africa & W Africa • 500 kW / W • Africa • 500 kW / N Africa & W Africa • 500 kW • ALT. FREQ. TO 13680 kHz / S • N Africa • 500 kW / W • C Africa & S Africa • 500 kW / S • Africa • 500 kW / W • W Africa • 250 kW

  †R FRANCE INTL, Via Moyabi, Gabon
GERMANY
  DEUTSCHE WELLE, Nauen — W • E Europe & Mideast • 500 kW
IRAN
  VO THE ISLAMIC REP, Sirjan — W Asia & S Asia • 500 kW
NETHERLANDS
  †R NEDERLAND, Via Neth Antilles — S • Australasia • 250 kW
ROMANIA
  †R ROMANIA INTL, Bucharest — S • W Europe • 250 kW / W • Mideast • 250 kW
UNITED KINGDOM
  BBC, Via Thailand — S Asia • 250 kW
USA
  †RFE-RL, Via Kavála, Greece — S • C Asia • 250 kW
  VOA, Via Philippines — W • E Asia • 250 kW
9795 CHINA
  †CHINA R INTL, Urümqi — W • Europe • 500 kW / E Europe • 500 kW / S • E Europe • 500 kW / S • S Europe • 500 kW

FRANCE
  †R FRANCE INTL, Via Tokyo, Japan — S • SE Asia • 300 kW • ALT. FREQ. TO 6120 kHz
GERMANY
  †DEUTSCHE WELLE, Via Sri Lanka — W • S Asia • 250 kW
HUNGARY
  †RADIO BUDAPEST, Jászberény — S • N America • 250 kW
NETHERLANDS
  †R NEDERLAND, Via Khabarovsk, Russia — W • E Asia & SE Asia • 100 kW
  †R NEDERLAND, Via Singapore — SE Asia • 100 kW / SE Asia • 250 kW

PHILIPPINES
  FEBC RADIO INTL, Bocaue — SE Asia • 100 kW • ALT. FREQ. TO 9490 kHz / SE Asia • 100 kW • ALT. FREQ. TO 9830 kHz

PORTUGAL
  †RDP INTERNATIONAL, Lisbon — Irr • W • Europe • 100 kW
RUSSIA
  VOICE OF RUSSIA, Moscow — S • Europe • 250 kW • ALT. FREQ. TO 7440 kHz
USA
  †KNLS-NEW LIFE STN, Anchor Pt, Alaska — S • E Asia • 100 kW
  R FARDA, Via Lampertheim, Germany — W • W Asia • 100 kW
  TRANS WORLD R, Via Fontbonne, France — • Europe • 100 kW / Su • Europe • 100 kW

  VOA, Via Philippines — W • E Asia • 250 kW
9800 BULGARIA
  †RADIO BULGARIA, Plovdiv — W • W Europe • 250 kW
CHINA
  †CHINA R INTL, Kashi — S America • 500 kW
  †CHINA R INTL, Urümqi — S • W Europe • 500 kW
CZECH REPUBLIC
  †RADIO PRAGUE, Litomyšl — S • W Africa & C Africa • 100 kW
FRANCE
  †R FRANCE INTL, Via French Guiana — W • C America • 500 kW • ALT. FREQ. TO 5995 kHz / S • C America • 500 kW

IRAN
  †VO THE ISLAMIC REP, Sirjan — S • S Africa • 500 kW
ITALY
  †RAI INTERNATIONAL, Rome — S • S Europe & N Africa • 100 kW
RUSSIA
  VOICE OF RUSSIA, Armavir — W • S Asia • 500 kW
UNITED KINGDOM
  †BBC, Via Oman — S • S Asia • 250 kW
USA
(con'd) ADVENTIST WORLD R, Via Austria — W • W Africa • 300 kW

0 1 2 3 4 5 6 7 8 9 10 11 12 13 14 15 16 17 18 19 20 21 22 23 24

ENGLISH ▬ ARABIC ▨ CHINESE ▫▫▫ FRENCH ▬ GERMAN ▬ RUSSIAN ═ SPANISH ▬ OTHER ▬

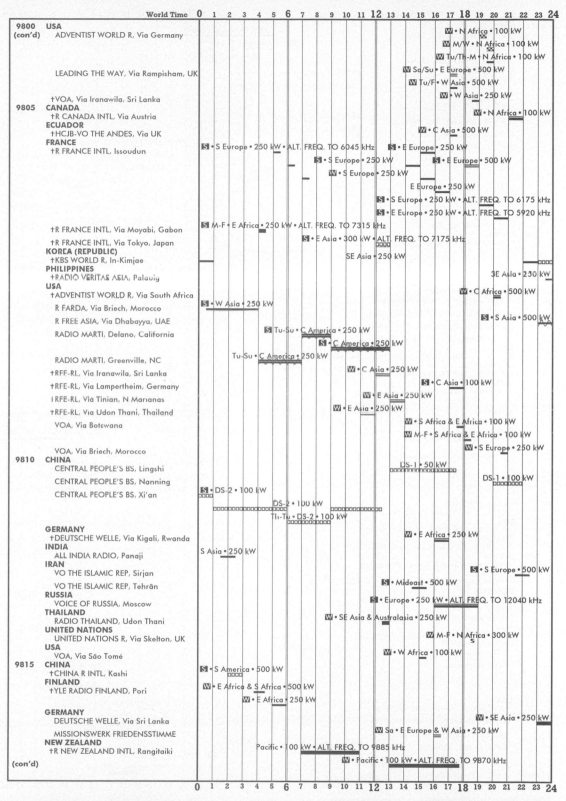

World Time	9800-9815 kHz schedule

9800 **USA**
(con'd) ADVENTIST WORLD R, Via Germany — W • N Africa • 100 kW / W M/W • N Africa • 100 kW / W Tu/Th-M • N Africa • 100 kW
LEADING THE WAY, Via Rampisham, UK — W Sa/Su • E Europe • 500 kW / W Tu/F • W Asia • 500 kW
†VOA, Via Iranawila, Sri Lanka — W • W Asia • 250 kW
9805 **CANADA**
†R CANADA INTL, Via Austria — W • N Africa • 100 kW
ECUADOR
†HCJB-VO THE ANDES, Via UK — W • C Asia • 500 kW
FRANCE
†R FRANCE INTL, Issoudun — S • S Europe • 250 kW • ALT. FREQ. TO 6045 kHz / S • E Europe • 250 kW
 — S • S Europe • 250 kW / S • E Europe • 500 kW
 — W • S Europe • 250 kW
 — E Europe • 250 kW
 — S • S Europe • 250 kW • ALT. FREQ. TO 6175 kHz
 — S • E Europe • 250 kW • ALT. FREQ. TO 5920 kHz
†R FRANCE INTL, Via Moyabi, Gabon — S M-F • E Africa • 250 kW • ALT. FREQ. TO 7315 kHz
†R FRANCE INTL, Via Tokyo, Japan — S • E Asia • 300 kW • ALT. FREQ. TO 7175 kHz
KOREA (REPUBLIC)
†KBS WORLD R, In-Kimjae — SE Asia • 250 kW
PHILIPPINES
†RADIO VERITAS ASIA, Palauig — 3E Asia • 230 kW
USA
†ADVENTIST WORLD R, Via South Africa — W • C Africa • 500 kW
R FARDA, Via Briech, Morocco — S • W Asia • 250 kW / S • S Asia • 500 kW
R FREE ASIA, Via Dhabayya, UAE
RADIO MARTI, Delano, California — S Tu-Su • C America • 250 kW / S • C America • 250 kW
RADIO MARTI, Greenville, NC — Tu-Su • C America • 250 kW
†RFE-RL, Via Iranawila, Sri Lanka — W • C Asia • 250 kW / S • C Asia • 100 kW
†RFE-RL, Via Lampertheim, Germany
†RFE-RL, Via Tinian, N Marianas — W • E Asia • 250 kW
†RFE-RL, Via Udon Thani, Thailand — W • E Asia • 250 kW
VOA, Via Botswana — W • S Africa & E Africa • 100 kW / W M-F • S Africa & E Africa • 100 kW
VOA, Via Briech, Morocco — W • S Europe • 250 kW
9810 **CHINA**
CENTRAL PEOPLE'S BS, Lingshi — DS-1 • 50 kW / DS-1 • 100 kW
CENTRAL PEOPLE'S BS, Nanning
CENTRAL PEOPLE'S BS, Xi'an — S • DS-2 • 100 kW
 — DS-2 • 100 kW
 — Th-Tu • DS-2 • 100 kW
GERMANY
†DEUTSCHE WELLE, Via Kigali, Rwanda — W • E Africa • 250 kW
INDIA
ALL INDIA RADIO, Panaji — S Asia • 250 kW
IRAN
VO THE ISLAMIC REP, Sirjan — S • S Europe • 500 kW
VO THE ISLAMIC REP, Tehrān — S • Mideast • 500 kW
RUSSIA
VOICE OF RUSSIA, Moscow — S • Europe • 250 kW • ALT. FREQ. TO 12040 kHz
THAILAND
RADIO THAILAND, Udon Thani — W • SE Asia & Australasia • 250 kW
UNITED NATIONS
UNITED NATIONS R, Via Skelton, UK — W M-F • N Africa • 300 kW
USA
VOA, Via São Tomé — W • W Africa • 100 kW
9815 **CHINA**
†CHINA R INTL, Kashi — S • S America • 500 kW
FINLAND
†YLE RADIO FINLAND, Pori — W • E Africa & S Africa • 500 kW / W • E Africa • 250 kW
GERMANY
DEUTSCHE WELLE, Via Sri Lanka — W • SE Asia • 250 kW
MISSIONSWERK FRIEDENSSTIMME — W Sa • E Europe & W Asia • 250 kW
NEW ZEALAND
†R NEW ZEALAND INTL, Rangitaiki — Pacific • 100 kW • ALT. FREQ. TO 9885 kHz
(con'd) — W • Pacific • 100 kW • ALT. FREQ. TO 9870 kHz

SEASONAL ⑤ OR ⑩   1-HR TIMESHIFT MIDYEAR ⊟ OR ⊡   JAMMING / OR ∧   EARLIEST HEARD ◁   LATEST HEARD ▷   NEW FOR 2006 †

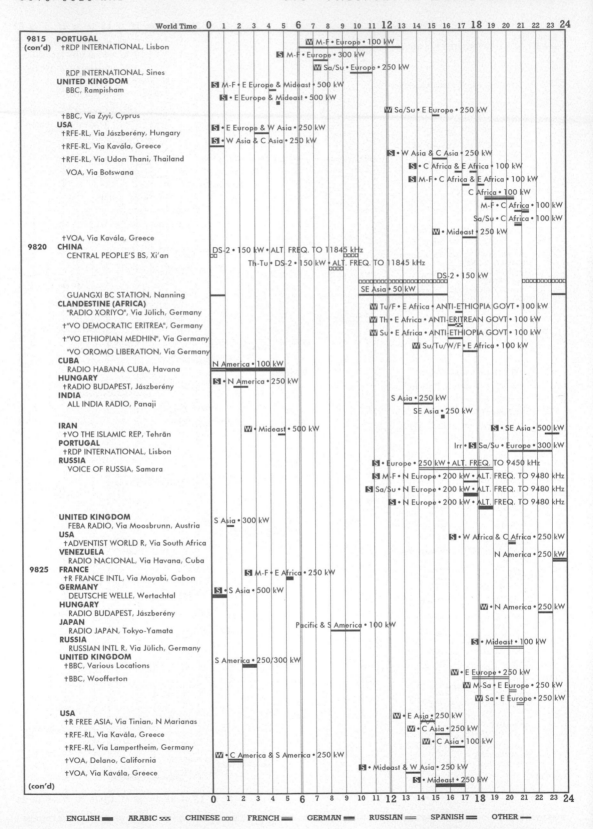

World Time	0 1 2 3 4 5 6 7 8 9 10 11 12 13 14 15 16 17 18 19 20 21 22 23 24
9815 (con'd) **PORTUGAL** †RDP INTERNATIONAL, Lisbon	W M-F • Europe • 100 kW / S M-F • Europe • 300 kW / W Sa/Su • Europe • 250 kW
RDP INTERNATIONAL, Sines **UNITED KINGDOM** BBC, Rampisham	S M-F • E Europe & Mideast • 500 kW / S • E Europe & Mideast • 500 kW
†BBC, Via Zyyi, Cyprus	W Sa/Su • E Europe • 250 kW
USA †RFE-RL, Via Jászberény, Hungary	S • E Europe & W Asia • 250 kW
†RFE-RL, Via Kavála, Greece	S • W Asia & C Asia • 250 kW
†RFE-RL, Via Udon Thani, Thailand	S • W Asia & C Asia • 250 kW
VOA, Via Botswana	S • C Africa & E Africa • 100 kW / S M-F • C Africa & E Africa • 100 kW / C Africa • 100 kW / M-F • C Africa • 100 kW / Sa/Su • C Africa • 100 kW
†VOA, Via Kavála, Greece	W • Mideast • 250 kW
9820 **CHINA** CENTRAL PEOPLE'S BS, Xi'an	DS-2 • 150 kW • ALT. FREQ. TO 11845 kHz / Th-Tu • DS-2 • 150 kW • ALT. FREQ. TO 11845 kHz / DS-2 • 150 kW
GUANGXI BC STATION, Nanning	SE Asia • 50 kW
CLANDESTINE (AFRICA) "RADIO XORIYO", Via Jülich, Germany	W Tu/F • E Africa • ANTI-ETHIOPIA GOVT • 100 kW
†"VO DEMOCRATIC ERITREA", Germany	W Th • E Africa • ANTI-ERITREAN GOVT • 100 kW
†"VO ETHIOPIAN MEDHIN", Via Germany	W Su • E Africa • ANTI-ETHIOPIA GOVT • 100 kW
"VO OROMO LIBERATION, Via Germany	W Su/Tu/W/F • E Africa • 100 kW
CUBA RADIO HABANA CUBA, Havana	N America • 100 kW
HUNGARY †RADIO BUDAPEST, Jászberény	S • N America • 250 kW
INDIA ALL INDIA RADIO, Panaji	S Asia • 250 kW / SE Asia • 250 kW
IRAN †VO THE ISLAMIC REP, Tehrān	W • Mideast • 500 kW / S • SE Asia • 500 kW
PORTUGAL †RDP INTERNATIONAL, Lisbon	Irr • S Sa/Su • Europe • 300 kW
RUSSIA VOICE OF RUSSIA, Samara	S • Europe • 250 kW • ALT. FREQ. TO 9450 kHz / S M-F • N Europe • 200 kW • ALT. FREQ. TO 9480 kHz / S Sa/Su • N Europe • 200 kW • ALT. FREQ. TO 9480 kHz / S • N Europe • 200 kW • ALT. FREQ. TO 9480 kHz
UNITED KINGDOM FEBA RADIO, Via Moosbrunn, Austria	S Asia • 300 kW
USA †ADVENTIST WORLD R, Via South Africa	S • W Africa & C Africa • 250 kW
VENEZUELA RADIO NACIONAL, Via Havana, Cuba	N America • 250 kW
9825 **FRANCE** †R FRANCE INTL, Via Moyabi, Gabon	S M-F • E Africa • 250 kW
GERMANY DEUTSCHE WELLE, Wertachtal	S • S Asia • 500 kW
HUNGARY RADIO BUDAPEST, Jászberény	W • N America • 250 kW
JAPAN RADIO JAPAN, Tokyo-Yamata	Pacific & S America • 100 kW
RUSSIA RUSSIAN INTL R, Via Jülich, Germany	S • Mideast • 100 kW
UNITED KINGDOM †BBC, Various Locations	S America • 250/300 kW
†BBC, Woofferton	W • E Europe • 250 kW / W M-Sa • E Europe • 250 kW / W Sa • E Europe • 250 kW
USA †R FREE ASIA, Via Tinian, N Marianas	W • E Asia • 250 kW
†RFE-RL, Via Kavála, Greece	W • C Asia • 250 kW
†RFE-RL, Via Lampertheim, Germany	W • C Asia • 100 kW
†VOA, Delano, California	W • C America & S America • 250 kW
†VOA, Via Kavála, Greece	S • Mideast & W Asia • 250 kW / S • Mideast • 250 kW
(con'd)	

0 1 2 3 4 5 6 7 8 9 10 11 12 13 14 15 16 17 18 19 20 21 22 23 24

ENGLISH ▬   ARABIC ⧖   CHINESE ▫▫▫   FRENCH ▬   GERMAN ▬   RUSSIAN ═   SPANISH ▬   OTHER ▬

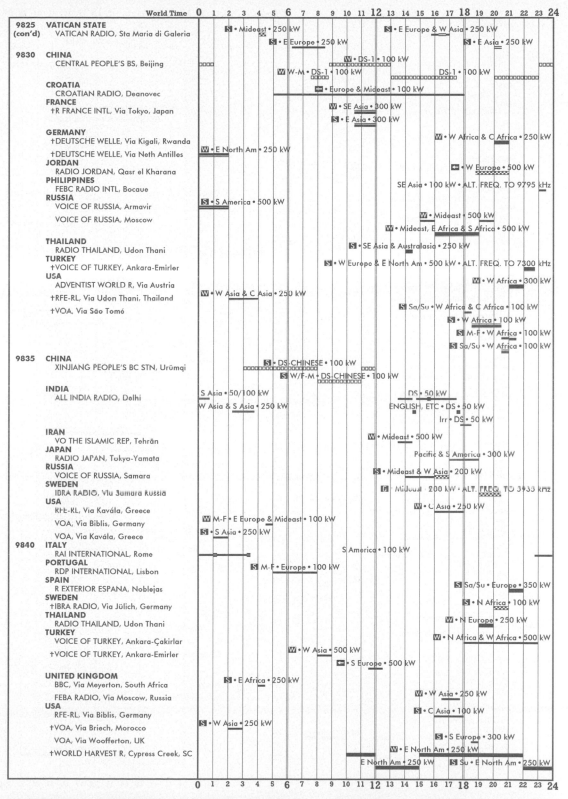

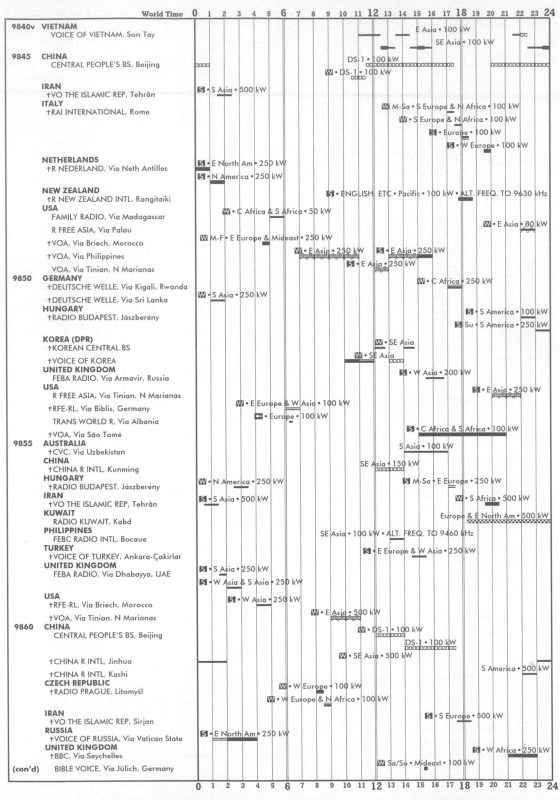

World Time 0 1 2 3 4 5 6 7 8 9 10 11 12 13 14 15 16 17 18 19 20 21 22 23 24

9840v VIETNAM
VOICE OF VIETNAM, Son Tay — E Asia • 100 kW / SE Asia • 100 kW

9845 CHINA
CENTRAL PEOPLE'S BS, Beijing — DS-1 • 100 kW / W • DS-1 • 100 kW

IRAN
†VO THE ISLAMIC REP, Tehrān — S • S Asia • 500 kW

ITALY
†RAI INTERNATIONAL, Rome — W • M-Sa • S Europe & N Africa • 100 kW / W • S Europe & N Africa • 100 kW / S • Europe • 100 kW / S • W Europe • 100 kW

NETHERLANDS
†R NEDERLAND, Via Neth Antilles — S • E North Am • 250 kW / S • N America • 250 kW

NEW ZEALAND
†R NEW ZEALAND INTL, Rangitaiki — S • ENGLISH, ETC • Pacific • 100 kW • ALT. FREQ. TO 9630 kHz

USA
FAMILY RADIO, Via Madagascar — W • C Africa & S Africa • 50 kW

R FREE ASIA, Via Palau — W • E Asia • 80 kW

†VOA, Via Briech, Morocco — W • M-F • E Europe & Mideast • 250 kW

†VOA, Via Philippines — W • E Asia • 250 kW / S • E Asia • 250 kW / S • E Asia • 250 kW

VOA, Via Tinian, N Marianas

9850 GERMANY
†DEUTSCHE WELLE, Via Kigali, Rwanda — W • C Africa • 250 kW

†DEUTSCHE WELLE, Via Sri Lanka — W • S Asia • 250 kW

HUNGARY
†RADIO BUDAPEST, Jászberény — S • S America • 100 kW / S • Su • S America • 250 kW

KOREA (DPR)
†KOREAN CENTRAL BS — W • SE Asia

†VOICE OF KOREA — W • SE Asia

UNITED KINGDOM
FEBA RADIO, Via Armavir, Russia — S • W Asia • 200 kW

USA
R FREE ASIA, Via Tinian, N Marianas — S • E Asia • 250 kW

†RFE-RL, Via Biblis, Germany — W • E Europe & W Asia • 100 kW

TRANS WORLD R, Via Albania — • Europe • 100 kW

†VOA, Via São Tomé — S • C Africa & S Africa • 100 kW

9855 AUSTRALIA
†CVC, Via Uzbekistan — S Asia • 100 kW

CHINA
†CHINA R INTL, Kunming — SE Asia • 150 kW

HUNGARY
†RADIO BUDAPEST, Jászberény — W • N America • 250 kW / S • M-Sa • E Europe • 250 kW

IRAN
†VO THE ISLAMIC REP, Tehrān — S • S Asia • 500 kW / W • S Africa • 500 kW

KUWAIT
RADIO KUWAIT, Kabd — Europe & E North Am • 500 kW

PHILIPPINES
FEBC RADIO INTL, Bocaue — SE Asia • 100 kW • ALT. FREQ. TO 9460 kHz

TURKEY
†VOICE OF TURKEY, Ankara-Çakirlar — S • E Europe & W Asia • 250 kW

UNITED KINGDOM
FEBA RADIO, Via Dhabayya, UAE — S • S Asia • 250 kW / S • W Asia & S Asia • 250 kW

USA
†RFE-RL, Via Briech, Morocco — S • W Asia • 250 kW

†VOA, Via Tinian, N Marianas — W • E Asia • 500 kW

9860 CHINA
CENTRAL PEOPLE'S BS, Beijing — W • DS-1 • 100 kW / DS-1 • 100 kW

†CHINA R INTL, Jinhua — W • SE Asia • 500 kW

†CHINA R INTL, Kashi — S America • 500 kW

CZECH REPUBLIC
†RADIO PRAGUE, Litomyšl — W • W Europe • 100 kW / W • W Europe & N Africa • 100 kW

IRAN
†VO THE ISLAMIC REP, Sirjan — S • S Europe • 500 kW

RUSSIA
†VOICE OF RUSSIA, Via Vatican State — S • E North Am • 250 kW

UNITED KINGDOM
†BBC, Via Seychelles — S • W Africa • 250 kW

(con'd) BIBLE VOICE, Via Jülich, Germany — W • Sa/Su • Mideast • 100 kW

0 1 2 3 4 5 6 7 8 9 10 11 12 13 14 15 16 17 18 19 20 21 22 23 24

ENGLISH ▬ ARABIC ░ CHINESE □□□ FRENCH ▬ GERMAN ▬ RUSSIAN ═ SPANISH ═ OTHER ─

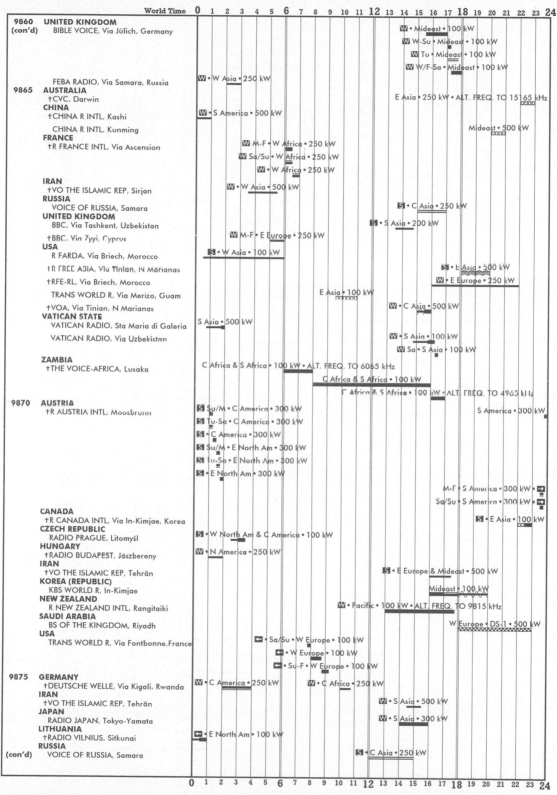

| World Time | 0 1 2 3 4 5 6 7 8 9 10 11 12 13 14 15 16 17 18 19 20 21 22 23 24 |

9860 UNITED KINGDOM
(con'd)   BIBLE VOICE, Via Jülich, Germany
- W • Mideast • 100 kW
- W-Su • Mideast • 100 kW
- Tu • Mideast • 100 kW
- W/F-Sa • Mideast • 100 kW

FEBA RADIO, Via Samara, Russia — W • W Asia • 250 kW

9865 AUSTRALIA
†CVC, Darwin — E Asia • 250 kW • ALT. FREQ. TO 15165 kHz

CHINA
†CHINA R INTL, Kashi — W • S America • 500 kW
CHINA R INTL, Kunming — Mideast • 500 kW

FRANCE
†R FRANCE INTL, Via Ascension
- W M-F • W Africa • 250 kW
- W Sa/Su • W Africa • 250 kW
- W • W Africa • 250 kW

IRAN
†VO THE ISLAMIC REP, Sirjan — W • W Asia • 500 kW

RUSSIA
VOICE OF RUSSIA, Samara — S • C Asia • 250 kW

UNITED KINGDOM
BBC, Via Tashkent, Uzbekistan — S • S Asia • 200 kW
†BBC, Via Zyyi, Cyprus — W M-F • E Europe • 250 kW

USA
R FARDA, Via Briech, Morocco — S • W Asia • 100 kW
†R FREE ASIA, Via Tinian, N Marianas — S • E Asia • 500 kW
†RFE-RL, Via Briech, Morocco — W • E Europe • 250 kW
TRANS WORLD R, Via Merizo, Guam — E Asia • 100 kW
†VOA, Via Tinian, N Marianas — W • C Asia • 500 kW

VATICAN STATE
VATICAN RADIO, Sta Maria di Galeria — S Asia • 500 kW
VATICAN RADIO, Via Uzbekistan
- W • S Asia • 100 kW
- W Sa • S Asia • 100 kW

ZAMBIA
†THE VOICE-AFRICA, Lusaka
- C Africa & S Africa • 100 kW • ALT. FREQ. TO 6065 kHz
- C Africa & S Africa • 100 kW
- C Africa & S Africa • 100 kW • ALT. FREQ. TO 4965 kHz

9870 AUSTRIA
†R AUSTRIA INTL, Moosbrunn
- S Su/M • C America • 300 kW
- S Tu-Sa • C America • 300 kW
- S • C America • 300 kW
- S Su/M • E North Am • 300 kW
- S Tu-Sa • E North Am • 300 kW
- S • E North Am • 300 kW
- S America • 300 kW
- M-F • S America • 300 kW •
- Sa/Su • S America • 300 kW •

CANADA
†R CANADA INTL, Via In-Kimjae, Korea — S • E Asia • 100 kW

CZECH REPUBLIC
RADIO PRAGUE, Litomyšl — S • W North Am & C America • 100 kW

HUNGARY
†RADIO BUDAPEST, Jászbereny — W • N America • 250 kW

IRAN
†VO THE ISLAMIC REP, Tehrān — S • E Europe & Mideast • 500 kW

KOREA (REPUBLIC)
KBS WORLD R, In-Kimjae — Mideast • 100 kW

NEW ZEALAND
R NEW ZEALAND INTL, Rangitaiki — W • Pacific • 100 kW • ALT. FREQ. TO 9815 kHz

SAUDI ARABIA
BS OF THE KINGDOM, Riyadh — W Europe • DS-1 • 500 kW

USA
TRANS WORLD R, Via Fontbonne, France
- Sa/Su • W Europe • 100 kW
- W Europe • 100 kW
- Su-F • W Europe • 100 kW

9875 GERMANY
†DEUTSCHE WELLE, Via Kigali, Rwanda
- W • C America • 250 kW
- W • C Africa • 250 kW

IRAN
†VO THE ISLAMIC REP, Tehrān — W • S Asia • 500 kW

JAPAN
RADIO JAPAN, Tokyo-Yamata — W • S Asia • 300 kW

LITHUANIA
†RADIO VILNIUS, Sitkunai — E North Am • 100 kW

RUSSIA
(con'd)   VOICE OF RUSSIA, Samara — S • C Asia • 250 kW

| 0 1 2 3 4 5 6 7 8 9 10 11 12 13 14 15 16 17 18 19 20 21 22 23 24 |

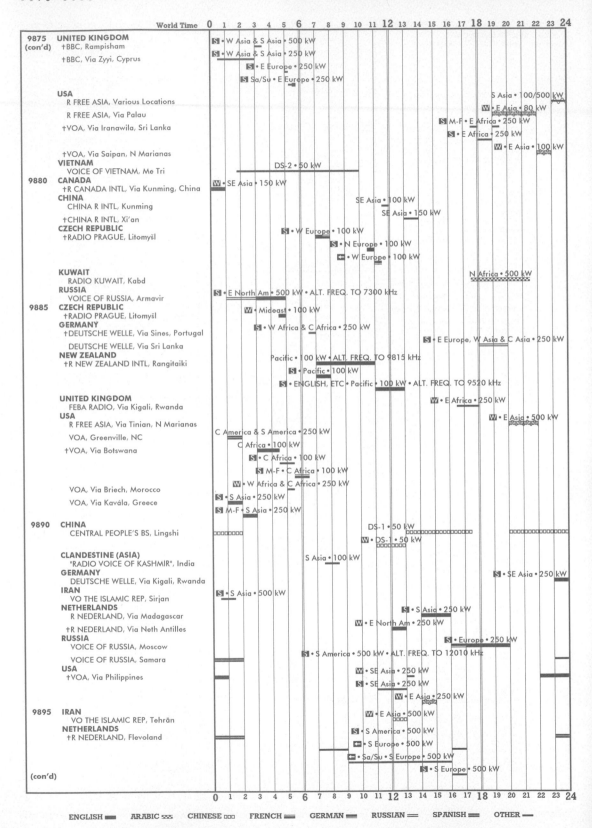

World Time — 0 1 2 3 4 5 6 7 8 9 10 11 12 13 14 15 16 17 18 19 20 21 22 23 24

9875 UNITED KINGDOM
(con'd) †BBC, Rampisham — S • W Asia & S Asia • 500 kW
 †BBC, Via Zyyi, Cyprus — S • W Asia & S Asia • 250 kW
 — S • E Europe • 250 kW
 — S Sa/Su • E Europe • 250 kW

USA
 R FREE ASIA, Various Locations — S Asia • 100/500 kW
 R FREE ASIA, Via Palau — W • E Asia • 80 kW
 †VOA, Via Iranawila, Sri Lanka — S M-F • E Africa • 250 kW
 — S • E Africa • 250 kW
 †VOA, Via Saipan, N Marianas — W • E Asia • 100 kW

VIETNAM
 VOICE OF VIETNAM, Me Tri — DS-2 • 50 kW

9880 CANADA
 †R CANADA INTL, Via Kunming, China — W • SE Asia • 150 kW

CHINA
 CHINA R INTL, Kunming — SE Asia • 100 kW
 — SE Asia • 150 kW
 †CHINA R INTL, Xi'an

CZECH REPUBLIC
 †RADIO PRAGUE, Litomyšl — S • W Europe • 100 kW
 — S • N Europe • 100 kW
 — ◻ • W Europe • 100 kW

KUWAIT
 RADIO KUWAIT, Kabd — N Africa • 500 kW

RUSSIA
 VOICE OF RUSSIA, Armavir — S • E North Am • 500 kW • ALT. FREQ. TO 7300 kHz

9885 CZECH REPUBLIC
 †RADIO PRAGUE, Litomyšl — W • Mideast • 100 kW

GERMANY
 †DEUTSCHE WELLE, Via Sines, Portugal — S • W Africa & C Africa • 250 kW
 DEUTSCHE WELLE, Via Sri Lanka — S • E Europe, W Asia & C Asia • 250 kW

NEW ZEALAND
 †R NEW ZEALAND INTL, Rangitaiki — Pacific • 100 kW • ALT. FREQ. TO 9815 kHz
 — S • Pacific • 100 kW
 — S • ENGLISH, ETC • Pacific • 100 kW • ALT. FREQ. TO 9520 kHz

UNITED KINGDOM
 FEBA RADIO, Via Kigali, Rwanda — W • E Africa • 250 kW

USA
 R FREE ASIA, Via Tinian, N Marianas — W • E Asia • 500 kW
 VOA, Greenville, NC — C America & S America • 250 kW
 †VOA, Via Botswana — C Africa • 100 kW
 — S • C Africa • 100 kW
 — S M-F • C Africa • 100 kW
 VOA, Via Briech, Morocco — W • W Africa & C Africa • 250 kW
 VOA, Via Kavála, Greece — S • S Asia • 250 kW
 — S M-F • S Asia • 250 kW

9890 CHINA
 CENTRAL PEOPLE'S BS, Lingshi — DS-1 • 50 kW
 — W • DS-1 • 50 kW

CLANDESTINE (ASIA)
 "RADIO VOICE OF KASHMIR", India — S Asia • 100 kW

GERMANY
 DEUTSCHE WELLE, Via Kigali, Rwanda — S • SE Asia • 250 kW

IRAN
 VO THE ISLAMIC REP, Sirjan — S • S Asia • 500 kW

NETHERLANDS
 R NEDERLAND, Via Madagascar — S • S Asia • 250 kW
 †R NEDERLAND, Via Neth Antilles — W • E North Am • 250 kW

RUSSIA
 VOICE OF RUSSIA, Moscow — S • Europe • 250 kW
 VOICE OF RUSSIA, Samara — S • S America • 500 kW • ALT. FREQ. TO 12010 kHz

USA
 †VOA, Via Philippines — W • SE Asia • 250 kW
 — S • SE Asia • 250 kW
 — W • E Asia • 250 kW

9895 IRAN
 VO THE ISLAMIC REP, Tehrān — W • E Asia • 500 kW

NETHERLANDS
 †R NEDERLAND, Flevoland — S • S America • 500 kW
 — ◻ • S Europe • 500 kW
 — ◻ • Sa/Su • S Europe • 500 kW
 — S • S Europe • 500 kW

(con'd)

0 1 2 3 4 5 6 7 8 9 10 11 12 13 14 15 16 17 18 19 20 21 22 23 24

ENGLISH ▬ ARABIC ▨ CHINESE ▢▢▢ FRENCH ═ GERMAN ▬ RUSSIAN ═ SPANISH ▬ OTHER ▬

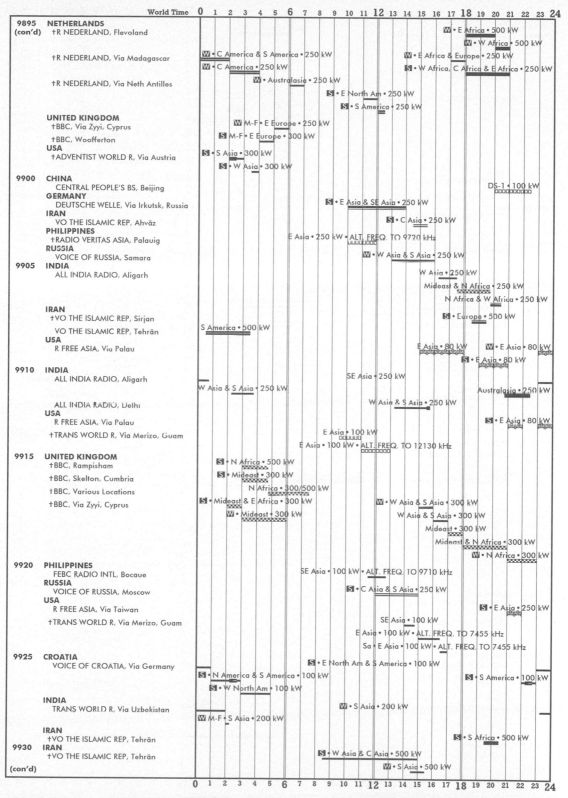

World Time scale: 0 1 2 3 4 5 6 7 8 9 10 11 12 13 14 15 16 17 18 19 20 21 22 23 24

9895 NETHERLANDS
(con'd) †R NEDERLAND, Flevoland
- W • E Africa • 500 kW
- W • W Africa • 500 kW

†R NEDERLAND, Via Madagascar
- W • C America & S America • 250 kW
- W • C America • 250 kW
- W • E Africa & Europe • 250 kW
- S • W Africa, C Africa & E Africa • 250 kW

†R NEDERLAND, Via Neth Antilles
- W • Australasia • 250 kW
- S • E North Am • 250 kW
- S • S America • 250 kW

UNITED KINGDOM
†BBC, Via Zyyi, Cyprus
- W M-F • E Europe • 250 kW

†BBC, Woofferton
- S M-F • E Europe • 300 kW

USA
†ADVENTIST WORLD R, Via Austria
- S • S Asia • 300 kW
- S • W Asia • 300 kW

9900 CHINA
CENTRAL PEOPLE'S BS, Beijing
- DS-1 • 100 kW

GERMANY
DEUTSCHE WELLE, Via Irkutsk, Russia
- S • E Asia & SE Asia • 250 kW

IRAN
VO THE ISLAMIC REP, Ahvāz
- S • C Asia • 250 kW

PHILIPPINES
†RADIO VERITAS ASIA, Palauig
- E Asia • 250 kW • ALT. FREQ. TO 9720 kHz

RUSSIA
VOICE OF RUSSIA, Samara
- W • W Asia & S Asia • 250 kW

9905 INDIA
ALL INDIA RADIO, Aligarh
- W Asia • 250 kW
- Mideast & N Africa • 250 kW
- N Africa & W Africa • 250 kW

IRAN
†VO THE ISLAMIC REP, Sirjan
- S • Europe • 500 kW

VO THE ISLAMIC REP, Tehrān
- S America • 500 kW

USA
R FREE ASIA, Via Palau
- E Asia • 80 kW
- W • E Asia • 80 kW
- S • E Asia • 80 kW

9910 INDIA
ALL INDIA RADIO, Aligarh
- SE Asia • 250 kW
- W Asia & S Asia • 250 kW
- Australasia • 250 kW

ALL INDIA RADIO, Delhi
- W Asia & S Asia • 250 kW

USA
R FREE ASIA, Via Palau
- S • E Asia • 80 kW

†TRANS WORLD R, Via Merizo, Guam
- E Asia • 100 kW
- E Asia • 100 kW • ALT. FREQ. TO 12130 kHz

9915 UNITED KINGDOM
†BBC, Rampisham
- S • N Africa • 500 kW

†BBC, Skelton, Cumbria
- S • Mideast • 300 kW

†BBC, Various Locations
- N Africa • 300/500 kW

†BBC, Via Zyyi, Cyprus
- S • Mideast & E Africa • 300 kW
- W • Mideast • 300 kW
- W • W Asia & S Asia • 300 kW
- W Asia & S Asia • 300 kW
- Mideast • 300 kW
- Mideast & N Africa • 300 kW
- W • N Africa • 300 kW

9920 PHILIPPINES
FEBC RADIO INTL, Bocaue
- SE Asia • 100 kW • ALT. FREQ. TO 9710 kHz

RUSSIA
VOICE OF RUSSIA, Moscow
- S • C Asia & S Asia • 250 kW

USA
R FREE ASIA, Via Taiwan
- S • E Asia • 250 kW

†TRANS WORLD R, Via Merizo, Guam
- SE Asia • 100 kW
- E Asia • 100 kW • ALT. FREQ. TO 7455 kHz
- Sa • E Asia • 100 kW • ALT. FREQ. TO 7455 kHz

9925 CROATIA
VOICE OF CROATIA, Via Germany
- S • E North Am & S America • 100 kW
- S • N America & S America • 100 kW
- S • S America • 100 kW
- S • W North Am • 100 kW

INDIA
TRANS WORLD R, Via Uzbekistan
- W • S Asia • 200 kW
- W M-F • S Asia • 200 kW

IRAN
†VO THE ISLAMIC REP, Tehrān
- S • S Africa • 500 kW

9930 IRAN
†VO THE ISLAMIC REP, Tehrān
- S • W Asia & C Asia • 500 kW
(con'd)
- W • S Asia • 500 kW

World Time scale: 0 1 2 3 4 5 6 7 8 9 10 11 12 13 14 15 16 17 18 19 20 21 22 23 24

SEASONAL S OR W   1-HR TIMESHIFT MIDYEAR ⟵ OR ⟶   JAMMING / OR ∧   EARLIEST HEARD ◁   LATEST HEARD ▷   NEW FOR 2006 †

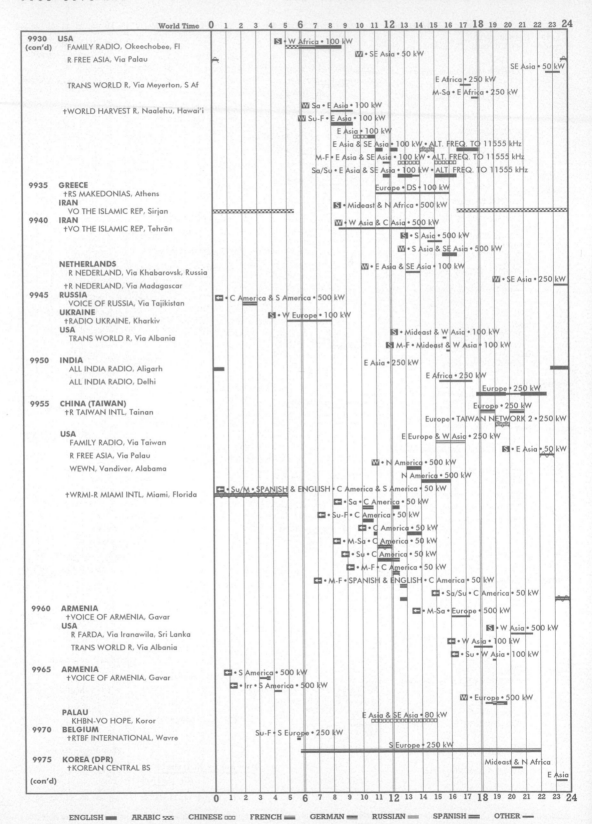

9930 (con'd)	**USA** FAMILY RADIO, Okeechobee, Fl	
	R FREE ASIA, Via Palau	
	TRANS WORLD R, Via Meyerton, S Af	
	†WORLD HARVEST R, Naalehu, Hawai'i	
9935	**GREECE** †RS MAKEDONIAS, Athens	
	IRAN VO THE ISLAMIC REP, Sirjan	
9940	**IRAN** †VO THE ISLAMIC REP, Tehrān	
	NETHERLANDS R NEDERLAND, Via Khabarovsk, Russia	
	†R NEDERLAND, Via Madagascar	
9945	**RUSSIA** VOICE OF RUSSIA, Via Tajikistan	
	UKRAINE †RADIO UKRAINE, Kharkiv	
	USA TRANS WORLD R, Via Albania	
9950	**INDIA** ALL INDIA RADIO, Aligarh	
	ALL INDIA RADIO, Delhi	
9955	**CHINA (TAIWAN)** †R TAIWAN INTL, Tainan	
	USA FAMILY RADIO, Via Taiwan	
	R FREE ASIA, Via Palau	
	WEWN, Vandiver, Alabama	
	†WRMI-R MIAMI INTL, Miami, Florida	
9960	**ARMENIA** †VOICE OF ARMENIA, Gavar	
	USA R FARDA, Via Iranawila, Sri Lanka	
	TRANS WORLD R, Via Albania	
9965	**ARMENIA** †VOICE OF ARMENIA, Gavar	
	PALAU KHBN-VO HOPE, Koror	
9970	**BELGIUM** †RTBF INTERNATIONAL, Wavre	
9975	**KOREA (DPR)** †KOREAN CENTRAL BS	
(con'd)		

ENGLISH ▬▬ ARABIC ▨▨ CHINESE ▢▢▢ FRENCH ▭▭ GERMAN ▬▬ RUSSIAN ══ SPANISH ▬▬ OTHER ──

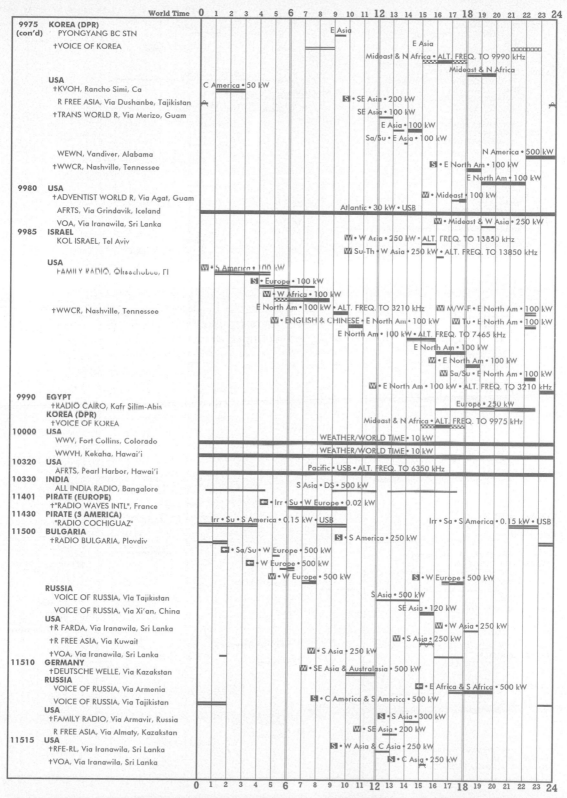

World Time: 0 1 2 3 4 5 6 7 8 9 10 11 12 13 14 15 16 17 18 19 20 21 22 23 24

Freq	Station	Schedule
9975 (con'd)	KOREA (DPR) — PYONGYANG BC STN	E Asia
	†VOICE OF KOREA	E Asia / Mideast & N Africa • ALT. FREQ. TO 9990 kHz / Mideast & N Africa
	USA — †KVOH, Rancho Simi, Ca	C America • 50 kW
	R FREE ASIA, Via Dushanbe, Tajikistan	S • SE Asia • 200 kW
	†TRANS WORLD R, Via Merizo, Guam	SE Asia • 100 kW / E Asia • 100 kW / Sa/Su • E Asia • 100 kW
	WEWN, Vandiver, Alabama	N America • 500 kW
	†WWCR, Nashville, Tennessee	S • E North Am • 100 kW / E North Am • 100 kW
9980	USA — †ADVENTIST WORLD R, Via Agat, Guam	W • Mideast • 100 kW
	AFRTS, Via Grindavik, Iceland	Atlantic • 30 kW • USB
	VOA, Via Iranawila, Sri Lanka	W • Mideast & W Asia • 250 kW
9985	ISRAEL — KOL ISRAEL, Tel Aviv	W • W Asia • 250 kW • ALT. FREQ. TO 13850 kHz / W Su-Th • W Asia • 250 kW • ALT. FREQ. TO 13850 kHz
	USA — FAMILY RADIO, Okeechobee, Fl	W • S America • 100 kW
		S • Europe • 100 kW
		W • W Africa • 100 kW
	†WWCR, Nashville, Tennessee	E North Am • 100 kW • ALT. FREQ. TO 3210 kHz / W M/W/F • E North Am • 100 kW / W • ENGLISH & CHINESE • E North Am • 100 kW / W Tu • E North Am • 100 kW / E North Am • 100 kW • ALT. FREQ. TO 7465 kHz / E North Am • 100 kW / W • E North Am • 100 kW / W Sa/Su • E North Am • 100 kW / W • E North Am • 100 kW • ALT. FREQ. TO 3210 kHz
9990	EGYPT — †RADIO CAIRO, Kafr Silim-Abis	Europe • 250 kW
	KOREA (DPR) — †VOICE OF KOREA	Mideast & N Africa • ALT. FREQ. TO 9975 kHz
10000	USA — WWV, Fort Collins, Colorado	WEATHER/WORLD TIME • 10 kW
	WWVH, Kekaha, Hawai'i	WEATHER/WORLD TIME • 10 kW
10320	USA — AFRTS, Pearl Harbor, Hawai'i	Pacific • USB • ALT. FREQ. TO 6350 kHz
10330	INDIA — ALL INDIA RADIO, Bangalore	S Asia • DS • 500 kW
11401	PIRATE (EUROPE) — †"RADIO WAVES INTL", France	Irr • Su • W Europe • 0.02 kW
11430	PIRATE (S AMERICA) — "RADIO COCHIGUAZ"	Irr • Su • S America • 0.15 kW • USB / Irr • Sa • S America • 0.15 kW • USB
11500	BULGARIA — †RADIO BULGARIA, Plovdiv	S • S America • 250 kW / Sa/Su • W Europe • 500 kW / W Europe • 500 kW / W • W Europe • 500 kW / S • W Europe • 500 kW
	RUSSIA — VOICE OF RUSSIA, Via Tajikistan	S Asia • 500 kW
	VOICE OF RUSSIA, Via Xi'an, China	SE Asia • 120 kW
	USA — †R FARDA, Via Iranawila, Sri Lanka	W • W Asia • 250 kW
	†R FREE ASIA, Via Kuwait	W • S Asia • 250 kW
	†VOA, Via Iranawila, Sri Lanka	W • S Asia • 250 kW
11510	GERMANY — †DEUTSCHE WELLE, Via Kazakstan	W • SE Asia & Australasia • 500 kW
	RUSSIA — VOICE OF RUSSIA, Via Armenia	S • E Africa & S Africa • 500 kW
	VOICE OF RUSSIA, Via Tajikistan	S • C America & S America • 500 kW
	USA — †FAMILY RADIO, Via Armavir, Russia	S • S Asia • 300 kW
	R FREE ASIA, Via Almaty, Kazakstan	W • SE Asia • 200 kW
11515	USA — †RFE-RL, Via Iranawila, Sri Lanka	S • W Asia & C Asia • 250 kW
	†VOA, Via Iranawila, Sri Lanka	S • C Asia • 250 kW

0 1 2 3 4 5 6 7 8 9 10 11 12 13 14 15 16 17 18 19 20 21 22 23 24

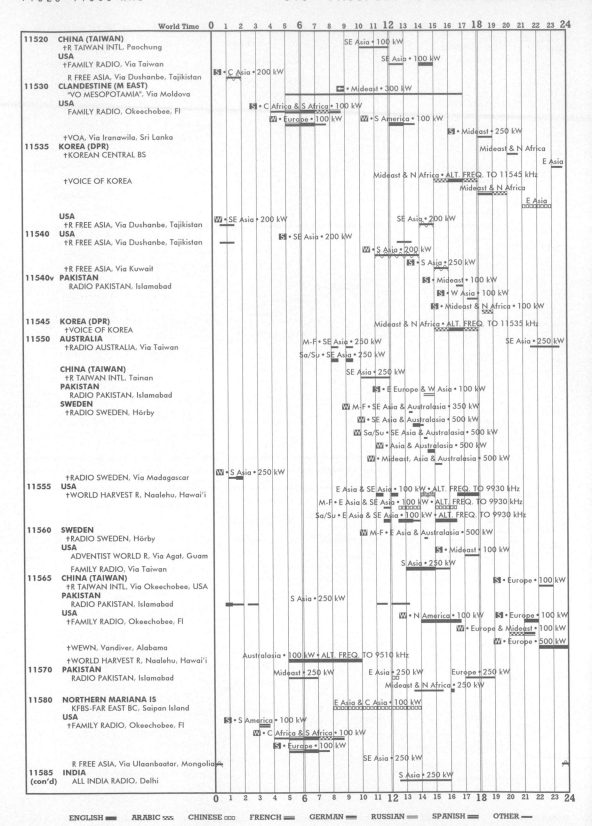

World Time

11520	CHINA (TAIWAN)	
	†R TAIWAN INTL, Paochung	SE Asia • 100 kW
	USA	
	†FAMILY RADIO, Via Taiwan	SE Asia • 100 kW
	R FREE ASIA, Via Dushanbe, Tajikistan	S • C Asia • 200 kW
11530	CLANDESTINE (M EAST)	
	"VO MESOPOTAMIA", Via Moldova	C • Mideast • 300 kW
	USA	
	FAMILY RADIO, Okeechobee, Fl	S • C Africa & S Africa • 100 kW
		W • Europe • 100 kW W • S America • 100 kW
	†VOA, Via Iranawila, Sri Lanka	S • Mideast • 250 kW
11535	KOREA (DPR)	
	†KOREAN CENTRAL BS	Mideast & N Africa
		E Asia
	†VOICE OF KOREA	Mideast & N Africa • ALT. FREQ. TO 11545 kHz
		Mideast & N Africa
		E Asia
	USA	
	†R FREE ASIA, Via Dushanbe, Tajikistan	W • SE Asia • 200 kW SE Asia • 200 kW
11540	USA	
	†R FREE ASIA, Via Dushanbe, Tajikistan	S • SE Asia • 200 kW
		W • S Asia • 200 kW
		S • S Asia • 250 kW
	†R FREE ASIA, Via Kuwait	S • Mideast • 100 kW
11540v	PAKISTAN	
	RADIO PAKISTAN, Islamabad	S • W Asia • 100 kW
		S • Mideast & N Africa • 100 kW
11545	KOREA (DPR)	
	†VOICE OF KOREA	Mideast & N Africa • ALT. FREQ. TO 11535 kHz
11550	AUSTRALIA	
	†RADIO AUSTRALIA, Via Taiwan	M-F • SE Asia • 250 kW SE Asia • 250 kW
		Sa/Su • SE Asia • 250 kW
	CHINA (TAIWAN)	
	†R TAIWAN INTL, Tainan	SE Asia • 250 kW
	PAKISTAN	
	RADIO PAKISTAN, Islamabad	S • E Europe & W Asia • 100 kW
	SWEDEN	
	†RADIO SWEDEN, Hörby	W M-F • SE Asia & Australasia • 350 kW
		W • SE Asia & Australasia • 500 kW
		W Sa/Su • SE Asia & Australasia • 500 kW
		W • Asia & Australasia • 500 kW
		W • Mideast, Asia & Australasia • 500 kW
	†RADIO SWEDEN, Via Madagascar	W • S Asia • 250 kW
11555	USA	
	†WORLD HARVEST R, Naalehu, Hawai'i	E Asia & SE Asia • 100 kW • ALT. FREQ. TO 9930 kHz
		M-F • E Asia & SE Asia • 100 kW • ALT. FREQ. TO 9930 kHz
		Sa/Su • E Asia & SE Asia • 100 kW • ALT. FREQ. TO 9930 kHz
11560	SWEDEN	
	†RADIO SWEDEN, Hörby	W M-F • E Asia & Australasia • 500 kW
	USA	
	ADVENTIST WORLD R, Via Agat, Guam	S • Mideast • 100 kW
	FAMILY RADIO, Via Taiwan	S Asia • 250 kW
11565	CHINA (TAIWAN)	
	†R TAIWAN INTL, Via Okeechobee, USA	S • Europe • 100 kW
	PAKISTAN	
	RADIO PAKISTAN, Islamabad	S Asia • 250 kW
	USA	
	†FAMILY RADIO, Okeechobee, Fl	W • N America • 100 kW S • Europe • 100 kW
		W • Europe & Mideast • 100 kW
		W • Europe • 500 kW
	†WEWN, Vandiver, Alabama	
	†WORLD HARVEST R, Naalehu, Hawai'i	Australasia • 100 kW • ALT. FREQ. TO 9510 kHz
11570	PAKISTAN	
	RADIO PAKISTAN, Islamabad	Mideast • 250 kW E Asia • 250 kW Europe • 250 kW
		Mideast & N Africa • 250 kW
11580	NORTHERN MARIANA IS	
	KFBS-FAR EAST BC, Saipan Island	E Asia & C Asia • 100 kW
	USA	
	†FAMILY RADIO, Okeechobee, Fl	S • S America • 100 kW
		W • C Africa & S Africa • 100 kW
		S • Europe • 100 kW
	R FREE ASIA, Via Ulaanbaatar, Mongolia	SE Asia • 250 kW
11585	INDIA	
(con'd)	ALL INDIA RADIO, Delhi	S Asia • 250 kW

ENGLISH ▬ ARABIC ⬚⬚⬚ CHINESE ⬚⬚⬚ FRENCH ▬ GERMAN ▬ RUSSIAN ═══ SPANISH ▬ OTHER ▬

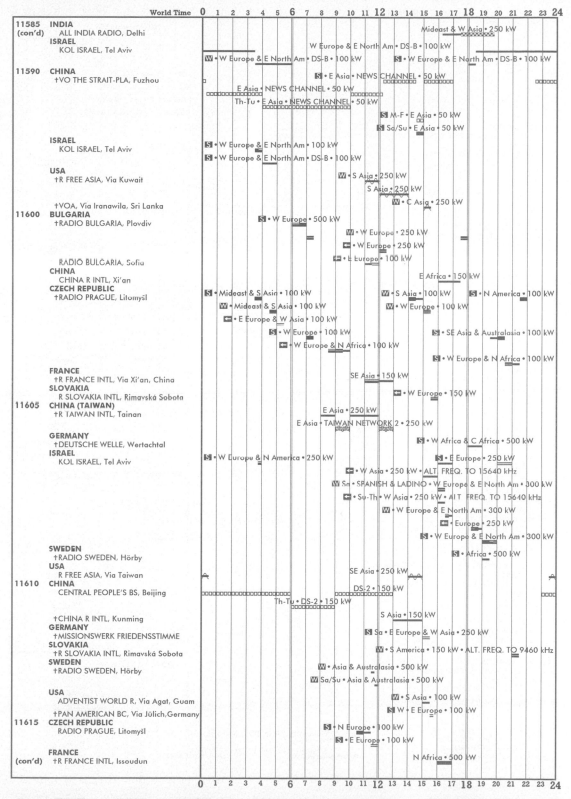

World Time 0 1 2 3 4 5 6 7 8 9 10 11 12 13 14 15 16 17 18 19 20 21 22 23 24

11585 **INDIA**
(con'd) ALL INDIA RADIO, Delhi — Mideast & W Asia • 250 kW
ISRAEL
KOL ISRAEL, Tel Aviv — W Europe & E North Am • DS-B • 100 kW
Ⓦ • W Europe & E North Am • DS-B • 100 kW — Ⓢ • W Europe & E North Am • DS-B • 100 kW

11590 **CHINA**
†VO THE STRAIT-PLA, Fuzhou — Ⓢ • E Asia • NEWS CHANNEL • 50 kW
E Asia • NEWS CHANNEL • 50 kW
Th-Tu • E Asia • NEWS CHANNEL • 50 kW
Ⓢ M-F • E Asia • 50 kW
Ⓢ Sa/Su • E Asia • 50 kW

ISRAEL
KOL ISRAEL, Tel Aviv — Ⓢ • W Europe & E North Am • 100 kW
Ⓢ • W Europe & E North Am • DS-B • 100 kW

USA
†R FREE ASIA, Via Kuwait — Ⓦ • S Asia • 250 kW
S Asia • 250 kW
†VOA, Via Iranawila, Sri Lanka — Ⓦ • C Asia • 250 kW

11600 **BULGARIA**
†RADIO BULGARIA, Plovdiv — Ⓢ • W Europe • 500 kW
Ⓦ • W Europe • 250 kW
⮂ • W Europe • 250 kW
⮂ • E Europe • 100 kW
RADIO BULGARIA, Sofia
CHINA — E Africa • 150 kW
CHINA R INTL, Xi'an
CZECH REPUBLIC
†RADIO PRAGUE, Litomyšl — Ⓢ • Mideast & S Asia • 100 kW / Ⓦ • S Asia • 100 kW / Ⓢ • N America • 100 kW
Ⓦ • Mideast & S Asia • 100 kW / Ⓦ • W Europe • 100 kW
⮂ • E Europe & W Asia • 100 kW
Ⓢ • W Europe • 100 kW / Ⓢ • SE Asia & Australasia • 100 kW
⮂ • W Europe & N Africa • 100 kW
Ⓢ • W Europe & N Africa • 100 kW

FRANCE
†R FRANCE INTL, Via Xi'an, China — SE Asia • 150 kW
SLOVAKIA
R SLOVAKIA INTL, Rimavská Sobota — ⮂ • W Europe • 150 kW

11605 **CHINA (TAIWAN)**
†R TAIWAN INTL, Tainan — E Asia • 250 kW
E Asia • TAIWAN NETWORK 2 • 250 kW

GERMANY
†DEUTSCHE WELLE, Wertachtal — Ⓢ • W Africa & C Africa • 500 kW
ISRAEL
KOL ISRAEL, Tel Aviv — Ⓢ • W Europe & N America • 250 kW / Ⓢ • E Europe • 250 kW
⮂ • W Asia • 250 kW • ALT. FREQ. TO 15640 kHz
Ⓦ Sa • SPANISH & LADINO • W Europe & E North Am • 300 kW
⮂ • Su-Th • W Asia • 250 kW • ALT. FREQ. TO 15640 kHz
Ⓦ • W Europe & E North Am • 300 kW
⮂ • Europe • 250 kW
Ⓢ • W Europe & E North Am • 300 kW

SWEDEN
†RADIO SWEDEN, Hörby — Ⓢ • Africa • 500 kW
USA
R FREE ASIA, Via Taiwan — SE Asia • 250 kW

11610 **CHINA**
CENTRAL PEOPLE'S BS, Beijing — DS-2 • 150 kW
Th-Tu • DS-2 • 150 kW
†CHINA R INTL, Kunming — S Asia • 150 kW
GERMANY
†MISSIONSWERK FRIEDENSSTIMME — Ⓢ Sa • E Europe & W Asia • 250 kW
SLOVAKIA
†R SLOVAKIA INTL, Rimavská Sobota — Ⓦ • S America • 150 kW • ALT. FREQ. TO 9460 kHz
SWEDEN
†RADIO SWEDEN, Hörby — Ⓦ • Asia & Australasia • 500 kW
Ⓦ Sa/Su • Asia & Australasia • 500 kW

USA
ADVENTIST WORLD R, Via Agat, Guam — Ⓦ • S Asia • 100 kW
†PAN AMERICAN BC, Via Jülich, Germany — Ⓢ W • E Europe • 100 kW

11615 **CZECH REPUBLIC**
RADIO PRAGUE, Litomyšl — Ⓢ • N Europe • 100 kW
Ⓢ • E Europe • 100 kW

FRANCE
(con'd) †R FRANCE INTL, Issoudun — N Africa • 500 kW

0 1 2 3 4 5 6 7 8 9 10 11 12 13 14 15 16 17 18 19 20 21 22 23 24

SEASONAL Ⓢ OR Ⓦ 1-HR TIMESHIFT MIDYEAR ⮂ OR ⮂ JAMMING / OR ∧ EARLIEST HEARD ◁ LATEST HEARD ▷ NEW FOR 2006 †

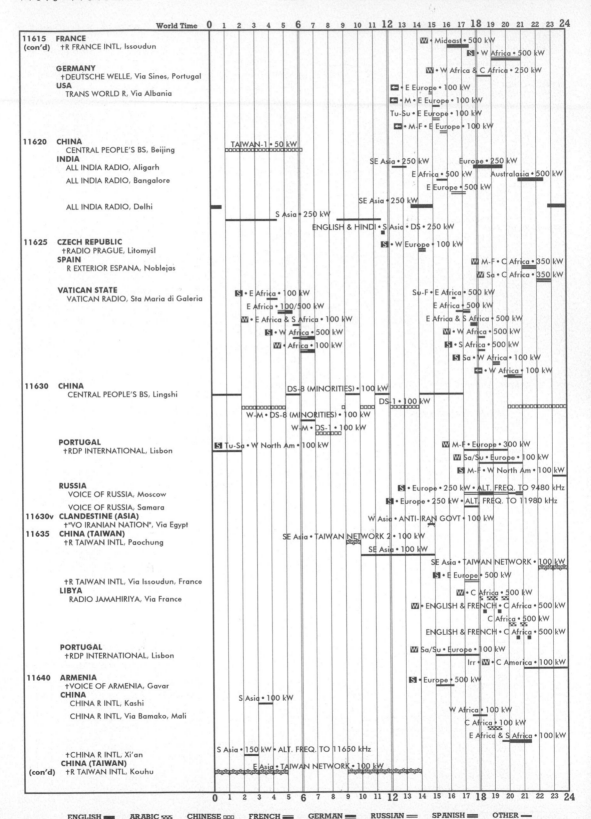

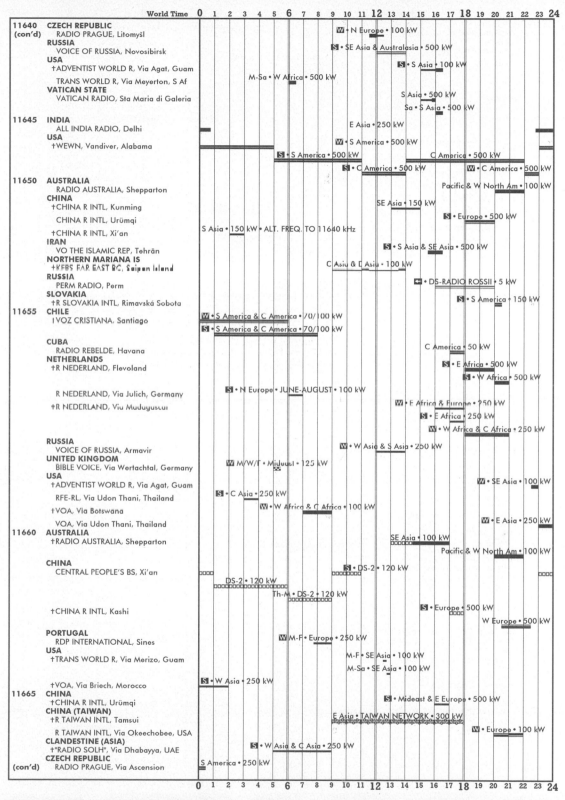

World Time scale: 0 1 2 3 4 5 6 7 8 9 10 11 12 13 14 15 16 17 18 19 20 21 22 23 24

Freq	Country / Station	Schedule
11640 (con'd)	CZECH REPUBLIC — RADIO PRAGUE, Litomyšl	W • N Europe • 100 kW
	RUSSIA — VOICE OF RUSSIA, Novosibirsk	S • SE Asia & Australasia • 500 kW
	USA — †ADVENTIST WORLD R, Via Agat, Guam	S • S Asia • 100 kW
	TRANS WORLD R, Via Meyerton, S Af	M-Sa • W Africa • 500 kW
	VATICAN STATE — VATICAN RADIO, Sta Maria di Galeria	S Asia • 500 kW / Sa • S Asia • 500 kW
11645	INDIA — ALL INDIA RADIO, Delhi	E Asia • 250 kW
	USA — †WEWN, Vandiver, Alabama	W • S America • 500 kW / S • S America • 500 kW / C America • 500 kW / S • C America • 500 kW / W • C America • 500 kW
11650	AUSTRALIA — RADIO AUSTRALIA, Shepparton	Pacific & W North Am • 100 kW
	CHINA — †CHINA R INTL, Kunming	SE Asia • 150 kW
	CHINA R INTL, Urümqi	S • Europe • 500 kW
	†CHINA R INTL, Xi'an	S Asia • 150 kW • ALT. FREQ. TO 11640 kHz
	IRAN — VO THE ISLAMIC REP, Tehrān	S • S Asia & SE Asia • 500 kW
	NORTHERN MARIANA IS — †KFBS FAR EAST BC, Saipan Island	C Asia & E Asia • 100 kW
	RUSSIA — PERM RADIO, Perm	• DS-RADIO ROSSII • 5 kW
	SLOVAKIA — †R SLOVAKIA INTL, Rimavská Sobota	S • S America • 150 kW
11655	CHILE — †VOZ CRISTIANA, Santiago	W • S America & C America • 70/100 kW / S • S America & C America • 70/100 kW
	CUBA — RADIO REBELDE, Havana	C America • 50 kW
	NETHERLANDS — †R NEDERLAND, Flevoland	S • E Africa • 500 kW / S • W Africa • 500 kW
	R NEDERLAND, Via Julich, Germany	S • N Europe • JUNE-AUGUST • 100 kW
	†R NEDERLAND, Via Madagascar	W • E Africa & Europe • 250 kW / S • E Africa • 250 kW / W • W Africa & C Africa • 250 kW
	RUSSIA — VOICE OF RUSSIA, Armavir	W • W Asia & S Asia • 250 kW
	UNITED KINGDOM — BIBLE VOICE, Via Wertachtal, Germany	W • M/W/F • Mideast • 125 kW
	USA — †ADVENTIST WORLD R, Via Agat, Guam	S • C Asia • 250 kW
	RFE-RL, Via Udon Thani, Thailand	W • SE Asia • 100 kW
	†VOA, Via Botswana	W • W Africa & C Africa • 100 kW
	VOA, Via Udon Thani, Thailand	W • E Asia • 250 kW
11660	AUSTRALIA — †RADIO AUSTRALIA, Shepparton	SE Asia • 100 kW / Pacific & W North Am • 100 kW
	CHINA — CENTRAL PEOPLE'S BS, Xi'an	S • DS-2 • 120 kW / DS-2 • 120 kW / Th-M • DS-2 • 120 kW
	†CHINA R INTL, Kashi	S • Europe • 500 kW / W Europe • 500 kW
	PORTUGAL — RDP INTERNATIONAL, Sines	W • M-F • Europe • 250 kW
	USA — †TRANS WORLD R, Via Merizo, Guam	M-F • SE Asia • 100 kW / M-Sa • SE Asia • 100 kW
	†VOA, Via Briech, Morocco	S • W Asia • 250 kW
11665	CHINA — †CHINA R INTL, Urümqi	S • Mideast & E Europe • 500 kW
	CHINA (TAIWAN) — †R TAIWAN INTL, Tamsui	E Asia • TAIWAN NETWORK • 300 kW
	R TAIWAN INTL, Via Okeechobee, USA	W • Europe • 100 kW
	CLANDESTINE (ASIA) — †"RADIO SOLH", Via Dhabayya, UAE	S • W Asia & C Asia • 250 kW
	CZECH REPUBLIC (con'd) — RADIO PRAGUE, Via Ascension	S America • 250 kW

World Time scale: 0 1 2 3 4 5 6 7 8 9 10 11 12 13 14 15 16 17 18 19 20 21 22 23 24

SEASONAL S OR W   1-HR TIMESHIFT MIDYEAR ⇐ OR ⇒   JAMMING / OR ∧   EARLIEST HEARD ◁   LATEST HEARD ▷   NEW FOR 2006 †

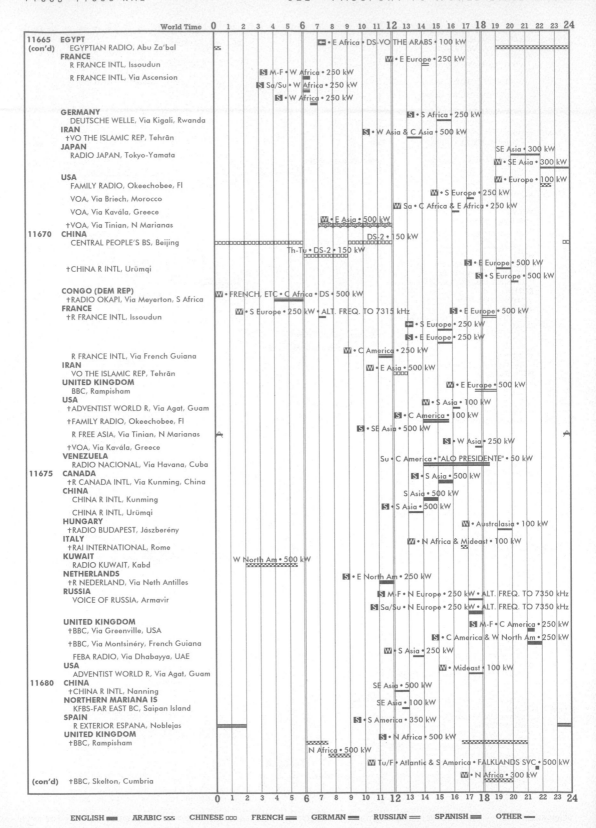

	World Time	0 1 2 3 4 5 6 7 8 9 10 11 12 13 14 15 16 17 18 19 20 21 22 23 24

11665 EGYPT
(con'd) EGYPTIAN RADIO, Abu Za'bal
• E Africa • DS-VO THE ARABS • 100 kW

FRANCE
R FRANCE INTL, Issoudun — W • E Europe • 250 kW

R FRANCE INTL, Via Ascension — S M-F • W Africa • 250 kW
S Sa/Su • W Africa • 250 kW
• W Africa • 250 kW

GERMANY
DEUTSCHE WELLE, Via Kigali, Rwanda — S • S Africa • 250 kW
IRAN
†VO THE ISLAMIC REP, Tehrān — S • W Asia & C Asia • 500 kW
JAPAN
RADIO JAPAN, Tokyo-Yamata — SE Asia • 300 kW
W • SE Asia • 300 kW

USA
FAMILY RADIO, Okeechobee, Fl — W • Europe • 100 kW

VOA, Via Briech, Morocco — W • S Europe • 250 kW

VOA, Via Kavála, Greece — W Sa • C Africa & E Africa • 250 kW

†VOA, Via Tinian, N Marianas — W • E Asia • 500 kW
11670 CHINA
CENTRAL PEOPLE'S BS, Beijing — DS-2 • 150 kW
Th-Tu • DS-2 • 150 kW

†CHINA R INTL, Urümqi — S • E Europe • 500 kW
S • S Europe • 500 kW

CONGO (DEM REP)
†RADIO OKAPI, Via Meyerton, S Africa — W • FRENCH, ETC • C Africa • DS • 500 kW
FRANCE
†R FRANCE INTL, Issoudun — W • S Europe • 250 kW • ALT. FREQ. TO 7315 kHz
S • E Europe • 500 kW
• S Europe • 250 kW
S • E Europe • 250 kW

R FRANCE INTL, Via French Guiana — W • C America • 250 kW
IRAN
VO THE ISLAMIC REP, Tehrān — W • E Asia • 500 kW
UNITED KINGDOM
BBC, Rampisham — W • E Europe • 500 kW
USA
†ADVENTIST WORLD R, Via Agat, Guam — W • S Asia • 100 kW

†FAMILY RADIO, Okeechobee, Fl — S • C America • 100 kW

R FREE ASIA, Via Tinian, N Marianas — S • SE Asia • 500 kW

†VOA, Via Kavála, Greece — S • W Asia • 250 kW
VENEZUELA
RADIO NACIONAL, Via Havana, Cuba — Su • C America • "ALO PRESIDENTE" • 50 kW
11675 CANADA
†R CANADA INTL, Via Kunming, China — S • S Asia • 500 kW
CHINA
CHINA R INTL, Kunming — S Asia • 500 kW

CHINA R INTL, Urümqi — S • S Asia • 500 kW
HUNGARY
†RADIO BUDAPEST, Jászberény — W • Australasia • 100 kW
ITALY
†RAI INTERNATIONAL, Rome — W • N Africa & Mideast • 100 kW
KUWAIT
RADIO KUWAIT, Kabd — W North Am • 500 kW
NETHERLANDS
†R NEDERLAND, Via Neth Antilles — S • E North Am • 250 kW
RUSSIA
VOICE OF RUSSIA, Armavir — S M-F • N Europe • 250 kW • ALT. FREQ. TO 7350 kHz
S Sa/Su • N Europe • 250 kW • ALT. FREQ. TO 7350 kHz

UNITED KINGDOM
†BBC, Via Greenville, USA — S M-F • C America • 250 kW

†BBC, Via Montsinéry, French Guiana — S • C America & W North Am • 250 kW

FEBA RADIO, Via Dhabayya, UAE — W • S Asia • 250 kW
USA
ADVENTIST WORLD R, Via Agat, Guam — W • Mideast • 100 kW
11680 CHINA
†CHINA R INTL, Nanning — SE Asia • 500 kW
NORTHERN MARIANA IS
KFBS-FAR EAST BC, Saipan Island — SE Asia • 100 kW
SPAIN
R EXTERIOR ESPANA, Noblejas — S • S America • 350 kW
UNITED KINGDOM
†BBC, Rampisham — S • N Africa • 500 kW

N Africa • 500 kW

W Tu/F • Atlantic & S America • FALKLANDS SVC • 500 kW

(con'd) †BBC, Skelton, Cumbria — W • N Africa • 300 kW

	0 1 2 3 4 5 6 7 8 9 10 11 12 13 14 15 16 17 18 19 20 21 22 23 24

ENGLISH ▬ ARABIC ░ CHINESE □□□ FRENCH ▬ GERMAN ▬ RUSSIAN ═ SPANISH ▬ OTHER ▬

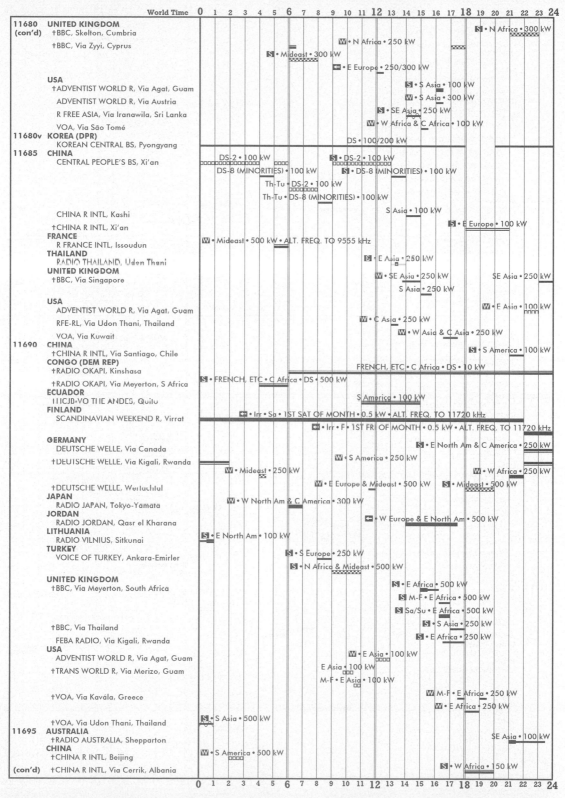

World Time: 0 1 2 3 4 5 6 7 8 9 10 11 12 13 14 15 16 17 18 19 20 21 22 23 24

11680 UNITED KINGDOM
(con'd) †BBC, Skelton, Cumbria — S • N Africa • 300 kW
†BBC, Via Zyyi, Cyprus — W • N Africa • 250 kW / S • Mideast • 300 kW / E Europe • 250/300 kW

USA
†ADVENTIST WORLD R, Via Agat, Guam — S • S Asia • 100 kW
ADVENTIST WORLD R, Via Austria — W • S Asia • 300 kW
R FREE ASIA, Via Iranawila, Sri Lanka — S • SE Asia • 250 kW
VOA, Via São Tomé — W • W Africa & C Africa • 100 kW

11680v KOREA (DPR)
KOREAN CENTRAL BS, Pyongyang — DS • 100/200 kW

11685 CHINA
CENTRAL PEOPLE'S BS, Xi'an — DS-2 • 100 kW / S • DS-2 • 100 kW
DS-8 (MINORITIES) • 100 kW / S • DS-8 (MINORITIES) • 100 kW
Th-Tu • DS-2 • 100 kW
Th-Tu • DS-8 (MINORITIES) • 100 kW

CHINA R INTL, Kashi — S Asia • 100 kW
†CHINA R INTL, Xi'an — S • E Europe • 100 kW
FRANCE
R FRANCE INTL, Issoudun — W • Mideast • 500 kW • ALT. FREQ. TO 9555 kHz
THAILAND
RADIO THAILAND, Udon Thani — E • E Asia • 250 kW
UNITED KINGDOM
†BBC, Via Singapore — W • SE Asia • 250 kW / SE Asia • 250 kW / S Asia • 250 kW

USA
ADVENTIST WORLD R, Via Agat, Guam — W • E Asia • 100 kW
RFE-RL, Via Udon Thani, Thailand — W • C Asia • 250 kW
VOA, Via Kuwait — W • W Asia & C Asia • 250 kW
11690 CHINA
†CHINA R INTL, Via Santiago, Chile — S • S America • 100 kW
CONGO (DEM REP)
†RADIO OKAPI, Kinshasa — FRENCH, ETC • C Africa • DS • 10 kW
†RADIO OKAPI, Via Meyerton, S Africa — S • FRENCH, ETC • C Africa • DS • 500 kW
ECUADOR
†HCJB-VO THE ANDES, Quito — S America • 100 kW
FINLAND
SCANDINAVIAN WEEKEND R, Virrat — Irr • Sa • 1ST SAT OF MONTH • 0.5 kW • ALT. FREQ. TO 11720 kHz
Irr • F • 1ST FRI OF MONTH • 0.5 kW • ALT. FREQ. TO 11720 kHz

GERMANY
DEUTSCHE WELLE, Via Canada — S • E North Am & C America • 250 kW
†DEUTSCHE WELLE, Via Kigali, Rwanda — W • S America • 250 kW / W • Mideast • 250 kW / W • W Africa • 250 kW
†DEUTSCHE WELLE, Wertachtal — W • E Europe & Mideast • 500 kW / S • Mideast • 500 kW
JAPAN
RADIO JAPAN, Tokyo-Yamata — W • W North Am & C America • 300 kW
JORDAN
RADIO JORDAN, Qasr el Kharana — W Europe & E North Am • 500 kW
LITHUANIA
RADIO VILNIUS, Sitkunai — S • E North Am • 100 kW
TURKEY
VOICE OF TURKEY, Ankara-Emirler — S • S Europe • 250 kW / S • N Africa & Mideast • 500 kW

UNITED KINGDOM
†BBC, Via Meyerton, South Africa — S • E Africa • 500 kW / S M-F • E Africa • 500 kW / S Sa/Su • E Africa • 500 kW

†BBC, Via Thailand — S • S Asia • 250 kW
FEBA RADIO, Via Kigali, Rwanda — S • E Africa • 250 kW
USA
ADVENTIST WORLD R, Via Agat, Guam — W • E Asia • 100 kW
†TRANS WORLD R, Via Merizo, Guam — E Asia • 100 kW / M-F • E Asia • 100 kW

†VOA, Via Kavála, Greece — W M-F • E Africa • 250 kW / W • E Africa • 250 kW

11695 †VOA, Via Udon Thani, Thailand — S • S Asia • 500 kW
AUSTRALIA
†RADIO AUSTRALIA, Shepparton — SE Asia • 100 kW
CHINA
†CHINA R INTL, Beijing — W • S America • 500 kW
(con'd) †CHINA R INTL, Via Cerrik, Albania — S • W Africa • 150 kW

0 1 2 3 4 5 6 7 8 9 10 11 12 13 14 15 16 17 18 19 20 21 22 23 24

SEASONAL S OR W   1-HR TIMESHIFT MIDYEAR ⊡ OR ⊐   JAMMING / OR ∧   EARLIEST HEARD ◁   LATEST HEARD ▷   NEW FOR 2006 †

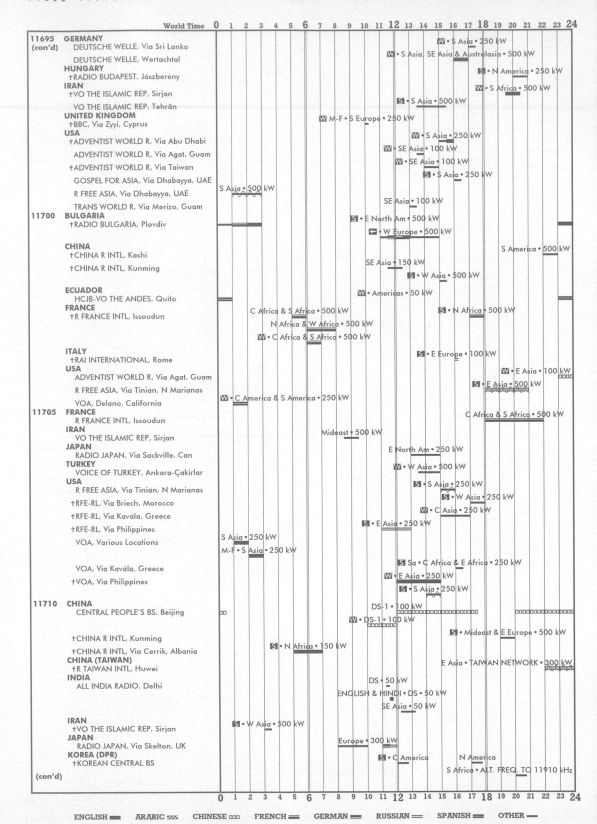

| World Time | 0 | 1 | 2 | 3 | 4 | 5 | 6 | 7 | 8 | 9 | 10 | 11 | 12 | 13 | 14 | 15 | 16 | 17 | 18 | 19 | 20 | 21 | 22 | 23 | 24 |

11695 GERMANY
(con'd) DEUTSCHE WELLE, Via Sri Lanka — W • S Asia • 250 kW

DEUTSCHE WELLE, Wertachtal — W • S Asia, SE Asia & Australasia • 500 kW

HUNGARY
†RADIO BUDAPEST, Jászberény — S • N America • 250 kW

IRAN
†VO THE ISLAMIC REP, Sirjan — W • S Africa • 500 kW

VO THE ISLAMIC REP, Tehrān — S • S Asia • 500 kW

UNITED KINGDOM
†BBC, Via Zyyi, Cyprus — W M-F • S Europe • 250 kW

USA
†ADVENTIST WORLD R, Via Abu Dhabi — W • S Asia • 250 kW

ADVENTIST WORLD R, Via Agat, Guam — W • SE Asia • 100 kW

†ADVENTIST WORLD R, Via Taiwan — W • SE Asia • 100 kW

GOSPEL FOR ASIA, Via Dhabayya, UAE — S • S Asia • 250 kW

R FREE ASIA, Via Dhabayya, UAE — S Asia • 500 kW

TRANS WORLD R, Via Merizo, Guam — SE Asia • 100 kW

11700 BULGARIA
†RADIO BULGARIA, Plovdiv — S • E North Am • 500 kW
— ← • W Europe • 500 kW
— S America • 500 kW

CHINA
†CHINA R INTL, Kashi — SE Asia • 150 kW

†CHINA R INTL, Kunming — S • W Asia • 500 kW

ECUADOR
HCJB-VO THE ANDES, Quito — W • Americas • 50 kW

FRANCE
†R FRANCE INTL, Issoudun — C Africa & S Africa • 500 kW
— S • N Africa • 500 kW
— N Africa & W Africa • 500 kW
— W • C Africa & S Africa • 500 kW

ITALY
†RAI INTERNATIONAL, Rome — S • E Europe • 100 kW

USA
ADVENTIST WORLD R, Via Agat, Guam — W • E Asia • 100 kW

R FREE ASIA, Via Tinian, N Marianas — S • E Asia • 500 kW

VOA, Delano, California — W • C America & S America • 250 kW

11705 FRANCE
R FRANCE INTL, Issoudun — C Africa & S Africa • 500 kW

IRAN
VO THE ISLAMIC REP, Sirjan — Mideast • 500 kW

JAPAN
RADIO JAPAN, Via Sackville, Can — E North Am • 250 kW

TURKEY
VOICE OF TURKEY, Ankara-Çakirlar — W • W Asia • 500 kW

USA
R FREE ASIA, Via Tinian, N Marianas — S • S Asia • 250 kW

†RFE-RL, Via Briech, Morocco — S • W Asia • 250 kW

†RFE-RL, Via Kavála, Greece — W • C Asia • 250 kW

†RFE-RL, Via Philippines — S • E Asia • 250 kW

VOA, Various Locations — S Asia • 250 kW
— M-F • S Asia • 250 kW

VOA, Via Kavála, Greece — S Sa • C Africa & E Africa • 250 kW

†VOA, Via Philippines — W • E Asia • 250 kW
— S • S Asia • 250 kW

11710 CHINA
CENTRAL PEOPLE'S BS, Beijing — DS-1 • 100 kW
— W • DS-1 • 100 kW

†CHINA R INTL, Kunming — S • Mideast & E Europe • 500 kW

†CHINA R INTL, Via Cerrik, Albania — S • N Africa • 150 kW

CHINA (TAIWAN)
†R TAIWAN INTL, Huwei — E Asia • TAIWAN NETWORK • 300 kW

INDIA
ALL INDIA RADIO, Delhi — DS • 50 kW
— ENGLISH & HINDI • DS • 50 kW
— SE Asia • 50 kW

IRAN
†VO THE ISLAMIC REP, Sirjan — S • W Asia • 500 kW

JAPAN
RADIO JAPAN, Via Skelton, UK — Europe • 300 kW

KOREA (DPR)
†KOREAN CENTRAL BS — S • C America   N America
— S Africa • ALT. FREQ. TO 11910 kHz

(con'd)

| World Time | 0 | 1 | 2 | 3 | 4 | 5 | 6 | 7 | 8 | 9 | 10 | 11 | 12 | 13 | 14 | 15 | 16 | 17 | 18 | 19 | 20 | 21 | 22 | 23 | 24 |

ENGLISH ▬   ARABIC ⋙   CHINESE ▢▢▢   FRENCH ▬   GERMAN ▬   RUSSIAN ═   SPANISH ═   OTHER —

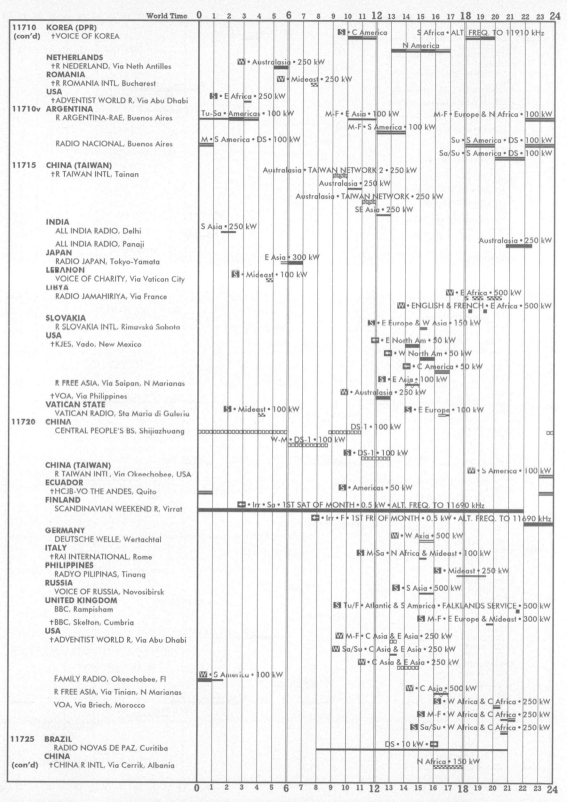

World Time 0 1 2 3 4 5 6 7 8 9 10 11 12 13 14 15 16 17 18 19 20 21 22 23 24

Freq	Station	
11710 (con'd)	**KOREA (DPR)** †VOICE OF KOREA	S • C America • S Africa • ALT. FREQ. TO 11910 kHz • N America
	NETHERLANDS †R NEDERLAND, Via Neth Antilles	W • Australasia • 250 kW
	ROMANIA †R ROMANIA INTL, Bucharest	W • Mideast • 250 kW
	USA †ADVENTIST WORLD R, Via Abu Dhabi	S • E Africa • 250 kW
11710v	**ARGENTINA** R ARGENTINA-RAE, Buenos Aires	Tu-Sa • Americas • 100 kW M-F • E Asia • 100 kW M-F • Europe & N Africa • 100 kW M-F • S America • 100 kW
	RADIO NACIONAL, Buenos Aires	M • S America • DS • 100 kW Su • S America • DS • 100 kW Sa/Su • S America • DS • 100 kW
11715	**CHINA (TAIWAN)** †R TAIWAN INTL, Tainan	Australasia • TAIWAN NETWORK 2 • 250 kW Australasia • 250 kW Australasia • TAIWAN NETWORK • 250 kW SE Asia • 250 kW
	INDIA ALL INDIA RADIO, Delhi	S Asia • 250 kW
	ALL INDIA RADIO, Panaji	Australasia • 250 kW
	JAPAN RADIO JAPAN, Tokyo-Yamata	E Asia • 300 kW
	LEBANON VOICE OF CHARITY, Via Vatican City	S • Mideast • 100 kW
	LIBYA RADIO JAMAHIRIYA, Via France	W • E Africa • 500 kW W • ENGLISH & FRENCH • E Africa • 500 kW
	SLOVAKIA R SLOVAKIA INTL, Rimavská Sobota	S • E Europe & W Asia • 150 kW
	USA †KJES, Vado, New Mexico	E North Am • 50 kW W North Am • 50 kW C America • 50 kW
	R FREE ASIA, Via Saipan, N Marianas	S • E Asia • 100 kW
	†VOA, Via Philippines	W • Australasia • 250 kW
	VATICAN STATE VATICAN RADIO, Sta Maria di Galeria	S • Mideast • 100 kW S • E Europe • 100 kW
11720	**CHINA** CENTRAL PEOPLE'S BS, Shijiazhuang	DS-1 • 100 kW W-M • DS-1 • 100 kW S • DS-1 • 100 kW
	CHINA (TAIWAN) R TAIWAN INTL, Via Okeechobee, USA	W • S America • 100 kW
	ECUADOR †HCJB-VO THE ANDES, Quito	S • Americas • 50 kW
	FINLAND SCANDINAVIAN WEEKEND R, Virrat	⇄ • Irr • Sa • 1ST SAT OF MONTH • 0.5 kW • ALT. FREQ. TO 11690 kHz ⇄ • Irr • F • 1ST FRI OF MONTH • 0.5 kW • ALT. FREQ. TO 11690 kHz
	GERMANY DEUTSCHE WELLE, Wertachtal	W • W Asia • 500 kW
	ITALY †RAI INTERNATIONAL, Rome	S • M-Sa • N Africa & Mideast • 100 kW
	PHILIPPINES RADYO PILIPINAS, Tinang	S • Mideast • 250 kW
	RUSSIA VOICE OF RUSSIA, Novosibirsk	S • S Asia • 500 kW
	UNITED KINGDOM BBC, Rampisham	S • Tu/F • Atlantic & S America • FALKLANDS SERVICE • 500 kW S • M-F • E Europe & Mideast • 300 kW
	†BBC, Skelton, Cumbria	
	USA †ADVENTIST WORLD R, Via Abu Dhabi	W • M-F • C Asia & E Asia • 250 kW W • Sa/Su • C Asia & E Asia • 250 kW W • C Asia & E Asia • 250 kW
	FAMILY RADIO, Okeechobee, Fl	W • S America • 100 kW
	R FREE ASIA, Via Tinian, N Marianas	W • C Asia • 500 kW
	VOA, Via Briech, Morocco	S • W Africa & C Africa • 250 kW S • M-F • W Africa & C Africa • 250 kW S • Sa/Su • W Africa & C Africa • 250 kW
11725	**BRAZIL** RADIO NOVAS DE PAZ, Curitiba	DS • 10 kW • ⇄
CHINA (con'd)	†CHINA R INTL, Via Cerrik, Albania	N Africa • 150 kW

World Time 0 1 2 3 4 5 6 7 8 9 10 11 12 13 14 15 16 17 18 19 20 21 22 23 24

World Time 0 1 2 3 4 5 6 7 8 9 10 11 12 13 14 15 16 17 18 19 20 21 22 23 24

11725 FRANCE
(con'd) R FRANCE INTL, Via Moyabi, Gabon — W • W Africa • 250 kW

NEW ZEALAND
†R NEW ZEALAND INTL, Rangitaiki — S • ENGLISH, ETC • Pacific • 100 kW

ROMANIA
R ROMANIA INTL, Galbeni — S • S America • 250 kW

USA
FAMILY RADIO, Okeechobee, Fl — W • C America • 100 kW

RFE-RL, Via Lampertheim, Germany — S • E Europe • 100 kW

VOA, Via Lampertheim, Germany — S • E Europe • 100 kW

VOA, Via Udon Thani, Thailand — S • S Asia • 250 kW ; S M-F • S Asia • 250 kW

11730 CHINA
†CHINA R INTL, Kunming — S Asia • 500 kW ; S • N Africa & Mideast • 500 kW ; W Africa & C Africa • 500 kW

INDIA
ALL INDIA RADIO, Aligarh — Irr • Mideast • HAJJ • 250 kW

ALL INDIA RADIO, Delhi — Mideast & W Asia • 250 kW

IRAN
VO THE ISLAMIC REP, Tehrān — S • W Asia & S Asia • 500 kW

JAPAN
RADIO JAPAN, Tokyo-Yamata — E Asia • 300 kW ; S • S Asia • 300 kW

PHILIPPINES
†RADIO VERITAS ASIA, Palauig — S Asia • 250 kW • ALT. FREQ. TO 11935 kHz

RADYO PILIPINAS, Tinang — W • Mideast • 250 kW

ROMANIA
†R ROMANIA INTL, Bucharest — W • E North Am • 250 kW

TUNISIA
†RTV TUNISIENNE, Sfax — ⇦ • W Europe • 500 kW

TURKEY
VOICE OF TURKEY, Ankara-Çakirlar — S • W Asia • 250 kW

UNITED KINGDOM
BBC, Via Seychelles — W • E Africa • 250 kW

USA
VOA, Via Iranawila, Sri Lanka — W • S Asia • 250 kW

11735 BELARUS
†BELARUSIAN R, Minsk — S • E Europe & W Asia • DS-1 • 250 kW

BRAZIL
†RADIO TRANS MUNDIAL, Santa Maria — DS • 50 kW • ⇨

INDIA
ALL INDIA RADIO, Aligarh — W Asia & S Asia • 250 kW

KOREA (DPR)
†KOREAN CENTRAL BS — S • SE Asia

†PYONGYANG BC STN — E Asia

†VOICE OF KOREA — C America ; E Asia ; S • SE Asia

TANZANIA
†VOICE OF TANZANIA, Dole, Zanzibar — DS • 50 kW

TURKEY
†VOICE OF TURKEY, Ankara-Emirler — W • S Asia, SE Asia & Australasia • 500 kW ; S • Mideast • 500 kW

USA
VOA, Via Iranawila, Sri Lanka — S • S Asia • 250 kW

VOA, Via Kavála, Greece — S M-F • E Europe & Mideast • 250 kW

11740 CHINA
CENTRAL PEOPLE'S BS, Beijing — W • DS-2 • 50 kW ; DS-2 • 50 kW

CHINA (TAIWAN)
R TAIWAN INTL, Via Okeechobee, USA — C America • 100 kW

INDIA
ALL INDIA RADIO, Panaji — SE Asia • 250 kW ; S Asia • 250 kW

JAPAN
RADIO JAPAN, Via Singapore — SE Asia • 250 kW

SAUDI ARABIA
BS OF THE KINGDOM, Riyadh — C Africa & W Africa • DS-HOLY KORAN • 500 kW

UNITED KINGDOM
†BBC, Skelton, Cumbria — S • E Europe • 300 kW

†BBC, Via Zyyi, Cyprus — S • Mideast • 300 kW

USA
FAMILY RADIO, Okeechobee, Fl — C America • 100 kW ; W • S America • 100 kW ; N America • 100 kW ; W • E North Am • 100 kW

R FREE ASIA, Via Tinian, N Marianas — S • E Asia • 500 kW ; W • E Asia • 500 kW

†RFE-RL, Via Lampertheim, Germany — W • C Asia • 100 kW

(con'd) †VOA, Via Kavála, Greece — S • Mideast & W Asia • 250 kW

ENGLISH ▬   ARABIC ▨   CHINESE ▫▫▫   FRENCH ▬   GERMAN ▬   RUSSIAN ▭   SPANISH ▬   OTHER ▬

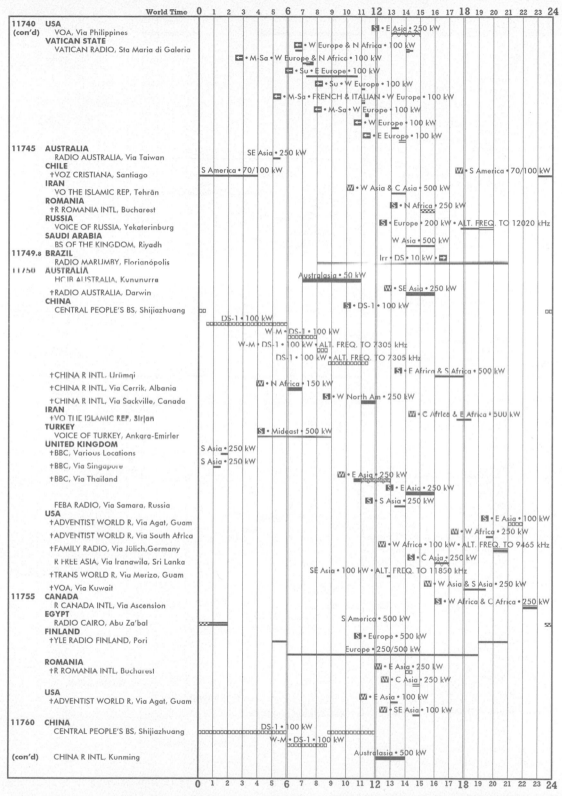

World Time   0 1 2 3 4 5 6 7 8 9 10 11 12 13 14 15 16 17 18 19 20 21 22 23 24

11740 **USA**
(con'd)   VOA, Via Philippines   S • E Asia • 250 kW
VATICAN STATE
  VATICAN RADIO, Sta Maria di Galeria   • W Europe & N Africa • 100 kW
   • M-Sa • W Europe & N Africa • 100 kW
   • Su • E Europe • 100 kW
   • Su • W Europe • 100 kW
   • M-Sa • FRENCH & ITALIAN • W Europe • 100 kW
   • M-Sa • W Europe • 100 kW
   • W Europe • 100 kW
   • E Europe • 100 kW

11745 **AUSTRALIA**
  RADIO AUSTRALIA, Via Taiwan   SE Asia • 250 kW
CHILE
  †VOZ CRISTIANA, Santiago   S America • 70/100 kW   W • S America • 70/100 kW
IRAN
  VO THE ISLAMIC REP, Tehrän   W • W Asia & C Asia • 500 kW
ROMANIA
  †R ROMANIA INTL, Bucharest   S • N Africa • 250 kW
RUSSIA
  VOICE OF RUSSIA, Yekaterinburg   S • Europe • 200 kW • ALT. FREQ. TO 12020 kHz
SAUDI ARABIA
  BS OF THE KINGDOM, Riyadh   W Asia • 500 kW
11749.8 BRAZIL
  RADIO MARUMBY, Florianópolis   Irr • DS • 10 kW •
11750 AUSTRALIA
  HCJB AUSTRALIA, Kununurra   Australasia • 50 kW

  †RADIO AUSTRALIA, Darwin   W • SE Asia • 250 kW
CHINA
  CENTRAL PEOPLE'S BS, Shijiazhuang   S • DS-1 • 100 kW
   DS-1 • 100 kW
   W-M • DS-1 • 100 kW
   W-M • DS-1 • 100 kW • ALT. FREQ. TO 7305 kHz
   DS-1 • 100 kW • ALT. FREQ. TO 7305 kHz

  †CHINA R INTL, Urümqi   S • E Africa & S Africa • 500 kW
  †CHINA R INTL, Via Cerrik, Albania   W • N Africa • 150 kW
  †CHINA R INTL, Via Sackville, Canada   S • W North Am • 250 kW
IRAN
  †VO THE ISLAMIC REP, Sirjan   W • C Africa & E Africa • 500 kW
TURKEY
  VOICE OF TURKEY, Ankara-Emirler   S • Mideast • 500 kW
UNITED KINGDOM
  †BBC, Various Locations   S Asia • 250 kW
  †BBC, Via Singapore   S Asia • 250 kW
  †BBC, Via Thailand   W • E Asia • 250 kW
   S • E Asia • 250 kW
  FEBA RADIO, Via Samara, Russia   W • S Asia • 250 kW
USA
  †ADVENTIST WORLD R, Via Agat, Guam   S • E Asia • 100 kW
  †ADVENTIST WORLD R, Via South Africa   W • W Africa • 250 kW
  †FAMILY RADIO, Via Jülich, Germany   W • W Africa • 100 kW • ALT. FREQ. TO 9465 kHz
  R FREE ASIA, Via Iranawila, Sri Lanka   S • C Asia • 250 kW
  †TRANS WORLD R, Via Merizo, Guam   SE Asia • 100 kW • ALT. FREQ. TO 11850 kHz
  †VOA, Via Kuwait   W • W Asia & S Asia • 250 kW
11755 CANADA
  R CANADA INTL, Via Ascension   S • W Africa & C Africa • 250 kW
EGYPT
  RADIO CAIRO, Abu Za'bal   S America • 500 kW
FINLAND
  †YLE RADIO FINLAND, Pori   S • Europe • 500 kW
   Europe • 250/500 kW
ROMANIA
  †R ROMANIA INTL, Bucharest   W • E Asia • 250 kW
   W • C Asia • 250 kW
USA
  †ADVENTIST WORLD R, Via Agat, Guam   W • E Asia • 100 kW
   W • SE Asia • 100 kW
11760 CHINA
  CENTRAL PEOPLE'S BS, Shijiazhuang   DS-1 • 100 kW
   W-M • DS-1 • 100 kW
(con'd)   CHINA R INTL, Kunming   Australasia • 500 kW

  0 1 2 3 4 5 6 7 8 9 10 11 12 13 14 15 16 17 18 19 20 21 22 23 24

SEASONAL S OR W   1-HR TIMESHIFT MIDYEAR ⊏ OR ⊐   JAMMING / OR ∧   EARLIEST HEARD ◁   LATEST HEARD ▷   NEW FOR 2006 †

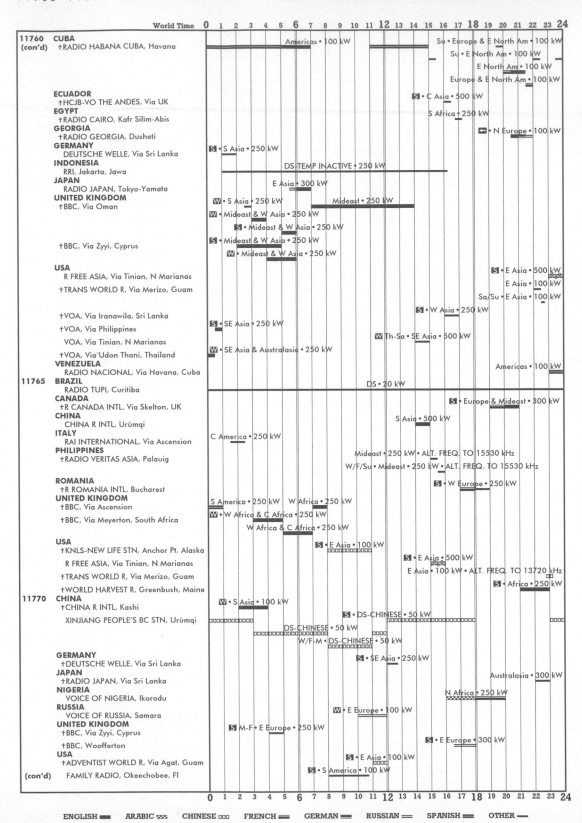

World Time scale: 0 1 2 3 4 5 6 7 8 9 10 11 12 13 14 15 16 17 18 19 20 21 22 23 24

11760
(con'd) CUBA
  †RADIO HABANA CUBA, Havana — Americas • 100 kW; Su • Europe & E North Am • 100 kW; Su • E North Am • 100 kW; E North Am • 100 kW; Europe & E North Am • 100 kW

ECUADOR
  †HCJB-VO THE ANDES, Via UK — S • C Asia • 500 kW
EGYPT
  †RADIO CAIRO, Kafr Silim-Abis — S Africa • 250 kW
GEORGIA
  †RADIO GEORGIA, Dusheti — N Europe • 100 kW
GERMANY
  DEUTSCHE WELLE, Via Sri Lanka — S • S Asia • 250 kW
INDONESIA
  RRI, Jakarta, Jawa — DS-TEMP INACTIVE • 250 kW
JAPAN
  RADIO JAPAN, Tokyo-Yamata — E Asia • 300 kW
UNITED KINGDOM
  †BBC, Via Oman — W • S Asia • 250 kW; Mideast • 250 kW; W • Mideast & W Asia • 250 kW; S • Mideast & W Asia • 250 kW
  †BBC, Via Zyyi, Cyprus — S • Mideast & W Asia • 250 kW; W • Mideast & W Asia • 250 kW

USA
  R FREE ASIA, Via Tinian, N Marianas — S • E Asia • 500 kW
  †TRANS WORLD R, Via Merizo, Guam — E Asia • 100 kW; Sa/Su • E Asia • 100 kW
  †VOA, Via Iranawila, Sri Lanka — S • W Asia • 250 kW
  †VOA, Via Philippines — S • SE Asia • 250 kW
  VOA, Via Tinian, N Marianas — W • Th-Sa • SE Asia • 500 kW
  †VOA, Via Udon Thani, Thailand — W • SE Asia & Australasia • 250 kW
VENEZUELA
  RADIO NACIONAL, Via Havana, Cuba — Americas • 100 kW
11765 BRAZIL
  RADIO TUPI, Curitiba — DS • 20 kW
CANADA
  †R CANADA INTL, Via Skelton, UK — S • Europe & Mideast • 300 kW
CHINA
  CHINA R INTL, Urümqi — S Asia • 500 kW
ITALY
  RAI INTERNATIONAL, Via Ascension — C America • 250 kW
PHILIPPINES
  †RADIO VERITAS ASIA, Palauig — Mideast • 250 kW • ALT. FREQ. TO 15530 kHz; W/F/Su • Mideast • 250 kW • ALT. FREQ. TO 15530 kHz
ROMANIA
  †R ROMANIA INTL, Bucharest — S • W Europe • 250 kW
UNITED KINGDOM
  †BBC, Via Ascension — S America • 250 kW; W Africa • 250 kW
  †BBC, Via Meyerton, South Africa — W • W Africa & C Africa • 250 kW; W Africa & C Africa • 250 kW
USA
  †KNLS-NEW LIFE STN, Anchor Pt, Alaska — S • E Asia • 100 kW
  R FREE ASIA, Via Tinian, N Marianas — S • E Asia • 500 kW
  †TRANS WORLD R, Via Merizo, Guam — E Asia • 100 kW • ALT. FREQ. TO 13720 kHz
  †WORLD HARVEST R, Greenbush, Maine — S • Africa • 250 kW
11770 CHINA
  †CHINA R INTL, Kashi — W • S Asia • 100 kW
  XINJIANG PEOPLE'S BC STN, Urümqi — S • DS-CHINESE • 50 kW; DS-CHINESE • 50 kW; W/F-M • DS-CHINESE • 50 kW
GERMANY
  †DEUTSCHE WELLE, Via Sri Lanka — S • SE Asia • 250 kW
JAPAN
  †RADIO JAPAN, Via Sri Lanka — Australasia • 300 kW
NIGERIA
  VOICE OF NIGERIA, Ikorodu — N Africa • 250 kW
RUSSIA
  VOICE OF RUSSIA, Samara — W • E Europe • 100 kW
UNITED KINGDOM
  †BBC, Via Zyyi, Cyprus — S • M-F • E Europe • 250 kW
  †BBC, Woofferton — S • E Europe • 300 kW
USA
  †ADVENTIST WORLD R, Via Agat, Guam — S • E Asia • 100 kW
(con'd) FAMILY RADIO, Okeechobee, Fl — S • S America • 100 kW

World Time scale: 0 1 2 3 4 5 6 7 8 9 10 11 12 13 14 15 16 17 18 19 20 21 22 23 24

ENGLISH ▰   ARABIC ░   CHINESE □□□   FRENCH ▭▭   GERMAN ▬   RUSSIAN ═   SPANISH ▬   OTHER ▬

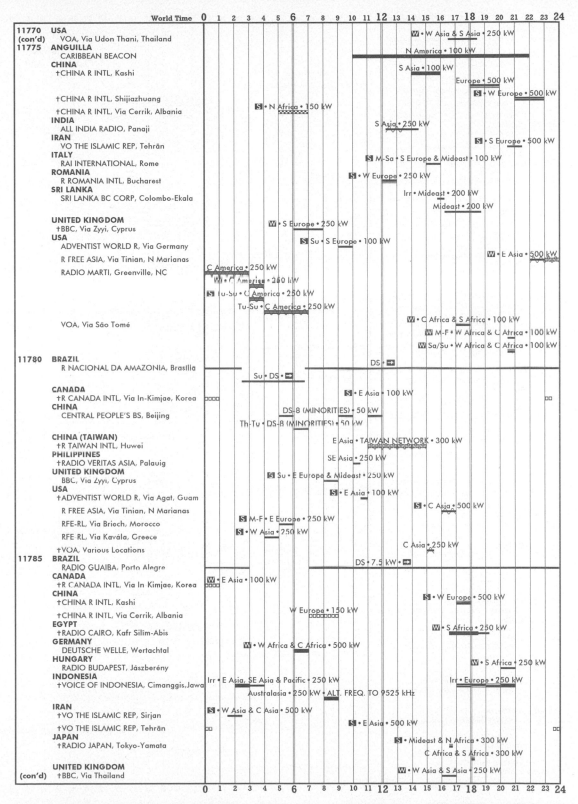

	World Time	0 1 2 3 4 5 6 7 8 9 10 11 12 13 14 15 16 17 18 19 20 21 22 23 24
11770	**USA**	
(con'd)	VOA, Via Udon Thani, Thailand	W • W Asia & S Asia • 250 kW
11775	**ANGUILLA**	
	CARIBBEAN BEACON	N America • 100 kW
	CHINA	
	†CHINA R INTL, Kashi	S Asia • 100 kW
		Europe • 500 kW
		S • W Europe • 500 kW
	†CHINA R INTL, Shijiazhuang	S • N Africa • 150 kW
	†CHINA R INTL, Via Cerrik, Albania	S Asia •
	INDIA	
	ALL INDIA RADIO, Panaji	S Asia • 250 kW
	IRAN	
	VO THE ISLAMIC REP, Tehrān	S • S Europe • 500 kW
	ITALY	
	RAI INTERNATIONAL, Rome	S M-Sa • S Europe & Mideast • 100 kW
	ROMANIA	
	R ROMANIA INTL, Bucharest	S • W Europe • 250 kW
	SRI LANKA	
	SRI LANKA BC CORP, Colombo-Ekala	Irr • Mideast • 200 kW
		Mideast • 200 kW
	UNITED KINGDOM	
	†BBC, Via Zyyi, Cyprus	W • S Europe • 250 kW
	USA	
	ADVENTIST WORLD R, Via Germany	S Su • S Europe • 100 kW
	R FREE ASIA, Via Tinian, N Marianas	W • E Asia • 500 kW
	RADIO MARTI, Greenville, NC	C America • 250 kW
		W • C America • 250 kW
		S Tu-Su • C America • 250 kW
		Tu-Su • C America • 250 kW
	VOA, Via São Tomé	W • C Africa & S Africa • 100 kW
		W M-F • W Africa & C Africa • 100 kW
		W Sa/Su • W Africa & C Africa • 100 kW
11780	**BRAZIL**	
	R NACIONAL DA AMAZONIA, Brasília	DS • ⇨
		Su • DS • ⇨
	CANADA	
	†R CANADA INTL, Via In-Kimjae, Korea	S • E Asia • 100 kW
	CHINA	
	CENTRAL PEOPLE'S BS, Beijing	DS-8 (MINORITIES) • 50 kW
		Th-Tu • DS-8 (MINORITIES) • 50 kW
	CHINA (TAIWAN)	
	†R TAIWAN INTL, Huwei	E Asia • TAIWAN NETWORK • 300 kW
	PHILIPPINES	
	†RADIO VERITAS ASIA, Palauig	SE Asia • 250 kW
	UNITED KINGDOM	
	BBC, Via Zyyi, Cyprus	S Su • E Europe & Mideast • 250 kW
	USA	
	†ADVENTIST WORLD R, Via Agat, Guam	S • E Asia • 100 kW
	R FREE ASIA, Via Tinian, N Marianas	S • C Asia • 500 kW
	RFE-RL, Via Briech, Morocco	S M-F • E Europe • 250 kW
	RFE-RL, Via Kavála, Greece	S • W Asia • 250 kW
	†VOA, Various Locations	C Asia • 250 kW
11785	**BRAZIL**	
	RADIO GUAIBA, Porto Alegre	DS • 7.5 kW • ⇨
	CANADA	
	†R CANADA INTL, Via In Kimjae, Korea	W • E Asia • 100 kW
	CHINA	
	†CHINA R INTL, Kashi	S • W Europe • 500 kW
	†CHINA R INTL, Via Cerrik, Albania	W Europe • 150 kW
	EGYPT	
	†RADIO CAIRO, Kafr Silîm-Abis	W • S Africa • 250 kW
	GERMANY	
	DEUTSCHE WELLE, Wertachtal	W • W Africa & C Africa • 500 kW
	HUNGARY	
	RADIO BUDAPEST, Jászberény	W • S Africa • 250 kW
	INDONESIA	
	†VOICE OF INDONESIA, Cimanggis,Jawa	Irr • E Asia, SE Asia & Pacific • 250 kW	Irr • Europe • 250 kW
		Australasia • 250 kW • ALT. FREQ. TO 9525 kHz
	IRAN	
	†VO THE ISLAMIC REP, Sirjan	S • W Asia & C Asia • 500 kW
	†VO THE ISLAMIC REP, Tehrān	S • E Asia • 500 kW
	JAPAN	
	†RADIO JAPAN, Tokyo-Yamata	S • Mideast & N Africa • 300 kW
		C Africa & S Africa • 300 kW
	UNITED KINGDOM	
(con'd)	†BBC, Via Thailand	W • W Asia & S Asia • 250 kW

	World Time	0 1 2 3 4 5 6 7 8 9 10 11 12 13 14 15 16 17 18 19 20 21 22 23 24

SEASONAL S OR W   1-HR TIMESHIFT MIDYEAR ⇦ OR ⇨   JAMMING / OR /\   EARLIEST HEARD ◁   LATEST HEARD ▷   NEW FOR 2006 †

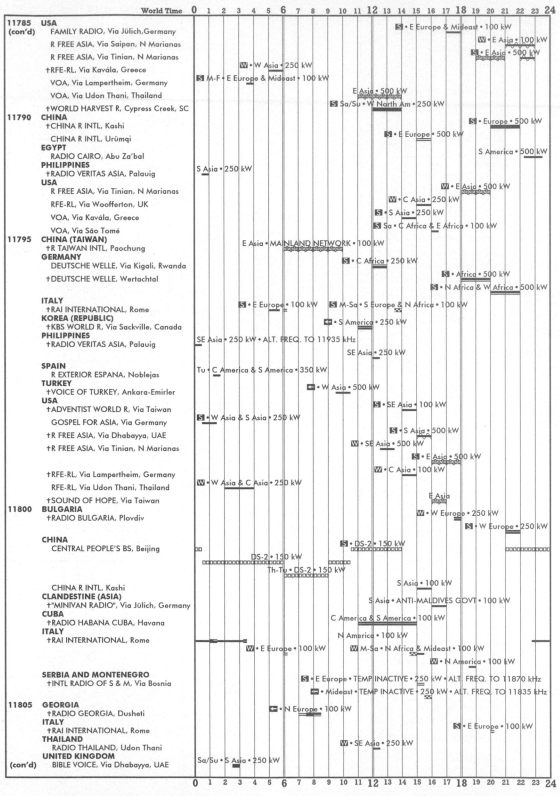

	World Time	0 1 2 3 4 5 6 7 8 9 10 11 12 13 14 15 16 17 18 19 20 21 22 23 24
11785 (con'd)	**USA**	
	FAMILY RADIO, Via Jülich, Germany	S • E Europe & Mideast • 100 kW
	R FREE ASIA, Via Saipan, N Marianas	W • E Asia • 100 kW
	R FREE ASIA, Via Tinian, N Marianas	S • E Asia • 500 kW
	†RFE-RL, Via Kavála, Greece	W • W Asia • 250 kW
	VOA, Via Lampertheim, Germany	S M-F • E Europe & Mideast • 100 kW
	VOA, Via Udon Thani, Thailand	E Asia • 500 kW
	†WORLD HARVEST R, Cypress Creek, SC	S Sa/Su • W North Am • 250 kW
11790	**CHINA**	
	†CHINA R INTL, Kashi	S • Europe • 500 kW
	CHINA R INTL, Urümqi	S • E Europe • 500 kW
	EGYPT	
	RADIO CAIRO, Abu Za'bal	S America • 500 kW
	PHILIPPINES	
	†RADIO VERITAS ASIA, Palauig	S Asia • 250 kW
	USA	
	R FREE ASIA, Via Tinian, N Marianas	W • E Asia • 500 kW
	RFE-RL, Via Woofferton, UK	W • C Asia • 250 kW
	VOA, Via Kavála, Greece	S • S Asia • 250 kW
	VOA, Via São Tomé	S Sa • C Africa & E Africa • 100 kW
11795	**CHINA (TAIWAN)**	
	†R TAIWAN INTL, Paochung	E Asia • MAINLAND NETWORK • 100 kW
	GERMANY	
	DEUTSCHE WELLE, Via Kigali, Rwanda	S • C Africa • 250 kW
	†DEUTSCHE WELLE, Wertachtal	S • Africa • 500 kW
		S • N Africa & W Africa • 500 kW
	ITALY	
	†RAI INTERNATIONAL, Rome	S • E Europe • 100 kW S M-Sa • S Europe & N Africa • 100 kW
	KOREA (REPUBLIC)	
	†KBS WORLD R, Via Sackville, Canada	S America • 250 kW
	PHILIPPINES	
	†RADIO VERITAS ASIA, Palauig	SE Asia • 250 kW • ALT. FREQ. TO 11935 kHz
		SE Asia • 250 kW
	SPAIN	
	R EXTERIOR ESPANA, Noblejas	Tu • C America & S America • 350 kW
	TURKEY	
	†VOICE OF TURKEY, Ankara-Emirler	W Asia • 500 kW
	USA	
	†ADVENTIST WORLD R, Via Taiwan	S • SE Asia • 100 kW
	GOSPEL FOR ASIA, Via Germany	S • W Asia & S Asia • 250 kW
	†R FREE ASIA, Via Dhabayya, UAE	S • S Asia • 500 kW
	†R FREE ASIA, Via Tinian, N Marianas	W • SE Asia • 500 kW
		S • E Asia • 500 kW
		W • C Asia • 100 kW
	†RFE-RL, Via Lampertheim, Germany	
	RFE-RL, Via Udon Thani, Thailand	W • W Asia & C Asia • 250 kW
	†SOUND OF HOPE, Via Taiwan	E Asia
11800	**BULGARIA**	
	†RADIO BULGARIA, Plovdiv	W • W Europe • 250 kW
		S • W Europe • 250 kW
	CHINA	
	CENTRAL PEOPLE'S BS, Beijing	S • DS-2 • 150 kW
		DS-2 • 150 kW
		Th-Tu • DS-2 • 150 kW
	CHINA R INTL, Kashi	S Asia • 100 kW
	CLANDESTINE (ASIA)	
	†"MINIVAN RADIO", Via Jülich, Germany	S Asia • ANTI-MALDIVES GOVT • 100 kW
	CUBA	
	†RADIO HABANA CUBA, Havana	C America & S America • 100 kW
	ITALY	
	†RAI INTERNATIONAL, Rome	N America • 100 kW
		W • E Europe • 100 kW W M-Sa • N Africa & Mideast • 100 kW
		W • N America • 100 kW
	SERBIA AND MONTENEGRO	
	†INTL RADIO OF S & M, Via Bosnia	S • E Europe • TEMP INACTIVE • 250 kW • ALT. FREQ. TO 11870 kHz
		• Mideast • TEMP INACTIVE • 250 kW • ALT. FREQ. TO 11835 kHz
11805	**GEORGIA**	
	†RADIO GEORGIA, Dusheti	N Europe • 100 kW
	ITALY	
	†RAI INTERNATIONAL, Rome	S • E Europe • 100 kW
	THAILAND	
	RADIO THAILAND, Udon Thani	W • SE Asia • 250 kW
	UNITED KINGDOM	
(con'd)	BIBLE VOICE, Via Dhabayya, UAE	Sa/Su • S Asia • 250 kW
		0 1 2 3 4 5 6 7 8 9 10 11 12 13 14 15 16 17 18 19 20 21 22 23 24

ENGLISH ▬   ARABIC ⬚⬚   CHINESE ▭▭▭   FRENCH ═══   GERMAN ▬▬   RUSSIAN ══   SPANISH ══   OTHER ──

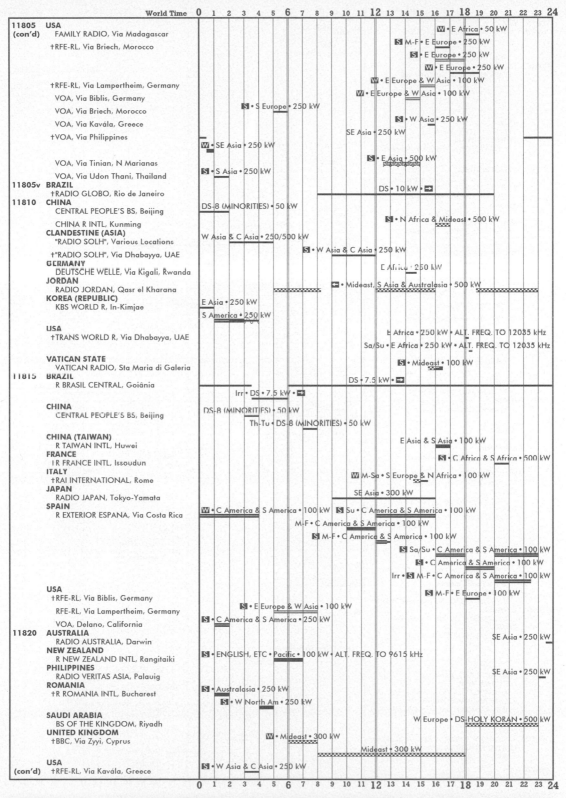

World Time | 0 1 2 3 4 5 6 7 8 9 10 11 12 13 14 15 16 17 18 19 20 21 22 23 24

11805 (con'd) **USA**	
FAMILY RADIO, Via Madagascar	W • E Africa • 50 kW
†RFE-RL, Via Briech, Morocco	S M-F • E Europe • 250 kW
	S • E Europe • 250 kW
	W • E Europe • 250 kW
†RFE-RL, Via Lampertheim, Germany	W • E Europe & W Asia • 100 kW
VOA, Via Biblis, Germany	W • E Europe & W Asia • 100 kW
VOA, Via Briech, Morocco	S • S Europe • 250 kW
VOA, Via Kavála, Greece	S • W Asia • 250 kW
†VOA, Via Philippines	SE Asia • 250 kW
VOA, Via Tinian, N Marianas	W • SE Asia • 250 kW
	S • E Asia • 500 kW
VOA, Via Udon Thani, Thailand	S • S Asia • 250 kW
11805v BRAZIL	
†RADIO GLOBO, Rio de Janeiro	DS • 10 kW • ➡
11810 CHINA	
CENTRAL PEOPLE'S BS, Beijing	DS-8 (MINORITIES) • 50 kW
CHINA R INTL, Kunming	S • N Africa & Mideast • 500 kW
CLANDESTINE (ASIA)	
"RADIO SOLH", Various Locations	W Asia & C Asia • 250/500 kW
†"RADIO SOLH", Via Dhabayya, UAE	S • W Asia & C Asia • 250 kW
GERMANY	
DEUTSCHE WELLE, Via Kigali, Rwanda	E Africa • 250 kW
JORDAN	
RADIO JORDAN, Qasr el Kharana	⬅ • Mideast, S Asia & Australasia • 500 kW
KOREA (REPUBLIC)	
KBS WORLD R, In-Kimjae	E Asia • 250 kW
	S America • 250 kW
USA	
†TRANS WORLD R, Via Dhabayya, UAE	E Africa • 250 kW • ALT. FREQ. TO 12035 kHz
	Sa/Su • E Africa 250 kW • ALT. FREQ. TO 12035 kHz
VATICAN STATE	
VATICAN RADIO, Sta Maria di Galeria	S • Mideast • 100 kW
11815 BRAZIL	
R BRASIL CENTRAL, Goiânia	DS • 7.5 kW • ➡
	Irr • DS • 7.5 kW • ➡
CHINA	
CENTRAL PEOPLE'S BS, Beijing	DS-8 (MINORITIES) • 50 kW
	Th-Tu • DS-8 (MINORITIES) • 50 kW
CHINA (TAIWAN)	
R TAIWAN INTL, Huwei	E Asia & S Asia • 100 kW
FRANCE	
I R FRANCE INTL, Issoudun	S • C Africa & S Africa • 500 kW
ITALY	
†RAI INTERNATIONAL, Rome	W M-Sa • S Europe & N Africa • 100 kW
JAPAN	
RADIO JAPAN, Tokyo-Yamata	SE Asia • 300 kW
SPAIN	
R EXTERIOR ESPANA, Via Costa Rica	W • C America & S America • 100 kW S Su • C America & S America • 100 kW
	M-F • C America & S America • 100 kW
	S M-F • C America & S America • 100 kW
	S Sa/Su • C America & S America • 100 kW
	C America & S America • 100 kW
	Irr • S M-F • C America & S America • 100 kW
	S M-F • E Europe • 100 kW
USA	
†RFE-RL, Via Biblis, Germany	S • E Europe & W Asia • 100 kW
RFE-RL, Via Lampertheim, Germany	S • C America & S America • 250 kW
VOA, Delano, California	
11820 AUSTRALIA	
RADIO AUSTRALIA, Darwin	SE Asia • 250 kW
NEW ZEALAND	
R NEW ZEALAND INTL, Rangitaiki	S • ENGLISH, ETC • Pacific • 100 kW • ALT. FREQ. TO 9615 kHz
PHILIPPINES	
RADIO VERITAS ASIA, Palauig	SE Asia • 250 kW
ROMANIA	
†R ROMANIA INTL, Bucharest	S • Australasia • 250 kW
	S • W North Am • 250 kW
SAUDI ARABIA	
BS OF THE KINGDOM, Riyadh	W Europe • DS-HOLY KORAN • 500 kW
UNITED KINGDOM	
†BBC, Via Zyyi, Cyprus	W • Mideast • 300 kW
	Mideast • 300 kW
USA	
(con'd) †RFE-RL, Via Kavála, Greece	S • W Asia & C Asia • 250 kW

0 1 2 3 4 5 6 7 8 9 10 11 12 13 14 15 16 17 18 19 20 21 22 23 24

SEASONAL S OR W   1-HR TIMESHIFT MIDYEAR ⬅ OR ➡   JAMMING / OR ∧   EARLIEST HEARD ◁   LATEST HEARD ▷   NEW FOR 2006 †

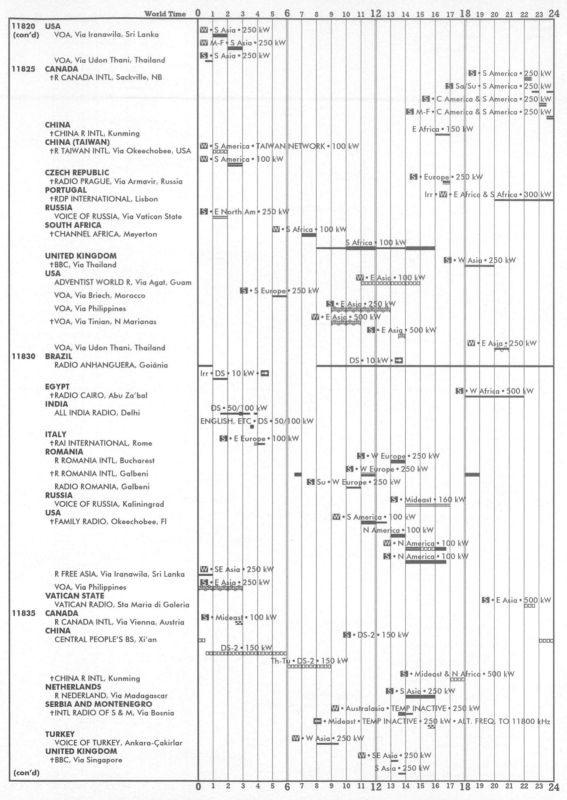

World Time 0 1 2 3 4 5 6 7 8 9 10 11 12 13 14 15 16 17 18 19 20 21 22 23 24

11820
(con'd)   **USA**
    VOA, Via Iranawila, Sri Lanka — W • S Asia • 250 kW / W M-F • S Asia • 250 kW
    VOA, Via Udon Thani, Thailand — S • S Asia • 250 kW
11825 **CANADA**
    †R CANADA INTL, Sackville, NB — S • S America • 250 kW / S Sa/Su • S America • 250 kW / S • C America & S America • 250 kW / S M-F • C America & S America • 250 kW

    CHINA
    †CHINA R INTL, Kunming — E Africa • 150 kW
    CHINA (TAIWAN)
    †R TAIWAN INTL, Via Okeechobee, USA — W • S America • TAIWAN NETWORK • 100 kW / W • S America • 100 kW
    CZECH REPUBLIC
    †RADIO PRAGUE, Via Armavir, Russia — S • Europe • 250 kW
    PORTUGAL
    †RDP INTERNATIONAL, Lisbon — Irr • W • E Africa & S Africa • 300 kW
    RUSSIA
    VOICE OF RUSSIA, Via Vatican State — S • E North Am • 250 kW
    SOUTH AFRICA
    †CHANNEL AFRICA, Meyerton — W • S Africa • 100 kW / S Africa • 100 kW

    UNITED KINGDOM
    †BBC, Via Thailand — S • W Asia • 250 kW
    USA
    ADVENTIST WORLD R, Via Agat, Guam — W • E Asia • 100 kW
    VOA, Via Briech, Morocco — S • S Europe • 250 kW
    VOA, Via Philippines — S • E Asia • 250 kW
    †VOA, Via Tinian, N Marianas — W • E Asia • 500 kW / S • E Asia • 500 kW

    VOA, Via Udon Thani, Thailand — W • E Asia • 250 kW
11830 **BRAZIL**
    RADIO ANHANGUERA, Goiânia — DS • 10 kW • ➡ / Irr • DS • 10 kW • ➡

    EGYPT
    †RADIO CAIRO, Abu Za'bal — S • W Africa • 500 kW
    INDIA
    ALL INDIA RADIO, Delhi — DS • 50/100 kW / ENGLISH, ETC • DS • 50/100 kW

    ITALY
    †RAI INTERNATIONAL, Rome — S • E Europe • 100 kW
    ROMANIA
    R ROMANIA INTL, Bucharest — S • W Europe • 250 kW
    †R ROMANIA INTL, Galbeni — S • W Europe • 250 kW
    RADIO ROMANIA, Galbeni — S Su • W Europe • 250 kW
    RUSSIA
    VOICE OF RUSSIA, Kaliningrad — S • Mideast • 160 kW
    USA
    †FAMILY RADIO, Okeechobee, Fl — W • S America • 100 kW / N America • 100 kW / W • N America • 100 kW / S • N America • 100 kW

    R FREE ASIA, Via Iranawila, Sri Lanka — W • SE Asia • 250 kW
    VOA, Via Philippines — S • E Asia • 250 kW
    VATICAN STATE
    VATICAN RADIO, Sta Maria di Galeria — S • E Asia • 500 kW
11835 **CANADA**
    R CANADA INTL, Via Vienna, Austria — S • Mideast • 100 kW
    CHINA
    CENTRAL PEOPLE'S BS, Xi'an — S • DS-2 • 150 kW / DS-2 • 150 kW / Th-Tu • DS-2 • 150 kW

    †CHINA R INTL, Kunming — S • Mideast & N Africa • 500 kW
    NETHERLANDS
    R NEDERLAND, Via Madagascar — S • S Asia • 250 kW
    SERBIA AND MONTENEGRO
    †INTL RADIO OF S & M, Via Bosnia — W • Australasia • TEMP INACTIVE • 250 kW / ➡ • Mideast • TEMP INACTIVE • 250 kW • ALT. FREQ. TO 11800 kHz

    TURKEY
    VOICE OF TURKEY, Ankara-Çakirlar — W • W Asia • 250 kW
    UNITED KINGDOM
    †BBC, Via Singapore — W • SE Asia • 250 kW / S Asia • 250 kW

(con'd)

World Time 0 1 2 3 4 5 6 7 8 9 10 11 12 13 14 15 16 17 18 19 20 21 22 23 24

ENGLISH ▬   ARABIC ▨   CHINESE ▯▯▯   FRENCH ▬   GERMAN ▬   RUSSIAN ═   SPANISH ▬   OTHER ▬

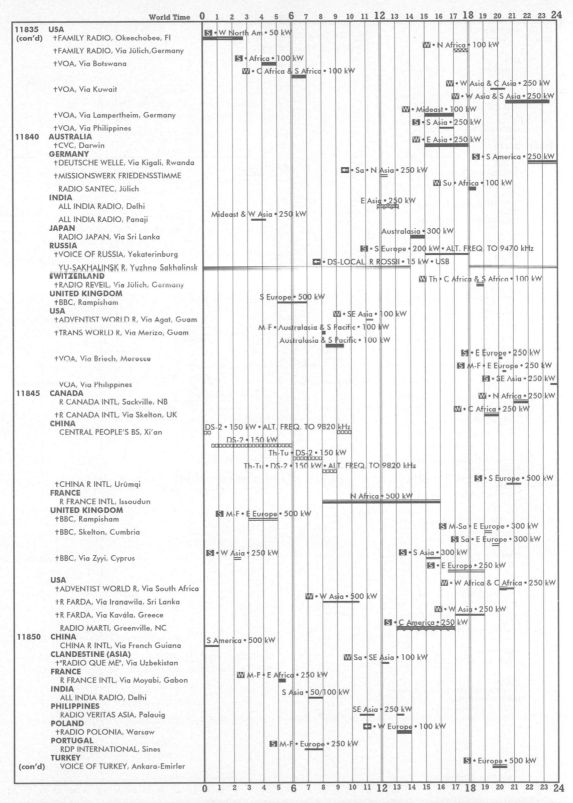

World Time 0 1 2 3 4 5 6 7 8 9 10 11 12 13 14 15 16 17 18 19 20 21 22 23 24

11835 USA
(con'd) †FAMILY RADIO, Okeechobee, Fl — S • W North Am • 50 kW
†FAMILY RADIO, Via Jülich, Germany — W • N Africa • 100 kW
†VOA, Via Botswana — S • Africa • 100 kW / W • C Africa & S Africa • 100 kW
†VOA, Via Kuwait — W • W Asia & C Asia • 250 kW / W • W Asia & S Asia • 250 kW
†VOA, Via Lampertheim, Germany — W • Mideast • 100 kW
†VOA, Via Philippines — S • S Asia • 250 kW

11840 AUSTRALIA
†CVC, Darwin — W • E Asia • 250 kW
GERMANY
†DEUTSCHE WELLE, Via Kigali, Rwanda — S • S America • 250 kW / Sa • N Asia • 250 kW
†MISSIONSWERK FRIEDENSSTIMME — W Su • Africa • 100 kW
RADIO SANTEC, Jülich — E Asia • 250 kW
INDIA
ALL INDIA RADIO, Delhi
ALL INDIA RADIO, Panaji — Mideast & W Asia • 250 kW
JAPAN
RADIO JAPAN, Via Sri Lanka — Australasia • 300 kW
RUSSIA
†VOICE OF RUSSIA, Yekaterinburg — S • S Europe • 200 kW • ALT. FREQ. TO 9470 kHz
YU-SAKHALINSK R, Yuzhno Sakhalinsk — DS-LOCAL R ROSSII • 15 kW • USB
SWITZERLAND
†RADIO REVEIL, Via Jülich, Germany — W Th • C Africa & S Africa • 100 kW
UNITED KINGDOM
†BBC, Rampisham — S Europe • 500 kW
USA
†ADVENTIST WORLD R, Via Agat, Guam — W • SE Asia • 100 kW
†TRANS WORLD R, Via Merizo, Guam — M-F • Australasia & S Pacific • 100 kW / Australasia & S Pacific • 100 kW
†VOA, Via Briech, Morocco — S • E Europe • 250 kW / S M-F • E Europe • 250 kW / S • SE Asia • 250 kW
VOA, Via Philippines

11845 CANADA
R CANADA INTL, Sackville, NB — W • N Africa • 250 kW
†R CANADA INTL, Via Skelton, UK — W • C Africa • 250 kW
CHINA
CENTRAL PEOPLE'S BS, Xi'an — DS-2 • 150 kW • ALT. FREQ. TO 9820 kHz / DS-2 • 150 kW / Th-Tu • DS-2 • 150 kW / Th-Tu • DS-2 • 150 kW • ALT. FREQ. TO 9820 kHz
†CHINA R INTL, Urümqi — S • S Europe • 500 kW
FRANCE
R FRANCE INTL, Issoudun — N Africa • 500 kW
UNITED KINGDOM
†BBC, Rampisham — S M-F • E Europe • 500 kW
†BBC, Skelton, Cumbria — S M-Sa • E Europe • 300 kW / S Sa • E Europe • 300 kW
†BBC, Via Zyyi, Cyprus — S • W Asia • 250 kW / S • S Asia • 300 kW / S • E Europe • 250 kW
USA
†ADVENTIST WORLD R, Via South Africa — W • W Africa & C Africa • 250 kW
†R FARDA, Via Iranawila, Sri Lanka — W • W Asia • 500 kW
†R FARDA, Via Kavála, Greece — W • W Asia • 250 kW
RADIO MARTI, Greenville, NC — S • C America • 250 kW

11850 CHINA
CHINA R INTL, Via French Guiana — S America • 500 kW
CLANDESTINE (ASIA)
†"RADIO QUE ME", Via Uzbekistan — W Sa • SE Asia • 100 kW
FRANCE
R FRANCE INTL, Via Moyabi, Gabon — W M-F • E Africa • 250 kW
INDIA
ALL INDIA RADIO, Delhi — S Asia • 50/100 kW
PHILIPPINES
RADIO VERITAS ASIA, Palauig — SE Asia • 250 kW
POLAND
†RADIO POLONIA, Warsaw — W Europe • 100 kW
PORTUGAL
RDP INTERNATIONAL, Sines — S M-F • Europe • 250 kW
TURKEY
(con'd) VOICE OF TURKEY, Ankara-Emirler — S • Europe • 500 kW

0 1 2 3 4 5 6 7 8 9 10 11 12 13 14 15 16 17 18 19 20 21 22 23 24

SEASONAL S OR W   1-HR TIMESHIFT MIDYEAR ⇐ OR ⇒   JAMMING / OR ∧   EARLIEST HEARD ◁   LATEST HEARD ▷   NEW FOR 2006 †

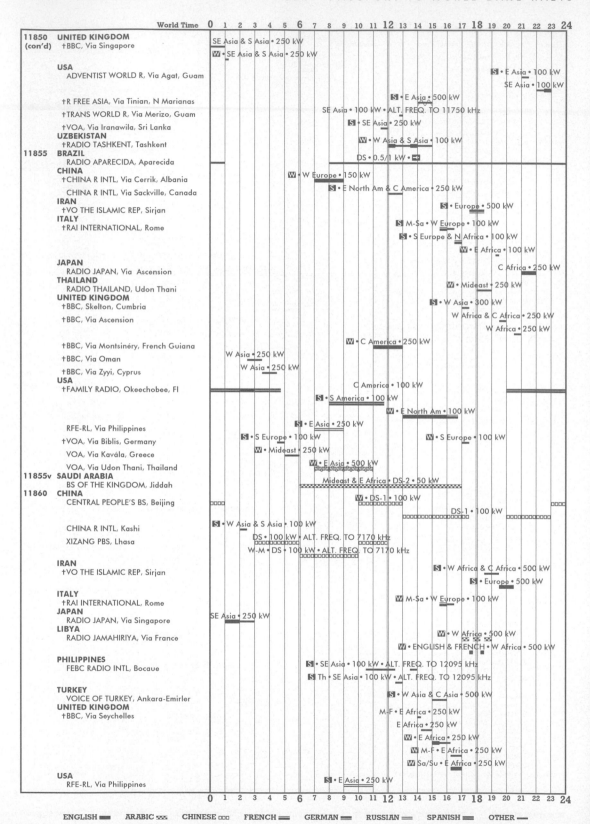

| | | | World Time | 0 | 1 | 2 | 3 | 4 | 5 | 6 | 7 | 8 | 9 | 10 | 11 | 12 | 13 | 14 | 15 | 16 | 17 | 18 | 19 | 20 | 21 | 22 | 23 | 24 |

11850 UNITED KINGDOM
(con'd) †BBC, Via Singapore — SE Asia & S Asia • 250 kW / W • SE Asia & S Asia • 250 kW

USA
ADVENTIST WORLD R, Via Agat, Guam — S • E Asia • 100 kW / SE Asia • 100 kW

†R FREE ASIA, Via Tinian, N Marianas — S • E Asia • 500 kW

†TRANS WORLD R, Via Merizo, Guam — SE Asia • 100 kW • ALT. FREQ. TO 11750 kHz

†VOA, Via Iranawila, Sri Lanka — S • SE Asia • 250 kW

UZBEKISTAN
†RADIO TASHKENT, Tashkent — W • W Asia & S Asia • 100 kW

11855 BRAZIL
RADIO APARECIDA, Aparecida — DS • 0.5/1 kW • S

CHINA
†CHINA R INTL, Via Cerrik, Albania — W • W Europe • 150 kW

CHINA R INTL, Via Sackville, Canada — S • E North Am & C America • 250 kW

IRAN
†VO THE ISLAMIC REP, Sirjan — S • Europe • 500 kW

ITALY
†RAI INTERNATIONAL, Rome — S M-Sa • W Europe • 100 kW / S • S Europe & N Africa • 100 kW / W • E Africa • 100 kW

JAPAN
RADIO JAPAN, Via Ascension — C Africa • 250 kW

THAILAND
RADIO THAILAND, Udon Thani — W • Mideast • 250 kW

UNITED KINGDOM
†BBC, Skelton, Cumbria — S • W Asia • 300 kW

†BBC, Via Ascension — W Africa & C Africa • 250 kW / W Africa • 250 kW

†BBC, Via Montsinéry, French Guiana — W • C America • 250 kW

†BBC, Via Oman — W Asia • 250 kW

†BBC, Via Zyyi, Cyprus — W Asia • 250 kW

USA
†FAMILY RADIO, Okeechobee, Fl — C America • 100 kW

S • S America • 100 kW

W • E North Am • 100 kW

RFE-RL, Via Philippines — S • E Asia • 250 kW

†VOA, Via Biblis, Germany — S • S Europe • 100 kW / W • S Europe • 100 kW

VOA, Via Kavála, Greece — W • Mideast • 250 kW

VOA, Via Udon Thani, Thailand — W • E Asia • 500 kW

11855v SAUDI ARABIA
BS OF THE KINGDOM, Jiddah — Mideast & E Africa • DS-2 • 50 kW

11860 CHINA
CENTRAL PEOPLE'S BS, Beijing — W • DS-1 • 100 kW / DS-1 • 100 kW

CHINA R INTL, Kashi — S • W Asia & S Asia • 100 kW

XIZANG PBS, Lhasa — DS • 100 kW • ALT. FREQ. TO 7170 kHz / W-M • DS • 100 kW • ALT. FREQ. TO 7170 kHz

IRAN
†VO THE ISLAMIC REP, Sirjan — S • W Africa & C Africa • 500 kW / S • Europe • 500 kW

ITALY
†RAI INTERNATIONAL, Rome — W M-Sa • W Europe • 100 kW

JAPAN
RADIO JAPAN, Via Singapore — SE Asia • 250 kW

LIBYA
RADIO JAMAHIRIYA, Via France — W • W Africa • 500 kW / W • ENGLISH & FRENCH • W Africa • 500 kW

PHILIPPINES
FEBC RADIO INTL, Bocaue — S • SE Asia • 100 kW • ALT. FREQ. TO 12095 kHz / S Th • SE Asia • 100 kW • ALT. FREQ. TO 12095 kHz

TURKEY
VOICE OF TURKEY, Ankara-Emirler — S • W Asia & C Asia • 500 kW

UNITED KINGDOM
†BBC, Via Seychelles — M-F • E Africa • 250 kW / E Africa • 250 kW / W • E Africa • 250 kW / W M-F • E Africa • 250 kW / W Sa/Su • E Africa • 250 kW

USA
RFE-RL, Via Philippines — S • E Asia • 250 kW

| | | | | 0 | 1 | 2 | 3 | 4 | 5 | 6 | 7 | 8 | 9 | 10 | 11 | 12 | 13 | 14 | 15 | 16 | 17 | 18 | 19 | 20 | 21 | 22 | 23 | 24 |

ENGLISH ▬▬   ARABIC ⬚⬚⬚   CHINESE ▫▫▫   FRENCH ▬▬   GERMAN ▬▬   RUSSIAN ══   SPANISH ▬▬   OTHER ▬

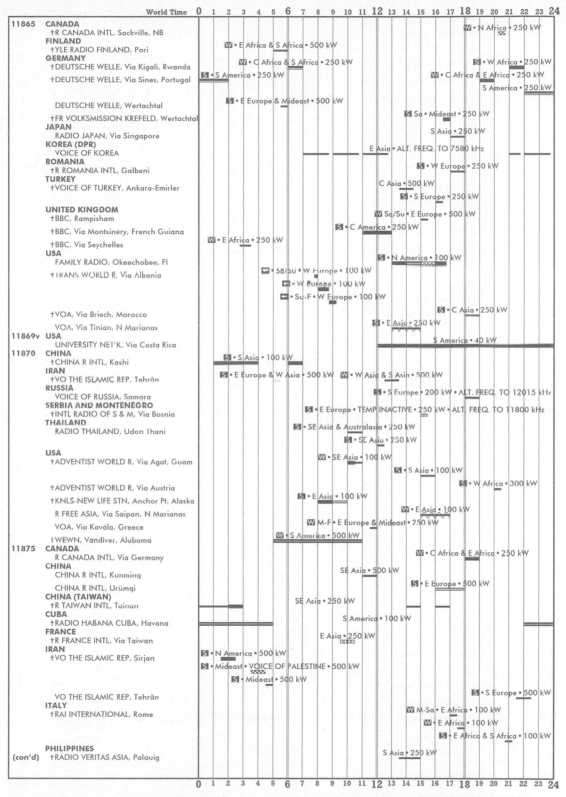

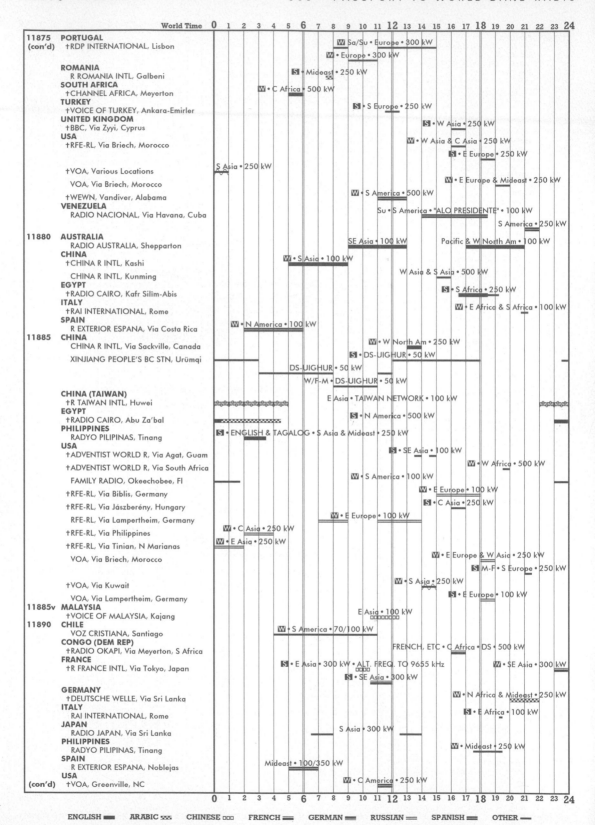

World Time 0 1 2 3 4 5 6 7 8 9 10 11 12 13 14 15 16 17 18 19 20 21 22 23 24

11875 PORTUGAL
(con'd) †RDP INTERNATIONAL, Lisbon   W • Sa/Su • Europe • 300 kW
                                              W • Europe • 300 kW

       ROMANIA
       R ROMANIA INTL, Galbeni   S • Mideast • 250 kW
       SOUTH AFRICA
       †CHANNEL AFRICA, Meyerton   W • C Africa • 500 kW
       TURKEY
       †VOICE OF TURKEY, Ankara-Emirler   S • S Europe • 250 kW
       UNITED KINGDOM
       †BBC, Via Zyyi, Cyprus   S • W Asia • 250 kW
       USA
       †RFE-RL, Via Briech, Morocco   W • W Asia & C Asia • 250 kW
                                             S • E Europe • 250 kW

       †VOA, Various Locations   S Asia • 250 kW
       VOA, Via Briech, Morocco   W • E Europe & Mideast • 250 kW

       †WEWN, Vandiver, Alabama   W • S America • 500 kW
       VENEZUELA
       RADIO NACIONAL, Via Havana, Cuba   Su • S America • "ALO PRESIDENTE" • 100 kW
                                                                    S America • 250 kW

11880 AUSTRALIA
       RADIO AUSTRALIA, Shepparton   SE Asia • 100 kW   Pacific & W North Am • 100 kW
       CHINA
       †CHINA R INTL, Kashi   W • S Asia • 100 kW

       CHINA R INTL, Kunming   W Asia & S Asia • 500 kW
       EGYPT
       †RADIO CAIRO, Kafr Silim-Abis   S • S Africa • 250 kW
       ITALY
       †RAI INTERNATIONAL, Rome   W • E Africa & S Africa • 100 kW
       SPAIN
       R EXTERIOR ESPANA, Via Costa Rica   W • N America • 100 kW
11885 CHINA
       CHINA R INTL, Via Sackville, Canada   W • W North Am • 250 kW
       XINJIANG PEOPLE'S BC STN, Urümqi   S • DS-UIGHUR • 50 kW

                                             DS-UIGHUR • 50 kW

                                             W/F-M • DS-UIGHUR • 50 kW

       CHINA (TAIWAN)
       †R TAIWAN INTL, Huwei   E Asia • TAIWAN NETWORK • 100 kW
       EGYPT
       †RADIO CAIRO, Abu Za'bal   S • N America • 500 kW
       PHILIPPINES
       RADYO PILIPINAS, Tinang   S • ENGLISH & TAGALOG • S Asia & Mideast • 250 kW
       USA
       †ADVENTIST WORLD R, Via Agat, Guam   S • SE Asia • 100 kW

       †ADVENTIST WORLD R, Via South Africa W • W Africa • 500 kW

       FAMILY RADIO, Okeechobee, Fl   W • S America • 100 kW

       †RFE-RL, Via Biblis, Germany   W • E Europe • 100 kW

       †RFE-RL, Via Jászberény, Hungary   S • C Asia • 250 kW

       RFE-RL, Via Lampertheim, Germany   W • E Europe • 100 kW

       †RFE-RL, Via Philippines   W • C Asia • 250 kW

       †RFE-RL, Via Tinian, N Marianas   W • E Asia • 250 kW

       VOA, Via Briech, Morocco   W • E Europe & W Asia • 250 kW
                                             S M-F • S Europe • 250 kW

       †VOA, Via Kuwait   W • S Asia • 250 kW

       VOA, Via Lampertheim, Germany   S • E Europe • 100 kW
11885v MALAYSIA
       †VOICE OF MALAYSIA, Kajang   E Asia • 100 kW
11890 CHILE
       VOZ CRISTIANA, Santiago   W • S America • 70/100 kW
       CONGO (DEM REP)
       †RADIO OKAPI, Via Meyerton, S Africa FRENCH, ETC • C Africa • DS • 500 kW
       FRANCE
       †R FRANCE INTL, Via Tokyo, Japan   S • E Asia • 300 kW • ALT. FREQ. TO 9655 kHz   W • SE Asia • 300 kW

                                             S • SE Asia • 300 kW

       GERMANY
       †DEUTSCHE WELLE, Via Sri Lanka   W • N Africa & Mideast • 250 kW
       ITALY
       RAI INTERNATIONAL, Rome   S • E Africa • 100 kW
       JAPAN
       RADIO JAPAN, Via Sri Lanka   S Asia • 300 kW
       PHILIPPINES
       RADYO PILIPINAS, Tinang   W • Mideast • 250 kW
       SPAIN
       R EXTERIOR ESPANA, Noblejas   Mideast • 100/350 kW
(con'd) †VOA, Greenville, NC   W • C America • 250 kW

World Time 0 1 2 3 4 5 6 7 8 9 10 11 12 13 14 15 16 17 18 19 20 21 22 23 24

ENGLISH ▬   ARABIC ▨   CHINESE ▭▭▭   FRENCH ▬▬   GERMAN ▬   RUSSIAN ═══   SPANISH ══   OTHER ▬

World Time 0 1 2 3 4 5 6 7 8 9 10 11 12 13 14 15 16 17 18 19 20 21 22 23 24

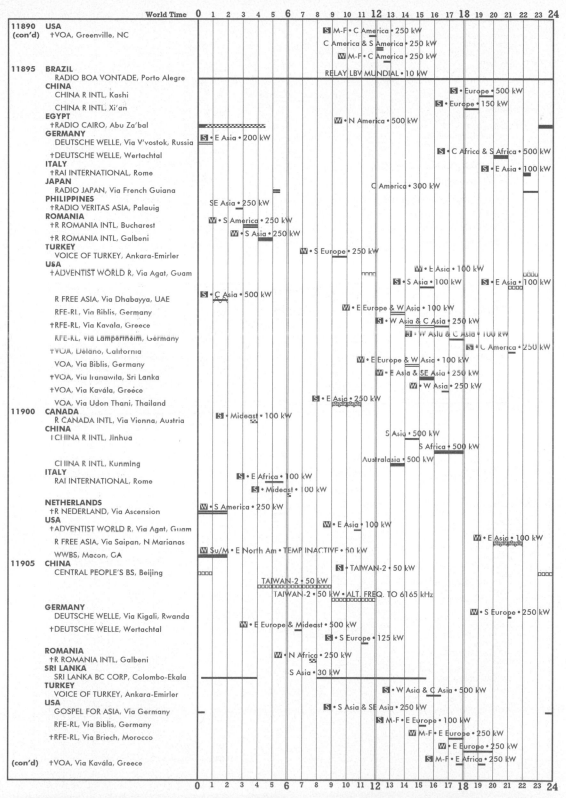

11890	USA	
(con'd)	†VOA, Greenville, NC	S • M-F • C America • 250 kW
		C America & S America • 250 kW
		W • M-F • C America • 250 kW
11895	BRAZIL	
	RADIO BOA VONTADE, Porto Alegre	RELAY LBV MUNDIAL • 10 kW
	CHINA	
	CHINA R INTL, Kashi	S • Europe • 500 kW
	CHINA R INTL, Xi'an	S • Europe • 150 kW
	EGYPT	
	†RADIO CAIRO, Abu Za'bal	W • N America • 500 kW
	GERMANY	
	DEUTSCHE WELLE, Via V'vostok, Russia	S • E Asia • 200 kW
	†DEUTSCHE WELLE, Wertachtal	S • C Africa & S Africa • 500 kW
	ITALY	
	†RAI INTERNATIONAL, Rome	S • E Asia • 100 kW
	JAPAN	
	RADIO JAPAN, Via French Guiana	C America • 300 kW
	PHILIPPINES	
	†RADIO VERITAS ASIA, Palauig	SE Asia • 250 kW
	ROMANIA	
	†R ROMANIA INTL, Bucharest	W • S America • 250 kW
	†R ROMANIA INTL, Galbeni	W • S Asia • 250 kW
	TURKEY	
	VOICE OF TURKEY, Ankara-Emirler	W • S Europe • 250 kW
	USA	
	†ADVENTIST WORLD R, Via Agat, Guam	W • E Asia • 100 kW
		S • S Asia • 100 kW	S • E Asia • 100 kW
	R FREE ASIA, Via Dhabayya, UAE	S • C Asia • 500 kW
	RFE-RL, Via Biblis, Germany	W • E Europe & W Asia • 100 kW
	†RFE-RL, Via Kavala, Greece	S • W Asia & C Asia • 250 kW
	RFE-RL, Via Lampertheim, Germany	S • W Asia & C Asia • 100 kW
	†VOA, Delano, California	S • C America • 250 kW
	VOA, Via Biblis, Germany	W • E Europe & W Asia • 100 kW
	†VOA, Via Iranawila, Sri Lanka	W • E Asia & SE Asia • 250 kW
	†VOA, Via Kavála, Greece	W • W Asia • 250 kW
	VOA, Via Udon Thani, Thailand	S • E Asia • 250 kW
11900	CANADA	
	R CANADA INTL, Via Vienna, Austria	S • Mideast • 100 kW
	CHINA	
	†CHINA R INTL, Jinhua	S Asia • 500 kW
		S Africa • 500 kW
	CHINA R INTL, Kunming	Australasia • 500 kW
	ITALY	
	RAI INTERNATIONAL, Rome	S • E Africa • 100 kW
		S • Mideast • 100 kW
	NETHERLANDS	
	†R NEDERLAND, Via Ascension	W • S America • 250 kW
	USA	
	†ADVENTIST WORLD R, Via Agat, Guam	W • E Asia • 100 kW
	R FREE ASIA, Via Saipan, N Marianas	W • E Asia • 100 kW
	WWBS, Macon, GA	W • Su/M • E North Am • TEMP INACTIVE • 50 kW
11905	CHINA	
	CENTRAL PEOPLE'S BS, Beijing	S • TAIWAN-2 • 50 kW
		TAIWAN-2 • 50 kW
		TAIWAN-2 • 50 kW • ALT. FREQ. TO 6165 kHz
	GERMANY	
	DEUTSCHE WELLE, Via Kigali, Rwanda	W • S Europe • 250 kW
	†DEUTSCHE WELLE, Wertachtal	W • E Europe & Mideast • 500 kW
		S • S Europe • 125 kW
	ROMANIA	
	†R ROMANIA INTL, Galbeni	W • N Africa • 250 kW
	SRI LANKA	
	SRI LANKA BC CORP, Colombo-Ekala	S Asia • 30 kW
	TURKEY	
	VOICE OF TURKEY, Ankara-Emirler	S • W Asia & C Asia • 500 kW
	USA	
	GOSPEL FOR ASIA, Via Germany	S • S Asia & SE Asia • 250 kW
	RFE-RL, Via Biblis, Germany	S • M-F • E Europe • 100 kW
	†RFE-RL, Via Briech, Morocco	W • M-F • E Europe • 250 kW
		W • E Europe • 250 kW
(con'd)	†VOA, Via Kavála, Greece	S • M-F • E Africa • 250 kW

0 1 2 3 4 5 6 7 8 9 10 11 12 13 14 15 16 17 18 19 20 21 22 23 24

SEASONAL S OR W 1-HR TIMESHIFT MIDYEAR ⇆ OR ⇄ JAMMING / OR ∧ EARLIEST HEARD ◁ LATEST HEARD ▷ NEW FOR 2006 †

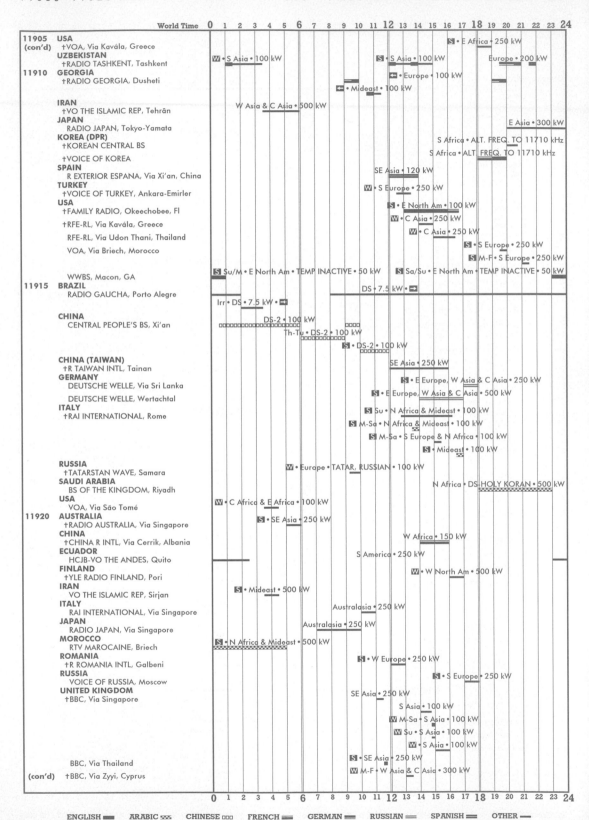

		World Time
11905 (con'd)	USA †VOA, Via Kavála, Greece	
	UZBEKISTAN †RADIO TASHKENT, Tashkent	
11910	GEORGIA †RADIO GEORGIA, Dusheti	
	IRAN †VO THE ISLAMIC REP, Tehrān	
	JAPAN RADIO JAPAN, Tokyo-Yamata	
	KOREA (DPR) †KOREAN CENTRAL BS	
	†VOICE OF KOREA	
	SPAIN R EXTERIOR ESPANA, Via Xi'an, China	
	TURKEY †VOICE OF TURKEY, Ankara-Emirler	
	USA †FAMILY RADIO, Okeechobee, Fl	
	†RFE-RL, Via Kavála, Greece	
	RFE-RL, Via Udon Thani, Thailand	
	VOA, Via Briech, Morocco	
	WWBS, Macon, GA	
11915	BRAZIL RADIO GAUCHA, Porto Alegre	
	CHINA CENTRAL PEOPLE'S BS, Xi'an	
	CHINA (TAIWAN) †R TAIWAN INTL, Tainan	
	GERMANY DEUTSCHE WELLE, Via Sri Lanka	
	DEUTSCHE WELLE, Wertachtal	
	ITALY †RAI INTERNATIONAL, Rome	
	RUSSIA †TATARSTAN WAVE, Samara	
	SAUDI ARABIA BS OF THE KINGDOM, Riyadh	
	USA VOA, Via São Tomé	
11920	AUSTRALIA †RADIO AUSTRALIA, Via Singapore	
	CHINA †CHINA R INTL, Via Cerrik, Albania	
	ECUADOR HCJB-VO THE ANDES, Quito	
	FINLAND †YLE RADIO FINLAND, Pori	
	IRAN VO THE ISLAMIC REP, Sirjan	
	ITALY RAI INTERNATIONAL, Via Singapore	
	JAPAN RADIO JAPAN, Via Singapore	
	MOROCCO RTV MAROCAINE, Briech	
	ROMANIA †R ROMANIA INTL, Galbeni	
	RUSSIA VOICE OF RUSSIA, Moscow	
	UNITED KINGDOM †BBC, Via Singapore	
	BBC, Via Thailand	
(con'd)	†BBC, Via Zyyi, Cyprus	

ENGLISH ▬ ARABIC ░ CHINESE ▫▫▫ FRENCH ═ GERMAN ▬ RUSSIAN ═ SPANISH ═ OTHER ▬

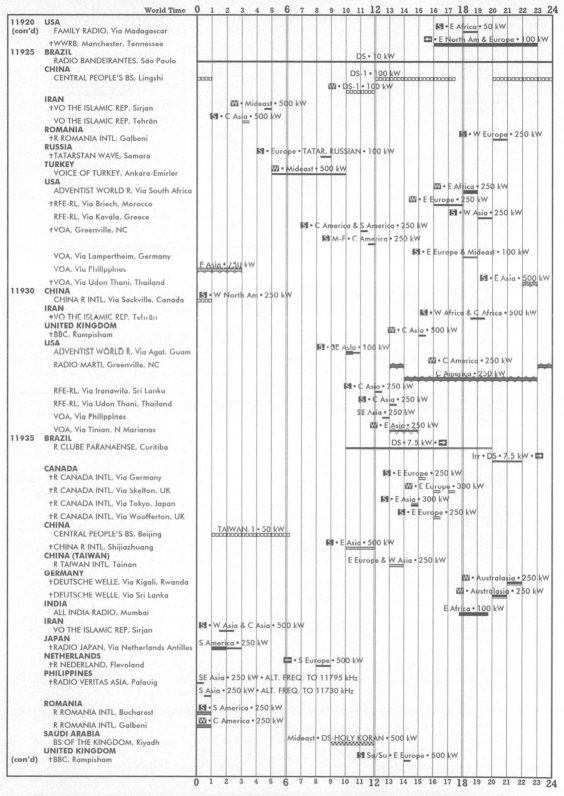

World Time | 0 1 2 3 4 5 6 7 8 9 10 11 12 13 14 15 16 17 18 19 20 21 22 23 24

11920 USA
(con'd) FAMILY RADIO, Via Madagascar — S • E Africa • 50 kW
†WWRB, Manchester, Tennessee — E North Am & Europe • 100 kW
11925 BRAZIL
RADIO BANDEIRANTES, São Paulo — DS • 10 kW
CHINA
CENTRAL PEOPLE'S BS, Lingshi — DS-1 • 100 kW / W • DS-1 • 100 kW
IRAN
†VO THE ISLAMIC REP, Sirjan — W • Mideast • 500 kW
VO THE ISLAMIC REP, Tehrān — S • C Asia • 500 kW
ROMANIA
†R ROMANIA INTL, Galbeni — S • W Europe • 250 kW
RUSSIA
†TATARSTAN WAVE, Samara — S • Europe • TATAR, RUSSIAN • 100 kW
TURKEY
VOICE OF TURKEY, Ankara-Emirler — W • Mideast • 500 kW
USA
ADVENTIST WORLD R, Via South Africa — W • E Africa • 250 kW
†RFE-RL, Via Briech, Morocco — W • E Europe • 250 kW
RFE-RL, Via Kavála, Greece — S • W Asia • 250 kW
†VOA, Greenville, NC — S • C America & S America • 250 kW
— S M-F • C America • 250 kW
VOA, Via Lampertheim, Germany — S • E Europe & Mideast • 100 kW
VOA, Via Philippines — E Asia • 250 kW
†VOA, Via Udon Thani, Thailand — S • E Asia • 500 kW
11930 CHINA
CHINA R INTL, Via Sackville, Canada — S • W North Am • 250 kW
IRAN
†VO THE ISLAMIC REP, Tehrān — S • W Africa & C Africa • 500 kW
UNITED KINGDOM
†BBC, Rampisham — W • C Asia • 500 kW
USA
ADVENTIST WORLD R, Via Agat, Guam — W • SE Asia • 100 kW
RADIO MARTI, Greenville, NC — W • C America • 250 kW
— C America • 250 kW
RFE-RL, Via Iranawila, Sri Lanka — S • C Asia • 250 kW
RFE-RL, Via Udon Thani, Thailand — S • C Asia • 250 kW
VOA, Via Philippines — SE Asia • 250 kW
VOA, Via Tinian, N Marianas — W • E Asia • 250 kW
11935 BRAZIL
R CLUBE PARANAENSE, Curitiba — DS • 7.5 kW •
— Irr • DS • 7.5 kW •
CANADA
†R CANADA INTL, Via Germany — S • E Europe • 250 kW
†R CANADA INTL, Via Skelton, UK — W • E Europe • 300 kW
†R CANADA INTL, Via Tokyo, Japan — S • E Asia • 300 kW
†R CANADA INTL, Via Woofferton, UK — S • E Europe • 250 kW
CHINA
CENTRAL PEOPLE'S BS, Beijing — TAIWAN-1 • 50 kW
†CHINA R INTL, Shijiazhuang — S • E Asia • 500 kW
CHINA (TAIWAN)
R TAIWAN INTL, Tainan — E Europe & W Asia • 250 kW
GERMANY
†DEUTSCHE WELLE, Via Kigali, Rwanda — W • Australasia • 250 kW
†DEUTSCHE WELLE, Via Sri Lanka — W • Australasia • 250 kW
INDIA
ALL INDIA RADIO, Mumbai — E Africa • 100 kW
IRAN
VO THE ISLAMIC REP, Sirjan — S • W Asia & C Asia • 500 kW
JAPAN
†RADIO JAPAN, Via Netherlands Antilles — S America • 250 kW
NETHERLANDS
†R NEDERLAND, Flevoland — S Europe • 500 kW
PHILIPPINES
†RADIO VERITAS ASIA, Palauig — SE Asia • 250 kW • ALT. FREQ. TO 11795 kHz
— S Asia • 250 kW • ALT. FREQ. TO 11730 kHz
ROMANIA
R ROMANIA INTL, Bucharest — S • S America • 250 kW
R ROMANIA INTL, Galbeni — W • C America • 250 kW
SAUDI ARABIA
BS OF THE KINGDOM, Riyadh — Mideast • DS-HOLY KORAN • 500 kW
UNITED KINGDOM
(con'd) †BBC, Rampisham — S Sa/Su • E Europe • 500 kW

0 1 2 3 4 5 6 7 8 9 10 11 12 13 14 15 16 17 18 19 20 21 22 23 24

SEASONAL S OR W   1-HR TIMESHIFT MIDYEAR ⮂ OR ⮀   JAMMING / OR ∧   EARLIEST HEARD ◁   LATEST HEARD ▷   NEW FOR 2006 †

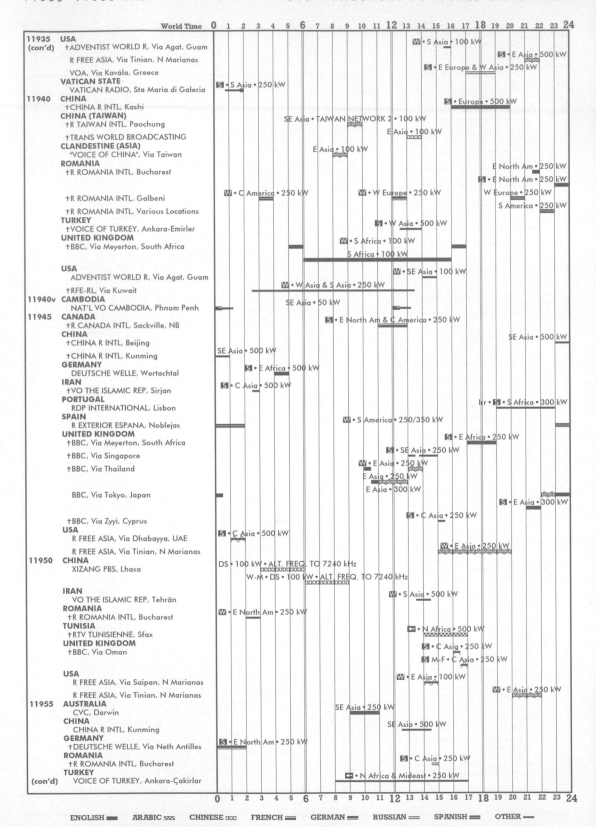

11935 (con'd)	**USA**
	†ADVENTIST WORLD R, Via Agat, Guam — W • S Asia • 100 kW
	R FREE ASIA, Via Tinian, N Marianas — S • E Asia • 500 kW
	VOA, Via Kavála, Greece — S • E Europe & W Asia • 250 kW
	VATICAN STATE
	VATICAN RADIO, Sta Maria di Galeria — S • S Asia • 250 kW
11940	**CHINA**
	†CHINA R INTL, Kashi — S • Europe • 500 kW
	CHINA (TAIWAN)
	†R TAIWAN INTL, Paochung — SE Asia • TAIWAN NETWORK 2 • 100 kW; E Asia • 100 kW
	†TRANS WORLD BROADCASTING
	CLANDESTINE (ASIA)
	"VOICE OF CHINA", Via Taiwan — E Asia • 100 kW
	ROMANIA
	†R ROMANIA INTL, Bucharest — E North Am • 250 kW; S • E North Am • 250 kW
	†R ROMANIA INTL, Galbeni — W • C America • 250 kW; W • W Europe • 250 kW; W Europe • 250 kW; S America • 250 kW
	†R ROMANIA INTL, Various Locations
	TURKEY
	†VOICE OF TURKEY, Ankara-Emirler — S • W Asia • 500 kW
	UNITED KINGDOM
	†BBC, Via Meyerton, South Africa — W • S Africa • 100 kW; S Africa • 100 kW
	USA
	ADVENTIST WORLD R, Via Agat, Guam — W • SE Asia • 100 kW
	†RFE-RL, Via Kuwait — W • W Asia & S Asia • 250 kW
11940v	**CAMBODIA**
	NAT'L VO CAMBODIA, Phnom Penh — SE Asia • 50 kW
11945	**CANADA**
	†R CANADA INTL, Sackville, NB — S • E North Am & C America • 250 kW
	CHINA
	†CHINA R INTL, Beijing — SE Asia • 500 kW
	†CHINA R INTL, Kunming — SE Asia • 500 kW
	GERMANY
	DEUTSCHE WELLE, Wertachtal — S • E Africa • 500 kW
	IRAN
	†VO THE ISLAMIC REP, Sirjan — S • C Asia • 500 kW
	PORTUGAL
	RDP INTERNATIONAL, Lisbon — Irr • S • S Africa • 300 kW
	SPAIN
	R EXTERIOR ESPANA, Noblejas — W • S America • 250/350 kW
	UNITED KINGDOM
	†BBC, Via Meyerton, South Africa — S • E Africa • 250 kW
	†BBC, Via Singapore — S • SE Asia • 250 kW
	†BBC, Via Thailand — W • E Asia • 250 kW; E Asia • 250 kW; E Asia • 300 kW
	BBC, Via Tokyo, Japan — S • E Asia • 300 kW
	†BBC, Via Zyyi, Cyprus — S • C Asia • 250 kW
	USA
	R FREE ASIA, Via Dhabayya, UAE — S • C Asia • 500 kW
	R FREE ASIA, Via Tinian, N Marianas — W • E Asia • 250 kW
11950	**CHINA**
	XIZANG PBS, Lhasa — DS • 100 kW • ALT. FREQ. TO 7240 kHz; W-M • DS • 100 kW • ALT. FREQ. TO 7240 kHz
	IRAN
	VO THE ISLAMIC REP, Tehrān — W • S Asia • 500 kW
	ROMANIA
	†R ROMANIA INTL, Bucharest — W • E North Am • 250 kW
	TUNISIA
	†RTV TUNISIENNE, Sfax — N Africa • 500 kW
	UNITED KINGDOM
	†BBC, Via Oman — S • C Asia • 250 kW; S M-F • C Asia • 250 kW
	USA
	R FREE ASIA, Via Saipan, N Marianas — W • E Asia • 100 kW
	R FREE ASIA, Via Tinian, N Marianas — W • E Asia • 250 kW
11955	**AUSTRALIA**
	CVC, Darwin — SE Asia • 250 kW
	CHINA
	CHINA R INTL, Kunming — SE Asia • 500 kW
	GERMANY
	†DEUTSCHE WELLE, Via Neth Antilles — S • E North Am • 250 kW
	ROMANIA
	†R ROMANIA INTL, Bucharest — S • C Asia • 250 kW
	TURKEY
(con'd)	VOICE OF TURKEY, Ankara-Çakirlar — N Africa & Mideast • 250 kW

World Time: 0 1 2 3 4 5 6 7 8 9 10 11 12 13 14 15 16 17 18 19 20 21 22 23 24

ENGLISH ▬   ARABIC ≈   CHINESE ▫▫▫   FRENCH ━   GERMAN ▭   RUSSIAN =   SPANISH ▬   OTHER ─

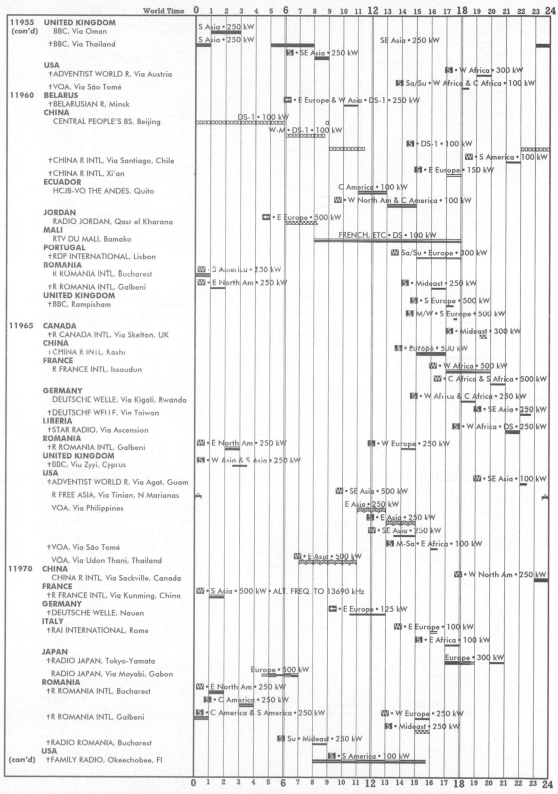

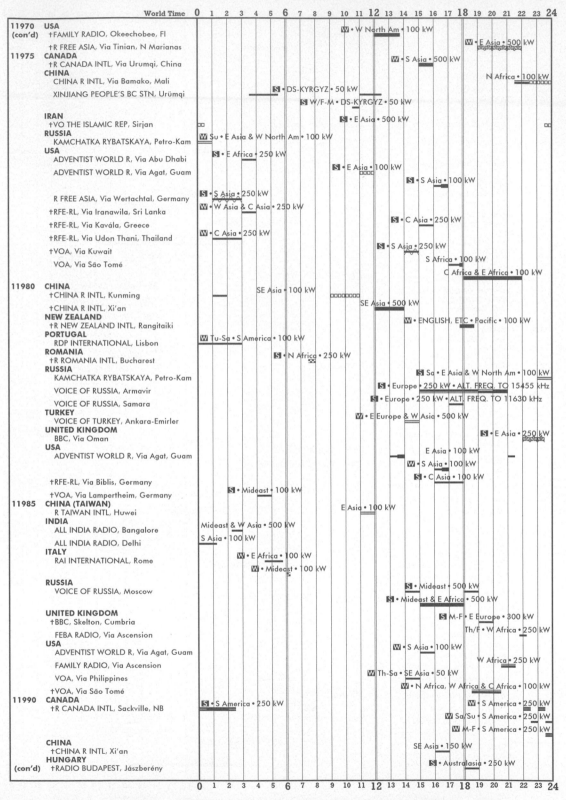

World Time   0 1 2 3 4 5 6 7 8 9 10 11 12 13 14 15 16 17 18 19 20 21 22 23 24

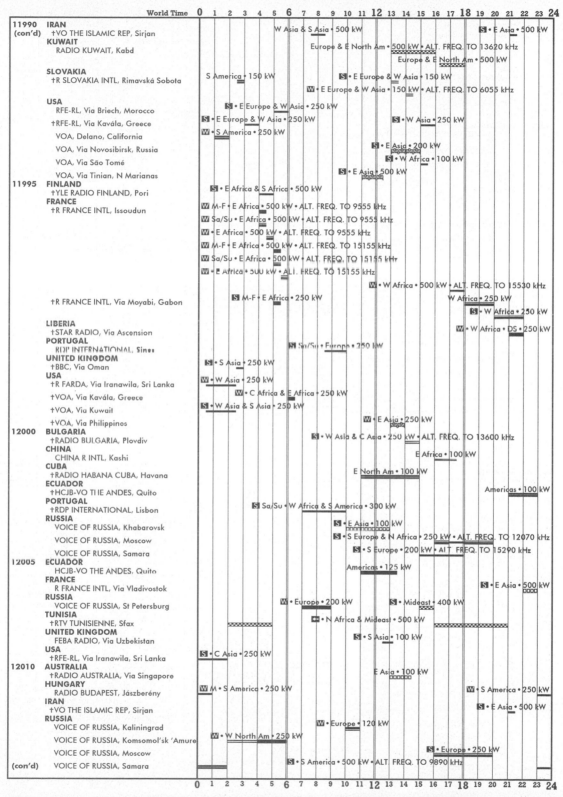

11990	IRAN
(con'd)	†VO THE ISLAMIC REP, Sirjan — W Asia & S Asia • 500 kW — S • E Asia • 500 kW
	KUWAIT
	RADIO KUWAIT, Kabd — Europe & E North Am • 500 kW • ALT. FREQ. TO 13620 kHz — Europe & E North Am • 500 kW
	SLOVAKIA
	†R SLOVAKIA INTL, Rimavská Sobota — S America • 150 kW — S • E Europe & W Asia • 150 kW — W • E Europe & W Asia • 150 kW • ALT. FREQ. TO 6055 kHz
	USA
	RFE-RL, Via Briech, Morocco — S • E Europe & W Asia • 250 kW
	†RFE-RL, Via Kavála, Greece — S • E Europe & W Asia • 250 kW — S • W Asia • 250 kW
	VOA, Delano, California — W • S America • 250 kW
	VOA, Via Novosibirsk, Russia — S • E Asia • 200 kW
	VOA, Via São Tomé — S • W Africa • 100 kW
	VOA, Via Tinian, N Marianas — S • E Asia • 500 kW
11995	FINLAND
	†YLE RADIO FINLAND, Pori — S • E Africa & S Africa • 500 kW
	FRANCE
	†R FRANCE INTL, Issoudun — W M-F • E Africa • 500 kW • ALT. FREQ. TO 9555 kHz
	— W Sa/Su • E Africa • 500 kW • ALT. FREQ. TO 9555 kHz
	— W • E Africa • 500 kW • ALT. FREQ. TO 9555 kHz
	— W M-F • E Africa • 500 kW • ALT. FREQ. TO 15155 kHz
	— W Sa/Su • E Africa • 500 kW • ALT. FREQ. TO 15155 kHz
	— W • E Africa • 500 kW • ALT. FREQ. TO 15155 kHz
	— W • W Africa • 500 kW • ALT. FREQ. TO 15530 kHz
	†R FRANCE INTL, Via Moyabi, Gabon — S M-F • E Africa • 250 kW — W Africa • 250 kW
	— S • W Africa • 250 kW
	— W • W Africa • DS • 250 kW
	LIBERIA
	†STAR RADIO, Via Ascension
	PORTUGAL
	RDP INTERNATIONAL, Sines — W Sa/Su • Europe • 250 kW
	UNITED KINGDOM
	†BBC, Via Oman — S • S Asia • 250 kW
	USA
	†R FARDA, Via Iranawila, Sri Lanka — W • W Asia • 250 kW
	†VOA, Via Kavála, Greece — W • C Africa & E Africa • 250 kW
	†VOA, Via Kuwait — S • W Asia & S Asia • 250 kW
	†VOA, Via Philippines — W • E Asia • 250 kW
12000	BULGARIA
	†RADIO BULGARIA, Plovdiv — S • W Asia & C Asia • 250 kW • ALT. FREQ. TO 13600 kHz
	CHINA
	CHINA R INTL, Kashi — E Africa • 100 kW
	CUBA
	†RADIO HABANA CUBA, Havana — E North Am • 100 kW
	ECUADOR
	†HCJB-VO THE ANDES, Quito — Americas • 100 kW
	PORTUGAL
	†RDP INTERNATIONAL, Lisbon — S Sa/Su • W Africa & S America • 300 kW
	RUSSIA
	VOICE OF RUSSIA, Khabarovsk — S • E Asia • 100 kW
	VOICE OF RUSSIA, Moscow — S • S Europe & N Africa • 250 kW • ALT. FREQ. TO 12070 kHz
	VOICE OF RUSSIA, Samara — S • S Europe • 200 kW • ALT. FREQ. TO 15290 kHz
12005	ECUADOR
	HCJB-VO THE ANDES, Quito — Americas • 125 kW
	FRANCE
	R FRANCE INTL, Via Vladivostok — S • E Asia • 500 kW
	RUSSIA
	VOICE OF RUSSIA, St Petersburg — W • Europe • 200 kW — S • Mideast • 400 kW
	TUNISIA
	†RTV TUNISIENNE, Sfax — N Africa & Mideast • 500 kW
	UNITED KINGDOM
	FEBA RADIO, Via Uzbekistan — S • S Asia • 100 kW
	USA
	†RFE-RL, Via Iranawila, Sri Lanka — S • C Asia • 250 kW
12010	AUSTRALIA
	†RADIO AUSTRALIA, Via Singapore — E Asia • 100 kW
	HUNGARY
	RADIO BUDAPEST, Jászberény — W M • S America • 250 kW — W • S America • 250 kW
	IRAN
	†VO THE ISLAMIC REP, Sirjan — S • E Asia • 500 kW
	RUSSIA
	VOICE OF RUSSIA, Kaliningrad — W • Europe • 120 kW
	VOICE OF RUSSIA, Komsomol'sk 'Amure — W • W North Am • 250 kW
	VOICE OF RUSSIA, Moscow — S • Europe • 250 kW
(con'd)	VOICE OF RUSSIA, Samara — S • S America • 500 kW • ALT. FREQ. TO 9890 kHz

  0 1 2 3 4 5 6 7 8 9 10 11 12 13 14 15 16 17 18 19 20 21 22 23 24

SEASONAL S OR W   1-HR TIMESHIFT MIDYEAR ⇐ OR ⇒   JAMMING / OR ∧   EARLIEST HEARD ◁   LATEST HEARD ▷   NEW FOR 2006 †

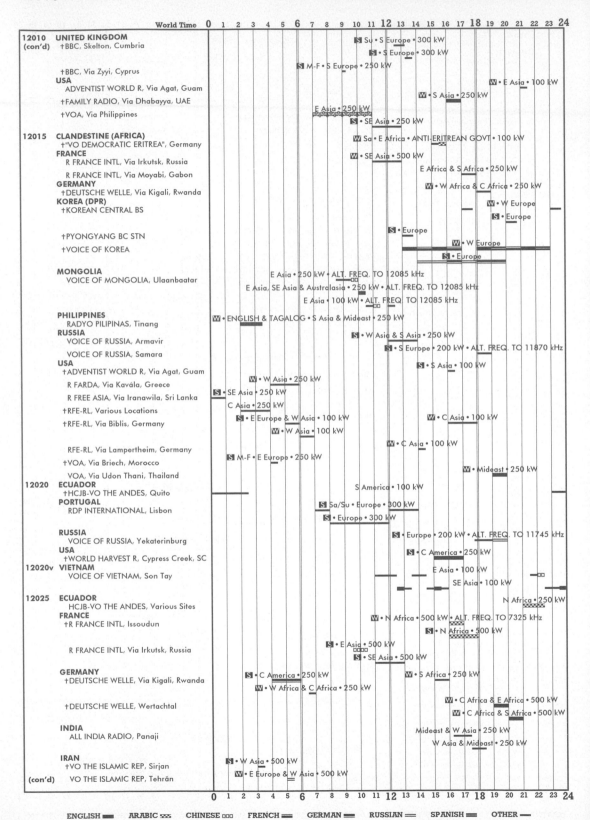

	World Time	0 1 2 3 4 5 6 7 8 9 10 11 12 13 14 15 16 17 18 19 20 21 22 23 24

12010 **UNITED KINGDOM**
(con'd) †BBC, Skelton, Cumbria — S · Su · S Europe · 300 kW; S · S Europe · 300 kW

†BBC, Via Zyyi, Cyprus — S · M-F · S Europe · 250 kW

USA
  ADVENTIST WORLD R, Via Agat, Guam — W · E Asia · 100 kW

†FAMILY RADIO, Via Dhabayya, UAE — W · S Asia · 250 kW

†VOA, Via Philippines — E Asia · 250 kW; S · SE Asia · 250 kW

12015 **CLANDESTINE (AFRICA)**
†"VO DEMOCRATIC ERITREA", Germany — W · Sa · E Africa · ANTI-ERITREAN GOVT · 100 kW

FRANCE
  R FRANCE INTL, Via Irkutsk, Russia — W · SE Asia · 500 kW

  R FRANCE INTL, Via Moyabi, Gabon — E Africa & S Africa · 250 kW

GERMANY
†DEUTSCHE WELLE, Via Kigali, Rwanda — W · W Africa & C Africa · 250 kW

KOREA (DPR)
†KOREAN CENTRAL BS — W · W Europe; S · Europe

†PYONGYANG BC STN — S · Europe

†VOICE OF KOREA — W · W Europe; S · Europe

MONGOLIA
  VOICE OF MONGOLIA, Ulaanbaatar — E Asia · 250 kW · ALT. FREQ. TO 12085 kHz; E Asia, SE Asia & Australasia · 250 kW · ALT. FREQ. TO 12085 kHz; E Asia · 100 kW · ALT. FREQ. TO 12085 kHz

PHILIPPINES
  RADYO PILIPINAS, Tinang — W · ENGLISH & TAGALOG · S Asia & Mideast · 250 kW

RUSSIA
  VOICE OF RUSSIA, Armavir — S · W Asia & S Asia · 250 kW; S · S Europe · 200 kW · ALT. FREQ. TO 11870 kHz

  VOICE OF RUSSIA, Samara — S · S Asia · 100 kW

USA
†ADVENTIST WORLD R, Via Agat, Guam — W · W Asia · 250 kW

  R FARDA, Via Kavála, Greece — S · SE Asia · 250 kW

  R FREE ASIA, Via Iranawila, Sri Lanka — C Asia · 250 kW

†RFE-RL, Various Locations — S · E Europe & W Asia · 100 kW; W · C Asia · 100 kW

†RFE-RL, Via Biblis, Germany — W · W Asia · 100 kW

  RFE-RL, Via Lampertheim, Germany — W · C Asia · 100 kW

†VOA, Via Briech, Morocco — S · M-F · E Europe · 250 kW

  VOA, Via Udon Thani, Thailand — W · Mideast · 250 kW

12020 **ECUADOR**
†HCJB-VO THE ANDES, Quito — S America · 100 kW

PORTUGAL
  RDP INTERNATIONAL, Lisbon — S · Sa/Su · Europe · 300 kW; S · Europe · 300 kW

RUSSIA
  VOICE OF RUSSIA, Yekaterinburg — S · Europe · 200 kW · ALT. FREQ. TO 11745 kHz

USA
†WORLD HARVEST R, Cypress Creek, SC — S · C America · 250 kW

12020v **VIETNAM**
  VOICE OF VIETNAM, Son Tay — E Asia · 100 kW; SE Asia · 100 kW

12025 **ECUADOR**
  HCJB-VO THE ANDES, Various Sites — N Africa · 250 kW

FRANCE
†R FRANCE INTL, Issoudun — W · N Africa · 500 kW · ALT. FREQ. TO 7325 kHz; S · N Africa · 500 kW

  R FRANCE INTL, Via Irkutsk, Russia — S · E Asia · 500 kW; S · SE Asia · 500 kW

GERMANY
†DEUTSCHE WELLE, Via Kigali, Rwanda — S · C America · 250 kW; W · W Africa & C Africa · 250 kW; W · S Africa · 250 kW

†DEUTSCHE WELLE, Wertachtal — W · C Africa & E Africa · 500 kW; W · C Africa & S Africa · 500 kW

INDIA
  ALL INDIA RADIO, Panaji — Mideast & W Asia · 250 kW; W Asia & Mideast · 250 kW

IRAN
†VO THE ISLAMIC REP, Sirjan — S · W Asia · 500 kW

(con'd) VO THE ISLAMIC REP, Tehrän — W · E Europe & W Asia · 500 kW

	0 1 2 3 4 5 6 7 8 9 10 11 12 13 14 15 16 17 18 19 20 21 22 23 24

ENGLISH ▬ ARABIC ▨ CHINESE □□□ FRENCH ▬ GERMAN ▬ RUSSIAN ═ SPANISH ▬ OTHER ▬

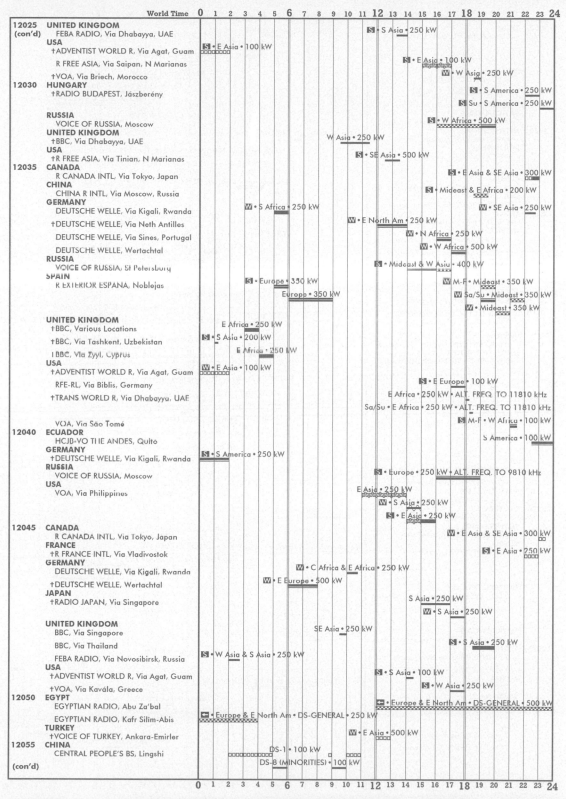

World Time   0 1 2 3 4 5 6 7 8 9 10 11 12 13 14 15 16 17 18 19 20 21 22 23 24

12025 UNITED KINGDOM
(con'd)   FEBA RADIO, Via Dhabayya, UAE — ⓈS Asia • 250 kW
USA
  †ADVENTIST WORLD R, Via Agat, Guam — E Asia • 100 kW
  R FREE ASIA, Via Saipan, N Marianas — Ⓢ • E Asia • 100 kW
  †VOA, Via Briech, Morocco — Ⓦ • W Asia • 250 kW
12030 HUNGARY
  †RADIO BUDAPEST, Jászberény — Ⓢ • S America • 250 kW / ⒮Su • S America • 250 kW
RUSSIA
  VOICE OF RUSSIA, Moscow — Ⓢ • W Africa • 500 kW
UNITED KINGDOM
  †BBC, Via Dhabayya, UAE — W Asia • 250 kW
USA
  †R FREE ASIA, Via Tinian, N Marianas — Ⓢ • SE Asia • 500 kW
12035 CANADA
  R CANADA INTL, Via Tokyo, Japan — Ⓢ • E Asia & SE Asia • 300 kW
CHINA
  CHINA R INTL, Via Moscow, Russia — Ⓢ • Mideast & E Africa • 200 kW
GERMANY
  DEUTSCHE WELLE, Via Kigali, Rwanda — Ⓦ • S Africa • 250 kW / Ⓦ • SE Asia • 250 kW
  †DEUTSCHE WELLE, Via Neth Antilles — Ⓦ • E North Am • 250 kW
  DEUTSCHE WELLE, Via Sines, Portugal — Ⓦ • N Africa • 250 kW
  DEUTSCHE WELLE, Wertachtal — Ⓦ • W Africa • 500 kW
RUSSIA
  VOICE OF RUSSIA, St Petersburg — Ⓢ • Mideast & W Asia • 400 kW
SPAIN
  R EXTERIOR ESPANA, Noblejas — Ⓢ • Europe • 350 kW / Europe • 350 kW / Ⓦ • M-F • Mideast • 350 kW / Ⓦ • Sa/Su • Mideast • 350 kW / Ⓦ • Mideast • 350 kW
UNITED KINGDOM
  †BBC, Various Locations — E Africa • 250 kW
  †BBC, Via Tashkent, Uzbekistan — Ⓢ • S Asia • 200 kW
  †BBC, Via Zyyi, Cyprus — E Africa • 250 kW
USA
  †ADVENTIST WORLD R, Via Agat, Guam — Ⓦ • E Asia • 100 kW
  RFE-RL, Via Biblis, Germany — Ⓢ • E Europe • 100 kW
  †TRANS WORLD R, Via Dhabayya, UAE — E Africa • 250 kW • ALT. FREQ. TO 11810 kHz / Sa/Su • E Africa • 250 kW • ALT. FREQ. TO 11810 kHz
  VOA, Via São Tomé — Ⓢ • M-F • W Africa • 100 kW
12040 ECUADOR
  HCJB-VOICE THE ANDES, Quito — S America • 100 kW
GERMANY
  †DEUTSCHE WELLE, Via Kigali, Rwanda — Ⓢ • S America • 250 kW
RUSSIA
  VOICE OF RUSSIA, Moscow — Ⓢ • Europe • 250 kW • ALT. FREQ. TO 9810 kHz
USA
  VOA, Via Philippines — E Asia • 250 kW / Ⓦ • S Asia • 250 kW / Ⓢ • E Asia • 250 kW
12045 CANADA
  R CANADA INTL, Via Tokyo, Japan — Ⓦ • E Asia & SE Asia • 300 kW
FRANCE
  †R FRANCE INTL, Via Vladivostok — Ⓢ • E Asia • 250 kW
GERMANY
  DEUTSCHE WELLE, Via Kigali, Rwanda — Ⓦ • C Africa & E Africa • 250 kW
  †DEUTSCHE WELLE, Wertachtal — Ⓦ • E Europe • 500 kW
JAPAN
  †RADIO JAPAN, Via Singapore — S Asia • 250 kW / Ⓦ • S Asia • 250 kW
UNITED KINGDOM
  BBC, Via Singapore — SE Asia • 250 kW
  BBC, Via Thailand — Ⓢ • S Asia • 250 kW
  FEBA RADIO, Via Novosibirsk, Russia — Ⓢ • W Asia & S Asia • 250 kW
USA
  †ADVENTIST WORLD R, Via Agat, Guam — Ⓢ • S Asia • 100 kW
  †VOA, Via Kavála, Greece — Ⓢ • W Asia • 250 kW
12050 EGYPT
  EGYPTIAN RADIO, Abu Za'bal — Europe & E North Am • DS-GENERAL • 500 kW
  EGYPTIAN RADIO, Kafr Silim-Abis — Europe & E North Am • DS-GENERAL • 250 kW
TURKEY
  †VOICE OF TURKEY, Ankara-Emirler — Ⓦ • E Asia • 500 kW
12055 CHINA
  CENTRAL PEOPLE'S BS, Lingshi — DS-1 • 100 kW / DS-8 (MINORITIES) • 100 kW
(con'd)

0 1 2 3 4 5 6 7 8 9 10 11 12 13 14 15 16 17 18 19 20 21 22 23 24

SEASONAL Ⓢ OR Ⓦ   1-HR TIMESHIFT MIDYEAR ⇦ OR ⇨   JAMMING / OR /\   EARLIEST HEARD ◁   LATEST HEARD ▷   NEW FOR 2006 †

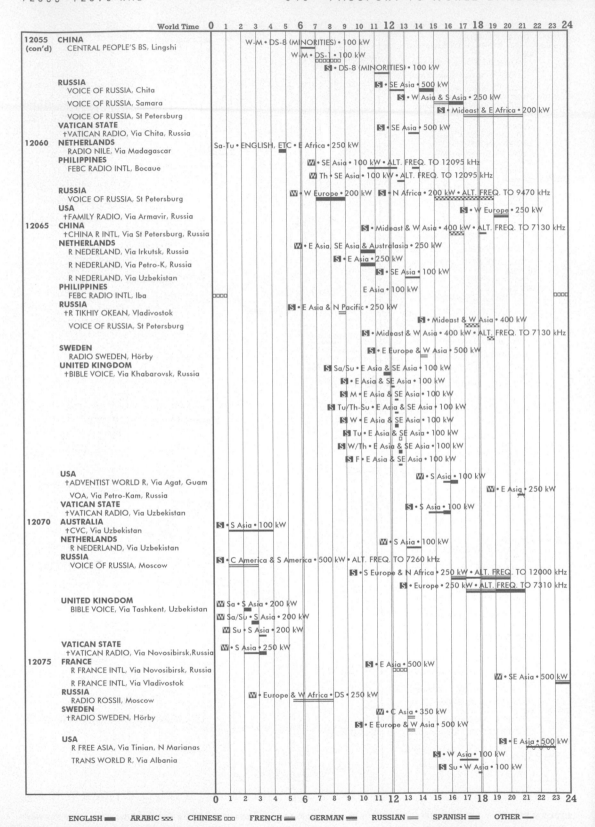

World Time	0 1 2 3 4 5 6 7 8 9 10 11 12 13 14 15 16 17 18 19 20 21 22 23 24
12055 (con'd) **CHINA** CENTRAL PEOPLE'S BS, Lingshi	W-M • DS-8 (MINORITIES) • 100 kW; W-M • DS-1 • 100 kW; S • DS-8 (MINORITIES) • 100 kW
RUSSIA VOICE OF RUSSIA, Chita	S • SE Asia • 500 kW
VOICE OF RUSSIA, Samara	S • W Asia & S Asia • 250 kW
VOICE OF RUSSIA, St Petersburg	S • Mideast & E Africa • 200 kW
VATICAN STATE †VATICAN RADIO, Via Chita, Russia	S • SE Asia • 500 kW
12060 **NETHERLANDS** RADIO NILE, Via Madagascar	Sa-Tu • ENGLISH, ETC • E Africa • 250 kW
PHILIPPINES FEBC RADIO INTL, Bocaue	W • SE Asia • 100 kW • ALT. FREQ. TO 12095 kHz; W Th • SE Asia • 100 kW • ALT. FREQ. TO 12095 kHz
RUSSIA VOICE OF RUSSIA, St Petersburg	W • W Europe • 200 kW; S • N Africa • 200 kW • ALT. FREQ. TO 9470 kHz
USA †FAMILY RADIO, Via Armavir, Russia	S • W Europe • 250 kW
12065 **CHINA** †CHINA R INTL, Via St Petersburg, Russia	S • Mideast & W Asia • 400 kW • ALT. FREQ. TO 7130 kHz
NETHERLANDS R NEDERLAND, Via Irkutsk, Russia	W • E Asia, SE Asia & Australasia • 250 kW
R NEDERLAND, Via Petro-K, Russia	S • E Asia • 250 kW
R NEDERLAND, Via Uzbekistan	S • SE Asia • 100 kW
PHILIPPINES FEBC RADIO INTL, Iba	E Asia • 100 kW
RUSSIA †R TIKHIY OKEAN, Vladivostok	S • E Asia & N Pacific • 250 kW
VOICE OF RUSSIA, St Petersburg	S • Mideast & W Asia • 400 kW; S • Mideast & W Asia • 400 kW • ALT. FREQ. TO 7130 kHz
SWEDEN RADIO SWEDEN, Hörby	S • E Europe & W Asia • 500 kW
UNITED KINGDOM †BIBLE VOICE, Via Khabarovsk, Russia	S Sa/Su • E Asia & SE Asia • 100 kW; S • E Asia & SE Asia • 100 kW; S M • E Asia & SE Asia • 100 kW; S Tu/Th-Su • E Asia & SE Asia • 100 kW; S W • E Asia & SE Asia • 100 kW; S Tu • E Asia & SE Asia • 100 kW; S W/Th • E Asia & SE Asia • 100 kW; S F • E Asia & SE Asia • 100 kW
USA †ADVENTIST WORLD R, Via Agat, Guam	W • S Asia • 100 kW
VOA, Via Petro-Kam, Russia	W • E Asia • 250 kW
VATICAN STATE †VATICAN RADIO, Via Uzbekistan	S • S Asia • 100 kW
12070 **AUSTRALIA** †CVC, Via Uzbekistan	S • S Asia • 100 kW
NETHERLANDS R NEDERLAND, Via Uzbekistan	W • S Asia • 100 kW
RUSSIA VOICE OF RUSSIA, Moscow	S • C America & S America • 500 kW • ALT. FREQ. TO 7260 kHz; S • S Europe & N Africa • 250 kW • ALT. FREQ. TO 12000 kHz; S • Europe • 250 kW • ALT. FREQ. TO 7310 kHz
UNITED KINGDOM BIBLE VOICE, Via Tashkent, Uzbekistan	W Sa • S Asia • 200 kW; W Sa/Su • S Asia • 200 kW; W Su • S Asia • 200 kW
VATICAN STATE †VATICAN RADIO, Via Novosibirsk, Russia	W • S Asia • 250 kW
12075 **FRANCE** R FRANCE INTL, Via Novosibirsk, Russia	S • E Asia • 500 kW
R FRANCE INTL, Via Vladivostok	W • SE Asia • 500 kW
RUSSIA RADIO ROSSII, Moscow	W • Europe & W Africa • DS • 250 kW
SWEDEN †RADIO SWEDEN, Hörby	W • C Asia • 350 kW; S • E Europe & W Asia • 500 kW
USA R FREE ASIA, Via Tinian, N Marianas	S • E Asia • 500 kW
TRANS WORLD R, Via Albania	S • W Asia • 100 kW; S Su • W Asia • 100 kW

0 1 2 3 4 5 6 7 8 9 10 11 12 13 14 15 16 17 18 19 20 21 22 23 24

ENGLISH ▬ ARABIC ▨ CHINESE ▫▫▫ FRENCH ▤ GERMAN ▭ RUSSIAN ═ SPANISH ▬ OTHER —

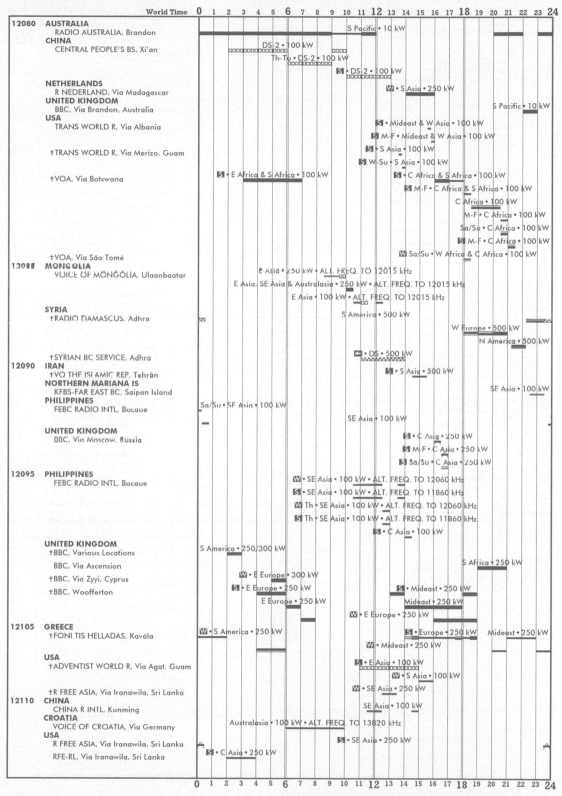

World Time 0 1 2 3 4 5 6 7 8 9 10 11 12 13 14 15 16 17 18 19 20 21 22 23 24

12080 **AUSTRALIA**
RADIO AUSTRALIA, Brandon
- S Pacific • 10 kW

CHINA
CENTRAL PEOPLE'S BS, Xi'an
- DS-2 • 100 kW
- Th-Tu • DS-2 • 100 kW
- [S] • DS-2 • 100 kW

NETHERLANDS
R NEDERLAND, Via Madagascar
- [W] • S Asia • 250 kW

UNITED KINGDOM
BBC, Via Brandon, Australia
- S Pacific • 10 kW

USA
TRANS WORLD R, Via Albania
- [S] • Mideast & W Asia • 100 kW
- [S] M-F • Mideast & W Asia • 100 kW

†TRANS WORLD R, Via Merizo, Guam
- [S] • S Asia • 100 kW
- [S] W-Su • S Asia • 100 kW

†VOA, Via Botswana
- [S] • E Africa & S Africa • 100 kW
- [S] • C Africa & S Africa • 100 kW
- [S] M-F • C Africa & S Africa • 100 kW
- C Africa • 100 kW
- M-F • C Africa • 100 kW
- Sa/Su • C Africa • 100 kW
- [S] M-F • C Africa • 100 kW

†VOA, Via São Tomé
- [W] Sa/Su • W Africa & C Africa • 100 kW

12085 **MONGOLIA**
VOICE OF MONGOLIA, Ulaanbaatar
- E Asia • 250 kW • ALT. FREQ. TO 12015 kHz
- E Asia, SE Asia & Australasia • 250 kW • ALT. FREQ. TO 12015 kHz
- E Asia • 100 kW • ALT. FREQ. TO 12015 kHz

SYRIA
†RADIO DAMASCUS, Adhra
- S America • 500 kW
- W Europe • 500 kW
- N America • 500 kW

†SYRIAN BC SERVICE, Adhra
- [⇦] • DS • 500 kW

12090 **IRAN**
†VO THE ISLAMIC REP, Tehrān
- [S] • S Asia • 500 kW

NORTHERN MARIANA IS
KFBS-FAR EAST BC, Saipan Island
- SE Asia • 100 kW

PHILIPPINES
FEBC RADIO INTL, Bocaue
- Sa/Su • SE Asia • 100 kW
- SE Asia • 100 kW

UNITED KINGDOM
BBC, Via Moscow, Russia
- [S] • C Asia • 250 kW
- [S] M-F • C Asia • 250 kW
- [S] Sa/Su • C Asia • 250 kW

12095 **PHILIPPINES**
FEBC RADIO INTL, Bocaue
- [W] • SE Asia • 100 kW • ALT. FREQ. TO 12060 kHz
- [S] • SE Asia • 100 kW • ALT. FREQ. TO 11860 kHz
- [W] Th • SE Asia • 100 kW • ALT. FREQ. TO 12060 kHz
- [S] Th • SE Asia • 100 kW • ALT. FREQ. TO 11860 kHz
- [S] • C Asia • 100 kW

UNITED KINGDOM
†BBC, Various Locations
- S America • 250/300 kW

BBC, Via Ascension
- S Africa • 250 kW

†BBC, Via Zyyi, Cyprus
- [W] • E Europe • 300 kW

†BBC, Woofferton
- [S] • E Europe • 250 kW
- [S] • Mideast • 250 kW
- E Europe • 250 kW
- Mideast • 250 kW
- [W] • E Europe • 250 kW

12105 **GREECE**
†FONI TIS HELLADAS, Kavála
- [W] • S America • 250 kW
- [S] • Europe • 250 kW
- Mideast • 250 kW
- [W] • Mideast • 250 kW

USA
†ADVENTIST WORLD R, Via Agat, Guam
- [S] • E Asia • 100 kW
- [W] • S Asia • 100 kW

†R FREE ASIA, Via Iranawila, Sri Lanka
- [W] • SE Asia • 250 kW

12110 **CHINA**
CHINA R INTL, Kunming
- SE Asia • 100 kW

CROATIA
VOICE OF CROATIA, Via Germany
- Australasia • 100 kW • ALT. FREQ. TO 13820 kHz

USA
R FREE ASIA, Via Iranawila, Sri Lanka
- [S] • SE Asia • 250 kW

RFE-RL, Via Iranawila, Sri Lanka
- [S] • C Asia • 250 kW

0 1 2 3 4 5 6 7 8 9 10 11 12 13 14 15 16 17 18 19 20 21 22 23 24

SEASONAL [S] OR [W] 1-HR TIMESHIFT MIDYEAR [⇦] OR [⇨] JAMMING / OR /\ EARLIEST HEARD ◁ LATEST HEARD ▷ NEW FOR 2006 †

World Time 0 1 2 3 4 5 6 7 8 9 10 11 12 13 14 15 16 17 18 19 20 21 22 23 24

| 12115 | **ICELAND** |
| | RIKISUTVARPID, Reykjavik |

Atlantic & Europe • DS-1 • 10 kW
Atlantic & E North Am • DS-1 • 10 kW

| | **USA** |
| | †RFE-RL, Via Iranawila, Sri Lanka |

S • C Asia • 250 kW

| 12120 | **CLANDESTINE (AFRICA)** |
| | "DEJEN RADIO", Via Samara, Russia |

Sa • E Africa • ANTI-ETHIOPIA GOVT • 250 kW

| | "VO ETHIOPIAN MEDHIN", Via Russia |

Su • E Africa • ANTI-ETHIOPIA GOVT • 250 kW

| | "VOICE OF LIBERTY", Via Samara, Russia |

W Su • E Africa • ANTI-ERITREA GOVT • 250 kW   S W • E Africa • ANTI-ERITREA GOVT • 250 kW

| | "VOICE OF OROMIYAA", Via Russia |

M/Th • E Africa • ANTI-ETHIOPIA GOVT • 200/250 kW • ALT. FREQ. TO 12125 kHz

| | **NORTHERN MARIANA IS** |
| | KFBS-FAR EAST BC, Saipan Island |

SE Asia • 100 kW

| | **USA** |
| | ADVENTIST WORLD R, Via Agat, Guam |

W • E Asia • 100 kW   S • E Asia • 100 kW

| | †ADVENTIST WORLD R, Via South Africa |

W • E Africa • 250 kW

| 12125 | **CLANDESTINE (AFRICA)** |
| | "VOICE OF OROMIYAA", Via Russia |

M/Th • E Africa • ANTI-ETHIOPIA GOVT • 200/250 kW • ALT. FREQ. TO 12120 kHz

| | **UNITED KINGDOM** |
| | FEBA RADIO, Via Meyerton, S Africa |

C Africa & E Africa • 250 kW
S • E Africa • 250 kW

| 12130 | **CLANDESTINE (AFRICA)** |
| | †"RADIO HORYAAL", Via Samara, Russia |

S Sa-Th • E Africa • 250 kW

| | †"VOICE OF DELINA", Via Armavir, Russia |

S Su • E Africa • 250 kW

| | **USA** |
| | †TRANS WORLD R, Via Merizo, Guam |

E Asia • 100 kW
E Asia • 100 kW • ALT. FREQ. TO 9910 kHz   F/Sa • E Asia • 100 kW
S Asia • 100 kW
Su-F • S Asia • 100 kW

| 12133.5 | **USA** |
| | AFRTS, Key West, Florida |

Americas • B kW • USB

| 12140 | **CLANDESTINE (AFRICA)** |
| | †"RADIO HORYAAL", Via Armavir, Russia |

W Sa-Th • E Africa • 250 kW

| | **USA** |
| | †RFE-RL, Via Kuwait |

S • W Asia & C Asia • 250 kW   W • W Asia & C Asia • 250 kW

| | †VOA, Via Iranawila, Sri Lanka |

W • W Asia • 250 kW

| | †VOA, Via Kuwait |

W Asia & S Asia • 250 kW
S • W Asia & S Asia • 250 kW

| 12150 | **USA** |
| | VOA, Via Iranawila, Sri Lanka |

W • S Asia • 250 kW

| 12155 | **USA** |
| | VOA, Via Iranawila, Sri Lanka |

S • S Asia • 250 kW

| 12160 | **USA** |
| | †WWCR, Nashville, Tennessee |

Irr • E North Am & Europe • 100 kW
E North Am & Europe • 100 kW
E North Am & Europe • 100 kW • ALT. FREQ. TO 5070 kHz

| 12257 | **PIRATE (EUROPE)** |
| | "WREKIN RADIO INTL", England |

• Irr • Su • W Europe • 0.03 kW

| 12579 | **USA** |
| | AFRTS, Via Diego Garcia |

S Asia • USB • ALT. FREQ. TO 4319 kHz

| 13362 | **USA** |
| | AFRTS, Via Guam |

Pacific • USB • ALT. FREQ. TO 5765 kHz

| 13570 | **USA** |
| | †WINB-WORLD INTL BC, Red Lion, Pa |

C America & W North Am • 50 kW
W • C America & W North Am • 50 kW

| 13575 | **GERMANY** |
| | †DEUTSCHE WELLE, Via Armavir, Russia |

S • W Asia & S Asia • 250 kW

| 13580 | **CZECH REPUBLIC** |
| | RADIO PRAGUE, Litomyšl |

S • N Europe • 100 kW
S • E Europe & W Asia • 100 kW
• W Europe • 100 kW
S • S Europe & N Africa • 100 kW

| | **SWEDEN** |
| | †RADIO SWEDEN, Hörby |

S Sa • Mideast • 500 kW   S • Mideast & W Africa • 500 kW
S Su • Mideast • 500 kW   S M-F • Mideast & W Africa • 500 kW
S • E Asia & Australasia • 500 kW
S Sa/Su • Mideast • 500 kW
W • W Europe & W Africa • 500 kW
W M-F • W Europe & W Africa • 500 kW
W • Mideast • 500 kW

| 13590 | **GERMANY** |
| | †DEUTSCHE WELLE, Wertachtal |

W • S Asia • 500 kW

| | **PORTUGAL** |
| | †RDP INTERNATIONAL, Lisbon |

S Sa/Su • Europe • 100 kW
S M-F • Europe • 300 kW

(con'd)

0 1 2 3 4 5 6 7 8 9 10 11 12 13 14 15 16 17 18 19 20 21 22 23 24

ENGLISH ▬   ARABIC ▩   CHINESE ▢▢▢   FRENCH ▬   GERMAN ▬   RUSSIAN ══   SPANISH ▬   OTHER ▬

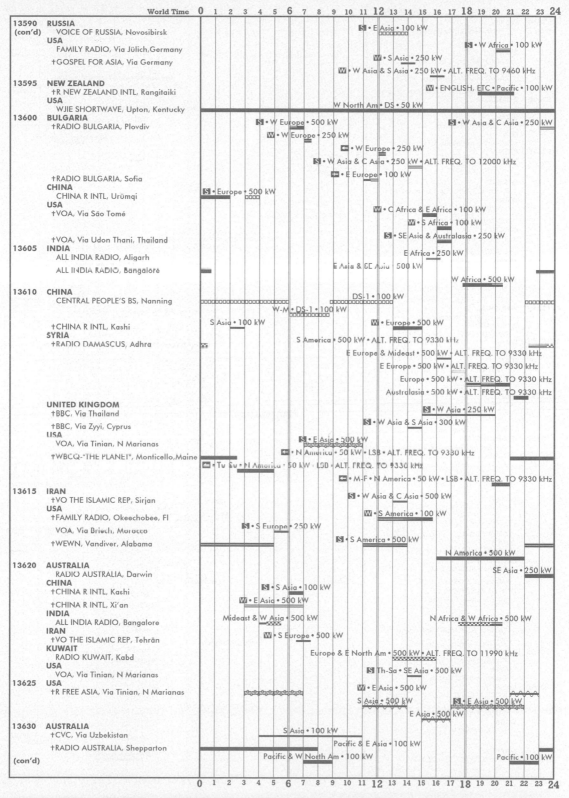

World Time 0 1 2 3 4 5 6 7 8 9 10 11 12 13 14 15 16 17 18 19 20 21 22 23 24

kHz	Country / Station	Schedule
13590 (con'd)	RUSSIA	
	VOICE OF RUSSIA, Novosibirsk	[S] • E Asia • 100 kW
	USA	
	FAMILY RADIO, Via Jülich,Germany	[S] • W Africa • 100 kW
	†GOSPEL FOR ASIA, Via Germany	[W] • S Asia • 250 kW
		[W] • W Asia & S Asia • 250 kW • ALT. FREQ. TO 9460 kHz
13595	NEW ZEALAND	
	†R NEW ZEALAND INTL, Rangitaiki	[W] • ENGLISH, ETC • Pacific • 100 kW
	USA	
	WJIE SHORTWAVE, Upton, Kentucky	W North Am • DS • 50 kW
13600	BULGARIA	
	†RADIO BULGARIA, Plovdiv	[S] • W Europe • 500 kW
		[S] • W Asia & C Asia • 250 kW
		[W] • W Europe • 250 kW
		⇐ • W Europe • 250 kW
		[S] • W Asia & C Asia • 250 kW • ALT. FREQ. TO 12000 kHz
	†RADIO BULGARIA, Sofia	⇐ • E Europe • 100 kW
	CHINA	
	CHINA R INTL, Urümqi	[S] • Europe • 500 kW
	USA	
	†VOA, Via São Tomé	[W] • C Africa & E Africa • 100 kW
		[W] • S Africa • 100 kW
	†VOA, Via Udon Thani, Thailand	[S] • SE Asia & Australasia • 250 kW
13605	INDIA	
	ALL INDIA RADIO, Aligarh	E Africa • 250 kW
	ALL INDIA RADIO, Bangalore	E Asia & SE Asia • 500 kW
		W Africa • 500 kW
13610	CHINA	
	CENTRAL PEOPLE'S BS, Nanning	DS-1 • 100 kW
		W-M • DS-1 • 100 kW
	†CHINA R INTL, Kashi	S Asia • 100 kW
		[W] • Europe • 500 kW
	SYRIA	
	†RADIO DAMASCUS, Adhra	S America • 500 kW • ALT. FREQ. TO 9330 kHz
		E Europe & Mideast • 500 kW • ALT. FREQ. TO 9330 kHz
		E Europe • 500 kW • ALT. FREQ. TO 9330 kHz
		Europe • 500 kW • ALT. FREQ. TO 9330 kHz
		Australasia • 500 kW • ALT. FREQ. TO 9330 kHz
	UNITED KINGDOM	
	†BBC, Via Thailand	[S] • W Asia • 250 kW
	†BBC, Via Zyyi, Cyprus	[S] • W Asia & S Asia • 300 kW
	USA	
	VOA, Via Tinian, N Marianas	[S] • E Asia • 500 kW
	†WBCQ-"THE PLANET", Monticello,Maine	⇐ • N America • 50 kW • LSB • ALT. FREQ. TO 9330 kHz
		⇐ • Tu-Su • N America • 50 kW • LSB • ALT. FREQ. TO 9330 kHz
		⇐ • M-F • N America • 50 kW • LSB • ALT. FREQ. TO 9330 kHz
13615	IRAN	
	†VO THE ISLAMIC REP, Sirjan	[S] • W Asia & C Asia • 500 kW
	USA	
	†FAMILY RADIO, Okeechobee, Fl	[W] • S America • 100 kW
	VOA, Via Briech, Morocco	[S] • S Europe • 250 kW
	†WEWN, Vandiver, Alabama	[S] • S America • 500 kW
		N America • 500 kW
13620	AUSTRALIA	
	RADIO AUSTRALIA, Darwin	SE Asia • 250 kW
	CHINA	
	†CHINA R INTL, Kashi	[S] • S Asia • 100 kW
	†CHINA R INTL, Xi'an	[W] • E Asia • 500 kW
	INDIA	
	ALL INDIA RADIO, Bangalore	Mideast & W Asia • 500 kW
		N Africa & W Africa • 500 kW
	IRAN	
	†VO THE ISLAMIC REP, Tehrān	[W] • S Europe • 500 kW
	KUWAIT	
	RADIO KUWAIT, Kabd	Europe & E North Am • 500 kW • ALT. FREQ. TO 11990 kHz
	USA	
	VOA, Via Tinian, N Marianas	[S] Th-Sa • SE Asia • 500 kW
13625	USA	
	†R FREE ASIA, Via Tinian, N Marianas	[W] • E Asia • 500 kW
		S Asia • 500 kW
		[S] • E Asia • 500 kW
		E Asia • 500 kW
13630	AUSTRALIA	
	†CVC, Via Uzbekistan	S Asia • 100 kW
	†RADIO AUSTRALIA, Shepparton	Pacific & E Asia • 100 kW
(con'd)		Pacific & W North Am • 100 kW
		Pacific • 100 kW

0 1 2 3 4 5 6 7 8 9 10 11 12 13 14 15 16 17 18 19 20 21 22 23 24

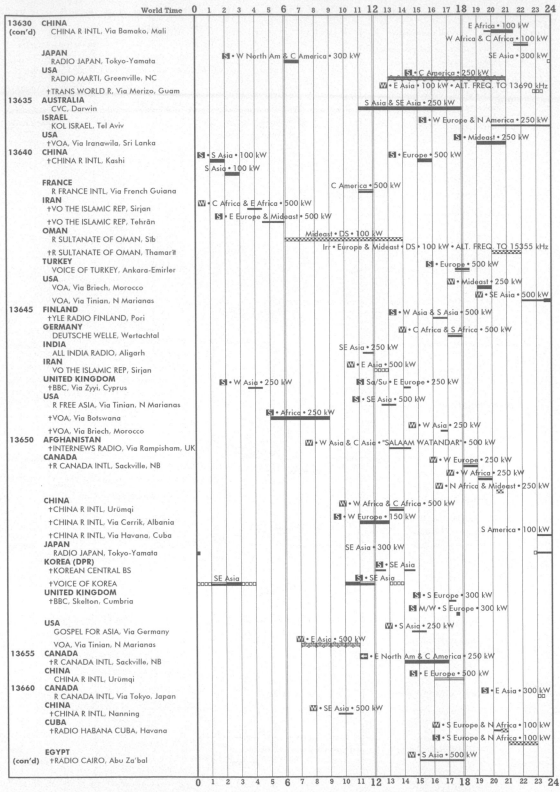

| | | World Time | 0 | 1 | 2 | 3 | 4 | 5 | 6 | 7 | 8 | 9 | 10 | 11 | 12 | 13 | 14 | 15 | 16 | 17 | 18 | 19 | 20 | 21 | 22 | 23 | 24 |

13630 CHINA
(con'd)   CHINA R INTL, Via Bamako, Mali — E Africa • 100 kW; W Africa & C Africa • 100 kW; SE Asia • 300 kW

JAPAN
   RADIO JAPAN, Tokyo-Yamata — S • W North Am & C America • 300 kW
USA
   RADIO MARTI, Greenville, NC — S • C America • 250 kW
   †TRANS WORLD R, Via Merizo, Guam — W • E Asia • 100 kW • ALT. FREQ. TO 13690 kHz

13635 AUSTRALIA
   CVC, Darwin — S Asia & SE Asia • 250 kW
ISRAEL
   KOL ISRAEL, Tel Aviv — S • W Europe & N America • 250 kW
USA
   †VOA, Via Iranawila, Sri Lanka — S • Mideast • 250 kW

13640 CHINA
   †CHINA R INTL, Kashi — S • S Asia • 100 kW; S Asia • 100 kW; S • Europe • 500 kW

FRANCE
   R FRANCE INTL, Via French Guiana — C America • 500 kW
IRAN
   †VO THE ISLAMIC REP, Sirjan — W • C Africa & E Africa • 500 kW
   †VO THE ISLAMIC REP, Tehrān — S • E Europe & Mideast • 500 kW
OMAN
   R SULTANATE OF OMAN, Sīb — Mideast • DS • 100 kW
   †R SULTANATE OF OMAN, Thamarīt — Irr • Europe & Mideast • DS • 100 kW • ALT. FREQ. TO 15355 kHz
TURKEY
   VOICE OF TURKEY, Ankara-Emirler — S • Europe • 500 kW
USA
   VOA, Via Briech, Morocco — W • Mideast • 250 kW
   VOA, Via Tinian, N Marianas — W • SE Asia • 500 kW

13645 FINLAND
   †YLE RADIO FINLAND, Pori — S • W Asia & S Asia • 500 kW
GERMANY
   DEUTSCHE WELLE, Wertachtal — W • C Africa & S Africa • 500 kW
INDIA
   ALL INDIA RADIO, Aligarh — SE Asia • 250 kW
IRAN
   VO THE ISLAMIC REP, Sirjan — W • E Asia • 500 kW
UNITED KINGDOM
   †BBC, Via Zyyi, Cyprus — S • W Asia • 250 kW; S Sa/Su • E Europe • 250 kW
USA
   R FREE ASIA, Via Tinian, N Marianas — S • SE Asia • 500 kW
   †VOA, Via Botswana — S • Africa • 250 kW
   †VOA, Via Briech, Morocco — W • W Asia • 250 kW

13650 AFGHANISTAN
   †INTERNEWS RADIO, Via Rampisham, UK — W • W Asia & C Asia • "SALAAM WATANDAR" • 500 kW
CANADA
   †R CANADA INTL, Sackville, NB — W • W Europe • 250 kW; W • W Africa • 250 kW; W • N Africa & Mideast • 250 kW

CHINA
   †CHINA R INTL, Urümqi — W • W Africa & C Africa • 500 kW
   †CHINA R INTL, Via Cerrik, Albania — S • W Europe • 150 kW
   †CHINA R INTL, Via Havana, Cuba — S America • 100 kW
JAPAN
   RADIO JAPAN, Tokyo-Yamata — SE Asia • 300 kW
KOREA (DPR)
   †KOREAN CENTRAL BS — S • SE Asia
   †VOICE OF KOREA — SE Asia; S • SE Asia
UNITED KINGDOM
   †BBC, Skelton, Cumbria — S • S Europe • 300 kW; S M/W • S Europe • 300 kW

USA
   GOSPEL FOR ASIA, Via Germany — W • S Asia • 250 kW
   VOA, Via Tinian, N Marianas — W • E Asia • 500 kW

13655 CANADA
   †R CANADA INTL, Sackville, NB — E North Am & C America • 250 kW
CHINA
   CHINA R INTL, Urümqi — S • E Europe • 500 kW

13660 CANADA
   R CANADA INTL, Via Tokyo, Japan — S • E Asia • 300 kW
CHINA
   †CHINA R INTL, Nanning — W • SE Asia • 500 kW
CUBA
   †RADIO HABANA CUBA, Havana — W • S Europe & N Africa • 100 kW; S • S Europe & N Africa • 100 kW

EGYPT
(con'd)   †RADIO CAIRO, Abu Za'bal — W • S Asia • 500 kW

| | | 0 | 1 | 2 | 3 | 4 | 5 | 6 | 7 | 8 | 9 | 10 | 11 | 12 | 13 | 14 | 15 | 16 | 17 | 18 | 19 | 20 | 21 | 22 | 23 | 24 |

ENGLISH ▬   ARABIC ▨   CHINESE ⬚⬚⬚   FRENCH ▬   GERMAN ▬   RUSSIAN ═   SPANISH ═   OTHER ▬

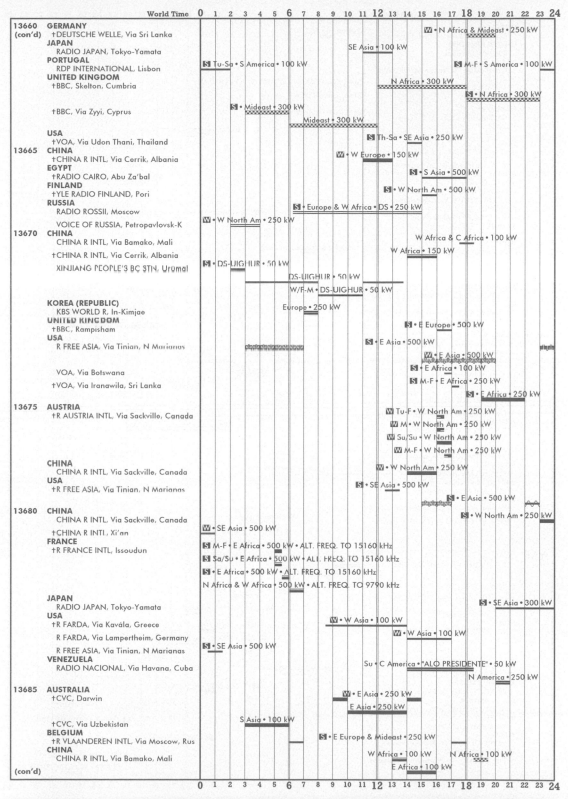

| | World Time | 0 | 1 | 2 | 3 | 4 | 5 | 6 | 7 | 8 | 9 | 10 | 11 | 12 | 13 | 14 | 15 | 16 | 17 | 18 | 19 | 20 | 21 | 22 | 23 | 24 |

13660 GERMANY
(con'd) †DEUTSCHE WELLE, Via Sri Lanka — Ⓦ • N Africa & Mideast • 250 kW
JAPAN
RADIO JAPAN, Tokyo-Yamata — SE Asia • 100 kW
PORTUGAL
RDP INTERNATIONAL, Lisbon — Ⓢ Tu-Sa • S America • 100 kW / Ⓢ M-F • S America • 100 kW
UNITED KINGDOM
†BBC, Skelton, Cumbria — N Africa • 300 kW / Ⓢ • N Africa • 300 kW

†BBC, Via Zyyi, Cyprus — Ⓢ • Mideast • 300 kW / Mideast • 300 kW

USA
†VOA, Via Udon Thani, Thailand — Ⓢ Th-Sa • SE Asia • 250 kW
13665 CHINA
†CHINA R INTL, Via Cerrik, Albania — Ⓦ • W Europe • 150 kW
EGYPT
†RADIO CAIRO, Abu Za'bal — Ⓢ • S Asia • 500 kW
FINLAND
†YLE RADIO FINLAND, Pori — Ⓢ • W North Am • 500 kW
RUSSIA
RADIO ROSSII, Moscow — Ⓢ • Europe & W Africa • DS • 250 kW

VOICE OF RUSSIA, Petropavlovsk-K — Ⓦ • W North Am • 250 kW
13670 CHINA
CHINA R INTL, Via Bamako, Mali — W Africa & C Africa • 100 kW

†CHINA R INTL, Via Cerrik, Albania — W Africa • 150 kW

XINJIANG PEOPLE'S BC STN, Ürümqi — Ⓢ • DS-UIGHUR • 50 kW
— DS-UIGHUR • 50 kW
— W/F-M • DS-UIGHUR • 50 kW

KOREA (REPUBLIC)
KBS WORLD R, In-Kimjae — Europe • 250 kW
UNITED KINGDOM
†BBC, Rampisham — Ⓢ • E Europe • 500 kW
USA
R FREE ASIA, Via Tinian, N Marianas — Ⓢ • E Asia • 500 kW / Ⓦ • E Asia • 500 kW

VOA, Via Botswana — Ⓢ • E Africa • 100 kW

†VOA, Via Iranawila, Sri Lanka — Ⓢ M-F • E Africa • 250 kW / Ⓢ • E Africa • 250 kW

13675 AUSTRIA
†R AUSTRIA INTL, Via Sackville, Canada — Ⓦ Tu-F • W North Am • 250 kW
— Ⓦ M • W North Am • 250 kW
— Ⓦ Su/Su • W North Am • 250 kW
— Ⓦ M-F • W North Am • 250 kW

CHINA
CHINA R INTL, Via Sackville, Canada — Ⓦ • W North Am • 250 kW
USA
†R FREE ASIA, Via Tinian, N Marianas — Ⓢ • SE Asia • 500 kW
— Ⓢ • E Asia • 500 kW
13680 CHINA
CHINA R INTL, Via Sackville, Canada — Ⓢ • W North Am • 250 kW

†CHINA R INTL, Xi'an — Ⓦ • SE Asia • 500 kW
FRANCE
†R FRANCE INTL, Issoudun — Ⓢ M-F • E Africa • 500 kW • ALT. FREQ. TO 15160 kHz
— Ⓢ Sa/Su • E Africa • 500 kW • ALT. FREQ. TO 15160 kHz
— Ⓢ • E Africa • 500 kW • ALT. FREQ. TO 15160 kHz
— N Africa & W Africa • 500 kW • ALT. FREQ. TO 9790 kHz

JAPAN
RADIO JAPAN, Tokyo-Yamata — Ⓢ • SE Asia • 300 kW
USA
†R FARDA, Via Kavála, Greece — Ⓦ • W Asia • 100 kW

R FARDA, Via Lampertheim, Germany — Ⓦ • W Asia • 100 kW

R FREE ASIA, Via Tinian, N Marianas — Ⓢ • SE Asia • 500 kW
VENEZUELA
RADIO NACIONAL, Via Havana, Cuba — Su • C America • "ALO PRESIDENTE" • 50 kW
— N America • 250 kW

13685 AUSTRALIA
†CVC, Darwin — Ⓦ • E Asia • 250 kW
— E Asia • 250 kW

†CVC, Via Uzbekistan — S Asia • 100 kW
BELGIUM
†R VLAANDEREN INTL, Via Moscow, Rus — Ⓢ • E Europe & Mideast • 250 kW
CHINA
CHINA R INTL, Via Bamako, Mali — W Africa • 100 kW / N Africa • 100 kW
— E Africa • 100 kW

(con'd)

| | 0 | 1 | 2 | 3 | 4 | 5 | 6 | 7 | 8 | 9 | 10 | 11 | 12 | 13 | 14 | 15 | 16 | 17 | 18 | 19 | 20 | 21 | 22 | 23 | 24 |

SEASONAL Ⓢ OR Ⓦ   1-HR TIMESHIFT MIDYEAR ⇦ OR ⇨   JAMMING / OR ∧   EARLIEST HEARD ◁   LATEST HEARD ▷   NEW FOR 2006 †

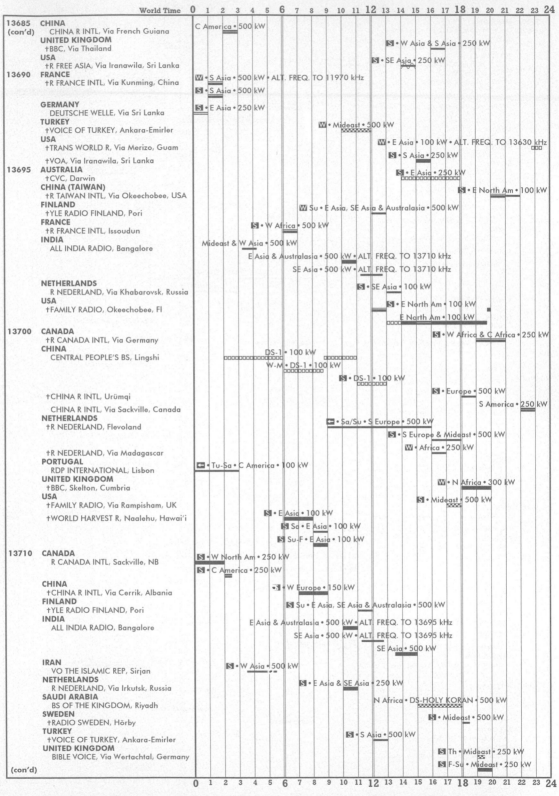

World Time 0 1 2 3 4 5 6 7 8 9 10 11 12 13 14 15 16 17 18 19 20 21 22 23 24

13685 CHINA
(con'd)   CHINA R INTL, Via French Guiana — C America • 500 kW
   UNITED KINGDOM
      †BBC, Via Thailand — S • W Asia & S Asia • 250 kW
   USA
      †R FREE ASIA, Via Iranawila, Sri Lanka — S • SE Asia • 250 kW
13690 FRANCE
      †R FRANCE INTL, Via Kunming, China — W • S Asia • 500 kW • ALT. FREQ. TO 11970 kHz
                                          S • S Asia • 500 kW
   GERMANY
      DEUTSCHE WELLE, Via Sri Lanka — S • E Asia • 250 kW
   TURKEY
      †VOICE OF TURKEY, Ankara-Emirler — W • Mideast • 500 kW
   USA
      †TRANS WORLD R, Via Merizo, Guam — W • E Asia • 100 kW • ALT. FREQ. TO 13630 kHz
      †VOA, Via Iranawila, Sri Lanka — S • S Asia • 250 kW
13695 AUSTRALIA
      †CVC, Darwin — S • E Asia • 250 kW
   CHINA (TAIWAN)
      †R TAIWAN INTL, Via Okeechobee, USA — S • E North Am • 100 kW
   FINLAND
      †YLE RADIO FINLAND, Pori — W Su • E Asia, SE Asia & Australasia • 500 kW
   FRANCE
      †R FRANCE INTL, Issoudun — S • W Africa • 500 kW
   INDIA
      ALL INDIA RADIO, Bangalore — Mideast & W Asia • 500 kW
                                   E Asia & Australasia • 500 kW • ALT. FREQ. TO 13710 kHz
                                   SE Asia • 500 kW • ALT. FREQ. TO 13710 kHz
   NETHERLANDS
      R NEDERLAND, Via Khabarovsk, Russia — S • SE Asia • 100 kW
   USA
      †FAMILY RADIO, Okeechobee, Fl — S • E North Am • 100 kW
                                      E North Am • 100 kW
13700 CANADA
      †R CANADA INTL, Via Germany — S • W Africa & C Africa • 250 kW
   CHINA
      CENTRAL PEOPLE'S BS, Lingshi — DS-1 • 100 kW
                                     W-M • DS-1 • 100 kW
                                     S • DS-1 • 100 kW
      †CHINA R INTL, Urümqi — S • Europe • 500 kW
      CHINA R INTL, Via Sackville, Canada — S America • 250 kW
   NETHERLANDS
      †R NEDERLAND, Flevoland — • Sa/Su • S Europe • 500 kW
                                S • S Europe & Mideast • 500 kW
      †R NEDERLAND, Via Madagascar — W • Africa • 250 kW
   PORTUGAL
      RDP INTERNATIONAL, Lisbon — • Tu-Sa • C America • 100 kW
   UNITED KINGDOM
      †BBC, Skelton, Cumbria — W • N Africa • 300 kW
   USA
      †FAMILY RADIO, Via Rampisham, UK — S • Mideast • 500 kW
      †WORLD HARVEST R, Naalehu, Hawai'i — S • E Asia • 100 kW
                                           S Sa • E Asia • 100 kW
                                           S Su-F • E Asia • 100 kW
13710 CANADA
      R CANADA INTL, Sackville, NB — S • W North Am • 250 kW
                                     S • C America • 250 kW
   CHINA
      †CHINA R INTL, Via Cerrik, Albania — • S • W Europe • 150 kW
   FINLAND
      †YLE RADIO FINLAND, Pori — S • Su • E Asia, SE Asia & Australasia • 500 kW
   INDIA
      ALL INDIA RADIO, Bangalore — E Asia & Australasia • 500 kW • ALT. FREQ. TO 13695 kHz
                                   SE Asia • 500 kW • ALT. FREQ. TO 13695 kHz
                                   SE Asia • 500 kW
   IRAN
      VO THE ISLAMIC REP, Sirjan — S • W Asia • 500 kW
   NETHERLANDS
      R NEDERLAND, Via Irkutsk, Russia — S • E Asia & SE Asia • 250 kW
   SAUDI ARABIA
      BS OF THE KINGDOM, Riyadh — N Africa • DS-HOLY KORAN • 500 kW
   SWEDEN
      †RADIO SWEDEN, Hörby — S • Mideast • 500 kW
   TURKEY
      †VOICE OF TURKEY, Ankara-Emirler — S • S Asia • 500 kW
   UNITED KINGDOM
      BIBLE VOICE, Via Wertachtal, Germany — S Th • Mideast • 250 kW
                                             S F-Su • Mideast • 250 kW
(con'd)

0 1 2 3 4 5 6 7 8 9 10 11 12 13 14 15 16 17 18 19 20 21 22 23 24

ENGLISH ▬   ARABIC ▦   CHINESE ▯▯▯   FRENCH ▬   GERMAN ▬   RUSSIAN ▭   SPANISH ▬   OTHER ▬

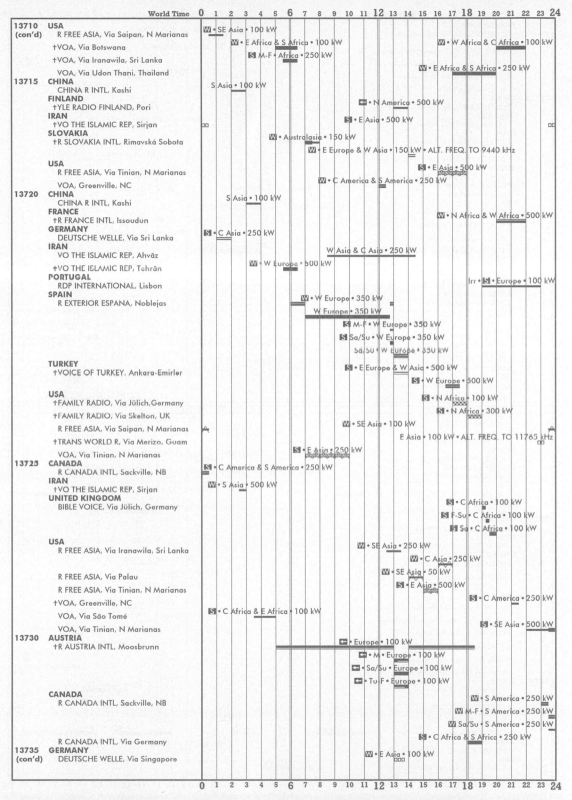

		World Time		

13710 USA
(con'd)
R FREE ASIA, Via Saipan, N Marianas — W • SE Asia • 100 kW
†VOA, Via Botswana — W • E Africa & S Africa • 100 kW / W • W Africa & C Africa • 100 kW
†VOA, Via Iranawila, Sri Lanka — S • M-F • Africa • 250 kW
VOA, Via Udon Thani, Thailand — W • E Africa & S Africa • 250 kW

13715 CHINA
CHINA R INTL, Kashi — S Asia • 100 kW
FINLAND
†YLE RADIO FINLAND, Pori — N America • 500 kW
IRAN
†VO THE ISLAMIC REP, Sirjan — S • E Asia • 500 kW
SLOVAKIA
†R SLOVAKIA INTL, Rimavská Sobota — W • Australasia • 150 kW
— W • E Europe & W Asia • 150 kW • ALT. FREQ. TO 9440 kHz

USA
R FREE ASIA, Via Tinian, N Marianas — S • E Asia • 500 kW
VOA, Greenville, NC — W • C America & S America • 250 kW

13720 CHINA
CHINA R INTL, Kashi — S Asia • 100 kW
FRANCE
†R FRANCE INTL, Issoudun — W • N Africa & W Africa • 500 kW
GERMANY
DEUTSCHE WELLE, Via Sri Lanka — S • C Asia • 250 kW
IRAN
VO THE ISLAMIC REP, Ahvāz — W Asia & C Asia • 250 kW
†VO THE ISLAMIC REP, Tehrān — W • W Europe • 500 kW
PORTUGAL
RDP INTERNATIONAL, Lisbon — Irr • S • Europe • 100 kW
SPAIN
R EXTERIOR ESPANA, Noblejas — W • W Europe • 350 kW
— W Europe • 350 kW
— S • M-F • W Europe • 350 kW
— S • Sa/Su • W Europe • 350 kW
— Sa/Su • W Europe • 350 kW

TURKEY
†VOICE OF TURKEY, Ankara-Emirler — S • E Europe & W Asia • 500 kW
— S • W Europe • 500 kW

USA
†FAMILY RADIO, Via Jülich, Germany — S • N Africa • 100 kW
†FAMILY RADIO, Via Skelton, UK — S • N Africa • 300 kW
R FREE ASIA, Via Saipan, N Marianas — W • SE Asia • 100 kW
†TRANS WORLD R, Via Merizo, Guam — E Asia • 100 kW • ALT. FREQ. TO 11765 kHz
VOA, Via Tinian, N Marianas — S • E Asia • 250 kW

13725 CANADA
R CANADA INTL, Sackville, NB — S • C America & S America • 250 kW
IRAN
†VO THE ISLAMIC REP, Sirjan — W • S Asia • 500 kW
UNITED KINGDOM
BIBLE VOICE, Via Jülich, Germany — S • C Africa • 100 kW
— S • F-Su • C Africa • 100 kW
— S • Sa • C Africa • 100 kW

USA
R FREE ASIA, Via Iranawila, Sri Lanka — W • SE Asia • 250 kW
— W • C Asia • 250 kW
R FREE ASIA, Via Palau — W • SE Asia • 50 kW
R FREE ASIA, Via Tinian, N Marianas — S • E Asia • 500 kW
†VOA, Greenville, NC — S • C America • 250 kW
VOA, Via São Tomé — S • C Africa & E Africa • 100 kW
VOA, Via Tinian, N Marianas — S • SE Asia • 500 kW

13730 AUSTRIA
†R AUSTRIA INTL, Moosbrunn — Europe • 100 kW
— M • Europe • 100 kW
— Sa/Su • Europe • 100 kW
— Tu-F • Europe • 100 kW

CANADA
R CANADA INTL, Sackville, NB — W • S America • 250 kW
— W • M-F • S America • 250 kW
— W • Sa/Su • S America • 250 kW
R CANADA INTL, Via Germany — S • C Africa & S Africa • 250 kW

13735 GERMANY
(con'd)
DEUTSCHE WELLE, Via Singapore — W • E Asia • 100 kW

SEASONAL S OR W   1-HR TIMESHIFT MIDYEAR ⇐ OR ⇒   JAMMING / OR ∧   EARLIEST HEARD ◁   LATEST HEARD ▷   NEW FOR 2006 †

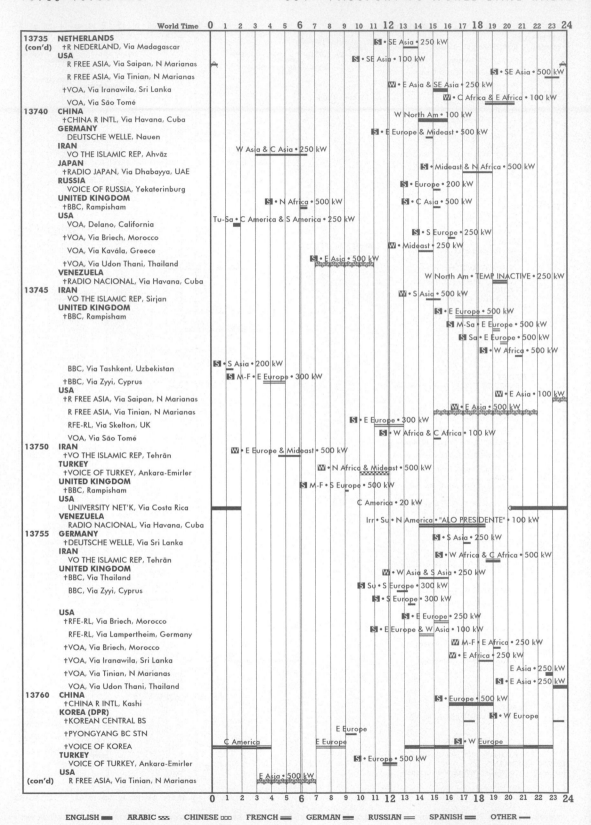

	World Time	0 1 2 3 4 5 6 7 8 9 10 11 12 13 14 15 16 17 18 19 20 21 22 23 24
13735	**NETHERLANDS**	
(con'd)	†R NEDERLAND, Via Madagascar	S • SE Asia • 250 kW
	USA	
	R FREE ASIA, Via Saipan, N Marianas	S • SE Asia • 100 kW
	R FREE ASIA, Via Tinian, N Marianas	S • SE Asia • 500 kW
	†VOA, Via Iranawila, Sri Lanka	W • E Asia & SE Asia • 250 kW
	VOA, Via São Tomé	W • C Africa & E Africa • 100 kW
13740	**CHINA**	
	†CHINA R INTL, Via Havana, Cuba	W North Am • 100 kW
	GERMANY	
	DEUTSCHE WELLE, Nauen	S • E Europe & Mideast • 500 kW
	IRAN	
	VO THE ISLAMIC REP, Ahvāz	W Asia & C Asia • 250 kW
	JAPAN	
	†RADIO JAPAN, Via Dhabayya, UAE	S • Mideast & N Africa • 500 kW
	RUSSIA	
	VOICE OF RUSSIA, Yekaterinburg	S • Europe • 200 kW
	UNITED KINGDOM	
	†BBC, Rampisham	S • C Africa • 500 kW
	USA	
	VOA, Delano, California	S • N Africa • 500 kW
		Tu-Sa • C America & S America • 250 kW
	†VOA, Via Briech, Morocco	S • S Europe • 250 kW
	VOA, Via Kavála, Greece	W • Mideast • 250 kW
	†VOA, Via Udon Thani, Thailand	S • E Asia • 500 kW
	VENEZUELA	
	†RADIO NACIONAL, Via Havana, Cuba	W North Am • TEMP INACTIVE • 250 kW
13745	**IRAN**	
	VO THE ISLAMIC REP, Sirjan	W • S Asia • 500 kW
	UNITED KINGDOM	
	†BBC, Rampisham	S • E Europe • 500 kW
		S M-Sa • E Europe • 500 kW
		S Sa • E Europe • 500 kW
		S • W Africa • 500 kW
	BBC, Via Tashkent, Uzbekistan	S • S Asia • 200 kW
	†BBC, Via Zyyi, Cyprus	S M-F • E Europe • 300 kW
	USA	
	†R FREE ASIA, Via Saipan, N Marianas	W • E Asia • 100 kW
	R FREE ASIA, Via Tinian, N Marianas	W • E Asia • 500 kW
	RFE-RL, Via Skelton, UK	S • E Europe • 300 kW
	VOA, Via São Tomé	S • W Africa & C Africa • 100 kW
13750	**IRAN**	
	†VO THE ISLAMIC REP, Tehrān	W • E Europe & Mideast • 500 kW
	TURKEY	
	†VOICE OF TURKEY, Ankara-Emirler	W • N Africa & Mideast • 500 kW
	UNITED KINGDOM	
	†BBC, Rampisham	S M-F • S Europe • 500 kW
	USA	
	UNIVERSITY NET'K, Via Costa Rica	C America • 20 kW
	VENEZUELA	
	RADIO NACIONAL, Via Havana, Cuba	Irr • Su • N America • "ALO PRESIDENTE" • 100 kW
13755	**GERMANY**	
	†DEUTSCHE WELLE, Via Sri Lanka	S • S Asia • 250 kW
	IRAN	
	VO THE ISLAMIC REP, Tehrān	S • W Africa & C Africa • 500 kW
	UNITED KINGDOM	
	†BBC, Via Thailand	W • W Asia & S Asia • 250 kW
	BBC, Via Zyyi, Cyprus	S Su • S Europe • 300 kW
		S • S Europe • 300 kW
	USA	
	†RFE-RL, Via Briech, Morocco	S • E Europe • 250 kW
	RFE-RL, Via Lampertheim, Germany	S • E Europe & W Asia • 100 kW
	†VOA, Via Briech, Morocco	W M-F • E Africa • 250 kW
	†VOA, Via Iranawila, Sri Lanka	W • E Africa • 250 kW
	†VOA, Via Tinian, N Marianas	E Asia • 250 kW
	VOA, Via Udon Thani, Thailand	S • E Asia • 250 kW
13760	**CHINA**	
	†CHINA R INTL, Kashi	S • Europe • 500 kW
	KOREA (DPR)	
	†KOREAN CENTRAL BS	S • W Europe
	†PYONGYANG BC STN	E Europe
	†VOICE OF KOREA	C America E Europe S • W Europe
	TURKEY	
	VOICE OF TURKEY, Ankara-Emirler	S • Europe • 500 kW
	USA	
(con'd)	R FREE ASIA, Via Tinian, N Marianas	E Asia • 500 kW
		0 1 2 3 4 5 6 7 8 9 10 11 12 13 14 15 16 17 18 19 20 21 22 23 24

ENGLISH ▬   ARABIC ⋙   CHINESE ▫▫▫   FRENCH ▬   GERMAN ▬   RUSSIAN ═   SPANISH ▬   OTHER ▬

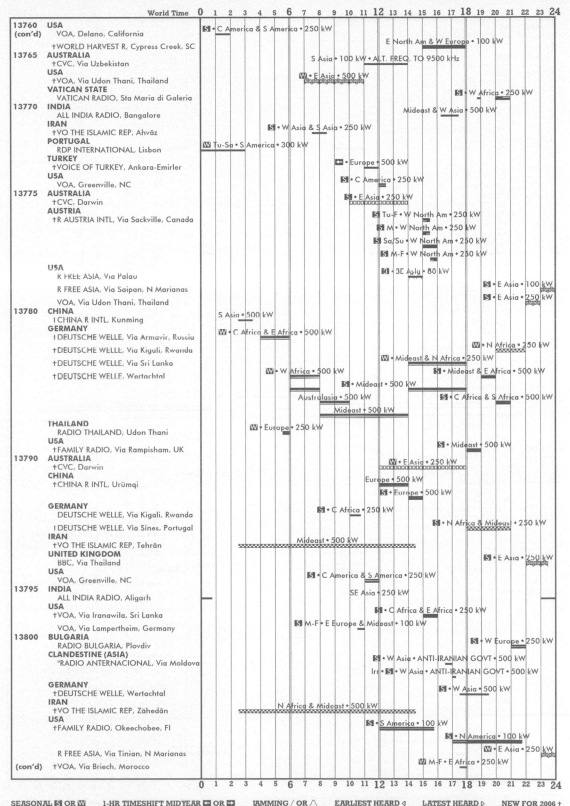

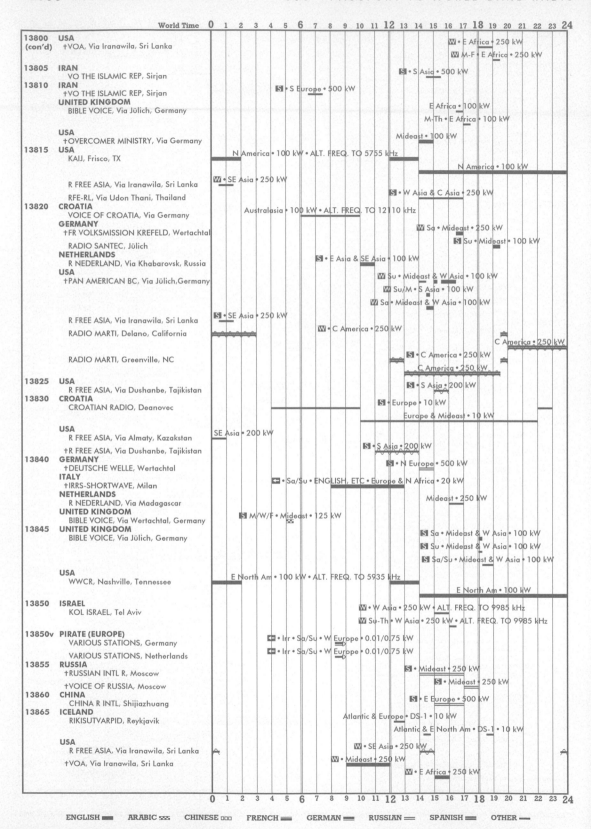

| | | World Time | 0 | 1 | 2 | 3 | 4 | 5 | 6 | 7 | 8 | 9 | 10 | 11 | 12 | 13 | 14 | 15 | 16 | 17 | 18 | 19 | 20 | 21 | 22 | 23 | 24 |

13800 (con'd) **USA**
†VOA, Via Iranawila, Sri Lanka
W • E Africa • 250 kW
W M-F • E Africa • 250 kW

13805 IRAN
VO THE ISLAMIC REP, Sirjan
S • S Asia • 500 kW

13810 IRAN
†VO THE ISLAMIC REP, Sirjan
S • S Europe • 500 kW

UNITED KINGDOM
BIBLE VOICE, Via Jülich, Germany
E Africa • 100 kW
M-Th • E Africa • 100 kW

USA
†OVERCOMER MINISTRY, Via Germany
Mideast • 100 kW

13815 USA
KAIJ, Frisco, TX
N America • 100 kW • ALT. FREQ. TO 5755 kHz
N America • 100 kW

R FREE ASIA, Via Iranawila, Sri Lanka
W • SE Asia • 250 kW

RFE-RL, Via Udon Thani, Thailand
S • W Asia & C Asia • 250 kW

13820 CROATIA
VOICE OF CROATIA, Via Germany
Australasia • 100 kW • ALT. FREQ. TO 12110 kHz

GERMANY
†FR VOLKSMISSION KREFELD, Wertachtal
W Sa • Mideast • 250 kW

RADIO SANTEC, Jülich
S Su • Mideast • 100 kW

NETHERLANDS
R NEDERLAND, Via Khabarovsk, Russia
S • E Asia & SE Asia • 100 kW

USA
†PAN AMERICAN BC, Via Jülich, Germany
W Su • Mideast & W Asia • 100 kW
W Su/M • S Asia • 100 kW
W Sa • Mideast & W Asia • 100 kW

R FREE ASIA, Via Iranawila, Sri Lanka
S • SE Asia • 250 kW

RADIO MARTI, Delano, California
W • C America • 250 kW
C America • 250 kW

RADIO MARTI, Greenville, NC
S • C America • 250 kW
C America • 250 kW

13825 USA
R FREE ASIA, Via Dushanbe, Tajikistan
S • S Asia • 200 kW

13830 CROATIA
CROATIAN RADIO, Deanovec
S • Europe • 10 kW
Europe & Mideast • 10 kW

USA
R FREE ASIA, Via Almaty, Kazakstan
SE Asia • 200 kW

†R FREE ASIA, Via Dushanbe, Tajikistan
S • S Asia • 200 kW

13840 GERMANY
†DEUTSCHE WELLE, Wertachtal
S • N Europe • 500 kW

ITALY
†IRRS-SHORTWAVE, Milan
• Sa/Su • ENGLISH, ETC • Europe & N Africa • 20 kW

NETHERLANDS
R NEDERLAND, Via Madagascar
Mideast • 250 kW

UNITED KINGDOM
BIBLE VOICE, Via Wertachtal, Germany
S M/W/F • Mideast • 125 kW

13845 UNITED KINGDOM
BIBLE VOICE, Via Jülich, Germany
S Sa • Mideast & W Asia • 100 kW
S Su • Mideast & W Asia • 100 kW
S Sa/Su • Mideast & W Asia • 100 kW

USA
WWCR, Nashville, Tennessee
E North Am • 100 kW • ALT. FREQ. TO 5935 kHz
E North Am • 100 kW

13850 ISRAEL
KOL ISRAEL, Tel Aviv
W • W Asia • 250 kW • ALT. FREQ. TO 9985 kHz
W Su-Th • W Asia • 250 kW • ALT. FREQ. TO 9985 kHz

13850v PIRATE (EUROPE)
VARIOUS STATIONS, Germany
• Irr • Sa/Su • W Europe • 0.01/0.75 kW

VARIOUS STATIONS, Netherlands
• Irr • Sa/Su • W Europe • 0.01/0.75 kW

13855 RUSSIA
†RUSSIAN INTL R, Moscow
S • Mideast • 250 kW

†VOICE OF RUSSIA, Moscow
S • Mideast • 250 kW

13860 CHINA
CHINA R INTL, Shijiazhuang
S • E Europe • 500 kW

13865 ICELAND
RIKISUTVARPID, Reykjavik
Atlantic & Europe • DS-1 • 10 kW
Atlantic & E North Am • DS-1 • 10 kW

USA
R FREE ASIA, Via Iranawila, Sri Lanka
W • SE Asia • 250 kW

†VOA, Via Iranawila, Sri Lanka
W • Mideast • 250 kW
W • E Africa • 250 kW

| | World Time | 0 | 1 | 2 | 3 | 4 | 5 | 6 | 7 | 8 | 9 | 10 | 11 | 12 | 13 | 14 | 15 | 16 | 17 | 18 | 19 | 20 | 21 | 22 | 23 | 24 |

ENGLISH ▬   ARABIC ▧   CHINESE ▯▯▯   FRENCH ▬   GERMAN ▬   RUSSIAN ═   SPANISH ▬   OTHER ▬

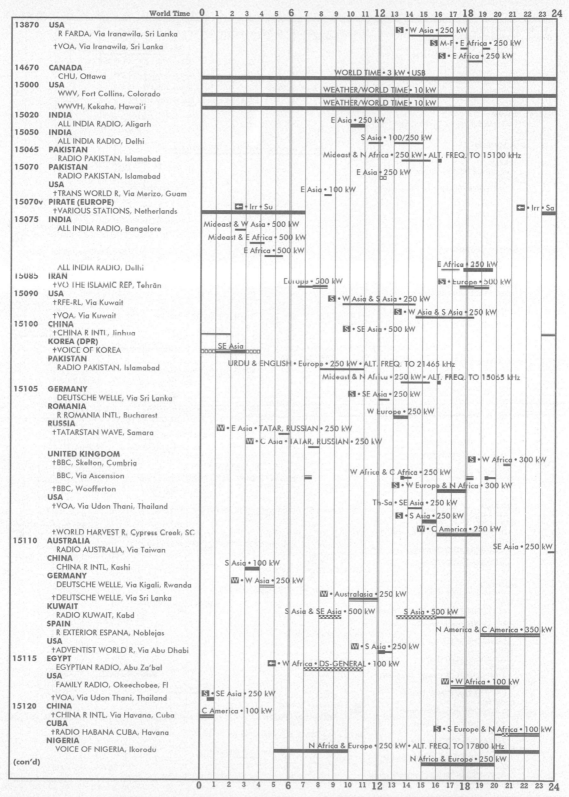

World Time	0 1 2 3 4 5 6 7 8 9 10 11 12 13 14 15 16 17 18 19 20 21 22 23 24
13870 **USA**	
R FARDA, Via Iranawila, Sri Lanka	S • W Asia • 250 kW
†VOA, Via Iranawila, Sri Lanka	S • M-F • E Africa • 250 kW
	S • E Africa • 250 kW
14670 **CANADA**	
CHU, Ottawa	WORLD TIME • 3 kW • USB
15000 **USA**	
WWV, Fort Collins, Colorado	WEATHER/WORLD TIME • 10 kW
WWVH, Kekaha, Hawai'i	WEATHER/WORLD TIME • 10 kW
15020 **INDIA**	
ALL INDIA RADIO, Aligarh	E Asia • 250 kW
15050 **INDIA**	
ALL INDIA RADIO, Delhi	S Asia • 100/250 kW
15065 **PAKISTAN**	
RADIO PAKISTAN, Islamabad	Mideast & N Africa • 250 kW • ALT. FREQ. TO 15100 kHz
15070 **PAKISTAN**	
RADIO PAKISTAN, Islamabad	E Asia • 250 kW
USA	
†TRANS WORLD R, Via Merizo, Guam	E Asia • 100 kW
15070v PIRATE (EUROPE)	
†VARIOUS STATIONS, Netherlands	⊏ • Irr • Su ⊏ • Irr • Sa
15075 **INDIA**	
ALL INDIA RADIO, Bangalore	Mideast & W Asia • 500 kW
	Mideast & E Africa • 500 kW
	E Africa • 500 kW
ALL INDIA RADIO, Delhi	E Africa • 250 kW
15085 **IRAN**	
†VO THE ISLAMIC REP, Tehrān	Europe • 500 kW S • Europe • 500 kW
15090 **USA**	
†RFE-RL, Via Kuwait	S • W Asia & S Asia • 250 kW
†VOA, Via Kuwait	S • W Asia & S Asia • 250 kW
15100 **CHINA**	
†CHINA R INTL, Jinhua	S • SE Asia • 500 kW
KOREA (DPR)	
†VOICE OF KOREA	SE Asia
PAKISTAN	
RADIO PAKISTAN, Islamabad	URDU & ENGLISH • Europe • 250 kW • ALT. FREQ. TO 21465 kHz
	Mideast & N Africa • 250 kW • ALT. FREQ. TO 15055 kHz
15105 **GERMANY**	
DEUTSCHE WELLE, Via Sri Lanka	S • SE Asia • 250 kW
ROMANIA	
R ROMANIA INTL, Bucharest	W Europe • 250 kW
RUSSIA	
†TATARSTAN WAVE, Samara	W • E Asia • TATAR, RUSSIAN • 250 kW
	W • C Asia • TATAR, RUSSIAN • 250 kW
UNITED KINGDOM	
†BBC, Skelton, Cumbria	S • W Africa • 300 kW
BBC, Via Ascension	W Africa & C Africa • 250 kW
†BBC, Woofferton	S • W Europe & N Africa • 300 kW
USA	
†VOA, Via Udon Thani, Thailand	Th-Sa • SE Asia • 250 kW
	S • S Asia • 250 kW
†WORLD HARVEST R, Cypress Creek, SC	W • C America • 250 kW
15110 **AUSTRALIA**	
RADIO AUSTRALIA, Via Taiwan	SE Asia • 250 kW
CHINA	
CHINA R INTL, Kashi	S Asia • 100 kW
GERMANY	
DEUTSCHE WELLE, Via Kigali, Rwanda	W • W Asia • 250 kW
†DEUTSCHE WELLE, Via Sri Lanka	W • Australasia • 250 kW
KUWAIT	
RADIO KUWAIT, Kabd	S Asia & SE Asia • 500 kW S Asia • 500 kW
SPAIN	
R EXTERIOR ESPANA, Noblejas	N America & C America • 350 kW
USA	
†ADVENTIST WORLD R, Via Abu Dhabi	W • S Asia • 250 kW
15115 **EGYPT**	
EGYPTIAN RADIO, Abu Za'bal	⊏ • W Africa • DS-GENERAL • 100 kW
USA	
FAMILY RADIO, Okeechobee, Fl	W • W Africa • 100 kW
†VOA, Via Udon Thani, Thailand	S • SE Asia • 250 kW
15120 **CHINA**	
†CHINA R INTL, Via Havana, Cuba	C America • 100 kW
CUBA	
†RADIO HABANA CUBA, Havana	S • S Europe & N Africa • 100 kW
NIGERIA	
VOICE OF NIGERIA, Ikorodu	N Africa & Europe • 250 kW • ALT. FREQ. TO 17800 kHz
(con'd)	N Africa & Europe • 250 kW

World Time	0 1 2 3 4 5 6 7 8 9 10 11 12 13 14 15 16 17 18 19 20 21 22 23 24

SEASONAL S OR W   1-HR TIMESHIFT MIDYEAR ⊏ OR ⊐   JAMMING / OR ∧   EARLIEST HEARD ◁   LATEST HEARD ▷   NEW FOR 2006 †

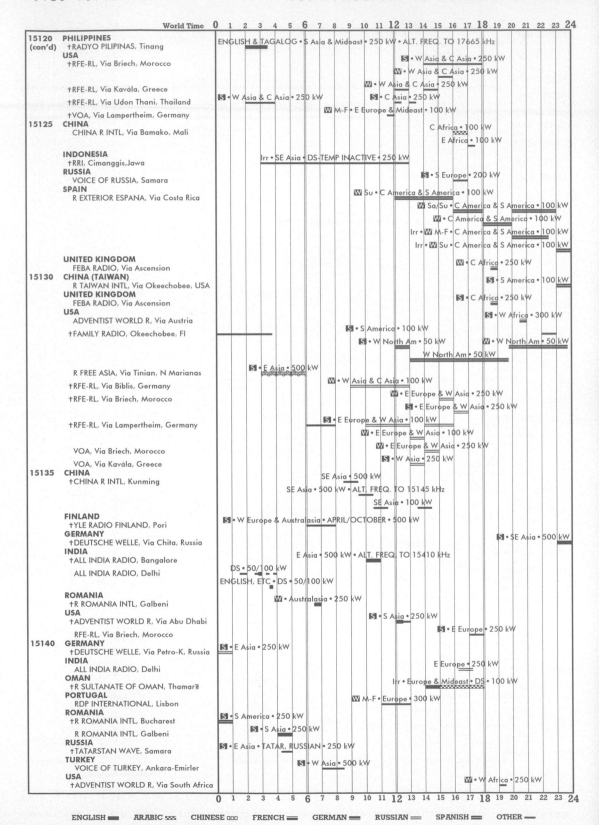

World Time 0 1 2 3 4 5 6 7 8 9 10 11 12 13 14 15 16 17 18 19 20 21 22 23 24

15120
(con'd) **PHILIPPINES**
   †RADYO PILIPINAS, Tinang — ENGLISH & TAGALOG • S Asia & Mideast • 250 kW • ALT. FREQ. TO 17665 kHz
USA
   †RFE-RL, Via Briech, Morocco — S • W Asia & C Asia • 250 kW
                                  — W • W Asia & C Asia • 250 kW
   †RFE-RL, Via Kavála, Greece — W • W Asia & C Asia • 250 kW
   †RFE-RL, Via Udon Thani, Thailand — S • W Asia & C Asia • 250 kW   S • C Asia • 250 kW
   †VOA, Via Lampertheim, Germany — W • M-F • E Europe & Mideast • 100 kW
15125 CHINA
   CHINA R INTL, Via Bamako, Mali — C Africa • 100 kW
                                  — E Africa • 100 kW

   INDONESIA
   †RRI, Cimanggis, Jawa — Irr • SE Asia • DS-TEMP INACTIVE • 250 kW
   RUSSIA
   VOICE OF RUSSIA, Samara — S • S Europe • 200 kW
   SPAIN
   R EXTERIOR ESPANA, Via Costa Rica — W • Su • C America & S America • 100 kW
                                      — W • Sa/Su • C America & S America • 100 kW
                                      — W • C America & S America • 100 kW
                                      — Irr • W • M-F • C America & S America • 100 kW
                                      — Irr • W • Su • C America & S America • 100 kW

   UNITED KINGDOM
   FEBA RADIO, Via Ascension — W • C Africa • 250 kW
15130 CHINA (TAIWAN)
   R TAIWAN INTL, Via Okeechobee, USA — S • S America • 100 kW
   UNITED KINGDOM
   FEBA RADIO, Via Ascension — S • C Africa • 250 kW
   USA
   ADVENTIST WORLD R, Via Austria — S • W Africa • 300 kW
   †FAMILY RADIO, Okeechobee, Fl — S • S America • 100 kW
                                  — S • W North Am • 50 kW   W • W North Am • 50 kW
                                  — W North Am • 50 kW
   R FREE ASIA, Via Tinian, N Marianas — S • E Asia • 500 kW
   †RFE-RL, Via Biblis, Germany — W • W Asia & C Asia • 100 kW
   †RFE-RL, Via Briech, Morocco — W • E Europe & W Asia • 250 kW
                                 — S • E Europe & W Asia • 250 kW
   †RFE-RL, Via Lampertheim, Germany — S • E Europe & W Asia • 100 kW
                                      — W • E Europe & W Asia • 100 kW
   VOA, Via Briech, Morocco — W • E Europe & W Asia • 250 kW
   VOA, Via Kavála, Greece — S • W Asia • 250 kW
15135 CHINA
   †CHINA R INTL, Kunming — SE Asia • 500 kW
                          — SE Asia • 500 kW • ALT. FREQ. TO 15145 kHz
                          — SE Asia • 100 kW
   FINLAND
   †YLE RADIO FINLAND, Pori — S • W Europe & Australasia • APRIL/OCTOBER • 500 kW
   GERMANY
   †DEUTSCHE WELLE, Via Chita, Russia — S • SE Asia • 500 kW
   INDIA
   †ALL INDIA RADIO, Bangalore — E Asia • 500 kW • ALT. FREQ. TO 15410 kHz
   ALL INDIA RADIO, Delhi — DS • 50/100 kW
                          — ENGLISH, ETC • DS • 50/100 kW
   ROMANIA
   †R ROMANIA INTL, Galbeni — W • Australasia • 250 kW
   USA
   †ADVENTIST WORLD R, Via Abu Dhabi — S • S Asia • 250 kW
                                      — S • E Europe • 250 kW
   RFE-RL, Via Briech, Morocco
15140 GERMANY
   †DEUTSCHE WELLE, Via Petro-K, Russia — S • E Asia • 250 kW
   INDIA
   ALL INDIA RADIO, Delhi — E Europe • 250 kW
   OMAN
   †R SULTANATE OF OMAN, Thamarīt — Irr • Europe & Mideast • DS • 100 kW
   PORTUGAL
   RDP INTERNATIONAL, Lisbon — W • M-F • Europe • 300 kW
   ROMANIA
   †R ROMANIA INTL, Bucharest — S • S America • 250 kW
   R ROMANIA INTL, Galbeni — S • S Asia • 250 kW
   RUSSIA
   †TATARSTAN WAVE, Samara — S • E Asia • TATAR, RUSSIAN • 250 kW
   TURKEY
   VOICE OF TURKEY, Ankara-Emirler — S • W Asia • 500 kW
   USA
   †ADVENTIST WORLD R, Via South Africa — W • W Africa • 250 kW

0 1 2 3 4 5 6 7 8 9 10 11 12 13 14 15 16 17 18 19 20 21 22 23 24

ENGLISH ▬   ARABIC ▨   CHINESE □□□   FRENCH ▭▭   GERMAN ▬▬   RUSSIAN ══   SPANISH ▭▭   OTHER ▬

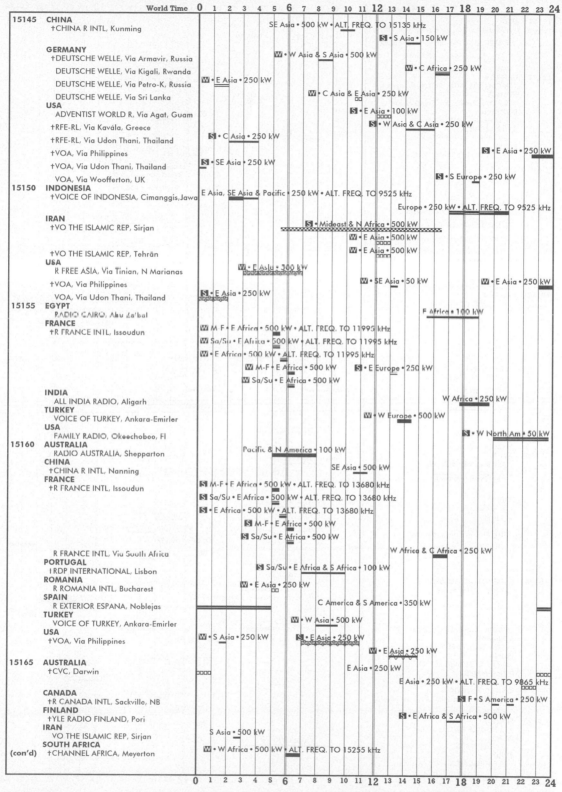

	World Time	0 1 2 3 4 5 6 7 8 9 10 11 12 13 14 15 16 17 18 19 20 21 22 23 24
15145	CHINA	
	†CHINA R INTL, Kunming	SE Asia • 500 kW • ALT. FREQ. TO 15135 kHz
		S • S Asia • 150 kW
	GERMANY	
	†DEUTSCHE WELLE, Via Armavir, Russia	W • W Asia & S Asia • 500 kW
	DEUTSCHE WELLE, Via Kigali, Rwanda	W • C Africa • 250 kW
	DEUTSCHE WELLE, Via Petro-K, Russia	W • E Asia • 250 kW
	DEUTSCHE WELLE, Via Sri Lanka	W • C Asia & E Asia • 250 kW
	USA	
	ADVENTIST WORLD R, Via Agat, Guam	S • E Asia • 100 kW
	†RFE-RL, Via Kavála, Greece	S • W Asia & C Asia • 250 kW
	†RFE-RL, Via Udon Thani, Thailand	S • C Asia • 250 kW
	†VOA, Via Philippines	S • E Asia • 250 kW
	†VOA, Via Udon Thani, Thailand	S • SE Asia • 250 kW
	VOA, Via Woofferton, UK	S • S Europe • 250 kW
15150	INDONESIA	
	†VOICE OF INDONESIA, Cimanggis, Jawa	E Asia, SE Asia & Pacific • 250 kW • ALT. FREQ. TO 9525 kHz
		Europe • 250 kW • ALT. FREQ. TO 9525 kHz
	IRAN	
	†VO THE ISLAMIC REP, Sirjan	S • Mideast & N Africa • 500 kW
		W • E Asia • 500 kW
	†VO THE ISLAMIC REP, Tehrān	W • E Asia • 500 kW
	USA	
	R FREE ASIA, Via Tinian, N Marianas	W • E Asia • 300 kW
	†VOA, Via Philippines	W • SE Asia • 50 kW W • E Asia • 250 kW
	VOA, Via Udon Thani, Thailand	S • E Asia • 250 kW
15155	EGYPT	
	RADIO CAIRO, Abu Za'bal	E Africa • 100 kW
	FRANCE	
	†R FRANCE INTL, Issoudun	W M-F • E Africa • 500 kW • ALT. FREQ. TO 11995 kHz
		W Sa/Su • E Africa • 500 kW • ALT. FREQ. TO 11995 kHz
		W • E Africa • 500 kW • ALT. FREQ. TO 11995 kHz
		W M-F • E Africa • 500 kW S • E Europe • 250 kW
		W Sa/Su • E Africa • 500 kW
	INDIA	
	ALL INDIA RADIO, Aligarh	W Africa • 250 kW
	TURKEY	
	VOICE OF TURKEY, Ankara-Emirler	W • W Europe • 500 kW
	USA	
	FAMILY RADIO, Okeechobee, Fl	S • W North Am • 50 kW
15160	AUSTRALIA	
	RADIO AUSTRALIA, Shepparton	Pacific & N America • 100 kW
	CHINA	
	†CHINA R INTL, Nanning	SE Asia • 500 kW
	FRANCE	
	†R FRANCE INTL, Issoudun	S M-F • E Africa • 500 kW • ALT. FREQ. TO 13680 kHz
		S Sa/Su • E Africa • 500 kW • ALT. FREQ. TO 13680 kHz
		S • E Africa • 500 kW • ALT. FREQ. TO 13680 kHz
		S M-F • E Africa • 500 kW
		S Sa/Su • E Africa • 500 kW
	R FRANCE INTL, Via South Africa	W Africa & C Africa • 250 kW
	PORTUGAL	
	†RDP INTERNATIONAL, Lisbon	S Sa/Su • E Africa & S Africa • 100 kW
	ROMANIA	
	R ROMANIA INTL, Bucharest	W • E Asia • 250 kW
	SPAIN	
	R EXTERIOR ESPANA, Noblejas	C America & S America • 350 kW
	TURKEY	
	VOICE OF TURKEY, Ankara-Emirler	W • W Asia • 500 kW
	USA	
	†VOA, Via Philippines	W • S Asia • 250 kW S • E Asia • 250 kW
		W • E Asia • 250 kW
15165	AUSTRALIA	
	†CVC, Darwin	E Asia • 250 kW
		E Asia • 250 kW • ALT. FREQ. TO 9865 kHz
	CANADA	
	†R CANADA INTL, Sackville, NB	S • S America • 250 kW
	FINLAND	
	†YLE RADIO FINLAND, Pori	S • E Africa & S Africa • 500 kW
	IRAN	
	VO THE ISLAMIC REP, Sirjan	S Asia • 500 kW
	SOUTH AFRICA	
(con'd)	†CHANNEL AFRICA, Meyerton	W • W Africa • 500 kW • ALT. FREQ. TO 15255 kHz

0 1 2 3 4 5 6 7 8 9 10 11 12 13 14 15 16 17 18 19 20 21 22 23 24

SEASONAL S OR W   1-HR TIMESHIFT MIDYEAR ⇦ OR ⇨   JAMMING / OR /\   EARLIEST HEARD ◁   LATEST HEARD ▷   NEW FOR 2006 †

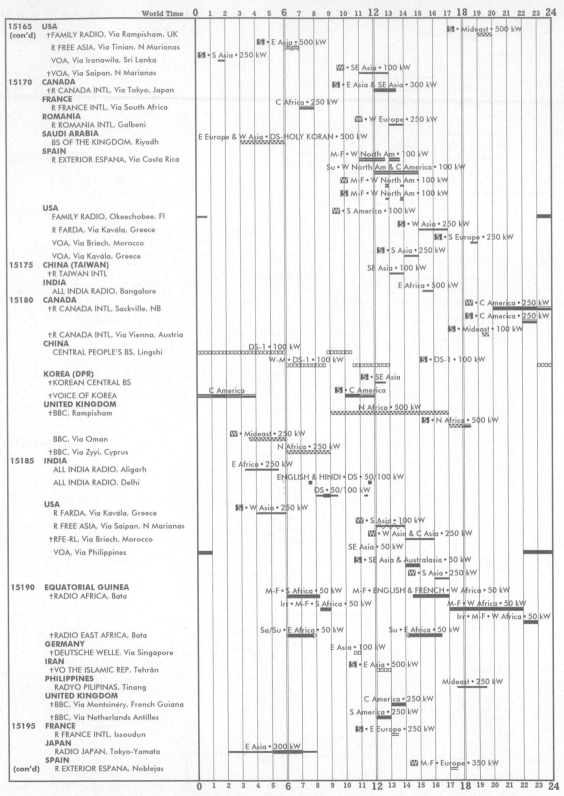

		World Time	
15165 (con'd)	USA	†FAMILY RADIO, Via Rampisham, UK	S • Mideast • 500 kW
		R FREE ASIA, Via Tinian, N Marianas	S • E Asia • 500 kW
		VOA, Via Iranawila, Sri Lanka	S • S Asia • 250 kW
		†VOA, Via Saipan, N Marianas	W • SE Asia • 100 kW
15170	CANADA	†R CANADA INTL, Via Tokyo, Japan	S • E Asia & SE Asia • 300 kW
	FRANCE	R FRANCE INTL, Via South Africa	C Africa • 250 kW
	ROMANIA	R ROMANIA INTL, Galbeni	W • W Europe • 250 kW
	SAUDI ARABIA	BS OF THE KINGDOM, Riyadh	E Europe & W Asia • DS-HOLY KORAN • 500 kW
	SPAIN	R EXTERIOR ESPANA, Via Costa Rica	M-F • W North Am • 100 kW
			Su • W North Am & C America • 100 kW
			W M-F • W North Am • 100 kW
			S M-F • W North Am • 100 kW
	USA	FAMILY RADIO, Okeechobee, Fl	W • S America • 100 kW
		R FARDA, Via Kavála, Greece	S • W Asia • 250 kW
		VOA, Via Briech, Morocco	S • S Europe • 250 kW
		VOA, Via Kavála, Greece	S • S Asia • 250 kW
15175	CHINA (TAIWAN)	†R TAIWAN INTL	SE Asia • 100 kW
	INDIA	ALL INDIA RADIO, Bangalore	E Africa • 500 kW
15180	CANADA	†R CANADA INTL, Sackville, NB	W • C America • 250 kW
			S • C America • 250 kW
		†R CANADA INTL, Via Vienna, Austria	S • Mideast • 100 kW
	CHINA	CENTRAL PEOPLE'S BS, Lingshi	DS-1 • 100 kW
			W-M • DS-1 • 100 kW
			S • DS-1 • 100 kW
	KOREA (DPR)	†KOREAN CENTRAL BS	S • SE Asia
		†VOICE OF KOREA	S • C America
			C America
	UNITED KINGDOM	†BBC, Rampisham	N Africa • 500 kW
			S • N Africa • 500 kW
		BBC, Via Oman	W • Mideast • 250 kW
		†BBC, Via Zyyi, Cyprus	N Africa • 250 kW
15185	INDIA	ALL INDIA RADIO, Aligarh	E Africa • 250 kW
		ALL INDIA RADIO, Delhi	ENGLISH & HINDI • DS • 50/100 kW
			DS • 50/100 kW
	USA	R FARDA, Via Kavála, Greece	S • W Asia • 250 kW
		R FREE ASIA, Via Saipan, N Marianas	W • S Asia • 100 kW
		†RFE-RL, Via Briech, Morocco	W • W Asia & C Asia • 250 kW
		VOA, Via Philippines	SE Asia • 50 kW
			S • SE Asia & Australasia • 50 kW
			W • S Asia • 250 kW
15190	EQUATORIAL GUINEA	†RADIO AFRICA, Bata	M-F • S Africa • 50 kW	M-F • ENGLISH & FRENCH • W Africa • 50 kW
			Irr • M-F • S Africa • 50 kW
			M-F • W Africa • 50 kW
			Irr • M-F • W Africa • 50 kW
		†RADIO EAST AFRICA, Bata	Sa/Su • E Africa • 50 kW	Su • E Africa • 50 kW
	GERMANY	†DEUTSCHE WELLE, Via Singapore	E Asia • 100 kW
	IRAN	†VO THE ISLAMIC REP, Tehrān	S • E Asia • 500 kW
	PHILIPPINES	RADYO PILIPINAS, Tinang	Mideast • 250 kW
	UNITED KINGDOM	†BBC, Via Montsinéry, French Guiana	C America • 250 kW
		†BBC, Via Netherlands Antilles	S America • 250 kW
15195	FRANCE	R FRANCE INTL, Issoudun	S • E Europe • 250 kW
	JAPAN	RADIO JAPAN, Tokyo-Yamata	E Asia • 300 kW
	SPAIN (con'd)	R EXTERIOR ESPANA, Noblejas	W M-F • Europe • 350 kW

ENGLISH ▬ ARABIC ⬚ CHINESE ⬚ FRENCH ▬ GERMAN ▬ RUSSIAN ═ SPANISH ▬ OTHER ▬

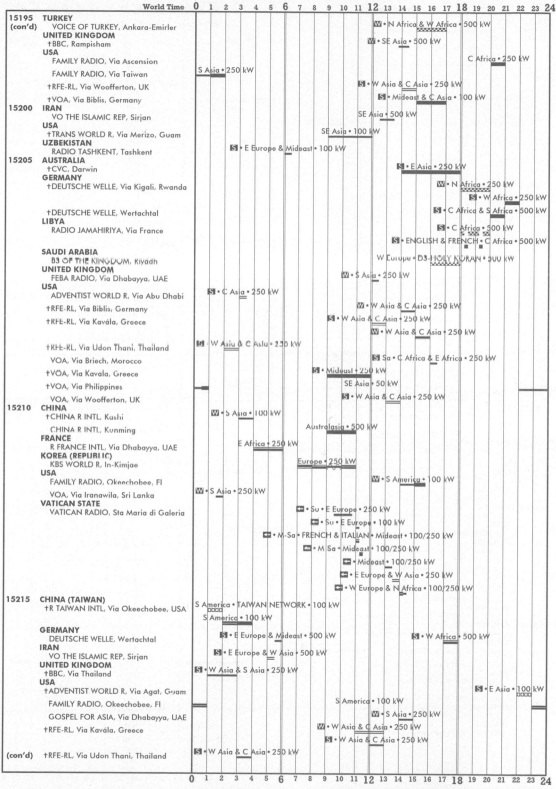

	World Time	0	1	2	3	4	5	6	7	8	9	10	11	12	13	14	15	16	17	18	19	20	21	22	23	24

15195 (con'd) TURKEY
VOICE OF TURKEY, Ankara-Emirler — W • N Africa & W Africa • 500 kW
UNITED KINGDOM
†BBC, Rampisham — W • SE Asia • 500 kW
USA
FAMILY RADIO, Via Ascension — C Africa • 250 kW
FAMILY RADIO, Via Taiwan — S Asia • 250 kW
†RFE-RL, Via Woofferton, UK — S • W Asia & C Asia • 250 kW
†VOA, Via Biblis, Germany — S • Mideast & C Asia • 100 kW

15200 IRAN
VO THE ISLAMIC REP, Sirjan — SE Asia • 500 kW
USA
†TRANS WORLD R, Via Merizo, Guam — SE Asia • 100 kW
UZBEKISTAN
RADIO TASHKENT, Tashkent — S • E Europe & Mideast • 100 kW

15205 AUSTRALIA
†CVC, Darwin — S • E Asia • 250 kW
GERMANY
†DEUTSCHE WELLE, Via Kigali, Rwanda — W • N Africa • 250 kW
— S • W Africa • 250 kW
†DEUTSCHE WELLE, Wertachtal — S • C Africa & S Africa • 500 kW
LIBYA
RADIO JAMAHIRIYA, Via France — S • C Africa • 500 kW
— S • ENGLISH & FRENCH • C Africa • 500 kW
SAUDI ARABIA
BS OF THE KINGDOM, Riyadh — W Europe • BS-HOLY KURAN • 500 kW
UNITED KINGDOM
FEBA RADIO, Via Dhabayya, UAE — W • S Asia • 250 kW
USA
ADVENTIST WORLD R, Via Abu Dhabi — S • C Asia • 250 kW
†RFE-RL, Via Biblis, Germany — W • W Asia & C Asia • 250 kW
†RFE-RL, Via Kavála, Greece — S • W Asia & C Asia • 250 kW
— W • W Asia & C Asia • 250 kW
†RFE-RL, Via Udon Thani, Thailand — W • W Asia & C Asia • 250 kW
VOA, Via Briech, Morocco — S • C Africa & E Africa • 250 kW
†VOA, Via Kavala, Greece — S • Mideast • 250 kW
†VOA, Via Philippines — SE Asia • 50 kW
VOA, Via Woofferton, UK — S • W Asia & C Asia • 250 kW

15210 CHINA
†CHINA R INTL, Kashi — W • S Asia • 100 kW
CHINA R INTL, Kunming — Australasia • 500 kW
FRANCE
R FRANCE INTL, Via Dhabayya, UAE — E Africa • 250 kW
KOREA (REPUBLIC)
KBS WORLD R, In-Kimjae — Europe • 250 kW
USA
FAMILY RADIO, Okeechobee, Fl — W • S America • 100 kW
VOA, Via Iranawila, Sri Lanka — W • S Asia • 250 kW
VATICAN STATE
VATICAN RADIO, Sta Maria di Galeria — ↔ • Su • E Europe • 250 kW
— ↔ • Su • E Europe • 100 kW
— ↔ • M-Sa • FRENCH & ITALIAN • Mideast • 100/250 kW
— ↔ • M-Sa • Mideast • 100/250 kW
— ↔ • Mideast • 100/250 kW
— ↔ • E Europe & W Asia • 250 kW
— ↔ • W Europe & N Africa • 100/250 kW

15215 CHINA (TAIWAN)
†R TAIWAN INTL, Via Okeechobee, USA — S America • TAIWAN NETWORK • 100 kW
— S America • 100 kW
GERMANY
DEUTSCHE WELLE, Wertachtal — S • E Europe & Mideast • 500 kW
— S • W Africa • 500 kW
IRAN
VO THE ISLAMIC REP, Sirjan — S • E Europe & W Asia • 500 kW
UNITED KINGDOM
†BBC, Via Thailand — S • W Asia & S Asia • 250 kW
USA
†ADVENTIST WORLD R, Via Agat, Guam — S • E Asia • 100 kW
FAMILY RADIO, Okeechobee, Fl — S America • 100 kW
GOSPEL FOR ASIA, Via Dhabayya, UAE — W • S Asia • 250 kW
†RFE-RL, Via Kavála, Greece — W • W Asia & C Asia • 250 kW
— S • W Asia & C Asia • 250 kW
(con'd) †RFE-RL, Via Udon Thani, Thailand — S • W Asia & C Asia • 250 kW

	0	1	2	3	4	5	6	7	8	9	10	11	12	13	14	15	16	17	18	19	20	21	22	23	24

SEASONAL S OR W   1-HR TIMESHIFT MIDYEAR ↔ OR ↔   JAMMING / OR ∧   EARLIEST HEARD ◁   LATEST HEARD ▷   NEW FOR 2006 †

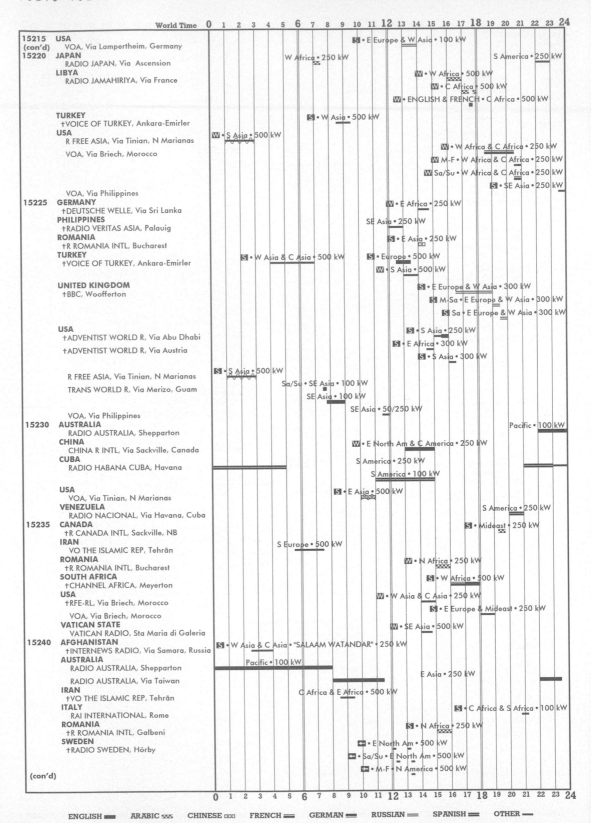

| | | | World Time | 0 | 1 | 2 | 3 | 4 | 5 | 6 | 7 | 8 | 9 | 10 | 11 | 12 | 13 | 14 | 15 | 16 | 17 | 18 | 19 | 20 | 21 | 22 | 23 | 24 |

15215 (con'd) USA VOA, Via Lampertheim, Germany — S • E Europe & W Asia • 100 kW

15220 JAPAN RADIO JAPAN, Via Ascension — W Africa • 250 kW ; S America • 250 kW

LIBYA RADIO JAMAHIRIYA, Via France — W • W Africa • 500 kW ; W • C Africa • 500 kW ; W • ENGLISH & FRENCH • C Africa • 500 kW

TURKEY †VOICE OF TURKEY, Ankara-Emirler — S • W Asia • 500 kW

USA R FREE ASIA, Via Tinian, N Marianas — W • S Asia • 500 kW

VOA, Via Briech, Morocco — W • W Africa & C Africa • 250 kW ; W M-F • W Africa & C Africa • 250 kW ; W Sa/Su • W Africa & C Africa • 250 kW ; S • SE Asia • 250 kW

VOA, Via Philippines

15225 GERMANY †DEUTSCHE WELLE, Via Sri Lanka — W • E Africa • 250 kW

PHILIPPINES †RADIO VERITAS ASIA, Palauig — SE Asia • 250 kW

ROMANIA †R ROMANIA INTL, Bucharest — S • E Asia • 250 kW

TURKEY †VOICE OF TURKEY, Ankara-Emirler — S • W Asia & C Asia • 500 kW ; S • Europe • 500 kW ; W • S Asia • 500 kW

UNITED KINGDOM †BBC, Woofferton — S • E Europe & W Asia • 300 kW ; S M-Sa • E Europe & W Asia • 300 kW ; S Sa • E Europe & W Asia • 300 kW

USA †ADVENTIST WORLD R, Via Abu Dhabi — S • S Asia • 250 kW ; S • E Africa • 300 kW

†ADVENTIST WORLD R, Via Austria — S • S Asia • 300 kW

R FREE ASIA, Via Tinian, N Marianas — S • S Asia • 500 kW

TRANS WORLD R, Via Merizo, Guam — Sa/Su • SE Asia • 100 kW ; SE Asia • 100 kW ; SE Asia • 50/250 kW

VOA, Via Philippines

15230 AUSTRALIA RADIO AUSTRALIA, Shepparton — Pacific • 100 kW

CHINA CHINA R INTL, Via Sackville, Canada — W • E North Am & C America • 250 kW

CUBA RADIO HABANA CUBA, Havana — S America • 250 kW ; S America • 100 kW

USA VOA, Via Tinian, N Marianas — S • E Asia • 500 kW

VENEZUELA RADIO NACIONAL, Via Havana, Cuba — S America • 250 kW

15235 CANADA †R CANADA INTL, Sackville, NB — S • Mideast • 250 kW

IRAN VO THE ISLAMIC REP, Tehrān — S Europe • 500 kW

ROMANIA †R ROMANIA INTL, Bucharest — W • N Africa • 250 kW

SOUTH AFRICA †CHANNEL AFRICA, Meyerton — S • W Africa • 500 kW

USA †RFE-RL, Via Briech, Morocco — W • W Asia & C Asia • 250 kW

VOA, Via Briech, Morocco — S • E Europe & Mideast • 250 kW

VATICAN STATE VATICAN RADIO, Sta Maria di Galeria — W • SE Asia • 500 kW

15240 AFGHANISTAN †INTERNEWS RADIO, Via Samara, Russia — S • W Asia & C Asia • "SALAAM WATANDAR" • 250 kW

AUSTRALIA RADIO AUSTRALIA, Shepparton — Pacific • 100 kW

RADIO AUSTRALIA, Via Taiwan — E Asia • 250 kW

IRAN †VO THE ISLAMIC REP, Tehrān — C Africa & E Africa • 500 kW

ITALY RAI INTERNATIONAL, Rome — S • C Africa & S Africa • 100 kW

ROMANIA †R ROMANIA INTL, Galbeni — S • N Africa • 250 kW

SWEDEN †RADIO SWEDEN, Hörby — • E North Am • 500 kW ; • Sa/Su • E North Am • 500 kW ; • M-F • N America • 500 kW

(con'd)

| | | | | 0 | 1 | 2 | 3 | 4 | 5 | 6 | 7 | 8 | 9 | 10 | 11 | 12 | 13 | 14 | 15 | 16 | 17 | 18 | 19 | 20 | 21 | 22 | 23 | 24 |

ENGLISH ▬   ARABIC ▨   CHINESE ▢▢▢   FRENCH ▬   GERMAN ▬   RUSSIAN ═   SPANISH ▬   OTHER ▬

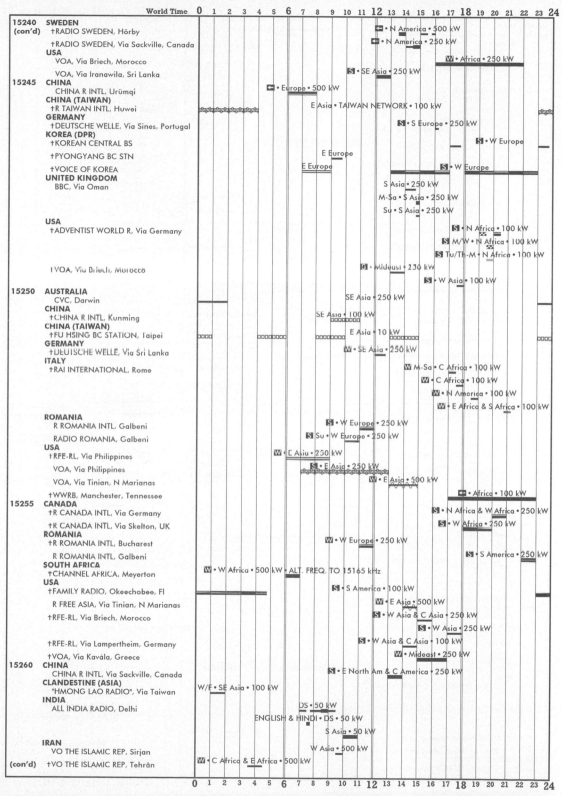

World Time   0 1 2 3 4 5 6 7 8 9 10 11 12 13 14 15 16 17 18 19 20 21 22 23 24

15240 SWEDEN
(con'd)   †RADIO SWEDEN, Hörby   ◻ • N America • 500 kW
   †RADIO SWEDEN, Via Sackville, Canada   ◻ • N America • 250 kW
USA
   VOA, Via Briech, Morocco   W • Africa • 250 kW
   VOA, Via Iranawila, Sri Lanka   S • SE Asia • 250 kW

15245 CHINA
   CHINA R INTL, Ürümqi   ◻ • Europe • 500 kW
CHINA (TAIWAN)
   †R TAIWAN INTL, Huwei   E Asia • TAIWAN NETWORK • 100 kW
GERMANY
   †DEUTSCHE WELLE, Via Sines, Portugal   S • S Europe • 250 kW
KOREA (DPR)
   †KOREAN CENTRAL BS   S • W Europe
   †PYONGYANG BC STN   E Europe
   †VOICE OF KOREA   E Europe   S • W Europe
UNITED KINGDOM
   BBC, Via Oman   S Asia • 250 kW
     M-Sa • S Asia • 250 kW
     Su • S Asia • 250 kW
USA
   †ADVENTIST WORLD R, Via Germany   S • N Africa • 100 kW
     S • M/W • N Africa • 100 kW
     S • Tu/Th-M • N Africa • 100 kW
   †VOA, Via Briech, Morocco   ◻ • Mideast • 250 kW
     S • W Asia • 100 kW

15250 AUSTRALIA
   CVC, Darwin   SE Asia • 250 kW
CHINA
   †CHINA R INTL, Kunming   SE Asia • 100 kW
CHINA (TAIWAN)
   †FU HSING BC STATION, Taipei   E Asia • 10 kW
GERMANY
   †DEUTSCHE WELLE, Via Sri Lanka   W • SE Asia • 250 kW
ITALY
   †RAI INTERNATIONAL, Rome   W M-Sa • C Africa • 100 kW
     W • C Africa • 100 kW
     W • N America • 100 kW
     W • E Africa & S Africa • 100 kW
ROMANIA
   R ROMANIA INTL, Galbeni   S • W Europe • 250 kW
   RADIO ROMANIA, Galbeni   S • Su • W Europe • 250 kW
USA
   †RFE-RL, Via Philippines   W • E Asia • 250 kW
   VOA, Via Philippines   S • E Asia • 250 kW
   VOA, Via Tinian, N Marianas   W • E Asia • 500 kW
   †WWRB, Manchester, Tennessee   ◻ • Africa • 100 kW

15255 CANADA
   †R CANADA INTL, Via Germany   S • N Africa & W Africa • 250 kW
   †R CANADA INTL, Via Skelton, UK   S • W Africa • 250 kW
ROMANIA
   †R ROMANIA INTL, Bucharest   W • W Europe • 250 kW
   R ROMANIA INTL, Galbeni   S • S America • 250 kW
SOUTH AFRICA
   †CHANNEL AFRICA, Meyerton   W • W Africa • 500 kW • ALT. FREQ. TO 15165 kHz
USA
   †FAMILY RADIO, Okeechobee, Fl   S • S America • 100 kW
   R FREE ASIA, Via Tinian, N Marianas   W • E Asia • 500 kW
   †RFE-RL, Via Briech, Morocco   S • W Asia & C Asia • 250 kW
     S • W Asia • 250 kW
   †RFE-RL, Via Lampertheim, Germany   S • W Asia & C Asia • 100 kW
   †VOA, Via Kavála, Greece   W • Mideast • 250 kW

15260 CHINA
   CHINA R INTL, Via Sackville, Canada   S • E North Am & C America • 250 kW
CLANDESTINE (ASIA)
   "HMONG LAO RADIO", Via Taiwan   W/F • SE Asia • 100 kW
INDIA
   ALL INDIA RADIO, Delhi   DS • 50 kW
     ENGLISH & HINDI • DS • 50 kW
     S Asia • 50 kW
IRAN
   VO THE ISLAMIC REP, Sirjan   W Asia • 500 kW
(con'd)   †VO THE ISLAMIC REP, Tehrän   W • C Africa & E Africa • 500 kW

0 1 2 3 4 5 6 7 8 9 10 11 12 13 14 15 16 17 18 19 20 21 22 23 24

SEASONAL S OR W   1-HR TIMESHIFT MIDYEAR ◻ OR ⬌   JAMMING / OR ∧   EARLIEST HEARD ◁   LATEST HEARD ▷   NEW FOR 2006 †

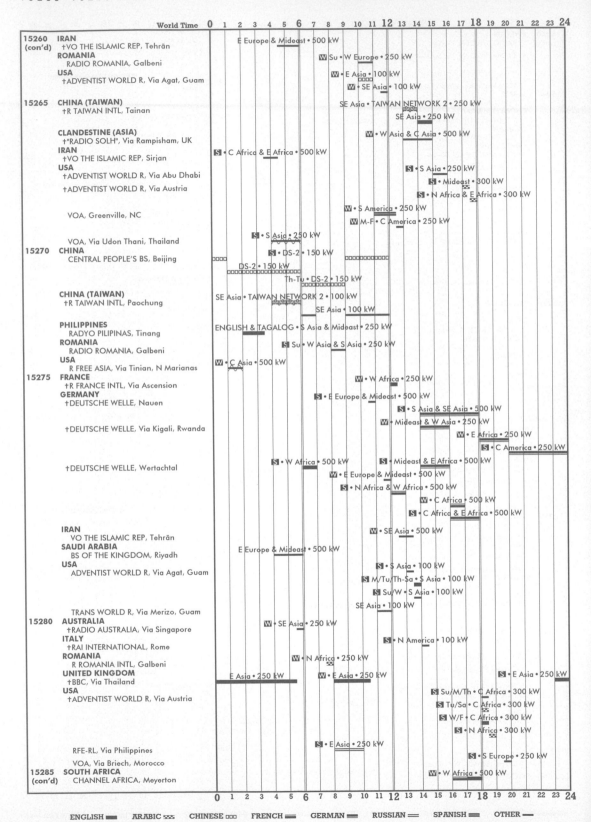

15260 (con'd) **IRAN** †VO THE ISLAMIC REP, Tehrān	E Europe & Mideast • 500 kW
ROMANIA RADIO ROMANIA, Galbeni	W Su • W Europe • 250 kW
USA †ADVENTIST WORLD R, Via Agat, Guam	W • E Asia • 100 kW
	W • SE Asia • 100 kW
15265 CHINA (TAIWAN) †R TAIWAN INTL, Tainan	SE Asia • TAIWAN NETWORK 2 • 250 kW
	SE Asia • 250 kW
CLANDESTINE (ASIA) †"RADIO SOLH", Via Rampisham, UK	W • W Asia & C Asia • 500 kW
IRAN †VO THE ISLAMIC REP, Sirjan	S • C Africa & E Africa • 500 kW
USA †ADVENTIST WORLD R, Via Abu Dhabi	S • S Asia • 250 kW
	S • Mideast • 300 kW
†ADVENTIST WORLD R, Via Austria	S • N Africa & E Africa • 300 kW
VOA, Greenville, NC	W • S America • 250 kW
	W M-F • C America • 250 kW
VOA, Via Udon Thani, Thailand	S • S Asia • 250 kW
15270 CHINA CENTRAL PEOPLE'S BS, Beijing	S • DS-2 • 150 kW
	DS-2 • 150 kW
	DS-2 • 150 kW
	Th-Tu • DS-2 • 150 kW
CHINA (TAIWAN) †R TAIWAN INTL, Paochung	SE Asia • TAIWAN NETWORK 2 • 100 kW
	SE Asia • 100 kW
PHILIPPINES RADYO PILIPINAS, Tinang	ENGLISH & TAGALOG • S Asia & Mideast • 250 kW
ROMANIA RADIO ROMANIA, Galbeni	S Su • W Asia & S Asia • 250 kW
USA R FREE ASIA, Via Tinian, N Marianas	W • C Asia • 500 kW
15275 FRANCE †R FRANCE INTL, Via Ascension	W • W Africa • 250 kW
GERMANY †DEUTSCHE WELLE, Nauen	S • E Europe & Mideast • 500 kW
	S • S Asia & SE Asia • 500 kW
†DEUTSCHE WELLE, Via Kigali, Rwanda	W • Mideast & W Asia • 250 kW
	W • E Africa • 250 kW
	S • C America • 250 kW
†DEUTSCHE WELLE, Wertachtal	S • W Africa • 500 kW
	S • Mideast & E Africa • 500 kW
	W • E Europe & Mideast • 500 kW
	S • N Africa & W Africa • 500 kW
	W • C Africa • 500 kW
	S • C Africa & E Africa • 500 kW
IRAN VO THE ISLAMIC REP, Tehrān	W • SE Asia • 500 kW
SAUDI ARABIA BS OF THE KINGDOM, Riyadh	E Europe & Mideast • 500 kW
USA ADVENTIST WORLD R, Via Agat, Guam	S • S Asia • 100 kW
	S M/Tu,Th-Sa • S Asia • 100 kW
	S Su • W • S Asia • 100 kW
	SE Asia • 100 kW
TRANS WORLD R, Via Merizo, Guam	
15280 AUSTRALIA †RADIO AUSTRALIA, Via Singapore	W • SE Asia • 250 kW
ITALY †RAI INTERNATIONAL, Rome	S • N America • 100 kW
ROMANIA R ROMANIA INTL, Galbeni	W • N Africa • 250 kW
UNITED KINGDOM †BBC, Via Thailand	E Asia • 250 kW W • E Asia • 250 kW S • E Asia • 250 kW
USA †ADVENTIST WORLD R, Via Austria	S Su/M/Th • C Africa • 300 kW
	S Tu/Sa • C Africa • 300 kW
	S W/F • C Africa • 300 kW
	S • N Africa • 300 kW
RFE-RL, Via Philippines	S • E Asia • 250 kW
VOA, Via Briech, Morocco	S • S Europe • 250 kW
15285 (con'd) **SOUTH AFRICA** CHANNEL AFRICA, Meyerton	W • W Africa • 500 kW

ENGLISH ▬   ARABIC ▨   CHINESE ▯▯▯   FRENCH ═   GERMAN ▬   RUSSIAN ═   SPANISH ═   OTHER ▬

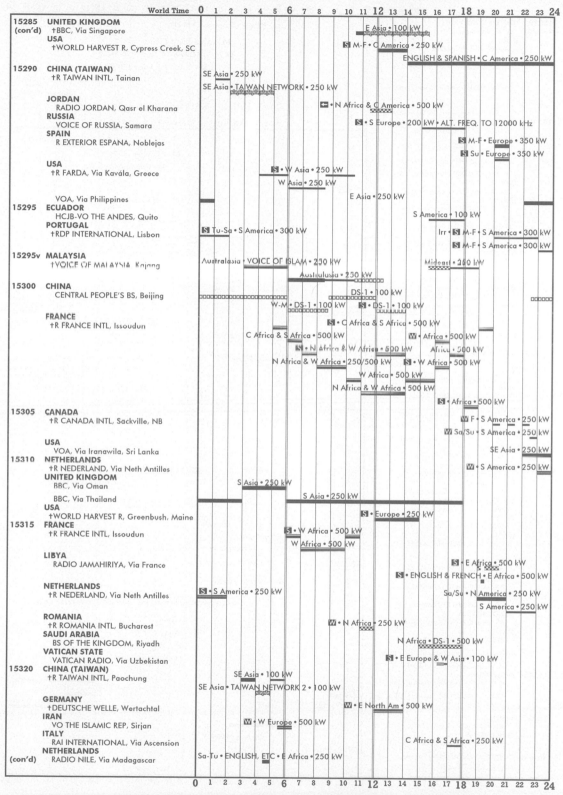

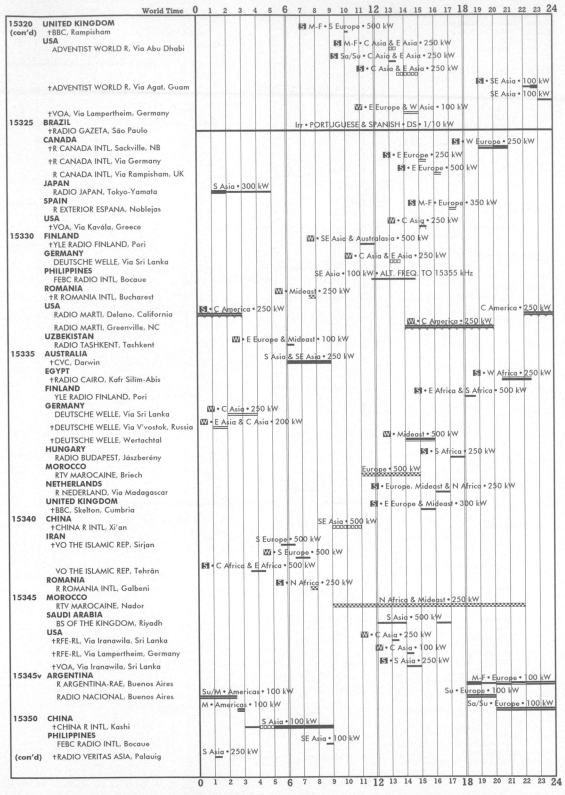

World Time 0 1 2 3 4 5 6 7 8 9 10 11 12 13 14 15 16 17 18 19 20 21 22 23 24

15320 UNITED KINGDOM
(con'd)   †BBC, Rampisham — S • M-F • S Europe • 500 kW
USA
ADVENTIST WORLD R, Via Abu Dhabi — S • M-F • C Asia & E Asia • 250 kW
S • Sa/Su • C Asia & E Asia • 250 kW
S • C Asia & E Asia • 250 kW

†ADVENTIST WORLD R, Via Agat, Guam — S • SE Asia • 100 kW
SE Asia • 100 kW

†VOA, Via Lampertheim, Germany — W • E Europe & W Asia • 100 kW
15325 BRAZIL
†RADIO GAZETA, São Paulo — Irr • PORTUGUESE & SPANISH • DS • 1/10 kW
CANADA
†R CANADA INTL, Sackville, NB — S • W Europe • 250 kW
†R CANADA INTL, Via Germany — S • E Europe • 250 kW
R CANADA INTL, Via Rampisham, UK — S • E Europe • 500 kW
JAPAN
RADIO JAPAN, Tokyo-Yamata — S Asia • 300 kW
SPAIN
R EXTERIOR ESPANA, Noblejas — S • M-F • Europe • 350 kW
USA
†VOA, Via Kavála, Greece — W • C Asia • 250 kW
15330 FINLAND
†YLE RADIO FINLAND, Pori — W • SE Asia & Australasia • 500 kW
GERMANY
DEUTSCHE WELLE, Via Sri Lanka — W • C Asia & E Asia • 250 kW
PHILIPPINES
FEBC RADIO INTL, Bocaue — SE Asia • 100 kW • ALT. FREQ. TO 15355 kHz
ROMANIA
†R ROMANIA INTL, Bucharest — W • Mideast • 250 kW
USA
RADIO MARTI, Delano, California — S • C America • 250 kW   C America • 250 kW
RADIO MARTI, Greenville, NC — W • C America • 250 kW
UZBEKISTAN
RADIO TASHKENT, Tashkent — W • E Europe & Mideast • 100 kW
15335 AUSTRALIA
†CVC, Darwin — S Asia & SE Asia • 250 kW
EGYPT
†RADIO CAIRO, Kafr Silim-Abis — S • W Africa • 250 kW
FINLAND
YLE RADIO FINLAND, Pori — S • E Africa & S Africa • 500 kW
GERMANY
DEUTSCHE WELLE, Via Sri Lanka — W • C Asia • 250 kW
†DEUTSCHE WELLE, Via V'vostok, Russia — W • E Asia & C Asia • 200 kW
†DEUTSCHE WELLE, Wertachtal — W • Mideast • 500 kW
HUNGARY
RADIO BUDAPEST, Jászberény — W • S Africa • 250 kW
MOROCCO
RTV MAROCAINE, Briech — Europe • 500 kW
NETHERLANDS
R NEDERLAND, Via Madagascar — S • Europe, Mideast & N Africa • 250 kW
UNITED KINGDOM
†BBC, Skelton, Cumbria — S • E Europe & Mideast • 300 kW
15340 CHINA
†CHINA R INTL, Xi'an — SE Asia • 500 kW
IRAN
†VO THE ISLAMIC REP, Sirjan — S Europe • 500 kW
W • S Europe • 500 kW

VO THE ISLAMIC REP, Tehrän — S • C Africa & E Africa • 500 kW
ROMANIA
R ROMANIA INTL, Galbeni — S • N Africa • 250 kW
15345 MOROCCO
RTV MAROCAINE, Nador — N Africa & Mideast • 250 kW
SAUDI ARABIA
BS OF THE KINGDOM, Riyadh — S Asia • 500 kW
USA
†RFE-RL, Via Iranawila, Sri Lanka — W • C Asia • 250 kW
†RFE-RL, Via Lampertheim, Germany — W • C Asia • 100 kW
†VOA, Via Iranawila, Sri Lanka — S • S Asia • 250 kW
15345v ARGENTINA
R ARGENTINA-RAE, Buenos Aires — M-F • Europe • 100 kW
RADIO NACIONAL, Buenos Aires — Su/M • Americas • 100 kW   Su • Europe • 100 kW
M • Americas • 100 kW   Sa/Su • Europe • 100 kW
15350 CHINA
†CHINA R INTL, Kashi — S Asia • 100 kW
PHILIPPINES
FEBC RADIO INTL, Bocaue — SE Asia • 100 kW
(con'd)   †RADIO VERITAS ASIA, Palauig — S Asia • 250 kW

0 1 2 3 4 5 6 7 8 9 10 11 12 13 14 15 16 17 18 19 20 21 22 23 24

ENGLISH ▬ ARABIC ▨ CHINESE ▢▢▢ FRENCH ═ GERMAN ▭ RUSSIAN = SPANISH ▭ OTHER ─

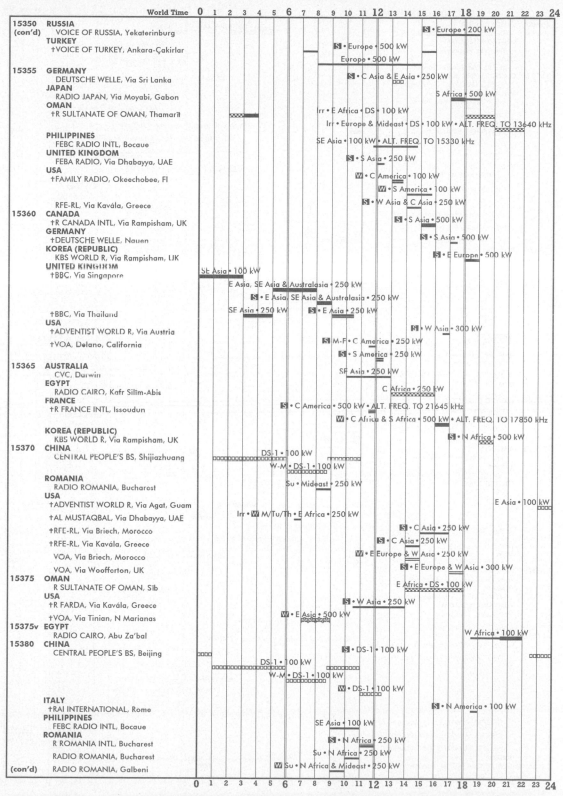

World Time 0 1 2 3 4 5 6 7 8 9 10 11 12 13 14 15 16 17 18 19 20 21 22 23 24

15350 RUSSIA
(con'd)   VOICE OF RUSSIA, Yekaterinburg — S • Europe • 200 kW
TURKEY
  †VOICE OF TURKEY, Ankara-Çakirlar — S • Europe • 500 kW / Europe • 500 kW

15355 GERMANY
  DEUTSCHE WELLE, Via Sri Lanka — S • C Asia & E Asia • 250 kW
JAPAN
  RADIO JAPAN, Via Moyabi, Gabon — S Africa • 500 kW
OMAN
  †R SULTANATE OF OMAN, Thamarīt — Irr • E Africa • DS • 100 kW / Irr • Europe & Mideast • DS • 100 kW • ALT. FREQ. TO 13640 kHz

PHILIPPINES
  FEBC RADIO INTL, Bocaue — SE Asia • 100 kW • ALT. FREQ. TO 15330 kHz
UNITED KINGDOM
  FEBA RADIO, Via Dhabayya, UAE — S • S Asia • 250 kW
USA
  †FAMILY RADIO, Okeechobee, Fl — W • C America • 100 kW / W • S America • 100 kW

  RFE-RL, Via Kavála, Greece — S • W Asia & C Asia • 250 kW
15360 CANADA
  †R CANADA INTL, Via Rampisham, UK — S • S Asia • 500 kW
GERMANY
  †DEUTSCHE WELLE, Nauen — S • S Asia • 500 kW
KOREA (REPUBLIC)
  KBS WORLD R, Via Rampisham, UK — S • E Europe • 500 kW
UNITED KINGDOM
  †BBC, Via Singapore — SE Asia • 100 kW / E Asia, SE Asia & Australasia • 250 kW / S • E Asia, SE Asia & Australasia • 250 kW

  †BBC, Via Thailand — SE Asia • 250 kW / S • E Asia • 250 kW
USA
  †ADVENTIST WORLD R, Via Austria — S • W Asia • 300 kW
  †VOA, Delano, California — S • M-F • C America • 250 kW / S • S America • 250 kW

15365 AUSTRALIA
  CVC, Darwin — SE Asia • 250 kW
EGYPT
  RADIO CAIRO, Kafr Silīm-Abis — C Africa • 250 kW
FRANCE
  †R FRANCE INTL, Issoudun — S • C America • 500 kW • ALT. FREQ. TO 21645 kHz / W • C Africa & S Africa • 500 kW • ALT. FREQ. TO 17850 kHz

KOREA (REPUBLIC)
  KBS WORLD R, Via Rampisham, UK — S • N Africa • 500 kW
15370 CHINA
  CENTRAL PEOPLE'S BS, Shijiazhuang — DS-1 • 100 kW / W-M • DS-1 • 100 kW

ROMANIA
  RADIO ROMANIA, Bucharest — Su • Mideast • 250 kW
USA
  †ADVENTIST WORLD R, Via Agat, Guam — E Asia • 100 kW
  †AL MUSTAQBAL, Via Dhabayya, UAE — Irr • W • M/Tu/Th • E Africa • 250 kW
  †RFE-RL, Via Briech, Morocco — S • C Asia • 250 kW
  †RFE-RL, Via Kavála, Greece — S • C Asia • 250 kW
  VOA, Via Briech, Morocco — W • E Europe & W Asia • 250 kW
  VOA, Via Woofferton, UK — S • E Europe & W Asia • 300 kW
15375 OMAN
  R SULTANATE OF OMAN, Sīb — E Africa • DS • 100 kW
USA
  †R FARDA, Via Kavála, Greece — S • W Asia • 250 kW
  †VOA, Via Tinian, N Marianas — W • E Asia • 500 kW
15375v EGYPT
  RADIO CAIRO, Abu Za'bal — W Africa • 100 kW
15380 CHINA
  CENTRAL PEOPLE'S BS, Beijing — S • DS-1 • 100 kW / DS-1 • 100 kW / W-M • DS-1 • 100 kW / W • DS-1 • 100 kW

ITALY
  †RAI INTERNATIONAL, Rome — S • N America • 100 kW
PHILIPPINES
  FEBC RADIO INTL, Bocaue — SE Asia • 100 kW
ROMANIA
  R ROMANIA INTL, Bucharest — S • N Africa • 250 kW
  RADIO ROMANIA, Bucharest — Su • N Africa • 250 kW
(con'd)   RADIO ROMANIA, Galbeni — W Su • N Africa & Mideast • 250 kW

World Time 0 1 2 3 4 5 6 7 8 9 10 11 12 13 14 15 16 17 18 19 20 21 22 23 24

SEASONAL S OR W   1-HR TIMESHIFT MIDYEAR ⇦ OR ⇨   JAMMING / OR ∧   EARLIEST HEARD ◁   LATEST HEARD ▷   NEW FOR 2006 †

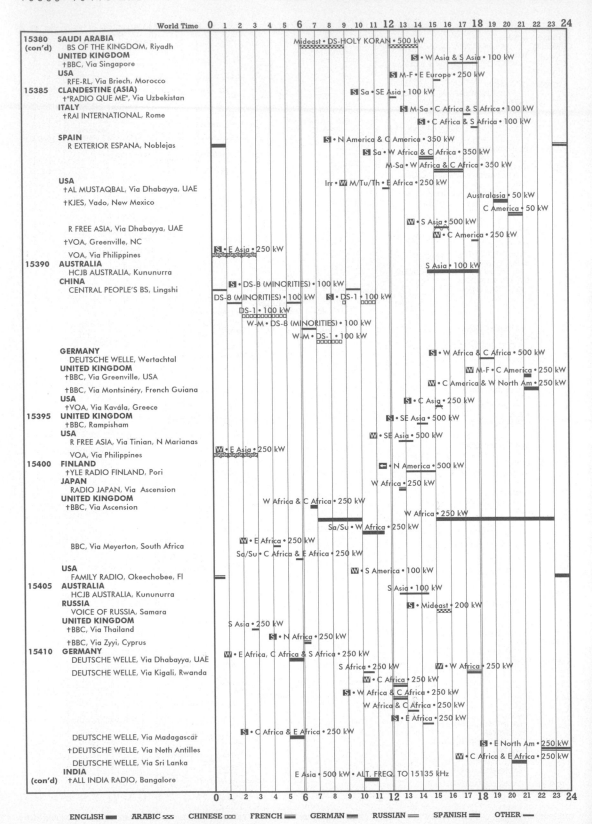

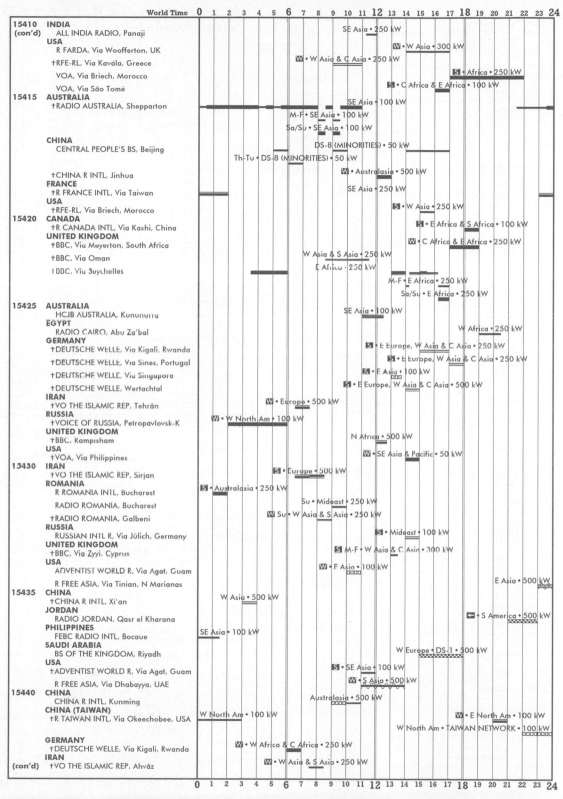

World Time   0 1 2 3 4 5 6 7 8 9 10 11 12 13 14 15 16 17 18 19 20 21 22 23 24

15410 INDIA
(con'd)   ALL INDIA RADIO, Panaji   SE Asia • 250 kW
USA
   R FARDA, Via Woofferton, UK   W • W Asia • 300 kW
   †RFE-RL, Via Kavála, Greece   W • W Asia & C Asia • 250 kW
   VOA, Via Briech, Morocco   S • Africa • 250 kW
   VOA, Via São Tomé   S • C Africa & E Africa • 100 kW
15415 AUSTRALIA
   †RADIO AUSTRALIA, Shepparton   SE Asia • 100 kW
     M-F • SE Asia • 100 kW
     Sa/Su • SE Asia • 100 kW
CHINA
   CENTRAL PEOPLE'S BS, Beijing   DS-8 (MINORITIES) • 50 kW
     Th-Tu • DS-8 (MINORITIES) • 50 kW
   †CHINA R INTL, Jinhua   W • Australasia • 500 kW
FRANCE
   †R FRANCE INTL, Via Taiwan   SE Asia • 250 kW
USA
   †RFE-RL, Via Briech, Morocco   S • W Asia • 250 kW
15420 CANADA
   †R CANADA INTL, Via Kashi, China   S • E Africa & S Africa • 100 kW
UNITED KINGDOM
   †BBC, Via Meyerton, South Africa   W • C Africa & E Africa • 250 kW
   †BBC, Via Oman   W Asia & S Asia • 250 kW
   †BBC, Via Seychelles   E Africa • 250 kW
     M-F • E Africa • 250 kW
     Sa/Su • E Africa • 250 kW
15425 AUSTRALIA
   HCJB AUSTRALIA, Kununurra   SE Asia • 100 kW
EGYPT
   RADIO CAIRO, Abu Za'bal   W Africa • 250 kW
GERMANY
   †DEUTSCHE WELLE, Via Kigali, Rwanda   S • E Europe, W Asia & C Asia • 250 kW
   †DEUTSCHE WELLE, Via Sines, Portugal   S • E Europe, W Asia & C Asia • 250 kW
   †DEUTSCHE WELLE, Via Singapore   S • E Asia • 100 kW
   †DEUTSCHE WELLE, Wertachtal   S • E Europe, W Asia & C Asia • 500 kW
IRAN
   †VO THE ISLAMIC REP, Tehrān   W • Europe • 500 kW
RUSSIA
   †VOICE OF RUSSIA, Petropavlovsk-K   W • W North Am • 100 kW
UNITED KINGDOM
   †BBC, Rampisham   N Africa • 500 kW
USA
   †VOA, Via Philippines   W • SE Asia & Pacific • 50 kW
15430 IRAN
   †VO THE ISLAMIC REP, Sirjan   S • Europe • 500 kW
ROMANIA
   R ROMANIA INTL, Bucharest   S • Australasia • 250 kW
   RADIO ROMANIA, Bucharest   Su • Mideast • 250 kW
   †RADIO ROMANIA, Galbeni   W Su • W Asia & S Asia • 250 kW
RUSSIA
   RUSSIAN INTL R, Via Jülich, Germany   S • Mideast • 100 kW
UNITED KINGDOM
   †BBC, Via Zyyi, Cyprus   S M-F • W Asia & C Asia • 300 kW
USA
   ADVENTIST WORLD R, Via Agat, Guam   W • E Asia • 100 kW
   R FREE ASIA, Via Tinian, N Marianas   E Asia • 500 kW
15435 CHINA
   †CHINA R INTL, Xi'an   W Asia • 500 kW
JORDAN
   RADIO JORDAN, Qasr el Kharana   ← S America • 500 kW
PHILIPPINES
   FEBC RADIO INTL, Bocaue   SE Asia • 100 kW
SAUDI ARABIA
   BS OF THE KINGDOM, Riyadh   W Europe • DS-1 • 500 kW
USA
   †ADVENTIST WORLD R, Via Agat, Guam   S • SE Asia • 100 kW
   R FREE ASIA, Via Dhabayya, UAE   W • S Asia • 500 kW
15440 CHINA
   CHINA R INTL, Kunming   Australasia • 500 kW
CHINA (TAIWAN)
   †R TAIWAN INTL, Via Okeechobee, USA   W North Am • 100 kW
     W • E North Am • 100 kW
     W North Am • TAIWAN NETWORK • 100 kW
GERMANY
   †DEUTSCHE WELLE, Via Kigali, Rwanda   W • W Africa & C Africa • 250 kW
IRAN
(con'd)   †VO THE ISLAMIC REP, Ahvāz   W • W Asia & S Asia • 250 kW

0 1 2 3 4 5 6 7 8 9 10 11 12 13 14 15 16 17 18 19 20 21 22 23 24

SEASONAL 🅢 OR 🅦   1-HR TIMESHIFT MIDYEAR ⇇ OR ⇉   JAMMING / OR ∧   EARLIEST HEARD ◁   LATEST HEARD ▷   NEW FOR 2006 †

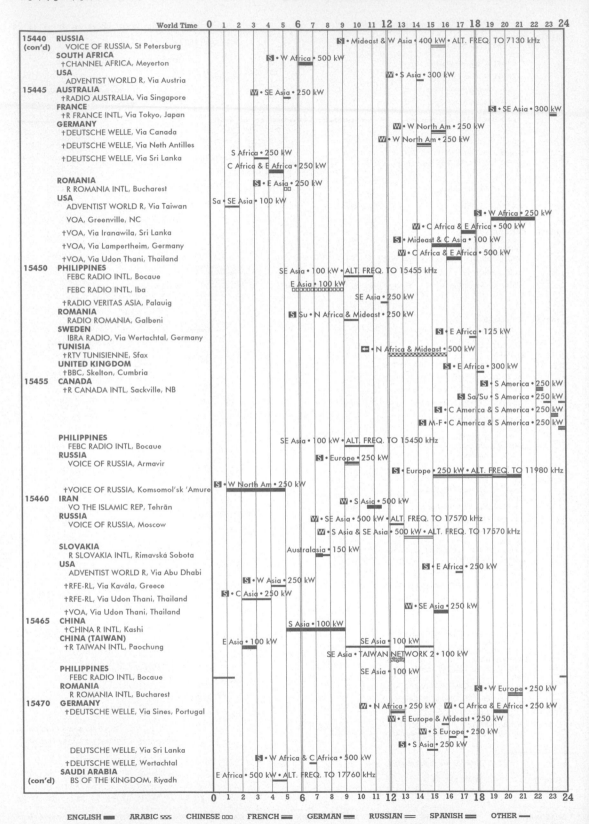

| | World Time | 0 | 1 | 2 | 3 | 4 | 5 | 6 | 7 | 8 | 9 | 10 | 11 | 12 | 13 | 14 | 15 | 16 | 17 | 18 | 19 | 20 | 21 | 22 | 23 | 24 |

15440 RUSSIA
(con'd) VOICE OF RUSSIA, St Petersburg — S • Mideast & W Asia • 400 kW • ALT. FREQ. TO 7130 kHz

SOUTH AFRICA
  †CHANNEL AFRICA, Meyerton — S • W Africa • 500 kW

USA
  ADVENTIST WORLD R, Via Austria — W • S Asia • 300 kW

15445 AUSTRALIA
  †RADIO AUSTRALIA, Via Singapore — W • SE Asia • 250 kW

FRANCE
  †R FRANCE INTL, Via Tokyo, Japan — S • SE Asia • 300 kW

GERMANY
  †DEUTSCHE WELLE, Via Canada — W • W North Am • 250 kW
  †DEUTSCHE WELLE, Via Neth Antilles — W • W North Am • 250 kW
  †DEUTSCHE WELLE, Via Sri Lanka — S Africa • 250 kW
                                  C Africa & E Africa • 250 kW

ROMANIA
  R ROMANIA INTL, Bucharest — S • E Asia • 250 kW

USA
  ADVENTIST WORLD R, Via Taiwan — Sa • SE Asia • 100 kW
  VOA, Greenville, NC — S • W Africa • 250 kW
  †VOA, Via Iranawila, Sri Lanka — W • C Africa & E Africa • 500 kW
  †VOA, Via Lampertheim, Germany — S • Mideast & C Asia • 100 kW
  †VOA, Via Udon Thani, Thailand — W • C Africa & E Africa • 500 kW

15450 PHILIPPINES
  FEBC RADIO INTL, Bocaue — SE Asia • 100 kW • ALT. FREQ. TO 15455 kHz
  FEBC RADIO INTL, Iba — E Asia • 100 kW
                       SE Asia • 250 kW
  †RADIO VERITAS ASIA, Palauig

ROMANIA
  RADIO ROMANIA, Galbeni — S Su • N Africa & Mideast • 250 kW

SWEDEN
  IBRA RADIO, Via Wertachtal, Germany — S • E Africa • 125 kW

TUNISIA
  †RTV TUNISIENNE, Sfax — ← • N Africa & Mideast • 500 kW

UNITED KINGDOM
  †BBC, Skelton, Cumbria — S • E Africa • 300 kW

15455 CANADA
  †R CANADA INTL, Sackville, NB — S • S America • 250 kW
                                  Sa/Su • S America • 250 kW
                                  S • C America & S America • 250 kW
                                  M-F • C America & S America • 250 kW

PHILIPPINES
  FEBC RADIO INTL, Bocaue — SE Asia • 100 kW • ALT. FREQ. TO 15450 kHz

RUSSIA
  VOICE OF RUSSIA, Armavir — S • Europe • 250 kW
                            S • Europe • 250 kW • ALT. FREQ. TO 11980 kHz
  †VOICE OF RUSSIA, Komsomol'sk 'Amure — S • W North Am • 250 kW

15460 IRAN
  VO THE ISLAMIC REP, Tehrān — W • S Asia • 500 kW

RUSSIA
  VOICE OF RUSSIA, Moscow — W • SE Asia • 500 kW • ALT. FREQ. TO 17570 kHz
                           W • S Asia & SE Asia • 500 kW • ALT. FREQ. TO 17570 kHz

SLOVAKIA
  R SLOVAKIA INTL, Rimavská Sobota — Australasia • 150 kW

USA
  ADVENTIST WORLD R, Via Abu Dhabi — S • E Africa • 250 kW
  †RFE-RL, Via Kavála, Greece — S • W Asia • 250 kW
  †RFE-RL, Via Udon Thani, Thailand — S • C Asia • 250 kW
  †VOA, Via Udon Thani, Thailand — W • SE Asia • 250 kW

15465 CHINA
  †CHINA R INTL, Kashi — S Asia • 100 kW

CHINA (TAIWAN)
  †R TAIWAN INTL, Paochung — E Asia • 100 kW
                            SE Asia • 100 kW
                            SE Asia • TAIWAN NETWORK 2 • 100 kW

PHILIPPINES
  FEBC RADIO INTL, Bocaue — SE Asia • 100 kW

ROMANIA
  R ROMANIA INTL, Bucharest — S • W Europe • 250 kW

15470 GERMANY
  †DEUTSCHE WELLE, Via Sines, Portugal — W • N Africa • 250 kW   W • C Africa & E Africa • 250 kW
                                         W • E Europe & Mideast • 250 kW
                                         W • S Europe • 250 kW
                                         S • S Asia • 250 kW
  DEUTSCHE WELLE, Via Sri Lanka
  †DEUTSCHE WELLE, Wertachtal — S • W Africa & C Africa • 500 kW

SAUDI ARABIA
(con'd) BS OF THE KINGDOM, Riyadh — E Africa • 500 kW • ALT. FREQ. TO 17760 kHz

| | | 0 | 1 | 2 | 3 | 4 | 5 | 6 | 7 | 8 | 9 | 10 | 11 | 12 | 13 | 14 | 15 | 16 | 17 | 18 | 19 | 20 | 21 | 22 | 23 | 24 |

ENGLISH ▬▬   ARABIC ⌇⌇⌇   CHINESE ▯▯▯   FRENCH ▬▬   GERMAN ▬▬   RUSSIAN ══   SPANISH ▬▬   OTHER ——

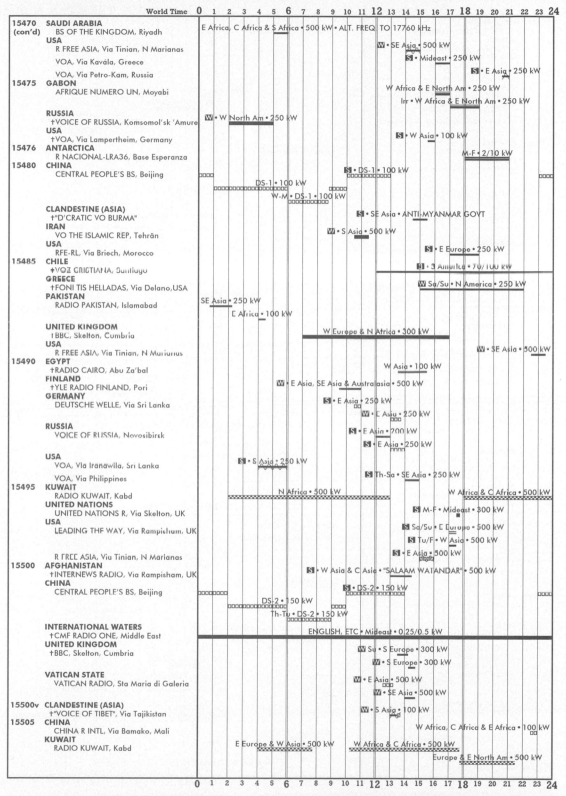

		World Time	0 1 2 3 4 5 6 7 8 9 10 11 12 13 14 15 16 17 18 19 20 21 22 23 24

15470 SAUDI ARABIA
(con'd) BS OF THE KINGDOM, Riyadh — E Africa, C Africa & S Africa • 500 kW • ALT. FREQ. TO 17760 kHz
USA
R FREE ASIA, Via Tinian, N Marianas — W • SE Asia • 500 kW
VOA, Via Kavála, Greece — S • Mideast • 250 kW
VOA, Via Petro-Kam, Russia — S • E Asia • 250 kW
15475 GABON
AFRIQUE NUMERO UN, Moyabi — W Africa & E North Am • 250 kW
Irr • W Africa & E North Am • 250 kW
RUSSIA
†VOICE OF RUSSIA, Komsomol'sk 'Amure — W • W North Am • 250 kW
USA
†VOA, Via Lampertheim, Germany — S • W Asia • 100 kW
15476 ANTARCTICA
R NACIONAL-LRA36, Base Esperanza — M-F • 2/10 kW
15480 CHINA
CENTRAL PEOPLE'S BS, Beijing — S • DS-1 • 100 kW
DS-1 • 100 kW
W-M • DS-1 • 100 kW
CLANDESTINE (ASIA)
†"D'CRATIC VO BURMA" — S • SE Asia • ANTI-MYANMAR GOVT
IRAN
VO THE ISLAMIC REP, Tehrān — W • S Asia • 500 kW
USA
RFE-RL, Via Briech, Morocco — S • E Europe • 250 kW
15485 CHILE
†VOZ CRISTIANA, Santiago — S • S America • 70/100 kW
GREECE
†FONI TIS HELLADAS, Via Delano, USA — W Sa/Su • N America • 250 kW
PAKISTAN
RADIO PAKISTAN, Islamabad — SE Asia • 250 kW
E Africa • 100 kW
UNITED KINGDOM
†BBC, Skelton, Cumbria — W Europe & N Africa • 300 kW
USA
R FREE ASIA, Via Tinian, N Marianas — W • SE Asia • 500 kW
15490 EGYPT
†RADIO CAIRO, Abu Za'bal — W Asia • 100 kW
FINLAND
†YLE RADIO FINLAND, Pori — W • E Asia, SE Asia & Australasia • 500 kW
GERMANY
DEUTSCHE WELLE, Via Sri Lanka — S • E Asia • 250 kW
W • C Asia • 250 kW
RUSSIA
VOICE OF RUSSIA, Novosibirsk — S • E Asia • 200 kW
S • E Asia • 250 kW
USA
VOA, Via Iranawila, Sri Lanka — S • S Asia • 250 kW
VOA, Via Philippines — S Th-Sa • SE Asia • 250 kW
15495 KUWAIT
RADIO KUWAIT, Kabd — N Africa • 500 kW / W Africa & C Africa • 500 kW
UNITED NATIONS
UNITED NATIONS R, Via Skelton, UK — S M-F • Mideast • 300 kW
USA
LEADING THE WAY, Via Rampisham, UK — S Sa/Su • E Europe • 500 kW
S Tu/F • W Asia • 500 kW
S • E Asia • 500 kW
R FREE ASIA, Via Tinian, N Marianas
15500 AFGHANISTAN
†INTERNEWS RADIO, Via Rampisham, UK — S • W Asia & C Asia • "SALAAM WATANDAR" • 500 kW
CHINA
CENTRAL PEOPLE'S BS, Beijing — S • DS-2 • 150 kW
DS-2 • 150 kW
Th-Tu • DS-2 • 150 kW
INTERNATIONAL WATERS
†CMF RADIO ONE, Middle East — ENGLISH, ETC • Mideast • 0.25/0.5 kW
UNITED KINGDOM
†BBC, Skelton, Cumbria — W Su • S Europe • 300 kW
W • S Europe • 300 kW
VATICAN STATE
VATICAN RADIO, Sta Maria di Galeria — W • E Asia • 500 kW
W • SE Asia • 500 kW
15500v CLANDESTINE (ASIA)
†"VOICE OF TIBET", Via Tajikistan — W • S Asia • 100 kW
15505 CHINA
CHINA R INTL, Via Bamako, Mali — W Africa, C Africa & E Africa • 100 kW
KUWAIT
RADIO KUWAIT, Kabd — E Europe & W Asia • 500 kW / W Africa & C Africa • 500 kW
Europe & E North Am • 500 kW

	World Time	0 1 2 3 4 5 6 7 8 9 10 11 12 13 14 15 16 17 18 19 20 21 22 23 24

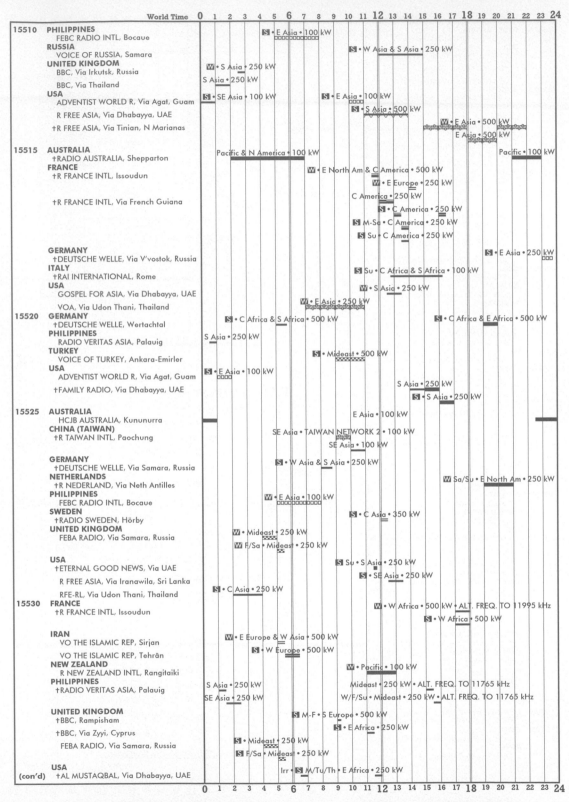

World Time 0 1 2 3 4 5 6 7 8 9 10 11 12 13 14 15 16 17 18 19 20 21 22 23 24

15510
PHILIPPINES
  FEBC RADIO INTL, Bocaue — S • E Asia • 100 kW
RUSSIA
  VOICE OF RUSSIA, Samara — S • W Asia & S Asia • 250 kW
UNITED KINGDOM
  BBC, Via Irkutsk, Russia — W • S Asia • 250 kW
  BBC, Via Thailand — S Asia • 250 kW
USA
  ADVENTIST WORLD R, Via Agat, Guam — S • SE Asia • 100 kW / S • E Asia • 100 kW
  R FREE ASIA, Via Dhabayya, UAE — S • S Asia • 500 kW
  †R FREE ASIA, Via Tinian, N Marianas — W • E Asia • 500 kW / E Asia • 500 kW

15515
AUSTRALIA
  †RADIO AUSTRALIA, Shepparton — Pacific & N America • 100 kW / Pacific • 100 kW
FRANCE
  †R FRANCE INTL, Issoudun — W • E North Am & C America • 500 kW / W • E Europe • 250 kW
  †R FRANCE INTL, Via French Guiana — C America • 250 kW / S • C America • 250 kW / S M-Sa • C America • 250 kW / S Su • C America • 250 kW
GERMANY
  †DEUTSCHE WELLE, Via V'vostok, Russia — S • E Asia • 250 kW
ITALY
  †RAI INTERNATIONAL, Rome — S Su • C Africa & S Africa • 100 kW
USA
  GOSPEL FOR ASIA, Via Dhabayya, UAE — W • S Asia • 250 kW
  VOA, Via Udon Thani, Thailand — W • E Asia • 250 kW

15520
GERMANY
  †DEUTSCHE WELLE, Wertachtal — S • C Africa & S Africa • 500 kW / S • C Africa & E Africa • 500 kW
PHILIPPINES
  RADIO VERITAS ASIA, Palauig — S Asia • 250 kW
TURKEY
  VOICE OF TURKEY, Ankara-Emirler — S • Mideast • 500 kW
USA
  ADVENTIST WORLD R, Via Agat, Guam — S • E Asia • 100 kW
  †FAMILY RADIO, Via Dhabayya, UAE — S Asia • 250 kW / S • S Asia • 250 kW

15525
AUSTRALIA
  HCJB AUSTRALIA, Kununurra — E Asia • 100 kW
CHINA (TAIWAN)
  †R TAIWAN INTL, Paochung — SE Asia • TAIWAN NETWORK 2 • 100 kW / SE Asia • 100 kW
GERMANY
  †DEUTSCHE WELLE, Via Samara, Russia — S • W Asia & S Asia • 250 kW
NETHERLANDS
  †R NEDERLAND, Via Neth Antilles — W Sa/Su • E North Am • 250 kW
PHILIPPINES
  FEBC RADIO INTL, Bocaue — W • E Asia • 100 kW
SWEDEN
  †RADIO SWEDEN, Hörby — S • C Asia • 350 kW
UNITED KINGDOM
  FEBA RADIO, Via Samara, Russia — W • Mideast • 250 kW / W F/Sa • Mideast • 250 kW
USA
  †ETERNAL GOOD NEWS, Via UAE — S Su • S Asia • 250 kW
  R FREE ASIA, Via Iranawila, Sri Lanka — S • SE Asia • 250 kW
  RFE-RL, Via Udon Thani, Thailand — S • C Asia • 250 kW

15530
FRANCE
  †R FRANCE INTL, Issoudun — W • W Africa • 500 kW • ALT. FREQ. TO 11995 kHz / S • W Africa • 500 kW
IRAN
  VO THE ISLAMIC REP, Sirjan — W • E Europe & W Asia • 500 kW
  VO THE ISLAMIC REP, Tehrān — S • W Europe • 500 kW
NEW ZEALAND
  R NEW ZEALAND INTL, Rangitaiki — W • Pacific • 100 kW
PHILIPPINES
  †RADIO VERITAS ASIA, Palauig — S Asia • 250 kW / Mideast • 250 kW • ALT. FREQ. TO 11765 kHz / SE Asia • 250 kW / W/F/Su • Mideast • 250 kW • ALT. FREQ. TO 11765 kHz
UNITED KINGDOM
  †BBC, Rampisham — S M-F • S Europe • 500 kW
  †BBC, Via Zyyi, Cyprus — S • E Africa • 250 kW
  FEBA RADIO, Via Samara, Russia — S • Mideast • 250 kW / S F/Sa • Mideast • 250 kW
USA
(con'd) †AL MUSTAQBAL, Via Dhabayya, UAE — Irr • S M/Tu/Th • E Africa • 250 kW

  0 1 2 3 4 5 6 7 8 9 10 11 12 13 14 15 16 17 18 19 20 21 22 23 24

ENGLISH ▬ ARABIC ▨ CHINESE □□□ FRENCH ▬ GERMAN ▬ RUSSIAN ═ SPANISH ▬ OTHER —

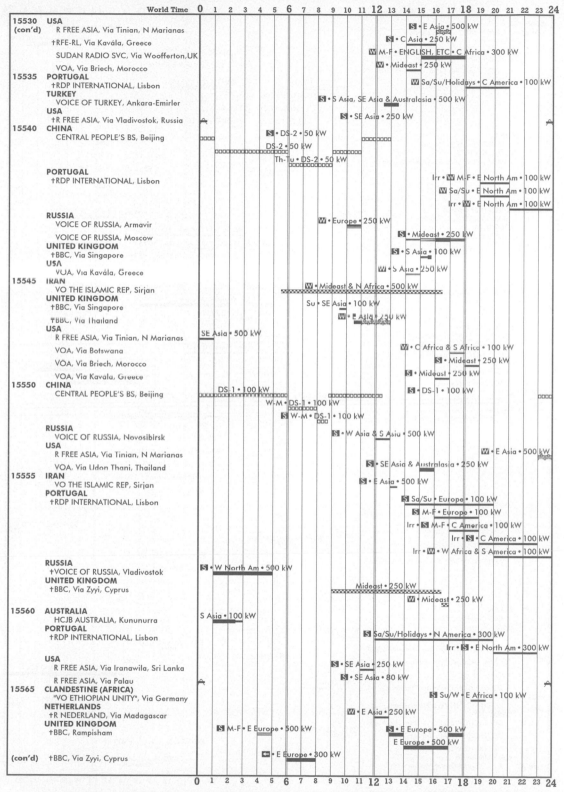

World Time		
15530 (con'd)	**USA**	
	R FREE ASIA, Via Tinian, N Marianas	S • E Asia • 500 kW
	†RFE-RL, Via Kavála, Greece	S • C Asia • 250 kW
	SUDAN RADIO SVC, Via Woofferton,UK	W M-F • ENGLISH, ETC • C Africa • 300 kW
	VOA, Via Briech, Morocco	W • Mideast • 250 kW
15535	**PORTUGAL**	
	†RDP INTERNATIONAL, Lisbon	W Sa/Su/Holidays • C America • 100 kW
	TURKEY	
	VOICE OF TURKEY, Ankara-Emirler	S • S Asia, SE Asia & Australasia • 500 kW
	USA	
	†R FREE ASIA, Via Vladivostok, Russia	S • SE Asia • 250 kW
15540	**CHINA**	
	CENTRAL PEOPLE'S BS, Beijing	S • DS-2 • 50 kW
		DS-2 • 50 kW
		Th-Tu • DS-2 • 50 kW
	PORTUGAL	
	†RDP INTERNATIONAL, Lisbon	Irr • W M-F • E North Am • 100 kW
		W Sa/Su • E North Am • 100 kW
		Irr • W • E North Am • 100 kW
	RUSSIA	
	VOICE OF RUSSIA, Armavir	W • Europe • 250 kW
	VOICE OF RUSSIA, Moscow	S • Mideast • 250 kW
	UNITED KINGDOM	
	†BBC, Via Singapore	S • S Asia • 100 kW
	USA	
	VOA, Via Kavála, Greece	W • S Asia • 250 kW
15545	**IRAN**	
	VO THE ISLAMIC REP, Sirjan	W • Mideast & N Africa • 500 kW
	UNITED KINGDOM	
	†BBC, Via Singapore	Su • SE Asia • 100 kW
	†BBC, Via Thailand	W • E Asia • 250 kW
	USA	
	R FREE ASIA, Via Tinian, N Marianas	SE Asia • 500 kW
	VOA, Via Botswana	W • C Africa & S Africa • 100 kW
	VOA, Via Briech, Morocco	S • Mideast • 250 kW
	VOA, Via Kavala, Greece	S • Mideast • 250 kW
15550	**CHINA**	
	CENTRAL PEOPLE'S BS, Beijing	DS-1 • 100 kW / S • DS-1 • 100 kW
		W-M • DS-1 • 100 kW
		S W-M • DS-1 • 100 kW
	RUSSIA	
	VOICE OF RUSSIA, Novosibirsk	S • W Asia & S Asia • 500 kW
	USA	
	R FREE ASIA, Via Tinian, N Marianas	W • E Asia • 500 kW
	VOA, Via Udon Thani, Thailand	S • SE Asia & Australasia • 250 kW
15555	**IRAN**	
	VO THE ISLAMIC REP, Sirjan	S • E Asia • 500 kW
	PORTUGAL	
	†RDP INTERNATIONAL, Lisbon	S Sa/Su • Europe • 100 kW
		S M-F • Europe • 100 kW
		Irr • S M-F • C America • 100 kW
		Irr • S • C America • 100 kW
		Irr • W • W Africa & S America • 100 kW
	RUSSIA	
	†VOICE OF RUSSIA, Vladivostok	S • W North Am • 500 kW
	UNITED KINGDOM	
	†BBC, Via Zyyi, Cyprus	Mideast • 250 kW
		W • Mideast • 250 kW
15560	**AUSTRALIA**	
	HCJB AUSTRALIA, Kununurra	S Asia • 100 kW
	PORTUGAL	
	†RDP INTERNATIONAL, Lisbon	S Sa/Su/Holidays • N America • 300 kW
		Irr • S • E North Am • 300 kW
	USA	
	R FREE ASIA, Via Iranawila, Sri Lanka	S • SE Asia • 250 kW
	R FREE ASIA, Via Palau	S • SE Asia • 80 kW
15565	**CLANDESTINE (AFRICA)**	
	"VO ETHIOPIAN UNITY", Via Germany	S Su/W • E Africa • 100 kW
	NETHERLANDS	
	†R NEDERLAND, Via Madagascar	W • E Asia • 250 kW
	UNITED KINGDOM	
	†BBC, Rampisham	S M-F • E Europe • 500 kW
		S • E Europe • 500 kW
		E Europe • 500 kW
(con'd)	†BBC, Via Zyyi, Cyprus	• E Europe • 300 kW

SEASONAL S OR W   1-HR TIMESHIFT MIDYEAR ◄► OR ►◄   JAMMING / OR ∧   EARLIEST HEARD ◄   LATEST HEARD ▷   NEW FOR 2006 †

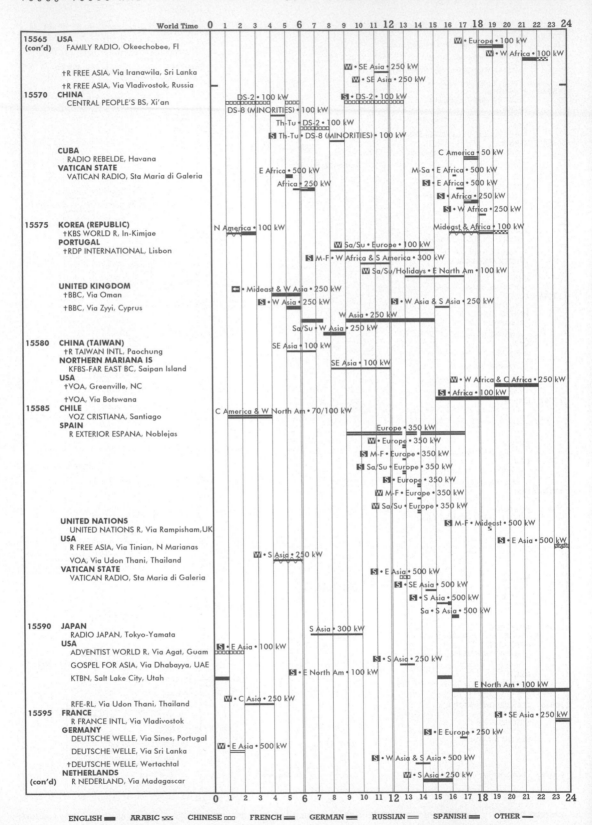

		World Time	0 1 2 3 4 5 6 7 8 9 10 11 12 13 14 15 16 17 18 19 20 21 22 23 24

15565 USA
(con'd) FAMILY RADIO, Okeechobee, Fl — W • Europe • 100 kW; W • W Africa • 100 kW

†R FREE ASIA, Via Iranawila, Sri Lanka — W • SE Asia • 250 kW

†R FREE ASIA, Via Vladivostok, Russia — W • SE Asia • 250 kW

15570 CHINA
CENTRAL PEOPLE'S BS, Xi'an — DS-2 • 100 kW; S • DS-2 • 100 kW; DS-8 (MINORITIES) • 100 kW; Th-Tu • DS-2 • 100 kW; S Th-Tu • DS-8 (MINORITIES) • 100 kW

CUBA
RADIO REBELDE, Havana — C America • 50 kW

VATICAN STATE
VATICAN RADIO, Sta Maria di Galeria — E Africa • 500 kW; M-Sa • E Africa • 500 kW; S • E Africa • 500 kW; Africa • 250 kW; S • Africa • 250 kW; S • W Africa • 250 kW

15575 KOREA (REPUBLIC)
†KBS WORLD R, In-Kimjae — N America • 100 kW; Mideast & Africa • 100 kW

PORTUGAL
†RDP INTERNATIONAL, Lisbon — W Sa/Su • Europe • 100 kW; S M-F • W Africa & S America • 300 kW; W Sa/Su/Holidays • E North Am • 100 kW

UNITED KINGDOM
†BBC, Via Oman — Mideast & W Asia • 250 kW

†BBC, Via Zyyi, Cyprus — S • W Asia • 250 kW; S • W Asia & S Asia • 250 kW; W Asia • 250 kW; Sa/Su • W Asia • 250 kW

15580 CHINA (TAIWAN)
†R TAIWAN INTL, Paochung — SE Asia • 100 kW

NORTHERN MARIANA IS
KFBS-FAR EAST BC, Saipan Island — SE Asia • 100 kW

USA
†VOA, Greenville, NC — W • W Africa & C Africa • 250 kW

†VOA, Via Botswana — S • Africa • 100 kW

15585 CHILE
VOZ CRISTIANA, Santiago — C America & W North Am • 70/100 kW

SPAIN
R EXTERIOR ESPANA, Noblejas — Europe • 350 kW; W • Europe • 350 kW; S M-F • Europe • 350 kW; S Sa/Su • Europe • 350 kW; S • Europe • 350 kW; W M-F • Europe • 350 kW; W Sa/Su • Europe • 350 kW

UNITED NATIONS
UNITED NATIONS R, Via Rampisham, UK — S M-F • Mideast • 500 kW

USA
R FREE ASIA, Via Tinian, N Marianas — S • E Asia • 500 kW

VOA, Via Udon Thani, Thailand — W • S Asia • 250 kW

VATICAN STATE
VATICAN RADIO, Sta Maria di Galeria — S • E Asia • 500 kW; S • SE Asia • 500 kW; S • S Asia • 500 kW; Sa • S Asia • 500 kW

15590 JAPAN
RADIO JAPAN, Tokyo-Yamata — S Asia • 300 kW

USA
ADVENTIST WORLD R, Via Agat, Guam — S • E Asia • 100 kW; S • S Asia • 250 kW

GOSPEL FOR ASIA, Via Dhabayya, UAE — S • E North Am • 100 kW

KTBN, Salt Lake City, Utah — E North Am • 100 kW

RFE-RL, Via Udon Thani, Thailand — W • C Asia • 250 kW

15595 FRANCE
R FRANCE INTL, Via Vladivostok — S • SE Asia • 250 kW

GERMANY
DEUTSCHE WELLE, Via Sines, Portugal — S • E Europe • 250 kW

DEUTSCHE WELLE, Via Sri Lanka — W • E Asia • 500 kW; S • W Asia & S Asia • 500 kW

†DEUTSCHE WELLE, Wertachtal

NETHERLANDS
(con'd) R NEDERLAND, Via Madagascar — W • S Asia • 250 kW

			0 1 2 3 4 5 6 7 8 9 10 11 12 13 14 15 16 17 18 19 20 21 22 23 24

ENGLISH ▬   ARABIC ▨   CHINESE ▫▫▫   FRENCH ▬   GERMAN ▬   RUSSIAN ═   SPANISH ═   OTHER ▬

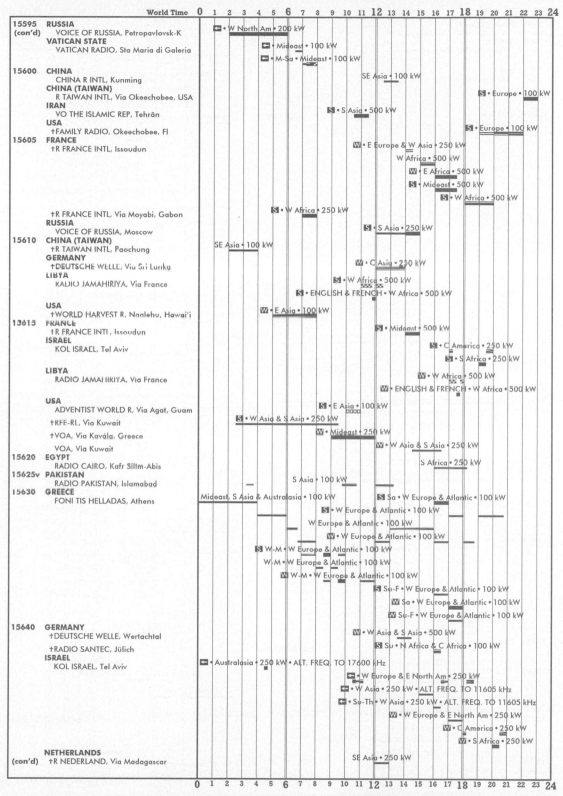

World Time

15595	RUSSIA	
(con'd)	VOICE OF RUSSIA, Petropavlovsk-K	⬅ • W North Am • 200 kW
	VATICAN STATE	
	VATICAN RADIO, Sta Maria di Galeria	S • Mideast • 100 kW
		S • M-Sa • Mideast • 100 kW
15600	CHINA	
	CHINA R INTL, Kunming	SE Asia • 100 kW
	CHINA (TAIWAN)	
	R TAIWAN INTL, Via Okeechobee, USA	S • Europe • 100 kW
	IRAN	
	VO THE ISLAMIC REP, Tehrān	S • S Asia • 500 kW
	USA	
	†FAMILY RADIO, Okeechobee, Fl	S • Europe • 100 kW
15605	FRANCE	
	†R FRANCE INTL, Issoudun	W • E Europe & W Asia • 250 kW
		W Africa • 500 kW
		W • E Africa • 500 kW
		S • Mideast • 500 kW
		S • W Africa • 500 kW
	†R FRANCE INTL, Via Moyabi, Gabon	S • W Africa • 250 kW
	RUSSIA	
	VOICE OF RUSSIA, Moscow	S • S Asia • 250 kW
15610	CHINA (TAIWAN)	
	†R TAIWAN INTL, Paochung	SE Asia • 100 kW
	GERMANY	
	†DEUTSCHE WELLE, Via Sri Lanka	W • C Asia • 250 kW
	LIBYA	
	RADIO JAMAHIRIYA, Via France	S • W Africa • 500 kW
		S • ENGLISH & FRENCH • W Africa • 500 kW
	USA	
	†WORLD HARVEST R, Naalehu, Hawai'i	W • E Asia • 100 kW
15615	FRANCE	
	†R FRANCE INTL, Issoudun	S • Mideast • 500 kW
	ISRAEL	
	KOL ISRAEL, Tel Aviv	S • C America • 250 kW
		S • S Africa • 250 kW
	LIBYA	
	RADIO JAMAHIRIYA, Via France	W • W Africa • 500 kW
		W • ENGLISH & FRENCH • W Africa • 500 kW
	USA	
	ADVENTIST WORLD R, Via Agat, Guam	S • E Asia • 100 kW
	†RFE-RL, Via Kuwait	S • W Asia & S Asia • 250 kW
	†VOA, Via Kavála, Greece	W • Mideast • 250 kW
	VOA, Via Kuwait	W • W Asia & S Asia • 250 kW
15620	EGYPT	
	RADIO CAIRO, Kafr Silim-Abis	S Africa • 250 kW
15625v	PAKISTAN	
	RADIO PAKISTAN, Islamabad	S Asia • 100 kW
15630	GREECE	
	FONI TIS HELLADAS, Athens	Mideast, S Asia & Australasia • 100 kW
		S Sa • W Europe & Atlantic • 100 kW
		S • W Europe & Atlantic • 100 kW
		W Europe & Atlantic • 100 kW
		W • W Europe & Atlantic • 100 kW
		S W-M • W Europe & Atlantic • 100 kW
		W-M • W Europe & Atlantic • 100 kW
		W W-M • W Europe & Atlantic • 100 kW
		S Su-F • W Europe & Atlantic • 100 kW
		W Sa • W Europe & Atlantic • 100 kW
		W Su-F • W Europe & Atlantic • 100 kW
15640	GERMANY	
	†DEUTSCHE WELLE, Wertachtal	W • W Asia & S Asia • 500 kW
	†RADIO SANTEC, Jülich	S Su • N Africa & C Africa • 100 kW
	ISRAEL	
	KOL ISRAEL, Tel Aviv	⬅ • Australasia • 250 kW • ALT. FREQ. TO 17600 kHz
		⬅ • W Europe & E North Am • 250 kW
		⬅ • W Asia • 250 kW • ALT. FREQ. TO 11605 kHz
		⬅ • Su-Th • W Asia • 250 kW • ALT. FREQ. TO 11605 kHz
		W • W Europe & E North Am • 250 kW
		W • C America • 250 kW
		W • S Africa • 250 kW
	NETHERLANDS	
(con'd)	†R NEDERLAND, Via Madagascar	SE Asia • 250 kW

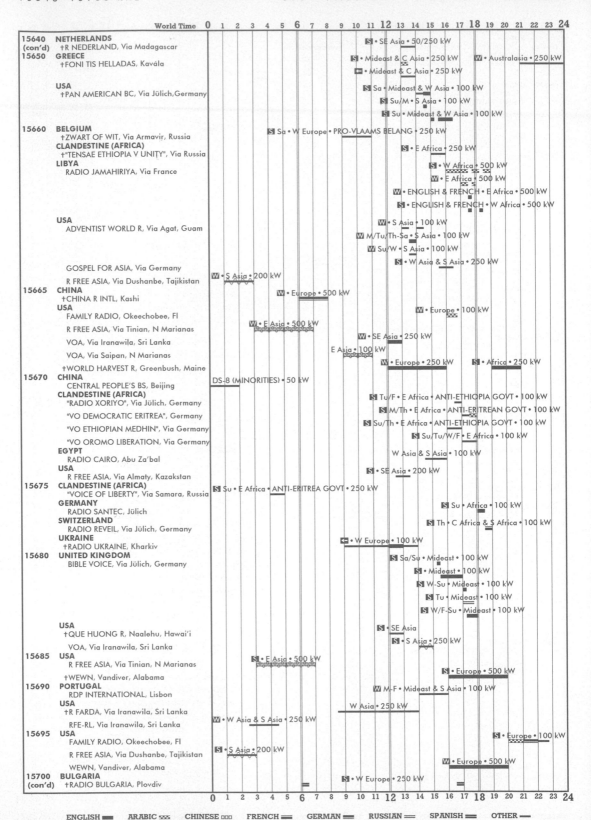

World Time   0 1 2 3 4 5 6 7 8 9 10 11 12 13 14 15 16 17 18 19 20 21 22 23 24

Frequency	Station	
15640 (con'd)	**NETHERLANDS** †R NEDERLAND, Via Madagascar	S • SE Asia • 50/250 kW
15650	**GREECE** †FONI TIS HELLADAS, Kavála	S • Mideast & C Asia • 250 kW / W • Australasia • 250 kW
		• Mideast & C Asia • 250 kW
	USA †PAN AMERICAN BC, Via Jülich, Germany	S Sa • Mideast & W Asia • 100 kW
		S Su/M • S Asia • 100 kW
		S Su • Mideast & W Asia • 100 kW
15660	**BELGIUM** †ZWART OF WIT, Via Armavir, Russia	S Sa • W Europe • PRO-VLAAMS BELANG • 250 kW
	CLANDESTINE (AFRICA) †"TENSAE ETHIOPIA V UNITY", Via Russia	S • E Africa • 250 kW
	LIBYA RADIO JAMAHIRIYA, Via France	S • W Africa • 500 kW
		W • E Africa • 500 kW
		W • ENGLISH & FRENCH • E Africa • 500 kW
		S • ENGLISH & FRENCH • W Africa • 500 kW
	USA ADVENTIST WORLD R, Via Agat, Guam	W • S Asia • 100 kW
		W M/Tu/Th-Sa • S Asia • 100 kW
		W Su/W • S Asia • 100 kW
	GOSPEL FOR ASIA, Via Germany	S • W Asia & S Asia • 250 kW
	R FREE ASIA, Via Dushanbe, Tajikistan	W • S Asia • 200 kW
15665	**CHINA** †CHINA R INTL, Kashi	W • Europe • 500 kW
	USA FAMILY RADIO, Okeechobee, Fl	W • Europe • 100 kW
	R FREE ASIA, Via Tinian, N Marianas	W • E Asia • 500 kW
	VOA, Via Iranawila, Sri Lanka	W • SE Asia • 250 kW
	VOA, Via Saipan, N Marianas	E Asia • 100 kW
	†WORLD HARVEST R, Greenbush, Maine	W • Europe • 250 kW / S • Africa • 250 kW
15670	**CHINA** CENTRAL PEOPLE'S BS, Beijing	DS-8 (MINORITIES) • 50 kW
	CLANDESTINE (AFRICA) "RADIO XORIYO", Via Jülich, Germany	S Tu/F • E Africa • ANTI-ETHIOPIA GOVT • 100 kW
	"VO DEMOCRATIC ERITREA", Germany	S M/Th • E Africa • ANTI-ERITREAN GOVT • 100 kW
	"VO ETHIOPIAN MEDHIN", Via Germany	S Su/Th • E Africa • ANTI-ETHIOPIA GOVT • 100 kW
	"VO OROMO LIBERATION, Via Germany	S Su/Tu/W/F • E Africa • 100 kW
	EGYPT RADIO CAIRO, Abu Za'bal	W Asia & S Asia • 100 kW
	USA R FREE ASIA, Via Almaty, Kazakstan	S • SE Asia • 200 kW
15675	**CLANDESTINE (AFRICA)** "VOICE OF LIBERTY", Via Samara, Russia	S Su • E Africa • ANTI-ERITREA GOVT • 250 kW
	GERMANY RADIO SANTEC, Jülich	S Su • Africa • 100 kW
	SWITZERLAND RADIO REVEIL, Via Jülich, Germany	S Th • C Africa & S Africa • 100 kW
	UKRAINE †RADIO UKRAINE, Kharkiv	• W Europe • 100 kW
15680	**UNITED KINGDOM** BIBLE VOICE, Via Jülich, Germany	S Sa/Su • Mideast • 100 kW
		S • Mideast • 100 kW
		S W-Su • Mideast • 100 kW
		S Tu • Mideast • 100 kW
		S W/F-Su • Mideast • 100 kW
	USA †QUE HUONG R, Naalehu, Hawai'i	S • SE Asia
	VOA, Via Iranawila, Sri Lanka	S • S Asia • 250 kW
15685	**USA** R FREE ASIA, Via Tinian, N Marianas	S • E Asia • 500 kW
	†WEWN, Vandiver, Alabama	S • Europe • 500 kW
15690	**PORTUGAL** RDP INTERNATIONAL, Lisbon	W M-F • Mideast & S Asia • 100 kW
	USA †R FARDA, Via Iranawila, Sri Lanka	W Asia • 250 kW
	RFE-RL, Via Iranawila, Sri Lanka	W • W Asia & S Asia • 250 kW
15695	**USA** FAMILY RADIO, Okeechobee, Fl	S • Europe • 100 kW
	R FREE ASIA, Via Dushanbe, Tajikistan	S • S Asia • 200 kW
	WEWN, Vandiver, Alabama	W • Europe • 500 kW
15700 (con'd)	**BULGARIA** †RADIO BULGARIA, Plovdiv	S • W Europe • 250 kW

0 1 2 3 4 5 6 7 8 9 10 11 12 13 14 15 16 17 18 19 20 21 22 23 24

ENGLISH ▬▬   ARABIC ▨▨   CHINESE ▫▫▫   FRENCH ▭▭   GERMAN ▬▬   RUSSIAN ══   SPANISH ▬▬   OTHER ──

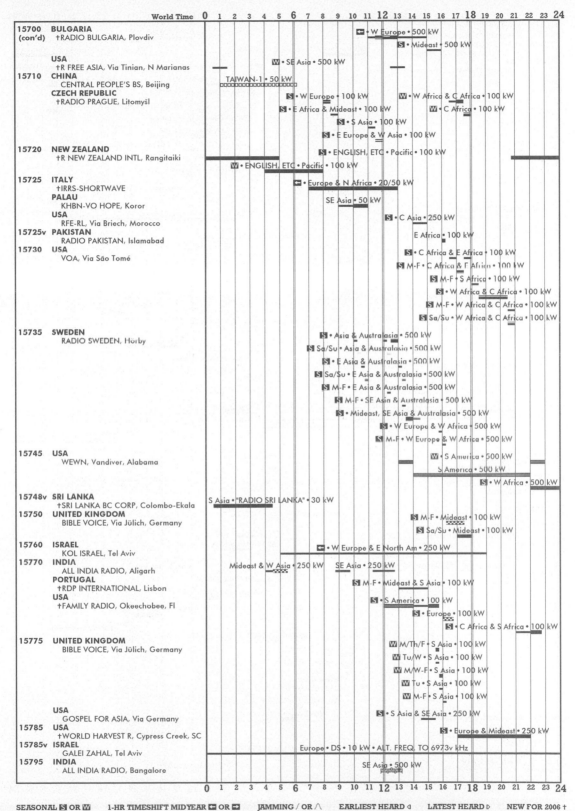

World Time 0 1 2 3 4 5 6 7 8 9 10 11 **12** 13 14 15 16 17 **18** 19 20 21 22 23 **24**

Freq	Station	Notes
15700 (con'd)	BULGARIA †RADIO BULGARIA, Plovdiv	⇐ • W Europe • 500 kW / S • Mideast • 500 kW
	USA †R FREE ASIA, Via Tinian, N Marianas	W • SE Asia • 500 kW
15710	CHINA CENTRAL PEOPLE'S BS, Beijing	TAIWAN-1 • 50 kW
	CZECH REPUBLIC †RADIO PRAGUE, Litomyšl	S • W Europe • 100 kW / W • W Africa & C Africa • 100 kW / S • E Africa & Mideast • 100 kW / W • C Africa • 100 kW / S • S Asia • 100 kW / S • E Europe & W Asia • 100 kW
15720	NEW ZEALAND †R NEW ZEALAND INTL, Rangitaiki	S • ENGLISH, ETC • Pacific • 100 kW / W • ENGLISH, ETC • Pacific • 100 kW
15725	ITALY †IRRS-SHORTWAVE	⇐ • Europe & N Africa • 20/50 kW
	PALAU KHBN-VO HOPE, Koror	SE Asia • 50 kW
	USA RFE-RL, Via Briech, Morocco	S • C Asia • 250 kW
15725v	PAKISTAN RADIO PAKISTAN, Islamabad	E Africa • 100 kW
15730	USA VOA, Via São Tomé	S • C Africa & E Africa • 100 kW / S M-F • C Africa & E Africa • 100 kW / S M-F • S Africa • 100 kW / S • W Africa & C Africa • 100 kW / S M-F • W Africa & C Africa • 100 kW / S Sa/Su • W Africa & C Africa • 100 kW
15735	SWEDEN RADIO SWEDEN, Hörby	S • Asia & Australasia • 500 kW / S Sa/Su • Asia & Australasia • 500 kW / S • E Asia & Australasia • 500 kW / S Sa/Su • E Asia & Australasia • 500 kW / S M-F • E Asia & Australasia • 500 kW / S M-F • SE Asia & Australasia • 500 kW / S • Mideast, SE Asia & Australasia • 500 kW / S • W Europe & W Africa • 500 kW / S M-F • W Europe & W Africa • 500 kW
15745	USA WEWN, Vandiver, Alabama	W • S America • 500 kW / S America • 500 kW / S • W Africa • 500 kW
15748v	SRI LANKA †SRI LANKA BC CORP, Colombo-Ekala	S Asia • "RADIO SRI LANKA" • 30 kW
15750	UNITED KINGDOM BIBLE VOICE, Via Jülich, Germany	S M-F • Mideast • 100 kW / S Sa/Su • Mideast • 100 kW
15760	ISRAEL KOL ISRAEL, Tel Aviv	⇐ • W Europe & E North Am • 250 kW
15770	INDIA ALL INDIA RADIO, Aligarh	Mideast & W Asia • 250 kW / SE Asia • 250 kW
	PORTUGAL †RDP INTERNATIONAL, Lisbon	S M-F • Mideast & S Asia • 100 kW
	USA †FAMILY RADIO, Okeechobee, Fl	S • S America • 100 kW / S • Europe • 100 kW / S • C Africa & S Africa • 100 kW
15775	UNITED KINGDOM BIBLE VOICE, Via Jülich, Germany	W M/Th/F • S Asia • 100 kW / W Tu/W • S Asia • 100 kW / W M/W-F • S Asia • 100 kW / W Tu • S Asia • 100 kW / W M-F • S Asia • 100 kW
	USA GOSPEL FOR ASIA, Via Germany	S • S Asia & SE Asia • 250 kW
15785	USA †WORLD HARVEST R, Cypress Creek, SC	S • Europe & Mideast • 250 kW
15785v	ISRAEL GALEI ZAHAL, Tel Aviv	Europe • DS • 10 kW • ALT. FREQ. TO 6973v kHz
15795	INDIA ALL INDIA RADIO, Bangalore	SE Asia • 500 kW

0 1 2 3 4 5 6 7 8 9 10 11 **12** 13 14 15 16 17 **18** 19 20 21 22 23 **24**

SEASONAL S OR W   1-HR TIMESHIFT MIDYEAR ⇐ OR ⇒   JAMMING / OR ∧   EARLIEST HEARD ◁   LATEST HEARD ▷   NEW FOR 2006 †

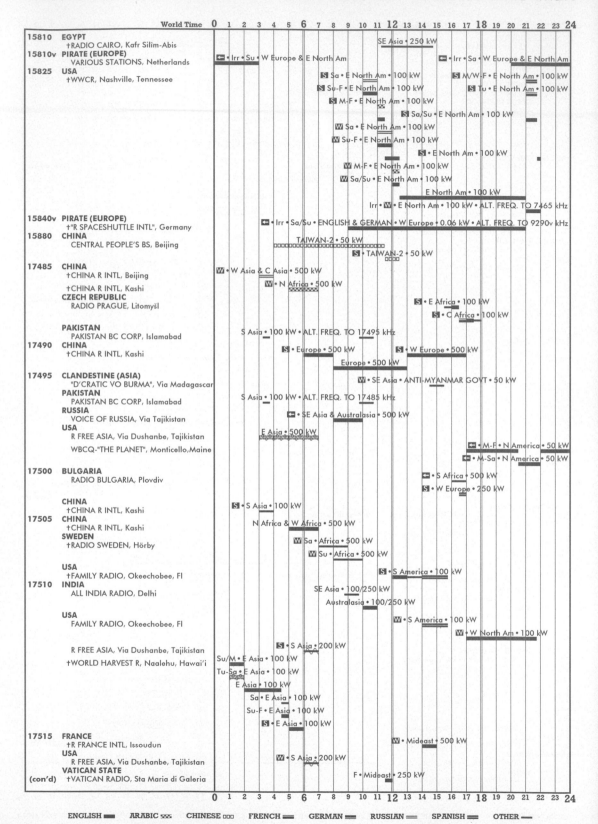

World Time			
0 1 2 3 4 5 6 7 8 9 10 11 12 13 14 15 16 17 18 19 20 21 22 23 24			

15810 EGYPT
  †RADIO CAIRO, Kafr Silim-Abis — SE Asia • 250 kW
15810v PIRATE (EUROPE)
  VARIOUS STATIONS, Netherlands — Irr • Su • W Europe & E North Am   Irr • Sa • W Europe & E North Am
15825 USA
  †WWCR, Nashville, Tennessee
    S • Sa • E North Am • 100 kW
    Su-F • E North Am • 100 kW
    S M/W-F • E North Am • 100 kW
    S Tu • E North Am • 100 kW
    S M-F • E North Am • 100 kW
    S Sa/Su • E North Am • 100 kW
    W Sa • E North Am • 100 kW
    W Su-F • E North Am • 100 kW
    S • E North Am • 100 kW
    W M-F • E North Am • 100 kW
    W Sa/Su • E North Am • 100 kW
    E North Am • 100 kW
    Irr • W • E North Am • 100 kW • ALT. FREQ. TO 7465 kHz

15840v PIRATE (EUROPE)
  †"R SPACESHUTTLE INTL", Germany — Irr • Sa/Su • ENGLISH & GERMAN • W Europe • 0.06 kW • ALT. FREQ. TO 9290v kHz
15880 CHINA
  CENTRAL PEOPLE'S BS, Beijing — TAIWAN-2 • 50 kW   S • TAIWAN-2 • 50 kW

17485 CHINA
  †CHINA R INTL, Beijing — W • W Asia & C Asia • 500 kW
  †CHINA R INTL, Kashi — W • N Africa • 500 kW
  CZECH REPUBLIC
  RADIO PRAGUE, Litomyšl — S • E Africa • 100 kW
    S • C Africa • 100 kW
  PAKISTAN
  PAKISTAN BC CORP, Islamabad — S Asia • 100 kW • ALT. FREQ. TO 17495 kHz
17490 CHINA
  †CHINA R INTL, Kashi — S • Europe • 500 kW   S • W Europe • 500 kW
    Europe • 500 kW

17495 CLANDESTINE (ASIA)
  "D'CRATIC VO BURMA", Via Madagascar — W • SE Asia • ANTI-MYANMAR GOVT • 50 kW
  PAKISTAN
  PAKISTAN BC CORP, Islamabad — S Asia • 100 kW • ALT. FREQ. TO 17485 kHz
  RUSSIA
  VOICE OF RUSSIA, Via Tajikistan — SE Asia & Australasia • 500 kW
  USA
  R FREE ASIA, Via Dushanbe, Tajikistan — E Asia • 500 kW
  WBCQ-"THE PLANET", Monticello, Maine — M-F • N America • 50 kW
    M-Sa • N America • 50 kW

17500 BULGARIA
  RADIO BULGARIA, Plovdiv — S Africa • 500 kW
    S • W Europe • 250 kW
  CHINA
  †CHINA R INTL, Kashi — S • S Asia • 100 kW
17505 CHINA
  †CHINA R INTL, Kashi — N Africa & W Africa • 500 kW
  SWEDEN
  †RADIO SWEDEN, Hörby — W Sa • Africa • 500 kW
    W Su • Africa • 500 kW
  USA
  †FAMILY RADIO, Okeechobee, Fl — S • S America • 100 kW
17510 INDIA
  ALL INDIA RADIO, Delhi — SE Asia • 100/250 kW
    Australasia • 100/250 kW
  USA
  FAMILY RADIO, Okeechobee, Fl — W • S America • 100 kW
    W • W North Am • 100 kW
  R FREE ASIA, Via Dushanbe, Tajikistan — S • S Asia • 200 kW
  †WORLD HARVEST R, Naalehu, Hawai'i — Su/M • E Asia • 100 kW
    Tu-Sa • E Asia • 100 kW
    E Asia • 100 kW
    Sa • E Asia • 100 kW
    Su-F • E Asia • 100 kW
    S • E Asia • 100 kW

17515 FRANCE
  †R FRANCE INTL, Issoudun — W • Mideast • 500 kW
  USA
  R FREE ASIA, Via Dushanbe, Tajikistan — W • S Asia • 200 kW
  VATICAN STATE
(con'd) †VATICAN RADIO, Sta Maria di Galeria — F • Mideast • 250 kW

0 1 2 3 4 5 6 7 8 9 10 11 12 13 14 15 16 17 18 19 20 21 22 23 24	

ENGLISH ▬ ARABIC ⧉ CHINESE □□□ FRENCH ▬ GERMAN ▬ RUSSIAN ══ SPANISH ▬ OTHER ▬

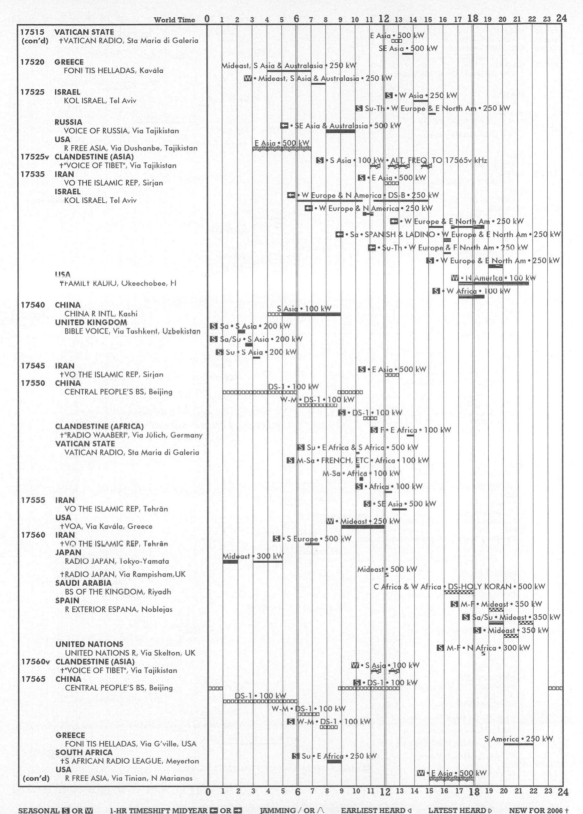

World Time	17515–17565 kHz broadcast schedule
17515 (con'd)	**VATICAN STATE** — †VATICAN RADIO, Sta Maria di Galeria — E Asia • 500 kW; SE Asia • 500 kW
17520	**GREECE** — FONI TIS HELLADAS, Kavála — Mideast, S Asia & Australasia • 250 kW; W • Mideast, S Asia & Australasia • 250 kW
17525	**ISRAEL** — KOL ISRAEL, Tel Aviv — S • W Asia • 250 kW; S Su-Th • W Europe & E North Am • 250 kW
	RUSSIA — VOICE OF RUSSIA, Via Tajikistan — SE Asia & Australasia • 500 kW
	USA — R FREE ASIA, Via Dushanbe, Tajikistan — E Asia • 500 kW
17525v	**CLANDESTINE (ASIA)** — †"VOICE OF TIBET", Via Tajikistan — S • S Asia • 100 kW • ALT. FREQ TO 17565v kHz
17535	**IRAN** — VO THE ISLAMIC REP, Sirjan — S • E Asia • 500 kW
	ISRAEL — KOL ISRAEL, Tel Aviv — W Europe & N America • DS-B • 250 kW; W Europe & N America • 250 kW; W Europe & E North Am • 250 kW; Sa • SPANISH & LADINO • W Europe & E North Am • 250 kW; Su-Th • W Europe & E North Am • 250 kW; S • W Europe & E North Am • 250 kW
	USA — †FAMILY RADIO, Okeechobee, Fl — W • N America • 100 kW; S • W Africa • 100 kW
17540	**CHINA** — CHINA R INTL, Kashi — S Asia • 100 kW
	UNITED KINGDOM — BIBLE VOICE, Via Tashkent, Uzbekistan — S Sa • S Asia • 200 kW; S Sa/Su • S Asia • 200 kW; S Su • S Asia • 200 kW
17545	**IRAN** — †VO THE ISLAMIC REP, Sirjan — S • E Asia • 500 kW
17550	**CHINA** — CENTRAL PEOPLE'S BS, Beijing — DS-1 • 100 kW; W-M • DS-1 • 100 kW; S • DS-1 • 100 kW
	CLANDESTINE (AFRICA) — †"RADIO WAABERI", Via Jülich, Germany — F • E Africa • 100 kW
	VATICAN STATE — VATICAN RADIO, Sta Maria di Galeria — S Su • E Africa & S Africa • 500 kW; S M-Sa • FRENCH, ETC • Africa • 100 kW; M-Sa • Africa • 100 kW; S • Africa • 100 kW
17555	**IRAN** — VO THE ISLAMIC REP, Tehrān — S • SE Asia • 500 kW
	USA — †VOA, Via Kavála, Greece — W • Mideast • 250 kW
17560	**IRAN** — †VO THE ISLAMIC REP, Tehrān — S • S Europe • 500 kW
	JAPAN — RADIO JAPAN, Tokyo-Yamata — Mideast • 300 kW; †RADIO JAPAN, Via Rampisham, UK — Mideast • 500 kW
	SAUDI ARABIA — BS OF THE KINGDOM, Riyadh — C Africa & W Africa • DS-HOLY KORAN • 500 kW
	SPAIN — R EXTERIOR ESPANA, Noblejas — S M-F • Mideast • 350 kW; S Sa/Su • Mideast • 350 kW; S • Mideast • 350 kW
	UNITED NATIONS — UNITED NATIONS R, Via Skelton, UK — S M-F • N Africa • 300 kW
17560v	**CLANDESTINE (ASIA)** — †"VOICE OF TIBET", Via Tajikistan — W • S Asia • 100 kW
17565	**CHINA** — CENTRAL PEOPLE'S BS, Beijing — S • DS-1 • 100 kW; DS-1 • 100 kW; W-M • DS-1 • 100 kW; S W-M • DS-1 • 100 kW
	GREECE — FONI TIS HELLADAS, Via G'ville, USA — S America • 250 kW
	SOUTH AFRICA — †S AFRICAN RADIO LEAGUE, Meyerton — S Su • E Africa • 250 kW
(con'd)	**USA** — R FREE ASIA, Via Tinian, N Marianas — W • E Asia • 500 kW

SEASONAL **S** OR **W**   1-HR TIMESHIFT MIDYEAR ⊡ OR ⊡   JAMMING / OR ∧   EARLIEST HEARD ◁   LATEST HEARD ▷   NEW FOR 2006 †

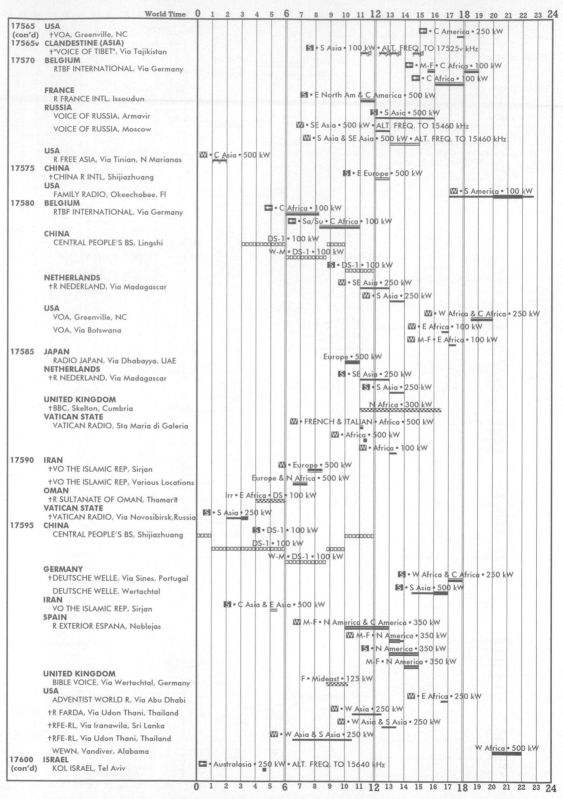

World Time 0 1 2 3 4 5 6 7 8 9 10 11 12 13 14 15 16 17 18 19 20 21 22 23 24

17565
(con'd) **USA**
  †VOA, Greenville, NC — C America • 250 kW
17565v CLANDESTINE (ASIA)
  †"VOICE OF TIBET", Via Tajikistan — S • S Asia • 100 kW • ALT. FREQ. TO 17525v kHz
17570 BELGIUM
  RTBF INTERNATIONAL, Via Germany — M-F • C Africa • 100 kW / C Africa • 100 kW

  FRANCE
  R FRANCE INTL, Issoudun — S • E North Am & C America • 500 kW
  RUSSIA
  VOICE OF RUSSIA, Armavir — S • S Asia • 500 kW
  VOICE OF RUSSIA, Moscow — W • SE Asia • 500 kW • ALT. FREQ. TO 15460 kHz
  — W • S Asia & SE Asia • 500 kW • ALT. FREQ. TO 15460 kHz

  USA
  R FREE ASIA, Via Tinian, N Marianas — W • C Asia • 500 kW
17575 CHINA
  †CHINA R INTL, Shijiazhuang — S • E Europe • 500 kW
  USA
  FAMILY RADIO, Okeechobee, Fl — W • S America • 100 kW
17580 BELGIUM
  RTBF INTERNATIONAL, Via Germany — C Africa • 100 kW
  — Sa/Su • C Africa • 100 kW

  CHINA
  CENTRAL PEOPLE'S BS, Lingshi — DS-1 • 100 kW
  — W-M • DS-1 • 100 kW
  — S • DS-1 • 100 kW

  NETHERLANDS
  †R NEDERLAND, Via Madagascar — W • SE Asia • 250 kW
  — W • S Asia • 250 kW

  USA
  VOA, Greenville, NC — W • W Africa & C Africa • 250 kW
  VOA, Via Botswana — W • E Africa • 100 kW
  — W M-F • E Africa • 100 kW

17585 JAPAN
  RADIO JAPAN, Via Dhabayya, UAE — Europe • 500 kW
  NETHERLANDS
  †R NEDERLAND, Via Madagascar — S • SE Asia • 250 kW
  — S • S Asia • 250 kW

  UNITED KINGDOM
  †BBC, Skelton, Cumbria — N Africa • 300 kW
  VATICAN STATE
  VATICAN RADIO, Sta Maria di Galeria — W • FRENCH & ITALIAN • Africa • 500 kW
  — W • Africa • 500 kW
  — W • Africa • 100 kW

17590 IRAN
  †VO THE ISLAMIC REP, Sirjan — W • Europe • 500 kW
  †VO THE ISLAMIC REP, Various Locations — Europe & N Africa • 500 kW
  OMAN
  †R SULTANATE OF OMAN, Thamarit — Irr • E Africa • DS • 100 kW
  VATICAN STATE
  †VATICAN RADIO, Via Novosibirsk, Russia — S • S Asia • 250 kW
17595 CHINA
  CENTRAL PEOPLE'S BS, Shijiazhuang — S • DS-1 • 100 kW
  — DS-1 • 100 kW
  — W-M • DS-1 • 100 kW

  GERMANY
  †DEUTSCHE WELLE, Via Sines, Portugal — S • W Africa & C Africa • 250 kW
  DEUTSCHE WELLE, Wertachtal — S • S Asia • 500 kW
  IRAN
  VO THE ISLAMIC REP, Sirjan — S • C Asia & E Asia • 500 kW
  SPAIN
  R EXTERIOR ESPANA, Noblejas — W M-F • N America & C America • 350 kW
  — W M-F • N America • 350 kW
  — S • N America • 350 kW
  — M-F • N America • 350 kW

  UNITED KINGDOM
  BIBLE VOICE, Via Wertachtal, Germany — F • Mideast • 125 kW
  USA
  ADVENTIST WORLD R, Via Abu Dhabi — W • E Africa • 250 kW
  †R FARDA, Via Udon Thani, Thailand — W • W Asia • 250 kW
  †RFE-RL, Via Iranawila, Sri Lanka — W • W Asia & S Asia • 250 kW
  †RFE-RL, Via Udon Thani, Thailand — W • W Asia & S Asia • 250 kW
  WEWN, Vandiver, Alabama — W Africa • 500 kW
17600 ISRAEL
(con'd) KOL ISRAEL, Tel Aviv — Australasia • 250 kW • ALT. FREQ. TO 15640 kHz

0 1 2 3 4 5 6 7 8 9 10 11 12 13 14 15 16 17 18 19 20 21 22 23 24

ENGLISH ▬ ARABIC ∾∾ CHINESE □□□ FRENCH ═ GERMAN ▭▭ RUSSIAN ══ SPANISH ▭▭ OTHER ▬

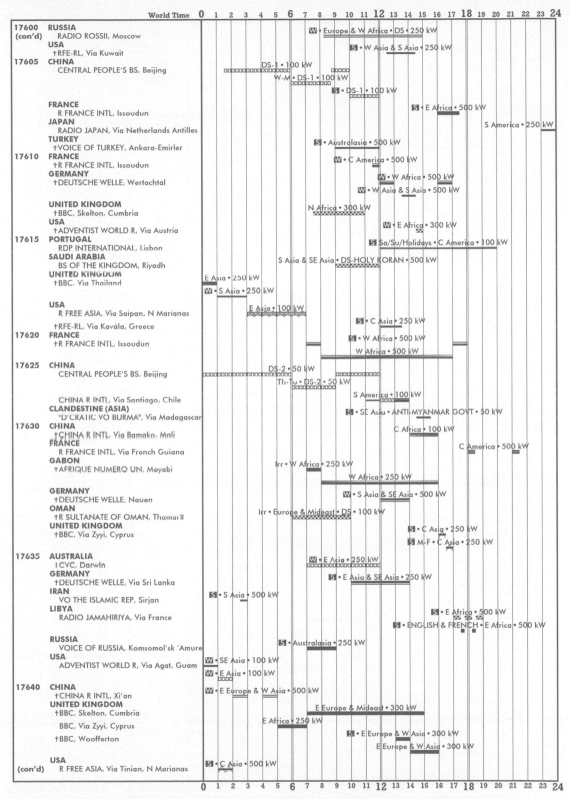

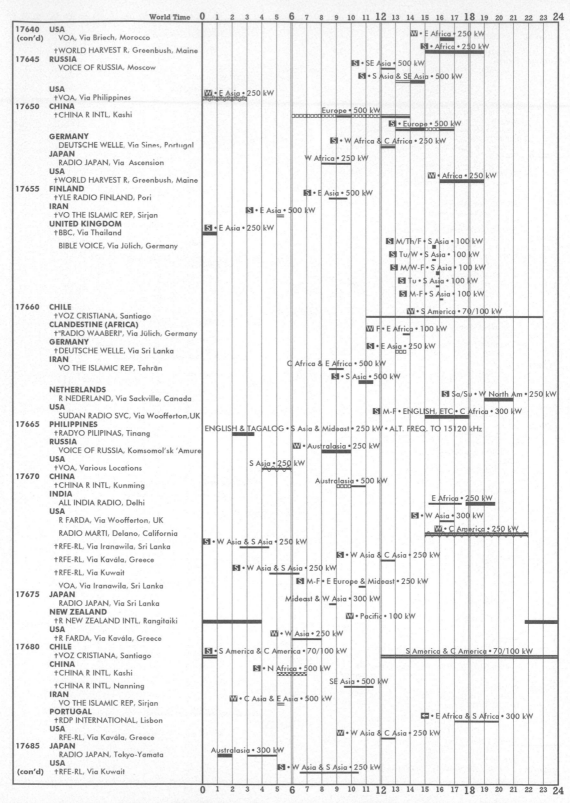

| | World Time | 0 | 1 | 2 | 3 | 4 | 5 | 6 | 7 | 8 | 9 | 10 | 11 | 12 | 13 | 14 | 15 | 16 | 17 | 18 | 19 | 20 | 21 | 22 | 23 | 24 |

17640 (con'd) USA
VOA, Via Briech, Morocco — W • E Africa • 250 kW
†WORLD HARVEST R, Greenbush, Maine — S • Africa • 250 kW

17645 RUSSIA
VOICE OF RUSSIA, Moscow — S • SE Asia • 500 kW; S • S Asia & SE Asia • 500 kW

USA
†VOA, Via Philippines — W • E Asia • 250 kW

17650 CHINA
†CHINA R INTL, Kashi — Europe • 500 kW; S • Europe • 500 kW

GERMANY
DEUTSCHE WELLE, Via Sines, Portugal — S • W Africa & C Africa • 250 kW

JAPAN
RADIO JAPAN, Via Ascension — W Africa • 250 kW

USA
†WORLD HARVEST R, Greenbush, Maine — W • Africa • 250 kW

17655 FINLAND
†YLE RADIO FINLAND, Pori — S • E Asia • 500 kW

IRAN
†VO THE ISLAMIC REP, Sirjan — S • E Asia • 500 kW

UNITED KINGDOM
†BBC, Via Thailand — S • E Asia • 250 kW

BIBLE VOICE, Via Jülich, Germany — S M/Th/F • S Asia • 100 kW; S Tu/W • S Asia • 100 kW; S M/W-F • S Asia • 100 kW; S Tu • S Asia • 100 kW; S M-F • S Asia • 100 kW

17660 CHILE
†VOZ CRISTIANA, Santiago — W • S America • 70/100 kW

CLANDESTINE (AFRICA)
†"RADIO WAABERI", Via Jülich, Germany — W F • E Africa • 100 kW

GERMANY
†DEUTSCHE WELLE, Via Sri Lanka — S • E Asia • 250 kW

IRAN
VO THE ISLAMIC REP, Tehrān — C Africa & E Africa • 500 kW; S • S Asia • 500 kW

NETHERLANDS
R NEDERLAND, Via Sackville, Canada — S Sa/Su • W North Am • 250 kW

USA
SUDAN RADIO SVC, Via Woofferton, UK — S M-F • ENGLISH, ETC • C Africa • 300 kW

17665 PHILIPPINES
†RADYO PILIPINAS, Tinang — ENGLISH & TAGALOG • S Asia & Mideast • 250 kW • ALT. FREQ. TO 15120 kHz

RUSSIA
VOICE OF RUSSIA, Komsomol'sk 'Amure — W • Australasia • 250 kW

USA
†VOA, Various Locations — S Asia • 250 kW

17670 CHINA
†CHINA R INTL, Kunming — Australasia • 500 kW

INDIA
ALL INDIA RADIO, Delhi — E Africa • 250 kW

USA
R FARDA, Via Woofferton, UK — S • W Asia • 300 kW

RADIO MARTI, Delano, California — W • C America • 250 kW

†RFE-RL, Via Iranawila, Sri Lanka — S • W Asia & S Asia • 250 kW

†RFE-RL, Via Kavála, Greece — S • W Asia & C Asia • 250 kW

†RFE-RL, Via Kuwait — S • W Asia & S Asia • 250 kW

VOA, Via Iranawila, Sri Lanka — S M-F • E Europe & Mideast • 250 kW

17675 JAPAN
RADIO JAPAN, Via Sri Lanka — Mideast & W Asia • 300 kW

NEW ZEALAND
†R NEW ZEALAND INTL, Rangitaiki — W • Pacific • 100 kW

USA
†R FARDA, Via Kavála, Greece — W • W Asia • 250 kW

17680 CHILE
†VOZ CRISTIANA, Santiago — S • S America & C America • 70/100 kW; S America & C America • 70/100 kW

CHINA
†CHINA R INTL, Kashi — S • N Africa • 500 kW

†CHINA R INTL, Nanning — SE Asia • 500 kW

IRAN
VO THE ISLAMIC REP, Sirjan — W • C Asia & E Asia • 500 kW

PORTUGAL
†RDP INTERNATIONAL, Lisbon — E Africa & S Africa • 300 kW

USA
RFE-RL, Via Kavála, Greece — W • W Asia & C Asia • 250 kW

17685 JAPAN
RADIO JAPAN, Tokyo-Yamata — Australasia • 300 kW

USA
(con'd) †RFE-RL, Via Kuwait — S • W Asia & S Asia • 250 kW

| | | 0 | 1 | 2 | 3 | 4 | 5 | 6 | 7 | 8 | 9 | 10 | 11 | 12 | 13 | 14 | 15 | 16 | 17 | 18 | 19 | 20 | 21 | 22 | 23 | 24 |

ENGLISH ▬▬   ARABIC ▨▨▨   CHINESE □□□   FRENCH ▬▬   GERMAN ▬▬   RUSSIAN ══   SPANISH ▭▭   OTHER ▬▬

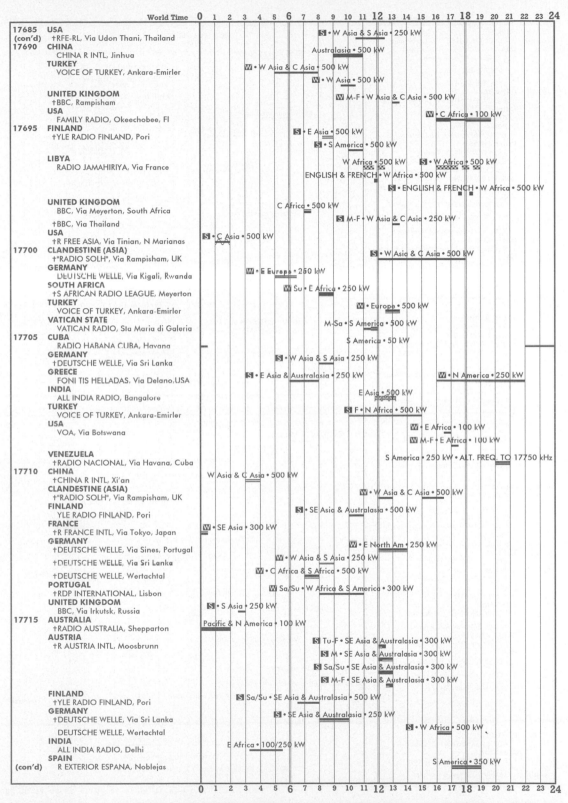

World Time 0 1 2 3 4 5 6 7 8 9 10 11 12 13 14 15 16 17 18 19 20 21 22 23 24

Freq	Country / Station	
17685 (con'd)	USA — †RFE-RL, Via Udon Thani, Thailand	S • W Asia & S Asia • 250 kW
17690	CHINA — CHINA R INTL, Jinhua	Australasia • 500 kW
	TURKEY — VOICE OF TURKEY, Ankara-Emirler	W • W Asia & C Asia • 500 kW
		W • W Asia • 500 kW
	UNITED KINGDOM — †BBC, Rampisham	W M-F • W Asia & C Asia • 500 kW
	USA — FAMILY RADIO, Okeechobee, Fl	W • C Africa • 100 kW
17695	FINLAND — †YLE RADIO FINLAND, Pori	S • E Asia • 500 kW
		S • S America • 500 kW
	LIBYA — RADIO JAMAHIRIYA, Via France	W Africa • 500 kW S • W Africa • 500 kW
		ENGLISH & FRENCH • W Africa • 500 kW
		S • ENGLISH & FRENCH • W Africa • 500 kW
	UNITED KINGDOM — BBC, Via Meyerton, South Africa	C Africa • 500 kW
	†BBC, Via Thailand	S M-F • W Asia & C Asia • 250 kW
	USA — †R FREE ASIA, Via Tinian, N Marianas	S • C Asia • 500 kW
17700	CLANDESTINE (ASIA) — †"RADIO SOLH", Via Rampisham, UK	S • W Asia & C Asia • 500 kW
	GERMANY — DEUTSCHE WELLE, Via Kigali, Rwanda	W • E Europe • 250 kW
	SOUTH AFRICA — †S AFRICAN RADIO LEAGUE, Meyerton	W Su • E Africa • 250 kW
	TURKEY — VOICE OF TURKEY, Ankara-Emirler	W • Europe • 500 kW
	VATICAN STATE — VATICAN RADIO, Sta Maria di Galeria	M-Sa • S America • 500 kW
17705	CUBA — RADIO HABANA CUBA, Havana	S America • 50 kW
	GERMANY — †DEUTSCHE WELLE, Via Sri Lanka	S • W Asia & S Asia • 250 kW
	GREECE — FONI TIS HELLADAS, Via Delano, USA	S • E Asia & Australasia • 250 kW W • N America • 250 kW
	INDIA — ALL INDIA RADIO, Bangalore	E Asia • 500 kW
	TURKEY — VOICE OF TURKEY, Ankara-Emirler	S F • N Africa • 500 kW
	USA — VOA, Via Botswana	W • E Africa • 100 kW
		W M-F • E Africa • 100 kW
	VENEZUELA — †RADIO NACIONAL, Via Havana, Cuba	S America • 250 kW • ALT. FREQ. TO 17750 kHz
17710	CHINA — †CHINA R INTL, Xi'an	W Asia & C Asia • 500 kW
	CLANDESTINE (ASIA) — †"RADIO SOLH", Via Rampisham, UK	W • W Asia & C Asia • 500 kW
	FINLAND — YLE RADIO FINLAND, Pori	S • SE Asia & Australasia • 500 kW
	FRANCE — †R FRANCE INTL, Via Tokyo, Japan	W • SE Asia • 300 kW
	GERMANY — †DEUTSCHE WELLE, Via Sines, Portugal	W • E North Am • 250 kW
	†DEUTSCHE WELLE, Via Sri Lanka	W • W Asia & S Asia • 250 kW
	†DEUTSCHE WELLE, Wertachtal	W • C Africa & S Africa • 500 kW
	PORTUGAL — †RDP INTERNATIONAL, Lisbon	W Sa/Su • W Africa & S America • 300 kW
	UNITED KINGDOM — BBC, Via Irkutsk, Russia	S • S Asia • 250 kW
17715	AUSTRALIA — †RADIO AUSTRALIA, Shepparton	Pacific & N America • 100 kW
	AUSTRIA — †R AUSTRIA INTL, Moosbrunn	S Tu-F • SE Asia & Australasia • 300 kW
		S M • SE Asia & Australasia • 300 kW
		S Sa/Su • SE Asia & Australasia • 300 kW
		S M-F • SE Asia & Australasia • 300 kW
	FINLAND — †YLE RADIO FINLAND, Pori	S Sa/Su • SE Asia & Australasia • 500 kW
	GERMANY — †DEUTSCHE WELLE, Via Sri Lanka	S • SE Asia & Australasia • 250 kW
	DEUTSCHE WELLE, Wertachtal	S • W Africa • 500 kW
	INDIA — ALL INDIA RADIO, Delhi	E Africa • 100/250 kW
(con'd)	SPAIN — R EXTERIOR ESPANA, Noblejas	S America • 350 kW

0 1 2 3 4 5 6 7 8 9 10 11 12 13 14 15 16 17 18 19 20 21 22 23 24

SEASONAL S OR W   1-HR TIMESHIFT MIDYEAR ⇐ OR ⇒   JAMMING / OR ∧   EARLIEST HEARD ◁   LATEST HEARD ▷   NEW FOR 2006 †

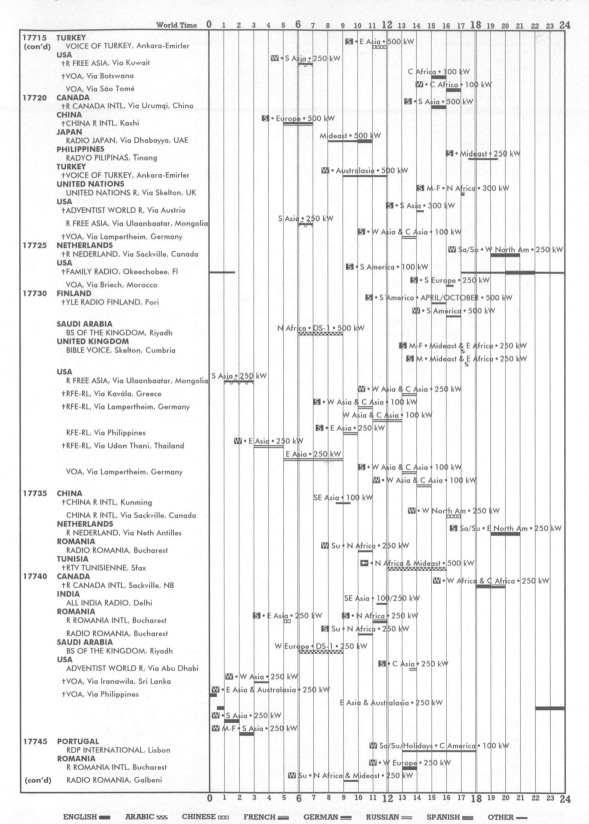

	World Time	0	1	2	3	4	5	6	7	8	9	10	11	12	13	14	15	16	17	18	19	20	21	22	23	24

17715 **TURKEY**
(con'd)   VOICE OF TURKEY, Ankara-Emirler — S • E Asia • 500 kW
USA
†R FREE ASIA, Via Kuwait — W • S Asia • 250 kW

†VOA, Via Botswana — C Africa • 100 kW

VOA, Via São Tomé — W • C Africa • 100 kW

17720 **CANADA**
†R CANADA INTL, Via Urumqi, China — S • S Asia • 500 kW
CHINA
†CHINA R INTL, Kashi — S • Europe • 500 kW
JAPAN
RADIO JAPAN, Via Dhabayya, UAE — Mideast • 500 kW
PHILIPPINES
RADYO PILIPINAS, Tinang — S • Mideast • 250 kW
TURKEY
†VOICE OF TURKEY, Ankara-Emirler — W • Australasia • 500 kW
UNITED NATIONS
UNITED NATIONS R, Via Skelton, UK — S M-F • N Africa • 300 kW
USA
†ADVENTIST WORLD R, Via Austria — S • S Asia • 300 kW

R FREE ASIA, Via Ulaanbaatar, Mongolia — S Asia • 250 kW

†VOA, Via Lampertheim, Germany — S • W Asia & C Asia • 100 kW
17725 **NETHERLANDS**
†R NEDERLAND, Via Sackville, Canada — W Sa/Su • W North Am • 250 kW
USA
†FAMILY RADIO, Okeechobee, Fl — S • S America • 100 kW

VOA, Via Briech, Morocco — S • S Europe • 250 kW
17730 **FINLAND**
†YLE RADIO FINLAND, Pori — S • S America • APRIL/OCTOBER • 500 kW

— W • S America • 500 kW

SAUDI ARABIA
BS OF THE KINGDOM, Riyadh — N Africa • DS-1 • 500 kW
UNITED KINGDOM
BIBLE VOICE, Skelton, Cumbria — S M-F • Mideast & E Africa • 250 kW

— S M • Mideast & E Africa • 250 kW

USA
R FREE ASIA, Via Ulaanbaatar, Mongolia — S Asia • 250 kW

†RFE-RL, Via Kavála, Greece — W • W Asia & C Asia • 250 kW

†RFE-RL, Via Lampertheim, Germany — S • W Asia & C Asia • 100 kW

— W Asia & C Asia • 100 kW

RFE-RL, Via Philippines — S • E Asia • 250 kW

†RFE-RL, Via Udon Thani, Thailand — W • E Asia • 250 kW

— E Asia • 250 kW

VOA, Via Lampertheim, Germany — S • W Asia & C Asia • 100 kW

— W • W Asia & C Asia • 100 kW

17735 **CHINA**
†CHINA R INTL, Kunming — SE Asia • 100 kW

CHINA R INTL, Via Sackville, Canada — W • W North Am • 250 kW
NETHERLANDS
R NEDERLAND, Via Neth Antilles — S Sa/Su • E North Am • 250 kW
ROMANIA
RADIO ROMANIA, Bucharest — W Su • N Africa • 250 kW
TUNISIA
†RTV TUNISIENNE, Sfax — N Africa & Mideast • 500 kW
17740 **CANADA**
†R CANADA INTL, Sackville, NB — W • W Africa & C Africa • 250 kW
INDIA
ALL INDIA RADIO, Delhi — SE Asia • 100/250 kW
ROMANIA
R ROMANIA INTL, Bucharest — S • E Asia • 250 kW   S • N Africa • 250 kW

RADIO ROMANIA, Bucharest — S Su • N Africa • 250 kW
SAUDI ARABIA
BS OF THE KINGDOM, Riyadh — W Europe • DS-1 • 250 kW
USA
ADVENTIST WORLD R, Via Abu Dhabi — S • C Asia • 250 kW

†VOA, Via Iranawila, Sri Lanka — W • W Asia • 250 kW

†VOA, Via Philippines — W • E Asia & Australasia • 250 kW

— E Asia & Australasia • 250 kW

— W • S Asia • 250 kW

— W M-F • S Asia • 250 kW

17745 **PORTUGAL**
RDP INTERNATIONAL, Lisbon — W Sa/Su/Holidays • C America • 100 kW
ROMANIA
R ROMANIA INTL, Bucharest — W • W Europe • 250 kW

(con'd)   RADIO ROMANIA, Galbeni — W Su • N Africa & Mideast • 250 kW

World Time	0	1	2	3	4	5	6	7	8	9	10	11	12	13	14	15	16	17	18	19	20	21	22	23	24

ENGLISH ▬ ARABIC ≋ CHINESE ▢▢▢ FRENCH ═ GERMAN ▬ RUSSIAN ══ SPANISH ▬ OTHER ▬

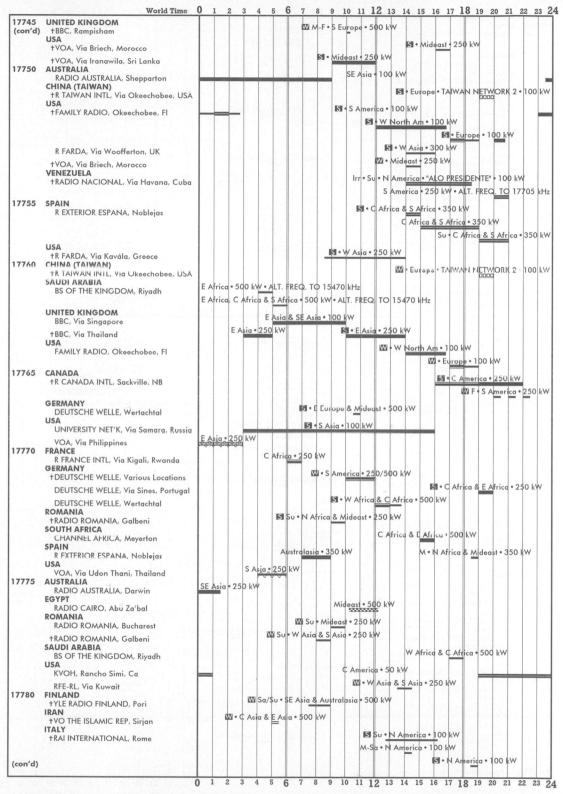

World Time 0 1 2 3 4 5 6 7 8 9 10 11 12 13 14 15 16 17 18 19 20 21 22 23 24

17745 **UNITED KINGDOM**
(con'd)   †BBC, Rampisham — W • M-F • S Europe • 500 kW
USA
   †VOA, Via Briech, Morocco — S • Mideast • 250 kW
   †VOA, Via Iranawila, Sri Lanka — S • Mideast • 250 kW

17750 **AUSTRALIA**
   RADIO AUSTRALIA, Shepparton — SE Asia • 100 kW
CHINA (TAIWAN)
   †R TAIWAN INTL, Via Okeechobee, USA — S • Europe • TAIWAN NETWORK 2 • 100 kW
USA
   †FAMILY RADIO, Okeechobee, Fl — S • S America • 100 kW
     S • W North Am • 100 kW
     S • Europe • 100 kW
   R FARDA, Via Woofferton, UK — S • W Asia • 300 kW
   †VOA, Via Briech, Morocco — W • Mideast • 250 kW
VENEZUELA
   †RADIO NACIONAL, Via Havana, Cuba — Irr • Su • N America • "ALO PRESIDENTE" • 100 kW
     S America • 250 kW • ALT. FREQ. TO 17705 kHz

17755 **SPAIN**
   R EXTERIOR ESPANA, Noblejas — S • C Africa & S Africa • 350 kW
     C Africa & S Africa • 350 kW
     Su • C Africa & S Africa • 350 kW
USA
   †R FARDA, Via Kavála, Greece — S • W Asia • 250 kW

17760 **CHINA (TAIWAN)**
   †R TAIWAN INTL, Via Okeechobee, USA — W • Europe • TAIWAN NETWORK 2 • 100 kW
SAUDI ARABIA
   BS OF THE KINGDOM, Riyadh — E Africa • 500 kW • ALT. FREQ. TO 15470 kHz
     E Africa, C Africa & S Africa • 500 kW • ALT. FREQ. TO 15470 kHz
UNITED KINGDOM
   BBC, Via Singapore — E Asia & SE Asia • 100 kW
   †BBC, Via Thailand — E Asia • 250 kW
     S • E Asia • 250 kW
USA
   FAMILY RADIO, Okeechobee, Fl — W • W North Am • 100 kW
     W • Europe • 100 kW

17765 **CANADA**
   †R CANADA INTL, Sackville, NB — S • C America • 250 kW
     W • F • S America • 250 kW
GERMANY
   DEUTSCHE WELLE, Wertachtal — S • E Europe & Mideast • 500 kW
USA
   UNIVERSITY NET'K, Via Samara, Russia — S • S Asia • 100 kW
   VOA, Via Philippines — E Asia • 250 kW

17770 **FRANCE**
   R FRANCE INTL, Via Kigali, Rwanda — C Africa • 250 kW
GERMANY
   †DEUTSCHE WELLE, Various Locations — W • S America • 250/500 kW
   DEUTSCHE WELLE, Via Sines, Portugal — S • C Africa & E Africa • 250 kW
   DEUTSCHE WELLE, Wertachtal — S • W Africa & C Africa • 500 kW
ROMANIA
   †RADIO ROMANIA, Galbeni — S • Su • N Africa & Mideast • 250 kW
SOUTH AFRICA
   CHANNEL AFRICA, Meyerton — C Africa & E Africa • 500 kW
SPAIN
   R EXTERIOR ESPANA, Noblejas — Australasia • 350 kW
     M • N Africa & Mideast • 350 kW
USA
   VOA, Via Udon Thani, Thailand — S Asia • 250 kW

17775 **AUSTRALIA**
   RADIO AUSTRALIA, Darwin — SE Asia • 250 kW
EGYPT
   RADIO CAIRO, Abu Za'bal — Mideast • 500 kW
ROMANIA
   RADIO ROMANIA, Bucharest — W • Su • Mideast • 250 kW
   †RADIO ROMANIA, Galbeni — W • Su • W Asia & S Asia • 250 kW
SAUDI ARABIA
   BS OF THE KINGDOM, Riyadh — W Africa & C Africa • 500 kW
USA
   KVOH, Rancho Simi, Ca — C America • 50 kW
   RFE-RL, Via Kuwait — W • W Asia & S Asia • 250 kW

17780 **FINLAND**
   †YLE RADIO FINLAND, Pori — W • Sa/Su • SE Asia & Australasia • 500 kW
IRAN
   †VO THE ISLAMIC REP, Sirjan — W • C Asia & E Asia • 500 kW
ITALY
   †RAI INTERNATIONAL, Rome — S • Su • N America • 100 kW
     M-Sa • N America • 100 kW
     S • N America • 100 kW

(con'd)

World Time 0 1 2 3 4 5 6 7 8 9 10 11 12 13 14 15 16 17 18 19 20 21 22 23 24

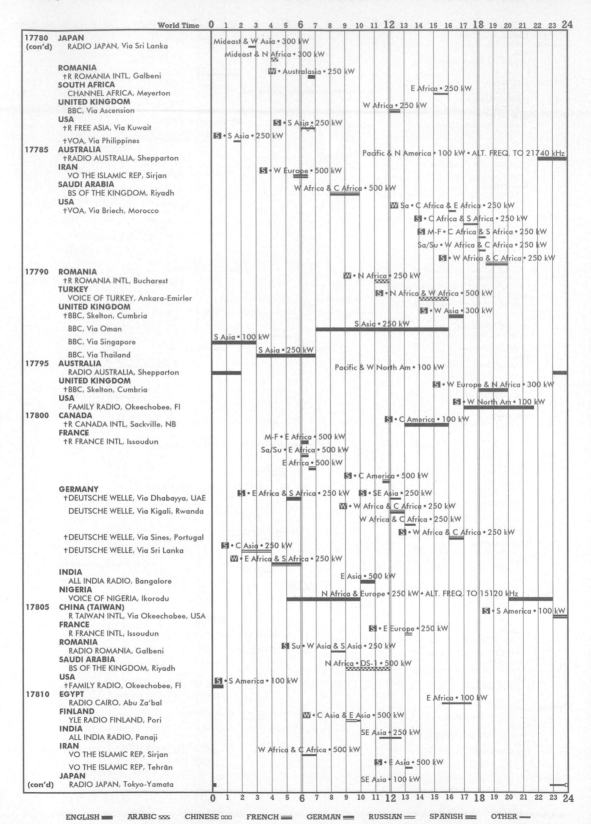

World Time 0 1 2 3 4 5 6 7 8 9 10 11 12 13 14 15 16 17 18 19 20 21 22 23 24

17780 JAPAN
(con'd)   RADIO JAPAN, Via Sri Lanka — Mideast & W Asia • 300 kW
Mideast & N Africa • 300 kW

ROMANIA
†R ROMANIA INTL, Galbeni — W • Australasia • 250 kW
SOUTH AFRICA
CHANNEL AFRICA, Meyerton — E Africa • 250 kW
UNITED KINGDOM
BBC, Via Ascension — W Africa • 250 kW
USA
†R FREE ASIA, Via Kuwait — S • S Asia • 250 kW
†VOA, Via Philippines — S • S Asia • 250 kW

17785 AUSTRALIA
†RADIO AUSTRALIA, Shepparton — Pacific & N America • 100 kW • ALT. FREQ. TO 21740 kHz
IRAN
VO THE ISLAMIC REP, Sirjan — S • W Europe • 500 kW
SAUDI ARABIA
BS OF THE KINGDOM, Riyadh — W Africa & C Africa • 500 kW
USA
†VOA, Via Briech, Morocco — W Sa • C Africa & E Africa • 250 kW
S • C Africa & S Africa • 250 kW
S M-F • C Africa & S Africa • 250 kW
Sa/Su • W Africa & C Africa • 250 kW
S • W Africa & C Africa • 250 kW

17790 ROMANIA
†R ROMANIA INTL, Bucharest — W • N Africa • 250 kW
TURKEY
VOICE OF TURKEY, Ankara-Emirler — S • N Africa & W Africa • 500 kW
UNITED KINGDOM
†BBC, Skelton, Cumbria — S • W Asia • 300 kW
BBC, Via Oman — S Asia • 250 kW
BBC, Via Singapore — S Asia • 100 kW
BBC, Via Thailand — S Asia • 250 kW

17795 AUSTRALIA
RADIO AUSTRALIA, Shepparton — Pacific & W North Am • 100 kW
UNITED KINGDOM
†BBC, Skelton, Cumbria — S • W Europe & N Africa • 300 kW
USA
FAMILY RADIO, Okeechobee, Fl — S • W North Am • 100 kW

17800 CANADA
†R CANADA INTL, Sackville, NB — S • C America • 100 kW
FRANCE
†R FRANCE INTL, Issoudun — M-F • E Africa • 500 kW
Sa/Su • E Africa • 500 kW
E Africa • 500 kW
S • C America • 500 kW

GERMANY
†DEUTSCHE WELLE, Via Dhabayya, UAE — S • E Africa & S Africa • 250 kW   S • SE Asia • 250 kW
DEUTSCHE WELLE, Via Kigali, Rwanda — W • W Africa & C Africa • 250 kW
W Africa & C Africa • 250 kW
†DEUTSCHE WELLE, Via Sines, Portugal — S • W Africa & C Africa • 250 kW
†DEUTSCHE WELLE, Via Sri Lanka — S • C Asia • 250 kW
W • E Africa & S Africa • 250 kW

INDIA
ALL INDIA RADIO, Bangalore — E Asia • 500 kW
NIGERIA
VOICE OF NIGERIA, Ikorodu — N Africa & Europe • 250 kW • ALT. FREQ. TO 15120 kHz

17805 CHINA (TAIWAN)
R TAIWAN INTL, Via Okeechobee, USA — S • S America • 100 kW
FRANCE
R FRANCE INTL, Issoudun — S • E Europe • 250 kW
ROMANIA
RADIO ROMANIA, Galbeni — S Su • W Asia & S Asia • 250 kW
SAUDI ARABIA
BS OF THE KINGDOM, Riyadh — N Africa • DS-1 • 500 kW
USA
†FAMILY RADIO, Okeechobee, Fl — S • S America • 100 kW

17810 EGYPT
RADIO CAIRO, Abu Za'bal — E Africa • 100 kW
FINLAND
YLE RADIO FINLAND, Pori — W • C Asia & E Asia • 500 kW
INDIA
ALL INDIA RADIO, Panaji — SE Asia • 250 kW
IRAN
VO THE ISLAMIC REP, Sirjan — W Africa & C Africa • 500 kW
VO THE ISLAMIC REP, Tehrān — S • E Asia • 500 kW
JAPAN
(con'd)   RADIO JAPAN, Tokyo-Yamata — SE Asia • 100 kW

0 1 2 3 4 5 6 7 8 9 10 11 12 13 14 15 16 17 18 19 20 21 22 23 24

ENGLISH ▬ ARABIC ▒ CHINESE ▯ FRENCH ▬ GERMAN ▬ RUSSIAN ═ SPANISH ▬ OTHER ▬

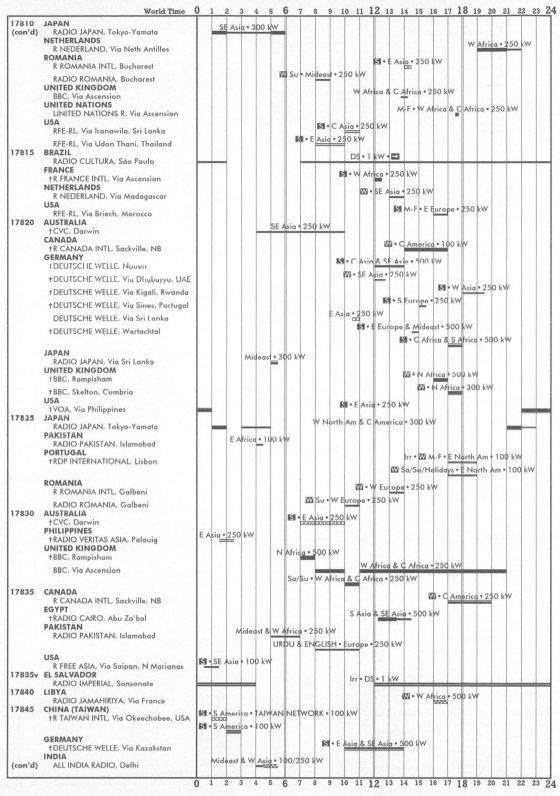

World Time: 0 1 2 3 4 5 6 7 8 9 10 11 12 13 14 15 16 17 18 19 20 21 22 23 24

17810 (con'd)
JAPAN
  RADIO JAPAN, Tokyo-Yamata — SE Asia • 300 kW
NETHERLANDS
  R NEDERLAND, Via Neth Antilles — W Africa • 250 kW
ROMANIA
  R ROMANIA INTL, Bucharest — S • E Asia • 250 kW
  RADIO ROMANIA, Bucharest — W • Su • Mideast • 250 kW
UNITED KINGDOM
  BBC, Via Ascension — W Africa & C Africa • 250 kW
UNITED NATIONS
  UNITED NATIONS R, Via Ascension — M-F • W Africa & C Africa • 250 kW
USA
  RFE-RL, Via Iranawila, Sri Lanka — S • C Asia • 250 kW
  RFE-RL, Via Udon Thani, Thailand — S • E Asia • 250 kW

17815
BRAZIL
  RADIO CULTURA, São Paulo — DS • 1 kW
FRANCE
  †R FRANCE INTL, Via Ascension — S • W Africa • 250 kW
NETHERLANDS
  R NEDERLAND, Via Madagascar — W • SE Asia • 250 kW
USA
  RFE-RL, Via Briech, Morocco — S M-F • E Europe • 250 kW

17820
AUSTRALIA
  †CVC, Darwin — SE Asia • 250 kW
CANADA
  †R CANADA INTL, Sackville, NB — W • C America • 100 kW
GERMANY
  †DEUTSCHE WELLE, Nauen — S • C Asia & SE Asia • 500 kW
  †DEUTSCHE WELLE, Via Dhabayya, UAE — W • SE Asia • 250 kW
  †DEUTSCHE WELLE, Via Kigali, Rwanda — S • W Asia • 250 kW
  †DEUTSCHE WELLE, Via Sines, Portugal — S • S Europe • 250 kW
  DEUTSCHE WELLE, Via Sri Lanka — E Asia • 250 kW
  †DEUTSCHE WELLE, Wertachtal — S • E Europe & Mideast • 500 kW
                                      S • C Africa & S Africa • 500 kW
JAPAN
  RADIO JAPAN, Via Sri Lanka — Mideast • 300 kW
UNITED KINGDOM
  †BBC, Rampisham — W • N Africa • 500 kW
  †BBC, Skelton, Cumbria — W • N Africa • 300 kW
USA
  †VOA, Via Philippines — S • E Asia • 250 kW

17825
JAPAN
  RADIO JAPAN, Tokyo-Yamata — W North Am & C America • 300 kW
PAKISTAN
  RADIO PAKISTAN, Islamabad — E Africa • 100 kW
PORTUGAL
  †RDP INTERNATIONAL, Lisbon — Irr • W • M-F • E North Am • 100 kW
                               W • Sa/Su/Holidays • E North Am • 100 kW
ROMANIA
  R ROMANIA INTL, Galbeni — W • W Europe • 250 kW
  RADIO ROMANIA, Galbeni — W • Su • W Europe • 250 kW

17830
AUSTRALIA
  †CVC, Darwin — S • E Asia • 250 kW
PHILIPPINES
  †RADIO VERITAS ASIA, Palauig — E Asia • 250 kW
UNITED KINGDOM
  †BBC, Rampisham — N Africa • 500 kW
  BBC, Via Ascension — W Africa & C Africa • 250 kW
                       Sa/Su • W Africa & C Africa • 250 kW

17835
CANADA
  R CANADA INTL, Sackville, NB — W • C America • 250 kW
EGYPT
  †RADIO CAIRO, Abu Za'bal — S Asia & SE Asia • 500 kW
PAKISTAN
  RADIO PAKISTAN, Islamabad — Mideast & W Africa • 250 kW
                             URDU & ENGLISH • Europe • 250 kW
USA
  R FREE ASIA, Via Saipan, N Marianas — S • SE Asia • 100 kW

17835v
EL SALVADOR
  RADIO IMPERIAL, Sonsonate — Irr • DS • 1 kW

17840
LIBYA
  RADIO JAMAHIRIYA, Via France — W • W Africa • 500 kW

17845
CHINA (TAIWAN)
  †R TAIWAN INTL, Via Okeechobee, USA — S • S America • TAIWAN NETWORK • 100 kW
                                        S • S America • 100 kW
GERMANY
  †DEUTSCHE WELLE, Via Kazakhstan — S • E Asia & SE Asia • 500 kW
INDIA
(con'd) ALL INDIA RADIO, Delhi — Mideast & W Asia • 100/250 kW

World Time: 0 1 2 3 4 5 6 7 8 9 10 11 12 13 14 15 16 17 18 19 20 21 22 23 24

SEASONAL S OR W   1-HR TIMESHIFT MIDYEAR ⇐ OR ⇒   JAMMING / OR ∧   EARLIEST HEARD ◁   LATEST HEARD ▷   NEW FOR 2006 †

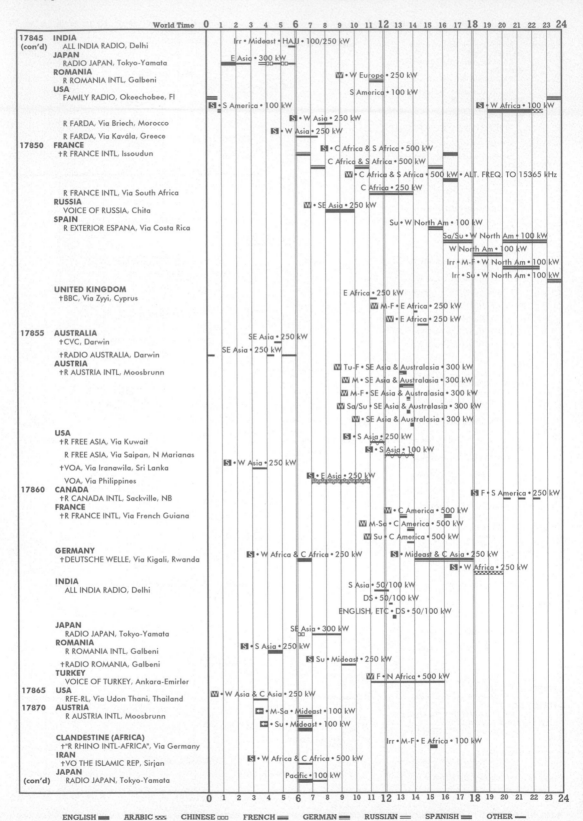

	World Time	0 1 2 3 4 5 6 7 8 9 10 11 12 13 14 15 16 17 18 19 20 21 22 23 24

17845 (con'd) **INDIA**
ALL INDIA RADIO, Delhi — Irr • Mideast • HAU • 100/250 kW
JAPAN
RADIO JAPAN, Tokyo-Yamata — E Asia • 300 kW
ROMANIA
R ROMANIA INTL, Galbeni — W • W Europe • 250 kW
USA
FAMILY RADIO, Okeechobee, Fl — S America • 100 kW
— S • S America • 100 kW — S • W Africa • 100 kW

R FARDA, Via Briech, Morocco — S • W Asia • 250 kW
R FARDA, Via Kavála, Greece — S • W Asia • 250 kW
17850 **FRANCE**
†R FRANCE INTL, Issoudun — S • C Africa & S Africa • 500 kW
C Africa & S Africa • 500 kW
W • C Africa & S Africa • 500 kW • ALT. FREQ. TO 15365 kHz
C Africa • 250 kW

R FRANCE INTL, Via South Africa
RUSSIA
VOICE OF RUSSIA, Chita — W • SE Asia • 250 kW
SPAIN
R EXTERIOR ESPANA, Via Costa Rica — Su • W North Am • 100 kW
Sa/Su • W North Am • 100 kW
W North Am • 100 kW
Irr • M-F • W North Am • 100 kW
Irr • Su • W North Am • 100 kW

UNITED KINGDOM
†BBC, Via Zyyi, Cyprus — E Africa • 250 kW
W M-F • E Africa • 250 kW
W • E Africa • 250 kW

17855 **AUSTRALIA**
†CVC, Darwin — SE Asia • 250 kW
†RADIO AUSTRALIA, Darwin — SE Asia • 250 kW
AUSTRIA
†R AUSTRIA INTL, Moosbrunn — W Tu-F • SE Asia & Australasia • 300 kW
W M • SE Asia & Australasia • 300 kW
W M-F • SE Asia & Australasia • 300 kW
W Sa/Su • SE Asia & Australasia • 300 kW
W • SE Asia & Australasia • 300 kW

USA
†R FREE ASIA, Via Kuwait — S • S Asia • 250 kW
R FREE ASIA, Via Saipan, N Marianas — S • S Asia • 100 kW
†VOA, Via Iranawila, Sri Lanka — S • W Asia • 250 kW
VOA, Via Philippines — S • E Asia • 250 kW
17860 **CANADA**
†R CANADA INTL, Sackville, NB — S F • S America • 250 kW
FRANCE
†R FRANCE INTL, Via French Guiana — W • C America • 500 kW
W M-Sa • C America • 500 kW
W Su • C America • 500 kW

GERMANY
†DEUTSCHE WELLE, Via Kigali, Rwanda — S • W Africa & C Africa • 250 kW
S • Mideast & C Asia • 250 kW
S • W Africa • 250 kW

INDIA
ALL INDIA RADIO, Delhi — S Asia • 50/100 kW
DS • 50/100 kW
ENGLISH, ETC • DS • 50/100 kW

JAPAN
RADIO JAPAN, Tokyo-Yamata — SE Asia • 300 kW
ROMANIA
R ROMANIA INTL, Galbeni — S • S Asia • 250 kW
†RADIO ROMANIA, Galbeni — S Su • Mideast • 250 kW
TURKEY
VOICE OF TURKEY, Ankara-Emirler — W F • N Africa • 500 kW
17865 **USA**
RFE-RL, Via Udon Thani, Thailand — W • W Asia & C Asia • 250 kW
17870 **AUSTRIA**
R AUSTRIA INTL, Moosbrunn — M-Sa • Mideast • 100 kW
Su • Mideast • 100 kW

CLANDESTINE (AFRICA)
†"R RHINO INTL-AFRICA", Via Germany — Irr • M-F • E Africa • 100 kW
IRAN
†VO THE ISLAMIC REP, Sirjan — S • W Africa & C Africa • 500 kW
JAPAN
(con'd) RADIO JAPAN, Tokyo-Yamata — Pacific • 100 kW

	0 1 2 3 4 5 6 7 8 9 10 11 12 13 14 15 16 17 18 19 20 21 22 23 24

ENGLISH ▬▬   ARABIC ⌇⌇⌇   CHINESE □□□   FRENCH ▬▬   GERMAN ▬▬   RUSSIAN ══   SPANISH ▬▬   OTHER ▬

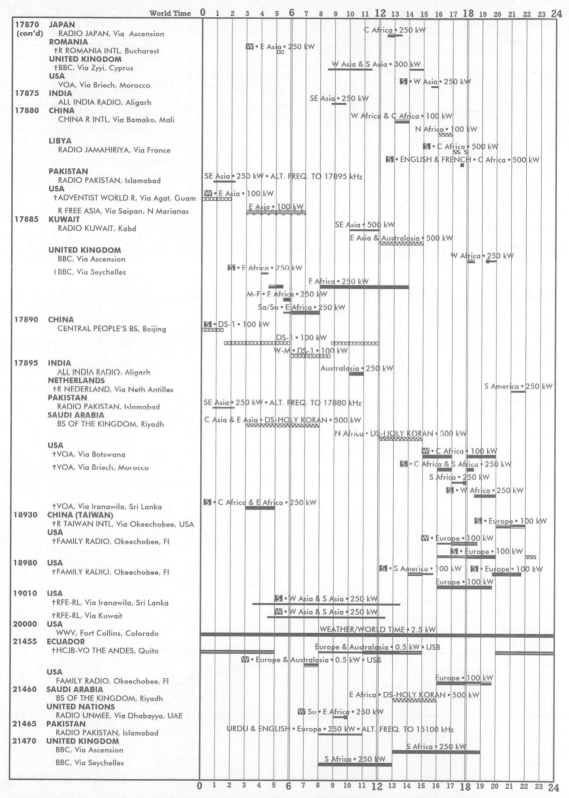

World Time 0 1 2 3 4 5 6 7 8 9 10 11 12 13 14 15 16 17 18 19 20 21 22 23 24

Freq	Country / Station	
17870 (con'd)	**JAPAN** RADIO JAPAN, Via Ascension	C Africa • 250 kW
	ROMANIA †R ROMANIA INTL, Bucharest	W • E Asia • 250 kW
	UNITED KINGDOM †BBC, Via Zyyi, Cyprus	W Asia & S Asia • 300 kW
	USA VOA, Via Briech, Morocco	S • W Asia • 250 kW
17875	**INDIA** ALL INDIA RADIO, Aligarh	SE Asia • 250 kW
17880	**CHINA** CHINA R INTL, Via Bamako, Mali	W Africa & C Africa • 100 kW
		N Africa • 100 kW
	LIBYA RADIO JAMAHIRIYA, Via France	S • C Africa • 500 kW
		S • ENGLISH & FRENCH • C Africa • 500 kW
	PAKISTAN RADIO PAKISTAN, Islamabad	SE Asia • 250 kW • ALT. FREQ. TO 17895 kHz
	USA †ADVENTIST WORLD R, Via Agat, Guam	W • E Asia • 100 kW
	R FREE ASIA, Via Saipan, N Marianas	E Asia • 100 kW
17885	**KUWAIT** RADIO KUWAIT, Kabd	SE Asia • 500 kW
		E Asia & Australasia • 500 kW
	UNITED KINGDOM BBC, Via Ascension	W Africa • 250 kW
	I BBC, Via Seychelles	S • E Africa • 250 kW
		E Africa • 250 kW
		M-F • E Africa • 250 kW
		Sa/Su • E Africa • 250 kW
17890	**CHINA** CENTRAL PEOPLE'S BS, Beijing	S • DS-1 • 100 kW
		DS-1 • 100 kW
		W-M • DS-1 • 100 kW
17895	**INDIA** ALL INDIA RADIO, Aligarh	Australasia • 250 kW
	NETHERLANDS †R NEDERLAND, Via Neth Antilles	S America • 250 kW
	PAKISTAN RADIO PAKISTAN, Islamabad	SE Asia • 250 kW • ALT. FREQ. TO 17880 kHz
	SAUDI ARABIA BS OF THE KINGDOM, Riyadh	C Asia & E Asia • DS-HOLY KORAN • 500 kW
		N Africa • DS-HOLY KORAN • 500 kW
	USA †VOA, Via Botswana	W • C Africa • 100 kW
	†VOA, Via Briech, Morocco	S • C Africa & S Africa • 250 kW
		S Africa • 250 kW
		S • W Africa • 250 kW
	†VOA, Via Iranawila, Sri Lanka	S • C Africa & E Africa • 250 kW
18930	**CHINA (TAIWAN)** †R TAIWAN INTL, Via Okeechobee, USA	S • Europe • 100 kW
	USA †FAMILY RADIO, Okeechobee, Fl	W • Europe • 100 kW
		S • Europe • 100 kW
18980	**USA** †FAMILY RADIO, Okeechobee, Fl	S • S America • 100 kW S • Europe • 100 kW
		Europe • 100 kW
19010	**USA** †RFE-RL, Via Iranawila, Sri Lanka	S • W Asia & S Asia • 250 kW
	†RFE-RL, Via Kuwait	W • W Asia & S Asia • 250 kW
20000	**USA** WWV, Fort Collins, Colorado	WEATHER/WORLD TIME • 2.5 kW
21455	**ECUADOR** †HCJB-VO THE ANDES, Quito	Europe & Australasia • 0.5 kW • USB
		W • Europe & Australasia • 0.5 kW • USB
	USA FAMILY RADIO, Okeechobee, Fl	Europe • 100 kW
21460	**SAUDI ARABIA** BS OF THE KINGDOM, Riyadh	E Africa • DS-HOLY KORAN • 500 kW
	UNITED NATIONS RADIO UNMEE, Via Dhabayya, UAE	W Su • E Africa • 250 kW
21465	**PAKISTAN** RADIO PAKISTAN, Islamabad	URDU & ENGLISH • Europe • 250 kW • ALT. FREQ. TO 15100 kHz
21470	**UNITED KINGDOM** BBC, Via Ascension	S Africa • 250 kW
	BBC, Via Seychelles	S Africa • 250 kW

0 1 2 3 4 5 6 7 8 9 10 11 12 13 14 15 16 17 18 19 20 21 22 23 24

SEASONAL 🅂 OR 🅆   1-HR TIMESHIFT MIDYEAR ⬅ OR ➡   JAMMING / OR ∧   EARLIEST HEARD ◁   LATEST HEARD ▷   NEW FOR 2006 †

World Time 0 1 2 3 4 5 6 7 8 9 10 11 12 13 14 15 16 17 18 19 20 21 22 23 24

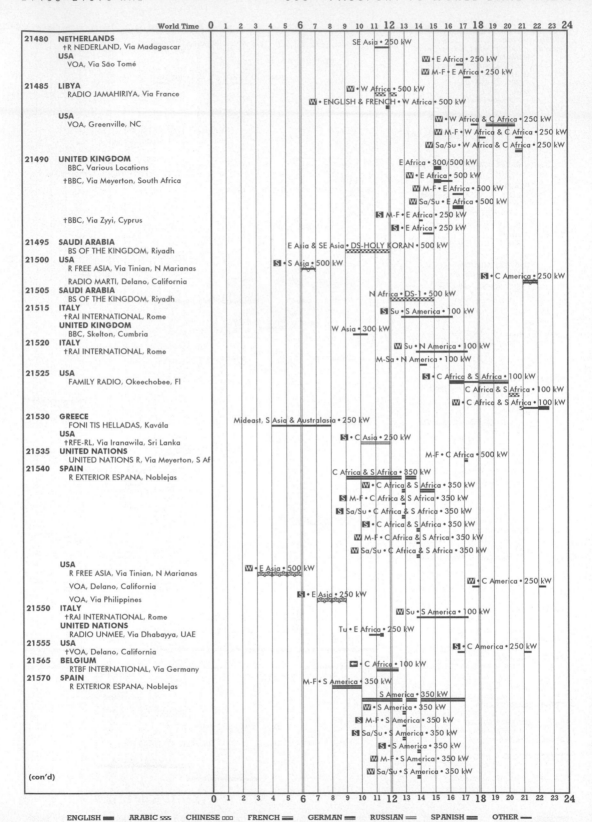

Freq	Country / Station	Notes
21480	**NETHERLANDS** †R NEDERLAND, Via Madagascar	SE Asia • 250 kW
	USA VOA, Via São Tomé	W • E Africa • 250 kW W M-F • E Africa • 250 kW
21485	**LIBYA** RADIO JAMAHIRIYA, Via France	W • W Africa • 500 kW W • ENGLISH & FRENCH • W Africa • 500 kW
	USA VOA, Greenville, NC	W • W Africa & C Africa • 250 kW W M-F • W Africa & C Africa • 250 kW W Sa/Su • W Africa & C Africa • 250 kW
21490	**UNITED KINGDOM** BBC, Various Locations	E Africa • 300/500 kW
	†BBC, Via Meyerton, South Africa	W • E Africa • 500 kW W M-F • E Africa • 500 kW W Sa/Su • E Africa • 500 kW
	†BBC, Via Zyyi, Cyprus	S M-F • E Africa • 250 kW S • E Africa • 250 kW
21495	**SAUDI ARABIA** BS OF THE KINGDOM, Riyadh	E Asia & SE Asia • DS-HOLY KORAN • 500 kW
21500	**USA** R FREE ASIA, Via Tinian, N Marianas	S • S Asia • 500 kW
	RADIO MARTI, Delano, California	S • C America • 250 kW
21505	**SAUDI ARABIA** BS OF THE KINGDOM, Riyadh	N Africa • DS-1 • 500 kW
21515	**ITALY** †RAI INTERNATIONAL, Rome	S • S America • 100 kW
	UNITED KINGDOM BBC, Skelton, Cumbria	W Asia • 300 kW
21520	**ITALY** †RAI INTERNATIONAL, Rome	W Su • N America • 100 kW M-Sa • N America • 100 kW
21525	**USA** FAMILY RADIO, Okeechobee, Fl	S • C Africa & S Africa • 100 kW C Africa & S Africa • 100 kW W • C Africa & S Africa • 100 kW
21530	**GREECE** FONI TIS HELLADAS, Kavála	Mideast, S Asia & Australasia • 250 kW
	USA †RFE-RL, Via Iranawila, Sri Lanka	S • C Asia • 250 kW
21535	**UNITED NATIONS** UNITED NATIONS R, Via Meyerton, S Af	M-F • C Africa • 500 kW
21540	**SPAIN** R EXTERIOR ESPANA, Noblejas	C Africa & S Africa • 350 kW W • C Africa & S Africa • 350 kW S M-F • C Africa & S Africa • 350 kW S Sa/Su • C Africa & S Africa • 350 kW S • C Africa & S Africa • 350 kW W M-F • C Africa & S Africa • 350 kW W Sa/Su • C Africa & S Africa • 350 kW
	USA R FREE ASIA, Via Tinian, N Marianas	W • E Asia • 500 kW
	VOA, Delano, California	W • C America • 250 kW
	VOA, Via Philippines	S • E Asia • 250 kW
21550	**ITALY** †RAI INTERNATIONAL, Rome	W Su • S America • 100 kW
	UNITED NATIONS RADIO UNMEE, Via Dhabayya, UAE	Tu • E Africa • 250 kW
21555	**USA** †VOA, Delano, California	S • C America • 250 kW
21565	**BELGIUM** RTBF INTERNATIONAL, Via Germany	C Africa • 100 kW
21570	**SPAIN** R EXTERIOR ESPANA, Noblejas	M-F • S America • 350 kW S America • 350 kW W • S America • 350 kW S M-F • S America • 350 kW S Sa/Su • S America • 350 kW S • S America • 350 kW W M-F • S America • 350 kW W Sa/Su • S America • 350 kW

(con'd)

0 1 2 3 4 5 6 7 8 9 10 11 12 13 14 15 16 17 18 19 20 21 22 23 24

ENGLISH ▬   ARABIC ▨   CHINESE ▫▫▫   FRENCH ═   GERMAN ▬   RUSSIAN ═   SPANISH ▬   OTHER ▬

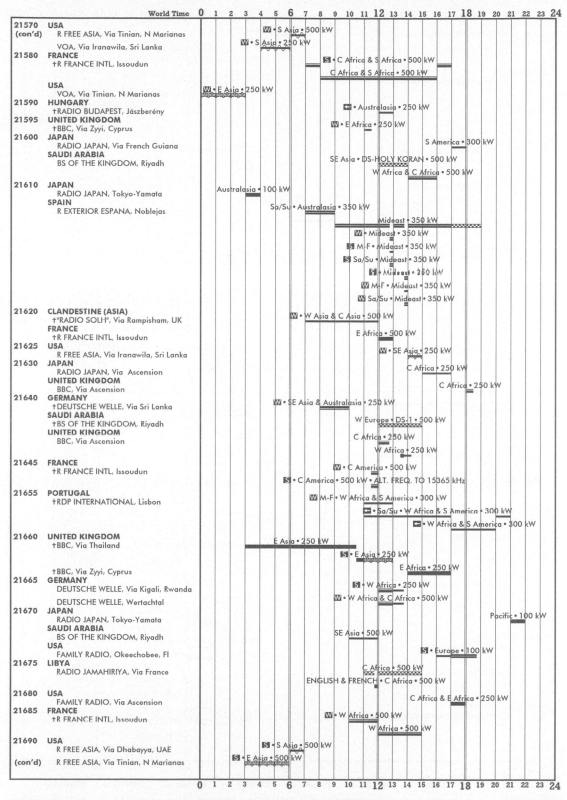

Freq	Station	
21570 (con'd)	**USA** R FREE ASIA, Via Tinian, N Marianas	W • S Asia • 500 kW
	VOA, Via Iranawila, Sri Lanka	W • S Asia • 250 kW
21580	**FRANCE** †R FRANCE INTL, Issoudun	S • C Africa & S Africa • 500 kW / C Africa & S Africa • 500 kW
	USA VOA, Via Tinian, N Marianas	W • E Asia • 250 kW
21590	**HUNGARY** †RADIO BUDAPEST, Jászberény	⇨ • Australasia • 250 kW
21595	**UNITED KINGDOM** †BBC, Via Zyyi, Cyprus	W • E Africa • 250 kW
21600	**JAPAN** RADIO JAPAN, Via French Guiana	S America • 300 kW
	SAUDI ARABIA BS OF THE KINGDOM, Riyadh	SE Asia • DS-HOLY KORAN • 500 kW / W Africa & C Africa • 500 kW
21610	**JAPAN** RADIO JAPAN, Tokyo-Yamata	Australasia • 100 kW
	SPAIN R EXTERIOR ESPANA, Noblejas	Sa/Su • Australasia • 350 kW / Mideast • 350 kW / W • Mideast • 350 kW / S M-F • Mideast • 350 kW / S Sa/Su • Mideast • 350 kW / S • Mideast • 350 kW / W M-F • Mideast • 350 kW / W Sa/Su • Mideast • 350 kW
21620	**CLANDESTINE (ASIA)** †"RADIO SOLH", Via Rampisham, UK	W • W Asia & C Asia • 500 kW
	FRANCE †R FRANCE INTL, Issoudun	E Africa • 500 kW
21625	**USA** R FREE ASIA, Via Iranawila, Sri Lanka	W • SE Asia • 250 kW
21630	**JAPAN** RADIO JAPAN, Via Ascension	C Africa • 250 kW
	UNITED KINGDOM BBC, Via Ascension	C Africa • 250 kW
21640	**GERMANY** †DEUTSCHE WELLE, Via Sri Lanka	W • SE Asia & Australasia • 250 kW
	SAUDI ARABIA †BS OF THE KINGDOM, Riyadh	W Europe • DS-1 • 500 kW
	UNITED KINGDOM BBC, Via Ascension	C Africa • 250 kW / W Africa • 250 kW
21645	**FRANCE** †R FRANCE INTL, Issoudun	W • C America • 500 kW / S • C America • 500 kW • ALT. FREQ. TO 15365 kHz
21655	**PORTUGAL** †RDP INTERNATIONAL, Lisbon	W M-F • W Africa & S America • 300 kW / ⇨ Sa/Su • W Africa & S America • 300 kW / ⇨ • W Africa & S America • 300 kW
21660	**UNITED KINGDOM** †BBC, Via Thailand	E Asia • 250 kW / S • E Asia • 250 kW
	†BBC, Via Zyyi, Cyprus	E Africa • 250 kW
21665	**GERMANY** DEUTSCHE WELLE, Via Kigali, Rwanda	S • W Africa • 250 kW
	DEUTSCHE WELLE, Wertachtal	W • W Africa & C Africa • 500 kW
21670	**JAPAN** RADIO JAPAN, Tokyo-Yamata	Pacific • 100 kW
	SAUDI ARABIA BS OF THE KINGDOM, Riyadh	SE Asia • 500 kW
	USA FAMILY RADIO, Okeechobee, Fl	S • Europe • 100 kW
21675	**LIBYA** RADIO JAMAHIRIYA, Via France	C Africa • 500 kW / ENGLISH & FRENCH • C Africa • 500 kW
21680	**USA** FAMILY RADIO, Via Ascension	C Africa & E Africa • 250 kW
21685	**FRANCE** †R FRANCE INTL, Issoudun	W • W Africa • 500 kW / W Africa • 500 kW
21690	**USA** R FREE ASIA, Via Dhabayya, UAE	S • S Asia • 500 kW
(con'd)	R FREE ASIA, Via Tinian, N Marianas	S • E Asia • 500 kW

SEASONAL S OR W   1-HR TIMESHIFT MIDYEAR ⇦ OR ⇨   JAMMING / OR ∧   EARLIEST HEARD ◁   LATEST HEARD ▷   NEW FOR 2006 †

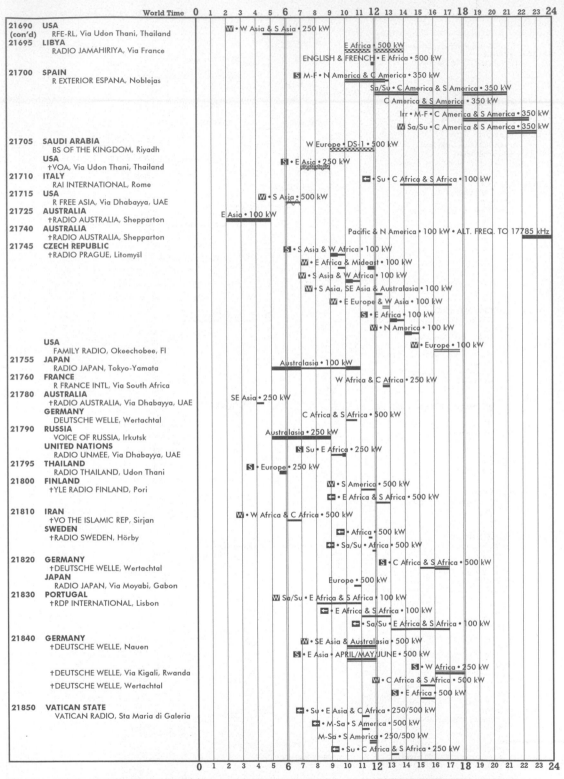

World Time	0 1 2 3 4 5 6 7 8 9 10 11 12 13 14 15 16 17 18 19 20 21 22 23 24
21690 (con'd) **USA** RFE-RL, Via Udon Thani, Thailand	W • W Asia & S Asia • 250 kW
21695 LIBYA RADIO JAMAHIRIYA, Via France	E Africa • 500 kW / ENGLISH & FRENCH • E Africa • 500 kW
21700 SPAIN R EXTERIOR ESPANA, Noblejas	S M-F • N America & C America • 350 kW / Sa/Su • C America & S America • 350 kW / C America & S America • 350 kW / Irr • M-F • C America & S America • 350 kW / W Sa/Su • C America & S America • 350 kW
21705 SAUDI ARABIA BS OF THE KINGDOM, Riyadh	W Europe • DS-1 • 500 kW
USA †VOA, Via Udon Thani, Thailand	S • E Asia • 250 kW
21710 ITALY RAI INTERNATIONAL, Rome	Su • C Africa & S Africa • 100 kW
21715 USA R FREE ASIA, Via Dhabayya, UAE	W • S Asia • 500 kW
21725 AUSTRALIA †RADIO AUSTRALIA, Shepparton	E Asia • 100 kW
21740 AUSTRALIA †RADIO AUSTRALIA, Shepparton	Pacific & N America • 100 kW • ALT. FREQ. TO 17785 kHz
21745 CZECH REPUBLIC †RADIO PRAGUE, Litomyšl	S • S Asia & W Africa • 100 kW / W • E Africa & Mideast • 100 kW / W • S Asia & W Africa • 100 kW / W • S Asia, SE Asia & Australasia • 100 kW / W • E Europe & W Asia • 100 kW / S • E Africa • 100 kW / W • N America • 100 kW
USA FAMILY RADIO, Okeechobee, Fl	W • Europe • 100 kW
21755 JAPAN RADIO JAPAN, Tokyo-Yamata	Australasia • 100 kW
21760 FRANCE R FRANCE INTL, Via South Africa	W Africa & C Africa • 250 kW
21780 AUSTRALIA †RADIO AUSTRALIA, Via Dhabayya, UAE	SE Asia • 250 kW
GERMANY DEUTSCHE WELLE, Wertachtal	C Africa & S Africa • 500 kW
21790 RUSSIA VOICE OF RUSSIA, Irkutsk	Australasia • 250 kW
UNITED NATIONS RADIO UNMEE, Via Dhabayya, UAE	S Su • E Africa • 250 kW
21795 THAILAND RADIO THAILAND, Udon Thani	S • Europe • 250 kW
21800 FINLAND †YLE RADIO FINLAND, Pori	W • S America • 500 kW / E Africa & S Africa • 500 kW
21810 IRAN †VO THE ISLAMIC REP, Sirjan	W • W Africa & C Africa • 500 kW
SWEDEN †RADIO SWEDEN, Hörby	Africa • 500 kW / Sa/Su • Africa • 500 kW
21820 GERMANY †DEUTSCHE WELLE, Wertachtal	S • C Africa & S Africa • 500 kW
JAPAN RADIO JAPAN, Via Moyabi, Gabon	Europe • 500 kW
21830 PORTUGAL †RDP INTERNATIONAL, Lisbon	W Sa/Su • E Africa & S Africa • 100 kW / E Africa & S Africa • 100 kW / Sa/Su • E Africa & S Africa • 100 kW
21840 GERMANY †DEUTSCHE WELLE, Nauen	W • SE Asia & Australasia • 500 kW / S • E Asia • APRIL/MAY/JUNE • 500 kW / S • W Africa • 250 kW
†DEUTSCHE WELLE, Via Kigali, Rwanda	W • C Africa & S Africa • 500 kW
†DEUTSCHE WELLE, Wertachtal	S • E Africa • 500 kW
21850 VATICAN STATE VATICAN RADIO, Sta Maria di Galeria	Su • E Asia & C Africa • 250/500 kW / M-Sa • S America • 500 kW / M-Sa • S America • 250/500 kW / Su • C Africa & S Africa • 250 kW

0 1 2 3 4 5 6 7 8 9 10 11 12 13 14 15 16 17 18 19 20 21 22 23 24

ENGLISH ▬ ARABIC ⬚⬚ CHINESE ▫▫▫ FRENCH ▭▭ GERMAN ▬ RUSSIAN ══ SPANISH ▭▭ OTHER ──